T4-ADM-754

CLAVIS COMMENTARIORUM
OF HEBREW LITURGICAL
POETRY IN MANUSCRIPT

CLAVIS COMMENTARIORUM
ANTIQUITATIS ET MEDII AEVI

General Editor

PROF. DR. THEOL. WILHELM GEERLINGS
Ruhr-Universität Bochum

Editors

PROF. DR. PHIL. SIEGMAR DÖPP
Universität Göttingen

PROF. DR. PHIL. RAINER JAKOBI
Martin-Luther-Universität Halle-Wittenberg

PROF. DR. RER. NAT. IRMGARD MÜLLER
Ruhr-Universität Bochum

VOLUME 4

CLAVIS COMMENTARIORUM OF HEBREW LITURGICAL POETRY IN MANUSCRIPT

BY

ELISABETH HOLLENDER

BRILL
LEIDEN · BOSTON
2005

This book is printed on acid-free paper.

Library of Congress Cataloging-in-Publication Data

A C.I.P. record for this book is available from the Library of Congress.

ISSN 1568–9999
ISBN 90 04 14640 7

© *Copyright 2005 by Koninklijke Brill NV, Leiden, The Netherlands*
Koninklijke Brill NV incorporates the imprints Brill Academic Publishers,
Martinus Nijhoff Publishers and VSP.

Cover design: Thorsten (Celine Ostendorf), Leiden

All rights reserved. No part of this publication may be reproduced, translated, stored in
a retrieval system, or transmitted in any form or by any means, electronic,
mechanical, photocopying, recording or otherwise, without prior written
permission from the publisher.

Authorization to photocopy items for internal or personal
use is granted by Brill provided that
the appropriate fees are paid directly to The Copyright
Clearance Center, 222 Rosewood Drive, Suite 910
Danvers MA 01923, USA.
Fees are subject to change.

PRINTED IN THE NETHERLANDS

As I complete this book, I am filled with memories of my sister, Mirjam. Each day, I miss her companionship even as I continue to feel her presence.
This volume is dedicated to her.

CONTENTS

Preface	ix
Transcription Table	xiii
Introduction	1
List of Manuscripts	21
Clavis Commentariorum	49
Bibliography	957
Index of Poets	963
Index of Commentators	971

PREFACE

The *Clavis Commentariorum of Hebrew Liturgical Poetry in Manuscript* is a key to commentaries on Hebrew liturgical poetry (piyyut) contained in manuscripts. The first parts of this work were byproducts of a major research into Ashkenazic and Tsarfatic piyyut-commentaries in the framework of my Habilitationsschrift "Mittelalterliche hebräische Kompilationsliteratur am Beispiel aschkenasischer und französischer Pijjutkommentare" presented at the Gerhard Mercator Universität GH Duisburg; and I am currently rewriting this thesis for publication in English with the working title "Ashkenazic and Tsarfatic Piyyut-Commentary as Compilatory Literature." For the Habilitationsschrift I had searched through approximately 150 manuscripts of Ashkenazic and Tsarfatic piyyut-commentary and had already then begun to feel the need for an index that included at least the main sources. When the editors of the series Clavis Commentariorum Antiquitatis et Medii Aevi, Prof. Wilhelm Geerlings and PD Dr. Christian Schulze, approached me with an invitation to complete my index and publish it for use by other scholars, I was delighted to be offered an opportunity to share my findings with the scholarly world. Once I had the time to collect all manuscripts of piyyut-commentary the project soon outgrew its original limitation to Ashkenazic piyyut-commentary. One of the reasons was the close connection between Ashkenazic, Tsarfatic and Italian piyyut-commentary that made it desirable to include all manuscripts containing piyyut-commentary from these countries. Once Italy was part of the collection it seemed right to include also the Maḥzorim and Siddurim of the Romaniote rite and the commentaries they offer, especially since many of the piyyutim commented on by the Romaniotes are included in the other European rites as well. On the other hand it seemed appropriate to include the תשלום אבודרהם, the only known and published piyyut-commentary from Sepharad. This gave rise to a search for further Sephardic commentaries, a few of which were found and included. Related to this are the commentaries on the Maḥzor Carpentras transmitted in several manuscripts. At this point it was obvious that the Clavis Commentariorum of Hebrew Liturgical Poetry should be enlarged to include all manuscript evidence of piyyut-commentary that could be located. This added also the large number Yemenite commentaries to the list, even though all Yementite Tiklal manuscripts extant were copied when printing had replaced handwritten transmission in the western Jewish communities. Beyond that I included a few manuscript commentaries on Hoshaanot and on the Azharot of Salomo Ibn Gabirol from Northern Africa and Karaite commentaries on Karaite piyyutim.

This project would not have been possible without the Institute for Hebrew Manuscripts on Microfilm at the Jewish National and University Library, Jerusalem. The entry "תפלה, פרשנות" in the card catalogue of the

Institute was the first source for my research, the electronic version of the catalogue brought even more manuscripts to my attention. The personnel at the Institute was always helpful and patient with my questions and made it possible for me to see most of the manuscripts in microform. I am grateful to all of them and also to those far-sighted scholars, who envisioned the need for a centralized collection of Hebrew manuscripts on microfilm, and elicited funds to establish this outstanding institution.

I also wish to express my gratitude to the librarians who allowed me to see some of the original manuscripts in their collections, at the Universitätsbibliothek Frankfurt am Main, the Staatsbibliothek Berlin, the library of the Jewish Theological Seminary of America, the Biblioteca Apostolica, the John Rylands Library, Manchester, the Biblioteca Palatina Parmense, the library of Yad ben Zvi, Jerusalem. I have received help whereever I needed it, often beyond what I dared to ask for. Thanks is also due to the staff at the Germania Judaica library in Köln that provided me with a working place outside of my study and generously offered coffee and moral support during the last crucial weeks of preparing this book.

I also wish to thank the many colleagues who encouraged me during the long and tedious work of preparing this index, who brought manuscripts to my attention and who encouraged me when I felt daunted by the enormity of this project. I cannot name them all, but would like to mention Prof. Shulamit Elizur, Jerusalem, who taught me so much about piyyut and who dissuaded me from starting this project when I first thought about it: if I had started 9 years earlier, the results would have been far less complete than they are now and I would not have finished my Habilitation; Prof. Dr. Wout van Bekkum, Groningen, who has taken interest in my research and has continuously encouraged me for many years now; Yehoshua Granat, Jerusalem, who was always willing to help when I had no access to the National and University Library, Jerusalem, and its treasures and who brought several manuscripts and publications to my attention; Hayyim Soloveitchik, New York, whose interest in my progress boosted my confidence so that I could actually finish the project, and all those others who asked me about piyyut-commentaries and made me understand that the *Clavis Commentariorum of Hebrew Liturgical Poetry* would indeed be a helpful tool for researchers.

Katja Soennecken proofread more than 900 pages of lists and the indices, Susan Oren corrected my English, I am deeply indebted to their help from which the book did greatly benefit. With great pleasure I also want to thank Notabene Associates, Inc., and their staff at technical support: without Notabene Lingua Workstation and Ibidem Plus I would not have been able to manage the huge amount of data, and when last minute technical questions arose, their solutions were fast, friendly, and successful.

My husband Ulrich Berzbach who has lived for years with piyyut-commentary as constant element in my working life has supported me throughout, even as this project continued to expand beyond anyone's expectations, in both scope and time frame. I could not have finished this project or any of my other endeavors without him.

Last but not least I wish to thank the editors of the series Clavis Commentariorum Antiquitatis et Medii Aevi, Prof. Wilhelm Geerlings and PD Dr. Christian Schulze, whose interest in my work initiated the Clavis Commentariorum of Hebrew Liturgical Poetry as published book. A grant from the Heisenberg program of the Deutsche Forschungsgemeinschaft (DFG) has enabled me to devote nearly two years of research to this project, an opportunity for which I am deeply grateful.

TRANSLITERATION TABLE

Comon names are not transliterated, instead their American spelling is used, e.g. Isaac for יצחק or Simon for שמעון. For other names, the following transliteration has been used:

א	not transliterated
ב	b/v
ג	g
ד	d
ה	h, not transliterated at end of word
ו	w, o, u
ז	z
ח	ḥ
ט	t
י	y, i
כ	k/kh
ל	l
מ	m
נ	n
ס	s
ע	not transliterated
פ	p/f
צ	ts
ק	q
ר	r
ש	sh
ת	t

INTRODUCTION

Poetic insertions are used to beautify religious services in most religions and Judaism is no exception to this rule. Psalms were sung during Temple liturgies and seem to have adorned synagogue services since earliest times. We do not know very much about the shape of synagogue services in the first centuries after the destruction of the Second Temple but it is safe to assume that they contained poetic texts. By the 4th century CE new poetic texts were added to the regular prayer and may have substituted for it partly. This kind of poetry developed over the next centuries into a genre with rules: some were applied to all Hebrew liturgical poetry and others were specifically linked to location and era of composition. The development had started in Byzantine Israel, where the new Hebrew word coined for liturgical poetry was an adapted form of the Greek ποίησις, namely פיוט, *piyyut*. Many important developments of piyyut took place during the 6th and 7th centuries CE in Byzantine Israel. Scholarship has termed this period the era of classical piyyut. The genre spread to all Jewish communities, and while acceptance varied–with some sages voicing strong concerns over the interruption in prayer by these piyyutim–there is not a single Jewish community that did not eventually adopt liturgical poetry to adorn its synagogue service. In addition to piyyutim received through tradition, poets in different times and places wrote new liturgical poetry according to the needs and the tastes of their communities. Hebrew liturgical poetry is therefore not a unified corpus, but a colorful mixture, strongly influenced by local and temporal aesthetics.

While it is assumed that in early times Hebrew liturgical poetry was composed for immediate use and was not codified, by the early Middle Ages we can detect local or regional rites that include variants in the standard prayers and individual selection of piyyutim. These rites were not completely stable and existing piyyutim were often replaced by newer compositions. Only with the wide distribution of printed prayerbooks, starting in the 16th century in Central Europe, were unified regional rites regularized, a process which began in Ashkenaz. Yet the differences among the local rites within these larger regions usually applied only to minor items and it has been customary to categorize the local rites within the regional rites.

A first description of the different Jewish liturgical rites, including piyyutim, was published by Leopold Zunz in 1858,[1] unfortunately it has not yet been replaced by a modern study that describes the historical development of all different rites and lists all piyyutim used by them. Zunz reviewed many of the manuscripts known in his time, but many more have become available to scholars since. The electronic catalogue of the Institute for

---

[1] L. Zunz, *Die Ritus des synagogalen Gottesdienstes, geschichtlich entwickelt*, Berlin, Louis Lamm, 1859.

Hebrew Manuscripts on Microfilm at the Jewish National and University Library Jerusalem (IHM) has made information available about all Hebrew manuscripts known and has enabled scholars to compare (microfilms of) manuscripts from distant collections at one place. With new palaeographic methods, manuscripts can be dated and located far more precisely than 150 years ago, and this may enable modern scholarship to add to Zunz's important work, especially where the development and change from local to regional rites is concerned. Davidson's Thesaurus of Medieval Hebrew Poetry (אוצר השירה והפיוט) cannot substitute for this, since it is limited to Hebrew poetry printed in Maḥzorim, Siddurim and other collections, plus unpublished texts that are mentioned in some early scholarly studies.[2] The presence and selection of piyyutim has yet to be studied for most rites. Minhag Ashkenaz is the only rite for which in-depth research is available, the festival liturgy of which have been published in five volumes as מחזור לפי מנהגי בני אשכנז לכל ענפיהם by L. Goldschmidt and Y. Fraenkel. The volumes represent the western Ashkenazic rites including Tsarfat and the eastern Ashkenazic rites.[3] The absence of similar works in other rites may be due to the lack of an audience for such prayerbooks outside of the scholarly world.

The status of liturgical poetry seems to have varied in the different Jewish communities, but generally it seems to have been high. In Ashkenaz (Germany, mainly the Rhineland) and Tsarfat (Northern France), the most famous poet of classical piyyut, Elazar birabbi Qallir (6th - 7th century CE, Israel), was regarded highly since he was assumed to be an early Talmudic authority, and doubts regarding the status of liturgical poetry that interrupts prayer were silenced with arguments pertaining to the ancient habit and scholarly contents of this sacred and traditional poetry.[4] While liturgical poetry never gained the authoritative status of Bible, Talmud, and Midrash (i.e. the written and the oral Torah), nevertheless the very fact that piyyutim were repeated in synagogue services every year and handed down from generation to generation created a de facto canon or at least a general acceptance of piyyutim as part of the cultural heritage of the communities that used them.

Piyyut-Commentary

Canonical written texts exist within a tension that creates itself, balancing the importance of both exact transmission and adapting the text's 'timeless truth' to the actual situation of the reader. Once a text is written down, understand-

---

[2] I. Davidson, *Thesaurus of Medieval Hebrew Poetry.* אוצר השירה והפיוט, New York, Jewish Theological Seminary, 1924–1933.

[3] An extension of this important project and the publication of a parallel Siddur is being prepared by Y. Fraenkel.

[4] R. Langer, Kalir was a Tanna. Rabbenu Tam's Invocation of Antiquity in Defense of the Ashkenazi Payyetanic Tradition, *HUCA*, 67, 1997, pp. 95–106; R. Langer, *To Worship God Properly. Tensions between Liturgical Customs and Halakha in Judaism*, Cincinnati, Hebrew Union College Press, 1998.

ing its message is not an unmediated act within a unified time and place any more. The 'stretching' of the communication in time and place calls for "cultures of application" that construct a new way of understanding the message within the cultural setting of the reader, or reconstruct the original setting of the text in order to make the message acceptable to the reader.[5] The privilege and duty of interpreting holy texts and ascribing meaning to them usually is the task of priests as a class within society.[6] In the Rabbinical Jewish societies rabbis and scholars assumed this task and created a new form of Judaism by writing and commenting on holy texts. J. Assman differentiates between three different approaches to the formation of a canon of cultural texts, but all of them emphasize the importance of taking the canonical text to heart and putting it into practice. Thus it is necessary that the text be understood, which underlies the impulse for creating commentaries. The main elements responsible for the development of commentaries are the closure of the text commented on, the semantic shift that provokes a new interpretation, and an accepted set of hermeneutical rules that govern the process of learning and understanding.[7] In the Middle Ages, commentaries were composed only on authoritative texts. They served both to maintain the meaning sense and to update the message of the texts. The dispute within the Jewish communities about the significance, meaning and status of piyyutim in the liturgy forced scholars in 12th-century Ashkenaz to legitimize the piyyutim contained in their Maḥzor and to safeguard the liturgical function of this poetry by writing commentaries. In their selection of what they commented on, they tried to determine which texts would be considered as obligatory parts of the liturgical culture in medieval Ashkenaz.

The very existence of commentaries on Hebrew liturgical poetry thus assigned status to this genre, while it enabled medieval and modern Judaism to continue using texts that were composed in a completely different cultural surrounding. As long as piyyutim were commented on, they could be part of synagogue service since their meaning could be adapted to the needs of their communities. L. Zunz had already published a list of 71 commentators and references to the commentaries ascribed to them or mentioning them. Most of the commentators are from Ashkenaz and Tsarfat, the remainder lived in Italy.[8] For this *Clavis Commentariorum of Hebrew Liturgical Poetry*, 415 manuscripts of piyyut-commentary were analyzed, 18,025 individual commentaries could be identified,[9] they comment on 2,088 piyyutim, 1,685 of them written by 209 poets, the other 403 piyyutim are transmitted anony-

---

[5] C. Epping-Jäger, *Die Inszenierung der Schrift. Der Literalisierungsprozeß und die Entstehungsgeschichte des Dramas*, Stuttgart, M. & P. Verlag für Wissenschaft und Forschung, 1996, p. 61.

[6] J. Assmann, Text und Kommentar. Einführung, in *Text und Kommentar*, Archäologie der literarischen Kommunikation IV, München, Fink, 1995, p. 26.

[7] Assmann, Einführung, 27–31.

[8] Zunz, *Ritus*, 194–201.

[9] Since some commentaries from the named manuscripts could not be identified, the overall number of piyyut-commentaries extant is slightly larger.

mously. The names of 69 commentators have been identified from rubrics and other ascriptions, though this number does not include all those to whom (single) explanations are ascribed in the text of the commentaries. Yet the vast majority of the commentaries are anonymous. Piyyut-commentaries in manuscript exist from the following rites: Ashkenaz, Tsarfat, AFM (Asti, Fossano, Moncalvo), Italia, Roma, Romania, Corfu, Sepharad, Carpentras, North Africa, Lurianic (haAri) and Yemen, additionally a Karaite commentary has been transmitted in several manuscripts and commentaries on the Azharot of Salomo Ibn Gabirol have been transmitted in communities such as Azerbeidjan and Persia. The fact that scholars, scribes and printers in almost all Jewish communities invested time and effort in the composition and transmission of commentaries on liturgical poetry proves the importance of this literature in different times and places.

The distribution of the extant commentaries among the different liturgical rites is anything but equal. About half of the individual commentaries listed are from Ashkenaz (more than 9,400), almost 2,500 are from Tsarfat. The related rites of Roma, Italia and Romania are represented by 340 individual commentaries, the Karaite commentary tradition makes up for almost 180 individual commentaries. Almost 500 commentaries were written in Sepharad, more than 800 in Carpentras, about 100 in North Africa, and more than 4,300 in Yemen.

This unequal distribution is largely due to the coincidences in transmission and the way manuscripts were collected. Liturgical manuscripts that could no longer be used were hidden in Genizot and/or buried. Manuscripts with the greatest likelihood of transmission across generations were those that were exceptionally well executed, contained beautiful illuminations, or were highly esteemed for another reason. Expulsions and economic hardships influenced the fate of manuscripts as well. Christian collections that started to include Hebrew manuscripts in the late Middle Ages and Early Modern Time were the first places where the uninterrupted transmission of Hebrew manuscripts was possible, since the manuscripts were used less often and did not suffer from expulsions and persecutions. But most Christian collectors were not interested in all Hebrew manuscripts: their interest lay with Bible manuscripts and a few related texts. It is therefore highly probable that a great number of manuscripts containing piyyut-commentary where destroyed or lost after the Middle Ages. But nevertheless it is obvious that far fewer piyyutim were commented on in the Romaniote tradition than in the Ashkenazic and Tsarfatic traditions which were the sources for many of the piyyutim and liturgical traditions of the Romaniotes. With only two manuscripts that are not copies of תשלום אבודרהם by David b. Josef Abudraham, Sepharad is definitely underrepresented and chance-transmission cannot sufficiently explain this. Obviously piyyut-commentary was far less popular in Sepharad than in Ashkenaz. The fact that only very few piyyut-commentary manuscripts are known from the Sephardic communities of the Ottoman empire further attests to a lack of interest in piyyut-commentary in that community.

If printed commentaries were taken into account as well, the results would differ only slightly. The sole addition to the corpus of piyyut-commentary would be the eastern Ashkenazic Minhagim, who inherited an interest in piyyut-commentary from their central Ashkenazic forefathers and are responsible for at least 250 editions of Maḥzor Ashkenaz with commentaries from the 16th to 18th centuries. Later commentaries on the Hoshaanot and the Azharot of Salomo Ibn Gabirol were printed in far smaller editions and less frequently in Constantinople for use in the Sephardic communities and for the kabbalists. A commentary on the Yotser for Shabbat Hanukka was printed in 1606 in Venice. Overall, Central Europe remained the productive center for piyyut-commentary, as it had been in the Middle Ages.

Commentaries were written for many piyyutim, regardless of genre. The most popular genres to be commented on were Azharot (poetic renderings of the 613 commandments and prohibitions traditionally counted in the Torah) and Hoshaanot (pleas for redemption used during Sukkot). This demonstrates the different purposes that piyyut-commentaries can have: Hoshaanot seem to have been mainly commented on in speculative and mystical ways, following the importance attached to them and their liturgical settings in kabbalistic circles. The Ashkenazic and Tsarfatic commentators and compilers also transmitted numerous commentaries on Hoshaanot, even though they rarely engaged in mystical or speculative explanations. Rather, they primarily focused on the plain meaning of the difficult language employed in classical Hoshaanot that were in use in their communities. Commentaries on Azharot were used to elaborate on the divine commandments and the additional rules derived from them. In addition to these genres, many commentaries were transmitted on the main genres of piyyut: Qerovot (compositions for the *Amida*) in all different forms, Yotserot (compositions for the *Shema Israel*), Selihot (penitential poems), Qinot (dirges), piyyutim for rain and dew and Sidre Avoda (describing the Temple service on Yom Kippur) were often commented on, as well as Reshuyot and Petihot (introductions for piyyutim). The distribution varies according to the different uses in the different communities. Thus we have commentaries on all genres from Ashkenaz, but commentaries mainly on Selihot and Qinot from Yemen. Within any one Jewish community, the style of commentary displays only a limited amount of variation, most of the distinctions are to be explained by the different styles and contents of the genres. In Ashkenaz, e. g., commentaries on most Selihot focused on the language, whereas commentaries on classical Qerovot and Yotserot, i.e. piyyutim that include many references to Rabbinical exegesis, refer to Talmud and Midrashim in order to explain the sometimes enigmatic references in the piyyutim. Most of the variation between the commentaries from different communities can be attributed to the diverse cultures of their compositions.

Ashkenazic and Tsarfatic Piyyut-Commentary

The piyyut-commentaries best known to modern scholarship are those that were composed in the high Middle Ages in Ashkenaz and Tsarfat. Piyyut-commentary served as an interface between the highly complicated and enigmatic piyyutim favored by the early Ashkenazic scholars who influenced the creation of a canon for the Ashkenazic Maḥzor and the medieval Jewish community. They define the medieval *status quaestionis* on piyyut-literature, dealing with single texts rather than with the genre. Given the fact that neither secular Jewish poetry nor theoretical treatises on poetry from Ashkenaz have come down to us, piyyut-commentary is the most important source for an assessment of the place of poetry in Jewish intellectual life in medieval western Europe. The diversity of the commentaries shows the varying criteria for a 'good' commentary defined by numerous groups within medieval Jewish society and thereby also attests to the vivid plurality of Ashkenaz.

Piyyut-commentary probably started with oral glosses on complicated or important piyyut-lines, transmitted in the study halls in Lotharingia and the Rhineland. It continued to be a literature of the study halls when it first was committed to writing in early 12th century Tsarfat. Rashi's younger contemporary and part time-student Josef Qara was probably the first scholar to write a piyyut-commentary, together with another member of Rashi's study hall, Shemaya, the secretary and student of Rashi.[10] Yet it may be that earlier written commentaries existed that were edited and incorporated into other texts so throughly that we cannot trace them at all, as might be concluded from the way Josef Qara quotes his uncle Menahem b. Ḥelbo. From Tsarfat action moved to Ashkenaz where Ephraim b. Jacob of Bonn and Eliezer b. Natan wrote their piyyut-commentaries in the middle of the 12th century, with Ḥasidei Ashkenaz like Elazar b. Yehuda of Worms and his pupil Abraham b. Azriel continuing and developing the genre in the 13th century. At the same time piyyut-commentaries were compiled and edited in Tsarfat as well. Both in Ashkenaz and in Tsarfat some of the authors/ compilers that we know by name were associated with the Tosafist movement, but most commentaries were transmitted without names of authors and compilers and cannot easily be attributed to a known group. After the 13th century, piyyut-commentaries continued to be copied and edited in Ashkenaz by compilers whose names are not known. When names are mentioned they can only rarely be associated with persons known from other sources. This is unique in Ashkenazic and Tsarfatic piyyut-commentary. In contrast, in most of the other rites the scholars who wrote piyyut-commentary are known for other literary works as well.

Few piyyut-commentaries from the Ashkenazic-Tsarfatic tradition have been edited by modern scholarship. After initial scholarly interest in the 19th century and the edition of ערוגת הבושם by E.E. Urbach in 1939, renewed research on these texts has only been appeared over the past two decades.

---

[10] A. Grossman, חכמי צרפת הראשונים, Jerusalem, Magnes, 1995, p. 529–531.

Best known among the Ashkenazic piyyut-commentaries is a work called ערוגת הבושם, the "Spice Garden", compiled by Abraham b. Azriel, a Bohemian follower of the Ḥasidei Ashkenaz movement, pupil of Yuda b. Samuel heḤasid and Elazar b. Yehuda of Worms and teacher of Isaac b. Mose of Vienna (author of the אור זרוע, "Light is Shed", Novellae). ערוגת הבושם, written in the first half of the 13th century, relies to a great extent on earlier compilations, while adding sources from the library of Ḥasidei Ashkenaz and many original interpretations. It owes its fame mainly to the fact that it was the first and the longest of the few published piyyut-commentaries and that its introductory volume was for a long time the only study of the historical development of piyyut-commentary.[11] Abraham b. Azriel belonged to a group that transmitted esoteric lore and showed a fondness for exegetical devices that are not meant to reveal the literal sense, including *gematriya* (comparison of numerical values) and *notarikon* (reading the word as abbreviation), as is reflected in the piyyut-commentary he edited. Compared to ערוגת הבושם, the bulk of Ashkenazic and Tsarfatic piyyut-commentary seems to be oriented more to the lexical meaning of single words or phrases and the reconstruction of the Biblical and Midrashic background to which a piyyut refers.[12] Very few Ashkenazic commentators used *gematriyot* and similar exegetical devices regularly, most *gematriyot* in piyyut-commentaries by non-Ḥasidei Ashkenaz commentators and compilers were taken from Midrashic sources. The importance of ערוגת הבושם cannot be denied. The fact that it is transmitted in two manuscripts—albeit with great variants both in the single commentaries and in the composition of the work—is only one of the factors that stress its importance. But the comparisons with other commentaries that Urbach began in his introductory volume need to be continued in a systematic way. Only then will we be able to to place Abraham b. Azriel and his work into his proper context of a fruitful genre that had already developed and changed for more than a century before him and continued to develop and change long after his time.

Some of Urbach's assumptions on piyyut-commentary and its authors have been challenged in recent years.[13] Especially the ascription of complete collections or even commentaries on single piyyutim to individual authors—

---

[11] D. Kaufmann, Aus der vatikanischen Handschrift von Abraham ben Asriel's Machsorcommentar, *Magazin für die Wissenschaft des Judenthums*, 13, 1886, pp. 129–160; E. E. Urbach (ed), ספר ערוגת הבושם. כולל פירושים לפיוטים, Jerusalem, Mekize Nirdamim, 1939; E. E. Urbach, מילואים ותיקונים לס' ערוגת הבושם ג' וד', *Qiryat Sefer*, 41, 1966, pp. 17–18.

[12] For a taxonomy of mainstream Ashkenazic and Tsarfatic piyyut-commentary cp. E. Hollender, Hebräische Kommentare hebräischer liturgischer Poesie: Eine Taxonomie der wichtigsten Kommentarelemente, in *Der Kommentar in Antike und Mittelalter. Beiträge zu seiner Erforschung*, Leiden, Boston, Köln, Brill, 2002, pp. 163–182, and my forthcoming monograph on Ashkenazic and Tsarfatic Piyyut-Commentary as Compilatory Literature.

[13] A. Grossman, הרקע לצמיחת פרשנות הפיוט בגרמניה ובצרפת במאה הי"א, in ספר יובל לשלמה סימונסון, Tel Aviv, Tel Aviv University, 1993, pp. 45–72.

even those brought forward by Urbach's critics—have to be reexamined very carefully. For example Hamburg Staats- und Universitaetsbibliothek Cod. hebr. 17/2 (Steinschneider 152) cannot be ascribed completely to Ephraim b. Jacob of Bonn—as Urbach did—even if it contains some of his commentaries and many of his liturgical rulings. Budapest Magyar tudomanyos akademia, MS. Kaufmann A 400 has been regarded as a parallel to Hamburg 17, which is true for many of the commentaries copied therein, but it does contain a different selection of commentaries and seems to reflect a slightly different local rite. The commentary in Maḥzor Nuremberg (MS Schocken 24100) is often closely related to ערוגת הבושם but the similarity is limited to certain piyyutim.[14] The commentaries on the Maḥzor attributed to Eliezer b. Natan in different manuscripts and printed Maḥzorim vary to such a degree that most of them cannot be ascribed to him, with the possible exception of the commentary on the Hoshaanot and a few yotserot that have usually been transmitted together.[15]

In the manuscripts, very few commentaries are directly ascribed to individual commentators in the rubrics. Since a comparison of different commentaries on the same piyyut ascribed to the same author can reveal vast differences, medieval ascription can not always be trusted. Ascriptions of single commentary elements in the manuscripts are more common and probably more reliable, since the elements were not changed by later editors. Only few commentators have developed a distinctive style that can be used to identify their works. Among them are Elazar b. Yehuda of Worms, whose abundant use of *gematriyot* and esoteric exegetical devices prevails not only in his prayer-commentaries but also in his piyyut-commentaries, and Ephraim b. Jacob of Bonn, whose commentaries combine a wealth of short references to Midrashim with quotes from rare narrative sources and discussions of grammatical questions that often criticize the מחברת of Menahem b. Saruq and in some cases even Dunash b. Labrat. A. Grossman has argued that the styles of Josef Qara and Shemaya are easily distinguishable as well. He claims a threefold pattern of commentary for Josef Qara that starts with the lexical explanation of the single words, continues with a paraphrase of the piyyutic line, and finally proceeds to the Midrashic context of the piyyutic line or stanza. Grossman also argued that Shemaya's commentary can be identified by the references to Rashi that are typically phrased אמר ר' where ר' is understood as abbreviation of רבי with the meaning of "my teacher" as opposed to the honorary title.[16] But since the commentaries of these important scholars are not transmitted in autographs but rather in edited versions, it is impossible to ascribe whole commentaries to either of them, as close comparison between different commentaries on the same piyyutim shows.[17]

---

[14] B. Ziemlich, *Das Machsor Nürnberg. Ein Beitrag zur Erforschung des Ritus und der Commentarliteratur des Deutschen Machsor*, Berlin, 1886, p. 47–76.

[15] I. Levine, פירוש על המחזור המיוחס לראב"ן, *Tarbiẓ*, 29, 1960, pp. 162–175.

[16] Grossman, *חכמי צרפת*, 383–385.

[17] Examples will be discussed in detail in my forthcoming monograph.

Ashkenazic and Tsarfatic piyyut-commentary was 'open text' in so far as it was edited by the compilers and copyists according to the needs of the audience, with little regard for the creative work of original commentators. Unlike the so-called Qara-commentary on Job and the Ḥizquni,[18] many individual piyyut-commentaries tend to be expanded and edited versions of one commentary-source that was supplemented by additional material from different sources, mostly Midrashim, Bible commentaries and grammatical treatises. Supplementary sources that can clearly be identified as piyyut-commentaries were also used. They can be introduced by phrases like פרוש אחר or עניין אחר, but they can also be inserted without marker. Only in a few cases where we have enough different commentaries detailed comparisons may allow for an identification of parts of a commentary-text as belonging to an assumed original commentary and its probable author or as belonging to a different source. This is one of the reasons why very few authors of Ashkenazic and Tsarfatic piyyut-commentaries have been named in this *Clavis Commentariorum of Hebrew Liturgical Poetry*, and even these ascriptions should be regarded cum grano salis—they may reflect earlier stages of the text than that transmitted in the commentary as is available today. Since the texts were open to all kinds of editing, we may assume that the exact shape a commentary has in any given manuscript was intended by the editor.

In a few cases, we can identify the compiler of a manuscript of piyyut-commentary who shaped the text from the manuscript itself. This ascription can rely on the identification of the editing copyist in the colophon or through insertions like "אני פלוני מצאתי" (I, so-and-so, have found ...) and similar phrases. Especially when this allows us to place the manuscript in an historical setting, such commentaries can be used for research on the development of Ashkenazic and Tsarfatic Judaism and its teachings. One example comes from Aaron b. Hayyim haKohen, who compiled a piyyut-commentary that is transmitted in autograph in Bodleian Library MS Laud. Or. 271 (Neubauer 1206), written in 1227.[19] A second manuscript (Bodleian Library MS Bodl. Or. 109 (Neubauer 1209)) is ascribed to him, which—if it is not an autograph—was copied in the 13th century. Aaron b. Hayyim haKohen was a nephew of the French Tosafist Jacob the Martyr of Corbeil, whose brother Yuda is supposed to have been a member of a circle of Ḥasidei Ashkenaz. Aaron b. Hayyim haKohen clearly lived in Northern France, and accordingly, the commentaries compiled by him have been assigned to Minhag Tsarfat in the Clavis Commentariorum of Hebrew Liturgical Poetry. In their combination of piyyutim his compilations often show more parallels to Minhag Ash-

---

[18] Cp. S. Japhet, The Nature and Distribution of Medieval Compilatory Commentaries in the Light of Rabbi Joseph Kara's Commentary on the Book of Job, in *The Midrashic Imagination. Jewish Exegesis, Thought, and History*, Albany, State University of New York Press, 1993, pp. 97–130, and S. Japhet, פירוש החזקוני לתורה, ספר היובל לרב מרדכי ברויאר. אסופת מאמרים במדעי היהדות, in דמותו שלל החיבור ולמטרתו, Jerusalem, Akademon, 1992, pp. 91–111.

[19] A. Grossman, פירוש הפיוטים לר' אהרון בר' חיים הכוהן, in *מחקרים בתרבות באורח חיים. ישראל מוגשים לאהרון מירסקי*, Lod, Habermann Institut, 1986, pp. 451–468.

kenaz than to later manuscripts of Minhag Tsarfat. However, in the choice of commentary elements to be transmitted they reflect the surrounding culture of early 13th-century France, including the knowledge of topics discussed in Christian theological circles in those days. For example Aaron b. Hayyim haKohen, who had a keen interest in Midrashim and narratives and knew the piyyut-commentaries of Ephraim b. Jacob of Bonn, did not include the well-known narrative of Amnon of Mayence in his commentaries on ונתנה תוקף, the famous piyyut for Musaf Rosh haShana. In contrast, it was transmitted in many Ashkenazic piyyut-commentaries from the same time and is—following the tradition in the אור זרוע—usually ascribed to Ephraim b. Jacob of Bonn.[20]

This is only one example of the differences between Ashkenazic and Tsarfatic piyyut-commentaries that have not yet been fully researched. Another characteristic of the Tsarfatic commentaries seems to be a greater disposition for polemics against Christianity, namely in the later Tsarfatic commentaries.[21] The different socio-political situation, and perhaps a greater familiarity among French Jewish scholars with Christian teachings, paved the road for more or less subtle polemics and counterdrafts. There is a high probability that in-depth research on Tsarfatic piyyut-commentary will find distinct characteristics both in content and in style that distinguish it from Ashkenazic piyyut-commentary and will thus shed new light on the cultural lines of communication and borders in medieval Europe.

All Ashkenazic and Tsarfatic piyyut-commentaries strive to explain the words of the piyyut to their audiences. Beyond that, they differ widely. Some commentaries focus on lexical explanations in Hebrew, some add explanations in Judeo-German or Judeo-French, rarely in Judeo-Slavic. Some commentaries simply identify Biblical references in piyyutim, while others add commentaries on these verses or place them into the historical narrative provided by Biblical exegesis. Some commentaries quote extensively from Midrashim; others seem to assume that the reader has the Midrashim at hand or knows them by heart after being reminded of the reference to a given Midrashic episode. Obviously, each compiler had his own interest when it came to the content of his commentaries, but the compilers also seem to have worked for different audiences and with various learning purposes in mind. Glossed Maḥzorim and Siddurim might have been used by Ḥazzanim when preparing for synagogue service, since correct pronunciation necessarily follows from understanding the text. Commentaries that quote Biblical verses in extenso, repeat large parts of Biblical exegesis, and copy out extensive passages from Talmud and Midrash seem to address an audience that is less learned but eager and willing to study. A possible Sitz im Leben could be the education of children or young people, similar to what S. Boynton assumes

---

[20] Cp. numbers 10937-10982 and the discussion of the Amnon-legend in L. Raspe, Jüdische Hagiographie im mittelalterlichen Aschkenas, forthcoming.

[21] Cp. A. Grossman, פולמוס אנטי־נוצרי בפירושיו של ר' יוסף קרא למקרא ולפיוט, *WCJS*, *9B 1*, 1986, pp. 71–78, for earlier polemics.

for Latin hymn-glosses.[22] Commentaries that refer to most Midrashim only briefly, quote rare works extensively, and discuss complicated grammatical questions were clearly addressed to a learned audience. The commentaries of Ephraim b. Jacob of Bonn exemplify this type. Many compilations—especially later ones—show an underlying tendency to dramatize the piyyutim and to resound their aggadic qualities by emphasizing the narrative aspect of piyyut-commentary. Commentaries in the tradition of Josef Qara, whose terse commentary-prose is saturated with lexical explanations, were later expanded into an often quite charming literature, uniting Midrashic episodes, *meshalim* and narratives from other sources with paraphrases and a limited number of lexical and grammatical explanations.[23] Elsewhere I have argued that this is a sign of shifting aesthetics: when the community was less likely to appreciate the complicated intellectual beauty of classic piyyutim, that is, when the intertextual references carefully concealed by the poets were not easily accessible to average member of the congregation, the sensuous enjoyment of piyyutim chanted in synagogue was enhanced by the intellectual pleasure of reading Midrashim, parables and narratives associated with and organized according to the piyyutim. The narrative commentaries took over part of the aesthetic value of the piyyutim.[24]

The differences between these types of piyyut-commentary are so great that they do not lead to a single explanation of why piyyutim were explained in writing and who was the audience of the commentaries. We have to assume a variety of different circumstances for the study of piyyut and accompanying commentary in Ashkenaz and Tsarfat. But the large number of manuscripts that contain piyyut-commentary gives ample evidence that a need for this genre was constantly felt in Ashkenaz and Tsarfat and that piyyutim were in fact studied and thereby understood.

The fact that hardly any manuscripts of piyyut-commentary from eastern Ashkenaz are known and none exist from later centers of eastern-European Jewish learning does not necessarily mean that piyyut was not studied there. Actually, very few liturgical manuscripts of any genre are extant from these areas, and from the 16th century printed books were used. Many printed Maḥzorim do contain piyyut-commentaries, about 250 editions were printed between the 16th and the 18th centuries and many more during the 19th century. Somewhere between the late Middle Ages and the Early Modern period, a change took place with regard to the audience for piyyut-commentary: this literature was no longer used in children's education and it disappeared from the studies of the scholars. The wide distribution of printed

---

[22] S. L. Boynton, *Glossed Hymns in Eleventh-Century Continental Hymnaries*, dissertation, Brandeis University, 1997.

[23] E. Hollender, Narrative Exegesis in Ashkenas and Zarfat: The Case of Piyyut-Commentary, in *Jewish Studies at the Turn of the Twentieth Century*, Proceedings of the 6th EAJS Congress, Leiden; Boston; Köln, Brill, 1999, pp. I, 429–435.

[24] E. Hollender, Eine permanente Renaissance? Zum status (quaestionis) von Pijjut-Kommentar, in *An der Schwelle zur Moderne. Juden in der Renaissance*, Leiden; Boston, Brill, 2003, pp. 25–50.

Maḥzorim with commentaries made piyyut-commentary a genre that was read in preparation for or during prayer services. It was popularized for a greater audience by dropping lexical and grammatical explanations in favour of paraphrases and narratives, and soon Yiddish commentaries and paraphrases of the piyyutim were added or even substituted for the commentaries. These were included in prayerbooks until the very end of the 19th century and helped those participants in synagogue services who did not understand linguistically complicated Hebrew poetry to enjoy its contents and beauty. These Yiddish commentaries and the Yiddish paraphrases that developed out of them soon spread to Germany as well, where they may have inspired the editors of 19th century Maḥzorim to include modern translations that ultimately took the place of commentaries.

Piyyut-Commentaries from other Communities

A different situation can be observed when it comes to piyyut-commentaries from other Jewish communities. Most of them are even less well-known to scholarly discourse today than those of the Ashkenazic tradition. The main commentary known from the Sephardic tradition was published in 1900, תשלום אבודרהם (The Completion of Abudraham, a commentary on piyyutim for Rosh haShana and Yom Kippur) by David b. Josef Abudarham.[25] He lived during the 14th century in Christian Andalusia and was probably a pupil of Jacob b. Asher, author of the ארבעה טורים. Jacob b. Asher had come from Ashkenaz to Toledo as a young person and is known to have brought Ashkenazic teaching to Sepharad. This connection of David b. Josef Abudraham to Ashkenazic teaching would account for his familiarity with a genre otherwise unknown in Sepharad. Abudarham is most famous for his commentary on the prayer-book, ספר אבודרהם (Book of Abudraham), which he wrote because "the customs connected with prayer have become varied from one country to another, and most of the people do not understand the words of the prayers, nor do they know the correct ritual procedures and the reasons for them." In his piyyut-commentary—as in his prayer-commentary—he drew on Ashkenazic and Sephardic sources. Stylistic similarities between his piyyut-commentary and the work of the Ashkenazic commentators of piyyut can easily be detected, although the mainly Sephardic piyyutim on which he commented generally required a different treatment than did the classical, Ashkenazic and Tsarfatic piyyutim commented on in central Europe.

Since the publication of תשלום אבודרהם in 1900 several more manuscripts of this text have been found which prove that the text was not greatly changed by later scribes, although commentaries on piyyutim that fell out of

---

[25] L. P. Prins (ed), ספר תשלום אבודרהם. והוא סדר עבודת יום הכפורים המיוחס ליוסי בן יוסי וגם פיוטים שונים של הפייטנים הגדולים עם פירוש גדול המפרשים רבינו דוד בר' יוסף בר' דוד אבודרהם, Berlin, Mekize Nirdamim, 1900.

INTRODUCTION

use seem to have been left out of later copies. Furthermore, a manuscript copied in North Africa contains commentaries that are not transmitted in the Sephardic manuscripts, which were probably added by later commentators. In the *Clavis Commentariorum of Hebrew Liturgical Poetry in Manuscript* these have nevertheless been ascribed to David b. Josef Abudarham, especially since no great variance in style could be detected. No research on this commentary has been published since the 1900 edition of the text, which contains variant readings and a few annotations by the editor, but lacks treatment of the piyyut-commentary, its method, its sources and the rite on which it is based. Even though a few other Sephardic piyyut-commentaries exist, most of them are generally unknown and have not yet been published,[26] which leaves the field of Sephardic piyyut-commentary *terra incognita* to be explored by future scholars.

One of the reasons why piyyut-commentary was less popular in Sepharad may have been this community's attitude towards the aesthetics of poetry. Sephardic poets began to write secular poetry in the Arabic style favored by the surrounding culture in Islamic Andalusia in the 10th century and continued the tradition of composing both secular and liturgical poetry for several centuries. Not all regulations for secular poetry were incorporated into Sephardic liturgical poetry, but some of these aesthetical guidelines were applied in Sephardic piyyutim and secular poetry. Following the model of the Arabs, Sephardic poets authored poetologies that offered criteria to judge literature and help on how to compose poetry. Sephardic poetology may have served one of the functions of Ashkenazic piyyut-commentary: it helped to decide what was good poetry. Additionally, the liturgical poetry of most Sephardic authors was far more biblical in its language and slightly less enigmatic than classical piyyutim, which is logical for an audience that knew biblical Hebrew well (and spoke another semitic language as *lingua franca*) and may not have needed that many explanations.

Even fewer commentaries from other communities have been published: the commentaries of Mose b. Hayyim Pesante on the Azharot of Salomo Ibn Gabirol and on the Hoshaanot according to the rite of Isaac Luria (haAri) were printed in the 16th century and have been transmitted in manuscript as well. The same holds true for the commentaries of Simon b. Tsemaḥ Duran from Algiers. His commentary on the Azharot of Salomo Ibn Gabirol, זוהר רקיע (Radiance of the Firmament), was transmitted in print and manuscript form, and even in an abridged version that survives in two manuscripts. Almost no Italian piyyut-commentaries were published, despite the fact that several commentators are known by name, including two from the late Middle Ages who commented on the Maḥzor according to Minhag Roma and several from Early Modern times who commented mainly on the Hoshaanot.

---

[26] For exemptions from this rule cp. S. Stern, קובץ מעשי, על סדר עבודה לר"י בן אביתור ידי גאונים קדמונים, J. Rosenberg, Berlin, Friedländer'sche Buchdruckerei, 1896, pp. 117–122, and Z. Malachi, and (ed), סדר עבודת יום הכפורים ליצחק אבן גיאת הספרדי, Lod, Habermann Institut, 1997, which also contains a medieval commentary on the Seder Avoda.

Italian printed Maḥzorim from the 16th and 17th centuries often contained commentaries, this practice was abandoned earlier than in central and eastern Europe. None of these commentaries have been studied by modern researchers. A few commentaries are extant in manuscripts and early prints of the Romaniote rite were used by the native Jewish communities of former Byzantium, but have not been researched. The same holds true for a 16th-century commentary on 13th-century Karaite piyyutim extant in four manuscripts.[27]

The commentary most often transmitted in manuscript is פעמון זהב ורמון (Golden Bell and Pomegranate), by the 17th-century Yemenite scholar and kabbalist Isaac b. Abraham Wanneh, who reformed the Yemenite prayer-book—called Tiklal—in accordance with the teachings of the Lurianic Kabbala and composed a commentary on prayers and piyyutim that was transmitted in many manuscripts. The commentary—usually called חידושין (Novellae)—combines lexical elements with homiletic and kabbalistic explanations. Since the Yemenite communities did not have access to printing presses, the Tiklal was first printed in Jerusalem in 1894-98. Manuscripts were copied into the 20th century. These manuscripts were included in the *Clavis Commentariorum of Hebrew Liturgical Poetry in Manuscript* even though they were produced in modern times. Other Yemenite scholars commented on the Maḥzor, as a whole or in part, and two manuscripts contain commentaries on the Yemenite *diwan*, mainly on the liturgical and paraliturgical poetry of the famous 17th-century poet Shalem Shabazi.

Yemenite piyyut-commentary as an active genre thrived mainly in the 17th century and is strongly influenced by the interest in pre-Lurianic and Lurianic Kabbala that prevailed in Yemen at that time. Since the Yemenite liturgy adopted piyyutim from various other traditions, Islamic Andalusia and Christian Ashkenaz among them, these commentaries invite research into the criteria that made piyyutim eligible for inclusion in the Tiklal. The hybrid character of these commentaries between lexical explanations and kabbalistic commentaries might yield insights into the intellectual history of Yemenite Judaism, even though these interesting piyyut-commentaries have not yet been published or been researched by contemporary scholars.[28]

Future Research

The *Clavis Commentariorum of Hebrew Liturgical Poetry in Manuscript* is a tool for further research, it aims to enable scholars to find manuscript com-

---

[27] The general lack of research on Karaite liturgy is even more regrettable when we take into account that an edition of many Karaite piyyutim has been available for many years now, cp. L. J. Weinberger, שירת הקודש לרבנים וקראים בדרום מזרח אירופה, Cincinnati, 1991.

[28] A first study of Wanneh's commentary on the Selihot contained in the Tiklal will hopefully evolve into a publication: P. Ghayyat, ראשית פרשנות הפיוט בתימן: פרשנותו של רבי יצחק ונה לפיוטי הסליחות, MA Thesis, Haifa, University of Haifa, 2003.

mentaries on piyyutim they know, commentaries on piyyutim by specific poets or commentaries written and compiled by particular scholars. As a tool it does not provide answers to scholarly questions concerning piyyut-commentary *per se*. Rather, as a register that encompasses commentaries from all different traditions in one large "bibliography", this work can serve as a starting point for new questions, among them those related to the liturgical rites represented in the various manuscripts. While the lists cannot substitute for a full study of the different liturgical rites and the piyyutim used therein, the *Clavis Commentariorum of Hebrew Liturgical Poetry in Manuscript* can help to clarify which piyyutim were considered to need of explanation by the different communities. It can provide first insights into the distribution of piyyutim within regional rites and across the borders of rites. One might ask why certain Sephardic piyyutim were commented on in later Tsarfatic commentaries and by the Yemenite commentators but never in Sepharad or Carpentras, where one would assume that they had been in use as well. A comparison of the different collections of commentaries from Tsarfat can provide material for a first sketch of how and when various piyyutim from Sepharad were introduced into Tsarfatic liturgy and which Ashkenazic piyyutim they replaced. A comparison of the number of extant copies of the commentary of Isaac b. Abraham Wanneh for different piyyutim might yield insights into the way the Tiklal developed and which of its parts were most popular.

On the other hand the lists of commentaries on some piyyutim invite research into the parallels and differences between the commentaries from unrelated communities. Piyyutim that were used in several communities might have been understood differently. On the other hand, some explanations might be so well known within the Hebrew-Aramaic textual tradition that they were employed in more than one commentary tradition. In the case of two commentators, both known for their interest in esoteric lore, who commented on the same piyyut in two geographically and historically separate communities, as happened with Abraham b. Azriel from 13th-century Ashkenaz and Isaac b. Abraham Wanneh from 17th-century Yemen, one might ask: did their interest in mysticism lead to similarities in their approach, unlike other commentaries that are not involved in speculative exegesis? Did Mordekhai b. Josef of Rocco Martino from Carpentras and Josef Garad from Sepharad, who lived in relatively close proximity to one another and wrote on similar piyyut–albeit in different times–, use similar methods and ask similar questions in their commentaries? Are there any similarities between the different non-Hebrew paraphrases of piyyutim? Were the same words glossed with non-Hebrew lexical explanations in different traditions of commentary?

On a regional level, one might ask how commentaries from the different branches of Minhag Ashkenaz differ. Which commentary elements were preferred by Ashkenazic commentators, which by Tsarfatic or Italian commentators? Have different sources been used, and can quotations from rare texts be used to describe the distribution of those texts? Within any regional tradition one could compare commentaries and attempt a reconstruction of transmission lines, to the extent possible given the limitations of the available data. How far were some commentaries known? If Abudarham's commentary was copied in North Africa and Simon b. Tsemaḥ Duran's commentary was transmitted in Yemen, what does this teach us about transcultural transmission? How closely were Ashkenaz and Sepharad connected? How many commentaries by Ephraim b. Jacob of Bonn did Aaron b. Hayyim haKohen know when he compiled his piyyut-commentary in 1227 in Tsarfat? B. Ziemlich tried to reconstruct the commentaries used by the compiler of the commentary in Maḥzor Nuremberg in 1884.[29] With the lists available now, it will be possible to conduct similar analyses for more Ashkenazic and Tsarfatic manuscripts and with the possibility to identify families of commentaries that share common traditions. We may be able to trace the movement of commentaries that were composed in Tsarfat, copied and edited in Ashkenaz, and then copied and reedited in Tsarfat.

Beyond questions concerned with the commentary itself piyyut-commentary may be used to study the variants of some piyyutim that were used in the different communities. It may even be possible to reconstruct piyyutim transmitted only partly or in illegible manuscripts.[30]

The *Clavis Commentariorum of Hebrew Liturgical Poetry in Manuscript* is a first survey of a vast literature hardly researched until now. May it serve as a key to uncover the hidden treasures of this long-neglected genre.

Disclaimer

The Clavis Commentariorum of Hebrew Liturgical Poetry in Manuscript is dedicated to the commentaries on Hebrew liturgical hymns (piyyutim) transmitted in manuscripts. It strives to include all commentaries of piyyutim transmitted in manuscripts that were meant for study and distribution, either in pre-print communities or as a substitute for printed editions that were rare or costly. The only deliberate exclusions are commentary manuscripts that were written by modern (18th-20th century) scholars in Europe and the US. These were typically written as preparations to editions of prayerbooks (like the commentaries of Wolf Heidenheim[31]) or as private notes for the understanding of the complicated poetic language and form.[32] With the exception

---

[29] Ziemlich, *Das Machsor Nürnberg*, 47–76.

[30] A first attempt at this was made by E. Hakohen, ח"י קרובה' אל תרחק ואסדך אמיתך', ספק קילירית לפורים, *קובץ על יד* N.S., *14*, 1998, pp. 1–40.

[31] E. g. Ms Amsterdam Rosenthaliana Rosenthal 139 (Fuks 103,2): Wolf Heidenheim, Notes on Yom Kippur Qatan, 19th century, IHM F. 3780.

[32] E. g. Warszaw - Zydowski Instytut Historyczny K 9/2, Baruch Isaak Lipschitz, Notes on Yotserot for Rosh haShana, 19th ct., IHM F. 11851; and Warszaw - Zydowski Instytut Historyczny 918, Meir Friedmann (איש שלום), G: On Prayers and Piyyutim, 19.-20. ct., IHM F. 30878.

of a few printed pages later bound into volumes of manuscripts, the *Clavis Commentariorum of Hebrew Liturgical Poetry in Manuscript* excludes all printed piyyut-commentaries. A Clavis Commentariorum for printed piyyut-commentary–or at least a detailed bibliography of printed Maḥzorim and Siddurim–is beyond the scope of this project but would merit its own volume.

This *Clavis Commentariorum of Hebrew Liturgical Poetry in Manuscript* does not include information on prayer-commentaries, since they represent a distinct, though related genre. It contains neither commentaries on the Pesaḥ-Haggada, nor commentaries on the "simanim," the rhymed mnemonics for the order of events during the Pesaḥ-Seder. The many commentaries on the prayers and the Pesaḥ-Haggada written throughout the ages and in different communities are separate genres and deserve complete and differentiated treatment.

Even though the *Clavis Commentariorum of Hebrew Liturgical Poetry in Manuscript* strives to be comprehensive by definition, it cannot be complete. The search for commentaries was conducted with the help of the Institute for Hebrew Manuscripts on Microfilm at the Jewish National and University Library, Jerusalem (IHM). This Institute constantly adds new sources of Hebrew manuscripts to its rich collection of microfilms. This volume represents the material catalogued at the IHM in September 2004. A few manuscripts that came to my knowledge later are listed in the appendix to the list of used manuscripts.

Some commentaries could not be identified since they do not indicate the piyyutim they comment on by incipits from the beginning of the piyyut, either because the scribe chose not to use incipits–because the commentary is transmitted only partly (in manuscript fragments, e.g. from bindings) , or because the commentator mixed prayers and piyyutim without indicating which texts he was referring to, like Isaac b. Todros of Barcelona in his commentary on the Sephardic Maḥzor.

I have tried to identify all piyyutim as accurately as possible. Nevertheless, mistakes are possible due to different reasons: (1) sometimes several piyyutim begin with the same words, (2) variants in the beginnings of piyyutim, and (3) lack of tools that might have helped to identify the piyyutim properly. I wish to acknowledge possible shortcomings in this work and invite readers to make their additions known to me (shira@rimon.de), to be published in the inevitable "Addenda" that characterize this kind of research.

How to read this Clavis Commentariorum?

The *Clavis Commentariorum of Hebrew Liturgical Poetry in Manuscript* is organized according to the works commented on, i.e. alphabetically according to the first line of each piyyut. This information is presented in Hebrew, followed by its identification number in Israel Davidson's אוצר השירה והפיוט, the name of the poet and the liturgical position of the piyyut. It is assumed that the reader is familiar with this type of information, therefore the entries in this volume do not elaborate on the piyyut beyond what can be found in the אוצר השירה והפיוט. In a few cases more than one liturgical position is indicated, since some piyyutim have been used in different positions. In particular the Yemenite Tiklal includes a great number of Sephardic piyyutim that were also used as Selihot.

After its initial identification, each piyyut is followed by a listing of manuscripts that include commentaries on it. Commentaries are ordered by liturgical rite. The identification of liturgical rites (Minhagim) for the manuscripts relies mainly on the data provided in the electronic catalogue of the Institute for Hebrew Manuscripts on Microfilm at the Jewish National and University Library, Jerusalem (IHM). Since many of the older (temporary) entries in this catalogue were copied from older printed catalogues without further verification, some of the ascriptions may be not completely accurate. Where mistakes in the Minhagim were obvious from the collection of piyyutim contained in the manuscripts, the identification was corrected. The specific Sephardic rites are not always differentiated; likewise, all manuscripts that were identified as belonging to a specific branch of the Ashkenazic rite like "Western Ashkenaz" or even "Worms" have been identified as "Ashkenaz." In some cases–especially with fragments–it is possible that manuscripts originally belonging to Minhag Tsarfat have been identified as Minhag Ashkenaz if sufficient data was lacking.

Minhag Tsarfat has been established as an independent rite, even though early Tsarfat used a rite that is very similar to Minhag Ashkenaz. But a tradition of piyyut-commentary can be established that reflects the relation of the French Jewish communities to their surrounding culture by the 13th century. Even manuscripts that were written in France but reflect the earlier French rite that contains more parallels with the rite of western Ashkenaz have been classified as "Tsarfat", since a difference in commentary style has to be assumed even in the early 13th century.

Within the rites, the manuscripts are sorted by their modern locations. Each manuscript is identified by the city and the collection where it is housed today, including call numbers and, in some cases, catalogue numbers that differ from the call numbers. The identification of the manuscripts follows the nomenclature of the manuscripts in the IHM catalogue: city - collection, call number." Cities are identified by their international names (e.g. Zurich instead of Zürich) and all accents in the names of collections have been omitted. Umlauts have been transcribed as ae, oe, ue. For the sake of easy identification, no abbreviations are used. The names of the manuscripts used in the *Clavis Commentariorum of Hebrew Liturgical Poetry in Manuscript* are usually identical to that in the electronic catalogue of the IHM, creating a unified system. General information on the manuscripts can be found in the list of manuscripts (p.21-46), where the call number of the microform of the manuscript kept at the IHM is also indicated. Since different types of copy exist, "F." indicates a microfilm, "PH" stands for "photostat" (this includes photocopies of Italian fragments) and "Fiche" is used for microfiche.

The identification of the manuscript is followed by its location in the manuscript. Wherever extant, the numbering within the body of the manuscript was used. Therefore, some manuscripts are counted by folio (f.) and side (a/b), others are counted by pages (p.). Page indication in manuscripts from the collection of the Biblioteca Palatina in Parma follows the external counter in the microfilms. If no page numbers exist in the manuscript, the pages were counted using the microfilm-frames. Occasional skipping of page-numbers has been noted. When a page-number was used more than once in a manuscript, this is indicated by bracketed small Roman numerals attached to the folio-number. In volumes that contain pages from more than one source, the reference identifies the complete volume, not the supposed sources.

The next item in each entry of the Clavis Commentariorum describes the general type of commentary. The abbreviations used are:
- C for "commentary": the commentary in a manuscript that does not generally contain the text of the piyyutim but only a commentary;
- M for "marginal commentary": a full commentary that accompanies a Maḥzor or Siddur or any other collection of piyyutim;
- G for "glosses": glosses on any number of phrases or words on the margins of a Maḥzor or Siddur;
- GI for "interlinear glosses": glosses on any number of phrases or words between the lines of a Maḥzor or Siddur;
- CG for "commentary glosses": a commentaries consist only of items that would be used as glosses in Maḥzor or Siddur-manuscripts;
- T for "translations": translations or paraphases of piyyutim into other Jewish languages, followed by the specific language. In a few cases, "T, Hebrew" describes the Hebrew paraphrase of an Aramaic piyyut. T and M often occur together, since some paraphrases were placed next to the piyyut. Non-Hebrew glosses were not marked as T unless they contained only lexical glosses.
- F for "fragment": added before the type of the commentary if the manuscript is a fragment. Fragments of piyyut-commentary have been found in various lengths, including single leaves from bindings, groups of single leaves, and even almost complete quires.

The name of the commentator is indicated only if the commentary is attributed to him in the manuscript or if other evidence clearly indicates his authorship. If a manuscript is ascribed to an author or compiler, all commentaries therein have been credited to this commentator, even if most Ashkenazic and Tsarfatic commentary manuscripts transmit compilations that draw from various sources. In these cases, the commentator is usually described as compiler. Not all compilers referred to in catalogue entries have been named, since their role in the shaping of the commentary is not often evident.

Multiple copies of a commentary by a single author will be grouped together as a distinct subgroup of the liturgical rite in question (e.g. Yemen, commentary by Isaac b. Abraham Wanneh). From the Ashkenazic rite, only Abraham b. Azriel, the compiler of ערוגת הבושם, and Eliezer b. Natan, have been singled out this way, since all other commentaries are compilations. Other commentators in this category are Mordekhai b. Josef of Rocco Martino, Eliyahu Carmi and Josef b. Abraham of Montelitz from Carpentras, Mose b. Hayyim Pesante, who commented on the Hoshaanot according to Minhag haAri; Simon b. Tsemaḥ Duran and some others who commented on Azharot; and several Yemenite commentators, most prominent among them Isaac b. Abraham Wanneh.

If the commentary is headed by a rubric, this will follow in the description of the commentary. Introductions, even short ones, have not been listed as rubrics, even if they serve that function in some cases.

Additional information is provided where this seemed necessary. The following information is usually given: (a) incipits that vary from the first word of the piyyut, (b) the lack of an incipit, (c) exeptionally short commentaries, (d) additional marginal notes that influence the appearance of the commentary, (e) if a commentary breaks off in the middle due to the end of a manuscript, and (f) those postscripts that do shed light onto the identity or the intentions of the commentator.

Commentaries that have been given scholarly editions or will appear as such soon have been annotated with brief information about the publications. Full information can be found in the bibliography. The main sources were two monographs, ערוגת הבושם, by Abraham b. Azriel, edited by E.E. Urbach, and תשלום אבודרהם, by David b. Josef Abudraham, published by L.Ph. Prins. A few commentaries have been published in articles in scholarly journals or collections. Despite my careful searching, there may be extant publications that have not been included in this volume. No annotations have been made to the facsimile-edition of Hamburg - Staats- und Universitaetsbibliothek Cod. hebr. 17 (Steinschneider 152) and Hamburg - Staats- und Universitaetsbibliothek Cod. hebr. 61 (Steinschneider 153), edited by Roth. For publications that cite short passages from piyyut-commentaries or deal with certain aspects of commentaries the reader is requested to consult the bibliography of this volume.

LIST OF MANUSCRIPTS

1. Alessandria - Archivio di Stato Fr. ebr. 12, Piyyut-commentary, fragment from binding, Minhag Ashkenaz, 13-14th ct., PH 7301.
2. Alessandria - Biblioteca Civica Fr. ebr. 2-9, Commentary on the Azharot of Eliyahu haZaqen b. Menahem, Minhag Ashkenaz, 13th ct., 37 fragmentary leafs, PH 7308.
3. Amsterdam - Universiteitsbibliotheek MS Rosenthal 190/2, f. 1a-9b (2nd count), לקוטי שמואל by Samuel b. David of Siena, commentary on אקדמות in Yiddish, Minhag Ashkenaz, 1771, F. 03794.
4. Berlin - Staatsbibliothek (Preussischer Kulturbesitz) Or. fol. 707 (Steinschneider 34), fragment from a piyyut-commentary, Minhag Ashkenaz, 13-14th ct., F. 02028.
5. Berlin - Staatsbibliothek (Preussischer Kulturbesitz) Or. Oct. 3567 (Berlin-Marburg 103), fragment of piyyut-commentary for Yom Kippur, Minhag Roma, not dated, F. 02014.
6. Berlin - Staatsbibliothek (Preussischer Kulturbesitz) Or. Qu. 361 (Steinschneider 51): Mahzor Ashkenaz with commentary, not dated, F. 17876.
7. Berlin - Staatsbibliothek (Preussischer Kulturbesitz) Or. Qu. 798-799 (Steinschneider 177): Mahzor Ashkenaz with commentary; 14-15th ct., F. 10053-54.
8. Berlin Staatsbibliothek (Preussischer Kulturbesitz) Or. Qu. 943, fragment of commentary on אם לפי בחרך, oriental, not dated, 2 leafs, Judeo-Arabic, F. 01861, F. 02192, PH 0011.
9. Berlin - Staatsbibliothek (Preussischer Kulturbesitz) Or. Qu. 1276 (Berlin-Tübingen 21): Piyyut-commentary, fragment from binding, Minhag Ashkenaz, not dated, F. 02191; PH 0270.
10. Bern - Burgerbibliothek A 409, Mahzor Tsarfat with mainly French glosses, 14-15th ct., F. 02298.
11. Bologna - Archivio di Stato MS Ebr. 253, Piyyut-Commentary, comparable to ערוגת הבושם, fragment from binding, Minhag Ashkenaz, 2 leafs, 14th ct., F. 47377, PH 6376.
12. Bologna - Archivio di Stato MS Ebr. 353, Piyyut-Commentary for Rosh haShana, fragment from binding, Minhag Ashkenaz, 2 leafs, 14th ct., F. 47377, PH 6375.
13. Braunschweig - Landesmuseum fuer Geschichte und Volkstum R 2386: Mahzor Ashkenaz with commentary (like printed edition Sulzbach 1699), 1741, F. 18894-5.
14. Brussels - Bibliotheque Royale de Belgique 4781/3, f. 177b-180b, Commentary on שיר היחוד, sephardic script, 1382, F. 03486.

15. Budapest - Magyar tudomanyos akademia, MS. Kaufmann A 384, Mahzor with commentary (Tripartite Mahzor I), Minhag Ashkenaz, 1322; F. 12668
16. Budapest - Magyar tudomanyos akademia, MS. Kaufmann A 399, Commentary on Mahzor Ashkenaz, compiled by Asher b. Jakob haLevi, not dated, Fiche 84.
17. Budapest - Magyar tudomanyos akademia, MS. Kaufmann A 400, Piyyut-Commentary, compiled by Asher b. Jakob haLevi, Minhag Ashkenaz, not dated, F. 12591.
18. Budapest - Magyar tudomanyos akademia, MS. Kaufmann A 405/2 , David b. Josef Abudarham, תשלום אבודרהם, Minhag Sepharad, not dated, F. 14727.
19. Cambridge - Trinity College F 12 16, f. 19b-60b, Mose b. Samuel Ibn Tibbon, Commentary on the Azharot of Salomo Ibn Gabirol, Minhag Sepharad, 15-16th ct., F. 12162.
20. Cambridge - University Library Add. 377,3/4 (Reif SCR 157), f. 55b-63b, Shabbetai b. Yeshayahu haKohen Bilbo, Piyyut-Commentary for Musaf of Pesah, Minhag Romania, 15th ct., F. 15872.
21. Cambridge - University Library Add. 394 (Reif SCR 461), 1) Commentary on Yotserot, Selihot, Hoshaanot, 2) Commentary on some Yotserot, 3) Fragment (1 leaf) of commentary on שושן עמק, Minhag Ashkenaz, 14-15th ct., F. 16312.
22. Cambridge - University Library Add. 504,1, Piyyut-Commentary, Minhag Ashkenaz, 14-15th ct., F. 16797.
23. Cambridge - University Library Add. 561.1 (Reif SCR 2258), Siddur Minhag Tsarfat with commentary on the margins, 14th ct., F. 16849.
24. Cambridge - University Library Add. 858,12/5 (f. 13b-46a), Prayer-commentary by Elazar b. Yehuda of Worms with commentary on Hoshaanot, Minhag Ashkenaz, 15th ct., F. 17013.
25. Cambridge - University Library Add. 858,2/5 (f. 15a-16b), Elazar b. Yehuda of Worms, Commentary on האוחז ביד מדת משפט, Minhag Ashkenaz, 14-15th ct., F. 17013
26. Cambridge - University Library Dd. 2.30, Selihot with short commentary on the margins, Minhag Ashkenaz, 14th ct., F. 15913.
27. Cambridge - University Library Oo. 6.71.6, Commentary on the Azharot of Salomo Ibn Gabirol, eastern Minhag, incomplete, 3 leafs, 17-18th ct., F. 16286.
28. Cambridge - University Library Or. 785, Mahzor Ashkenaz for Rosh haShana, Yom Kippur, Sukkot, with glosses, 14-15th ct., F. 18716
29. Cambridge - University Library Or. 790, Commentary on prayers and Hoshaanot, Minhag Ashkenaz, 13-14th ct., end missing, F. 18721.
30. Cambridge - University Library, Taylor Schechter Collection Misc. 33/3, Mahzor Minhag Ashkenaz without Rosh haShana and Yom Kippur with glosses by later hand, 14th ct., incomplete, F. 19672.
31. Cambridge (Mass.) - Harvard University 067, Mahzor Yamim Noraim with glosses, Minhag haAri, 1819 (?), F. 34476.

32. Chicago-Spertus College of Judaica D 1, Tiklal with commentary פעמון זהב ורמון by Isaac b. Abraham Wanneh, Minhag Yemen, 1664, F. 40251.
33. Chicago-Spertus College of Judaica D 10, Tiklal with commentary on the Azharot of Salomo Ibn Gabirol and on the Hoshaanot, Minhag Yemen, 18th ct., F. 40259.
34. Chicago-Spertus College of Judaica D 2, 2nd part of Tiklal with commentary פעמון זהב ורמון by Isaac b. Abraham Wanneh, Minhag Yemen, 1660, F. 40252.
35. Cincinatti - Hebrew Union Collge 291, Piyyut-Commentary סדרא דקדושה by Josef b. Abraham of Montelitz; Minhag Carpentras, 18th ct., F. 18242.
36. Cincinnati - Hebrew Union College 199, Tiklal with glosses on the margins, Minhag Yemen, 1646, F. 50839.
37. Cincinnati - Hebrew Union College 246/1, Mordekhai b. Josef of Rocco Martino, Commentary of piyyutim for the 4 fastdays and the 4 parashiyot, Minhag Carpentras, 1783, F. 18197.
38. Cincinnati - Hebrew Union College 275, Collection, contains מנחת יעקב, a commentary on the shabbat-songs of Isaac Luria by Jacob b. Raphael haLevi, Minhag haAri, 19th ct., F. 18226.
39. Cincinnati - Hebrew Union College 357/1, Siddur Rosh haShana with commentary אליהו זוטא by Eliyahu Carmi and סדרא דקדושא by Josef b. Abraham of Montelitz, Minhag Carpentras, 1733, F. 18330.
40. Cincinnati - Hebrew Union College 392, Mahzor Minhag Carpentras Yom Kippur with short commentary, 1683, F. 18674.
41. Cincinnati - Hebrew Union College 398, Diwan of R. Shalem Shabazi with commentaries by Yehuda b. Josef Guzpan and Shalom Shekh, Minhag Yemen, 18-19th ct., F. 18680.
42. Cincinnati - Hebrew Union College 429/1, f. 1a-57b: Mahzor Minhag Carpentras for Rosh haShana with short commentary, 17th ct., F. 18790.
43. Cincinnati - Hebrew Union College 436, Siddur Minhag Ashkenaz with some glosses, 1435, F. 18797.
44. Cincinnati - Hebrew Union Collge 490, David b. Joseph Abudarham, תשלום אבודרהם for Yom Kippur, Minhag Sepharad, 15th ct., F. 19025.
45. Cincinnati - Hebrew Union College 559/2, Ephraim b. Jacob of. Bonn, תא שמע מארי עלמא צלותא שפירא with Hebrew paraphrase, Minhag Italia, 18th ct., F. 19484.
46. Copenhagen - The Royal Library Cod. Sim. Hebr. 94, Commentary on אחד מי יודע, Minhag Ashkenaz, 18th ct., F. 06904.
47. Cremona - Archivio di Stato (Archiva Notarile) 68, Ephraim b. Jacob of Bonn, Prayer-Commentary, fragment containing commentary on Hoshaanot, Minhag Ashkenaz, 14th ct., F. 34136, PH 4915.
48. Darmstadt - Hessisches Landes- und Hochschulbibliothek Cod. Or. 15, Mahzor Ashkenaz with commentary for some piyyutim for Rosh haShana, Frankfurt am Main, 1728, F. 12701

49. Darmstadt - Hessisches Landes- und Hochschulbibliothek Cod. Or. 25/55, f. 110a, Commentary on האוחז ביד מדת משפט, esoteric, Minhag Ashkenaz, 14th ct., F. 12695.
50. Erlangen - Universitaetsbibliothek 1270/6 (Roth 88), Fragment of piyyut-commentary, Minhag Ashkenaz, 13-14th ct., F. 35867.
51. Erlangen - Universitaetsbibliothek 2601 (Roth 67), Mahzor Ashkenaz with marginal commentary by later hand, margins cut, 14-15th ct., F. 35872.
52. Firenze - Biblioteca Medicea Laurentiana Plut. 44.13/6, f. 92a-92b, Elazar b. Yehuda of Worms, Commentary on האוחז ביד מדת משפט, esoteric, Minhag Ashkenaz, 15-16th ct., F. 17831.
53. Forli - Archivio di Stato 4, Fragment of Commentary on Selihot, Minhag Ashkenaz, 14th ct., PH 6977.
54. Frankfurt a M - Stadt- und Universitaetsbibliothek Fol. 16 (Merzbacher 95), Abraham b. Azriel, ערוגת הבושם, 13-14th ct., F. 41160.
55. Frankfurt a M - Stadt- und Universitaetsbibliothek Oct. 121/1 (Merzbacher 105), f. 2b-25a, Commentary on שיר היחוד, Minhag Ashkenaz, 15th ct., F. 26467.
56. Frankfurt a M - Stadt- und Universitaetsbibliothek Oct. 227, f. 2a-182a, Siddur Minhag Ashkenaz with marginal commentary, 15-16th ct., F. 23165.
57. Frankfurt a M - Stadt- und Universitaetsbibliothek Oct. 134, Siddur Minhag Sepharad, includes Azharot by Salomo Ibn Gabirol with commentary by Isaak ben Todros, Minhag Sepharad, 15th ct., F. 23152.
58. Friedberg - Stadbibliothek und Stadtarchiv Fragm. Hebr. 20, Fragment of piyyut-commentary, Minhag Ashkenaz, 14th ct., F. 27934.
59. Fulda - Hessische Landesbibliothek A 3 II, Piyyut-commentary for Yom Kippur and Sukkot, compiled by Josef, Minhag Ashkenaz, 12th ct., F. 02143.
60. Goettingen - Niedersaechsische Staats -und Universitaetsbibliothek Fragm. 788, Commentary on אדיר דר מתוחים for Shabbat haGadol, Minhag Ashkenaz, 13-14th ct., F. 18700.
61. Graz - Universitaetsbibliothek 1703\195, Commentary on Selihot for Erev Rosh haShana, Fragment, 13-14th ct., F. 30369, PH 0404\27.
62. Hamburg - Staats- und Universitaetsbibliothek Cod. hebr. 12 (Steinschneider 102); Mahzor for Yamim Noraim, Minhag Ashkenaz, 14-15th ct., F. 26276.
63. Hamburg - Staats- und Universitaetsbibliothek Cod. hebr. 17/2 (Steinschneider 152), f. 6b-178b, Piyyut-Commentary, Minhag Ashkenaz, 1318, F. 26278.[1]
64. Hamburg - Staats- und Universitaetsbibliothek Cod. hebr. 40b (Steinschneider 110), Mahzor Ashkenaz for Yamim Noraim and Sukkot, with glosses, 14th ct., F. 00891.

---

[1] E. Roth (ed), *Staats- und Universitätsbibliothek Hamburg Handschrift Hebr 17 (Steinschneider 152–153)*, Faksimile, Jerusalem, 1972.

65. Hamburg - Staats- und Universitaetsbibliothek Cod. hebr. 40c (Steinschneider 111), Mahzor Ashkenaz with short commentaries in the margins, 15th ct., F. 00892.
66. Hamburg - Staats- und Universitaetsbibliothek Cod. hebr. 61 (Steinschneider 153): Eliezer b. Natan, Commentary on prayers and piyyutim, Minhag Ashkenaz, not dated, F. 26298.[2]
67. Hamburg - Staats- und Universitaetsbibliothek Cod. hebr. 62 (Steinschneider 154): Commentary on prayers and piyyutim, Minhag Ashkenaz, not dated, F. 26299.
68. Hamburg - Staats- und Universitaetsbibliothek Cod. hebr. 132 (Steinschneider 155): Commentary on prayers and piyyutim for Yamim Noraim and Sukkot, Minhag Ashkenaz, not dated, F. 26315.
69. Hamburg - Staats- und Universitaetsbibliothek Cod. hebr. 139 (Steinschneider 115), Mahzor Minhag Ashkenaz with commentary, 14-15th ct., F. 00971.
70. Hamburg - Staats- und Universitaetsbibliothek Cod. hebr. 225 : Mahzor Ashkenaz for Hanukka to Shavuot with commentary, 14th ct., F. 01035.
71. Hamburg - Staats- und Universitaetsbibliothek Cod. hebr. 233/2, f. 67a-99b, Qinot Tisha beAv with commentary, 14th ct., Minhag Ashkenaz, F. 01039.
72. Hamburg - Staats- und Universitaetsbibliothek Cod. hebr. 239a (Steinschneider 130), Piyyutim, partly with glosses, Minhag Ashkenaz, not dated, F. 01044.
73. Hamburg - Staats- und Universitaetsbibliothek Cod. hebr. 299/2, f. 3a, Commentary on the piyyut אדיר דר מתוחים, Minhag Ashkenaz, 17-18th ct., F. 26355.
74. Hamburg - Staats- und Universitaetsbibliothek, Ms. Levy 78/11, f. 288a-302a, Commentary on אלהים בישראל גדול יחודך, esoteric, not located, 1594, F. 01539.
75. Hamburg - Staats- und Universitaetsbibliothek, Ms. Levy 111, Simon b. Tsemaḥ Duran, ספר זוהר הרקיע (Commentary on the Azharot of Salomo Ibn Gabirol), 17th ct., eastern Minhag, F. 01557.
76. Holon - Yehuda Nahum 278, David b. Josef Abudraham, ספר אבודרהם, fragments, including commentary on Hoshaanot, not dated, F. 42096.
77. Jerusalem - Benayahu ז 25, Mahzor Minhag Sepharad Yom Kippur, כתר מלכות with commentary, 19th ct., F. 43920.
78. Jerusalem - Benayahu ז 26, Mahzor Minhag Sepharad Yom Kippur, כתר מלכות with commentary, 19th ct., F. 43921.
79. Jerusalem - Benayahu ז 27, Mahzor Minhag North Africa for Sukkot with commentary on the Hoshaanot, 19th ct., F. 43922.

---

[2] E. Roth (ed), *Staats- und Universitätsbibliothek Hamburg Handschrift Hebr 17 (Steinschneider 152–153)*, Faksimile, Jerusalem, 1972. Page numbering in the Clavis Commentariorum according to the resorted order by Roth.

80. Jerusalem - Benayahu ע 41, Yehoshua Raphael b. Israel Benvenisti, עבודה תמה, Commentary on Seder Avoda, esstern Minhag, 18-19th ct., F. 44762.
81. Jerusalem - Benayahu צ 155/2, f. 19b-25a, Commentary on חד גדיא in kabbalistic collection, Minhag Ashkenaz, 19-20th ct., F. 43654.
82. Jerusalem - Benayahu ק 165, kabbalistic collection, contains commentary on לך דודי, eastern Minhag, not dated, F. 72372.
83. Jerusalem - Benayahu ת 88, Tiklal with commentary, Minhag Yemen, not dated, F. 44883.
84. Jerusalem - Benayahu ת 261, Tiklal with commentary פעמון זהב ורמון by Isaac b. Abraham Wanneh, Minhag Yemen, 17th ct., F. 44213.
85. Jerusalem - Benayahu ת 282, Tiklal with commentary פעמון זהב ורמון by Isaac b. Abraham Wanneh, Minhag Yemen, Rada'a 1660, F. 44392.
86. Jerusalem - Benayahu ת 283, incomplete Tiklal with commentary פעמון זהב ורמון by Isaac b. Abraham Wanneh and parts of another commentary, Minhag Yemen, 17th ct., F. 44210.
87. Jerusalem - Benayahu ת 301, Tiklal with commentary, Minhag Yemen, 1611, F. 44216.
88. Jerusalem - Benayahu ת 414, Tiklal with commentary, Minhag Yemen, 1649, F. 73030.
89. Jerusalem - Israel Museum 180/78: Hoshaanot with commentary by Isaac b. Abraham Wanneh, Minhag Yemen, Saana, 19th ct., F. 34718.
90. Jerusalem - Jewish National and University Library Ms Heb 8° 3037: Mahzor Ashkenaz with commentary, 13th ct., (B 116).
91. Jerusalem - Jewish National and University Library Ms Heb 8° 4153: Commentary on yotserot and piyyutim compiled by Daniel ben Salomo haRofe, Minhag Roma, ca. 1480, (B 828) [= Pitigliano - Comunita' Israelitica 3, F. 02337].
92. Jerusalem - Makhon Ben Zvi 1156 (Tubi 155), Tiklal with commentary פעמון זהב ורימון by Isaac b. Abraham Wanneh, Minhag Yemen, 1661, F. 26699.
93. Jerusalem - Makhon b. Zvi 1168 (Tubi 157), incomplete Tiklal with commentary, Minhag Yemen, ca. 1650, F. 38105.
94. Jerusalem - Makhon Ben Zvi 1169 (Tubi 159), Tiklal with excerpts from commentary פעמון זהב ורימון by Isaac b. Abraham Wanneh, Minhag Yemen, 1661, F. 36052.
95. Jerusalem - Makhon Ben Zvi 1174 (Tubi 154), Tiklal with commentary פעמון זהב ורימון by Isaac b. Abraham Wanneh, Minhag Yemen, 1656, F. 38109.
96. Jerusalem - Makhon ben Zvi 1186 (Tubi 205), Hosha anot with commentary by Isaac b. Abraham Wanneh, Minhag Yemen, 19th ct., F. 36020.
97. Jerusalem - Makhon Ben Zvi 2464/1, Rahamim Nissim Yehuda Siroga, Commentary on Seder Avoda, Minhag Yemen, not dated, F. 36144.

98. Jerusalem - Makhon ben Zvi 2808, Samḥun b. Salomo Ḥaloah, פועל ישועות, Commentary on Hoshaanot, Minhag Yemen, 1886, F. 27627.
99. Jerusalem - Makhon Ben Zvi 4509, תפסיר כתר מלכות, Minhag Yemen, not dated, F. 37953.
100. Jerusalem - Makhon Ben Zvi 921, incomplete Commentary on כתר מלכות, only beginning, eastern Minhag, 19th ct., F. 38178.
101. Jerusalem - Michael Krupp 604, Tiklal with commentary פעמון זהב ורימון by Isaac b. Abraham Wanneh, Minhag Yemen, 17-18th ct., F. 71874.
102. Jerusalem - Michael Krupp 1758, Hoshaanot and Seder Simhat Tora, with commentary on Hoshaanot, Minhag Yemen, 19th ct., F. 73512.
103. Jerusalem - Michael Krupp 1990, Tiklal with commentary פעמון זהב ורימון by Isaac b. Abraham Wanneh, Minhag Yemen, 19th ct., F. 31533.
104. Jerusalem - Michael Krupp 2807, Piyyutim with commentary, Minhag Yemen, 19th ct., F. 73516
105. Jerusalem - Michael Krupp 2818, Piyyutim with commentary by Meir b. Mose Buchritz (בוכריץ), eastern Minhag, 19-20th ct., F. 73622.
106. Jerusalem - Michael Krupp 3391, Hoshaanot with commentary, Minhag Yemen, 19th ct., F.73891.
107. Jerusalem - Musad haRav Kook 325, Tiklal with commentary פעמון זהב ורימון by Isaac b. Abraham Wanneh, Minhag Yemen, 17th ct., F. 20812.
108. Jerusalem - Musad haRav Kook 327, Tiklal with commentary פעמון זהב ורימון by Isaac b. Abraham Wanneh, Minhag Yemen, 17th ct., F. 20815.
109. Jerusalem - Musad haRav Kook 330, Tiklal with commentary פעמון זהב ורימון by Isaac b. Abraham Wanneh, Minhag Yemen, 17th ct., F. 20809.
110. Jerusalem - Musad haRav Kook 334, Tiklal with commentaries, mainly extracted from פעמון זהב ורימון by Isaac b. Abraham Wanneh, Minhag Yemen, 17-18th ct., F. 22331.
111. Jerusalem - Musad haRav Kook 335, Tiklal with commentaries, Minhag Yemen, 1651, F. 22326.
112. Jerusalem - Musad haRav Kook 347, Tiklal with excerpts from פעמון זהב ורימון by Isaac b. Abraham Wanneh, Minhag Yemen, 17th ct., F. 20816.
113. Jerusalem - Musad haRav Kook 478: Benjamin b. Abraham Anav: פירוש אלפבטין, incomplete, Minhag Ashkenaz, 19-20th ct., F. 22786.
114. Jerusalem - Musad haRav Kook 952, Tikkun Hoshaanot with commentary, Minhag Yemen, 19th ct., F. 22792.
115. Jerusalem - Musad haRav Kook 1129, Azharot of Isaac b. Ruben Albargeloni with commentary, eastern Minhag, 18th ct., F. 21479.
116. Jerusalem - Safrai 1/4, Yehuda Leib Karlburg, אמרי דעת, Commentary on Brit Mila and its piyyutim, Minhag Ashkenaz, 19th ct., F. 32879.

117. Jerusalem - Sassoon 264, Tiklal with commentary, Minhag Yemen, 17th ct., F. 09898.
118. Jerusalem - Sassoon 902, Tiklal with commentary, Minhag Yemen, 17th ct., F. 09877.
119. Jerusalem - Sassoon 1158, Tiklal with commentary פעמון זהב ורימון by Isaac b. Abraham Wanneh, Minhag Yemen, 17th ct., F. 09826.³
120. Jerusalem - Sassoon 1174, Tiklal with commentary פעמון זהב ורימון by Isaac b. Abraham Wanneh, Minhag Yemen, 17th ct., F. 09778
121. Jerusalem - Sassoon 1216, Mose Nigrin, מלאכת עבודת הקדש (Commentary on סדר עבודה), Minhag Sepharad, 18-19th ct., F. 09218.⁴
122. Jerusalem - Schocken Institute 15791/7 (f. 56a-65b): Kabbalistic commentary on the piyyutim of Elazar birabbi Qallir for Rosh haShana and Yom Kippur, Minhag Ashkenaz, 15-16th ct., F. 45414.
123. Jerusalem - Schocken Institute 19623, Siddur Minhag Tsarfat (Troyes) with commentaries by Yehuda b. Eliezer Zvi, 1405-1407, F. 71912
124. Jerusalem - Schocken Institute 24100 / Mahzor Nuremberg with commentary, Minhag Ashkenaz, 1331, no microform at IHM, photostats at Schocken Library, Jerusalem.
125. Jerusalem - Schocken Institute 70014, Mahzor Minhag Sepharad Yom Kippur with commentaries, 17-18th ct., F. 45405.
126. Jerusalem - Schocken Institute 70027, Mahzor Minhag Corfu, contains one commentary, Venice, 16-17th ct., F. 45423.
127. Jerusalem - Schocken Institute 70028, Tiklal with commentaries, incomplete, Minhag Yemen, 1656, F. 45331.
128. Jerusalem - Yehiel haLevi 4, Tiklal with commentary פעמון זהב ורמון by Isaac b. Abraham Wanneh, Minhag Yemen, 17th ct., F. 39593.
129. Jerusalem - Yehoshua Yakobovitz 2, Commentary on Seder Avoda Yom Kippur, not dated, F. 73875.
130. Karlsruhe - Badische Landesbibliothek, Schwarzach 20 (Roth 226): Fragment of commentary on Selihot, Minhag Ashkenaz, 14th ct., F. 18772; PH 3819.
131. Klosterneuburg - Stiftsbibliothek St. Augustini 271, Fragment of Mahzor-commentary, Minhag Ashkenaz, not dated, F. 09991, PH 2171/9.
132. Koblenz - Staatsarchiv Abt. 701, Nr. 759,5,7: Fragment of Mahzor-commentary, Minhag Ashkenaz, 14th ct., F. 18668.
133. Koblenz - Staatsarchiv Abt. 701, Nr. 759,5,8: Fragment of Mahzor-commentary, Minhag Ashkenaz, 14th ct., F. 18668.
134. Krakow - Biblioteka Jagiellonska Fr. 4: Fragment of piyyut-commentary, Minhag Ashkenaz, 14th ct., F. 41995; PH 5402.

---

³ The manuscript also commentaries on dirges (pp. 276-283) and on poetical versions for the ceremony of circumcision (oo. 445-449), but these are not contained in the Clavis Commentariorum.

⁴ Cp. the edition ספר מלאכת קדש, Lakewood 1999, and the edition אתה כוננת, published 1991 in Toronto.

135. Krakow - Biblioteka Jagiellonska Fr. 629: Fragment of piyyut-commentary, Minhag Ashkenaz, 14th ct., F. 41995; F. 35747; PH 5402.
136. Leeds - Brotherton Library, MS Roth 60, Brit Shalom, including the piyyut שמע נא קהלי והקשיב לקולי with commentary, Minhag Italia, Pesaro, 17-18th ct., F. 15292.
137. Leeds - Brotherton Library, MS Roth 711/6, f. 40b-42b: Mose Nahman, Commentary on חד גדיא, Minhag Italia, 17-18th ct., F. 15523.
138. Leiden - Bibliotheek der Rijksuniversiteit Cod. Or. 4772, Azharot of Menahem b. Mose Tamar with commentary and preface by the author, Minhag Romania, 16th ct., F. 17373.
139. Linz - Oberoesterreichische Landesbibliothek 570, fragment of Mahzor Ashkenaz, with commentary, from binding, 14th ct., F. 30710, PH 4256.
140. London - Beth Din & Beth Hamidrash 6,9, f. 148ff: Benjamin b. Abraham Anaw, פירוש אלפבטין (Pijjut ארכין שלית עליאה ותתאה); 13. Jh.; F. 04675.
141. London - British Library Add. 11639 (Margoliouth 1056): Siddur Minhag Tsarfat with commentaries, late 13th ct., F. 04948 G.[5]
142. London - British Library Add. 18695 (Margoliouth 683): Piyyut-commentary in Yiddish, Minhag Ashkenaz, 16-17th ct., F. 04981.
143. London - British Library Add. 19778, f. 35b-38a, Commentary of Meir haMeili of Narbonne on the difficult words in the Hoshaanot of Josef Ibn Abitur, Minhag Narbonne, 1476, F. 04998.[6]
144. London - British Library Add. 19787 (Margolioth 697), Collection, 1 (f. 1a-2b), Commentary on the Azharot of Salomo Ibn Gabirol, incomplete, 2 (f. 3a-62b), Isaak ben Todros of Barcelona, Commentary on the Azharot of Salomo Ibn Gabirol, 3 (f. 63a-99), Simon b. Tsemaḥ Duran, ספר זוהר הרקיע (commentary on the Azharot of Salomo Ibn Gabirol), incomplete, 5 (f. 114a-119b): Natan b. Isaac, Commentary on the piyyut יום יצאה כלת עדנים by Zeraḥya b. Isaac haLevi, Minhag Sepharad, 15th ct., F. 05002.
145. London - British Library Add. 22431 (Margoliouth 662a), Mahzor Minhag Ashkenaz for Shavuot and Sukkot with commentary (Tripartite Mahzor II), 14th ct., F. 05061.
146. London - British Library Add. 27208 (Margolioth 654), Siddur Minhag Ashkenaz with commentary on Hoshaanot,14th ct., F. 05874.
147. London - British Library Add. 27556, Siddur Minhag Ashkenaz with commentary, 13-14th ct., F. 06091.
148. London - British Library Or. 10105/1, Azharot of Salomo Ibn Gabirol with commentary, Minhag Romania, 15-16th ct., F. 07467.

---

[5] Cp. S.Z. Leiman, JQR, 74 (1983-4), pp. 174-195. Facsimile edition with essays on the MS: The North French Hebrew miscellany, London: Facsimile Editions, 2003.

[6] Published within Sepher haMikhtam, ed. A. Sofer, NY 1959, pp. 150-163.

149. London - British Library Or. 10415, Mose b. Mordekhai Zakut, אדני אלהי ישראל אבינו with kabbalistic commentary, Minhag Italia, 18-19th ct., F. 07777.
150. London - British Library Or. 1054/7 (f. 31b) (Margolioth 1094/7), Astrological tabels on the yotser אלהינו אלהים אמת, Minhag Ashkenaz, 14th ct., F. 05933.
151. London - British Library Or. 11121/4, f. 113a-140b, Isaac b. Abraham Wanneh, פעמון זהב ורמון, Minhag Yemen, 17-18th ct., F. 08337, F. 06634.
152. London - British Library Or. 11122, Tiklal with commentary פעמון זהב ורמון by Isaac b. Abraham Wanneh and commentary תולעת יעאב by Meir Ibn Gabbai, Minhag Yemen, Radaa, 17th ct., F. 08338, F. 06953.
153. London - British Library Or. 11318/1, f. 1a-173a, Commentary on the prayers and piyyutim for Rosh haShana, Yom Kippur, and Sukkot, Minhag Ashkenaz, 1557, F. 08345, F. 06954.
154. London - British Library Or. 2735 (Margoliouth 663), Mahzor Tsarfat with commentary, 13-14th ct., F. 06386
155. London - British Library Or. 5066, Simon b. Tsemaḥ Duran, ספר זוהר הרקיע (Commentary on the Azharot of Salomo Ibn Gabirol), Minhag Sepharad, incomplete, 15-16th ct., F. 06469
156. London - British Library Or. 5554 B/14 (f. 23a-24b), Isaac b. Samuel haSephardi, Introduction and commentary on אם לפי בחרך צורנו באדם הזה הדל by Saadia Gaon, incomplete, Minhag Sepharad, not dated, F. 06517 G, PH 0468.[7]
157. London - British Library Or. 8682, Mahzor Minhag Tsarfat with interlinear glosses, 17th ct., F. 06570.
158. London - British Library Or. 9598, Mahzor Minhag Corfu, Musaf Yom Kippur with commentary, 18-19th ct., F. 06616.
159. London - British Library Or. 9951,2 (f. 18a-47b), Raphael Salomo b. Yakob haKohen Prato, Commentary on the Azharot of Salomo Ibn Gabirol, (shortened version of ספר זורה הרקיע by Simon b. Tsemaḥ Duran), Minhag Italia, 1535, F. 07010.
160. London - David Sofer 5, Commentary on prayer and piyyutim, Minhag Tsarfat, 1301, F. 70553, F. 72147.[8]
161. London - Hirschler - Dzialowski (bookdealers), Mahzor Minhag Ashkenaz for Yamim Noraim with commentary by Ḥ at Hazzan of Padova, 16th ct., F. 04484.
162. London - London School of Jewish Studies. Asher I.Myers collection 9, Mahzor Minhag Romania with commenatries, 14th ct., F. 05420.
163. London - Montefiore Library 124/21 (f. 110a-110b), Commentary on אלהינו אלהים אמת, Minhag Italia, 16th ct., F. 04636.

---

[7] Y. Tubi published the complete introduction in תעודה 14 (1998), p. 67.

[8] Cp. A. Z. Schwarz, Die hebräischen Handschriften in Österreich (ausserhalb der Nationalbibliothek in Wien), Leipzig, Verlag Karl W. Hiersemann, 1931, p. 146–151.

164. London - Montefiore Library 261, Eliezer b. Natan, Commentary on the Mahzor, Minhag Ashkenaz, 13-14th ct., F. 05226.
165. London - Montefiore Library 263, Isaak b. Todros of Barcelona, Commentary on the Azharot of Salomo Ibn Gabirol, copied from Paris - Biblioteque National Ms heb. 273 by Ber Goldberg, 19th ct., F. 05228.
166. London - Montefiore Library 297 (f. 2a-49a), Mose b. Samuel Ibn Tibbon, Commentary on the Azharot of Salomo Ibn Gabirol, Minhag Sepharad, 15-16th ct., F. 05249.
167. London - Montefiore Library 419 (f. 7a-8a), excerpt from Azharot with commentary, Minhag Romania, 15th ct., F. 05352.
168. London - Montefiore Library 479/22 (f. 410a-410b), Samuel b. Elisha of Schaar Arie, Commentary on the Yotser for Shabbat Hanukka, Minhag Italia, 1670, F. 06111.
169. London - Montefiore Library 50/2 (f. 67a-82b), Josef b. Josef Ibn Nahmiash, Commentary on Seder Avoda, Minhag Sepharad, 15th ct., F. 04570.
170. London - Valmadonna Trust 13, Tiklal with commentary פעמון זהב ורמון by Isaac b. Abraham Wanneh, Minhag Yemen, 1646, F. 09896.
171. London - Valmadonna Trust 267/19 (f. 149a-153b), Commentary on אלהינו אלהים אמת, Minhag Ashkenaz, 14th ct., F. 49133.
172. Lund - Universitetsbibliothek Ms. L.O. 2, Siddur Minhag Ashkenaz with commentary, 1407, F. 34100.
173. Manchester - John Rylands University Library, Ms. Gaster 4, Tiklal with commentary on Azharot of Salomo Ibn Gabirol and a few other piyyutim, Minhag Yemen, ca. 1637, F. 15984.
174. Manchester - John Rylands University Library, Ms. Gaster 5, Tiklal with commentary פעמון זהב ורמון by Isaac b. Abrahm Wanneh, Minhag Yemen, 1769, F. 15976.[9]

---

[9] The original Gaster card catalogue of the items from the Gaster collection that were aquired by the John Rylands Library does not include a number 5, the manuscript clearly bears a pencilled 5 on the first leaf. In addition to that number, a (newer?) pencilled "51" appears on the left upper corner of the first leaf. The conservator therefore marked the box containing the manuscript as "51". Alexander Samely, in his draft version of "A Preliminary Catalogue of the Hebrew Manuscripts in the John Rylands University Library", 1997, mentions that a lead pencil number "4" is found on each of the card boards between cover boards and paper, the one on the front carton board is crossed out and changed to "5". In Gaster's handlist, the entry for ms 5 reads "מחזיר Rome", and it is marked as being in the British Library; for ms 6 the entry reads "Siddur Yemen [very similar to 4] 315 fol; also this item is marked BM (British Museum). According to the description in W. H. Greenburg, The Haggadah according to the Rite of Yemen ..., London (David Nutt) 1896, pp. xxiii-xxvi ms Gaster 6 is not identical with this manuscript. Samely decided to designate it as Gaster 5Add, cp. Samely, "The Interpreted Text", note 12.

175. Manchester - John Rylands University Library, Ms. Gaster 733, Mahzor Tsarfat with commentary on a few piyyutim, 13-14th ct., F. 16013.
176. Marseille - Mlle. Odette Valabregue [1], 3 (f. 37a-51a): Mose b. Samuel ibn Tibbon, Commentary on the Azharot of Salomo Ibn Gabirol, 4 (f. 51a-80a): Isaak b. Mordekhai Qimhi, Commentary on his Azharot, Minhag Carpentras, 1745, F. 34204.[10]
177. Milano - Ambrosiana X 230 Sup., Mahzor Minhag Italia with commentary by Ḥat Hazzan of Padova, 1584, F. 12646.
178. Modena - Archivio Capitolare di Modena 98.1, Fragment from Mahzor Minhag Ashkenaz with commentary, 13-14th ct., PH 6738, F. 72450.
179. Modena - Archivio della Curia Arcivescovile di Modena 58, Fragment from Siddur Minhag Ashkenaz with commentary, 13-14th ct., PH 6776.
180. Modena - Archivio di Stato 27, Fragment of Mahzor Roma with commentary, 14-15th ct., PH 7161.
181. Montreal - Elberg 203, Fragment from Tiklal with commentary עץ חיים by Yiḥya b. Josef Tsalaḥ, Minhag Yemen, 19th ct., F. 40728.
182. Moscow - Russian State Library, Ms. Guenzburg 111/10 (f. 181a-217b), Mose b. Samuel Ibn Tibbon, Commentary on the Azharot of Salomo Ibn Gabirol, incomplete, Minhag Sepharad, 1468, PH 3999, F. 06791.
183. Moscow - Russian State Library, Ms. Guenzburg 1274, Samuel b. Salomo of Faliza, Commentary on the halakhot for Pesah according to the piyyutim of Josef Tov Elem, Minhag Ashkenaz, 16th ct., F. 48372.
184. Moscow - Russian State Library, Ms. Guenzburg 134/8 (f. 78b-81b), Commentary on prayers for Rosh haShana, Minhag Italia, 15th c.t, kabbalistic, F. 06814.
185. Moscow - Russian State Library, Ms. Guenzburg 1401/2 (f. 10a-19b), Piyyut-Commentary, Minhag Ashkenaz, 15th ct., F. 48472.
186. Moscow - Russian State Library, Ms. Guenzburg 1594/3 (f. 24a-25b), Commentary on Hoshaanot, Minhag Italia, 1479, F. 48641.
187. Moscow - Russian State Library, Ms. Guenzburg 1665, Mahzor Minhag Tsarfat with commentary, 14th ct., F. 48679.
188. Moscow - Russian State Library, Ms. Guenzburg 190, Selihot Minhag Ashkenaz with short commentary, 13th ct., F. 6868.
189. Moscow - Russian State Library, Ms. Guenzburg 191, Mahzor Ashkenaz for Rosh haShana and Yom Kippur with commentary, incomplete, 14th ct., F. 06869.
190. Moscow - Russian State Library, Ms. Guenzburg 206, Siddur Minhag Ashkenaz with commentary, 14-15th ct., F. 45723.

---

[10] Cp. Archives Juives 12 (1976), pp. 61-70.

LIST OF MANUSCRIPTS 33

191. Moscow - Russian State Library, Ms. Guenzburg 211 (f. 48a-107b), Azharot with commentaries, Minhag Italia, 16-17th ct., F. 47615.
192. Moscow - Russian State Library, Ms. Guenzburg 249/10 (f. 242a-249a), Mordekhai b. Yehuda Dato, Piyyutim, some with commentary, Mńinhag Italia, 1582, F. 16876.
193. Moscow - Russian State Library, Ms. Guenzburg 363/8 (f. 120a-129b), Mystical commentary on prayers and piyyutim, Minhag Italia, 16-17th ct., F. 27972.
194. Moscow - Russian State Library, Ms. Guenzburg 482/3 (f. 28a-37a): Mahzor Minhag Ashkenaz Rosh haShana with commentary, 15-16th ct., F. 45724.
195. Moscow - Russian State Library, Ms. Guenzburg 522, Mahzor Minhag Ashkenaz for Yamim Noraim with commentary by Ḥat Hazzan of Padova, Minhag Italia, late 16th ct., F. 47811.
196. Moscow - Russian State Library, Ms. Guenzburg 533/1 (f. 1a-62b) Yehoshua Segre, ספר חביט חביט, Commentary on Hoshaanot, Minhag Italia, 1791, F. 18341.
197. Moscow - Russian State Library, Ms. Guenzburg 615, Commentary on Mahzor Ashkenaz, 13-14th ct., F. 43927.
198. Moscow - Russian State Library, Ms. Guenzburg 674/2 (f. 40a-58a), Mordekhai b. Yehuda Dato, Piyyutim with commentary of the author, Minhag Italia, 16th ct., F. 47964.
199. Moscow - Russian State Library, Ms. Guenzburg 710, Mahzor Minhag Carpentras for Shavuot with Azharot of Isaak Qimhi with commentary, 1662, F. 47971.
200. Moscow - Russian State Library, Ms. Guenzburg 775/4 (f. 292b-300b), Mose b. Samuel Ibn Tibbon, Commentary on theAzahrot of Salomo Ibn Gabirol, Minhag Sepharad, 14-15th ct, F. 04194.
201. Muenchen - Bayerische Staatsbibliothek, Cod. hebr. 153 X, Fragment of piyyut-commentary, Minhag Ashkenaz, from binding, not dated, F. 25997, F. 01274, PH 1544.
202. Muenchen - Bayerische Staatsbibliothek, Cod. hebr. 21: Mahzor Minhag Ashkenaz with commentary, 13-14th ct., F. 01173.
203. Muenchen - Bayerische Staatsbibliothek, Cod. hebr. 273,1, Commentary on the piyyut אלהינו אלהים אמת, Minhag Ashkenaz, 15th ct., F. 01687.
204. Muenchen - Bayerische Staatsbibliothek, Cod. hebr. 346: Collection of piyyut-commentaries, Minhag Ashkenaz, bound together in the Middle Ages, average age: 14th century; F. 23140.
205. Muenchen - Bayerische Staatsbibliothek, Cod. hebr. 393,9: Commentary on yotserot and piyyutim for shabbatot, Minhag Ashkenaz, 1527, F. 01124.
206. Muenchen - Bayerische Staatsbibliothek, Cod. hebr. 422: Mahzor Minhag Ashkenaz with short glosses, 14th ct., F. 25983.

207. Muenchen - Bayerische Staatsbibliothek, Cod. hebr. 472 , Tiklal with commentary פעמון זהב ורמון by Isaac b. Abraham Wanneh, Minhag Yemen, 1662, F. 37744.
208. Muenchen - Bayerische Staatsbibliothek, Cod. hebr. 69, Mahzor Minhag Ashkenaz with commentary, 14th ct., F. 01620.
209. Muenchen - Bayerische Staatsbibliothek, Cod. hebr. 86, Mahzor Minhag Ashkenaz, partly with commentary, 13-14th ct, F. 23121.
210. Muenchen - Bayerische Staatsbibliothek, Cod. hebr. 88, Mahzor Minhag Ashkenaz with glosses, not dated, F. 01673.
211. Muenchen - Bayerische Staatsbibliothek, Cod. hebr. 92/12, Elazar b. Yehuda v. Worms, Commentary on משפט מדת ביד האוחז, Minhag Ashkenaz, 16th ct., F. 23122.
212. Nahariya - Menahem and Saida Yaakob 187, Tiklal with commentary, Minhag Yemen, not dated, F. 73887.
213. Nahariya - Menahem and Saida Yaakob 284, Hoshaanot with commentary פעמון זהב ורמון by Isaac b. Abraham Wanneh, Minhag Yemen, 19th ct., F. 73351.
214. New Haven - Yale University, Beinecke Rare Book and MS Library, MS Heb. 52, Mahzor Asti, Fossano, Moncalvo for Yamim Noraim with commentary, 19th ct., F. 12764.
215. New York - Alfred Moldovan HH, Seder Hoshaano with commentary, Minhag Yemen, 18th ct., F. 40458.
216. New York - Columbia University X 893 G 11, Azahrot of Isaac b. Mordekhai Kimhi with commentary of the author, Minhag Italia, 16th ct., F. 23309.
217. New York - Columbia University X 893 J 558, Siddur Minhag haAri, Hoshaanot with two commentaries: רשב"ץ and Mose b. Hayim Pesanti, 18th ct., F. 23376.
218. New York - Columbia University X 893 J 724, Yehoshua Raphael b. Israel Benvenisti, עבודה תמה (Commentary on Seder Avoda), Minhag Sepharad, not dated, F. 52658.
219. New York - Columbia University X 893.1 BE P 43, Greek glossary for yotser Shabbat Zakhor and Azharot of Salomo Ibn Gabirol, Minhag Romania, 1872, F. 27430.
220. New York - Columbia X893 Ab 93: David b. Josef Abudraham, תשלום אבודרהם, Minhag Sepharad, 15-16th ct., F. 20663.
221. New York - Jewish Theological Seminary Benaim 130, Mose Muati, ישיר משה (commentary on the Azharot of Isaac b. Ruben al-Bargeloni), Minhag North Africa, 18th ct., F. 24408.
222. New York - Jewish Theological Seminary Benaim 68, Azharot with commentaries, Minhag North Africa, 18th ct., manuscript burned and damaged, F. 24347.
223. New York - Jewish Theological Seminary Lutzki 888 /3 (f. 61a-79a) Isaak b. Salomo Ḥadab, Commentary on the Azharot of Salomo Ibn Gabirol, Minhag Sepharad, 15-16th ct., F. 24110.

LIST OF MANUSCRIPTS

224. New York - Jewish Theological Seminary Ms. 1393/2 (f. 36a-72b), Tafsir Keter Malkhut in Persian, not dated, F. 28315.
225. New York - Jewish Theological Seminary Ms. 1609/13 (f. 98a-100b), Commentary on Hoshaanot, Minhag Carpentras, 14th ct., F. 10707.
226. New York - Jewish Theological Seminary Ms. 1639, Piyyut-commentary by Salomo b. Samuel Rofe, Minhag Roma, 17th ct., F. 10737.
227. New York - Jewish Theological Seminary Ms. 1670, Fragment of commentary on the Azharot of Salomo Ibn Gabirol, Minhag Italia, on the binding, 14-15th ct., F. 10768.
228. New York - Jewish Theological Seminary Ms. 1725/3 (f. 6b-7a), Commentary on piyyutim for Teqiat haShofar, Minhag Yemen, not dated, F. 10823.
229. New York - Jewish Theological Seminary Ms. 2269/5 (f. 43), Fragment of piyyut-commentary, Minhag Ashkenaz, F. 28522.
230. New York - Jewish Theological Seminary Ms. 2577/3 (f. 40a-41b), Josef b. Yehuda Ibn Shimon, רשות לברכו, prayers and piyyutim with commentary, Minhag Ashkenaz, 19th ct., F. 28830.
231. New York - Jewish Theological Seminary Ms. 3011, David b. Josef. Abudraham, תשלום אבודרהם, Minhag Sepharad, 15th ct., F. 29048.
232. New York - Jewish Theological Seminary Ms. 3013, Tiklal with commentary פעמון זהב ורמון by Isaac b. Abraham Wanneh, Minhag Yemen, 1675 (?)., F. 29050.
233. New York - Jewish Theological Seminary Ms. 3028, Tiklal with commentaries in Hebrew and Arabic, Minhag Yemen, 17th ct., F. 29065.
234. New York - Jewish Theological Seminary Ms. 3052: Selihot Minhag Yemen with commentary, 1652, F. 29089.
235. New York - Jewish Theological Seminary Ms. 3060, Azharot of Isaac b. Ruben al-Bargeloni with commentary by Mose Muati, Minhag North Africa, 1790, F. 29097.
236. New York - Jewish Theological Seminary Ms. 3061, Mose Muati, ישיר משה (commentary on the Azharot of Isaac b. Ruben alBargeloni with additions by the copyist, Minhag North Africa, 18th ct., F. 29098.
237. New York - Jewish Theological Seminary Ms. 3068, Azharot of Isaac b. Ruben al-Bargeloni with commentaries by Mose Muati and Amram Alqayim, incomplete, Minhag North Africa, 16th ct., F. 29105.
238. New York - Jewish Theological Seminary Ms. 3108, Tiklal with commentary on the Hoshaanot, partly by Isaac b. Abraham Wanneh, Minhag Yemen, 17th ct., F. 29145.
239. New York - Jewish Theological Seminary Ms. 3109, Tiklal with commentary פעמון זהב ורמון by Isaac b. Abraham Wanneh, Minhag Yemen and additional explanations, 1654, F. 29146.
240. New York - Jewish Theological Seminary Ms. 3151, Mahzor Minhag Carpentras for Rosh haShana with commentary by Eliyahu Carmi (הצאן), 17th ct., F. 29188.

241. New York - Jewish Theological Seminary Ms. 3183, Azharot of Isaac b. Ruben al-Bargeloni with commentary by Amram Alqayim, Minhag North Africa, Sefrou 1826, F. 29220.
242. New York - Jewish Theological Seminary Ms. 3193, Tiklal with commentaries, Minhag Yemen, 1679, F. 29230.
243. New York - Jewish Theological Seminary Ms. 3294, פעמון זהב ורמון by Isaac b. Abrahm Wanneh, excerpts, Minhag Yemen, 18th ct., F. 29331.
244. New York - Jewish Theological Seminary Ms. 3295, Tiklal with commentary פעמון זהב ורמון by Isaac b. Abraham Wanneh, Minhag Yemen, 18-19th ct., F. 29332.
245. New York - Jewish Theological Seminary Ms. 3367: Berakha b. Josef haKohen, ספר טוב טעם, commentary on the piyyutim of the Karaite poet Aaron b. Josef haRofe, 18th ct., F. 32052.
246. New York - Jewish Theological Seminary Ms. 4121, Seder Hallel Musaf Sukkot with Hoshaanot and commentary by Simon b. Tsemaḥ Duran, Minhag North Africa, 1829, F. 25023.
247. New York - Jewish Theological Seminary Ms. 4195, Hoshaanot with commentary פעמון זהב ורמון by Isaac b. Abraham Wanneh, Minhag Yemen, 1746, F. 25097.
248. New York - Jewish Theological Seminary Ms. 4197, Mahzor Minhag Carpentras for Yom Kippur with commentary קדושא דסדרא by Josef b. Abraham of Montelitz, 1666, F. 25099.
249. New York - Jewish Theological Seminary Ms. 4268, Azharot with commentary, Minhag Carpentras, not dated, F. 25171.
250. New York - Jewish Theological Seminary Ms. 4300, Yehuda Toledano, Perush Hoshaanot, Minhag North Africa, F. 25203.
251. New York - Jewish Theological Seminary Ms. 4361, Fragment of Mahzor Romania, Azharot of Salomo Ibn Gabirol with commentary by Mose b. Samuel Ibn Tibbon, incomplete, 15th ct., F. 25263.
252. New York - Jewish Theological Seminary Ms. 4362/1 (f. 1a-6a), Commentary on a qallirian qedushta, ascribed to Tobia b. Eliezer, Minhag Romania, 13-14th ct., F. 25264.[11]
253. New York - Jewish Theological Seminary Ms. 4392, Siddur Minhag Ashkenaz for Yamim Noraim with commentary by Ḥet Hazzan of Padova, Minhag Italia, Cremona 1588, F. 25294.
254. New York - Jewish Theological Seminary Ms. 4416, Mahzor Minhag Roma, with leafs from Mahzor Ashkenaz with commentary, not dated, F. 25318.
255. New York - Jewish Theological Seminary Ms. 4460/1 (f. 1a-98b), Siddur Minhag Tsarfat with commentary, 14th ct., F. 25362.

---

[11] L. Ginzberg, גנזי שכטר. ספר א: קטעי מדרש ואגדה, New York, Jewish Theological Seminary, 1928, p. 246–297.

LIST OF MANUSCRIPTS

256. New York - Jewish Theological Seminary Ms. 4466: Mahzor Minhag Ashkenaz with commentary, not dated, F. 25368.[12]
257. New York - Jewish Theological Seminary Ms. 4488, Tiklal with commentary, Minhag Yemen, 1653, F. 25402.
258. New York - Jewish Theological Seminary Ms. 4663; Fragment from Mahzor Minhag Ashkenaz with commentary, 14-15th ct., F. 25566.
259. New York - Jewish Theological Seminary Ms. 4687/1 (f. 1a-79a), Azharot of Salomo Ibn Gabirol with commentary, Minhag North Africa, 1809, F. 25591.
260. New York - Jewish Theological Seminary Ms. 4696, 1 (f. 1a-25a), Mose b. Hayim Pesante, ישע אלהים (Commentary on Hoshaanot), 2 (f. 34a-104a) Azharot of Salomo Ibn Gabirol with commentary נר מצוה by Mose b. Hayyim Pesante, Minhag haAri, F. 25600.
261. New York - Jewish Theological Seminary Ms. 4746, Mahzor Minhag Carpentras for Rosh haShana with commentary סדרא דקדושה by Josef b. Abraham of Montelitz 1656, F. 25647.
262. New York - Jewish Theological Seminary Ms. 4799, Azharot with commentary, Minhag Yemen, not dated, F. 25700.
263. New York - Jewish Theological Seminary Ms. 4821, Mahzor Minhag Corfu for Pesah with commentary, not dated, F. 25722.
264. New York - Jewish Theological Seminary Ms. 4823, Fragments from Mahzor Romania with commentary, not dated, F. 25724
265. New York - Jewish Theological Seminary Ms. 4824, Fragment of Mahzor Minhag Ashkenas with commentary, not dated, F. 25725.
266. New York - Jewish Theological Seminary Ms. 4826: Fragment of Mahzor Ashkenaz with short commentary, not dated, F. 25727.
267. New York - Jewish Theological Seminary Ms. 5086, Persian commentary on אדון עולם אשר מלאך, not dated, F. 29883.
268. New York - Jewish Theological Seminary Ms. 5426: Mahzor Minhag North Africa with תשלום אבודרהם by David b. Josef Abudraham, 18-19th ct., F. 37170.
269. New York - Jewish Theological Seminary Ms. 8097, Commentary onYotserot, Minahg Ashkenaz, not dated, F. 25802, F. 31841.
270. New York - Jewish Theological Seminary Ms. 8169, Mahzor Ashkenaz with commentary, 14th ct., F. 40101, F. 25806.
271. New York - Jewish Theological Seminary Ms. 8753, Fragment of piyyut commentary, Minhag Ashkenaz, 14th ct., F. 49446.
272. New York - Jewish Theological Seminary Ms. 8767, Tiklal with commentary on Hoshaanot, Minhag Yemen, 1622, F. 49451.
273. New York - Jewish Theological Seminary Ms. 9325, Tiklal with commentary on Azharot and Hoshaanot, Minhag Yemen, 1713, F. 49718.

---

[12] H. Gross, Ein anonymer Handschriftlicher Kommentar zum Machsor, Zeitschrift für hebräische Bibliographie, 11, 1907, pp. 169–181; S. J. Schachter, The liturgical Commentary of Mahzor Ashkenaz (Jewish Theological Seminary of America Ms. # 4466), dissertation, New York, The Graduate School of the Jewish Theological Seminary of America, 1986.

274. New York - Jewish Theological Seminary Rab. 1077/4 (f. 21a-21b), Piyyut-commentary, Minhag Ashkenaz, 14th ct., F. 43192.
275. New York - Jewish Theological Seminary Rab. 1493/2 (f. 48-105), Mose b. Samuel Ibn Tibbon, Commentary on the Azharot of Salomo Ibn Gabirol, Minhag Sepharad, 15th ct., F. 43257.
276. New York - Jewish Theological Seminary Rab. 1853 (f. 90b-91a?), Alexander Sander b. Natan Faber, Commentary on Selihot of Ḥebra Qadisha, Minhag Ashkenaz, 1751-1780, F. 50153.
277. New York - Jewish Theological Seminary Rab. 2027, at the end piyyutim by Mordekhai b. Mose and a commentary thereon, Minhag North Africa, 1860, F. 50184.
278. New York - Jewish Theological Seminary Rab. 949 (f. 116-142), Commentaries on liturgical texts by Yehuda b. Meir Toledano (compiler), Minhag North Africa, 1814, F. 37456.
279. New York - M. Lehmann 274, Yemenite Poems by Shalem Shabazi and others with short kabbalistic commentaries, Minhag Yemen, 19-20th ct., F. 24598.
280. New York - M. Lehmann Fr. 9.5, Fragment of piyyut-commentary, Minhag Ashkenaz, 14-15th ct., F. 72815.
281. New York - M. Lehmann FR 10.4, Fragment of piyyut-commentary, Minhag Ashkenaz, not dated, F. 72811.
282. New York - M. Lehmann FR 17.4, Fragment of piyyut-commentary, Minhag Ashkenaz, 14-15th ct., F. 72814.
283. New York - Public Library, Heb. Ms. 10, Tiklal with commentary פעמון זהב ורמון by Isaac b. Abraham Wanneh, Minhag Yemen, 1658, jemen., F. 31099.
284. New York - Public Library, Heb. Ms. 9, Tiklal with commentary פעמון זהב ורמון by Isaac b. Abraham Wanneh, Minhag Yemen, 17th ct., F. 31098.
285. New York - Public Library, Jewish Items 2, Tiklal with commentary פעמון זהב ורמון by Isaac b. Abraham Wanneh, Minhag Yemen, incomplete, 18-19th ct., F. 31129.
286. Nuernberg - Stadtbibliothek, Amberger 173 fol., Fragment of piyyut-commentary, Minhag Ashkenaz, 13th ct., from binding, cp. to ערוגת הבושם (Urbach vol I, pp. 167-168), PH 4976.
287. Oxford - Bodleian Library Heb.e.10 (Neubauer 2746/1), Commentary on piyyutim to 4 parashiyot by Josef Garad, Minhag Sepharad, 1402, F. 22713.
288. Oxford - Bodleian Library Heb.e.13 (Cowley 2747/1), Mose b. Samuel Ibn Tibbon, Commentary on the Azharot of Salomo Ibn Gabirol, Geniza, F. 22714.
289. Oxford - Bodleian Library Heb.e.20 (Neubauer 2748): Piyyutim, partly with commentary, Minhag Italia, not dated, late, F. 22715.
290. Oxford - Bodleian Library MS Bodl. Or. 109 (Neubauer 1209), Commentary on prayers and piyyutim, compiled by Aaron b. Hayyim haKohen, Minhag Tsarfat, 13th ct., F. 16669.

LIST OF MANUSCRIPTS

291. Oxford - Bodleian Library MS Can. Or. 1 (Neubauer 1104), Siddur Minhag Ashkenaz with commentary, 14th ct., F. 17710.
292. Oxford - Bodleian Library MS Can. Or. 70 (Neubauer 1147), Piyyutim Isaak haNaqdan and Qinot with commentary, Minhag Ashkenaz, 14. ct., F. 16608.
293. Oxford - Bodleian Library MS Can. Or. 82 (Neubauer 1148), Yotserot with commentary, Minhag Ashkenaz, 14th ct., F. 16609.
294. Oxford - Bodleian Library MS Laud. Or. 106 (Neubauer 1178/1), Azharot of Salomo Ibn Gabirol with commentaries by Isaac b. Todros of Barcelona and "Ibn Shushan", Minhag North Africa, 1509, F. 16635.
295. Oxford - Bodleian Library MS Laud. Or. 271 (Neubauer 1206), Commentary on prayers and piyyutim compiled by Aaron b. Hayyim haKohen, Minhag Tsarfat, 1227, F. 16666.
296. Oxford - Bodleian Library MS Mich. 190/9 (Neubauer 914), f. 145a-148b, Criticism on the Azharot of Eliyahu haZaqen, Minhag Italia, 15th ct., F. 21873.
297. Oxford - Bodleian Library MS Mich. 312,1 (Neubauer 2276,1), Piyyut-commentary, Minhag Roma, 16th ct., F. 20968.
298. Oxford - Bodleian Library MS Mich. 344 (Neubauer 1177), Simon b. Tsemaḥ Duran, ספר זוהר הרקיע (Commentary on the Azharot of Salomo Ibn Gabirol) Minhag Sepharad, 15th ct., F. 16636.
299. Oxford - Bodleian Library MS Mich. 365 (Neubauer 1208), numbers 3 and 5, Piyyut-commentary, Minhag Ashkenaz, 15-16th ct., F. 16668
300. Oxford - Bodleian Library MS Mich. 543 (Neubauer 1212), Commentary on 136 Selihot compiled by Isaac b. Jakob, Minhag Ashkenaz, 14th ct., F. 16672.
301. Oxford - Bodleian Library MS Mich. 573 (Neubauer 1099), Siddur Minhag Ashkenaz with commentary on prayers and Hoshaanot, 13. ct., F. 17705
302. Oxford - Bodleian Library MS Opp. 12 (Neubauer 1029), Mahzor Ashkenaz with some marginal glosses, 13.-14. ct., F. 22615.
303. Oxford - Bodleian Library MS Opp 160 (Neubauer 1204), Elazar b. Yehuda of Worms, Prayer-commentary, includes commentary on Hoshaanot, Minhag Ashkenaz, 13th ct., F. 16664.
304. Oxford - Bodleian Library MS Opp. 169 (Neubauer 1151), Yotserot with short commentary, Minhag Ashkenaz, 14th ct., F. 16611.
305. Oxford - Bodleian Library MS Opp. 170 (Neubauer 1205), Commentary on prayers and piyyutim, Minhag Ashkenaz, 13th ct., F. 16665.
306. Oxford - Bodleian Library MS Opp. 171 (Neubauer 1207), Piyyut-commentary, Minhag Ashkenaz, 13th ct., F. 16667.
307. Oxford - Bodleian Library MS Opp. 172 (Neubauer 1211), Piyyut-commentary for Yamim Noraim and Sukkot, Minhag Ashkenaz, 15-16th ct., F. 16671.

308. Oxford - Bodleian Library MS Opp. 498 (Neubauer 1930), Naftali Hirsch Trebitsh, Mystical commentary on prayers and piyyutim for Yamim Noraim, Minhag Ashkenaz, Gelnhausen 1562, F. 18863.
309. Oxford - Bodleian Library MS Opp. 521/1 (Neubauer 1936) (f. 1a-5b), Kabbalistic commentary on חד גדיא, Minhag Ashkenaz, 17-18th ct., F. 18868.
310. Oxford - Bodleian Library MS Opp. 525,18 (Neubauer 1598/18) (f. 103a-104a), Elazar b. Yehuda of Worms, COmmentary on three piyyutim, Minhag Ashkenaz, 17th ct., F. 17176.
311. Oxford - Bodleian Library MS Opp. 619 (Neubauer 2374), Mahzor Minhag Ashkenaz with commentary (Tripartite Mahzor III), 14th ct., F. 21437.
312. Oxford - Bodleian Library MS Opp. 675 (Neubauer 1210), Piyyut-commentary, Minhag Ashkenaz, 16th ct., F. 16670.
313. Oxford - Bodleian Library MS Opp. 677 (Neubauer 1167), Seliha by Uri b. Raphael of Erburga with marginal commentary, Minhag Ashkenaz, 16th ct., F. 16626.
314. Oxford - Bodleian Library MS Opp. 681 (Neubauer 1213), Commentary on Selihot, Minhag Ashkenaz, 15th ct., F. 16673.
315. Oxford - Bodleian Library MS Opp. 696/13 (Neubauer 2253) (f. 244b-250a), Commentary on האדרת והאמונה, Minhag Ashkenaz, 16-17th ct., F. 20536.[13]
316. Oxford - Bodleian Library MS Opp. Add. fol. 58 (Neubauer 2498), Tiklal with commentary פעמון זהב ורמון by Isaac b. Abraham Wanneh, Minhag Yemen, 1678, F. 22210.
317. Oxford - Bodleian Library MS Reggio 63/3 (Neubauer 1081/3) (f. 341a-374b), Marginal commentary on Seder Avoda, Minhag Sepharad, 15th ct., F. 17688.
318. Padova - Biblioteca del Seminario Vescovile Cod. 218, Selihot with commentary, Minhag Ashkenaz, 1460; F. 00775.
319. Palo Alto L.U. Berman [2]/2, Qinot for Tisha beAb, one with commentary, Minhag North Africa, 18-19th ct., F. 34374.
320. Paris - Alliance Israelite Universelle H 10 A/11 (f. 117a-125a), Commentary on the piyyut יקדש בכוס ישועות ושמחה, Minhag Ashkenaz, 16th ct., F. 02746, F. 03030.
321. Paris - Alliance Israelite Universelle H 133 A, Siddur Minhag Ashkenaz with commentary, 13-14th ct., F. 03205.
322. Paris - Alliance Israelite Universelle H 422 A, Mahzor Minhag Carpentras, Rosh haShana with commentary by Josef b. Abraham of Montelitz, 17th ct., F. 03323.
323. Paris - Alliance Israelite Universelle III B 1, Commentary on the Azharot of Salomo Ibn Gabirol, incomplete, Minhag Sepharad, 13-14th ct., Geniza, F. 03357, PH 0916.

---

[13] On this commentary cp. J. Dan, פירושי 'האדרת והאמונה' של חסידי אשכנז, Tarbiz 50 (1981), p. 398-399.

324. Paris - Bibliotheque Nationale heb. 1408/22, Elazar b. Yehuda of Worms, Commentary on the Selihot of Meir b. Isaac, Minhag Ashkenaz, 14th ct., F. 24886; PH 3755.
325. Paris - Bibliotheque Nationale heb. 273/2 (f. 150a-203b), Isaak b. Todros of Barcelona, Commentary on the Azharot of Salomo Ibn Gabirol, incomplete, Minhag Sepharad, 15-16th ct., F. 04292.
326. Paris - Bibliotheque Nationale heb. 327/2 (f. 33a-51b), Eliezer b. Natan, Commentary on the Mahzor, including Hoshaanot, Minhag Ashkenaz, 1386, F. 04336.
327. Paris - Bibliotheque Nationale heb. 445/9 (f. 55a-89b): Piyyut-commentary, Minhag Tsarfat, 14-15th ct., F. 04468.
328. Paris - Bibliotheque Nationale heb. 635, Mahzor for Shabbat Zakhor and Pesach with one marginal commentary, Minhag Tsarfat, 15th ct., F. 31300.
329. Paris - Bibliotheque Nationale heb. 653, Mahzor Ashkenaz with commentary, 14th ct., F. 11546.
330. Paris - Bibliotheque Nationale heb. 709, Piyyut-commentary, Minhag Ashkenaz, 15th ct., F. 11597.
331. Paris - Bibliotheque Nationale heb. 842, Teil 9, f. 131a-160b, Kommentar zu den Azahrot des Salomo Ibn Gabirol, Oran, 1464, F. 14471.
332. Paris - Ecole Rabbinique 31: Mahzor Minhag Carpentras for Rosh haShana Minhag with commentaries by Eliyahu Carmi and Josef b. Abraham of Montelitz, 18th ct., F. 04011.
333. Paris - Ecole Rabbinique 32: Mahzor Minhag Carpentras for Rosh haShana with commentary by Josef b. Abraham of Montelitz, 16th ct., F. 04012.
334. Paris - G. Epstein 23/57, Isaac b. Abraham Wanneh, Commentary on Hoshaanot, Minhag Yemen, 18-18th ct., F. 07277.
335. Parma - Biblioteca Palatin Cod. Parm. 2248 (de Rossi 149/2), Commentary on Yotserot, Minhag Italia, late 15th ct., F. 13413.
336. Parma - Biblioteca Palatina Cod. Parm. 1002 (Ta 24), Mahzor Ashkenaz with commentary, 14th ct., F. 27555.
337. Parma - Biblioteca Palatina Cod. Parm. 1264, Mahsor Tsarfat for Sukkot with glosses, early 14th ct., F. 27556.
338. Parma - Biblioteca Palatina Cod. Parm. 1794 (de Rossi 1061), Mahzor Tsarfat for Rosh haShana and Yom kippur with commentary, ca. 1400, F. 13018.
339. Parma - Biblioteca Palatina Cod. Parm. 1902 (de Rossi 403), Mahzor Tsarfat with commentary, ca. 1470, F. 13059.
340. Parma - Biblioteca Palatina Cod. Parm. 1923/2 (f. 121a-280a), Mahzor Minhag Provence with commentary on the Azharot of Salomo Ibn Gabirol, 15th ct., F. 13079.
341. Parma - Biblioteca Palatina Cod. Parm. 2125 (de Rossi 812), Piyyut-commentary, Minhag tsarfat, late 14th ct., F. 13344.
342. Parma - Biblioteca Palatina Cod. Parm. 2224 (de Rossi 1028), Mahzor Roma with commentary on one piyyut, 14th ct., F. 13390.

343. Parma - Biblioteca Palatina Cod. Parm. 2290/1 (f. 3b-5a), Isaac b. Mose Duran, Commentary on the piyyut אחד לבדו באין סמוך לו of Abraham Ibn Ezra, Minhag North Africa, 17th ct., F. 17804.
344. Parma - Biblioteca Palatina Cod. Parm. 2342/17 (de Rossi 541,14), Commentary on the piyyut שמיני אותותיו שלו, Minhag Ashkenaz, late 13th ct., F. 13218.
345. Parma - Biblioteca Palatina Cod. Parm. 2351/5 (f. 123a-140b), Hayyim b. Gallipapa, Commentary on the Seder Avoda אל אלהים יצדקו בך צדוק of Josef Ibn Abitur, Minhag Sepharad, 14-15th ct., F. 13223.[14]
346. Parma - Biblioteca Palatina Cod. Parm. 2404 (de Rossi 1104), Mahzor Ashkenaz with commentary, copied from printed edition Saloniki 1550 (Benjamin b. Meir Levi), late 16th ct., F. 13269.
347. Parma - Bibliotcca Palatina Cod. Parm. 2430/14 (de Rossi 1138/15) (f.79r-81r), Elazar b. Yehuda of Worms, Commentary on the piyyut האוחז ביד מדת משפט, Minhag Ashkenaz, late 14th ct., F. 13434.
348. Parma - Biblioteca Palatina Cod. Parm. 2574 (de Rossi 159), Simha b. Samuel, Mahzor Vitry, incomplete, Minhag Tsarfat, 12-13th ct., F. 13582.
349. Parma - Biblioteca Palatina Cod. Parm. 2577 (de Rossi 310), Mahzor Roma with glosses, 14th ct., F. 13585.
350. Parma - Biblioteca Palatina Cod. Parm. 2736 (de Rossi 804), Mahzor Roma with glosses on Azharot, late 14th ct., F. 13671.
351. Parma - Biblioteca Palatina Cod. Parm. 2737 (de Rossi 804), Mahzor Roma with commentary on one piyyut, late 14th ct., F. 13672.
352. Parma - Biblioteca Palatina Cod. Parm. 2886 (de Rossi 585), Mahzor Ashkenaz with commentary on a few piyyutim, 14th ct., F. 13779.
353. Parma - Biblioteca Palatina Cod. Parm. 2890 (de Rossi 856), Mahzor Tsarfat for Yom Kippur with commentary, late 13th ct., F. 13783.
354. Parma - Biblioteca Palatina Cod. Parm. 2895 (de Rossi 653), Siddur Minhag Ashkenaz with commentary, 1450-1453, F. 13788.
355. Parma - Biblioteca Palatina Cod. Parm 3000 (de Rossi 378), Mahzor Ashkenaz with commentary, 14th ct., F. 13736
356. Parma - Biblioteca Palatina Cod. Parm. 3002 (de Rossi 407), Machsor Ashkenaz with commentary on some piyyutim, 14th ct., F. 13726.
357. Parma - Biblioteca Palatina Cod. Parm. 3006 (de Rossi 654,1), Mahzor Tsarfat for Yamim Noraim with commentary, Part I, Tallard, 1304, F. 13730.
358. Parma - Biblioteca Palatina Cod. Parm. 3007 (de Rossi 654,2), Mahzor Tsarfat for Yamim Noraim with commentary, Part II, Tallard 1304, F. 13731.

---

[14] Published by S. Stern, על סדר עבודה לר"יי בן אביתור, *קובץ מעשי ידי גאונים קדמונים*, J. Rosenberg (ed.), Berlin 1896, pp. 117-122.

359. Parma - Biblioteca Palatina Cod. Parm. 3057/12 (de Rossi 1033/10) (f. 121v-152r), Eliezer b. Natan, Commentary on Yotserot, Minhag Ashkenaz, early 14th ct., F. 13823.
360. Parma - Biblioteca Palatina Cod. Parm. 3057.9 (de Rossi 1033) (f. 90v-100r), Commentary on Hoshaanot, Minhag Ashkenaz, early 14th ct., F. 13823.
361. Parma - Biblioteca Palatina Cod. Parm. 3136 (de Rossi 405), Mahzor Tsarfat with commentary, 13th ct., F. 13878.
362. Parma - Biblioteca Palatina Cod. Parm. 3141 (de Rossi 767), Mahzor Roma with commentary on a few piyyutim, 1462/63, F. 13883.
363. Parma - Biblioteca Palatina Cod. Parm. 3175/13 (f. 40a-40b), Josef b. Yehuda Ibn Shimon, רשות לברכו, Prayers and piyyutim with commentary, Minhag Carpentras, 14-15th ct., F. 13913.
364. Parma - Biblioteca Palatina Cod. Parm. 3205 (de Rossi 655), Piyyut-commentary, Minhag Ashkenaz, 13-14th ct., F. 13920.
365. Parma - Biblioteca Palatina Cod. Parm. 3266/6 (f. 60a-61a), Commentary on prayers and piyyutim for Rosh haShana, Minhag Ashkenaz, 14th ct., F. 34168.
366. Parma - Biblioteca Palatina Cod. Parm. 3269, Mahzor Ashkenaz with commentary on a few piyyutim, 13-14th ct., F. 13953.
367. Parma - Biblioteca Palatina Cod. Parm. 3270 (de Rossi 1215), Mahzor Ashkenaz with commentary, 14th ct., F. 13954.
368. Parma - Biblioteca Palatina Cod. Parm. 3271 (de Rossi 1216), Mahzor Ashkenaz for Yom Kipuur with glosses, 14th ct., F. 13955.
369. Parma - Biblioteca Palatina Cod. Parm. 3491: Azharot with commentary, Minhag Carpentras, 1659, F. 13999.
370. Parma - Biblioteca Palatina Cod. Parm. 3507 (Perreau 27), Piyyut-commentary, Minhag Ashkenaz, 1386, F. 14015.
371. Parma - Biblioteca Palatina Cod. Parm. 3515 (Perreau 16), Mahzor Roma with commentary on two stanzas from the piyyut אלהינו אלהים אמת, 15th ct., F. 14023.
372. Philadelphia - University of Pennsylvania HB 2, Tiklal with commentary פעמון זהב ורמון by Isaac b. Abraham Wanneh, Minhag Yemen, 1763, F. 38358.
373. Ramat Gan - Universitat BarIlan 62, Tiklal with commentaries, Minhag Yemen, 17th ct., F. 36828.
374. Ramat Gan - Universitat Bar Ilan 63, Tiklal with commentaries, Minhag Yemen, 1657, F. 36827.
375. Ramat Gan - Universitat Bar Ilan 703, Tiklal with commentary פעמון זהב ורמון by Isaac b. Abraham Wanneh, Minhag Yemen, 1876, F. 36824.
376. Roma - Collegio Rabbinico Italiano 110, Hoshaanot with commentary, Minhag Romania, 18-19th ct., F. 42993.
377. Salzburg - Universitaetsbibliothek M II 342, Fragment of piyyut-commentary, Minhag Ashkenaz, 14th ct., PH 4942, PH 0045, F. 02196.

378. San Francisco - California State Library, Sutro Branch MS 154 (Brinner 125), Tiklal with commentary פעמון זהב ורמון by Isaac b. Abraham Wanneh, Minhag Yemen, 1611, F. 34650.
379. Skokie - Hebrew Theological College 3, Prayers of Yamim Noraim and Selihot with commentary, Minhag Sepharad, combined out of two manuscripts with indepent page count, not dated, F. 40050.
380. St. Petersburg - Inst. of Oriental Studies of the Russian Academy A 133, תפסיר כתר מלכות, Persian, 1854, F. 52372.
381. St. Petersburg - Inst. of Oriental Studies of the Russian Academy A 33, Salomo Ibn Gabirol, כתר מלכות with commentary, Minhag Sepharad, 15th ct., F. 52292.
382. St. Petersburg - Inst. of Oriental Studies of the Russian Academy B 431, Berakha b. Josef, טוב טעם (Commentary on the piyyutim of Aaron b. Josef haRofe), Karaite, 19-20th ct., F. 53617.
383. St. Petersburg - Inst. of Oriental Studies of the Russian Academy B 483, Berakha b. Josef, Commentary on the piyyutim of Aaron b. Josef haRofe, Karaite, 18-19th ct., F. 53717.
384. St. Petersburg - Inst. of Oriental Studies of the Russian Academy C 14/10 (f. 91b-92b), Kabbalistic commentary on the piyyut אחד באין סמוך לו of Abraham Ibn Ezra, Minhag Romania, 15th ct., F. 69265.
385. St. Petersburg - Russian National Library Evr. IV 148/2, Gershon ben Ruven (compiler), Exempla, includes commentary on חד גדיא (f. 34b), Minhag Azerbeidjan, 1864-65, F. 69557.
386. St. Petersburg - Russian National Library, Evr. IV 50: Berakha b. Josef, אמרי נועם (Commentary on the piyyutim of Aaron b. Josef haRofe), Karaite, 19th ct., F 69500.
387. Strasbourg - Bibliotheque Nationale et Universitaire 3965 (Landauer 39), Tiklal with commentary פעמון זהב ורמון by Isaac b. Abraham Wanneh, Minhag Yemen, Demar 1651, F. 02859.
388. Strasbourg - Bibliotheque Nationale et Universitaire 4081, Mahzor Carpentras for Yom Kippur with commentary by Josef b. Abraham of Montelitz, 1660, F. 03958.
389. Tel Aviv - Bill Gross 291, Azharot of Isaac b. Ruben al-Bargeloni wth commentary ישיר משה by Mose Muati, Minhag North Africa, copied from printed edition Amsterdam 1735, incomplete, 18-19th ct., F. 70628.
390. Torino - Archivio Terracini 1492: Mahzor Ashkenaz for Yamim Noraim with commentary on some piyyutim, 18th ct., F. 41739.
391. Torino - Archivio Terracini 1499, Zakharya David Shabbetai Segr e, קול רנה וישועה (Commentary on prayers and piyyutim for Sukkot), Minhag Italia, Vercelli 1849, F. 41742.
392. Toronto - University of Toronto, MS Friedberg 3-014, Siddur Minhag Ashkenaz with commentary, 13th ct., F. 70569.
393. Uppsala - Universitetsbibliotek O.Heb.22, Mahzor Ashkenaz with commentary on Hoshaanot and some piyyutim, not dated, F. 18026.

LIST OF MANUSCRIPTS 45

394. Vatican - Biblioteca Apostolica ebr. 213/4 (f. 120a-165a), Commentary on Seder Avoda אל אל אשא דעי of Isaac Ibn Giat, incomplete, Minhag Sepharad, 15th ct., F. 00272.
395. Vatican - Biblioteca Apostolica ebr. 228/10 (f. 105a-112a), Elazar b. Yehuda of Worms, Commentary on the piyyut האדרת והאמונה, Minhag Ashkenaz, 15th ct., F. 00285.
396. Vatican - Biblioteca Apostolica ebr. 232/2 (f. 23a-44b), Commentary on the wedding-song ראשון טלה of David b. Yedidya, Minhag Sepharad, 15th ct., F. 00289.
397. Vatican - Biblioteca Apostolica ebr. 266/2: (f. 138b-155b) Samuel b. Salomo of Faliza, Commentary on the piyyut אלהי הרוחות of Josef Tov Elem, Minhag Ashkenaz, 14th ct., F. 00323.
398. Vatican - Biblioteca Apostolica ebr. 274/4 (f. 167a-184b), Commentary on שיר היחוד, kabbalistic, Minhag Romania, 1437/8, F. 00331.
399. Vatican - Biblioteca Apostolica ebr. 285/30, Fragment of commentary on Mahzor Romania for Sukkot, 14th ct., F. 08632.
400. Vatican - Biblioteca Apostolica ebr. 288/10, Elazar b. Yehuda of Worms, Commentary on the piyyut האדרת והאמונה, Minhag Ashkenaz, 15th ct., F. 00285.
401. Vatican - Bibliotheca Apostolica ebr. 298/1, Piyyut-Commentary, Minhag Ashkenaz, 15-16th ct., F. 00353.
402. Vatican - Biblioteca Apostolica ebr. 301,1, Abraham b. Azriel, ערוגת הבושם, Minhag Ashkenaz, 14th ct., F. 08702.
403. Vatican - Biblioteca Apostolica ebr. 305,1, Commentary on piyyutim of Elazar birabbi Qallir, Minhag Ashkenaz, 13th ct., F. 00356.
404. Vatican - Biblioteca Apostolica ebr. 306, Piyyut-commentary, Minhag Tsarfat, 14th ct., F. 00357.
405. Vatican - Biblioteca Apostolica ebr. 308, Commentary on Selihot and piyyutim for Rosh haShana, compiled by David b. Mose, Minhag Ashkenaz, 1440, F. 00359.
406. Vatican - Biblioteca Apostolica ebr. 312, Qinot for Tisha beAv with commentary, Minhag Ashkenaz, 15th ct., F. 00362.
407. Vatican - Biblioteca Apostolica ebr. 318, Mahzor Ashkenaz with interlinear glosses, 15th ct., F. 00368.
408. Vatican - Biblioteca Apostolica ebr. 320, Mahzor Romania for Rosh haShana, Yom Kippur, and Sukkot with commentary, 14-15th ct., F. 00370.
409. Vatican - Biblioteca Apostolica ebr. 422, Piyyut-commentary, Minhag Ashkenaz, 14th ct., F. 00497.
410. Verona - Seminario Maggiore 34, Siddur Minhag Ashkenaz with commentary, 14th ct., F. 32864.
411. Warszaw - Uniwersytet, Inst. Orientalistyczny 258/3 (f. 132a-209b), Eliezer b. Natan, Commentary on prayers and Hoshaanot, Minhag Ashkenaz, 14-15th ct., F. 32500.

412. Warszaw - Zydowski Instytut Historyczny 838, Benjamin b. Abraham Anav, Commentary on Aramaic piyyutim, Minhag Ashkenaz, incomplete, 19th ct., F. 30854.
413. Wien - Oesterreichische Nationalbibliothek Cod hebr. 111 /2 (f. 81a-112b), Raphael Salomo b. Jakob haKohen Prato, Commentary on the Azharot of Salomo Ibn Gabirol, shortened version of ספר זוהר הרקיע by Simon b. Tsemaḥ Duran, Minhag Italia, autograph, 1525, F. 01387.
414. Wolfenbuettel - Niedersaechsisches Staatsarchiv VII B Hs. 192, Fragment of piyyut-commentary, Minhag Ashkenaz, 14th ct., F. 44284, PH 5436.
415. Zurich - Zentralbibliothek Heid. 139, 1: piyyut-commentary (פרישה קטנה) with many marginal notes probably by the same hand, 2: Elazar b. Yehuda of Worms, Commentary on the Mahzor, Minhag Ashkenaz, 14th ct., F. 02681.

ADDENDA
NOT ANALYZED FOR CLAVIS COMMENTARIORUM

- Marseille - Mlle. Odette Valabregue [1], 2 (f. 28a-37a): Eliyahu Carmi, Commentary on Mahzor Carpentras for Rosh haShana, 5 (f. 87b-101a), Josef b. Abraham von Montelitz, Piyyut-commentary, Minhag Carpentras, 1745, F. 34204.
- Muenchen - Bayerische Staatsbibliothek, Cod. hebr. 43/2 (f. 17b-21a), Commentary on one piyyut, Minhag Ashkenaz, 16th ct., F. 01150.
- Paris - Bibliotheque Nationale heb. 839/11 (f. 191a-225b), Isaac b. Todros of Barcelona, Commentary on Mahzor Sepharad, kabbalistic, 14th ct., F. 14468.
- Torino - Archivio Terracini 1486: Mahzor Asti, Fossano, Moncalvo for Yamim Noraim with commentary, 1696, F. 41639.

CLAVIS COMMENTARIORUM

אאביך ביום מבך עוגל חצי גרני (א 3), אלעזר ברבי קליר, קרובה לתשע באב

Ashkenaz
1. Berlin - Staatsbibliothek (Preussischer Kulturbesitz) Or. Qu. 798-799 (Steinschneider 177), II, f. 181b-184b, M.אל׳כסח.
2. Budapest - Magyar tudomanyos akademia, MS. Kaufmann A 400, p. 193-200, C, rubric: קינות ליום ט׳ באב דר׳ אלעזר קליר.
3. Hamburg - Staats- und Universitaetsbibliothek Cod. hebr. 17/2 (Steinschneider 152), f. 91b-93b, C, rubric: קינות ליום ט׳ באב.
4. Hamburg - Staats- und Universitaetsbibliothek Cod. hebr. 61 (Steinschneider 153), f. 45b, C, commentator: Eliezer b. Natan, rubric: וזה פירוש מקינות, only beginning, manuscript ends here.
5. Hamburg - Staats- und Universitaetsbibliothek Cod. hebr. 233, f. 68a-70b, G.
6. London - British Library Add. 18695 (Margoliouth 683), f. 98b-101b, T, Yiddish, rubric: דש קרובוץ זגט מן צו מורגש אם תשעה באב אם שמונה עשרה.
7. Lund - Universitetsbibliothek Ms. L.O. 2, f. 124b, M, the manuscript breaks off in this commentary.
8. Oxford - Bodleian Library MS Can. Or. 70 (Neubauer 1147,8), f. 107b-111a, M.
9. Oxford - Bodleian Library MS Opp. 170 (Neubauer 1205), f. 262a-266b, C.
10. Parma - Biblioteca Palatina Cod. Parm. 3205 (de Rossi 655), f. 190a-192a, C, rubric: קרובץ ביום ט לאב.
11. Vatican - Biblioteca Apostolica ebr. 318, f. 220a-224b, GI.

Ashkenaz, commentary by Abraham b. Azriel[1]

12. Vatican - Biblioteca Apostolica ebr. 301,1, f. 133a-133b, C.

Tsarfat
13. Oxford - Bodleian Library MS Laud. Or. 271 (Neubauer 1206), f. 136a-138b, C, commentator: Aaron b. Hayyim haKohen (compiler).

אאגרה בני איש המשורר בטל (א 4), אלעזר ברבי קליר, מוסף א׳ דפסח

Ashkenaz
14. Berlin - Staatsbibliothek (Preussischer Kulturbesitz) Or. Qu. 798-799 (Steinschneider 177), II, f. 65a-66b, M.

---

[1] Edited by Urbach, ערוגת הבושם, vol. III, p. 246-256.

15. Braunschweig - Landesmuseum fuer Geschichte und Volkstum R 2386, vol. I, f. 24b-26a, M.
16. Budapest - Magyar tudomanyos akademia, MS. Kaufmann A 384, f. 139a-141a, M.
17. Budapest - Magyar tudomanyos akademia, MS. Kaufmann A 400, p. 109-115, C, no incipit.
18. Budapest - Magyar tudomanyos akademia, MS. Kaufmann A 400, p. 383-388, C.
19. Hamburg - Staats- und Universitaetsbibliothek Cod. hebr. 17/2 (Steinschneider 152), f. 56a-58b, C.
20. Hamburg - Staats- und Universitaetsbibliothek Cod. hebr. 225, f. 70a-73a, G.
21. Jerusalem - Schocken Institute 24100 / Mahzor Nuremberg, f. 84a-85b, M.
22. Koblenz - Staatsarchiv Abt. 701, Nr. 759,5,7, f. 1b-2b, FC.
23. London - British Library Add. 18695 (Margoliouth 683), f. 27a-28b, T, Yiddish.
24. Moscow - Russian State Library, Ms. Guenzburg 615, f. 11a-14a, C, rubric: רהוטא. למוסף את זה קרובוץ. קול רינה וישועה באהלי צדיקים.
25. Muenchen - Bayerische Staatsbibliothek, Cod. hebr. 393, f. 127a, C, no incipit, very short.
26. New York - Jewish Theological Seminary Ms. 4466, f. 58b-61a, M.
27. Oxford - Bodleian Library MS Opp. 170 (Neubauer 1205), f. 63b-66b, C.
28. Paris - Bibliotheque Nationale heb. 709, f. 78a-82b, C, rubric: אלפא ביתא אחרת.
29. Parma - Biblioteca Palatina Cod. Parm. 3507 (Perreau 27), f. 52a-54a, C.
30. Parma - Biblioteca Palatina Cod. Parm 3000 (de Rossi 378), f. 58b-61b, M.
31. Parma - Biblioteca Palatina Cod. Parm. 3205 (de Rossi 655), f. 85a-87a, C.
32. Parma - Biblioteca Palatina Cod. Parm. 1002 (Ta 24), f. 98a-99b, M.
33. Zurich - Zentralbibliothek Heid. 139, f. 29b-31a, C, additional marginal notes.

Romania
34. Cambridge - University Library Add. 377,3, f. 56b-59a, C.
35. New York - Jewish Theological Seminary Ms. 4823, f. 1a-1b, FM, only end of commentary.

Tsarfat
36. London - British Library Add. 11639 (Margoliouth 1056), f. 657a-659a, M.
37. Moscow - Russian State Library, Ms. Guenzburg 1665, f. 62a-63a, M.

38. Oxford - Bodleian Library MS Laud. Or. 271 (Neubauer 1206), f. 64b-66a, C, commentator: Aaron b. Hayyim haKohen (compiler).
39. Parma - Biblioteca Palatina Cod. Parm. 3136 (de Rossi 405), f. 84b-85b, M, partly bleached.
40. Vatican - Biblioteca Apostolica ebr. 306, f. 142a-144a, C, no incipit.

אאדה עד חוג שמים אאלה אתי שמים (א 5), אלעזר ברבי קליר, קינה

Ashkenaz
41. Berlin - Staatsbibliothek (Preussischer Kulturbesitz) Or. Qu. 798-799 (Steinschneider 177), II, f. 186b-187b, M.
42. Budapest - Magyar tudomanyos akademia, MS. Kaufmann A 400, p. 207-209, C, rubric: אחרת.
43. Hamburg - Staats- und Universitaetsbibliothek Cod. hebr. 17/2 (Steinschneider 152), f. 95a-95b, C.
44. Jerusalem - Schocken Institute 24100 / Mahzor Nuremberg, f. 195a-195b, M.
45. Oxford - Bodleian Library MS Can. Or. 70 (Neubauer 1147,8), f. 125a-126a, M.
46. Oxford - Bodleian Library MS Opp. 170 (Neubauer 1205), f. 268a-269a, C.
47. Parma - Biblioteca Palatina Cod. Parm. 2886 (de Rossi 585), f. 116a-116b, M, later hand, margins cut.
48. Parma - Biblioteca Palatina Cod. Parm. 3205 (de Rossi 655), f. 194b-195a, C.
49. Vatican - Biblioteca Apostolica ebr. 312, f. 45a, G.
50. Vatican - Biblioteca Apostolica ebr. 318, f. 227a-228a, GI.

Ashkenaz, commentary by Abraham b. Azriel[2]
51. Vatican - Biblioteca Apostolica ebr. 301,1, f. 134b, C.

אאמיץ לנורא ואיום (א 13), אלעזר ברבי קליר, יוצר ב' דסכות

Ashkenaz
52. Berlin - Staatsbibliothek (Preussischer Kulturbesitz) Or. Qu. 798-799 (Steinschneider 177), I, f. 196b-197b, M.
53. Braunschweig - Landesmuseum fuer Geschichte und Volkstum R 2386, vol. I, f. 131b-132b, M.
54. Hamburg - Staats- und Universitaetsbibliothek Cod. hebr. 62 (Steinschneider 154), f. 36a-36b, C, rubric: יוצר ליום שיני.
55. Hamburg - Staats- und Universitaetsbibliothek Cod. hebr. 132 (Steinschneider 155), f. 55a-56b, C.
56. Jerusalem - Jewish National and University Library Ms Heb 8° 3037, f. 251b-253a, M.

---

[2] Edited by Urbach, ערוגת הבושם, vol. III, 261-262.

57. Jerusalem - Schocken Institute 24100 / Mahzor Nuremberg , f. 479b-480b, M.
58. London - British Library Add. 18695 (Margoliouth 683), f. 115b-116b, T, Yiddish, rubric: יוצר צו דעם אנדרן טג.
59. London - British Library Add. 22431 (Margoliouth 662a), f. 99a-100a, M.
60. London - British Library Or. 11318/1, f. 133a, C.
61. London - Montefiore Library 261 , f. 69a-69b, C, commentator: Eliezer b. Natan?.
62. New York - Jewish Theological Seminary Ms. 4466, f. 442b-444a, M.
63. Oxford - Bodleian Library MS Mich. 365 (Neubauer 1208) , f. 100a-100b, C, rubric: יוצר ליום שיני.
64. Oxford - Bodleian Library MS Opp. 172 (Neubauer 1211), f. 91a, C, rubric: יוצר ליום שני.
65. Parma - Biblioteca Palatina Cod. Parm. 3507 (Perreau 27), f. 175b, C.
66. Vatican - Biblioteca Apostolica ebr. 305,1, f. 40a-40b, C, rubric: יוצר ליום שיני.
67. Vatican - Biblioteca Apostolica ebr. 422/1, f. 21a-21b, C, rubric: יוצר ליום שיני.
68. Zurich - Zentralbibliothek Heid. 139 , f. 92b, C, rubric: יוצר ליום שיני, additional marginal notes.

Romania
69. London - London School of Jewish Studies. Asher I.Myers collection 9, f. 217b-218b, M, rubric: יוצר ליום שני. לחן מלך אזור גבורה. וגם לחן ויהי הכל במאם׳.
70. Vatican - Biblioteca Apostolica ebr. 320, f. 427b-428a, M.

Tsarfat
71. London - David Sofer 5, f. 178a-178b, C, rubric: זה פירוש מסוכות של יום ראשון.
72. Moscow - Russian State Library, Ms. Guenzburg 1665, f. 169a-169b, M.
73. Parma - Biblioteca Palatina Cod. Parm. 1264, f. 49b-50b, G.

אאמיר אותך סלה (א 18), אלעזר ברבי קליר, אופן א׳ או ב׳ דסכות

Ashkenaz
74. Berlin - Staatsbibliothek (Preussischer Kulturbesitz) Or. Qu. 798-799 (Steinschneider 177), I, f. 189b-190a, M.
75. Braunschweig - Landesmuseum fuer Geschichte und Volkstum R 2386, vol. I, f. 120a-120b, M.
76. Braunschweig - Landesmuseum fuer Geschichte und Volkstum R 2386, vol. I, f. 132b, M.
77. Hamburg - Staats- und Universitaetsbibliothek Cod. hebr. 62 (Steinschneider 154), f. 33a, C, rubric: אופן, very short.

78. Jerusalem - Jewish National and University Library Ms Heb 8° 3037, f. 233b, M, very short.
79. Jerusalem - Schocken Institute 24100 / Mahzor Nuremberg, f. 475b, M, very short.
80. London - British Library Add. 18695 (Margoliouth 683), f. 110b, T, Yiddish.
81. London - British Library Or. 11318/1, f. 129b, C, short.
82. London - Montefiore Library 261, f. 65a, C, commentator: Eliezer b. Natan?.
83. Oxford - Bodleian Library MS Mich. 365 (Neubauer 1208), f. 94b, C, rubric: אופן, very short.
84. Vatican - Biblioteca Apostolica ebr. 422/1, f. 20a, C, very short.
85. Zurich - Zentralbibliothek Heid. 139, f. 89b, C, rubric: אופן, short.

Romania

86. London - London School of Jewish Studies. Asher I.Myers collection 9, f. 201a, M, rubric: אופן.

אאמיר אל עליון

Sepharad, commentary by Josef Garad

87. Oxford - Bodleian Library Heb.e.10 (Neubauer 2746/1), f. 23a, C, rubric: מגן לאל, very short, no incipit.

אאמיר מסתתר במעון חביון (א 21), יוסף ב"ר שמואל טוב עלם, יוצר לשבת הגדול

Ashkenaz, commentary by Abraham b. Azriel[3]

88. Frankfurt a M - Stadt- und Universitaetsbibliothek Fol. 16 (Merzbacher 95), f. 49b-50(i)a, C, rubric: יוצר דשבת שלפני שבת הגדול.

אאפיד נזר איום בשלוש קדושה ביום (א 25), אלעזר ברבי קליר, חלק ז', קדושתא א' דראש השנה

Ashkenaz

89. Berlin - Staatsbibliothek (Preussischer Kulturbesitz) Or. Qu. 798-799 (Steinschneider 177), I, f. 8a, M.
90. Braunschweig - Landesmuseum fuer Geschichte und Volkstum R 2386, vol. II, f. 82a-82b, M.
91. Budapest - Magyar tudomanyos akademia, MS. Kaufmann A 400, p. 254, C, no incipit, ecclectic.
92. Cambridge - University Library Or. 785, f. 20b, G.
93. Darmstadt - Hessisches Landes- und Hochschulbibliothek Cod. Or. 15, f. 7b, M.
94. Hamburg - Staats- und Universitaetsbibliothek Cod. hebr. 12 (Steinschneider 102), f. 7a, G.

---

[3] Edited by Urbach, ערוגת הבושם, vol. III, p. 532-533.

95. Hamburg - Staats- und Universitaetsbibliothek Cod. hebr. 17/2 (Steinschneider 152), f. 108b, C.
96. Hamburg - Staats- und Universitaetsbibliothek Cod. hebr. 40b (Steinschneider 110), f. 7b, G.
97. Hamburg - Staats- und Universitaetsbibliothek Cod. hebr. 40c (Steinschneider 111), f. 133b, G.
98. Hamburg - Staats- und Universitaetsbibliothek Cod. hebr. 132 (Steinschneider 155), f. 7a-7b, C.
99. Hamburg - Staats- und Universitaetsbibliothek Cod. hebr. 139 (Steinschneider 115), f. 22a-22b, G.
100. Hamburg - Staats- und Universitaetsbibliothek Cod. hebr. 225, f. 220b-221a, G.
101. Jerusalem - Jewish National and University Library Ms Heb 8° 3037, f. 10a-10b, M.
102. Jerusalem - Schocken Institute 15791/7, f. 59b-60a, C, no incipit, kabbalistic.
103. Jerusalem - Schocken Institute 24100 / Mahzor Nuremberg, f. 325a, M.
104. London - British Library Or. 11318/1, f. 12a-12b, C.
105. Moscow - Russian State Library, Ms. Guenzburg 1401/2, f. 16b, C.
106. Moscow - Russian State Library, Ms. Guenzburg 615, f. 59a, C.
107. New York - Jewish Theological Seminary Ms. 4466, f. 213a, M.
108. New York - Jewish Theological Seminary Ms. 8097, f. 59b, C, additional glosses in the margins.
109. New York - Jewish Theological Seminary Ms. 8169 (Acc. 0016), f. 6b-7b, M.
110. Oxford - Bodleian Library MS Opp. 170 (Neubauer 1205), f. 106b-107a, C.
111. Oxford - Bodleian Library MS Opp. 172 (Neubauer 1211), f. 4b-5a, C.
112. Oxford - Bodleian Library MS Opp. 619 (Neubauer 2374), f. 12b-13a, M.
113. Oxford - Bodleian Library MS Opp. 675 (Neubauer 1210), f. 17a-17b, C, no incipit.
114. Paris - Bibliotheque Nationale heb. 653, f. 10b, G.
115. Parma - Biblioteca Palatina Cod. Parm. 3507 (Perreau 27), f. 112b-113a, C, first incipit מלך, then אאפיד.
116. Parma - Biblioteca Palatina Cod. Parm. 3270 (de Rossi 1215), f. 21b, M.
117. Parma - Biblioteca Palatina Cod. Parm. 3205 (de Rossi 655), f. 205b, C.
118. Vatican - Biblioteca Apostolica ebr. 308, f. 34a-34b, C, commentator: David b. Mose (compiler).
119. Vatican - Biblioteca Apostolica ebr. 422/1, f. 8b, C, short.

120. Zurich - Zentralbibliothek Heid. 139, f. 59a-59b, C, additional marginal notes.

Asti, Fossano, Moncalvo

121. New Haven - Yale University, Beinecke Rare Book and MS Library, MS Heb. 52, f. 20b, M.

Romania

122. Vatican - Biblioteca Apostolica ebr. 320, f. 151b-152a, M.

Tsarfat

123. Parma - Biblioteca Palatina Cod. Parm. 2125 (de Rossi 812), f. 10b-11a, C, first incipit מלך, second incipit אאפיד.
124. London - British Library Or. 8682, f. 12a, G.
125. London - David Sofer 5, f. 110b-111a, C.
126. Oxford - Bodleian Library MS Laud. Or. 271 (Neubauer 1206), f. 141a-141b, C, commentator: Aaron b. Hayyim haKohen (compiler), additional marginal notes.
127. Oxford - Bodleian Library MS Opp. 171 (Neubauer 1207), f. 59a, C, rubric: פזמון, incipit מלך.
128. Paris - Bibliotheque Nationale heb. 445,9, f. 65b-66a, C.
129. Parma - Biblioteca Palatina Cod. Parm. 1794 (de Rossi 1061), f. 64a-64b, M, incipit מלך.
130. Parma - Biblioteca Palatina Cod. Parm. 3006 (de Rossi 654,1), f. 27a-27b, M.
131. Vatican - Biblioteca Apostolica ebr. 306, f. 49b-50a, C, no incipit.

אאריא מתילי ואחיון (א 26), רשות ארמי לדבור שמיני בשבועות

Ashkenaz

132. Hamburg - Staats- und Universitaetsbibliothek Cod. hebr. 17/2 (Steinschneider 152), f. 73a-73b, C.
133. Oxford - Bodleian Library MS Opp. 170 (Neubauer 1205), f. 99a-100b, C.
134. Parma - Biblioteca Palatina Cod. Parm. 3205 (de Rossi 655), f. 186-187a, C.

Ashkenaz, commentary by Benjamin b. Abraham Anaw

135. Jerusalem - Musad haRav Kook 478, p. 55-66, C, rubric: אלפא ביתא יא.
136. London - Beth Din & Beth Hamidrash 6,9, f. 182a-188b, C, rubric: אלפא ביט.

אב הרחמים אשר הסליחה עמך (א 39), סעדיה גאון, סליחה

Yemen

137. New York - Jewish Theological Seminary Ms. 3193, f. 139b-140a, M.

Yemen, commentary by Isaac b. Abraham Wanneh

138. Chicago-Spertus College of Judaica D 2, 2, f. 228a-228b, M, no incipit.

56 CLAVIS COMMENTARIORUM

139. Jerusalem - Sassoon 1158, p. 315, M, no incipit.
140. London - British Library Or. 11122, f. 204b-205a, M, rubric: אל מלך, no incipit.

אב ידעך מנוער בחנתו בעשר בל עבור בראש תער (א 47), אלעזר ברקבי קליר, קרובה לנעילה
Ashkenaz
141. Berlin - Staatsbibliothek (Preussischer Kulturbesitz) Or. Qu. 798-799 (Steinschneider 177), I, f. 179b-180b, M.
142. Braunschweig - Landesmuseum fuer Geschichte und Volkstum R 2386, vol. II, f. 269b-270a, M.
143. Cambridge - University Library Add. 394,1 (Reif SCR 461), f. 73a, C.
144. Fulda - Hessische Landesbibliothek A 3 II, f. 129a-129b, C, commentator: Josef.
145. Hamburg - Staats- und Universitaetsbibliothek Cod. hebr. 17/2 (Steinschneider 152), f. 161a-161b, C, rubric: לנעילה.
146. Hamburg - Staats- und Universitaetsbibliothek Cod. hebr. 62 (Steinschneider 154), f. 22a-23a, C, rubric: לנעילה.
147. Hamburg - Staats- und Universitaetsbibliothek Cod. hebr. 132 (Steinschneider 155), f. 50a, C, short.
148. Jerusalem - Jewish National and University Library Ms Heb 8° 3037, f. 225b, M.
149. Jerusalem - Schocken Institute 24100 / Mahzor Nuremberg, f. 461b, M, only on the first three Berakhot.
150. London - British Library Or. 11318/1, f. 126a-127a, C, .
151. London - Montefiore Library 261, f. 64b, C, commentator: Eliezer b. Natan?.
152. Moscow - Russian State Library, Ms. Guenzburg 615, f. 109a, C, rubric: לנעילה, incomplete.
153. Muenchen - Bayerische Staatsbibliothek, Cod. hebr. 346, f. 88b-89a, C.
154. New York - Jewish Theological Seminary Ms. 4466, f. 425a-425b, M, rubric: קרובה לנעילה.
155. Oxford - Bodleian Library MS Mich. 365 (Neubauer 1208), f. 93b-94a, C, rubric: לנעילה.
156. Oxford - Bodleian Library MS Opp. 170 (Neubauer 1205), f. 182a, C, rubric: קרובה לנעילה.
157. Oxford - Bodleian Library MS Opp. 619 (Neubauer 2374), f. 277a-277b, M.
158. Oxford - Bodleian Library MS Opp. 172 (Neubauer 1211), f. 86a-86b, C, rubric: זו תפילת נעילה, no incipit.
159. Paris - Bibliotheque Nationale heb. 653, f. 117a, G.
160. Parma - Biblioteca Palatina Cod. Parm. 3205 (de Rossi 655), f. 238a, C, rubric: לנעילה.

161. Parma - Biblioteca Palatina Cod. Parm. 3270 (de Rossi 1215), f. 238a, M, rubric: קרובה לנעילה.
162. Parma - Biblioteca Palatina Cod. Parm. 3507 (Perreau 27), f. 172b-173a, C.
163. Vatican - Biblioteca Apostolica ebr. 308, f. 145(ii)b-146a, C, commentator: David b. Mose (compiler), rubric: ובכאן אתחיל נעילה בע"ה.
164. Vatican - Biblioteca Apostolica ebr. 422/1, f. 19b, C, rubric: סליחות לנעילה.
165. Zurich - Zentralbibliothek Heid. 139, f. 89a, C, rubric: לנעילה, short, additional marginal notes.

Roma
166. Oxford - Bodleian Library MS Mich. 312,1 (Neubauer 2276,1), f. 9a, C, rubric: בנעילה באב ידעך, no incipit, begins. בחנתו כל עבור בראש תער.

Tsarfat
167. London - David Sofer 5, f. 171b-172a, C, rubric: זה פירוש מקרובה אחרת של נעילה מיום הכפורים.
168. Oxford - Bodleian Library MS Bodl. Or. 109 (Neubauer 1209), f. 42b-43a, C, commentator: Aaron b. Hayyim haKohen (compiler), no incipit.
169. Oxford - Bodleian Library MS Laud. Or. 271 (Neubauer 1206), f. 118b-119a, C, commentator: Aaron b. Hayyim haKohen (compiler), rubric: לנעילה, no incipit.
170. Vatican - Biblioteca Apostolica ebr. 306, f. 111b-112a, C, rubric: סדר נעילה. קרובה.

אב לרחם ורב סלוח (א 53), שלמה הבבלי, סליחה

Ashkenaz
171. Budapest - Magyar tudomanyos akademia, MS. Kaufmann A 400, p. 435-436, C, rubric: סליחה שלמונית.
172. Cambridge - University Library Dd. 2.30, f. 58b-59a, G.
173. Hamburg - Staats- und Universitaetsbibliothek Cod. hebr. 17/2 (Steinschneider 152), f. 130a-130b, C, rubric: סליחה שלמונית.
174. Jerusalem - Schocken Institute 24100 / Mahzor Nuremberg, f. 397b-398a, M.
175. Moscow - Russian State Library, Ms. Guenzburg 190, f. 22b-23a, G.
176. Moscow - Russian State Library, Ms. Guenzburg 615, f. 156a-157a, C, rubric: אל מלך.
177. Muenchen - Bayerische Staatsbibliothek, Cod. hebr. 346, f. 139a-140a, C, rubric: אחרת.
178. Oxford - Bodleian Library MS Mich. 543 (Neubauer 1212), f. 67a-67b, C, commentator: Isaac b. Jacob (compiler).
179. Oxford - Bodleian Library MS Opp. 170 (Neubauer 1205), f. 225a-226a, C.

180. Oxford - Bodleian Library MS Opp. 172 (Neubauer 1211), f. 56a-56b, C.
181. Oxford - Bodleian Library MS Opp. 681 (Neubauer 1213), f. 50b-52a, C.
182. Padova - Biblioteca del Seminario Vescovile Cod. 218, f. 151a-151b, M.
183. Padova - Biblioteca del Seminario Vescovile Cod. 218, f. 151b-152a, M.
184. Parma - Biblioteca Palatina Cod. Parm. 3205 (de Rossi 655), f. 254b-255a, C.
185. Vatican - Biblioteca Apostolica ebr. 308, f. 111a-112a, C, commentator: David b. Mose (compiler).
186. Vatican - Biblioteca Apostolica ebr. 422/1, f. 27a, C, very short.
187. Vatican - Biblioteca Apostolica ebr. 422/1, f. 40b, CG, no incipit.

Ashkenaz, commentary by Abraham b. Azriel[4]

188. Vatican - Biblioteca Apostolica ebr. 301,1, f. 157b-158a, C, rubric: אחרת.

Tsarfat

189. London - British Library Add. 11639 (Margoliouth 1056), f. 462b, M.
190. London - David Sofer 5, f. 166b-167a, C, rubric: סליחה.
191. Oxford - Bodleian Library MS Laud. Or. 271 (Neubauer 1206), f. 176a-176b, C, commentator: Aaron b. Hayyim haKohen (compiler).
192. Oxford - Bodleian Library MS Opp. 171 (Neubauer 1207), f. 96b-97a, C, rubric: אחרת.
193. Parma - Biblioteca Palatina Cod. Parm. 1794 (de Rossi 1061), f. 30a-31a, M.
194. Parma - Biblioteca Palatina Cod. Parm. 3006 (de Rossi 654,1), f. 204a-204b, M.
195. Vatican - Biblioteca Apostolica ebr. 306, f. 89b-90b, C.

אב רחמן מלא רחמים חטאנו לפניך רחם עלינו (א 59), סליחה

Yemen, commentary by Isaac b. Abraham Wanneh

196. Jerusalem - Sassoon 1158, p. 300, M, here as אדון הסליחות בוחן לבבות.

אב שמעון יקול יא כאלקי (א 62), שלם שבזי

Yemen

197. Cincinnati - Hebrew Union College 398, f. 45b-46b, M.

אב שמעון קאל קלבי (א 63), שלם שבזי

Yemen

198. Cincinnati - Hebrew Union College 398, f. 44a-44b, M.

---

[4] Edited by Urbach, ערוגת הבושם, vol. III, p. 414-416.

HEBREW LITURGICAL POETRY 59

אבאר קצת פלאי אלהים (א 73), יהודה הלוי, סליחה

Yemen
199. Cincinnati - Hebrew Union College 199, f. 77b, G.
200. Jerusalem - Benayahu ת 414, f. 133a, M.
201. Jerusalem - Musad haRav Kook 334, f. 135a-136a, M.
202. Jerusalem - Sassoon 902, p. 380-381, M.
203. New York - Jewish Theological Seminary Ms. 3052, f. 47b-49b, M, rubric: אל מלך.
204. New York - Jewish Theological Seminary Ms. 3109, f. 73b-74a, M.

Yemen, commentary by Isaac b. Abraham Wanneh
205. Chicago-Spertus College of Judaica D 2, 2, f. 207b-208a, M, no incipit.
206. Jerusalem - Benayahu ת 282, f. 127b-128b, M, rubric: אל מלך.
207. Jerusalem - Benayahu ת 261, f. 144b-145a, M, rubric: אל מלך.
208. Jerusalem - Makhon Ben Zvi 1156 (Tubi 155), f. 127a-127b, M, rubric: אל מלך.
209. Jerusalem - Makhon Ben Zvi 1174 (Tubi 154), f. 100a, M, rubric: אל מלך.
210. Jerusalem - Michael Krupp 604, f. 161a-161b, M, rubric: אל מלך.
211. Jerusalem - Musad haRav Kook 325, f. 160b-161a, M.
212. Jerusalem - Sassoon 1158, p. 392-393, M, no incipit.
213. Jerusalem - Sassoon 1174, p. 245-246, M.
214. Jerusalem - Yehiel haLevi 4, f. 141a-141b, G.
215. London - British Library Or. 11122, f. 197b-198b, M, no incipit.
216. Manchester - John Rylands University Library, Ms. Gaster 5, f. 182b-183a, M.
217. Muenchen - Bayerische Staatsbibliothek, Cod. hebr. 472, f. 174b-175b, M, rubric: אל מלך.
218. New York - Jewish Theological Seminary Ms. 3013, f. 110a, M, rubric: אל מלך.
219. New York - Jewish Theological Seminary Ms. 3294, f. 4b-5a, C.
220. New York - Public Library, Heb. Ms. 9, f. 119a, M.
221. Philadelphia - University of Pennsylvania HB 2, f. 122b-123a, M, rubric: אל מלך.
222. Strasbourg - Bibliotheque Nationale et Universitaire 3965 (Landauer 39), p. 336, M, rubric: אל מלך.

אבדא בתוחיד רבי, שלם שבזי?

Yemen
223. Cincinnati - Hebrew Union College 398, f. 10a-11a, M.

אבדה ממנו אמונה (א 83), יצחק השנירי
Carpentras, commentary by Mordekhai b. Josef of Rocco Martino
224. Cincinnati - Hebrew Union College 246/1, f. 82a-82b, C, rubric: פי׳ רהוטה אבדה ממנו.

אבדו חכמי גזית יושבי גנים (א 85), אליה ב"ר שמעיה, סליחה
Ashkenaz
225. Padova - Biblioteca del Seminario Vescovile Cod. 218, f. 159a-160a, M.
226. Vatican - Biblioteca Apostolica ebr. 308/1, f. 6a-6b, C, commentator: David b. Mose (compiler).
227. Vatican - Biblioteca Apostolica ebr. 422/1, f. 30a, C.
228. Vatican - Biblioteca Apostolica ebr. 422/1, f. 44a, CG, no incipit.

Ashkenaz, commentary by Abraham b. Azriel[5]
229. Frankfurt a M - Stadt- und Universitaetsbibliothek Fol. 16 (Merzbacher 95), f. 103b, C.
230. Frankfurt a M - Stadt- und Universitaetsbibliothek Fol. 16 (Merzbacher 95), f. 109b-110a, C.
231. Vatican - Biblioteca Apostolica ebr. 301,1, f. 148b-149a, C, rubric: לא מצאתי יותר postscript אחרת.

אבדו ישרי חומותי ושורי, סליחה
Yemen, commentary by Isaac b. Abraham Wanneh
232. Chicago-Spertus College of Judaica D 2, 2, f. 242a-242b, M, no incipit.
233. London - British Library Or. 11122, f. 219a-219b, M, no incipit.

אבדנו ארץ טובה בהפזון (א 86), גרשום ב"ר יהודה מאור הגולה, סליחה
Ashkenaz
234. Budapest - Magyar tudomanyos akademia, MS. Kaufmann A 400, p. 507-508, C, rubric: גרש׳ דרב׳ ברית. זכור.
235. Jerusalem - Schocken Institute 24100 / Mahzor Nuremberg, f. 261b-262a, M, begins זכור ברית אברהם ועקידת יצחק.
236. Jerusalem - Schocken Institute 24100 / Mahzor Nuremberg, f. 468b, M, begins זכור ברית אהברהם, incipit אבדנו.
237. London - British Library Add. 18695 (Margoliouth 683), f. 168b-169a, T, Yiddish, begins זכור ברית אהברהם.
238. Moscow - Russian State Library, Ms. Guenzburg 190, f. 108b-109b, G.
239. Muenchen - Bayerische Staatsbibliothek, Cod. hebr. 346, f. 121b-123a, C, rubric: גרשם דרבנא פיזמון begins זכור ברית אהברהם.

---
[5] Edited by Urbach, ערוגת הבושם, vol. III, p. 353-355.

240. Padova - Biblioteca del Seminario Vescovile Cod. 218, f. 112a-112b, M, begins זכור ברית אהברהם.
241. Parma - Biblioteca Palatina Cod. Parm. 3205 (de Rossi 655), f. 272a-273a, C.

Ashkenaz, commentary by Abraham b. Azriel[6]

242. Vatican - Biblioteca Apostolica ebr. 301,1, f. 164a-164b, C.

Tsarfat

243. London - David Sofer 5, f. 148a-149a, C, rubric: זכור.
244. Oxford - Bodleian Library MS Laud. Or. 271 (Neubauer 1206), f. 127a-127b, C, commentator: Aaron b. Hayyim haKohen (compiler).
245. Oxford - Bodleian Library MS Opp. 171 (Neubauer 1207), f. 104a-105a, C, rubric: אחרת.
246. Parma - Biblioteca Palatina Cod. Parm. 3006 (de Rossi 654,1), f. 165b-166a, M.
247. Parma - Biblioteca Palatina Cod. Parm. 3007 (de Rossi 654,2), f. 6b-7b, M.
248. Vatican - Biblioteca Apostolica ebr. 306, f. 183b-184b, C.

אבו יהודה יעורר ציר תעודה (א 92), שלם שבזי

Yemen

249. Cincinnati - Hebrew Union College 398, f. 186b-188a, M.

אבו יהודה יקול פי ראי מעקול (א 93), שלם שבזי

Yemen

250. Cincinnati - Hebrew Union College 398, f. 185b-186a, M.

אבו יהודא יקול אלבי תפכד (א 94), שלם שבזי

Yemen

251. Cincinnati - Hebrew Union College 398, f. 185a-185b, M.

אבוא בחיל להתיצבה (א 106), יוסף ב"ר שמואל טוב עלם, חלק ה', קדושתא לשבת הגדול

Ashkenaz

252. Jerusalem - Schocken Institute 24100 / Mahzor Nuremberg, f. 73b, M.
253. Muenchen - Bayerische Staatsbibliothek, Cod. hebr. 88, f. 51b-52a, G.
254. Parma - Biblioteca Palatina Cod. Parm. 3507 (Perreau 27), f. 34b, C.

Tsarfat

255. Moscow - Russian State Library, Ms. Guenzburg 1665, f. 47a, M.
256. Parma - Biblioteca Palatina Cod. Parm. 3136 (de Rossi 405), f. 60b-61a, M.

---

[6] Edited by Urbach, ערוגת הבושם, vol. III, p. 453-459.

257. Vatican - Biblioteca Apostolica ebr. 306, f. 165a, C, rubric: לשבת הגדול של פסח.

אבואה ואשתחוה ואכרעה (א 129), סליחה

Ashkenaz
258. Berlin - Staatsbibliothek (Preussischer Kulturbesitz) Or. Qu. 798-799 (Steinschneider 177), I, f. 169b-170a, M.
259. Oxford - Bodleian Library MS Opp. 681 (Neubauer 1213), f. 45b, C.
260. Padova - Biblioteca del Seminario Vescovile Cod. 218, f. 211b-212a, M, short.

Ashkenaz, commentary by Abraham b. Azriel[7]
261. Frankfurt a M - Stadt- und Universitaetsbibliothek Fol. 16 (Merzbacher 95), f. 107a, C.

Tsarfat
262. London - David Sofer 5, f. 173a-173b, C, rubric: זה פירוש מסליחות של נעילה.
263. Oxford - Bodleian Library MS Bodl. Or. 109 (Neubauer 1209), f. 43b-44a, C, commentator: Aaron b. Hayyim haKohen (compiler).
264. Parma - Biblioteca Palatina Cod. Parm. 3006 (de Rossi 654,1), f. 246a, M.
265. Vatican - Biblioteca Apostolica ebr. 306, f. 203a, C.

אבונן דבשמיא ובריין (א 139), מאיר ב"ר יצחק, ראשות לתרגום

Tsarfat
266. Oxford - Bodleian Library MS Laud. Or. 271 (Neubauer 1206), f. 78b-79a, C, commentator: Aaron b. Hayyim haKohen (compiler).

אבותי כרבת ריבם (א 148), אליה ב"ר שמעיה, סליחה

Ashkenaz
267. Budapest - Magyar tudomanyos akademia, MS. Kaufmann A 400, p. 514-515, C, rubric: חטאנו דרבינו גרשם.
268. Moscow - Russian State Library, Ms. Guenzburg 190, f. 117a-118b, G.
269. Oxford - Bodleian Library MS Mich. 543 (Neubauer 1212), f. 84a-84b, C, commentator: Isaac b. Jacob (compiler).
270. Oxford - Bodleian Library MS Opp. 170 (Neubauer 1205), f. 240(ii)a-241a, C.
271. Oxford - Bodleian Library MS Opp. 681 (Neubauer 1213), f. 91a-92a, C.
272. Parma - Biblioteca Palatina Cod. Parm. 3205 (de Rossi 655), f. 275a-275b, C.

---

[7] Edited by Urbach, ערוגת הבושם, vol. III, p. 556.

273. Vatican - Biblioteca Apostolica ebr. 422/1, f. 45a-45b, CG, no incipit.
Romania
274. Vatican - Biblioteca Apostolica ebr. 320, f. 393a-394a, M.
Tsarfat
275. London - British Library Add. 11639 (Margoliouth 1056), f. 489b-491a, M.
276. London - David Sofer 5, f. 170a-171a, C, rubric: חטאנו.
277. Oxford - Bodleian Library MS Laud. Or. 271 (Neubauer 1206), f. 126a-127a, C, commentator: Aaron b. Hayyim haKohen (compiler).
278. Oxford - Bodleian Library MS Opp. 171 (Neubauer 1207), f. 115b-116a, C, rubric: אחרת.
279. Parma - Biblioteca Palatina Cod. Parm. 2890 (de Rossi 856), f. 138a-139a, M.
280. Parma - Biblioteca Palatina Cod. Parm. 3007 (de Rossi 654,2), f. 10a-11a, M.
281. Vatican - Biblioteca Apostolica ebr. 306, f. 176b-177b, C.

אבי אביון יהי הגיון (א 163), שמשון, סליחה
Ashkenaz
282. Moscow - Russian State Library, Ms. Guenzburg 190, f. 68a-68b, G.
283. Vatican - Biblioteca Apostolica ebr. 422/1, f. 41a, CG, no incipit.
Tsarfat
284. London - David Sofer 5, f. 100b-101a, C.
285. Parma - Biblioteca Palatina Cod. Parm. 2890 (de Rossi 856), f. 134a-134b, M.
286. Parma - Biblioteca Palatina Cod. Parm. 3007 (de Rossi 654,2), f. 103a-103b, M.
287. Vatican - Biblioteca Apostolica ebr. 306, f. 210b-211a, C.

אבי התעודה לבש ענוה (א 173), אהרן בן יוסף הרופא, פרשת וארא
Karaite, commentary by Berakha b. Josef haKohen
288. New York - Jewish Theological Seminary Ms. 3367, f. 66a-68b, C, rubric: פרוש פרשת וארא.
289. St. Petersburg - Inst. of Oriental Studies of the Russian Academy B 431, f. 48b-50a, C, rubric: פרשת וארא.
290. St. Petersburg - Russian National Library, Evr. IV 50, f. 47b-49a, C, rubric: וארא.

אבי כל חוזה חל בו במחזה (א 181), אלעזר ברבי קליר, חלק ד', קדושתא החדש
Ashkenaz
291. Berlin - Staatsbibliothek (Preussischer Kulturbesitz) Or. Qu. 798-799 (Steinschneider 177), II, f. 41a-41b, M.

292. Budapest - Magyar tudomanyos akademia, MS. Kaufmann A 384, f. 90b-91a, M.
293. Erlangen - Universitaetsbibliothek 2601 (Roth 67), f. 51a, M.
294. Hamburg - Staats- und Universitaetsbibliothek Cod. hebr. 17/2 (Steinschneider 152), f. 28b, C.
295. Jerusalem - Schocken Institute 24100 / Mahzor Nuremberg, f. 65b-66a, M.
296. London - British Library Add. 18695 (Margoliouth 683), f. 4a-5a, T, Yiddish.
297. Muenchen - Bayerische Staatsbibliothek, Cod. hebr. 88, f. 44a-44b, G.
298. Muenchen - Bayerische Staatsbibliothek, Cod. hebr. 393, f. 104b-105a, C, no incipit.
299. New York - Jewish Theological Seminary Ms. 4466, f. 21b-22b, M.
300. Oxford - Bodleian Library MS Opp. 170 (Neubauer 1205), f. 34b-35a, C.
301. Paris - Bibliotheque Nationale heb. 709, f. 40b-41b, C.
302. Parma - Biblioteca Palatina Cod. Parm. 1002 (Ta 24), f. 68b, M.
303. Parma - Biblioteca Palatina Cod. Parm 3000 (de Rossi 378), f. 21b-22b, M.
304. Parma - Biblioteca Palatina Cod. Parm. 3205 (de Rossi 655), f. 40a-41b, C.
305. Parma - Biblioteca Palatina Cod. Parm. 3507 (Perreau 27), f. 30b-31a, C.
306. Vatican - Biblioteca Apostolica ebr. 305,1, f. 26a-26b, C, no incipit.
307. Zurich - Zentralbibliothek Heid. 139, f. 9b-10a, C, additional marginal notes.

Tsarfat
308. London - British Library Add. 11639 (Margoliouth 1056), f. 277a-277b, M.
309. London - David Sofer 5, f. 33b-35a, C.
310. Moscow - Russian State Library, Ms. Guenzburg 1665, f. 40a-40b, M.
311. Oxford - Bodleian Library MS Laud. Or. 271 (Neubauer 1206), f. 47a-47b, C, commentator: Aaron b. Hayyim haKohen (compiler).
312. Parma - Biblioteca Palatina Cod. Parm. 3136 (de Rossi 405), f. 54b-55a, M.
313. Vatican - Biblioteca Apostolica ebr. 306, f. 154a-154b, C, no incipit.

אבי עבור על רשעי התדרוש לעון בצעי (א 187), אברהם אבן עזרא, תוכחה
Sepharad, commentary by David b. Josef Abudarham[8]
314. Budapest - Magyar tudomanyos akademia, MS. Kaufmann A 405/2, p. 210, C, rubric: תוכחה לאברהם ן' זרא ז"ל.

---
[8] Edited by Prins, תשלום אבודרהם, p. 104-105.

315. New York - Columbia X893 Ab 93, f. 13(ii)a, C, rubric: תוכחה לאברהם
ן׳ עזרא ז״ל.

אביוני עמך עניים ודלים (א 204), בנימין ב״ר זרח, סליחה
Ashkenaz
316. Muenchen - Bayerische Staatsbibliothek, Cod. hebr. 346, f. 164b, C.
317. Oxford - Bodleian Library MS Mich. 543 (Neubauer 1212), f. 16b-17a, C, commentator: Isaac b. Jacob (compiler).
318. Oxford - Bodleian Library MS Opp. 681 (Neubauer 1213), f. 43b-44a, C.
319. Parma - Bibliotheca Palatina Cod. Parm. 3205 (de Rossi 655), f. 287a, C.
320. Vatican - Biblioteca Apostolica ebr. 422/1, f. 30a, C.
321. Vatican - Biblioteca Apostolica ebr. 422/1, f. 44b, CG, no incipit.

אבינו מלך אנקת עמך ישראל ושועתו (א 212), משה ב״ר חסדאי, סליחה
Ashkenaz
322. Muenchen - Bayerische Staatsbibliothek, Cod. hebr. 346, f. 138a-138b, C, rubric: אחרת.
323. Muenchen - Bayerische Staatsbibliothek, Cod. hebr. 346, f. 149a, C, rubric: אחרת, short.
324. Oxford - Bodleian Library MS Opp. 172 (Neubauer 1211), f. 85a, C.
325. Vatican - Biblioteca Apostolica ebr. 308, f. 142b-143a, C, commentator: David b. Mose (compiler).
Ashkenaz, commentary by Abraham b. Azriel[9]
326. Frankfurt a M - Stadt- und Universitaetsbibliothek Fol. 16 (Merzbacher 95), f. 108a, C.

אביר אזרחים לאור עולם (א 248), מנחם, חלק א׳, קדושתא שחרית יום ב׳ דראש השנה
Carpentras
327. Cincinnati - Hebrew Union College 429/1, f. 21b-22b, M, no incipit.
Carpentras, commentary by Josef b. Abraham of Montelitz
328. Cincinnati - Hebrew Union College 357, f. 98b-99b, M.
329. Paris - Ecole Rabbinique 31, f. 137b-138a, M.

אביר הגביר אשר העביר (א 250), אברהם, אופן שבת וראש חדש
Ashkenaz
330. Jerusalem - Schocken Institute 24100 / Mahzor Nuremberg, f. 11a, M.
Ashkenaz, commentary by Abraham b. Azriel[10]
331. Frankfurt a M - Stadt- und Universitaetsbibliothek Fol. 16 (Merzbacher 95), f. 74b-75b, C, rubric: אופן.

---

[9] Edited by Urbach, ערוגת הבושם, vol. III, p. 559-560.
[10] Edited by Urbach, ערוגת הבושם, vol. III, p. 72-78.

332. Vatican - Biblioteca Apostolica ebr. 301,1, f. 105b-106b, C, rubric: אופן.

אביר יום העשור לכל המיחלים (א 252), סעדיה, סליחה

Yemen
333. New York - Jewish Theological Seminary Ms. 3028, f. 98b-99a, G.
334. New York - Jewish Theological Seminary Ms. 3193, f. 138b-139a, M.

Yemen, commentary by Isaac b. Abraham Wanneh
335. Chicago-Spertus College of Judaica D 2, 2, f. 227b-228a, M, no incipit.
336. Jerusalem - Sassoon 1158, p. 314-315, M, no incipit.
337. London - British Library Or. 11122, f. 204b, M, no incipit.

אבירי ארץ יאמירו במרץ (א 259), יוסף אבן אביתור, חלק ג', קדושתא ראש השנה

Tsarfat
338. London - David Sofer 5, f. 124b-125a, C.
339. Parma - Biblioteca Palatina Cod. Parm. 3006 (de Rossi 654,1), f. 90a, M.

אבכה בלב מר נכאה ונדכה (א 266), אליה, קינה

Carpentras, commentary by Mordekhai b. Josef of Rocco Martino
340. Cincinnati - Hebrew Union College 246/1, f. 73b-74a, C, rubric: פי' קינה אבכה בלב מר.

אבכה ועל שוד זבולי זבולי עיני בריכות כאולי (א 279), קינה

Yemen, commentary by Isaac b. Abraham Wanneh
341. Jerusalem - Sassoon 1158, p. 170, M.
342. London - British Library Or. 11122, f. 102a, M.

אבל אנחנו חטאים ואשמים (א 287), בנימין ב"ר זרח, סליחה

Ashkenaz
343. Berlin - Staatsbibliothek (Preussischer Kulturbesitz) Or. Qu. 798-799 (Steinschneider 177), I, f. 141a-141b, M.
344. Braunschweig - Landesmuseum fuer Geschichte und Volkstum R 2386, vol. II, f. 242a, M.
345. Jerusalem - Schocken Institute 24100 / Mahzor Nuremberg, f. 427a-427b, M.
346. Muenchen - Bayerische Staatsbibliothek, Cod. hebr. 346, f. 137b, C, rubric: אחרת, short.
347. New York - Jewish Theological Seminary Ms. 4466, f. 396b-397a, M.
348. New York - Jewish Theological Seminary Ms. 8097, f. 84a, C, short.
349. Oxford - Bodleian Library MS Mich. 543 (Neubauer 1212), f. 25a-25b, C, commentator: Isaac b. Jacob (compiler).

350. Oxford - Bodleian Library MS Opp. 172 (Neubauer 1211), f. 71b-72a, C.
351. Oxford - Bodleian Library MS Opp. 619 (Neubauer 2374), f. 227a-228a, M.
352. Oxford - Bodleian Library MS Opp. 681 (Neubauer 1213), f. 24b-25b, C.
353. Padova - Biblioteca del Seminario Vescovile Cod. 218, f. 190a-191a, M.
354. Vatican - Biblioteca Apostolica ebr. 308, f. 131(ii)b-132a, C, commentator: David b. Mose (compiler).
355. Vatican - Biblioteca Apostolica ebr. 422/1, f. 24b, C, very short.
356. Vatican - Biblioteca Apostolica ebr. 422/2, f. 39a, CG, no incipit, very short.

Ashkenaz, commentary by Abraham b. Azriel[11]
357. Frankfurt a M - Stadt- und Universitaetsbibliothek Fol. 16 (Merzbacher 95), f. 106b, C.

Asti, Fossano, Moncalvo
358. New Haven - Yale University, Beinecke Rare Book and MS Library, MS Heb. 52, f. 150b-151a, M.

Tsarfat
359. Oxford - Bodleian Library MS Bodl. Or. 109 (Neubauer 1209), f. 65a-65b, C, commentator: Aaron b. Hayyim haKohen (compiler).

אבל אשמים אנחנו און זרענו ועמל קצרנו (א 1920), יהודה הלוי, סליחה

Yemen
360. Jerusalem - Sassoon 902, p. 404-405, M.

Yemen, commentary by Isaac b. Abraham Wanneh
361. Chicago-Spertus College of Judaica D 2, 2, f. 204a, M, no incipit.
362. Jerusalem - Benayahu ת 261, f. 138a, M, rubric: אל מלך.
363. Jerusalem - Benayahu ת 282, f. 121b, M, rubric: אל מלך, no incipit.
364. Jerusalem - Makhon Ben Zvi 1156 (Tubi 155), f. 120a-120b, M, rubric: אל מלך.
365. Jerusalem - Makhon Ben Zvi 1174 (Tubi 154), f. 123a, M.
366. Jerusalem - Michael Krupp 604, f. 151b-152a, M, rubric: אל מלך, no incipit.
367. Jerusalem - Musad haRav Kook 325, f. 179a, M, rubric: אל מלך.
368. Jerusalem - Musad haRav Kook 347, f. 84b-85a, G.
369. Jerusalem - Sassoon 1158, p. 350, M, rubric: סים׳ אני יהודה הלוי.
370. Jerusalem - Sassoon 1174, p. 231, M, no incipit.
371. Jerusalem - Yehiel haLevi 4, f. 153a-153b, G.
372. London - British Library Or. 11122, f. 173b-174a, M, rubric: אל מלך.

---

[11] Edited by Urbach, ערוגת הבושם, vol. III, p. 554-555.

68 CLAVIS COMMENTARIORUM

373. Manchester - John Rylands University Library, Ms. Gaster 5, f. 195a-195b, M.
374. Muenchen - Bayerische Staatsbibliothek, Cod. hebr. 472, f. 164a-164b, M, rubric: אל מלך.
375. New York - Jewish Theological Seminary Ms. 3013, f. 120a, M, rubric: אל מלך.
376. Philadelphia - University of Pennsylvania HB 2, f. 131b-132a, M.
377. Strasbourg - Bibliotheque Nationale et Universitaire 3965 (Landauer 39), p. 372, M, rubric: אל מלך.

אבל חטאנו ועוינו ופשענו אנחנו ואבותינו, יהודה בן זרובבל, וידוי
Yemen, commentary by Isaac b. Abraham Wanneh
378. Chicago-Spertus College of Judaica D 2, 2, f. 180b, M.

אבלה יהודה והיתה נדודה, סליחה
Yemen
379. New York - Jewish Theological Seminary Ms. 3028, f. 81b, G.
Yemen, commentary by Isaac b. Abraham Wanneh
380. Chicago-Spertus College of Judaica D 2,2, f. 243b-244a, M, no incipit.
381. London - British Library Or. 11122, f. 222a, M, no incipit.

אבלה נפשי וחשך תארי (א 304), סעדיה גאון, סליחה
Ashkenaz
382. Braunschweig - Landesmuseum fuer Geschichte und Volkstum R 2386, vol. II, f. 125b, M, .
383. Muenchen - Bayerische Staatsbibliothek, Cod. hebr. 346, f. 121a, C.
384. Oxford - Bodleian Library MS Mich. 543 (Neubauer 1212), f. 33a-33b, C, commentator: Isaac b. Jacob (compiler).
385. Oxford - Bodleian Library MS Opp. 681 (Neubauer 1213), f. 8b-9a, C.
386. Padova - Biblioteca del Seminario Vescovile Cod. 218, f. 117b-118a, M.
387. Vatican - Biblioteca Apostolica ebr. 308, f. 22a, C, commentator: David b. Mose (compiler).

אבן בוחן פנה מיוקרת (א 309), שלמה אבן גברול, חלק ב', קדושתא לשהרית יום כפור
Sepharad, commentary by David b. Josef Abudarham[12]
388. Budapest - Magyar tudomanyos akademia, MS. Kaufmann A 405/2, p. 188-190, C, rubric: פזמון לר' שלמן ן' גבירול.
389. Cincinnati - Hebrew Union College 490, f. 4a-4b, C.

---

[12] Edited by Prins, תשלום אבודרהם, p. 17-19.

390. Holon - Yehuda Nahum 278, f. 13a, FC, only end of commentary.
391. Holon - Yehuda Nahum 278, f. 23a-23b, FC, rubric: מגן, incomplete.
392. New York - Columbia X893 Ab 93, f. 5b-6b, C.
393. New York - Jewish Theological Seminary Ms. 3011, f. 5a-5b, C, rubric: מגן.

אבן הראשה לעיים לחרישה (א 313), אברהם בן מנחם, סליחה

Ashkenaz
394. Oxford - Bodleian Library MS Opp. 681 (Neubauer 1213), f. 33a-33b, C.
395. Padova - Biblioteca del Seminario Vescovile Cod. 218, f. 246a-246b, M.
396. Vatican - Biblioteca Apostolica ebr. 422/1, f. 45a, CG, no incipit, very short.

Ashkenaz, commentary by Abraham b. Azriel[13]
397. Vatican - Biblioteca Apostolica ebr. 301,1, f. 140a, C.

אבן חוג מצוק נשיה (א 314), אלעזר ברבי קליר, חלק ג', קדושתא לשחרית ביום א' של ראש השנה

Ashkenaz
398. Berlin - Staatsbibliothek (Preussischer Kulturbesitz) Or. Qu. 798-799 (Steinschneider 177), I, f. 6b-7a, M.
399. Braunschweig - Landesmuseum fuer Geschichte und Volkstum R 2386, vol. II, f. 81b-82a, M.
400. Budapest - Magyar tudomanyos akademia, MS. Kaufmann A 400, p. 249-252, C, no incipit.
401. Cambridge - University Library Or. 785, f. 19b, G.
402. Darmstadt - Hessisches Landes- und Hochschulbibliothek Cod. Or. 15, f. 6b-7a, M.
403. Hamburg - Staats- und Universitaetsbibliothek Cod. hebr. 12 (Steinschneider 102), f. 6a-6b, G.
404. Hamburg - Staats- und Universitaetsbibliothek Cod. hebr. 17/2 (Steinschneider 152), f. 107b-108a, C.
405. Hamburg - Staats- und Universitaetsbibliothek Cod. hebr. 40c (Steinschneider 111), f. 133a, G.
406. Hamburg - Staats- und Universitaetsbibliothek Cod. hebr. 40b (Steinschneider 110), f. 6b, G.
407. Hamburg - Staats- und Universitaetsbibliothek Cod. hebr. 132 (Steinschneider 155), f. 5b-6b, C.
408. Hamburg - Staats- und Universitaetsbibliothek Cod. hebr. 139 (Steinschneider 115), f. 21a-21b, G.

---

[13] Edited by Urbach, ערוגת הבושם, vol. III, p. 298-299.

409. Hamburg - Staats- und Universitaetsbibliothek Cod. hebr. 225, f. 219a-219b, G.
410. Jerusalem - Jewish National and University Library Ms Heb 8° 3037, f. 8b-9b, M.
411. Jerusalem - Schocken Institute 24100 / Mahzor Nuremberg, f. 324a-324b, M.
412. London - British Library Or. 11318/1, f. 11a-11b, C.
413. Moscow - Russian State Library, Ms. Guenzburg 1401/2, f. 16a-16b, C.
414. Moscow - Russian State Library, Ms. Guenzburg 615, f. 57a-58b, C.
415. Muenchen - Bayerische Staatsbibliothek, Cod. hebr. 346, f. 2b-4a, C, no incipit, marginal glosses by later hand.
416. Muenchen - Bayerische Staatsbibliothek, Cod. hebr. 422, f. 73a, G.
417. New York - Jewish Theological Seminary Ms. 4466, f. 211b-212b, M.
418. New York - Jewish Theological Seminary Ms. 8097, f. 59a, C, additional glosses in the margin.
419. New York - Jewish Theological Seminary Ms. 8169 (Acc. 0016), f. 4b-5a, M.
420. New York - Jewish Theological Seminary Rab. 1077/4 (Acc. 02505), f. 21b, FC, only beginning.
421. Oxford - Bodleian Library MS Opp. 170 (Neubauer 1205), f. 104b-106a, C.
422. Oxford - Bodleian Library MS Opp. 172 (Neubauer 1211), f. 3b-4a, C.
423. Oxford - Bodleian Library MS Opp. 619 (Neubauer 2374), f. 11b-12a, M.
424. Oxford - Bodleian Library MS Opp. 675 (Neubauer 1210), f. 15a-16a, C, no incipit.
425. Paris - Bibliotheque Nationale heb. 653, f. 9b-10a, G.
426. Parma - Biblioteca Palatina Cod. Parm. 2404 (de Rossi 1104), f. 126b, M, copied from printed edition Saloniki 1550 (Benyamin b. Meir Levi).
427. Parma - Biblioteca Palatina Cod. Parm. 3205 (de Rossi 655), f. 204b-205a, C.
428. Parma - Biblioteca Palatina Cod. Parm. 3270 (de Rossi 1215), f. 20b-21a, M.
429. Parma - Biblioteca Palatina Cod. Parm. 3507 (Perreau 27), f. 110b-112a, C.
430. Vatican - Bibliotheca Apostolica ebr. 298/1, f. 9a-10a, C, no incipit.
431. Vatican - Biblioteca Apostolica ebr. 308, f. 30b-32a, C, commentator: David b. Mose (compiler).
432. Vatican - Biblioteca Apostolica ebr. 422/1, f. 8a, C.
433. Zurich - Zentralbibliothek Heid. 139, f. 102a, C, commentator: Elazar b. Yehuda of Worms, no incipit, short, esoteric.

Asti, Fossano, Moncalvo
434. New Haven - Yale University, Beinecke Rare Book and MS Library, MS Heb. 52, f. 19a, M.

Romania
435. Vatican - Biblioteca Apostolica ebr. 320, f. 149a-149b, M.

Tsarfat
436. Parma - Biblioteca Palatina Cod. Parm. 2125 (de Rossi 812), f. 8a-9b, M.
437. London - British Library Add. 11639 (Margoliouth 1056), f. 709a, M.
438. London - British Library Or. 8682, f. 10b, G.
439. London - David Sofer 5, f. 109a, C.
440. Manchester - John Rylands University Library, Ms. Gaster 733, f. 81a, C, commentary block in Mahzor, manuscript damaged.
441. Oxford - Bodleian Library MS Laud. Or. 271 (Neubauer 1206), f. 140b-141a, C, commentator: Aaron b. Hayyim haKohen (compiler), additional marginal notes.
442. Oxford - Bodleian Library MS Opp. 171 (Neubauer 1207), f. 56b-57b, C.
443. Paris - Bibliotheque Nationale heb. 445,9, f. 63b-65a, C, additional commentary in separate textblocks.
444. Parma - Biblioteca Palatina Cod. Parm. 1794 (de Rossi 1061), f. 58b-60a, M.
445. Parma - Biblioteca Palatina Cod. Parm. 3006 (de Rossi 654,1), f. 25a-25b, M.
446. Vatican - Biblioteca Apostolica ebr. 306, f. 48a-49a, C, no incipit.

אבן מעמסה עמוס ולאל תמאסה (א 315), משלש, נעילה

Ashkenaz
447. Berlin - Staatsbibliothek (Preussischer Kulturbesitz) Or. Qu. 798-799 (Steinschneider 177), I, f. 182b-183a, M, short.
448. Jerusalem - Jewish National and University Library Ms Heb 8° 3037, f. 227b-228a, M, short.
449. Jerusalem - Schocken Institute 24100 / Mahzor Nuremberg, f. 470a, M, short.
450. London - British Library Or. 11318/1, f. 127b, C.
451. London - Montefiore Library 261, f. 64b, C, commentator: Eliezer b. Natan?, very short.
452. Oxford - Bodleian Library MS Mich. 365 (Neubauer 1208), f. 94a, C, short.
453. Vatican - Biblioteca Apostolica ebr. 308, f. 151a, C, commentator: David b. Mose (compiler).

Tsarfat
454. Oxford - Bodleian Library MS Bodl. Or. 109 (Neubauer 1209), f. 43a, C, commentator: Aaron b. Hayyim haKohen (compiler), short.

אבן שתיה בית הבחירה גורן ארונן (א 319), הושענא

Ashkenaz

455. Berlin - Staatsbibliothek (Preussischer Kulturbesitz) Or. Qu. 361 (Steinschneider 51), f. 116a-116b, M.
456. Berlin - Staatsbibliothek (Preussischer Kulturbesitz) Or. Qu. 798-799 (Steinschneider 177), I, f. 204b-205a, M.
457. Budapest - Magyar tudomanyos akademia, MS. Kaufmann A 399 , p. 298-299, C.
458. Budapest - Magyar tudomanyos akademia, MS. Kaufmann A 400 , p. 532-533, C.
459. Cambridge - University Library Add. 394,1 (Reif SCR 461) , f. 74b-75a, C, rubric: הושענא.
460. Cambridge - University Library Or. 790, f. 32a-32b, C.
461. Cremona - Archivio di Stato 68, f. 1b, FC, beginning missing.
462. Frankfurt a M - Stadt- und Universitaetsbibliothek Oct. 227 , f. 112b-113a, M.
463. Hamburg - Staats- und Universitaetsbibliothek Cod. hebr. 17/2 (Steinschneider 152), f. 166a, C, rubric: וכן אחרת.
464. Jerusalem - Schocken Institute 24100 / Mahzor Nuremberg , f. 493a, M.
465. London - British Library Add. 18695 (Margoliouth 683), f. 149b-150a, T, Yiddish.
466. London - British Library Add. 22431 (Margoliouth 662a), f. 119b, M.
467. London - British Library Add. 27208 (Margolioth 654), f. 266a-266b, M.
468. London - British Library Add. 27556, f. 128a, M.
469. Lund - Universitetsbibliothek Ms. L.O. 2, f. 86b-87a, M.
470. Moscow - Russian State Library, Ms. Guenzburg 615, f. 128b, C, rubric: אחרת, short.
471. New York - Jewish Theological Seminary Ms. 4466, f. 478(i)b, M.
472. Oxford - Bodleian Library MS Can. Or. 1 (Neubauer 1104), f. 25a-25b, M.
473. Oxford - Bodleian Library MS Mich. 573 (Neubauer 1099), f. 17b, M.
474. Oxford - Bodleian Library MS Opp 160 (Neubauer 1204), f. 235a-235b, C, commentator: Elazar b. Yehuda of Worms.[14]
475. Oxford - Bodleian Library MS Opp. 170 (Neubauer 1205), f. 200b-201a, C.
476. Parma - Biblioteca Palatina Cod. Parm. 2895, p. 211, M.
477. Parma - Biblioteca Palatina Cod. Parm. 2895 , p. 215, M, very short, wrong position.
478. Parma - Biblioteca Palatina Cod. Parm. 3057.9 (de Rossi 1033), f. 92a-92b, C.

---

[14] Edited by Katzenellenbogen, פירוש ההושענות, p. 31-33.

479. Parma - Biblioteca Palatina Cod. Parm. 3205 (de Rossi 655), f. 249b-250a, C.
480. Uppsala - Universitetsbibliotek O.Heb.22, f. 110a, M.
481. Vatican - Biblioteca Apostolica ebr. 305,1, f. 43b, C, no incipit.
482. Vatican - Biblioteca Apostolica ebr. 308, f. 155b-156a, C, commentator: David b. Mose (compiler).
483. Verona - Seminario Maggiore 34, f. 168a, M.

Ashkenaz, commentary by Eliezer bar Natan

484. Hamburg - Staats- und Universitaetsbibliothek Cod. hebr. 61 (Steinschneider 153), f. 22b, C.
485. London - Montefiore Library 261, f. 86a-86b, C.
486. Paris - Bibliotheque Nationale heb. 327/2, f. 38a-38b, C.
487. Warszaw - Uniwersytet, Inst. Orientalistyczny 258, f. 195b-196a, C.

Italia

488. Moscow - Russian State Library, Ms. Guenzburg 533, f. 12b-17b, C, commentator: Yehoshua Segre, rubric: לימוד ט.
489. Moscow - Russian State Library, Ms. Guenzburg 1594, f. 24a, C, no incipit.
490. Torino - Archivio Terracini 1499, p. 94-100, C, commentator: Zakharya David Shabbetai Segre, rubric: פירוש אבן שתיה.

Roma

491. Jerusalem - Jewish National and University Library Ms Heb 8° 4153, f. 141b-142a, C, commentator: Daniel ben Salomo haRofe (compiler).
492. Oxford - Bodleian Library MS Mich. 312,1 (Neubauer 2276,1), f. 10a, C.

Romania

493. London - London School of Jewish Studies. Asher I.Myers collection 9, f. 210b-211a, M.
494. Roma - Collegio Rabbinico Italiano 110, f. 11b-12b, M.
495. Vatican - Biblioteca Apostolica ebr. 285/30, f. 235b, C.
496. Vatican - Biblioteca Apostolica ebr. 320, f. 446a, M.

Tsarfat

497. Cambridge - University Library Add. 561.1, f. 114b, M.
498. Jerusalem - Schocken Institute 19623, f. 126a, M, commentator: Yehuda b. Eliezer Zvi.
499. London - British Library Or. 2735 (Margoliouth 663), f. 148a, M.
500. London - David Sofer 5, f. 192b, C.
501. Moscow - Russian State Library, Ms. Guenzburg 1665, f. 181a-181b, M.
502. New York - Jewish Theological Seminary Ms. 4460, f. 81b, G.
503. Parma - Biblioteca Palatina Cod. Parm. 1264, f. 95b-96a, M.
504. Parma - Biblioteca Palatina Cod. Parm. 1902, f. 178a-179a, M.
505. Vatican - Biblioteca Apostolica ebr. 306, f. 122a-122b, C.

אבני קדש ומצוקי ארץ (א 323), יצחק גיאת, חלק ב, קדושתא למוסף י"כ
Sepharad, commentary by David b. Josef Abudarham[15]
506. Budapest - Magyar tudomanyos akademia, MS. Kaufmann A 405/2, p. 242, C, rubric: מחיה.
507. New York - Columbia X893 Ab 93, f. 26b, C, rubric: מחיה.

אברהם שמח בשמחת תורה, שמחת תורה
Ashkenaz
508. London - British Library Add. 18695 (Margoliouth 683), f. 142a-142b, T, Yiddish, incipit אגיל.

אברות יונה שפתים דחופה (א 335), יוסף ב"ר שמואל טוב עלם, קדושתא לפסח
Tsarfat
509. Parma - Biblioteca Palatina Cod. Parm. 3136 (de Rossi 405), f. 89b-90a, M.

אברך בורא נפרדים עשר מעלות עומדים, סליחה
Yemen, commentary by Isaac b. Abraham Wanneh
510. Chicago-Spertus College of Judaica D 2, 2, 223a-223b, M, no incipit.
511. Jerusalem - Sassoon 1158, p. 396-397, M, no incipit.
512. London - British Library Or. 11122, f. 200a-200b, M, no incipit.

אברם הוא אברהם (א 396), מנחם ורדימשי ברבי פרץ, עקדה
Tsarfat
513. Oxford - Bodleian Library MS Laud. Or. 271 (Neubauer 1206), f. 131a-135a, C, commentator: Aaron b. Hayyim haKohen (compiler), postscript סליק העקידה שפייט רבנו מנחם הוורדמסי בן הזקן ר' פרץ נ"ע.

אגגי בעמיק מחשבת זוממו (א 401), יוסף, סליחה תענית אסתר
Carpentras, commentary by Mordekhai b. Josef of Rocco Martino
514. Cincinnati - Hebrew Union College 246/1, f. 92b-93b, C, rubric: פי' רהוטה אנוש וכו'.

אגן הסהר נוקשת שערר (א 447), בנימין ב"ר שמואל, חלק א', קדושתא למוסף ר"ה
Ashkenaz
515. Alessandria - Archivio di Stato Fr. ebr. 12, , FC.
516. Moscow - Russian State Library, Ms. Guenzburg 191, f. 48a-49b, M.
517. New York - Jewish Theological Seminary Ms. 8169 (Acc. 0016), f. 44b-45a, M.

---

[15] Edited by Prins, תשלום אבודרהם, p. 77-78.

Tsarfat
518. London - British Library Add. 11639 (Margoliouth 1056), f. 710b, M, rubric: ליום שיני.
519. London - British Library Or. 8682, f. 43a-43b, GI.
520. London - David Sofer 5, f. 123a-123b, C.
521. Oxford - Bodleian Library MS Opp. 171 (Neubauer 1207), f. 68b-69a, C.
522. Parma - Biblioteca Palatina Cod. Parm. 1794 (de Rossi 1061), f. 80b-81b, M.
523. Parma - Biblioteca Palatina Cod. Parm. 2125 (de Rossi 812), f. 31b-32a, C.
524. Parma - Biblioteca Palatina Cod. Parm. 3006 (de Rossi 654,1), f. 86a-86b, M.
525. Vatican - Biblioteca Apostolica ebr. 306, f. 68b-69b, C.

אדאג מחטאתי ואגיד עוני (א 455), יעקב ב"ר חזקיה, סליחה

Ashkenaz
526. Oxford - Bodleian Library MS Opp. 681 (Neubauer 1213), f. 46a-47a, C, rubric: לי"ז בתמוז.

אדברה וירוח ליי כי רוחי הציקתני (א 470), בנימין ב"ר זרח, סליחה י' בטבת

Ashkenaz
527. Oxford - Bodleian Library MS Opp. 681 (Neubauer 1213), f. 32b-33a, C, rubric: לעשרה בטבת.
528. Padova - Biblioteca del Seminario Vescovile Cod. 218, f. 245a-245b, M.
529. Padova - Biblioteca del Seminario Vescovile Cod. 218, f. 245b, M, short.

Ashkenaz, commentary by Abraham b. Azriel[16]
530. Vatican - Biblioteca Apostolica ebr. 301,1, f. 142a, C.

Tsarfat
531. London - David Sofer 5, f. 102a, C, short.
532. Parma - Biblioteca Palatina Cod. Parm. 3007 (de Rossi 654,2), f. 30a-30b, M.
533. Vatican - Biblioteca Apostolica ebr. 306, f. 96b-97a, C.

אדברה תחנונים כרש ואבכה (א 473), קלונימוס ב"ר יהודה, חטאנו

Ashkenaz
534. Berlin - Staatsbibliothek (Preussischer Kulturbesitz) Or. Qu. 798-799 (Steinschneider 177), I, f. 106a-107b, M.

---

[16] Edited by Urbach, ערוגת הבושם, vol. III, p. 310-312.

535. Braunschweig - Landesmuseum fuer Geschichte und Volkstum R 2386, vol. II, f. 215a-217a, M.
536. Hamburg - Staats- und Universitaetsbibliothek Cod. hebr. 62 (Steinschneider 154), f. 21a-22a, C.
537. Jerusalem - Schocken Institute 24100 / Mahzor Nuremberg , f. 401b-402b, M.
538. London - British Library Or. 11318/1, f. 96a-97a, C.
539. Muenchen - Bayerische Staatsbibliothek, Cod. hebr. 346 , f. 88a-88b, C.
540. New York - Jewish Theological Seminary Ms. 4466, f. 350b,351b-352b,353b, M.
541. Oxford - Bodleian Library MS Mich. 365 (Neubauer 1208), f. 91b-92b, C, postscript 'מר.
542. Oxford - Bodleian Library MS Mich. 543 (Neubauer 1212), f. 23a-23b (margin), C, commentator: Isaac b. Jacob (compiler).
543. Oxford - Bodleian Library MS Opp. 172 (Neubauer 1211), f. 58a-59a, C.
544. Oxford - Bodleian Library MS Opp. 619 (Neubauer 2374), f. 186b-188a, M, very ecclectic.
545. Oxford - Bodleian Library MS Opp. 681 (Neubauer 1213), f. 94b-96b, C.
546. Parma - Biblioteca Palatina Cod. Parm. 3205 (de Rossi 655), f. 286a-286b, C.
547. Parma - Biblioteca Palatina Cod. Parm. 3507 (Perreau 27), f. 160a-161a, C.
548. Vatican - Biblioteca Apostolica ebr. 308, f. 115a-116a, C, commentator: David b. Mose (compiler).
549. Vatican - Biblioteca Apostolica ebr. 422/1, f. 33a-33b, C.
550. Vatican - Biblioteca Apostolica ebr. 422/1 , f. 45a, CG, no incipit, short.
551. Vatican - Biblioteca Apostolica ebr. 422/2, f. 38b-39a, CG, no incipit.
Asti, Fossano, Moncalvo
552. New Haven - Yale University, Beinecke Rare Book and MS Library, MS Heb. 52, f. 126a-127a, M.
Tsarfat
553. Oxford - Bodleian Library MS Bodl. Or. 109 (Neubauer 1209), f. 12b-14a, C, commentator: Aaron b. Hayyim haKohen (compiler).

אדון אימנני (א 484), שמעון ב"ר יצחק, יוצר לשבועות

Ashkenaz
554. Berlin - Staatsbibliothek (Preussischer Kulturbesitz) Or. Qu. 798-799 (Steinschneider 177), II, f. 113a-114a, M.
555. Braunschweig - Landesmuseum fuer Geschichte und Volkstum R 2386, vol. I, f. 70a-70b, M.

556. Budapest - Magyar tudomanyos akademia, MS. Kaufmann A 400, p. 148-151, C, rubric: בשם יי לו הגדולה והתפארת. אתחיל לכתוב פירושי עצרת.
557. Erlangen - Universitaetsbibliothek 2601 (Roth 67), f. 145b, M.
558. Hamburg - Staats- und Universitaetsbibliothek Cod. hebr. 17/2 (Steinschneider 152), f. 69b-70b, C, rubric: יוצר לשבועות דר' שמעון.
559. Jerusalem - Schocken Institute 24100 / Mahzor Nuremberg, f. 145a-145b, M, short.
560. London - British Library Add. 18695 (Margoliouth 683), f. 62b-63b, T, Yiddish, rubric: יוצר צום ערשטן טג בון שבועות.
561. London - British Library Add. 22431 (Margoliouth 662a), f. 3a-4a, M.
562. Moscow - Russian State Library, Ms. Guenzburg 615, f. 43a-46a, C, commentator: Elazar b. Yehuda of Worms.
563. Muenchen - Bayerische Staatsbibliothek, Cod. hebr. 88, f. 114b, G.
564. New York - Jewish Theological Seminary Ms. 4466, f. 120b-122b, M.
565. Oxford - Bodleian Library MS Opp. 170 (Neubauer 1205), f. 83a-85a, C, rubric: בשם יי לנו למושעות אכתוב פירוש של שבועות.
566. Paris - Bibliotheque Nationale heb. 709, f. 116b-119a, C.
567. Parma - Biblioteca Palatina Cod. Parm. 1002 (Ta 24), f. 173b-174b, M.
568. Parma - Biblioteca Palatina Cod. Parm. 3002 (de Rossi 407), f. 120b, M, page from printed Mahzor bound into Ms.
569. Parma - Biblioteca Palatina Cod. Parm. 3205 (de Rossi 655), f. 118a-119a, C.
570. Parma - Biblioteca Palatina Cod. Parm. 3507 (Perreau 27), f. 85b-87a, C.
571. Zurich - Zentralbibliothek Heid. 139, f. 48a-49a, C, rubric: בשם שוכן מעונות. אתחיל קרובוץ דשבועות, additional marginal notes.

Tsarfat

572. London - David Sofer 5, f. 49a-50a, C, rubric: זה פירוש מקרובוץ של שבועות.
573. Moscow - Russian State Library, Ms. Guenzburg 1665, f. 115a-115b, M.
574. Oxford - Bodleian Library MS Laud. Or. 271 (Neubauer 1206), f. 83b-85a, C, commentator: Aaron b. Hayyim haKohen (compiler), rubric: אחל קרובץ של שבועות.
575. Oxford - Bodleian Library MS Opp. 171 (Neubauer 1207), f. 42a-43b, C, rubric: ואתחיל פירושי קרובצס של שבועות בשם אל. ואני אליהו בר' בנימן הכותבם יעזור אדוני האל. ובעזרתי יהי גבריאל.
576. Oxford - Bodleian Library MS Opp. 171 (Neubauer 1207), f. 43b-44a, C.
577. Parma - Biblioteca Palatina Cod. Parm. 3136 (de Rossi 405), f. 147a-148a, M.
578. Vatican - Biblioteca Apostolica ebr. 306, f. 221b-225a, C, rubric: יוצר.

אדון אמתך היא מבצר לכל המחזיקי׳, מי כמוך לשבת שקלים

Tsarfat
579. London - David Sofer 5, f. 16b-17b, C, rubric: מי כמוך.

אדון בינה הגיגינו (א 492), סליחה

Ashkenaz
580. Braunschweig - Landesmuseum fuer Geschichte und Volkstum R 2386, vol. II, f. 43a, M.
581. Oxford - Bodleian Library MS Mich. 543 (Neubauer 1212), f. 86a-86b, C, commentator: Isaac b. Jacob (compiler).
582. Oxford - Bodleian Library MS Opp. 681 (Neubauer 1213), f. 96b, C.
583. Padova - Biblioteca del Seminario Vescovile Cod. 218, f. 59b-60b, M.
584. Padova - Biblioteca del Seminario Vescovile Cod. 218, f. 242a-242b, M.
585. Padova - Biblioteca del Seminario Vescovile Cod. 218, f. 248b-249a, M.
586. Vatican - Biblioteca Apostolica ebr. 422/1, f. 32b, C.

אדון בכל וחי עולם ועד אין סוף תהלתו (א *140), מרדכי דאטו

Italia
587. Oxford - Bodleian Library Heb.e.20 (Neubauer 2748), f. 3a-3b, M, rubric: ר״ת אברהם מיכאל.

אדון בפוקדך אנוש לבקרים (א 496), יצחק הכהן החבר, סליחה

Ashkenaz
588. Berlin - Staatsbibliothek (Preussischer Kulturbesitz) Or. Qu. 798-799 (Steinschneider 177), I, f. 101b-102a, M.
589. Braunschweig - Landesmuseum fuer Geschichte und Volkstum R 2386, vol. II, f. 61b-62a, M.
590. Jerusalem - Schocken Institute 24100 / Mahzor Nuremberg, f. 399a, M.
591. London - British Library Add. 18695 (Margoliouth 683), f. 161a-161b, T, Yiddish.
592. Muenchen - Bayerische Staatsbibliothek, Cod. hebr. 346, f. 126b, C, rubric: אחרת.
593. New York - Jewish Theological Seminary Ms. 4466, f. 348b-349a, M.
594. New York - Jewish Theological Seminary Ms. 8097, f. 82a, C.
595. Oxford - Bodleian Library MS Mich. 543 (Neubauer 1212), f. 15a, C, commentator: Isaac b. Jacob (compiler).
596. Oxford - Bodleian Library MS Opp. 172 (Neubauer 1211), f. 57a-57b, C.
597. Oxford - Bodleian Library MS Opp. 619 (Neubauer 2374), f. 178a-178b, M, short.

598. Oxford - Bodleian Library MS Opp. 681 (Neubauer 1213) , f. 2a-2b, C.
599. Padova - Biblioteca del Seminario Vescovile Cod. 218, f. 93b-94a, M.
600. Padova - Biblioteca del Seminario Vescovile Cod. 218, f. 204b-205a, M.
601. Vatican - Biblioteca Apostolica ebr. 308 , f. 110b, C, commentator: David b. Mose (compiler).
602. Vatican - Biblioteca Apostolica ebr. 422/1, f. 24a, C, very short.
603. Vatican - Biblioteca Apostolica ebr. 422/2 , f. 38b, CG, no incipit, very short.

Ashkenaz, commentary by Abraham b. Azriel[17]

604. Frankfurt a M - Stadt- und Universitaetsbibliothek Fol. 16 (Merzbacher 95), f. 109a, C.
605. Vatican - Biblioteca Apostolica ebr. 301,1, f. 146a, C, rubric: אחרת.

Asti, Fossano, Moncalvo

606. New Haven - Yale University, Beinecke Rare Book and MS Library, MS Heb. 52, f. 165b, M, ecclectic.

Tsarfat

607. Oxford - Bodleian Library MS Bodl. Or. 109 (Neubauer 1209), f. 59b-60a, C, commentator: Aaron b. Hayyim haKohen (compiler).

אדון בשפטך אנוש רמה (א 498), אליה ב"ר שמעיה, סליחה

Ashkenaz

608. Berlin - Staatsbibliothek (Preussischer Kulturbesitz) Or. Qu. 798-799 (Steinschneider 177), f. 100b-101a, M.
609. Braunschweig - Landesmuseum fuer Geschichte und Volkstum R 2386, vol. II, f. 62a-62b, M.
610. Jerusalem - Schocken Institute 24100 / Mahzor Nuremberg , f. 254a, M.
611. Jerusalem - Schocken Institute 24100 / Mahzor Nuremberg , f. 435b-436a, M.
612. London - British Library Add. 18695 (Margoliouth 683) , f. 161a, T, Yiddish.
613. Muenchen - Bayerische Staatsbibliothek, Cod. hebr. 346 , f. 120a, C, very short.
614. Muenchen - Bayerische Staatsbibliothek, Cod. hebr. 346, f. 126b-127a, C.
615. New York - Jewish Theological Seminary Ms. 4466, f. 401a-401b, M.
616. Oxford - Bodleian Library MS Mich. 543 (Neubauer 1212), f. 15a-16a, C, commentator: Isaac b. Jacob (compiler).
617. Oxford - Bodleian Library MS Opp. 172 (Neubauer 1211), f. 77b, C.

---

[17] Edited by Urbach, ערוגת הבושם, vol. III, p. 333-334.

618. Oxford - Bodleian Library MS Opp. 619 (Neubauer 2374), f. 261b, M.
619. Oxford - Bodleian Library MS Opp. 681 (Neubauer 1213), f. 3a-3b, C.
620. Padova - Biblioteca del Seminario Vescovile Cod. 218, f. 94a-94b, M.
621. Padova - Biblioteca del Seminario Vescovile Cod. 218, f. 175a-175b, M.
622. Vatican - Biblioteca Apostolica ebr. 308, f. 134a, C, commentator: David b. Mose (compiler).
623. Vatican - Biblioteca Apostolica ebr. 308, f. 163a, C, commentator: David b. Mose (compiler).
624. Vatican - Biblioteca Apostolica ebr. 422/1, f. 24a, C, very short.
625. Vatican - Biblioteca Apostolica ebr. 422/2, f. 38b, CG, no incipit, very short.

Ashkenaz, commentary by Abraham b. Azriel[18]
626. Frankfurt a M - Stadt- und Universitaetsbibliothek Fol. 16 (Merzbacher 95), f. 109a-109b, C.

Asti, Fossano, Moncalvo
627. New Haven - Yale University, Beinecke Rare Book and MS Library, MS Heb. 52, f. 120b-121a, M.

Tsarfat
628. Oxford - Bodleian Library MS Bodl. Or. 109 (Neubauer 1209), f. 77b-78a, C, commentator: Aaron b. Hayyim haKohen (compiler).

אדון דין אם ידקדק (א 499), זבדיה, סליחה

Ashkenaz
629. Berlin - Staatsbibliothek (Preussischer Kulturbesitz) Or. Qu. 798-799 (Steinschneider 177), I, f. 103a, M.
630. Jerusalem - Schocken Institute 24100 / Mahzor Nuremberg, f. 398a-398b, M.
631. London - British Library Add. 18695 (Margoliouth 683), f. 161b, T, Yiddish.
632. Muenchen - Bayerische Staatsbibliothek, Cod. hebr. 346, f. 137a, C, rubric: אחרת, short.
633. Muenchen - Bayerische Staatsbibliothek, Cod. hebr. 346, f. 147b, C, rubric: אחרת, short.
634. New York - Jewish Theological Seminary Ms. 8097, f. 82a, C.
635. Oxford - Bodleian Library MS Mich. 543 (Neubauer 1212), f. 18b, C, commentator: Isaac b. Jacob (compiler).
636. Oxford - Bodleian Library MS Opp. 172 (Neubauer 1211), f. 56b, C.
637. Oxford - Bodleian Library MS Opp. 619 (Neubauer 2374), f. 180a, M.

---

[18] Edited by Urbach, ערוגת הבושם, vol. III, p. 564-565.

638. Oxford - Bodleian Library MS Opp. 681 (Neubauer 1213), f. 5a-5b, C.
639. Padova - Biblioteca del Seminario Vescovile Cod. 218, f. 98a-98b, M.
640. Padova - Biblioteca del Seminario Vescovile Cod. 218, f. 195a, M.
641. Vatican - Biblioteca Apostolica ebr. 308, f. 112a, C, commentator: David b. Mose (compiler).
642. Vatican - Biblioteca Apostolica ebr. 422/1, f. 24a, C, very short.
643. Vatican - Biblioteca Apostolica ebr. 422/2, f. 38b, CG, no incipit, very short.

Ashkenaz, commentary by Abraham b. Azriel[19]
644. Frankfurt a M - Stadt- und Universitaetsbibliothek Fol. 16 (Merzbacher 95), f. 110a-110b.

Asti, Fossano, Moncalvo
645. New Haven - Yale University, Beinecke Rare Book and MS Library, MS Heb. 52, f. 153a, M.

Tsarfat
646. London - David Sofer 5, f. 134a, C.
647. Oxford - Bodleian Library MS Bodl. Or. 109 (Neubauer 1209), f. 60a-60b, C, commentator: Aaron b. Hayyim haKohen (compiler).
648. Parma - Biblioteca Palatina Cod. Parm. 2890 (de Rossi 856), f. 127b, M.
649. Parma - Biblioteca Palatina Cod. Parm. 3006 (de Rossi 654,1), f. 202b, M.

אדון היושב אל חוג הארץ (א 509), משה אבן עזרא, חלק א', קדושתא נעילה

Carpentras
650. Cincinnati - Hebrew Union College 392, f. 115a, M, no incipit.

Carpentras, commentary by Josef b. Abraham of Montelitz
651. Cincinnati - Hebrew Union College 291, f. 58a-58b, C, rubric: פי' אדון היושב וכו'.
652. New York - Jewish Theological Seminary Ms. 4197, f. 266a-266b, M.
653. Paris - Ecole Rabbinique 32, f. 274b-275a, M.
654. Strasbourg - Bibliotheque Nationale et Universitaire 4081, f. 245a-245b, M.

אדון המושיע בלתך אין להושיע גבור (א 523), הושענא

Ashkenaz
655. Berlin - Staatsbibliothek (Preussischer Kulturbesitz) Or. Qu. 361 (Steinschneider 51), f. 114b-115a, M.
656. Berlin - Staatsbibliothek (Preussischer Kulturbesitz) Or. Qu. 798-799 (Steinschneider 177), I, f. 204a-204b, M.

---

[19] Edited by Urbach, ערוגת הבושם, vol. III, p. 570.

657. Budapest - Magyar tudomanyos akademia, MS. Kaufmann A 399 , p. 298, C.
658. Budapest - Magyar tudomanyos akademia, MS. Kaufmann A 400 , p. 531, C.
659. Cambridge - University Library Add. 394,1 (Reif SCR 461), f. 74b, C, rubric: הושענא, short.
660. Cambridge - University Library Or. 790, f. 31b-32a, C.
661. Frankfurt a M - Stadt- und Universitaetsbibliothek Oct. 227 , f. 113b, M.
662. Hamburg - Staats- und Universitaetsbibliothek Cod. hebr. 17/2 (Steinschneider 152), f. 165b-166a, C, rubric: אחרת.
663. Jerusalem - Schocken Institute 24100 / Mahzor Nuremberg , f. 493b, M.
664. London - British Library Add. 18695 (Margoliouth 683) , f. 150b, T, Yiddish.
665. London - British Library Add. 22431 (Margoliouth 662a), f. 120b, M.
666. London - British Library Add. 27208 (Margolioth 654), f. 265a, M.
667. London - British Library Add. 27556, f. 128a, M.
668. Lund - Universitetsbibliothek Ms. L.O. 2, f. 85b-86a, M.
669. Moscow - Russian State Library, Ms. Guenzburg 615, f. 128b, C, rubric: אחרת, short.
670. New York - Jewish Theological Seminary Ms. 4416, f. 13a, M.
671. New York - Jewish Theological Seminary Ms. 4466, f. 478a, M.
672. Oxford - Bodleian Library MS Mich. 573 (Neubauer 1099), f. 18a, M.
673. Oxford - Bodleian Library MS Opp 160 (Neubauer 1204), f. 236a-236b, C, commentator: Elazar b. Yehuda of Worms, additional note on margin.[20]
674. Oxford - Bodleian Library MS Opp. 170 (Neubauer 1205), f. 200a-200b, C.
675. Parma - Biblioteca Palatina Cod. Parm. 2895, p. 216, M.
676. Parma - Biblioteca Palatina Cod. Parm. 3057.9 (de Rossi 1033), f. 91a, C.
677. Parma - Biblioteca Palatina Cod. Parm. 3205 (de Rossi 655), f. 249b, C.
678. Uppsala - Universitetsbibliotek O.Heb.22, f. 111b, M.
679. Vatican - Biblioteca Apostolica ebr. 308 , f. 155a, C, commentator: David b. Mose (compiler).
680. Verona - Seminario Maggiore 34, f. 168b-169a, M, very short.

Ashkenaz, commentary by Eliezer b. Natan

681. Hamburg - Staats- und Universitaetsbibliothek Cod. hebr. 61 (Steinschneider 153), f. 22a, C.
682. London - Montefiore Library 261, f. 85b-86a, C.

---

[20] Edited by Katzenellenbogen, פירוש ההושענות, p. 35-36.

683. Paris - Bibliotheque Nationale heb. 327/2, f. 37b, C.
684. Warszaw - Uniwersytet, Inst. Orientalistyczny 258, f. 195b, C.

Italia
685. Moscow - Russian State Library, Ms. Guenzburg 533, f. 17b-22a, C, commentator: Yehoshua Segre, rubric: לימוד י'.
686. Moscow - Russian State Library, Ms. Guenzburg 1594, f. 24a, C, no incipit.
687. Torino - Archivio Terracini 1499, p. 163, C, commentator: Zakharya David Shabbetai Segre, rubric: פירוש אדון המושיע.

Roma
688. Jerusalem - Jewish National and University Library Ms Heb 8° 4153, f. 141a-141b, C, commentator: Daniel ben Salomo haRofe (compiler).
689. Oxford - Bodleian Library MS Mich. 312,1 (Neubauer 2276,1), f. 10a, C, rubric: הושענות.

Romania
690. London - London School of Jewish Studies. Asher I.Myers collection 9, f. 210a-210b, M.
691. Roma - Collegio Rabbinico Italiano 110, f. 7a-7b, M.
692. Vatican - Biblioteca Apostolica ebr. 285/30, f. 235a, C.
693. Vatican - Biblioteca Apostolica ebr. 320, f. 446a, M.

Tsarfat
694. Cambridge - University Library Add. 561.1, f. 114a-114b, M.
695. Jerusalem - Schocken Institute 19623, f. 125a, M, commentator: Yehuda b. Eliezer Zvi, short.
696. London - British Library Or. 2735 (Margoliouth 663), f. 146b-147a, M.
697. London - David Sofer 5, f. 192b, C.
698. Moscow - Russian State Library, Ms. Guenzburg 1665, f. 180b, M.
699. Parma - Biblioteca Palatina Cod. Parm. 1264, f. 96a, M.
700. Vatican - Biblioteca Apostolica ebr. 306, f. 122a, C.

אדון חסדך בל יחדל (א 536), יהודה הלוי, יוצר לשבת זכור

Carpentras, commentary by Mordekhai b. Josef of Rocco Martino
701. Cincinnati - Hebrew Union College 246/1, f. 19b-22a, C, rubric: פי' מי כמוך ואין כמוך וכו'.

Romania
702. New York - Columbia University X 893.1 BE P 43, f. 57a-62a, T, Greek.

Sepharad, commentary by Josef Garad
703. Oxford - Bodleian Library Heb.e.10 (Neubauer 2746/1), f. 7a-7b, C, rubric: מי כמוך.
704. Oxford - Bodleian Library Heb.e.10 (Neubauer 2746/1), f. 18a, C, rubric: אדון חסדך, no incipit.

אדון כל הבריאות הנשגב בהודו (א 544), אהרן ב"ר יוסף הרופא, פרשת לך לך
Karaite, commentary by Berakha b. Josef haKohen

705. New York - Jewish Theological Seminary Ms. 3367, f. 25a-29a, C, rubric: פרוש פר' לך לך.
706. St. Petersburg - Inst. of Oriental Studies of the Russian Academy B 431, f. 20a-23a, C, rubric: פרשת לך לך.
707. St. Petersburg - Russian National Library, Evr. IV 50, f. 18a-21a, C.

אדון כתקח מועד לשפוט מישרים (א 549), יוסף ב"ר יצחק, סליחה

Ashkenaz
708. Braunschweig - Landesmuseum fuer Geschichte und Volkstum R 2386, vol. II, f. 62b-63a, M.
709. Hamburg - Staats- und Universitaetsbibliothek Cod. hebr. 40c (Steinschneider 111), f. 285b-286a, G.
710. Jerusalem - Schocken Institute 24100 / Mahzor Nuremberg, f. 466a, M.
711. London - British Library Add. 18695 (Margoliouth 683), f. 160b-161a, T, Yiddish.
712. Muenchen - Bayerische Staatsbibliothek, Cod. hebr. 346, f. 138b, C, rubric: אחרת, very short.
713. Muenchen - Bayerische Staatsbibliothek, Cod. hebr. 346, f. 147b-148a, C, rubric: אחרת.
714. New York - Jewish Theological Seminary Ms. 8097, f. 87a, C.
715. Oxford - Bodleian Library MS Mich. 543 (Neubauer 1212), f. 14a-15a, C, commentator: Isaac b. Jacob (compiler).
716. Oxford - Bodleian Library MS Opp. 619 (Neubauer 2374), f. 262a-263a, M.
717. Oxford - Bodleian Library MS Opp. 681 (Neubauer 1213), f. 1b-2a, C, rubric: לערב ר"ה ולערב י"כ.
718. Padova - Biblioteca del Seminario Vescovile Cod. 218, f. 92a-93a, M.
719. Vatican - Biblioteca Apostolica ebr. 308, f. 146a-146b, C, commentator: David b. Mose (compiler).
720. Vatican - Biblioteca Apostolica ebr. 422/1, f. 25b, C.
721. Vatican - Biblioteca Apostolica ebr. 422/1, f. 41b, CG, no incipit, very short.

Tsarfat
722. Oxford - Bodleian Library MS Bodl. Or. 109 (Neubauer 1209), f. 58a-59b, C, commentator: Aaron b. Hayyim haKohen (compiler).

אדון מקדם תכנו ראש (א 561), אלעזר ברבי קליר, הלק ו', קדושתא החדש

Ashkenaz
723. Berlin - Staatsbibliothek (Preussischer Kulturbesitz) Or. Qu. 798-799 (Steinschneider 177), II, f. 41b-42a, M, incipit ראשון.

724. Budapest - Magyar tudomanyos akademia, MS. Kaufmann A 384, f. 91b-92a, M.
725. Hamburg - Staats- und Universitaetsbibliothek Cod. hebr. 17/2 (Steinschneider 152), f. 28b-29a, C.
726. Jerusalem - Schocken Institute 24100 / Mahzor Nuremberg, f. 66a, M.
727. London - British Library Add. 18695 (Margoliouth 683), f. 5a-5b, T, Yiddish.
728. Muenchen - Bayerische Staatsbibliothek, Cod. hebr. 88, f. 44b-45a, G.
729. Muenchen - Bayerische Staatsbibliothek, Cod. hebr. 393, f. 105a, C, no incipit.
730. New York - Jewish Theological Seminary Ms. 4466, f. 22b-23a, M.
731. Oxford - Bodleian Library MS Opp. 170 (Neubauer 1205), f. 35a-35b, C.
732. Paris - Bibliotheque Nationale heb. 709, f. 41b-42a, C, rubric: פיזמון.
733. Parma - Biblioteca Palatina Cod. Parm 3000 (de Rossi 378), f. 22b-23a, M.
734. Parma - Biblioteca Palatina Cod. Parm. 1002 (Ta 24), f. 69a, M.
735. Parma - Biblioteca Palatina Cod. Parm. 3205 (de Rossi 655), f. 41b-42b, C.
736. Parma - Biblioteca Palatina Cod. Parm. 3507 (Perreau 27), f. 31a-31b, C.
737. Vatican - Biblioteca Apostolica ebr. 305,1, f. 26b-27a, C, no incipit.
738. Zurich - Zentralbibliothek Heid. 139, f. 10a-11a, C, rubric: סילוק, no incipit, additional marginal notes.

Tsarfat
739. London - British Library Add. 11639 (Margoliouth 1056), f. 278a, M.
740. London - David Sofer 5, f. 35a-36b, C.
741. Moscow - Russian State Library, Ms. Guenzburg 1665, f. 40b-41a, M.
742. Oxford - Bodleian Library MS Laud. Or. 271 (Neubauer 1206), f. 47b-48a, C, commentator: Aaron b. Hayyim haKohen (compiler).
743. Parma - Biblioteca Palatina Cod. Parm. 3136 (de Rossi 405), f. 55a-56a, M.
744. Vatican - Biblioteca Apostolica ebr. 306, f. 154b-155b, C, no incipit.

אדון משפט בקרבך (א 563), שמואל, סליחה

Ashkenaz
745. Oxford - Bodleian Library MS Mich. 543 (Neubauer 1212), f. 86b-88b, C, commentator: Isaac b. Jacob (compiler).

אדון עבדיו הריץ (א 569)

Sepharad, commentary by Josef Garad
746. Oxford - Bodleian Library Heb.e.10 (Neubauer 2746/1), f. 8b, C, rubric: עשיריה.

אדון עולם אברח ממך (א 6377), משה אבן עזרא, חלק ה', קדושתא מוסף י"כ

Carpentras
747. Cincinnati - Hebrew Union College 392, f. 89b-90a, M, no incipit.
Carpentras, commentary by Josef b. Abraham of Montelitz
748. New York - Jewish Theological Seminary Ms. 4197, f. 202b-203b, M.
749. Paris - Ecole Rabbinique 32, f. 210b-211a, M.
750. Strasbourg - Bibliotheque Nationale et Universitaire 4081, f. 185a-186b, M.

אדון עולם אשר מלאך (א 575)

Persian
751. New York - Jewish Theological Seminary Ms. 5086, f. 2b-3b, T, Persian.

אדון צור ישעי (א 609), הושענא

Romania
752. Vatican - Biblioteca Apostolica ebr. 285/30, f. 235b, C, very short.
Tsarfat
753. London - British Library Or. 2735 (Margoliouth 663), f. 148b, M, ecclectic.

אדון רבון העולמים, סליחה

Ashkenaz
754. Oxford - Bodleian Library MS Opp. 172 (Neubauer 1211), f. 88a-88b, C.

אדון שעה תחן (א 614)

Tsarfat
755. Vatican - Biblioteca Apostolica ebr. 306, f. 54a, C.

יי אבינו בך בטחו אבותינו

Tsarfat
756. Oxford - Bodleian Library MS Bodl. Or. 109 (Neubauer 1209), f. 57b-58a, C, commentator: Aaron b. Hayyim haKohen (compiler).

יי יי רחום וחנון ארך אפים, סליחה

Tsarfat
757. London - David Sofer 5, f. 168a, C, rubric: פזמון.

יי אורי וישעי (א 640), יוסף, סליחה

Tsarfat
758. London - David Sofer 5, f. 134a-134b, C.
759. Parma - Biblioteca Palatina Cod. Parm. 1794 (de Rossi 1061), f. 10b, M.
760. Parma - Biblioteca Palatina Cod. Parm. 3007 (de Rossi 654,2), f. 24b-25a, M.

יי אל נמצא בעיני מזימה (א 654), ליום כפור

Sepharad, commentary by David b. Josef Abudarham[21]
761. Budapest - Magyar tudomanyos akademia, MS. Kaufmann A 405/2, p. 181, C, rubric: פזמון. יי אדוננו מה אדיר שמך בכל הארץ.
762. Cincinnati - Hebrew Union College 490, f. 2a, C, rubric: פזמון. יי אדוננו מה אדיר שמך בכל הארץ.
763. New York - Columbia X893 Ab 93, f. 2b-3a, C, rubric: פזמון. יי אדוננו מה אדיר שמך בכל הארץ.

יי אלהא את אמרת לכנשתא דישראל עתידנא לנחמותיך, סליחה

Yemen, commentary by Isaac b. Abraham Wanneh
764. Chicago-Spertus College of Judaica D 2, 2, f. 246a-246b, M, no incipit.
765. Jerusalem - Sassoon 1158, p. 424-425, M, no incipit.
766. London - British Library Or. 11122, f. 219b, M, no incipit.

יי אלהא די כוסייה שביבין דנורא, סליחה

Yemen, commentary by Isaac b. Abraham Wanneh
767. Chicago-Spertus College of Judaica D 2, 2, f. 247a, M, no incipit.
768. Jerusalem - Sassoon 1158, p. 425-426, M, no incipit.
769. London - British Library Or. 11122, f. 220a-220b, M, no incipit.

יי אלהא דכל דמטמד קדמוהי, סליחה

Yemen, commentary by Isaac b. Abraham Wanneh
770. Chicago-Spertus College of Judaica D 2, 2, f. 238b, M, no incipit.
771. Jerusalem - Benayahu ת 261, f. 166a, M, short.
772. Jerusalem - Makhon Ben Zvi 1156 (Tubi 155), f. 138b, M, no incipit.
773. Jerusalem - Makhon Ben Zvi 1156 (Tubi 155), f. 139b, M, no incipit.
774. Jerusalem - Makhon Ben Zvi 1174 (Tubi 154), f. 138a, M, short.

---

[21] Edited by Prins, תשלום אבודרהם, p. 32-33.

775. Jerusalem - Musad haRav Kook 325, f. 195a, M, very short.
776. Jerusalem - Sassoon 1158, p. 417, M, no incipit.
777. Jerusalem - Sassoon 1174, p. 271, M, no incipit, short.
778. London - British Library Or. 11122, f. 215b, M, no incipit, short.
779. Muenchen - Bayerische Staatsbibliothek, Cod. hebr. 472, f. 195a, M, short.
780. New York - Jewish Theological Seminary Ms. 3013, f. 134a, M, no incipit, very short.
781. New York - Jewish Theological Seminary Ms. 3294, f. 17b, C.
782. Strasbourg - Bibliotheque Nationale et Universitaire 3965 (Landauer 39), p. 413, M, short.

יי אלהא דשכינתיה בשמי מרומיי, סליחה
Yemen, commentary by Isaac b. Abraham Wanneh
783. Jerusalem - Sassoon 1158, p. 424, M, no incipit.
784. London - British Library Or. 11122, f. 219b, M, no incipit.

יי אלהי אברהם יצחק וישראל (א 663), מאיר ב"ר יצחק, סליחה
Tsarfat
785. Oxford - Bodleian Library MS Bodl. Or. 109 (Neubauer 1209), f. 55a-57a, C, commentator: Aaron b. Hayyim haKohen (compiler).

יי אלהי הסליחות צדיק אתה, סליחה
Tsarfat
786. Oxford - Bodleian Library MS Opp. 171 (Neubauer 1207), f. 96b, C, rubric: אחרת.

יי אלהי הצבאות יושב הכרובים (א 682), סליהה
Ashkenaz
787. Berlin - Staatsbibliothek (Preussischer Kulturbesitz) Or. Qu. 798-799 (Steinschneider 177), I, f. 56a-56b, M.
788. Braunschweig - Landesmuseum fuer Geschichte und Volkstum R 2386, vol. II, f. 61b, M.
789. Cambridge - University Library Add. 394,1 (Reif SCR 461), f. 95b-96a, C, rubric: בשם יי אלהי הצבאות אחל לפרש הסליחות.
790. Hamburg - Staats- und Universitaetsbibliothek Cod. hebr. 17/2 (Steinschneider 152), f. 145b-146a, C.
791. Moscow - Russian State Library, Ms. Guenzburg 190, f. 5a-5b, M.
792. Muenchen - Bayerische Staatsbibliothek, Cod. hebr. 346, f. 142b, C, rubric: אחרת.
793. New York - Jewish Theological Seminary Ms. 8097, f. 83b, C.
794. Oxford - Bodleian Library MS Mich. 365 (Neubauer 1208), f. 63a-63b, C.

795. Oxford - Bodleian Library MS Mich. 543 (Neubauer 1212), f. 7b, C, commentator: Isaac b. Jacob (compiler), short.
796. Oxford - Bodleian Library MS Opp. 619 (Neubauer 2374), f. 107a, M.
797. Padova - Biblioteca del Seminario Vescovile Cod. 218, f. 90b, M.
798. Parma - Biblioteca Palatina Cod. Parm. 3205 (de Rossi 655), f. 278b, C, rubric: פתיחה.
799. Vatican - Biblioteca Apostolica ebr. 308, f. 12a, C, commentator: David b. Mose (compiler), rubric: אתחיל סליחות של ערה ר"ה.
800. Vatican - Biblioteca Apostolica ebr. 422/2, f. 40a, CG, no incipit, very short.

Ashkenaz, commentary by Abraham b. Azriel[22]

801. Frankfurt a M - Stadt- und Universitaetsbibliothek Fol. 16 (Merzbacher 95), f. 103a, C, short.
802. Vatican - Biblioteca Apostolica ebr. 301,1, f. 142b, C, rubric: פתיחות, short.

Tsarfat

803. London - David Sofer 5, f. 83a, C, rubric: זה פירוש מסליחות מעשרת ימי תשובה.
804. Parma - Biblioteca Palatina Cod. Parm. 3007 (de Rossi 654,2), f. 22b-23a, M.
805. Vatican - Biblioteca Apostolica ebr. 306, f. 192a-192b, C.

Yemen

806. Jerusalem - Benayahu ת 88, f. 108a, M.
807. New York - Jewish Theological Seminary Ms. 3193, f. 114a, M.

Yemen, commentary by Isaac b. Abraham Wanneh

808. Chicago-Spertus College of Judaica D 2, 2, f. 176b-177a, M.
809. Jerusalem - Sassoon 1158, p. 292, M.
810. London - British Library Or. 11122, f. 153b, M.
811. Philadelphia - University of Pennsylvania HB 2, f. 113b, M.

יי אלהי הצבאות נורא בעליונים (א 686), שלמה ב"ר יצחק, סליחה

Ashkenaz

812. Braunschweig - Landesmuseum fuer Geschichte und Volkstum R 2386, vol. II, f. 149b, M.
813. Hamburg - Staats- und Universitaetsbibliothek Cod. hebr. 17/2 (Steinschneider 152), f. 146a-146b, C, rubric: אחרת.
814. London - British Library Add. 18695 (Margoliouth 683), f. 173b, T, Yiddish.
815. Moscow - Russian State Library, Ms. Guenzburg 190, f. 6a-7a, M.
816. Muenchen - Bayerische Staatsbibliothek, Cod. hebr. 346, f. 119a, C.

---

[22] Edited by Urbach, ערוגת הבושם, vol. III, p. 312.

817. Oxford - Bodleian Library MS Mich. 543 (Neubauer 1212), f. 7a-7b, C, commentator: Isaac b. Jacob (compiler), rubric: אחרת.
818. Padova - Biblioteca del Seminario Vescovile Cod. 218, f. 91a-91b, M.
819. Parma - Biblioteca Palatina Cod. Parm. 3205 (de Rossi 655), f. 258b-259a, C.
820. Vatican - Biblioteca Apostolica ebr. 308, f. 163a, C, commentator: David b. Mose (compiler), short.
821. Vatican - Biblioteca Apostolica ebr. 422/1, f. 25b, C.
822. Vatican - Biblioteca Apostolica ebr. 422/1, f. 43b-44a, CG, no incipit.

Ashkenaz, commentary by Abraham b. Azriel[23]
823. Vatican - Biblioteca Apostolica ebr. 301,1, f. 142b, C, rubric: אחרת, incipit 'יי אלהי ישר.

Tsarfat
824. London - David Sofer 5, f. 131b-132a, C, rubric: פירוש של סליחות מליל כפור.
825. Parma - Biblioteca Palatina Cod. Parm. 3006 (de Rossi 654,1), f. 110b-111b, M.
826. Vatican - Biblioteca Apostolica ebr. 306, f. 168a-168b, C, rubric: סליחות ותחנונים.

יי אלהי הצבאות צג בין ההדסים (א 688), סליחה

Ashkenaz
827. Jerusalem - Schocken Institute 24100 / Mahzor Nuremberg, f. 393a-393b, M.
828. Muenchen - Bayerische Staatsbibliothek, Cod. hebr. 346, f. 145a, C.
829. Muenchen - Bayerische Staatsbibliothek, Cod. hebr. 346, f. 149a, C, rubric: אחרת.
830. Oxford - Bodleian Library MS Mich. 543 (Neubauer 1212), f. 7a, C, commentator: Isaac b. Jacob (compiler).
831. Oxford - Bodleian Library MS Opp. 172 (Neubauer 1211), f. 53b, C.
832. Vatican - Biblioteca Apostolica ebr. 308, f. 107(ii)b-108(ii)a, C, commentator: David b. Mose (compiler), rubric: אתחיל סליחות לצומא רבא לשחרית.

Ashkenaz, commentary by Abraham b. Azriel[24]
833. Frankfurt a M - Stadt- und Universitaetsbibliothek Fol. 16 (Merzbacher 95), f. 110a, C.

יי אלהי ישראל אבינו (א 701), משה זכות

Italia, commentary by Mose Zakut
834. London - British Library Or. 10415, f. 12a-25b, C, rubric: פירוש.

---
[23] Edited by Urbach, ערוגת הבושם, vol. II, p. 312-314.
[24] Edited by Urbach, ערוגת הבושם, vol. III, p. 567-568.

יי אלהי ישראל צדיק אתה אלוה הסליחות (א 703), סליחה

Ashkenaz
835. Budapest - Magyar tudomanyos akademia, MS. Kaufmann A 400 , p. 492-493, C, rubric: אחרת.
836. Cambridge - University Library Dd. 2.30, f. 14b-15a, G.
837. Moscow - Russian State Library, Ms. Guenzburg 615, f. 161b, C, rubric: אל מלך.
838. Muenchen - Bayerische Staatsbibliothek, Cod. hebr. 346, f. 105a, C.
839. Oxford - Bodleian Library MS Opp. 170 (Neubauer 1205), f. 230b-231a, C, rubric: אחרת.
840. Oxford - Bodleian Library MS Opp. 681 (Neubauer 1213), f. 37b-38a, C.
841. Vatican - Biblioteca Apostolica ebr. 422/1, f. 31a, C.

Ashkenaz, commentary by Abraham b. Azriel[25]
842. Vatican - Biblioteca Apostolica ebr. 301,1, f. 160b, C, rubric: אחרת.

Tsarfat
843. London - David Sofer 5, f. 175a, C, rubric: סליחה.
844. Oxford - Bodleian Library MS Bodl. Or. 109 (Neubauer 1209), f. 53b-55a, C, commentator: Aaron b. Hayyim haKohen (compiler).
845. Oxford - Bodleian Library MS Laud. Or. 271 (Neubauer 1206), f. 123b, C, commentator: Aaron b. Hayyim haKohen (compiler).
846. Oxford - Bodleian Library MS Opp. 171 (Neubauer 1207), f. 116b, C, rubric: אחרת.
847. Parma - Biblioteca Palatina Cod. Parm. 3007 (de Rossi 654,2), f. 23a-23b, M.
848. Vatican - Biblioteca Apostolica ebr. 306, f. 201b-202a, C.

יי אלהי ישראל שוב מחרון אפיך (א 708), סליחה

Yemen, commentary by Isaac b. Abraham Wanneh
849. Chicago-Spertus College of Judaica D 2, 2, f. 183a-184a, M.
850. London - British Library Or. 11122, f. 160a, M, rubric: תחנה ליום שלישי.

יי אלהי רבת צררוני מנעורי (א 717), דוד בר שמואל הלוי, סליחה

Ashkenaz
851. Berlin - Staatsbibliothek (Preussischer Kulturbesitz) Or. Qu. 798-799 (Steinschneider 177), I, f. 103b-104a, M.
852. Berlin - Staatsbibliothek (Preussischer Kulturbesitz) Or. Qu. 798-799 (Steinschneider 177), I, f. 147a-148a, M.
853. Cambridge - University Library Dd. 2.30, f. 13b-14b, G.

---

[25] Edited by Urbach, ערוגת הבושם, vol. III, p. 430-432.

854. London - British Library Add. 18695 (Margoliouth 683), f. 164a-164b, T, Yiddish.
855. New York - Jewish Theological Seminary Ms. 8097, f. 87a, C, incipit רבת.
856. Oxford - Bodleian Library MS Mich. 543 (Neubauer 1212), f. 25b-26a, C, commentator: Isaac b. Jacob (compiler).
857. Oxford - Bodleian Library MS Opp. 619 (Neubauer 2374), f. 181b-182b, M.
858. Oxford - Bodleian Library MS Opp. 619 (Neubauer 2374), f. 266a-267a, M.
859. Oxford - Bodleian Library MS Opp. 681 (Neubauer 1213), f. 44b, C, short.
860. Padova - Biblioteca del Seminario Vescovile Cod. 218, f. 101b-102b, M.
861. Padova - Biblioteca del Seminario Vescovile Cod. 218, f. 180a-181a, M.
862. Padova - Biblioteca del Seminario Vescovile Cod. 218, f. 197a-198a, M.
863. Padova - Biblioteca del Seminario Vescovile Cod. 218, f. 213b-214b, M.
864. Vatican - Biblioteca Apostolica ebr. 422/1, f. 25b, C.
865. Vatican - Biblioteca Apostolica ebr. 422/1, f. 44b, CG, no incipit, very short.

Tsarfat
866. Oxford - Bodleian Library MS Bodl. Or. 109 (Neubauer 1209), f. 57a-57b, C, commentator: Aaron b. Hayyim haKohen (compiler).

אדוני אלהים אתה החלות להראות לי שערי גבוהים (א 723), שמחה יצחק בן משה?
או אהרן בן יוסף הרופא, פרשת אתחנן

Karaite, commentary by Berakha b. Josef haKohen
867. New York - Jewish Theological Seminary Ms. 3367, f. 141a-144a, C, rubric: פרוש פרשת ואתחנן.
868. St. Petersburg - Inst. of Oriental Studies of the Russian Academy B 483, f. 12b, C, rubric: פרשת ואתחנן.
869. St. Petersburg - Inst. of Oriental Studies of the Russian Academy B 431, f. 95b-97a, C, rubric: פרשת ואתחנן.
870. St. Petersburg - Russian National Library, Evr. IV 50, f. 109b-112a, C, rubric: ואתחנן.

יי אלהים הלא עיניך לאמונה (א 725), ליום כפור

Ashkenaz
871. Berlin - Staatsbibliothek (Preussischer Kulturbesitz) Or. Qu. 798-799 (Steinschneider 177), I, f. 149b-150a, M.

יי אם גדל עוני מנשוא והסכלתי (א 749), דוד, סליחה

Sepharad
872. Skokie - Hebrew Theological College 3, f. 18a-18b, G.
Yemen, commentary by Isaac b. Abraham Wanneh
873. Chicago-Spertus College of Judaica D 2, 2, f. 183b-184a, M, rubric: תחנה ליום רביעי.
874. London - British Library Or. 11122, f. 160a, M, rubric: תחנה ליום רביעי.

יי ארץ אשתחוה לך (א 763), סליחה

Ashkenaz
875. Jerusalem - Schocken Institute 24100 / Mahzor Nuremberg, f. 254b-255a, M, short marginal notes by later hand only.
876. Vatican - Biblioteca Apostolica ebr. 308, f. 14b, C, commentator: David b. Mose (compiler).

יי אתה הוא עד לא עולם נברא, סליחה

Yemen, commentary by Isaac b. Abraham Wanneh
877. Chicago-Spertus College of Judaica D 2, 2, f. 218b, M, no incipit.
878. Jerusalem - Michael Krupp 604, f. 163b, M.
879. Jerusalem - Sassoon 1158, p. 373-374, M, no incipit.
880. London - British Library Or. 11122, f. 186b-187a, M, rubric: אל מלך.

יי בצר פקדנוך (א 779), סליחה

Tsarfat
881. London - David Sofer 5, f. 134b-135a, C.
882. Parma - Biblioteca Palatina Cod. Parm. 3006 (de Rossi 654,1), f. 249a-249b, M.

יי בקול שופר (א 782), יעקב, סליחה

Carpentras
883. Cincinnati - Hebrew Union College 429/1, f. 9b, M, no incipit.
884. Cincinnati - Hebrew Union College 429/1, f. 29b, M, no incipit.
Carpentras, commentary by Josef b. Abraham of Montelitz
885. Cincinnati - Hebrew Union College 357, f. 56b-57a, M.
886. New York - Jewish Theological Seminary Ms. 4746, f. 14b, M.
887. Paris - Alliance Israelite Universelle H 422 A, f. 34a-34b, M.
888. Paris - Alliance Israelite Universelle H 422 A, f. 93a, M.
889. Paris - Ecole Rabbinique 31, f. 103a, M.
Yemen
890. New York - Jewish Theological Seminary Ms. 1725, f. 6b-7a, M.
891. New York - Jewish Theological Seminary Ms. 3052, f. 42b-43a, M, rubric: אל מלך.

892. Ramat Gan - Universitat Bar Ilan 62, f. 40a, G.

Yemen, commentary by Isaac b. Abraham Wanneh

893. Chicago-Spertus College of Judaica D 2, 2, f. 217b, M, no incipit.
894. Jerusalem - Benayahu ת 261, f. 143a-143b, M, rubric: אל מלך.
895. Jerusalem - Benayahu ת 282, f. 126a-126b, M, rubric: אל מלך.
896. Jerusalem - Makhon Ben Zvi 1156 (Tubi 155), f. 125a-125b, M, rubric: אל מלך.
897. Jerusalem - Makhon Ben Zvi 1156 (Tubi 155), f. 125b-127a, M, rubric: אל מלך.
898. Jerusalem - Makhon Ben Zvi 1174 (Tubi 154), f. 108b, M, rubric: אל מלך.
899. Jerusalem - Musad haRav Kook 325, f. 160a, M.
900. Jerusalem - Sassoon 1174, p. 240, M, no incipit.
901. London - British Library Or. 11122, f. 194b, M, no incipit.
902. Muenchen - Bayerische Staatsbibliothek, Cod. hebr. 472, f. 172a, M, rubric: אל מלך.
903. New York - Jewish Theological Seminary Ms. 3013, f. 109a, M, rubric: אל מלך, short.
904. New York - Jewish Theological Seminary Ms. 3109, f. 72a-72b, M, rubric: אל מלך.
905. New York - Jewish Theological Seminary Ms. 3294, f. 4a, C.
906. New York - Public Library, Heb. Ms. 9, f. 113a, M.
907. Philadelphia - University of Pennsylvania HB 2, f. 122a, M, incipit חזיון.
908. Strasbourg - Bibliotheque Nationale et Universitaire 3965 (Landauer 39), p. 333, M, rubric: אל מלך.

יי דבידיה אסו לכל מחתא, סליחה

Yemen, commentary by Isaac b. Abraham Wanneh

909. Chicago-Spertus College of Judaica D 2, 2, f. 236a, M, no incipit.
910. Jerusalem - Sassoon 1158, p. 413, M, no incipit.

יי דלו עיני למרום (א 794), דוד בן אלעזר בקודה, סליחה

Sepharad

911. Skokie - Hebrew Theological College 3, f. 17b-18a, G.

Yemen, commentary by Isaac b. Abraham Wanneh

912. Chicago-Spertus College of Judaica D 2, 2, f. 183b, M, rubric: תחנה ליום שלישי.

יי דסגיאין רחמוהי על כל בריתא, סליחה

Yemen, commentary by Isaac b. Abraham Wanneh

913. Chicago-Spertus College of Judaica D 2, 2, f. 236a, M, no incipit.
914. Jerusalem - Sassoon 1158, p. 413, M, no incipit.

יי דקריב לכל מאן דקרי ליה, סליחה

Yemen
915. New York - Jewish Theological Seminary Ms. 3052, f. 85b-86a, M.
Yemen, commentary by Isaac b. Abraham Wanneh
916. Chicago-Spertus College of Judaica D 2, 2, f. 238b, M, no incipit.
917. Jerusalem - Benayahu ת 261, f. 166a, M.
918. Jerusalem - Benayahu ת 282, f. 141b-142a, M.
919. Jerusalem - Makhon Ben Zvi 1156 (Tubi 155), f. 138b, M, no incipit.
920. Jerusalem - Makhon Ben Zvi 1156 (Tubi 155), f. 139b, M, no incipit.
921. Jerusalem - Michael Krupp 604, f. 176b, M, short.
922. Jerusalem - Musad haRav Kook 325, f. 195a, M, very short.
923. Jerusalem - Sassoon 1158, p. 417, M, no incipit.
924. Jerusalem - Sassoon 1174, p. 271, M, no incipit, very short.
925. London - British Library Or. 11122, f. 215b, M, no incipit, short.
926. Muenchen - Bayerische Staatsbibliothek, Cod. hebr. 472, f. 194b-195a, M, very short.
927. New York - Jewish Theological Seminary Ms. 3013, f. 134a, M, very short, no incipit.
928. New York - Jewish Theological Seminary Ms. 3294, f. 17b, C.
929. Strasbourg - Bibliotheque Nationale et Universitaire 3965 (Landauer 39), p. 413, M, very short.

אדוני האדונים השקיפה ממעונים ורחם אביונים (א 801), סליחה

Ashkenaz
930. Moscow - Russian State Library, Ms. Guenzburg 190, f. 106a-106b, G.
Romania
931. Vatican - Biblioteca Apostolica ebr. 320, f. 351b-352a, M.
Tsarfat
932. London - David Sofer 5, f. 101a-101b, C.
933. Parma - Biblioteca Palatina Cod. Parm. 3006 (de Rossi 654,1), f. 229a-229b, M.
934. Vatican - Biblioteca Apostolica ebr. 306, f. 207a, C.
Yemen
935. Jerusalem - Benayahu ת 414, f. 155a, M.
936. Jerusalem - Sassoon 902, p. 442, M.
Yemen, commentary by Isaac b. Abraham Wanneh
937. Chicago-Spertus College of Judaica D 2, 2, f. 192a, M, no incipit.
938. Jerusalem - Michael Krupp 604, f. 148b, M, rubric: אל מלך.
939. Jerusalem - Musad haRav Kook 330, f. 103b-104a, G.
940. Jerusalem - Sassoon 1158, p. 355, M, rubric: אל מלך, no incipit.
941. Jerusalem - Yehiel haLevi 4, f. 154b, G.
942. London - British Library Or. 11122, f. 176b, M.

943. New York - Jewish Theological Seminary Ms. 3109 , f. 65a, M, rubric: אל מלך.

יי זעקתי בחבלי (א 815), זרחיה, סליחה
Carpentras, commentary by Mordekhai b. Josef of Rocco Martino
944. Cincinnati - Hebrew Union College 246/1, f. 62a-62b, C, rubric: פי' תחינה ה' זעקתי בחבלי.

יי יגוני קראוני אל אבל (א 831), יהודה הלוי, סליחה
Carpentras, commentary by Mordekhai b. Josef of Rocco Martino
945. Cincinnati - Hebrew Union College 246/1, f. 89b-90a, C, rubric: פי' התחנה.

יי יום לך אערוך תחנה (א 849), יהודה הלוי, בקשה
Carpentras
946. Cincinnati - Hebrew Union College 429/1, f. 16b, M, no incipit.
Carpentras, commentary by Josef b. Abraham of Montelitz
947. Cincinnati - Hebrew Union College 357, f. 89b-90a, M, rubric: פירוש.
948. New York - Jewish Theological Seminary Ms. 4746, f. 25a-25b, M.
949. Paris - Alliance Israelite Universelle H 422 A, f. 60a-60b, M.
950. Paris - Ecole Rabbinique 31, f. 130a-130b, M.
Sepharad
951. Skokie - Hebrew Theological College 3, f. 82a-82b, M.

יי יחיד לבות כל בני אדם חוקר (א 861), יהודה הלוי, סליחה
Sepharad
952. Skokie - Hebrew Theological College 3, f. 17b, G.
Yemen, commentary by Isaac b. Abraham Wanneh
953. Chicago-Spertus College of Judaica D 2, 2, f. 183b, M, rubric: תחנה ליום שני.
954. London - British Library Or. 11122, f. 159b-160a, M.

יי מה אדם אנושים וענושים בקשים (א 6521), שלמה אבן גבירול
Sepharad, commentary by David b. Josef Abudarham[26]
955. Budapest - Magyar tudomanyos akademia, MS. Kaufmann A 405/2 , p. 197-199, C, rubric: מסטאג'יב.
956. New York - Columbia X893 Ab 93, f. 9a-10a, C, rubric: ובכן מסתאגיב. מה אדם ותדעהו ובן אנוש ותחשבהו.

---

[26] Edited by Prins, תשלום אבודרהם, p. 87-91.

יי מה אדם הלֹא בשר ודם (א 886), שלמה אבן גבירול, פזמון

Sepharad
957. Skokie - Hebrew Theological College 3, f. 19a, G.

Sepharad, commentary by David b. Josef Abudarham[27]
958. Budapest - Magyar tudomanyos akademia, MS. Kaufmann A 405/2, p. 200, C, rubric: פזמון.
959. Cincinnati - Hebrew Union College 490, f. 6a, C.
960. Holon - Yehuda Nahum 278, f. 2b, FC, rubric: פזמון.
961. Holon - Yehuda Nahum 278, f. 5a-5b, FC, rubric: מסתאגיב.
962. New York - Columbia X893 Ab 93, f. 10a-10b, C, rubric: פזמון.
963. New York - Jewish Theological Seminary Ms. 3011, f. 8a-9b, C, rubric: מסתאגיב.

Yemen
964. Jerusalem - Sassoon 902, p. 420, M.
965. New York - Jewish Theological Seminary Ms. 3052, f. 18a-19b, M, rubric: אל מלך.

Yemen, commentary by Isaac b. Abraham Wanneh
966. Chicago-Spertus College of Judaica D 2, 2, f. 184a, M, rubric: תחנה ליום ששי.
967. Chicago-Spertus College of Judaica D 2, 2, f. 195a-195b, M.
968. Jerusalem - Michael Krupp 604, f. 146a-146b, M.
969. Jerusalem - Sassoon 1158, p. 356-357, M, rubric: אל מלך.
970. London - British Library Or. 11122, f. 160a-160b, M, rubric: תחנה ליום ששי.
971. London - British Library Or. 11122, f. 177a, M, rubric: אל מלך.

יי מעון אתה אמון קנית, סליחה

Yemen, commentary by Isaac b. Abraham Wanneh
972. Chicago-Spertus College of Judaica D 2, 2, f. 210b, M, no incipit.
973. Jerusalem - Michael Krupp 604, f. 164b-165a, M.
974. Jerusalem - Sassoon 1158, p. 385, M, no incipit.
975. London - British Library Or. 11122, f. 192b-193a, M, no incipit.

יי נגדיך כל תאותי ואם לא אעלנה על שפתי (א 920), יהודה הלוי, בקשה

Carpentras
976. Cincinnati - Hebrew Union College 392, f. 21b-22a, M.

Carpentras, commentary by Josef b. Abraham of Montelitz
977. Cincinnati - Hebrew Union College 291, f. 10b-11a, C, rubric: פי' בקשה ה' נגדך כל תאותי.
978. New York - Jewish Theological Seminary Ms. 4197, f. 49a-50a, M.
979. Paris - Ecole Rabbinique 32, f. 72b-73a, M.

---

[27] Edited by Prins, תשלום אבודרהם, p. 91-92.

980. Strasbourg - Bibliotheque Nationale et Universitaire 4081, f. 52a-53a, M.

Yemen, commentary by Isaac b. Abraham Wanneh
981. Chicago-Spertus College of Judaica D 2, 2, f. 182b-183a, M.
982. Jerusalem - Sassoon 1158, p. 302, M.

אדוני נתן אמר להקדיש קרואיו (א 936), אהרן ב"ר יוסף הרופא, פרשת נשוא

Karaite, commentary by Berakha b. Josef haKohen
983. New York - Jewish Theological Seminary Ms. 3367, f. 119a-121b, C, rubric: פרוש פרשת נשוא.
984. St. Petersburg - Inst. of Oriental Studies of the Russian Academy B 431, f. 82a-83a, C, rubric: פרשת נשוא.
985. St. Petersburg - Russian National Library, Evr. IV 50, f. 92a-93b, C, rubric: נשוא.

יי צבאות שם כבוד מלכותך (א +952), יהודה הלוי, חלק ב' אל אלהים אל מי אמשילך

Carpentras, commentary by Josef b. Abraham of Montelitz
986. Cincinnati - Hebrew Union College 357, f. 108b-111a, M.

יי קנני ראשית דרכו (א +958), אלעזר בקברי קליר, חלק ו', קדושתא לשבועות

Ashkenaz
987. Muenchen - Bayerische Staatsbibliothek, Cod. hebr. 88, f. 140b-143b, G.
988. Berlin - Staatsbibliothek (Preussischer Kulturbesitz) Or. Qu. 798-799 (Steinschneider 177), II, f. 141a-144b, M.
989. Braunschweig - Landesmuseum fuer Geschichte und Volkstum R 2386, vol. I, f. 97b-100a, M.
990. Hamburg - Staats- und Universitaetsbibliothek Cod. hebr. 17/2 (Steinschneider 152), f. 86a-87b, C.
991. Hamburg - Staats- und Universitaetsbibliothek Cod. hebr. 225, f. 190a, 196a, G.
992. London - British Library Add. 18695 (Margoliouth 683), f. 86b-90a, T, Yiddish, rubric: דר נוך היבט דער חזן אן ובכן יי קנני ראשית דרכו אישט אין טויצן.
993. London - British Library Add. 22431 (Margoliouth 662a), f. 57a-61b, M.
994. Moscow - Russian State Library, Ms. Guenzburg 615, f. 42b, C, no incipit, very short.
995. New York - Jewish Theological Seminary Ms. 4466, f. 168a-169a, 171a-172b, M.
996. Paris - Bibliotheque Nationale heb. 709, f. 136b-137a, C.
997. Parma - Biblioteca Palatina Cod. Parm. 2886 (de Rossi 585), f. 65b-70b, M, later hand, margins cut.

998. Parma - Biblioteca Palatina Cod. Parm. 3205 (de Rossi 655), f. 127b-128a, C.
999. Parma - Biblioteca Palatina Cod. Parm. 3507 (Perreau 27), f. 89b-92a, C.
1000. Zurich - Zentralbibliothek Heid. 139, f. 55a, C, additional marginal notes.

יי שומרי לביתך נאוה (א 1017), אפרים ב"ר יצחק מרגנסבורג, סליחה

Ashkenaz
1001. Braunschweig - Landesmuseum fuer Geschichte und Volkstum R 2386, vol. II, f. 148b-149a, M, ecclectic, short.
1002. Padova - Biblioteca del Seminario Vescovile Cod. 218, f. 169b-171b, M.
1003. Parma - Bibliotheca Palatina Cod. Parm. 3205 (de Rossi 655), f. 289b-290b, C.

יי שועת עמך הקשיבה (א 1019), שמואל, סליחה

Sepharad
1004. Skokie - Hebrew Theological College 3, f. 17a, G.

יי שמענא את קולינו חוסה וגם רחם עלינו (א 1030), אברהם, סליחה

Yemen, commentary by Isaac b. Abraham Wanneh
1005. Chicago-Spertus College of Judaica D 2, 2, f. 195a, M.
1006. Jerusalem - Musad haRav Kook 330, f. 104a, G.
1007. Jerusalem - Musad haRav Kook 347, f. 80a, G.
1008. Jerusalem - Sassoon 1158, p. 353, M, no incipit.
1009. London - British Library Or. 11122, f. 175b-176a, M.

יי שמעה יי סלחה יי הקשיבה (א+ 1031), סליחה

Ashkenaz
1010. Berlin - Staatsbibliothek (Preussischer Kulturbesitz) Or. Qu. 798-799 (Steinschneider 177), I, f. 149a, M, very short.
1011. Braunschweig - Landesmuseum fuer Geschichte und Volkstum R 2386, vol. II, f. 52b, M.
1012. Padova - Biblioteca del Seminario Vescovile Cod. 218, f. 87b, M.
1013. Vatican - Biblioteca Apostolica ebr. 422/1, f. 32a, C, very short.
1014. Vatican - Biblioteca Apostolica ebr. 422/2, f. 40a, CG, no incipit.

יי שעה נודד מקנו (א 1045), שמואל, סליחה

Sepharad
1015. Skokie - Hebrew Theological College 3, f. 18b, G.

Yemen, commentary by Isaac b. Abraham Wanneh
1016. Chicago-Spertus College of Judaica D 2, 2, f. 184a, M, rubric: תחנה ליום חמישי.
1017. London - British Library Or. 11122, f. 160a, M, rubric: תחנה ליום חמישי.

יי שפתי תפתח ופי יגיד תהלתך יהיו לרצון אמרי פי
Carpentras
1018. Cincinnati - Hebrew Union College 429/1, f. 1b, M, very short.

אדורי משבעים זעומי שבועים (א 1055), אלעזר ברבי קליר, חלק ה', קדושתא שמיני עצרת
Tsarfat
1019. London - David Sofer 5, f. 184b, C, incipit אדירי.
1020. Oxford - Bodleian Library MS Opp. 171 (Neubauer 1207), f. 162a-163a, C, incipit אדירי.

אדיר אשר עולם בראת (א 1063), משה אבן עזרא, סילוק, קדושתא מנחה יום כפור
Carpentras
1021. Cincinnati - Hebrew Union College 392, f. 103b-104a, M, no incipit.
Carpentras, commentary by Josef b. Abraham of Montelitz
1022. Paris - Ecole Rabbinique 32, f. 247b-248a, M, no incipit.
1023. Strasbourg - Bibliotheque Nationale et Universitaire 4081, f. 219b-220b, M, no incipit.

אדיר בועודו ברום ותחת הודו (א 1068), אלעזר ברבי קליר, חלק ח', קדושתא למוסף יום כפור
Ashkenaz
1024. Cambridge - University Library Add. 394,1 (Reif SCR 461), f. 69b, C, short.
1025. Jerusalem - Schocken Institute 24100 / Mahzor Nuremberg, f. 412a-412b, M, very short.
1026. London - Montefiore Library 261, f. 55b-56a, C, commentator: Eliezer b. Natan?.
1027. Moscow - Russian State Library, Ms. Guenzburg 191, f. 118a-118b, M.
1028. Muenchen - Bayerische Staatsbibliothek, Cod. hebr. 346, f. 77b, C.
1029. New York - Jewish Theological Seminary Ms. 8097, f. 79a, C, very short.
1030. Oxford - Bodleian Library MS Mich. 365 (Neubauer 1208), f. 83a-83b, C.
1031. Oxford - Bodleian Library MS Opp. 172 (Neubauer 1211), f. 61a, C, short.

1032. Vatican - Biblioteca Apostolica ebr. 308, f. 118a, C, commentator: David b. Mose (compiler), very short.
1033. Parma - Biblioteca Palatina Cod. Parm. 3507 (Perreau 27), f. 163b, C, short.

Roma
1034. Berlin - Staatsbibliothek (Preussischer Kulturbesitz) Or. Oct. 3567, f. 8a, FC, short.

Tsarfat
1035. Parma - Biblioteca Palatina Cod. Parm. 3006 (de Rossi 654,1), f. 182a, M.
1036. London - David Sofer 5, f. 151b, C.

אדיר בעברו על אדמת סינים (א 1076), יוסף ב"ר שמואל טוב עלם, חלק ו', קדושתא ליום ז' של פסח

Tsarfat
1037. Parma - Biblioteca Palatina Cod. Parm. 3136 (de Rossi 405), f. 110b-111a, M, incipit יופיע.

אדיר דר מתוחים (א 1082), מנחם?, מוסף שבת הגדול

Ashkenaz
1038. Berlin - Staatsbibliothek (Preussischer Kulturbesitz) Or. Qu. 798-799 (Steinschneider 177), II, f. 49b-52a, M.
1039. Budapest - Magyar tudomanyos akademia, MS. Kaufmann A 384, f. 112a-115a, M.
1040. Erlangen - Universitaetsbibliothek 2601 (Roth 67), f. 59b-60a, M.
1041. Goettingen - Niedersaechsische Staats -und Universitaetsbibliothek Fragm. 788, f. 1a-4b, FC, incomplete.
1042. Hamburg - Staats- und Universitaetsbibliothek Cod. hebr. 17/2 (Steinschneider 152), f. 31b-33a, C, rubric: סדר.
1043. Hamburg - Staats- und Universitaetsbibliothek Cod. hebr. 299/2, f. 3a, C.
1044. London - British Library Add. 18695 (Margoliouth 683), f. 13a-16a, T, Yiddish, rubric: צו מוסף.
1045. Muenchen - Bayerische Staatsbibliothek, Cod. hebr. 393, f. 109a-112b, C.
1046. New York - Jewish Theological Seminary Ms. 4466, f. 35b-45b, continued f. 205a-206b, M.
1047. Paris - Bibliotheque Nationale heb. 709, f. 44b-62b, C, rubric: זה סדר של פסח.
1048. Parma - Biblioteca Palatina Cod. Parm. 1002 (Ta 24), f. 75a-82a, M, wrong position.
1049. Parma - Biblioteca Palatina Cod. Parm. 3205 (de Rossi 655), f. 46b-57a, C, rubric: סדר.

1050. Zurich - Zentralbibliothek Heid. 139, f. 14b-18a, C, additional marginal notes on first part.

Tsarfat

1051. Oxford - Bodleian Library MS Laud. Or. 271 (Neubauer 1206), f. 50b-51b, C, commentator: Aaron b. Hayyim haKohen (compiler), rubric: ‏סדר. סדר נקרא על שם שסידר בו הפייט איסור והיתר על שם‎ ...

‏אדיר ונאה בקודש‎ (‏א‎ 1092), ‏מאיר ב"ר יצחק, יוצר שבת אחרי שבועות‎

Ashkenaz

1052. Jerusalem - Schocken Institute 24100 / Mahzor Nuremberg, f. 183b-184b, M.
1053. Muenchen - Bayerische Staatsbibliothek, Cod. hebr. 69, f. 54a-56a, M.
1054. Muenchen - Bayerische Staatsbibliothek, Cod. hebr. 88, f. 150b-151b, G.

Ashkenaz, commentary by Abraham b. Azriel[28]

1055. Nuernberg - Stadtbibliothek, Amberger 173 fol., FC, incomplete, equals Ed. Urbach, vol. I, p. 167-168.
1056. Vatican - Biblioteca Apostolica ebr. 301,1, f. 23a-32a, C, rubric: ‏יוצר‎.

‏אדיר ונאור בורא דוק וחלד‎ (‏א‎ 1095), ‏מוסף יום כפור‎

Ashkenaz

1057. Berlin - Staatsbibliothek (Preussischer Kulturbesitz) Or. Qu. 798-799 (Steinschneider 177), I, f. 156b-157a, M.

Sepharad

1058. Jerusalem - Benayahu ‏ז‎ 25, f. 104a, M.
1059. Jerusalem - Schocken Institute 70014, f. 55b, M.
1060. Skokie - Hebrew Theological College 3, f. 2.24b-25a, M.

‏אדיר ונשגב קורא הדורות, יוסף ב"ר שמואל טוב עלם, חלק ה', קדושתא לשבועות‎

Tsarfat

1061. Parma - Biblioteca Palatina Cod. Parm. 3136 (de Rossi 405), f. 170b-171a, M, no incipit.

‏אדירי איומה יאדירו בקול יי‎ (‏א‎ 1133), ‏אלעזר ברבי קליר, חלק ח', קדושתא ר"ה‎

Ashkenaz

1062. Berlin - Staatsbibliothek (Preussischer Kulturbesitz) Or. Qu. 798-799 (Steinschneider 177), I, f. 8a-8b, M.
1063. Braunschweig - Landesmuseum fuer Geschichte und Volkstum R 2386, vol. II, f. 82b-83a, M.

---

[28] Edited by Urbach, ‏ערוגת הבושם‎, vol. I, p. 146-197.

1064. Budapest - Magyar tudomanyos akademia, MS. Kaufmann A 400, p. 254, C, no incipit, ecclectic.
1065. Cambridge - University Library Or. 785, f. 21a, G.
1066. Darmstadt - Hessisches Landes- und Hochschulbibliothek Cod. Or. 15, f. 8a, M.
1067. Hamburg - Staats- und Universitaetsbibliothek Cod. hebr. 17/2 (Steinschneider 152), f. 108b-109a, C.
1068. Hamburg - Staats- und Universitaetsbibliothek Cod. hebr. 40c (Steinschneider 111), f. 134a, G.
1069. Hamburg - Staats- und Universitaetsbibliothek Cod. hebr. 132 (Steinschneider 155), f. 7b-8a, C.
1070. Jerusalem - Jewish National and University Library Ms Heb 8° 3037, f. 10b-11a, M.
1071. Jerusalem - Schocken Institute 15791/7, f. 60a-60b, C, no incipit, kabbalistic.
1072. Jerusalem - Schocken Institute 24100 / Mahzor Nuremberg, f. 325a-325b, M.
1073. London - British Library Or. 11318/1, f. 12b, C.
1074. Moscow - Russian State Library, Ms. Guenzburg 615, f. 59a-59b, C, rubric: יי מל׳ יי מל׳ יי ימלוך לעו׳ ועד.
1075. Moscow - Russian State Library, Ms. Guenzburg 1401/2, f. 16b, C.
1076. New York - Jewish Theological Seminary Ms. 4466, f. 213a-213b, M.
1077. New York - Jewish Theological Seminary Ms. 8097, f. 59b-60a, C, additional glosses in the margins.
1078. Oxford - Bodleian Library MS Opp. 170 (Neubauer 1205), f. 107a-107b, C, followed by esoteric abstracts from the works of Elazar b. Yehuda of Worms in smaller hand.
1079. Oxford - Bodleian Library MS Opp. 172 (Neubauer 1211), f. 5a, C.
1080. Oxford - Bodleian Library MS Opp. 619 (Neubauer 2374), f. 13a-13b, M.
1081. Oxford - Bodleian Library MS Opp. 675 (Neubauer 1210), f. 17b, C, double commentary.
1082. Paris - Bibliotheque Nationale heb. 653, f. 10b-11a, G.
1083. Parma - Biblioteca Palatina Cod. Parm. 3205 (de Rossi 655), f. 205b-206a, C.
1084. Parma - Biblioteca Palatina Cod. Parm. 3270 (de Rossi 1215), f. 22a, M.
1085. Parma - Biblioteca Palatina Cod. Parm. 3507 (Perreau 27), f. 113a-113b, C.
1086. Vatican - Bibliotheca Apostolica ebr. 298/1, f. 10b, C, no incipit.
1087. Vatican - Biblioteca Apostolica ebr. 308, f. 34b-35a, C, commentator: David b. Mose (compiler).
1088. Vatican - Biblioteca Apostolica ebr. 422/1, f. 8b, C, short.
1089. Zurich - Zentralbibliothek Heid. 139, f. 59b-60a, C, additional marginal notes.

Asti, Fossano, Moncalvo
1090. New Haven - Yale University, Beinecke Rare Book and MS Library, MS Heb. 52, f. 21a-21b, M.
Romania
1091. Vatican - Biblioteca Apostolica ebr. 320, f. 152b-153a, C.
Tsarfat
1092. London - British Library Or. 8682, f. 12a-12b, GI.
1093. London - David Sofer 5, f. 111a, C.
1094. Manchester - John Rylands University Library, Ms. Gaster 733, f. 81b, C, commentary block in Mahzor, manuscript damaged.
1095. Oxford - Bodleian Library MS Laud. Or. 271 (Neubauer 1206), f. 141b, C, commentator: Aaron b. Hayyim haKohen (compiler).
1096. Paris - Bibliotheque Nationale heb. 445,9, f. 66a, C.
1097. Parma - Biblioteca Palatina Cod. Parm. 2125 (de Rossi 812), f. 11a-11b, C.
1098. Parma - Biblioteca Palatina Cod. Parm. 3006 (de Rossi 654,1), f. 27b-28a, M.
1099. Vatican - Biblioteca Apostolica ebr. 306, f. 50a, C.

אדירי ישורון יברכו בקול' יי מלך (א 1134), יצחק בן יהודה גירונדי, א' דר"ה
Carpentras
1100. Cincinnati - Hebrew Union College 429/1, f. 11a, M, no incipit.
Carpentras, commentary by Josef b. Abraham of Montelitz
1101. Cincinnati - Hebrew Union College 357, f. 59b, M, rubric: פירוש, no incipit.
1102. New York - Jewish Theological Seminary Ms. 4746, f. 16b, M, no incipit.
1103. Paris - Alliance Israelite Universelle H 422 A, f. 36a-37b, M, no incipit.
1104. Paris - Ecole Rabbinique 31, f. 105b, M, no incipit.

אדם איך יזכה בכל יום למות מחכה (א 1138), סליחה
Ashkenaz
1105. Jerusalem - Schocken Institute 24100 / Mahzor Nuremberg, f. 253b, M.
1106. Jerusalem - Schocken Institute 24100 / Mahzor Nuremberg, f. 435a-435b, M.
1107. Muenchen - Bayerische Staatsbibliothek, Cod. hebr. 346, f. 148a-148b, C, rubric: אחרת.
1108. Oxford - Bodleian Library MS Opp. 172 (Neubauer 1211), f. 77a-77b, C.

אדם בקום עלינו חיל אחזתנו (א 1158), מנחם ב"ר מכיר, סליחה תענית אסתר
Ashkenaz
1109. Muenchen - Bayerische Staatsbibliothek, Cod. hebr. 88, f. 27b-28b, G.
1110. Oxford - Bodleian Library MS Opp. 681 (Neubauer 1213), f. 34a-34b, C.
1111. Padova - Biblioteca del Seminario Vescovile Cod. 218, f. 252a-253a, M.
1112. Vatican - Biblioteca Apostolica ebr. 422/1, f. 45a, CG, no incipit.
Ashkenaz, commentary by Abraham b. Azriel[29]
1113. Vatican - Biblioteca Apostolica ebr. 301,1, f. 140b-141a, C, rubric: סליחות לתענית אסתר.

אדם ובהמה בשר ורוח ונשמה (א 1165), אלעזר ברבי קליר, הושענא
Ashkenaz
1114. Berlin - Staatsbibliothek (Preussischer Kulturbesitz) Or. Qu. 361 (Steinschneider 51), f. 115b, M.
1115. Berlin - Staatsbibliothek (Preussischer Kulturbesitz) Or. Qu. 798-799 (Steinschneider 177), I, 205a-205b, M.
1116. Budapest - Magyar tudomanyos akademia, MS. Kaufmann A 399, p. 300, C.
1117. Budapest - Magyar tudomanyos akademia, MS. Kaufmann A 400, p. 533, C.
1118. Cambridge - University Library Add. 394,1 (Reif SCR 461), f. 75a, C, rubric: הושענא.
1119. Cambridge - University Library Or. 790, f. 33a, C.
1120. Frankfurt a M - Stadt- und Universitaetsbibliothek Oct. 227, f. 113b-114a, M.
1121. Hamburg - Staats- und Universitaetsbibliothek Cod. hebr. 17/2 (Steinschneider 152), f. 166b, C, rubric: אחרת.
1122. Jerusalem - Schocken Institute 24100 / Mahzor Nuremberg, f. 493b-494a, M.
1123. London - British Library Add. 18695 (Margoliouth 683), f. 150b-151a, T, Yiddish.
1124. London - British Library Add. 22431 (Margoliouth 662a), f. 121a, M.
1125. London - British Library Add. 27208 (Margoliouth 654), f. 266b-267a, M.
1126. London - British Library Add. 27556, f. 128a-128b, M.
1127. Lund - Universitetsbibliothek Ms. L.O. 2, f. 86b, M.
1128. Moscow - Russian State Library, Ms. Guenzburg 615, f. 129a, C, short.

---

[29] Edited by Urbach, ערוגת הבושם, vol. III, p. 302-306.

1129. New York - Jewish Theological Seminary Ms. 4416, f. 13b, M.
1130. New York - Jewish Theological Seminary Ms. 4466, f. 478(i)b-478(ii)a, M.
1131. Oxford - Bodleian Library MS Can. Or. 1 (Neubauer 1104), f. 26b, M.
1132. Oxford - Bodleian Library MS Can. Or. 1 (Neubauer 1104), f. 27b-28a, M.
1133. Oxford - Bodleian Library MS Mich. 573 (Neubauer 1099), f. 18a, M.
1134. Oxford - Bodleian Library MS Opp 160 (Neubauer 1204), f. 236a, C, commentator: Elazar b. Yehuda of Worms, additional marginal note.[30]
1135. Oxford - Bodleian Library MS Opp. 170 (Neubauer 1205), f. 201b-202a, C.
1136. Parma - Biblioteca Palatina Cod. Parm. 3057.9 (de Rossi 1033), f. 92b-93a, C.
1137. Parma - Biblioteca Palatina Cod. Parm. 3205 (de Rossi 655), f. 250a, C.
1138. Uppsala - Universitetsbibliotek O.Heb.22, f. 110a-110b, M, no incipit.
1139. Vatican - Biblioteca Apostolica ebr. 308, f. 156a-156b, C, commentator: David b. Mose (compiler).
1140. Vatican - Biblioteca Apostolica ebr. 318, f. 199a-199b, Gl.
1141. Verona - Seminario Maggiore 34, f. 169b-170a, M, short.

Ashkenaz, commentary by Eliezer b. Natan

1142. Hamburg - Staats- und Universitaetsbibliothek Cod. hebr. 61 (Steinschneider 153), f. 23a.
1143. London - Montefiore Library 261, f. 86b, C.
1144. Paris - Bibliotheque Nationale heb. 327/2, f. 39a, C.
1145. Warszaw - Uniwersytet, Inst. Orientalistyczny 258, f. 196a-196b, C.

Italia

1146. Moscow - Russian State Library, Ms. Guenzburg 533, f. 26a-30a, C, commentator: Yehoshua Segre, rubric: לימוד י"ב.
1147. Moscow - Russian State Library, Ms. Guenzburg 1594, f. 24b, C, no incipit.
1148. Parma - Biblioteca Palatina Cod. Parm. 2895, p. 217, M.
1149. Torino - Archivio Terracini 1499, p. 119-123, C, commentator: Zakharya David Shabbetai Segre, rubric: פירוש אדם ובהמה.

Roma

1150. Jerusalem - Jewish National and University Library Ms Heb 8° 4153, f. 142a, C, commentator: Daniel ben Salomo haRofe (compiler).
1151. Oxford - Bodleian Library MS Mich. 312,1 (Neubauer 2276,1), f. 10a-10b, C.

---

[30] Edited by Katzenellenbogen, פירוש ההושענות, p. 34-35.

Romania
1152. London - London School of Jewish Studies. Asher I.Myers collection 9, f. 210a, M.
1153. Roma - Collegio Rabbinico Italiano 110, f. 5a-5b, M.
1154. Vatican - Biblioteca Apostolica ebr. 285/30, f. 235a, C.
1155. Vatican - Biblioteca Apostolica ebr. 320, f. 445b, M.

Tsarfat
1156. Jerusalem - Schocken Institute 19623, f. 125b, M, commentator: Yehuda b. Eliezer Zvi.
1157. London - British Library Or. 2735 (Margoliouth 663), f. 147a-147b, M.
1158. London - British Library Or. 2735 (Margoliouth 663), f. 147b, M.
1159. London - David Sofer 5, f. 192a-192b, C.
1160. Moscow - Russian State Library, Ms. Guenzburg 1665, f. 181a, M.
1161. Parma - Biblioteca Palatina Cod. Parm. 1264, f. 96b-97a, M.
1162. Parma - Biblioteca Palatina Cod. Parm. 1902, f. 177a-177b, M.
1163. Vatican - Biblioteca Apostolica ebr. 306, f. 121b-122a, C.

אדמה מארר בהמה ממשכלת גורן מגזם (א 1198), אלעזר ברבי קליר, הושענא

Ashkenaz
1164. Berlin - Staatsbibliothek (Preussischer Kulturbesitz) Or. Qu. 361 (Steinschneider 51), f. 117a, M.
1165. Berlin - Staatsbibliothek (Preussischer Kulturbesitz) Or. Qu. 798-799 (Steinschneider 177), I, f. 205a, M.
1166. Budapest - Magyar tudomanyos akademia, MS. Kaufmann A 399, p. 300-301, C.
1167. Budapest - Magyar tudomanyos akademia, MS. Kaufmann A 400, p. 533, C.
1168. Cambridge - University Library Or. 790, f. 33a, C.
1169. Cremona - Archivio di Stato 68, f. 1b, FC, commentator: Ephraim b. Jacob of Bonn, end missing.
1170. Frankfurt a M - Stadt- und Universitaetsbibliothek Oct. 227, f. 114a, M.
1171. Hamburg - Staats- und Universitaetsbibliothek Cod. hebr. 17/2 (Steinschneider 152), f. 166a-166b, C, rubric: אחרת.
1172. Jerusalem - Schocken Institute 24100 / Mahzor Nuremberg, f. 494a, M.
1173. London - British Library Add. 18695 (Margoliouth 683), f. 150a-150b, T, Yiddish.
1174. London - British Library Add. 22431 (Margoliouth 662a), f. 121b, M.
1175. London - British Library Add. 27208 (Margolioth 654), f. 267a-267b, M.
1176. London - British Library Add. 27556, f. 128b, M.
1177. Lund - Universitetsbibliothek Ms. L.O. 2, f. 86a, M.

1178. Moscow - Russian State Library, Ms. Guenzburg 615, f. 128b, C, very short.
1179. New York - Jewish Theological Seminary Ms. 4416, f. 13a, M, incomplete: beginning missing.
1180. Oxford - Bodleian Library MS Can. Or. 1 (Neubauer 1104), f. 27a-27b, M.
1181. Oxford - Bodleian Library MS Mich. 573 (Neubauer 1099), f. 18b, M.
1182. Oxford - Bodleian Library MS Opp 160 (Neubauer 1204), f. 235b-236a, C, commentator: Elazar b. Yehuda of Worms, additional marginal note.[31]
1183. Oxford - Bodleian Library MS Opp. 170 (Neubauer 1205), f. 201a, C.
1184. Parma - Biblioteca Palatina Cod. Parm. 2895, p. 212, M.
1185. Parma - Biblioteca Palatina Cod. Parm. 3205 (de Rossi 655), f. 250a, C.
1186. Parma - Biblioteca Palatina Cod. Parm. 3057.9 (de Rossi 1033), f. 91a-91b, C.
1187. Uppsala - Universitetsbibliotek O.Heb.22, f. 110b, M.
1188. Vatican - Biblioteca Apostolica ebr. 305,1, f. 43b, C, no incipit.
1189. Vatican - Biblioteca Apostolica ebr. 308, f. 156a, C, commentator: David b. Mose (compiler).
1190. Verona - Seminario Maggiore 34, f. 169b, M, very short.

Ashkenaz, commentary by Eliezer b. Natan

1191. Hamburg - Staats- und Universitaetsbibliothek Cod. hebr. 61 (Steinschneider 153), f. 22b-23a, C.
1192. London - Montefiore Library 261, f. 86b, C.
1193. Paris - Bibliotheque Nationale heb. 327/2, f. 38b-39a, C.
1194. Warszaw - Uniwersytet, Inst. Orientalistyczny 258, f. 196a, C.

Italia

1195. Moscow - Russian State Library, Ms. Guenzburg 1594, f. 24a-24b, C, no incipit.
1196. Torino - Archivio Terracini 1499, p. 107-110, C, commentator: Zakharya David Shabbetai Segre, rubric: פירוש אדמה מארר.

Romania

1197. Vatican - Biblioteca Apostolica ebr. 285/30, f. 235a-235b, C, incipit אדם.

Tsarfat

1198. Cambridge - University Library Add. 561.1, f. 114b-115a, M.
1199. Jerusalem - Schocken Institute 19623, f. 125b-126a, M, commentator: Yehuda b. Eliezer Zvi.
1200. Moscow - Russian State Library, Ms. Guenzburg 1665, f. 181a, M.
1201. Parma - Biblioteca Palatina Cod. Parm. 1264, f. 97a, M.
1202. Parma - Biblioteca Palatina Cod. Parm. 1902, f. 177b-178a, M.

---

[31] Edited by Katzenellenbogen, פירוש ההושענות, p. 33-34.

1203. Vatican - Biblioteca Apostolica ebr. 306, f. 126b-127a, C.

אדני חלד עד לא טבועים (א 1200), משולם ב"ר קלונימוס, חלק ד', קדושתא ליום ח'
של פסח

Ashkenaz

1204. Parma - Biblioteca Palatina Cod. Parm. 3507 (Perreau 27), f. 73a-73b, C.
1205. Berlin - Staatsbibliothek (Preussischer Kulturbesitz) Or. Qu. 798-799 (Steinschneider 177), II, f. 92a, M.
1206. Braunschweig - Landesmuseum fuer Geschichte und Volkstum R 2386, vol. I, f. 61b, M.
1207. Budapest - Magyar tudomanyos akademia, MS. Kaufmann A 384, f. 203b-204a, M.
1208. Budapest - Magyar tudomanyos akademia, MS. Kaufmann A 400, p. 138-139, C, very short.
1209. Hamburg - Staats- und Universitaetsbibliothek Cod. hebr. 17/2 (Steinschneider 152), f. 67a, C.
1210. Jerusalem - Schocken Institute 24100 / Mahzor Nuremberg, f. 122b, M.
1211. Moscow - Russian State Library, Ms. Guenzburg 615, f. 25a, C, incipit אל נא, short.
1212. Muenchen - Bayerische Staatsbibliothek, Cod. hebr. 88, f. 83a, G.
1213. Muenchen - Bayerische Staatsbibliothek, Cod. hebr. 393, f. 135a, C, incipit אל נא.
1214. New York - Jewish Theological Seminary Ms. 4466, f. 109a-109b, M.
1215. Oxford - Bodleian Library MS Opp. 170 (Neubauer 1205), f. 76a-76b, C, incipit אל נא.
1216. Paris - Bibliotheque Nationale heb. 709, f. 102b, C, rubric: אל נא.
1217. Parma - Biblioteca Palatina Cod. Parm. 3205 (de Rossi 655), f. 109a, C.
1218. Zurich - Zentralbibliothek Heid. 139, f. 46a, C, no incipit, additional marginal notes.

Tsarfat

1219. London - David Sofer 5, f. 41b-42a, C, incipit אל נא, additional glosses.
1220. London - David Sofer 5, f. 46a-46b, C, incipit אל נא.
1221. Moscow - Russian State Library, Ms. Guenzburg 1665, f. 90b, M, incipit אל נא.
1222. Moscow - Russian State Library, Ms. Guenzburg 1665, f. 106a, M.
1223. Oxford - Bodleian Library MS Laud. Or. 271 (Neubauer 1206), f. 81a, C, commentator: Aaron b. Hayyim haKohen (compiler).
1224. Parma - Biblioteca Palatina Cod. Parm. 3136 (de Rossi 405), f. 124b, M, incipit אל נא.
1225. Vatican - Biblioteca Apostolica ebr. 306, f. 218a, C, no incipit.

אדעה כי אין זולתך לגאול (א 1204), מנחם ב"ר מכיר, זולת שבת שובה

Ashkenaz

1226. Jerusalem - Schocken Institute 24100 / Mahzor Nuremberg, f. 358b-356(ii)a, M.
1227. London - Montefiore Library 261, f. 83b-84a, C, commentator: Eliezer b. Natan?, rubric: זולת.
1228. Muenchen - Bayerische Staatsbibliothek, Cod. hebr. 69, f. 71a-71b, M.
1229. Muenchen - Bayerische Staatsbibliothek, Cod. hebr. 88, f. 209b-210b, G.

Ashkenaz, commentary by Abraham b. Azriel[32]

1230. Frankfurt a M - Stadt- und Universitaetsbibliothek Fol. 16 (Merzbacher 95), f. 46b-48b, C, rubric: זולת.
1231. Vatican - Biblioteca Apostolica ebr. 301,1, f. 71a-73a, C, rubric: זולת.

אדר בתואר כמון (א 1206), אלעזר ברבי קליר, חלק ד', קדושתא למנחה יום כפור

Ashkenaz

1232. Fulda - Hessische Landesbibliothek A 3 II, f. 128a-128b, C, commentator: Josef, incipit אמונת.
1233. Hamburg - Staats- und Universitaetsbibliothek Cod. hebr. 132 (Steinschneider 155), f. 49b, C, no incipit.
1234. Jerusalem - Schocken Institute 24100 / Mahzor Nuremberg, f. 444a-444b, M, incipit אמונת.
1235. London - British Library Or. 11318/1, f. 123a-124a, C, incipit אמונת.
1236. London - Montefiore Library 261, f. 63b-64a, C, commentator: Eliezer b. Natan?, incipit אמונת.
1237. Moscow - Russian State Library, Ms. Guenzburg 615, f. 108a, C, rubric: והפיזמון הזה יסד ר' אלע' קליר, incipit אמונת, incomplete.
1238. Muenchen - Bayerische Staatsbibliothek, Cod. hebr. 21, f. 240a, G.
1239. Muenchen - Bayerische Staatsbibliothek, Cod. hebr. 346, f. 87b, C, no incipit, begins אמונת.
1240. New York - Jewish Theological Seminary Ms. 4466, f. 414a-415a, M, incipit אמונת.
1241. Oxford - Bodleian Library MS Mich. 365 (Neubauer 1208), f. 93a-93b, C, incipit אמונת.
1242. Oxford - Bodleian Library MS Opp. 172 (Neubauer 1211), f. 82a, C.
1243. Parma - Biblioteca Palatina Cod. Parm. 3205 (de Rossi 655), f. 237a-237b, C, incipit אמונת.
1244. Vatican - Biblioteca Apostolica ebr. 308, f. 140a, C, commentator: David b. Mose (compiler).

---

[32] Edited by Urbach, ערוגת הבושם, vol. II, p. 139-153.

1245. Zurich - Zentralbibliothek Heid. 139, f. 88b-89a, C, no incipit, very short, additional marginal notes.

Tsarfat

1246. London - David Sofer 5, f. 165b, margin, C, incipit אמונת.
1247. Oxford - Bodleian Library MS Bodl. Or. 109 (Neubauer 1209), f. 41b-42a, C, commentator: Aaron b. Hayyim haKohen (compiler), incipit אמונת.
1248. Oxford - Bodleian Library MS Laud. Or. 271 (Neubauer 1206), f. 118a-118b, C, commentator: Aaron b. Hayyim haKohen (compiler), incipit אמונת, postscript יסד הקליר ואילך יסד ר' אליה ומכאן עד כאן יסד.

אדר והוד אתן בצביון (א 1210; ש 1461), שמעון ב"ר יצחק, חלק ד', קדושתא לר"ה

Ashkenaz

1249. Berlin - Staatsbibliothek (Preussischer Kulturbesitz) Or. Qu. 798-799 (Steinschneider 177), I, 37a-38b, M, 1st incipit שמו.
1250. Braunschweig - Landesmuseum fuer Geschichte und Volkstum R 2386, vol. II, f. 111b-112b (112a empty page), M.
1251. Cambridge - University Library Or. 785, f. 61a-62b, G, ecclectic.
1252. Darmstadt - Hessisches Landes- und Hochschulbibliothek Cod. Or. 15, f. 35b-36b, M, ecclectic.
1253. Hamburg - Staats- und Universitaetsbibliothek Cod. hebr. 17/2 (Steinschneider 152), f. 122a, C, rubric: פזמון.
1254. Hamburg - Staats- und Universitaetsbibliothek Cod. hebr. 40b (Steinschneider 110), f. 41a-42a, G.
1255. Hamburg - Staats- und Universitaetsbibliothek Cod. hebr. 40c (Steinschneider 111), f. 149a-149b, G.
1256. Hamburg - Staats- und Universitaetsbibliothek Cod. hebr. 132 (Steinschneider 155), f. 24b-25a, C, no incipit.
1257. Hamburg - Staats- und Universitaetsbibliothek Cod. hebr. 225, f. 255b-257b, G.
1258. Jerusalem - Jewish National and University Library Ms Heb 8° 3037, f. 54a-55a, M, 1st incipit שמו, 2nd incipit אדר.
1259. Jerusalem - Schocken Institute 24100 / Mahzor Nuremberg, f. 342a-343a, M, 1st incipit שמו, 2nd incipit אדר.
1260. London - British Library Or. 11318/1, f. 41a-42a, C, 1st incipit שמו, 2nd incipit אדר.
1261. London - Montefiore Library 261, f. 28a-29a, C, commentator: Eliezer b. Natan?.
1262. Moscow - Russian State Library, Ms. Guenzburg 191, f. 37a-38a, M.
1263. Moscow - Russian State Library, Ms. Guenzburg 615, f. 86b-87a, C, 1st incipit שמו, 2nd incipit אדר והוד.
1264. Muenchen - Bayerische Staatsbibliothek, Cod. hebr. 21, f. 179b-180a, G.

112 CLAVIS COMMENTARIORUM

1265. Muenchen - Bayerische Staatsbibliothek, Cod. hebr. 86, f. 66a-68b, G.
1266. Muenchen - Bayerische Staatsbibliothek, Cod. hebr. 346, f. 36a, C, no incipit, begins דיע ישימו.
1267. New York - Jewish Theological Seminary Ms. 4466, f. 252b-254b, M, 1st incipit שמו, 2nd incipit אדר.
1268. New York - Jewish Theological Seminary Ms. 8097, f. 65b-66a, C, 1st incipit שמו, 2nd incipit אדר.
1269. New York - Jewish Theological Seminary Ms. 8169 (Acc. 0016), f. 36a-37a, M, short.
1270. Oxford - Bodleian Library MS Mich. 365 (Neubauer 1208), f. 50a-50b, C, rubric: פזמון.
1271. Oxford - Bodleian Library MS Opp. 172 (Neubauer 1211), f. 22a-22b, C.
1272. Oxford - Bodleian Library MS Opp. 619 (Neubauer 2374), f. 60a-62a, M, short.
1273. Oxford - Bodleian Library MS Opp. 675 (Neubauer 1210), f. 51a-52a, C, no incipit.
1274. Paris - Bibliotheque Nationale heb. 653, f. 29b-30b, G.
1275. Parma - Biblioteca Palatina Cod. Parm. 3205 (de Rossi 655), f. 217b, C, incipits for some of the refrain-stanzas.
1276. Parma - Biblioteca Palatina Cod. Parm. 3507 (Perreau 27), f. 132b-133a, C.
1277. Vatican - Biblioteca Apostolica ebr. 422/1, f. 12b-13a, C.
1278. Vatican - Biblioteca Apostolica ebr. 308, f. 76a-77b, C, commentator: David b. Mose (compiler), incipits for refrain stanzas.
1279. Zurich - Zentralbibliothek Heid. 139, f. 71a, C, incipit שבטי, short, additional marginal notes.

Asti, Fossano, Moncalvo
1280. New Haven - Yale University, Beinecke Rare Book and MS Library, MS Heb. 52, f. 54a-54b, M.

Romania
1281. Vatican - Biblioteca Apostolica ebr. 320, f. 183a-184b, M.

Tsarfat
1282. London - British Library Or. 8682, f. 37b-38a, G.
1283. London - David Sofer 5, f. 120b, C.
1284. London - David Sofer 5, f. 120b-121a, C.
1285. Oxford - Bodleian Library MS Laud. Or. 271 (Neubauer 1206), f. 157a-157b, C, commentator: Aaron b. Hayyim haKohen (compiler), 1st incipit שמו, 2nd incipit אדר והוד.
1286. Oxford - Bodleian Library MS Opp. 171 (Neubauer 1207), f. 67b-68a, C, rubric: פזמון.
1287. Parma - Biblioteca Palatina Cod. Parm. 2125 (de Rossi 812), f. 30a, C, 1st incipit שמו, 2nd incipit אדר.

1288. Parma - Biblioteca Palatina Cod. Parm. 3006 (de Rossi 654,1), f. 71a-71b, M.
1289. Vatican - Biblioteca Apostolica ebr. 306, f. 67a-67b, C, incipit שמו.

אדר יקר אלי אחוה בארש מלולי (א 1211), משולם ב"ר קלונימוס, חלק ו', קדושתא שחרית ליום כפור
Ashkenaz

1290. Berlin - Staatsbibliothek (Preussischer Kulturbesitz) Or. Qu. 798-799 (Steinschneider 177), I, f. 74a-74b, M.
1291. Braunschweig - Landesmuseum fuer Geschichte und Volkstum R 2386, vol. II, f. 186b-187a, M, no incipit.
1292. Budapest - Magyar tudomanyos akademia, MS. Kaufmann A 400, p. 311, C.
1293. Hamburg - Staats- und Universitaetsbibliothek Cod. hebr. 17/2 (Steinschneider 152), f. 151a, C.
1294. Hamburg - Staats- und Universitaetsbibliothek Cod. hebr. 132 (Steinschneider 155), f. 33b, C.
1295. Jerusalem - Jewish National and University Library Ms Heb 8° 3037, f. 117a, M.
1296. Jerusalem - Schocken Institute 24100 / Mahzor Nuremberg, f. 376b-377a, M.
1297. London - British Library Or. 11318/1, f. 73a-73b, C.
1298. London - Montefiore Library 261, f. 43a-43b, C, commentator: Eliezer b. Natan?.
1299. Moscow - Russian State Library, Ms. Guenzburg 191, f. 86a-86b, M.
1300. Muenchen - Bayerische Staatsbibliothek, Cod. hebr. 86, f. 102a-102b, Gl.
1301. Muenchen - Bayerische Staatsbibliothek, Cod. hebr. 346, f. 52b-53a, C, no incipit, begins אביע, short.
1302. Muenchen - Bayerische Staatsbibliothek, Cod. hebr. 393, f. 141b, C.
1303. New York - Jewish Theological Seminary Ms. 4466, f. 306b-307a, M.
1304. New York - Jewish Theological Seminary Ms. 8097, f. 71b, C.
1305. New York - Jewish Theological Seminary Ms. 8169 (Acc. 0016), f. 67a-67b, M.
1306. Oxford - Bodleian Library MS Mich. 365 (Neubauer 1208), f. 69a, C, very short.
1307. Oxford - Bodleian Library MS Opp. 172 (Neubauer 1211), f. 37b-38a, C.
1308. Oxford - Bodleian Library MS Opp. 619 (Neubauer 2374), f. 141b-142b, M, ecclectic.
1309. Parma - Biblioteca Palatina Cod. Parm. 3205 (de Rossi 655), f. 225b, C, short.
1310. Parma - Biblioteca Palatina Cod. Parm. 3271 (de Rossi 1216), f. 36b-37a, G.

1311. Vatican - Biblioteca Apostolica ebr. 308, f. 99a-99b, C, commentator: David b. Mose (compiler).
1312. Vatican - Biblioteca Apostolica ebr. 422/1, f. 15a, C, very short.
1313. Zurich - Zentralbibliothek Heid. 139, f. 76a-76b, C, no incipit, additional marginal notes.

Asti, Fossano, Moncalvo

1314. New Haven - Yale University, Beinecke Rare Book and MS Library, MS Heb. 52, f. 103b-104a, M.

Romania

1315. Vatican - Biblioteca Apostolica ebr. 320, f. 280b-281a, M.

Tsarfat

1316. Bern - Burgerbibliothek A 409, f. 79a-79b, G.
1317. London - British Library Or. 8682, f. 66b-67a, G.
1318. London - David Sofer 5, f. 137a-137b, C.
1319. Oxford - Bodleian Library MS Bodl. Or. 109 (Neubauer 1209), f. 19b, C, commentator: Aaron b. Hayyim haKohen (compiler), short, incipit מלך.
1320. Oxford - Bodleian Library MS Laud. Or. 271 (Neubauer 1206), f. 112b, C, commentator: Aaron b. Hayyim haKohen (compiler), rubric: פיזמון אחר, no incipit, begins לעמו מחיש, short.
1321. Parma - Biblioteca Palatina Cod. Parm. 1794 (de Rossi 1061), f. 116b-117a, M.
1322. Parma - Biblioteca Palatina Cod. Parm. 2125 (de Rossi 812), f. 39b, C.
1323. Parma - Biblioteca Palatina Cod. Parm. 2890 (de Rossi 856), f. 26a, M, incipit מלך.
1324. Vatican - Biblioteca Apostolica ebr. 306, f. 76b-77b, C, incipit מלך.

אדרוש בוטח בורא רוחי (א 1218), סעדיה, סליחה

Yemen

1325. New York - Jewish Theological Seminary Ms. 3052, f. 80a-80b, M, no incipit.

Yemen, commentary by Isaac b. Abraham Wanneh

1326. Chicago-Spertus College of Judaica D 2, 2, f. 236b, M, no incipit.
1327. Jerusalem - Benayahu ת 261, f. 164b, M.
1328. Jerusalem - Benayahu ת 282, f. 140a, M.
1329. Jerusalem - Makhon Ben Zvi 1156 (Tubi 155), f. 137b, M.
1330. Jerusalem - Makhon Ben Zvi 1174 (Tubi 154), f. 135a, M.
1331. Jerusalem - Michael Krupp 604, f. 174b, M, no incipit.
1332. Jerusalem - Musad haRav Kook 325, f. 193a, M.
1333. Jerusalem - Sassoon 1158, p. 414, M, no incipit.
1334. Jerusalem - Sassoon 1174, p. 268, M, no incipit.
1335. London - British Library Or. 11122, f. 213b, M, no incipit.

1336. Manchester - John Rylands University Library, Ms. Gaster 5, f. 222a, M.
1337. Muenchen - Bayerische Staatsbibliothek, Cod. hebr. 472, f. 192a, M.
1338. New York - Jewish Theological Seminary Ms. 3013, f. 132a, M, no incipit.
1339. New York - Jewish Theological Seminary Ms. 3294, f. 16b, C.
1340. New York - Public Library, Heb. Ms. 9, f. 128a-128b, M, no incipit.
1341. Strasbourg - Bibliotheque Nationale et Universitaire 3965 (Landauer 39), p. 406, M.

אדרת ממלכה על מה הושלכה (א 1224), אלעזר ברבי קליר, חלק ה', קדושתא לר"ה
Ashkenaz

1342. Berlin - Staatsbibliothek (Preussischer Kulturbesitz) Or. Qu. 798-799 (Steinschneider 177), I, f. 7a-8a, M.
1343. Budapest - Magyar tudomanyos akademia, MS. Kaufmann A 400, p. 252-254, C, 1st incipit תריע, 2nd incipit אדרת.
1344. Cambridge - University Library Or. 785, f. 20a-20b, G.
1345. Darmstadt - Hessisches Landes- und Hochschulbibliothek Cod. Or. 15, f. 7a-7b, M.
1346. Hamburg - Staats- und Universitaetsbibliothek Cod. hebr. 12 (Steinschneider 102), f. 6b-7a, G.
1347. Hamburg - Staats- und Universitaetsbibliothek Cod. hebr. 17/2 (Steinschneider 152), f. 108a-108b, C, 1st incipit תריע, 2nd incipit אדרת.
1348. Hamburg - Staats- und Universitaetsbibliothek Cod. hebr. 40b (Steinschneider 110), f. 7a-7b, G.
1349. Hamburg - Staats- und Universitaetsbibliothek Cod. hebr. 40c (Steinschneider 111), f. 133a-133b, G.
1350. Hamburg - Staats- und Universitaetsbibliothek Cod. hebr. 132 (Steinschneider 155), f. 6b-7a, C.
1351. Hamburg - Staats- und Universitaetsbibliothek Cod. hebr. 139 (Steinschneider 115), f. 21b-22a, G.
1352. Hamburg - Staats- und Universitaetsbibliothek Cod. hebr. 225, f. 219b-220b, G.
1353. Jerusalem - Jewish National and University Library Ms Heb 8° 3037, f. 9b-10a, M.
1354. Jerusalem - Schocken Institute 15791/7, f. 59a-59b, C, kabbalistic.
1355. Jerusalem - Schocken Institute 24100 / Mahzor Nuremberg, f. 324b-325a, M.
1356. London - British Library Or. 11318/1, f. 11b-12a, C.
1357. Modena - Archivio Capitolare di Modena 98.1, FM.
1358. Moscow - Russian State Library, Ms. Guenzburg 615, f. 58b, C, 1st incipit תריע, 2nd incipit אדרת.
1359. Moscow - Russian State Library, Ms. Guenzburg 1401/2, f. 16b, C.

1360. Muenchen - Bayerische Staatsbibliothek, Cod. hebr. 346, f. 4a-5a, C, 1st incipit תריע, 2nd incipit אדרת.
1361. New York - Jewish Theological Seminary Ms. 4466, f. 212b-213a, M.
1362. New York - Jewish Theological Seminary Ms. 8097, f. 59b, C, additional glosses in the margins.
1363. New York - Jewish Theological Seminary Ms. 8169 (Acc. 0016), f. 6a-6b.
1364. Oxford - Bodleian Library MS Opp. 12 (Neubauer 1029), f. 267b-268a, G.
1365. Oxford - Bodleian Library MS Opp. 170 (Neubauer 1205), f. 106a-106b, C, 1st incipit תריע, 2nd incipit אדרת.
1366. Oxford - Bodleian Library MS Opp. 172 (Neubauer 1211), f. 4a-4b, C, 1st incipit תריע, 2nd incipit אדרת.
1367. Oxford - Bodleian Library MS Opp. 619 (Neubauer 2374), f. 12a-12b, M.
1368. Oxford - Bodleian Library MS Opp. 675 (Neubauer 1210), f. 16a-16b, C, incipit תריע.
1369. Parma - Biblioteca Palatina Cod. Parm. 3205 (de Rossi 655), f. 205a-205b, C, 1st incipit תריע, 2nd incipit אדרת.
1370. Parma - Biblioteca Palatina Cod. Parm. 3270 (de Rossi 1215), f. 21a, M.
1371. Parma - Biblioteca Palatina Cod. Parm. 3507 (Perreau 27), f. 112a, C.
1372. Vatican - Bibliotheca Apostolica ebr. 298/1, f. 10a-10b, C, no incipit.
1373. Vatican - Bibliotheca Apostolica ebr. 308, f. 33a-34a, C, commentator: David b. Mose (compiler), first incipit תעיר, second incipit אדרת.
1374. Vatican - Bibliotheca Apostolica ebr. 422/1, f. 8a-8b, C.
1375. Zurich - Zentralbibliothek Heid. 139, f. 58b-59a, C, 1st incipit תריע, 2nd incipit אדרת, additional marginal notes.

Romania

1376. Vatican - Biblioteca Apostolica ebr. 320, f. 151a-151b, M, 1st incipit תריע, 2nd incipit אדרת.

Tsarfat

1377. Oxford - Bodleian Library MS Opp. 171 (Neubauer 1207), f. 59a-59b, C, rubric: פזמון.
1378. London - British Library Add. 11639 (Margoliouth 1056), f. 709a-709b, M.
1379. London - David Sofer 5, f. 110a-110b, C.
1380. Oxford - Bodleian Library MS Laud. Or. 271 (Neubauer 1206), f. 141a, C, commentator: Aaron b. Hayyim haKohen (compiler), 1st incipit תריע, 2nd incipit אדרת, additional glosses.
1381. Paris - Bibliotheque Nationale heb. 445,9, f. 65a-65b, C, 1st incipit תריע, 2nd incipit אדרת, additional halakhic remarks in seperate field.
1382. Parma - Biblioteca Palatina Cod. Parm. 1794 (de Rossi 1061), f. 62a-63a, M.

1383. Parma - Biblioteca Palatina Cod. Parm. 2125 (de Rossi 812), f. 9b-10a, C, 1st incipit תריע, 2nd incipit אדרת.
1384. Parma - Biblioteca Palatina Cod. Parm. 3006 (de Rossi 654,1), f. 26a-26b, M.
1385. Vatican - Biblioteca Apostolica ebr. 306, f. 49a-49b, C.

אדרת תלבושת (א 1225), שלמה הבבלי, סדר עבודה

Corfu
1386. Jerusalem - Schocken Institute 70027, vol. II, f. 50a-59a, M.
1387. London - British Library Or. 9598, f. 5a-13a, M, here the piyyut is attributed to Salomo Ibn Gabirol.

Tsarfat
1388. Oxford - Bodleian Library MS Opp. 171 (Neubauer 1207), f. 125a-139a, C.

אדרת תפארתי כותרת התורה (א 1745), אליעזר ב"ר נתן, קינה

Ashkenaz
1389. Berlin - Staatsbibliothek (Preussischer Kulturbesitz) Or. Qu. 798-799 (Steinschneider 177), II, f. 199b-200b, M.

אהבו את יי דור ישרים (א 1234), אהרן בן יוסף הרופא, פרשת שופטים

Karaite, commentary by Berakha b. Josef haKohen
1390. New York - Jewish Theological Seminary Ms. 3367, f. 147a-150a, C, rubric: פרוש פרשת שופטים.
1391. St. Petersburg - Inst. of Oriental Studies of the Russian Academy B 431, f. 99a-101a, C, rubric: פרשת שופטים.
1392. St. Petersburg - Russian National Library, Evr. IV 50, f. 115a-117b, C, rubric: שופטים.

אהבו את יי כל חיסדיו (א 1235), אהרן בן יוסף הרופא, פרשת קורח

Karaite, commentary by Berakha b. Josef haKohen
1393. New York - Jewish Theological Seminary Ms. 3367, f. 125b-127b, C, rubric: פרוש פרשת קרח.
1394. St. Petersburg - Inst. of Oriental Studies of the Russian Academy B 431, f. 86a-87a, C, rubric: פרשת קרח.
1395. St. Petersburg - Inst. of Oriental Studies of the Russian Academy B 483, f. 4a-5a, C, rubric: פרשת קרח.
1396. St. Petersburg - Russian National Library, Evr. IV 50, f. 96b-98a, C, rubric: קרח.

אהבוך נפש להדך (א 1236), שלמה הבבלי, זולת, א' דפסח

Ashkenaz
1397. Braunschweig - Landesmuseum fuer Geschichte und Volkstum R 2386, vol. I, f. 20a-21a, M.
1398. Budapest - Magyar tudomanyos akademia, MS. Kaufmann A 384, f. 128b-130a, M.
1399. Budapest - Magyar tudomanyos akademia, MS. Kaufmann A 384, II, f. 60b-62b, M.
1400. Budapest - Magyar tudomanyos akademia, MS. Kaufmann A 400, p. 96-104, C.
1401. Cambridge - University Library Add. 394,1 (Reif SCR 461), f. 53a-55a, C, commentator: Josef Qara (attributed in rubric), rubric: זולת יסד ר' יוסף קרא בהיותו בטרויססש.
1402. Erlangen - Universitaetsbibliothek 2601 (Roth 67), f. 68b, M.
1403. Hamburg - Staats- und Universitaetsbibliothek Cod. hebr. 17/2 (Steinschneider 152), f. 53b-55a, C, rubric: זולת.
1404. Hamburg - Staats- und Universitaetsbibliothek Cod. hebr. 225, f. 65b-66b, G.
1405. Jerusalem - Schocken Institute 24100 / Mahzor Nuremberg, f. 81b-82b, M.
1406. London - British Library Add. 18695 (Margoliouth 683), f. 23b-25a, T, Yiddish, rubric: זולת.
1407. Moscow - Russian State Library, Ms. Guenzburg 615, f. 4a-7a, C, rubric: זולת.
1408. Muenchen - Bayerische Staatsbibliothek, Cod. hebr. 88, f. 60a-60b, G.
1409. Muenchen - Bayerische Staatsbibliothek, Cod. hebr. 393, f. 122a-125a, C.
1410. New York - Jewish Theological Seminary Ms. 4466, f. 53b-55b, M.
1411. Oxford - Bodleian Library MS Opp. 170 (Neubauer 1205), f. 56b-59b, C, rubric: זולת.
1412. Paris - Bibliotheque Nationale heb. 709, f. 71b-74a, C, rubric: זולת.
1413. Parma - Biblioteca Palatina Cod. Parm. 1002 (Ta 24), f. 92a-93a, M.
1414. Parma - Biblioteca Palatina Cod. Parm. 3205 (de Rossi 655), f. 80a-83a, C, rubric: זולת.
1415. Parma - Biblioteca Palatina Cod. Parm. 3507 (Perreau 27), f. 47a-49a, C, rubric: זולת.
1416. Zurich - Zentralbibliothek Heid. 139, f. 25b-28a, C, additional marginal notes.

Italia
1417. Parma - Biblioteca Palatin Cod. Parm. 2248 (de Rossi 149/2), f. 34b-37a, C, rubric: זולת.

Tsarfat
1418. London - British Library Add. 11639 (Margoliouth 1056), f. 289a-290b, M, rubric: זולת.
1419. Moscow - Russian State Library, Ms. Guenzburg 1665, f. 56b-57a, M.
1420. Oxford - Bodleian Library MS Laud. Or. 271 (Neubauer 1206), f. 60a-63b, C, commentator: Josef Qara (attributed in rubric), Aaron b. Hayyim haKohen (compiler), rubric: יסוד ר' יוסי קרא בהיותו בטרוייש.
1421. Parma - Biblioteca Palatina Cod. Parm. 3136 (de Rossi 405), f. 80a-81a, M.
1422. Vatican - Biblioteca Apostolica ebr. 306, f. 137a-140a, C.

אהבת דוד חפצי וגם חשקי (א 1244), שלם שבזי

Yemen
1423. Cincinnati - Hebrew Union College 398, f. 15a-15b, M.

אהבת יום שבת מנוחה תנחני (א 1252), שלם שבזי

Yemen
1424. Cincinnati - Hebrew Union College 398, f. 15b-19a, M, very long.

אהבת עוז ותוקף חיבה (א 1258), בנימין ב"ר זרח, עקדה

Ashkenaz
1425. Berlin - Staatsbibliothek (Preussischer Kulturbesitz) Or. Qu. 798-799 (Steinschneider 177), I, f. 141b-142b, M.
1426. Cambridge - University Library Dd. 2.30, f. 40a-40b, G.
1427. Moscow - Russian State Library, Ms. Guenzburg 190, f. 101a-101b, G.
1428. New York - Jewish Theological Seminary Ms. 8097, f. 85b, C.
1429. Oxford - Bodleian Library MS Mich. 543 (Neubauer 1212), f. 38a-39b, C, commentator: Isaac b. Jacob (compiler), rubric: זו עקידה ואגב גרר' אכתו' בעו' הש'' כל העקידות ובידו כל הנשמות ופקדות.
1430. Oxford - Bodleian Library MS Opp. 619 (Neubauer 2374), f. 240a-240b, M.
1431. Oxford - Bodleian Library MS Opp. 681 (Neubauer 1213), f. 70b, C.
1432. Oxford - Bodleian Library MS Opp. 681 (Neubauer 1213), f. 70b-71b, C, rubric: פי' אחרת.
1433. Padova - Biblioteca del Seminario Vescovile Cod. 218, f. 200a-200b, M.
1434. Parma - Biblioteca Palatina Cod. Parm. 3205 (de Rossi 655), f. 265b, C.
1435. Vatican - Biblioteca Apostolica ebr. 422/1, f. 24b, C, very short.
1436. Vatican - Biblioteca Apostolica ebr. 422/2, f. 39b, CG, no incipit, very short.

Ashkenaz, commentary by Abraham b. Azriel[33]
1437. Vatican - Biblioteca Apostolica ebr. 301,1, f. 146a-146b, C, rubric: אחרת.

Tsarfat
1438. London - David Sofer 5, f. 169b-170a, C, rubric: סליחה.
1439. Oxford - Bodleian Library MS Bodl. Or. 109 (Neubauer 1209), f. 77b-78b, C, commentator: Aaron b. Hayyim haKohen (compiler).
1440. Parma - Biblioteca Palatina Cod. Parm. 3006 (de Rossi 654,1), f. 119a-119b, M.
1441. Vatican - Biblioteca Apostolica ebr. 306, f. 182a-183a, C.

אהבת עלמות עלמות מוגרה לאנשים (א 1259), מאיר ב"ר יצחק, זולת חתונה

Ashkenaz
1442. Budapest - Magyar tudomanyos akademia, MS. Kaufmann A 399, p. 344-349, C, rubric: זולתו של זה יוצר.
1443. Oxford - Bodleian Library MS Opp. 170 (Neubauer 1205), f. 250b-251b, C, rubric: זולת.

Ashkenaz, commentary by Abraham b. Azriel[34]
1444. Frankfurt a M - Stadt- und Universitaetsbibliothek Fol. 16 (Merzbacher 95), f. 99b-101a, C, rubric: אחר.
1445. Vatican - Biblioteca Apostolica ebr. 301,1, f. 116a, C, rubric: אחר.

אהבת צבייה חן אשר גלתה (א 1261), שלם שבזי

Yemen
1446. Cincinnati - Hebrew Union College 398, f. 13b-15a, M.

אהבתי מעון בית משכנותיך (א 1271), יוסף ב"ר יעקב, חלק א, קדושתא לנעילה

Tsarfat
1447. London - David Sofer 5, f. 171a-171b, C, rubric: זה פירוש של תסילות מיום הכפורים של נעילה.
1448. Parma - Biblioteca Palatina Cod. Parm. 3006 (de Rossi 654,1), f. 239b, M.

אהבתיך אהבה כלולה ומכתרת (א 1273), אמתי ב"ר שפטיה, זולת

Ashkenaz
1449. Budapest - Magyar tudomanyos akademia, MS. Kaufmann A 399, p. 424, C.
1450. Oxford - Bodleian Library MS Can. Or. 82 (Neubauer 1148), f. 22a-23a, M.

---

[33] Edited by Urbach, ערוגת הבושם, vol. III, p. 335-337.
[34] Edited by Urbach, ערוגת הבושם, vol. III, p. 137-143.

1451. Parma - Biblioteca Palatina Cod. Parm. 3205 (de Rossi 655), f. 150a-151a, C.

אהה ירד על ספרד רע מן השמים (א 1301), אברהם אבן עזרא, קינה
Yemen, commentary by Isaac b. Abraham Wanneh
1452. Jerusalem - Sassoon 1158, p. 174-175, M, rubric: אהה ירד סים׳ אברהם.
1453. London - British Library Or. 11122, f. 104b, M, no incipit.

אהוב לבי שמח במצות נכתבו (א 1358), שלם שבזי
Yemen
1454. Cincinnati - Hebrew Union College 398, f. 43b-44a, M.

אהוביך אוהביך מישרים (א 1387), שמעון ב"ר יצחק, יוצר שבת וחול המועד פסח
Ashkenaz
1455. Berlin - Staatsbibliothek (Preussischer Kulturbesitz) Or. Qu. 798-799 (Steinschneider 177), II, f. 82a-83b, M.
1456. Braunschweig - Landesmuseum fuer Geschichte und Volkstum R 2386, vol. I, f. 39b-41b, M.
1457. Budapest - Magyar tudomanyos akademia, MS. Kaufmann A 384, f. 173a-176b, M.
1458. Budapest - Magyar tudomanyos akademia, MS. Kaufmann A 400, p. 135-137, C, rubric: יוצר דרבי שמעון לחולו של מועד, breaks off after stanza 16.
1459. Hamburg - Staats- und Universitaetsbibliothek Cod. hebr. 17/2 (Steinschneider 152), f. 66a-67a, C, rubric: פירוש יוצר דרבי שמעון לחולו של מועד.
1460. London - British Library Add. 18695 (Margoliouth 683), f. 49a-51b, T, Yiddish, rubric: יוצר שבת און חולו של מועד אים פסח.
1461. Muenchen - Bayerische Staatsbibliothek, Cod. hebr. 88, f. 75a-76b, G.
1462. Muenchen - Bayerische Staatsbibliothek, Cod. hebr. 393, f. 131a-132a, C, beginning missing.
1463. New York - Jewish Theological Seminary Ms. 4466, f. 78b-81b, M.
1464. Paris - Bibliotheque Nationale heb. 709, f. 110a-114b, C, rubric: יוצר לשבת בחולו של מועד של פסח.
1465. Parma - Biblioteca Palatina Cod. Parm. 1002 (Ta 24), f. 125b-127b, M.
1466. Parma - Biblioteca Palatina Cod. Parm. 3205 (de Rossi 655), f. 103b-105b, C.
1467. Parma - Biblioteca Palatina Cod. Parm. 3507 (Perreau 27), f. 66a-69a, C, rubric: יוצר לשבת חול המועד.
1468. Zurich - Zentralbibliothek Heid. 139, f. 39a-40a, C, rubric: לחול המועד, additional marginal notes.

Tsarfat
1469. Moscow - Russian State Library, Ms. Guenzburg 1665, f. 75b-77a, M.
1470. Oxford - Bodleian Library MS Laud. Or. 271 (Neubauer 1206), f. 74a-74b, C, commentator: Aaron b. Hayyim haKohen (compiler), rubric: לשבת חול מועד.
1471. Parma - Biblioteca Palatina Cod. Parm. 3136 (de Rossi 405), f. 104a-105a, M.

אהובת נוער כלבבך מצאתה, אברהם אבן עזרא, מחיה לנעילה
Sepharad, commentary by David b. Josef Abudarham
1472. New York - Columbia X893 Ab 93, f. 33a, C, rubric: מחיה.

אהול מנוער אהל בתומתו (א 1410), מנחם, חלק ג', קרובה שחרית ראש השנה
Carpentras
1473. Cincinnati - Hebrew Union College 429/1, f. 24a-24b, M, no incipit.
Carpentras, commentary by Josef b. Abraham of Montelitz
1474. Cincinnati - Hebrew Union College 357, f. 102b-103b, M, no incipit.
1475. New York - Jewish Theological Seminary Ms. 4746, f. 35a-35b, M, no incipit.
1476. Paris - Alliance Israelite Universelle H 422 A, f. 82b-83b, M, no incipit.
1477. Paris - Ecole Rabbinique 31, f. 141a-142b, M, no incipit.

אהלי אשר תאבת עד לא בראשית (א 1432), אלעזר ברבי קליר, קינה
Ashkenaz
1478. Berlin - Staatsbibliothek (Preussischer Kulturbesitz) Or. Qu. 798-799 (Steinschneider 177), II, f. 193b-194a, M.
1479. Budapest - Magyar tudomanyos akademia, MS. Kaufmann A 400, p. 216-217, C, rubric: אחרת.
1480. Hamburg - Staats- und Universitaetsbibliothek Cod. hebr. 17/2 (Steinschneider 152), f. 97a, C.
1481. Jerusalem - Schocken Institute 24100 / Mahzor Nuremberg, f. 198b, M.
1482. Oxford - Bodleian Library MS Can. Or. 70 (Neubauer 1147,8), f. 118b-119a, M.
1483. Oxford - Bodleian Library MS Opp. 170 (Neubauer 1205), f. 260a-260b, C, rubric: אחרת.
1484. Parma - Biblioteca Palatina Cod. Parm. 3205 (de Rossi 655), f. 195a-195b, C, rubric: אחרת.
1485. Vatican - Biblioteca Apostolica ebr. 318, f. 229b-230a, Gl.

Ashkenaz, commentary by Abraham b. Azriel[35]
1486. Vatican - Biblioteca Apostolica ebr. 301,1, f. 137a, C, rubric: אחרת.

אהלל אלהי ואשמח בו ואשימה תקותי בו (א 1453)
Ashkenaz
1487. Berlin - Staatsbibliothek (Preussischer Kulturbesitz) Or. Qu. 798-799 (Steinschneider 177), I, f. 231a, M.

אהלל בצלצלי שמע אל אלהים יי (א 1459), בנימין ב"ר זרח, יוצר לשבת לפני שבועות
Ashkenaz
1488. Jerusalem - Schocken Institute 24100 / Mahzor Nuremberg, f. 140b-141a, M, commentary starts only in the middle of the piyyut.
1489. Muenchen - Bayerische Staatsbibliothek, Cod. hebr. 88, f. 113a-114a, G.
1490. Muenchen - Bayerische Staatsbibliothek, Cod. hebr. 69, f. 49a-50b, M.
1491. Oxford - Bodleian Library MS Opp. 169 (Neubauer 1151), f. 27a-28a, M, commentary starts only in the middle of the piyyut.

Ashkenaz, commentary by Abraham b. Azriel[36]
1492. Vatican - Biblioteca Apostolica ebr. 301,1, f. 19b-21b, C, rubric: יוצר דר' בנימין הדוש מלא.

אהללה אלהי אשירה עזו אספרה כבודו (א 1494), יוסי בן יוסי, תקיעתא, ב' בראש השנה
Ashkenaz
1493. Berlin - Staatsbibliothek (Preussischer Kulturbesitz) Or. Qu. 798-799 (Steinschneider 177), I, f. 44b-46b, M.
1494. Braunschweig - Landesmuseum fuer Geschichte und Volkstum R 2386, vol. II, f. 118a-119b, M.
1495. Budapest - Magyar tudomanyos akademia, MS. Kaufmann A 400, p. 286-292, C.
1496. Cambridge - University Library Add. 858, 1, f. 15a, C, commentator: Elazar b. Yehuda of Worms, very short.
1497. Cambridge - University Library Or. 785, f. 72b-74a, G, ecclectic.
1498. Darmstadt - Hessisches Landes- und Hochschulbibliothek Cod. Or. 15, f. 54a-56b, M.
1499. Darmstadt - Hessisches Landes- und Hochschulbibliothek Cod. Or. 15, f. 59b-61a, M, ecclectic.

---

[35] Edited by Urbach, ערוגת הבושם, vol. III, p. 279-280.
[36] Edited by Urbach, ערוגת הבושם, vol. I, p.122-136.

1500. Hamburg - Staats- und Universitaetsbibliothek Cod. hebr. 17/2 (Steinschneider 152), f. 122b-124a, C, rubric: סדר תקיעות דר׳ יוסי בר אביתור היתום.
1501. Hamburg - Staats- und Universitaetsbibliothek Cod. hebr. 40b (Steinschneider 110), f. 57b-60a, G.
1502. Hamburg - Staats- und Universitaetsbibliothek Cod. hebr. 40c (Steinschneider 111), f. 156b-157b, G.
1503. Hamburg - Staats- und Universitaetsbibliothek Cod. hebr. 132 (Steinschneider 155), f. 26a-27a, C.
1504. Hamburg - Staats- und Universitaetsbibliothek Cod. hebr. 225, f. 270b-272b, G.
1505. Jerusalem - Jewish National and University Library Ms Heb 8° 3037, f. 75a-77a, M.
1506. Jerusalem - Schocken Institute 24100 / Mahzor Nuremberg, f. 347b-349a, M.
1507. London - British Library Or. 11318/1, f. 47a-51b, C, includes esoteric insert.
1508. London - Montefiore Library 261, f. 16b-20a, C, commentator: Eliezer b. Natan?.
1509. Moscow - Russian State Library, Ms. Guenzburg 191, f. 61b-64a, M.
1510. Moscow - Russian State Library, Ms. Guenzburg 615, f. 85b, C, rubric: יום הרת.
1511. Muenchen - Bayerische Staatsbibliothek, Cod. hebr. 86, f. 79a-80a, M, ecclectic.
1512. Muenchen - Bayerische Staatsbibliothek, Cod. hebr. 346, f. 38a-38b, C.
1513. Muenchen - Bayerische Staatsbibliothek, Cod. hebr. 346, f. 38b-40b, C, new source, beginning missing.
1514. New York - Jewish Theological Seminary Ms. 4466, f. 266a-269a, M.
1515. New York - Jewish Theological Seminary Ms. 8097, f. 67b-68a, C.
1516. New York - Jewish Theological Seminary Ms. 8169 (Acc. 0016), f. 51b-53b, M.
1517. New York - Jewish Theological Seminary Ms. 8753, FC.
1518. Oxford - Bodleian Library MS Mich. 365 (Neubauer 1208), f. 52a-57a, C, rubric: תקיעתא.
1519. Oxford - Bodleian Library MS Opp. 12 (Neubauer 1029), f. 244b-245a, G.
1520. Oxford - Bodleian Library MS Opp. 170 (Neubauer 1205), f. 144b-149b, C, commentator: Salomo b. Isaac (Rashi)?, rubric: תקיעתות יתומיות מר׳ יוסף היתום בר׳ אביתור ואני מצאתי כתוב מכתיבת הח׳ר׳ אברההם החזן שקבל מר׳ מיכאל מאירוי והוא מאחר ואחר מאחר עד עשרה שאילן התקיעתות יוסף הכהן בן גוריון עשאם ועל כך נקראו יתומיות שהעולם היה אזי יתום שנחרב בית שיני ואין מחזיק ואין מנהל י׳ב׳ר׳א׳.

1521. Oxford - Bodleian Library MS Opp. 172 (Neubauer 1211), f. 25a-27a, C.
1522. Oxford - Bodleian Library MS Opp. 619 (Neubauer 2374), f. 86a-88a, M.
1523. Oxford - Bodleian Library MS Opp. 675 (Neubauer 1210), f. 62b-63b, C, no incipit.
1524. Paris - Bibliotheque Nationale heb. 653, f. 36b, G.
1525. Parma - Biblioteca Palatina Cod. Parm. 3205 (de Rossi 655), f. 218a-220a, C.
1526. Parma - Biblioteca Palatina Cod. Parm. 3270 (de Rossi 1215), f. 65a-67a, M.
1527. Parma - Biblioteca Palatina Cod. Parm. 3507 (Perreau 27), f. 135a-138a, C.
1528. Vatican - Biblioteca Apostolica ebr. 308, f. 80b-83b, C, commentator: David b. Mose (compiler).
1529. Vatican - Biblioteca Apostolica ebr. 422/1, f. 13b-14a, C.
1530. Zurich - Zentralbibliothek Heid. 139, f. 71a-72a, C, rubric: תקיעתות, additional marginal notes.

Asti, Fossano, Moncalvo

1531. New Haven - Yale University, Beinecke Rare Book and MS Library, MS Heb. 52, f. 73a-74a, M.

Tsarfat

1532. London - British Library Add. 11639 (Margoliouth 1056), f. 714b-715b, M, rubric: אתחיל שלישית.
1533. London - David Sofer 5, f. 125b-126a, C.
1534. Oxford - Bodleian Library MS Bodl. Or. 109 (Neubauer 1209), f. 1a-3a, C, commentator: Aaron b. Hayyim haKohen (compiler), beginning missing.
1535. Oxford - Bodleian Library MS Laud. Or. 271 (Neubauer 1206), f. 157b-159b, C, commentator: Aaron b. Hayyim haKohen (compiler).
1536. Oxford - Bodleian Library MS Opp. 171 (Neubauer 1207), f. 77a-77b, C.
1537. Parma - Biblioteca Palatina Cod. Parm. 1794 (de Rossi 1061), f. 87b-100a, M.
1538. Parma - Biblioteca Palatina Cod. Parm. 2125 (de Rossi 812), f. 33a-35a, C, rubric: תקיעתות שניות.
1539. Parma - Biblioteca Palatina Cod. Parm. 3006 (de Rossi 654,1), f. 96b-98a, M.
1540. Vatican - Biblioteca Apostolica ebr. 306, f. 70b-72a, C.

אהללך בקול רם מגן אברהם (א 1506), אלעזר ברבי קליר, סליחה

Ashkenaz

1541. Berlin - Staatsbibliothek (Preussischer Kulturbesitz) Or. Qu. 798-799 (Steinschneider 177), I, f. 112a-112b, M.

אודה חסדו הפלא (א 1549), מנחם ב"ר יעקב, מעריז, ז' דפסח

Ashkenaz
1542. Budapest - Magyar tudomanyos akademia, MS. Kaufmann A 399, p. 217-218, C.
1543. Frankfurt a M - Stadt- und Universitaetsbibliothek Oct. 227, f. 124b-127b, M.
1544. London - British Library Add. 18695 (Margoliouth 683), f. 45a-46a, T, Yiddish.
1545. Parma - Biblioteca Palatina Cod. Parm. 2895, p. 321-325, M.

אודה יי מאוד כי בתוך רבים, שיר לפורים

Mizrah, commentary by Meir b. Mose Buchritz
1546. Jerusalem - Michael Krupp 2818, f. 1a-2b, M.

אודה עלי חטאתי פני צור ישועתי (א 1595), סליחה

Ashkenaz
1547. Padova - Biblioteca del Seminario Vescovile Cod. 218, f. 264a-264b, M.

אודה עלי פשעי (א 1603), משה בן שמואל בן אבשלום, סליחה

Ashkenaz
1548. Braunschweig - Landesmuseum fuer Geschichte und Volkstum R 2386, vol. II, f. 140b, M.
1549. Budapest - Magyar tudomanyos akademia, MS. Kaufmann A 400, p. 510-511, C, rubric: חטאנו אחרת.
1550. Moscow - Russian State Library, Ms. Guenzburg 190, f. 111b-112b, G.
1551. New York - M. Lehmann FR 10/4, f. 1a-1b, FC, only beginning.
1552. Oxford - Bodleian Library MS Mich. 543 (Neubauer 1212), f. 83a-84a, C, commentator: Isaac b. Jacob (compiler).
1553. Oxford - Bodleian Library MS Opp. 170 (Neubauer 1205), f. 240(i)a-240(ii)a, C.
1554. Oxford - Bodleian Library MS Opp. 681 (Neubauer 1213), f. 87b-88b, C.
1555. Padova - Biblioteca del Seminario Vescovile Cod. 218, f. 65a-66a, M.
1556. Padova - Biblioteca del Seminario Vescovile Cod. 218, f. 165b-167a, M.
1557. Parma - Biblioteca Palatina Cod. Parm. 3205 (de Rossi 655), f. 274b-275a, C.

Tsarfat
1558. London - British Library Add. 11639 (Margoliouth 1056), f. 488b-489b, M.
1559. London - David Sofer 5, f. 149a-150a, C, rubric: חטאנו.

1560. Oxford - Bodleian Library MS Laud. Or. 271 (Neubauer 1206), f. 127b-128a, C, commentator: Aaron b. Hayyim haKohen (compiler).
1561. Oxford - Bodleian Library MS Opp. 171 (Neubauer 1207), f. 105b-106a, C.
1562. Parma - Biblioteca Palatina Cod. Parm. 3006 (de Rossi 654,1), f. 123b-124b, M, additional notes by later hand.
1563. Parma - Biblioteca Palatina Cod. Parm. 3007 (de Rossi 654,2), f. 8b-9a, M.
1564. Vatican - Biblioteca Apostolica ebr. 306, f. 92b-93a, C.

אודות באר המים אות היא לאזרחיים (א 1616), יוסף ב"ר נתן, חלק ו' ממעריב לשמיני עצרת

Ashkenaz
1565. Braunschweig - Landesmuseum fuer Geschichte und Volkstum R 2386, vol. I, f. 147b, M, very short.
1566. London - British Library Add. 18695 (Margoliouth 683), f. 124a-125b, T, Yiddish.
1567. Oxford - Bodleian Library MS Mich. 365 (Neubauer 1208), f. 12b-14a, C.

אודיעך חטאתי על פשעי בהתודי, סליחה

Yemen
1568. New York - Jewish Theological Seminary Ms. 3028, f. 71a, G.
1569. New York - Jewish Theological Seminary Ms. 3052, f. 83b-84b, M.
1570. Ramat Gan - Universitat Bar Ilan 62, f. 52b, G, margins damaged.
Yemen, commentary by Isaac b. Abraham Wanneh
1571. Chicago-Spertus College of Judaica D 2, 2, f. 237b-238a, M, no incipit.
1572. Jerusalem - Benayahu ת 261, f. 165b, M.
1573. Jerusalem - Benayahu ת 282, f. 141a, M.
1574. Jerusalem - Makhon Ben Zvi 1156 (Tubi 155), f. 138b-139a, M, no incipit.
1575. Jerusalem - Makhon Ben Zvi 1174 (Tubi 154), f. 137b, M.
1576. Jerusalem - Michael Krupp 604, f. 175b-176a, M.
1577. Jerusalem - Sassoon 1174, p. 270, M, no incipit.
1578. London - British Library Or. 11122, f. 215a, M, no incipit.
1579. Manchester - John Rylands University Library, Ms. Gaster 5, f. 224a, M, incipit סופר.
1580. Muenchen - Bayerische Staatsbibliothek, Cod. hebr. 472, f. 193b-194a, M.
1581. New York - Jewish Theological Seminary Ms. 3013, f. 133b, M, no incipit, beginns סופר.
1582. New York - Jewish Theological Seminary Ms. 3294, f. 18a, C.

1583. New York - Public Library, Heb. Ms. 9, f. 130a-130b, M, no incipit.
1584. Strasbourg - Bibliotheque Nationale et Universitaire 3965 (Landauer 39), p. 411, M.

אודך יי בכל לבבי ואכבדה שמך לעולם (א 1619), חלק הוידוי
Carpentras
1585. Cincinnati - Hebrew Union College 429/1, f. 1a, M, short.
Carpentras, commentary by Eliyahu Carmi
1586. New York - Jewish Theological Seminary Ms. 3151, f. 29b, M.
Carpentras, commentary by Josef b. Abraham of Montelitz
1587. Cincinnati - Hebrew Union College 357, f. 34a-35a, M, rubric: פירוש.
1588. New York - Jewish Theological Seminary Ms. 4746, f. 3a-4a, M.
1589. Paris - Alliance Israelite Universelle H 422 A, f. 7b-8b, M.
1590. Paris - Ecole Rabbinique 31, f. 78b-80a, M.

אודך כי אנפת בי ותשוב (א 1651), יוסף ב"ר שלמה, יוצר לשבת ראשון בחנוכה
Ashkenaz
1591. Berlin - Staatsbibliothek (Preussischer Kulturbesitz) Or. Qu. 798-799 (Steinschneider 177), II, f. 1a-4a, M.
1592. Budapest - Magyar tudomanyos akademia, MS. Kaufmann A 384, f. 18a-22a, M.
1593. Budapest - Magyar tudomanyos akademia, MS. Kaufmann A 399, p. 397-405, C, rubric: פירוש של יוצר החנוכה.
1594. Cambridge - University Library Add. 394,1 (Reif SCR 461), f. 40b-41b, C, rubric: פי' של יוצרות.
1595. Cambridge - University Library Add. 394,1 (Reif SCR 461), f. 78b-81b, C, rubric: יוצר לשבת של חנוכה.
1596. Cambridge - University Library Add. 504,1, f. 17a-20b, C.
1597. Erlangen - Universitaetsbibliothek 2601 (Roth 67), f. 23a-23b, M.
1598. Frankfurt a M - Stadt- und Universitaetsbibliothek Oct. 227, f. 141b-145b, M.
1599. Hamburg - Staats- und Universitaetsbibliothek Cod. hebr. 17/2 (Steinschneider 152), f. 6b-8a, C.
1600. Hamburg - Staats- und Universitaetsbibliothek Cod. hebr. 17/2 (Steinschneider 152), f. 8a-8b, C.
1601. Jerusalem - Schocken Institute 24100 / Mahzor Nuremberg, f. 18b-20b, M.
1602. Krakow - Biblioteka Jagiellonska Fr. 4, f. 1a-1b, FC, only end of commentary.
1603. Muenchen - Bayerische Staatsbibliothek, Cod. hebr. 88, f. 1a-4a, G.
1604. Oxford - Bodleian Library MS Can. Or. 82 (Neubauer 1148), f. 9b-13a, M.

1605. Oxford - Bodleian Library MS Mich. 365 (Neubauer 1208), f. 16a-18a, C.
1606. Oxford - Bodleian Library MS Opp. 170 (Neubauer 1205), f. 271a-275a, C.
1607. Parma - Biblioteca Palatina Cod. Parm. 1002 (Ta 24), f. 10b-13a, M.
1608. Parma - Biblioteca Palatina Cod. Parm. 2895, p. 375-381, M, margins cut, text damaged.
1609. Parma - Biblioteca Palatina Cod. Parm. 3205 (de Rossi 655), f. 2a-4b, C.
1610. Parma - Biblioteca Palatina Cod. Parm. 3205 (de Rossi 655), f. 7a-8b, C.
1611. Parma - Biblioteca Palatina Cod. Parm. 3507 (Perreau 27), f. 189b-192a, C, rubric: יוצר חנוכה.
1612. Vatican - Biblioteca Apostolica ebr. 318, f. 211b-215a, GI.

Italia

1613. London - Montefiore Library 479/22, f. 410a-410b, C, commentator: Samuel b. Elisha of Schear Arie.
1614. Parma - Biblioteca Palatin Cod. Parm. 2248 (de Rossi 149/2), f. 10a-16b, C, rubric: פירוש יוצר מחנוכה.

Roma

1615. Jerusalem - Jewish National and University Library Ms Heb 8° 4153, f. 151a-156a, C, commentator: Daniel ben Salomo haRofe (compiler), rubric: פירוש יוצר מחנוכה, additional glosses.
1616. New York - Jewish Theological Seminary Ms. 1639, f. 7b-15a, C, commentator: Salomo b. Samuel Rofe, rubric: הפירוש יוצר מחנוכה.
1617. Oxford - Bodleian Library MS Mich. 312,1 (Neubauer 2276,1), f. 18a-21b, C, rubric: פי' יוצר משבת וחנוכה.
1618. Parma - Biblioteca Palatina Cod. Parm. 2577 (de Rossi 310), f. 120a-122b, G.

Tsarfat

1619. London - British Library Add. 11639 (Margoliouth 1056), f. 261b-263b, M.
1620. London - David Sofer 5, f. 1b-4a, C.
1621. Moscow - Russian State Library, Ms. Guenzburg 1665, f. 3a-5a, M.
1622. Oxford - Bodleian Library MS Laud. Or. 271 (Neubauer 1206), f. 1a-2b, C, commentator: Aaron b. Hayyim haKohen (compiler), beginning missing.
1623. Oxford - Bodleian Library MS Opp. 171 (Neubauer 1207), f. 1a-1b, C.
1624. Oxford - Bodleian Library MS Opp. 171 (Neubauer 1207), f. 1b-2b, C.
1625. Parma - Biblioteca Palatina Cod. Parm. 3136 (de Rossi 405), f. 16b-18a, C.

אודך כי עניתני וחייתני (א 1654), מנחם ב"ר מכיר, זולת לשבת שני בחנוכה
Ashkenaz
1626. Frankfurt a M - Stadt- und Universitaetsbibliothek Oct. 227 , f. 146a-147a, M.
1627. Jerusalem - Schocken Institute 24100 / Mahzor Nuremberg, f. 22b-23b, M.
1628. Parma - Biblioteca Palatina Cod. Parm. 2895, p. 385-389, M, margins cut, text damaged.

Ashkenaz, commentary by Abraham b. Azriel[37]
1629. Frankfurt a M - Stadt- und Universitaetsbibliothek Fol. 16 (Merzbacher 95), f. 54a-56a, C, rubric: יוצר דחנוכה לשבת שנייה.
1630. Vatican - Biblioteca Apostolica ebr. 301,1, f. 84b-86b, C, rubric: יוצר דחנוכה.

אודך כי עניתני מועד (א 1655), משולם ב"ר קלונימוס, זולת ליום ב' של פסח
Ashkenaz
1631. Berlin - Staatsbibliothek (Preussischer Kulturbesitz) Or. Qu. 798-799 (Steinschneider 177), II, f. 77a-77b, M.
1632. Braunschweig - Landesmuseum fuer Geschichte und Volkstum R 2386, vol. I, f. 35b, M.
1633. Budapest - Magyar tudomanyos akademia, MS. Kaufmann A 384 , f. 160a-160b, M.
1634. Hamburg - Staats- und Universitaetsbibliothek Cod. hebr. 17/2 (Steinschneider 152), f. 35a, C, commentator: Ephraim b. Jacob of Bonn?, postscript: אי איפשר שחיסר פייט זה מאני לדודי עד לא ידעתי נפשי ח' פסוקי' ונראה שפיוט אחר יסד באילו ח' פסוקים החסירין כע"א מצאתי במחזור ישן בפיוט סדר דשיר השירים של רבי שמעון לפנים.
1635. Jerusalem - Schocken Institute 24100 / Mahzor Nuremberg, f. 93a-93b, M.
1636. London - British Library Add. 18695 (Margoliouth 683) , f. 39b-40b, T, Yiddish, rubric: זולת.
1637. Moscow - Russian State Library, Ms. Guenzburg 615 , f. 21a-22a, C, rubric: זולת.
1638. Muenchen - Bayerische Staatsbibliothek, Cod. hebr. 88, f. 71b, G.
1639. Muenchen - Bayerische Staatsbibliothek, Cod. hebr. 393, f. 128b-129a, C, no incipit.
1640. New York - Jewish Theological Seminary Ms. 4466, f. 71b-72b, M.
1641. Oxford - Bodleian Library MS Opp. 170 (Neubauer 1205), f. 74a-75a, C, rubric: זולת.
1642. Paris - Bibliotheque Nationale heb. 709, f. 96a-97b, C, rubric: זולת.

---

[37] Edited by Urbach, ערוגת הבושם, vol. II, p. 232-247.

1643. Parma - Biblioteca Palatina Cod. Parm. 1002 (Ta 24), f. 115b-116b, M.
1644. Parma - Biblioteca Palatina Cod. Parm. 3205 (de Rossi 655), f. 98b-100b, C.
1645. Parma - Biblioteca Palatina Cod. Parm. 3507 (Perreau 27), f. 63b-64a, C, rubric: זולת.
1646. Zurich - Zentralbibliothek Heid. 139, f. 36b-37a, C, additional marginal notes.

Tsarfat
1647. Moscow - Russian State Library, Ms. Guenzburg 1665, f. 70a-71a, M.
1648. Oxford - Bodleian Library MS Laud. Or. 271 (Neubauer 1206), f. 72a-72b, C, commentator: Aaron b. Hayyim haKohen (compiler), short.
1649. Parma - Biblioteca Palatina Cod. Parm. 3136 (de Rossi 405), f. 101a, M.

אודך על כי נוראות נפלאתה מעודי (א 1658), משה ב"ר משולם, זולת

Ashkenaz
1650. Budapest - Magyar tudomanyos akademia, MS. Kaufmann A 399, p. 424, C.
1651. Oxford - Bodleian Library MS Can. Or. 82 (Neubauer 1148), f. 20b-21a, M.
1652. Parma - Biblioteca Palatina Cod. Parm. 3205 (de Rossi 655), f. 146b-147b, C, rubric: זולת אחר.

אווי סכת דוד הנופלת (א 1689), אלעזר ברבי קליר, חלק ג', קדושתא ליום ב' של סוכות

Ashkenaz
1653. Berlin - Staatsbibliothek (Preussischer Kulturbesitz) Or. Qu. 798-799 (Steinschneider 177), I, f. 191b-192a, M.
1654. Braunschweig - Landesmuseum fuer Geschichte und Volkstum R 2386, vol. I, f. 135a, M.
1655. Budapest - Magyar tudomanyos akademia, MS. Kaufmann A 400, p. 376-377, C, includes schematic drawing.
1656. Fulda - Hessische Landesbibliothek A 3 II, f. 131b-132b, C, commentator: Josef, includes schematic drawing.
1657. Hamburg - Staats- und Universitaetsbibliothek Cod. hebr. 17/2 (Steinschneider 152), f. 162b-163a, C, includes schematic drawing.
1658. Hamburg - Staats- und Universitaetsbibliothek Cod. hebr. 62 (Steinschneider 154), f. 38b-39b, C, no incipit.
1659. Hamburg - Staats- und Universitaetsbibliothek Cod. hebr. 132 (Steinschneider 155), f. 52a-52b, C, no incipit.
1660. Jerusalem - Jewish National and University Library Ms Heb 8° 3037, f. 254b-255a, M, no incipit.

1661. Jerusalem - Schocken Institute 24100 / Mahzor Nuremberg, f. 48b, M.
1662. London - British Library Add. 18695 (Margoliouth 683), f. 117b-118a, T, Yiddish.
1663. London - British Library Add. 22431 (Margoliouth 662a), f. 91b-92a, M.
1664. London - British Library Or. 11318/1, f. 134b-135b, C.
1665. London - Montefiore Library 261, f. 71b-72a, C, commentator: Eliezer b. Natan?.
1666. Moscow - Russian State Library, Ms. Guenzburg 615, f. 112a-112b, C.
1667. New York - Jewish Theological Seminary Ms. 4466, f. 446b-447a, M.
1668. New York - Jewish Theological Seminary Ms. 4826, f. 2b-3a, FM, margins damaged.
1669. Oxford - Bodleian Library MS Mich. 365 (Neubauer 1208), f. 102b-103b, C.
1670. Oxford - Bodleian Library MS Opp. 170 (Neubauer 1205), f. 183b-184b, C.
1671. Parma - Biblioteca Palatina Cod. Parm. 3205 (de Rossi 655), f. 240a-240b, C, no incipit.
1672. Parma - Biblioteca Palatina Cod. Parm. 3507 (Perreau 27), f. 178a-178b, C.
1673. Vatican - Biblioteca Apostolica ebr. 305,1, f. 41a-42a, C, no incipit.
1674. Vatican - Biblioteca Apostolica ebr. 422/1, f. 20b, C.
1675. Zurich - Zentralbibliothek Heid. 139, f. 90b-91a, C, no incipit, additional marginal notes.

Romania

1676. London - London School of Jewish Studies. Asher I.Myers collection 9, f. 219b-220a, M.
1677. Vatican - Biblioteca Apostolica ebr. 320, f. 430b-431a, M.

Tsarfat

1678. London - David Sofer 5, f. 182a-182b, C.
1679. Moscow - Russian State Library, Ms. Guenzburg 1665, f. 163a-163b, M.
1680. Oxford - Bodleian Library MS Laud. Or. 271 (Neubauer 1206), f. 95b-96a, C, commentator: Aaron b. Hayyim haKohen (compiler), no incipit.
1681. Oxford - Bodleian Library MS Opp. 171 (Neubauer 1207), f. 145b-146a, C, no incipit.
1682. Parma - Biblioteca Palatina Cod. Parm. 1264, f. 55b-56a, M.

אוחזי בידים ארבעה מינים (א 1691), יוסף ב"ר שמואל טוב עלם, מעריב סוכות

Ashkenaz

1683. Berlin - Staatsbibliothek (Preussischer Kulturbesitz) Or. Qu. 798-799 (Steinschneider 177), I, f. 188a-188b, M.

1684. London - British Library Add. 18695 (Margoliouth 683), f. 109a-109b, T, Yiddish.
1685. Lund - Universitetsbibliothek Ms. L.O. 2, f. 69b, M.

Tsarfat

1686. London - British Library Or. 2735 (Margoliouth 663), f. 97b-98a, M.
1687. London - David Sofer 5, f. 177b-178a, C, rubric: וזה פירוש ממעריב ראשון של יום מסוכות.

אוחילה לאיום בעדונים קדוש גאולתי יחדש, סליחה

Yemen, commentary by Isaac b. Abraham Wanneh

1688. London - British Library Or. 11122, f. 213b-214a, M, no incipit.

אוחילה לאל אחלה פניו (א 1701), רשות

Ashkenaz

1689. Braunschweig - Landesmuseum fuer Geschichte und Volkstum R 2386, vol. II, f. 99a, M, short.
1690. Cambridge - University Library Add. 858,1, f. 15a, C, commentator: Elazar b. Yehuda of Worms?, rubric: סוד אוחילה, short, gematriot.
1691. Darmstadt - Hessisches Landes- und Hochschulbibliothek Cod. Or. 15, f. 21a, M, short.
1692. Jerusalem - Jewish National and University Library Ms Heb 8° 3037, f. 34b, M, short.
1693. London - British Library Or. 11318/1, f. 108b-109a, C.
1694. London - Montefiore Library 261, f. 16b, C, commentator: Eliezer b. Natan?, short.
1695. Moscow - Russian State Library, Ms. Guenzburg 191, f. 61b, M.
1696. Muenchen - Bayerische Staatsbibliothek, Cod. hebr. 86, f. 36a-36b, G.
1697. Muenchen - Bayerische Staatsbibliothek, Cod. hebr. 346, f. 37b-38a, C.
1698. New York - Jewish Theological Seminary Ms. 8097, f. 63a, C.
1699. Oxford - Bodleian Library MS Opp. 498 (Neubauer 1930), f. 21b, M, commentator: Naftali Hirsh Trebitsh (compiler), esoteric.
1700. Oxford - Bodleian Library MS Opp. 675 (Neubauer 1210), f. 62b, C, no incipit, short.
1701. Parma - Biblioteca Palatina Cod. Parm. 3205 (de Rossi 655), f. 211b-212a, C.
1702. Parma - Biblioteca Palatina Cod. Parm. 3205 (de Rossi 655), f. 218a, C.
1703. Parma - Biblioteca Palatina Cod. Parm. 3507 (Perreau 27), f. 124b, C.
1704. Vatican - Biblioteca Apostolica ebr. 308, f. 58b-59a, C, commentator: David b. Mose (compiler).

Ashkenaz, commentary by Abraham b. Azriel[38]
1705. Frankfurt a M - Stadt- und Universitaetsbibliothek Fol. 16 (Merzbacher 95), f. 111a, C.
1706. Vatican - Biblioteca Apostolica ebr. 301,1, f. 166b, C.

Asti, Fossano, Moncalvo
1707. New Haven - Yale University, Beinecke Rare Book and MS Library, MS Heb. 52, f. 39b, M.
1708. New Haven - Yale University, Beinecke Rare Book and MS Library, MS Heb. 52, f. 143b, M.

Tsarfat
1709. London - British Library Or. 8682, f. 90a-90b, G.
1710. Paris - Bibliotheque Nationale heb. 445,9, f. 83a, C.

אוחילה לאל חי לו אשברה (א 1703), רשות לאזהרות ליום ב' שבועות

Carpentras
1711. Parma - Biblioteca Palatina Cod. Parm. 3491, f. 29a, M.

Italia
1712. Moscow - Russian State Library, Ms. Guenzburg 211, f. 72a, M.

אוחילה לקדוש בעד עם קדוש, סליחה

Yemen
1713. New York - Jewish Theological Seminary Ms. 3052, f. 80b-81a, M, no incipit.

Yemen, commentary by Isaac b. Abraham Wanneh
1714. Chicago-Spertus College of Judaica D 2, 2, f. 236b-237a, M, no incipit.
1715. Jerusalem - Makhon Ben Zvi 1156 (Tubi 155), f. 137b, M, no incipit.
1716. Jerusalem - Makhon Ben Zvi 1174 (Tubi 154), f. 135b, M.
1717. Jerusalem - Musad haRav Kook 325, f. 193b, M.
1718. Jerusalem - Sassoon 1174, p. 268, M, no incipit.
1719. Manchester - John Rylands University Library, Ms. Gaster 5, f. 222b, M.
1720. Muenchen - Bayerische Staatsbibliothek, Cod. hebr. 472, f. 192a-192b, M.
1721. New York - Jewish Theological Seminary Ms. 3013, f. 132a, M, no incipit.
1722. New York - Public Library, Heb. Ms. 9, f. 128b, M, no incipit.
1723. Strasbourg - Bibliotheque Nationale et Universitaire 3965 (Landauer 39), p. 407, M.

---

[38] Edited by Urbach, ערוגת הבושם, vol. III, p. 475-476.

אוחילה מעי גיה (א 1708), שמעון ב"ר יצחק, סליחה

Ashkenaz
1724. Budapest - Magyar tudomanyos akademia, MS. Kaufmann A 400, p. 523-525, C, rubric: אחרת.
1725. Jerusalem - Schocken Institute 24100 / Mahzor Nuremberg, f. 316a-316b, M.
1726. Oxford - Bodleian Library MS Mich. 543 (Neubauer 1212), f. 81b-82a, C, commentator: Isaac b. Jacob (compiler).
1727. Oxford - Bodleian Library MS Opp. 170 (Neubauer 1205), f. 238a-238b, C.
1728. Parma - Biblioteca Palatina Cod. Parm. 3205 (de Rossi 655), f. 285b-286a, C.
1729. Vatican - Biblioteca Apostolica ebr. 422/1, f. 42b, CG, no incipit, short.

Tsarfat
1730. Oxford - Bodleian Library MS Laud. Or. 271 (Neubauer 1206), f. 169a-169b, C, commentator: Aaron b. Hayyim haKohen (compiler).
1731. Oxford - Bodleian Library MS Opp. 171 (Neubauer 1207), f. 88b-89a, C, rubric: אחרת.
1732. Vatican - Biblioteca Apostolica ebr. 306, f. 214a-215a, C.

אוי כי ירד אש מן השמים (א 1718), קינה

Carpentras, commentary by Mordekhai b. Josef of Rocco Martino
1733. Cincinnati - Hebrew Union College 246/1, f. 70a, C, rubric: פי' קינה אוי כי ירד.

Yemen, commentary by Isaac b. Abraham Wanneh
1734. Jerusalem - Sassoon 1158, p. 161, M.
1735. London - British Library Or. 11122, f. 97b, M.

אוי כי קינה רבת מפי בן ומפי בת (א 1726), קינה

Carpentras, commentary by Mordekhai b. Josef of Rocco Martino
1736. Cincinnati - Hebrew Union College 246/1, f. 66a, C, rubric: פי' קינה אחרת למוצאי שבת.

Yemen, commentary by Isaac b. Abraham Wanneh
1737. Jerusalem - Sassoon 1158, p. 162, M.
1738. London - British Library Or. 11122, f. 98a, M.

אוי מאן דאיתתא (א 1753), לשבועות

Ashkenaz
1739. Cambridge - University Library Add. 394,1 (Reif SCR 461), f. 64a-64b, C.
1740. Oxford - Bodleian Library MS Can. Or. 1 (Neubauer 1104), f. 120a-121b, M.

Tsarfat
1741. London - David Sofer 5, f. 65a-66a, C.
1742. London - British Library Add. 11639 (Margoliouth 1056), f. 682a-683a, M.
1743. London - British Library Or. 2735 (Margoliouth 663), f. 40a-42a, M.

אויה ליך נפשי (א 1791), יהודה הכהן, סליחה
Ashkenaz, commentary by Abraham b. Azriel[39]
1744. Vatican - Biblioteca Apostolica ebr. 301,1, f. 150b, C, rubric: אחרת.

אוילי המתעה ומרגיז ומחטיא (א 1807), שמעון ב"ר יצחק, סליחה
Ashkenaz
1745. Bologna - Archivio di Stato MS Ebr. 253, f. 2b, FC.
1746. Budapest - Magyar tudomanyos akademia, MS. Kaufmann A 400, p. 515-516, C, rubric: רהוטה שמעונית.
1747. Cambridge - University Library Dd. 2.30, f. 44a-44b, G.
1748. Forli - Archivio di Stato 4, FC.
1749. Hamburg - Staats- und Universitaetsbibliothek Cod. hebr. 40c (Steinschneider 111), f. 285a, G.
1750. Jerusalem - Schocken Institute 24100 / Mahzor Nuremberg, f. 268b, M.
1751. London - British Library Add. 18695 (Margoliouth 683), f. 163b-164a, T, Yiddish.
1752. Moscow - Russian State Library, Ms. Guenzburg 615, f. 162a-162b, C, rubric: אל מלך.
1753. Muenchen - Bayerische Staatsbibliothek, Cod. hebr. 346, f. 120b-121a, C, rubric: מפרישה אחרת, on the margin a second commentary with the rubric מפריש' ראשונה.
1754. Muenchen - Bayerische Staatsbibliothek, Cod. hebr. 346, f. 125a-125b, C, rubric: אחרת.
1755. Oxford - Bodleian Library MS Mich. 543 (Neubauer 1212), f. 68a-68b, C, commentator: Isaac b. Jacob (compiler), rubric: רהיטה שמעונית.
1756. Oxford - Bodleian Library MS Opp. 170 (Neubauer 1205), f. 231b-232a, C.
1757. Oxford - Bodleian Library MS Opp. 681 (Neubauer 1213), f. 4b-5a, C.
1758. Padova - Biblioteca del Seminario Vescovile Cod. 218, f. 96b-97a, M.
1759. Parma - Biblioteca Palatina Cod. Parm. 3205 (de Rossi 655), f. 276b, C.
1760. Vatican - Biblioteca Apostolica ebr. 308/1, f. 5b-6a, C, commentator: David b. Mose (compiler).

---

[39] Edited by Urbach, ערוגת הבושם, vol. III, p. 364-365.

Ashkenaz, commentary by Abraham b. Azriel[40]
1761. Vatican - Biblioteca Apostolica ebr. 301,1, f. 162a-162b, C, rubric: אחרת.

Tsarfat
1762. London - British Library Add. 11639 (Margoliouth 1056), f. 475a, M, short.
1763. London - David Sofer 5, f. 90b, C.
1764. Oxford - Bodleian Library MS Bodl. Or. 109 (Neubauer 1209), f. 78a-78b, C, commentator: Aaron b. Hayyim haKohen (compiler).
1765. Oxford - Bodleian Library MS Laud. Or. 271 (Neubauer 1206), f. 174b-175a, C, commentator: Aaron b. Hayyim haKohen (compiler).
1766. Parma - Biblioteca Palatina Cod. Parm. 3007 (de Rossi 654,2), f. 32a, M.
1767. Vatican - Biblioteca Apostolica ebr. 306, f. 191b-192a, C.

אוילים מדרך פשעם זכרו (א 1810), לוי בן יעקב, סליחה

Carpentras
1768. Cincinnati - Hebrew Union College 392, f. 4a-4b, M.

Carpentras, commentary by Josef b. Abraham of Montelitz
1769. Marseille - Mlle. Odette Valabregue [1], f. 87a, C.
1770. New York - Jewish Theological Seminary Ms. 4197, f. 4a-5a, M.
1771. Paris - Ecole Rabbinique 32, f. 7b-8b, M.
1772. Strasbourg - Bibliotheque Nationale et Universitaire 4081, f. 6b-7b, M.

אוימתי בחיל כיפור בעותה בחשבון הספור (א 1813), אלעזר ברבי קליר, קדושתא ליום א' של סוכות

Ashkenaz
1773. Berlin - Staatsbibliothek (Preussischer Kulturbesitz) Or. Qu. 798-799 (Steinschneider 177), I, f. 197b-198a, M.
1774. Braunschweig - Landesmuseum fuer Geschichte und Volkstum R 2386, vol. I, f. 122a, M.
1775. Budapest - Magyar tudomanyos akademia, MS. Kaufmann A 400, p. 369, C, rubric: קרובה מסוכות.
1776. Fulda - Hessische Landesbibliothek A 3 II, f. 135b-136a, C, commentator: Josef, rubric: ליום שיני.
1777. Hamburg - Staats- und Universitaetsbibliothek Cod. hebr. 17/2 (Steinschneider 152), f. 164a-164b, C, rubric: ליום שיני דר' אלעזר.
1778. Hamburg - Staats- und Universitaetsbibliothek Cod. hebr. 62 (Steinschneider 154), f. 33a-33b, C, rubric: קרובה.

---

[40] Edited by Urbach, ערוגת הבושם, vol. III, p. 441-442.

1779. Hamburg - Staats- und Universitaetsbibliothek Cod. hebr. 132 (Steinschneider 155), f. 55b, C.
1780. Jerusalem - Jewish National and University Library Ms Heb 8° 3037, f. 236, M.
1781. Jerusalem - Schocken Institute 24100 / Mahzor Nuremberg, f. 475b-476a, M.
1782. London - British Library Add. 18695 (Margoliouth 683), f. 111a, T, Yiddish, rubric: קרובץ.
1783. London - British Library Add. 22431 (Margoliouth 662a), f. 100b-101a, M.
1784. London - British Library Or. 11318/1, f. 130a-130b, C.
1785. London - Montefiore Library 261, f. 65a-65b, C, commentator: Eliezer b. Natan?.
1786. Moscow - Russian State Library, Ms. Guenzburg 615, f. 115a-115b, C, rubric: קרוב' ליום שיני.
1787. New York - Jewish Theological Seminary Ms. 4466, f. 437b-438a, M.
1788. Oxford - Bodleian Library MS Mich. 365 (Neubauer 1208), f. 94b-95a, C, rubric: קרובה.
1789. Oxford - Bodleian Library MS Opp. 170 (Neubauer 1205), f. 187b, C, rubric: קרובה ליום שיני.
1790. Oxford - Bodleian Library MS Opp. 172 (Neubauer 1211), f. 90a, C, rubric: קדושתין, short.
1791. Paris - Bibliotheque Nationale heb. 653, f. 120b-121a, G.
1792. Parma - Biblioteca Palatina Cod. Parm. 3205 (de Rossi 655), f. 241b-242a, C.
1793. Parma - Biblioteca Palatina Cod. Parm. 3507 (Perreau 27), f. 173b-174a, C.
1794. Vatican - Biblioteca Apostolica ebr. 305,1, f. 39a, C.
1795. Vatican - Biblioteca Apostolica ebr. 422/1, f. 21b, C, very short.
1796. Zurich - Zentralbibliothek Heid. 139, f. 92b-93a, C, additional marginal notes.

Romania
1797. London - London School of Jewish Studies. Asher I.Myers collection 9, f. 201b, M.
1798. Vatican - Biblioteca Apostolica ebr. 320, f. 411a, M.

Tsarfat
1799. London - David Sofer 5, f. 178b-179a, C.
1800. Moscow - Russian State Library, Ms. Guenzburg 1665, f. 169b, M.
1801. Oxford - Bodleian Library MS Laud. Or. 271 (Neubauer 1206), f. 97b, C, commentator: Aaron b. Hayyim haKohen (compiler), rubric: קרובה ליום שיני.
1802. Parma - Biblioteca Palatina Cod. Parm. 1264, f. 26b-27a, M.

אויירי ערץ עד לא באהלו (א 1815), יהודה, ראש השנה

Ashkenaz
1803. Moscow - Russian State Library, Ms. Guenzburg 191, f. 14a-14b, M.
1804. New York - Jewish Theological Seminary Ms. 8169 (Acc. 0016), f. 19a-19b, M.
1805. Torino - Archivio Terracini 1492, f. 34a, M.

Tsarfat
1806. London - British Library Add. 11639 (Margoliouth 1056), f. 711a, M, rubric: פזמון, very short.
1807. London - British Library Or. 8682, f. 39b-40a, GI.
1808. London - David Sofer 5, f. 115a, C.
1809. Parma - Biblioteca Palatina Cod. Parm. 3006 (de Rossi 654,1), f. 46b-47a, M.
1810. Vatican - Biblioteca Apostolica ebr. 306, f. 56a-56b, C.

אויתיך קויתיך מארץ מרחקים (א 1816), אליה ב"ר שמעיה, סליחה

Ashkenaz
1811. Braunschweig - Landesmuseum fuer Geschichte und Volkstum R 2386, vol. II, f. 52a, M.
1812. Jerusalem - Schocken Institute 24100 / Mahzor Nuremberg, f. 243a, M, very very short, later hand.
1813. Moscow - Russian State Library, Ms. Guenzburg 190, f. 20a-20b, G.
1814. Muenchen - Bayerische Staatsbibliothek, Cod. hebr. 346, f. 95a-97b, C.
1815. Oxford - Bodleian Library MS Mich. 543 (Neubauer 1212), f. 48a, C, commentator: Isaac b. Jacob (compiler).
1816. Padova - Biblioteca del Seminario Vescovile Cod. 218, f. 80b-81a, M.
1817. Padova - Biblioteca del Seminario Vescovile Cod. 218, f. 239b, M.
1818. Vatican - Biblioteca Apostolica ebr. 422/1, f. 26b, C, very short.

Ashkenaz, commentary by Abraham b. Azriel[41]
1819. Vatican - Biblioteca Apostolica ebr. 301,1, f. 144b, C.

Tsarfat
1820. London - David Sofer 5, f. 85a, C.
1821. Parma - Biblioteca Palatina Cod. Parm. 3007 (de Rossi 654,2), f. 32a-32b, M.
1822. Vatican - Biblioteca Apostolica ebr. 306, f. 202a-202b, C.

אום אני חומה ברה כחמה (א 1829), הושענא

Ashkenaz
1823. Berlin - Staatsbibliothek (Preussischer Kulturbesitz) Or. Qu. 361 (Steinschneider 51), f. 117a-117b, M.

---

[41] Edited by Urbach, ערוגת הבושם, vol. III, p. 325.

1824. Berlin - Staatsbibliothek (Preussischer Kulturbesitz) Or. Qu. 798-799 (Steinschneider 177), I, f. 204b, M.
1825. Budapest - Magyar tudomanyos akademia, MS. Kaufmann A 399 , p. 299-300, C.
1826. Budapest - Magyar tudomanyos akademia, MS. Kaufmann A 400 , p. 531-532, C.
1827. Cambridge - University Library Or. 790, f. 32a, C.
1828. Frankfurt a M - Stadt- und Universitaetsbibliothek Oct. 227 , f. 113a-113b, M.
1829. Hamburg - Staats- und Universitaetsbibliothek Cod. hebr. 17/2 (Steinschneider 152), f. 166a, C, rubric: אחרת.
1830. London - British Library Add. 18695 (Margoliouth 683), f. 149a-149b, T, Yiddish.
1831. London - British Library Add. 22431 (Margoliouth 662a), f. 120a, M.
1832. London - British Library Add. 27556, f. 127b, M.
1833. London - British Library Add. 27208 (Margolioth 654), f. 265b, M.
1834. Moscow - Russian State Library, Ms. Guenzburg 615 , f. 128b-129a, C, short.
1835. New York - Jewish Theological Seminary Ms. 4466, f. 478(ii)a-478(ii)b, M.
1836. Oxford - Bodleian Library MS Opp 160 (Neubauer 1204), f. 234b-235a, C, commentator: Elazar b. Yehuda of Worms.[42]
1837. Oxford - Bodleian Library MS Can. Or. 1 (Neubauer 1104), f. 27a, M.
1838. Oxford - Bodleian Library MS Mich. 573 (Neubauer 1099), f. 18a-18b, M.
1839. Oxford - Bodleian Library MS Opp. 170 (Neubauer 1205), f. 201a-201b, C.
1840. Parma - Biblioteca Palatina Cod. Parm. 2895, p. 211, M.
1841. Parma - Biblioteca Palatina Cod. Parm. 2895, p. 216, M.
1842. Parma - Biblioteca Palatina Cod. Parm. 3057.9 (de Rossi 1033), f. 91b, C.
1843. Parma - Biblioteca Palatina Cod. Parm. 3205 (de Rossi 655), f. 250a, C.
1844. Uppsala - Universitetsbibliotek O.Heb.22, f. 109b, M, no incipit.
1845. Vatican - Biblioteca Apostolica ebr. 305,1, f. 44b, C, no incipit.
1846. Vatican - Biblioteca Apostolica ebr. 308, f. 155a-155b, C, commentator: David b. Mose (compiler).
1847. Verona - Seminario Maggiore 34, f. 169b, M, short.

Ashkenaz, commentary by Eliezer b. Natan

1848. Hamburg - Staats- und Universitaetsbibliothek Cod. hebr. 61 (Steinschneider 153), f. 22a, C.
1849. London - Montefiore Library 261, f. 86a, C.

---

[42] Edited by Katzenellenbogen, פירוש ההושענות, p. 30-31.

1850. Paris - Bibliotheque Nationale heb. 327/2, f. 37b-38a, C.
1851. Warszaw - Uniwersytet, Inst. Orientalistyczny 258, f. 195b, C.
Italia
1852. Moscow - Russian State Library, Ms. Guenzburg 1594, f. 24a, C, no incipit.
1853. Torino - Archivio Terracini 1499, p. 85-87, C, commentator: Zakharya David Shabbetai Segre, rubric: פירוש אום אני חומה, no incipit.
Tsarfat
1854. Parma - Biblioteca Palatina Cod. Parm. 1264, f. 96b, M.
1855. Vatican - Biblioteca Apostolica ebr. 306, f. 127a, C.

אום אשר בך דבוקה (א 1830), אלעזר ברבי קילר, יוצר לשבת פרה
Ashkenaz
1856. Berlin - Staatsbibliothek (Preussischer Kulturbesitz) Or. Qu. 798-799 (Steinschneider 177), II, f. 31a-32a, M.
1857. Budapest - Magyar tudomanyos akademia, MS. Kaufmann A 384, f. 73a-74a, M.
1858. Cambridge - University Library Add. 394,1 (Reif SCR 461), f. 43a-43b, C, rubric: לפרשת פרה.
1859. Jerusalem - Schocken Institute 24100 / Mahzor Nuremberg, f. 60a-60b, M.
1860. Muenchen - Bayerische Staatsbibliothek, Cod. hebr. 393, f. 100a-100b, C, rubric: לפרשת פרה.
1861. Muenchen - Bayerische Staatsbibliothek, Cod. hebr. 88, f. 37a-37b, G.
1862. New York - Jewish Theological Seminary Ms. 4466, f. 6a-7a, M.
1863. Oxford - Bodleian Library MS Opp. 170 (Neubauer 1205), f. 27a-28b, C, rubric: בשם נשגב ונורא . אתחיל לכתוב פירושי פרה.
1864. Paris - Bibliotheque Nationale heb. 709, f. 33b-35a, C, rubric: יוצר לפרה אדומה.
1865. Parma - Biblioteca Palatina Cod. Parm. 1002 (Ta 24), f. 52a, M, very short.
1866. Parma - Biblioteca Palatina Cod. Parm. 3205 (de Rossi 655), f. 57b-58a, C, rubric: יוצר לפרה אדומה.
1867. Parma - Biblioteca Palatina Cod. Parm. 3507 (Perreau 27), f. 26a-27a, C, rubric: אתחיל פרשת פרה אדומה.
1868. Vatican - Biblioteca Apostolica ebr. 305,1, f. 38a, C, rubric: יוצר לפרה אדומה.
1869. Zurich - Zentralbibliothek Heid. 139, f. 4b, C, rubric: לפרשת פרה, additional marginal notes.
Italia
1870. Parma - Biblioteca Palatin Cod. Parm. 2248 (de Rossi 149/2), f. 19a-21a, M, rubric: ביאור יוצר פרשת פרה.

Roma

1871. Jerusalem - Jewish National and University Library Ms Heb 8° 4153, f. 156b-157a, C, commentator: Daniel ben Salomo haRofe (compiler), rubric: פי' יוצר דפרה, additional glosses.
1872. New York - Jewish Theological Seminary Ms. 1639, f. 17b-19a, C, commentator: Salomo b. Samuel Rofe, rubric: ביאור דיוצר פרשת פרה.
1873. Oxford - Bodleian Library MS Mich. 312,1 (Neubauer 2276,1), f. 22b, C, rubric: פי' יוצר דפרה.

Tsarfat

1874. Moscow - Russian State Library, Ms. Guenzburg 1665, f. 33a-33b, M.
1875. Parma - Biblioteca Palatina Cod. Parm. 3136 (de Rossi 405), f. 47b, M.
1876. Vatican - Biblioteca Apostolica ebr. 306, f. 147b-148a, C, rubric: שבת פרה.

אום כאישון ננצרת (א 1835), יוצר לשמיני עצרת

Ashkenaz

1877. Berlin - Staatsbibliothek (Preussischer Kulturbesitz) Or. Qu. 798-799 (Steinschneider 177), I, f. 212a-212b, M.
1878. Braunschweig - Landesmuseum fuer Geschichte und Volkstum R 2386, vol. I, f. 149a, M, short.
1879. Cambridge - University Library Add. 394,1 (Reif SCR 461), f. 73b, C, rubric: לשמיני עצרת, short.
1880. Jerusalem - Jewish National and University Library Ms Heb 8° 3037, f. 280b-281a, M.
1881. London - British Library Add. 18695 (Margoliouth 683), f. 125b-126a, T, Yiddish, rubric: יוצר צו שמיני עצרת.
1882. London - Montefiore Library 261, f. 73a, C, commentator: Eliezer b. Natan?.
1883. New York - Jewish Theological Seminary Ms. 4466, f. 456a-457a, M.
1884. Vatican - Biblioteca Apostolica ebr. 422/1, f. 22b, C, rubric: יוצר ליום שמיני עצרת.
1885. Zurich - Zentralbibliothek Heid. 139, f. 93b-94a, C, rubric: יוצר ליום אחרון (in margin), additional marginal notes.

Roma

1886. Jerusalem - Jewish National and University Library Ms Heb 8° 4153, f. 146a, C, commentator: Daniel ben Salomo haRofe (compiler).
1887. Oxford - Bodleian Library MS Mich. 312,1 (Neubauer 2276,1), f. 14a, C, short.

Romania

1888. London - London School of Jewish Studies. Asher I. Myers collection 9, f. 230a, M.
1889. Vatican - Biblioteca Apostolica ebr. 320, f. 457b-458b, M, ecclectic.

Tsarfat

1890. London - David Sofer 5, f. 183a-183b, C, rubric: פירוש מיוצר של שביעי מסוכות, short.
1891. Moscow - Russian State Library, Ms. Guenzburg 1665, f. 186a-186b, M, short.
1892. Oxford - Bodleian Library MS Laud. Or. 271 (Neubauer 1206), f. 191a, C, commentator: Aaron b. Hayyim haKohen (compiler), rubric: יוצר ליום שמיני של חג, short.
1893. Vatican - Biblioteca Apostolica ebr. 306, f. 112a, C, rubric: יוצר לשמיני עצרת, short.

אום נצורה כבבת בונה בהלכות שבת (א 1838), הושענא לשבת

Ashkenaz

1894. Berlin - Staatsbibliothek (Preussischer Kulturbesitz) Or. Qu. 361 (Steinschneider 51), f. 118a-118b, M.
1895. Berlin - Staatsbibliothek (Preussischer Kulturbesitz) Or. Qu. 798-799 (Steinschneider 177), I, f. 206a-206b, M.
1896. Budapest - Magyar tudomanyos akademia, MS. Kaufmann A 399, p. 308-309, C, rubric: הושע נא של שבת.
1897. Budapest - Magyar tudomanyos akademia, MS. Kaufmann A 400, p. 535, C.
1898. Cambridge - University Library Or. 790, f. 33b-34a, C.
1899. Cremona - Archivio di Stato 68, f. 1a, FC, commentator: Ephraim b. Jacob of Bonn.
1900. Frankfurt a M - Stadt- und Universitaetsbibliothek Oct. 227, f. 114a-114b, M.
1901. Hamburg - Staats- und Universitaetsbibliothek Cod. hebr. 17/2 (Steinschneider 152), f. 176a, C, rubric: אחרת לשבת.
1902. Hamburg - Staats- und Universitaetsbibliothek Cod. hebr. 132 (Steinschneider 155), f. 57a-57b, C.
1903. Jerusalem - Schocken Institute 24100 / Mahzor Nuremberg, f. 493a, M.
1904. London - British Library Add. 18695 (Margoliouth 683), f. 152b-153a, T, Yiddish, rubric: הושע נא של שבת.
1905. London - British Library Add. 22431 (Margoliouth 662a), f. 117a, M.
1906. London - British Library Add. 27208 (Margolioth 654), f. 269a, M.
1907. London - British Library Add. 27556, f. 130b-131a, M.
1908. Moscow - Russian State Library, Ms. Guenzburg 615, f. 129a, C, rubric: לשבת.
1909. New York - Jewish Theological Seminary Ms. 4466, f. 485b-486a, M.
1910. Oxford - Bodleian Library MS Can. Or. 1 (Neubauer 1104), f. 29a-29b, M.
1911. Oxford - Bodleian Library MS Mich. 573 (Neubauer 1099), f. 19a, M.

1912. Oxford - Bodleian Library MS Opp 160 (Neubauer 1204), f. 236b-237b, C, commentator: Elazar b. Yehuda of Worms, rubric: לשבת.[43]
1913. Oxford - Bodleian Library MS Opp. 170 (Neubauer 1205), f. 202b-203a, C.
1914. Parma - Biblioteca Palatina Cod. Parm. 2895, p. 212-213, M.
1915. Parma - Biblioteca Palatina Cod. Parm. 3057.9 (de Rossi 1033), f. 93a, C.
1916. Parma - Biblioteca Palatina Cod. Parm. 3205 (de Rossi 655), f. 250b, C.
1917. Uppsala - Universitetsbibliotek O.Heb.22, f. 110b-111a, M, no incipit.
1918. Vatican - Biblioteca Apostolica ebr. 308, f. 157a-157b, C, commentator: David b. Mose (compiler).
1919. Verona - Seminario Maggiore 34, f. 170a, M.

Ashkenaz, commentary by Eliezer b. Natan
1920. Hamburg - Staats- und Universitaetsbibliothek Cod. hebr. 61 (Steinschneider 153), f. 24a, C.
1921. London - Montefiore Library 261, f. 87a-87b, C.
1922. Paris - Bibliotheque Nationale heb. 327/2, f. 39b-40a, C, rubric: בשבת אום׳.
1923. Warszaw - Uniwersytet, Inst. Orientalistyczny 258, f. 196b, C.

haAri, commentary by Mose b. Hayyim Pesante
1924. New York - Columbia University X 893 J 558, f. 206b-207a, M.
1925. New York - Jewish Theological Seminary Ms. 4696, f. 19b-20a, C, rubric: לשבת.

Italia
1926. Moscow - Russian State Library, Ms. Guenzburg 1594, f. 24b, C, no incipit.

Italia, commentary by Zakharya David Shabbetai Segre
1927. Torino - Archivio Terracini 1499, p. 131-133, C, rubric: פירוש אום נצורה כבבת, no incipit.
1928. Torino - Archivio Terracini 1499, p. 135-137, C, rubric: פירוש הושענא של שבת כמנהג הספרדים, no incipit.

North Africa, commentary by Simon b. Tsemaḥ Duran?
1929. New York - Jewish Theological Seminary Ms. 4121, f. 48a, C, rubric: ביאור קצת מלות ליום השבת.

North Africa, commentary by Yehuda Toledano
1930. New York - Jewish Theological Seminary Ms. 4300, f. 36a-37a, C.

Romania
1931. Vatican - Biblioteca Apostolica ebr. 285/30, f. 232b-233a, C.

Tsarfat
1932. Cambridge - University Library Add. 561.1, f. 113b-114a, M.

---

[43] Edited by Katzenellenbogen, פירוש ההושענות, p. 36-37.

1933. Jerusalem - Schocken Institute 19623, f. 124a, M, commentator: Yehuda b. Eliezer Zvi.
1934. London - British Library Or. 2735 (Margoliouth 663), f. 141a-141b, M.
1935. London - David Sofer 5, f. 192a, C.
1936. Moscow - Russian State Library, Ms. Guenzburg 1665, f. 179a-179b, M.
1937. Parma - Biblioteca Palatina Cod. Parm. 1264, f. 93b-94a, M.
1938. Parma - Biblioteca Palatina Cod. Parm. 1902, f. 172b-173a, M.
1939. Vatican - Biblioteca Apostolica ebr. 306, f. 127a-127b, C.

Yemen
1940. Chicago-Spertus College of Judaica D 10, f. 140b, M, rubric: פירוש, short.
1941. Jerusalem - Benayahu ת 283, f. 97b, M.
1942. Jerusalem - Sassoon 264, f. 97a, M, rubric: פרוש, short.

Yemen, commentary by Isaac b. Abraham Wanneh
1943. Jerusalem - Benayahu ת 261, f. 85a, M, rubric: פירוש.
1944. Jerusalem - Benayahu ת 282, f. 78a-78b, M.
1945. Jerusalem - Makhon Ben Zvi 1156 (Tubi 155), f. 77a, M, no incipit.
1946. Jerusalem - Makhon Ben Zvi 1174 (Tubi 154), f. 87b, M, no incipit.
1947. Jerusalem - Michael Krupp 604, f. 95b, M, short.
1948. Jerusalem - Musad haRav Kook 325, f. 111a, M, rubric: חידושין.
1949. Jerusalem - Musad haRav Kook 325, f. 127a, M.
1950. Jerusalem - Sassoon 1158, p. 219, M, no incipit.
1951. Jerusalem - Sassoon 1174, p. 148, M, rubric: פירוש, short.
1952. London - British Library Or. 11122, f. 124a, M, short.
1953. Manchester - John Rylands University Library, Ms. Gaster 5, f. 152a, M, short.
1954. Muenchen - Bayerische Staatsbibliothek, Cod. hebr. 472, f. 102a, M, short.
1955. New York - Jewish Theological Seminary Ms. 3028, f. 250b, C, rubric: פירוש הושענות לשבת.
1956. New York - Jewish Theological Seminary Ms. 3108, f. 83a, C, rubric: פירוש הושענות לשבת.
1957. New York - Jewish Theological Seminary Ms. 3193, f. 169a, M, rubric: הושענות לשבת.
1958. New York - Jewish Theological Seminary Ms. 3295, f. 94b, M, no incipit.
1959. Ramat Gan - Universitat Bar Ilan 703, f. 198a, M, rubric: ליום שבת, short.
1960. Strasbourg - Bibliotheque Nationale et Universitaire 3965 (Landauer 39), p. 247, M, short.

Yemen, commentary by Samḥun b. Salomo Ḥaloah
1961. Jerusalem - Makhon ben Zvi 2808, f. 153a-159b, C.

Yemen, commentary by Simon b. Tsemaḥ Duran?
1962. Jerusalem - Michael Krupp 1758, f. 20a, M, rubric: פירוש, no incipit.

אום קרואה חבצלת השרון (א 1839), סליחה
Ashkenaz
1963. Muenchen - Bayerische Staatsbibliothek, Cod. hebr. 346 , f. 163b, C, short.
1964. Oxford - Bodleian Library MS Opp. 681 (Neubauer 1213), f. 45b-46a, C, rubric: לעשרה בטבת.
1965. Padova - Biblioteca del Seminario Vescovile Cod. 218, f. 243b-244b, M.
1966. Vatican - Biblioteca Apostolica ebr. 422/1, f. 27b, C.
1967. Vatican - Biblioteca Apostolica ebr. 422/1, f. 41a, CG, no incipit.

אומן אמונת אמן בפיו בקומו ובשבתו (א 1850), אהרן בן יוסף הרופא, פרשת ואלה הדברים
Karaite, commentary by Berakha b. Josef haKohen
1968. New York - Jewish Theological Seminary Ms. 3367, f. 139a-141a, C, rubric: ספר ואלה הדברים. פרוש פרשת דברים.
1969. St. Petersburg - Inst. of Oriental Studies of the Russian Academy B 431, f. 94b-95b, C, rubric: ספר ואלֹה הדברים.
1970. St. Petersburg - Inst. of Oriental Studies of the Russian Academy B 483, f. 12a-12b, C, incomplete, beginning missing.
1971. St. Petersburg - Russian National Library, Evr. IV 50 , f. 108a-109b, C, rubric: ספר ואלה הדברים.

אומן בחזות כבוד אל והשיג מדוותיו (א 1852), אהרן בן יוסף הרופא, פרשת ויקהל
Karaite, commentary by Berakha b. Josef haKohen
1972. New York - Jewish Theological Seminary Ms. 3367, f. 88b-90a, C, rubric: פירוש פרשת ויקהל.
1973. St. Petersburg - Inst. of Oriental Studies of the Russian Academy B 431, f. 62b-63b, C, rubric: פרשת ויקהל.
1974. St. Petersburg - Russian National Library, Evr. IV 50 , f. 65b-66b, C, rubric: ויקהל.

אומן בעמדו להתחנן לפניך (א 1854), יוסף, סליחה
Ashkenaz
1975. Vatican - Biblioteca Apostolica ebr. 422/1, f. 41b, CG, no incipit.

אומן בשומע כי תאש ראש (א 1855), אלעזר ברבי קליר, חלק ד׳, קדושתא לשבת שקלים

Ashkenaz
1976. Berlin - Staatsbibliothek (Preussischer Kulturbesitz) Or. Qu. 798-799 (Steinschneider 177), II, f. 14b-15a, M.
1977. Budapest - Magyar tudomanyos akademia, MS. Kaufmann A 384, f. 39a-39b, M.
1978. Budapest - Magyar tudomanyos akademia, MS. Kaufmann A 400, p. 8-12, C.
1979. Cambridge - University Library Add. 504,1, f. 5a-6a, C.
1980. Erlangen - Universitaetsbibliothek 2601 (Roth 67), f. 28a-28b, M.
1981. Jerusalem - Schocken Institute 24100 / Mahzor Nuremberg, f. 35b, M.
1982. Muenchen - Bayerische Staatsbibliothek, Cod. hebr. 88, f. 16a, G.
1983. Muenchen - Bayerische Staatsbibliothek, Cod. hebr. 393, f. 86a-86b, C, no incipit.
1984. Oxford - Bodleian Library MS Opp. 170 (Neubauer 1205), f. 5a-5b, C.
1985. Paris - Bibliotheque Nationale heb. 709, f. 6b-7b, C.
1986. Parma - Biblioteca Palatina Cod. Parm. 3205 (de Rossi 655), f. 13a-14a, C.
1987. Parma - Biblioteca Palatina Cod. Parm. 1002 (Ta 24), f. 24b-25a, M.
1988. Parma - Biblioteca Palatina Cod. Parm. 3507 (Perreau 27), f. 4b-5b, C, no incipit.
1989. Vatican - Biblioteca Apostolica ebr. 305,1, f. 4b-5a, C.

Tsarfat
1990. London - British Library Add. 11639 (Margoliouth 1056), f. 265a-265b, M.
1991. London - David Sofer 5, f. 11a-11b, C.
1992. Moscow - Russian State Library, Ms. Guenzburg 1665, f. 14b-15a, M.
1993. Oxford - Bodleian Library MS Laud. Or. 271 (Neubauer 1206), 11a-12a, C, commentator: Aaron b. Hayyim haKohen (compiler).
1994. Oxford - Bodleian Library MS Opp. 171 (Neubauer 1207), f. 7b-8b, C.
1995. Parma - Biblioteca Palatina Cod. Parm. 3136 (de Rossi 405), f. 23b-24a, M.
1996. Vatican - Biblioteca Apostolica ebr. 306, f. 158a-159b, C, no incipit.

אומן חסדך, סליחה

Ashkenaz
1997. Vatican - Biblioteca Apostolica ebr. 422/1, f. 41b, CG, no incipit.

אומן ישעך בא קול דודי הנה זה בא (א 1857), אלעזר ברבי קליר, הושענא
Ashkenaz
1998. Berlin - Staatsbibliothek (Preussischer Kulturbesitz) Or. Qu. 798-799 (Steinschneider 177), I, f. 211b, M.
1999. Budapest - Magyar tudomanyos akademia, MS. Kaufmann A 399, p. 308, C, incipit קול מבשר.
2000. Budapest - Magyar tudomanyos akademia, MS. Kaufmann A 400, p. 541-542, C, incipit קול מבשר.
2001. Cambridge - University Library Add. 394,1 (Reif SCR 461), f. 78b, C, incipit קול מבשר.
2002. Frankfurt a M - Stadt- und Universitaetsbibliothek Oct. 227, f. 117b, M, incipit קול מבשר.
2003. Hamburg - Staats- und Universitaetsbibliothek Cod. hebr. 17/2 (Steinschneider 152), f. 169a, C, incipit קול מבשר.
2004. Jerusalem - Schocken Institute 24100 / Mahzor Nuremberg, f. 496b, M.
2005. London - British Library Add. 18695 (Margoliouth 683), f. 157b-158a, T, Yiddish.
2006. London - British Library Add. 22431 (Margoliouth 662a), f. 127a-128a, M, incipit קול מבשר.
2007. London - British Library Add. 27208 (Margolioth 654), f. 282b-283b, M.
2008. London - British Library Add. 27556, f. 136a, M.
2009. Moscow - Russian State Library, Ms. Guenzburg 615, f. 131a, C, incipit קול מבשר.
2010. Oxford - Bodleian Library MS Can. Or. 1 (Neubauer 1104), f. 35a, M, incipit קול מבשר.
2011. Oxford - Bodleian Library MS Mich. 573 (Neubauer 1099), f. 25a-25b, M, incipit קול מבשר.
2012. Oxford - Bodleian Library MS Opp 160 (Neubauer 1204), f. 248b, C, commentator: Elazar b. Yehuda of Worms, starts קול מבשר.[44]
2013. Oxford - Bodleian Library MS Opp. 170 (Neubauer 1205), f. 206a-206b, C, incipit קול מבשר.
2014. Parma - Biblioteca Palatina Cod. Parm. 2895, p. 230-231, M, incipit קול מבשר.
2015. Parma - Biblioteca Palatina Cod. Parm. 3205 (de Rossi 655), f. 253a, C.
2016. Parma - Biblioteca Palatina Cod. Parm. 3057.9 (de Rossi 1033), f. 99b-100a, C, incipit קול מבשר.
2017. Vatican - Biblioteca Apostolica ebr. 305,1, f. 45a, C, no incipit, starts אומר לצאן וגו'.

---

[44] Edited by Katzenellenbogen, פירוש ההושענות, p. 66-70.

2018. Vatican - Biblioteca Apostolica ebr. 308, f. 161a, C, commentator: David b. Mose (compiler), incipit קול מבשר.
2019. Verona - Seminario Maggiore 34, f. 173a-173b, M, incipit קול מבשר.

Ashkenaz, commentary by Eliezer b. Natan

2020. Hamburg - Staats- und Universitaetsbibliothek Cod. hebr. 61 (Steinschneider 153), f. 26b, C, incipit קול מבשר.
2021. Warszaw - Uniwersytet, Inst. Orientalistyczny 258, f. 199a-199b, C, incipit קול מבשר.

Italia, commentary by Yehoshua Segre

2022. Moscow - Russian State Library, Ms. Guenzburg 533, f. 54a-60a, C, rubric: לימד כב.

Italia, commentary by Zakharya David Shabbetai Segre

2023. Torino - Archivio Terracini 1499, p. 255-256, C, rubric: פירוש אומן ישעך בא, incipit קול מבשר.

Roma

2024. Jerusalem - Jewish National and University Library Ms Heb 8° 4153, f. 146a, C, commentator: Daniel ben Salomo haRofe (compiler), incipit קול מבשר.
2025. Oxford - Bodleian Library MS Mich. 312,1 (Neubauer 2276,1), f. 13b, C, incipit קול מבשר.

Romania

2026. London - London School of Jewish Studies. Asher I.Myers collection 9, f. 216a, M, incipit קול מבשר.
2027. Vatican - Biblioteca Apostolica ebr. 285/30, f. 237b, C, incipit קול מבשר.
2028. Vatican - Biblioteca Apostolica ebr. 320, f. 454a, M.

Tsarfat

2029. Cambridge - University Library Add. 561.1, f. 117a-117b, M, variant reading: אומץ ישעך בא.
2030. Jerusalem - Schocken Institute 19623, f. 130b-131a, M, commentator: Yehuda b. Eliezer Zvi.
2031. London - David Sofer 5, f. 193b, C, very short.
2032. London - David Sofer 5, f. 194a, C, incipit קול.
2033. Moscow - Russian State Library, Ms. Guenzburg 1665, f. 185a, M, incipit .
2034. Parma - Biblioteca Palatina Cod. Parm. 1264, f. 101b-102a, M, incipit קול.
2035. Parma - Biblioteca Palatina Cod. Parm. 1902, f. 185b-187a, M, incipit קול מבשר.
2036. Vatican - Biblioteca Apostolica ebr. 306, f. 126b, C, incipit מבשר.

אומנות אבותי תפשתי (א 1863), אפרים ב"ר יצחק מרגנסבורג, סליחה
Ashkenaz
2037. Vatican - Biblioteca Apostolica ebr. 308, f. 12b-13b, C, commentator: David b. Mose (compiler).

אומנות הדורות סדורה (א 1865), מאיר ב"ר יצחק, לשבת חתונה
Ashkenaz
2038. Budapest - Magyar tudomanyos akademia, MS. Kaufmann A 399 , p. 338-344, C, rubric: יוצר לחתן.
2039. Oxford - Bodleian Library MS Can. Or. 82 (Neubauer 1148) , f. 60b-62a, M.
2040. Oxford - Bodleian Library MS Opp. 170 (Neubauer 1205), f. 248b-250b, C, rubric: גם זה יוצר דחת' שלו ואין על עפו' משלו.
2041. Parma - Biblioteca Palatina Cod. Parm. 3205 (de Rossi 655), f. 175b-176a, C.

Ashkenaz, commentary by Abraham b. Azriel[45]
2042. Frankfurt a M - Stadt- und Universitaetsbibliothek Fol. 16 (Merzbacher 95), f. 95b-98b, C, rubric: יוצר.
2043. Vatican - Biblioteca Apostolica ebr. 301,1, f. 112a-113b, C, rubric: יוצר אחר.

אומץ אדירי כל חפץ (א 1868), אלעזר ברבי קליר, חלק ה', קדושתא לראש השנה
Ashkenaz
2044. Berlin - Staatsbibliothek (Preussischer Kulturbesitz) Or. Qu. 798-799 (Steinschneider 177), I, 16a-17a, M.
2045. Braunschweig - Landesmuseum fuer Geschichte und Volkstum R 2386, vol. II, f. 92b-93a, M, no incipit.
2046. Budapest - Magyar tudomanyos akademia, MS. Kaufmann A 400 , p. 262-265, C.
2047. Darmstadt - Hessisches Landes- und Hochschulbibliothek Cod. Or. 15, f. 14b-15a, M.
2048. Hamburg - Staats- und Universitaetsbibliothek Cod. hebr. 12 (Steinschneider 102), f. 15a-15b, G.
2049. Hamburg - Staats- und Universitaetsbibliothek Cod. hebr. 17/2 (Steinschneider 152), f. 111b-113a, C.
2050. Hamburg - Staats- und Universitaetsbibliothek Cod. hebr. 40b (Steinschneider 110), f. 15a-16a, G.
2051. Hamburg - Staats- und Universitaetsbibliothek Cod. hebr. 40c (Steinschneider 111), f. 137b-138a, G.
2052. Hamburg - Staats- und Universitaetsbibliothek Cod. hebr. 132 (Steinschneider 155), f. 12a-13a, C.

---

[45] Edited by Urbach, ערוגת הבושם, vol. III, p. 110-122.

2053. Hamburg - Staats- und Universitaetsbibliothek Cod. hebr. 139 (Steinschneider 115), f. 29b-30a, G.
2054. Hamburg - Staats- und Universitaetsbibliothek Cod. hebr. 225, f. 227b, G.
2055. Jerusalem - Jewish National and University Library Ms Heb 8° 3037, f. 26b-28a, M.
2056. Jerusalem - Schocken Institute 24100 / Mahzor Nuremberg , f. 330b-331a, M.
2057. London - British Library Or. 11318/1, f. 15a-16a, C.
2058. London - Montefiore Library 261, f. 8a-9b, C, commentator: Eliezer b. Natan?.
2059. Moscow - Russian State Library, Ms. Guenzburg 191, f. 10b-11a, M.
2060. Moscow - Russian State Library, Ms. Guenzburg 615, f. 66a-68a, C.
2061. Moscow - Russian State Library, Ms. Guenzburg 1401/2, f. 18a-18b, C.
2062. Muenchen - Bayerische Staatsbibliothek, Cod. hebr. 86, f. 22a-24a, M.
2063. Muenchen - Bayerische Staatsbibliothek, Cod. hebr. 346 , f. 11a-13b, C.
2064. Muenchen - Bayerische Staatsbibliothek, Cod. hebr. 422 , f. 77a-77b, G.
2065. New York - Jewish Theological Seminary Ms. 4466, f. 223a-224b, M.
2066. New York - Jewish Theological Seminary Ms. 8097, f. 61a-62a, C.
2067. New York - Jewish Theological Seminary Ms. 8169 (Acc. 0016), f. 16b-17b, M.
2068. Oxford - Bodleian Library MS Opp. 170 (Neubauer 1205), f. 118a-120a, C.
2069. Oxford - Bodleian Library MS Opp. 172 (Neubauer 1211), f. 9b-10b, C.
2070. Oxford - Bodleian Library MS Opp. 619 (Neubauer 2374), f. 28a-29a, M.
2071. Oxford - Bodleian Library MS Opp. 675 (Neubauer 1210), f. 23a-24a, C, no incipit.
2072. Paris - Bibliotheque Nationale heb. 653, f. 15a-15b, G.
2073. Parma - Biblioteca Palatina Cod. Parm. 3205 (de Rossi 655), f. 206b-207b, C.
2074. Parma - Biblioteca Palatina Cod. Parm. 3270 (de Rossi 1215), f. 30b-31b, M.
2075. Parma - Biblioteca Palatina Cod. Parm. 3507 (Perreau 27), f. 118a-119b, C.
2076. Salzburg - Universitsetsbibliothek M II 342 , f. 2a-2b, FM, incomplete.
2077. Torino - Archivio Terracini 1492, f. 21a-21b, M.

2078. Vatican - Biblioteca Apostolica ebr. 308, f. 47b-49b, C, commentator: David b. Mose (compiler).
2079. Vatican - Biblioteca Apostolica ebr. 422/1, f. 9b-10a, C.
2080. Zurich - Zentralbibliothek Heid. 139, f. 61b-62b, C, incipit אדירי, additional marginal notes.
2081. Zurich - Zentralbibliothek Heid. 139, f. 102a-102b, C, commentator: Elazar b. Yehuda of Worms, short, esoteric.

Asti, Fossano, Moncalvo

2082. New Haven - Yale University, Beinecke Rare Book and MS Library, MS Heb. 52, f. 32a-33a, M.

Tsarfat

2083. London - British Library Or. 8682, f. 20b-21a, G.
2084. London - British Library Add. 11639 (Margoliouth 1056), f. 709b, M, short.
2085. London - David Sofer 5, f. 114a-114b, C.
2086. Oxford - Bodleian Library MS Laud. Or. 271 (Neubauer 1206), f. 145a-146a, C, commentator: Aaron b. Hayyim haKohen (compiler).
2087. Paris - Bibliotheque Nationale heb. 445,9, f. 72b-75(i)a, C.
2088. Parma - Biblioteca Palatina Cod. Parm. 2125 (de Rossi 812), f. 16a-17b, C, page 16a damaged.
2089. Parma - Biblioteca Palatina Cod. Parm. 3006 (de Rossi 654,1), f. 44a-45b, M.

אומץ גבורותיך הלפאתה בפסח (א 1871), אלעזר ברבי קליר, חלק ה', קדושתא ליום א' של פסח

Ashkenaz

2090. Berlin - Staatsbibliothek (Preussischer Kulturbesitz) Or. Qu. 798-799 (Steinschneider 177), II, f. 80a-80b, M.
2091. Braunschweig - Landesmuseum fuer Geschichte und Volkstum R 2386, vol. I, f. 37b, M.
2092. Budapest - Magyar tudomanyos akademia, MS. Kaufmann A 384, f. 164b-165a, M.
2093. Budapest - Magyar tudomanyos akademia, MS. Kaufmann A 399, p. 190, C, rubric: לליל שיני של פסח.
2094. Cambridge - University Library Add. 394.2 (Reif SCR 462), f. 103b, C, rubric: ביאור אומץ גבורתך שאומרי' ג"כ בליל פסח לי"ח.
2095. Cincinnati - Hebrew Union College 436, f. 73b-74a, G.
2096. Frankfurt a M - Stadt- und Universitaetsbibliothek Oct. 227, f. 74a-75a, M.
2097. Hamburg - Staats- und Universitaetsbibliothek Cod. hebr. 17/2 (Steinschneider 152), f. 35b-36b, C.
2098. London - British Library Add. 18695 (Margoliouth 683), f. 43a-43b, T, Yiddish.

2099. Moscow - Russian State Library, Ms. Guenzburg 1401/2, f. 15a-15b, C.
2100. Muenchen - Bayerische Staatsbibliothek, Cod. hebr. 69, f. 35b-36a, G.
2101. Muenchen - Bayerische Staatsbibliothek, Cod. hebr. 88, f. 74a, G.
2102. Paris - Bibliotheque Nationale heb. 709, f 99a-99b, C.
2103. Zurich - Zentralbibliothek Heid. 139, f. 38a, C.

Italia

2104. Parma - Biblioteca Palatina Cod. Parm. 2248 (de Rossi 149/2), f. 40b-41a, C.

Roma

2105. New York - Jewish Theological Seminary Ms. 1639, f. 20b-21b, C, commentator: Salomo b. Samuel Rofe, rubric: ביאור אומץ שאומרים גם כן בליל פסח.

Tsarfat

2106. Oxford - Bodleian Library MS Laud. Or. 271 (Neubauer 1206), f. 73b, C, commentator: Aaron b. Hayyim haKohen (compiler), short.

אומץ גבורותיך מי ימלל (א 1872), משה בן קלונימוס, סילוק, קדושתא לשחרית יום כפור

Ashkenaz

2107. Berlin - Staatsbibliothek (Preussischer Kulturbesitz) Or. Qu. 798-799 (Steinschneider 177), II, f. 97a-99a, M.
2108. Braunschweig - Landesmuseum fuer Geschichte und Volkstum R 2386, vol. I, f. 65a-67a, M.
2109. Budapest - Magyar tudomanyos akademia, MS. Kaufmann A 384, f. 211a-213a, M.
2110. Budapest - Magyar tudomanyos akademia, MS. Kaufmann A 400, p. 145-147, C, rubric: סילוק.
2111. Hamburg - Staats- und Universitaetsbibliothek Cod. hebr. 17/2 (Steinschneider 152), f. 69a-69b, C.
2112. Jerusalem - Schocken Institute 24100 / Mahzor Nuremberg, f. 126a-127b, M.
2113. London - British Library Add. 18695 (Margoliouth 683), f. 61a-63a, T, Yiddish.
2114. Moscow - Russian State Library, Ms. Guenzburg 615, f. 27b-28b, C, rubric: סילוק, incipit כי מי.
2115. Muenchen - Bayerische Staatsbibliothek, Cod. hebr. 393, f. 136b-137a, C.
2116. New York - Jewish Theological Seminary Ms. 4466, f. 118a-120a, M, incipit להתפאר.
2117. New York - Jewish Theological Seminary Ms. 4663, f. 1b-3b, FM.
2118. Oxford - Bodleian Library MS Opp. 170 (Neubauer 1205), f. 78b-79b, C, rubric: סילוק, incipit כי.

2119. Paris - Bibliotheque Nationale heb. 709, f. 105b-106b, C, rubric: סילוק, incipit להתפאר.
2120. Parma - Biblioteca Palatina Cod. Parm. 1002 (Ta 24), f. 145b-146b, M.
2121. Parma - Biblioteca Palatina Cod. Parm. 3205 (de Rossi 655), f. 110b-111a, C, rubric: סילוק.
2122. Parma - Biblioteca Palatina Cod. Parm. 3507 (Perreau 27), f. 77a-77b, C, rubric: סילוק.
2123. Zurich - Zentralbibliothek Heid. 139, f. 47a-47b, C, additional marginal notes.

Tsarfat
2124. Oxford - Bodleian Library MS Laud. Or. 271 (Neubauer 1206), f. 83a-83b, C, commentator: Aaron b. Hayyim haKohen (compiler), rubric: סילוק.

אומץ דר חזקים אבאר לפי ספוקים (א 1873), שלמה הבבלי, יוצר
Ashkenaz
2125. Budapest - Magyar tudomanyos akademia, MS. Kaufmann A 399, p. 443-444, C, rubric: יוצר לשלישי של נחמו.
2126. Cambridge - University Library Add. 504,1, f. 52b-53b, C, rubric: 'ר שלמה יסד זה וחתום בסוף הזולת שפר.
2127. Oxford - Bodleian Library MS Can. Or. 82 (Neubauer 1148), f. 34b-36a, M.
2128. Parma - Biblioteca Palatina Cod. Parm. 3205 (de Rossi 655), f. 162b-163b, C.

אומץ דתותי וסדרי עניני (א 1874), יוסף ב"ר שמואל טוב עלם, זולת
Ashkenaz
2129. Budapest - Magyar tudomanyos akademia, MS. Kaufmann A 399, p. 446, C, rubric: זולת לנצבים.
2130. Cambridge - University Library Add. 504,1, f. 54b-55a, C, rubric: זולת ט'ע', לאתם נצבים רבי יוסף, short.
2131. Oxford - Bodleian Library MS Can. Or. 82 (Neubauer 1148), f. 37b-38a, M.
2132. Parma - Biblioteca Palatina Cod. Parm. 3205 (de Rossi 655), f. 165a-165b, C, rubric: זולת לנצבים.

אומץ יוסיף וטהר ידים (א 1878), יוסף, סליחה
Ashkenaz
2133. Berlin - Staatsbibliothek (Preussischer Kulturbesitz) Or. Qu. 798-799 (Steinschneider 177), I, f. 165a-166a, M.

2134. Budapest - Magyar tudomanyos akademia, MS. Kaufmann A 400 , p. 475-481, C, commentator: Elazar b. Yehuda of Worms, rubric: אחרת דר' מאיר שליח ציבור.
2135. Budapest - Magyar tudomanyos akademia, MS. Kaufmann A 400 , p. 481-482, C, rubric: סליחה אחרת.
2136. Cambridge - University Library Dd. 2.30, f. 24b-25b, G.
2137. Jerusalem - Schocken Institute 24100 / Mahzor Nuremberg , f. 247b, M, very few marginal notes by later hand only.
2138. Moscow - Russian State Library, Ms. Guenzburg 190, f. 12b-13a, M.
2139. Muenchen - Bayerische Staatsbibliothek, Cod. hebr. 346, f. 121b, C.
2140. Muenchen - Bayerische Staatsbibliothek, Cod. hebr. 346, f. 164a, C.
2141. Oxford - Bodleian Library MS Mich. 543 (Neubauer 1212), f. 12b-14a, C, commentator: Isaac b. Jacob (compiler), rubric: 'ואחריכן פותחי במדין' בשלמונית שנתקנה על יום כיפור. וזו היא.
2142. Oxford - Bodleian Library MS Opp. 619 (Neubauer 2374), f. 229b-230a, M.
2143. Oxford - Bodleian Library MS Opp. 681 (Neubauer 1213), f. 30a-31a, C.
2144. Paris - Bibliotheque Nationale heb. 1408/22, f. 123a-125a, C, commentator: Elazar b. Yehuda of Worms, rubric: סליחה זו גם היא מיסודו .והפירוש כתב רבינו ר' אלעזר בן רבינו יהודה.
2145. Parma - Biblioteca Palatina Cod. Parm. 3205 (de Rossi 655), f. 276b-277a, C.
2146. Vatican - Biblioteca Apostolica ebr. 308/1, f. 4b-5b, C, commentator: David b. Mose (compiler).
2147. Vatican - Biblioteca Apostolica ebr. 422/1, f. 25a, C, short.
2148. Vatican - Biblioteca Apostolica ebr. 422/2 , f. 39b, CG, no incipit, very short.

Ashkenaz, commentary by Abraham b. Azriel[46]

2149. Vatican - Biblioteca Apostolica ebr. 301,1, f. 142b-143a, C.

Tsarfat

2150. London - British Library Or. 2735 (Margoliouth 663) , f. 155b-156b, M.
2151. London - David Sofer 5, f. 92a-92b, C.
2152. London - David Sofer 5, f. 168a-168b, C, rubric: סליחה.
2153. Oxford - Bodleian Library MS Bodl. Or. 109 (Neubauer 1209), f. 73a-73b, C, commentator: Aaron b. Hayyim haKohen (compiler).
2154. Oxford - Bodleian Library MS Bodl. Or. 109 (Neubauer 1209), f. 75b-77a, C, commentator: Aaron b. Hayyim haKohen (compiler).
2155. Oxford - Bodleian Library MS Opp. 171 (Neubauer 1207), f. 115a-115b, C, rubric: אחרת.

---

[46] Edited by Urbach, ערוגת הבושם, vol. III, p. 315-316.

2156. Oxford - Bodleian Library MS Laud. Or. 271 (Neubauer 1206), f. 129b-130a, C, commentator: Aaron b. Hayyim haKohen (compiler).
2157. Parma - Biblioteca Palatina Cod. Parm. 3007 (de Rossi 654,2), f. 32b-33a, M.
2158. Vatican - Biblioteca Apostolica ebr. 306, f. 203a-204a, C.

אומץ קצות דרכיך אין מי יבין (א 1879), יוצר ליום ב' של סוכות

Roma

2159. Jerusalem - Jewish National and University Library Ms Heb 8° 4153, f. 147b-148a, C, commentator: Daniel ben Salomo haRofe (compiler), rubric: יוצר ליו' שני.
2160. Oxford - Bodleian Library MS Mich. 312,1 (Neubauer 2276,1), f. 14a, C.

אומר וגומר הכל באמרה (א 1891), אהרן בן יוסף הרופא, יוצר בראשית

Karaite, commentary by Berakha b. Josef haKohen

2161. New York - Jewish Theological Seminary Ms. 3367, f. 6a-10a, C.
2162. St. Petersburg - Inst. of Oriental Studies of the Russian Academy B 431, f. 8a-11a, C.

אומרה לאל סלעי (א 1912), שלמה הבבלי, סליחה

Ashkenaz

2163. Budapest - Magyar tudomanyos akademia, MS. Kaufmann A 400, p. 493-494, C, rubric: אחרת.
2164. Moscow - Russian State Library, Ms. Guenzburg 190, f. 31b-32a, G.
2165. Muenchen - Bayerische Staatsbibliothek, Cod. hebr. 346, f. 125b, C, rubric: אחרת.
2166. Oxford - Bodleian Library MS Opp. 170 (Neubauer 1205), f. 231a, C.
2167. Vatican - Biblioteca Apostolica ebr. 422/1, f. 6a-6b, C, rubric: אחרת.
2168. Vatican - Biblioteca Apostolica ebr. 422/1, f. 31a, C.
2169. Vatican - Biblioteca Apostolica ebr. 422/1, f. 41a, CG, no incipit.

Ashkenaz, commentary by Abraham b. Azriel[47]

2170. Vatican - Biblioteca Apostolica ebr. 301,1, f. 161a, C, rubric: אחרת.

Tsarfat

2171. London - British Library Add. 11639 (Margoliouth 1056), f. 478b-479b, M.
2172. Oxford - Bodleian Library MS Laud. Or. 271 (Neubauer 1206), f. 123b-124a, C, commentator: Aaron b. Hayyim haKohen (compiler).

---

[47] Edited by Urbach, ערוגת הבושם, vol. III, p. 433-435.

אומרה לאל סלעי למה אהיה עבד לבן אמה (א 1914), אברהם, סליחה

Ashkenaz
2173. Moscow - Russian State Library, Ms. Guenzburg 615, f. 161b-162a, C, rubric: אל מלך.
2174. Oxford - Bodleian Library MS Mich. 543 (Neubauer 1212), f. 68a, C, commentator: Isaac b. Jacob (compiler).
2175. Parma - Biblioteca Palatina Cod. Parm. 3205 (de Rossi 655), f. 270a-270b, C.

Tsarfat
2176. London - David Sofer 5, f. 100a-100b, C.
2177. Parma - Biblioteca Palatina Cod. Parm. 3007 (de Rossi 654,2), f. 33a-33b, M.
2178. Vatican - Biblioteca Apostolica ebr. 306, f. 174a-174b, C.

אומרים לאדרך הושענא באים לברכך (א 1917), הושענא

Italia, commentary by Yehoshua Segre
2179. Moscow - Russian State Library, Ms. Guenzburg 533, f. 22a-26a, C, rubric: לימוד י"א.

אומרת אני מעשי למלך (א 1918), בנימין ב"ר זרח, זולת

Ashkenaz
2180. Berlin - Staatsbibliothek (Preussischer Kulturbesitz) Or. Qu. 798-799 (Steinschneider 177), II, f. 46a-47b, M, rubric: זולת.
2181. Budapest - Magyar tudomanyos akademia, MS. Kaufmann A 384, f. 106b-107b, M.
2182. Hamburg - Staats- und Universitaetsbibliothek Cod. hebr. 17/2 (Steinschneider 152), f. 30b-31a, C, commentator: Ephraim b. Jacob of Bonn, rubric: זולת.
2183. London - British Library Add. 18695 (Margoliouth 683), f. 9b-11a, T, Yiddish, rubric: זולת.
2184. Muenchen - Bayerische Staatsbibliothek, Cod. hebr. 393, f. 107b-108a, C.
2185. Zurich - Zentralbibliothek Heid. 139, f. 13a-13b, C, additional marginal notes.

און זרענו ועמל קצירנו (א 1920), יהודה הלוי, סליחה

Yemen
2186. New York - Jewish Theological Seminary Ms. 3052, f. 28a-30a, M, rubric: אל מלך, starts אבל אשמים אנחנו און זרענו.

אוני פטרי רחמתים בתקת במשלי חמורתים (א 1921), יניי, קדושתא ליום א' של פסח
Ashkenaz
2187. Berlin - Staatsbibliothek (Preussischer Kulturbesitz) Or. Qu. 798-799 (Steinschneider 177), II, f. 47b, M.
2188. Budapest - Magyar tudomanyos akademia, MS. Kaufmann A 384, f. 108a, M.
2189. Erlangen - Universitaetsbibliothek 2601 (Roth 67), f. 57b, M, very short.
2190. Hamburg - Staats- und Universitaetsbibliothek Cod. hebr. 17/2 (Steinschneider 152), f. 31a, C, rubric: אוני פטרי רחמתים ואום' העולם שהיא יסוד ר' יניי רבו של רב אלעזר בר קליר אבל בכל ארץ לומברדיאה אין אום' אותה כי אומרים עליו שנתקנא בר' אלעזר תלמידו והטיל עקרב במנעלו והרגו יסלח יי לכל האומרין עליו אם לא כן היה.
2191. London - British Library Add. 18695 (Margoliouth 683), f. 11a, T, Yiddish, rubric: קרובוץ.
2192. Muenchen - Bayerische Staatsbibliothek, Cod. hebr. 393, f. 108a-108b, C.
2193. New York - Jewish Theological Seminary Ms. 4466, f. 32b-35a, M, rubric: קרובה.
2194. Oxford - Bodleian Library MS Opp. 170 (Neubauer 1205), f. 37b, C, rubric: האלך פירוש מקרובהח של שבת הגדול, additional marginal notes.
2195. Paris - Bibliotheque Nationale heb. 709, f. 44a-44b, C, rubric: לשבת הגדול.
2196. Parma - Biblioteca Palatina Cod. Parm. 3205 (de Rossi 655), f. 46a-46b, C, rubric: קרובה.
2197. Parma - Biblioteca Palatina Cod. Parm. 3507 (Perreau 27), f. 32b-33a, C, rubric: קרובה לשבת הגדול.
2198. Zurich - Zentralbibliothek Heid. 139, f. 13b-14a, C, additional marginal notes.
Tsarfat
2199. Oxford - Bodleian Library MS Laud. Or. 271 (Neubauer 1206), f. 50a-50b, C, commentator: Aaron b. Hayyim haKohen (compiler).

אופל אלמנה תאיר (א 4805), סליחה
Ashkenaz
2200. Berlin - Staatsbibliothek (Preussischer Kulturbesitz) Or. Qu. 798-799 (Steinschneider 177), I, f. 138b-139a, M.
2201. Hamburg - Staats- und Universitaetsbibliothek Cod. hebr. 62 (Steinschneider 154), f. 21a, C, short.
2202. London - Montefiore Library 261, f. 62b-63a, C, commentator: Eliezer b. Natan?, short.
2203. Muenchen - Bayerische Staatsbibliothek, Cod. hebr. 346, f. 144a, C, short.

2204. Oxford - Bodleian Library MS Mich. 365 (Neubauer 1208), f. 91b, C.
2205. Oxford - Bodleian Library MS Opp. 172 (Neubauer 1211), f. 69b, C, short.
2206. Oxford - Bodleian Library MS Opp. 619 (Neubauer 2374), f. 225b, M, short.
2207. Vatican - Biblioteca Apostolica ebr. 308, f. 128b-129a, C, commentator: David b. Mose (compiler).

Ashkenaz, commentary by Abraham b. Azriel[48]

2208. Vatican - Biblioteca Apostolica ebr. 301,1, f. 168b, C, short.

Tsarfat

2209. Oxford - Bodleian Library MS Bodl. Or. 109 (Neubauer 1209), f. 41a, C, commentator: Aaron b. Hayyim haKohen (compiler), short.

אופן אחד בארץ (א 1929), שלמה ב"ר יצחק, סליחה

Ashkenaz, commentary by Abraham b. Azriel[49]

2210. Vatican - Biblioteca Apostolica ebr. 301,1, f. 140a, C, rubric: סליחה שיסד רבי' שלמה.

אור זרוע זורח כבודו (א 1951), מנחם ב"ר מכיר, יוצר להפסקה

Ashkenaz

2211. Berlin - Staatsbibliothek (Preussischer Kulturbesitz) Or. Qu. 361 (Steinschneider 51), f. 164b-166b, M, no incipit.
2212. Berlin - Staatsbibliothek (Preussischer Kulturbesitz) Or. Qu. 798-799 (Steinschneider 177), I, f. 245b-248b, M.
2213. Budapest - Magyar tudomanyos akademia, MS. Kaufmann A 384, f. 47a-48b, M.
2214. Budapest - Magyar tudomanyos akademia, MS. Kaufmann A 399, p. 413-420, C, rubric: יוצר להפסקה.
2215. Cambridge - University Library Add. 504,1, f. 36a-39b, C, rubric: להפסקה מר' מנחם המכירי אחיו של ר' גרשום מאור הגולה.
2216. Frankfurt a M - Stadt- und Universitaetsbibliothek Oct. 227, f. 154a-155b, M.
2217. Hamburg - Staats- und Universitaetsbibliothek Cod. hebr. 17/2 (Steinschneider 152), f. 44a-44b, C.
2218. Jerusalem - Schocken Institute 24100 / Mahzor Nuremberg, f. 38b-39a, M.
2219. Lund - Universitetsbibliothek Ms. L.O. 2, f. 120b-122b, M.
2220. Muenchen - Bayerische Staatsbibliothek, Cod. hebr. 393, f. 178a-182a, C, rubric: להפסקה.
2221. New York - Jewish Theological Seminary Ms. 4466, f. 27b-29b, M.

---

[48] Edited by Urbach, ערוגת הבושם, vol. III, p. 488.
[49] Edited by Urbach, ערוגת הבושם, vol. III, p. 297-298.

2222. Oxford - Bodleian Library MS Can. Or. 82 (Neubauer 1148) , f. 17a-18b, M.
2223. Oxford - Bodleian Library MS Mich. 365 (Neubauer 1208), f. 26b-28a, C.
2224. Oxford - Bodleian Library MS Opp. 169 (Neubauer 1151) , f. 3b-6a, M.
2225. Parma - Biblioteca Palatina Cod. Parm. 2895, p. 392-395, M, margins cut, text damaged.
2226. Parma - Biblioteca Palatina Cod. Parm. 3205 (de Rossi 655), f. 141a-144a, C, rubric: יוצר להפסקה.
2227. Vatican - Biblioteca Apostolica ebr. 318, f. 128a-129b, GI.

Ashkenaz, commentary by Abraham b. Azriel[50]

2228. Vatican - Biblioteca Apostolica ebr. 301,1, f. 87b-95a, C, rubric: יוצר.
2229. Frankfurt a M - Stadt- und Universitaetsbibliothek Fol. 16 (Merzbacher 95), f. 57a-61b, C, rubric: יוצר להפסקה.

Ashkenaz, commentary by Eliezer b. Natan

2230. Parma - Biblioteca Palatina Cod. Parm. 3057.12 (de Rossi 1033/10), f. 130b-133b, C, rubric: יוצר להפסקה.
2231. Warszaw - Uniwersytet, Inst. Orientalistyczny 258, f. 185a-187a, C, rubric: יוצר להפסקה.
2232. Hamburg - Staats- und Universitaetsbibliothek Cod. hebr. 61 (Steinschneider 153), f. 39a-41a, C, rubric: יוצר להפסקה.

אור יום הנף (א 1958), מאיר ב"ר יצחק, חלק ב' מן מעריב ליום ב' של פסח

Ashkenaz

2233. Berlin - Staatsbibliothek (Preussischer Kulturbesitz) Or. Qu. 361 (Steinschneider 51), f. 137a-139a, M, no incipit, postscript לא מצאתי עוד פירוש.
2234. Berlin - Staatsbibliothek (Preussischer Kulturbesitz) Or. Qu. 798-799 (Steinschneider 177), II, f. 73b-74b, M.
2235. Braunschweig - Landesmuseum fuer Geschichte und Volkstum R 2386, vol. I, f. 32a-32b, M.
2236. Budapest - Magyar tudomanyos akademia, MS. Kaufmann A 384 , f. 151b-153a, M.
2237. Budapest - Magyar tudomanyos akademia, MS. Kaufmann A 399 , p. 208-215, C.
2238. Erlangen - Universitaetsbibliothek 2601 (Roth 67), f. 85b, M.
2239. Hamburg - Staats- und Universitaetsbibliothek Cod. hebr. 17/2 (Steinschneider 152), f. 45a-47a, C, rubric: פירוש העומר.
2240. Hamburg - Staats- und Universitaetsbibliothek Cod. hebr. 225, f. 82a-83b, G.

---

[50] Edited by Urbach, ערוגת הבושם, vol. II, p. 253-299.

2241. Jerusalem - Schocken Institute 24100 / Mahzor Nuremberg, f. 89b-90b, M.
2242. London - British Library Add. 18695 (Margoliouth 683), f. 34a-35b, T, Yiddish, rubric: ביכור.
2243. Lund - Universitetsbibliothek Ms. L.O. 2, f. 63b-65a, M.
2244. Muenchen - Bayerische Staatsbibliothek, Cod. hebr. 88, f. 67a-67b, G.
2245. Muenchen - Bayerische Staatsbibliothek, Cod. hebr. 393, f. 212a-217b, C.
2246. New York - Jewish Theological Seminary Ms. 4466, f. 198b-201a, M.
2247. Oxford - Bodleian Library MS Can. Or. 1 (Neubauer 1104), f. 63b-65a, M.
2248. Oxford - Bodleian Library MS Opp. 170 (Neubauer 1205), f. 41a-43b, C, rubric: ביכור לליל שני מר' נהוראי.
2249. Parma - Biblioteca Palatina Cod. Parm. 2895, p. 317-320, M, margins cut, text damaged.
2250. Parma - Biblioteca Palatina Cod. Parm. 3205 (de Rossi 655), f. 63b-68a, C.
2251. Parma - Biblioteca Palatina Cod. Parm. 3507 (Perreau 27), f. 59b-60b, C.
2252. Verona - Seminario Maggiore 34, f. 189b, M, very short.
2253. Warszaw - Uniwersytet, Inst. Orientalistyczny 258, f. 206a-208a, C, commentator: Eliezer b. Natan.

Ashkenaz, commentary by Abraham b. Azriel[51]

2254. Vatican - Biblioteca Apostolica ebr. 301,1, f. 153a-154a, C, rubric: עומר דר' מאיר שליח ציבור.

Romania

2255. Vatican - Biblioteca Apostolica ebr. 285/30, f. 228b-231a, C, very short.

Tsarfat

2256. Jerusalem - Schocken Institute 19623, f. 87a-88b, M, commentator: Yehuda b. Eliezer Zvi.
2257. London - British Library Or. 2735 (Margoliouth 663), f. 80a-82b, M.
2258. Moscow - Russian State Library, Ms. Guenzburg 1665, f. 66b-67a, M.
2259. Oxford - Bodleian Library MS Laud. Or. 271 (Neubauer 1206), f. 69b-71a, C, commentator: Aaron b. Hayyim haKohen (compiler).
2260. Parma - Biblioteca Palatina Cod. Parm. 1902, f. 105a-107a, M.
2261. Parma - Biblioteca Palatina Cod. Parm. 3136 (de Rossi 405), f. 88b, M.

---

[51] Edited by Urbach, ערוגת הבושם, vol. III, p. 385-389.

אור ישע מאושרים (א 1962), שלמה הבבלי, יוצר ליום א' של פסח

Ashkenaz

2262. Berlin - Staatsbibliothek (Preussischer Kulturbesitz) Or. Qu. 798-799 (Steinschneider 177), II, f. 55b-58a, M.
2263. Braunschweig - Landesmuseum fuer Geschichte und Volkstum R 2386, vol. I, f. 16b-18a, M.
2264. Budapest - Magyar tudomanyos akademia, MS. Kaufmann A 384, f. 120a-123b, M.
2265. Budapest - Magyar tudomanyos akademia, MS. Kaufmann A 400, p. 80-87, C.
2266. Cambridge - University Library Add. 394,1 (Reif SCR 461), f. 45b-49a, C, rubric: יוצרות של פסח.
2267. Erlangen - Universitaetsbibliothek 2601 (Roth 67), f. 63b-64b, M.
2268. Hamburg - Staats- und Universitaetsbibliothek Cod. hebr. 17/2 (Steinschneider 152), f. 48b-51b, C, rubric: קבלה שר' שלמ' הבבלי פייט אור ישע שנה אחת ופיללו ביום ראשון ורבי' משלם היה תלמידו ואם' לו אני רוצה עד למחר לפייט כזה וכן עשה ושיבחו אור ישע מלאכת שנה ביותר מפי מורי אבי הרב' זצולה"ה.
2269. Hamburg - Staats- und Universitaetsbibliothek Cod. hebr. 225, f. 59b-60a, G.
2270. Jerusalem - Schocken Institute 24100 / Mahzor Nuremberg, f. 78a-80a (leaf 80 missing, leaf 78 separate, owned by Schocken), M.
2271. London - British Library Add. 18695 (Margoliouth 683), f. 19a-21b, T, Yiddish, rubric: יוצר צו דעם ערשטן טג בון פסח.
2272. Muenchen - Bayerische Staatsbibliothek, Cod. hebr. 88, f. 58a-58b, G.
2273. Muenchen - Bayerische Staatsbibliothek, Cod. hebr. 393, f. 112b-119a, C.
2274. New York - Jewish Theological Seminary Ms. 4466, f. 46a-50b, M.
2275. Oxford - Bodleian Library MS Opp. 170 (Neubauer 1205), f. 43b-52a, C, rubric: יוצר ליום ראשון של פסח מרבינו שלמה הבבלי.
2276. Paris - Bibliotheque Nationale heb. 709, f. 62b-67b, C, rubric: בעזרת משפיל ומרים אתחיל אור ישע מאושרים.
2277. Parma - Biblioteca Palatina Cod. Parm. 1002 (Ta 24), f. 86b-88b, M.
2278. Parma - Biblioteca Palatina Cod. Parm. 3205 (de Rossi 655), f. 69a-75b, C.
2279. Parma - Biblioteca Palatina Cod. Parm. 3507 (Perreau 27), f. 39a-44b, C, rubric: יוצר לפסח.
2280. Zurich - Zentralbibliothek Heid. 139, f. 18a-23a, C, additional marginal notes.

Italia

2281. Parma - Biblioteca Palatin Cod. Parm. 2248 (de Rossi 149/2), f. 23a-30b, C, rubric: ביאור יוצר אור מיושרים.

Roma
2282. Jerusalem - Jewish National and University Library Ms Heb 8° 4153, f. 157b-165a, C, commentator: Daniel ben Salomo haRofe (compiler), rubric: פי' יוצר ליום רשון של פסח.
2283. New York - Jewish Theological Seminary Ms. 1639, f. 27a-39b, C, commentator: Salomo b. Samuel Rofe, rubric: ביאור יוצר אור ישע מאושרים.
2284. Oxford - Bodleian Library MS Mich. 312,1 (Neubauer 2276,1), f. 23b-29a, C, rubric: פי' יוצר ליום רשון של פסח.
2285. Parma - Biblioteca Palatina Cod. Parm. 3141 (de Rossi 767), f. 108b-112a, M, rubric: פרוש אור ישע מאושרים.

Tsarfat
2286. London - British Library Add. 11639 (Margoliouth 1056), f. 285b-287b, M.
2287. Moscow - Russian State Library, Ms. Guenzburg 1665, f. 53a-55a, M.
2288. Oxford - Bodleian Library MS Laud. Or. 271 (Neubauer 1206), f. 52b-56a, C, commentator: Aaron b. Hayyim haKohen (compiler), rubric: אתחיל יוצר דפסח.
2289. Paris - Bibliotheque Nationale heb. 635, f. 18b-23a, M.
2290. Parma - Biblioteca Palatina Cod. Parm. 3136 (de Rossi 405), f. 76b-78b, M.
2291. Vatican - Biblioteca Apostolica ebr. 306, f. 127b-133b, C.

אור ישראל וקדושו בפארן הופיע (א 1965), יוסף ב"ר שמואל טוב עלם, זולת

Ashkenaz
2292. Jerusalem - Schocken Institute 24100 / Mahzor Nuremberg, f. 186a, M, short.
2293. Muenchen - Bayerische Staatsbibliothek, Cod. hebr. 69, f. 57b, M.
2294. Oxford - Bodleian Library MS Can. Or. 70 (Neubauer 1147,7), f. 85a-85b, M, rubric: אחרת.

Ashkenaz, commentary by Abraham b. Azriel[52]
2295. Vatican - Biblioteca Apostolica ebr. 301,1, f. 23a, C, rubric: זולת.

Tsarfat
2296. London - David Sofer 5, f. 67a-67b, C, rubric: זולת, short.
2297. Parma - Biblioteca Palatina Cod. Parm. 3136 (de Rossi 405), f. 168a-168b, M.

אור מסות אור בראו, יצחק הלוי בן זרחיה גירונדי, חלק ב' קדושתא לשבת החדש

Sepharad, commentary by Josef Garad
2298. Oxford - Bodleian Library Heb.e.10 (Neubauer 2746/1), f. 21a, C, rubric: יה אור, no incipit.

---

[52] Edited by Urbach, ערוגת הבושם, vol. I, p. 144-146.

אור נוגה עטית מעילו (א 1977), יוחנן הכהן, חלק ו׳, קדושתא למוסף יום כפור
Ashkenaz
2299. Cambridge - University Library Add. 394,1 (Reif SCR 461), f. 70b-71a, C.
2300. Moscow - Russian State Library, Ms. Guenzburg 191, f. 120b-121a, M.
Romania
2301. Vatican - Biblioteca Apostolica ebr. 320, f. 324a, M, very short.
Tsarfat
2302. London - British Library Or. 8682, f. 85a, Gl.
2303. London - David Sofer 5, f. 152a, C.
2304. Parma - Biblioteca Palatina Cod. Parm. 1794 (de Rossi 1061), f. 174a-174b, M.
2305. Parma - Biblioteca Palatina Cod. Parm. 3006 (de Rossi 654,1), f. 183a, M.

אור נכון מוצאו ולבי לכבוד נוראו (א 1979), שמואל בן יהודה, יוצר לסוכות
Tsarfat
2306. Moscow - Russian State Library, Ms. Guenzburg 1665, f. 172a-172b, M.

אור עולם אוצר חיים (א 1981), יוסי בן יוסי, חלק מיוצר לשחרית ראש השנה
Ashkenaz
2307. Jerusalem - Schocken Institute 15791/7, f. 56b, C.
Carpentras, commentary by Josef b. Abraham of Montelitz
2308. Cincinnati - Hebrew Union College 357, f. 42b, M, rubric: פירוש.
2309. New York - Jewish Theological Seminary Ms. 4746, f. 8a, M.
2310. Paris - Alliance Israelite Universelle H 422 A, f. 15b, M.

אור עולם קראו אחריו תלכו למוראו (א 1982), אליעזר ב״ר נתן, יוצר לשבת שובה
Ashkenaz
2311. Berlin - Staatsbibliothek (Preussischer Kulturbesitz) Or. Qu. 798-799 (Steinschneider 177), I, f. 53a-54(i)a, M.
2312. Braunschweig - Landesmuseum fuer Geschichte und Volkstum R 2386, vol. II, f. 123b-124a, M.
2313. Budapest - Magyar tudomanyos akademia, MS. Kaufmann A 399, p. 448-449, C, rubric: לאים טובה שנה עלינו יחדש דשובה לשבת יוצר א׳בן מרבי הבינה.
2314. Cambridge - University Library Add. 504,1, f. 55a-56b, C, rubric: יוצר בא כסא לעשור מר׳ אליעזר בר׳ נתן וחקוק באופן
2315. Frankfurt a M - Stadt- und Universitaetsbibliothek Oct. 227, f. 165a-166a, M.
2316. Lund - Universitetsbibliothek Ms. L.O. 2, f. 117a-117b, M.

2317. Modena - Archivio della Curia Arcivescovile di Modena 58, FM, incomplete.
2318. Muenchen - Bayerische Staatsbibliothek, Cod. hebr. 393, f. 171b-173b, C, rubric: יוצר שבת תשובה.
2319. Oxford - Bodleian Library MS Can. Or. 82 (Neubauer 1148), f. 38a-39a, M.
2320. Oxford - Bodleian Library MS Mich. 365 (Neubauer 1208), f. 8a-9a, C.
2321. Parma - Biblioteca Palatina Cod. Parm. 2895, p. 409-411, M, margins cut, text damaged
2322. Parma - Biblioteca Palatina Cod. Parm. 3205 (de Rossi 655), f. 165b-167a, C, rubric: יוצר לשבת שובה.

אור תורה הבהיקה (א 1993), קלונימוס ב"ר יהודה, יוצר לברית מילה
Ashkenaz

2323. Berlin - Staatsbibliothek (Preussischer Kulturbesitz) Or. Qu. 798-799 (Steinschneider 177), I, f. 259b-260a, M.
2324. Parma - Biblioteca Palatina Cod. Parm. 3205 (de Rossi 655), f. 177a-178a, C, rubric: לברית מילה.

אורות מאופל הזריח מהודו (א 2004), מאיר בן ברוך, יוצר להפסקה שנית
Ashkenaz

2325. Frankfurt a M - Stadt- und Universitaetsbibliothek Oct. 227, f. 155a-158b, M.
2326. Parma - Biblioteca Palatina Cod. Parm. 2895, p. 395-400, 402, M, margins cut, text damaged.

אורח חיים (א 2010), שמעון ב"ר יצחק, קדושתא ליום ב' של שבועות
Ashkenaz

2327. Berlin - Staatsbibliothek (Preussischer Kulturbesitz) Or. Qu. 798-799 (Steinschneider 177), II, f. 115a-115b, M.
2328. Braunschweig - Landesmuseum fuer Geschichte und Volkstum R 2386, vol. I, f. 73a, M.
2329. Budapest - Magyar tudomanyos akademia, MS. Kaufmann A 400, p. 154-155, C.
2330. Erlangen - Universitaetsbibliothek 2601 (Roth 67), f. 148b, M.
2331. Hamburg - Staats- und Universitaetsbibliothek Cod. hebr. 17/2 (Steinschneider 152), f. 82a, C.
2332. Jerusalem - Schocken Institute 24100 / Mahzor Nuremberg, f. 146b-147a, M.[53]

---

[53] Edited by J. Adler, פירוש מחזור נירנברג לקרובה "אורח חיים מוסר תוכחת" לחג השבועות לרבי שמעון בן יצחק, Sinai, 83, 1978, p. 237-258.

2333. London - British Library Add. 18695 (Margoliouth 683), f. 65a-65b, T, Yiddish, rubric: קרובץ.
2334. London - British Library Add. 22431 (Margoliouth 662a), f. 7b-8a, M.
2335. Moscow - Russian State Library, Ms. Guenzburg 615, f. 28b-29b, C.
2336. Muenchen - Bayerische Staatsbibliothek, Cod. hebr. 88, f. 115b-116a, G.
2337. New York - Jewish Theological Seminary Ms. 4466, f. 125a-126a, M, rubric: קדושתא.
2338. Paris - Bibliotheque Nationale heb. 709, f. 120b-121a, C.
2339. Parma - Biblioteca Palatina Cod. Parm. 1002 (Ta 24), f. 177a, M.
2340. Parma - Biblioteca Palatina Cod. Parm. 3205 (de Rossi 655), f. 120a-120b, C, rubric: קדושתא.
2341. Parma - Biblioteca Palatina Cod. Parm. 3507 (Perreau 27), f. 96a-96b, C.
2342. Zurich - Zentralbibliothek Heid. 139, f. 50a, C, additional marginal notes.

Tsarfat

2343. London - David Sofer 5, f. 50b, C.
2344. Moscow - Russian State Library, Ms. Guenzburg 1665, f. 117a, M.
2345. Oxford - Bodleian Library MS Laud. Or. 271 (Neubauer 1206), f. 85b-86a, C, commentator: Aaron b. Hayyim haKohen (compiler), ecclectic.
2346. Parma - Biblioteca Palatina Cod. Parm. 3136 (de Rossi 405), f. 148a-149a, M.
2347. Vatican - Biblioteca Apostolica ebr. 306, f. 227a-227b, C, rubric: קרובא.

אורח צדקה ועלמות נהיית דבריך (א 2016), שלמה הבבלי, סליחה

Ashkenaz

2348. Berlin - Staatsbibliothek (Preussischer Kulturbesitz) Or. Qu. 1276, FC.
2349. Braunschweig - Landesmuseum fuer Geschichte und Volkstum R 2386, vol. II, f. 126b, M.
2350. Budapest - Magyar tudomanyos akademia, MS. Kaufmann A 400, p. 419-425, C, rubric: פירוש הסליחות. זאת יסד ר' שלמה הבבלי.
2351. Cambridge - University Library Dd. 2.30, f. 59a-60a, G.
2352. Forli - Archivio di Stato 4, FC.
2353. Hamburg - Staats- und Universitaetsbibliothek Cod. hebr. 17/2 (Steinschneider 152), f. 126b-128a, C, rubric: פירוש הסליחות. זאת יסד ר' שלמה הבבלי.
2354. Jerusalem - Schocken Institute 24100 / Mahzor Nuremberg, f. 274b-275b, M.

2355. Jerusalem - Schocken Institute 24100 / Mahzor Nuremberg, f. 434a-434b, M.
2356. Moscow - Russian State Library, Ms. Guenzburg 190, f. 23b-24b, G.
2357. Moscow - Russian State Library, Ms. Guenzburg 615, f. 142b-146b, C, rubric: אחרת. אל מלך.
2358. Muenchen - Bayerische Staatsbibliothek, Cod. hebr. 21, f. 242a-243b, M.
2359. Muenchen - Bayerische Staatsbibliothek, Cod. hebr. 346, f. 140a-140b, C, rubric: אחרת.
2360. Oxford - Bodleian Library MS Mich. 543 (Neubauer 1212), f. 52b-55b, C, commentator: Isaac b. Jacob (compiler).
2361. Oxford - Bodleian Library MS Opp. 170 (Neubauer 1205), f. 206b-211b, C, rubric: ובעזרת בורא כל הרוחות . אתחיל לכתוב פיר' סליחות. חזק אמן ואמץ.
2362. Oxford - Bodleian Library MS Opp. 172 (Neubauer 1211), f. 76a-77a, C.
2363. Oxford - Bodleian Library MS Opp. 681 (Neubauer 1213), f. 60a-65b, C.
2364. Oxford - Bodleian Library MS Opp. 681 (Neubauer 1213), f. 65b-67a, C, rubric: פי' אחרת בקיצור.
2365. Padova - Biblioteca del Seminario Vescovile Cod. 218, f. 130a-131b, M.
2366. Parma - Biblioteca Palatina Cod. Parm. 3205 (de Rossi 655), f. 266a-167a, C.
2367. Vatican - Biblioteca Apostolica ebr. 422/1, f. 26b, C.
2368. Vatican - Biblioteca Apostolica ebr. 422/1, f. 40b, CG, no incipit.

Ashkenaz, commentary by Abraham b. Azriel[54]
2369. Vatican - Biblioteca Apostolica ebr. 301,1, f. 158a-159a, C, rubric: אחרת.

Tsarfat
2370. London - British Library Add. 11639 (Margoliouth 1056), f. 480b-482b, M.
2371. London - David Sofer 5, f. 85b-86b, C.
2372. Oxford - Bodleian Library MS Laud. Or. 271 (Neubauer 1206), f. 163b-164b, C, commentator: Aaron b. Hayyim haKohen (compiler), rubric: בעזרת אלהי הרוחות אחל פירוש סליחות.
2373. Oxford - Bodleian Library MS Opp. 171 (Neubauer 1207), f. 97b-99a, C, rubric: אחרת.
2374. Parma - Biblioteca Palatina Cod. Parm. 3007 (de Rossi 654,2), f. 34a-36a, M.
2375. Vatican - Biblioteca Apostolica ebr. 306, f. 95a-96a, C.

---

[54] Edited by Urbach, ערוגת הבושם, vol. III, p. 416-421.

אורחות אראלים יקדישו ברדתו בסיני (א 2017), אופן

Ashkenaz
2376. Berlin - Staatsbibliothek (Preussischer Kulturbesitz) Or. Qu. 798-799 (Steinschneider 177), II, f. 138b, M.
2377. London - British Library Add. 18695 (Margoliouth 683), f. 84a-84b, T, Yiddish, rubric: דש אישט דער אופן.

אורי וישעי אליך אזעק על גלות המר האריכות (א 2021), אורי ב״ר רפאל מענגבורגו, סליחה

Ashkenaz
2378. Oxford - Bodleian Library MS Opp. 677 (Neubauer 1167), f. 1a-4a, M.

אורי וישעי על הים נגלה (א 2026), מנחם ב״ר יעקב, מעריב ליום ז׳ של פסח

Ashkenaz
2379. Berlin - Staatsbibliothek (Preussischer Kulturbesitz) Or. Qu. 798-799 (Steinschneider 177), II, f. 86b-88a, M.
2380. Budapest - Magyar tudomanyos akademia, MS. Kaufmann A 399, p. 217; 218-219, C, short.
2381. London - British Library Add. 18695 (Margoliouth 683), f. 45a, 46b, T, Yiddish.
2382. Lund - Universitetsbibliothek Ms. L.O. 2, f. 65a-66b, M.
2383. New York - Jewish Theological Seminary Ms. 4466, f. 201a-203a, M.
2384. Parma - Biblioteca Palatina Cod. Parm. 2895, p. 320-321, M, short.

אורך ואמתך שלח (א 2035), שמעון ב״ר יצחק, סליחה

Ashkenaz
2385. Braunschweig - Landesmuseum fuer Geschichte und Volkstum R 2386, vol. II, f. 66a, M.
2386. London - British Library Add. 18695 (Margoliouth 683), f. 162b-163a, T, Yiddish.
2387. New York - Jewish Theological Seminary Ms. 8097, f. 82b, C.
2388. Oxford - Bodleian Library MS Mich. 543 (Neubauer 1212), f. 19a, C, commentator: Isaac b. Jacob (compiler).
2389. Oxford - Bodleian Library MS Opp. 681 (Neubauer 1213), f. 68b-69a, C.
2390. Padova - Biblioteca del Seminario Vescovile Cod. 218, f. 99a-99b, M.
2391. Vatican - Biblioteca Apostolica ebr. 422/1, f. 27a, C, very short.
2392. Vatican - Biblioteca Apostolica ebr. 422/1, f. 40b, CG, no incipit.

Tsarfat
2393. Oxford - Bodleian Library MS Bodl. Or. 109 (Neubauer 1209), f. 80b-81b, C, commentator: Aaron b. Hayyim haKohen (compiler).

אורך תזריח לחשוכה (א 4806), הוספה לסדר עבודה "אמיץ כח"
Ashkenaz
2394. Berlin - Staatsbibliothek (Preussischer Kulturbesitz) Or. Qu. 798-799 (Steinschneider 177), I, f. 138a-138b, M.
2395. Braunschweig - Landesmuseum fuer Geschichte und Volkstum R 2386, vol. II, f. 240b, M.
2396. London - Montefiore Library 261, f. 62b, C, commentator: Eliezer b. Natan?.
2397. Muenchen - Bayerische Staatsbibliothek, Cod. hebr. 346, f. 154a-154b, C.
2398. Oxford - Bodleian Library MS Opp. 172 (Neubauer 1211), f. 69b, C.
2399. Vatican - Biblioteca Apostolica ebr. 308, f. 129a, C, commentator: David b. Mose (compiler).

אות ברית ישראל ושבת והתורה (א 2046), אברהם בן יצחק הכהן, זולת לברית מילה
Ashkenaz, commentary by Abraham b. Azriel[55]
2400. Vatican - Biblioteca Apostolica ebr. 301,1, f. 126b, C, rubric: זולת.

אות ברית שלישתי למרפא לעולם (א 2047), אליעזר ב"ר נתן, זולת לברית מילה
Ashkenaz
2401. Berlin - Staatsbibliothek (Preussischer Kulturbesitz) Or. Qu. 798-799 (Steinschneider 177), I, f. 258b-259a, M.
2402. Cambridge - University Library Add. 504,1, f. 66a-67a, C, rubric: זולת.
2403. Muenchen - Bayerische Staatsbibliothek, Cod. hebr. 393,9, f. 191b-192b, C, rubric: זולת.
2404. Oxford - Bodleian Library MS Can. Or. 82 (Neubauer 1148), f. 70b-71a, M.

אות בריתות שלש עשרה (א 2048), אברהם בן יצחק הכהן, יוצר לברית מילה
Ashkenaz, commentary by Abraham b. Azriel[56]
2405. Vatican - Biblioteca Apostolica ebr. 301,1, f. 118a-126b, C, rubric: יוצר אחר.

אות ומופת קדשת להראות לשלוחיך (א 2050), יוסף ב"ר שמואל טוב עלם, יוצר לשבועות
Tsarfat
2406. London - David Sofer 5, f. 67a, C, rubric: זה פיר' מקרו' של יום שיני משבועות.

---

[55] Edited by Urbach, ערוגת הבושם, vol. III, p. 204-206.
[56] Edited by Urbach, ערוגת הבושם, vol. III, p. 148-203.

2407. Moscow - Russian State Library, Ms. Guenzburg 1665, f. 140a-140b, M.
2408. Parma - Biblioteca Palatina Cod. Parm. 3136 (de Rossi 405), f. 167b-168a, M.

אות זה החודש אצתה מכל לקדש (א 2051), אלעזר ברבי קילר, יוצר לשבת החדש
Ashkenaz
2409. Berlin - Staatsbibliothek (Preussischer Kulturbesitz) Or. Qu. 798-799 (Steinschneider 177), II, f. 38b, M.
2410. Budapest - Magyar tudomanyos akademia, MS. Kaufmann A 384, f. 85b-86a, M.
2411. Cambridge - University Library Add. 394,1 (Reif SCR 461), f. 43b, C, rubric: לפרשת החדש.
2412. Erlangen - Universitaetsbibliothek 2601 (Roth 67), f. 48b, M.
2413. Hamburg - Staats- und Universitaetsbibliothek Cod. hebr. 17/2 (Steinschneider 152), f. 27a-27b, C, rubric: פי' היוצר של פרשת החדש.
2414. Muenchen - Bayerische Staatsbibliothek, Cod. hebr. 88, f. 42b-43a, G.
2415. Muenchen - Bayerische Staatsbibliothek, Cod. hebr. 393, f. 103a-103b, C, rubric: יוצר וקרובץ לפרשת החדש, no incipit.
2416. New York - Jewish Theological Seminary Ms. 4466, f. 17b-18b, M.
2417. Parma - Biblioteca Palatina Cod. Parm. 1002 (Ta 24), f. 64a-64b, M.
2418. Parma - Biblioteca Palatina Cod. Parm 3000 (de Rossi 378), f. 18a, M.
2419. Parma - Biblioteca Palatina Cod. Parm. 3205 (de Rossi 655), f. 37a-37b, C.
2420. Parma - Biblioteca Palatina Cod. Parm. 3507 (Perreau 27), f. 29b, C.
2421. Vatican - Biblioteca Apostolica ebr. 305,1, f. 38a-38b, C, rubric: יוצר.
2422. Zurich - Zentralbibliothek Heid. 139, f. 8a-8b, C, rubric: לפרשת החדש, additional marginal notes.
Italia
2423. Parma - Biblioteca Palatin Cod. Parm. 2248 (de Rossi 149/2), f. 21a-21b, M, rubric: ביאור יוצר פרשת החדש.
Roma
2424. Jerusalem - Jewish National and University Library Ms Heb 8° 4153, f. 157a-157b, C, commentator: Daniel ben Salomo haRofe (compiler), rubric: פי' יוצר דהחדש, additional glosses.
2425. New York - Jewish Theological Seminary Ms. 1639, f. 19b-20a, C, rubric: ביאור יוצר פרשת החדש.
2426. Oxford - Bodleian Library MS Mich. 312,1 (Neubauer 2276,1), f. 22b-23a, C, rubric: פי' יוצר דפרשת החדש.
2427. Parma - Biblioteca Palatina Cod. Parm. 2577 (de Rossi 310), f. 136a-136b, G.

Tsarfat

2428. Moscow - Russian State Library, Ms. Guenzburg 1665, f. 37b-38a, M.
2429. Parma - Biblioteca Palatina Cod. Parm. 3136 (de Rossi 405), f. 52b, M.
2430. Vatican - Biblioteca Apostolica ebr. 306, f. 151b, C.

אות לי חד טלייא

Ashkenaz, commentary by Benjamin b. Abraham Anaw

2431. Jerusalem - Musad haRav Kook 478, p. 52-55, C, rubric: אלפא ביתא י.
2432. London - Beth Din & Beth Hamidrash 6,9, f. 180a-181b, C, rubric: אלפא ביט.

אות מבראשית הוכתרה (א 2053), מאיר הכהן, ברכת המזון לשבת נישווין

Ashkenaz

2433. Parma - Biblioteca Palatina Cod. Parm. 3205 (de Rossi 655), f. 172b-173a, C.

אותה נפשי אל מקום נעשה (א 2058), משה אבן עזרא

Carpentras

2434. Cincinnati - Hebrew Union College 392, f. 13b-14a, M.

Carpentras, commentary by Josef b. Abraham of Montelitz

2435. Cincinnati - Hebrew Union College 291, f. 7b-8b, C, rubric: פי' מסתגיאיב אותה נפשי וכו'.
2436. New York - Jewish Theological Seminary Ms. 4197, f. 27b-29a, M.
2437. Paris - Ecole Rabbinique 32, f. 32b-34a, M.
2438. Strasbourg - Bibliotheque Nationale et Universitaire 4081, f. 30a-31a, M.

אותו מבהלת חתום לו גחלת (א 2061), אלעזר ברבי קליר, קרובה לפורים, פיוט הרכבה

Ashkenaz

2439. Berlin - Staatsbibliothek (Preussischer Kulturbesitz) Or. Qu. 798-799 (Steinschneider 177), II, f. 28a-28b, M.
2440. Budapest - Magyar tudomanyos akademia, MS. Kaufmann A 384, f. 67b-68a, M.
2441. Budapest - Magyar tudomanyos akademia, MS. Kaufmann A 400, p. 68-70, C.
2442. Hamburg - Staats- und Universitaetsbibliothek Cod. hebr. 17/2 (Steinschneider 152), f. 23a-23b, C.
2443. Jerusalem - Schocken Institute 24100 / Mahzor Nuremberg, f. 50a, M.
2444. Muenchen - Bayerische Staatsbibliothek, Cod. hebr. 88, f. 34b-35a, G.
2445. Muenchen - Bayerische Staatsbibliothek, Cod. hebr. 393, f. 97a-98a, C, no incipit.

2446. New York - Jewish Theological Seminary Ms. 4466, f. 1b, M, only end.
2447. Oxford - Bodleian Library MS Opp. 170 (Neubauer 1205), f. 23a-24a, C.
2448. Paris - Bibliotheque Nationale heb. 709, f. 30a-30b, C.
2449. Parma - Biblioteca Palatina Cod. Parm. 1002 (Ta 24), f. 47b, M.
2450. Parma - Biblioteca Palatina Cod. Parm. 3205 (de Rossi 655), f. 30a-30b, C.
2451. Parma - Biblioteca Palatina Cod. Parm. 3507 (Perreau 27), f. 23b-24a, C.
2452. Vatican - Biblioteca Apostolica ebr. 305,1, f. 34a-35a, C.
2453. Zurich - Zentralbibliothek Heid. 139, f. 1a-2a, C, additional marginal notes.

Tsarfat
2454. London - British Library Add. 11639 (Margoliouth 1056), f. 273b-274a, M, no incipit.
2455. Moscow - Russian State Library, Ms. Guenzburg 1665, f. 23a-23b, M.
2456. Oxford - Bodleian Library MS Laud. Or. 271 (Neubauer 1206), f. 34b-35b, C, commentator: Aaron b. Hayyim haKohen (compiler).
2457. Oxford - Bodleian Library MS Opp. 171 (Neubauer 1207), f. 30a-31a, C, postscript: עד כאן יסד ר' אלעזר דברי גזית ושבח מפואר אספרה אל חוק, אמל ורבך, יסוד אחרים הוא אצלו.
2458. Parma - Biblioteca Palatina Cod. Parm. 3136 (de Rossi 405), f. 36b-37a, M, no incipit.

אותות אלהינו מעולם נודעו (א 2064), אהרן בן יוסף הרופא, פרשת מסעי
Karaite, commentary by Berakha b. Josef haKohen
2459. New York - Jewish Theological Seminary Ms. 3367, f. 136b-139a, C, rubric: פרוש פרשת מסעי.
2460. St. Petersburg - Inst. of Oriental Studies of the Russian Academy B 431, f. 92b-94a, C, rubric: פרשת מסעי.
2461. St. Petersburg - Inst. of Oriental Studies of the Russian Academy B 483, f. 10b-11a, C, rubric: פרשת מסעי.
2462. St. Petersburg - Russian National Library, Evr. IV 50, f. 107a, C, rubric: מסעי.

אותות באר המים אות היא לאזרחיים, סליחה
Ashkenaz
2463. Parma - Biblioteca Palatina Cod. Parm. 2895, p. 360-362, M, margins cut, text damaged.

אותותיך אז ראינו (א 2075), שמעון ב"ר יצחק, קדושתא לשבת וחול המועד של פסח

Ashkenaz

2464. Berlin - Staatsbibliothek (Preussischer Kulturbesitz) Or. Qu. 798-799 (Steinschneider 177), II, f. 101b, M.
2465. Braunschweig - Landesmuseum fuer Geschichte und Volkstum R 2386, vol. I, f. 49b-50a, M.
2466. Budapest - Magyar tudomanyos akademia, MS. Kaufmann A 384, f. 233a-233b, M, rubric: קדושתא.
2467. Hamburg - Staats- und Universitaetsbibliothek Cod. hebr. 17/2 (Steinschneider 152), f. 38a, C, rubric: קדושתא.
2468. Jerusalem - Schocken Institute 24100 / Mahzor Nuremberg, f. 109a, M, very short.
2469. London - British Library Add. 18695 (Margoliouth 683), f. 54a, T, Yiddish, rubric: מעריב צו שביעי בון פסח.
2470. Muenchen - Bayerische Staatsbibliothek, Cod. hebr. 88, f. 94b, G.
2471. New York - Jewish Theological Seminary Ms. 4466, f. 88a-88b, M.
2472. Paris - Bibliotheque Nationale heb. 709, f. 107b-108a, C, rubric: קדושתא.
2473. Parma - Biblioteca Palatina Cod. Parm. 1002 (Ta 24), f. 157a, M.
2474. Parma - Biblioteca Palatina Cod. Parm. 3205 (de Rossi 655), f. 114a, C, very short.
2475. Parma - Biblioteca Palatina Cod. Parm. 3507 (Perreau 27), f. 78a-78b, C, rubric: קדושתא.
2476. Zurich - Zentralbibliothek Heid. 139, f. 42a, C.

Tsarfat

2477. London - David Sofer 5, f. 45b, C.
2478. Moscow - Russian State Library, Ms. Guenzburg 1665, f. 104b-105a, M.
2479. Oxford - Bodleian Library MS Laud. Or. 271 (Neubauer 1206), f. 76a-76b, C, commentator: Ephraim b. Jacob of Bonn (mainly), Aaron b. Hayyim haKohen (compiler).
2480. Parma - Biblioteca Palatina Cod. Parm. 3136 (de Rossi 405), f. 123a-123b, M.

אותך אדרוש ואליך אתודע (א 2082), שמעון ב"ר יצחק, סליחה

Ashkenaz

2481. Berlin - Staatsbibliothek (Preussischer Kulturbesitz) Or. Qu. 798-799 (Steinschneider 177), I, f. 61a-62b, M, rubric: חטאנו דר' שמעון ליום כיפור.
2482. Braunschweig - Landesmuseum fuer Geschichte und Volkstum R 2386, vol. II, f. 162a-163b, M.
2483. Budapest - Magyar tudomanyos akademia, MS. Kaufmann A 400, p. 508-510, C, rubric: חטאנו ליום כפור.

2484. Forli - Archivio di Stato 4, FC, rubric: לצום כיפור יאומרו זה.
2485. Hamburg - Staats- und Universitaetsbibliothek Cod. hebr. 17/2 (Steinschneider 152), f. 178a-178b, C, rubric: חטאנו ליום הכיפורים.
2486. Jerusalem - Jewish National and University Library Ms Heb 8° 3037, f. 97a-99b, M.
2487. Jerusalem - Schocken Institute 24100 / Mahzor Nuremberg, f. 358(ii)b-359b, M.
2488. London - British Library Or. 11318/1, f. 65a-67a, C.
2489. Moscow - Russian State Library, Ms. Guenzburg 190, f. 118b-119b, G.
2490. Moscow - Russian State Library, Ms. Guenzburg 615, f. 91a-92a, C, rubric: חטאנו צורינו.
2491. Muenchen - Bayerische Staatsbibliothek, Cod. hebr. 346, f. 71a-73a, C.
2492. Muenchen - Bayerische Staatsbibliothek, Cod. hebr. 393, f. 137b-138b, C, no incipit
2493. New York - Jewish Theological Seminary Ms. 4466, f. 288b-290b, M.
2494. New York - Jewish Theological Seminary Ms. 8097, f. 70a-70b, C.
2495. Oxford - Bodleian Library MS Mich. 365 (Neubauer 1208), f. 66a-66b, C.
2496. Oxford - Bodleian Library MS Opp. 170 (Neubauer 1205), f. 164a-164(ii)b, C, rubric: חטאנו צורינו.
2497. Oxford - Bodleian Library MS Opp. 172 (Neubauer 1211), f. 32a-33a, C.
2498. Oxford - Bodleian Library MS Opp. 619 (Neubauer 2374), f. 112a-114b, M.
2499. Oxford - Bodleian Library MS Opp. 681 (Neubauer 1213), f. 92a-93a, C.
2500. Paris - Bibliotheque Nationale heb. 653, f. 46b, G.
2501. Parma - Biblioteca Palatina Cod. Parm. 3205 (de Rossi 655), f. 275b-276a, C.
2502. Parma - Biblioteca Palatina Cod. Parm. 3270 (de Rossi 1215), f. 87b-89b, M.
2503. Parma - Biblioteca Palatina Cod. Parm. 3271 (de Rossi 1216), f. 14a-15b, G.
2504. Parma - Biblioteca Palatina Cod. Parm. 3507 (Perreau 27), f. 145a-146a, C.
2505. Vatican - Biblioteca Apostolica ebr. 308, f. 93a-94a, C, commentator: David b. Mose (compiler).
2506. Vatican - Biblioteca Apostolica ebr. 422/1, f. 33a, C.
2507. Wolfenbuettel - Niedersaechsisches Staatsarchiv VII B Hs. 192, FC.
2508. Zurich - Zentralbibliothek Heid. 139, f. 74a, C, additional marginal notes.

Asti, Fossano, Moncalvo
2509. New Haven - Yale University, Beinecke Rare Book and MS Library, MS Heb. 52, f. 91b-92a, M.

Tsarfat
2510. London - British Library Add. 11639 (Margoliouth 1056), f. 491a-492b, M, rubric: חטאנו צורינו.
2511. London - David Sofer 5, f. 135a-135b, C, rubric: חטאנו.
2512. Oxford - Bodleian Library MS Bodl. Or. 109 (Neubauer 1209), f. 12a-12b, C, commentator: Aaron b. Hayyim haKohen (compiler).
2513. Oxford - Bodleian Library MS Laud. Or. 271 (Neubauer 1206), f. 175b, C, commentator: Aaron b. Hayyim haKohen (compiler), rubric: לצום כיפור.
2514. Oxford - Bodleian Library MS Opp. 171 (Neubauer 1207), f. 106a-106b, C, rubric: אחרת ליום כיפור דר' שמעון הגדול.
2515. Parma - Biblioteca Palatina Cod. Parm. 1794 (de Rossi 1061), f. 14a-16a, M.
2516. Parma - Biblioteca Palatina Cod. Parm. 3006 (de Rossi 654,1), f. 166b-167b, M.
2517. Vatican - Biblioteca Apostolica ebr. 306, f. 196a-197b, C.

אותך כל היום קוינו (א 2084), אפרים ב"ר יצחק מרגנסבורג, זולת

Ashkenaz
2518. Oxford - Bodleian Library MS Can. Or. 82 (Neubauer 1148), f. 45a-45b, M.

אז אמרתי הנה באתי (א 2087), אפרים ב"ר יעקב מבון, קינה

Ashkenaz
2519. New York - Jewish Theological Seminary Ms. 8169 (Acc. 0016), f. 37b-38a, M.
2520. Torino - Archivio Terracini 1492, f. 21b, M.
2521. London - British Library Or. 8682, f. 45a-45b, G.

אז אמרתי הנה באתי לחלותך, אלעזר ברבי קליר?, מוסף ר"ה

Tsarfat
2522. London - British Library Or. 8682, f. 19b-20a, GI.

אז בבית שביינו צר לא הניח לנו (א 2091), קינה

Yemen
2523. Ramat Gan - Universitat Bar Ilan 62, f. 21b-22a, G.

Yemen, commentary by Isaac b. Abraham Wanneh
2524. Jerusalem - Makhon b. Zvi 1168 (Tubi 157), f. 18b, M, margins damaged.
2525. Jerusalem - Sassoon 1158, p. 179-180, M.

2526. London - British Library Or. 11122, f. 106b-107a, M.

אז בהלוך ירימיה על קברי אבות (א 2098), אלעזר ברבי קליר, קינה

Ashkenaz

2527. Berlin - Staatsbibliothek (Preussischer Kulturbesitz) Or. Qu. 798-799 (Steinschneider 177), II, f. 197b-198a, M.
2528. Budapest - Magyar tudomanyos akademia, MS. Kaufmann A 400, p. 185, C, rubric: אחרת, short.

אז בהר המור דץ יונת אלם (א 2101), שלמה אבן גבירול, מחיה, באשכנז: סליחה

Ashkenaz

2529. Braunschweig - Landesmuseum fuer Geschichte und Volkstum R 2386, vol. II, f. 145a, M.
2530. Muenchen - Bayerische Staatsbibliothek, Cod. hebr. 346, f. 148b-149a, C, rubric: אחרת.
2531. Muenchen - Bayerische Staatsbibliothek, Cod. hebr. 346, f. 164b, C, short.
2532. Oxford - Bodleian Library MS Mich. 543 (Neubauer 1212), f. 41b-42b, C, commentator: Isaac b. Jacob (compiler), rubric: עקיד'.
2533. Oxford - Bodleian Library MS Opp. 681 (Neubauer 1213), f. 69a-69b, C, rubric: עקידות.
2534. Padova - Biblioteca del Seminario Vescovile Cod. 218, f. 121b-122b, M, rubric: עקיד'.
2535. Vatican - Biblioteca Apostolica ebr. 422/1, f. 26a, C, very short.
2536. Vatican - Biblioteca Apostolica ebr. 422/2, f. 39b, CG, no incipit.

Ashkenaz, commentary by Abraham b. Azriel[57]

2537. Vatican - Biblioteca Apostolica ebr. 301,1, f. 144b-145a, C, rubric: אחרת.

Sepharad, commentary by David b. Josef Abudarham[58]

2538. Budapest - Magyar tudomanyos akademia, MS. Kaufmann A 405/2, p. 191-192, C, rubric: מחיה לר' שלמה ן' גבירול ז"ל.
2539. Cincinnati - Hebrew Union College 490, f. 4b-5a, C.
2540. Holon - Yehuda Nahum 278, f. 1b, FC, rubric: מחיה, incomplete
2541. Holon - Yehuda Nahum 278, f. 13a-13b, FC, rubric: מחיה, incomplete.
2542. New York - Columbia X893 Ab 93, f. 6b-7a, C, rubric: מחיה לר' שלמה גבירול ז"ל.
2543. New York - Jewish Theological Seminary Ms. 3011, f. 5b-6a, C, rubric: מחיה.

---

[57] Edited by Urbach, ערוגת הבושם, vol. III, p. 325-328.
[58] Edited by Prins, תשלום אבודרהם, p. 20-22.

Tsarfat

2544. Oxford - Bodleian Library MS Bodl. Or. 109 (Neubauer 1209), f. 50a-51a, C, commentator: Aaron b. Hayyim haKohen (compiler).

אז בהר המור קרא אל לעניו (א 2102), אהרן בן יוסף הרופא, פרשת כי תשא

Karaite, commentary by Berakha b. Josef haKohen

2545. New York - Jewish Theological Seminary Ms. 3367, f. 85b-88b, C, rubric: פרוש פרשת כי תשא.
2546. St. Petersburg - Inst. of Oriental Studies of the Russian Academy B 483, f. 1a-4a, C, rubric: פרשת כי תשא.
2547. St. Petersburg - Inst. of Oriental Studies of the Russian Academy B 431, f. 61a-62b, C, rubric: פרשת כי תשא.
2548. St. Petersburg - Russian National Library, Evr. IV 50, f. 63a-65a, C, rubric: כי תשא.

אז בחטאינו חרב מקדש (א 2104), קינה

Ashkenaz

2549. Berlin - Staatsbibliothek (Preussischer Kulturbesitz) Or. Qu. 798-799 (Steinschneider 177), II, f. 180b-181a, M.
2550. Budapest - Magyar tudomanyos akademia, MS. Kaufmann A 400, p. 192-193, C, rubric: עד אנא בכיה בציון.
2551. Hamburg - Staats- und Universitaetsbibliothek Cod. hebr. 17/2 (Steinschneider 152), f. 91b, C, rubric: עד אנא בכיה בציון.
2552. Hamburg - Staats- und Universitaetsbibliothek Cod. hebr. 233, f. 67a-68a, G.
2553. Jerusalem - Schocken Institute 24100 / Mahzor Nuremberg, f. 193b, M, incipit עד.
2554. Jerusalem - Schocken Institute 24100 / Mahzor Nuremberg, f. 219a-219b, M, incipit עד.
2555. Oxford - Bodleian Library MS Can. Or. 70 (Neubauer 1147,8), f. 106b-107b, M, incipit עד אנא בכייה.
2556. Parma - Biblioteca Palatina Cod. Parm. 2886 (de Rossi 585), f. 109b-110b, M, later hand, margins cut.
2557. Parma - Biblioteca Palatina Cod. Parm. 3205 (de Rossi 655), f. 189b-190a, C.
2558. Vatican - Biblioteca Apostolica ebr. 318, f. 219a-219b, GI.

Ashkenaz, commentary by Abraham b. Azriel[59]

2559. Vatican - Biblioteca Apostolica ebr. 301,1, f. 137b, C, rubric: אחרת, incipit עד.

---

[59] Edited by Urbach, ערוגת הבושם, vol. III, p. 283-284.

Carpentras, commentary by Mordekhai b. Josef of Rocco Martino
2560. Cincinnati - Hebrew Union College 246/1, f. 67a-67b, C, rubric: פי' אז בחטאינו.

Yemen, commentary by Isaac b. Abraham Wanneh
2561. Jerusalem - Sassoon 1158, p. 162-163, M.
2562. London - British Library Or. 11122, f. 98a-98b, M.

אז ביום השביעי נחת (א 2105), שיר היחוד לשבת

Ashkenaz
2563. Moscow - Russian State Library, Ms. Guenzburg 1401/2, f. 12a-12b, C.
2564. Moscow - Russian State Library, Ms. Guenzburg 1401/2, f. 12b-13a, C, rubric: פירוש אחר.

אז ביום כיפור סליחה הורית (א 2106), יוצר ליום כפור

Ashkenaz
2565. Berlin - Staatsbibliothek (Preussischer Kulturbesitz) Or. Qu. 798-799 (Steinschneider 177), I, f. 67b-68a, M.
2566. Braunschweig - Landesmuseum fuer Geschichte und Volkstum R 2386, vol. II, f. 179a-180b, M.
2567. Budapest - Magyar tudomanyos akademia, MS. Kaufmann A 400, p. 301-302, C.
2568. Cambridge - University Library Add. 394,1 (Reif SCR 461), f. 66b-67a, C, rubric: ליום כיפור.
2569. Cambridge - University Library Or. 785, f. 106a-107a, G, rubric: ליום כיפור.
2570. Hamburg - Staats- und Universitaetsbibliothek Cod. hebr. 17/2 (Steinschneider 152), f. 150a, C, rubric: למחרתו.
2571. Hamburg - Staats- und Universitaetsbibliothek Cod. hebr. 40c (Steinschneider 111), f. 174b-175a, G.
2572. Hamburg - Staats- und Universitaetsbibliothek Cod. hebr. 62 (Steinschneider 154), f. 1a-2a, C, rubric: יוצר ליום כפור.
2573. Hamburg - Staats- und Universitaetsbibliothek Cod. hebr. 132 (Steinschneider 155), f. 31b-32a, C.
2574. Jerusalem - Jewish National and University Library Ms Heb 8° 3037, f. 105b-106a, M, rubric: ליום צום כפור.
2575. Jerusalem - Schocken Institute 24100 / Mahzor Nuremberg, f. 372b, M.
2576. London - Montefiore Library 261, f. 40b-41a, C, commentator: Eliezer b. Natan?.
2577. Moscow - Russian State Library, Ms. Guenzburg 191, f. 80b-81a, M.
2578. Muenchen - Bayerische Staatsbibliothek, Cod. hebr. 86, f. 95b-96b, G.

2579. Muenchen - Bayerische Staatsbibliothek, Cod. hebr. 346, f. 49b, C.
2580. Muenchen - Bayerische Staatsbibliothek, Cod. hebr. 346 , f. 50a-51a, C, rubric: מפרישה אחרת.
2581. Muenchen - Bayerische Staatsbibliothek, Cod. hebr. 393 , f. 138b-139a, C.
2582. New York - Jewish Theological Seminary Ms. 4466, f. 299b-300b, M.
2583. New York - Jewish Theological Seminary Ms. 8097, f. 70b, C.
2584. New York - Jewish Theological Seminary Ms. 8169 (Acc. 0016), f. 62b-63a, M.
2585. Oxford - Bodleian Library MS Mich. 365 (Neubauer 1208), f. 66b-67b, C.
2586. Oxford - Bodleian Library MS Opp. 170 (Neubauer 1205), f. 164b, C.
2587. Oxford - Bodleian Library MS Opp. 172 (Neubauer 1211), f. 33b-34b, C.
2588. Oxford - Bodleian Library MS Opp. 619 (Neubauer 2374), f. 130a-130b, M.
2589. Paris - Bibliotheque Nationale heb. 653, f. 52a-52b, G.
2590. Parma - Biblioteca Palatina Cod. Parm. 3205 (de Rossi 655), f. 224a, C.
2591. Parma - Biblioteca Palatina Cod. Parm. 3271 (de Rossi 1216), f. 26b-27a, G.
2592. Parma - Biblioteca Palatina Cod. Parm. 3507 (Perreau 27), f. 143a-144a, C.
2593. Vatican - Biblioteca Apostolica ebr. 308, f. 96a-96b, C, commentator: David b. Mose (compiler), rubric: אתחיל לכתו' פי' ליום צומא רבה.
2594. Vatican - Biblioteca Apostolica ebr. 422/1, f. 14b, C, short.
2595. Wolfenbuettel - Niedersaechsisches Staatsarchiv VII B Hs. 192, FC.
2596. Zurich - Zentralbibliothek Heid. 139 , f. 74a-75b, C, rubric: ליום כפור, additional marginal notes.

Roma

2597. Berlin - Staatsbibliothek (Preussischer Kulturbesitz) Or. Oct. 3567, f. 4a, FC, rubric: ליום צום כפור.
2598. Jerusalem - Jewish National and University Library Ms Heb 8° 4153, f. 138a-138b, C, commentator: Daniel ben Salomo haRofe (compiler).
2599. Oxford - Bodleian Library MS Mich. 312,1 (Neubauer 2276,1), f. 9b, C, rubric: פי' יוצר לצום כפור.

Romania

2600. Vatican - Biblioteca Apostolica ebr. 320, f. 269b-270b, M.

Tsarfat

2601. Bern - Burgerbibliothek A 409, f. 73b-744, G.
2602. London - British Library Add. 11639 (Margoliouth 1056), f. 721a-721b, M.
2603. London - David Sofer 5, f. 135b-136a, C, rubric: זה פירוש מקרובוץ של יום הכפורים.

2604. Oxford - Bodleian Library MS Bodl. Or. 109 (Neubauer 1209), f. 17a, C, commentator: Aaron b. Hayyim haKohen (compiler).
2605. Oxford - Bodleian Library MS Laud. Or. 271 (Neubauer 1206), f. 111a, C, commentator: Aaron b. Hayyim haKohen (compiler).
2606. Parma - Biblioteca Palatina Cod. Parm. 1794 (de Rossi 1061), f. 107b-109a, M.
2607. Parma - Biblioteca Palatina Cod. Parm. 2125 (de Rossi 812), f. 38a, C.
2608. Parma - Biblioteca Palatina Cod. Parm. 2890 (de Rossi 856), f. 17b, M.
2609. Parma - Biblioteca Palatina Cod. Parm. 3006 (de Rossi 654,1), f. 129b-130a, M.
2610. Vatican - Biblioteca Apostolica ebr. 306, f. 75a, C.

אז בכתב אשורית (א 2107), אלעזר ברבי קליר, חלק ה׳, קדושתא לשבועות
Ashkenaz

2611. Berlin - Staatsbibliothek (Preussischer Kulturbesitz) Or. Qu. 798-799 (Steinschneider 177), II, f. 140a-141a, M.
2612. Braunschweig - Landesmuseum fuer Geschichte und Volkstum R 2386, vol. I, 97a-97b, M.
2613. Budapest - Magyar tudomanyos akademia, MS. Kaufmann A 400, p. 178-179, C.
2614. Hamburg - Staats- und Universitaetsbibliothek Cod. hebr. 17/2 (Steinschneider 152), f. 86a, C.
2615. Hamburg - Staats- und Universitaetsbibliothek Cod. hebr. 225, f. 188b, G.
2616. Jerusalem - Schocken Institute 24100 / Mahzor Nuremberg, f. 172b, M.
2617. London - British Library Add. 18695 (Margoliouth 683), f. 86a-86b, T, Yiddish.
2618. London - British Library Add. 22431 (Margoliouth 662a), f. 56b-57a, M.
2619. Moscow - Russian State Library, Ms. Guenzburg 615, f. 41b-42b, C.
2620. New York - Jewish Theological Seminary Ms. 4466, f. 167b-168a, M.
2621. Oxford - Bodleian Library MS Opp. 170 (Neubauer 1205), f. 87a-87b, C.
2622. Paris - Bibliotheque Nationale heb. 709, f. 136a-136b, C.
2623. Parma - Biblioteca Palatina Cod. Parm. 1002 (Ta 24), f. 205a, M.
2624. Parma - Biblioteca Palatina Cod. Parm. 2886 (de Rossi 585), f. 64b-65b, M, later hand, margins cut.
2625. Parma - Biblioteca Palatina Cod. Parm. 3205 (de Rossi 655), f. 127b, C, no incipit.
2626. Parma - Biblioteca Palatina Cod. Parm. 3507 (Perreau 27), f. 89a-89b, C.

2627. Zurich - Zentralbibliothek Heid. 139, f. 54b-55a, C.

אז במלאת ספק יפה כתרצה (א 2108), אלעזר ברבי קליר, קינה
Ashkenaz
2628. Berlin - Staatsbibliothek (Preussischer Kulturbesitz) Or. Qu. 798-799 (Steinschneider 177), II, f. 203a, M.
2629. Budapest - Magyar tudomanyos akademia, MS. Kaufmann A 400, p. 185, C, rubric: אחרת, very short.
2630. Muenchen - Bayerische Staatsbibliothek, Cod. hebr. 88, f. 188a-189a, G, mainly variant readings.

אז בקשב ענו עלה אל הר העברים (א 2120), משה בן שמואל בן אבשלום, זולת שמחת תורה
Ashkenaz
2631. London - British Library Add. 18695 (Margoliouth 683), f. 136a-136b, T, Yiddish, rubric: זולת.
2632. London - Montefiore Library 261, f. 82a-82b, C, commentator: Eliezer b. Natan?.
2633. Parma - Biblioteca Palatina Cod. Parm. 2895, p. 425-427, M, margins cut, text damaged.
2634. Vatican - Biblioteca Apostolica ebr. 305,1, f. 52a, C, commentator: Isaac of Bohemia, rubric: זולת זה פירש הרב ר' יצחק מבהם.

אז דברת תמים דעים (א 2123), משה אבן עזרא, זולת ליום כפור
Carpentras
2635. Cincinnati - Hebrew Union College 392, f. 42a-43a, M, no incipit.
Carpentras, commentary by Josef b. Abraham of Montelitz
2636. Cincinnati - Hebrew Union College 291, f. 18a-19a, C, rubric: פי' אז דברת תמים רעים וכו'.
2637. New York - Jewish Theological Seminary Ms. 4197, f. 98a-99a, M, no incipit.
2638. Paris - Ecole Rabbinique 32, f. 120b-121b, M, no incipit.
2639. Strasbourg - Bibliotheque Nationale et Universitaire 4081, f. 97b-98b, M, no incipit.

אז היתה חנית סוכו (א 2125), אלעזר ברבי קליר, חלק ה', קדושתא ליום א' דסוכות
Ashkenaz
2640. Krakow - Biblioteka Jagiellonska Fr. 629, f. 1a-1b, FC.
2641. London - Montefiore Library 261, f. 67b-68a, C, commentator: Eliezer b. Natan?.
2642. Oxford - Bodleian Library MS Mich. 365 (Neubauer 1208), f. 97b-98b, C.

2643. Oxford - Bodleian Library MS Opp. 172 (Neubauer 1211), f. 90b, C, very short.
2644. Parma - Biblioteca Palatina Cod. Parm. 3507 (Perreau 27), f. 174b-175a, C, no incipit.
2645. Vatican - Biblioteca Apostolica ebr. 305,1, f. 39b, C, no incipit, very short.

אז טרם נוסדו (א 2129), יוחנן הכהן, חלק ד' מקדושתא לשבועות

Ashkenaz
2646. Budapest - Magyar tudomanyos akademia, MS. Kaufmann A 400 , p. 179-182, C, rubric: במקום יי קנני ראשית דרכו מצאתי זה.
2647. Oxford - Bodleian Library MS Opp. 170 (Neubauer 1205), f. 87b-89a, C.

אז טרם נמתחו נבלי שבבים (א 2130), שלמה ב"ר יצחק, סליחה

Ashkenaz
2648. Braunschweig - Landesmuseum fuer Geschichte und Volkstum R 2386, vol. II, f. 141b, M.
2649. Hamburg - Staats- und Universitaetsbibliothek Cod. hebr. 17/2 (Steinschneider 152), f. 146b, C, rubric: אחרת.
2650. Muenchen - Bayerische Staatsbibliothek, Cod. hebr. 346 , f. 119a, C, short.
2651. Oxford - Bodleian Library MS Mich. 543 (Neubauer 1212), f. 5b-7a, C, commentator: Isaac b. Jacob (compiler), rubric: אחרת.
2652. Padova - Biblioteca del Seminario Vescovile Cod. 218, f. 157a-157b, M.
2653. Parma - Bibliotheca Palatina Cod. Parm. 3205 (de Rossi 655), f. 288a-288b, C.
2654. Vatican - Biblioteca Apostolica ebr. 308/1, f. 3a-3b, C, commentator: David b. Mose (compiler), short.

Ashkenaz, commentary by Abraham b. Azriel[60]
2655. Frankfurt a M - Stadt- und Universitaetsbibliothek Fol. 16 (Merzbacher 95), f. 103a, C.

אז כארסת בתולה במהר (א 2137), יוסף ב"ר שמואל טוב עלם, זולת

Ashkenaz
2656. Jerusalem - Schocken Institute 24100 / Mahzor Nuremberg, f. 70b, M, very short.
2657. London - British Library Or. 2735 (Margoliouth 663) , f. 174a-175b, M, margins partly damaged.
2658. London - David Sofer 5, f. 40b-41a, C, additional glosses.

---

[60] Edited by Urbach, ערוגת הבושם, vol. III, p. 541-543.

HEBREW LITURGICAL POETRY

Ashkenaz, commentary Abraham b. Azriel[61]
2659. Frankfurt a M - Stadt- und Universitaetsbibliothek Fol. 16 (Merzbacher 95), f. 50(i)a, C, rubric: זולת.

אז כעברת בארץ פתרוסים (א 2141), קלונימוס ב"ר יהודה, זולת לברית מילה
Ashkenaz
2660. Berlin - Staatsbibliothek (Preussischer Kulturbesitz) Or. Qu. 798-799 (Steinschneider 177), I, f. 261a-262a, M.

אז כעיני עבדים אל יד אדונים באנו לפניך נדונים (א 2142), הושענא
Ashkenaz
2661. Berlin - Staatsbibliothek (Preussischer Kulturbesitz) Or. Qu. 798-799 (Steinschneider 177), I, f. 211a-211b, M, incipit רחם.
2662. Budapest - Magyar tudomanyos akademia, MS. Kaufmann A 399, p. 307-308, C.
2663. Budapest - Magyar tudomanyos akademia, MS. Kaufmann A 400, p. 541, C, incipit רחם נא.
2664. Cambridge - University Library Add. 394,1 (Reif SCR 461), f. 78a-78b, C, rubric: הושענא.
2665. Frankfurt a M - Stadt- und Universitaetsbibliothek Oct. 227, f. 117a-117b, M.
2666. Hamburg - Staats- und Universitaetsbibliothek Cod. hebr. 17/2 (Steinschneider 152), f. 169a, C.
2667. Jerusalem - Schocken Institute 24100 / Mahzor Nuremberg, f. 496a-496b, M.
2668. London - British Library Add. 18695 (Margoliouth 683), f. 157a-157b, T, Yiddish.
2669. London - British Library Add. 22431 (Margoliouth 662a), f. 126b-127a, M.
2670. London - British Library Add. 27208 (Margolioth 654), f. 281a-282a, M.
2671. London - British Library Add. 27556, f. 135a-136a, M.
2672. New York - Jewish Theological Seminary Ms. 4466, f. 483b-484a, M.
2673. Oxford - Bodleian Library MS Can. Or. 1 (Neubauer 1104), f. 33b-34a, M.
2674. Oxford - Bodleian Library MS Mich. 573 (Neubauer 1099), f. 24b-25a, M.
2675. Oxford - Bodleian Library MS Opp 160 (Neubauer 1204), f. 247a-248b, C, commentator: Elazar b. Yehuda of Worms.[62]

---

[61] Edited by Urbach, ערוגת הבושם, vol. III, p. 533-534.
[62] Edited by Katzenellenbogen, פירוש ההושענות, p. 65-66.

2676. Oxford - Bodleian Library MS Opp. 170 (Neubauer 1205), f. 205b-206a, C.
2677. Parma - Biblioteca Palatina Cod. Parm. 2895, p. 228-230, M.
2678. Parma - Biblioteca Palatina Cod. Parm. 3057.9 (de Rossi 1033), f. 95b-96a, C.
2679. Parma - Biblioteca Palatina Cod. Parm. 3205 (de Rossi 655), f. 253a, C.
2680. Vatican - Biblioteca Apostolica ebr. 308, f. 160b, C, commentator: David b. Mose (compiler).
2681. Verona - Seminario Maggiore 34, f. 172b-173a, M, margins partly damaged, very short.

Ashkenaz, commentary by Eliezer b. Natan

2682. Hamburg - Staats- und Universitaetsbibliothek Cod. hebr. 61 (Steinschneider 153), f. 26a-26b, C.
2683. Warszaw - Uniwersytet, Inst. Orientalistyczny 258, f. 199a, C, incipit רחם נא קהל.

Italia, commentary by Yehoshua Segre

2684. Moscow - Russian State Library, Ms. Guenzburg 533, f. 47b-49a, C, rubric: לימוד י"ח.

Italia, commentary by Zakharya David Shabbetai Segre

2685. Torino - Archivio Terracini 1499, p. 247-248, C, rubric: פירוש אז כעיני עבדים.

Roma

2686. Oxford - Bodleian Library MS Mich. 312,1 (Neubauer 2276,1), f. 13b, C, short.

Romania

2687. London - London School of Jewish Studies. Asher I.Myers collection 9, f. 214a-214b, M.
2688. Vatican - Biblioteca Apostolica ebr. 285/30, f. 237b, C.
2689. Vatican - Biblioteca Apostolica ebr. 320, f. 450b-451a, M.

Tsarfat

2690. Jerusalem - Schocken Institute 19623, f. 129b-130a, M, commentator: Yehuda b. Eliezer Zvi.
2691. London - British Library Or. 2735 (Margoliouth 663), f. 155a-155b, M.
2692. London - David Sofer 5, f. 193b, C.
2693. London - David Sofer 5, f. 193b-194a, C, incipit חרחם.
2694. Moscow - Russian State Library, Ms. Guenzburg 1665, f. 184b-185a, M.
2695. Parma - Biblioteca Palatina Cod. Parm. 1264, f. 101a-101b, M.
2696. Vatican - Biblioteca Apostolica ebr. 306, f. 126a, C.

אז לפנות ערב דפקנו הומים על שערי מלך (א 2146), סליחה

Ashkenaz
2697. Berlin - Staatsbibliothek (Preussischer Kulturbesitz) Or. Qu. 798-799 (Steinschneider 177), I, f. 182a-182b, M.
2698. Jerusalem - Jewish National and University Library Ms Heb 8° 3037, f. 227a, M.

אז מאז אימנת, סליחה

Tsarfat
2699. Vatican - Biblioteca Apostolica ebr. 306, f. 80b-81a, C.

אז מאז כל מפעל הבנת (א 2148), ליום א' של ראש השנה

Tsarfat
2700. London - David Sofer 5, f. 112b, C.
2701. Parma - Biblioteca Palatina Cod. Parm. 3006 (de Rossi 654,1), f. 30b-31a, M.

אז מאז זמות בכל פועל (א 2149), אלעזר ברבי קליר, קדושתא לשבת שקלים

Ashkenaz
2702. Berlin - Staatsbibliothek (Preussischer Kulturbesitz) Or. Qu. 798-799 (Steinschneider 177), II, f. 12b-13a, M.
2703. Budapest - Magyar tudomanyos akademia, MS. Kaufmann A 384, f. 37a-37b, M.
2704. Budapest - Magyar tudomanyos akademia, MS. Kaufmann A 400, p. 1-4, C, beginning missing.
2705. Cambridge - University Library Add. 504,1, f. 1b-2b, C.
2706. Erlangen - Universitaetsbibliothek 2601 (Roth 67), f. 27a, M.
2707. Hamburg - Staats- und Universitaetsbibliothek Cod. hebr. 17/2 (Steinschneider 152), f. 10b-12a, C.
2708. Hamburg - Staats- und Universitaetsbibliothek Cod. hebr. 225, f. 10a, G.
2709. Jerusalem - Schocken Institute 24100 / Mahzor Nuremberg, f. 34a-34b, M.
2710. Muenchen - Bayerische Staatsbibliothek, Cod. hebr. 88, f. 14b-15a, G.
2711. Muenchen - Bayerische Staatsbibliothek, Cod. hebr. 393, f. 84b, C, no incipit.
2712. Oxford - Bodleian Library MS Opp. 170 (Neubauer 1205), f. 3a-4a, C.
2713. Paris - Bibliotheque Nationale heb. 709, f. 3b-4b, C, rubric: קרובה.
2714. Parma - Biblioteca Palatina Cod. Parm. 1002 (Ta 24), f. 23a-23b, M.
2715. Parma - Biblioteca Palatina Cod. Parm. 3205 (de Rossi 655), f. 10b-11b, C.

2716. Parma - Biblioteca Palatina Cod. Parm. 3269, f. 8b, G, later hand.
2717. Parma - Biblioteca Palatina Cod. Parm. 3507 (Perreau 27), f. 2a-2b, C, rubric: קדושתא.
2718. Vatican - Biblioteca Apostolica ebr. 305,1, f. 2b-3a, C, no incipit.

Tsarfat

2719. London - British Library Add. 11639 (Margoliouth 1056), f. 264a, M.
2720. London - British Library Add. 11639 (Margoliouth 1056), f. 710a, M, rubric: קדושתא.
2721. London - David Sofer 5, f. 8b-9b, C.
2722. Moscow - Russian State Library, Ms. Guenzburg 1665, f. 13b, M.
2723. Oxford - Bodleian Library MS Laud. Or. 271 (Neubauer 1206), f. 6a-11a, C, commentator: Aaron b. Hayyim haKohen (compiler).
2724. Oxford - Bodleian Library MS Opp. 171 (Neubauer 1207), f. 4b-5b, C, rubric: קרובה.
2725. Parma - Biblioteca Palatina Cod. Parm. 3136 (de Rossi 405), f. 21b-22a, M.
2726. Vatican - Biblioteca Apostolica ebr. 306, f. 157a-157b, C, no incipit.

אז מאז כל מפעל סקרת (א 2150), אלעזר ברבי קליר, קדושה, שחרית ראש השנה

Ashkenaz

2727. Moscow - Russian State Library, Ms. Guenzburg 191, f. 4a-4b, M.
2728. New York - Jewish Theological Seminary Ms. 8169 (Acc. 0016), f. 11a-11b, M.
2729. Torino - Archivio Terracini 1492, f. 13a-13b, M.

Asti, Fossano, Moncalvo

2730. New Haven - Yale University, Beinecke Rare Book and MS Library, MS Heb. 52, f. 23b, M.

Tsarfat

2731. London - British Library Or. 8682, f. 14a-14b, GI.
2732. London - David Sofer 5, f. 112b, C, rubric: קדושות.
2733. Oxford - Bodleian Library MS Laud. Or. 271 (Neubauer 1206), f. 114a, C, commentator: Aaron b. Hayyim haKohen (compiler), rubric: אופן.
2734. Parma - Biblioteca Palatina Cod. Parm. 1794 (de Rossi 1061), f. 72a-72b, M.
2735. Parma - Biblioteca Palatina Cod. Parm. 3006 (de Rossi 654,1), f. 30b, M.

אז מלפני בראשית אבות ובנים השית (א 2152), אלעזר ברבי קליר, חלק ט"ו, קדושתא למוסף יום כפור

Ashkenaz

2736. Budapest - Magyar tudomanyos akademia, MS. Kaufmann A 400, p 361-362, C, incipit אבות.

2737. London - British Library Or. 11318/1, f. 106b-107a, C.
2738. Muenchen - Bayerische Staatsbibliothek, Cod. hebr. 346 , f. 79b-80b, C, no incipit.
2739. Parma - Biblioteca Palatina Cod. Parm. 3270 (de Rossi 1215), f. 175a, M.
2740. Oxford - Bodleian Library MS Bodl. Or. 109 (Neubauer 1209), f. 33b-34b, C, commentator: Aaron b. Hayyim haKohen (compiler), no incipit.

אז מלפני בראשית דת וכס השית (א 2153), אלעזר ברבי קליר, חלק ט"ו, קדושתא למוסף יום כפור

Ashkenaz
2741. Budapest - Magyar tudomanyos akademia, MS. Kaufmann A 400 , p. 360-361, C, rubric: קדושה.
2742. Hamburg - Staats- und Universitaetsbibliothek Cod. hebr. 40c (Steinschneider 111), f. 218a-218b, G.
2743. Jerusalem - Jewish National and University Library Ms Heb 8° 3037, f. 184a-184b, M.
2744. Jerusalem - Schocken Institute 24100 / Mahzor Nuremberg , f. 414a-414b, M.
2745. London - British Library Or. 11318/1, f. 105b-106b, C.
2746. London - Montefiore Library 261 , f. 56b-57a, C, commentator: Eliezer b. Natan?.
2747. Muenchen - Bayerische Staatsbibliothek, Cod. hebr. 346 , f. 79a-79b, C.
2748. New York - Jewish Theological Seminary Ms. 4466, f. 376b-377b, M.
2749. New York - Jewish Theological Seminary Ms. 8097, f. 79a, C.
2750. Oxford - Bodleian Library MS Mich. 365 (Neubauer 1208), f. 84b-85b, C, rubric: אופן.
2751. Oxford - Bodleian Library MS Opp. 172 (Neubauer 1211), f. 61a-61b, C.
2752. Parma - Biblioteca Palatina Cod. Parm. 3270 (de Rossi 1215), f. 174b, M.
2753. Parma - Biblioteca Palatina Cod. Parm. 3271 (de Rossi 1216), f. 111b-112a, G.
2754. Parma - Biblioteca Palatina Cod. Parm. 3507 (Perreau 27), f. 164b-165a, C.
2755. Vatican - Biblioteca Apostolica ebr. 308, f. 118a-118b, C, commentator: David b. Mose (compiler).

Tsarfat
2756. Oxford - Bodleian Library MS Bodl. Or. 109 (Neubauer 1209), f. 33a-33b, C, commentator: Aaron b. Hayyim haKohen (compiler).

אז מלפני בראשית נוה יונון הׁשית (א 2154), אלעזר ברבי קליר, חלק ט"ז, קדושתא למוסף יום כפור

Ashkenaz
2757. Budapest - Magyar tudomanyos akademia, MS. Kaufmann A 400, p. 362, C, incipit נוה.
2758. Hamburg - Staats- und Universitaetsbibliothek Cod. hebr. 40c (Steinschneider 111), f. 218b, G.
2759. Jerusalem - Jewish National and University Library Ms Heb 8° 3037, f. 185a, M.
2760. Jerusalem - Schocken Institute 24100 / Mahzor Nuremberg, f. 414b, M, incipit נוה.
2761. London - British Library Or. 11318/1, f. 107a, C.
2762. London - Montefiore Library 261, f. 57a-57b, C, commentator: Eliezer b. Natan?, incipit נוה.
2763. Muenchen - Bayerische Staatsbibliothek, Cod. hebr. 346, f. 80b-81b, C, no incipit.
2764. New York - Jewish Theological Seminary Ms. 4466, f. 377b-378a, M, incipit נוה.
2765. New York - Jewish Theological Seminary Ms. 8097, f. 79a, C.
2766. Oxford - Bodleian Library MS Mich. 365 (Neubauer 1208), f. 85b-86a, C, no incipit.
2767. Oxford - Bodleian Library MS Opp. 172 (Neubauer 1211), f. 61b-62a, C.
2768. Parma - Biblioteca Palatina Cod. Parm. 3270 (de Rossi 1215), f. 175b, M.
2769. Parma - Biblioteca Palatina Cod. Parm. 3507 (Perreau 27), f. 165a-165b, C, incipit נוה.
2770. Vatican - Biblioteca Apostolica ebr. 308, f. 118b-119a, C, commentator: David b. Mose (compiler), no incipit.

Tsarfat
2771. Oxford - Bodleian Library MS Bodl. Or. 109 (Neubauer 1209), f. 34b-35a, C, commentator: Aaron b. Hayyim haKohen (compiler), no incipit.

אז מלפני בראשית שבעה אלה השית (א 2155), אלעזר ברבי קליר, חלק ט"ז, קדושתא למוסף יום כפור

Ashkenaz
2772. Budapest - Magyar tudomanyos akademia, MS. Kaufmann A 400, p. 362-363, C, incipit שבעה.
2773. Jerusalem - Jewish National and University Library Ms Heb 8° 3037, f. 185b, M.
2774. Jerusalem - Schocken Institute 24100 / Mahzor Nuremberg, f. 414b-415a, M, incipit שבעה.

2775. London - British Library Or. 11318/1, f. 107b, C.
2776. London - Montefiore Library 261, f. 57b, C, commentator: Eliezer b. Natan?, incipit שבעה.
2777. Muenchen - Bayerische Staatsbibliothek, Cod. hebr. 346, f. 81b, C.
2778. New York - Jewish Theological Seminary Ms. 4466, f. 378a-378b, M, incipit שבעה.
2779. New York - Jewish Theological Seminary Ms. 8097, f. 79b, C.
2780. Oxford - Bodleian Library MS Mich. 365 (Neubauer 1208), f. 86a, 87a, C, no incipit.
2781. Oxford - Bodleian Library MS Opp. 172 (Neubauer 1211), f. 62a, C.
2782. Parma - Biblioteca Palatina Cod. Parm. 3507 (Perreau 27), f. 165b-166a, C, no incipit.
2783. Vatican - Biblioteca Apostolica ebr. 308, f. 119a, C, commentator: David b. Mose (compiler).

Tsarfat

2784. Oxford - Bodleian Library MS Bodl. Or. 109 (Neubauer 1209), f. 35a-35b, C, commentator: Aaron b. Hayyim haKohen (compiler).

אז מקדם הקדמת תשובה (א 2159), בנימין ב"ר זרח, סליחה

Ashkenaz

2785. Moscow - Russian State Library, Ms. Guenzburg 190, f. 14a-14b, G, beginns with petiha הורית.

Ashkenaz, commentary by Abraham b. Azriel[63]

2786. Vatican - Biblioteca Apostolica ebr. 301,1, f. 170a, C, no incipit.

Romania

2787. Vatican - Biblioteca Apostolica ebr. 320, f. 217b, M.

אז מראשית כל מפעל יצירה (א 2163), יוסף ב"ר שמואל טוב עלם, חלק ז' מקדושתא לשבועות

Tsarfat

2788. London - David Sofer 5, f. 69a-70a, C.
2789. Moscow - Russian State Library, Ms. Guenzburg 1665, f. 143a-146a, M.
2790. Parma - Biblioteca Palatina Cod. Parm. 3136 (de Rossi 405), f. 172a-174b, M.

אז נקשוב עניו עלה אל הר העברים, זולת

Ashkenaz

2791. Berlin - Staatsbibliothek (Preussischer Kulturbesitz) Or. Qu. 798-799 (Steinschneider 177), I, f. 227a-228a, M.

---

[63] Edited by Urbach, ערוגת הבושם, vol. III, p. 496.

2792. Lund - Universitetsbibliothek Ms. L.O. 2, f. 92a-92b, M.

אז על כל חיות יער נשאת שור (א 2169), אלעזר ברבי קליר, חלק ה', קדושתא לפסח
Ashkenaz
2793. Braunschweig - Landesmuseum fuer Geschichte und Volkstum R 2386, vol. I, f. 37a, M.
2794. Berlin - Staatsbibliothek (Preussischer Kulturbesitz) Or. Qu. 798-799 (Steinschneider 177), II, f. 79b-80a, M.
2795. Budapest - Magyar tudomanyos akademia, MS. Kaufmann A 384 , f. 163b-164a, M.
2796. Budapest - Magyar tudomanyos akademia, MS. Kaufmann A 400 , p. 132-133, C.
2797. Hamburg - Staats- und Universitaetsbibliothek Cod. hebr. 17/2 (Steinschneider 152), f. 65a-65b, C.
2798. Jerusalem - Schocken Institute 24100 / Mahzor Nuremberg, f. 95a, M.
2799. London - British Library Add. 18695 (Margoliouth 683), f. 42a-43a, T, Yiddish.
2800. Moscow - Russian State Library, Ms. Guenzburg 615, f. 23a-23b, C.
2801. Muenchen - Bayerische Staatsbibliothek, Cod. hebr. 21, f. 33b, M.
2802. Muenchen - Bayerische Staatsbibliothek, Cod. hebr. 88, f. 73a-73b, G.
2803. Muenchen - Bayerische Staatsbibliothek, Cod. hebr. 393 , f. 130a-130b, C.
2804. New York - Jewish Theological Seminary Ms. 4466, f. 75a-76a, M.
2805. Paris - Bibliotheque Nationale heb. 709, f. 98a-98b, C, no incipit.
2806. Parma - Biblioteca Palatina Cod. Parm. 1002 (Ta 24), f. 118b-119a, M.
2807. Parma - Biblioteca Palatina Cod. Parm. 3205 (de Rossi 655), f. 102b, C.
2808. Parma - Biblioteca Palatina Cod. Parm. 3507 (Perreau 27), f. 65a, C, no incipit.
2809. Zurich - Zentralbibliothek Heid. 139, f. 38a-38b, C, no incipit, additional marginal notes.
Tsarfat
2810. London - British Library Add. 11639 (Margoliouth 1056), f. 293b, M.
2811. Moscow - Russian State Library, Ms. Guenzburg 1665, f. 71b-72a, M.
2812. Oxford - Bodleian Library MS Laud. Or. 271 (Neubauer 1206), f. 73a-73b, C, commentator: Aaron b. Hayyim haKohen (compiler).
2813. Oxford - Bodleian Library MS Opp. 171 (Neubauer 1207), f. 41b, C.

אז קשתי וחרבי (א 2173), שלמה הבבלי, סליחה

Ashkenaz
2814. Budapest - Magyar tudomanyos akademia, MS. Kaufmann A 400 , p. 459-464, C, rubric: חטאנו שלמונית.
2815. Hamburg - Staats- und Universitaetsbibliothek Cod. hebr. 17/2 (Steinschneider 152), f. 136b-138a, C, rubric: חטאנו שלמונית.
2816. Moscow - Russian State Library, Ms. Guenzburg 190 , f. 112b-114a, G.
2817. Oxford - Bodleian Library MS Mich. 543 (Neubauer 1212), f. 88b, C, commentator: Isaac b. Jacob (compiler), breaks off in the middle.
2818. Oxford - Bodleian Library MS Opp. 681 (Neubauer 1213), f. 88b-91a, C.
2819. Padova - Biblioteca del Seminario Vescovile Cod. 218, f. 71a-72b, M.
2820. Parma - Biblioteca Palatina Cod. Parm. 3205 (de Rossi 655), f. 273a-274b, C.

Tsarfat
2821. London - British Library Add. 11639 (Margoliouth 1056), f. 485a-488b, M.
2822. London - David Sofer 5, f. 164a-165a, C, rubric: חטאנו.
2823. Oxford - Bodleian Library MS Laud. Or. 271 (Neubauer 1206), f. 168a-169a, C, commentator: Aaron b. Hayyim haKohen (compiler).
2824. Oxford - Bodleian Library MS Opp. 171 (Neubauer 1207), f. 106b-108a, C, rubric: אחרת.
2825. Parma - Biblioteca Palatina Cod. Parm. 3007 (de Rossi 654,2) , f. 9a-10a, M.
2826. Vatican - Biblioteca Apostolica ebr. 306, f. 93a-95a, C.

אז ראית וספרת והכנת (א 2174), אלעזר ברבי קליר, סילוק, קדושתא לשבת שקלים

Ashkenaz
2827. Berlin - Staatsbibliothek (Preussischer Kulturbesitz) Or. Qu. 798-799 (Steinschneider 177), II, f. 15b-17b, M.
2828. Budapest - Magyar tudomanyos akademia, MS. Kaufmann A 384 , f. 40a-42b, M.
2829. Budapest - Magyar tudomanyos akademia, MS. Kaufmann A 400 , p. 15-25, C.
2830. Cambridge - University Library Add. 504,1, f. 7b-8b, C.
2831. Hamburg - Staats- und Universitaetsbibliothek Cod. hebr. 17/2 (Steinschneider 152), f. 13b-16a, C.
2832. Jerusalem - Schocken Institute 24100 / Mahzor Nuremberg, f. 36a-36b, M.
2833. Muenchen - Bayerische Staatsbibliothek, Cod. hebr. 88, f. 16b-18a, G.

2834. Muenchen - Bayerische Staatsbibliothek, Cod. hebr. 393, f. 87a-88a, C, no incipit.
2835. Oxford - Bodleian Library MS Opp. 170 (Neubauer 1205), f. 6a-7a, C.
2836. Paris - Bibliotheque Nationale heb. 709, f. 9a-14b, C, rubric: סילוק.
2837. Parma - Biblioteca Palatina Cod. Parm. 1002 (Ta 24), f. 25b-27a, M.
2838. Parma - Biblioteca Palatina Cod. Parm. 3205 (de Rossi 655), f. 15a-17b, C, rubric: סילוק.
2839. Parma - Biblioteca Palatina Cod. Parm. 3507 (Perreau 27), f. 6b-10b, C, rubric: סילוק, no incipit.
2840. Vatican - Biblioteca Apostolica ebr. 305,1, f. 6a-9a, C, rubric: סילוק.

Tsarfat
2841. London - David Sofer 5, f. 12a-16a, C, rubric: סילוק.
2842. Oxford - Bodleian Library MS Laud. Or. 271 (Neubauer 1206), f. 13a-15b, C, commentator: Aaron b. Hayyim haKohen (compiler), rubric: סילוק.
2843. Oxford - Bodleian Library MS Opp. 171 (Neubauer 1207), f. 9a-12b, C.

אז רוב ניסים הפלאת בלילה (א 2175), יניי, חלק ה', קדושתא לפסח

Ashkenaz
2844. Berlin - Staatsbibliothek (Preussischer Kulturbesitz) Or. Qu. 798-799 (Steinschneider 177), II, f. 49a, M.
2845. Budapest - Magyar tudomanyos akademia, MS. Kaufmann A 384, f. 109b-110a, M.
2846. Budapest - Magyar tudomanyos akademia, MS. Kaufmann A 399, p. 189-190, C.
2847. Cambridge - University Library Add. 394.2 (Reif SCR 462), f. 103a-103b, C, rubric: ביאור אז רוב ניסים שאומרי' בליל פסח לי"ח.
2848. Erlangen - Universitaetsbibliothek 2601 (Roth 67), f. 59a, M, very short.
2849. Frankfurt a M - Stadt- und Universitaetsbibliothek Oct. 227, f. 73b-74a, M.
2850. Hamburg - Staats- und Universitaetsbibliothek Cod. hebr. 17/2 (Steinschneider 152), f. 31b, C.
2851. London - British Library Add. 18695 (Margoliouth 683), f. 12b-13a, T, Yiddish.
2852. Moscow - Russian State Library, Ms. Guenzburg 1401/2, f. 15a, C, short.
2853. Muenchen - Bayerische Staatsbibliothek, Cod. hebr. 69, f. 35a, G.
2854. Muenchen - Bayerische Staatsbibliothek, Cod. hebr. 88, f. 51a-51b, G.
2855. Muenchen - Bayerische Staatsbibliothek, Cod. hebr. 393, f. 108b-109a, C.

2856. Vatican - Biblioteca Apostolica ebr. 318, f. 164a, G.
2857. Zurich - Zentralbibliothek Heid. 139, f. 14a-14b, C, additional marginal notes.

Italia

2858. Parma - Biblioteca Palatin Cod. Parm. 2248 (de Rossi 149/2), f. 40a-40b, C, rubric: ביאור אז רוב נסים שאום׳ בליל פסח.

Roma

2859. New York - Jewish Theological Seminary Ms. 1639, f. 20a-20b, C, commentator: Salomo b. Samuel Rofe, rubric: ביאור אז רוב ניסים שאוי׳ בליל פסח.

Tsarfat

2860. Oxford - Bodleian Library MS Laud. Or. 271 (Neubauer 1206), f. 50b, C, commentator: Aaron b. Hayyim haKohen (compiler), short.

אז תשע מכות (א 2182), יניי, חלק ד׳, קדושתא לפסח

Ashkenaz

2861. Berlin - Staatsbibliothek (Preussischer Kulturbesitz) Or. Qu. 798-799 (Steinschneider 177), II, f. 48b, M.
2862. Budapest - Magyar tudomanyos akademia, MS. Kaufmann A 384, f. 109a-109b, M.
2863. London - British Library Add. 18695 (Margoliouth 683), f. 12a, T, Yiddish.
2864. Paris - Bibliotheque Nationale heb. 709, f. 44b, C, incipit דנתה.

אזדהר משהדות שקר ולישנא בישא (א 2185), רשות בארמית לדבור שלישי

Ashkenaz

2865. Hamburg - Staats- und Universitaetsbibliothek Cod. hebr. 17/2 (Steinschneider 152), f. 73b-74a, C.
2866. Parma - Biblioteca Palatina Cod. Parm. 3205 (de Rossi 655), f. 187a-187b, C.

Ashkenaz, commentary by Benjamin b. Abraham Anaw

2867. Jerusalem - Musad haRav Kook 478, p. 72-80, C, rubric: אלפא ביתא יג.
2868. London - Beth Din & Beth Hamidrash 6,9, f. 192b-196b, C, rubric: אלפא בית.

אזהרת ראשית לעמך נתתה (א 2186), אזהרות דרבנן

Ashkenaz

2869. Berlin - Staatsbibliothek (Preussischer Kulturbesitz) Or. Qu. 798-799 (Steinschneider 177), II, f. 150b-152a, M.
2870. Braunschweig - Landesmuseum fuer Geschichte und Volkstum R 2386, vol. I, f. 106b-107b, M.
2871. Cambridge - University Library Add. 394,1 (Reif SCR 461), f. 55b-56a, C, rubric: למוסף.

2872. Hamburg - Staats- und Universitaetsbibliothek Cod. hebr. 225, f. 208b-209b, G.
2873. Hamburg - Staats- und Universitaetsbibliothek Cod. hebr. 17/2 (Steinschneider 152), f. 89b-90b, C, rubric: אזהרת דמתיבתא קדישא דרבנן דפומבדיתא אזהרת בגימטריא הרי"ג.
2874. Jerusalem - Schocken Institute 24100 / Mahzor Nuremberg, f. 182b-183a, M.
2875. London - British Library Add. 18695 (Margoliouth 683), f. 96a-96b, T, Yiddish, rubric: און צו מוסף זעגט מן דש איין אין מפני חטאינו און היבט אן אזהרת ראשית.
2876. London - British Library Add. 22431 (Margoliouth 662a), f. 80b-81b, M.
2877. Moscow - Russian State Library, Ms. Guenzburg 615, f. 49a-52b, C, commentator: Elazar b. Yehuda of Worms.
2878. Muenchen - Bayerische Staatsbibliothek, Cod. hebr. 88, f. 149b-150a, G.
2879. New York - Jewish Theological Seminary Ms. 4466, f. 180b-181b, M.
2880. Paris - Bibliotheque Nationale heb. 709, f. 139a-139b, C.
2881. Parma - Biblioteca Palatina Cod. Parm. 1002 (Ta 24), f. 226b-227a, M, short.
2882. Parma - Biblioteca Palatina Cod. Parm. 2886 (de Rossi 585), f. 87b, M, later hand, margins cut, only beginning.
2883. Parma - Biblioteca Palatina Cod. Parm. 3205 (de Rossi 655), f. 128b-129a, C.
2884. Parma - Biblioteca Palatina Cod. Parm. 3507 (Perreau 27), f. 105b-106b, C.

Tsarfat
2885. London - David Sofer 5, f. 66a-66b, C, incomplete.
2886. Moscow - Russian State Library, Ms. Guenzburg 1665, f. 152a-152b, M, only beginning.
2887. Oxford - Bodleian Library MS Laud. Or. 271 (Neubauer 1206), f. 93b-94a, C, commentator: Aaron b. Hayyim haKohen (compiler).
2888. Parma - Biblioteca Palatina Cod. Parm. 3136 (de Rossi 405), f. 166a-167a, M.

אזון שלש עשרה מדות מקוראי מעבר (א 2191), סעדיה, סליחה

Yemen
2889. New York - Jewish Theological Seminary Ms. 3028, f. 95b, G.
2890. New York - Jewish Theological Seminary Ms. 3193, f. 135a-135b, M.

Yemen, commentary by Isaac b. Abraham Wanneh
2891. Chicago-Spertus College of Judaica D 2, 2, f. 226a-226b, M, no incipit.
2892. Jerusalem - Sassoon 1158, p. 311-312, M, no incipit.

2893. London - British Library Or. 11122, f. 203a, M, rubric: אל מלך, no incipit.

אזון תחן והסכת עתידה (א 2192), סליחה
Ashkenaz
2894. Braunschweig - Landesmuseum fuer Geschichte und Volkstum R 2386, vol. II, f. 54b-55b, M.
2895. Budapest - Magyar tudomanyos akademia, MS. Kaufmann A 400, p. 483-484, C, rubric: אחרת.
2896. Cambridge - University Library Dd. 2.30, f. 5b-7a, G.
2897. Jerusalem - Schocken Institute 24100 / Mahzor Nuremberg, f. 243b, M, short.
2898. Moscow - Russian State Library, Ms. Guenzburg 190, f. 11a-11b, G.
2899. Moscow - Russian State Library, Ms. Guenzburg 615, f. 158a-158b, C, rubric: אל מלך.
2900. Muenchen - Bayerische Staatsbibliothek, Cod. hebr. 346, f. 127b-128a, C.
2901. Muenchen - Bayerische Staatsbibliothek, Cod. hebr. 346, f. 162a, C.
2902. Oxford - Bodleian Library MS Mich. 543 (Neubauer 1212), f. 51a, C, commentator: Isaac b. Jacob (compiler), rubric: אכתוב פירושי סליחות בשם אלהי הרוחות.
2903. Oxford - Bodleian Library MS Opp. 170 (Neubauer 1205), f. 227a-227b, C.
2904. Padova - Biblioteca del Seminario Vescovile Cod. 218, f. 57a, M.
2905. Padova - Biblioteca del Seminario Vescovile Cod. 218, f. 57a-58a, M, rubric: אחרת.
2906. Padova - Biblioteca del Seminario Vescovile Cod. 218, f. 233b, M.
2907. Padova - Biblioteca del Seminario Vescovile Cod. 218, f. 233b-234a, M.
2908. Parma - Biblioteca Palatina Cod. Parm. 3205 (de Rossi 655), f. 258a, C.
2909. Vatican - Biblioteca Apostolica ebr. 308/1, f. 9b-10a, C, commentator: David b. Mose (compiler).
2910. Vatican - Biblioteca Apostolica ebr. 422/1, f. 6a, C, rubric: אחרת.
2911. Vatican - Biblioteca Apostolica ebr. 422/1, f. 26a, C, very short.
2912. Vatican - Biblioteca Apostolica ebr. 422/2, f. 40a, CG, no incipit.
Ashkenaz, commentary by Abraham b. Azriel[64]
2913. Vatican - Biblioteca Apostolica ebr. 301,1, f. 155a, C, rubric: אחרת.
Tsarfat
2914. London - David Sofer 5, f. 167b-168a, C, rubric: סליחה.

---

[64] Edited by Urbach, ערוגת הבושם, vol. III, p. 397-398.

2915. Oxford - Bodleian Library MS Laud. Or. 271 (Neubauer 1206), f. 172b-173a, C, commentator: Aaron b. Hayyim haKohen (compiler).
2916. Oxford - Bodleian Library MS Opp. 171 (Neubauer 1207), f. 93a-93b, C, rubric: אחרת.
2917. Parma - Biblioteca Palatina Cod. Parm. 3006 (de Rossi 654,1), f. 226a-226b, M.
2918. Vatican - Biblioteca Apostolica ebr. 306, f. 192b, C.

אזור נא קנאות בגוים שית מוראיך (א 2197), משה, זולת
Ashkenaz
2919. Budapest - Magyar tudomanyos akademia, MS. Kaufmann A 399 , p. 424, C, very short.
2920. Oxford - Bodleian Library MS Can. Or. 82 (Neubauer 1148) , f. 21b-22a, M.
2921. Parma - Biblioteca Palatina Cod. Parm. 3205 (de Rossi 655), f. 145b-146a, C, rubric: זולת אחר.

אזורי איומה (א 2200), אליעזר ב"ר נתן, אופן לברית מילה
Ashkenaz
2922. Berlin - Staatsbibliothek (Preussischer Kulturbesitz) Or. Qu. 798-799 (Steinschneider 177), I, f. 258a-258b, M.
2923. Cambridge - University Library Add. 504,1, f. 66a, C, no incipit.

אזיל מעין דמעות כמו עין ואזעק מקץ, סליחה
Yemen, commentary by Isaac b. Abraham Wanneh
2924. Chicago-Spertus College of Judaica D 2, 2, f. 238a-238b, M, no incipit.
2925. Jerusalem - Benayahu ת 261, f. 166a, M.
2926. Jerusalem - Benayahu ת 282, f. 141b, M.
2927. Jerusalem - Makhon Ben Zvi 1156 (Tubi 155), f. 139a-139b, M.
2928. Jerusalem - Makhon Ben Zvi 1174 (Tubi 154), f. 138a, M.
2929. Jerusalem - Michael Krupp 604, f. 176b, M.
2930. Jerusalem - Musad haRav Kook 325, f. 195a, M.
2931. Jerusalem - Sassoon 1174, p. 270-271, M, no incipit.
2932. London - British Library Or. 11122, f. 215b, M, no incipit.
2933. Muenchen - Bayerische Staatsbibliothek, Cod. hebr. 472, f. 194b, M.
2934. New York - Jewish Theological Seminary Ms. 3013, f. 134a, M, very short, no incipit.
2935. New York - Jewish Theological Seminary Ms. 3294, f. 17b, C.
2936. New York - Public Library, Heb. Ms. 9, f. 131a, M, no incipit.
2937. Strasbourg - Bibliotheque Nationale et Universitaire 3965 (Landauer 39), p. 412, M.

אזכור אהבו אביהו רע יחשוב על אחיהו, לשבת זכור

Carpentras, commentary by Mordekhai b. Josef of Rocco Martino
2938. Cincinnati - Hebrew Union College 246/1, f. 24b-25b, C, rubric: פי'
פיוט להוצאת התורה.

אזכור ברעד מעללי יה (א 2270), יוסף ב"ר שמואל טוב עלם, יוצר ליום ב' של פסח

Tsarfat
2939. Parma - Biblioteca Palatina Cod. Parm. 3136 (de Rossi 405), f. 89a-89b, M.

אזכיר סלה זכרון מעשיך (א2249), אלעזר ברבי קליר, קדושתא שבת זכור

Ashkenaz
2940. Berlin - Staatsbibliothek (Preussischer Kulturbesitz) Or. Qu. 798-799 (Steinschneider 177), II, f. 20a-20b, M.
2941. Budapest - Magyar tudomanyos akademia, MS. Kaufmann A 384, f. 52b-53a, M.
2942. Budapest - Magyar tudomanyos akademia, MS. Kaufmann A 400, p. 29-38, C, rubric: שבח לאל אלים קדושתא שני.
2943. Cambridge - University Library Add. 504,1, f. 11b-13a, C.
2944. Erlangen - Universitaetsbibliothek 2601 (Roth 67), f. 34a, M.
2945. Hamburg - Staats- und Universitaetsbibliothek Cod. hebr. 17/2 (Steinschneider 152), f. 17a-18a, C, rubric: קדושתא לפרש זכור.
2946. Jerusalem - Schocken Institute 24100 / Mahzor Nuremberg, f. 40b-41a, M.
2947. Muenchen - Bayerische Staatsbibliothek, Cod. hebr. 88, f. 23b-24a, G.
2948. Muenchen - Bayerische Staatsbibliothek, Cod. hebr. 393, f. 89b-90a, C, no incipit.
2949. Oxford - Bodleian Library MS Opp. 170 (Neubauer 1205), f. 9a-10a, C, rubric: לפרשת זכור.
2950. Paris - Bibliotheque Nationale heb. 709, f. 16b-18b, C, rubric: קרובה של פרשת זכור.
2951. Parma - Biblioteca Palatina Cod. Parm. 1002 (Ta 24), f. 35a-35b, M.
2952. Parma - Biblioteca Palatina Cod. Parm. 3205 (de Rossi 655), f. 18a-19a, C, rubric: קרובה לפרשה זכור ולא מצאתי פירוש היוצר. היוצר תמצא אחרי שבת הגדול.
2953. Parma - Biblioteca Palatina Cod. Parm. 3507 (Perreau 27), f. 12a-13a, C, rubric: קרובץ, no incipit.
2954. Vatican - Biblioteca Apostolica ebr. 305,1, f. 11a-12a, C.

Tsarfat
2955. London - British Library Add. 11639 (Margoliouth 1056), f. 266b-267b, M.
2956. London - David Sofer 5, f. 17b-18b, C.

2957. Moscow - Russian State Library, Ms. Guenzburg 1665, f. 17b-18a, M.
2958. Oxford - Bodleian Library MS Laud. Or. 271 (Neubauer 1206), f. 17a-19a, C, commentator: Aaron b. Hayyim haKohen (compiler), rubric: פרשת זכור.
2959. Oxford - Bodleian Library MS Opp. 171 (Neubauer 1207), f. 13b-14b, C, rubric: ואתחיל פרשת זכור.
2960. Parma - Biblioteca Palatina Cod. Parm. 3136 (de Rossi 405), f. 30b-31a, M.
2961. Vatican - Biblioteca Apostolica ebr. 306, f. 161a-162a, C, no incipit.

אזכיר תהילות אלהי קדם משנה, יצחק הנקדן, יוצר לחתן

Ashkenaz
2962. Oxford - Bodleian Library MS Can. Or. 70 (Neubauer 1147,7), f. 87b-92a, M, rubric: יוצר של חתונה דילגתי למעלה.

אזכירה סדר עבודה אזכירה תהלות יי (א 2267), אברהם אבן עזרא, רשות לסדר עבורדה

Carpentras
2963. Cincinnati - Hebrew Union College 392, f. 66a-66b, C, rubric: פירוש סדר עבודה.

Carpentras, commentary by Josef b. Abraham of Montelitz
2964. New York - Jewish Theological Seminary Ms. 4197, f. 160a, M.
2965. Paris - Ecole Rabbinique 32, f. 172a, M.
2966. Strasbourg - Bibliotheque Nationale et Universitaire 4081, f. 149a-149b, M.

Yemen
2967. Ramat Gan - Universitat Bar Ilan 62, f. 53b, G.

Yemen, commentary by Isaac b. Abraham Wanneh
2968. Chicago-Spertus College of Judaica D 2, 2, f. 247b-248a, M, rubric: פירוש.
2969. Jerusalem - Sassoon 1158, p. 328, M, rubric: וזה פירושא.
2970. London - British Library Or. 11122, f. 225b, M, rubric: פירוש. סדר עבודה.

אזכר סלה לשם פה לאדם (א 2272), יוחנן הכהן, סדר עבודה

Roma
2971. Jerusalem - Jewish National and University Library Ms Heb 8° 4153, f. 137a-137b, C, commentator: Daniel ben Salomo haRofe (compiler), rubric: בסדר עבודה, only a few words explained.
2972. Parma - Biblioteca Palatina Cod. Parm. 2737 (de Rossi 804), f. 110b-112b, M, added by later hand.

אזכרה אלהים ואהימה (א 2275), אמתי, סליחה

Ashkenaz
2973. Berlin - Staatsbibliothek (Preussischer Kulturbesitz) Or. Qu. 798-799 (Steinschneider 177), I, f. 172a-172b, M.
2974. Braunschweig - Landesmuseum fuer Geschichte und Volkstum R 2386, vol. II, f. 55b-56a, M.
2975. Jerusalem - Schocken Institute 24100 / Mahzor Nuremberg, f. 468a, M.
2976. Moscow - Russian State Library, Ms. Guenzburg 190, f. 12a, G.
2977. Muenchen - Bayerische Staatsbibliothek, Cod. hebr. 346, f. 124a, C, commentator: Abraham Ḥaldiq, rubric: זה מפריש׳ הר׳ר׳ אברהם חלדיק זצ״ל.
2978. New York - Jewish Theological Seminary Ms. 4466, f. 400a-400b, M, incipit יי׳.
2979. Oxford - Bodleian Library MS Mich. 543 (Neubauer 1212), f. 9a-9b, C, commentator: Isaac b. Jacob (compiler).
2980. Oxford - Bodleian Library MS Opp. 172 (Neubauer 1211), f. 89a-89b, C, rubric: פזמון, incipit יי׳.
2981. Oxford - Bodleian Library MS Opp. 681 (Neubauer 1213), f. 75b, C, short.
2982. Oxford - Bodleian Library MS Opp. 681 (Neubauer 1213), f. 75b, C, rubric: פי׳ אחרת, very short.
2983. Padova - Biblioteca del Seminario Vescovile Cod. 218, f. 58b, M, short.
2984. Padova - Biblioteca del Seminario Vescovile Cod. 218, f. 59a, M, rubric: אחרת.
2985. Padova - Biblioteca del Seminario Vescovile Cod. 218, f. 230a, M.
2986. Padova - Biblioteca del Seminario Vescovile Cod. 218, f. 230b, M.
2987. Vatican - Biblioteca Apostolica ebr. 308, f. 150b, C, commentator: David b. Mose (compiler), incipit יי׳.
2988. Vatican - Biblioteca Apostolica ebr. 308, f. 150b-151a, C, commentator: David b. Mose (compiler).
2989. Vatican - Biblioteca Apostolica ebr. 422/1, f. 31b, C, very short.
2990. Vatican - Biblioteca Apostolica ebr. 422/1, f. 45b, CG, no incipit, very short.

Ashkenaz, commentary by Abraham b. Azriel[65]
2991. Frankfurt a M - Stadt- und Universitaetsbibliothek Fol. 16 (Merzbacher 95), f. 107b, C, incipit יי׳, short.
2992. Vatican - Biblioteca Apostolica ebr. 301,1, f. 139a-139b, C, rubric: אחר, incipit יי׳.

Tsarfat
2993. London - David Sofer 5, f. 168a, C, margin, incipit יי׳.

---

[65] Edited by Urbach, ערוגת הבושם, vol. III, p. 294 (one stanza) and p. 558.

אזכרה ימים מקדם ימי חמלתך, סליחה

Ashkenaz

2996. Oxford - Bodleian Library MS Mich. 543 (Neubauer 1212), f. 73a, C, commentator: Isaac b. Jacob (compiler).

Ashkenaz, commentary by Abraham b. Azriel[66]

2997. Vatican - Biblioteca Apostolica ebr. 301,1, f. 147b-148a, C, rubric: אחרת.

2998. Vatican - Biblioteca Apostolica ebr. 301,1, f. 160a, C, rubric: אחרת.

Tsarfat

2999. Oxford - Bodleian Library MS Laud. Or. 271 (Neubauer 1206), f. 174b, C, commentator: Aaron b. Hayyim haKohen (compiler).

3000. Oxford - Bodleian Library MS Opp. 171 (Neubauer 1207), f. 101a, C, rubric: אחרת.

3001. Vatican - Biblioteca Apostolica ebr. 306, f. 211a-211b, C.

אזכרה מצוק אשר קראני (א 2287), יוסף ב"ר שמואל טוב עלם, סליחה

Ashkenaz

3002. Oxford - Bodleian Library MS Opp. 681 (Neubauer 1213), f. 33b, C.

Ashkenaz, commentary by Abraham b. Azriel[67]

3003. Vatican - Biblioteca Apostolica ebr. 301,1, f. 141b-142a, C, rubric: וזהו סליחות לעשרה בטבת.

אזכרה מקדם פלאיך (א 2292), יצחק, זולת לשבת וחול המועד סוכות

Ashkenaz

3004. Budapest - Magyar tudomanyos akademia, MS. Kaufmann A 399, p. 453-454, C, rubric: זולת.

3005. Cambridge - University Library Add. 504,1, f. 61b-63a, C, rubric: וזהו זולתו.

3006. London - British Library Add. 18695 (Margoliouth 683), f. 147b-148a, T, Yiddish.

3007. Lund - Universitetsbibliothek Ms. L.O. 2, f. 114a-114b, M, rubric: זולת.

3008. New York - Jewish Theological Seminary Ms. 4466, f. 455a-456a, M.

3009. Oxford - Bodleian Library MS Can. Or. 82 (Neubauer 1148), f. 44a-45a, M, rubric: זולת.

---

[66] Edited by Urbach, ערוגת הבושם, vol. III, p. 347-348.
[67] Edited by Urbach, ערוגת הבושם, vol. III, p. 309-310.

3010. Parma - Biblioteca Palatina Cod. Parm. 2895, p. 417-418, M, margins cut, text damaged.

אזכרה שנות עולמים (א 2302), מאיר ב"ר יצחק, תוספת למעריב לליל א' של פסח
Ashkenaz

3011. Berlin - Staatsbibliothek (Preussischer Kulturbesitz) Or. Qu. 361 (Steinschneider 51), f. 133b-134b, M, no incipit.
3012. Berlin - Staatsbibliothek (Preussischer Kulturbesitz) Or. Qu. 798-799 (Steinschneider 177), II, f. 54b-55a, M.
3013. Braunschweig - Landesmuseum fuer Geschichte und Volkstum R 2386, vol. I, f. 15a-15b, M.
3014. Budapest - Magyar tudomanyos akademia, MS. Kaufmann A 384, f. 118b-119a, M.
3015. Budapest - Magyar tudomanyos akademia, MS. Kaufmann A 399, p. 195-199, C.
3016. Hamburg - Staats- und Universitaetsbibliothek Cod. hebr. 17/2 (Steinschneider 152), f. 44b-45a, C, rubric: מעריב לליל ראשון של פסח. לשומר ישראל.
3017. Jerusalem - Schocken Institute 24100 / Mahzor Nuremberg, f. 77a-77b, M.
3018. London - British Library Add. 18695 (Margoliouth 683), f. 18a-19a, T, Yiddish.
3019. Moscow - Russian State Library, Ms. Guenzburg 615, f. 170b-173a, C, rubric: אתחיל בסם'.
3020. Muenchen - Bayerische Staatsbibliothek, Cod. hebr. 88, f. 57b-58a, G.
3021. Muenchen - Bayerische Staatsbibliothek, Cod. hebr. 393,9, f. 201b-204b, C, no incipit.
3022. New York - Jewish Theological Seminary Ms. 4466, f. 193a-194b, M.
3023. Oxford - Bodleian Library MS Can. Or. 1 (Neubauer 1104), f. 46b-48b, M.
3024. Oxford - Bodleian Library MS Opp. 170 (Neubauer 1205), f. 39b-41a, C.
3025. Parma - Biblioteca Palatina Cod. Parm. 2895, p. 309-310, M, margins cut, text damaged.
3026. Parma - Biblioteca Palatina Cod. Parm. 3205 (de Rossi 655), f. 58b-59b, C, incipit זבח.
3027. Parma - Biblioteca Palatina Cod. Parm. 3507 (Perreau 27), f. 37b-39a, C.
3028. Verona - Seminario Maggiore 34, f. 188a-189b, M, rubric: תוספת ליל ראשון של פסח.
3029. Warszaw - Uniwersytet, Inst. Orientalistyczny 258, f. 200a-201b, C, commentator: Eliezer b. Natan.

Ashkenaz, commentary by Abraham b. Azriel[68]
3030. Vatican - Biblioteca Apostolica ebr. 301,1, f. 152a, C.
Tsarfat
3031. Oxford - Bodleian Library MS Laud. Or. 271 (Neubauer 1206), f. 52a-52b, C, commentator: Aaron b. Hayyim haKohen (compiler), rubric: תוספת לליל ראשון.

אזכרך דודי מארץ ירדן וחרמונים (א 2304), משולם ב"ר קלונימוס, זולת
Ashkenaz
3032. Budapest - Magyar tudomanyos akademia, MS. Kaufmann A 399, p. 422-423, C, rubric: זולתות שין פסח לעצרת. תיכן שמי בזרת.
3033. Cambridge - University Library Add. 504,1, f. 39b-40b, C, rubric: משלם יסד זה.
3034. Hamburg - Staats- und Universitaetsbibliothek Cod. hebr. 239a (Steinschneider 130), f. 22b-23a, G.
3035. Lund - Universitetsbibliothek Ms. L.O. 2, f. 96b-97a, M.
3036. Muenchen - Bayerische Staatsbibliothek, Cod. hebr. 393,9, f. 197a-197b, C, rubric: זולתות.
3037. Oxford - Bodleian Library MS Can. Or. 82 (Neubauer 1148), f. 19a, M.
3038. Parma - Biblioteca Palatina Cod. Parm. 2895, p. 402, M, short.
3039. Parma - Biblioteca Palatina Cod. Parm. 3205 (de Rossi 655), f. 146a-146b, C, rubric: זולת אחר.
Ashkenaz, commentary by Abraham b. Azriel[69]
3040. Vatican - Biblioteca Apostolica ebr. 301,1, f. 17b-18a, C, rubric: זולת.

אזמר בשבחין למיעל גו פתחין (א 2322), יחצק לוריא, זמר לשבת
haAri, commentary by Jacob b. Raphael haLevi
3041. Cincinnati - Hebrew Union College 275, f. 2b-3b, C, rubric: פי' מנחת יעקב על הזמר אזמר בשבחין לסעודה ראשית של שבת.

אזמרך עליון בשובי ברציון (א 2351), סעדיה, סליחה
Yemen
3042. New York - Jewish Theological Seminary Ms. 3052, f. 80b, M, short.
Yemen, commentary by Isaac b. Abraham Wanneh
3043. Chicago-Spertus College of Judaica D 2, 2, f. 236b, M, no incipit, short.
3044. Jerusalem - Benayahu ת 261, f. 164b, M.
3045. Jerusalem - Benayahu ת 282, f. 140a, M.
3046. Jerusalem - Makhon Ben Zvi 1156 (Tubi 155), f. 137b, M, no incipit.

---
[68] Edited by Urbach, ערוגת הבושם, vol. III, p. 376-377.
[69] Edited by Urbach, ערוגת הבושם, vol. I, p. 109-112.

3047. Jerusalem - Makhon Ben Zvi 1174 (Tubi 154), f. 135b, M.
3048. Jerusalem - Michael Krupp 604, f. 174b, M, no incipit, short.
3049. Jerusalem - Musad haRav Kook 325, f. 193a, M.
3050. Jerusalem - Sassoon 1158, p. 414-415, M, no incipit, short.
3051. Jerusalem - Sassoon 1174, p. 268, M, no incipit.
3052. London - British Library Or. 11122, f. 213b, M, no incipit, short.
3053. Muenchen - Bayerische Staatsbibliothek, Cod. hebr. 472, f. 192a, M.
3054. New York - Jewish Theological Seminary Ms. 3013, f. 132a, M, no incipit.
3055. New York - Public Library, Heb. Ms. 9, f. 128b, M, no incipit.
3056. Strasbourg - Bibliotheque Nationale et Universitaire 3965 (Landauer 39), p. 406, M.

אזעק אל אלהים קולי (א 2360), שלמה בן נחמן, סליחה
Ashkenaz

3057. Oxford - Bodleian Library MS Opp. 681 (Neubauer 1213), f. 68b, C, very short.
3058. Vatican - Biblioteca Apostolica ebr. 422/1, f. 26b, C.
3059. Vatican - Biblioteca Apostolica ebr. 422/1, f. 40b, CG, no incipit.

אזרח בט חוץ בכסל גהוץ (א ++2368), אלעזר ברבי קליר, קרובה לפורים, פיוט הרכבה
Ashkenaz

3060. Berlin - Staatsbibliothek (Preussischer Kulturbesitz) Or. Qu. 798-799 (Steinschneider 177), II, f. 26b-27b, M.
3061. Budapest - Magyar tudomanyos akademia, MS. Kaufmann A 384, f. 65b-66b, M.
3062. Budapest - Magyar tudomanyos akademia, MS. Kaufmann A 400, p. 59-64, C.
3063. Erlangen - Universitaetsbibliothek 2601 (Roth 67), f. 40a-40b, M, no incipit.
3064. Hamburg - Staats- und Universitaetsbibliothek Cod. hebr. 17/2 (Steinschneider 152), f. 22a-22b, C.
3065. Hamburg - Staats- und Universitaetsbibliothek Cod. hebr. 40c (Steinschneider 111), f. 14b-15a, G.
3066. Jerusalem - Schocken Institute 24100 / Mahzor Nuremberg, f. 49a-49b, M.
3067. Muenchen - Bayerische Staatsbibliothek, Cod. hebr. 88, f. 32b-33a, G.
3068. Muenchen - Bayerische Staatsbibliothek, Cod. hebr. 393, f. 94b-96a, C.
3069. Oxford - Bodleian Library MS Opp. 170 (Neubauer 1205), f. 19b-21b, C.
3070. Paris - Bibliotheque Nationale heb. 709, f. 27a-28b, C.

3071. Parma - Biblioteca Palatina Cod. Parm. 1002 (Ta 24), f. 46a-46b, M.
3072. Parma - Biblioteca Palatina Cod. Parm. 3205 (de Rossi 655), f. 29a-29b, C.
3073. Parma - Biblioteca Palatina Cod. Parm. 3507 (Perreau 27), f. 21b-22b, C, no incipit.
3074. Vatican - Biblioteca Apostolica ebr. 305,1, f. 31b-33a, C.

Tsarfat
3075. London - British Library Add. 11639 (Margoliouth 1056), f. 272b-273a, M.
3076. London - David Sofer 5, f. 25a-26a, C, additional glosses.
3077. Moscow - Russian State Library, Ms. Guenzburg 1665, f. 22a-22b, M.
3078. Oxford - Bodleian Library MS Laud. Or. 271 (Neubauer 1206), f. 30b-32b, C, commentator: Aaron b. Hayyim haKohen (compiler).
3079. Oxford - Bodleian Library MS Opp. 171 (Neubauer 1207), f. 26b-28b, C.
3080. Parma - Biblioteca Palatina Cod. Parm. 3136 (de Rossi 405), f. 35b-36b, M.

אזרח רענן פרח כשושנה (א 2372), משה אבן עזרא, חלק ב', קדושתא לשחרית יום כפור

Carpentras
3081. Cincinnati - Hebrew Union College 392, f. 44b-45a, M, no incipit.

Carpentras, commentary by Josef b. Abraham of Montelitz
3082. Cincinnati - Hebrew Union College 291, f. 20a-21b, C, rubric: פי' אזרח רענן וכו'.
3083. New York - Jewish Theological Seminary Ms. 4197, f. 102b-104a, M, no incipit.
3084. Paris - Ecole Rabbinique 32, f.124b-125b, M, no incipit.
3085. Strasbourg - Bibliotheque Nationale et Universitaire 4081, f. 101b-102a, M, no incipit.

אזרחי מעבר הנהר (א 2375), סליחה

Ashkenaz
3086. Braunschweig - Landesmuseum fuer Geschichte und Volkstum R 2386, vol. II, f. 127b, M, short.
3087. Muenchen - Bayerische Staatsbibliothek, Cod. hebr. 346, f. 164a, C, short.
3088. Oxford - Bodleian Library MS Mich. 543 (Neubauer 1212), f. 43b-44a, C, commentator: Isaac b. Jacob (compiler), rubric: עקידה.
3089. Oxford - Bodleian Library MS Opp. 681 (Neubauer 1213), f. 75b-76a, C.
3090. Padova - Biblioteca del Seminario Vescovile Cod. 218, f. 152a-152b, M.
3091. Vatican - Biblioteca Apostolica ebr. 422/1, f. 26a, C, very short.

3092. Vatican - Biblioteca Apostolica ebr. 422/2, f. 39b, CG, no incipit, very short.

Tsarfat

3093. Oxford - Bodleian Library MS Bodl. Or. 109 (Neubauer 1209), f. 47b-48a, C, commentator: Aaron b. Hayyim haKohen (compiler).

אח ועבד הדימוני ויתנו ארצי שממה (א 2379), אברהם אבן עזרא, קינה
Yemen, commentary by Isaac b. Abraham Wanneh

3094. Jerusalem - Sassoon 1158, p. 174, M, rubric: קינה סים׳ אברהם.
3095. London - British Library Or. 11122, f. 104b, M, no incipit.

אחבר שיר ביום ששי לנקדשי, שלמה
Yemen

3096. New York - M. Lehmann 274, f. 126b-127b, M, kabbalistic.

אחד אלהינו בשמים עידותנו בכל יום פעמים, סליחה
Yemen, commentary by Isaac b. Abraham Wanneh

3097. Chicago-Spertus College of Judaica D 2, 2, f. 181a, M, very short.

אחד לבדו באין סמוך לו (א 2411), אברהם אבן עזרא, סילוק, קדושתא למנחה יום כפור
North Africa

3098. Parma - Biblioteca Palatina Cod. Parm. 2290, f. 3b-5a, M, commentator: Isaac b. Mose Duran, rubric: פיוט לחכם השלם אבן עזרא ז״ל והוא סלוק מנחת הצום הנכבד צום כפור וביאורו.

Romania

3099. St. Petersburg - Inst. of Oriental Studies of the Russian Academy C 14/10, f. 91b-92b, C, philosophical and kabbalistic, rubric: זה השיר שחבר אברהם ב״ר אבן עזרה ובספרד מתפללים בו ביום הכפורים.

אחד מי יודע (א 2414), זמר לפסח
Ashkenaz

3100. Copenhagen - The Royal Library Cod. Sim. Hebr. 94, f. 46a-47a, M, rubric: ביאור אחד מי יודע.

אחד קדוש אש אוכלה אש (א 2418), קדושה
Ashkenaz

3101. London - British Library Or. 11318/1, f. 158a-158b, C.
3102. Moscow - Russian State Library, Ms. Guenzburg 191, f. 99b-100a, M.
3103. New York - Jewish Theological Seminary Ms. 8169 (Acc. 0016), f. 43a-43b, M.
3104. Oxford - Bodleian Library MS Opp. 172 (Neubauer 1211), f. 7a-7b, C, no incipit.

3105. Oxford - Bodleian Library MS Opp. 675 (Neubauer 1210), f. 61a, C, no incipit.
3106. Salzburg - Universitsetsbibliothek M II 342, f. 1b, FM, no incipit.
Tsarfat
3107. London - David Sofer 5, f. 122a-122b, C.
3108. Paris - Bibliotheque Nationale heb. 445,9, f. 69b-70a, C.
3109. Parma - Biblioteca Palatina Cod. Parm. 1794 (de Rossi 1061), f. 76a-77b, M.
3110. Parma - Biblioteca Palatina Cod. Parm. 1794 (de Rossi 1061), f. 143b, M.
3111. Parma - Biblioteca Palatina Cod. Parm. 2125 (de Rossi 812), f. 30b-31a, C, rubric: קדושה.
3112. Parma - Biblioteca Palatina Cod. Parm. 2890 (de Rossi 856), f. 38b, M.
3113. Parma - Biblioteca Palatina Cod. Parm. 3006 (de Rossi 654,1), f. 76a-76b, M.
3114. Parma - Biblioteca Palatina Cod. Parm. 3006 (de Rossi 654,1), f. 150a-150b, M.

אחד קדוש המדבר שלום לחסידיו (א 2419), יצחק בן אליעזר, אופן לחתן
Ashkenaz
3115. Budapest - Magyar tudomanyos akademia, MS. Kaufmann A 399, p. 369-370, C, rubric: אופנו.
Ashkenaz, commentary by Abraham b. Azriel[70]
3116. Frankfurt a M - Stadt- und Universitaetsbibliothek Fol. 16 (Merzbacher 95), f. 93b-94b, C, rubric: אופן אחר.
3117. Vatican - Biblioteca Apostolica ebr. 301,1, f. 111a-112a, C, rubric: אופן.

אחדת יום זה (א 2427), משולם ב"ר קלונימוס, חלק ג', קדושתא לשחרית יום כפור
Ashkenaz
3118. Berlin - Staatsbibliothek (Preussischer Kulturbesitz) Or. Qu. 798-799 (Steinschneider 177), I, 72a-73a, M.
3119. Braunschweig - Landesmuseum fuer Geschichte und Volkstum R 2386, vol. II, f. 185a-185b, M.
3120. Budapest - Magyar tudomanyos akademia, MS. Kaufmann A 400, p. 308-309, C.
3121. Hamburg - Staats- und Universitaetsbibliothek Cod. hebr. 17/2 (Steinschneider 152), f. 151a, C.
3122. Hamburg - Staats- und Universitaetsbibliothek Cod. hebr. 62 (Steinschneider 154), f. 3a-3b, C.

---

[70] Edited by Urbach, ערוגת הבושם, vol. III, p. 105-110.

3123. Hamburg - Staats- und Universitaetsbibliothek Cod. hebr. 40b (Steinschneider 110), f. 91a, G.
3124. Hamburg - Staats- und Universitaetsbibliothek Cod. hebr. 132 (Steinschneider 155), f. 33a, C.
3125. Jerusalem - Jewish National and University Library Ms Heb 8° 3037, f. 115b-116a, M.
3126. Jerusalem - Schocken Institute 24100 / Mahzor Nuremberg , f. 375b-376a, M.
3127. London - British Library Or. 11318/1, f. 71b-72a, C.
3128. London - Montefiore Library 261, f. 42b-43a, C, commentator: Eliezer b. Natan?.
3129. Moscow - Russian State Library, Ms. Guenzburg 191, f. 84a-84b, M.
3130. Muenchen - Bayerische Staatsbibliothek, Cod. hebr. 86, f. 100a-100b, G.
3131. Muenchen - Bayerische Staatsbibliothek, Cod. hebr. 346, f. 52a-52b, C, later marginal glosses.
3132. Muenchen - Bayerische Staatsbibliothek, Cod. hebr. 393, f. 140b-141a, C, no incipit.
3133. New York - Jewish Theological Seminary Ms. 4466, f. 304b-305a, M.
3134. New York - Jewish Theological Seminary Ms. 8097, f. 71a-72b, C, additional glosses in the margins.
3135. New York - Jewish Theological Seminary Ms. 8169 (Acc. 0016), f. 65b-66a, M.
3136. Oxford - Bodleian Library MS Mich. 365 (Neubauer 1208), f. 68b, C.
3137. Oxford - Bodleian Library MS Opp. 172 (Neubauer 1211), f. 36b-37b, C.
3138. Oxford - Bodleian Library MS Opp. 619 (Neubauer 2374), f. 139b-140a, M.
3139. Parma - Biblioteca Palatina Cod. Parm. 3205 (de Rossi 655), f. 225a, C.
3140. Parma - Biblioteca Palatina Cod. Parm. 3270 (de Rossi 1215), f. 103a, M.
3141. Parma - Biblioteca Palatina Cod. Parm. 3271 (de Rossi 1216), f. 34b, G.
3142. Parma - Bibliotcca Palatina Cod. Parm. 3507 (Perreau 27), f. 146b, C.
3143. Vatican - Biblioteca Apostolica ebr. 308, f. 98(ii)a-98(ii)b, C, commentator: David b. Mose (compiler).
3144. Vatican - Biblioteca Apostolica ebr. 422/1, f. 15a, C, short.
3145. Zurich - Zentralbibliothek Heid. 139, f. 76a, C, additional marginal notes.

Asti, Fossano, Moncalvo
3146. New Haven - Yale University, Beinecke Rare Book and MS Library, MS Heb. 52, f. 102a, M.

Romania
3147. Vatican - Biblioteca Apostolica ebr. 320, f. 278a-279a, M.
Tsarfat
3148. Bern - Burgerbibliothek A 409, f. 78a-79a, G.
3149. London - British Library Or. 8682, f. 65b, G.
3150. London - David Sofer 5, f. 136b, C.
3151. London - David Sofer 5, f. 136b, C, rubric: פירוש אחר.
3152. Oxford - Bodleian Library MS Bodl. Or. 109 (Neubauer 1209), f. 18b-19a, C, commentator: Aaron b. Hayyim haKohen (compiler).
3153. Oxford - Bodleian Library MS Laud. Or. 271 (Neubauer 1206), f. 112a-112b, C, commentator: Aaron b. Hayyim haKohen (compiler), no incipit.
3154. Parma - Biblioteca Palatina Cod. Parm. 1794 (de Rossi 1061), f. 112b-113a, M.
3155. Parma - Biblioteca Palatina Cod. Parm. 2125 (de Rossi 812), f. 39a, C.
3156. Parma - Biblioteca Palatina Cod. Parm. 2890 (de Rossi 856), f. 23b, M.
3157. Parma - Biblioteca Palatina Cod. Parm. 3006 (de Rossi 654,1), f. 137a-137b, M.
3158. Parma - Biblioteca Palatina Cod. Parm. 3006 (de Rossi 654,1), f. 137b-138a, M.

אחור וקדם מפה ומפה לכל דור ודור (א 2444), אלעזר ברבי קליר, פתיחה לקינה
Ashkenaz
3159. Berlin - Staatsbibliothek (Preussischer Kulturbesitz) Or. Qu. 798-799 (Steinschneider 177), II. f. 194a-196a, M.
3160. Budapest - Magyar tudomanyos akademia, MS. Kaufmann A 400, S. 217-223, C.
3161. Hamburg - Staats- und Universitaetsbibliothek Cod. hebr. 17/2 (Steinschneider 152), f. 97b-98b, C.
3162. Oxford - Bodleian Library MS Can. Or. 70 (Neubauer 1147,8), f. 119a-122b, M.
3163. Oxford - Bodleian Library MS Opp. 170 (Neubauer 1205), f. 260b-261a, C, rubric: אחרת.
3164. Parma - Biblioteca Palatina Cod. Parm. 3205 (de Rossi 655), f. 201a-201b, C.
3165. Vatican - Biblioteca Apostolica ebr. 312, f. 48a-49b, G.
3166. Vatican - Biblioteca Apostolica ebr. 318, f. 230b-231b, GI.

אחור וקדם צרתה ארחי ורבעי זריתה (א 2445), מנחם ב"ר מכיר, זולת הפסקה

Ashkenaz
3167. Jerusalem - Schocken Institute 24100 / Mahzor Nuremberg, f. 39b-40a, M.
3168. Oxford - Bodleian Library MS Opp. 169 (Neubauer 1151), f. 6a-7a, M.

Ashkenaz, commentary by Abraham b. Azriel[71]
3169. Frankfurt a M - Stadt- und Universitaetsbibliothek Fol. 16 (Merzbacher 95), f. 62a-64b, C, rubric: זולת.
3170. Vatican - Biblioteca Apostolica ebr. 301,1, f. 95b-97b, C, rubric: זולת.

אחות אשר לך כספת (א 2446), אלעזר ברבי קליר, קדושתא לשמיני עצרת

Ashkenaz
3171. Muenchen - Bayerische Staatsbibliothek, Cod. hebr. 153 X, FC, incomplete.

Romania
3172. Vatican - Biblioteca Apostolica ebr. 320, f. 459a, M.

Tsarfat
3173. London - David Sofer 5, f. 183b, C.
3174. Moscow - Russian State Library, Ms. Guenzburg 1665, f. 187a, M.
3175. Oxford - Bodleian Library MS Opp. 171 (Neubauer 1207), f. 161b, C, rubric: לשמחת תורה.
3176. Vatican - Biblioteca Apostolica ebr. 306, f. 112a-112b, C, rubric: קדושתא.

אחות קטנה תפלותיה עורכה (א 2451), אברהם גירונדי, מעריב, יום א' של ראש השנה

Carpentras
3177. Cincinnati - Hebrew Union College 429/1, f. 56a-56b, M, no incipit.

Carpentras, commentary by Eliyahu Carmi
3178. Cincinnati - Hebrew Union College 357, f. 3b, M, rubric: תנא דרבי אלהו.
3179. New York - Jewish Theological Seminary Ms. 3151, f. 1a-1b, M.
3180. Paris - Ecole Rabbinique 31, f. 42a, M.

Carpentras, commentary by Josef b. Abraham of Montelitz
3181. Cincinnati - Hebrew Union College 357, f. 3a-3b, M, rubric: פירוש.
3182. New York - Jewish Theological Seminary Ms. 4746, f. 2a-2b, M.
3183. Paris - Alliance Israelite Universelle H 422 A, f. 130a-130b, M.
3184. Paris - Ecole Rabbinique 31, f. 41b-42b, M.

haAri
3185. Harvard University 067, vol. II, f. 5b-8b, M, lexical explanations in Hebrew and Ladino.

---

[71] Edited by Urbach, ערוגת הבושם, vol. III, p. 5-18.

Sepharad

3186. Skokie - Hebrew Theological College 3, f. 25a-26a, M.

אחזתי בקאתי אשר הייתי מודד, סליחה

Yemen, commentary by Isaac b. Abraham Wanneh

3187. Chicago-Spertus College of Judaica D 2, 2, f. 241b-242a, M.
3188. Jerusalem - Sassoon 1158, p. 421-423, M, no incipit.
3189. London - British Library Or. 11122, f. 218a-218b, M, no incipit.

אחלה אל יי אולי אכפרה (א 2515), מנחם ב"ר מכיר, סליחה

Ashkenaz

3190. Jerusalem - Schocken Institute 24100 / Mahzor Nuremberg, f. 448b, M.
3191. Muenchen - Bayerische Staatsbibliothek, Cod. hebr. 346, f. 137b-138a, C, rubric: אחרת, short.
3192. Oxford - Bodleian Library MS Opp. 172 (Neubauer 1211), f. 83a, C, short.

Ashkenaz, commentary by Abraham b. Azriel[72]

3193. Frankfurt a M - Stadt- und Universitaetsbibliothek Fol. 16 (Merzbacher 95), f. 107a-107b, C.

אחלה בתחנוני אליך יי ולך אשא עיני, סליחה

Yemen

3194. New York - Jewish Theological Seminary Ms. 3028, f. 81a, G.
3195. New York - Jewish Theological Seminary Ms. 3109, f. 14a, G.

אחנן מעשה בראשית, ליום א' של ראש השנה

Tsarfat

3196. London - David Sofer 5, f. 109a-109b, C.

אחננה לך רחום כי בך אושע (א 2540), סעדיה גאון, סליחה

Yemen

3197. New York - Jewish Theological Seminary Ms. 3028, f. 100b-101a, G, wenig.
3198. New York - Jewish Theological Seminary Ms. 3193, f. 140a-140b, M.

Yemen, commentary by Isaac b. Abraham Wanneh

3199. Chicago-Spertus College of Judaica D 2, 2, f. 228b, M, no incipit.
3200. Jerusalem - Sassoon 1158, p. 315-316, M, no incipit.
3201. London - British Library Or. 11122, f. 205a, M, no incipit.

---

[72] Edited by Urbach, ערוגת הבושם, vol. III, p. 556-557.

אחר שלישים במועצות (א 2573), יצחק בן אליעזר, יוצר לחתן

Ashkenaz

3202. Budapest - Magyar tudomanyos akademia, MS. Kaufmann A 399, p. 363-366, C.

אחרי בוא ישורון בקדש ברנע (א 2579), אהרן בן יוסף הרופא, פרשת שלח לך

Karaite, commentary by Berakha b. Josef haKohen

3203. New York - Jewish Theological Seminary Ms. 3367, f. 123b-125b, C, rubric: פרוש פרשת שלח לך.

3204. St. Petersburg - Russian National Library, Evr. IV 50, f. 95a-96b, C, rubric: שלח לך.

3205. St. Petersburg - Inst. of Oriental Studies of the Russian Academy B 431, f. 84b-86a, C, rubric: פרשת שלח לך.

אחרי בוא ענו בתוך אש ולהב (א 2580), אהרן בן יוסף הרופא, פרשת תרומה

Karaite, commentary by Berakha b. Josef haKohen

3206. New York - Jewish Theological Seminary Ms. 3367, f. 80a-83a, C, rubric: פירוש פרשת תרומה.

3207. St. Petersburg - Inst. of Oriental Studies of the Russian Academy B 431, f. 57b-59b, C, rubric: פרשת תרומה.

3208. St. Petersburg - Russian National Library, Evr. IV 50, f. 58b-61a, C, rubric: פ׳ תרומה.

אחריך נרוצה משכוני מונח בידיך, זולת

Ashkenaz, commentary by Abraham b. Azriel[73]

3209. Frankfurt a M - Stadt- und Universitaetsbibliothek Fol. 16 (Merzbacher 95), f. 98b-99b, C, rubric: זולת.

3210. Vatican - Biblioteca Apostolica ebr. 301,1, f. 115a-116a, C, rubric: זולת.

אחרי נמכר גאולה תהיה לו (א 2587), ברוך ב״ר שמואל, זולת שבת בהר

Ashkenaz

3211. Oxford - Bodleian Library MS Can. Or. 82 (Neubauer 1148), f. 73a-73b, M.

אחריש ואתאפק ולבי חלל (א 2592), בנימין ב״ר זרח, סליחה

Ashkenaz

3212. Muenchen - Bayerische Staatsbibliothek, Cod. hebr. 346, f. 162b, C.

3213. Oxford - Bodleian Library MS Opp. 681 (Neubauer 1213), f. 42a-42b, C.

---

[73] Edited by Urbach, ערוגת הבושם, vol. III, p. 132-137.

3214. Parma - Bibliotheca Palatina Cod. Parm. 3205 (de Rossi 655), f. 288a, C.

אחרית ותקוה ישלח אלהים (א 2593), משה אבן עזרא, סליחה
Ashkenaz

3215. Parma - Bibliotheca Palatina Cod. Parm. 3205 (de Rossi 655), f. 288a, C.

Carpentras

3216. Cincinnati - Hebrew Union College 392, f. 108b, M, no incipit, very short.

Carpentras, commentary by Josef b. Abraham of Montelitz

3217. New York - Jewish Theological Seminary Ms. 4197, f. 254b, M, no incipit, very short.
3218. Paris - Ecole Rabbinique 32, f. 263b, M, no incipit, very short.
3219. Strasbourg - Bibliotheque Nationale et Universitaire 4081, f. 234b, M, no incipit, very short.

אחשבה לדעת עמל (א 2595), שלמה הבבלי, זולת לשבת בראשית
Ashkenaz

3220. Berlin - Staatsbibliothek (Preussischer Kulturbesitz) Or. Qu. 361 (Steinschneider 51), f. 160a-161b, M, no incipit.
3221. Berlin - Staatsbibliothek (Preussischer Kulturbesitz) Or. Qu. 798-799 (Steinschneider 177), I, f. 234b-237a, M.
3222. Budapest - Magyar tudomanyos akademia, MS. Kaufmann A 399, p. 322-325, C.
3223. Cambridge - University Library Add. 504,1, f. 28a-31a, C, rubric: זה יסד שלמו לסוף חתום שלמה הקטון יגדל בתורה בשפוט לטרוף טרף תחילת החתימה.
3224. Frankfurt a M - Stadt- und Universitaetsbibliothek Oct. 227, f. 138b-140a, M, rubric: זולת.
3225. Jerusalem - Schocken Institute 24100 / Mahzor Nuremberg, f. 9b-10a, M.
3226. Lund - Universitetsbibliothek Ms. L.O. 2, f. 119a-120a, M, rubric: זולת.
3227. Moscow - Russian State Library, Ms. Guenzburg 615, f. 134b, C, rubric: זולת.
3228. Oxford - Bodleian Library MS Can. Or. 82 (Neubauer 1148), f. 3b-5a, M.
3229. Oxford - Bodleian Library MS Mich. 365 (Neubauer 1208), f. 21a-21b, C, rubric: זולת.
3230. Parma - Biblioteca Palatina Cod. Parm. 2895, p. 372-374, M, rubric: זולת.
3231. Parma - Biblioteca Palatina Cod. Parm. 3205 (de Rossi 655), f. 132a-133b, C, rubric: זולת.

3232. Uppsala - Universitetsbibliotek O.Heb.22, f. 127a-129a, M.
Ashkenaz, commentary by Abraham b. Azriel[74]
3233. Frankfurt a M - Stadt- und Universitaetsbibliothek Fol. 16 (Merzbacher 95), f. 52b-54a, C, rubric: זולת.
3234. Vatican - Biblioteca Apostolica ebr. 301,1, f. 82a-84a, C, rubric: זולת.
Ashkenaz, commentary by Eliezer b. Natan
3235. Parma - Biblioteca Palatina Cod. Parm. 3057.12 (de Rossi 1033/10), f. 146a-148b, C, rubric: שיתו לב לעבור זולת.
3236. Hamburg - Staats- und Universitaetsbibliothek Cod. hebr. 61 (Steinschneider 153), f. 27b-29b, C, rubric: זולת לשבת בראשית.
3237. Warszaw - Uniwersytet, Inst. Orientalistyczny 258, f. 177a-179a, C, rubric: זולת.

Tsarfat
3238. Oxford - Bodleian Library MS Laud. Or. 271 (Neubauer 1206), f. 183b-185b, C, commentator: Aaron b. Hayyim haKohen (compiler).
3239. Oxford - Bodleian Library MS Opp. 171 (Neubauer 1207), f. 33b-35b, C, rubric: פרשה פרה אדומה. פירוש מיוצר לא מצאתי. והא לך פירוש מזולת קלירית.
3240. Parma - Biblioteca Palatina Cod. Parm. 1264, f. 164b-165b, M.

אטתי מטתי מתוך צוקה ותוגה (א 2616), אליה ב"ר שמעיה, סליחה

Ashkenaz
3241. Cambridge - University Library Dd. 2.30, f. 33b-34a, G.
3242. Oxford - Bodleian Library MS Mich. 543 (Neubauer 1212), f. 49b-50a, C, commentator: Isaac b. Jacob (compiler).
3243. Oxford - Bodleian Library MS Opp. 681 (Neubauer 1213), f. 32a, C.
3244. Padova - Biblioteca del Seminario Vescovile Cod. 218, f. 138a-138b, M.
3245. Vatican - Biblioteca Apostolica ebr. 422/1, f. 29a-29b, C.
3246. Vatican - Biblioteca Apostolica ebr. 422/1, f. 43b, CG, no incipit.

אי זה מקום בינה אי מה זה (א 2620), יצחק ב"ר ראובן אלברגלוני, אזהרות

Mizrah
3247. Jerusalem - Musad haRav Kook 1129, f. 4b-56a, M, commentator: Amram b. Elqayim, no incipit.
3248. Tel Aviv - Bill Gross 291, f. 1a-6b, M, commentator: Mose Muati, incomplete.

North Africa
3249. New York - Jewish Theological Seminary Benaim 68, f. 1a-97a, M, Ms burned and badly damaged.

---

[74] Edited by Urbach, ערוגת הבושם, vol. II, p. 216-228.

3250. New York - Jewish Theological Seminary Ms. 3183, f. 6b-68b, M. North Africa, commentary by Mose Muati
3251. New York - Jewish Theological Seminary Benaim 68, f. 1a-97a, M, Ms burned and badly damaged.
3252. New York - Jewish Theological Seminary Benaim 130, f. 82a-99a, C.
3253. New York - Jewish Theological Seminary Ms. 3060, f. 2a-7b, M, only on beginning of the Azharot.
3254. New York - Jewish Theological Seminary Ms. 3061, f. 1a-51a, 54a-79b, M, additions by Salomo Ibn Tsur, incomplete, only prohibitions, beginning and end missing.
3255. New York - Jewish Theological Seminary Ms. 3068, f. 1b-45b, M, incomplete, only prohibitions, beginning and end missing.

אי כה אומר כורת לאב בפצח (א 2624), אלעזר ברבי קליר, קינה
Ashkenaz
3256. Berlin - Staatsbibliothek (Preussischer Kulturbesitz) Or. Qu. 798-799 (Steinschneider 177), II, f. 196a-196b, M.
3257. Jerusalem - Schocken Institute 24100 / Mahzor Nuremberg, f. 199b-200a, M.
3258. Oxford - Bodleian Library MS Can. Or. 70 (Neubauer 1147,8), f. 122b-123b, M.
3259. Vatican - Biblioteca Apostolica ebr. 312, f. 49b-50a, G.
3260. Vatican - Biblioteca Apostolica ebr. 318, f. 233b-234a, GI.
Ashkenaz, commentary by Abraham b. Azriel[75]
3261. Vatican - Biblioteca Apostolica ebr. 301,1, f. 136a-136b, C, rubric: אחר'.

אי פתרוס (א 2628), שמעון ב"ר יצחק, זולת ליום ז' של פסח
Ashkenaz
3262. Berlin - Staatsbibliothek (Preussischer Kulturbesitz) Or. Qu. 798-799 (Steinschneider 177), II, f. 89b-90a, M.
3263. Budapest - Magyar tudomanyos akademia, MS. Kaufmann A 384, f. 200a-201a, M.
3264. Erlangen - Universitaetsbibliothek 2601 (Roth 67), f. 114a, M, very short.
3265. Hamburg - Staats- und Universitaetsbibliothek Cod. hebr. 17/2 (Steinschneider 152), f. 37b-38a, C.
3266. Jerusalem - Schocken Institute 24100 / Mahzor Nuremberg, f. 108a-108b, M.
3267. London - British Library Add. 18695 (Margoliouth 683), f. 48a-48b, T, Yiddish, rubric: זולת.

---

[75] Edited by Urbach, ערוגת הבושם, vol. III, p. 274-275.

3268. Muenchen - Bayerische Staatsbibliothek, Cod. hebr. 88, f. 81a-81b, G.
3269. Muenchen - Bayerische Staatsbibliothek, Cod. hebr. 393, f. 133a-134a, C, no incipit.
3270. New York - Jewish Theological Seminary Ms. 4466, f. 87a-88a, M.
3271. Paris - Bibliotheque Nationale heb. 709, f. 101a-102a, C.
3272. Parma - Biblioteca Palatina Cod. Parm. 1002 (Ta 24), f. 137b-138a, M.
3273. Parma - Biblioteca Palatina Cod. Parm. 3205 (de Rossi 655), f. 107b-108b, C, rubric: זולת.
3274. Parma - Biblioteca Palatina Cod. Parm. 3507 (Perreau 27), f. 71b-72a, C, rubric: זולת.
3275. Zurich - Zentralbibliothek Heid. 139, f. 41a-42a, C, additional marginal notes.

Tsarfat
3276. London - David Sofer 5, f. 45a-45b, C.
3277. Moscow - Russian State Library, Ms. Guenzburg 1665, f. 104a-104b, M.
3278. Oxford - Bodleian Library MS Laud. Or. 271 (Neubauer 1206), f. 76b, C, commentator: Ephraim b. Jakob of Bonn?, Aaron b. Hayyim haKohen (compiler).
3279. Parma - Biblioteca Palatina Cod. Parm. 3136 (de Rossi 405), f. 108a-108b, M.

איברא קדמאה כד הוה נפיק מפום קודשא בריך הוא, תרגום דיבור ראשון

Ashkenaz
3280. Oxford - Bodleian Library MS Opp. 170 (Neubauer 1205), f. 95a-95b, C.

איה כל נלפאותיך הגדולות (א 2651), גרשום ב"ר יהודה מאור הגולה, סליחה

Ashkenaz
3281. Braunschweig - Landesmuseum fuer Geschichte und Volkstum R 2386, vol. II, f. 49b-50a, M.
3282. Budapest - Magyar tudomanyos akademia, MS. Kaufmann A 400, p. 489-490, C, rubric: אחרת דרבינו גרשם.
3283. Cambridge - University Library Dd. 2.30, f. 12b-13b, G.
3284. Jerusalem - Schocken Institute 24100 / Mahzor Nuremberg, f. 245b, M.
3285. Moscow - Russian State Library, Ms. Guenzburg 190, f. 21b-22b, G.
3286. Moscow - Russian State Library, Ms. Guenzburg 615, f. 159b-160a, C, rubric: אל מלך.
3287. Muenchen - Bayerische Staatsbibliothek, Cod. hebr. 346, f. 125a, C, short.

3288. Oxford - Bodleian Library MS Mich. 543 (Neubauer 1212), f. 51a-51b, C, commentator: Isaac b. Jakob (compiler).
3289. Oxford - Bodleian Library MS Opp. 170 (Neubauer 1205), f. 228b-229a, C.
3290. Padova - Biblioteca del Seminario Vescovile Cod. 218, f. 61b-62a, M.
3291. Padova - Biblioteca del Seminario Vescovile Cod. 218, f. 62a-62b, M, rubric: אחרת.
3292. Parma - Biblioteca Palatina Cod. Parm. 3205 (de Rossi 655), f. 268b-269a, C.
3293. Vatican - Biblioteca Apostolica ebr. 308, f. 13b, C, commentator: David b. Mose (compiler).
3294. Vatican - Biblioteca Apostolica ebr. 422/1, f. 28a, C.
3295. Vatican - Biblioteca Apostolica ebr. 422/1, f. 42a, CG, very short.

Ashkenaz, commentary by Abraham b. Azriel[76]

3296. Frankfurt a M - Stadt- und Universitaetsbibliothek Fol. 16 (Merzbacher 95), f. 111b-112a, C.
3297. Vatican - Biblioteca Apostolica ebr. 301,1, f. 147b, C, rubric: אחרת.

Tsarfat

3298. London - British Library Add. 11639 (Margoliouth 1056), f. 469a-469b, M.
3299. London - David Sofer 5, f. 84a-84b, C.
3300. Oxford - Bodleian Library MS Laud. Or. 271 (Neubauer 1206), f. 171b, C, commentator: Aaron b. Hayyim haKohen (compiler), rubric: דרבנא גרשום.
3301. Oxford - Bodleian Library MS Opp. 171 (Neubauer 1207), f. 103a-103b, C.
3302. Parma - Biblioteca Palatina Cod. Parm. 3007 (de Rossi 654,2), f. 39a-39b, M.
3303. Vatican - Biblioteca Apostolica ebr. 306, f. 194b-195b, C.

איה קנאתך וגבורתך העצומות (א 2660), בנימין ב"ר זרח, סליחה

Ashkenaz

3304. Muenchen - Bayerische Staatsbibliothek, Cod. hebr. 346, f. 164a, C, very short.
3305. Oxford - Bodleian Library MS Mich. 543 (Neubauer 1212), f. 73a, C, commentator: Isaac b. Jakob (compiler), short.

---

[76] Edited by Urbach, ערוגת הבושם, vol. III, p. 344-346.

HEBREW LITURGICAL POETRY 217

איום אמצה עשירייה (א 2665), אלעזר ברבי קליר, קדושתא לשמיני עצרת
Tsarfat[77]
3306. Oxford - Bodleian Library MS Opp. 171 (Neubauer 1207), f. 149a-152a, C.

איום ונורא מי לא יראך (א 2668), משולם ב"ר קלונימוס, חלק ג' קדושתא לשחרית יום כפור
Ashkenaz
3307. Berlin - Staatsbibliothek (Preussischer Kulturbesitz) Or. Qu. 798-799 (Steinschneider 177), II, f. 91a-91b, M.
3308. Braunschweig - Landesmuseum fuer Geschichte und Volkstum R 2386, vol. I, f. 61a-61b, M, no incipit.
3309. Budapest - Magyar tudomanyos akademia, MS. Kaufmann A 384, f. 203a-203b, M.
3310. Budapest - Magyar tudomanyos akademia, MS. Kaufmann A 400, p. 138, C, no incipit, short.
3311. Hamburg - Staats- und Universitaetsbibliothek Cod. hebr. 17/2 (Steinschneider 152), f. 67a, C, very short.
3312. Jerusalem - Schocken Institute 24100 / Mahzor Nuremberg, f. 122a, M, short.
3313. Moscow - Russian State Library, Ms. Guenzburg 615, f. 25a, C, very short, no incipit.
3314. Muenchen - Bayerische Staatsbibliothek, Cod. hebr. 88, f. 82b-83a, G.
3315. Muenchen - Bayerische Staatsbibliothek, Cod. hebr. 393, f. 134b-135a, C, no incipit.
3316. New York - Jewish Theological Seminary Ms. 4466, f. 108b-109a, M, short.
3317. Paris - Bibliotheque Nationale heb. 709, f. 102a-102b, C, no incipit.
3318. Parma - Biblioteca Palatina Cod. Parm. 3205 (de Rossi 655), f. 108b-109a, C.
3319. Parma - Biblioteca Palatina Cod. Parm. 3507 (Perreau 27), f. 73a, C, no incipit.
3320. Zurich - Zentralbibliothek Heid. 139, f. 46a, C, no incipit, additional marginal notes.
Tsarfat
3321. London - David Sofer 5, f. 41b, C, additional glosses.
3322. Moscow - Russian State Library, Ms. Guenzburg 1665, f. 90a, M, no incipit.
3323. Vatican - Biblioteca Apostolica ebr. 306, f. 217b-218a, C, no incipit.

---

[77] An edition of this commentary by being prepared by E. Hollender.

איום זכור נא לשואלי מים (א 2675), מוסף לשמיני עצרת

Ashkenaz

3324. Berlin - Staatsbibliothek (Preussischer Kulturbesitz) Or. Qu. 798-799 (Steinschneider 177), I, f. 221a-221b, M.
3325. Budapest - Magyar tudomanyos akademia, MS. Kaufmann A 400, p. 411, C.
3326. Hamburg - Staats- und Universitaetsbibliothek Cod. hebr. 17/2 (Steinschneider 152), f. 176b, C.
3327. London - British Library Add. 22431 (Margoliouth 662a), f. 143b-144a, M.
3328. London - British Library Or. 11318/1, f. 152b-153a, C.
3329. Zurich - Zentralbibliothek Heid. 139, f. 100a-100b, C.

Tsarfat

3330. Oxford - Bodleian Library MS Laud. Or. 271 (Neubauer 1206), f. 105a, C, commentator: Aaron b. Hayyim haKohen (compiler), no incipit.

איום תמים דעי (א 2682), בנימין ב"ר שמואל, חלק ח', קדושתא למוסף ראש השנה

Tsarfat

3331. London - British Library Or. 8682, f. 44b-45a, GI.

איומה את פני דודך תחלי (א 2684), שלם שבזי

Yemen

3332. Cincinnati - Hebrew Union College 398, f. 183a-185a, M.

איומה בהר המור עלי לך ובשרי ונשיר בשיר מזמור בניגון ליוצרי ונעלה להר תבור (א 2686), שלם שבזי

Yemen

3333. Cincinnati - Hebrew Union College 398, f. 28a-30a, M.

איומה בהר המור עלי לך ובשרי ונשיר בשיר מזמור בניגון ליוצרי וצמח ארי גבור (א 2688), שלם שבזי

Yemen

3334. Cincinnati - Hebrew Union College 398, f. 31b-32b, M.

איומה בוערה שפוך למולך עתרת, יוסף אבן אביתור, הושענא

Narbonne, commentary by Meir Meili of Narbonne[78]

3335. London - British Library Add. 19778, f. 37b, C, rubric: ליום שבת.

---

[78] Edited by Sofer, ספר המכתם, p. 161-162.

איומה בחר ילבין כצמר צחר (א 2689/ה 478), יוסף אבן אביתור, יוצר ליום כפור

Ashkenaz
3336. Jerusalem - Schocken Institute 24100 / Mahzor Nuremberg, f. 377a-377b, M.
3337. Oxford - Bodleian Library MS Opp. 172 (Neubauer 1211), f. 38a, C.

איומה המשי דגלי המוני ממצולה (א 2691), שלם שבזי

Yemen
3338. Cincinnati - Hebrew Union College 398, f. 26a, M.

איומה חשוקה יפה כלבנה (א 2693), יוסף ב"ר שמואל טוב עלם, חלק ז', קדושתא לשבועות

Tsarfat
3339. London - David Sofer 5, f. 68b-69a, C.
3340. Parma - Biblioteca Palatina Cod. Parm. 3136 (de Rossi 405), f. 171a, M.

איומה לדוד חכי מלכי (א 2698), שלם שבזי

Yemen
3341. Cincinnati - Hebrew Union College 398, f. 12b-13b, M.

איומה נאוה ושחורה (א 2702), יהודה הלוי, מאורה

Carpentras, commentary by Mordekhai b. Josef of Rocco Martino
3342. Cincinnati - Hebrew Union College 246/1, f. 16a-17b, C, rubric: פי' מאורה איומה וכו'.

Sepharad, commentary by Josef Garad
3343. Oxford - Bodleian Library Heb.e.10 (Neubauer 2746/1), f. 6a-7a, C, rubric: פרשת זכור . מאורה.
3344. Oxford - Bodleian Library Heb.e.10 (Neubauer 2746/1), f. 17b-18a, C, rubric: איומה נאוה, no incipit.

איומתי בהר מור תסובב היכלי (א 716*), שלם שבזי

Yemen
3345. Cincinnati - Hebrew Union College 398, f. 27a, M.

איומתי תעורר אהבתי להזכיר שיר לנורא על תהלות (א 2718), שלם שבזי

Yemen
3346. Cincinnati - Hebrew Union College 398, f. 192b-194a, M.

איומתי תעורר הישנים (א 2719), שלם שבזי

Yemen
3347. Cincinnati - Hebrew Union College 398, f. 175b-178b, M.

איומתך סודרת קילוסך (א 2721), אליהו בן צדוק, מעריב ליום ב' של סוכות

Tsarfat
3348. London - British Library Or. 2735 (Margoliouth 663), f. 99b-100a, M.
3349. London - David Sofer 5, f. 180a-181a, C, rubric: מעריב לליל שיני.

אייהו אל חצן אלמסמא (א 2734), שלם שבזי

Yemen
3350. Cincinnati - Hebrew Union College 398, f. 23a-24a, M.

אייהו אל קצר אלימצאני (א 2735), שלם שבזי

Yemen
3351. Cincinnati - Hebrew Union College 398, f. 24b-25a, M.

אייהו צבי אל שרוד, שלם שבזי

Yemen
3352. Cincinnati - Hebrew Union College 398, f. 22a-23a, M.

אייוס אפתינטין ואבזרי אורייתא, פיוט בארמית לשבועות

Ashkenaz, commentary by Benjamin b. Abraham Anaw
3353. Jerusalem - Musad haRav Kook 478, p. 66-72, C, rubric: אלפא ביתא אחרן יב.
3354. London - Beth Din & Beth Hamidrash 6,9, f. 188b-192a, C, rubric: אלפא בית אחרן.

אייחד שם שוכן תרשימים (א 2730), שמעון ב"ר יצחק, יוצר לחתן

Ashkenaz
3355. Berlin - Staatsbibliothek (Preussischer Kulturbesitz) Or. Qu. 798-799 (Steinschneider 177), I, f. 263a-264a, M.
3356. Budapest - Magyar tudomanyos akademia, MS. Kaufmann A 399, p. 349-352, C, rubric: יוצר לחתן מדרבנא שמעון הגדול זצ"ל.
3357. Frankfurt a M - Stadt- und Universitaetsbibliothek Oct. 227, f. 147b-148b, M.
3358. Jerusalem - Schocken Institute 24100 / Mahzor Nuremberg, f. 223b-224a, M.
3359. Lund - Universitetsbibliothek Ms. L.O. 2, f. 110b-111a, M.
3360. Muenchen - Bayerische Staatsbibliothek, Cod. hebr. 69, f. 78b-79b, M.
3361. Muenchen - Bayerische Staatsbibliothek, Cod. hebr. 393, f. 224b-226b, C.
3362. Muenchen - Bayerische Staatsbibliothek, Cod. hebr. 393,9, f. 182a-183b, C, no incipit.
3363. Oxford - Bodleian Library MS Can. Or. 82 (Neubauer 1148), f. 47a-48a, M.

3364. Oxford - Bodleian Library MS Mich. 365 (Neubauer 1208), f. 35a-35b, C, rubric: יוצר לנישואין.
3365. Parma - Biblioteca Palatina Cod. Parm. 2895, p. 448-451, M, margins cut, text damaged.
3366. Parma - Biblioteca Palatina Cod. Parm. 3205 (de Rossi 655), f. 168b-170b, C.

Ashkenaz, commentary by Abraham b. Azriel[79]
3367. Frankfurt a M - Stadt- und Universitaetsbibliothek Fol. 16 (Merzbacher 95), f. 75b-77b, C.
3368. Vatican - Biblioteca Apostolica ebr. 301,1, f. 110a-111a, C, rubric: יוצר דחתן.

Tsarfat
3369. London - British Library Or. 2735 (Margoliouth 663), f. 172a-173b, M, margins partly damaged.

איך אוכל לבא עדיך ועובדי זולתיך (א 2745), יצחק בן סעדיה, סליחה

Ashkenaz
3370. Jerusalem - Schocken Institute 24100 / Mahzor Nuremberg, f. 248b-249a, M, few marginal notes by later hand only.
3371. Muenchen - Bayerische Staatsbibliothek, Cod. hebr. 346, f. 126a-126b, C, rubric: אחרת.
3372. Oxford - Bodleian Library MS Mich. 543 (Neubauer 1212), f. 56a-56b, Margin, C, commentator: Isaac b. Jakob (compiler), rubric: שלמונית.
3373. Oxford - Bodleian Library MS Opp. 681 (Neubauer 1213), f. 18b-19a, C.
3374. Vatican - Biblioteca Apostolica ebr. 308, f. 12a-12b, C, commentator: David b. Mose (compiler).
3375. Vatican - Biblioteca Apostolica ebr. 422/1, f. 29b, C.
3376. Vatican - Biblioteca Apostolica ebr. 422/1, f. 44a-44b, CG, no incipit.

Ashkenaz, commentary by Abraham b. Azriel[80]
3377. Vatican - Biblioteca Apostolica ebr. 301,1, f. 145b-146a, C, rubric: אחרת.

Tsarfat
3378. Oxford - Bodleian Library MS Bodl. Or. 109 (Neubauer 1209), f. 52b-53b, C, commentator: Aaron b. Hayyim haKohen (compiler).

---
[79] Edited by Urbach, ערוגת הבושם, vol. III, p. 97-105.
[80] Edited by Urbach, ערוגת הבושם, vol. III, p. 332-333.

איך אפתח לפניך, סליחה

Ashkenaz
3379. Parma - Biblioteca Palatina Cod. Parm. 3205 (de Rossi 655), f. 278b-279a, C, rubric: פתיחה.
Tsarfat
3380. Parma - Biblioteca Palatina Cod. Parm. 3007 (de Rossi 654,2), f. 25b, M.

איך אפתח פי בחין לחלותיך (א 2763), סליחה

Ashkenaz
3381. Vatican - Biblioteca Apostolica ebr. 422/1, f. 25b-26a, C, very short.
Tsarfat
3382. London - David Sofer 5, f. 83b, C.
3383. London - David Sofer 5, f. 101b-102a, C.
3384. Vatican - Biblioteca Apostolica ebr. 306, f. 168b, C.

איך אשא ראש (א 2767), שמעון ב"ר יצחק, סליחה

Ashkenaz
3385. Braunschweig - Landesmuseum fuer Geschichte und Volkstum R 2386, vol. II, f. 241a-241b, M.
3386. Cambridge - University Library Dd. 2.30, f. 76a-76b, G.
3387. Jerusalem - Schocken Institute 24100 / Mahzor Nuremberg, f. 426b-427a, M.
3388. London - British Library Or. 11318/1, f. 120a-121b, C.
3389. Moscow - Russian State Library, Ms. Guenzburg 190, f. 17b-18a, G.
3390. Muenchen - Bayerische Staatsbibliothek, Cod. hebr. 346, f. 119b, C, commentator: Abraham Ḥaldiq, rubric: 'זאת הסליח' מפריש' הר' אברה' חלדיק זע"ל והיא שייכא למוסף דיום הכפורים.
3391. Muenchen - Bayerische Staatsbibliothek, Cod. hebr. 346, f. 119b-120a, C, rubric: .
3392. New York - Jewish Theological Seminary Ms. 4466, f. 395a-396a, M.
3393. New York - Jewish Theological Seminary Ms. 8097, f. 85a-85b, C.
3394. Oxford - Bodleian Library MS Mich. 543 (Neubauer 1212), f. 29b-30b, C, commentator: Isaac b. Jakob (compiler).
3395. Oxford - Bodleian Library MS Opp. 172 (Neubauer 1211), f. 70b-71b, C.
3396. Oxford - Bodleian Library MS Opp. 619 (Neubauer 2374), f. 226a-227a, M.
3397. Oxford - Bodleian Library MS Opp. 681 (Neubauer 1213), f. 20b-22a, C.
3398. Padova - Biblioteca del Seminario Vescovile Cod. 218, f. 189a-190a, M.

3399. Parma - Biblioteca Palatina Cod. Parm. 3205 (de Rossi 655), f. 280a, C.
3400. Vatican - Biblioteca Apostolica ebr. 308, f. 129b-131a, C, commentator: David b. Mose (compiler).
3401. Vatican - Biblioteca Apostolica ebr. 308, f. 131a-131(ii)b, C, commentator: David b. Mose (compiler).
3402. Vatican - Biblioteca Apostolica ebr. 422/1, f. 24b, C, very short.
3403. Vatican - Biblioteca Apostolica ebr. 422/2, f. 39a, C, no incipit, very short.

Ashkenaz, commentary by Abraham b. Azriel[81]
3404. Frankfurt a M - Stadt- und Universitaetsbibliothek Fol. 16 (Merzbacher 95), f. 110b-111a, .
3405. Frankfurt a M - Stadt- und Universitaetsbibliothek Fol. 16 (Merzbacher 95), f. 113b, C, commentator: Abraham Ḥaldiq; rubric: זאת הסליחה מפריש הר' ר' אברהם חלדיק זצ"ל והיא שייכא למוסף דיום הכיפורים.
3406. Vatican - Biblioteca Apostolica ebr. 301,1, f. 143b-144a, C.

Asti, Fossano, Moncalvo
3407. New Haven - Yale University, Beinecke Rare Book and MS Library, MS Heb. 52, f. 150a, M.

Romania
3408. Vatican - Biblioteca Apostolica ebr. 320, f. 397b-398a, M.

Tsarfat
3409. London - David Sofer 5, f. 142b-143b, C, rubric: סליחות מיום הכפורים לתפילת השחר.
3410. Oxford - Bodleian Library MS Bodl. Or. 109 (Neubauer 1209), f. 67b-69b, C, commentator: Aaron b. Hayyim haKohen (compiler).
3411. Parma - Biblioteca Palatina Cod. Parm. 1794 (de Rossi 1061), f. 21a-22a, M.
3412. Parma - Biblioteca Palatina Cod. Parm. 2890 (de Rossi 856), f. 46a-47a, M.
3413. Parma - Biblioteca Palatina Cod. Parm. 3006 (de Rossi 654,1), f. 157b-158a, M.
3414. Vatican - Biblioteca Apostolica ebr. 306, f. 200b-201b, C.

איך זרים אכזרים כדבורים סבבוני (א 2780), סליחה לתענית אסתר

Carpentras, commentary by Mordekhai b. Josef of Rocco Martino
3415. Cincinnati - Hebrew Union College 246/1, f. 92a-92b, C, rubric: פי' סליחה איך זרים אכזרים.

---

[81] Edited by Urbach, ערוגת הבושם, vol. III, p. 318-322 and p. 579.

איך ידידות נפש מקנה נדדה (א 2783), סליחה
Yemen, commentary by Isaac b. Abraham Wanneh
3416. Jerusalem - Sassoon 1158, p. 167-168, M, rubric: וסימני דאלפא ביתא צאתי ממץ'.
3417. London - British Library Or. 11122, f. 101a-101b, M, rubric: וסימני דאלפא ביתא צאתי ממץ'.

איך נוי חטאתי השמימה (א 2828), קינה
Yemen, commentary by Isaac b. Abraham Wanneh
3418. Jerusalem - Sassoon 1158, p. 169, M.
3419. London - British Library Or. 11122, f. 101b-102a, M.

איך נוי שודד ודודי עף ונדד (א 2829), קינה
Carpentras, commentary by Mordekhai b. Josef of Rocco Martino
3420. Cincinnati - Hebrew Union College 246/1, f. 70a-71a, C, rubric: פי' קינה איך נוי שודד.
Yemen, commentary by Isaac b. Abraham Wanneh
3421. Jerusalem - Sassoon 1158, p. 166, M.
3422. London - British Library Or. 11122, f. 100b, M.

איך נפתח לפניך דר מתוחים (א 2838), בנימין ב"ר זרח, פתיחה
Ashkenaz
3423. Hamburg - Staats- und Universitaetsbibliothek Cod. hebr. 17/2 (Steinschneider 152), f. 145b, C, rubric: פי' של פתיחות.
3424. Moscow - Russian State Library, Ms. Guenzburg 190, f. 5b, M, short.
3425. Muenchen - Bayerische Staatsbibliothek, Cod. hebr. 346, f. 119a, C, very short.
3426. Oxford - Bodleian Library MS Mich. 543 (Neubauer 1212), f. 4b-5a, C, commentator: Isaac b. Jakob (compiler), rubric: אתחיל לכתוב הפתיחות זאת הפתיחה ליום א'.
3427. Padova - Biblioteca del Seminario Vescovile Cod. 218, f. 40b-41a, M.
3428. Vatican - Biblioteca Apostolica ebr. 308/1, f. 3a, C, commentator: David b. Mose (compiler), short, additional marginal note.
3429. Vatican - Biblioteca Apostolica ebr. 422/2, f. 40a, CG, no incipit, very short.
Ashkenaz, commentary by Abraham b. Azriel[82]
3430. Frankfurt a M - Stadt- und Universitaetsbibliothek Fol. 16 (Merzbacher 95), f. 103b, C, rubric: אחרת.
3431. Vatican - Biblioteca Apostolica ebr. 301,1, f. 142b, C, rubric: אחרת.

---

[82] Edited by Urbach, ערוגת הבושם, vol. III, p. 314-316.

3432. Vatican - Biblioteca Apostolica ebr. 301,1, f. 168b-169a, C, rubric: פתיחה.

איך תנחמוני הבל (א 2860), אלעזר ברבי קליר, סליחה
Ashkenaz
3433. Berlin - Staatsbibliothek (Preussischer Kulturbesitz) Or. Qu. 798-799 (Steinschneider 177), II, f. 202a-202b, M.
3434. Budapest - Magyar tudomanyos akademia, MS. Kaufmann A 400, p. 238-239, C.
3435. Hamburg - Staats- und Universitaetsbibliothek Cod. hebr. 17/2 (Steinschneider 152), f. 103a, C.
3436. Jerusalem - Schocken Institute 24100 / Mahzor Nuremberg, f. 200b-201a, M, additional marginal glosses.
3437. Muenchen - Bayerische Staatsbibliothek, Cod. hebr. 88, f. 182b-183a, G.
3438. Parma - Biblioteca Palatina Cod. Parm. 3205 (de Rossi 655), f. 201b-202a, C, rubric: אחרת.
3439. Vatican - Biblioteca Apostolica ebr. 318, f. 255a-256a, GI.
Ashkenaz, commentary by Abraham b. Azriel[83]
3440. Vatican - Biblioteca Apostolica ebr. 301,1, f. 137b-138a, C, rubric: אחרת.

איכה אלי קוננו מאליו (א 2871), אלעזר ברבי קליר, קינה
Ashkenaz
3441. Berlin - Staatsbibliothek (Preussischer Kulturbesitz) Or. Qu. 798-799 (Steinschneider 177), II, f. 197a-197b, M, no incipit.
3442. Budapest - Magyar tudomanyos akademia, MS. Kaufmann A 400, p. 214-216, C, rubric: אחרת. ויותקונן ירמיהו על יאשיהו.
3443. Hamburg - Staats- und Universitaetsbibliothek Cod. hebr. 17/2 (Steinschneider 152), f. 96b-97a, C, rubric: ויותקונן ירמיהו על יאשיהו.
3444. Jerusalem - Schocken Institute 24100 / Mahzor Nuremberg, f. 198a, M, no incipit.
3445. Parma - Biblioteca Palatina Cod. Parm. 3205 (de Rossi 655), f. 199b-201a, C, rubric: ויקונן ירמיהו incipit, וזה קינה התחלה באיכה נתונה לעיל.
3446. Vatican - Biblioteca Apostolica ebr. 312, f. 47a-47b, G.
3447. Vatican - Biblioteca Apostolica ebr. 318, f. 232b-233b, GI.
Ashkenaz, commentary by Abraham b. Azriel[84]
3448. Vatican - Biblioteca Apostolica ebr. 301,1, f. 138a, C, rubric: אחרת.

---

[83] Edited by Urbach, ערוגת הבושם, vol. III, p. 284-285.
[84] Edited by Urbach, ערוגת הבושם, vol. III, p. 285-287.

איכה אצת באפך לאבד ביד אדומים (א 2875), אלעזר ברבי קליר, קינה
Ashkenaz
3449. Berlin - Staatsbibliothek (Preussischer Kulturbesitz) Or. Qu. 798-799 (Steinschneider 177), II, f. 186a, M.
3450. Budapest - Magyar tudomanyos akademia, MS. Kaufmann A 400 , p. 205-206, C, rubric: אחרת.
3451. Hamburg - Staats- und Universitaetsbibliothek Cod. hebr. 17/2 (Steinschneider 152), f. 94b, C.
3452. Hamburg - Staats- und Universitaetsbibliothek Cod. hebr. 233, f. 72a-72b, G.
3453. Jerusalem - Schocken Institute 24100 / Mahzor Nuremberg , f. 195a, M.
3454. Parma - Biblioteca Palatina Cod. Parm. 2886 (de Rossi 585), f. 115a-116a, M, later hand, margins cut.
3455. Parma - Biblioteca Palatina Cod. Parm. 3205 (de Rossi 655), f. 193a-193b, C, rubric: אחרת.
3456. Vatican - Biblioteca Apostolica ebr. 312, f. 43b-44a, G.
3457. Vatican - Biblioteca Apostolica ebr. 318, f. 226b-227a, GI.
Ashkenaz, commentary by Abraham b. Azriel[85]
3458. Vatican - Biblioteca Apostolica ebr. 301,1, f. 134a-134b, C, rubric: אחרת, short.

איכה אשפתו פתוח כקבר (א 2881), אלעזר ברבי קליר, קינה
Ashkenaz
3459. Berlin - Staatsbibliothek (Preussischer Kulturbesitz) Or. Qu. 798-799 (Steinschneider 177), II, f. 204a-206b, M.
3460. Budapest - Magyar tudomanyos akademia, MS. Kaufmann A 400 , p. 231-238, , rubric: אחרת משונה בניגון.
3461. Hamburg - Staats- und Universitaetsbibliothek Cod. hebr. 17/2 (Steinschneider 152), f. 100b-103a, C.
3462. Hamburg - Staats- und Universitaetsbibliothek Cod. hebr. 233, f. 75a, G.
3463. Jerusalem - Schocken Institute 24100 / Mahzor Nuremberg , f. 206b-207b, M.
3464. Muenchen - Bayerische Staatsbibliothek, Cod. hebr. 88, f. 176a-178a, G.
3465. Oxford - Bodleian Library MS Can. Or. 70 (Neubauer 1147,8), f. 112b-118a, M.
3466. Oxford - Bodleian Library MS Opp. 170 (Neubauer 1205), f. 256a-260a, C, rubric: אחרת.

---

[85] Edited by Urbach, ערוגת הבושם, vol. III, p. 260.

3467. Parma - Biblioteca Palatina Cod. Parm. 3205 (de Rossi 655), f. 197b-199b, C, rubric: אחרת.
3468. Vatican - Biblioteca Apostolica ebr. 318, f. 240a-243b, GI.

Ashkenaz, commentary by Abraham b. Azriel[86]

3469. Vatican - Biblioteca Apostolica ebr. 301,1, f. 135a-135b, C, rubric: אחרת.

איכה את אשר כבר עשוהו (א 2882), אלעזר ברבי קליר, קינה

Ashkenaz

3470. Budapest - Magyar tudomanyos akademia, MS. Kaufmann A 400, p. 223-225, , rubric: אחרת.
3471. Hamburg - Staats- und Universitaetsbibliothek Cod. hebr. 17/2 (Steinschneider 152), f. 98b-99a, C.
3472. Jerusalem - Schocken Institute 24100 / Mahzor Nuremberg, f. 198b-199b, M.
3473. Muenchen - Bayerische Staatsbibliothek, Cod. hebr. 88, f. 166b-168a, G.
3474. Oxford - Bodleian Library MS Opp. 170 (Neubauer 1205), f. 261a-262b, C.
3475. Parma - Biblioteca Palatina Cod. Parm. 3205 (de Rossi 655), f. 195b-196a, C, rubric: אחרת.

Ashkenaz, commentary by Abraham b. Azriel[87]

3476. Vatican - Biblioteca Apostolica ebr. 301,1, f. 135b-136a, C, rubric: אחרת.

איכה ישבה חבצלת השרון (א 2904), אלעזר ברבי קליר, קינה

Ashkenaz

3477. Berlin - Staatsbibliothek (Preussischer Kulturbesitz) Or. Qu. 798-799 (Steinschneider 177), II, f. 189b-190b, M.
3478. Budapest - Magyar tudomanyos akademia, MS. Kaufmann A 400, p. 209-214, C, rubric: אחרת.
3479. Hamburg - Staats- und Universitaetsbibliothek Cod. hebr. 17/2 (Steinschneider 152), f. 95b-96b, C.
3480. Hamburg - Staats- und Universitaetsbibliothek Cod. hebr. 233, f. 72b-74a, G.
3481. Jerusalem - Schocken Institute 24100 / Mahzor Nuremberg, f. 196b-197b, M.
3482. Modena - Archivio della Curia Arcivescovile di Modena 58, FM, incomplete.

---

[86] Edited by Urbach, ערוגת הבושם, vol. III, p. 264-268.
[87] Edited by Urbach, ערוגת הבושם, vol. III, p. 270-274.

3483. Oxford - Bodleian Library MS Opp. 170 (Neubauer 1205), f. 269a-271b, C.
3484. Parma - Biblioteca Palatina Cod. Parm. 3205 (de Rossi 655), f. 193b-194b, C, rubric: איכה.
3485. Vatican - Biblioteca Apostolica ebr. 312, f. 46a-47a, G.
3486. Vatican - Biblioteca Apostolica ebr. 318, f. 235a-236b, GI.
Ashkenaz, commentary b. Abraham b. Azriel[88]
3487. Vatican - Biblioteca Apostolica ebr. 301,1, f. 135b, C, rubric: אחרת.

איכה צאן ההריגה (א 2916), יהודה, קינה
Yemen, commentary by Isaac b. Abraham Wanneh
3488. Jerusalem - Sassoon 1158, p. 174, M.
3489. London - British Library Or. 11122, f. 104a, M.

איכה תפארתי מראשותי השליכי (א 2923), אלעזר ברבי קליר, קינה
Ashkenaz
3490. Berlin - Staatsbibliothek (Preussischer Kulturbesitz) Or. Qu. 798-799 (Steinschneider 177), II, f. 187b-188b, M.
3491. Budapest - Magyar tudomanyos akademia, MS. Kaufmann A 400, p. 184-185, C.
3492. Jerusalem - Schocken Institute 24100 / Mahzor Nuremberg, f. 196a-196b, M.
3493. Vatican - Biblioteca Apostolica ebr. 318, f. 228a-229b, GI.
3494. Vatican - Biblioteca Apostolica ebr. 312, f. 45(i)b-45(ii)b, G.
Ashkenaz, commentary by Abraham b. Azriel[89]
3495. Vatican - Biblioteca Apostolica ebr. 301,1, f. 134b-135a, C, rubric: אחרת.

איככה אוכל פנים להרים פנים (א 2927), יוסף ב"ר שמואל טוב עלם, רשות למוסף ביום ב' של ראש השנה
Ashkenaz
3496. Moscow - Russian State Library, Ms. Guenzburg 191, f. 48b, M.
Tsarfat
3497. London - David Sofer 5, f. 122b-123a, C.
3498. Parma - Biblioteca Palatina Cod. Parm. 3006 (de Rossi 654,1), f. 85b, M.

---
[88] Edited by Urbach, ערוגת הבושם, vol. III, p. 268-270.
[89] Edited by Urbach, ערוגת הבושם, vol. III, p. 262-264.

איככה אפצה פה ואיך אשא עין (א 2928), אליה ב"ר שמעיה, סליחה

Ashkenaz
3499. Braunschweig - Landesmuseum fuer Geschichte und Volkstum R 2386, vol. II, f. 142b-143b, M.
3500. Cambridge - University Library Dd. 2.30, f. 15b-16a, G.
3501. Jerusalem - Schocken Institute 24100 / Mahzor Nuremberg, f. 393b-394a, M.
3502. Moscow - Russian State Library, Ms. Guenzburg 190, f. 39b-40a, G.
3503. Muenchen - Bayerische Staatsbibliothek, Cod. hebr. 346, f. 119a, C.
3504. Muenchen - Bayerische Staatsbibliothek, Cod. hebr. 346, f. 163a, C.
3505. Oxford - Bodleian Library MS Mich. 543 (Neubauer 1212), f. 47b-48a, C, commentator: Isaac b. Jakob (compiler).
3506. Oxford - Bodleian Library MS Opp. 172 (Neubauer 1211), f. 53b-54a, C.
3507. Oxford - Bodleian Library MS Opp. 681 (Neubauer 1213), f. 45a-45b, C.
3508. Padova - Biblioteca del Seminario Vescovile Cod. 218, f. 73a-73b, M.
3509. Parma - Biblioteca Palatina Cod. Parm. 3205 (de Rossi 655), f. 284b, C.
3510. Vatican - Biblioteca Apostolica ebr. 308, f. 141a-141b, C, commentator: David b. Mose (compiler), rubric: כאן אתחיל סליחות של נעילה.
3511. Vatican - Biblioteca Apostolica ebr. 422/1, f. 29b, C.
3512. Vatican - Biblioteca Apostolica ebr. 422/1, f. 44a, CG.

Tsarfat
3513. London - David Sofer 5, f. 133a-133b, C.
3514. Parma - Biblioteca Palatina Cod. Parm. 2890 (de Rossi 856), f. 98a-98b, M.
3515. Parma - Biblioteca Palatina Cod. Parm. 3006 (de Rossi 654,1), f. 156b-157a, M.

איל אחד נאחז בסבך בקרניו (א 2931), קלונימוס ב"ר יהודה, סליחה

Tsarfat
3516. Oxford - Bodleian Library MS Bodl. Or. 109 (Neubauer 1209), f. 48b-50a, C, commentator: Aaron b. Hayyim haKohen (compiler).

אילו פומי נימי (א 2935), מאיר ב"ר יצחק, רשות לדיבור ז'

Ashkenaz
3517. Berlin - Staatsbibliothek (Preussischer Kulturbesitz) Or. Qu. 798-799 (Steinschneider 177), II, f. 167b, M.
3518. Muenchen - Bayerische Staatsbibliothek, Cod. hebr. 393, f. 153a-154b, C, no incipit.
3519. New York - Jewish Theological Seminary Ms. 4466, f. 190a-191a, M.

3520. Oxford - Bodleian Library MS Opp. 170 (Neubauer 1205), f. 79b-80a, C, rubric: בסדר אילי הצדק זהו שיעבוד תניין פיר׳ שמעב׳ מצר׳ שהיה תניץ בן שיני של אן׳ ובניהם נוש ומצרים. ראית׳ כת׳ משם של הח׳ ר׳ יוסף מצרפת זצ״ל המכו׳ מולטון רש׳ למוש׳ הר׳ מאי׳ שך׳ ציבו׳ מגרמיז זצ״ל.
Tsarfat

3521. Oxford - Bodleian Library MS Laud. Or. 271 (Neubauer 1206), f. 78a-78b, C, commentator: Aaron b. Hayyim haKohen (compiler), rubric: אגלוף רשות ליווש ע.

אילותינו לעזרתנו חושה למהרה (א 2939), שמעון ב״ר יצחק, סליחה
Ashkenaz

3522. Muenchen - Bayerische Staatsbibliothek, Cod. hebr. 346, f. 127a, C, rubric: אחרת, no incipit.

אילי הצדק ידועים (א 2941), שמעון ב״ר יצחק, חלק ה׳, קדושתא לשבועות
Ashkenaz

3523. New York - Jewish Theological Seminary Ms. 4663, f. 1a-1b, FM, only end.
3524. Berlin - Staatsbibliothek (Preussischer Kulturbesitz) Or. Qu. 798-799 (Steinschneider 177), II, f. 104b-108a, M.
3525. Braunschweig - Landesmuseum fuer Geschichte und Volkstum R 2386, vol. I, f. 52a-54a, M.
3526. Budapest - Magyar tudomanyos akademia, MS. Kaufmann A 384, f. 237a-242b, M.
3527. Hamburg - Staats- und Universitaetsbibliothek Cod. hebr. 17/2 (Steinschneider 152), f. 39b-40b, C, commentator: Ephraim b. Jakob of Bonn.
3528. Jerusalem - Schocken Institute 24100 / Mahzor Nuremberg, f. 111a-113b, M, short, ecclectic.
3529. London - British Library Add. 18695 (Margoliouth 863), f. 57b-59b, T, Yiddish, breaks off after a few stanzas.
3530. Muenchen - Bayerische Staatsbibliothek, Cod. hebr. 88, f. 98b-101a, G.
3531. New York - Jewish Theological Seminary Ms. 4466, f. 93a-98b, M, ecclectic.
3532. Paris - Bibliotheque Nationale heb. 709, f. 109a-110a, C, rubric: סדר.
3533. Parma - Biblioteca Palatina Cod. Parm. 1002 (Ta 24), f. 159a, M, very short.
3534. Parma - Biblioteca Palatina Cod. Parm. 3205 (de Rossi 655), f. 115a-115b, C.
3535. Parma - Biblioteca Palatina Cod. Parm. 3507 (Perreau 27), f. 81a-84b, C.

3536. Zurich - Zentralbibliothek Heid. 139, f. 43a-44b, C, additional marginal notes.

Tsarfat

3537. London - David Sofer 5, f. 47a-48b, C, short, ecclectic.
3538. Moscow - Russian State Library, Ms. Guenzburg 1665, f. 107b-110b, M.
3539. Oxford - Bodleian Library MS Laud. Or. 271 (Neubauer 1206), f. 77a-78a, C, commentator: Ephraim b. Jakob of Bonn (mainly), Aaron b. Hayyim haKohen (compiler).
3540. Parma - Biblioteca Palatina Cod. Parm. 3136 (de Rossi 405), f. 126a-128b, M.

אילי הצדק עברו בשערים (א 2943), משה אבן עזרא, חלק ג', קדושתא לנעילה

Carpentras

3541. Cincinnati - Hebrew Union College 392, f. 115b, M, no incipit.

Carpentras, commentary by Josef b. Abraham of Montelitz

3542. Paris - Ecole Rabbinique 32, f. 275b, M, no incipit.
3543. Strasbourg - Bibliotheque Nationale et Universitaire 4081, f. 246a, M, no incipit.

אילי מרום אומרים הלולו (א +2944), אלעזר ברבי קליר, חלק ט"ו, קדושתא למוסף יום כפור

Ashkenaz

3544. Berlin - Staatsbibliothek (Preussischer Kulturbesitz) Or. Qu. 798-799 (Steinschneider 177), I, f. 122a-122b, M, incipit זה.
3545. Braunschweig - Landesmuseum fuer Geschichte und Volkstum R 2386, vol. II, f. 228b-229a, M.
3546. Budapest - Magyar tudomanyos akademia, MS. Kaufmann A 400, p. 357-359, C.
3547. Cambridge - University Library Add. 394,1 (Reif SCR 461), f. 70b, C, incipit זה.
3548. Jerusalem - Schocken Institute 24100 / Mahzor Nuremberg, f. 413a-413b, M, incipit זה.
3549. London - British Library Or. 11318/1, f. 103b-104a, C, incipit זה.
3550. London - Montefiore Library 261, f. 56a-56b, C, commentator: Eliezer b. Natan?.
3551. Muenchen - Bayerische Staatsbibliothek, Cod. hebr. 346, f. 78b-79a, C.
3552. Muenchen- Bayrische Staatsbibliothek, Cod. hebr. 393, f. 149a-149b, C, no incipit, short.
3553. New York - Jewish Theological Seminary Ms. 4466, f. 374a-374b, M, very ecclectic.
3554. New York - Jewish Theological Seminary Ms. 8097, f. 79a, C.

3555. Oxford - Bodleian Library MS Mich. 365 (Neubauer 1208), f. 83b-84a, C.
3556. Oxford - Bodleian Library MS Opp. 172 (Neubauer 1211), f. 61a, C.
3557. Parma - Biblioteca Palatina Cod. Parm. 3270 (de Rossi 1215), f. 172a-172b, M.
3558. Parma - Biblioteca Palatina Cod. Parm. 3271 (de Rossi 1216), f. 109a-109b, G.
3559. Parma - Biblioteca Palatina Cod. Parm. 3507 (Perreau 27), f. 164a-164b, C.
3560. Vatican - Biblioteca Apostolica ebr. 422/1, f. 18a, C, very short.
3561. Zurich - Zentralbibliothek Heid. 139, f. 84b, C, incipit זה.

Roma

3562. Berlin - Staatsbibliothek (Preussischer Kulturbesitz) Or. Oct. 3567, f. 8b, FC, rubric: זה אל זה שואלים והוא אלי מרום.

Tsarfat

3563. Oxford - Bodleian Library MS Bodl. Or. 109 (Neubauer 1209), f. 32b, C, commentator: Aaron b. Hayyim haKohen (compiler), incipit זה, short.

אילי שחק הצובי להבים (א 2946), משולם ב"ר קלונימוס, חלק כ"ב, קדושתא לשחרית יום כפור

Ashkenaz

3564. Berlin - Staatsbibliothek (Preussischer Kulturbesitz) Or. Qu. 798-799 (Steinschneider 177), I, f. 81a-81b, M.
3565. Braunschweig - Landesmuseum fuer Geschichte und Volkstum R 2386, vol. II, f. 193a-194a, M.
3566. Budapest - Magyar tudomanyos akademia, MS. Kaufmann A 400, p. 320-323, C.
3567. Cambridge - University Library Or. 785, f. 123a-124a, G.
3568. Hamburg - Staats- und Universitaetsbibliothek Cod. hebr. 17/2 (Steinschneider 152), f. 152b-153a, C.
3569. Hamburg - Staats- und Universitaetsbibliothek Cod. hebr. 40b (Steinschneider 110), f. 98b-99b, G.
3570. Hamburg - Staats- und Universitaetsbibliothek Cod. hebr. 132 (Steinschneider 155), f. 35b-36a, C, no incipit.
3571. Jerusalem - Jewish National and University Library Ms Heb 8° 3037, f. 125b-126a, M.
3572. Jerusalem - Schocken Institute 24100 / Mahzor Nuremberg, f. 381a-381b, M.
3573. London - British Library Or. 11318/1, f. 77b-79a, C.
3574. London - Montefiore Library 261, f. 46a, C, commentator: Eliezer b. Natan?.
3575. Moscow - Russian State Library, Ms. Guenzburg 191, f. 92b-93b, M.

3576. Muenchen - Bayerische Staatsbibliothek, Cod. hebr. 346 , f. 54a-55a, C.
3577. New York - Jewish Theological Seminary Ms. 4466, f. 317a-318b, M.
3578. New York - Jewish Theological Seminary Ms. 8097, f. 72b-73a, C.
3579. New York - Jewish Theological Seminary Ms. 8169 (Acc. 0016), f. 73b-74b, M.
3580. Oxford - Bodleian Library MS Mich. 365 (Neubauer 1208), f. 70a-70b, C.
3581. Oxford - Bodleian Library MS Opp. 172 (Neubauer 1211), f. 41b-42b, C.
3582. Oxford - Bodleian Library MS Opp. 619 (Neubauer 2374), f. 153a-154a, M.
3583. Parma - Biblioteca Palatina Cod. Parm. 3205 (de Rossi 655), f. 226a, C.
3584. Parma - Biblioteca Palatina Cod. Parm. 3271 (de Rossi 1216), f. 44a-45a, G.
3585. Parma - Biblioteca Palatina Cod. Parm. 3507 (Perreau 27), f. 151b-152a, C.
3586. Vatican - Biblioteca Apostolica ebr. 308, f. 103b-104a, C, commentator: David b. Mose (compiler).
3587. Vatican - Biblioteca Apostolica ebr. 422/1, f. 15b-16a, C.
3588. Zurich - Zentralbibliothek Heid. 139, f. 77a, C, additional marginal notes.

Asti, Fossano, Moncalvo
3589. New Haven - Yale University, Beinecke Rare Book and MS Library, MS Heb. 52, f. 109a-109b, M.

Romania
3590. Vatican - Biblioteca Apostolica ebr. 320, f. 287b-288b, M.

Tsarfat
3591. Bern - Burgerbibliothek A 409, f. 86b-87b, G.
3592. London - British Library Or. 8682, f. 70b-71a, G.
3593. London - David Sofer 5, f. 139a, C.
3594. Oxford - Bodleian Library MS Bodl. Or. 109 (Neubauer 1209), f. 22a-22b, C, commentator: Aaron b. Hayyim haKohen (compiler), incipit ליושב.
3595. Oxford - Bodleian Library MS Laud. Or. 271 (Neubauer 1206), f. 113a-113b, C, commentator: Aaron b. Hayyim haKohen (compiler), no incipit.
3596. Parma - Biblioteca Palatina Cod. Parm. 1794 (de Rossi 1061), f. 129b-131a, M.
3597. Parma - Biblioteca Palatina Cod. Parm. 2890 (de Rossi 856), f. 31b, M.
3598. Parma - Biblioteca Palatina Cod. Parm. 3006 (de Rossi 654,1), f. 145a-145b, M.

3599. Vatican - Biblioteca Apostolica ebr. 306, f. 78a-78b, C.

אילת אהבים מתנת סיני (א 2960), שמעון ב"ר יצחק, יוצר ליום ב' של שבועות
Ashkenaz
3600. Berlin - Staatsbibliothek (Preussischer Kulturbesitz) Or. Qu. 798-799 (Steinschneider 177), II, f. 137b-138a, M.
3601. Braunschweig - Landesmuseum fuer Geschichte und Volkstum R 2386, vol. I, f. 94b-95a, M.
3602. London - British Library Add. 18695 (Margoliouth 683), f. 83b-84a, T, Yiddish, rubric: יוצר און' קרוביץ כום אנדרן טג בון שבועות.
3603. London - British Library Add. 22431 (Margoliouth 662a), f. 50a-51a, M.
3604. Moscow - Russian State Library, Ms. Guenzburg 615, f. 39b-40b, C, rubric: יום שיני.
3605. Muenchen - Bayerische Staatsbibliothek, Cod. hebr. 88, f. 138a-138b, G.
3606. Parma - Biblioteca Palatina Cod. Parm. 1002 (Ta 24), f. 200b, M, very short.
3607. Parma - Biblioteca Palatina Cod. Parm. 2886 (de Rossi 585), f. 58a-59a, M, later hand, margins cut.
3608. Parma - Biblioteca Palatina Cod. Parm. 3507 (Perreau 27), f. 95b-96a, C, rubric: ליום שיני.
3609. Zurich - Zentralbibliothek Heid. 139, f. 54a, C, very short.

אילת אהבים נגידו אומר תצביא (א 2961), משה אבן עזרא, חלק ב', קדושתא למוסף יום כפור
Carpentras
3610. Cincinnati - Hebrew Union College 392, f. 86a, M, no incipit.
Carpentras, commentary by Josef b. Abraham of Montelitz
3611. New York - Jewish Theological Seminary Ms. 4197, f. 195b-196b, M.
3612. Paris - Ecole Rabbinique 32, f. 204b-205b, M.
3613. Strasbourg - Bibliotheque Nationale et Universitaire 4081, f. 180a-180b, M.

אילת השחר אורה בהצחר (א 2963), מאיר ב"ר יצחק, יוצר לשבת וראש חדש
Ashkenaz
3614. Budapest - Magyar tudomanyos akademia, MS. Kaufmann A 399, p. 332-338, C, rubric: יוצר אחר לראש חדש.
3615. Jerusalem - Schocken Institute 24100 / Mahzor Nuremberg, f. 10a-11a, M.
3616. Oxford - Bodleian Library MS Can. Or. 82 (Neubauer 1148), f. 7b-8a, M, postscript לא מצאתי יותר.

3617. Parma - Biblioteca Palatina Cod. Parm. 3205 (de Rossi 655), f. 136a-137b, C.

Ashkenaz, commentary by Abraham b. Azriel[90]

3618. Frankfurt a M - Stadt- und Universitaetsbibliothek Fol. 16 (Merzbacher 95), f. 83b-87a, C, rubric: יוצר דראש חדש.
3619. Vatican - Biblioteca Apostolica ebr. 301,1, f. 103b-105b, C, rubric: יוצר.

אילת חן בגלות תסמכני (א 2966), שלם שבזי

Yemen

3620. Cincinnati - Hebrew Union College 398, f. 178b-181a, M.

אימות עלי נפלו ושעיפו בי נבהלו (א 2973), אברהם אבן עזרא, תוכחה

Sepharad, commentary by David b. Josef Abudarham[91]

3621. Budapest - Magyar tudomanyos akademia, MS. Kaufmann A 405/2, p. 244, C, rubric: תוכחה.
3622. New York - Columbia X893 Ab 93, f. 27a-27b, C, rubric: תוכחה.

אימיך נשאתי חין בערכי (א 2976), משולם ב"ר קלונימוס, קדושתא לשחרית יום כפור

Ashkenaz

3623. Berlin - Staatsbibliothek (Preussischer Kulturbesitz) Or. Qu. 798-799 (Steinschneider 177), I, 70a-70b, M.
3624. Braunschweig - Landesmuseum fuer Geschichte und Volkstum R 2386, vol. II, f. 183a, M.
3625. Budapest - Magyar tudomanyos akademia, MS. Kaufmann A 400, p. 303-304, C.
3626. Hamburg - Staats- und Universitaetsbibliothek Cod. hebr. 17/2 (Steinschneider 152), f. 150b, C.
3627. Hamburg - Staats- und Universitaetsbibliothek Cod. hebr. 40c (Steinschneider 111), f. 175b, G.
3628. Hamburg - Staats- und Universitaetsbibliothek Cod. hebr. 62 (Steinschneider 154), f. 2a, C, rubric: קדושתא.
3629. Hamburg - Staats- und Universitaetsbibliothek Cod. hebr. 132 (Steinschneider 155), f. 32a-32b, C.
3630. Jerusalem - Jewish National and University Library Ms Heb 8° 3037, f. 113a, M.
3631. Jerusalem - Schocken Institute 24100 / Mahzor Nuremberg, f. 374b, M.
3632. London - British Library Or. 11318/1, f. 69a-70b, C.

---

[90] Edited by Urbach, ערוגת הבושם, vol. III, p. 58-72.
[91] Edited by Prins, תשלום אבודרהם, p. 112-113.

3633. London - Montefiore Library 261, f. 41b, C, commentator: Eliezer b. Natan.?
3634. Moscow - Russian State Library, Ms. Guenzburg 191, f. 82a-82b, M.
3635. Moscow - Russian State Library, Ms. Guenzburg 615, f. 92a-92b, C, rubric: קרובא ליוצר.
3636. Muenchen - Bayerische Staatsbibliothek, Cod. hebr. 86, f. 97b, G.
3637. Muenchen - Bayerische Staatsbibliothek, Cod. hebr. 346, f. 51a-51b, C.
3638. Muenchen - Bayerische Staatsbibliothek, Cod. hebr. 393, f. 139a-139b, C.
3639. New York - Jewish Theological Seminary Ms. 4466, f. 301b-302a, M.
3640. New York - Jewish Theological Seminary Ms. 8097, f. 70b-71a, C.
3641. New York - Jewish Theological Seminary Ms. 8169 (Acc. 0016), f. 64a, M.
3642. Oxford - Bodleian Library MS Mich. 365 (Neubauer 1208), f. 67b-68a, C, rubric: קדושתא.
3643. Oxford - Bodleian Library MS Opp. 170 (Neubauer 1205), f. 164(ii)b, C.
3644. Oxford - Bodleian Library MS Opp. 172 (Neubauer 1211), f. 35a-35b, C.
3645. Oxford - Bodleian Library MS Opp. 619 (Neubauer 2374), f. 136b-137a, M.
3646. Paris - Bibliotheque Nationale heb. 653, f. 53a, G.
3647. Parma - Biblioteca Palatina Cod. Parm. 3205 (de Rossi 655), f. 224b, C.
3648. Parma - Biblioteca Palatina Cod. Parm. 3271 (de Rossi 1216), f. 32a, G.
3649. Parma - Biblioteca Palatina Cod. Parm. 3507 (Perreau 27), f. 146a-146b, C.
3650. Vatican - Biblioteca Apostolica ebr. 308, f. 97a-97b, C, commentator: David b. Mose (compiler).
3651. Vatican - Biblioteca Apostolica ebr. 422/1, f. 14b-15a, C, incipit אמיך, short.
3652. Zurich - Zentralbibliothek Heid. 139, f. 74b-75a, C.

Asti, Fossano, Moncalvo
3653. New Haven - Yale University, Beinecke Rare Book and MS Library, MS Heb. 52, f. 101a, M.

Romania
3654. Vatican - Biblioteca Apostolica ebr. 320, f. 276a-276b, M.

Tsarfat
3655. Bern - Burgerbibliothek A 409, f. 76b-77a, G.
3656. London - British Library Or. 8682, f. 64b, G.
3657. London - David Sofer 5, f. 136a, C, rubric: רשות.

3658. Oxford - Bodleian Library MS Bodl. Or. 109 (Neubauer 1209), f. 17b, C, commentator: Aaron b. Hayyim haKohen (compiler).
3659. Oxford - Bodleian Library MS Laud. Or. 271 (Neubauer 1206), f. 111a-111b, C, commentator: Aaron b. Hayyim haKohen (compiler), rubric: רשות לקדושתא.
3660. Parma - Biblioteca Palatina Cod. Parm. 1794 (de Rossi 1061), f. 109a-109b, M.
3661. Parma - Biblioteca Palatina Cod. Parm. 2125 (de Rossi 812), f. 38a, C, rubric: רשות לעמידה.
3662. Parma - Biblioteca Palatina Cod. Parm. 2890 (de Rossi 856), f. 22a, M.
3663. Parma - Biblioteca Palatina Cod. Parm. 3006 (de Rossi 654,1), f. 135b, M.
3664. Vatican - Biblioteca Apostolica ebr. 306, f. 75b, C.

אימת נוראותיך בשדה צוען (א 2979), משה בן קלונימוס, קדושתא ליום ח' של פסח
Ashkenaz

3665. Berlin - Staatsbibliothek (Preussischer Kulturbesitz) Or. Qu. 798-799 (Steinschneider 177), II, f. 90a-90b, M.
3666. Braunschweig - Landesmuseum fuer Geschichte und Volkstum R 2386, vol. I, f. 60a-60b, M.
3667. Budapest - Magyar tudomanyos akademia, MS. Kaufmann A 384, f. 201b-202a, M.
3668. Budapest - Magyar tudomanyos akademia, MS. Kaufmann A 400, p. 137, C, rubric: קדושתא ליום שביעי של פסח דרבנא משה בר קלונימוס, very short.
3669. Hamburg - Staats- und Universitaetsbibliothek Cod. hebr. 17/2 (Steinschneider 152), f. 67a, C, rubric: קדושתא ליום שביעי דרבנא משה ב"ר קלונימוס, very short.
3670. Jerusalem - Schocken Institute 24100 / Mahzor Nuremberg, f. 121b, M.
3671. Moscow - Russian State Library, Ms. Guenzburg 615, f. 25a, C, rubric: קרובה, very short.
3672. Muenchen - Bayerische Staatsbibliothek, Cod. hebr. 88, f. 81b-82a, G.
3673. Muenchen - Bayerische Staatsbibliothek, Cod. hebr. 393, f. 134a-134b, C.
3674. New York - Jewish Theological Seminary Ms. 4466, f. 107a, M, very ecclectic.
3675. New York - Jewish Theological Seminary Ms. 4663, f. 6b, FM, only beginning.
3676. Oxford - Bodleian Library MS Opp. 170 (Neubauer 1205), f. 76a, C, rubric: קדושתא.
3677. Paris - Bibliotheque Nationale heb. 709, f. 102a, C, rubric: קדושתא.

3678. Parma - Biblioteca Palatina Cod. Parm. 3205 (de Rossi 655), f. 108a-108b, C, rubric: זולת.
3679. Parma - Biblioteca Palatina Cod. Parm. 3507 (Perreau 27), f. 72a-72b, C.
3680. Zurich - Zentralbibliothek Heid. 139, f. 45b, C.
Tsarfat
3681. London - David Sofer 5, f. 41a, C, additional glosses.
3682. Moscow - Russian State Library, Ms. Guenzburg 1665, f. 89a-89b, M.
3683. Oxford - Bodleian Library MS Laud. Or. 271 (Neubauer 1206), f. 81a, C, commentator: Aaron b. Hayyim haKohen (compiler).
3684. Vatican - Biblioteca Apostolica ebr. 306, f. 216b-217a, C, no incipit.

אין אומר ואין דברים (א 2984), יוסף ב"ר שמואל טוב עלם, סליחה
Tsarfat
3685. Parma - Biblioteca Palatina Cod. Parm. 3007 (de Rossi 654,2), f. 41a-42a, M.

אין זולתך ואפס דוגמתך (א 3005), מאיר ב"ר יצחק, זולת
Ashkenaz
3686. Muenchen - Bayerische Staatsbibliothek, Cod. hebr. 88, f. 142b-143a, G.
Ashkenaz, commentary by Abraham b. Azriel[92]
3687. Frankfurt a M - Stadt- und Universitaetsbibliothek Fol. 16 (Merzbacher 95), f. 1a-4b, C, beginning missing.
3688. Vatican - Biblioteca Apostolica ebr. 301,1, f. 35b-39a, C, rubric: זולת.

אין כאלהינו נורא עלילות (א 3021), אהרן בן יוסף הרופא, פרשת אחרי מות
Karaite, commentary by Berakha b. Josef haKohen
3689. New York - Jewish Theological Seminary Ms. 3367, f. 105a-107b, C, rubric: פרוש פרשת אחרי מות.
3690. St. Petersburg - Inst. of Oriental Studies of the Russian Academy B 431, f. 73a-74b, C, rubric: פרשת אחרי מות.
3691. St. Petersburg - Russian National Library, Evr. IV 50, f. 80a-82a, C, rubric: אחרי מות.

אין כמדת בשר מידתך (א 3022), שלמה הבבלי, סליחה
Ashkenaz
3692. Braunschweig - Landesmuseum fuer Geschichte und Volkstum R 2386, vol. II, f. 48a-48b, M.
3693. Budapest - Magyar tudomanyos akademia, MS. Kaufmann A 400, p. 455-459, C, rubric: אחרת שלמונית.

---

[92] Edited by Urbach, ערוגת הבושם, vol. I, p. 217-238.

3694. Hamburg - Staats- und Universitaetsbibliothek Cod. hebr. 17/2 (Steinschneider 152), f. 135b-136b, C, rubric: אחרת שלמונית.
3695. Jerusalem - Schocken Institute 24100 / Mahzor Nuremberg , f. 241b-242a, M.
3696. Moscow - Russian State Library, Ms. Guenzburg 190, f. 13a-13b, G.
3697. Moscow - Russian State Library, Ms. Guenzburg 615 , f. 153b-155b, C, rubric: אל מלך.
3698. Muenchen - Bayerische Staatsbibliothek, Cod. hebr. 88, f. 158b-159a, G.
3699. Oxford - Bodleian Library MS Mich. 543 (Neubauer 1212), f. 65a-66b, C, commentator: Isaac b. Jakob (compiler).
3700. Oxford - Bodleian Library MS Opp. 170 (Neubauer 1205), f. 223a-224b, C.
3701. Padova - Biblioteca del Seminario Vescovile Cod. 218, f. 56b-57b, M.
3702. Padova - Biblioteca del Seminario Vescovile Cod. 218, f. 228a-229a, M.
3703. Parma - Biblioteca Palatina Cod. Parm. 3205 (de Rossi 655), f. 260a-261a, C.
3704. Vatican - Biblioteca Apostolica ebr. 308/1, f. 8a-9a, C, commentator: David b. Mose (compiler).
3705. Vatican - Biblioteca Apostolica ebr. 422/1, f. 28b, C.
3706. Vatican - Biblioteca Apostolica ebr. 422/1, f. 42b, CG, no incipit.
Ashkenaz, commentary by Abraham b. Azriel[93]
3707. Vatican - Biblioteca Apostolica ebr. 301,1, f. 156a-157a, C, rubric: אחרת.

Tsarfat
3708. London - British Library Add. 11639 (Margoliouth 1056), f. 467a-467b, M.
3709. London - David Sofer 5, f. 86b-87b, C.
3710. Oxford - Bodleian Library MS Laud. Or. 271 (Neubauer 1206), f. 120a-121a, C, commentator: Aaron b. Hayyim haKohen (compiler).
3711. Oxford - Bodleian Library MS Opp. 171 (Neubauer 1207), f. 95a-96b, C, rubric: אחרת.
3712. Vatican - Biblioteca Apostolica ebr. 306, f. 170a-172a, C.

אין כמוך באדירי מעלה (א 3026), משולם ב"ר קלונימוס, חלק ט"ו, קדושתא לשחרית יום כפור

Ashkenaz
3713. Braunschweig - Landesmuseum fuer Geschichte und Volkstum R 2386, vol. II, f. 191a, M.
3714. Budapest - Magyar tudomanyos akademia, MS. Kaufmann A 400 , p. 316, C, incipit באדירי, short.

---

[93] Edited by Urbach, ערוגת הבושם, vol. III, p. 404-409.

3715. Jerusalem - Schocken Institute 24100 / Mahzor Nuremberg, f. 379b, M, very short.
3716. London - British Library Or. 11318/1, f. 75b, C, very short.
3717. London - Montefiore Library 261, f. 44a, C, commentator: Eliezer b. Natan?, very short.
3718. Moscow - Russian State Library, Ms. Guenzburg 191, f. 91b, M.
3719. Muenchen - Bayerische Staatsbibliothek, Cod. hebr. 346, f. 130a-131a, C, rubric: אחרת.
3720. Muenchen - Bayerische Staatsbibliothek, Cod. hebr. 393, f. 142a-142b, C, no incipit, short.
3721. Oxford - Bodleian Library MS Opp. 172 (Neubauer 1211), f. 39a, C, short.
3722. Vatican - Biblioteca Apostolica ebr. 422/1, f. 15b, C, very short

Asti, Fossano, Moncalvo
3723. New Haven - Yale University, Beinecke Rare Book and MS Library, MS Heb. 52, f. 107a, M.

Tsarfat
3724. Bern - Burgerbibliothek A 409, f. 84b, G..

אין כמוך גואל ישראל דר בשחקים (א 3030), אהרן בן יוסף הרופא, פרשת בהר סיני
Karaite, commentary by Berakha b. Josef haKohen
3725. New York - Jewish Theological Seminary Ms. 3367, f. 112a-113b, C, rubric: פרוש פרשת בהר סיני.
3726. St. Petersburg - Inst. of Oriental Studies of the Russian Academy B 431, f. 77a-78b, C, rubric: בהר סיני.
3727. St. Petersburg - Russian National Library, Evr. IV 50, f. 85b-86b, C, rubric: בהר סיני.

אין לנו מצח (א 3052), סליחה
Ashkenaz
3728. Berlin - Staatsbibliothek (Preussischer Kulturbesitz) Or. Qu. 798-799 (Steinschneider 177), I, f. 144a-145a, M.
3729. Oxford - Bodleian Library MS Opp. 681 (Neubauer 1213), f. 37a-37b, C.
3730. Vatican - Biblioteca Apostolica ebr. 422/1, f. 31a, C, very short.
3731. Vatican - Biblioteca Apostolica ebr. 422/1, f. 41a, CG, no incipit, very short.

Ashkenaz, commentary by Abraham b. Azriel[94]
3732. Frankfurt a M - Stadt- und Universitaetsbibliothek Fol. 16 (Merzbacher 95), f. 106a-106b, C.

---

[94] Edited by Urbach, ערוגת הבושם, vol. III, p. 559.

3733. Frankfurt a M - Stadt- und Universitaetsbibliothek Fol. 16 (Merzbacher 95), f. 108a, C, short.

אין לשוחה עוצם נפלאות (א 3056), אלעזר ברבי קליר, סילוק, קדושתא לשבת פרה
Ashkenaz
3734. Berlin - Staatsbibliothek (Preussischer Kulturbesitz) Or. Qu. 798-799 (Steinschneider 177), II, f. 35a-37a, M.
3735. Budapest - Magyar tudomanyos akademia, MS. Kaufmann A 384, f. 79b-81b, M.
3736. Erlangen - Universitaetsbibliothek 2601 (Roth 67), f. 47a, M.
3737. Hamburg - Staats- und Universitaetsbibliothek Cod. hebr. 17/2 (Steinschneider 152), f. 26a-27a, C, rubric: סילוק.
3738. Hamburg - Staats- und Universitaetsbibliothek Cod. hebr. 225, f. 41b-44b, M.
3739. Jerusalem - Schocken Institute 24100 / Mahzor Nuremberg, f. 63b-64b, M.
3740. Muenchen - Bayerische Staatsbibliothek, Cod. hebr. 88, f. 39b-40b, G.
3741. New York - Jewish Theological Seminary Ms. 4466, f. 12a-14a, M.
3742. Oxford - Bodleian Library MS Opp. 170 (Neubauer 1205), f. 31a-32b, C, rubric: סילוק.
3743. Paris - Bibliotheque Nationale heb. 709, f. 37b-39a, C, rubric: סילוק.
3744. Parma - Biblioteca Palatina Cod. Parm. 3205 (de Rossi 655), f. 35b-36b, C, rubric: סילוק.
3745. Parma - Biblioteca Palatina Cod. Parm. 3507 (Perreau 27), f. 28b-29a, C, rubric: סילוק.
3746. Vatican - Biblioteca Apostolica ebr. 305,1, f. 22a-24a, C, rubric: סילוק.
3747. Zurich - Zentralbibliothek Heid. 139, f. 7b-8a, C, rubric: סילוק, additional marginal notes.

Tsarfat
3748. Oxford - Bodleian Library MS Laud. Or. 271 (Neubauer 1206), f. 41a-42b, C, commentator: Aaron b. Hayyim haKohen (compiler), rubric: סילוק אתחיל.
3749. Oxford - Bodleian Library MS Opp. 171 (Neubauer 1207), f. 39a-40b, C, rubric: סילוק.

אין מושיע וגואל (א 3058), מנחם ב"ר מכיר, זולת, שבת שני בחנוכה
Ashkenaz
3750. Jerusalem - Schocken Institute 24100 / Mahzor Nuremberg, f. 25b-26a, M.
3751. Parma - Biblioteca Palatina Cod. Parm. 2895, p. 389-392, M, margins cut, text damaged.

Ashkenaz, commentary by Abraham b. Azriel[95]
3752. Frankfurt a M - Stadt- und Universitaetsbibliothek Fol. 16 (Merzbacher 95), f. 56a-57a, C, rubric: זולת.
3753. Vatican - Biblioteca Apostolica ebr. 301,1, f. 86b-87b, C, rubric: זולת בניגון אף לפי בגולה וכולו מסדרים בפסוקים.

אין מי בשחק יערך לו (א 3059), משלם ב"ר קלונימוס, חלק י', קדושתא לשחרית יום כפור

Ashkenaz
3754. Berlin - Staatsbibliothek (Preussischer Kulturbesitz) Or. Qu. 798-799 (Steinschneider 177), I, f. 77a, M.
3755. Hamburg - Staats- und Universitaetsbibliothek Cod. hebr. 62 (Steinschneider 154), f. 4a, C, short.
3756. Jerusalem - Jewish National and University Library Ms Heb 8° 3037, f. 120b-121a, M, very short.
3757. Jerusalem - Schocken Institute 24100 / Mahzor Nuremberg, f. 378b, M, short.
3758. London - British Library Or. 11318/1, f. 74b, C, short.
3759. London - Montefiore Library 261, f. 43b, C, commentator: Eliezer b. Natan?, short.
3760. Moscow - Russian State Library, Ms. Guenzburg 191, f. 89b-90a, M, short.
3761. Muenchen - Bayerische Staatsbibliothek, Cod. hebr. 393, f. 142a, C, no incipit, very short.
3762. New York - Jewish Theological Seminary Ms. 8097, f. 72a, C.
3763. New York - Jewish Theological Seminary Ms. 8169 (Acc. 0016), f. 70a-70b, M, short.
3764. Oxford - Bodleian Library MS Mich. 365 (Neubauer 1208), f. 69b, C, short.
3765. Oxford - Bodleian Library MS Opp. 172 (Neubauer 1211), f. 38b, C, short.
3766. Oxford - Bodleian Library MS Opp. 619 (Neubauer 2374), f. 146b-147b, M.
3767. Parma - Biblioteca Palatina Cod. Parm. 3271 (de Rossi 1216), f. 40a-40b, G.
3768. Vatican - Biblioteca Apostolica ebr. 308, f. 100a-100b, C, commentator: David b. Mose (compiler).
3769. Vatican - Biblioteca Apostolica ebr. 422/1, f. 15b, C, very short.
3770. Zurich - Zentralbibliothek Heid. 139, f. 76b, C, additional marginal notes.

---

[95] Edited by Urbach, ערוגת הבושם, vol. II, p. 247-252.

Asti, Fossano, Moncalvo
3771. New Haven - Yale University, Beinecke Rare Book and MS Library, MS Heb. 52, f. 106a, M.
Romania
3772. Vatican - Biblioteca Apostolica ebr. 320, f. 284a-284b, M.
Tsarfat
3773. Bern - Burgerbibliothek A 409, f. 83a-83b, G.
3774. London - David Sofer 5, f. 138a, C.
3775. London - David Sofer 5, f. 138a, C, second commentary on margin, short.
3776. Oxford - Bodleian Library MS Bodl. Or. 109 (Neubauer 1209), f. 20a, C, commentator: Aaron b. Hayyim haKohen (compiler), short.
3777. Parma - Biblioteca Palatina Cod. Parm. 1794 (de Rossi 1061), f. 122b-123a, M.
3778. Parma - Biblioteca Palatina Cod. Parm. 2125 (de Rossi 812), f. 40a, C.
3779. Parma - Biblioteca Palatina Cod. Parm. 2125 (de Rossi 812), f. 40a-41a, C.
3780. Parma - Biblioteca Palatina Cod. Parm. 2890 (de Rossi 856), f. 28a, M.
3781. Parma - Biblioteca Palatina Cod. Parm. 3006 (de Rossi 654,1), f. 142a, M.
3782. Vatican - Biblioteca Apostolica ebr. 306, f. 77a, C.

אין מי יקרא בצדק (א 3060), שלמה הבבלי, סליחה

Ashkenaz
3783. Bologna - Archivio di Stato MS Ebr. 253, f. 1a-1b, FC.
3784. Braunschweig - Landesmuseum fuer Geschichte und Volkstum R 2386, vol. II, f. 53b-54a, M.
3785. Budapest - Magyar tudomanyos akademia, MS. Kaufmann A 400, p. 446-448, C, rubric: אחרת שלמונית.
3786. Cambridge - University Library Dd. 2.30, f. 7a-8a, G.
3787. Hamburg - Staats- und Universitaetsbibliothek Cod. hebr. 17/2 (Steinschneider 152), f. 133a-133b, C, rubric: אחרת שלמונית.
3788. Jerusalem - Schocken Institute 24100 / Mahzor Nuremberg, f. 394b-395a, M.
3789. Karlsruhe - Badische Landesbibliothek, Schwarzach 20, f. 2a-2b, FC, end missing.
3790. Moscow - Russian State Library, Ms. Guenzburg 190, f. 30a-30b, G.
3791. Moscow - Russian State Library, Ms. Guenzburg 615, f. 153a-153b, C, rubric: אל מלך.
3792. Oxford - Bodleian Library MS Mich. 543 (Neubauer 1212), f. 54b-65a, C, commentator: Isaac b. Jakob (compiler).

3793. Oxford - Bodleian Library MS Opp. 170 (Neubauer 1205), f. 222b-223a, C.
3794. Oxford - Bodleian Library MS Opp. 172 (Neubauer 1211), f. 54a-54b, C.
3795. Padova - Biblioteca del Seminario Vescovile Cod. 218, f. 45a-46a, M.
3796. Padova - Biblioteca del Seminario Vescovile Cod. 218, f. 229a-230a, M.
3797. Parma - Biblioteca Palatina Cod. Parm. 3205 (de Rossi 655), f. 257a-257b, C.
3798. Vatican - Biblioteca Apostolica ebr. 308, f. 108(ii)b-109a, C, commentator: David b. Mose (compiler).
3799. Vatican - Biblioteca Apostolica ebr. 422/1, f. 1a, C.
3800. Vatican - Biblioteca Apostolica ebr. 422/1, f. 26a, C, very short.
3801. Vatican - Biblioteca Apostolica ebr. 422/2, f. 40a, CG, no incipit, short.

Ashkenaz, commentary by Abraham b. Azriel[96]

3802. Frankfurt a M - Stadt- und Universitaetsbibliothek Fol. 16 (Merzbacher 95), f. 115b-116a, C, manuscript partly damaged.
3803. Vatican - Biblioteca Apostolica ebr. 301,1, f. 154b, C, very short.

Tsarfat

3804. London - British Library Add. 11639 (Margoliouth 1056), f. 462a, M.
3805. London - David Sofer 5, f. 145a-145b, C, rubric: סליחה.
3806. Oxford - Bodleian Library MS Laud. Or. 271 (Neubauer 1206), f. 121a-121b, C, commentator: Aaron b. Hayyim haKohen (compiler).
3807. Oxford - Bodleian Library MS Opp. 171 (Neubauer 1207), f. 92a, C, rubric: אחרת.
3808. Vatican - Biblioteca Apostolica ebr. 306, f. 101a-102a, C.

אין מלה בלשוני מפני כובד זדוני (א 3061), אברהם אבן עזרא, תוכחה

Sepharad, commentary by David b. Josef Abudarham[97]

3809. Budapest - Magyar tudomanyos akademia, MS. Kaufmann A 405/2, p. 244-245, C, rubric: תוכחה.
3810. New York - Columbia X893 Ab 93, f. 27b, C, rubric: תוכחה.
3811. New York - Jewish Theological Seminary Ms. 3011, f. 21b, C, rubric: תוכחה.

אין מנחה רחוקה (א 3062), חייא, פזמון

Sepharad, commentary by David b. Josef Abudarham[98]

3812. Budapest - Magyar tudomanyos akademia, MS. Kaufmann A 405/2, p. 255-256, C, rubric: פזמון.

---

[96] Edited by Urbach, ערוגת הבושם, vol. III, p. 393-395.
[97] Edited by Prins, תשלום אבודרהם, p. 114-115.
[98] Edited by Prins, תשלום אבודרהם, p. 159-169.

3813. New York - Columbia X893 Ab 93, f. 31b, C, rubric: פזמון.

אין מספר לגדודי צבא חילו (א 3063), משולם ב"ר קלונימוס, חלק כ"ג, קדושתא לשחרית יום כפור

Ashkenaz

3814. Berlin - Staatsbibliothek (Preussischer Kulturbesitz) Or. Qu. 798-799 (Steinschneider 177), I, f. 82a-82b, M.
3815. Braunschweig - Landesmuseum fuer Geschichte und Volkstum R 2386, vol II, f. 194a-195a, M.
3816. Budapest - Magyar tudomanyos akademia, MS. Kaufmann A 400, p. 323-325, C, incipit זה.
3817. Hamburg - Staats- und Universitaetsbibliothek Cod. hebr. 17/2 (Steinschneider 152), f. 153a, C, incipit זה.
3818. Hamburg - Staats- und Universitaetsbibliothek Cod. hebr. 40b (Steinschneider 110), f. 100a, G.
3819. Jerusalem - Jewish National and University Library Ms Heb 8° 3037, f. 126b-127a, M.
3820. Jerusalem - Schocken Institute 24100 / Mahzor Nuremberg, f. 381b-382a, M, short.
3821. London - British Library Or. 11318/1, f. 79a-79b, C.
3822. London - Montefiore Library 261, f. 46a, C, commentator: Eliezer b. Natan?, incipit זה.
3823. Moscow - Russian State Library, Ms. Guenzburg 191, f. 94a-94b, M.
3824. New York - Jewish Theological Seminary Ms. 4466, f. 318b-319a, M, incipit שרפים.
3825. New York - Jewish Theological Seminary Ms. 8097, f. 72b, C, very short.
3826. New York - Jewish Theological Seminary Ms. 8169 (Acc. 0016), f. 74b-75a, M.
3827. Oxford - Bodleian Library MS Mich. 365 (Neubauer 1208), f. 70b, C, short.
3828. Oxford - Bodleian Library MS Opp. 172 (Neubauer 1211), f. 42b-43a, C.
3829. Oxford - Bodleian Library MS Opp. 619 (Neubauer 2374), f. 154a-154b, M.
3830. Parma - Biblioteca Palatina Cod. Parm. 3205 (de Rossi 655), f. 226b, C, incipit זה.
3831. Parma - Biblioteca Palatina Cod. Parm. 3271 (de Rossi 1216), f. 45b-46a, G.
3832. Vatican - Biblioteca Apostolica ebr. 308, f. 104b, C, commentator: David b. Mose (compiler).
3833. Zurich - Zentralbibliothek Heid. 139, f. 77a-, C, incipit זה, additional marginal notes.

Asti, Fossano, Moncalvo
3834. New Haven - Yale University, Beinecke Rare Book and MS Library, MS Heb. 52, f. 110a-110b, M.

Romania
3835. Vatican - Biblioteca Apostolica ebr. 320, f. 288b-289b, M.

Tsarfat
3836. Bern - Burgerbibliothek A 409, f. 87b-88a, G.
3837. London - British Library Or. 8682, f. 71b, GI.
3838. London - David Sofer 5, f. 139a-139b, C, 1st incipit זה, 2nd incipit אין.
3839. Oxford - Bodleian Library MS Bodl. Or. 109 (Neubauer 1209), f. 22b, C, commentator: Aaron b. Hayyim haKohen (compiler), incipit זה.
3840. Oxford - Bodleian Library MS Laud. Or. 271 (Neubauer 1206), f. 113b, C, commentator: Aaron b. Hayyim haKohen (compiler), no incipit.
3841. Parma - Biblioteca Palatina Cod. Parm. 1794 (de Rossi 1061), f. 131b-132b, M.
3842. Parma - Biblioteca Palatina Cod. Parm. 3006 (de Rossi 654,1), f. 145b-146a, M.
3843. Parma - Biblioteca Palatina Cod. Parm. 2890 (de Rossi 856), f. 32b, M, short.
3844. Vatican - Biblioteca Apostolica ebr. 306, f. 78b, C, incipit זה.

אין ערוך אליך (א 3071), אלעזר ברבי קליר, חלק ה', קדושתא למוסף יום כפור

Ashkenaz
3845. Berlin - Staatsbibliothek (Preussischer Kulturbesitz) Or. Qu. 798-799 (Steinschneider 177), I, f. 118b-119a, M.
3846. Braunschweig - Landesmuseum fuer Geschichte und Volkstum R 2386, vol. II, f. 226a, M, very short.
3847. Cambridge - University Library Add. 394,1 (Reif SCR 461), f. 69b, C, short.
3848. Hamburg - Staats- und Universitaetsbibliothek Cod. hebr. 132 (Steinschneider 155), f. 44b, C, no incipit.
3849. Jerusalem - Jewish National and University Library Ms Heb 8° 3037, f. 177b, M, short.
3850. Jerusalem - Schocken Institute 24100 / Mahzor Nuremberg, f. 410a, M.
3851. London - British Library Or. 11318/1, f. 102a-102b, C.
3852. London - Montefiore Library 261, f. 55a-55b, C, commentator: Eliezer b. Natan?.
3853. Moscow - Russian State Library, Ms. Guenzburg 191, f. 116b-117a, M.
3854. Muenchen - Bayerische Staatsbibliothek, Cod. hebr. 393, f. 148b, C, rubric: חסר ג"כ במוסף בתוך הפיוט המתחיל אין ערך אליך.
3855. New York - Jewish Theological Seminary Ms. 4466, f. 369a-369b, M.

3856. New York - Jewish Theological Seminary Ms. 8097, f. 78b, C.
3857. New York - Jewish Theological Seminary Ms. 8169 (Acc. 0016), f. 91a-91b, M.
3858. Oxford - Bodleian Library MS Opp. 172 (Neubauer 1211), f. 60b, C.
3859. Oxford - Bodleian Library MS Opp. 619 (Neubauer 2374), f. 204b-205a, M.
3860. Parma - Biblioteca Palatina Cod. Parm. 3271 (de Rossi 1216), f. 105a-105b, G.
3861. Parma - Biblioteca Palatina Cod. Parm. 3507 (Perreau 27), f. 163a, C, no incipit.
3862. Vatican - Biblioteca Apostolica ebr. 308, f. 118a, C, commentator: David b. Mose (compiler).
3863. Zurich - Zentralbibliothek Heid. 139, f. 84a, C, incipit את, short.

Asti, Fossano, Moncalvo
3864. New Haven - Yale University, Beinecke Rare Book and MS Library, MS Heb. 52, f. 134b-135a, M.

Roma
3865. Berlin - Staatsbibliothek (Preussischer Kulturbesitz) Or. Oct. 3567, f. 7a-7b, FC, incipit את.
3866. Jerusalem - Jewish National and University Library Ms Heb 8° 4153, f. 140a-140b, C, commentator: Daniel ben Salomo haRofe (compiler), no incipit, short.
3867. Oxford - Bodleian Library MS Mich. 312,1 (Neubauer 2276,1), f. 7b, C, short.

Tsarfat
3868. London - David Sofer 5, f. 151a-151b, C, incipit את.
3869. London - British Library Or. 8682, f. 83a, GI.
3870. Oxford - Bodleian Library MS Bodl. Or. 109 (Neubauer 1209), f. 31b, C, commentator: Aaron b. Hayyim haKohen (compiler), incipit את.
3871. Oxford - Bodleian Library MS Laud. Or. 271 (Neubauer 1206), f. 115a, C, commentator: Aaron b. Hayyim haKohen (compiler), rubric: פיזמון אחר, no incipit.
3872. Parma - Biblioteca Palatina Cod. Parm. 1794 (de Rossi 1061), f. 162a-162b, M.
3873. Parma - Biblioteca Palatina Cod. Parm. 3006 (de Rossi 654,1), f. 180a-180b, M, incipit את.
3874. Vatican - Biblioteca Apostolica ebr. 306, f. 105a, C, incipit את.

אין ערוך אליך להגיד ולדבר (א 3072), יוסף ב"ר שמואל טוב עלם, חלק ד', קדושתא לשבת הגדול

Ashkenaz
3875. Muenchen - Bayerische Staatsbibliothek, Cod. hebr. 88, f. 54a-56a, G.

אין ערוך לאל יה ומעשה פלאו (א 3073), אהרן בן יוסף הרופא, פרשת ויקרא
Karaite, commentary by Berakha b. Josef haKohen

3876. New York - Jewish Theological Seminary Ms. 3367, f. 93b-96b, C, rubric: ספר ויקרא. פירוש פרשת ויקרא.
3877. St. Petersburg - Inst. of Oriental Studies of the Russian Academy B 431, f. 66a-67b, C, rubric: ספר ויקרא.
3878. St. Petersburg - Russian National Library, Evr. IV 50, f. 70a-72b, C, rubric: ספר ויקרא.

אין פה להשיב ולישא פנים (א 3076), אפרים ב"ר יקר, סליחה
Ashkenaz

3879. Jerusalem - Schocken Institute 24100 / Mahzor Nuremberg, f. 425b-426a, M.
3880. Muenchen - Bayerische Staatsbibliothek, Cod. hebr. 346, f. 144b-145a, C, rubric: פתיחה, short.
3881. Oxford - Bodleian Library MS Opp. 172 (Neubauer 1211), f. 70b, C, rubric: פתיחה.
3882. Vatican - Biblioteca Apostolica ebr. 308, f. 129a-129b, C, commentator: David b. Mose (compiler), rubric: אתחיל סליחות למוסף בעזרה ואסיים.

אין צור חלף (א 3079), שלמה הבבלי, זולת לשבת ראשון בחנוכה
Ashkenaz

3883. Berlin - Staatsbibliothek (Preussischer Kulturbesitz) Or. Qu. 798-799 (Steinschneider 177), II, f. 6b-8b, M.
3884. Budapest - Magyar tudomanyos akademia, MS. Kaufmann A 384, f. 23b-24b, M.
3885. Budapest - Magyar tudomanyos akademia, MS. Kaufmann A 399, p. 407-413, C.
3886. Cambridge - University Library Add. 504,1, f. 21b-25a, C, rubric: שלמה הקטן יסד זה.
3887. Erlangen - Universitaetsbibliothek 2601 (Roth 67), f. 25b, M.
3888. Hamburg - Staats- und Universitaetsbibliothek Cod. hebr. 17/2 (Steinschneider 152), f. 8b-10a, C, commentator: R. Samuel heHazzan of Erfurt, rubric: משם ר' שמואל חזן הנהרג על קידוש השם בערפורט.
3889. Jerusalem - Schocken Institute 24100 / Mahzor Nuremberg, f. 21b-22a, M.
3890. Krakow - Biblioteka Jagiellonska Fr. 4, f. 1b, FC, only beginning.
3891. Ms Oxford Bodleana Opp 170 (Neubauer 1205), f. 275b-278b, C.
3892. Muenchen - Bayerische Staatsbibliothek, Cod. hebr. 88, f. 5a-5b, G.
3893. Oxford - Bodleian Library MS Can. Or. 82 (Neubauer 1148), f. 14a-15b, M.

3894. Oxford - Bodleian Library MS Mich. 365 (Neubauer 1208), f. 18a-19b, C.
3895. Parma - Biblioteca Palatina Cod. Parm. 1002 (Ta 24), f. 15a-15b, M.
3896. Parma - Biblioteca Palatina Cod. Parm. 2895, p. 382-384, M, rubric: זולת, margins cut, text damaged.
3897. Parma - Biblioteca Palatina Cod. Parm. 3205 (de Rossi 655), f. 8b-10a, C, rubric: זולת.
3898. Parma - Biblioteca Palatina Cod. Parm. 3507 (Perreau 27), f. 192a-193b, C, rubric: זולת.
3899. Vatican - Biblioteca Apostolica ebr. 318, f. 215b-216b, GI.

Ashkenaz, commentary by Abraham b. Azriel[99]

3900. Vatican - Biblioteca Apostolica ebr. 301,1, f. 154a-154b, C, rubric: זולת.

Tsarfat

3901. London - David Sofer 5, f. 4b-7b, C, rubric: זולת, .
3902. Moscow - Russian State Library, Ms. Guenzburg 1665, f. 5b-6b, M.
3903. Oxford - Bodleian Library MS Laud. Or. 271 (Neubauer 1206), f. 2b-5a, C, commentator: Aaron b. Hayyim haKohen (compiler).
3904. Oxford - Bodleian Library MS Opp. 171 (Neubauer 1207), f. 2b-4a, C, rubric: זולת.

אין תליה לראש אם לפי מעוה (א 3091), אליה ב"ר שמעיה, סליחה

Ashkenaz

3905. Vatican - Biblioteca Apostolica ebr. 308/1, f. 5b, C, commentator: David b. Mosc (compiler).

איש אלהים ברך לשבטי ישורון הברורים (א 3115), אהרן בן יוסף הרופא, פרשת וזאת הברכה

Karaite, commentary by Berakha b. Josef haKohen

3906. New York - Jewish Theological Seminary Ms. 3367, f. 159b-165b, C, rubric: פרוש פרשת וזאת הברכה.
3907. St. Petersburg - Inst. of Oriental Studies of the Russian Academy B 431, f. 108a-112b, C, rubric: וזאת הברכה.
3908. St. Petersburg - Inst. of Oriental Studies of the Russian Academy B 483, f. 20a- 21b, C, rubric: וזאת הברכה.
3909. St. Petersburg - Russian National Library, Evr. IV 50, f. 127a-131b, C, rubric: וזאת הברכה.

---

[99] Edited by Urbach, ערוגת הבושם, vol. III, p. 389-393.

איש חלק ישב במגורי אביו (א 3135), אהרן בן יוסף הרופא, פרשת וישב
Karaite, commentary by Berakha b. Josef haKohen
3910. New York - Jewish Theological Seminary Ms. 3367, f. 49b-53a, C, rubric: פרשת וישב.
3911. St. Petersburg - Inst. of Oriental Studies of the Russian Academy B 431, f. 35b-37b, C, rubric: פרשת וישב.
3912. St. Petersburg - Russian National Library, Evr. IV 50 , f. 36b-38b, C, rubric: וישב.

איש תם בלכתו במהללכיו (א 3175), אהרן בן יוסף הרופא, פרשת וישלח
Karaite, commentary by Berakha b. Josef haKohen
3913. New York - Jewish Theological Seminary Ms. 3367, f. 46b-49b, C, rubric: פרשת וישלח.
3914. St. Petersburg - Inst. of Oriental Studies of the Russian Academy B 431, f. 33b-35b, C, rubric: פרשת וישלח.
3915. St. Petersburg - Russian National Library, Evr. IV 50 , f. 34a-36a, C, rubric: וישלח.

איש תם יושב אהלי תושיה (א 3174), שלמה אבן גבירול, חלק ד', קדושתא לשחרית יום כפור
Sepharad, commentary by David b. Josef Abudarham[100]
3916. Budapest - Magyar tudomanyos akademia, MS. Kaufmann A 405/2 , p. 193-194, C, rubric: משלו לר' שלמה בן גיבירול ז"ל.
3917. Cincinnati - Hebrew Union College 490, f. 5a-5b, C.
3918. New York - Columbia X893 Ab 93, f. 7b-8a, C, rubric: משלש לר' שלמה ן' גיבירול ז"ל.
3919. New York - Jewish Theological Seminary Ms. 3011, f. 6b-7a, C, rubric: משלש.

אית חזותא ודוגמא (א 3195), מאיר בן אלעזר מלומבארד, רשות לתרגום התורה בפסח
Ashkenaz
3920. Oxford - Bodleian Library MS Opp. 170 (Neubauer 1205), f. 80a-81a, C.
Tsarfat
3921. Oxford - Bodleian Library MS Laud. Or. 271 (Neubauer 1206), f. 78b, C, commentator: Aaron b. Hayyim haKohen (compiler), short.

איתגבר בחיליה אדוניה בר חגית (א 3197), פיוט בארמית לשבועות
Ashkenaz
3922. Berlin - Staatsbibliothek (Preussischer Kulturbesitz) Or. Qu. 798-799 (Steinschneider 177), II, f. 163b-164a, M.

---

[100] Edited by Prins, תשלום אבודרהם, p. 23-25.

3923. Cambridge - University Library Add. 394,1 (Reif SCR 461), f. 63a, C.
3924. Jerusalem - Schocken Institute 24100 / Mahzor Nuremberg, f. 162b-163b, M, very short.
3925. Moscow - Russian State Library, Ms. Guenzburg 206, f. 90b, M.
3926. Muenchen - Bayerische Staatsbibliothek, Cod. hebr. 21, f. 84a-86a, M.
3927. Muenchen - Bayerische Staatsbibliothek, Cod. hebr. 393, f. 152b-153a, C, no incipit.
3928. Oxford - Bodleian Library MS Can. Or. 1 (Neubauer 1104), f. 117b-118b, M.
3929. Oxford - Bodleian Library MS Opp. 170 (Neubauer 1205), f. 98b, C, very short.
3930. Parma - Biblioteca Palatina Cod. Parm. 3205 (de Rossi 655), f. 185b-186a, C.

Ashkenaz, commentary by Benjamin b. Abraham Anaw
3931. Jerusalem - Musad haRav Kook 478, p. 50-52, C, rubric: אלפא ביתא ט, very short.
3932. London - Beth Din & Beth Hamidrash 6,9, f. 179a-179b, C, rubric: אלפא ביט, short.

Tsarfat
3933. Cambridge - University Library Add. 561.1, f. 81b-82a, MT, Hebrew.
3934. Jerusalem - Schocken Institute 19623, f. 185b-187a, M, commentator: Yehuda b. Eliezer Zvi, very short.
3935. London - British Library Add. 11639 (Margoliouth 1056), f. 680b-681a, M, very short.
3936. London - British Library Or. 2735 (Margoliouth 663), f. 35b-36b, M.
3937. London - David Sofer 5, f. 63b, C, very short.
3938. Moscow - Russian State Library, Ms. Guenzburg 1665, f. 128b-129a, M.
3939. New York - Jewish Theological Seminary Ms. 4460, f. 65b-66a, M, pages damaged.
3940. Parma - Biblioteca Palatina Cod. Parm. 1902, f. 149a-149b, M.
3941. Parma - Biblioteca Palatina Cod. Parm. 2574, f. 121a-121b, G, commentator: Simḥa b. Samuel, cp. Mahzor Vitry.
3942. Parma - Biblioteca Palatina Cod. Parm. 3136 (de Rossi 405), f. 162b-163a, M.

איתו כרועו לצלם (א 3198), פיוט בארמית לשבועות

Ashkenaz, commentary by Benjamin b. Abraham Anaw
3943. Jerusalem - Musad haRav Kook 478, p. 27-31, C, rubric: אלפא ביתא אוחרן ה.
3944. London - Beth Din & Beth Hamidrash 6,9, f. 165a-167a, C, rubric: אלפא ביט אוחרן.

איתן אחר כלות בריתו וברית כל המוניו (א 3201), אהרן בן יוסף הרופא, פרשת וירא
Karaite, commentary by Berakha b. Josef haKohen

3945. New York - Jewish Theological Seminary Ms. 3367, f. 29a-34a, C, rubric: פרוש פיוט פרשת וירא.
3946. St. Petersburg - Inst. of Oriental Studies of the Russian Academy B 431, f. 23a-26a, C, rubric: פרשת וירא.
3947. St. Petersburg - Russian National Library, Evr. IV 50, f. 21b-25b, C.

איתן הכיר אמונתך (א 3204), אליה ברבי מרדכי, קדושתא למנחה יום פכור
Ashkenaz

3948. Berlin - Staatsbibliothek (Preussischer Kulturbesitz) Or. Qu. 798-799 (Steinschneider 177), I, f. 160b-161a, M.
3949. Braunschweig - Landesmuseum fuer Geschichte und Volkstum R 2386, vol. II, f. 254a, M.
3950. Fulda - Hessische Landesbibliothek A 3 II, f. 127b, C, commentator: Josef, rubric: למנחה, short.
3951. Hamburg - Staats- und Universitaetsbibliothek Cod. hebr. 17/2 (Steinschneider 152), f. 160b, C, rubric: למנחה.
3952. Hamburg - Staats- und Universitaetsbibliothek Cod. hebr. 62 (Steinschneider 154), f. 22a, C, rubric: למנחה.
3953. Hamburg - Staats- und Universitaetsbibliothek Cod. hebr. 132 (Steinschneider 155), f. 49a-49b, C.
3954. Jerusalem - Jewish National and University Library Ms Heb 8° 3037, f. 214a-214b, M.
3955. Jerusalem - Schocken Institute 24100 / Mahzor Nuremberg, f. 443b, M, short.
3956. London - British Library Or. 11318/1, f. 122a, C.
3957. London - Montefiore Library 261, f. 63a-63b, C, commentator: Eliezer b. Natan?, rubric: למנחה.
3958. Moscow - Russian State Library, Ms. Guenzburg 191, f. 144a, M.
3959. Moscow - Russian State Library, Ms. Guenzburg 615, f. 108a, C, rubric: למנחה.
3960. Muenchen - Bayerische Staatsbibliothek, Cod. hebr. 21, f. 239b, M.
3961. Muenchen - Bayerische Staatsbibliothek, Cod. hebr. 346, f. 87a, C.
3962. New York - Jewish Theological Seminary Ms. 4466, f. 412b-413a, M.
3963. New York - Jewish Theological Seminary Ms. 8169 (Acc. 0016), f. 114b, M.
3964. Oxford - Bodleian Library MS Mich. 365 (Neubauer 1208), f. 92b, C, rubric: למנחה דר' אליה בר מכיר.
3965. Oxford - Bodleian Library MS Opp. 170 (Neubauer 1205), f. 180b, C, rubric: הא לך פירוש של מנחה.
3966. Oxford - Bodleian Library MS Opp. 172 (Neubauer 1211), f. 81b, C.

3967. Oxford - Bodleian Library MS Opp. 619 (Neubauer 2374), f. 254a, M.
3968. Parma - Biblioteca Palatina Cod. Parm. 3205 (de Rossi 655), f. 237a, C, short.
3969. Parma - Biblioteca Palatina Cod. Parm. 3270 (de Rossi 1215), f. 212a-212b, M.
3970. Parma - Biblioteca Palatina Cod. Parm. 3507 (Perreau 27), f. 171b-172a, C.
3971. Vatican - Biblioteca Apostolica ebr. 308, f. 139b, C, commentator: David b. Mose (compiler), rubric: אתחיל מנחה בעזה אסיים.
3972. Vatican - Biblioteca Apostolica ebr. 422/1, f. 19b, C, very short.
3973. Zurich - Zentralbibliothek Heid. 139, f. 88b, C, rubric: למנחה, additional marginal notes.

Asti, Fossano, Moncalvo

3974. New Haven - Yale University, Beinecke Rare Book and MS Library, MS Heb. 52, f. 160b, M.

Tsarfat

3975. London - David Sofer 5, f. 165a, C, rubric: פירוש מקרובוץ של מנחה של יום הכפורים.
3976. Oxford - Bodleian Library MS Bodl. Or. 109 (Neubauer 1209), f. 41a-41b, C, commentator: Aaron b. Hayyim haKohen (compiler).
3977. Oxford - Bodleian Library MS Laud. Or. 271 (Neubauer 1206), f. 118a, C, commentator: Aaron b. Hayyim haKohen (compiler), rubric: למנחה דר' אליה, short.
3978. Parma - Biblioteca Palatina Cod. Parm. 3006 (de Rossi 654,1), f. 219a, M.
3979. Vatican - Biblioteca Apostolica ebr. 306, f. 102a, C, rubric: למנחה.

איתן למד דעת (א 3207), סליחה

Ashkenaz

3980. Braunschweig - Landesmuseum fuer Geschichte und Volkstum R 2386, vol. II, f. 131b, M.
3981. Cambridge - University Library Dd. 2.30, f. 45b, G.
3982. Muenchen - Bayerische Staatsbibliothek, Cod. hebr. 346, f. 123b, C.
3983. Muenchen - Bayerische Staatsbibliothek, Cod. hebr. 346, f. 164a, C, very short.
3984. Oxford - Bodleian Library MS Mich. 543 (Neubauer 1212), f. 40b-41a, C, commentator: Isaac b. Jakob (compiler), rubric: עקידה.
3985. Oxford - Bodleian Library MS Mich. 543 (Neubauer 1212), f. 41a-41b, C, commentator: Isaac b. Jakob (compiler), rubric: גם זו עקידה.
3986. Oxford - Bodleian Library MS Opp. 681 (Neubauer 1213), f. 73a-73b, C.
3987. Oxford - Bodleian Library MS Opp. 681 (Neubauer 1213), f. 74a-74b, C.

3988. Padova - Biblioteca del Seminario Vescovile Cod. 218, f. 142a, M.
3989. Padova - Biblioteca del Seminario Vescovile Cod. 218, f. 142a-142b, M.
3990. Vatican - Biblioteca Apostolica ebr. 422/1, f. 30a, C, short.
3991. Vatican - Biblioteca Apostolica ebr. 422/1, f. 44b, CG, no incipit, very short.

Tsarfat

3992. Oxford - Bodleian Library MS Bodl. Or. 109 (Neubauer 1209), f. 48a-48b, C, commentator: Aaron b. Hayyim haKohen (compiler).
3993. Oxford - Bodleian Library MS Bodl. Or. 109 (Neubauer 1209), f. 51b-52a, C, commentator: Aaron b. Hayyim haKohen (compiler).

אך אומרים בחין לפניך (א 3211), אלעזר ברבי קליר, חלק י"ד, קדושתא למוסף יום כפור

Roma

3994. Berlin - Staatsbibliothek (Preussischer Kulturbesitz) Or. Oct. 3567, f. 8b, FC.

אך אין לנו אלוה מבלעדיך (א 3213), אלעזר ברבי קליר, חלק ז', קדושתא למוסף יום כפור

Ashkenaz

3995. Berlin - Staatsbibliothek (Preussischer Kulturbesitz) Or. Qu. 798-799 (Steinschneider 177), I, f. 119b-120a, M.
3996. Zurich - Zentralbibliothek Heid. 139, f. 84a, C, very short.

אך אתים בחין לפניך (א 3215), משולם ב"ר קלונימוס, חלק ח', קדושתא לשחרית יום כפור

Ashkenaz

3997. Berlin - Staatsbibliothek (Preussischer Kulturbesitz) Or. Qu. 798-799 (Steinschneider 177), I, f. 75a, M, short.
3998. Braunschweig - Landesmuseum fuer Geschichte und Volkstum R 2386, vol. II, f. 187b-188a, M.
3999. Budapest - Magyar tudomanyos akademia, MS. Kaufmann A 400, p. 312, C.
4000. Cambridge - University Library Or. 785, f. 116a-116b, G.
4001. Hamburg - Staats- und Universitaetsbibliothek Cod. hebr. 17/2 (Steinschneider 152), f. 151a, C.
4002. Hamburg - Staats- und Universitaetsbibliothek Cod. hebr. 62 (Steinschneider 154), f. 4a, C.
4003. Hamburg - Staats- und Universitaetsbibliothek Cod. hebr. 132 (Steinschneider 155), f. 34a, C.
4004. Jerusalem - Jewish National and University Library Ms Heb 8° 3037, f. 118b, M, short.

4005. Jerusalem - Schocken Institute 24100 / Mahzor Nuremberg , f. 377b, M.
4006. London - British Library Or. 11318/1, f. 73b-74a, C.
4007. Moscow - Russian State Library, Ms. Guenzburg 191, f. 87a-87b, M.
4008. Muenchen - Bayerische Staatsbibliothek, Cod. hebr. 86, f. 103b-104a, GI.
4009. Muenchen - Bayerische Staatsbibliothek, Cod. hebr. 393 , f. 142a, C, no incipit, short.
4010. Muenchen - Bayerische Staatsbibliothek, Cod. hebr. 393 , f. 149a, C, excerpt only, no incipit.
4011. New York - Jewish Theological Seminary Ms. 4466, f. 308a-308b, M, no incipit.
4012. New York - Jewish Theological Seminary Ms. 8097 , f. 72a, C, additional glosses in the margins, short.
4013. Oxford - Bodleian Library MS Mich. 365 (Neubauer 1208), f. 69a, C, short.
4014. Oxford - Bodleian Library MS Opp. 172 (Neubauer 1211), f. 38a-38b, C, short.
4015. Oxford - Bodleian Library MS Opp. 619 (Neubauer 2374), f. 143a-143b, M, short.
4016. Parma - Biblioteca Palatina Cod. Parm. 3205 (de Rossi 655), f. 225b, C, short.
4017. Parma - Biblioteca Palatina Cod. Parm. 3271 (de Rossi 1216), f. 37b-38a, G.
4018. Zurich - Zentralbibliothek Heid. 139, f. 76b, C, additional marginal notes.

Asti, Fossano, Moncalvo
4019. New Haven - Yale University, Beinecke Rare Book and MS Library, MS Heb. 52, f. 104b, M.

Romania
4020. Vatican - Biblioteca Apostolica ebr. 320, f. 282a-282b, M, short.

Tsarfat
4021. London - British Library Or. 8682, f. 67a-67b, GI.
4022. London - David Sofer 5, f. 137b, C, second commentary on margin, short.
4023. London - David Sofer 5, f. 137b, C, short.
4024. Oxford - Bodleian Library MS Bodl. Or. 109 (Neubauer 1209), f. 19b, C, commentator: Aaron b. Hayyim haKohen (compiler), short.
4025. Oxford - Bodleian Library MS Laud. Or. 271 (Neubauer 1206), f. 112b, C, commentator: Aaron b. Hayyim haKohen (compiler), no incipit.
4026. Parma - Biblioteca Palatina Cod. Parm. 1794 (de Rossi 1061), f. 118b-119a, M.

4027. Parma - Biblioteca Palatina Cod. Parm. 2125 (de Rossi 812), f. 39b, C.
4028. Parma - Biblioteca Palatina Cod. Parm. 3006 (de Rossi 654,1), f. 140a-140b, M.
4029. Parma - Biblioteca Palatina Cod. Parm. 3006 (de Rossi 654,1), f. 140b, M, short.
4030. Vatican - Biblioteca Apostolica ebr. 306, f. 77a, C.

אך בך לדל מעוז (א 3218), שלמה הבבלי, סליחה
Ashkenaz

4031. Berlin - Staatsbibliothek (Preussischer Kulturbesitz) Or. Qu. 798-799 (Steinschneider 177), I, f. 102b-103a, M.
4032. Braunschweig - Landesmuseum fuer Geschichte und Volkstum R 2386, vol. II, f. 64a-64b, M.
4033. Budapest - Magyar tudomanyos akademia, MS. Kaufmann A 400, p. 494, C, rubric: תוספת מן המדרש לסליחות אך בך לכל מזעו.
4034. Cambridge - University Library Dd. 2.30, f. 41a, G.
4035. Hamburg - Staats- und Universitaetsbibliothek Cod. hebr. 17/2 (Steinschneider 152), f. 177a-177b, C, rubric: אחרת.
4036. Jerusalem - Schocken Institute 24100 / Mahzor Nuremberg, f. 398b-399a, M.
4037. London - British Library Add. 18695 (Margoliouth 683), f. 163a-163b, T, Yiddish.
4038. Moscow - Russian State Library, Ms. Guenzburg 615, f. 149a-150b, C, rubric: אל מלך.
4039. Muenchen - Bayerische Staatsbibliothek, Cod. hebr. 346, f. 120a-120b, C.
4040. New York - Jewish Theological Seminary Ms. 8097, f. 82a-82b, C.
4041. Oxford - Bodleian Library MS Mich. 543 (Neubauer 1212), f. 58a-58b, C, commentator: Isaac b. Jakob (compiler).
4042. Oxford - Bodleian Library MS Opp. 172 (Neubauer 1211), f. 56b-57a, C.
4043. Oxford - Bodleian Library MS Opp. 619 (Neubauer 2374), f. 232a-232b, M.
4044. Oxford - Bodleian Library MS Opp. 681 (Neubauer 1213), f. 3b-4b, C.
4045. Padova - Biblioteca del Seminario Vescovile Cod. 218, f. 95b-96a, M.
4046. Padova - Biblioteca del Seminario Vescovile Cod. 218, f. 212a-213a, M.
4047. Parma - Biblioteca Palatina Cod. Parm. 3205 (de Rossi 655), f. 256a-256b, C.
4048. Vatican - Biblioteca Apostolica ebr. 308, f. 110b-111a, C, commentator: David b. Mose (compiler).
4049. Vatican - Biblioteca Apostolica ebr. 422/1, f. 30a, C, very short.

4050. Vatican - Biblioteca Apostolica ebr. 422/2, f. 38b, CG, no incipit, very short.

Ashkenaz, commentary by Abraham b. Azriel[101]

4051. Vatican - Biblioteca Apostolica ebr. 301,1, f. 155b-156a, C, rubric: אחרת.

Asti, Fossano, Moncalvo

4052. New Haven - Yale University, Beinecke Rare Book and MS Library, MS Heb. 52, f. 167b, M.

Tsarfat

4053. London - British Library Add. 11639 (Margoliouth 1056), f. 469b-470a, M, rubric: תוספת מן המדרש לסליחות אך בך לכל מזעו.
4054. London - David Sofer 5, f. 85a-85b, C.
4055. Oxford - Bodleian Library MS Bodl. Or. 109 (Neubauer 1209), f. 52a-52b, C, commentator: Aaron b. Hayyim haKohen (compiler).
4056. Oxford - Bodleian Library MS Laud. Or. 271 (Neubauer 1206), f. 177b-178a, C, commentator: Aaron b. Hayyim haKohen (compiler).
4057. Oxford - Bodleian Library MS Opp. 171 (Neubauer 1207), f. 111b, C, rubric: אחרת.
4058. Parma - Biblioteca Palatina Cod. Parm. 3006 (de Rossi 654,1), f. 227b-228a, M.
4059. Vatican - Biblioteca Apostolica ebr. 306, f. 169b-170a, C.

אך בך מקוה ישראל (א 3220), שלמה הבבלי, סליחה

Ashkenaz

4060. Bologna - Archivio di Stato MS Ebr. 253, f. 2b, FC, only beginning.
4061. Braunschweig - Landesmuseum fuer Geschichte und Volkstum R 2386, vol. II, f. 137b-138a, M.
4062. Budapest - Magyar tudomanyos akademia, MS. Kaufmann A 400, p. 428-433, C, rubric: סליחה שלמונית.
4063. Cambridge - University Library Dd. 2.30, f. 8b-9b, G.
4064. Hamburg - Staats- und Universitaetsbibliothek Cod. hebr. 17/2 (Steinschneider 152), f. 128b-129b, C, rubric: סליחה שלמונית.
4065. Jerusalem - Schocken Institute 24100 / Mahzor Nuremberg, f. 271a-271b, M.
4066. Moscow - Russian State Library, Ms. Guenzburg 190, f. 26b-27b, G.
4067. Moscow - Russian State Library, Ms. Guenzburg 615, f. 152a-153a, C, rubric: אל מלך.
4068. Muenchen - Bayerische Staatsbibliothek, Cod. hebr. 346, f. 161b-162a, C.
4069. Oxford - Bodleian Library MS Mich. 543 (Neubauer 1212), f. 63a-64a, C, commentator: Isaac b. Jakob (compiler).

---

[101] Edited by Urbach, ערוגת הבושם, vol. III, p. 402-404.

4070. Oxford - Bodleian Library MS Opp. 170 (Neubauer 1205), f. 214a-215a, C.
4071. Oxford - Bodleian Library MS Opp. 170 (Neubauer 1205), f. 220b-222a, C.
4072. Padova - Biblioteca del Seminario Vescovile Cod. 218, f. 67a-67b, M.
4073. Padova - Biblioteca del Seminario Vescovile Cod. 218, f. 67b-68b, M, rubric: אחרת.
4074. Parma - Biblioteca Palatina Cod. Parm. 3205 (de Rossi 655), f. 262a-263a, C.
4075. Vatican - Biblioteca Apostolica ebr. 308/1, f. 7b-8a, C, commentator: David b. Mose (compiler).
4076. Vatican - Biblioteca Apostolica ebr. 422/1, f. 3a-4a, C, rubric: אחרת.
4077. Vatican - Biblioteca Apostolica ebr. 422/1, f. 24a, C, very short.
4078. Vatican - Biblioteca Apostolica ebr. 422/1, f. 29a, C.
4079. Vatican - Biblioteca Apostolica ebr. 422/1, f. 43a, CG, no incipit.
4080. Vatican - Biblioteca Apostolica ebr. 422/2, f. 38b, CG, no incipit, short.

Ashkenaz, commentary by Abraham b. Azriel[102]
4081. Frankfurt a M - Stadt- und Universitaetsbibliothek Fol. 16 (Merzbacher 95), f. 112b-113b, C.

Tsarfat
4082. London - British Library Add. 11639 (Margoliouth 1056), f. 470b-472a, M.
4083. London - David Sofer 5, f. 147b-148a, C.
4084. Oxford - Bodleian Library MS Bodl. Or. 109 (Neubauer 1209), f. 60b-61b, C, commentator: Aaron b. Hayyim haKohen (compiler).
4085. Oxford - Bodleian Library MS Laud. Or. 271 (Neubauer 1206), f. 121b-122b, C, commentator: Aaron b. Hayyim haKohen (compiler).
4086. Oxford - Bodleian Library MS Opp. 171 (Neubauer 1207), f. 94b-95a, C, rubric: אחרת.
4087. Parma - Biblioteca Palatina Cod. Parm. 2890 (de Rossi 856), f. 54a-55a, M.
4088. Parma - Biblioteca Palatina Cod. Parm. 3007 (de Rossi 654,2), f. 43b-44a, M.
4089. Vatican - Biblioteca Apostolica ebr. 306, f. 91b-92b, C.

אך במתח דין ומרוץ חבל בני אמוניך (א 3221), סליחה

Ashkenaz
4090. Berlin - Staatsbibliothek (Preussischer Kulturbesitz) Or. Qu. 798-799 (Steinschneider 177), I, f. 99a, M.
4091. Braunschweig - Landesmuseum fuer Geschichte und Volkstum R 2386, vol. II, f. 63a-63b, M.

---

[102] Edited by Urbach, ערוגת הבושם, vol. III, p. 574-579.

4092. London - British Library Add. 18695 (Margoliouth 683), f. 163a, T, Yiddish.
4093. Muenchen - Bayerische Staatsbibliothek, Cod. hebr. 346, f. 120a, C, rubric: לערב ראש האשנה, short.
4094. New York - Jewish Theological Seminary Ms. 8097, f. 83b-84a, C.
4095. Oxford - Bodleian Library MS Mich. 543 (Neubauer 1212), f. 16a-16b, C, commentator: Isaac b. Jakob (compiler).
4096. Oxford - Bodleian Library MS Opp. 619 (Neubauer 2374), f. 179a, M.
4097. Oxford - Bodleian Library MS Opp. 681 (Neubauer 1213), f. 2b-3a, C.
4098. Padova - Biblioteca del Seminario Vescovile Cod. 218, f. 95a-95b, M.
4099. Padova - Biblioteca del Seminario Vescovile Cod. 218, f. 195b-196a, M.
4100. Parma - Bibliotheca Palatina Cod. Parm. 3205 (de Rossi 655), f. 287b, C.
4101. Vatican - Biblioteca Apostolica ebr. 422/1, f. 24b, C, very short.
4102. Vatican - Biblioteca Apostolica ebr. 422/1, f. 44b, CG, no incipit.

Ashkenaz, commentary by Abraham b. Azriel[103]
4103. Vatican - Biblioteca Apostolica ebr. 301,1, f. 146a, C, rubric: אחרת.

Asti, Fossano, Moncalvo
4104. New Haven - Yale University, Beinecke Rare Book and MS Library, MS Heb. 52, f. 153a-153b, M.

Tsarfat
4105. Oxford - Bodleian Library MS Bodl. Or. 109 (Neubauer 1209), f. 61b-62a, C, commentator: Aaron b. Hayyim haKohen (compiler).

אך זה היום יום פקודת חובי (א 3223), קינה

Yemen, commentary by Isaac b. Abraham Wanneh
4106. Jerusalem - Sassoon 1158, p. 165, M.

אך טוב אלהים לישראל (א 3225), ברכת המזון לחתונה

Ashkenaz
4107. Parma - Biblioteca Palatina Cod. Parm. 3205 (de Rossi 655), f. 173b-174b, C.

אכן אין כאלהינו ואין צור כאדוננו (א 3271), אהרן בן יוסף הרופא, פרשת אמור

Karaite, commentary by Berakha b. Josef haKohen
4108. New York - Jewish Theological Seminary Ms. 3367, f. 110a-112a, C, rubric: פרוש פרשת אמור.

---

[103] Edited by Urbach, ערוגת הבושם, vol. III, p. 334-335.

4109. St. Petersburg - Inst. of Oriental Studies of the Russian Academy B 431, f. 76a-77a, C, rubric: פרשת אמור.
4110. St. Petersburg - Russian National Library, Evr. IV 50, f. 84a-85a, C, rubric: אמור.

אכן אתה אל מסתתר (א 3274), בנימין ב"ר שמואל, סילוק, קדושתא לראש השנה
Ashkenaz
4111. Moscow - Russian State Library, Ms. Guenzburg 191, f. 54b-57a, M.
4112. New York - Jewish Theological Seminary Ms. 8169 (Acc. 0016), f. 49a-50b, M.

Tsarfat
4113. London - David Sofer 5, f. 125a-125b, C, rubric: סילוק.
4114. Parma - Biblioteca Palatina Cod. Parm. 1794 (de Rossi 1061), f. 88b-89b, M.
4115. Parma - Biblioteca Palatina Cod. Parm. 2125 (de Rossi 812), f. 32b, C.
4116. Parma - Biblioteca Palatina Cod. Parm. 3006 (de Rossi 654,1), f. 90b-92a, M.
4117. Vatican - Biblioteca Apostolica ebr. 306, f. 70b, C.

אכן אתה אל מסתתר וגולה רזים בנהורא את שתי במאמר חוזים, סליחה
Yemen
4118. New York - Jewish Theological Seminary Ms. 3052, f. 88b, M.
Yemen, commentary by Isaac b. Abraham Wanneh
4119. Chicago-Spertus College of Judaica D 2, 2, f. 239b, M, no incipit.
4120. Jerusalem - Benayahu ת 261, f. 167a, M, short.
4121. Jerusalem - Benayahu ת 282, f. 143a, M.
4122. Jerusalem - Makhon Ben Zvi 1156 (Tubi 155), f. 140b, M, no incipit.
4123. Jerusalem - Michael Krupp 604, f. 177b, M.
4124. Jerusalem - Musad haRav Kook 325, f. 196a, M, short.
4125. Jerusalem - Sassoon 1158, p. 419, M, no incipit.
4126. Jerusalem - Sassoon 1174, p. 272, M, no incipit.
4127. London - British Library Or. 11122, f. 216b-217a, M, no incipit.
4128. Muenchen - Bayerische Staatsbibliothek, Cod. hebr. 472, f. 196a, M.
4129. New York - Jewish Theological Seminary Ms. 3013, f. 135b, M, short.
4130. New York - Jewish Theological Seminary Ms. 3294, f. 18b, C.
4131. New York - Public Library, Heb. Ms. 9, f. 132a, M.
4132. Strasbourg - Bibliotheque Nationale et Universitaire 3965 (Landauer 39), p. 417, M.

אכן אתה אל מסתתר וגולה רזים בשמך יגילונם ולדי חוזים, סליחה

Yemen
4133. New York - Jewish Theological Seminary Ms. 3052, f. 88a-88b, M.
Yemen, commentary by Isaac b. Abraham Wanneh
4134. Chicago-Spertus College of Judaica D 2, 2, f. 239b, M, no incipit.
4135. Jerusalem - Benayahu ת 261, f. 166b-167a, M.
4136. Jerusalem - Benayahu ת 282, f. 142b, M.
4137. Jerusalem - Makhon Ben Zvi 1156 (Tubi 155), f. 140a-140b, M, no incipit.
4138. Jerusalem - Makhon Ben Zvi 1174 (Tubi 154), f. 139b, M.
4139. Jerusalem - Michael Krupp 604, f. 177b, M.
4140. Jerusalem - Musad haRav Kook 325, f. 195b, M.
4141. Jerusalem - Sassoon 1158, p. 419, M, no incipit.
4142. Jerusalem - Sassoon 1174, p. 272, M, no incipit.
4143. London - British Library Or. 11122, f. 216b, M, no incipit.
4144. Muenchen - Bayerische Staatsbibliothek, Cod. hebr. 472, f. 196a, M.
4145. New York - Jewish Theological Seminary Ms. 3013, f. 135a, M, no incipit.
4146. New York - Jewish Theological Seminary Ms. 3294, f. 19a, C.
4147. New York - Public Library, Heb. Ms. 9, f. 132a, M, no incipit.
4148. Strasbourg - Bibliotheque Nationale et Universitaire 3965 (Landauer 39), p. 417, M.

אכפרה פני מלך רב (א 3288), אליעזר ב"ר נתן, סליחה

Ashkenaz
4149. Braunschweig - Landesmuseum fuer Geschichte und Volkstum R 2386, vol. II, f. 242b-243a, M.
4150. New York - Jewish Theological Seminary Ms. 8097, f. 84a-85a, C.
4151. Oxford - Bodleian Library MS Mich. 543 (Neubauer 1212), f. 30b-31b, C, commentator: Isaac b. Jakob (compiler).
4152. Oxford - Bodleian Library MS Opp. 619 (Neubauer 2374), f. 228a-229a, M.
4153. Oxford - Bodleian Library MS Opp. 681 (Neubauer 1213), f. 25b-26a, C.
4154. Padova - Biblioteca del Seminario Vescovile Cod. 218, f. 191a-192b, M.
4155. Vatican - Biblioteca Apostolica ebr. 422/1, f. 25a-25b, C.
4156. Vatican - Biblioteca Apostolica ebr. 422/2, f. 39a, CG, no incipit.
Asti, Fossano, Moncalvo
4157. New Haven - Yale University, Beinecke Rare Book and MS Library, MS Heb. 52, f. 151a-151b, M.

Tsarfat

4158. Oxford - Bodleian Library MS Bodl. Or. 109 (Neubauer 1209), f. 71a-72a, C, commentator: Aaron b. Hayyim haKohen (compiler).

אכר אלליל אתפק (א 3289), שלם שבזי

Yemen

4159. Cincinnati - Hebrew Union College 398, f. 67b-69a, M, long.

אכר אלליל יא מחב, שלם שבזי

Yemen

4160. Cincinnati - Hebrew Union College 398, f. 69a-70b, M.

אכר אלליל יא פתא אנתבה ושד באזלי (א* 851), שלם שבזי

Yemen

4161. Cincinnati - Hebrew Union College 398, f. 70b-72b, M.

אכתיר זר תהילה (א 3301), אלעזר ברבי קליר?, יוצר לסוכות

Ashkenaz

4162. Berlin - Staatsbibliothek (Preussischer Kulturbesitz) Or. Qu. 798-799 (Steinschneider 177), I, f. 189a-189b, M.

4163. Braunschweig - Landesmuseum fuer Geschichte und Volkstum R 2386, vol. I, f. 119a-119b, M.

4164. Cambridge - University Library Add. 394,1 (Reif SCR 461), f. 73b, C, rubric: לסוכות, short.

4165. Hamburg - Staats- und Universitaetsbibliothek Cod. hebr. 62 (Steinschneider 154), f. 32b-33a, C, rubric: יוצר ליום ראשון של סוכות.

4166. Hamburg - Staats- und Universitaetsbibliothek Cod. hebr. 132 (Steinschneider 155), f. 50a-51a, C.

4167. Jerusalem - Jewish National and University Library Ms Heb 8° 3037, f. 232a-232b, M.

4168. Jerusalem - Schocken Institute 24100 / Mahzor Nuremberg, f. 475a, M.

4169. London - British Library Add. 18695 (Margoliouth 683), f. 109b-110b, T, Yiddish, rubric: יוצר צו דעם ערשטן טג בון סכות.

4170. London - British Library Add. 22431 (Margoliouth 662a), f. 86a-87a, M.

4171. London - British Library Or. 11318/1, f. 128a-129b, C, rubric: בכאן אתחיל לכתוב קרובץ של סוכת.

4172. London - Montefiore Library 261, f. 64b-65a, C, commentator: Eliezer b. Natan?, rubric: לסוכות.

4173. New York - Jewish Theological Seminary Ms. 4466, f. 435b-436b, M.

4174. Oxford - Bodleian Library MS Mich. 365 (Neubauer 1208), f. 94a-94b, C, rubric: יוצר ליום ראשון של סוכות.

4175. Oxford - Bodleian Library MS Opp. 172 (Neubauer 1211), f. 89b, C, rubric: זהא לך יוצר מיום ראשון של סוכות.
4176. Parma - Biblioteca Palatina Cod. Parm. 3507 (Perreau 27), f. 173a-173b, C.
4177. Vatican - Biblioteca Apostolica ebr. 305,1, f. 38b-39a, C, rubric: יוצר לחג הסוכות.
4178. Vatican - Biblioteca Apostolica ebr. 422/1, f. 20a, C, short.
4179. Zurich - Zentralbibliothek Heid. 139, f. 89a-89b, C, rubric: לסוכות, additional marginal notes.

Roma

4180. Jerusalem - Jewish National and University Library Ms Heb 8° 4153, f. 141a, C, commentator: Daniel ben Salomo haRofe (compiler), rubric: פירוש אכתיר זיר תהילה.
4181. Jerusalem - Jewish National and University Library Ms Heb 8° 4153, f. 147b, C, commentator: Daniel ben Salomo haRofe (compiler), rubric: יוצר ליו' ראשו' של סוכות.
4182. Oxford - Bodleian Library MS Mich. 312,1 (Neubauer 2276,1), f. 9b-10a, C, rubric: פי' יוצר ראשון של סוכות שהוא אכתיר.
4183. Oxford - Bodleian Library MS Mich. 312,1 (Neubauer 2276,1), f. 13b-14a, C.

Romania

4184. London - London School of Jewish Studies. Asher I.Myers collection 9, f. 200b-201a, M, rubric: ומתחיל זה היוצר לחן מלך אזור גדולה.
4185. Vatican - Biblioteca Apostolica ebr. 320, f. 407b-408a, M.

Tsarfat

4186. London - David Sofer 5, f. 181a-181b, C, rubric: פירו' מיוצר ש' שיני של יום סוכות.
4187. Moscow - Russian State Library, Ms. Guenzburg 1665, f. 162a, M.
4188. Parma - Biblioteca Palatina Cod. Parm. 1264, f. 19b-20a, M.

אל אדון על כל המעשים בחפת חתנים (א 3219), לחתונה

Ashkenaz

4189. Oxford - Bodleian Library MS Can. Or. 82 (Neubauer 1148), f. 48a-48b, M.

אל אדון על כל המעשים ברוך ומבורך בפי כל נשמה (א 3320), שחרית שבת

Tsarfat

4190. Parma - Biblioteca Palatina Cod. Parm. 1902, f. 210b-212a, M, commentator: Natan b. Yehuda, ספר המחכים.

אל אדיר מיכאל מימא׳ ממלל, סוכות

Tsarfat
4191. Parma - Biblioteca Palatina Cod. Parm. 3006 (de Rossi 654,1), f. 220a-220b, M.

אל אדיר רב חילו (א 3339), אלעזר ברבי קליר, חלק ז׳, קדושתא למנחה יום כפור

Ashkenaz
4192. New York - Jewish Theological Seminary Ms. 8169 (Acc. 0016), f. 116b-117a, M.

Tsarfat
4193. London - David Sofer 5, f. 172b, C, rubric: רהיטים.
4194. Oxford - Bodleian Library MS Laud. Or. 271 (Neubauer 1206), f. 118b, C, commentator: Aaron b. Hayyim haKohen (compiler), no incipit, very short.

אל אדני שמע בקולי שלח לפני מלאכי וגואלי, לנוסעים

Ashkenaz
4195. Oxford - Bodleian Library MS Opp. 696/13 (Neubauer 2253), f. 252a-254b, M.

אל אחד אהיה אשר אהיה (א 3347), אהרן בן יוסף הרופא, פרשת חיי שרה

Karaite, commentary by Berakha b. Josef haKohen
4196. New York - Jewish Theological Seminary Ms. 3367, f. 34a-36b, C, rubric: פרוש פיוט פרשת ויהיו חיי שרה.
4197. St. Petersburg - Inst. of Oriental Studies of the Russian Academy B 431, f. 26a-27b, C, rubric: פרשת חיי שרה.
4198. St. Petersburg - Russian National Library, Evr. IV 50, f. 25b-27b, C, rubric: פ׳ חיי שרה.

אל אל אשא דעי (א 3362), יצחק גיאת, סדר עבודה

Sepharad[104]
4199. Vatican - Biblioteca Apostolica ebr. 213, f. 120a-163a, C, commentary on the text begins f. 128a, incomplete.

אל אל חי ארנן (א 3377), שמעון ב"ר יצחק, יוצר

Ashkenaz
4200. Budapest - Magyar tudomanyos akademia, MS. Kaufmann A 399, p. 421-422, C, rubric: זולתות בין י"ז בתמוז לט׳ באב.
4201. Cambridge - University Library Add. 504,1, f. 42a-43a, C, rubric: זולתות בין י"ז לתמוז לט׳ באב. ר׳ שמעון בר׳ יצחק יסד זה וחתום בחרו׳ שלח.

---

[104] Edited by Z. Malachi, סדר עבודת יום הכפורים לר׳ יצחק אבן גיאת הספרדי, Lod 1997.

4202. Frankfurt a M - Stadt- und Universitaetsbibliothek Oct. 227, f. 161b-162a, M.
4203. Hamburg - Staats- und Universitaetsbibliothek Cod. hebr. 62 (Steinschneider 154), f. 27b-28a, C, rubric: זולת אחר.
4204. Jerusalem - Schocken Institute 24100 / Mahzor Nuremberg, f. 135a-135b, M.
4205. Muenchen - Bayerische Staatsbibliothek, Cod. hebr. 88, f. 105b-106a, G.
4206. Muenchen - Bayerische Staatsbibliothek, Cod. hebr. 393,9, f. 198b, C, short.
4207. New York - Jewish Theological Seminary Ms. 4824, f. 3a-3b, FM.
4208. Oxford - Bodleian Library MS Can. Or. 82 (Neubauer 1148), f. 25a-26b, M.
4209. Parma - Biblioteca Palatina Cod. Parm. 3205 (de Rossi 655), f. 152b-153b, C.
4210. Vatican - Biblioteca Apostolica ebr. 318, f. 100b-101b, GI.

Ashkenaz, commentary by Abraham b. Azriel[105]

4211. Vatican - Biblioteca Apostolica ebr. 301,1, f. 13a-14a, C, rubric: זולת.

אל אל שדי ארנן (א 3383), מנחם ב"ר מכיר, יוצר לשבת נחמו

Ashkenaz

4212. Jerusalem - Schocken Institute 24100 / Mahzor Nuremberg, f. 219b-220b, M.
4213. Muenchen - Bayerische Staatsbibliothek, Cod. hebr. 69, f. 58b-60b, M.

Ashkenaz, commentary by Abraham b. Azriel[106]

4214. Frankfurt a M - Stadt- und Universitaetsbibliothek Fol. 16 (Merzbacher 95), f. 5b-13b, C, rubric: יוצר אחר.
4215. Vatican - Biblioteca Apostolica ebr. 301,1, f. 40a-46a, C, rubric: יוצר.

אל אלהים יי דברויקרא ארץ (א 3424), אליעזר ב"ר נתן, מעריב ליום ב' של שבועות

Ashkenaz

4216. Braunschweig - Landesmuseum fuer Geschichte und Volkstum R 2386, vol. I, f. 91b-94a, M.
4217. Budapest - Magyar tudomanyos akademia, MS. Kaufmann A 399, p. 222-228, C.
4218. Frankfurt a M - Stadt- und Universitaetsbibliothek Oct. 227, f. 127b-132b, M, rubric: לשבועות.
4219. London - British Library Add. 18695 (Margoliouth 683), f. 78b-81a, T, Yiddish.

---

[105] Edited by Urbach, ערוגת הבושם, vol. I, p. 84-91.
[106] Edited by Urbach, ערוגת הבושם, vol. I, p. 244-280.

4220. New York - Jewish Theological Seminary Ms. 4466, f. 156b-159b, M.
4221. Parma - Biblioteca Palatina Cod. Parm. 2895, p. 336-342, M, margins cut, text damaged.
4222. Parma - Biblioteca Palatina Cod. Parm. 3205 (de Rossi 655), f. 116a-116b, C.

אל אלהים בך יצדקו צדוק (א 4626), יוסף אבן אביתור, סדר עבודה

Sepharad or Provence, commentary by Hayyim Galipapa[107]

4223. Parma - Biblioteca Palatina Cod. Parm. 2351, f. 122a-139b, C, rubric: פרוש סדר עבודה לר' חיים ז"ל בן גליפפה.

אל אלהים זלפה עיני (א 3393), יואל ב"ר יצחק הלוי, סליחה

Ashkenaz

4224. Vatican - Biblioteca Apostolica ebr. 308, f. 13b-14a, C, commentator: David b. Mose (compiler).
4225. Vatican - Biblioteca Apostolica ebr. 308, f. 163a, C, commentator: David b. Mose (compiler).

אל אלהינו נשוב בצר לנו בגלותינו (א 3452), אליעזר ב"ר נתן, זולת לשבת שובה

Ashkenaz

4226. Braunschweig - Landesmuseum fuer Geschichte und Volkstum R 2386, vol. II, f. 124b-125a, M, no incipit.

אל אלוה דלפה נפש קורא (א 3392), פזמון

Sepharad, commentary by David b. Josef Abudarham[108]

4227. Budapest - Magyar tudomanyos akademia, MS. Kaufmann A 405/2, p. 205-206, C, rubric: פזמון.
4228. New York - Columbia X893 Ab 93, f. 12b, C, rubric: פזמון.

אל אמונה עזרה הבה (א 3460), אליה, סליחה

Ashkenaz

4229. Jerusalem - Schocken Institute 24100 / Mahzor Nuremberg, f. 251b, G.
4230. Vatican - Biblioteca Apostolica ebr. 308, f. 14a, C, commentator: David b. Mose (compiler).

---

[107] Partly published by S. Stern, *קובץ מעשי ידי גאונים*, על סדר עבודה לר"י בן אביתור *קדמונים*, J. Rosenberg (ed), Berlin, Friedländer'sche Buchdruckerei, 1896, p. 117-122.

[108] Edited by Prins, תשלום אבודרהם, p. 151-152.

אל באפך פן תמעיט בצר פקדוך צקון לחש (א 3487), סליחה

Ashkenaz
4231. Berlin - Staatsbibliothek (Preussischer Kulturbesitz) Or. Qu. 798-799 (Steinschneider 177), I, f. 101a-101b, M.
4232. Budapest - Magyar tudomanyos akademia, MS. Kaufmann A 400, p. 483, C, rubric: אחרת, short.
4233. Graz - Universitaetsbibliothek 1703\195, f. 2b, FC, only beginning.
4234. Hamburg - Staats- und Universitaetsbibliothek Cod. hebr. 17/2 (Steinschneider 152), f. 177a, C, rubric: אילו פירוש של סליחות שכתבתי לעיל.
4235. London - British Library Add. 18695 (Margoliouth 683), f. 163a, T, Yiddish.
4236. Moscow - Russian State Library, Ms. Guenzburg 615, f. 158b, C, rubric: אל מלך, short.
4237. Muenchen - Bayerische Staatsbibliothek, Cod. hebr. 346, f. 121a, C, rubric: זו פריש׳ ראשונה, short.
4238. Oxford - Bodleian Library MS Mich. 543 (Neubauer 1212), f. 70a, C, commentator: Isaac b. Jakob (compiler), short.
4239. Oxford - Bodleian Library MS Opp. 170 (Neubauer 1205), f. 227b, C, short.
4240. Oxford - Bodleian Library MS Opp. 681 (Neubauer 1213), f. 4b, C.
4241. Padova - Biblioteca del Seminario Vescovile Cod. 218, f. 96a-96b, M.
4242. Padova - Biblioteca del Seminario Vescovile Cod. 218, f. 212b-213a, M.
4243. Parma - Biblioteca Palatina Cod. Parm. 3205 (de Rossi 655), f. 259b-260a, C.

Ashkenaz, commentary by Abraham b. Azriel[109]
4244. Vatican - Biblioteca Apostolica ebr. 301,1, f. 157a, C, rubric: אחרת.

Tsarfat
4245. London - British Library Add. 11639 (Margoliouth 1056), f. 470a, M, very short.
4246. London - David Sofer 5, f. 91a-92b, C, short.
4247. Oxford - Bodleian Library MS Bodl. Or. 109 (Neubauer 1209), f. 84b-85a, C, commentator: Aaron b. Hayyim haKohen (compiler).
4248. Oxford - Bodleian Library MS Laud. Or. 271 (Neubauer 1206), f. 120a, C, commentator: Aaron b. Hayyim haKohen (compiler).
4249. Parma - Biblioteca Palatina Cod. Parm. 3007 (de Rossi 654,2), f. 47a, M, short.
4250. Vatican - Biblioteca Apostolica ebr. 306, f. 170a, C, short.

---

[109] Edited by Urbach, ערוגת הבושם, vol. III, p. 411-412.

אל בית המלך לבא נקראתי (א 3503), אברהם אבן עזרא, פזמון, בתימן: סליחה
Sepharad, commentary by David b. Josef Abudarham[110]

4251. Budapest - Magyar tudomanyos akademia, MS. Kaufmann A 405/2, p. 213, C, rubric: פזמון.
4252. Cincinnati - Hebrew Union College 490, f. 14b, C.
4253. New York - Columbia X893 Ab 93, f. 14b, C, rubric: פזמון.
4254. New York - Jewish Theological Seminary Ms. 3011, f. 21a-21b, C, rubric: פזמון.

Yemen
4255. Jerusalem - Sassoon 902, p. 419, M.

Yemen, commentary by Isaac b. Abraham Wanneh
4256. Chicago-Spertus College of Judaica D 2, 2, f. 195b, M, no incipit.
4257. Jerusalem - Sassoon 1158, p. 354, M, no incipit.
4258. London - British Library Or. 11122, f. 176a, M, rubric: אל מלך, no incipit.

אל בעשותו נוראות כיפה וכשירה, יוסף ב"ר שמואל טוב עלם, חלק ז, קדושתא לפסח
Tsarfat
4259. Parma - Biblioteca Palatina Cod. Parm. 3136 (de Rossi 405), f. 111a-111b, M.

אל ברוב עצות תכן את רוח (א 3513), משולם ב"ר קלונימוס, חלק כ"ה, קדושתא לשחרית יום כפור
Ashkenaz
4260. Berlin - Staatsbibliothek (Preussischer Kulturbesitz) Or. Qu. 798-799 (Steinschneider 177), I, f. 86b-87a, M.
4261. Braunschweig - Landesmuseum fuer Geschichte und Volkstum R 2386, vol. II, f. 199a-199b, M.
4262. Budapest - Magyar tudomanyos akademia, MS. Kaufmann A 400, p. 332-335, C.
4263. Cambridge - University Library Add. 394,1 (Reif SCR 461), f. 71b-72a, Margin, C.
4264. Cambridge - University Library Add. 394,1 (Reif SCR 461), f. 72a-72b, C.
4265. Hamburg - Staats- und Universitaetsbibliothek Cod. hebr. 62 (Steinschneider 154), f. 9a-10a, C, rubric: ויקרא זה אל זה ואמ' ק'ק'ק'.
4266. Hamburg - Staats- und Universitaetsbibliothek Cod. hebr. 132 (Steinschneider 155), f. 37b-38a, C.
4267. Jerusalem - Jewish National and University Library Ms Heb 8° 3037, f. 133a-133b, M.

---

[110] Edited by Prins, תשלום אבודרהם, p. 108-109.

4268. Jerusalem - Schocken Institute 24100 / Mahzor Nuremberg , f. 384b-385a, M.
4269. London - British Library Or. 11318/1, f. 83a-83b, C.
4270. London - Montefiore Library 261 , f. 48a-48b, C, commentator: Eliezer b. Natan?.
4271. Moscow - Russian State Library, Ms. Guenzburg 191 , f. 123b-124a, M.
4272. Muenchen - Bayerische Staatsbibliothek, Cod. hebr. 346 , f. 57b-58b, C,no incipit.
4273. New York - Jewish Theological Seminary Ms. 4466, f. 326b-327b, M.
4274. New York - Jewish Theological Seminary Ms. 8169 (Acc. 0016), f. 100a, M.
4275. Oxford - Bodleian Library MS Mich. 365 (Neubauer 1208), f. 72b-73a, C, rubric: אופן בעמידה.
4276. Oxford - Bodleian Library MS Opp. 172 (Neubauer 1211), f. 45b-46a, C.
4277. Paris - Bibliotheque Nationale heb. 653, f. 66b, G.
4278. Parma - Biblioteca Palatina Cod. Parm. 3205 (de Rossi 655), f. 226b-227a, C, rubric: קדושה.
4279. Parma - Bibliotheca Palatina Cod. Parm. 3205 (de Rossi 655), f. 292a-292b, C.
4280. Parma - Biblioteca Palatina Cod. Parm. 3271 (de Rossi 1216), f. 52a-52b, G.
4281. Parma - Biblioteca Palatina Cod. Parm. 3507 (Perreau 27), f. 153b-154a, C.
4282. Vatican - Biblioteca Apostolica ebr. 308, f. 107a-108a, C, commentator: David b. Mose (compiler).
4283. Vatican - Biblioteca Apostolica ebr. 422/1, f. 16b, C, incipit לכפר.
4284. Zurich - Zentralbibliothek Heid. 139 , f. 78a-78b, C, additional marginal notes.

Asti, Fossano, Moncalvo
4285. New Haven - Yale University, Beinecke Rare Book and MS Library, MS Heb. 52, f. 139a-139b, M.

Roma
4286. Jerusalem - Jewish National and University Library Ms Heb 8° 4153, f. 140b, C, commentator: Daniel ben Salomo haRofe (compiler), no incipit, short.
4287. Oxford - Bodleian Library MS Mich. 312,1 (Neubauer 2276,1), f. 8b, C, short.

Tsarfat
4288. London - David Sofer 5, f. 153a-153b, C.
4289. Oxford - Bodleian Library MS Bodl. Or. 109 (Neubauer 1209), f. 24a-24b, C, commentator: Aaron b. Hayyim haKohen (compiler), rubric: קדושה.

4290. Parma - Biblioteca Palatina Cod. Parm. 1794 (de Rossi 1061), f. 180b, M.
4291. Parma - Biblioteca Palatina Cod. Parm. 2890 (de Rossi 856), f. 79a, M.
4292. Parma - Biblioteca Palatina Cod. Parm. 3006 (de Rossi 654,1), f. 185a-185b, M.

אל ברוך ומבורך בפי כלם (א 3520), אהרן בן יוסף הרופא, פרשת ויצא
Karaite, commentary by Berakha b. Josef haKohen
4293. New York - Jewish Theological Seminary Ms. 3367, f. 40a-46b, C, rubric: פרוש פרשת ויצא יעקב.
4294. St. Petersburg - Inst. of Oriental Studies of the Russian Academy B 431, f. 30a-33b, C, rubric: פרשת ויצא יעקב.
4295. St. Petersburg - Russian National Library, Evr. IV 50, f. 30b-34a, C, rubric: ויצא יעקב.

אל דביר קדשך (א 3542), יוסף, סליחה
Ashkenaz
4296. Bologna - Archivio di Stato MS Ebr. 253, f. 2a-2b, FC.
4297. Budapest - Magyar tudomanyos akademia, MS. Kaufmann A 400, p. 492, C, rubric: אחרת.
4298. Moscow - Russian State Library, Ms. Guenzburg 190, f. 33a-33b, G.
4299. Moscow - Russian State Library, Ms. Guenzburg 615, f. 158b-159a, C, rubric: אל מלך.
4300. Muenchen - Bayerische Staatsbibliothek, Cod. hebr. 346, f. 127b, C.
4301. Oxford - Bodleian Library MS Mich. 543 (Neubauer 1212), f. 70a-70b, C, commentator: Isaac b. Jakob (compiler).
4302. Oxford - Bodleian Library MS Opp. 170 (Neubauer 1205), f. 227b-228a, C.
4303. Oxford - Bodleian Library MS Opp. 681 (Neubauer 1213), f. 41a-41b, C.
4304. Parma - Biblioteca Palatina Cod. Parm. 3205 (de Rossi 655), f. 258a-258b, C.
Ashkenaz, commentary by Abraham b. Azriel[111]
4305. Frankfurt a M - Stadt- und Universitaetsbibliothek Fol. 16 (Merzbacher 95), f. 116b-117a, C, manuscript partly damaged.
4306. Vatican - Biblioteca Apostolica ebr. 301,1, f. 157a, C, rubric: אחרת.
Tsarfat
4307. London - David Sofer 5, f. 161b-162a, C, rubric: סליחה.
4308. Oxford - Bodleian Library MS Laud. Or. 271 (Neubauer 1206), f. 170b-171a, C, commentator: Aaron b. Hayyim haKohen (compiler).

---

[111] Edited by Urbach, ערוגת הבושם, vol. III, p. 410-411.

4309. Oxford - Bodleian Library MS Opp. 171 (Neubauer 1207), f. 93b, C, rubric: אחרת.
4310. Parma - Biblioteca Palatina Cod. Parm. 1794 (de Rossi 1061), f. 32b-34a, M.
4311. Parma - Biblioteca Palatina Cod. Parm. 2890 (de Rossi 856), f. 102b-103a, M.
4312. Parma - Biblioteca Palatina Cod. Parm. 3007 (de Rossi 654,2), f. 47a-47b, M, incipit missing.
4313. Vatican - Biblioteca Apostolica ebr. 306, f. 168b-169b, C.
4314. Vatican - Biblioteca Apostolica ebr. 306, f. 193b-194a, C.

אל דמי לכם ילדי איתני (א 3550), משה אבן עזרא, סליחה

Yemen
4315. Jerusalem - Sassoon 902, p. 427, M, short.
4316. New York - Jewish Theological Seminary Ms. 3052, f. 32b-33a, M, rubric: אל מלך.

Yemen, commentary by Isaac b. Abraham Wanneh
4317. Chicago-Spertus College of Judaica D 2, 2, f. 201a, M.
4318. Jerusalem - Benayahu ת 261, f. 140a-141a, M, rubric: אל מלך.
4319. Jerusalem - Makhon Ben Zvi 1156 (Tubi 155), f. 122a, M, rubric: אל מלך, short.
4320. Jerusalem - Michael Krupp 604, f. 155a, M, rubric: אל מלך.
4321. Jerusalem - Musad haRav Kook 325, f. 184a, M, rubric: אל מלך.
4322. Jerusalem - Sassoon 1174, p. 235, M, no incipit, short.
4323. Manchester - John Rylands University Library, Ms. Gaster 5, f. 198b-199a, M.
4324. Muenchen - Bayerische Staatsbibliothek, Cod. hebr. 472, f. 167a, M, rubric: אל מלך, short.
4325. New York - Jewish Theological Seminary Ms. 3013, f. 123a, M, rubric: אל מלך.
4326. New York - Jewish Theological Seminary Ms. 3294, f. 11a, C.
4327. Strasbourg - Bibliotheque Nationale et Universitaire 3965 (Landauer 39), p. 383, M, rubric: אל מלך, short.

אל הר המור גבעת הוריה (א 3603), מאיר ב"ר יצחק, סליחה

Ashkenaz
4328. Berlin - Staatsbibliothek (Preussischer Kulturbesitz) Or. Qu. 798-799 (Steinschneider 177), I, f. 169a-169b, M.
4329. Cambridge - University Library Dd. 2.30, f. 88a-88b, G.
4330. Jerusalem - Schocken Institute 24100 / Mahzor Nuremberg, f. 467b-468a, M.
4331. Oxford - Bodleian Library MS Mich. 543 (Neubauer 1212), f. 42b-43a, C, commentator: Isaac b. Jakob (compiler), rubric: עקיד'.

4332. Oxford - Bodleian Library MS Opp. 172 (Neubauer 1211), f. 78b-79a, C, rubric: עקידה.
4333. Oxford - Bodleian Library MS Opp. 681 (Neubauer 1213), f. 72a-73a, C.
4334. Padova - Biblioteca del Seminario Vescovile Cod. 218, f. 131b, M.
4335. Padova - Biblioteca del Seminario Vescovile Cod. 218, f. 131b-132a, M.
4336. Padova - Biblioteca del Seminario Vescovile Cod. 218, f. 132a, M.
4337. Vatican - Biblioteca Apostolica ebr. 308, f. 135a-135b, C, commentator: David b. Mose (compiler).
4338. Vatican - Biblioteca Apostolica ebr. 422/1, f. 26a, C, very short.
4339. Vatican - Biblioteca Apostolica ebr. 422/2, f. 39b, CG, no incipit, short.

Ashkenaz, commentary by Abraham b. Azriel[112]

4340. Frankfurt a M - Stadt- und Universitaetsbibliothek Fol. 16 (Merzbacher 95), f. 107b, C.
4341. Vatican - Biblioteca Apostolica ebr. 301,1, f. 145a-145b, C, rubric: אחר'.

Tsarfat

4342. London - David Sofer 5, f. 145b-146a, C, rubric: עקידה.
4343. Oxford - Bodleian Library MS Bodl. Or. 109 (Neubauer 1209), f. 51a-51b, C, commentator: Aaron b. Hayyim haKohen (compiler).
4344. Parma - Biblioteca Palatina Cod. Parm. 3007 (de Rossi 654,2), f. 50a-50b, M.

אל חי נגלה, יצחק הנקדן

Ashkenaz

4345. Oxford - Bodleian Library MS Can. Or. 70 (Neubauer 1147,7), f. 86b-87a, M, rubric: אחרת.

אל טוב וסלח אדמתנו בטוב הצלח (א 3678), הושענא

Italia, commentary by Yehoshua Segre

4346. Moscow - Russian State Library, Ms. Guenzburg 533, f. 45a-46b, C, rubric: לימוד י"ז.

Tsarfat

4347. London - David Sofer 5, f. 193b, C.
4348. Parma - Biblioteca Palatina Cod. Parm. 1902, f. 184b-185a, M.

---

[112] Edited by Urbach, ערוגת הבושם, vol. III, p. 330-332.

אל ימעטו לפניך את כל התלאה (א 3713), משה בר שמואל, סליחה
Ashkenaz
4349. Budapest - Magyar tudomanyos akademia, MS. Kaufmann A 400 , p. 491, C, rubric: אחרת.
4350. Moscow - Russian State Library, Ms. Guenzburg 615, f. 159a, C, rubric: אל מלך.
4351. Muenchen - Bayerische Staatsbibliothek, Cod. hebr. 346 , f. 127a, C, short.
4352. Oxford - Bodleian Library MS Mich. 543 (Neubauer 1212), f. 70b, C, commentator: Isaac b. Jakob (compiler), short.
4353. Oxford - Bodleian Library MS Opp. 170 (Neubauer 1205), f. 228a, C.
4354. Padova - Biblioteca del Seminario Vescovile Cod. 218, f. 85a-85b, M.
4355. Parma - Biblioteca Palatina Cod. Parm. 3205 (de Rossi 655), f. 268a-268b, C.
4356. Vatican - Biblioteca Apostolica ebr. 422/1, f. 28a-28b, C.
4357. Vatican - Biblioteca Apostolica ebr. 422/1, f. 42a, CG, no incipit.
Ashkenaz, commentary by Abraham b. Azriel[113]
4358. Frankfurt a M - Stadt- und Universitaetsbibliothek Fol. 16 (Merzbacher 95), f. 111b, C.
4359. Vatican - Biblioteca Apostolica ebr. 301,1, f. 147b, C, rubric: אחרת.
Tsarfat
4360. London - David Sofer 5, f. 89b, C.
4361. London - David Sofer 5, f. 146b-147a, C, rubric: סליחה.
4362. Oxford - Bodleian Library MS Laud. Or. 271 (Neubauer 1206), f. 171a, C, commentator: Aaron b. Hayyim haKohen (compiler).
4363. Oxford - Bodleian Library MS Opp. 171 (Neubauer 1207), f. 102b-103a, C, rubric: אחרת.
4364. Parma - Biblioteca Palatina Cod. Parm. 3007 (de Rossi 654,2), f. 56a-56b, M, ecclectic, partly censored.
4365. Vatican - Biblioteca Apostolica ebr. 306, f. 90b-91a, C.

אל ישעך צמאתי (א 3733), יצחק בר ואליק, הושענא
haAri, commentary by Mose b. Hayyim Pesante
4366. New York - Columbia University X 893 J 558, f. 200a-200b, M.
4367. New York - Jewish Theological Seminary Ms. 4696, f. 10b-11a, C.
haAri, commentary by Simon b. Tsemah Duran
4368. New York - Columbia University X 893 J 558, f. 200a-200b, M.
North Africa, commentary by Yehuda Toledona
4369. New York - Jewish Theological Seminary Ms. 4300, f. 6a-8b, C.

---

[113] Edited by Urbach, ערוגת הבושם, vol. III, p. 347.

Yemen, commentary by Samḥun b. Salomo Ḥaloah
4370. Jerusalem - Makhon ben Zvi 2808, f. 17a-21b, C.

אל ישראל נקראת לפנים (א 3735), אברהם אבן עזרא, גאולה ליום כפור
Ashkenaz
4371. Budapest - Magyar tudomanyos akademia, MS. Kaufmann A 399 , p. 361, C, rubric: פיוט קודם שמונה עשרה.
4372. Oxford - Bodleian Library MS Can. Or. 82 (Neubauer 1148) , f. 51a-51b, M, short.

אל לבבינו נשוב בצר לנו בגלותינו, אליעזר ב"ר נתן, זולת
Ashkenaz
4373. Berlin - Staatsbibliothek (Preussischer Kulturbesitz) Or. Qu. 798-799 (Steinschneider 177), I, f. 54(i)b-54(ii)a, M.
4374. Frankfurt a M - Stadt- und Universitaetsbibliothek Oct. 227 , f. 166a, M.
4375. Oxford - Bodleian Library MS Can. Or. 82 (Neubauer 1148) , f. 40a-41a, M.
4376. Parma - Biblioteca Palatina Cod. Parm. 2895 , p. 412-414, M, rubric: זולת.
4377. Parma - Biblioteca Palatina Cod. Parm. 3205 (de Rossi 655), f. 167b-168a, C, rubric: זולת.

אל לבבם עמך ישראל השיבו (א 3750), סליחה
Ashkenaz
4378. New York - Jewish Theological Seminary Ms. 4466, f. 286b, M, very ecclectic.
4379. Parma - Bibliotheca Palatina Cod. Parm. 3205 (de Rossi 655), f. 287a, C.

אל למושעות בארבע שבועות (א 3754), הושענא
Ashkenaz
4380. Berlin - Staatsbibliothek (Preussischer Kulturbesitz) Or. Qu. 361 (Steinschneider 51), f. 115a-115b, M.
4381. Berlin - Staatsbibliothek (Preussischer Kulturbesitz) Or. Qu. 798-799 (Steinschneider 177), I, f. 203b-204a, M.
4382. Budapest - Magyar tudomanyos akademia, MS. Kaufmann A 399 , p. 297-298, C.
4383. Cambridge - University Library Add. 394,1 (Reif SCR 461) , f. 74a-74b, C, rubric: הושענות.
4384. Cambridge - University Library Or. 790, f. 31a-31b, C.
4385. Frankfurt a M - Stadt- und Universitaetsbibliothek Oct. 227 , f. 113a, M.

4386. Hamburg - Staats- und Universitaetsbibliothek Cod. hebr. 17/2 (Steinschneider 152), f. 165b, C, rubric: הושענות.
4387. Jerusalem - Schocken Institute 24100 / Mahzor Nuremberg, f. 493a-493b, M.
4388. London - British Library Add. 18695 (Margoliouth 683), f. 149a, T, Yiddish.
4389. London - British Library Add. 22431 (Margoliouth 662a), f. 119a, M.
4390. London - British Library Add. 27208 (Margolioth 654), f. 268a-268b, M.
4391. London - British Library Add. 27556, f. 127b, M.
4392. Lund - Universitetsbibliothek Ms. L.O. 2, f. 86a-86b, M.
4393. New York - Jewish Theological Seminary Ms. 4466, f. 477b, M.
4394. Oxford - Bodleian Library MS Can. Or. 1 (Neubauer 1104), f. 25b-26b, M.
4395. Oxford - Bodleian Library MS Mich. 573 (Neubauer 1099), f. 17b-18a, M, rubric: הושענות.
4396. Oxford - Bodleian Library MS Opp 160 (Neubauer 1204), f. 234a-234b, C, commentator: Elazar b. Yehuda of Worms.[114]
4397. Oxford - Bodleian Library MS Opp. 170 (Neubauer 1205), f. 199b-200a, C, rubric: הושענות.
4398. Parma - Biblioteca Palatina Cod. Parm. 2895, p. 210, M.
4399. Parma - Biblioteca Palatina Cod. Parm. 3205 (de Rossi 655), f. 249a-249b, C.
4400. Uppsala - Universitetsbibliotek O.Heb.22, f. 109a-109b, M.
4401. Vatican - Biblioteca Apostolica ebr. 305,1, f. 43a-43b, C, rubric: פירושי הושענות, no incipit.
4402. Vatican - Biblioteca Apostolica ebr. 308, f. 154a-154b, C, commentator: David b. Mose (compiler).
4403. Verona - Seminario Maggiore 34, f. 168a-168b, M, rubric: פירוש על הושענות.

Ashkenaz, commentary by Eliezer b. Natan
4404. Hamburg - Staats- und Universitaetsbibliothek Cod. hebr. 61 (Steinschneider 153), f. 23a-23b, C.
4405. London - Montefiore Library 261, f. 85a-85b, C.
4406. Paris - Bibliotheque Nationale heb. 327/2, f. 36b-37b, C.
4407. Warszaw - Uniwersytet, Inst. Orientalistyczny 258, f. 195a-195b, C, rubric: אתחיל הושענות.

Italia
4408. Moscow - Russian State Library, Ms. Guenzburg 533, f. 30a-34b, C, commentator: Yehoshua Segre, rubric: לימוד י"ג.

---

[114] Edited by Katzenellenbogen, פירוש ההושענות, p. 27-30.

4409. Torino - Archivio Terracini 1499, p. 67-79, C, commentator: Zakharya David Shabbetai Segre, rubric: הקדמה לפירוש אל למושעות (67), פירוש אל למושעות (74).

Roma

4410. Jerusalem - Jewish National and University Library Ms Heb 8° 4153, f. 142a-142b, C, commentator: Daniel ben Salomo haRofe (compiler).
4411. Oxford - Bodleian Library MS Mich. 312,1 (Neubauer 2276,1), f. 10b, C.

Romania

4412. London - London School of Jewish Studies. Asher I.Myers collection 9, f. 209b-210a, M.
4413. Roma - Collegio Rabbinico Italiano 110, f. 2a-2b, M.
4414. Vatican - Biblioteca Apostolica ebr. 285/30, f. 234b-235a, C.
4415. Vatican - Biblioteca Apostolica ebr. 320, f. 445a-445b, M.

Tsarfat

4416. Cambridge - University Library Add. 561.1, f. 115a-115b, M.
4417. Jerusalem - Schocken Institute 19623, f. 125a-125b, M, commentator: Yehuda b. Eliezer Zvi.
4418. London - British Library Or. 2735 (Margoliouth 663), f. 146a-146b, M.
4419. London - David Sofer 5, f. 192a, C.
4420. Moscow - Russian State Library, Ms. Guenzburg 1665, f. 181a, M.
4421. New York - Jewish Theological Seminary Ms. 4460, f. 81b, G, only on end of Hoshaana.
4422. Parma - Biblioteca Palatina Cod. Parm. 1264, f. 96a, M.
4423. Parma - Biblioteca Palatina Cod. Parm. 1902, f. 175a-176a, M.
4424. Vatican - Biblioteca Apostolica ebr. 306, f. 121a-121b, C.

אל לקחני לנחלה כי גם יום וגם לילה (א 3761), אברהם אבן עזרא, פזמון

Tsarfat

4425. Parma - Biblioteca Palatina Cod. Parm. 3136 (de Rossi 405), f. 60b, M.

אל מי נמשילך ואין עדוך אליך (א 3788), אברהם אבן עזרא, סליחה

Yemen

4426. Jerusalem - Sassoon 902, p. 440, M.
4427. New York - Jewish Theological Seminary Ms. 3028, f. 46b-47a, G. Yemen, commentary by Isaac b. Abraham Wanneh
4428. Chicago-Spertus College of Judaica D 2, 2, f. 221b, M, no incipit.
4429. Jerusalem - Michael Krupp 604, f. 159a-159b, M.
4430. Jerusalem - Sassoon 1158, p. 384-385, M, no incipit.
4431. London - British Library Or. 11122, f. 192a-192b, M, no incipit.

אל מי תדמיון אל ומה דמות תערכו לו, אהרן בן יוסף הרופא, פרשת בהעלתך
Karaite, commentary by Berakha b. Josef haKohen
4432. New York - Jewish Theological Seminary Ms. 3367, f. 121b-123b, C, rubric: פרוש פרשת בהעלותך.
4433. St. Petersburg - Inst. of Oriental Studies of the Russian Academy B 431, f. 83b-84b, C, rubric: פרשת בהעלותך.
4434. St. Petersburg - Russian National Library, Evr. IV 50 , f. 93b-95a, C, rubric: בהעלותך.

אל מי תדמיון אל ומעשיו לו עדים (א 3790), אהרן בן יוסף הרופא, פרשת ויגש
Karaite, commentary by Berakha b. Josef haKohen
4435. New York - Jewish Theological Seminary Ms. 3367, f. 56b-59a, C, rubric: פרוש פרשת ויגש.
4436. St. Petersburg - Inst. of Oriental Studies of the Russian Academy B 431, f. 40a-41b, C, rubric: פרשת ויגש.
4437. St. Petersburg - Russian National Library, Evr. IV 50 , f. 41b-43a, C, rubric: ויגש.

אל מיום פקודה יחילו ברואיך, זולת
Tsarfat
4438. Oxford - Bodleian Library MS Opp. 171 (Neubauer 1207), f. 53b-54a, C, rubric: זולת.

אל מלך היושב בשמים המשגיח (א 3815), אהרן בן יוסף הרופא, פרשת נח
Karaite, commentary by Berakha b. Josef haKohen
4439. New York - Jewish Theological Seminary Ms. 3367, f. 19a-25a, C, rubric: פרוש פיוט פרשת נח.
4440. St. Petersburg - Inst. of Oriental Studies of the Russian Academy B 431, f. 16b-20a, C, rubric: פרשת נח.
4441. St. Petersburg - Russian National Library, Evr. IV 50 , f. 14a-17b, C, rubric: ועתה אחל פ' נוח '' בעזר נותן ליעף כוח.

אל מלך יושב אל כסא רחמים (א 3822), פתיחה לשלוש עשרה מדות
Ashkenaz
4442. London - British Library Or. 11318/1, f. 63a-64a, C.
4443. Padova - Biblioteca del Seminario Vescovile Cod. 218, f. 42b-45a, M.

אל מנת חלקנו הנמצא רצונך (א 3832)
Carpentras, commentary by Josef b. Abraham of Montelitz
4444. Cincinnati - Hebrew Union College 357, f. 111a, M.
4445. New York - Jewish Theological Seminary Ms. 4746, f. 41a, M.
4446. Paris - Alliance Israelite Universelle H 422 A, f. 88a, M.
4447. Paris - Ecole Rabbinique 31, f. 150a, M.

אל מסתתר בחביון עוזו, סליחה
Ashkenaz, commentary by Abraham b. Azriel[115]
4448. Frankfurt a M - Stadt- und Universitaetsbibliothek Fol. 16 (Merzbacher 95), f. 103a, C, short.

אל מעמדי שבתי לעמוד (א 3843), אברהם אבן עזרא, חלק ב׳, קדושתא למוסף יום כפור
Carpentras, commentary by Josef b. Abraham of Montelitz
4449. Cincinnati - Hebrew Union College 291, f. 44b-45a, C, rubric: פי׳ פזמון אל מעמדי וכו׳.
4450. New York - Jewish Theological Seminary Ms. 4197, f. 194b-195b, M.
4451. Paris - Ecole Rabbinique 32, f. 204a-204b, M.
4452. Strasbourg - Bibliotheque Nationale et Universitaire 4081, f. 179a-179b, M.

אל מתנשא לכל לראש (א 3853), אלעזר ברבי קילר, יוצר לשבת שקלים
Ashkenaz
4453. Berlin - Staatsbibliothek (Preussischer Kulturbesitz) Or. Qu. 798-799 (Steinschneider 177), II, f. 11b-12b, M.
4454. Budapest - Magyar tudomanyos akademia, MS. Kaufmann A 384, f. 34a-34b, M.
4455. Cambridge - University Library Add. 394,1 (Reif SCR 461), f. 41b-42b, C, rubric: יוצר לפרשת שקלים.
4456. Cambridge - University Library Add. 504,1, f. 1a, C.
4457. Erlangen - Universitaetsbibliothek 2601 (Roth 67), f. 26a-26b, M.
4458. Hamburg - Staats- und Universitaetsbibliothek Cod. hebr. 17/2 (Steinschneider 152), f. 10a-10b, C, rubric: חסלת.
4459. Hamburg - Staats- und Universitaetsbibliothek Cod. hebr. 225, f. 8a-9a, G.
4460. Jerusalem - Schocken Institute 24100 / Mahzor Nuremberg, f. 33b-34a, M.
4461. Muenchen - Bayerische Staatsbibliothek, Cod. hebr. 88, f. 13a, G.
4462. Muenchen - Bayerische Staatsbibliothek, Cod. hebr. 393, f. 84a-84b, C.
4463. Oxford - Bodleian Library MS Mich. 573 (Neubauer 1099), f. 49a-50a, M.
4464. Oxford - Bodleian Library MS Opp. 170 (Neubauer 1205), f. 1b-3a, C.
4465. Paris - Bibliotheque Nationale heb. 709, f. 1a-3a, C.
4466. Parma - Biblioteca Palatina Cod. Parm. 1002 (Ta 24), f. 20a-20b, M.
4467. Parma - Biblioteca Palatina Cod. Parm. 3205 (de Rossi 655), f. 10a-10b, C, rubric: לארבע פרשיו׳.

---

[115] Edited by Urbach, ערוגת הבושם, vol. III, p. 543.

4468. Parma - Biblioteca Palatina Cod. Parm. 3269, f. 7b-8a, G, later hand.
4469. Parma - Biblioteca Palatina Cod. Parm. 3507 (Perreau 27), f. 1a-2a, C.
4470. Vatican - Biblioteca Apostolica ebr. 305,1, f. 37b-38a, C.

Italia
4471. Parma - Biblioteca Palatin Cod. Parm. 2248 (de Rossi 149/2), f. 17a-18b, C, rubric: ביאור יוצר פרשת שקלים.

Roma
4472. Jerusalem - Jewish National and University Library Ms Heb 8° 4153, f. 156a-156b, C, commentator: Daniel ben Salomo haRofe (compiler), rubric: פירוש יוצר דכי תשא, additional glosses.
4473. New York - Jewish Theological Seminary Ms. 1639, f. 15a-16b, C, commentator: Salomo b. Samuel Rofe, rubric: ביאור יוצר פרשת שקלים.
4474. Oxford - Bodleian Library MS Mich. 312,1 (Neubauer 2276,1), f. 21b-22a, C.

Tsarfat
4475. London - David Sofer 5, f. 7b-8a, C, rubric: יוצר לפרשת שקלים.
4476. London - David Sofer 5, f. 11b-12a, C, rubric: פירוש אחר מקרובץ של פר' שקלים.
4477. Moscow - Russian State Library, Ms. Guenzburg 1665, f. 12a-12b, M.
4478. Oxford - Bodleian Library MS Laud. Or. 271 (Neubauer 1206), f. 5a-6a, C, commentator: Aaron b. Hayyim haKohen (compiler), rubric: פרשת שקלים.
4479. Oxford - Bodleian Library MS Opp. 171 (Neubauer 1207), f. 4a-4b, C, rubric: ואילו פירוש של ארבעה פרשיות.
4480. Parma - Biblioteca Palatina Cod. Parm. 3136 (de Rossi 405), f. 20b, C.
4481. Vatican - Biblioteca Apostolica ebr. 306, f. 155b-156a, C, rubric: פרשת שקלים.

אל נא אוצרך הטוב פתח (א 3856), יוסף אבן אביתור, הושענא

haAri, commentary by Mose b. Hayyim Pesante
4482. New York - Jewish Theological Seminary Ms. 4696, f. 24a, C, incipit השיג.

North Africa
4483. Jerusalem - Benayahu ז 27, f. 129a-129b, M, incipit השיג.
4484. New York - Jewish Theological Seminary Ms. 4121, f. 49a-50a, C, commentator: Simon b. Tsemaḥ Duran?, rubric: אלל נא אוצרך הטוב פתח, incipit השיג.
4485. New York - Jewish Theological Seminary Ms. 4300, f. 57a-58b, C, commentator: Yehuda Toledano.

Yemen, commentary by Samḥun b. Salomo Ḥaloah
4486. Jerusalem - Makhon ben Zvi 2808, f. 207a-216b, C, incipit השיג.

אל נא הטיבה יי לטובים בעצרת שמחים (א 3861), אלעזר ברבי קליר, חלק ד',
קדושתא לשמיני עצרת

Romania
4487. Vatican - Biblioteca Apostolica ebr. 320, f. 460a, M, incipit אל נא.

Tsarfat
4488. Moscow - Russian State Library, Ms. Guenzburg 1665, f. 187b, M, incipit אל נא.

אל נא יום זה על קץ תפסיע (א 3866), יוסף אבן אביתור, הושענא
haAri, commentary by Mose b. Hayyim Pesante
4489. New York - Jewish Theological Seminary Ms. 4696, f. 24a, C, incipit תפסיע.

North Africa
4490. Jerusalem - Benayahu ז 27, f. 130a, M, incipit תפסיע.
4491. New York - Jewish Theological Seminary Ms. 4300, f. 58b-59b, C, commentator: Yehuda Toledano.

Yemen, commentary by Samḥun b. Salomo Ḥaloah
4492. Jerusalem - Makhon ben Zvi 2808, f. 216b-222b, C, incipit תפסיע.

אל נא קרב תשועת מצפיך (א 3874), סליחה
Yemen, commentary by Isaac b. Abraham Wanneh
4493. Jerusalem - Musad haRav Kook 330, f. 93a, M, short.

אל נא רפא נא תחלואי פוריה (א 3875), חטאנו
Ashkenaz
4494. Braunschweig - Landesmuseum fuer Geschichte und Volkstum R 2386, vol. II, f. 55b, M.
4495. Oxford - Bodleian Library MS Mich. 543 (Neubauer 1212), f. 86a, C, commentator: Isaac b. Jakob (compiler), very short.
4496. Oxford - Bodleian Library MS Opp. 172 (Neubauer 1211), f. 86a, C, rubric: חטאנו, very short.
4497. Oxford - Bodleian Library MS Opp. 681 (Neubauer 1213), f. 96b, C, manuscript breaks off after 2 lines of this commentary.
4498. Padova - Biblioteca del Seminario Vescovile Cod. 218, f. 77a-77b, M.
4499. Vatican - Biblioteca Apostolica ebr. 422/1, f. 32b-33a, C.

אל נא תעינו כשה אובד (א 3886), הושענא
Ashkenaz
4500. Berlin - Staatsbibliothek (Preussischer Kulturbesitz) Or. Qu. 361 (Steinschneider 51), f. 120b-121a, M.
4501. Berlin - Staatsbibliothek (Preussischer Kulturbesitz) Or. Qu. 798-799 (Steinschneider 177), I, f. 208b, M.

4502. Budapest - Magyar tudomanyos akademia, MS. Kaufmann A 399 , p. 303-304, C.
4503. Budapest - Magyar tudomanyos akademia, MS. Kaufmann A 400 , p. 536-537, C.
4504. Cambridge - University Library Add. 394,1 (Reif SCR 461) , f. 76a-76b, C, rubric: הושענא.
4505. Cambridge - University Library Or. 790, f. 34b-35a, C.
4506. Frankfurt a M - Stadt- und Universitaetsbibliothek Oct. 227 , f. 115b-116a, M.
4507. Hamburg - Staats- und Universitaetsbibliothek Cod. hebr. 17/2 (Steinschneider 152), f. 167b, C, rubric: אחרת.
4508. Jerusalem - Schocken Institute 24100 / Mahzor Nuremberg , f. 494b-495a, M.
4509. London - British Library Add. 18695 (Margoliouth 683), f. 154a-154b, T, Yiddish.
4510. London - British Library Add. 22431 (Margoliouth 662a), f. 124a, M.
4511. London - British Library Add. 27208 (Margolioth 654), f. 273b-274b, M, ecclectic.
4512. London - British Library Add. 27556, f. 132a-132b, M, short.
4513. Lund - Universitetsbibliothek Ms. L.O. 2, f. 88a, M.
4514. Oxford - Bodleian Library MS Mich. 573 (Neubauer 1099), f. 21b-22a, M.
4515. Oxford - Bodleian Library MS Opp 160 (Neubauer 1204), f. 242a-243a, C, commentator: Elazar b. Yehuda of Worms.[116]
4516. Parma - Biblioteca Palatina Cod. Parm. 2895, p. 223, M.
4517. Parma - Biblioteca Palatina Cod. Parm. 3205 (de Rossi 655), f. 252b, C.
4518. Uppsala - Universitetsbibliotek O.Heb.22 , f. 113b-114a, M, no incipit.
4519. Vatican - Biblioteca Apostolica ebr. 305,1, f. 44b, C, no incipit.
4520. Vatican - Biblioteca Apostolica ebr. 308 , f. 158b, C, commentator: David b. Mose (compiler), incipit אנא.

Ashkenaz, commentary by Eliezer b. Natan
4521. Hamburg - Staats- und Universitaetsbibliothek Cod. hebr. 61 (Steinschneider 153), f. 24b.
4522. Paris - Bibliotheque Nationale heb. 327/2, f. 40b, C.
4523. Warszaw - Uniwersytet, Inst. Orientalistyczny 258, f. 197a-197b, C.
4524. Warszaw - Uniwersytet, Inst. Orientalistyczny 258, f. 197b-198b, C.

Italia
4525. Moscow - Russian State Library, Ms. Guenzburg 533 , f. 51a-52b, C, commentator: Yehoshua Segre, rubric: לימוד כ'.

---

[116] Edited by Katzenellenbogen, פירוש ההושענות, p. 53-55.

4526. Torino - Archivio Terracini 1499, p. 232-233, C, commentator: Zakharya David Shabbetai Segre, rubric: פירוש אל נא תעינו כשה אובד.

Roma

4527. Jerusalem - Jewish National and University Library Ms Heb 8° 4153, f. 145a-145b, C, commentator: Daniel ben Salomo haRofe (compiler), incipit הושענא.

4528. Oxford - Bodleian Library MS Mich. 312,1 (Neubauer 2276,1), f. 13a, C, incipit הושענא.

Romania

4529. Vatican - Biblioteca Apostolica ebr. 285/30, f. 236a, C.

4530. Vatican - Biblioteca Apostolica ebr. 320, f. 447b-448a, M.

Tsarfat

4531. Cambridge - University Library Add. 561.1, f. 115b, M.

4532. Jerusalem - Schocken Institute 19623, f. 127a-127b, M, commentator: Yehuda b. Eliezer Zvi.

4533. London - British Library Or. 2735 (Margoliouth 663), f. 150b-151a, M.

4534. London - David Sofer 5, f. 192b, C.

4535. Moscow - Russian State Library, Ms. Guenzburg 1665, f. 183b, M, incipit תעינו.

4536. Parma - Biblioteca Palatina Cod. Parm. 1264, f. 98b, M.

4537. Parma - Biblioteca Palatina Cod. Parm. 1902, f. 176b-177a, M.

4538. Parma - Biblioteca Palatina Cod. Parm. 1902, f. 180b-181a, M.

אל נגלה במדות שלש עשרה בסיני (א 3900), שלמה בן יצחק גירונדי

Carpentras

4539. Cincinnati - Hebrew Union College 392, f. 17b-18a, M.

Carpentras, commentary by Josef b. Abraham of Montelitz

4540. Cincinnati - Hebrew Union College 291, f. 9b-10a, C, rubric: פי׳ אל נגלה במדות וכו׳.

4541. Paris - Ecole Rabbinique 32, f. 41a-42b, M.

4542. Strasbourg - Bibliotheque Nationale et Universitaire 4081, f. 36a, M.

אל נורא עלילה המצא לנו מחילה (א 3911), משה אבן עזרא, לנעילה

Carpentras, commentary by Josef b. Abraham of Montelitz

4543. Cincinnati - Hebrew Union College 291, f. 57b-58a, C, rubric: פי׳ אל נורא וכו׳.

4544. New York - Jewish Theological Seminary Ms. 4197, f. 257b, M.

4545. Paris - Ecole Rabbinique 32, f. 266b, M.

Yemen, commentary by Isaac b. Abraham Wanneh

4546. Jerusalem - Sassoon 1158, p. 203, M, rubric: אל מלך. סים׳ דוד.

4547. London - British Library Or. 11122, f. 206b, M, rubric: אל מלך.

אל נערץ בסוד מלאכי שביבו (א 3928), אהרן בן יוסף הרופא, פרשת עקב
Karaite, commentary by Berakha b. Josef haKohen
4548. New York - Jewish Theological Seminary Ms. 3367, f. 144a-145b, C, rubric: פרוש פרשת עקב.
4549. St. Petersburg - Inst. of Oriental Studies of the Russian Academy B 431, f. 97a-98a, C, rubric: פרשת עקב.
4550. St. Petersburg - Russian National Library, Evr. IV 50, f. 112a-113b, C, rubric: עקב.

אל נערץ בסוד קדושים רבה ברך אום מיוחדת (א 3934), הושענא
Narbonne, commentary by Meir Meili of Narbonne[117]
4551. London - British Library Add. 19778, f. 35a, C.
Romania
4552. Vatican - Biblioteca Apostolica ebr. 285/30, f. 231b, C, short.
Tsarfat
4553. London - British Library Or. 2735 (Margoliouth 663), f. 138a-138b, M, ecclectic.
4554. London - British Library Or. 2735 (Margoliouth 663), f. 140a, M, ecclectic, no incipit.

אל נערץ בסוד קדושים רבת מזמור (א 3937), יוסף אבן אביתור, הושענא
haAri, commentary by Mose b. Hayyim Pesante
4555. New York - Columbia University X 893 J 558, f. 207a-207b, M.
4556. New York - Jewish Theological Seminary Ms. 4696, f. 20a-20b, C.
North Africa, commentary by Yehuda Toledano
4557. New York - Jewish Theological Seminary Ms. 4300, f. 37a-38a, C.
Tsarfat
4558. London - David Sofer 5, f. 191a-191b, C, rubric: אתחיל הושענות.
Yemen, commentary by Isaac b. Abraham Wanneh
4559. Jerusalem - Benayahu ת 282, f. 78b, M.
4560. Jerusalem - Makhon Ben Zvi 1156 (Tubi 155), f. 77b, M, short.
4561. Jerusalem - Makhon Ben Zvi 1174 (Tubi 154), f. 87b, M, short.
4562. Jerusalem - Michael Krupp 604, f. 96a, M, rubric: פירוש, short.
4563. Jerusalem - Musad haRav Kook 325, f. 111a, M.
4564. Jerusalem - Musad haRav Kook 325, f. 127a, M.
4565. Jerusalem - Sassoon 1158, p. 219, M, short.
4566. Jerusalem - Sassoon 1174, p. 148, M, rubric: פירוש, short.
4567. London - British Library Or. 11122, f. 124a-124b, M.
4568. Muenchen - Bayerische Staatsbibliothek, Cod. hebr. 472, f. 102b, M, short.

---

[117] Edited by Sofer, ספר המכתם, p. 150-151.

4569. New York - Jewish Theological Seminary Ms. 3193, f. 169a, M.
4570. New York - Jewish Theological Seminary Ms. 3295, f. 94b, M, no incipit, short.
4571. Ramat Gan - Universitat Bar Ilan 703, f. 198a-198b, M, short.
4572. Strasbourg - Bibliotheque Nationale et Universitaire 3965 (Landauer 39), p. 247, M, short.

Yemen, commentary by Samḥun b. Salomo Ḥaloah
4573. Jerusalem - Makhon ben Zvi 2808, f. 159b-162a, C.

אל נשא ארנן בהתעלסה (א 3945), שלמה הבבלי, יוצר לשבת בראשית

Ashkenaz
4574. Berlin - Staatsbibliothek (Preussischer Kulturbesitz) Or. Qu. 361 (Steinschneider 51), f. 158b-159b, M, no incipit.
4575. Berlin - Staatsbibliothek (Preussischer Kulturbesitz) Or. Qu. 798-799 (Steinschneider 177), I, f. 232a-233a, M.
4576. Budapest - Magyar tudomanyos akademia, MS. Kaufmann A 399, p. 313-316, C.
4577. Cambridge - University Library Add. 504,1, f. 25a-27b, C, rubric: לשבת בראשית אום׳ יוצר זה שלמה יסד וחתום בשיתו לס לעבוד.
4578. Frankfurt a M - Stadt- und Universitaetsbibliothek Oct. 227, f. 138a-138b, M.
4579. Jerusalem - Schocken Institute 24100 / Mahzor Nuremberg, f. 8a-8b, M.
4580. Lund - Universitetsbibliothek Ms. L.O. 2, f. 118a-118b, M, rubric: לשבת בראשית.
4581. Moscow - Russian State Library, Ms. Guenzburg 615, f. 131a-132a, C, rubric: לשבת בראשית.
4582. Oxford - Bodleian Library MS Can. Or. 82 (Neubauer 1148), f. 1b-2a, M.
4583. Oxford - Bodleian Library MS Mich. 365 (Neubauer 1208), f. 19b-21a, C.
4584. Parma - Biblioteca Palatina Cod. Parm. 2895, p. 368-371, M, margins cut, text damaged.
4585. Parma - Biblioteca Palatina Cod. Parm. 3205 (de Rossi 655), f. 129b-130a, C, rubric: אתחיל פירוש של יוצרות וזולתות.
4586. Vatican - Biblioteca Apostolica ebr. 318, f. 108b-109b, GI.

Ashkenaz, commentary by Abraham b. Azriel[118]
4587. Frankfurt a M - Stadt- und Universitaetsbibliothek Fol. 16 (Merzbacher 95), f. 50(ii)b-52a, C.
4588. Vatican - Biblioteca Apostolica ebr. 301,1, f. 79b-81a, C.

---

[118] Edited by Urbach, ערוגת הבושם, vol. II, p. 199-208.

Ashkenaz, commentary by Eliezer b. Natan
4589. Hamburg - Staats- und Universitaetsbibliothek Cod. hebr. 61 (Steinschneider 153), f. 26b-27b, C.
4590. Warszaw - Uniwersytet, Inst. Orientalistyczny 258, f. 176a-177a, C, rubric: פירושים של יוצרות.

Tsarfat
4591. Oxford - Bodleian Library MS Laud. Or. 271 (Neubauer 1206), f. 186a-187a, C, commentator: Aaron b. Hayyim haKohen (compiler).
4592. Parma - Biblioteca Palatina Cod. Parm. 1264, f. 164a-164b, M.

אל עבדיך המצא (א 3947), אהרן, סליחה

Ashkenaz
4593. Berlin - Staatsbibliothek (Preussischer Kulturbesitz) Or. Qu. 798-799 (Steinschneider 177), I, f. 100a-100b, M.
4594. Klosterneuburg - Stiftsbibliothek St. Augustini 271, FC, incomplete.
4595. Oxford - Bodleian Library MS Opp. 681 (Neubauer 1213), f. 36a, C.
4596. Vatican - Biblioteca Apostolica ebr. 422/1, f. 26b, C.
4597. Vatican - Biblioteca Apostolica ebr. 422/2, f. 39a, CG, no incipit, very short.

Ashkenaz, commentary by Abraham b. Azriel[119]
4598. Frankfurt a M - Stadt- und Universitaetsbibliothek Fol. 16 (Merzbacher 95), f. 104a, C.

אל עושה נפלאות בעבורם עשית נוראות (א 3955), זולת, שבת החדש

Ashkenaz
4599. Parma - Biblioteca Palatina Cod. Parm. 3205 (de Rossi 655), f. 58a, C, rubric: זולת לפרש׳ החדש, short.
4600. Zurich - Zentralbibliothek Heid. 139, f. 8b, C.

אל עליון רומך צדק מגיד מישרים, אהרן בן יוסף הרופא, פרשת תצוה

Karaite, commentary by Berakha b. Josef haKohen
4601. New York - Jewish Theological Seminary Ms. 3367, f. 83a-85b, C, rubric: פירוש פרשת ואתה תצוה.
4602. St. Petersburg - Inst. of Oriental Studies of the Russian Academy B 431, f. 59b-60b, C, rubric: פרשת תצוה.
4603. St. Petersburg - Inst. of Oriental Studies of the Russian Academy B 483, f. 14a-14b, C, incomplete, beginning and end missing.
4604. St. Petersburg - Russian National Library, Evr. IV 50, f. 61a-63a, C, rubric: תצוה.

---

[119] Edited by Urbach, ערוגת הבושם, vol. III, p.545.

אל פתחת ירון שה אובד (א 3991), יוסף אבן אביתור, הושענא
haAri, commentary by Mose b. Hayyim Pesante
4605. New York - Columbia University X 893 J 558, f. 204a, M.
North Africa
4606. Jerusalem - Benayahu ז 27, f. 69a-69b, M.
4607. New York - Jewish Theological Seminary Ms. 4300, f. 23a-24a, C, commentator: Yehuda Toledano.
Yemen, commentary by Samḥun b. Salomo Ḥaloah
4608. Jerusalem - Makhon ben Zvi 2808, f. 89b-92a, C.

אל רחום שמך (א 4019), סליחה
Ashkenaz
4609. London - British Library Add. 18695 (Margoliouth 683), f. 169b-170a, T, Yiddish.
North Africa, commentary by David b. Josef Abudarham
4610. New York - Jewish Theological Seminary Ms. 5426, f. 60b-61a, M.
Sepharad
4611. Skokie - Hebrew Theological College 3, f. 13a-13b, G.
4612. Skokie - Hebrew Theological College 3, f. 2.20a, M.

אל שוכן רום הדיצה נאמי, סליחה
Yemen
4613. New York - Jewish Theological Seminary Ms. 3052, f. 86b, M.
4614. Ramat Gan - Universitat Bar Ilan 62, f. 51b, G.
Yemen, commentary by Isaac b. Abraham Wanneh
4615. Chicago-Spertus College of Judaica D 2, 2, f. 239a, M, no incipit.
4616. Jerusalem - Benayahu ת 261, f. 166a-166b, M.
4617. Jerusalem - Benayahu ת 282, f. 142a-142b, M.
4618. Jerusalem - Makhon Ben Zvi 1156 (Tubi 155), f. 139b, M, no incipit.
4619. Jerusalem - Makhon Ben Zvi 1174 (Tubi 154), f. 138b, M.
4620. Jerusalem - Michael Krupp 604, f. 176b-177a, M, no incipit.
4621. Jerusalem - Sassoon 1158, p. 418, M, no incipit.
4622. Jerusalem - Sassoon 1174, p. 271, M, no incipit.
4623. London - British Library Or. 11122, f. 216a, M, no incipit.
4624. Manchester - John Rylands University Library, Ms. Gaster 5, f. 225a, M.
4625. Muenchen - Bayerische Staatsbibliothek, Cod. hebr. 472, f. 195a-195b, M.
4626. New York - Jewish Theological Seminary Ms. 3013, f. 134b, M.
4627. New York - Jewish Theological Seminary Ms. 3294, f. 18a, C.
4628. New York - Public Library, Heb. Ms. 9, f. 131a-131b, M, no incipit.
4629. Strasbourg - Bibliotheque Nationale et Universitaire 3965 (Landauer 39), p. 414, M.

אל תזכר לנו עונותינו (א 4131), אלעזר ברבי קליר, חלק ז', קדושתא למוסף יום כפור
Ashkenaz
4630. Zurich - Zentralbibliothek Heid. 139, f. 84a, C, short, incipit אתהה.

אל תסתיר פנים ועין אל תעלים (א 4192), סעדיה, סליחה
Yemen
4631. New York - Jewish Theological Seminary Ms. 3028, f. 97b, G.
4632. New York - Jewish Theological Seminary Ms. 3193, f. 137b-138a, M. Yemen, commentary by Isaac b. Abraham Wanneh
4633. Chicago-Spertus College of Judaica D 2, 2, f. 227b, M, no incipit.
4634. Jerusalem - Sassoon 1158, p. 314, M, no incipit.
4635. London - British Library Or. 11122, f. 204a-204b, M, no incipit.

אל תעזבנו יי ואל דמי לך (א 4196), אליהו, סליחה
Ashkenaz
4636. Vatican - Biblioteca Apostolica ebr. 422/2, f. 39b, CG, no incipit.

אל תתעלם מתחינתי כי דרשתיך (א 4257), סעדיה, סליחה
Yemen
4637. New York - Jewish Theological Seminary Ms. 3028, f. 98b, G.
4638. New York - Jewish Theological Seminary Ms. 3193, f. 138a-138b, M. Yemen, commentary by Isaac b. Abraham Wanneh
4639. Chicago-Spertus College of Judaica D 2, 2, f. 227b, M, no incipit.
4640. Jerusalem - Sassoon 1158, p. 314, M, no incipit.
4641. London - British Library Or. 11122, f. 204a, M, no incipit.

אלבש היום מדי חילי (א 4266)
Sepharad, commentary by David b. Josef Abudarham[120]
4642. Budapest - Magyar tudomanyos akademia, MS. Kaufmann A 405/2, p. 204-205, C, rubric: סתג׳׳ב. ביי תתהלל נפשי.
4643. New York - Columbia X893 Ab 93, f. 12a, C, rubric: מסתאג׳׳ב. ביי תתהלל נפשי.

אלה אזכרה את אשר נעשה (א 4267), אלעזר ברבי קליר, חלק ו', קדושתא לשבת שקלים
Ashkenaz
4644. Berlin - Staatsbibliothek (Preussischer Kulturbesitz) Or. Qu. 798-799 (Steinschneider 177), II, f. 15a-15b, M.
4645. Budapest - Magyar tudomanyos akademia, MS. Kaufmann A 384, f. 39b-40a, M.

---

[120] Edited by Prins, תשלום אבודרהם, p. 148-151.

4646. Budapest - Magyar tudomanyos akademia, MS. Kaufmann A 400 , p. 13-15, C.
4647. Cambridge - University Library Add. 504,1, f. 6b-7b, C.
4648. Hamburg - Staats- und Universitaetsbibliothek Cod. hebr. 17/2 (Steinschneider 152), f. 13a-13b, C.
4649. Jerusalem - Schocken Institute 24100 / Mahzor Nuremberg, f. 35b-36a, M.
4650. Muenchen - Bayerische Staatsbibliothek, Cod. hebr. 88, f. 16b, G.
4651. Muenchen - Bayerische Staatsbibliothek, Cod. hebr. 393 , f. 86b-87a, C, no incipit.
4652. Oxford - Bodleian Library MS Opp. 170 (Neubauer 1205) , f. 5b-6a, C.
4653. Paris - Bibliotheque Nationale heb. 709, f. 8a-9a, C.
4654. Parma - Biblioteca Palatina Cod. Parm. 1002 (Ta 24), f. 25a-25b, M.
4655. Parma - Biblioteca Palatina Cod. Parm. 3205 (de Rossi 655) , f. 14b-15a, C.
4656. Parma - Biblioteca Palatina Cod. Parm. 3507 (Perreau 27) , f. 5b-6b, C, no incipit.
4657. Vatican - Biblioteca Apostolica ebr. 305,1, f. 5a-6a, C, no incipit.

Tsarfat
4658. London - British Library Add. 11639 (Margoliouth 1056), f. 265b-266b, M.
4659. Moscow - Russian State Library, Ms. Guenzburg 1665, f. 15a, M.
4660. Oxford - Bodleian Library MS Laud. Or. 271 (Neubauer 1206) , 12a-13a, C, commentator: Aaron b. Hayyim haKohen (compiler).
4661. Oxford - Bodleian Library MS Opp. 171 (Neubauer 1207) , f. 8b-9a, C.
4662. Parma - Biblioteca Palatina Cod. Parm. 3136 (de Rossi 405) , f. 24a-25a, M.

אלה אזכרה ונפשי עלי אשפכה (א 4273), יהודה, סליחה

Ashkenaz
4663. Berlin - Staatsbibliothek (Preussischer Kulturbesitz) Or. Qu. 798-799 (Steinschneider 177), I, f. 150b-152a, M.
4664. Braunschweig - Landesmuseum fuer Geschichte und Volkstum R 2386, vol. II, f. 70b-71b, M.
4665. London - British Library Add. 18695 (Margoliouth 683), f. 167a-168a, T, Yiddish.
4666. Moscow - Russian State Library, Ms. Guenzburg 190 , f. 119b-121b, G.
4667. Muenchen - Bayerische Staatsbibliothek, Cod. hebr. 346, f. 87a, C, short.
4668. New York - Jewish Theological Seminary Ms. 8097, f. 87b, C, short.

4669. Oxford - Bodleian Library MS Mich. 543 (Neubauer 1212), f. 23a-24b, C, commentator: Isaac b. Jakob (compiler).
4670. Oxford - Bodleian Library MS Opp. 172 (Neubauer 1211), f. 81a-81b, C, rubric: חטאנו.
4671. Oxford - Bodleian Library MS Opp. 619 (Neubauer 2374), f. 241b-243a, M.
4672. Oxford - Bodleian Library MS Opp. 681 (Neubauer 1213), f. 93a-94a, C.
4673. Padova - Biblioteca del Seminario Vescovile Cod. 218, f. 110a-111a, M.
4674. Padova - Biblioteca del Seminario Vescovile Cod. 218, f. 219a-220a, M.
4675. Vatican - Biblioteca Apostolica ebr. 308, f. 138a-138b, C, commentator: David b. Mose (compiler).
4676. Vatican - Biblioteca Apostolica ebr. 422/1, f. 33b, C.
4677. Zurich - Zentralbibliothek Heid. 139, f. 103b, C, commentator: Elazar b. Yehuda of Worms, rubric: לכיפור, no incipit, short.

Asti, Fossano, Moncalvo
4678. New Haven - Yale University, Beinecke Rare Book and MS Library, MS Heb. 52, f. 170a-171a, M.

Carpentras, commentary by Mordekhai b. Josef of Rocco Martino
4679. Cincinnati - Hebrew Union College 246/1, f. 71a-73a; 83a-84a, C, rubric: פי׳ קינה עשרה הרוגי מלוכה.

Tsarfat
4680. London - David Sofer 5, f. 91b, C, rubric: אלה סליחה.
4681. Oxford - Bodleian Library MS Bodl. Or. 109 (Neubauer 1209), f. 14a-14b, C, commentator: Aaron b. Hayyim haKohen (compiler).
4682. Parma - Biblioteca Palatina Cod. Parm. 3006 (de Rossi 654,1), f. 208b-209a, M.
4683. Parma - Biblioteca Palatina Cod. Parm. 3007 (de Rossi 654,2), f. 12a-12b, 13b, M, only beginning.
4684. Vatican - Biblioteca Apostolica ebr. 306, f. 210a-210b, C.

Yemen, commentary by Isaac b. Abraham Wanneh
4685. Jerusalem - Sassoon 1158, p. 178-179, M.
4686. London - British Library Or. 11122, f. 106a-106b, M, no incipit.

אלה ברכב ואלה בסוסים (א 4279), שמעון ב״ר יצחק, סליחה

Ashkenaz
4687. Budapest - Magyar tudomanyos akademia, MS. Kaufmann A 400, p. 505-506, C, rubric: פיזמן בבלי.
4688. Oxford - Bodleian Library MS Opp. 170 (Neubauer 1205), f. 245b-246a, C.

Tsarfat
4689. London - David Sofer 5, f. 99a-99b, C.

4690. Oxford - Bodleian Library MS Laud. Or. 271 (Neubauer 1206), f. 129a-129b, C, commentator: Aaron b. Hayyim haKohen (compiler).
4691. Oxford - Bodleian Library MS Opp. 171 (Neubauer 1207), f. 108a-108b, C, rubric: אחרת.

אלה בשלישמו ואלה בפרשימו, שלמה, סליחה
Tsarfat
4692. Parma - Biblioteca Palatina Cod. Parm. 3007 (de Rossi 654,2), f. 107a-107b, M.

אלה החקים בחירים כשחקים (א 4281), יצחק בן מרדכי קמחי, חתימה לאזהרות
Carpentras
4693. New York - Jewish Theological Seminary Ms. 4268, f. 30a, C, rubric: פירוש החתימה.

אלה העדות והחוקים (א 4243), אלעזר ברבי קליר, סילוק, קדושתא לשבועות
Ashkenaz
4694. Berlin - Staatsbibliothek (Preussischer Kulturbesitz) Or. Qu. 798-799 (Steinschneider 177), II, f. 148b-150b, M.
4695. Braunschweig - Landesmuseum fuer Geschichte und Volkstum R 2386, vol. 103a-105a, M.
4696. Hamburg - Staats- und Universitaetsbibliothek Cod. hebr. 17/2 (Steinschneider 152), f. 88b-89a, C.
4697. London - British Library Add. 18695 (Margoliouth 683), f. 94b-96a, T, Yiddish.
4698. London - British Library Add. 22431 (Margoliouth 662a), f. 67b-69b, M.
4699. Parma - Biblioteca Palatina Cod. Parm. 3002 (de Rossi 407), f. 179b-181b, M, pages from printed Mahzor bound into Ms.
4700. Parma - Biblioteca Palatina Cod. Parm. 3507 (Perreau 27), f. 95a-95b, C, rubric: סילוק.

אלה וכאלה (א 4284), שמעון ב"ר יצחק, זולת לשבת וחול המועד של פסח
Ashkenaz
4701. Berlin - Staatsbibliothek (Preussischer Kulturbesitz) Or. Qu. 798-799 (Steinschneider 177), II, f. 85a-85b, M.
4702. Braunschweig - Landesmuseum fuer Geschichte und Volkstum R 2386, vol. I, f. 42b-43a, C.
4703. Budapest - Magyar tudomanyos akademia, MS. Kaufmann A 384, f. 179b-180b, M.
4704. Hamburg - Staats- und Universitaetsbibliothek Cod. hebr. 17/2 (Steinschneider 152), f. 36b-37a, C, rubric: זולת.

HEBREW LITURGICAL POETRY 291

4705. London - British Library Add. 18695 (Margoliouth 683), f. 52b-53a, T, Yiddish, rubric: זולת.
4706. Muenchen - Bayerische Staatsbibliothek, Cod. hebr. 88, f. 77b-78a, G.
4707. Muenchen - Bayerische Staatsbibliothek, Cod. hebr. 393, f. 132a, C, no incipit.
4708. New York - Jewish Theological Seminary Ms. 4466, f. 83b-84b, M.
4709. Paris - Bibliotheque Nationale heb. 709, f. 115a-115b, C.
4710. Parma - Biblioteca Palatina Cod. Parm. 1002 (Ta 24), f. 130b-131a, M.
4711. Parma - Biblioteca Palatina Cod. Parm. 3205 (de Rossi 655), f. 106a-106b, C, rubric: זולת.
4712. Parma - Biblioteca Palatina Cod. Parm. 3507 (Perreau 27), f. 70a-70b, C, rubric: זולת.
4713. Zurich - Zentralbibliothek Heid. 139, f. 40b, C, additional marginal notes.

Tsarfat

4714. London - David Sofer 5, f. 38b-39a, C, additional glosses.
4715. Moscow - Russian State Library, Ms. Guenzburg 1665, f. 78b-79a, M.
4716. Oxford - Bodleian Library MS Laud. Or. 271 (Neubauer 1206), f. 75a-75b, C, commentator: Aaron b. Hayyim haKohen (compiler), short.
4717. Parma - Biblioteca Palatina Cod. Parm. 3136 (de Rossi 405), f. 105b-106a, M.

אלה עשיתם ואל תעשו, אלעזר ברבי קליר, סילוק, קדושתא לשמיני עצרת

Tsarfat

4718. Oxford - Bodleian Library MS Opp. 171 (Neubauer 1207), f. 163b-164b, C.

אלהא דישראל ומארי נהודיה, סליחה

Yemen

4719. New York - Jewish Theological Seminary Ms. 3052, f. 83a-83b, M.
4720. Ramat Gan - Universitat Bar Ilan 62, f. 52a, G.

Yemen, commentary by Isaac b. Abraham Wanneh

4721. Chicago-Spertus College of Judaica D 2, 2, f. 237b, M, no incipit.
4722. Jerusalem - Benayahu ת 261, f. 165a, M, short.
4723. Jerusalem - Benayahu ת 282, f. 141a, M.
4724. Jerusalem - Makhon Ben Zvi 1174 (Tubi 154), f. 137a, M.
4725. Jerusalem - Michael Krupp 604, f. 175b, M.
4726. Jerusalem - Sassoon 1174, p. 269, M, no incipit.
4727. London - British Library Or. 11122, f. 215a, M, no incipit.
4728. Muenchen - Bayerische Staatsbibliothek, Cod. hebr. 472, f. 193b, M.

4729. New York - Jewish Theological Seminary Ms. 3013, f. 133a, M, no incipit, short.
4730. New York - Jewish Theological Seminary Ms. 3294, f. 17a, C.
4731. New York - Public Library, Heb. Ms. 9, f. 130a, M, no incipit, short.
4732. Strasbourg - Bibliotheque Nationale et Universitaire 3965 (Landauer 39), p. 410, M.

אלהא דמלקדמין שירה רבוא, סליחה
Ashkenaz
4733. Oxford - Bodleian Library MS Opp. 170 (Neubauer 1205), f. 81b-83a, C, rubric: יסוד מר׳ נהוראי זץ״ל.

אלהא מקמא בעינא רשותא (א 4338), שלמה ב״ר שמואל, פיוט בארמית לשבועות
Ashkenaz
4734. Oxford - Bodleian Library MS Can. Or. 1 (Neubauer 1104), f. 121b-122b, M.

אלהא עלם דמלקדמין במימרה עלמא ברא (א 4321), מאיר ב״ר יצחק, רשות בארמית לשבועות
Ashkenaz
4735. Parma - Biblioteca Palatina Cod. Parm. 3205 (de Rossi 655), f. 188a-188b, C.

אלהא תקיפא רבא וגברא (א 4344), יקותיאל ב״ר יוסף, רשות לקריאת התורה ביום ז׳ של פסח
Ashkenaz
4736. Oxford - Bodleian Library MS Opp. 170 (Neubauer 1205), f. 81a-81b, C, rubric: פיוט מר׳ יקוטיאל בר יוסף.
4737. Parma - Biblioteca Palatina Cod. Parm. 3205 (de Rossi 655), f. 187b-188a, C.
Tsarfat
4738. Oxford - Bodleian Library MS Laud. Or. 271 (Neubauer 1206), f. 79a-79b, C, commentator: Aaron b. Hayyim haKohen (compiler).

אלהי אזכורה ושינה אסירה (א 4356), סליחה
Yemen, commentary by Isaac b. Abraham Wanneh
4739. Chicago-Spertus College of Judaica D 2, 2, f. 243a-243b, M, no incipit.
4740. Jerusalem - Sassoon 1158, p. 428-429, M, no incipit.
4741. London - British Library Or. 11122, f. 221a-221b, M, no incipit.

אלהי אל תדינני כמעלי (א 4362), סליחה

Carpentras
4742. Cincinnati - Hebrew Union College 429/1, f. 2a-2b, M.
Carpentras, commentary Eliyahu Carmi
4743. Cincinnati - Hebrew Union College 357, f. 35b-37a, M, rubric: תנא דרבי אליהו.
4744. New York - Jewish Theological Seminary Ms. 3151, f. 30b-31a, M.
Carpentras, commentary by Josef b. Abraham of Montelitz
4745. Cincinnati - Hebrew Union College 357, f. 35b-37a, M, rubric: פירוש.
4746. New York - Jewish Theological Seminary Ms. 4746, f. 4a-5a, M.
4747. Paris - Alliance Israelite Universelle H 422 A, f. 9a-10a, M.
4748. Paris - Ecole Rabbinique 31, f. 80a-81a, M.

אלהי בך אחבק (א 4397), אפרים ב"ר יצחק מרגנסבורג, זולת

Ashkenaz
4749. Jerusalem - Schocken Institute 24100 / Mahzor Nuremberg, f. 139a-139b, M.
4750. Muenchen - Bayerische Staatsbibliothek, Cod. hebr. 88, f. 109a-109b, G.
Ashkenaz, commentary by Abraham b. Azriel[121]
4751. Vatican - Biblioteca Apostolica ebr. 301,1, f. 18a-18b, C, rubric: זולת.

אלהי בשר עמך מפחדך סמר (א 4403), אליעזר ב"ר יצחק הלוי, סליחה

Ashkenaz
4752. Muenchen - Bayerische Staatsbibliothek, Cod. hebr. 346, f. 138a, C, rubric: אחרת, very short.
4753. Oxford - Bodleian Library MS Opp. 172 (Neubauer 1211), f. 85a, C, short.
4754. Vatican - Biblioteca Apostolica ebr. 308, f. 143a, C, commentator: David b. Mose (compiler).
Ashkenaz, commentary by Abraham b. Azriel[122]
4755. Frankfurt a M - Stadt- und Universitaetsbibliothek Fol. 16 (Merzbacher 95), f. 107b-108a, C, short

אלהי האלהים ואדוני האדונים באנו בשברון רוח (א 4409), מאיר ב"ר משה, סליחה

Ashkenaz
4756. Oxford - Bodleian Library MS Opp. 681 (Neubauer 1213), f. 84b-85b, C.

---

[121] Edited by Urbach, ערוגת הבושם, vol. I, p. 112-116.
[122] Edited by Urbach, ערוגת הבושם, vol. III, p. 559.

אלהי האלהים ואדוני האדונים מלך על כל מלכים (א 4410), משולם ב"ר קלונימוס, חלק כ"ד, קדושתא לשחרית יום כפור

Tsarfat

4757. Oxford - Bodleian Library MS Laud. Or. 271 (Neubauer 1206), f. 113b-114b, C, commentator: Aaron b. Hayyim haKohen (compiler), no incipit, ecclectic.

4758. Parma - Biblioteca Palatina Cod. Parm. 1794 (de Rossi 1061), f. 134b-142b, M.

אלהי הודיעני את אורח החיים (א 4412), אברהם אבן עזרא, סליחה

Yemen

4759. Jerusalem - Sassoon 902, p. 418, M.

Yemen, commentary by Isaac b. Abraham Wanneh

4760. Chicago-Spertus College of Judaica D 2, 2, f. 202a, M, no incipit.

4761. Jerusalem - Michael Krupp 604, f. 147b, M, rubric: אל מלך.

4762. Jerusalem - Sassoon 1158, p. 362, M, no incipit.

4763. London - British Library Or. 11122, f. 180b, M, no incipit.

אלהי העברים נקרא בכל דברים (א 4415), אפרים ב"ר יצחק מרגנסבורג, סליחה

Ashkenaz

4764. Muenchen - Bayerische Staatsbibliothek, Cod. hebr. 346, f. 147a-147b, C, rubric: אחרת.

4765. Oxford - Bodleian Library MS Opp. 172 (Neubauer 1211), f. 73a-73b, C, incipit אלקי.

4766. Oxford - Bodleian Library MS Opp. 681 (Neubauer 1213), f. 27b-28a, C.

4767. Padova - Biblioteca del Seminario Vescovile Cod. 218, f. 214b-216a, M.

4768. Vatican - Biblioteca Apostolica ebr. 308, f. 133b-134a, C, commentator: David b. Mose (compiler).

אלהי הרוחות לכל בשר אתה וחכמת בטוחות (א 4426), אברהם אבן עזרא, קדיש לשבועות

Carpentras

4769. Cincinnati - Hebrew Union College 429/1, f. 18b-19b, M, no incipit.

Carpentras, commentary by Josef b. Abraham of Montelitz

4770. New York - Jewish Theological Seminary Ms. 4746, f. 28a, M.

4771. Paris - Alliance Israelite Universelle H 422 A, f. 64b-65a, M.

4772. Paris - Ecole Rabbinique 31, f. 133a-133b, M.

אלהי הרוחות לכל בשר חק לעמו מסר (א 4428), יוסף ב"ר שמואל טוב עלם, סדר, קדושתא לשבת הגדול

Ashkenaz

4773. Jerusalem - Schocken Institute 24100 / Mahzor Nuremberg, f. 73b-75a, M.
4774. Muenchen - Bayerische Staatsbibliothek, Cod. hebr. 88, f. 52a-54a, G.
4775. Parma - Biblioteca Palatina Cod. Parm 3000 (de Rossi 378), f. 30a-35b, M.
4776. Parma - Biblioteca Palatina Cod. Parm. 3507 (Perreau 27), f. 34b-35b, C.

Ashkenaz, commentary by Samuel b. Salomo of Faliza[123]

4777. Moscow - Russian State Library, Ms. Guenzburg 1274, f. 2a-6a, M.
4778. Vatican - Biblioteca Apostolica ebr. 266/2, f. 138b-155b, C.

Tsarfat

4779. London - British Library Add. 11639 (Margoliouth 1056), f. 673b-674a, M, rubric: וזהו הסדר.
4780. Moscow - Russian State Library, Ms. Guenzburg 1665, f. 47b-49b, M.
4781. Parma - Biblioteca Palatina Cod. Parm. 3136 (de Rossi 405), f. 61a-62a, M.
4782. Vatican - Biblioteca Apostolica ebr. 306, f. 165a-166b, C, no incipit.

אלהי ימי ושנותי כלו (4447), יוסף שבתי בן יצחק, אהבה

Ashkenaz

4783. Jerusalem - Schocken Institute 24100 / Mahzor Nuremberg, f. 141b-142a, M.
4784. Muenchen - Bayerische Staatsbibliothek, Cod. hebr. 69, f. 51a-51b.
4785. Oxford - Bodleian Library MS Opp. 169 (Neubauer 1151), f. 28a, M.

Ashkenaz, commentary by Abraham b. Azriel[124]

4786. Vatican - Biblioteca Apostolica ebr. 301,1, f. 11a-12a, C, rubric: אהבה.

אלהי ישראל צדיק אתה אלוה סליחות (א 1192*), אליה ב"ר שמעיה, סליחה

Ashkenaz

4787. Jerusalem - Schocken Institute 24100 / Mahzor Nuremberg, f. 277a, M.
4788. Oxford - Bodleian Library MS Mich. 543 (Neubauer 1212), f. 67b-68a, C, commentator: Isaac b. Jakob (compiler).

---

[123] Commentary mainly on the Halakhot contained in the piyyut. This commentary is also included in אור זרוע by R. Isaac of Vienna, part II, § 256, it was published from the Vatican manuscript by G. Zinner, ספר אוצר פסקי הראשונים, Brooklyn 1985, p. 15-172.

[124] Edited by Urbach, ערוגת הבושם, vol. I, p. 71-75.

4789. Parma - Biblioteca Palatina Cod. Parm. 3205 (de Rossi 655), f. 279b-280a, C.

Tsarfat

4790. Vatican - Biblioteca Apostolica ebr. 306, f. 191a-191b, C.

אלהי ישראל רומה היום והופיע (א 4461), משה אבן עזרא, סילוק ב׳, קדושתא למוסף יום כפור

Carpentras, commentary by Josef b. Abraham of Montelitz

4791. New York - Jewish Theological Seminary Ms. 4197, f. 153b-154b, M.
4792. Paris - Ecole Rabbinique 32, f. 217a-218b, M.
4793. Strasbourg - Bibliotheque Nationale et Universitaire 4081, f. 191a-192a, M.

אלהי מה נורא מעשיך ליודעים (א 4484), אהרן בן יוסף הרופא, פרשת מטות

Karaite, commentary by Berakha b. Josef haKohen

4794. New York - Jewish Theological Seminary Ms. 3367, f. 134b-136b, C, rubric: פרוש פרשת ראשי מטות.
4795. St. Petersburg - Inst. of Oriental Studies of the Russian Academy B 431, f. 91b-92b, C, rubric: פרשת מטות.
4796. St. Petersburg - Inst. of Oriental Studies of the Russian Academy B 483, f. 9b-10b, C, rubric: פרשת מטות.
4797. St. Petersburg - Russian National Library, Evr. IV 50, f. 104b-106b, C, rubric: מטות.

אלהי מעשיו מה נפלאים (א 4490), יהודה הלוי, זולת

Carpentras

4798. Cincinnati - Hebrew Union College 429/1, f. 5b-6b, M.

Carpentras, commentary by Eliyahu Carmi

4799. New York - Jewish Theological Seminary Ms. 3151, f. 44b-45a, M.

Carpentras, commentary by Josef b. Abraham of Montelitz

4800. Cincinnati - Hebrew Union College 357, f. 51a-52a, M.
4801. New York - Jewish Theological Seminary Ms. 4746, f. 9a-10b, M.
4802. Paris - Alliance Israelite Universelle H 422 A, f. 28a-29b, M.
4803. Paris - Ecole Rabbinique 31, f. 97a-98a, M.

אלהי עולם העושה כל מאפס (א 4516), אהרן בן יוסף הרופא, פרשת והיה כי תבא

Karaite, commentary by Berakha b. Josef haKohen

4804. New York - Jewish Theological Seminary Ms. 3367, f. 152a-154a, C, rubric: פרוש פרשת והיה כי תבוא.
4805. St. Petersburg - Inst. of Oriental Studies of the Russian Academy B 431, f. 103a-104b, C, rubric: פרשת כי אבוא.
4806. St. Petersburg - Inst. of Oriental Studies of the Russian Academy B 483, f. 16a-16b, C, rubric: פרשת כי תבוא.

4807. St. Petersburg - Russian National Library, Evr. IV 50, f. 119b-121b, C rubric: והיה כי אבוא.

אלהי עושי נוצרי ויוצרי (א 4522), יצחק בן מאיר, סליחה

Ashkenaz
4808. Jerusalem - Schocken Institute 24100 / Mahzor Nuremberg, f. 453b-454a, M, rubric: אלוה.
4809. Oxford - Bodleian Library MS Opp. 172 (Neubauer 1211), f. 84a-84b, C.

אלהי קדם מעונה ישובב יונה הגלה (א 4544), אברהם אבן עזרא, סליחה

Yemen
4810. Jerusalem - Benayahu ת 301, f. 48b, G.
4811. Jerusalem - Sassoon 902, p. 417, M.
4812. New York - Jewish Theological Seminary Ms. 3028, f. 33a, G, margins damaged.
4813. Ramat Gan - Universitat Bar Ilan 62, f. 43b, G, margins damaged.

Yemen, commentary by Isaac b. Abraham Wanneh
4814. Jerusalem - Michael Krupp 604, f. 147b, M, rubric: אל מלך.
4815. Jerusalem - Musad haRav Kook 330, f. 104b-105a, G.
4816. Jerusalem - Sassoon 1158, p. 353, M, no incipit.
4817. Jerusalem - Yehiel haLevi 4, f. 164a, G.
4818. London - British Library Or. 11122, f. 175b, M.
4819. New York - Jewish Theological Seminary Ms. 3013, f. 125a-125b, M, rubric: אל מלך.

אלהי קדם על אדירים שכנת (א 4548), סדר עבודה

Ashkenaz
4820. Muenchen - Bayerische Staatsbibliothek, Cod. hebr. 393, f. 143b-144b, C, several parts of the Avoda, starting with לארז בלבנון.

אלהיכם יי צבאות השלים קוראים קדושתו, יצחק הנקדן, קדושה

Ashkenaz
4821. Oxford - Bodleian Library MS Can. Or. 70 (Neubauer 1147,7), f. 95a-95b, M, rubric: אחרת.

אלהיכם יוסיף ידו לקבץ נפוצותיכם (א 4577), יהודה בן שמואל החסיד, קדושה לשבת נחמו

Ashkenaz
4822. Berlin - Staatsbibliothek (Preussischer Kulturbesitz) Or. Qu. 798-799 (Steinschneider 177), I, f. 256a, M.
4823. Lund - Universitetsbibliothek Ms. L.O. 2, f. 108b, M, short.

אלהיכם יוסיף ידו שנית (א 4578), יוסף ב"ר נתן, קדושה למוסף שבת חתונה
Ashkenaz

4824. London - British Library Add. 18695 (Margoliouth 683), f. 148a, T, Yiddish, rubric: דש אלהיכם זגט מן צו מוסף אין דער קדושה אלז הינטרשט פון דער קדושה.

אלהיכם יזריח שמשו (א 4581), יהודה, יוצר לשבת וראש חדש
Ashkenaz

4825. Berlin - Staatsbibliothek (Preussischer Kulturbesitz) Or. Qu. 798-799 (Steinschneider 177), I, f. 245a, M.

4826. Lund - Universitetsbibliothek Ms. L.O. 2, f. 120b, M.

אלהיכם יחכה לחננכם, יצחק הנקדן, קדושה
Ashkenaz

4827. Oxford - Bodleian Library MS Can. Or. 70 (Neubauer 1147,7), f. 96b-97a, M, rubric: אחרת.

אלהיכם ישיב שלם סוכו ומעונתו (א 4588), יהודה בן שמואל, קדושה לשבת וחול המועד סוכות
Ashkenaz

4828. London - British Library Add. 18695 (Margoliouth 683), f. 148b, T, Yiddish, rubric: אן מיין טייל אורטירן זגט מן דש אלהיכם.

אלהיכם ישכיל עבדו יכון כסאו (א 4489), יהודה בן שמואל, יוצר לשבת בראשית
Ashkenaz

4829. Berlin - Staatsbibliothek (Preussischer Kulturbesitz) Or. Qu. 798-799 (Steinschneider 177), I, f. 237b, M.

אלהיכם נערץ בקדש בסוד עשר ספירות (א 4597), נקדן ב"ר שמואל, קדושה לשבת חנוכה
Ashkenaz

4830. Oxford - Bodleian Library MS Can. Or. 70 (Neubauer 1147,7), f. 97a-98a, M, rubric: אחרת.

אלהיכם עשה את הכל יפה בעיתו, יצחק הנקדן
Ashkenaz

4831. Oxford - Bodleian Library MS Can. Or. 70 (Neubauer 1147,7), f. 95b-96b, M, rubric: אחרת.

אלהים יי חילי ותושע לי ימינו הנאדרת (א 4609), יצחק השנירי, זולת לשבת זכור
Carpentras, commentary by Mordekhai b. Josef of Rocco Martino
4832. Cincinnati - Hebrew Union College 246/1, f. 17b-19b, C, rubric: 'פי זולת אלקים ה' חילי וכו'.

אלהים יי חילי יוצרי ומחוללי (א 4610), אפרים ב"ר יצחק מרגנסבורג, סליחה
Ashkenaz
4833. Vatican - Biblioteca Apostolica ebr. 308, f. 16a, C, commentator: David b. Mose (compiler).
4834. Vatican - Biblioteca Apostolica ebr. 308, f. 163b, C, commentator: David b. Mose (compiler).

אלהים אין בלתיך (א 4620), זבדיה, סליחה
Ashkenaz
4835. Moscow - Russian State Library, Ms. Guenzburg 190, f. 35a-36a, G.
4836. Oxford - Bodleian Library MS Mich. 543 (Neubauer 1212), f. 19a-19b, C, commentator: Isaac b. Jakob (compiler).
4837. Oxford - Bodleian Library MS Opp. 681 (Neubauer 1213), f. 6a, C.
4838. Padova - Biblioteca del Seminario Vescovile Cod. 218, f. 119b-120b, M.
4839. Parma - Biblioteca Palatina Cod. Parm. 3205 (de Rossi 655), f. 286b, C, very short.
4840. Vatican - Biblioteca Apostolica ebr. 422/1, f. 44b, CG, no incipit.
Tsarfat
4841. Oxford - Bodleian Library MS Bodl. Or. 109 (Neubauer 1209), f. 82b, C, commentator: Aaron b. Hayyim haKohen (compiler), very short.
4842. Parma - Biblioteca Palatina Cod. Parm. 1794 (de Rossi 1061), f. 12a, M.
4843. Vatican - Biblioteca Apostolica ebr. 306, f. 96b, C.

אלהים אל דומי לדמי אל תחרש (א 4626), דוד בן משולם, סליחה
Ashkenaz
4844. Berlin - Staatsbibliothek (Preussischer Kulturbesitz) Or. Qu. 798-799 (Steinschneider 177), I, f. 146a-147a, M.
4845. Jerusalem - Schocken Institute 24100 / Mahzor Nuremberg, f. 429b-430a, M.
4846. London - British Library Add. 18695 (Margoliouth 683), f. 164b-165a, T, Yiddish.
4847. Muenchen - Bayerische Staatsbibliothek, Cod. hebr. 21, f. 230a-230b, M.
4848. Muenchen - Bayerische Staatsbibliothek, Cod. hebr. 346, f. 120a, C, short.
4849. New York - Jewish Theological Seminary Ms. 8097, f. 85b-86a, C.

4850. Oxford - Bodleian Library MS Can. Or. 82 (Neubauer 1148), f. 19b-20a, M.
4851. Oxford - Bodleian Library MS Mich. 543 (Neubauer 1212), f. 20a-22a, C, commentator: Isaac b. Jakob (compiler).
4852. Oxford - Bodleian Library MS Opp. 681 (Neubauer 1213), f. 7b-8a, C.
4853. Oxford - Bodleian Library MS Opp. 172 (Neubauer 1211), f. 73b-74a, C, incipit אלקים.
4854. Padova - Biblioteca del Seminario Vescovile Cod. 218, f. 103a-104a, M.
4855. Padova - Biblioteca del Seminario Vescovile Cod. 218, f. 210a-211a, M.
4856. Vatican - Biblioteca Apostolica ebr. 308, f. 135b-136b, C, commentator: David b. Mose (compiler).
4857. Vatican - Biblioteca Apostolica ebr. 422/1, f. 24b-25a, C.
4858. Vatican - Biblioteca Apostolica ebr. 422/2, f. 39b, CG, no incipit, very short.
4859. Vatican - Biblioteca Apostolica ebr. 422/2, f. 39b, CG, no incipit, second longer commentary.

Ashkenaz, commentary by Abraham b. Azriel[125]

4860. Frankfurt a M - Stadt- und Universitaetsbibliothek Fol. 16 (Merzbacher 95), f. 104b, C.
4861. Vatican - Biblioteca Apostolica ebr. 301,1, f. 146b-147a, C, rubric: לא מצאתי יותר, postscript אחרת.

Tsarfat
4862. London - David Sofer 5, f. 102a-102b, C.
4863. Oxford - Bodleian Library MS Bodl. Or. 109 (Neubauer 1209), f. 83b-84b, C, commentator: Aaron b. Hayyim haKohen (compiler).
4864. Parma - Biblioteca Palatina Cod. Parm. 3007 (de Rossi 654,2), f. 48a-49a, M.

אלהים אל דמי לך אל תשקוט ואל תחרש (א 4628), בנימין ב"ר זרח, זולת

Ashkenaz
4865. Budapest - Magyar tudomanyos akademia, MS. Kaufmann A 399, p. 423, C, short.
4866. Cambridge - University Library Add. 504,1, f. 41b-42a, C, rubric: זולת לשמעו דבר יי בנימין יסדו.
4867. Hamburg - Staats- und Universitaetsbibliothek Cod. hebr. 239a (Steinschneider 130), f. 23a-24a, G.
4868. Lund - Universitetsbibliothek Ms. L.O. 2, f. 96a-96b, M, rubric: זולת אחר.

---

[125] Edited by Urbach, ערוגת הבושם, vol. III, p. 337-340.

4869. Muenchen - Bayerische Staatsbibliothek, Cod. hebr. 393,9, f. 198a-198b, C.
4870. Parma - Biblioteca Palatina Cod. Parm. 3205 (de Rossi 655), f. 144b-145a, C.
4871. Parma - Biblioteca Palatina Cod. Parm. 3205 (de Rossi 655), f. 153b-154b, C.

אלהים אל דמי לך כקול מים רבים נשמע קולך (א 4632), אלעזר ברבי קליר, סילוק, קדושתא לשבת זכור

Ashkenaz
4872. Berlin - Staatsbibliothek (Preussischer Kulturbesitz) Or. Qu. 798-799 (Steinschneider 177), II, f. 23a-25a, M.
4873. Budapest - Magyar tudomanyos akademia, MS. Kaufmann A 384, f. 56a-58b, M.
4874. Budapest - Magyar tudomanyos akademia, MS. Kaufmann A 400, p. 46-51, C.
4875. Cambridge - University Library, Taylor Schechter Collection Misc. 33/3, f. 23b-24a, G.
4876. Erlangen - Universitaetsbibliothek 2601 (Roth 67), f. 36b-37b, M, ecclectic.
4877. Hamburg - Staats- und Universitaetsbibliothek Cod. hebr. 17/2 (Steinschneider 152), f. 20a-21a, C, rubric: סילוק.
4878. Hamburg - Staats- und Universitaetsbibliothek Cod. hebr. 225, f. 27a-28b, G.
4879. Jerusalem - Schocken Institute 24100 / Mahzor Nuremberg, f. 43a-44b, M.
4880. Muenchen - Bayerische Staatsbibliothek, Cod. hebr. 88, f. 26a-27b, G.
4881. Muenchen - Bayerische Staatsbibliothek, Cod. hebr. 393, f. 92a-93a, C, no incipit.
4882. Oxford - Bodleian Library MS Opp. 170 (Neubauer 1205), f. 14a-15a, C, rubric: סילוק, incipit פליט.
4883. Paris - Bibliotheque Nationale heb. 709, f. 23b-24b, C, rubric: סילוק, commentary crossed out.
4884. Parma - Biblioteca Palatina Cod. Parm. 1002 (Ta 24), f. 38a-39b, M, partly censored.
4885. Parma - Biblioteca Palatina Cod. Parm. 3205 (de Rossi 655), f. 24a-26a, C, rubric: סילוק.
4886. Parma - Biblioteca Palatina Cod. Parm. 3507 (Perreau 27), f. 17b-18b, C, rubric: סילוק.
4887. Vatican - Biblioteca Apostolica ebr. 305,1, f. 17a-19a, C.

Tsarfat

4888. Oxford - Bodleian Library MS Laud. Or. 271 (Neubauer 1206), f. 23b-25a, C, commentator: Aaron b. Hayyim haKohen (compiler), rubric: ובכן ולך תעלה אלהים אל דמי לך.

4889. Oxford - Bodleian Library MS Opp. 171 (Neubauer 1207), f. 20b-23a, C.

אלהים אל מי אמשליך ואין ערוך אליך (א 4635), יהודה הלוי, סילוק, קדושתא לשחרית יום כפור

Carpentras

4890. Cincinnati - Hebrew Union College 429/1, f. 27a-28a, M, no incipit.

Carpentras, commentary by Josef b. Abraham of Montelitz

4891. Cincinnati - Hebrew Union College 357, f. 107b-108b, M, no incipit.

4892. New York - Jewish Theological Seminary Ms. 4746, f. 39a-41a, M, no incipit.

4893. Paris - Alliance Israelite Universelle H 422 A, f. 72a-74a, M, no incipit.

4894. Paris - Ecole Rabbinique 31, f. 146b-150a, M, no incipit.

haAri

4895. Harvard University 067, f. 53a, 54b, 56a, 58b-59a, 60b, 61b, 63a-b, M, lexical explanations in Hebrew and Ladino.

North Africa, commentary by David b. Josef Abudarham

4896. New York - Jewish Theological Seminary Ms. 5426, f. 63b-65b, M, rubric: ובכן ולך תעלה הקדושה.

Sepharad

4897. Jerusalem - Benayahu ז 25, f. 87b-88b, 89b-91b, M.

Sepharad, commentary by David b. Josef Abudarham[126]

4898. Budapest - Magyar tudomanyos akademia, MS. Kaufmann A 405/2, p. 183-187, C, rubric: 'ובכן ולך תעלה הקדוש'.

4899. Cincinnati - Hebrew Union College 490, f. 2b-3b, C.

4900. New York - Columbia X893 Ab 93, f. 3b-5a, C.

4901. New York - Jewish Theological Seminary Ms. 3011, f. 3a-4a, C.

אלהים אל נורא מאוד ואיום (א 4636), משה אבן עזרא, ליום כפור

Carpentras, commentary by Josef b. Abraham of Montelitz

4902. Cincinnati - Hebrew Union College 291, f. 11b-12b, C, rubric: פירוש אל נורא וכו'.

4903. New York - Jewish Theological Seminary Ms. 4197, f. 55b-57b, M, first stanzas of piyyut missing.

4904. Paris - Ecole Rabbinique 32, f. 78a-79b, M.

---

[126] Edited by Prins, תשלום אבודרהם, p. 10-14.

4905. Strasbourg - Bibliotheque Nationale et Universitaire 4081, f. 58a-59b, M, first stanzas of piyyut missing.

אלהים אלי אתה אשחריך בסוד סגלתך (א 4649), שלמה אבן גבירול, רשות לנשמת יום כפור

haAri
4906. Harvard University 067, f. 120b-121a, 122a, 123a-123b, 124b, G, lexical explanations in Hebrew and Ladino.
Sepharad
4907. Jerusalem - Benayahu ז 25, f. 61b-62a, M.

אלהים אלי אתה אשחרך מארץ שביי ופזורי (א 4651), יוסף אבן אביתור, הושענא

haAri, commentary by Mose b. Hayyim Pesante
4908. New York - Columbia University X 893 J 558, f. 201b-202a, M.
North Africa, commentary by Yehuda Toledano
4909. New York - Jewish Theological Seminary Ms. 4300, f. 13a-14a, C.
Yemen, commentary by Samḥun b. Salomo
4910. Jerusalem - Makhon ben Zvi 2808, f. 45a-50b, C.

אלהים אמת אלהים חיים ומלך מיוחד (א 4661), מאיר ב"ר יצחק, שבעתא לשבת פרה

Ashkenaz
4911. New York - Jewish Theological Seminary Ms. 4466, f. 14b-17b, M.
4912. Parma - Biblioteca Palatina Cod. Parm. 3205 (de Rossi 655), f. 36b-37a, C, rubric: שבעתא לפרש' פרה.
Tsarfat
4913. Oxford - Bodleian Library MS Laud. Or. 271 (Neubauer 1206), f. 42b-45a, C, commentator: Aaron b. Hayyim haKohen (compiler), rubric: שבעתא דפרה דר' מאיר שליח ציבור זצ"ל.

אלהים אתה ידעת לאולתי ואשמתי (א 4670), סליחה

Sepharad
4914. Skokie - Hebrew Theological College 3, f. 11b, G.
Yemen, commentary by Isaac b. Abraham Wanneh
4915. Chicago-Spertus College of Judaica D 2, 2, f. 181a-181b, M.
4916. Jerusalem - Sassoon 1158, p. 299, M.
4917. London - British Library Or. 11122, f. 157b, M.

אלהים באזננו שמענו (א 4678), אליעזר ב"ר נתן, זולת לשבת איכה

Ashkenaz
4918. Frankfurt a M - Stadt- und Universitaetsbibliothek Oct. 227, f. 159b-161a, M.
4919. Lund - Universitetsbibliothek Ms. L.O. 2, f. 98b-100b, M, rubric: זולת אחר, including commentary to the inserted stanzas.

4920. Muenchen - Bayerische Staatsbibliothek, Cod. hebr. 393,9, f. 199a, C, short.
4921. Oxford - Bodleian Library MS Can. Or. 82 (Neubauer 1148), f. 24a-25a, M, rubric: זולת לגזירה בשבת שלפני ה' בתמוז.
4922. Parma - Biblioteca Palatina Cod. Parm. 3205 (de Rossi 655), f. 151a-152a, C.

אלהים בישראל גדול יחודך (א 4683), יהודה בן שמואל החסיד, סליחה

Ashkenaz
4923. Hamburg - Staats- und Universitaetsbibliothek, Ms. Levy 78/11, f. 288a-302a, C, esoteric.

אלהים בישראל גדול נודעת (א 4685), סליחה

Ashkenaz
4924. Braunschweig - Landesmuseum fuer Geschichte und Volkstum R 2386, vol. II, f. 59b, M.
4925. Vatican - Biblioteca Apostolica ebr. 422/1, f. 27b, C, short.
4926. Vatican - Biblioteca Apostolica ebr. 422/1, f. 41a, CG, no incipit.

Asti, Fossano, Moncalvo
4927. New Haven - Yale University, Beinecke Rare Book and MS Library, MS Heb. 52, f. 166b-167a, M.

Tsarfat
4928. Oxford - Bodleian Library MS Bodl. Or. 109 (Neubauer 1209), f. 83a-83b, C, commentator: Aaron b. Hayyim haKohen (compiler).

אלהים ביתה מושב יחידים (א 4686), אברהם בן יהודה הכהן, מעריב לשבועות

Ashkenaz
4929. Berlin - Staatsbibliothek (Preussischer Kulturbesitz) Or. Qu. 798-799 (Steinschneider 177), II, f. 135b-137a, M.
4930. Lund - Universitetsbibliothek Ms. L.O. 2, f. 67b, M.

אלהים בצעדך הכות פתרוס (א 4691), יוסף ב"ר שמואל טוב עלם, קדושתא לשבת הגדול

Ashkenaz
4931. Jerusalem - Schocken Institute 24100 / Mahzor Nuremberg, f. 71b, M, very short.
4932. Muenchen - Bayerische Staatsbibliothek, Cod. hebr. 88, f. 49b, G.
4933. Parma - Biblioteca Palatina Cod. Parm 3000 (de Rossi 378), f. 26b-27a, C.
4934. Parma - Biblioteca Palatina Cod. Parm. 3507 (Perreau 27), f. 33a-33b, C, rubric: קרובה לשבת הגדול מזה המלכות.

Tsarfat
4935. London - British Library Add. 11639 (Margoliouth 1056), f. 672b, M.

4936. Moscow - Russian State Library, Ms. Guenzburg 1665, f. 45a, M.
4937. Parma - Biblioteca Palatina Cod. Parm. 3136 (de Rossi 405), f. 58b-59a, M.

אלֹהים בקדש חזיתיך (א 4692), יהודה הלוי, מי כמוך לשבת החדש, בתימן: סליחה
Yemen
4938. Cincinnati - Hebrew Union College 199, f. 78b, G.
4939. Jerusalem - Benayahu ת 414, f. 136a, M.
4940. Jerusalem - Musad haRav Kook 334, f. 137b, M.
4941. Jerusalem - Sassoon 264, f. 156a, M.
4942. Jerusalem - Sassoon 902, p. 387, M.
4943. New York - Jewish Theological Seminary Ms. 3052, f. 50b-53a, M, rubric: אל מלך.
4944. New York - Jewish Theological Seminary Ms. 3109, f. 79a-79b, M.
Yemen, commentary by Isaac b. Abraham Wanneh
4945. Chicago-Spertus College of Judaica D 2, 2, f. 219a-219b, M, no incipit.
4946. Jerusalem - Benayahu ת 261, f. 145a-146a, M, rubric: אל מלך.
4947. Jerusalem - Benayahu ת 282, f. 128b-129b, M, rubric: אל מלך.
4948. Jerusalem - Makhon Ben Zvi 1156 (Tubi 155), f. 128a-129a, M, rubric: אל מלך.
4949. Jerusalem - Makhon Ben Zvi 1174 (Tubi 154), f. 111b-112a, M, rubric: אל מלך.
4950. Jerusalem - Michael Krupp 604, f. 162b-163a, M, rubric: אל מלך.
4951. Jerusalem - Musad haRav Kook 325, f. 162b-163a, M.
4952. Jerusalem - Sassoon 1158, p. 390-391, M, no incipit.
4953. Jerusalem - Sassoon 1174, p. 246--248, M, no incipit.
4954. London - British Library Or. 11122, f. 196b-197a, M, no incipit.
4955. Manchester - John Rylands University Library, Ms. Gaster 5, f. 184b-185b, M.
4956. Muenchen - Bayerische Staatsbibliothek, Cod. hebr. 472, f. 177a-178a, M, rubric: אל מלך.
4957. New York - Jewish Theological Seminary Ms. 3013, f. 111b, M, rubric: אל מלך.
4958. New York - Jewish Theological Seminary Ms. 3294, f. 5b-6a, C.
4959. New York - Public Library, Heb. Ms. 9, f. 120b-121a, M.
4960. Philadelphia - University of Pennsylvania HB 2, f. 124a-125a, M, rubric: אל מלך.
4961. Strasbourg - Bibliotheque Nationale et Universitaire 3965 (Landauer 39), p. 339, M, rubric: אל מלך.

אלהים יראה לו שה פזורה (א 4738), יואל ב"ר יצחק הלוי, סליחה
Ashkenaz
4962. Vatican - Biblioteca Apostolica ebr. 308, f. 14b-15a, C, commentator: David b. Mose (compiler).
4963. Vatican - Biblioteca Apostolica ebr. 308, f. 163b, C, commentator: David b. Mose (compiler).

אלהים לא אדע זולתך (א 4742), אפרים ב"ר יצחק מרגנסבורג, זולת
Ashkenaz
4964. Jerusalem - Schocken Institute 24100 / Mahzor Nuremberg, f. 137b-138a, M.
Ashkenaz, commentary by Abraham b. Azriel[127]
4965. Vatican - Biblioteca Apostolica ebr. 301,1, f. 15a-16b, C, rubric: זולת לר' אפרים.

אלהים למשפטיך עמדנו היום (א 4752), משה אבן עזרא, קדוש
Carpentras
4966. Cincinnati - Hebrew Union College 392, f. 85a-85b, M, no incipit.
Carpentras, commentary by Josef b. Abraham of Montelitz
4967. New York - Jewish Theological Seminary Ms. 4197, f. 194a, M.
4968. Paris - Ecole Rabbinique 32, f. 203a-203b, G.
4969. Strasbourg - Bibliotheque Nationale et Universitaire 4081, f. 178b, M.

אלהים מה טובו מחנות מגרשיך (א 4758), יצחק גיאת, פזמון
Sepharad, commentary by David b. Josef Abudarham[128]
4970. Budapest - Magyar tudomanyos akademia, MS. Kaufmann A 405/2, p. 241-242, C, rubric: פזמון.
4971. New York - Columbia X893 Ab 93, f. 26a-26b, C, rubric: פזמון.

אלהים צוית לידיך (א 4781), אפרים ב"ר יעקב מבון, ברכת מזון לברית מילה
Ashkenaz
4972. Jerusalem - Safrai 1/4, f. 2a-7a, C, commentator: Yehuda Leib Karlburg, no incipit.
4973. Muenchen - Bayerische Staatsbibliothek, Cod. hebr. 393,9, f. 192b-194a, C, rubric: ברכת המזון.

אלהים צמאה לך נפש גולים (א 4782), אברהם ב"ר חייא, חלק ב', קדושתא לשבת פרה
Carpentras, commentary by Josef b. Abraham of Montelitz
4974. Cincinnati - Hebrew Union College 291, f. 59a, C, rubric: פי' פיוט אלהים צמאו לך וכו'.

---
[127] Edited by Urbach, ערוגת הבושם, vol. I, p. 96-104.
[128] Edited by Prins, תשלום אבודרהם, p. 78-80.

4975. New York - Jewish Theological Seminary Ms. 4197, f. 269a, M.
Carpentras, commentary by Mordekhai b. Josef of Rocco Martino
4976. Cincinnati - Hebrew Union College 246/1, f. 28b-29a, C, rubric: פי'
פזמון אלקים צמאה וכו', rubric for Ḥatima: פי' אל כרוג.
Sepharad, commentary by Josef Garad
4977. Oxford - Bodleian Library Heb.e.10 (Neubauer 2746/1), f. 11a-11b, C, rubric: פזמון.
4978. Oxford - Bodleian Library Heb.e.10 (Neubauer 2746/1), f. 19b, C, rubric: אלהים צמאו, no incipit. very short.

אלהים שחרתיך ונגדך אשפוך שיחי (א 4788), יהודה הלוי, סליחה

Carpentras
4979. Cincinnati - Hebrew Union College 392, f. 12b, M.
Carpentras, commentary by Josef b. Abraham of Montelitz
4980. Cincinnati - Hebrew Union College 291, f. 7a-7b, C, rubric: פי' הסליחה אלדים שחרתיך.
4981. New York - Jewish Theological Seminary Ms. 4197, f. 26b, M.
4982. Paris - Ecole Rabbinique 32, f. 30b-31b, M.
4983. Strasbourg - Bibliotheque Nationale et Universitaire 4081, f. 28b-29a, M.
Yemen
4984. Jerusalem - Sassoon 902, p. 385, M.
4985. New York - Jewish Theological Seminary Ms. 3052, f. 3b-4a, M, rubric: אל מלך.
4986. New York - Jewish Theological Seminary Ms. 3109, f. 78b, M.
4987. Ramat Gan - Universitat Bar Ilan 62, f. 45a, G.
Yemen, commentary by Isaac b. Abraham Wanneh
4988. Chicago-Spertus College of Judaica D 2, 2, f. 188a-188b, M, no incipit.
4989. Jerusalem - Benayahu ת 261, f. 125b, M, rubric: אל מלך, .
4990. Jerusalem - Benayahu ת 282, f. 110b-111a, M, no incipit.
4991. Jerusalem - Makhon Ben Zvi 1156 (Tubi 155), f. 108b, M, rubric: אל מלך, .
4992. Jerusalem - Makhon Ben Zvi 1174 (Tubi 154), f. 115a, M.
4993. Jerusalem - Michael Krupp 604, f. 137b, M, rubric: אל מלך.
4994. Jerusalem - Musad haRav Kook 325, f. 167a, M.
4995. Jerusalem - Musad haRav Kook 330, f. 99a-99b, G.
4996. Jerusalem - Sassoon 1158, p. 338-339, M, rubric: אל מלך, .
4997. Jerusalem - Sassoon 1174, p. 209-210, M no incipit.
4998. Jerusalem - Yehiel haLevi 4, f. 147a, G.
4999. London - British Library Or. 11122, f. 167b-168a, M, no incipit.
5000. Manchester - John Rylands University Library, Ms. Gaster 5, f. 188a, M.

5001. Muenchen - Bayerische Staatsbibliothek, Cod. hebr. 472, f. 147a-147b, M, rubric: אל מלך.
5002. New York - Jewish Theological Seminary Ms. 3013, f. 114a, M, rubric: אל מלך.
5003. New York - Jewish Theological Seminary Ms. 3294, f. 7b-8a, C.
5004. New York - Public Library, Heb. Ms. 9, f. 104b, M.
5005. Philadelphia - University of Pennsylvania HB 2, f. 127a, M, rubric: אל מלך.
5006. Strasbourg - Bibliotheque Nationale et Universitaire 3965 (Landauer 39), p. 348, M rubric: אל מלך.

אלהינו אלהים אמת (א 4794), בנימין ב"ר זרח, יוצר לשבת בראשית או לשבת וראש חדש

Ashkenaz

5007. Berlin - Staatsbibliothek (Preussischer Kulturbesitz) Or. Qu. 361 (Steinschneider 51), f. 161b-163b, M, no incipit.
5008. Berlin - Staatsbibliothek (Preussischer Kulturbesitz) Or. Qu. 798-799 (Steinschneider 177), I, f. 237b-241b, M.
5009. Budapest - Magyar tudomanyos akademia, MS. Kaufmann A 399, p. 325-328, C, rubric: יוצר דשבת וראש חודש.
5010. Cambridge - University Library Add. 394.2 (Reif SCR 462), f. 100a-102a, C, rubric: ביאור יוצר בראשית.
5011. Cambridge - University Library Add. 504.1, f. 31a-33b, C, rubric: יוסף יסד וחתום בכן נפש בו יושב מכון לשבת ור"ח אום' זה.
5012. Frankfurt a M - Stadt- und Universitaetsbibliothek Oct. 227, f. 140a-141b, M.
5013. Hamburg - Staats- und Universitaetsbibliothek Cod. hebr. 239a (Steinschneider 130), f. 5b-7a, G.
5014. London - British Library Or. 1054/7 (Margolioth 1094/7), f. 31b, C.
5015. London - Valmadonna Trust 267/19, f. 149a-153b, C.
5016. Muenchen - Bayerische Staatsbibliothek, Cod. hebr. 273,1, f. 1a-8b, C, rubric: בשם אדוני האדונים אתחיל פי' אלהינו אלהים.
5017. Muenchen - Bayerische Staatsbibliothek, Cod. hebr. 393,9, f. 173b-176a, C, rubric: לשבת וראש חודש.
5018. Oxford - Bodleian Library MS Can. Or. 82 (Neubauer 1148), f. 5b-7a, M.
5019. Oxford - Bodleian Library MS Mich. 365 (Neubauer 1208), f. 22a-24b, C, rubric: לשבת ור"ח.
5020. Oxford - Bodleian Library MS Mich. 573 (Neubauer 1099), f. 52b, M.
5021. Parma - Biblioteca Palatina Cod. Parm. 2895, p. 435-438, M, margins cut, text damaged.
5022. Parma - Biblioteca Palatina Cod. Parm. 3205 (de Rossi 655), f. 134a-135b, C, rubric: לשבת וראש חודש.
5023. Uppsala - Universitetsbibliotek O.Heb.22, f. 129a-132b, M.

5024. Vatican - Biblioteca Apostolica ebr. 318, f. 111b-113b, GI.
Ashkenaz, commentary by Abraham b. Azriel[129]

5025. Frankfurt a M - Stadt- und Universitaetsbibliothek Fol. 16 (Merzbacher 95), f. 70a-74b, C, rubric: יוצר לשבת וראש חדש דרבי' בנימין חסיד.

5026. Vatican - Biblioteca Apostolica ebr. 301,1, f. 99b-103b, C, rubric: יוצר דרבי בנימין חסר. ובזולת אנא השקיפה כתי' למה חסר.
Ashkenaz, commentary by Eliezer b. Natan

5027. Hamburg - Staats- und Universitaetsbibliothek Cod. hebr. 61 (Steinschneider 153), f. 29b-32a, C, rubric: וזה פירוש מיוצר של ראש חדש.

5028. Parma - Biblioteca Palatina Cod. Parm. 3057.12 (de Rossi 1033/10), f. 121b-125b, C, rubric: אתחיל פירוש של יוצרות.

5029. Warszaw - Uniwersytet, Inst. Orientalistyczny 258, f. 179a-182a, C, rubric: פירוש יוצר של ראש חדש.

Italia

5030. Parma - Biblioteca Palatin Cod. Parm. 2248 (de Rossi 149/2), f. 6b-9b, C, rubric: ביאור יוצר בראשית.

Roma

5031. Jerusalem - Jewish National and University Library Ms Heb 8° 4153, f. 148a-151a, C, commentator: Daniel ben Salomo haRofe (compiler), rubric: פי' יוצר לשבת בראשית.

5032. London - Montefiore Library 124/21, f. 110a-110b, FC.

5033. New York - Jewish Theological Seminary Ms. 1639, f. 3a-7b, C, commentator: Salomo b. Samuel Rofe, rubric: ביאור יוצר בראשית.

5034. Oxford - Bodleian Library MS Mich. 312,1 (Neubauer 2276,1), f. 15a-18a, C, rubric: פי' יוצר של שבת ברשית.

5035. Parma - Biblioteca Palatina Cod. Parm. 3515 (Perreau 16), before Isaac Dura on איסור והיתר (no count in ms), C, rubric: פירוש מיוצר של בראשית.

אלהינו בושנו במעשינו ונכלמו בעונותינו (א 4798), סליחה
Yemen, commentary by Isaac b. Abraham Wanneh

5036. Chicago-Spertus College of Judaica D 2, 2, f. 231a, M, no incipit.

אלהינו ואלהי אבותינו אל תעש עמנו כלה (א 4808), סליחה
Ashkenaz

5037. Berlin - Staatsbibliothek (Preussischer Kulturbesitz) Or. Qu. 798-799 (Steinschneider 177), I, f. 137b, M.

5038. Hamburg - Staats- und Universitaetsbibliothek Cod. hebr. 62 (Steinschneider 154), f. 20b-21a, C.

5039. London - Montefiore Library 261, f. 62b, C, commentator: Eliezer b. Natan?, very short.

---

[129] Edited by Urbach, ערוגת הבושם, vol. III, p. 32-57.

5040. Muenchen - Bayerische Staatsbibliothek, Cod. hebr. 346, f. 86b-87a, C.
5041. Muenchen - Bayerische Staatsbibliothek, Cod. hebr. 346, f. 144a, C, short.
5042. Oxford - Bodleian Library MS Opp. 172 (Neubauer 1211), f. 69a-69b, C.
5043. Vatican - Biblioteca Apostolica ebr. 308, f. 129a, C, commentator: David b. Mose (compiler).

Ashkenaz, commentary by Abraham b. Azriel[130]

5044. Vatican - Biblioteca Apostolica ebr. 301,1, f. 168b, C, short.

Sepharad

5045. Skokie - Hebrew Theological College 3, f. 8b-9a, M.
5046. Skokie - Hebrew Theological College 3, f. 2.22a, M.

Tsarfat

5047. Oxford - Bodleian Library MS Bodl. Or. 109 (Neubauer 1209), f. 40b-41a, C, commentator: Aaron b. Hayyim haKohen (compiler).

Yemen, commentary by Isaac b. Abraham Wanneh

5048. Chicago-Spertus College of Judaica D 2, 2, f. 179b-180a, M.
5049. Jerusalem - Yehiel haLevi 4, f. 132a, M.

אלהינו ואלהי אבותינו אם תעינו לא תתענו (א 4809), הוספה לסדר עבודה

Ashkenaz

5050. Berlin - Staatsbibliothek (Preussischer Kulturbesitz) Or. Qu. 798-799 (Steinschneider 177), I, f. 136a-136b, M.
5051. Braunschweig - Landesmuseum fuer Geschichte und Volkstum R 2386, vol. II, f. 239b, M, short.
5052. London - Montefiore Library 261, f. 62a-62b, C, commentator: Eliezer b. Natan?, very short.
5053. Muenchen - Bayerische Staatsbibliothek, Cod. hebr. 346, f. 153b-154a, C.
5054. Oxford - Bodleian Library MS Opp. 172 (Neubauer 1211), f. 70a, C.

אלהינו ואלהי אבותינו היה עם פיפיות שלוחי עמך (א 4821), רשות למוסף ראשה השנה ומוסף יום כפור

Ashkenaz

5055. Oxford - Bodleian Library MS Opp. 172 (Neubauer 1211), f. 14a, C, no incipit.
5056. Oxford - Bodleian Library MS Opp. 619 (Neubauer 2374), f. 37b, M, short.
5057. Oxford - Bodleian Library MS Opp. 675 (Neubauer 1210), f. 32a, C, no incipit.

---

[130] Edited by Urbach, ערוגת הבושם, vol. III, p. 487-488.

5058. Oxford - Bodleian Library MS Opp. 675 (Neubauer 1210), f. 62b, C, no incipit.
5059. Parma - Biblioteca Palatina Cod. Parm. 3205 (de Rossi 655), f. 211b, C.
5060. Parma - Biblioteca Palatina Cod. Parm. 3507 (Perreau 27), f. 134b, C, rubric: למוסף, .
5061. Parma - Biblioteca Palatina Cod. Parm. 3507 (Perreau 27), f. 166a-166b, C.
5062. Vatican - Biblioteca Apostolica ebr. 422/1, f. 10b, C, very short.
5063. Zurich - Zentralbibliothek Heid. 139, f. 66a (inserted leaf, commentary inserted between commentary to משפט מדת ביד האוחז), C.
5064. Zurich - Zentralbibliothek Heid. 139, f. 102b, C, commentator: Elazar b. Yehuda of Worms, no incipit, very short.

Ashkenaz, commentary by Abraham b. Azriel[131]
5065. Vatican - Biblioteca Apostolica ebr. 301,1, f. 166b, C.

Tsarfat
5066. Vatican - Biblioteca Apostolica ebr. 306, f. 58b, C

אלהינו ואלהי אבותינו טל תן לרצות ארצך (א 4823), אלעזר ברבי קליר, תפלת טל
Ashkenaz
5067. Berlin - Staatsbibliothek (Preussischer Kulturbesitz) Or. Qu. 798-799 (Steinschneider 177), II, f. 71b-72a, M.
5068. New York - Jewish Theological Seminary Ms. 4466, f. 66b, M

אלהינו ואלהי אבותינו הושיענו למען שמך בצר לנו קראנוך (א 4829), סליחה
Yemen
5069. Jerusalem - Benayahu ת 88, f. 127a, M.

אלהינו ואלהי אבותינו סלח־נא אשמות ופשעי לאומך (א 4832), סליחה
Ashkenaz
5070. Berlin - Staatsbibliothek (Preussischer Kulturbesitz) Or. Qu. 798-799 (Steinschneider 177), I, 57b, M.
5071. Braunschweig - Landesmuseum fuer Geschichte und Volkstum R 2386, vol. II, f. 160b-161a, M.
5072. Hamburg - Staats- und Universitaetsbibliothek Cod. hebr. 40b (Steinschneider 110), f. 74a, G.
5073. Jerusalem - Jewish National and University Library Ms Heb 8° 3037, f. 94a-94b, M.
5074. Jerusalem - Schocken Institute 24100 / Mahzor Nuremberg, f. 357(ii)b, M.

---

[131] Edited by Urbach, ערוגת הבושם, vol. III, p. 474-475.

5075. Muenchen - Bayerische Staatsbibliothek, Cod. hebr. 346, f. 146a, C, rubric: אחרת.
5076. Oxford - Bodleian Library MS Opp. 172 (Neubauer 1211), f. 31b, C.
5077. Oxford - Bodleian Library MS Opp. 681 (Neubauer 1213), f. 44a-44b, C.
5078. Parma - Biblioteca Palatina Cod. Parm. 3271 (de Rossi 1216), f. 9a, G.

Ashkenaz, commentary by Abraham b. Azriel[132]

5079. Frankfurt a M - Stadt- und Universitaetsbibliothek Fol. 16 (Merzbacher 95), f. 103b, C, incipit סלח.
5080. Frankfurt a M - Stadt- und Universitaetsbibliothek Fol. 16 (Merzbacher 95), f. 111a, C, incipit סלח.

Tsarfat

5081. Parma - Biblioteca Palatina Cod. Parm. 3007 (de Rossi 654,2), f. 156a, M.

אלהינו ואלהי אבותינו תאמר למחות אשמינו (א 4838), ליום כפור

Ashkenaz

5082. Berlin - Staatsbibliothek (Preussischer Kulturbesitz) Or. Qu. 798-799 (Steinschneider 177), I, f. 137b-138a, M.
5083. Braunschweig - Landesmuseum fuer Geschichte und Volkstum R 2386, vol. II, f. 240b, M, very short.
5084. London - Montefiore Library 261, f. 62b, C, commentator: Eliezer b. Natan?, very short.
5085. Muenchen - Bayerische Staatsbibliothek, Cod. hebr. 346, f. 154a, C.
5086. Oxford - Bodleian Library MS Opp. 172 (Neubauer 1211), f. 70a, C, very short.
5087. Vatican - Biblioteca Apostolica ebr. 308, f. 128b, C, commentator: David b. Mose (compiler).

אלהינו שבשמים שמע קולינו וקבל תפלתינו (א+ 4858), סליחה

Yemen

5088. Jerusalem - Benayahu ת 88, f. 117b, M.

Yemen, commentary by Isaac b. Abraham Wanneh

5089. Chicago-Spertus College of Judaica D 2, 2, f. 181a, M.

אלוה כשן מרומות אלף ציר אחרי מות, שלמה, קיקלר

Sepharad, commentary by David b. Josef Abudarham[133]

5090. Holon - Yehuda Nahum 278, f. 9a, FC, rubric: ובכן למדני דתך, incomplete.

---

[132] Edited by Urbach, ערוגת הבושם, vol. III, p. 543, 571.
[133] Edited by Prins, תשלום אבודרהם, p. 84-86.

5091. New York - Columbia X893 Ab 93, f. 8b-9a, C, rubric: ובכן למדני דתך.
5092. New York - Jewish Theological Seminary Ms. 3011, f. 7b-8a, C, rubric: ובכן למדני דתך.

אלוה פקד גפן פוריה (א 4322), משה אבן עזרא, חלק ד׳, קדושתא לשחרית יום כפור
Carpentras
5093. Cincinnati - Hebrew Union College 392, f. 46a-46b, M, no incipit.
Carpentras, commentary by Josef b. Abraham of Montelitz
5094. Cincinnati - Hebrew Union College 291, f. 22a-23a, C, rubric: פי׳ אלוה פקד וכו׳.
5095. New York - Jewish Theological Seminary Ms. 4197, f. 105b-107a, M, no incipit.
5096. Paris - Ecole Rabbinique 32, f. 127a-128b, M, no incipit.
5097. Strasbourg - Bibliotheque Nationale et Universitaire 4081, f. 104a-105a, M, no incipit.

אלוף מסובל (א 4875), שמעון ב״ר יצחק, חלק ז׳, קדושתא לשבועות
Ashkenaz
5098. Berlin - Staatsbibliothek (Preussischer Kulturbesitz) Or. Qu. 798-799 (Steinschneider 177), II, f. 121b-126b, M.
5099. Braunschweig - Landesmuseum fuer Geschichte und Volkstum R 2386, vol. I, f. 77b-81a, M.
5100. Budapest - Magyar tudomanyos akademia, MS. Kaufmann A 400, p. 159-163, C.
5101. Hamburg - Staats- und Universitaetsbibliothek Cod. hebr. 17/2 (Steinschneider 152), f. 83b-85a, C.
5102. Jerusalem - Schocken Institute 24100 / Mahzor Nuremberg, f. 150b-153a, M, ecclectic.
5103. London - British Library Add. 18695 (Margoliouth 683), f. 69a-72a, T, Yiddish.
5104. London - British Library Add. 22431 (Margoliouth 662a), f. 15a-20b, M.
5105. Moscow - Russian State Library, Ms. Guenzburg 615, f. 34a-36b, C.
5106. Muenchen - Bayerische Staatsbibliothek, Cod. hebr. 88, f. 119a-123b, G.
5107. New York - Jewish Theological Seminary Ms. 4466, f. 136b-141b, M, very ecclectic.
5108. Paris - Bibliotheque Nationale heb. 709, f. 122b-125a, C.
5109. Parma - Biblioteca Palatina Cod. Parm. 1002 (Ta 24), f. 183a-184a, 185a-185a, M, short, ecclectic.
5110. Parma - Biblioteca Palatina Cod. Parm. 3205 (de Rossi 655), f. 121a-121b, C, rubric: סדר.

5111. Parma - Biblioteca Palatina Cod. Parm. 3507 (Perreau 27), f. 101a-104b, C.

5112. Zurich - Zentralbibliothek Heid. 139, f. 51a-51b, C, additional marginal notes.

Tsarfat

5113. London - David Sofer 5, f. 52b-54a, C.

5114. Moscow - Russian State Library, Ms. Guenzburg 1665, f. 121b-124b, M.

5115. Oxford - Bodleian Library MS Laud. Or. 271 (Neubauer 1206), f. 86b-87a, C, commentator: Aaron b. Hayyim haKohen (compiler), rubric: סדר.

5116. Parma - Biblioteca Palatina Cod. Parm. 3136 (de Rossi 405), f. 153a-155b, M.

5117. Vatican - Biblioteca Apostolica ebr. 306, f. 234b-241a, C, no incipit.

אלי עדתי והליל יום בו נפל כלילי (א 4969), קינה

Yemen, commentary by Isaac b. Abraham Wanneh

5118. Jerusalem - Sassoon 1158, p. 167, M.

5119. London - British Library Or. 11122, f. 100b-101a, M.

אלי צורי איחדו בורא ואין בלעדו, סליחה

Tsarfat

5120. Parma - Biblioteca Palatina Cod. Parm. 3006 (de Rossi 654,1), f. 89a-89b, M, incipit צבאות.

אלי שמעך שמעו רחוקים (א 4985), אהרן בן יוסף הרופא, פרשת יתרו

Karaite, commentary by Berakha b. Josef haKohen

5121. New York - Jewish Theological Seminary Ms. 3367, f. 73b-76b, C, rubric: פרוש פרשת יתרו.

5122. St. Petersburg - Inst. of Oriental Studies of the Russian Academy B 431, f. 53b-55a, C, rubric: פרשת יתרו.

5123. St. Petersburg - Russian National Library, Evr. IV 50, f. 53a-55a, C, rubric: יתרו.

אליהו הנביא איש אשר קנא לשם האל (א 5001), זמר לשבת

Yemen

5124. Cincinnati - Hebrew Union College 199, f. 13a, M.

אליו נערוג כאייל וקומתינו נשוחחה, סליחה

Yemen

5125. Jerusalem - Benayahu ת 88, f. 147b, M.

אליך יי אקרא אוים ונורא (א 5012), גרשום ב"ר יהודה מאור הגולה, סליחה

Ashkenaz
5126. Oxford - Bodleian Library MS Opp. 681 (Neubauer 1213), f. 10b, C, short.
5127. Padova - Biblioteca del Seminario Vescovile Cod. 218, f. 158a-158b, M.
5128. Vatican - Biblioteca Apostolica ebr. 422/1, f. 42a, CG, no incipit, short.

אליך יי אקרא משגב לעתות בצרה (א 5020), שמריה, סליחה

Yemen
5129. New York - Jewish Theological Seminary Ms. 3193, f. 116a, M.
5130. Ramat Gan - Universitat Bar Ilan 62, f. 35a, G.
Yemen, commentary by Isaac b. Abraham Wanneh
5131. Jerusalem - Yehiel haLevi 4, f. 131a, M.

אליך יי נשאנו עינינו יהמו רחמיך מהה כעב, סליחה

Yemen, commentary by Isaac b. Abraham Wanneh
5132. Chicago-Spertus College of Judaica D 2, 2, f. 216a, M, no incipit.
5133. Jerusalem - Sassoon 1158, p. 368, M, no incipit.
5134. London - British Library Or. 11122, f. 184a-184b, M, rubric: אל מלך, no incipit.

אליך יי נשאתי עיני (א 5029), סליחה

Sepharad
5135. Skokie - Hebrew Theological College 3, f. 21a-22a, G.
Yemen
5136. Jerusalem - Sassoon 264, f. 148a, M.
5137. Jerusalem - Sassoon 902, p. 372, M.
5138. New York - Jewish Theological Seminary Ms. 3108, f. 19a, M, short.
Yemen, commentary by Isaac b. Abraham Wanneh
5139. Chicago-Spertus College of Judaica D 1, f. 228b-229a, M, rubric: 'פ.
5140. Chicago-Spertus College of Judaica D 2, 2, f. 184b-185b, M.
5141. Jerusalem - Sassoon 1158, p. 308, M, no incipit.
5142. Jerusalem - Yehiel haLevi 4, f. 136b-137a, M.
5143. London - British Library Or. 11122, f. 225a, M, no incipit.
5144. New York - Jewish Theological Seminary Ms. 3013, f. 102a, M, short.

אליך יי שועתי (א 5030), זולת

Ashkenaz
5145. Budapest - Magyar tudomanyos akademia, MS. Kaufmann A 399, p. 423, C.

5146. Oxford - Bodleian Library MS Can. Or. 82 (Neubauer 1148), f. 20a-20b, M.

5147. Parma - Biblioteca Palatina Cod. Parm. 3205 (de Rossi 655), f. 145a-145b, C, rubric: זולת אחר.

אליך יי שועתי בצר לי קראתי (א 5032), משה בר שמואל, סליחה

Ashkenaz

5148. Padova - Biblioteca del Seminario Vescovile Cod. 218, f. 129b, M.

5149. Parma - Biblioteca Palatina Cod. Parm. 3205 (de Rossi 655), f. 254a, C.

אליך אלכה ועיני למעוניך (א 5041), יהודה הלוי, סליחה

Yemen

5150. Jerusalem - Sassoon 902, p. 400, M.

5151. New York - Jewish Theological Seminary Ms. 3028, f. 17b, G, Arabic.

5152. New York - Jewish Theological Seminary Ms. 3052, f. 15a-16b, M, rubric: אל מלך.

5153. Ramat Gan - Universitat Bar Ilan 62, f. 41b, G, margins damaged.

Yemen, commentary by Isaac b. Abraham Wanneh

5154. Chicago-Spertus College of Judaica D 2, 2, f. 198b-199a, M, no incipit.

5155. Jerusalem - Benayahu ת 261, f. 131b-132a, M, rubric: אל מלך.

5156. Jerusalem - Benayahu ת 282, f. 116b-117a, M, rubric: אל מלך, no incipit.

5157. Jerusalem - Makhon Ben Zvi 1156 (Tubi 155), f. 114b-115a, M, rubric: אל מלך.

5158. Jerusalem - Makhon Ben Zvi 1174 (Tubi 154), f. 117b-118a, M.

5159. Jerusalem - Michael Krupp 604, f. 144a-145a, M, rubric: אל מלך.

5160. Jerusalem - Musad haRav Kook 325, f. 170b, M, rubric: אל מלך.

5161. Jerusalem - Sassoon 1158, p. 363, M, rubric: אל מלך, no incipit.

5162. Jerusalem - Sassoon 1174, p. 220-221, M, no incipit.

5163. Jerusalem - Yehiel haLevi 4, f. 151a, G.

5164. London - British Library Or. 11122, f. 181a-181b, M, no incipit.

5165. Manchester - John Rylands University Library, Ms. Gaster 5, f. 190b, M.

5166. Muenchen - Bayerische Staatsbibliothek, Cod. hebr. 472, f. 155a-156a, M, rubric: אל מלך.

5167. New York - Jewish Theological Seminary Ms. 3013, f. 116a, M, rubric: אל מלך.

5168. New York - Jewish Theological Seminary Ms. 3109, f. 96b, M, rubric: אל מלך, no incipit.

5169. New York - Public Library, Heb. Ms. 9, f. 111a, M.

5170. Strasbourg - Bibliotheque Nationale et Universitaire 3965 (Landauer 39), p. 355-356, M, rubric: אל מלך.

אליך אקרא, סליחה

Ashkenaz

5171. Muenchen - Bayerische Staatsbibliothek, Cod. hebr. 346, f. 162b, C, short.
5172. Vatican - Biblioteca Apostolica ebr. 422/1, f. 28a, C.

אליך אקרא יומם ולילה, סליחה

Yemen, commentary by Isaac b. Abraham Wanneh

5173. Jerusalem - Sassoon 1158, p. 431, M, no incipit.
5174. London - British Library Or. 11122, f. 225a, M, no incipit.

אליך אתודה על עונות ופשעים (א 5054), סליחה

Yemen, commentary by Isaac b. Abraham Wanneh

5175. Chicago-Spertus College of Judaica D 2, 2, f. 244b-245a, M, no incipit.
5176. London - British Library Or. 11122, f. 222b-223a, M, no incipit.

אליך אתודה שוכן מעונים (א 5055), סליחה

Yemen

5177. New York - Jewish Theological Seminary Ms. 3052, f. 82a-82b, M.
5178. Ramat Gan - Universitat Bar Ilan 62, f. 52b, G.

Yemen, commentary by Isaac b. Abraham Wanneh

5179. Chicago-Spertus College of Judaica D 2, 2, f. 237a-237b, M, no incipit.
5180. Jerusalem - Benayahu ת 282, f. 140b, M, short.
5181. Jerusalem - Makhon Ben Zvi 1156 (Tubi 155), f. 138a-138b, M, no incipit.
5182. Jerusalem - Makhon Ben Zvi 1174 (Tubi 154), f. 136b, M.
5183. Jerusalem - Michael Krupp 604, f. 175a-175b, M, no incipit.
5184. Jerusalem - Musad haRav Kook 325, f. 194b, M.
5185. Jerusalem - Sassoon 1158, p. 416, M, no incipit.
5186. Jerusalem - Sassoon 1174, p. 269, M, no incipit.
5187. London - British Library Or. 11122, f. 214b, M, no incipit.
5188. Muenchen - Bayerische Staatsbibliothek, Cod. hebr. 472, f. 193a, M.
5189. New York - Jewish Theological Seminary Ms. 3013, f. 133a, M, short.
5190. New York - Jewish Theological Seminary Ms. 3294, f. 17a, C.
5191. New York - Public Library, Heb. Ms. 9, f. 129a, M, no incipit.
5192. Strasbourg - Bibliotheque Nationale et Universitaire 3965 (Landauer 39), p. 409, M.

אליך האל עיני כל יציר תלויות (א 5059), בנימין ב"ר זרח, סליחה

Ashkenaz

5193. Cambridge - University Library Dd. 2.30, f. 30a, G.
5194. Padova - Biblioteca del Seminario Vescovile Cod. 218, f. 263b, M.

Asti, Fossano, Moncalvo

5195. New Haven - Yale University, Beinecke Rare Book and MS Library, MS Heb. 52, f. 123b, M.
5196. New Haven - Yale University, Beinecke Rare Book and MS Library, MS Heb. 52, f. 154a, M, ecclectic.
5197. New Haven - Yale University, Beinecke Rare Book and MS Library, MS Heb. 52, f. 168a, M, ecclectic.

אליך ועדיך יבא כל בשר (א 5062), אלעזר ברבי קליר, פיוט אחרי הקדושה, קדושתא למוסף יום כפור

Ashkenaz

5198. Berlin - Staatsbibliothek (Preussischer Kulturbesitz) Or. Qu. 798-799 (Steinschneider 177), I, f. 87b-88a, M.
5199. Braunschweig - Landesmuseum fuer Geschichte und Volkstum R 2386, vol. II, f. 200a-200b, M.
5200. Budapest - Magyar tudomanyos akademia, MS. Kaufmann A 400 , p. 336-337, C.
5201. Jerusalem - Jewish National and University Library Ms Heb 8° 3037, f. 134b-135a, M, no inicpit.
5202. Jerusalem - Schocken Institute 24100 / Mahzor Nuremberg , f. 385a-385b, M.
5203. London - Montefiore Library 261 , f. 48b-49a, C, commentator: Eliezer b. Natan?.
5204. Moscow - Russian State Library, Ms. Guenzburg 191 , f. 124b-125a, M.
5205. New York - Jewish Theological Seminary Ms. 4466, f. 327b-328b, M.
5206. New York - Jewish Theological Seminary Ms. 8169 (Acc. 0016), f. 100b-101a, M.
5207. Oxford - Bodleian Library MS Opp. 172 (Neubauer 1211), f. 46b, C.
5208. Parma - Bibliotheca Palatina Cod. Parm. 3205 (de Rossi 655), f. 294a-295a, C.
5209. Parma - Biblioteca Palatina Cod. Parm. 3271 (de Rossi 1216), f. 53a-53b, G.
5210. Vatican - Biblioteca Apostolica ebr. 308 , f. 108b, C, commentator: David b. Mose (compiler).

Asti, Fossano, Moncalvo

5211. New Haven - Yale University, Beinecke Rare Book and MS Library, MS Heb. 52, f. 140a, M.

Roma
5212. Jerusalem - Jewish National and University Library Ms Heb 8° 4153, f. 140b, C, commentator: Daniel ben Salomo haRofe (compiler), no incipit, very short.
5213. Oxford - Bodleian Library MS Mich. 312,1 (Neubauer 2276,1), f. 8b, C, very short.

Tsarfat
5214. Oxford - Bodleian Library MS Bodl. Or. 109 (Neubauer 1209), f. 25a-25b, C, commentator: Aaron b. Hayyim haKohen (compiler).
5215. Parma - Biblioteca Palatina Cod. Parm. 1794 (de Rossi 1061), f. 182b-183a, M, no incipit.
5216. Parma - Biblioteca Palatina Cod. Parm. 2890 (de Rossi 856), f. 80a, M.
5217. Parma - Biblioteca Palatina Cod. Parm. 3006 (de Rossi 654,1), f. 186a-186b, M.

אליך לב ונפש אשפוך כמים (א 5066), אליה ב"ר שמעיה, סליחה

Ashkenaz
5218. Muenchen - Bayerische Staatsbibliothek, Cod. hebr. 346, f. 118b-119a, C, rubric: אתחיל סליחות. פתיחה, very short.
5219. Vatican - Biblioteca Apostolica ebr. 308/1, f. 3b, C, commentator: David b. Mose (compiler), very short.

אליך נשואות עינינו (א 5081), סליחה

Ashkenaz
5220. Braunschweig - Landesmuseum fuer Geschichte und Volkstum R 2386, vol. II, f. 51a, M, short.
5221. Jerusalem - Schocken Institute 24100 / Mahzor Nuremberg, f. 242b, M, very short.
5222. Muenchen - Bayerische Staatsbibliothek, Cod. hebr. 346, f. 124a, C, very short.
5223. Padova - Biblioteca del Seminario Vescovile Cod. 218, f. 75a, M, very short.
5224. Padova - Biblioteca del Seminario Vescovile Cod. 218, f. 238b-239a, M, short.
5225. Vatican - Biblioteca Apostolica ebr. 422/1, f. 26b, C, very short.
5226. Vatican - Biblioteca Apostolica ebr. 422/1, f. 40b, CG, no incipit, very short.

Ashkenaz, commentary by Abraham b. Azriel[134]
5227. Vatican - Biblioteca Apostolica ebr. 301,1, f. 144a, C, rubric: אחרת.

---

[134] Edited by Urbach, ערוגת הבושם, vol. III, p. 322-323.

אליך פנינו בושנו להרים (א 5086), אליה ב"ר שמעיה, סליחה

Ashkenaz
5228. Jerusalem - Schocken Institute 24100 / Mahzor Nuremberg, f. 395a-395b, M.
5229. Muenchen - Bayerische Staatsbibliothek, Cod. hebr. 346, f. 124a, C, rubric: 'מפריש' ראשון, very short.
5230. Muenchen - Bayerische Staatsbibliothek, Cod. hebr. 346, f. 146a, C, rubric: אחרת.
5231. Oxford - Bodleian Library MS Opp. 172 (Neubauer 1211), f. 54b-55a, C.
5232. Vatican - Biblioteca Apostolica ebr. 308, f. 109a-109b, C, commentator: David b. Mose (compiler).

Ashkenaz, commentary by Abraham b. Azriel[135]
5233. Frankfurt a M - Stadt- und Universitaetsbibliothek Fol. 16 (Merzbacher 95), f. 110a, C.

Tsarfat
5234. Vatican - Biblioteca Apostolica ebr. 306, f. 202b, C.

אליך צורי כפי שטחתי (א 5087), אליהו, סליחה

Ashkenaz
5235. Braunschweig - Landesmuseum fuer Geschichte und Volkstum R 2386, vol. II, f. 263a, M, very short.
5236. Oxford - Bodleian Library MS Mich. 543 (Neubauer 1212), f. 84b-85a, C, commentator: Isaac b. Jacob (compiler).
5237. Oxford - Bodleian Library MS Opp. 681 (Neubauer 1213), f. 94a-94b, C.
5238. Padova - Biblioteca del Seminario Vescovile Cod. 218, f. 88b-90a, M.
5239. Vatican - Biblioteca Apostolica ebr. 422/1, f. 33b-34a, C.

אליך תלויות עינינו (א 5095), אלעזר ברבי קליר, חלק י"ב, קדושתא למוסף יום כפור

Ashkenaz
5240. Berlin - Staatsbibliothek (Preussischer Kulturbesitz) Or. Qu. 798-799 (Steinschneider 177), I, f. 88a-88b, M.
5241. Berlin - Staatsbibliothek (Preussischer Kulturbesitz) Or. Qu. 798-799 (Steinschneider 177), I, f. 124b, M.
5242. Berlin - Staatsbibliothek (Preussischer Kulturbesitz) Or. Qu. 798-799 (Steinschneider 177), I, f. 163a-163b, M.
5243. Braunschweig - Landesmuseum fuer Geschichte und Volkstum R 2386, vol. II, f. 200b, M.
5244. Budapest - Magyar tudomanyos akademia, MS. Kaufmann A 400, p. 337-338, C.

---

[135] Edited by Urbach, ערוגת הבושם, vol. III, p. 568-569.

5245. Cambridge - University Library Add. 394,1 (Reif SCR 461), f. 72b-73a, C.
5246. Cambridge - University Library Add. 394,1 (Reif SCR 461), f. 72b-73a margin, C.
5247. Jerusalem - Jewish National and University Library Ms Heb 8° 3037, f. 135a, M, no incipit.
5248. Jerusalem - Schocken Institute 24100 / Mahzor Nuremberg, f. 385b-386a, M, short.
5249. London - British Library Or. 11318/1, f. 84b, C, short, no incipit.
5250. London - Montefiore Library 261, f. 49a, C, commentator: Eliezer b. Natan?.
5251. New York - Jewish Theological Seminary Ms. 4466, f. 328b, M, very ecclectic.
5252. Oxford - Bodleian Library MS Opp. 172 (Neubauer 1211), f. 46b-47a, C.
5253. Parma - Biblioteca Palatina Cod. Parm. 3507 (Perreau 27), f. 154b, C, no incipit, short.
5254. Vatican - Biblioteca Apostolica ebr. 308, f. 108b, C, commentator: David b. Mose (compiler).

Tsarfat
5255. London - David Sofer 5, f. 154a, C.

אליכם אקרא אישים (א 5111), אהרן בן יוסף הרופא, פרשת קדושים
Karaite, commentary by Berakha b. Josef haKohen
5256. New York - Jewish Theological Seminary Ms. 3367, f. 107b-110a, C, rubric: פרוש פרשת קדושים.
5257. St. Petersburg - Inst. of Oriental Studies of the Russian Academy B 431, f. 74b-76a, C, rubric: פרשת קדושים.
5258. St. Petersburg - Russian National Library, Evr. IV 50, f. 82a-84a, C, rubric: קדושים.

אליכם עדה קדושה אשאל מכם שאלות (א 5120), קינה
Carpentras, commentary by Mordekhai b. Josef of Rocco Martino
5259. Cincinnati - Hebrew Union College 246/1, f. 65b-66a, C, rubric: פי' קינה אליכם עדה קדישה.
Yemen, commentary by Isaac b. Abraham Wanneh
5260. Jerusalem - Sassoon 1158, p. 161, M.

אלים ביום מחוסן (א 5126), אלעזר ברבי קליר, מוסף ליום א' של פסח
Ashkenaz
5261. Berlin - Staatsbibliothek (Preussischer Kulturbesitz) Or. Qu. 798-799 (Steinschneider 177), II, f. 68a-71a, M.

5262. Braunschweig - Landesmuseum fuer Geschichte und Volkstum R 2386, vol. I, f. 27a-28b, M.
5263. Budapest - Magyar tudomanyos akademia, MS. Kaufmann A 384, f. 142a-145b, M.
5264. Budapest - Magyar tudomanyos akademia, MS. Kaufmann A 400, p. 118-122, C, no incipit.
5265. Budapest - Magyar tudomanyos akademia, MS. Kaufmann A 400, p. 390-393, C.
5266. Hamburg - Staats- und Universitaetsbibliothek Cod. hebr. 17/2 (Steinschneider 152), f. 59b-62b, C, rubric: מכאן ואילך מסדר והולך החדשים והמזלות וכנגדם האבות והשבטים בחרוז׳ אחת החודש ועמו צדיק אחר ובחרוזה אחרת מזל של אותו החודש וצדיק אחד עמו כלום׳ רחם על זה בזכות זה נמצאת השנה מבוכרת ומוצלחת.
5267. Hamburg - Staats- und Universitaetsbibliothek Cod. hebr. 225, f. 73b-77a, G.
5268. Jerusalem - Schocken Institute 24100 / Mahzor Nuremberg, f. 86b-88b, M.
5269. London - British Library Add. 18695 (Margoliouth 683), f. 29b-31b, T, Yiddish.
5270. Moscow - Russian State Library, Ms. Guenzburg 615, f. 15b-17a, C, rubric: סדר.
5271. Muenchen - Bayerische Staatsbibliothek, Cod. hebr. 88, f. 63b-65a, G.
5272. New York - Jewish Theological Seminary Ms. 4466, f. 62b-66a, M.
5273. Oxford - Bodleian Library MS Opp. 170 (Neubauer 1205), f. 68a-69b, C.
5274. Paris - Bibliotheque Nationale heb. 709, f. 84b-90b, C.
5275. Parma - Biblioteca Palatina Cod. Parm. 1002 (Ta 24), f. 100b-103a, M.
5276. Parma - Biblioteca Palatina Cod. Parm 3000 (de Rossi 378), f. 63b-67a, M.
5277. Parma - Biblioteca Palatina Cod. Parm. 3205 (de Rossi 655), f. 88a-88b, C.
5278. Parma - Biblioteca Palatina Cod. Parm. 3507 (Perreau 27), f. 55a-56b, C, no incipit.
5279. Zurich - Zentralbibliothek Heid. 139, f. 31b-33b, C, additional marginal notes.

Romania
5280. Cambridge - University Library Add. 377,3, f. 60a-63b, C.

Tsarfat
5281. London - British Library Add. 11639 (Margoliouth 1056), f. 660a-662b, M.
5282. Moscow - Russian State Library, Ms. Guenzburg 1665, f. 64a-66a, M.

5283. Oxford - Bodleian Library MS Laud. Or. 271 (Neubauer 1206), f. 67a-68b, C, commentator: Aaron b. Hayyim haKohen (compiler).
5284. Parma - Biblioteca Palatina Cod. Parm. 3136 (de Rossi 405), f. 86a-88a, M.
5285. Vatican - Biblioteca Apostolica ebr. 306, f. 145b-147b, C, no incipit.

אלים כהשעין אב תחת עץ בסוכה (א 5127), אלעזר ברבי קליר, חלק ה', קדושתא ליום א' של סוכות

Ashkenaz
5286. Berlin - Staatsbibliothek (Preussischer Kulturbesitz) Or. Qu. 798-799 (Steinschneider 177), I, f. 192a-193a, M.
5287. Braunschweig - Landesmuseum fuer Geschichte und Volkstum R 2386, vol. I, f. 135b-136a, M.
5288. Budapest - Magyar tudomanyos akademia, MS. Kaufmann A 400, p. 377-378, C.
5289. Fulda - Hessische Landesbibliothek A 3 II, f. 132b-134a, C, commentator: Josef.
5290. Hamburg - Staats- und Universitaetsbibliothek Cod. hebr. 17/2 (Steinschneider 152), f. 163a-b, C.
5291. Hamburg - Staats- und Universitaetsbibliothek Cod. hebr. 62 (Steinschneider 154), f. 40a-40b, C, no incipit.
5292. Hamburg - Staats- und Universitaetsbibliothek Cod. hebr. 132 (Steinschneider 155), f. 53a-54a, C.
5293. Jerusalem - Jewish National and University Library Ms Heb 8° 3037, f. 255b-256a, M.
5294. Jerusalem - Schocken Institute 24100 / Mahzor Nuremberg, f. 482a, M.
5295. London - British Library Add. 18695 (Margoliouth 683), f. 118b-119b, T, Yiddish.
5296. London - British Library Add. 22431 (Margoliouth 662a), f. 92b-93a, M.
5297. London - British Library Or. 11318/1, f. 136a-136b, C.
5298. London - Montefiore Library 261, f. 72a, C, commentator: Eliezer b. Natan?.
5299. New York - Jewish Theological Seminary Ms. 4466, f. 447b-448b, M.
5300. New York - Jewish Theological Seminary Ms. 4826, f. 3b, FM, only beginning, margins damaged.
5301. Oxford - Bodleian Library MS Mich. 365 (Neubauer 1208), f. 104a-104b, C.
5302. Oxford - Bodleian Library MS Opp. 170 (Neubauer 1205), f. 185a-185b, C.
5303. Parma - Biblioteca Palatina Cod. Parm. 3205 (de Rossi 655), f. 240b-241a, C, no incipit.

5304. Parma - Biblioteca Palatina Cod. Parm. 3507 (Perreau 27), f. 178b-179a, C, no incipit.
5305. Vatican - Biblioteca Apostolica ebr. 305,1, f. 42a-42b, C.
5306. Vatican - Biblioteca Apostolica ebr. 422/1, f. 20b-21a, C.
5307. Zurich - Zentralbibliothek Heid. 139, f. 91a-92a, C, additional marginal notes.

Romania

5308. London - London School of Jewish Studies. Asher I.Myers collection 9, f. 220b-221a, M.
5309. Vatican - Biblioteca Apostolica ebr. 320, f. 432b-433a, M.

Tsarfat

5310. London - David Sofer 5, f. 179b-180a, C, rubric: זה פירוש מפזמון.
5311. Moscow - Russian State Library, Ms. Guenzburg 1665, f. 163b-164a, M.
5312. Oxford - Bodleian Library MS Laud. Or. 271 (Neubauer 1206), f. 96a-96b, C, commentator: Aaron b. Hayyim haKohen (compiler).
5313. Oxford - Bodleian Library MS Opp. 171 (Neubauer 1207), f. 146b-147a, C.
5314. Parma - Biblioteca Palatina Cod. Parm. 1264, f. 56b, M.

אלכה ואשובה אל אישי הראשון (א 5138), יצחק, סליחה

Ashkenaz

5315. Cambridge - University Library Add. 394,1 (Reif SCR 461), f. 96a-96b, C.
5316. Oxford - Bodleian Library MS Opp. 681 (Neubauer 1213), f. 35a-36a, C.

Ashkenaz, commentary by Abraham b. Azriel[136]

5317. Vatican - Biblioteca Apostolica ebr. 301,1, f. 148a, C, rubric: אחרת.

Roma

5318. Berlin - Staatsbibliothek (Preussischer Kulturbesitz) Or. Oct. 3567, f. 2a-2b, FC.

Tsarfat

5319. London - David Sofer 5, f. 99b-100a, C.
5320. Parma - Biblioteca Palatina Cod. Parm. 3007 (de Rossi 654,2), f. 55a-55b, M.

אלכס אלנור קטר אלכואכב, שלם שבזי

Yemen

5321. Cincinnati - Hebrew Union College 398, f. 62a-63b, M.

---

[136] Edited by Urbach, ערוגת הבושם, vol. III, p. 348-350.

אלכס אלנור קטר אלתרייא, שלם שבזי

Yemen
5322. Cincinnati - Hebrew Union College 398, f. 60a-61b, M.

אלכס אלנור קצר אלהוייה חין אשרק, שלם שבזי

Yemen
5323. Cincinnati - Hebrew Union College 398, f. 58a-60a, M.

אללי אללי צרים סמך עלי (א 5146), אברהם אבן עזרא, קינה

Yemen, commentary by Isaac b. Abraham Wanneh
5324. Jerusalem - Sassoon 1158, p. 175, M, rubric: אחרת סים׳ אברהם.
5325. London - British Library Or. 11122, f. 104b, M, no incipit.

אללי לי אללי על רוע (א 5150), קינה

Carpentras, commentary by Mordekhai b. Josef of Rocco Martino
5326. Cincinnati - Hebrew Union College 246/1, f. 69a-70a, C, rubric: פי׳ קינה אללי לי.
Yemen, commentary by Isaac b. Abraham Wanneh
5327. Jerusalem - Sassoon 1158, p. 176-177, M.
5328. London - British Library Or. 11122, f. 105a, M, no incipit.

אלף אלפת לחני ואלנצאם (א 5165), שלם שבזי

Yemen
5329. Cincinnati - Hebrew Union College 398, f. 52b-55a, M, very long.

אלף אלפת קולי בתרתיב אלמעאני (א 5166), שלם שבזי

Yemen
5330. Cincinnati - Hebrew Union College 398, f. 55a-57a, M, very long.

אלף אלפת קלבי (א 5167), שלם שבזי

Yemen
5331. Cincinnati - Hebrew Union College 398, f. 50b-51b, M.

אלפי רבבותיך שילוש קדושתיך (א 5178), אמיתי בן שפטיה, אופן

Ashkenaz
5332. Parma - Biblioteca Palatina Cod. Parm 3000 (de Rossi 378), f. 12a, M.

אלפתנו לטהר על כן נודה לך (א 5182), אברהם ב״ר חייא, סילוק, קדושתא לשבת פרה

Carpentras, commentary by Mordekhai b. Josef of Rocco Martino
5333. Cincinnati - Hebrew Union College 246/1, f. 32b-34b, C, rubric: פי׳ סליק ובכן וכו׳.

Sepharad, commentary by Josef Garad

5334. Oxford - Bodleian Library Heb.e.10 (Neubauer 2746/1), f. 12a-13a, C, rubric: סלוק.

5335. Oxford - Bodleian Library Heb.e.10 (Neubauer 2746/1), f. 20a-20b, C, rubric: אלפתנו, no incipit.

אם אויבי יאמרו רע לי (א 5195), אברהם אבן עזרא, סליחה

Yemen

5336. Jerusalem - Sassoon 902, p. 417, M.

5337. New York - Jewish Theological Seminary Ms. 3052, f. 36a-37a, M, rubric: אל מלך.

Yemen, commentary by Isaac b. Abraham Wanneh

5338. Chicago-Spertus College of Judaica D 2, 2, f. 209b, M, no incipit.

5339. Jerusalem - Benayahu ת 261, f. 141a-141b, M, rubric: אל מלך.

5340. Jerusalem - Benayahu ת 282, f. 124a, M, rubric: אל מלך.

5341. Jerusalem - Makhon Ben Zvi 1156 (Tubi 155), f. 123a, M, rubric: אל מלך.

5342. Jerusalem - Makhon Ben Zvi 1174 (Tubi 154), f. 126b-127a, M, beginns מטה רגלי.

5343. Jerusalem - Michael Krupp 604, f. 156b-157a, M, rubric: אל מלך.

5344. Jerusalem - Musad haRav Kook 325, f. 183b-184a, M, rubric: אל מלך.

5345. Jerusalem - Sassoon 1158, p. 353-354, M, no incipit.

5346. Jerusalem - Sassoon 1174, p. 237, M, no incipit.

5347. London - British Library Or. 11122, f. 175b, M.

5348. Manchester - John Rylands University Library, Ms. Gaster 5, f. 198b, M.

5349. Muenchen - Bayerische Staatsbibliothek, Cod. hebr. 472, f. 169a, M, rubric: אל מלך.

5350. New York - Jewish Theological Seminary Ms. 3013, f. 123b, M, rubric: אל מלך, very short.

5351. New York - Jewish Theological Seminary Ms. 3294, f. 12a, C.

5352. New York - Public Library, Heb. Ms. 9, f. 113b-114a, M.

5353. Strasbourg - Bibliotheque Nationale et Universitaire 3965 (Landauer 39), p. 382-383, M, rubric: אל מלך.

אם אמרי אשכחה מרי שיחי (א 5215), שלמה הבבלי, סליחה

Ashkenaz

5354. Budapest - Magyar tudomanyos akademia, MS. Kaufmann A 400, p. 490-491, C, rubric: אחרת.

5355. Cambridge - University Library Dd. 2.30, f. 18b-19a, G.

5356. Jerusalem - Schocken Institute 24100 / Mahzor Nuremberg, f. 240b, M.

5357. Moscow - Russian State Library, Ms. Guenzburg 190, f. 25b-26a, G.

HEBREW LITURGICAL POETRY 327

5358. Moscow - Russian State Library, Ms. Guenzburg 615, f. 157b-158a, C, rubric: אל מלך.
5359. Muenchen - Bayerische Staatsbibliothek, Cod. hebr. 346, f. 136a-136b, C, rubric: אחרת.
5360. Oxford - Bodleian Library MS Mich. 543 (Neubauer 1212), f. 71a-71b, C, commentator: Isaac b. Jacob (compiler).
5361. Oxford - Bodleian Library MS Opp. 170 (Neubauer 1205), f. 226b-227a, C.
5362. Oxford - Bodleian Library MS Opp. 681 (Neubauer 1213), f. 17a-18a, C.
5363. Padova - Biblioteca del Seminario Vescovile Cod. 218, f. 127b-128a, M.
5364. Parma - Biblioteca Palatina Cod. Parm. 3205 (de Rossi 655), f. 263a-263b, C.
5365. Vatican - Biblioteca Apostolica ebr. 422/1, f. 43a-43b, CG, no incipit.

Ashkenaz, commentary by Abraham b. Azriel[137]
5366. Frankfurt a M - Stadt- und Universitaetsbibliothek Fol. 16 (Merzbacher 95), f. 112a, C.
5367. Vatican - Biblioteca Apostolica ebr. 301,1, f. 159b-160a, C, rubric: אחרת.

Tsarfat
5368. London - David Sofer 5, f. 90b-91a, C.
5369. Oxford - Bodleian Library MS Laud. Or. 271 (Neubauer 1206), f. 171b-172a, C, commentator: Aaron b. Hayyim haKohen (compiler).
5370. Oxford - Bodleian Library MS Opp. 171 (Neubauer 1207), f. 100b-101a, C, rubric: אחרת.
5371. Parma - Biblioteca Palatina Cod. Parm. 3007 (de Rossi 654,2), f. 58a-58b, M.
5372. Vatican - Biblioteca Apostolica ebr. 306, f. 91a-91b, C.

אם אפס רובע הקן (א 5226), אפרים ב"ר יצחק מרגנסבורג, עקדה

Ashkenaz
5373. Muenchen - Bayerische Staatsbibliothek, Cod. hebr. 346, f. 164b, C, very short.

North Africa, commentary by David b. Josef Abudarham
5374. New York - Jewish Theological Seminary Ms. 5426, f. 61a, M.

Sepharad
5375. Skokie - Hebrew Theological College 3, f. 14b-15b, G.

Tsarfat
5376. London - David Sofer 5, f. 100b, C.
5377. Parma - Biblioteca Palatina Cod. Parm. 2890 (de Rossi 856), f. 135a, M.

---
[137] Edited by Urbach, ערוגת הבושם, vol. III, p. 426-428.

5378. Parma - Biblioteca Palatina Cod. Parm. 3007 (de Rossi 654,2), f. 58b-59a, M.

Yemen

5379. New York - Jewish Theological Seminary Ms. 3193, f. 123a, M.

Yemen, commentary by Isaac b. Abraham Wanneh

5380. Chicago-Spertus College of Judaica D 2, 2, f. 182b, M.
5381. Jerusalem - Sassoon 1158, p. 301-302, M.
5382. London - British Library Or. 11122, f. 158b-159a, M.
5383. Manchester - John Rylands University Library, Ms. Gaster 5, f. 177b, M.

אם אשמנו כתולע האדים יי (א 5235), סליחה

Sepharad

5384. Skokie - Hebrew Theological College 3, f. 19a-19b, G.

Yemen

5385. New York - Jewish Theological Seminary Ms. 3193, f. 125a, M.

Yemen, commentary by Isaac b. Abraham Wanneh

5386. Chicago-Spertus College of Judaica D 2, 2, f. 184a-184b, M.
5387. London - British Library Or. 11122, f. 160b, M.

אם אשר בצדק (א 5239), אלעזר ברבי קליר, חלק ו', קדושתא לראש השנה

Ashkenaz

5388. Jerusalem - Schocken Institute 24100 / Mahzor Nuremberg, f. 324b, M.
5389. New York - Jewish Theological Seminary Ms. 8169 (Acc. 0016), f. 5b-6a, M.
5390. Oxford - Bodleian Library MS Opp. 172 (Neubauer 1211), f. 4b, C.
5391. Oxford - Bodleian Library MS Opp. 675 (Neubauer 1210), f. 16b-17a, C.
5392. Torino - Archivio Terracini 1492, f. 10b-11a, M.
5393. Vatican - Biblioteca Apostolica ebr. 308, f. 32a-32b, C, commentator: David b. Mose (compiler).
5394. Zurich - Zentralbibliothek Heid. 139, f. 63b (extra leaf bound into volume), C, rubric: שייך לעיל קודם אאפיד.

Romania

5395. Vatican - Biblioteca Apostolica ebr. 320, f. 399b, M.

Tsarfat

5396. London - British Library Add. 11639 (Margoliouth 1056), f. 709b, M.
5397. London - British Library Or. 8682, f. 11a, G.
5398. London - David Sofer 5, f. 110b, C.
5399. Manchester - John Rylands University Library, Ms. Gaster 733, f. 81a, C, commentary block in Mahzor, manuscript damaged.

5400. Oxford - Bodleian Library MS Opp. 171 (Neubauer 1207), f. 57b, C, rubric: פזמון.
5401. Paris - Bibliotheque Nationale heb. 445,9, f. 63b, C.
5402. Parma - Biblioteca Palatina Cod. Parm. 1794 (de Rossi 1061), f. 63a-63b, M.
5403. Parma - Biblioteca Palatina Cod. Parm. 2125 (de Rossi 812), f. 10a-10b, C.
5404. Parma - Biblioteca Palatina Cod. Parm. 3006 (de Rossi 654,1), f. 43b-44a, M.

אם הרבינו פשע (א 5310), אמתי בן שפטיה, סליחה

Ashkenaz
5405. Moscow - Russian State Library, Ms. Guenzburg 615, f. 162b-163a, C, rubric: אל מלך.
5406. Oxford - Bodleian Library MS Mich. 543 (Neubauer 1212), f. 68b-69a, C, commentator: Isaac b. Jacob (compiler).
5407. Oxford - Bodleian Library MS Opp. 170 (Neubauer 1205), f. 237a, C.

Ashkenaz, commentary by Abraham b. Azriel[138]
5408. Vatican - Biblioteca Apostolica ebr. 301,1, f. 162b, C, rubric: אחר.

Tsarfat
5409. London - British Library Add. 11639 (Margoliouth 1056), f. 276b-278b, M.
5410. Oxford - Bodleian Library MS Laud. Or. 271 (Neubauer 1206), f. 128b-129a, C, commentator: Aaron b. Hayyim haKohen (compiler).
5411. Oxford - Bodleian Library MS Opp. 171 (Neubauer 1207), f. 116b, C.
5412. Parma - Biblioteca Palatina Cod. Parm. 3007 (de Rossi 654,2), f. 107b-108a, M.

אם חובי אנה בי, סליחה

Yemen, commentary by Isaac b. Abraham Wanneh
5413. London - British Library Or. 11122, f. 103b, M.

אם חסדך שכחנו ותורתך זנחנו (א 5323), משה אבן עזרא, תוכחה

Sepharad, commentary by David b. Josef Abudarham[139]
5414. Budapest - Magyar tudomanyos akademia, MS. Kaufmann A 405/2, p. 212-213, C, rubric: תוכחה.
5415. New York - Columbia X893 Ab 93, f. 14a-14b, C, rubric: תוכחה.

---

[138] Edited by Urbach, ערוגת הבושם, vol. III, p. 443.
[139] Edited by Prins, תשלום אבודרהם, p. 106-108.

אם לא אמריך הנעימים (א 5372), שמעון ב"ר יצחק, חלק ד', קדושתא לשבועות

Ashkenaz

5416. Berlin - Staatsbibliothek (Preussischer Kulturbesitz) Or. Qu. 798-799 (Steinschneider 177), II, f. 117a-117b, M.
5417. Braunschweig - Landesmuseum fuer Geschichte und Volkstum R 2386, vol. I, f. 74a-74b, M.
5418. Hamburg - Staats- und Universitaetsbibliothek Cod. hebr. 17/2 (Steinschneider 152), f. 82b, C.
5419. Jerusalem - Schocken Institute 24100 / Mahzor Nuremberg, f. 148a, M, very short.
5420. London - British Library Add. 18695 (Margoliouth 683), f. 66a-66b, T, Yiddish.
5421. London - British Library Add. 22431 (Margoliouth 662a), f. 9b-10a, M, no incipit.
5422. Moscow - Russian State Library, Ms. Guenzburg 615, f. 31a-31b, C.
5423. New York - Jewish Theological Seminary Ms. 4466, f. 128a, M, incipit ונגלה, ecclectic, short.
5424. Parma - Biblioteca Palatina Cod. Parm. 3205 (de Rossi 655), f. 121a, C, incipit אל נא.
5425. Parma - Biblioteca Palatina Cod. Parm. 3507 (Perreau 27), f. 97b-98a, C.

Tsarfat

5426. London - David Sofer 5, f. 51a, C, short.
5427. Moscow - Russian State Library, Ms. Guenzburg 1665, f. 118a, M, incipit אל נא.
5428. Parma - Biblioteca Palatina Cod. Parm. 3136 (de Rossi 405), f. 149b-150a, M, partly bleached.
5429. Vatican - Biblioteca Apostolica ebr. 306, f. 229b-230a, C, incipit אל נא.

אם לא למעננו יעש, לראש השנה

Tsarfat

5430. Oxford - Bodleian Library MS Opp. 171 (Neubauer 1207), f. 58a-59a, C, rubric: פזמון.
5431. Manchester - John Rylands University Library, Ms. Gaster 733, f. 81b, C, commentary block in Mahzor, manuscript damaged.
5432. Vatican - Biblioteca Apostolica ebr. 306, f. 56b-58a, C.

אם לא תדעי נפשי אחריתך (א 5375), אברהם אבן עזרא, תוכחה

Sepharad, commentary by David b. Josef Abudarham[140]

5433. Budapest - Magyar tudomanyos akademia, MS. Kaufmann A 405/2, p. 246, C, rubric: תוכחה לר' אברהרם ן' עזרא ז"ל.

5434. New York - Columbia X893 Ab 93, f. 28a, C, rubric: תוכחה לר' אברהרם ן' עזרא ז"ל.

אם לפי בחרך צורנו באדם הזה הדל (א 5390), סעדיה גאון, תוכחה

Mizrah

5435. Berlin - Staatsbibliothek (Preussischer Kulturbesitz) Or. Qu. 943, 1a-2b, FC, only stanzas ה to ט and כ to ל, Judeo-Arabic.

5436. London - British Library Or. 5554 B/14, f. 23a-24b, C, commentator: Isaac b. Samuel haSephardi, introduction and commentary on stanza א.

אם ננעלו דלתי נדיבים (א 5407), שלם שבזי

Yemen

5437. Cincinnati - Hebrew Union College 398, f. 19b-20b, M.

5438. New York - M. Lehmann 274, f. 65a, M, kabbalistic.

אם עברנו תורות וחלפנו חוקים (א 5444), סליחה

Ashkenaz

5439. Berlin - Staatsbibliothek (Preussischer Kulturbesitz) Or. Qu. 798-799 (Steinschneider 177), I, f. 149a-149b, M.

5440. Moscow - Russian State Library, Ms. Guenzburg 615, f. 142a-142b, C, rubric: אחרת.

5441. New York - Jewish Theological Seminary Ms. 4466, f. 403a, M.

5442. Oxford - Bodleian Library MS Mich. 543 (Neubauer 1212), f. 9a-9b margin, C, commentator: Isaac b. Jacob (compiler).

5443. Oxford - Bodleian Library MS Opp. 619 (Neubauer 2374), f. 268a-268b, M.

5444. Vatican - Biblioteca Apostolica ebr. 422/1, f. 32a, C, short.

Asti, Fossano, Moncalvo

5445. New Haven - Yale University, Beinecke Rare Book and MS Library, MS Heb. 52, f. 156a, M, ecclectic.

אם עונות ענו בנו (א 5456), שלמה הבבלי, סליחה

Ashkenaz

5446. Budapest - Magyar tudomanyos akademia, MS. Kaufmann A 400, p. 425-428, C, rubric: פזמון שלמוני.

5447. Forli - Archivio di Stato 4, FC, rubric: פיזמון הבבלי בניגון לך יי הצדקה.

---

[140] Edited by Prins, תשלום אבודרהם, p. 115-116.

5448. Hamburg - Staats- und Universitaetsbibliothek Cod. hebr. 17/2 (Steinschneider 152), f. 128a-128b, C, rubric: פזמון שלמוני.
5449. Jerusalem - Schocken Institute 24100 / Mahzor Nuremberg, f. 437b-438a, M.
5450. Moscow - Russian State Library, Ms. Guenzburg 190, f. 43b-44b, G.
5451. Moscow - Russian State Library, Ms. Guenzburg 615, f. 164b-166b, C.
5452. Muenchen - Bayerische Staatsbibliothek, Cod. hebr. 346, f. 107b-110a, C, rubric: אתחיל לכתוב סליחות.
5453. Oxford - Bodleian Library MS Mich. 543 (Neubauer 1212), f. 73a-74b, C, commentator: Isaac b. Jacob (compiler), rubric: פיזמונים.
5454. Oxford - Bodleian Library MS Opp. 170 (Neubauer 1205), f. 234a-236a, C.
5455. Oxford - Bodleian Library MS Opp. 172 (Neubauer 1211), f. 79b-81a, C, rubric: פזמון.
5456. Oxford - Bodleian Library MS Opp. 681 (Neubauer 1213), f. 82a-84b, C.
5457. Parma - Bibliotheca Palatina Cod. Parm. 3205 (de Rossi 655), f. 290b-292a, C.
5458. Vatican - Biblioteca Apostolica ebr. 308/1, f. 6b-7a, C, commentator: David b. Mose (compiler).
5459. Vatican - Biblioteca Apostolica ebr. 308, f. 144(ii)b-145(ii)b, C, commentator: David b. Mose (compiler).
5460. Vatican - Biblioteca Apostolica ebr. 422/1, f. 28b, C.
5461. Vatican - Biblioteca Apostolica ebr. 422/1, f. 42b-43a, CG, no incipit, short.

Ashkenaz, commentary by Abraham b. Azriel[141]

5462. Frankfurt a M - Stadt- und Universitaetsbibliothek Fol. 16 (Merzbacher 95), f. 113b-114a, C, manuscript partly damaged.

Tsarfat

5463. London - David Sofer 5, f. 88a-89a, C.
5464. Oxford - Bodleian Library MS Laud. Or. 271 (Neubauer 1206), f. 166b-167b, C, commentator: Aaron b. Hayyim haKohen (compiler).
5465. Oxford - Bodleian Library MS Laud. Or. 271 (Neubauer 1206), f. 175a-175b, C, commentator: Aaron b. Hayyim haKohen (compiler), rubric: פיזמון הבבלי בניגון הצדקה.
5466. Oxford - Bodleian Library MS Opp. 171 (Neubauer 1207), f. 90b-91b, C, rubric: פזמון.
5467. Oxford - Bodleian Library MS Opp. 171 (Neubauer 1207), f. 91b-92a, C, rubric: אחרת.
5468. Parma - Bibliotheca Palatina Cod. Parm. 3007 (de Rossi 654,2), f. 108a-109a, M.

---

[141] Edited by Urbach, ערוגת הבושם, vol. III, p. 580-584.

5469. Vatican - Biblioteca Apostolica ebr. 306, f. 180a-182a, C.

אם עונות יענו בנו והרחיקו צור ממנו (א 5457), סליחה

Yemen
5470. New York - Jewish Theological Seminary Ms. 3052, f. 30a, M, rubric: אל מלך.

Yemen, commentary by Isaac b. Abraham Wanneh
5471. Chicago-Spertus College of Judaica D 2, 2, f. 200a, M.
5472. Jerusalem - Benayahu ת 261, f. 139a, M, rubric: אל מלך, short.
5473. Jerusalem - Benayahu ת 282, f. 122a-122b, M, rubric: אל מלך.
5474. Jerusalem - Makhon Ben Zvi 1156 (Tubi 155), f. 120b, M, rubric: אל מלך, short.
5475. Jerusalem - Makhon Ben Zvi 1174 (Tubi 154), f. 125b, M, short.
5476. Jerusalem - Michael Krupp 604, f. 153a, M, rubric: אל מלך.
5477. Jerusalem - Musad haRav Kook 325, f. 182b, M, rubric: אל מלך, short.
5478. Jerusalem - Musad haRav Kook 347, f. 83b, G.
5479. Jerusalem - Sassoon 1158, p. 359, M, no incipit.
5480. Jerusalem - Sassoon 1174, p. 232-233, M, no incipit.
5481. Manchester - John Rylands University Library, Ms. Gaster 5, f. 197a-197b, M.
5482. Muenchen - Bayerische Staatsbibliothek, Cod. hebr. 472, f. 165a-165b, M, rubric: אל מלך, short.
5483. New York - Jewish Theological Seminary Ms. 3013, f. 122a, M, rubric: אל מלך, very short.
5484. New York - Jewish Theological Seminary Ms. 3294, f. 10b, C.
5485. Strasbourg - Bibliotheque Nationale et Universitaire 3965 (Landauer 39), p. 379, M, rubric: אל מלך, short.

אם עונינו ענו בנו כעדים, סליחה

Yemen, commentary by Isaac b. Abraham Wanneh
5486. Chicago-Spertus College of Judaica D 2, 2, f. 242b-243a, M, no incipit.
5487. Jerusalem - Sassoon 1158, p. 427-428, M, no incipit.
5488. London - British Library Or. 11122, f. 220b-221a, M, no incipit.
5489. New York - Jewish Theological Seminary Ms. 3109, f. 112b-113a, M, rubric: אל מלך, no incipit.

אם עונינו רבו והפשע גבר בחסדך בטחנו, סליחה

Yemen, commentary by Isaac b. Abraham Wanneh
5490. Chicago-Spertus College of Judaica D 2, 2, f. 247b, M, no incipit.
5491. Jerusalem - Sassoon 1158, p. 426, M, no incipit.
5492. London - British Library Or. 11122, f. 220b, M, no incipit.

אם עונינו רבו להגדיל (א 5459), שלמה הבבלי, סליחה

Ashkenaz

5493. Bologna - Archivio di Stato MS Ebr. 253, f. 1a, FC, incomplete, beginning missing.
5494. Budapest - Magyar tudomanyos akademia, MS. Kaufmann A 400, p. 450-451, C, rubric: אחרת שלמונית.
5495. Cambridge - University Library Dd. 2.30, f. 7a, G.
5496. Hamburg - Staats- und Universitaetsbibliothek Cod. hebr. 17/2 (Steinschneider 152), f. 134a-134b, C, rubric: אחרת שלמונית.
5497. Jerusalem - Schocken Institute 24100 / Mahzor Nuremberg, f. 241a, M.
5498. Karlsruhe - Badische Landesbibliothek, Schwarzach 20, f. 1b-2a, FC.
5499. Moscow - Russian State Library, Ms. Guenzburg 190, f. 29a-29b, G.
5500. Muenchen - Bayerische Staatsbibliothek, Cod. hebr. 346, f. 135a-135b, C, rubric: אחרת.
5501. Oxford - Bodleian Library MS Mich. 543 (Neubauer 1212), f. 64a-64b, C, commentator: Isaac b. Jacob (compiler).
5502. Oxford - Bodleian Library MS Opp. 170 (Neubauer 1205), f. 222a-222b, C.
5503. Padova - Biblioteca del Seminario Vescovile Cod. 218, f. 66a-66b, M.
5504. Padova - Biblioteca del Seminario Vescovile Cod. 218, f. 232b-233b, M.
5505. Parma - Biblioteca Palatina Cod. Parm. 3205 (de Rossi 655), f. 269b-270a, C.
5506. Vatican - Biblioteca Apostolica ebr. 422/1, f. 4a-4b, C, rubric: אחרת.

Ashkenaz, commentary by Abraham b. Azriel[142]

5507. Frankfurt a M - Stadt- und Universitaetsbibliothek Fol. 16 (Merzbacher 95), f. 115a-115b, C, incipit כי.

Tsarfat

5508. London - British Library Add. 11639 (Margoliouth 1056), f. 479b-480b, M.
5509. London - David Sofer 5, f. 89a-89b, C.
5510. Oxford - Bodleian Library MS Laud. Or. 271 (Neubauer 1206), f. 167b-168a, C, commentator: Aaron b. Hayyim haKohen (compiler).
5511. Parma - Biblioteca Palatina Cod. Parm. 3006 (de Rossi 654,1), f. 159a, M.
5512. Vatican - Biblioteca Apostolica ebr. 306, f. 195b-196a, C.

אם תאהב דרך אמת (א 5492), אברהם אבן עזרא, סליחה

Yemen

5513. New York - Jewish Theological Seminary Ms. 3193, f. 127a, M.

---

[142] Edited by Urbach, ערוגת הבושם, vol. III, p. 589-591.

Yemen, commentary by Isaac b. Abraham Wanneh
5514. Chicago-Spertus College of Judaica D 2, 2, f. 185b, M.
5515. Jerusalem - Sassoon 1158, p. 310, M, no incipit.
5516. Jerusalem - Yehiel haLevi 4, f. 138a, M, short.

אם תאכלנה נשים פרים (א 5503), אלעזר ברבי קליר, קינה

Ashkenaz
5517. Berlin - Staatsbibliothek (Preussischer Kulturbesitz) Or. Qu. 798-799 (Steinschneider 177), II, f. 188b-189a, M.
5518. Budapest - Magyar tudomanyos akademia, MS. Kaufmann A 400, p. 228-229, C, rubric: קינה אחרת.
5519. Hamburg - Staats- und Universitaetsbibliothek Cod. hebr. 17/2 (Steinschneider 152), f. 99b-100a, C.
5520. Jerusalem - Schocken Institute 24100 / Mahzor Nuremberg, f. 196b, M.
5521. Oxford - Bodleian Library MS Can. Or. 70 (Neubauer 1147,8), f. 118a-118b, M.
5522. Parma - Biblioteca Palatina Cod. Parm. 3205 (de Rossi 655), f. 196b-197a, C, rubric: אחרת.
5523. Vatican - Biblioteca Apostolica ebr. 312, f. 50b-51a, G.
5524. Vatican - Biblioteca Apostolica ebr. 318, f. 234a-235a, GI.
Ashkenaz, commentary by Abraham b. Azriel[143]
5525. Vatican - Biblioteca Apostolica ebr. 301,1, f. 137a-137b, C, rubric: אחרת.

אם תחפצה בן איש לסודות נבחרו (א 5531), שלם שבזי

Yemen
5526. Cincinnati - Hebrew Union College 398, f. 181b-182b, M.

אמגן מומי לא תשתבע (א 5566), רשות בארמית לדבור שלישי

Ashkenaz
5527. Hamburg - Staats- und Universitaetsbibliothek Cod. hebr. 17/2 (Steinschneider 152), f. 72b-73a, C.
5528. Oxford - Bodleian Library MS Opp. 170 (Neubauer 1205), f. 97a-98a, C.
Ashkenaz, commentary by Benjamin b. Abraham Anaw
5529. Jerusalem - Musad haRav Kook 478, p. 31-40, C, rubric: אלפא ביתא ו.
5530. London - Beth Din & Beth Hamidrash 6,9, f. 167b-172b, C, rubric: אלפא בית.

---

[143] Edited by Urbach, ערוגת הבושם, vol. III, p. 281-282.

אמהות עת נכבשה (א 5573), שמעון ב"ר יצחק, זולת לחתן
Ashkenaz
5531. Berlin - Staatsbibliothek (Preussischer Kulturbesitz) Or. Qu. 798-799 (Steinschneider 177), I, f. 265a-266a, M.
5532. Budapest - Magyar tudomanyos akademia, MS. Kaufmann A 399 , p. 354-356, C, rubric: זולת.
5533. Frankfurt a M - Stadt- und Universitaetsbibliothek Oct. 227 , f. 149a-149b, M.
5534. Jerusalem - Schocken Institute 24100 / Mahzor Nuremberg , f. 225b-226a, M.
5535. Lund - Universitetsbibliothek Ms. L.O. 2, f. 111b-112a, M.
5536. Muenchen - Bayerische Staatsbibliothek, Cod. hebr. 393,9, f. 184a-185b, C, no incipit.
5537. Oxford - Bodleian Library MS Can. Or. 82 (Neubauer 1148) , f. 50a-51a, M.
5538. Parma - Biblioteca Palatina Cod. Parm. 2895, p. 452-454, M, margins cut, text slightly damaged.
5539. Parma - Biblioteca Palatina Cod. Parm. 3205 (de Rossi 655), f. 170b-172a, C, rubric: זולת לר' שמעון.
Ashkenaz, commentary by Abraham b. Azriel[144]
5540. Vatican - Biblioteca Apostolica ebr. 301,1, f. 9b-10b, C, rubric: זולת.
Tsarfat
5541. Parma - Biblioteca Palatina Cod. Parm. 3136 (de Rossi 405), f. 122b-123a, M.
5542. Vatican - Biblioteca Apostolica ebr. 306, f. 151b-152b, C, rubric: זולת.

אמון היתה תורה אצל נורא ואיום (א 5578), אהרן בן יוסף הרופא, פרשת חוקת
Karaite, commentary by Berakha b. Josef haKohen
5543. New York - Jewish Theological Seminary Ms. 3367, f. 127b-130a, C, rubric: פרוש פרשת חקת התורה.
5544. St. Petersburg - Inst. of Oriental Studies of the Russian Academy B 431, f. 87a-88b, C, rubric: פרשת חקת.
5545. St. Petersburg - Inst. of Oriental Studies of the Russian Academy B 483, f. 5a-6b, C, rubric: פרשת חקת.
5546. St. Petersburg - Russian National Library, Evr. IV 50, f. 98a-100b, C, rubric: חקת.

אמון יום זה נחלו עם זה (א 5582), דוד בן אלעזר בקודה, רשות לאזהרות
Carpentras
5547. New York - Jewish Theological Seminary Ms. 4268, f. 3a-3b, G.

---

[144] Edited by Urbach, ערוגת הבושם, vol. I, pp.62-66.

5548. Parma - Biblioteca Palatina Cod. Parm. 3491, f. 5a-5b, M, rubric: ביאור המלות.

Italia

5549. Moscow - Russian State Library, Ms. Guenzburg 211, f. 48a-49a, G.
5550. New York - Columbia University X 893 G 11, f. 1a-2a, G.

Romania

5551. London - British Library Or. 10105, f. 2a, .
5552. New York - Columbia University X 893.1 BE P 43, f. 109a-110a, T, Greek.

Yemen

5553. Chicago-Spertus College of Judaica D 10, f. 42a, M, rubric: פירוש.
5554. Jerusalem - Benayahu ת 88, f. 92a-92b, M.
5555. New York - Jewish Theological Seminary Ms. 3193, f. 141a, M.

Yemen, commentary by Isaac b. Abraham Wanneh

5556. New York - Jewish Theological Seminary Ms. 3295, f. 35a, M.

Yemen commentary by Yiḥya b. Josef Tsalaḥ

5557. Montreal - Elberg 203, f. 18b-19a, M.

אמון נוא הובא (א 5586), מנחם ב"ר יעקב?, זולת לשבת הגדול

Ashkenaz, commentary by Abraham b. Azriel[145]

5558. Frankfurt a M - Stadt- und Universitaetsbibliothek Fol. 16 (Merzbacher 95), f. 101a-102b (f. 102a more than half empty, but ruled), C, rubric: אחר, commentary breaks off in the middle of a sentence.
5559. Vatican - Biblioteca Apostolica ebr. 301,1, f. 117a-118a, C, rubric: אחר.

אמונה יצרה יסוד היסודות (א 5596), יחיא אלץ'הארי, לשמחת תורה

Yemen, commentary by Yiḥya b. Josef Tsalaḥ

5560. Montreal - Elberg 203, f. 38a-39b, M.

אמוני לבב הבינו מהנראה סוד נעלם (א 5607), אברהם אבן עזרא, סדר עבודה

Carpentras

5561. Cincinnati - Hebrew Union College 392, f. 66b-69b, 70b-72a, M, no incipit.

Carpentras, commentary by Josef b. Abraham of Montelitz

5562. Cincinnati - Hebrew Union College 291, f. 35b-42a, C, rubric: פירוש סדר עבודה.
5563. New York - Jewish Theological Seminary Ms. 4197, f. 160b-169a, M.
5564. Paris - Ecole Rabbinique 32, f. 172b-180a, M.
5565. Strasbourg - Bibliotheque Nationale et Universitaire 4081, f. 150a-158a, M.

---

[145] Edited by Urbach, ערוגת הבושם, vol. III, p. 143-148

Yemen
5566. Jerusalem - Benayahu ת 301, f. 64a-66a, G.
5567. Jerusalem - Makhon Ben Zvi 2464, f. 1a-11a, C, commentator: Rahamim Nissim Yehuda Siroga.
5568. Jerusalem - Musad haRav Kook 325, f. 197a-198a, G.
5569. Jerusalem - Musad haRav Kook 330, f. 126a-128a, G, very few glosses.
5570. Jerusalem - Musad haRav Kook 334, f. 159a-161b, G.
5571. Jerusalem - Musad haRav Kook 347, f. 95b-97b, G.
5572. Jerusalem - Yehiel haLevi 4, f. 183a-186a, G.
5573. New York - Jewish Theological Seminary Ms. 3028, f. 112a-116b, G.
5574. New York - Jewish Theological Seminary Ms. 4488, f. 126a-127b, G.
5575. New York - Public Library, Heb. Ms. 10, f. 99a-100b, G.
5576. Ramat Gan - Universitat Bar Ilan 62, f. 53b-55a, G.

Yemen, commentary by Isaac b. Abraham Wanneh
5577. Chicago-Spertus College of Judaica D 2, 2, f. 248a-251a, M, rubric: סדר עבודה.
5578. Jerusalem - Sassoon 1158, p. 328-335, M, rubric: סדר עבודה.
5579. London - British Library Or. 11122, f. 225b-228b, M, rubric: סדר עבודה.

אמוני נבונים בתקעם בירח איתנים (א 5611), מעריב ליום א' של ראש השנה

Tsarfat
5580. London - David Sofer 5, f. 107a, C.
5581. Parma - Biblioteca Palatina Cod. Parm. 1902, f. 112a-112b, C.
5582. Parma - Biblioteca Palatina Cod. Parm. 3006 (de Rossi 654,1), f. 13b, M.

אמוני עתים ישולח לקדיש, ליום כפור

Tsarfat
5583. London - British Library Or. 8682, f. 92a-92b, GI.
5584. Parma - Biblioteca Palatina Cod. Parm. 2125 (de Rossi 812), f. 46b-50b, C.

אמוני שלומי ישראל גזרתם כשהם (א 5616), הלל ב"ר יעקב מבון, סליחה

Ashkenaz
5585. Oxford - Bodleian Library MS Opp. 172 (Neubauer 1211), f. 78a-78b, C.
5586. Vatican - Biblioteca Apostolica ebr. 308, f. 162b-163a, C, commentator: David b. Mose (compiler).

Ashkenaz, commentary by Abraham b. Azriel[146]
5587. Vatican - Biblioteca Apostolica ebr. 301,1, f. 150b, C, rubric: אחרת.

אמוניך בתחננים לחבוש מחצם (א 5620), יצחק (או יוסף אבן אביתור), הושענא
haAri, commentary by Mose b. Hayyim Pesante
5588. New York - Columbia University X 893 J 558, f. 204b-205a, M.
5589. New York - Jewish Theological Seminary Ms. 4696, f. 17b, C.
haAri, commentary by Simon b. Tsemaḥ Duran
5590. New York - Columbia University X 893 J 558, f. 204b-205a, M.
North African, commentary by Yehuda Toledano
5591. New York - Jewish Theological Seminary Ms. 4300, f. 28a-28b, C.
Yemen, commentary by Samḥun b. Salomo Ḥaloah
5592. Jerusalem - Makhon ben Zvi 2808, f. 116a-120b, C.

אמונים אשר נאספו (א 5622), זולת לשמיני עצרת
Ashkenaz
5593. Berlin - Staatsbibliothek (Preussischer Kulturbesitz) Or. Qu. 798-799 (Steinschneider 177), I, f. 213a, M, short.
5594. Jerusalem - Jewish National and University Library Ms Heb 8° 3037, f. 281a, M.
5595. London - British Library Add. 18695 (Margoliouth 683), f. 126a-126b, T, Yiddish, rubric: זולת.
5596. London - Montefiore Library 261, f. 73a, C, commentator: Eliezer b. Natan?.
5597. Zurich - Zentralbibliothek Heid. 139, f. 94a, C, very short.
Romania
5598. London - London School of Jewish Studies. Asher I.Myers collection 9, f. 230b, M, very short.

אמונים בני מאמינים הנאמנים בבריתך (א 5627), בנימין ב"ר זרח, סליחה
Ashkenaz
5599. Berlin - Staatsbibliothek (Preussischer Kulturbesitz) Or. Qu. 798-799 (Steinschneider 177), I, f. 171b-172a, M.
5600. Braunschweig - Landesmuseum fuer Geschichte und Volkstum R 2386, vol. II, f. 69a, M.
5601. Budapest - Magyar tudomanyos akademia, MS. Kaufmann A 400, p. 483, C, rubric: אחרת, short.
5602. Cambridge - University Library Dd. 2.30, f. 39a-39b, G.
5603. Hamburg - Staats- und Universitaetsbibliothek Cod. hebr. 17/2 (Steinschneider 152), f. 177a, C, rubric: אחרת.

---

[146] Edited by Urbach, ערוגת הבושם, vol. III, p. 365-366.

5604. Jerusalem - Jewish National and University Library Ms Heb 8° 3037, f. 149b-150a, M.
5605. Jerusalem - Schocken Institute 24100 / Mahzor Nuremberg, f. 455b-456a, M.
5606. London - British Library Add. 18695 (Margoliouth 683), f. 165b, T, Yiddish.
5607. Moscow - Russian State Library, Ms. Guenzburg 190, f. 100a-100b, G.
5608. Moscow - Russian State Library, Ms. Guenzburg 615, f. 162a, C, rubric: אל מלך, short.
5609. Muenchen - Bayerische Staatsbibliothek, Cod. hebr. 346, f. 123b-124a, C, short.
5610. New York - Jewish Theological Seminary Ms. 4466, f. 346b-347a, M.
5611. New York - Jewish Theological Seminary Ms. 8097, f. 82b-83a, C.
5612. Oxford - Bodleian Library MS Mich. 543 (Neubauer 1212), f. 72a, C, commentator: Isaac b. Jacob (compiler), rubric: אל נא, short.
5613. Oxford - Bodleian Library MS Mich. 543 (Neubauer 1212), f. 72a margin, C, commentator: Isaac b. Jacob (compiler), rubric: אל נא, short.
5614. Oxford - Bodleian Library MS Opp. 170 (Neubauer 1205), f. 231a-231b, C.
5615. Oxford - Bodleian Library MS Opp. 172 (Neubauer 1211), f. 79a-79b, C, rubric: עקידה.
5616. Oxford - Bodleian Library MS Opp. 619 (Neubauer 2374), f. 183a-183b, M.
5617. Oxford - Bodleian Library MS Opp. 681 (Neubauer 1213), f. 7a-7b, C.
5618. Padova - Biblioteca del Seminario Vescovile Cod. 218, f. 107a-107b, M.
5619. Parma - Biblioteca Palatina Cod. Parm. 3205 (de Rossi 655), f. 258b, C, short.
5620. Vatican - Biblioteca Apostolica ebr. 308, f. 143b, C, commentator: David b. Mose (compiler).
5621. Vatican - Biblioteca Apostolica ebr. 422/1, f. 24a, C, very short.
5622. Vatican - Biblioteca Apostolica ebr. 422/2, f. 38b, CG, no incipit, very short.

Ashkenaz, commentary by Abraham b. Azriel[147]

5623. Frankfurt a M - Stadt- und Universitaetsbibliothek Fol. 16 (Merzbacher 95), f. 108a, C.
5624. Vatican - Biblioteca Apostolica ebr. 301,1, f. 144a, C.

---

[147] Edited by Urbach, ערוגת הבושם, vol. III, p. 323-324.

Asti, Fossano, Moncalvo
5625. New Haven - Yale University, Beinecke Rare Book and MS Library, MS Heb. 52, f. 90a, M.

Tsarfat
5626. London - British Library Add. 11639 (Margoliouth 1056), f. 469b, M, short.
5627. London - David Sofer 5, f. 148a, C, rubric: עקידה.
5628. Oxford - Bodleian Library MS Bodl. Or. 109 (Neubauer 1209), f. 62a-63a, C, commentator: Aaron b. Hayyim haKohen (compiler).
5629. Oxford - Bodleian Library MS Laud. Or. 271 (Neubauer 1206), f. 173a, C, commentator: Aaron b. Hayyim haKohen (compiler).
5630. Oxford - Bodleian Library MS Opp. 171 (Neubauer 1207), f. 93b-94a, C, rubric: אחרת.
5631. Parma - Biblioteca Palatina Cod. Parm. 3007 (de Rossi 654,2), f. 59b-60a, M, plus additional explanation in later hand.
5632. Vatican - Biblioteca Apostolica ebr. 306, f. 97b, C.

אמונת אום נוטרת (א +5635), אלעזר ברבי קליר, חרוז חוזר אשר נשתמש בתוך קדושתא למנחה יום כפור של אליה ב"ר מרדכי

Ashkenaz
5633. Parma - Biblioteca Palatina Cod. Parm. 3507 (Perreau 27), f. 172a, C.

Tsarfat
5634. London - David Sofer 5, f. 165b, C margin.

אמונת אומן עצות מרחק (א 5638), יצחק, סליחה

Ashkenaz
5635. Berlin - Staatsbibliothek (Preussischer Kulturbesitz) Or. Qu. 798-799 (Steinschneider 177), I, f. 142b-143b, M.
5636. Oxford - Bodleian Library MS Mich. 543 (Neubauer 1212), f. 39b-40b, C, commentator: Isaac b. Jacob (compiler), rubric: ועוד זו עקידה.
5637. Oxford - Bodleian Library MS Opp. 681 (Neubauer 1213), f. 73b-74a, C.
5638. Padova - Biblioteca del Seminario Vescovile Cod. 218, f. 216b-217a, M.

Tsarfat
5639. Oxford - Bodleian Library MS Bodl. Or. 109 (Neubauer 1209), f. 63a-63b, C, commentator: Aaron b. Hayyim haKohen (compiler).

אמונת עתים אצלו אמון (א 5647), אברהם, יוצר

Roma
5640. Jerusalem - Jewish National and University Library Ms Heb 8° 4153, f. 165a, C, commentator: Daniel ben Salomo haRofe (compiler), rubric: פי' יוצר שבת קודם שבועות, starts מחצצים.

5641. Oxford - Bodleian Library MS Mich. 312,1 (Neubauer 2276,1), f. 29a, C, rubric: פי' יוצר שבת קודם שבועות, starts מחצצים.

אמונתך אמיתי רבה (א 5652), מאיר ב"ר יצחק, יוצר לשבת וראש חדש
Ashkenaz
5642. Berlin - Staatsbibliothek (Preussischer Kulturbesitz) Or. Qu. 361 (Steinschneider 51), f. 164a-164b, M, no incipit.
5643. Berlin - Staatsbibliothek (Preussischer Kulturbesitz) Or. Qu. 798-799 (Steinschneider 177), I, f. 243a-245a, M.
5644. Budapest - Magyar tudomanyos akademia, MS. Kaufmann A 399, p. 329-332, C, rubric: זולת מראש חודש (later hand).
5645. Cambridge - University Library Add. 504,1, f. 33b-36a, C, rubric: שליח ציבור יסד זה. כאן שייך איילת הסחר ולך אלים. לאופן.
5646. Hamburg - Staats- und Universitaetsbibliothek Cod. hebr. 239a (Steinschneider 130), f. 8b-9a, G.
5647. Jerusalem - Schocken Institute 24100 / Mahzor Nuremberg, f. 11b, M.
5648. Muenchen - Bayerische Staatsbibliothek, Cod. hebr. 393,9, f. 176b-178a, C.
5649. Oxford - Bodleian Library MS Can. Or. 82 (Neubauer 1148), f. 8b-9a, M.
5650. Oxford - Bodleian Library MS Mich. 365 (Neubauer 1208), f. 24b-26a, C, rubric: זולת.
5651. Parma - Biblioteca Palatina Cod. Parm. 2895, p. 440-441, M, margins cut, text damaged.
5652. Parma - Biblioteca Palatina Cod. Parm. 3205 (de Rossi 655), f. 138a-139b, C, rubric: זולת.
5653. Uppsala - Universitetsbibliotek O.Heb.22, f. 133b-135a, M.
5654. Vatican - Biblioteca Apostolica ebr. 318, f. 114a-115a, GI.
Ashkenaz, commentary by Abraham b. Azriel[148]
5655. Frankfurt a M - Stadt- und Universitaetsbibliothek Fol. 16 (Merzbacher 95), f. 87a-90b, C, rubric: זולת.
5656. Vatican - Biblioteca Apostolica ebr. 301,1, f. 107b-110a, C, rubric: זולת.
Ashkenaz, commentary by Eliezer b. Natan
5657. Hamburg - Staats- und Universitaetsbibliothek Cod. hebr. 61 (Steinschneider 153), f. 33b-35a, C, rubric: זולת.
5658. Parma - Biblioteca Palatina Cod. Parm. 3057.12 (de Rossi 1033/10), f. 128a-130b, C.
5659. Warszaw - Uniwersytet, Inst. Orientalistyczny 258, f. 183b-185a, C, rubric: זולת.

---

[148] Edited by Urbach, ערוגת הבושם, vol. III, p. 82-97.

אמונתך בעליונים (א 5656), משולם ב"ר קלונימוס, חלק כ', קדושתא לשחרית יום כפור
Ashkenaz
5660. Berlin - Staatsbibliothek (Preussischer Kulturbesitz) Or. Qu. 798-799 (Steinschneider 177), I, f. 80a-80b, M.
5661. Braunschweig - Landesmuseum fuer Geschichte und Volkstum R 2386, vol. II, f. 193a, M.
5662. Budapest - Magyar tudomanyos akademia, MS. Kaufmann A 400, p. 319-320, C.
5663. Hamburg - Staats- und Universitaetsbibliothek Cod. hebr. 17/2 (Steinschneider 152), f. 152b, C.
5664. Hamburg - Staats- und Universitaetsbibliothek Cod. hebr. 62 (Steinschneider 154), f. 6b-7a, C, very short.
5665. Jerusalem - Jewish National and University Library Ms Heb 8° 3037, f. 124b, M, very short.
5666. London - Montefiore Library 261, f. 45b, C, commentator: Eliezer b. Natan?, very short.
5667. New York - Jewish Theological Seminary Ms. 8097, f. 72b, C, very short.
5668. Oxford - Bodleian Library MS Opp. 172 (Neubauer 1211), f. 41b, C, very short.
5669. Vatican - Biblioteca Apostolica ebr. 308, f. 103b, C, commentator: David b. Mose (compiler), very short.
5670. Vatican - Biblioteca Apostolica ebr. 422/1, f. 15b, C, very short.
Asti, Fossano, Moncalvo
5671. New Haven - Yale University, Beinecke Rare Book and MS Library, MS Heb. 52, f. 108b, M.
Tsarfat
5672. London - David Sofer 5, f. 138b, C.
5673. London - David Sofer 5, f. 138b, C, second commentary on the margin.

אמונתך יודיעו יחודך יבוננו בני אלים (א 5658), אברהם אבן עזרא, סליחה
Yemen
5674. Jerusalem - Sassoon 902, p. 442-443, M.

אמור ישועתך לנפש (א 5671), אפרים ב"ר יצחק מרגנסבורג, זולת לשבת חנוכה
Ashkenaz, commentary by Abraham b. Azriel[149]
5675. Vatican - Biblioteca Apostolica ebr. 301,1, f. 14a-15a, C, rubric: זולת.

---

[149] Edited by Urbach, ערוגת הבושם, vol. I, p. 91-94.

אמיץ שיתין לרומא (א 5697), לשבועות

Ashkenaz

5676. Jerusalem - Schocken Institute 24100 / Mahzor Nuremberg, f. 155b-156a, M.
5677. Muenchen - Bayerische Staatsbibliothek, Cod. hebr. 21, f. 79a-81a, M.
5678. Oxford - Bodleian Library MS Can. Or. 1 (Neubauer 1104), f. 122b-123a, M.

Ashkenaz, commentary by Benjamin b. Abraham Anaw

5679. Jerusalem - Musad haRav Kook 478, p. 19-27, C, rubric: אלפא ביתא ד.
5680. London - Beth Din & Beth Hamidrash 6,9, f. 160a-165a, C, rubric: אלפא ביט.

אמיץ אשר לו הגדולה (א 5698), דוד בן אלעזר בקודה, סליחה

Yemen, commentary by Isaac b. Abraham Wanneh

5681. Chicago-Spertus College of Judaica D 2, 2, f. 211b-212a, M, no incipit.
5682. Jerusalem - Michael Krupp 604, f. 157b-158a, M.
5683. Jerusalem - Sassoon 1158, p. 382-383, M, no incipit.
5684. London - British Library Or. 11122, f. 191b, M, rubric: אל מלך.

אמיץ כח גביר ורב אונים (א 5703), משולם ב"ר קלונימוס, סדר עבודה

Ashkenaz

5685. Berlin - Staatsbibliothek (Preussischer Kulturbesitz) Or. fol. 707 (Steinschneider 34), f. 16a-16b, FC, on line 57-65.
5686. Berlin - Staatsbibliothek (Preussischer Kulturbesitz) Or. Qu. 798-799 (Steinschneider 177), I, f. 128a-132b, M.
5687. Braunschweig - Landesmuseum fuer Geschichte und Volkstum R 2386, vol. II, f. 233b-237b, C.
5688. Budapest - Magyar tudomanyos akademia, MS. Kaufmann A 400, p. 356-357, C.
5689. Budapest - Magyar tudomanyos akademia, MS. Kaufmann A 400, p. 366-369, C, rubric: סדר.
5690. Fulda - Hessische Landesbibliothek A 3 II, f. 123b-127b, C, commentator: Josef, rubric: סדר.
5691. Hamburg - Staats- und Universitaetsbibliothek Cod. hebr. 12 (Steinschneider 102), f. 170b-172a, G.
5692. Hamburg - Staats- und Universitaetsbibliothek Cod. hebr. 17/2 (Steinschneider 152), f. 158a-160b, C, rubric: סדר.
5693. Hamburg - Staats- und Universitaetsbibliothek Cod. hebr. 40c (Steinschneider 111), f. 222a-224b, G.
5694. Hamburg - Staats- und Universitaetsbibliothek Cod. hebr. 62 (Steinschneider 154), f. 17a-20b, C, beginning missing.

5695. Hamburg - Staats- und Universitaetsbibliothek Cod. hebr. 132 (Steinschneider 155), f. 45a-49a, C.
5696. Hamburg - Staats- und Universitaetsbibliothek Cod. hebr. 139 (Steinschneider 115), f. 135b-136a, G.
5697. Jerusalem - Jewish National and University Library Ms Heb 8° 3037, f. 190b-195a, M.
5698. Jerusalem - Schocken Institute 24100 / Mahzor Nuremberg, f. 416b-419a, M.
5699. London - British Library Or. 11318/1, f. 109a-118a, C, rubric: זו העבודה של יום כיפור.
5700. London - Montefiore Library 261, f. 57b-61b, C, commentator: Eliezer b. Natan?.
5701. Moscow - Russian State Library, Ms. Guenzburg 615, f. 103b-107b, C, rubric: סדר.
5702. Muenchen - Bayerische Staatsbibliothek, Cod. hebr. 86, f. 167a-173b, G.
5703. Muenchen - Bayerische Staatsbibliothek, Cod. hebr. 346, f. 81b-86b, C,.
5704. New York - Jewish Theological Seminary Ms. 4466, f. 384a-389a, M.
5705. New York - Jewish Theological Seminary Ms. 8097, f. 80a-82a, C.
5706. Oxford - Bodleian Library MS Mich. 365 (Neubauer 1208), f. 87a-91b, C, rubric: סדר.
5707. Oxford - Bodleian Library MS Opp. 170 (Neubauer 1205), f. 175b-180b, C, rubric: והא לך הסדר של מוסף.
5708. Oxford - Bodleian Library MS Opp. 619 (Neubauer 2374), f. 216a-220b, M.
5709. Paris - Bibliotheque Nationale heb. 653, f. 96a-98b, G.
5710. Parma - Biblioteca Palatina Cod. Parm. 2404 (de Rossi 1104), f. 279a-289b, M, copied from printed edition Saloniki 1550 (Benyamin b. Meir Levi), rubric: פירוש, commentary only on beginning of piyyut.
5711. Parma - Biblioteca Palatina Cod. Parm. 3205 (de Rossi 655), f. 234b-237a, C.
5712. Parma - Biblioteca Palatina Cod. Parm. 3270 (de Rossi 1215), f. 180a-183b, M, rubric: והא לך הסדר של מוסף.
5713. Parma - Biblioteca Palatina Cod. Parm. 3271 (de Rossi 1216), f. 119b-124a, G.
5714. Parma - Biblioteca Palatina Cod. Parm. 3507 (Perreau 27), f. 169a-171b; 173a, C, 2nd part on f. 173a introduced by כה אמיץ לסדר שייך זה.
5715. Vatican - Biblioteca Apostolica ebr. 422/1, f. 18b-19b, C.
5716. Zurich - Zentralbibliothek Heid. 139, f. 84b-88b, C, rubric: סדר של כג, additional marginal notes.

Ashkenaz, commentary by Abraham b. Azriel[150]
5717. Vatican - Biblioteca Apostolica ebr. 301,1, f. 173b-176a, C.

Tsarfat
5718. Oxford - Bodleian Library MS Bodl. Or. 109 (Neubauer 1209), f. 35b-40a, C, commentator: Aaron b. Hayyim haKohen (compiler).
5719. Oxford - Bodleian Library MS Laud. Or. 271 (Neubauer 1206), f. 115b-118a, C, commentator: Aaron b. Hayyim haKohen (compiler).

אמיצי שחק ופליאי תבל (א 5707), יוסף ב"ר שמואל טוב עלם, חלק ג', קדושתא לשבועות

Tsarfat
5720. London - David Sofer 5, f. 68a, C.
5721. Moscow - Russian State Library, Ms. Guenzburg 1665, f. 141b-142a, M, no incipit.
5722. Parma - Biblioteca Palatina Cod. Parm. 3136 (de Rossi 405), f. 169b, M.

אמיצי שחקים ממעל (א 5708), אלעזר ברבי קליר, חלק י"ב, קדושתא למוסף יום כפור

Ashkenaz
5723. Berlin - Staatsbibliothek (Preussischer Kulturbesitz) Or. Qu. 798-799 (Steinschneider 177), I, f. 121a-122a, M.
5724. Braunschweig - Landesmuseum fuer Geschichte und Volkstum R 2386, vol. II, f. 228a-228b, M.
5725. Cambridge - University Library Add. 394,1 (Reif SCR 461), f. 69b-70a, C.
5726. Jerusalem - Schocken Institute 24100 / Mahzor Nuremberg, f. 412b, M, short.
5727. London - British Library Or. 11318/1, f. 103a-103b, C.
5728. London - Montefiore Library 261, f. 56a, C, commentator: Eliezer b. Natan?.
5729. Moscow - Russian State Library, Ms. Guenzburg 191, f. 119b-120b, M.
5730. Muenchen - Bayerische Staatsbibliothek, Cod. hebr. 346, f. 78a-78b, C.
5731. Muenchen - Bayerische Staatsbibliothek, Cod. hebr. 393, f. 149a, C, no incipit, short.
5732. New York - Jewish Theological Seminary Ms. 4466, f. 372b-374b, M, very ecclectic.
5733. New York - Jewish Theological Seminary Ms. 8097, f. 79a, C, short.
5734. New York - Jewish Theological Seminary Ms. 8169 (Acc. 0016), f. 95b-96b, M.

---

[150] Edited by Urbach, ערוגת הבושם, vol. III, p. 518-530.

5735. Oxford - Bodleian Library MS Mich. 365 (Neubauer 1208), f. 83b, C.
5736. Parma - Biblioteca Palatina Cod. Parm. 3507 (Perreau 27), f. 164a, C.
5737. Vatican - Biblioteca Apostolica ebr. 308, f. 118a, C, commentator: David b. Mose (compiler), short.
5738. Zurich - Zentralbibliothek Heid. 139, f. 84a-84b, C, short.

Asti, Fossano, Moncalvo

5739. New Haven - Yale University, Beinecke Rare Book and MS Library, MS Heb. 52, f. 136b-137a, M.

Roma

5740. Berlin - Staatsbibliothek (Preussischer Kulturbesitz) Or. Oct. 3567, f. 8a, FC.
5741. Berlin - Staatsbibliothek (Preussischer Kulturbesitz) Or. Oct. 3567, f. 8a-8b, FC, rubric: פי' אחר ליושב תהלות והוא אמיצי שחקים.
5742. Oxford - Bodleian Library MS Mich. 312,1 (Neubauer 2276,1), f. 7b-8b, C.

Romania

5743. Vatican - Biblioteca Apostolica ebr. 320, f. 322b-323b, M.

Tsarfat

5744. London - British Library Or. 8682, f. 84a-84b, GI.
5745. London - David Sofer 5, f. 151b-152a, C.
5746. Oxford - Bodleian Library MS Bodl. Or. 109 (Neubauer 1209), f. 32a-32b, C, commentator: Aaron b. Hayyim haKohen (compiler).
5747. Oxford - Bodleian Library MS Laud. Or. 271 (Neubauer 1206), f. 115b, C, commentator: Aaron b. Hayyim haKohen (compiler), no incipit.
5748. Parma - Biblioteca Palatina Cod. Parm. 1794 (de Rossi 1061), f. 171b-174a, M.
5749. Parma - Biblioteca Palatina Cod. Parm. 2890 (de Rossi 856), f. 75b, M.
5750. Parma - Biblioteca Palatina Cod. Parm. 3006 (de Rossi 654,1), f. 182a-183a, M.
5751. Vatican - Biblioteca Apostolica ebr. 306, f. 105a-105b, C.

אמל ורבך חמישי כהנבך (א 5713), אלעזר ברבי קליר, קרובה לפורים, פיוט הרכבה

Ashkenaz

5752. Berlin - Staatsbibliothek (Preussischer Kulturbesitz) Or. Qu. 798-799 (Steinschneider 177), II, f. 29b-30a, M.
5753. Budapest - Magyar tudomanyos akademia, MS. Kaufmann A 384, f. 69a-69b, M.
5754. Budapest - Magyar tudomanyos akademia, MS. Kaufmann A 400, p. 73-75, C, no incipit.
5755. Hamburg - Staats- und Universitaetsbibliothek Cod. hebr. 17/2 (Steinschneider 152), f. 23b-24a, C.

5756. Jerusalem - Schocken Institute 24100 / Mahzor Nuremberg, f. 51a, M.
5757. Muenchen - Bayerische Staatsbibliothek, Cod. hebr. 393, f. 98b-99b, C, no incipit.
5758. New York - Jewish Theological Seminary Ms. 4466, f. 3a-3b, M.
5759. Oxford - Bodleian Library MS Opp. 170 (Neubauer 1205), f. 25a-26a, C.
5760. Paris - Bibliotheque Nationale heb. 709, f. 31b-32b, C.
5761. Parma - Biblioteca Palatina Cod. Parm. 1002 (Ta 24), f. 48b-49a, M.
5762. Parma - Biblioteca Palatina Cod. Parm 3000 (de Rossi 378), f. 3a, M.
5763. Parma - Biblioteca Palatina Cod. Parm. 3205 (de Rossi 655), f. 31a-31b, C.
5764. Parma - Biblioteca Palatina Cod. Parm. 3507 (Perreau 27), f. 24b-25a, C.
5765. Vatican - Biblioteca Apostolica ebr. 305,1, f. 35b-36b, C.
5766. Zurich - Zentralbibliothek Heid. 139, f. 3a-3b, C, additional marginal notes.

Tsarfat

5767. London - British Library Add. 11639 (Margoliouth 1056), f. 274a, M.
5768. Moscow - Russian State Library, Ms. Guenzburg 1665, f. 24a-24b, M.
5769. Oxford - Bodleian Library MS Laud. Or. 271 (Neubauer 1206), f. 36b-37a, C, commentator: Aaron b. Hayyim haKohen (compiler).
5770. Oxford - Bodleian Library MS Opp. 171 (Neubauer 1207), f. 31b-32b, C.
5771. Parma - Biblioteca Palatina Cod. Parm. 3136 (de Rossi 405), f. 37b-38a, M.

אמנה גדולה היתה בעם (א 5730), יוסף ב"ר שמואל טוב עלם, חלק ד' קדושתא לשבת הגדול

Ashkenaz

5772. Jerusalem - Schocken Institute 24100 / Mahzor Nuremberg, f. 73a, M.
5773. Muenchen - Bayerische Staatsbibliothek, Cod. hebr. 88, f. 51a, G.
5774. Parma - Biblioteca Palatina Cod. Parm. 3507 (Perreau 27), f. 34b, C, no incipit.

Tsarfat

5775. London - British Library Add. 11639 (Margoliouth 1056), f. 673a-673b, M.
5776. Moscow - Russian State Library, Ms. Guenzburg 1665, f. 46b, M.
5777. Parma - Biblioteca Palatina Cod. Parm. 3136 (de Rossi 405), f. 60a-60b, M.

אמנם אלהי עולם בגד בדגנו בך, סליחה

Romania

5778. Vatican - Biblioteca Apostolica ebr. 320, f. 220a, M.

אמנם אלהי עולם בגדנו במצותיך בגלוי ונעם (א 5737), סליחה

Ashkenaz
5779. Oxford - Bodleian Library MS Mich. 543 (Neubauer 1212), f. 29a, C, commentator: Isaac b. Jacob (compiler).
5780. Oxford - Bodleian Library MS Opp. 619 (Neubauer 2374), f. 260a-260b, M.
5781. Oxford - Bodleian Library MS Opp. 681 (Neubauer 1213), f. 22b-23a, C, short.
5782. Padova - Biblioteca del Seminario Vescovile Cod. 218, f. 177a-177b, M, short.

Ashkenaz, commentary by Abraham b. Azriel[151]
5783. Vatican - Biblioteca Apostolica ebr. 301,1, f. 162a, C, rubric: אחרת.

Tsarfat
5784. London - David Sofer 5, f. 89a, C.
5785. Oxford - Bodleian Library MS Bodl. Or. 109 (Neubauer 1209), f. 63b-64a, C, commentator: Aaron b. Hayyim haKohen (compiler).
5786. Vatican - Biblioteca Apostolica ebr. 306, f. 190b-191a, C.

אמנם אם עונינו הגדולים, סליחה

Yemen
5787. New York - Jewish Theological Seminary Ms. 3028, f. 70a-70b, G.
5788. New York - Jewish Theological Seminary Ms. 3052, f. 87b-88a, M.

Yemen, commentary by Isaac b. Abraham Wanneh
5789. Chicago-Spertus College of Judaica D 2, 2, f. 239a-239b, M, no incipit.
5790. Jerusalem - Benayahu ת 261, f. 166b, M.
5791. Jerusalem - Benayahu ת 282, f. 142b, M.
5792. Jerusalem - Makhon Ben Zvi 1156 (Tubi 155), f. 140a, M, no incipit.
5793. Jerusalem - Makhon Ben Zvi 1174 (Tubi 154), f. 139a-139b, M.
5794. Jerusalem - Michael Krupp 604, f. 177a-177b, M.
5795. Jerusalem - Sassoon 1158, p. 418-419, M, no incipit.
5796. Jerusalem - Sassoon 1174, p. 272, M, no incipit.
5797. London - British Library Or. 11122, f. 216b, M, no incipit.
5798. Muenchen - Bayerische Staatsbibliothek, Cod. hebr. 472, f. 196a, M.
5799. New York - Jewish Theological Seminary Ms. 3013, f. 135a, M, short.
5800. New York - Jewish Theological Seminary Ms. 3294, f. 18b, C.
5801. New York - Public Library, Heb. Ms. 9, f. 132a, M, no incipit.
5802. Strasbourg - Bibliotheque Nationale et Universitaire 3965 (Landauer 39), p. 416, M.

---

[151] Edited by Urbach, ערוגת הבושם, vol. III, p. 441.

אמנם אנחנו חטאנו והעוינו (א 5743), גרשום ב"ר יהודה מאור הגולה, סליחה

Ashkenaz

5803. Berlin - Staatsbibliothek (Preussischer Kulturbesitz) Or. Qu. 798-799 (Steinschneider 177), I, f. 139a-139b, M.

5804. Braunschweig - Landesmuseum fuer Geschichte und Volkstum R 2386, vol. II, f. 244a, M, short.

5805. Budapest - Magyar tudomanyos akademia, MS. Kaufmann A 400, p. 486, C, rubric: אחרת דרבנא גרשם.

5806. Cambridge - University Library Dd. 2.30, f. 82b-83a, G.

5807. Hamburg - Staats- und Universitaetsbibliothek Cod. hebr. 17/2 (Steinschneider 152), f. 177a, C, rubric: אחרת.

5808. Jerusalem - Jewish National and University Library Ms Heb 8° 3037, f. 148a, M.

5809. Jerusalem - Schocken Institute 24100 / Mahzor Nuremberg, f. 283b, M, short.

5810. Moscow - Russian State Library, Ms. Guenzburg 615, f. 158b, C, rubric: אל מלך, short.

5811. Muenchen - Bayerische Staatsbibliothek, Cod. hebr. 346, f. 124b, C, short.

5812. New York - Jewish Theological Seminary Ms. 4466, f. 344b-345a, M.

5813. New York - Jewish Theological Seminary Ms. 8097, f. 83b, C.

5814. Oxford - Bodleian Library MS Mich. 543 (Neubauer 1212), f. 29a-29b, C, commentator: Isaac b. Jacob (compiler).

5815. Oxford - Bodleian Library MS Mich. 543 (Neubauer 1212), f. 70a, C, commentator: Isaac b. Jacob (compiler), rubric: רבנא גרשם, short.

5816. Oxford - Bodleian Library MS Opp. 170 (Neubauer 1205), f. 227b, C.

5817. Oxford - Bodleian Library MS Opp. 681 (Neubauer 1213), f. 25b, C, short.

5818. Padova - Biblioteca del Seminario Vescovile Cod. 218, f. 196a-197a, M.

5819. Parma - Biblioteca Palatina Cod. Parm. 3205 (de Rossi 655), f. 258b, C.

5820. Parma - Biblioteca Palatina Cod. Parm. 3270 (de Rossi 1215), f. 142b, M.

5821. Vatican - Biblioteca Apostolica ebr. 422/1, f. 24a, C, very short.

Ashkenaz, commentary by Abraham b. Azriel[152]

5822. Frankfurt a M - Stadt- und Universitaetsbibliothek Fol. 16 (Merzbacher 95), f. 117a, C.

5823. Vatican - Biblioteca Apostolica ebr. 301,1, f. 157a, C, rubric: אחרת, short.

---

[152] Edited by Urbach, ערוגת הבושם, vol. III, p. 410.

Asti, Fossano, Moncalvo
5824. New Haven - Yale University, Beinecke Rare Book and MS Library, MS Heb. 52, f. 153b-154a, M, ecclectic.

Tsarfat
5825. London - David Sofer 5, f. 91b, C, short.
5826. London - David Sofer 5, f. 161a, C, rubric: סליחה.
5827. London - David Sofer 5, f. 174a-174b, C, rubric: סליחה.
5828. Oxford - Bodleian Library MS Bodl. Or. 109 (Neubauer 1209), f. 44a, C, commentator: Aaron b. Hayyim haKohen (compiler).
5829. Oxford - Bodleian Library MS Bodl. Or. 109 (Neubauer 1209), f. 64a-65a, C, commentator: Aaron b. Hayyim haKohen (compiler).
5830. Oxford - Bodleian Library MS Laud. Or. 271 (Neubauer 1206), f. 170b, C, commentator: Aaron b. Hayyim haKohen (compiler), rubric: דרבנא גרשם, short.
5831. Oxford - Bodleian Library MS Opp. 171 (Neubauer 1207), f. 93b, C, rubric: אחרת.
5832. Parma - Biblioteca Palatina Cod. Parm. 3006 (de Rossi 654,1), f. 228b-229a, M.
5833. Parma - Biblioteca Palatina Cod. Parm. 3007 (de Rossi 654,2), f. 60a, M.
5834. Vatican - Biblioteca Apostolica ebr. 306, f. 88a-88b, C, rubric: סליחות.

אמנם אשמנו עצמו מספר (א 5748), יוסי בן יוסי, מעריב ליום פכור

Ashkenaz
5835. Berlin - Staatsbibliothek (Preussischer Kulturbesitz) Or. Qu. 798-799 (Steinschneider 177), I, f. 58b-61a, M.
5836. Budapest - Magyar tudomanyos akademia, MS. Kaufmann A 400, p. 299-301, C.
5837. Hamburg - Staats- und Universitaetsbibliothek Cod. hebr. 17/2 (Steinschneider 152), f. 148b-150a, C, rubric: לליל כיפורים דר' יוסי בר אביתור היתום.
5838. Jerusalem - Jewish National and University Library Ms Heb 8° 3037, f. 92a-93b, M.
5839. Jerusalem - Schocken Institute 24100 / Mahzor Nuremberg, f. 356(ii)b-(357(ii)a, M.
5840. London - British Library Or. 11318/1, f. 60a-63a, C.
5841. London - Montefiore Library 261, f. 38b-40a, C, commentator: Eliezer b. Natan?.
5842. Moscow - Russian State Library, Ms. Guenzburg 615, f. 88b-91a, C.
5843. Muenchen - Bayerische Staatsbibliothek, Cod. hebr. 346, f. 47b-49b, C.
5844. Muenchen - Bayerische Staatsbibliothek, Cod. hebr. 393, f. 137b, C, very short.
5845. New York - Jewish Theological Seminary Ms. 4466, f. 282b-285a, M.

5846. Oxford - Bodleian Library MS Mich. 365 (Neubauer 1208), f. 64a-66a, C.
5847. Oxford - Bodleian Library MS Opp. 170 (Neubauer 1205), f. 161b-164a, C, rubric: סליחות, incipit דרכך.
5848. Oxford - Bodleian Library MS Opp. 172 (Neubauer 1211), f. 31a-31b, C.
5849. Oxford - Bodleian Library MS Opp. 619 (Neubauer 2374), f. 108a-110a, M.
5850. Paris - Bibliotheque Nationale heb. 653, f. 43b, G.
5851. Parma - Biblioteca Palatina Cod. Parm. 3205 (de Rossi 655), f. 222b-224a, C.
5852. Parma - Biblioteca Palatina Cod. Parm. 3270 (de Rossi 1215), f. 86a, M.
5853. Parma - Biblioteca Palatina Cod. Parm. 3271 (de Rossi 1216), f. 10a-10b, G.
5854. Parma - Biblioteca Palatina Cod. Parm. 3507 (Perreau 27), f. 144a-145a, C.
5855. Vatican - Biblioteca Apostolica ebr. 308, f. 90b-92b, C, commentator: David b. Mose (compiler).
5856. Wolfenbuettel - Niedersaechsisches Staatsarchiv VII B Hs. 192, FC, incomplete, only end.

Tsarfat
5857. London - David Sofer 5, f. 132a-133a, C.
5858. Oxford - Bodleian Library MS Bodl. Or. 109 (Neubauer 1209), f. 9a-10b, C, commentator: Aaron b. Hayyim haKohen (compiler).
5859. Oxford - Bodleian Library MS Opp. 171 (Neubauer 1207), f. 101a-102b, C, rubric: אחרת.
5860. Oxford - Bodleian Library MS Laud. Or. 271 (Neubauer 1206), f. 178a-179b, C, commentator: Aaron b. Hayyim haKohen (compiler), rubric: שמו כלילי צום כיפור .
5861. Parma - Biblioteca Palatina Cod. Parm. 2890 (de Rossi 856), f. 3b-5a, M.
5862. Parma - Biblioteca Palatina Cod. Parm. 3006 (de Rossi 654,1), f. 121a-122b, M.
5863. Vatican - Biblioteca Apostolica ebr. 306, f. 197b-200a, C.

אמנם ידעתי כי אתה (א 5758), שמואל ב"ר קלונימוס?, שיר היחוד ליום ג'

Ashkenaz
5864. Braunschweig - Landesmuseum fuer Geschichte und Volkstum R 2386, vol. II, f. 169b-171a, M, no incipit.
5865. Frankfurt a M - Stadt- und Universitaetsbibliothek Oct. 121/1 (Merzbacher 105), f. 10a-16a, C, no incipit.
5866. Paris - Alliance Israelite Universelle H 133 A, f. 8b-9b, M.

Romania

5867. Vatican - Biblioteca Apostolica ebr. 274, f. 172a-176b, M, kabbalistic, no incipit.

Sepharad

5868. Brussels - Bibliotheque Royale de Belgique 4781, f. 179a-180a, C, no incipit.

אמנם כי דברך לדור ודור קיים (א 5762), אברהם אבן עזרא, פזמון

Sepharad, commentary by David b. Josef Abudarham[153]

5869. Budapest - Magyar tudomanyos akademia, MS. Kaufmann A 405/2, p. 243-244, C, rubric: פזמון רפ״ס עניין שבר וכתישה.
5870. New York - Columbia X893 Ab 93, f. 27a, C, rubric: פזמון.

אמנם כן וצר סוכן בנו (א 5763), סליחה ליום כפור

Ashkenaz

5871. Jerusalem - Schocken Institute 24100 / Mahzor Nuremberg, f. 358(ii)a, M, short.
5872. Muenchen - Bayerische Staatsbibliothek, Cod. hebr. 346, f. 146b, C, rubric: אחרת, short.
5873. Oxford - Bodleian Library MS Opp. 172 (Neubauer 1211), f. 31b-32a, C.

Ashkenaz, commentary by Abraham b. Azriel[154]

5874. Frankfurt a M - Stadt- und Universitaetsbibliothek Fol. 16 (Merzbacher 95), f. 105b, C.

אמנם מפי מונה כוכב בוקר תדנה (א 5767), שמואל בן יהודה, יוצר לשמיני עצרת, נשתמש גם כחלק ו׳, קדושרא ליום ב׳ של סוכות

Tsarfat

5875. London - British Library Or. 2735 (Margoliouth 663), f. 166a-167b, M.
5876. Moscow - Russian State Library, Ms. Guenzburg 1665, f. 171a-171b, M.

אמנם מצוה גוררת מצות (א 5768), אלעזר ברבי קליר, חלק ו׳, קדושתא ליום א׳ של סוכות

Ashkenaz

5877. Berlin - Staatsbibliothek (Preussischer Kulturbesitz) Or. Qu. 798-799 (Steinschneider 177), I, f. 193a-193b, M.
5878. Braunschweig - Landesmuseum fuer Geschichte und Volkstum R 2386, vol. I, f. 136a-136b, M.

---

[153] Edited by Prins, תשלום אבודרהם, p. 111-112.
[154] Edited by Urbach, ערוגת הבושם, vol. III, p. 552.

5879. Budapest - Magyar tudomanyos akademia, MS. Kaufmann A 400 , p. 378-379, C.
5880. Fulda - Hessische Landesbibliothek A 3 II, f. 134a-134b, C, commentator: Josef.
5881. Hamburg - Staats- und Universitaetsbibliothek Cod. hebr. 17/2 (Steinschneider 152), f. 163b-164a, C.
5882. Hamburg - Staats- und Universitaetsbibliothek Cod. hebr. 62 (Steinschneider 154), f. 40b-41a, C, no incipit.
5883. Hamburg - Staats- und Universitaetsbibliothek Cod. hebr. 132 (Steinschneider 155), f. 54a-54b, C, starts לסוככי, incipit afterwards גוררת.
5884. Jerusalem - Jewish National and University Library Ms Heb 8° 3037, f. 256a-256b, M, no incipit.
5885. Jerusalem - Schocken Institute 24100 / Mahzor Nuremberg , f. 482a-482b, M.
5886. London - British Library Add. 18695 (Margoliouth 683), f. 119b-120a, T, Yiddish.
5887. London - British Library Add. 22431 (Margoliouth 662a), f. 93a-93b, M.
5888. London - British Library Or. 11318/1, f. 136b-137b, C.
5889. London - Montefiore Library 261 , f. 72a-72b, C, commentator: Eliezer b. Natan?.
5890. Moscow - Russian State Library, Ms. Guenzburg 615 , f. 113a-113b, C.
5891. Moscow - Russian State Library, Ms. Guenzburg 615 , f. 113b-114a, C.
5892. New York - Jewish Theological Seminary Ms. 4466, f. 448b-449b, M.
5893. Oxford - Bodleian Library MS Mich. 365 (Neubauer 1208) , f. 104b-105b, C.
5894. Oxford - Bodleian Library MS Opp. 170 (Neubauer 1205), f. 185b-186a, C.
5895. Parma - Biblioteca Palatina Cod. Parm. 3205 (de Rossi 655), f. 241a-241b, C, no incipit.
5896. Parma - Biblioteca Palatina Cod. Parm. 3507 (Perreau 27), f. 179a-179b, C, no incipit.
5897. Vatican - Biblioteca Apostolica ebr. 305,1, f. 42b, C, no incipit, starts לסוככי.
5898. Vatican - Biblioteca Apostolica ebr. 422/1, f. 21a, C.
5899. Zurich - Zentralbibliothek Heid. 139 , f. 92a, C, no incipit, additional marginal notes.

Romania
5900. London - London School of Jewish Studies. Asher I.Myers collection 9, f. 221a-221b, M.
5901. Vatican - Biblioteca Apostolica ebr. 320, f. 433a-433b, M.

Tsarfat
5902. London - David Sofer 5, f. 182b, C, rubric: פירוש מאל נא ימצא לעיל יום ראשון של סוכות.
5903. Oxford - Bodleian Library MS Laud. Or. 271 (Neubauer 1206), f. 96b-97a, C, commentator: Aaron b. Hayyim haKohen (compiler), no incipit.
5904. Oxford - Bodleian Library MS Opp. 171 (Neubauer 1207), f. 147a-147b, C, incipit לסוככי למוסכי.
5905. Parma - Biblioteca Palatina Cod. Parm. 1264, f. 57a-57b, M.

אמנם פסו מעדני (א 5776), יוסף ב"ר שמואל טוב עלם, זולת
Ashkenaz, commentary by Abraham b. Azriel[155]
5906. Vatican - Biblioteca Apostolica ebr. 301,1, f. 15a, C, rubric: זולת.

אמנת מאז ארשת ניב שפתים (א 5780), בנימין ב"ר זרח, סליחה
Ashkenaz
5907. Braunschweig - Landesmuseum fuer Geschichte und Volkstum R 2386, vol. II, f. 126a, M.
5908. Jerusalem - Schocken Institute 24100 / Mahzor Nuremberg, f. 267b, M, short.
5909. Muenchen - Bayerische Staatsbibliothek, Cod. hebr. 346, f. 121a, C, rubric: לצום גדליה, very short.
5910. Oxford - Bodleian Library MS Mich. 543 (Neubauer 1212), f. 32b-33a, C, commentator: Isaac b. Jacob (compiler), rubric: אתחיל לכתו' הפי' מצום גדליה.
5911. Oxford - Bodleian Library MS Opp. 681 (Neubauer 1213), f. 8a-8b, C, rubric: סליחות לצום גדליה.
5912. Padova - Biblioteca del Seminario Vescovile Cod. 218, f. 116b-117a, M.
5913. Vatican - Biblioteca Apostolica ebr. 308, f. 21b-22a, C, commentator: David b. Mose (compiler), rubric: אתחיל לכתו' פי' מסליחות שך צום גדליה.
5914. Vatican - Biblioteca Apostolica ebr. 422/1, fr. 29b-30a, C, short.
5915. Vatican - Biblioteca Apostolica ebr. 422/1, f. 44b, CG, no incipit.

אמנת תעל לנהרים (א 5782), אלעזר ברבי קליר, קדושתא לשבת שובה
Tsarfat
5916. Oxford - Bodleian Library MS Opp. 171 (Neubauer 1207), f. 80b-81b, C, rubric: ואתחיל קרובה של עשרת ימי תשובה.

---

[155] Edited by Urbach, ערוגת הבושם, vol. I, p. 94-96.

אמצני אלהי במועדי וחגיגי (א 5791), יוסף אבן אביתור, הושענא
North Africa
5917. Jerusalem - Benayahu ז 27, f. 66a-66b, M.
5918. New York - Jewish Theological Seminary Ms. 4300, f. 19a-20a, C, commentator: Yehuda Toledano.
Yemen, commentary by Samḥun b. Salomo Ḥaloah
5919. Jerusalem - Makhon ben Zvi 2808, f. 64a-67a, C.

אמצת עשור לכפור תמה (א 5793), משולם ב"ר קלונימוס, חלק א', קדושתא לשחרית יום כפור
Ashkenaz
5920. Berlin - Staatsbibliothek (Preussischer Kulturbesitz) Or. Qu. 798-799 (Steinschneider 177), I, f. 70b-71a, M.
5921. Braunschweig - Landesmuseum fuer Geschichte und Volkstum R 2386, vol. II, f. 183a-183b, M.
5922. Budapest - Magyar tudomanyos akademia, MS. Kaufmann A 400, p. 304-305, C.
5923. Hamburg - Staats- und Universitaetsbibliothek Cod. hebr. 40c (Steinschneider 111), f. 175b, G.
5924. Hamburg - Staats- und Universitaetsbibliothek Cod. hebr. 62 (Steinschneider 154), f. 2a-2b, C.
5925. Hamburg - Staats- und Universitaetsbibliothek Cod. hebr. 132 (Steinschneider 155), f. 32b, C.
5926. Jerusalem - Jewish National and University Library Ms Heb 8° 3037, f. 113b-114a, M.
5927. Jerusalem - Schocken Institute 24100 / Mahzor Nuremberg, f. 374b-375a, M.
5928. London - British Library Or. 11318/1, f. 69b-70a, C, no incipit.
5929. London - Montefiore Library 261, f. 41b-42a, C, commentator: Eliezer b. Natan?.
5930. Moscow - Russian State Library, Ms. Guenzburg 191, f. 82b-83a, M.
5931. Moscow - Russian State Library, Ms. Guenzburg 615, f. 92b, C.
5932. Muenchen - Bayerische Staatsbibliothek, Cod. hebr. 86, f. 98a-98b, G.
5933. Muenchen - Bayerische Staatsbibliothek, Cod. hebr. 346, f. 51b, C.
5934. Muenchen - Bayerische Staatsbibliothek, Cod. hebr. 393, f. 139b, C, no incipit.
5935. New York - Jewish Theological Seminary Ms. 4466, f. 302a, M.
5936. New York - Jewish Theological Seminary Ms. 8097, f. 71a, C.
5937. New York - Jewish Theological Seminary Ms. 8169 (Acc. 0016), f. 64b, M.
5938. Oxford - Bodleian Library MS Mich. 365 (Neubauer 1208), f. 68a, C, no incipit.

5939. Oxford - Bodleian Library MS Opp. 170 (Neubauer 1205), f. 164(ii)b-165a, C, rubric: קדושתא.
5940. Oxford - Bodleian Library MS Opp. 172 (Neubauer 1211), f. 35b, C.
5941. Oxford - Bodleian Library MS Opp. 619 (Neubauer 2374), f. 137a-137b, M.
5942. Paris - Bibliotheque Nationale heb. 653, f. 53b, G.
5943. Parma - Biblioteca Palatina Cod. Parm. 3205 (de Rossi 655), f. 224b, C.
5944. Parma - Biblioteca Palatina Cod. Parm. 3271 (de Rossi 1216), f. 32a-32b, G.
5945. Vatican - Biblioteca Apostolica ebr. 308, f. 97b-98a, C, commentator: David b. Mose (compiler).
5946. Vatican - Biblioteca Apostolica ebr. 422/1, f. 15a, C, short.
5947. Zurich - Zentralbibliothek Heid. 139, f. 75a-75b, C.

Asti, Fossano, Moncalvo
5948. New Haven - Yale University, Beinecke Rare Book and MS Library, MS Heb. 52, f. 101a, M.

Romania
5949. Vatican - Biblioteca Apostolica ebr. 320, f. 276b, M, rubric: קדושתא מק׳ משולם בר קלונימוס.

Tsarfat
5950. Bern - Burgerbibliothek A 409, f. 77a-77b, G.
5951. London - British Library Or. 8682, f. 64b, Gl.
5952. London - David Sofer 5, f. 136a, C.
5953. Oxford - Bodleian Library MS Bodl. Or. 109 (Neubauer 1209), f. 17b-18a, C, commentator: Aaron b. Hayyim haKohen (compiler), rubric: קדושתא.
5954. Oxford - Bodleian Library MS Laud. Or. 271 (Neubauer 1206), f. 111b, C, commentator: Aaron b. Hayyim haKohen (compiler), no incipit.
5955. Parma - Biblioteca Palatina Cod. Parm. 1794 (de Rossi 1061), f. 110a-110b, M.
5956. Parma - Biblioteca Palatina Cod. Parm. 2125 (de Rossi 812), f. 38b, C.
5957. Parma - Biblioteca Palatina Cod. Parm. 2890 (de Rossi 856), f. 22a, M.
5958. Parma - Biblioteca Palatina Cod. Parm. 3006 (de Rossi 654,1), f. 136a, M.
5959. Vatican - Biblioteca Apostolica ebr. 306, f. 75b-76a, C.

אמר אויב ארדוף כאריה (א 5798), יהודה הלוי, חלק ז׳, קדושתא לשבת זכור
Carpentras, commentary by Mordekhai b. Josef of Rocco Martino
5960. Cincinnati - Hebrew Union College 246/1, f. 23b-24b, C, rubric: פי׳ סליק אמר אויב וכו׳.

Sepharad, commentary by Josef Garad
5961. Oxford - Bodleian Library Heb.e.10 (Neubauer 2746/1), f. 8b-9a, C, rubric: סלוק.

אמר יצחק לאברהם אבוהי (א 5812), רשות בארמית לדיבור חמישי

Ashkenaz
5962. Berlin - Staatsbibliothek (Preussischer Kulturbesitz) Or. Qu. 798-799 (Steinschneider 177), II, f. 162b-163b, M.
5963. Cambridge - University Library Add. 394,1 (Reif SCR 461), f. 62b-63a, C.
5964. Jerusalem - Schocken Institute 24100 / Mahzor Nuremberg, f. 162a, M, rubric: פי' לדברא.
5965. Moscow - Russian State Library, Ms. Guenzburg 206, f. 90b, M.
5966. Muenchen - Bayerische Staatsbibliothek, Cod. hebr. 21, f. 84a-84b, M.
5967. Muenchen - Bayerische Staatsbibliothek, Cod. hebr. 393, f. 152b, C, no incipit.
5968. Oxford - Bodleian Library MS Can. Or. 1 (Neubauer 1104), f. 116a-117b, M.
5969. Oxford - Bodleian Library MS Opp. 170 (Neubauer 1205), f. 98b, C.
5970. Parma - Biblioteca Palatina Cod. Parm. 3205 (de Rossi 655), f. 185a-185b, C.

Ashkenaz, commentary by Benjamin b. Abraham Anaw
5971. Jerusalem - Musad haRav Kook 478, p. 47-50, C, rubric: אלפא ביתא ח.
5972. London - Beth Din & Beth Hamidrash 6,9, f. 177a-178b, C, rubric: אלפא ביט.

Tsarfat
5973. Cambridge - University Library Add. 561.1, f. 80b-81a, MT, Hebrew.
5974. Jerusalem - Schocken Institute 19623, f. 182a-183a, M, commentator: Yehuda b. Eliezer Zvi, rubric: פי' לדברא.
5975. London - British Library Add. 11639 (Margoliouth 1056), f. 680a-680b, M.
5976. London - British Library Or. 2735 (Margoliouth 663), f. 33b-34b, M.
5977. London - David Sofer 5, f. 62b-63a, C.
5978. Moscow - Russian State Library, Ms. Guenzburg 1665, f. 128a-128b, M.
5979. New York - Jewish Theological Seminary Ms. 4460, f. 65a-65b, M, pages damaged.
5980. Parma - Biblioteca Palatina Cod. Parm. 1902, f. 147b-149a, M.
5981. Parma - Biblioteca Palatina Cod. Parm. 2574, f. 120b-121a, G, commentator: Simḥa b. Samuel, cp. Mahzor Vitry.
5982. Parma - Biblioteca Palatina Cod. Parm. 3136 (de Rossi 405), f. 162b, M.

אמר משה נביא (א 5818), פיוט בארמית לשבועות

Ashkenaz
5983. Berlin - Staatsbibliothek (Preussischer Kulturbesitz) Or. Qu. 798-799 (Steinschneider 177), II, f. 160b-161b, M.
5984. Cambridge - University Library Add. 394,1 (Reif SCR 461), f. 61a-61b, C.
5985. Jerusalem - Schocken Institute 24100 / Mahzor Nuremberg, f. 160a-161a, M.
5986. Moscow - Russian State Library, Ms. Guenzburg 206, f. 89b-90a, M.
5987. Muenchen - Bayerische Staatsbibliothek, Cod. hebr. 21, f. 82a-83a, M.
5988. Oxford - Bodleian Library MS Can. Or. 1 (Neubauer 1104), f. 113a-114a, M.

Tsarfat
5989. Cambridge - University Library Add. 561.1, f. 79a-80a, MT, Hebrew.
5990. Jerusalem - Schocken Institute 19623, f. 181b-182b, M, commentator: Yehuda b. Eliezer Zvi.
5991. London - British Library Add. 11639 (Margoliouth 1056), f. 678b-679b, M.
5992. London - British Library Or. 2735 (Margoliouth 663), f. 27b-29a, M.
5993. London - David Sofer 5, f. 61a-61b, C.
5994. New York - Jewish Theological Seminary Ms. 4460, f. 63b, M, page damaged.
5995. Parma - Biblioteca Palatina Cod. Parm. 1902, f. 144b-146a, M.
5996. Parma - Biblioteca Palatina Cod. Parm. 2574, f. 119a-119b, G, commentator: Simḥa b. Samuel, cp. Mahzor Vitry.

אמרה גולה וסורה (א 5828), שלמה אבן גבירול, לשבת נצבים, בתימן: סליחה

Yemen, commentary by Isaac b. Abraham Wanneh
5997. Chicago-Spertus College of Judaica D 2, 2, f. 205b-206a, M, no incipit.
5998. Jerusalem - Michael Krupp 604, f. 156a-156b, M, rubric: אל מלך.
5999. Jerusalem - Sassoon 1158, p. 391-392, M, no incipit.
6000. London - British Library Or. 11122, f. 197a-197b, M, no incipit.

אמרה סנונה וצרופה (א 5831), אלעזר ברבי קליר, חלק ו', קדושתא לשבת פרה

Ashkenaz
6001. Berlin - Staatsbibliothek (Preussischer Kulturbesitz) Or. Qu. 798-799 (Steinschneider 177), II, f. 34a-34b, M.
6002. Budapest - Magyar tudomanyos akademia, MS. Kaufmann A 384, f. 79a-79b, M.
6003. Hamburg - Staats- und Universitaetsbibliothek Cod. hebr. 17/2 (Steinschneider 152), f. 25b-26a, C.

6004. Hamburg - Staats- und Universitaetsbibliothek Cod. hebr. 225, f. 40a-41a, G.
6005. Jerusalem - Schocken Institute 24100 / Mahzor Nuremberg, f. 63a-63b, M.
6006. Muenchen - Bayerische Staatsbibliothek, Cod. hebr. 88, f. 39a-39b, G.
6007. Muenchen - Bayerische Staatsbibliothek, Cod. hebr. 393, f. 101b-102b, C, no incipit.
6008. Muenchen - Bayerische Staatsbibliothek, Cod. hebr. 393, f. 102b-103a, C, no incipit.
6009. New York - Jewish Theological Seminary Ms. 4466, f. 10a-11b, M.
6010. Oxford - Bodleian Library MS Opp. 170 (Neubauer 1205), f. 30b-31a, C.
6011. Paris - Bibliotheque Nationale heb. 709, f. 37a-37b, C.
6012. Parma - Biblioteca Palatina Cod. Parm. 1002 (Ta 24), f. 56b, M.
6013. Parma - Biblioteca Palatina Cod. Parm 3000 (de Rossi 378), f. 16a-17a, M.
6014. Parma - Biblioteca Palatina Cod. Parm. 3205 (de Rossi 655), f. 34b-35b, C.
6015. Vatican - Biblioteca Apostolica ebr. 305,1, f. 21b-22a, C, no incipit.
6016. Zurich - Zentralbibliothek Heid. 139, f. 6a-7a, C, no incipit, additional marginal notes.

Tsarfat
6017. London - British Library Add. 11639 (Margoliouth 1056), f. 275b-276a, M, rubric: פזמון.
6018. London - David Sofer 5, f. 28b-29b, C.
6019. Moscow - Russian State Library, Ms. Guenzburg 1665, f. 35a-35b, M.
6020. Oxford - Bodleian Library MS Laud. Or. 271 (Neubauer 1206), f. 40b-41a, C, commentator: Aaron b. Hayyim haKohen (compiler).
6021. Oxford - Bodleian Library MS Opp. 171 (Neubauer 1207), f. 38a-39a, C, rubric: פזמון.
6022. Parma - Biblioteca Palatina Cod. Parm. 3136 (de Rossi 405), f. 49b-50a, M.
6023. Vatican - Biblioteca Apostolica ebr. 306, f. 150b-151b, C.

אמרה ציון איך יצאוני בני בצאתם (א 5832), אברהם אבן עזרא, קינה
Carpentras, commentary by Mordekhai b. Josef of Rocco Martino
6024. Cincinnati - Hebrew Union College 246/1, f. 68b-69a, C, rubric: פי' קינה אמרה ציון.

Yemen, commentary by Isaac b. Abraham Wanneh
6025. Jerusalem - Sassoon 1158, p. 176, M.
6026. London - British Library Or. 11122, f. 105a, M, no incipit.

אמרו לאלהים אדירים (כעל גמולות) (א 5859), שמעון ב"ר יצחק, חלק ו', קדושתא ליום
ז' של פסח

Ashkenaz
6027. Berlin - Staatsbibliothek (Preussischer Kulturbesitz) Or. Qu. 798-799 (Steinschneider 177), II, f. 103b-104b, M.
6028. Braunschweig - Landesmuseum fuer Geschichte und Volkstum R 2386, vol. I, f. 51a-51b, M.
6029. Budapest - Magyar tudomanyos akademia, MS. Kaufmann A 384 , f. 235b-236b, M.
6030. Hamburg - Staats- und Universitaetsbibliothek Cod. hebr. 17/2 (Steinschneider 152), f. 39a-39b, C, commentator: Ephraim b. Jacob of Bonn, rubric: רבינו גרשם הקשה לרבינו שמעון והלא פסוק אז הוחל לקרוא בשם יי ופסוק הקורא למי הים וישפכם נדרש בבראשי' רבא על דור אנוש איך יסדתם אתה על דור המבול. ושמעתי שיסד רבי' גרשם חרוזה אחת במקומה ולא ראיתי' עד הנה. אפרים.
6031. Jerusalem - Schocken Institute 24100 / Mahzor Nuremberg , f. 110b, M, short.
6032. London - British Library Add. 18695 (Margoliouth 683) , f. 56b-57b, T, Yiddish.
6033. Muenchen - Bayerische Staatsbibliothek, Cod. hebr. 88, f. 96b-98a, G.
6034. New York - Jewish Theological Seminary Ms. 4466, f. 91a-93a, M, no incipit, ecclectic.
6035. Paris - Bibliotheque Nationale heb. 709 , f. 108a-109a, C, incipit כעל גמילות.
6036. Parma - Biblioteca Palatina Cod. Parm. 3205 (de Rossi 655), f. 114b-115a, C.
6037. Parma - Biblioteca Palatina Cod. Parm. 3507 (Perreau 27), f. 79b-81a, C.
6038. Zurich - Zentralbibliothek Heid. 139, f. 42b-43a, C, incipit כעל, additional marginal notes.

Tsarfat
6039. London - David Sofer 5, f. 46b-47a, C, short commentary on the refrain in smaller letters before the commentary on the piyyut.
6040. Moscow - Russian State Library, Ms. Guenzburg 1665, f. 106a-107a, M.
6041. Oxford - Bodleian Library MS Laud. Or. 271 (Neubauer 1206), f. 76b-77a, C, commentator: Ephraim b. Jacob of Bonn (mainly), Aaron b. Hayyim haKohen (compiler).
6042. Parma - Biblioteca Palatina Cod. Parm. 3136 (de Rossi 405), f. 124b-126a, M, incipit כעל.

אמרו לאלהים אמת וישר פעלו (א 5861), פיוט למוסף יום כפור

Tsarfat

6043. Oxford - Bodleian Library MS Laud. Or. 271 (Neubauer 1206), f. 115a, C, commentator: Aaron b. Hayyim haKohen (compiler).

אמרו לאלהים ארך אפים (א 5862), משולם ב"ר קלונימוס, חלק ט', קדושתא לשחרית יום כפור

Ashkenaz

6044. Berlin - Staatsbibliothek (Preussischer Kulturbesitz) Or. Qu. 798-799 (Steinschneider 177), I, f. 75b-76b, M.
6045. Braunschweig - Landesmuseum fuer Geschichte und Volkstum R 2386, vol. II, f. 188a-189b, M.
6046. Budapest - Magyar tudomanyos akademia, MS. Kaufmann A 400, p. 312-314, C.
6047. Hamburg - Staats- und Universitaetsbibliothek Cod. hebr. 17/2 (Steinschneider 152), f. 151a, C.
6048. Hamburg - Staats- und Universitaetsbibliothek Cod. hebr. 62 (Steinschneider 154), f. 4a, C, short.
6049. Hamburg - Staats- und Universitaetsbibliothek Cod. hebr. 132 (Steinschneider 155), f. 36a, C.
6050. Jerusalem - Jewish National and University Library Ms Heb 8° 3037, f. 119a-120b, M.
6051. Jerusalem - Schocken Institute 24100 / Mahzor Nuremberg, f. 378a-378b, M, short.
6052. London - British Library Or. 11318/1, f. 74a-74b, C.
6053. London - Montefiore Library 261, f. 43b, C, commentator: Eliezer b. Natan?, short.
6054. Moscow - Russian State Library, Ms. Guenzburg 191, f. 88a-89b, M.
6055. Muenchen - Bayerische Staatsbibliothek, Cod. hebr. 346, f. 53a-53b, C.
6056. Muenchen - Bayerische Staatsbibliothek, Cod. hebr. 393, f. 142a, C, no incipit, very short.
6057. New York - Jewish Theological Seminary Ms. 8169 (Acc. 0016), f. 69a-70a, M, short.
6058. Oxford - Bodleian Library MS Mich. 365 (Neubauer 1208), f. 69b, C, short.
6059. Oxford - Bodleian Library MS Opp. 172 (Neubauer 1211), f. 38b, C.
6060. Oxford - Bodleian Library MS Opp. 619 (Neubauer 2374), f. 144a-146a, M, ecclectic.
6061. Parma - Biblioteca Palatina Cod. Parm. 3205 (de Rossi 655), f. 225b-226a, C.
6062. Parma - Biblioteca Palatina Cod. Parm. 3271 (de Rossi 1216), f. 38a-39b, G.

6063. Parma - Biblioteca Palatina Cod. Parm. 3507 (Perreau 27), f. 147a-147b, C.
6064. Vatican - Biblioteca Apostolica ebr. 308, f. 100a, C, commentator: David b. Mose (compiler).
6065. Vatican - Biblioteca Apostolica ebr. 422/1, f. 15b, C, short.

Asti, Fossano, Moncalvo
6066. New Haven - Yale University, Beinecke Rare Book and MS Library, MS Heb. 52, f. 104b-105b, M.

Romania
6067. Vatican - Biblioteca Apostolica ebr. 320, f. 282b-284a, M, short.

Tsarfat
6068. Bern - Burgerbibliothek A 409, f. 81b-82b, G.
6069. London - David Sofer 5, f. 137b-138a, C.
6070. Ms London British Library Or. 8682, f. 67b-68b, GI.
6071. Oxford - Bodleian Library MS Bodl. Or. 109 (Neubauer 1209), f. 19b-20a, C, commentator: Aaron b. Hayyim haKohen (compiler).
6072. Oxford - Bodleian Library MS Laud. Or. 271 (Neubauer 1206), f. 112b-113a, C, commentator: Aaron b. Hayyim haKohen (compiler), no incipit.
6073. Parma - Biblioteca Palatina Cod. Parm. 1794 (de Rossi 1061), f. 119b-122a, M.
6074. Parma - Biblioteca Palatina Cod. Parm. 2890 (de Rossi 856), f. 27a-27b, M, short.
6075. Parma - Biblioteca Palatina Cod. Parm. 3006 (de Rossi 654,1), f. 140b-141b, M.

אמרות יי אמרות טהורות (א 5900), יוסף ב"ר שמואל טוב עלם, קדושתא לשבועות

Tsarfat
6076. London - David Sofer 5, f. 67b-68a, C.
6077. Moscow - Russian State Library, Ms. Guenzburg 1665, f. 141a-141b, M.
6078. Parma - Biblioteca Palatina Cod. Parm. 3136 (de Rossi 405), f. 168b-169a, M.

אמרות יי אמרות תמימות (א 5903), אהרן בן יוסף הרופא, פרשת מצורע

Karaite, commentary by Berakha b. Josef haKohen
6079. New York - Jewish Theological Seminary Ms. 3367, f. 103a-105a, C, rubric: פירוש פרשת המצורע.
6080. St. Petersburg - Inst. of Oriental Studies of the Russian Academy B 431, f. 71b-73a, C, rubric: פרשת מצורע.
6081. St. Petersburg - Russian National Library, Evr. IV 50, f. 78a-80a, C, rubric: מצורע.

אמרות האל טהורות מפנינים הם יקרות (א 5909), יהודה הלוי, מאורה

Ashkenaz

6082. Muenchen - Bayerische Staatsbibliothek, Cod. hebr. 69, f. 68a-68b, M.

אמרות טהורות בהרצותך (א 5910), דוד בן גדליה, יוצר לשבועות

Ashkenaz

6083. New York - Jewish Theological Seminary Ms. 4466, f. 161b-163a, M.
6084. Parma - Biblioteca Palatina Cod. Parm. 3205 (de Rossi 655), f. 126b-127a, C.

אמרנו נגזרנו לנו (א 5943), שלמה הבבלי, סליחה

Ashkenaz

6085. Budapest - Magyar tudomanyos akademia, MS. Kaufmann A 400, p. 442-446, C, rubric: אחרת שלמונית.
6086. Cambridge - University Library Dd. 2.30, f. 56b-57b, G.
6087. Hamburg - Staats- und Universitaetsbibliothek Cod. hebr. 17/2 (Steinschneider 152), f. 131b-133a, C, rubric: אחרת שלמונית.
6088. Jerusalem - Schocken Institute 24100 / Mahzor Nuremberg, f. 275b-276a, M.
6089. Jerusalem - Schocken Institute 24100 / Mahzor Nuremberg, f. 434b-435a, M.
6090. Karlsruhe - Badische Landesbibliothek, Schwarzach 20, f. 1a-1b, FC, only end.
6091. Moscow - Russian State Library, Ms. Guenzburg 190, f. 24b-25b, G.
6092. Moscow - Russian State Library, Ms. Guenzburg 615, f. 138a-139b, C, rubric: בשם הדר בערבות אתחיל פי׳ מסליחות.
6093. Muenchen - Bayerische Staatsbibliothek, Cod. hebr. 346, f. 129b-130a, C.
6094. Muenchen - Bayerische Staatsbibliothek, Cod. hebr. 346, f. 161b, C.
6095. Oxford - Bodleian Library MS Mich. 543 (Neubauer 1212), f. 61b-63a, C, commentator: Isaac b. Jacob (compiler).
6096. Oxford - Bodleian Library MS Opp. 170 (Neubauer 1205), f. 219a-220b, C.
6097. Oxford - Bodleian Library MS Opp. 172 (Neubauer 1211), f. 75a-76a, C.
6098. Oxford - Bodleian Library MS Opp. 681 (Neubauer 1213), f. 47b-50b, C.
6099. Parma - Biblioteca Palatina Cod. Parm. 3205 (de Rossi 655), f. 267a-268a, C.
6100. Vatican - Biblioteca Apostolica ebr. 422/1, f. 27a, C.
6101. Vatican - Biblioteca Apostolica ebr. 422/1, f. 40b, CG, no incipit, short.

Ashkenaz, commentary by Abraham b. Azriel[156]
6102. Frankfurt a M - Stadt- und Universitaetsbibliothek Fol. 16 (Merzbacher 95), f. 114a-115a, C, incipit צפו מים.

Tsarfat
6103. London - British Library Add. 11639 (Margoliouth 1056), f. 465b-467a, M.
6104. London - David Sofer 5, f. 159b-160b, C, rubric: סליחות של מוסף.
6105. Oxford - Bodleian Library MS Laud. Or. 271 (Neubauer 1206), f. 122b-123a, C, commentator: Aaron b. Hayyim haKohen (compiler).
6106. Oxford - Bodleian Library MS Opp. 171 (Neubauer 1207), f. 110b-111b, C, rubric: אחרת.
6107. Parma - Biblioteca Palatina Cod. Parm. 1794 (de Rossi 1061), f. 26a-27b, M.
6108. Parma - Biblioteca Palatina Cod. Parm. 3006 (de Rossi 654,1), f. 198b-199b, M.
6109. Vatican - Biblioteca Apostolica ebr. 306, f. 173a-173b, C.

אמרר בבכי מפני יד שלוחה (א 5946), מנחם ב"ר מכיר, סליחה

Ashkenaz
6110. Muenchen - Bayerische Staatsbibliothek, Cod. hebr. 88, f. 157a-157b, G.

Ashkenaz, commentary by Abraham b. Azriel[157]
6111. Vatican - Biblioteca Apostolica ebr. 301,1, f. 140a-140b, C.

אמרת לעבדיך, סליחה

Ashkenaz
6112. Oxford - Bodleian Library MS Mich. 543 (Neubauer 1212), f. 5a-6a, C, commentator: Isaac b. Jacob (compiler).

אמרת רנן ארוכה (א 5954), יהודה בן מנחם, יוצר לשבת וזאת הברכה

Ashkenaz
6113. Cambridge - University Library Add. 394.2 (Reif SCR 462), f. 102a-103a, C, rubric: פי' יוצר וזאת הברכה.

Italia
6114. Parma - Biblioteca Palatin Cod. Parm. 2248 (de Rossi 149/2), f. 38a-40a, C, rubric: פירוש יוצר וזאת הברכה.

Roma
6115. Jerusalem - Jewish National and University Library Ms Heb 8° 4153, f. 146b-147b, C, commentator: Daniel ben Salomo haRofe (compiler), rubric: פי' יוצר לזאת ברכה.

---

[156] Edited by Urbach, ערוגת הבושם, vol. III, p. 584-589.
[157] Edited by Urbach, ערוגת הבושם, vol. III, p. 299-301.

אמרתי אוי לי כי נא לי כי יסף יי מוטה עלי, סליחה

Yemen, commentary by Isaac b. Abraham Wanneh
6117. Chicago-Spertus College of Judaica D 2, 2, f. 244a-244b, M.
6118. London - British Library Or. 11122, f. 222a-222b, M.

אמרתי אחכמה והיא רחוקה (א 5955), אלעזר ברבי קליר, חלק ד, קדושתא לשבת פרה

Ashkenaz
6119. Berlin - Staatsbibliothek (Preussischer Kulturbesitz) Or. Qu. 798-799 (Steinschneider 177), II, f. 33b, M, short.
6120. Budapest - Magyar tudomanyos akademia, MS. Kaufmann A 384, f. 77b, M.
6121. Hamburg - Staats- und Universitaetsbibliothek Cod. hebr. 17/2 (Steinschneider 152), f. 25a, C.
6122. Jerusalem - Schocken Institute 24100 / Mahzor Nuremberg, f. 61b, M, short.
6123. Muenchen - Bayerische Staatsbibliothek, Cod. hebr. 88, f. 38b, G.
6124. Muenchen - Bayerische Staatsbibliothek, Cod. hebr. 393, f. 101a-101b, C, no incipit.
6125. New York - Jewish Theological Seminary Ms. 4466, f. 9b, M, incipit בחרות.
6126. Oxford - Bodleian Library MS Opp. 170 (Neubauer 1205), f. 29b-30a, C.
6127. Paris - Bibliotheque Nationale heb. 709, f. 36b, C, incipit אל נא.
6128. Parma - Biblioteca Palatina Cod. Parm. 1002 (Ta 24), f. 56a, M, incipit אל נא.
6129. Parma - Biblioteca Palatina Cod. Parm 3000 (de Rossi 378), f. 15a, M, incipit אל נא.
6130. Parma - Biblioteca Palatina Cod. Parm. 3205 (de Rossi 655), f. 34a, C.
6131. Vatican - Biblioteca Apostolica ebr. 305,1, f. 21a, C, no incipit.
6132. Zurich - Zentralbibliothek Heid. 139, f. 5b, C, no incipit, additional marginal notes.

Tsarfat
6133. London - British Library Add. 11639 (Margoliouth 1056), f. 275a, M.
6134. Moscow - Russian State Library, Ms. Guenzburg 1665, f. 34b, M, incipit אל נא.
6135. Oxford - Bodleian Library MS Laud. Or. 271 (Neubauer 1206), f. 39b, C, commentator: Aaron b. Hayyim haKohen (compiler).
6136. Oxford - Bodleian Library MS Opp. 171 (Neubauer 1207), f. 37a-37b, C, incipit אל נא.

6137. Parma - Biblioteca Palatina Cod. Parm. 3136 (de Rossi 405), f. 49a, M, incipit אל.

6138. Vatican - Biblioteca Apostolica ebr. 306, f. 149b-150a, C, incipit אל נא.

אמרתי לפושעים אכלה פשעים (א 5965), סליחה

Ashkenaz

6139. Berlin - Staatsbibliothek (Preussischer Kulturbesitz) Or. Qu. 798-799 (Steinschneider 177), I, f. 110b-111a, M.

6140. New York - Jewish Theological Seminary Ms. 4466, f. 359b, M, short.

6141. Vatican - Biblioteca Apostolica ebr. 422/1, f. 17b, C, short.

Tsarfat

6142. Oxford - Bodleian Library MS Bodl. Or. 109 (Neubauer 1209), f. 29a, C, commentator: Aaron b. Hayyim haKohen (compiler), short.

אמרתי נגזרתי בחרוב בית תפארתי (א 5967), סעדיה, סליחה

Yemen

6143. New York - Jewish Theological Seminary Ms. 3028, f. 101a, G.

6144. New York - Jewish Theological Seminary Ms. 3193, f. 140b-141a, M.

Yemen, commentary by Isaac b. Abraham Wanneh

6145. Chicago-Spertus College of Judaica D 2, 2, f. 228b-229a, M, no incipit.

6146. Jerusalem - Sassoon 1158, p. 316-317, M, no incipit.

6147. London - British Library Or. 11122, f. 205a-205b, M, no incipit.

אמרתי שעו מני אמרר (א 5971), קלונימוס ב"ר יהודה, סליחה

Ashkenaz

6148. Berlin - Staatsbibliothek (Preussischer Kulturbesitz) Or. Qu. 798-799 (Steinschneider 177), II, f. 198a-199b, M.

6149. Budapest - Magyar tudomanyos akademia, MS. Kaufmann A 400, p. 187-188, C.

6150. Jerusalem - Schocken Institute 24100 / Mahzor Nuremberg, f. 204b, M, short.

אמרתך צרופה ועדותיך צדק (א 5973), שמעון ב"ר יצחק, חלק א', קדושתא לראש השנה

Ashkenaz

6151. Berlin - Staatsbibliothek (Preussischer Kulturbesitz) Or. Qu. 798-799 (Steinschneider 177), I, f. 34b-35b, M.

6152. Braunschweig - Landesmuseum fuer Geschichte und Volkstum R 2386, vol. II, f. 110b, M, no incipit.

6153. Cambridge - University Library Or. 785, f. 58b-59a, G.

6154. Darmstadt - Hessisches Landes- und Hochschulbibliothek Cod. Or. 15, f. 33b-34a, M.
6155. Hamburg - Staats- und Universitaetsbibliothek Cod. hebr. 17/2 (Steinschneider 152), f. 121b-122a, C, rubric: קדושתא גם משלו.
6156. Hamburg - Staats- und Universitaetsbibliothek Cod. hebr. 40c (Steinschneider 111), f. 146b, G.
6157. Hamburg - Staats- und Universitaetsbibliothek Cod. hebr. 132 (Steinschneider 155), f. 23b-24a, C, no incipit.
6158. Hamburg - Staats- und Universitaetsbibliothek Cod. hebr. 225, f. 151b, G.
6159. Jerusalem - Jewish National and University Library Ms Heb 8° 3037, f. 51b-52a, M.
6160. London - British Library Or. 11318/1, f. 39b-40a, C.
6161. London - Montefiore Library 261, f. 27b, C, commentator: Eliezer b. Natan?.
6162. Moscow - Russian State Library, Ms. Guenzburg 191, f. 34a-34b, M.
6163. Moscow - Russian State Library, Ms. Guenzburg 615, f. 86a, C, short.
6164. Muenchen - Bayerische Staatsbibliothek, Cod. hebr. 86, f. 61b-62b, G.
6165. Muenchen - Bayerische Staatsbibliothek, Cod. hebr. 346, f. 35b, C.
6166. New York - Jewish Theological Seminary Ms. 4466, f. 249b-250b, M, short.
6167. New York - Jewish Theological Seminary Ms. 8097, f. 65a, C.
6168. New York - Jewish Theological Seminary Ms. 8169 (Acc. 0016), f. 33a, M.
6169. Oxford - Bodleian Library MS Mich. 365 (Neubauer 1208), f. 49b, C.
6170. Oxford - Bodleian Library MS Opp. 170 (Neubauer 1205), f. 143b, C, short.
6171. Oxford - Bodleian Library MS Opp. 172 (Neubauer 1211), f. 20b, C.
6172. Oxford - Bodleian Library MS Opp. 619 (Neubauer 2374), f. 57b-58a, M, short.
6173. Parma - Biblioteca Palatina Cod. Parm. 3205 (de Rossi 655), f. 217a, C, short.
6174. Parma - Biblioteca Palatina Cod. Parm. 3507 (Perreau 27), f. 131b-132a, C, short.
6175. Vatican - Biblioteca Apostolica ebr. 308, f. 74b-75a, C, commentator: David b. Mose (compiler).
6176. Vatican - Biblioteca Apostolica ebr. 422/1, f. 12b, C, short.
6177. Zurich - Zentralbibliothek Heid. 139, f. 70b, C, short, no incipit, additional marginal notes.

Asti, Fossano, Moncalvo
6178. New Haven - Yale University, Beinecke Rare Book and MS Library, MS Heb. 52, f. 52a-52b, M.

Romania
6179. Vatican - Biblioteca Apostolica ebr. 320, f. 179b-180b, M.
Tsarfat
6180. London - British Library Or. 8682, f. 35b-36a, Gl.
6181. London - David Sofer 5, f. 119b-120a, C.
6182. Oxford - Bodleian Library MS Laud. Or. 271 (Neubauer 1206), f. 156b-157a, C, commentator: Aaron b. Hayyim haKohen (compiler), no incipit.
6183. Oxford - Bodleian Library MS Opp. 171 (Neubauer 1207), f. 67a, C, short.
6184. Parma - Biblioteca Palatina Cod. Parm. 2125 (de Rossi 812), f. 29b, C, short.
6185. Parma - Biblioteca Palatina Cod. Parm. 3006 (de Rossi 654,1), f. 68b-69a, M.
6186. Vatican - Biblioteca Apostolica ebr. 306, f. 66a-66b, C, no incipit.

אמת אבאר הלכות סוכה (א 5977), יצחק השנירי, זולת
Narbonne, commentary by Meir Meili of Narbonne[158]
6187. London - British Library Add. 19778, f. 35b, C, no incipit.

אמת אל מאין ליש בחסדו המציאנו (א 5983), אהרן בן יוסף הרופא, פרשת תזריע
Karaite, commentary by Berakha b. Josef haKohen
6188. New York - Jewish Theological Seminary Ms. 3367, f. 100b-103a, C, rubric: פירוש פרשת תזריע.
6189. St. Petersburg - Inst. of Oriental Studies of the Russian Academy B 431, f. 70a-71b, C, rubric: פרשת תזריע.
6190. St. Petersburg - Russian National Library, Evr. IV 50, f. 76a-78a, C, rubric: תזריע.

אמת אתה הוא ראשון (א 5992), יואל ב"ר יצחק הלוי, סליחה
Ashkenaz
6191. Vatican - Biblioteca Apostolica ebr. 308, f. 15a-15b, C, commentator: David b. Mose (compiler).
6192. Vatican - Biblioteca Apostolica ebr. 308, f. 163b, C, commentator: David b. Mose (compiler).

אמת בספרך בראתך עולמרך (א 5998), אברהם אבן עזרא, פזמון
Sepharad, commentary by David b. Josef Abudarham[159]
6193. Budapest - Magyar tudomanyos akademia, MS. Kaufmann A 405/2, p. 259, C, rubric: ובכן ולך תעלה קדוש' וכו'. אמת ספרך.

---
[158] Edited by Sofer, ספר המכתם, p. 152.
[159] Edited by Prins, תשלום אבודרהם, p. 139-140.

6194. Holon - Yehuda Nahum 278, f. 1b, C, very short.
6195. New York - Columbia X893 Ab 93, f. 32b, C, rubric: ובכן ולך תעלה קדוש' כי אתה אלהינו.

אמת השמים כסאך והארץ הדום רגליך (א 6009), אהרן בן יוסף הרופא, פרשת פקודי
Karaite, commentary by Berakha b. Josef haKohen
6196. New York - Jewish Theological Seminary Ms. 3367, f. 90a-93b, C, rubric: פירוש פרשת אלה פקודי.
6197. St. Petersburg - Inst. of Oriental Studies of the Russian Academy B 431, f. 63b-65b, C, rubric: פרשת פקודי.
6198. St. Petersburg - Russian National Library, Evr. IV 50 , f. 66b-69a, C, rubric: פ' פקודי.

אמת יהגה חכי משפטי יי אדוני (א 6022), אליהו ב"ר מנחם הזקן, אזהרות
Ashkenaz
6199. Alessandria - Biblioteca Civica Fr. ebr. 2-9, FC.[160]
6200. Erlangen - Universitaetsbibliothek 1270/6 (Roth 88), f. 1a-1b, FC, versus the end of the Azharot.
Italia
6201. Oxford - Bodleian Library MS Mich. 190/9 (Neubauer 914), f. 145a-148b, C, critique rather than commentary.
Tsarfat
6202. London - British Library Add. 11639 (Margoliouth 1056), f. 647b-656a, M.
6203. London - David Sofer 5, f. 71a-78a, C.
6204. Moscow - Russian State Library, Ms. Guenzburg 1665, f. 132a-139a, M.
6205. Oxford - Bodleian Library MS Opp. 171 (Neubauer 1207), f. 44a-52b, C.
6206. Parma - Biblioteca Palatina Cod. Parm. 3136 (de Rossi 405), f. 177b-186a, M.
6207. Vatican - Biblioteca Apostolica ebr. 306, f. 1a-45b, C.[161]

אמת משל היה באמיתות קדמוני משליך (א 6060), מאיר ב"ר יצחק, זולת לשבת נחמו
Ashkenaz
6208. Berlin - Staatsbibliothek (Preussischer Kulturbesitz) Or. Qu. 798-799 (Steinschneider 177), I, f. 254b-255b, M.
6209. Budapest - Magyar tudomanyos akademia, MS. Kaufmann A 399 , p. 432-436, C, rubric: זולת לנחמו.

---

[160] M. Perani prepares a publication of this manuscript.
[161] E. Kupfer, פרוש אזהרות דרבנא אליהו הזקן בר מנחם ממנש, מאת חכם אחד מחוג בניו של רבנו חיים בר חננאל הכהן קובץ על יד N.S., 11, 1989, p. 109–207.

6210. Cambridge - University Library Add. 504,1 , f. 49a-50a, C, rubric: 'ר מאיר ב'ר' יצחק חזק ואמץ יסד זה וחתום בסוף.
6211. Frankfurt a M - Stadt- und Universitaetsbibliothek Oct. 227 , f. 164b-165a, M.
6212. Jerusalem - Schocken Institute 24100 / Mahzor Nuremberg , f. 222a, M.
6213. Lund - Universitetsbibliothek Ms. L.O. 2, f. 107b-108b, M.
6214. Muenchen - Bayerische Staatsbibliothek, Cod. hebr. 69, f. 62b, M.
6215. Oxford - Bodleian Library MS Can. Or. 82 (Neubauer 1148) , f. 31b-32a, M, rubric: זולת.
6216. Oxford - Bodleian Library MS Mich. 365 (Neubauer 1208), f. 32a-32b, C.
6217. Oxford - Bodleian Library MS Opp. 170 (Neubauer 1205), f. 248a-248b, C.
6218. Parma - Biblioteca Palatina Cod. Parm. 2895 , p. 407-408, M, rubric: זולת.
6219. Parma - Biblioteca Palatina Cod. Parm. 3205 (de Rossi 655), f. 159b-160b, C, rubric: זולת.
6220. Vatican - Biblioteca Apostolica ebr. 318, f. 117b-118a, GI.

Ashkenaz, commentary by Abraham b. Azriel[162]

6221. Frankfurt a M - Stadt- und Universitaetsbibliothek Fol. 16 (Merzbacher 95), f. 16b-18b, C, rubric: זולת.
6222. Vatican - Biblioteca Apostolica ebr. 301,1, f. 48b-50a, C, rubric: זולת.

Ashkenaz, commentary by Eliezer b. Natan

6223. Hamburg - Staats- und Universitaetsbibliothek Cod. hebr. 61 (Steinschneider 153), f. 38b-39a, C, rubric: זולת לשבת נחמו.
6224. Parma - Biblioteca Palatina Cod. Parm. 3057.12 (de Rossi 1033/10), f. 143a-146a, C, rubric: זולת.
6225. Warszaw - Uniwersytet, Inst. Orientalistyczny 258 , f. 188b-189a, C, rubric: זולת.

Tsarfat

6226. Oxford - Bodleian Library MS Laud. Or. 271 (Neubauer 1206), f. 188b, 192a, C, commentator: Aaron b. Hayyim haKohen (compiler).

אנא אדון בינה הגיגי, סליחה

Ashkenaz, commentary by Abraham b. Azriel[163]

6227. Frankfurt a M - Stadt- und Universitaetsbibliothek Fol. 16 (Merzbacher 95), f. 110a, C.

---

[162] Edited by Urbach, ערוגת הבושם, vol. I, p. 296-304.
[163] Edited by Urbach, ערוגת הבושם, vol. III, p. 569-570.

אנא אדון הסליחות (א 6099), סליחה

Ashkenaz

6228. Muenchen - Bayerische Staatsbibliothek, Cod. hebr. 346, f. 145a, C, very short.

6229. Oxford - Bodleian Library MS Opp. 172 (Neubauer 1211), f. 77b-78a, C.

6230. Vatican - Biblioteca Apostolica ebr. 308, f. 110a, C, commentator: David b. Mose (compiler).

6231. Vatican - Biblioteca Apostolica ebr. 422/1, f. 31a, C.

אנא אדון הרחמים השקיפה ממרומים (א 6103), סליחה

Ashkenaz

6232. Muenchen - Bayerische Staatsbibliothek, Cod. hebr. 346, f. 145a, C, very short.

6233. Oxford - Bodleian Library MS Opp. 172 (Neubauer 1211), f. 87a, C, no incipit.

אנא אדון מלא רחמים עגומים, סליחה

Ashkenaz

6234. Muenchen - Bayerische Staatsbibliothek, Cod. hebr. 346, f. 137a, C, rubric: אחרת, short.

אנא יי האל הגדול והגובור והנורא (א 6150), בנימין ב"ר זרח, סליחה

Ashkenaz

6235. Berlin - Staatsbibliothek (Preussischer Kulturbesitz) Or. Qu. 798-799 (Steinschneider 177), I, f. 148a-149a, M.

6236. Jerusalem - Schocken Institute 24100 / Mahzor Nuremberg, f. 396a-396b, M.

6237. New York - Jewish Theological Seminary Ms. 8097, f. 82b, C, very short.

6238. Oxford - Bodleian Library MS Opp. 681 (Neubauer 1213), f. 31a-32a, C.

6239. Vatican - Biblioteca Apostolica ebr. 308, f. 110a, C, commentator: David b. Mose (compiler), short.

Ashkenaz, commentary by Abraham b. Azriel[164]

6240. Frankfurt a M - Stadt- und Universitaetsbibliothek Fol. 16 (Merzbacher 95), f. 107a, C.

אנא יי רחמיך יראו (א 6167), סליחה

North Africa, commentary by David b. Josef Abudarham

6241. New York - Jewish Theological Seminary Ms. 5426, f. 60a-60b, C.

---

[164] Edited by Urbach, ערוגת הבושם, vol. III, p. 555-556.

6242. New York - Jewish Theological Seminary Ms. 5426, f. 61b, M, rubric: פירוש פזמון.
Sepharad, commentary by David b. Josef Abudarham[165]
6243. Budapest - Magyar tudomanyos akademia, MS. Kaufmann A 405/2, p. 178, C, rubric: ליל יום הכפירים.
6244. Cincinnati - Hebrew Union College 490, f. 1a, C, rubric: ליל יום הכפורים.
6245. New York - Columbia X893 Ab 93, f. 1b, C, rubric: ליל יום הכפירים.
6246. New York - Jewish Theological Seminary Ms. 3011, f. 1a, C, rubric: ליל יום הכפירים.

אנא אזון חין תאבי ישעך (6171 א), הושענא
Ashkenaz
6247. Berlin - Staatsbibliothek (Preussischer Kulturbesitz) Or. Qu. 361 (Steinschneider 51), f. 120a-120b, M.
6248. Berlin - Staatsbibliothek (Preussischer Kulturbesitz) Or. Qu. 798-799 (Steinschneider 177), I, f. 208a, M.
6249. Budapest - Magyar tudomanyos akademia, MS. Kaufmann A 399, p. 303, C.
6250. Budapest - Magyar tudomanyos akademia, MS. Kaufmann A 400, p. 535-536, C.
6251. Cambridge - University Library Add. 394,1 (Reif SCR 461), f. 76a, C, rubric: הושענא.
6252. Cambridge - University Library Or. 790, f. 34a-34b, C.
6253. Frankfurt a M - Stadt- und Universitaetsbibliothek Oct. 227, f. 115b, M.
6254. Hamburg - Staats- und Universitaetsbibliothek Cod. hebr. 17/2 (Steinschneider 152), f. 167a-167b, C.
6255. Jerusalem - Schocken Institute 24100 / Mahzor Nuremberg, f. 494b, M.
6256. London - British Library Add. 18695 (Margoliouth 683), f. 153b-154a, T, Yiddish.
6257. London - British Library Add. 22431 (Margoliouth 662a), f. 123b, M.
6258. London - British Library Add. 27208 (Margolioth 654), f. 272b-273b, M.
6259. London - British Library Add. 27556, f. 131b-132a, M.
6260. Lund - Universitetsbibliothek Ms. L.O. 2, f. 88a, M.
6261. Moscow - Russian State Library, Ms. Guenzburg 615, f. 129a, C, rubric: אחרת.
6262. New York - Jewish Theological Seminary Ms. 4466, f. 480b-481a, M.
6263. Oxford - Bodleian Library MS Can. Or. 1 (Neubauer 1104), f. 29b-30a, M.

---

[165] Edited by Prins, תשלום אבודרהם, p. 3.

6264. Oxford - Bodleian Library MS Mich. 573 (Neubauer 1099), f. 21a-21b, M.
6265. Oxford - Bodleian Library MS Opp 160 (Neubauer 1204), f. 241a-242a, C, commentator: Elazar b. Yehuda of Worms.[166]
6266. Oxford - Bodleian Library MS Opp. 170 (Neubauer 1205), f. 203a, C.
6267. Parma - Biblioteca Palatina Cod. Parm. 2895, p. 222-223, M.
6268. Parma - Biblioteca Palatina Cod. Parm. 3057.9 (de Rossi 1033), f. 96b-97a, C.
6269. Parma - Biblioteca Palatina Cod. Parm. 3205 (de Rossi 655), f. 251a, C.
6270. Uppsala - Universitetsbibliotek O.Heb.22, f. 113a-113b, M.
6271. Vatican - Biblioteca Apostolica ebr. 305,1, f. 44a-44b, C, no incipit.
6272. Vatican - Biblioteca Apostolica ebr. 308, f. 158a-158b, C, commentator: David b. Mose (compiler).
6273. Verona - Seminario Maggiore 34, f. 170a-170b, M.

Ashkenaz, commentary by Eliezer b. Natan

6274. Hamburg - Staats- und Universitaetsbibliothek Cod. hebr. 61 (Steinschneider 153), f. 24a-24b, C.
6275. London - Montefiore Library 261, f. 87b, C.
6276. Paris - Bibliotheque Nationale heb. 327/2, f. 40a-40b, C.
6277. Warszaw - Uniwersytet, Inst. Orientalistyczny 258, f. 196b-197a, C.

Italia

6278. Moscow - Russian State Library, Ms. Guenzburg 533, f. 34b-37b, C, commentator: Yehoshua Segre, rubric: לימוד י"ד.
6279. Moscow - Russian State Library, Ms. Guenzburg 1594, f. 24b-25a, C, no incipit.
6280. Torino - Archivio Terracini 1499, p. 229-230, C, commentator: Zakharya David Shabbetai Segre, rubric: פירוש אנא אזון.

Roma

6281. Jerusalem - Jewish National and University Library Ms Heb 8° 4153, f. 142b-143a, C, commentator: Daniel ben Salomo haRofe (compiler).
6282. Oxford - Bodleian Library MS Mich. 312,1 (Neubauer 2276,1), f. 10b-11a, C.

Romania

6283. London - London School of Jewish Studies. Asher I.Myers collection 9, f. 211b-212a, M.
6284. Roma - Collegio Rabbinico Italiano 110, f. 14b, M.
6285. Vatican - Biblioteca Apostolica ebr. 285/30, f. 235b-236a, C.

Tsarfat

6286. Jerusalem - Schocken Institute 19623, f. 126b-127a, M, commentator: Yehuda b. Eliezer Zvi.

---

[166] Edited by Katzenellenbogen, פירוש ההושענות, p. 50-53.

HEBREW LITURGICAL POETRY   375

6287. London - British Library Or. 2735 (Margoliouth 663), f. 150a-150b, M.
6288. London - David Sofer 5, f. 192b, C.
6289. Moscow - Russian State Library, Ms. Guenzburg 1665, f. 183a, M.
6290. Parma - Biblioteca Palatina Cod. Parm. 1264, f. 98a, M.
6291. Parma - Biblioteca Palatina Cod. Parm. 1902, f. 179b-180a, M.
6292. Vatican - Biblioteca Apostolica ebr. 306, f. 123b, C.

אנא אזון שועת חנון (א 6175), אלעזר ברבי קליר, חלק ו', קדושתא למוסף יום כפור
Ashkenaz
6293. Berlin - Staatsbibliothek (Preussischer Kulturbesitz) Or. Qu. 798-799 (Steinschneider 177), I, f. 119a-119b, M.
6294. Hamburg - Staats- und Universitaetsbibliothek Cod. hebr. 132 (Steinschneider 155), f. 44b, C, incipit only, no commentary.
6295. Jerusalem - Jewish National and University Library Ms Heb 8° 3037, f. 178a, M.
6296. London - Montefiore Library 261, f. 55b, C, commentator: Eliezer b. Natan?.
6297. Muenchen - Bayerische Staatsbibliothek, Cod. hebr. 346, f. 77a-77b, C.
6298. Oxford - Bodleian Library MS Mich. 365 (Neubauer 1208), f. 82b-83a, C.
6299. Oxford - Bodleian Library MS Opp. 619 (Neubauer 2374), f. 205a-205b, M, short.
6300. Parma - Biblioteca Palatina Cod. Parm. 3507 (Perreau 27), f. 163a-163b, C.
6301. Vatican - Biblioteca Apostolica ebr. 422/2, f. 40a, CG, no incipit, very short.
6302. Zurich - Zentralbibliothek Heid. 139, f. 84a, C, short.

Asti, Fossano, Moncalvo
6303. New Haven - Yale University, Beinecke Rare Book and MS Library, MS Heb. 52, f. 135a, M, ecclectic.

Tsarfat
6304. London - British Library Or. 8682, f. 83a-83b, GI.
6305. Parma - Biblioteca Palatina Cod. Parm. 3006 (de Rossi 654,1), f. 180b-181a, M.

אנא אל אחד הנקדש בקדושות שלשה (א 6180), הושענא
haAri, commentary by Mose b. Hayyim Pesante
6306. New York - Jewish Theological Seminary Ms. 4696, f. 11b-16a, C.

North Africa
6307. Jerusalem - Benayahu ז 27, f. 65b, M, no incipit.

Sepharad, commentary by Josef Garad
6308. Oxford - Bodleian Library Heb.e.10 (Neubauer 2746/1), f. 26a, C, rubric: הושענות, no incipit.

Yemen
6309. Chicago-Spertus College of Judaica D 10, f. 123b-124a, M, no incipit.
6310. Jerusalem - Benayahu ת 414, f. 86a-86b, M, no incipit.
6311. Jerusalem - Musad haRav Kook 327, f. 80a, M, beginning missing.
6312. Jerusalem - Musad haRav Kook 334, f. 88a, M.
6313. Jerusalem - Musad haRav Kook 335, f. 94a, M.
6314. Jerusalem - Musad haRav Kook 952, f. 8b-9b, M, rubric: הושענא.
6315. Jerusalem - Sassoon 264, f. 93b, M, no incipit.
6316. Jerusalem - Sassoon 902, p. 174, M, no incipit.
6317. New York - Jewish Theological Seminary Ms. 4488, f. 68a, M.
6318. New York - Jewish Theological Seminary Ms. 9325, f. 74b-75a, M.
6319. New York - Public Library, Heb. Ms. 10, f. 58a, M, no incipit.
6320. Ramat Gan - Universitat Bar Ilan 62, f. 28a-28b, G, margins damaged.
6321. Ramat Gan - Universitat Bar Ilan 63, f. 21b, G, margins damaged.

Yemen, commentary by Isaac b. Abraham Wanneh
6322. Jerusalem - Benayahu ת 261, f. 81a, M, rubric: הושענא.
6323. Jerusalem - Benayahu ת 282, f. 74a-74b, M, rubric: הושענא, no incipit.
6324. Jerusalem - Israel Museum 180/78, f. 10b-11a, C, rubric: הושענא.
6325. Jerusalem - Makhon Ben Zvi 1156 (Tubi 155), f. 71b, M, rubric: הושענא.
6326. Jerusalem - Makhon Ben Zvi 1169 (Tubi 159), f. 62a, M.
6327. Jerusalem - Makhon Ben Zvi 1174 (Tubi 154), f. 83a, M, rubric: הושענא.
6328. Jerusalem - Makhon ben Zvi 1186 (Tubi 205), f. 4b, M, incipit 'הושע בקדושות.
6329. Jerusalem - Michael Krupp 604, f. 91b, M, rubric: הושענא, no incipit.
6330. Jerusalem - Michael Krupp 1990, f. 98b-99a, M, rubric: הושענא, margins damaged.
6331. Jerusalem - Musad haRav Kook 325, f. 121a-121b, M, rubric: הושענא, no incipit.
6332. Jerusalem - Musad haRav Kook 330, f. 67a-67b, M.
6333. Jerusalem - Musad haRav Kook 347, f. 57b, M, no incipit.
6334. Jerusalem - Sassoon 1158, p. 213, M, rubric: הושענא.
6335. Jerusalem - Sassoon 1174, p. 141-142, M, rubric: הושענא.
6336. Jerusalem - Schocken Institute 70028, f. 187b, M, rubric: הושענא.
6337. Jerusalem - Yehiel haLevi 4, f. 87a, M, no incipit.
6338. London - British Library Or. 11122, f. 121a, M, rubric: הושענא.
6339. Manchester - John Rylands University Library, Ms. Gaster 5, f. 147a-147b, M, rubric: הושענא.

6340. Muenchen - Bayerische Staatsbibliothek, Cod. hebr. 472, f. 98a-98b, M, rubric: הושענא.
6341. Nahariya - Menahem and Saida Yaakob 284, f. 9b-10a, M.
6342. New York - Jewish Theological Seminary Ms. 3013, f. 73b-74a, M, rubric: הושענא, margins damaged.
6343. New York - Jewish Theological Seminary Ms. 3028, f. 245a-246b, C, rubric: ליום שלישי, no incipit.
6344. New York - Jewish Theological Seminary Ms. 3108, f. 78b-79a (plus one uncounted folio), C, rubric: ליום שלישי, no incipit.
6345. New York - Jewish Theological Seminary Ms. 3193, f. 161a-161b, M, rubric: הוש׳.
6346. New York - Jewish Theological Seminary Ms. 3295, f. 89a, M, rubric: הושענא.
6347. New York - Jewish Theological Seminary Ms. 4195, f. 13a-14a, M, incipit שהנקד.
6348. New York - Public Library, Heb. Ms. 9, f. 71a-71b, M, rubric: הוש׳.
6349. Oxford - Bodleian Library MS Opp. Add. fol. 58 (Neubauer 2498), f. 141a, M, rubric: הושענא.
6350. Paris - G. Epstein 23/57, f. 100b-101a, C, no incipit.
6351. Philadelphia - University of Pennsylvania HB 2, f. 97b, M, rubric: הושענא.
6352. Ramat Gan - Universitat Bar Ilan 703, f. 193a-193b, M, rubric: הושענא.
6353. San Francisco - California State Library, Sutro Branch MS 154 (Brinner 125), f. 107a-108a, C, rubric: ליום שלישי, no incipit.
6354. Strasbourg - Bibliotheque Nationale et Universitaire 3965 (Landauer 39), p. 235-236, M, rubric: הושענא.

Yemen, commentary by Samḥun b. Salomo Ḥaloah
6355. Jerusalem - Makhon ben Zvi 2808, f. 58a-63a, C.

Yemen, commentary by Simon b. Tsemaḥ Duran
6356. Jerusalem - Michael Krupp 1758, f. 7a-7b, M, rubric: פירוש.

אנא אל אחד ומבייש אומרים שנים (א 6181), הושענא

Carpentras
6357. New York - Jewish Theological Seminary Ms. 1609, f. 98a, C, kabbalistic, no incipit.

haAri, commentary by Mose b. Hayyim Pesante
6358. New York - Columbia University X 893 J 558, f. 201a, C.
6359. New York - Jewish Theological Seminary Ms. 4696, f. 11b, C.

haAri, commentary by Simon b. Tsemaḥ Duran
6360. New York - Columbia University X 893 J 558, f. 201a, C.

Italia

6361. Torino - Archivio Terracini 1499, p. 81-83, C, commentator: Zakharya David Shabbetai Segre, rubric: פירוש אנא אל אחד ומבייש אומרים שנים.

Narbonne, commentary by Meir Meili of Narbonne[167]

6362. London - British Library Add. 19778, f. 35b, C, rubric: ליום שני.

North Africa, commentary by Simon b. Tsemaḥ Duran

6363. New York - Jewish Theological Seminary Ms. 4121, f. 41b-42b, C, rubric: ליום שני, .

6364. New York - Jewish Theological Seminary Ms. 4121, f. 42b-44a, M, rubric: ליום שלישי.

North Africa, commentary by Yehuda Toledano

6365. New York - Jewish Theological Seminary Ms. 4300, f. 10b-13a, C.

Yemen

6366. New York - Alfred Moldovan HH, f. 7a-7b, M, rubric: הושענא.
6367. Chicago-Spertus College of Judaica D 10, f. 122a-122b, M, incipit אומרי.
6368. Jerusalem - Benayahu ת 414, f. 84b, M.
6369. Jerusalem - Benayahu ת 414, f. 85b, M.
6370. Jerusalem - Michael Krupp 3391, f. 4b, M.
6371. Jerusalem - Musad haRav Kook 334, f. 87b, M.
6372. Jerusalem - Musad haRav Kook 952, f. 7a-7b, M, rubric: הושענא.
6373. Jerusalem - Sassoon 264, f. 92b-93a, M, no incipit.
6374. Jerusalem - Sassoon 902, p. 173-174, M, no incipit.
6375. New York - Jewish Theological Seminary Ms. 4488, f. 67b, M.
6376. New York - Jewish Theological Seminary Ms. 9325, f. 72b, M.
6377. New York - Public Library, Heb. Ms. 10, f. 57a-57b, M, margins damaged.
6378. Ramat Gan - Universitat Bar Ilan 62, f. 28a, G, margins damaged.
6379. Ramat Gan - Universitat Bar Ilan 63, f. 21a, G, margins damaged.

Yemen, commentary by Isaac b. Abraham Wanneh

6380. Chicago-Spertus College of Judaica D 1, f. 194b, M.
6381. Jerusalem - Benayahu ת 261, f. 80b, M, rubric: הושענא.
6382. Jerusalem - Benayahu ת 282, f. 73b-74a, M, rubric: הושענא.
6383. Jerusalem - Israel Museum 180/78, f. 8a-8b, M, rubric: הושענא, no incipit.
6384. Jerusalem - Makhon Ben Zvi 1156 (Tubi 155), f. 71a, M, rubric: הושענא.
6385. Jerusalem - Makhon Ben Zvi 1168 (Tubi 157), f. 24a, M, margins damaged.
6386. Jerusalem - Makhon Ben Zvi 1174 (Tubi 154), f. 82a-82b, M, rubric: הושענא.

---

[167] Edited by Sofer, ספר המכתם, p. 152-153.

6387. Jerusalem - Makhon ben Zvi 1186 (Tubi 205), f. 3b-4a, M, rubric: הושענא, incipit ומבייש.
6388. Jerusalem - Michael Krupp 604, f. 91a, M, rubric: הושענא.
6389. Jerusalem - Michael Krupp 1990, f. 97b-98a, M, rubric: הושענא, margins damaged.
6390. Jerusalem - Musad haRav Kook 325, f. 102b, M, rubric: חידושין.
6391. Jerusalem - Musad haRav Kook 325, f. 120b, M.
6392. Jerusalem - Musad haRav Kook 330, f. 66b-67a, M.
6393. Jerusalem - Musad haRav Kook 347, f. 57a, M.
6394. Jerusalem - Sassoon 1158, p. 212, M, rubric: הושענא.
6395. Jerusalem - Sassoon 1174, p. 140-141, M, rubric: הושענא.
6396. Jerusalem - Schocken Institute 70028, f. 186b, M, rubric: הושענא.
6397. Jerusalem - Yehiel haLevi 4, f. 86b, M.
6398. London - British Library Or. 11122, f. 120b-121a, M, rubric: הושענא.
6399. London - British Library Or. 11121, f. 131b, C, rubric: הושענא, no incipit.
6400. Manchester - John Rylands University Library, Ms. Gaster 5, f. 146a-146b, M, rubric: הושענא.
6401. Muenchen - Bayerische Staatsbibliothek, Cod. hebr. 472, f. 97b, M, rubric: הושענא.
6402. Nahariya - Menahem and Saida Yaakob 284, f. 7a, M.
6403. New York - Jewish Theological Seminary Ms. 3013, f. 73a-73b, M, margins damaged.
6404. New York - Jewish Theological Seminary Ms. 3028, f. 244a-245a, C, rubric: ליום שני.
6405. New York - Jewish Theological Seminary Ms. 3108, f. 77a-78b, C, rubric: ליום שני.
6406. New York - Jewish Theological Seminary Ms. 3193, f. 160a-160b, M, rubric: 'הושע.
6407. New York - Jewish Theological Seminary Ms. 3295, f. 88a-88b, M, rubric: הושענא.
6408. New York - Jewish Theological Seminary Ms. 4195, f. 9a-10a, M, incipit מבייש.
6409. New York - Public Library, Heb. Ms. 9, f. 70b, M, rubric: 'הוש, no incipit.
6410. Oxford - Bodleian Library MS Opp. Add. fol. 58 (Neubauer 2498), f. 140a, M, rubric: הושענא.
6411. Paris - G. Epstein 23/57, f. 99a-99b, C, no incipit.
6412. Philadelphia - University of Pennsylvania HB 2, f. 97a, M, rubric: הושענא, short.
6413. Ramat Gan - Universitat Bar Ilan 703, f. 192a-192b, M, rubric: הושענא.
6414. San Francisco - California State Library, Sutro Branch MS 154 (Brinner 125), f. 106b-107, C, rubric: ליום שני.

6415. Strasbourg - Bibliotheque Nationale et Universitaire 3965 (Landauer 39), p. 233-234, M, rubric: הושענא.

Yemen, commentary by Samḥun b. Salomo Ḥaloah

6416. Jerusalem - Makhon ben Zvi 2808, f. 33a-34a, C, no incipit.

6417. Jerusalem - Makhon ben Zvi 2808, f. 34a-43a, C

Yemen, commentary by Simon b. Tsemaḥ Duran

6418. Jerusalem - Michael Krupp 1758, f. 5a-6a, M, rubric: פירוש.

Yemen, commentary by Yiḥya b. Josef Tsalaḥ

6419. Montreal - Elberg 203, f. 4b-5a, M, no incipit.

הושענא, (6182 א) אנא אל' אחד ושמו אחד

Carpentras

6420. New York - Jewish Theological Seminary Ms. 1609, f. 98a, C, kabbalistic, rubric: יום א', no incipit.

haAri, commentary by Mose b. Hayyim Pesante

6421. New York - Columbia University X 893 J 558, f. 199b, M.

6422. New York - Jewish Theological Seminary Ms. 4696, f. 10a-10b, C.

haAri, commentary by Simon b. Tsemaḥ Duran

6423. New York - Columbia University X 893 J 558, f. 199b, M.

Italia

6424. Torino - Archivio Terracini 1499, p. 51-54, C, commentator: Zakharya David Shabbetai Segre, rubric: פירוש הושענא אנא אל אחד ושמו אחד.

Narbonne, commentary by Meir Meili of Narbonne[168]

6425. London - British Library Add. 19778, f. 35a, C.

North Africa

6426. Jerusalem - Benayahu ב 27, f. 54a, M, no incipit.

North Africa, commentary by Yehuda Toledano

6427. New York - Jewish Theological Seminary Ms. 4300, f. 1a-5b, C, no incipit.

North Africa, commentary by Simon b. Tsemaḥ Duran

6428. New York - Jewish Theological Seminary Ms. 4121, f. 40a-41a, M, rubric: הושענות ליום ראשון.

Yemen

6429. Chicago-Spertus College of Judaica D 10, f. 120a-120b, M, no incipit.

6430. Jerusalem - Michael Krupp 3391, f. 3a, M.

6431. Jerusalem - Musad haRav Kook 334, f. 86b, M.

6432. Jerusalem - Musad haRav Kook 335, f. 92b, M.

6433. Jerusalem - Musad haRav Kook 952, f. 3b-4a, M, incipit קרא.

6434. Jerusalem - Sassoon 264, f. 91b-92a, M, no incipit.

6435. Jerusalem - Sassoon 902, p. 170-171, M, no incipit.

6436. New York - Alfred Moldovan HH, f. 4a-5a, M, rubric: הושענא.

---

[168] Edited by Sofer, ספר המכתם, p. 151.

6437. New York - Jewish Theological Seminary Ms. 4488, f. 66b, M.
6438. New York - Jewish Theological Seminary Ms. 9325, f. 70b-71a, M.
6439. New York - Public Library, Heb. Ms. 10, f. 56b, M, rubric: הושענא.
Yemen, commentary by Isaac b. Abraham Wanneh
6440. Jerusalem - Israel Museum 180/78, f. 4b, M.
6441. Jerusalem - Makhon Ben Zvi 1156 (Tubi 155), f. 70b-71a, M, rubric: הושענא, no incipit.
6442. Jerusalem - Makhon Ben Zvi 1169 (Tubi 159), f. 61a, M, very short.
6443. Jerusalem - Makhon Ben Zvi 1174 (Tubi 154), f. 81a-81b, M, rubric: הושענא, no incipit.
6444. Jerusalem - Makhon ben Zvi 1186 (Tubi 205), f. 1b-2a, M, incipit קרא.
6445. Jerusalem - Michael Krupp 1990, f. 97a, M, rubric: הושענא.
6446. Jerusalem - Michael Krupp 604, f. 90b, M, rubric: הושענא.
6447. Jerusalem - Musad haRav Kook 325, f. 101a-101b, M, rubric: הושענא.
6448. Jerusalem - Musad haRav Kook 325, f. 119b, M, rubric: הושענא.
6449. Jerusalem - Musad haRav Kook 330, f. 66a, M.
6450. Jerusalem - Musad haRav Kook 347, f. 56a, M.
6451. Jerusalem - Sassoon 1158, p. 211, M, no incipit.
6452. Jerusalem - Sassoon 1174, p. 140, M, rubric: הושענא.
6453. Jerusalem - Schocken Institute 70028, f. 185b, M, no incipit.
6454. Jerusalem - Yehiel haLevi 4, f. 85b, M.
6455. London - British Library Or. 11121, f. 131a, C, incipit תבנה.
6456. London - British Library Or. 11122, f. 120a-120b, M, rubric: הושענא.
6457. Manchester - John Rylands University Library, Ms. Gaster 5, f. 145b, M, rubric: הושענא.
6458. Muenchen - Bayerische Staatsbibliothek, Cod. hebr. 472, f. 96b-97a, M, rubric: הושענא.
6459. Nahariya - Menahem and Saida Yaakob 284, f. 3a-4a, M, rubric: הושענא.
6460. New York - Jewish Theological Seminary Ms. 3013, f. 72b, M, rubric: הושענא.
6461. New York - Jewish Theological Seminary Ms. 3028, f. 243a-244a, C, rubric: פירוש הושענות לסכות.
6462. New York - Jewish Theological Seminary Ms. 3108, f. 75b-77a, C, rubric: פירוש הושענות לסכות.
6463. New York - Jewish Theological Seminary Ms. 3193, f. 159b, M, rubric: הושענא.
6464. New York - Jewish Theological Seminary Ms. 4195, f. 3b-4b, M, incipit תבנה.
6465. New York - Public Library, Heb. Ms. 9, f. 70a, M, no incipit.
6466. Paris - G. Epstein 23/57, f. 97a-97b, C, no incipit.
6467. Philadelphia - University of Pennsylvania HB 2, f. 96a-96b, M, rubric: הושענא.

6468. Ramat Gan - Universitat Bar Ilan 703, f. 191a-191b, M, incipit תבנה.
6469. Strasbourg - Bibliotheque Nationale et Universitaire 3965 (Landauer 39), p. 231, M, rubric: הושענא.

Yemen, commentary by Samḥun b. Salomo Ḥaloah
6470. Jerusalem - Makhon ben Zvi 2808, f. 11b-12b, C

Yemen, commentary by Simon b. Tsemaḥ Duran
6471. Jerusalem - Michael Krupp 1758, f. 3a-3b, M, rubric: פירוש.

Yemen, commentary by Yiḥya b. Josef Tsalaḥ
6472. Montreal - Elberg 203, f. 2b-3a, M, no incipit.

אנא אל אחרון וראשון (א 6183), הושענא

haAri, commentary by Mose b. Hayyim Pesante
6473. New York - Columbia University X 893 J 558, f. 200b, M.
6474. New York - Jewish Theological Seminary Ms. 4696, f. 11a, C.

haAri, commentary by Simon b. Tsemaḥ Duran
6475. New York - Columbia University X 893 J 558, f. 200b, M.

North Africa, commentary by Yehuda Toledano
6476. New York - Jewish Theological Seminary Ms. 4300, f. 8b-9a, C.

Yemen, commentary by Samḥun b. Salomo Ḥaloah
6477. Jerusalem - Makhon ben Zvi 2808, f. 22a-23b, C.

אנא אל הנא דר במרומי רומה, סליחה

Yemen, commentary by Isaac b. Abraham Wanneh
6478. Chicago-Spertus College of Judaica D 2, 2, f. 247a-247b, M, no incipit.
6479. Jerusalem - Sassoon 1158, p. 426, M, no incipit.
6480. London - British Library Or. 11122, f. 220b, M, no incipit.

אנא אלהי תהלתי אשפוך (א 6217), מאיר, סליחה

Ashkenaz
6481. Jerusalem - Schocken Institute 24100 / Mahzor Nuremberg, f. 396b, M, no incipit, very short.
6482. Muenchen - Bayerische Staatsbibliothek, Cod. hebr. 346, f. 137a, C, rubric: אחרת.
6483. Oxford - Bodleian Library MS Opp. 172 (Neubauer 1211), f. 86b-87a, C.
6484. Vatican - Biblioteca Apostolica ebr. 308, f. 147b-148a (two leafs numbered 147), C, commentator: David b. Mose (compiler).

Ashkenaz, commentary by Abraham b. Azriel[169]
6485. Frankfurt a M - Stadt- und Universitaetsbibliothek Fol. 16 (Merzbacher 95), f. 110a, C, short.

---

[169] Edited by Urbach, ערוגת הבושם, vol. III, p. 569.

Tsarfat
6486. Oxford - Bodleian Library MS Bodl. Or. 109 (Neubauer 1209), f. 67a-67b, C, commentator: Aaron b. Hayyim haKohen (compiler).

אנא אלהים חיים (א 6219), משולם ב"ר קלונימוס, חלק ז', קדושתא לשחרית יום כפור
Ashkenaz
6487. Berlin - Staatsbibliothek (Preussischer Kulturbesitz) Or. Qu. 798-799 (Steinschneider 177), I, f. 74b-75a, M.
6488. Braunschweig - Landesmuseum fuer Geschichte und Volkstum R 2386, vol. II, f. 187a, M.
6489. Budapest - Magyar tudomanyos akademia, MS. Kaufmann A 400, p. 311-312, C.
6490. Hamburg - Staats- und Universitaetsbibliothek Cod. hebr. 17/2 (Steinschneider 152), f. 151a, C.
6491. Hamburg - Staats- und Universitaetsbibliothek Cod. hebr. 62 (Steinschneider 154), f. 4a, C.
6492. Jerusalem - Jewish National and University Library Ms Heb 8° 3037, f. 118a, M, short.
6493. Jerusalem - Schocken Institute 24100 / Mahzor Nuremberg, f. 377a, M.
6494. London - British Library Or. 11318/1, f. 73b, C.
6495. London - Montefiore Library 261, f. 43b, C, commentator: Eliezer b. Natan?.
6496. Moscow - Russian State Library, Ms. Guenzburg 191, f. 86b-87a, M.
6497. Muenchen Bayerische Staatsbibliothek, Cod. hebr. 86, f. 102b-103a, Gl.
6498. Muenchen - Bayerische Staatsbibliothek, Cod. hebr. 346, f. 53a, C, no incipit.
6499. Muenchen - Bayerische Staatsbibliothek, Cod. hebr. 393, f. 141b-142a, C, no incipit, short.
6500. New York - Jewish Theological Seminary Ms. 4466, f. 307b-308a, M, no incipit.
6501. New York - Jewish Theological Seminary Ms. 8097, f. 71b-72a, C, short.
6502. New York - Jewish Theological Seminary Ms. 8169 (Acc. 0016), f. 68a-68b, M.
6503. Oxford - Bodleian Library MS Mich. 365 (Neubauer 1208), f. 69a, C, very short.
6504. Oxford - Bodleian Library MS Opp. 172 (Neubauer 1211), f. 38a, C, short.
6505. Oxford - Bodleian Library MS Opp. 619 (Neubauer 2374), f. 142b-143a, M, short.
6506. Parma - Biblioteca Palatina Cod. Parm. 3205 (de Rossi 655), f. 225b, C, short.

6507. Vatican - Biblioteca Apostolica ebr. 308, f. 99b-100a, C, commentator: David b. Mose (compiler).
6508. Vatican - Biblioteca Apostolica ebr. 422/1, f. 15a-15b, C, very short.
6509. Zurich - Zentralbibliothek Heid. 139, f. 76b, C, no incipit, additional marginal notes.

Asti, Fossano, Moncalvo

6510. New Haven - Yale University, Beinecke Rare Book and MS Library, MS Heb. 52, f. 104a, M.

Romania

6511. Vatican - Biblioteca Apostolica ebr. 320, f. 281b-282a, M.

Tsarfat

6512. Bern - Burgerbibliothek A 409, f. 79b-81a, G.
6513. London - British Library Or. 8682, f. 67a, Gl.
6514. London - David Sofer 5, f. 137b, C.
6515. London - David Sofer 5, f. 137b, C, second commentary on the margin.
6516. Oxford - Bodleian Library MS Bodl. Or. 109 (Neubauer 1209), f. 19b, C, commentator: Aaron b. Hayyim haKohen (compiler), short.
6517. Oxford - Bodleian Library MS Laud. Or. 271 (Neubauer 1206), f. 113b, C, commentator: Aaron b. Hayyim haKohen (compiler), very short.
6518. Parma - Biblioteca Palatina Cod. Parm. 1794 (de Rossi 1061), f. 117b-118a, M.
6519. Parma - Biblioteca Palatina Cod. Parm. 2125 (de Rossi 812), f. 39b, C.
6520. Parma - Biblioteca Palatina Cod. Parm. 2890 (de Rossi 856), f. 26a, M, short.
6521. Parma - Biblioteca Palatina Cod. Parm. 3006 (de Rossi 654,1), f. 139a-139b, M.
6522. Parma - Biblioteca Palatina Cod. Parm. 3006 (de Rossi 654,1), f. 139b-140a, M.
6523. Vatican - Biblioteca Apostolica ebr. 306, f. 77a, C.

אנא אתקינת עלמא בתבונה (א 6237), רשות לדיבור ראשון

Ashkenaz

6524. Berlin - Staatsbibliothek (Preussischer Kulturbesitz) Or. Qu. 798-799 (Steinschneider 177), II, f. 156b-157b, M.
6525. Jerusalem - Schocken Institute 24100 / Mahzor Nuremberg, f. 155a-155b, M.
6526. Muenchen - Bayerische Staatsbibliothek, Cod. hebr. 393, f. 151a-151b, C, no incipit.

אנא בכוח גדולת ימינך תתיר צרורה (א 6242), בקשה

Yemen
6527. Manchester - John Rylands University Library, Ms. Gaster 4, f. 87b, M.
6528. New York - Jewish Theological Seminary Ms. 3108, f. 21a, M, short.
Yemen, commentary by Isaac b. Abraham Wanneh
6529. Chicago-Spertus College of Judaica D 2, 2, f. 185b, M.
6530. Jerusalem - Sassoon 1158, p. 310, M, no incipit.

אנא בקראנו לקול שוענו יי שמעה (א 6245), דוד בן אלעזר בקודה, סליחה

North Africa, commentary by David b. Josef Abudarham
6531. New York - Jewish Theological Seminary Ms. 5426, f. 62a-62b, M.
Sepharad
6532. Skokie - Hebrew Theological College 3, f. 2.15a, M.
Sepharad, commentary by David b. Josef Abudarham[170]
6533. Budapest - Magyar tudomanyos akademia, MS. Kaufmann A 405/2, p. 181-182, C.
6534. Cincinnati - Hebrew Union College 490, f. 2a, C.
6535. New York - Columbia X893 Ab 93, f. 3a, C.

אנא בשעיר שתליה בפארן שכליל הילכה, הושענא

Yemen, commentary by Isaac b. Abraham Wanneh
6536. Jerusalem - Israel Museum 180/78, f. 34b-36a, M.

אנא האל הנקדש בקדושות שלשה (א 6263), הושענא

Carpentras
6537. New York - Jewish Theological Seminary Ms. 1609, f. 98b, C, kabbalistic, rubric: יום ג', no incipit.
haAri, commentary by Mose b. Hayyim Pesante
6538. New York - Columbia University X 893 J 558, f. 202b-203a, M.
Italia, commentary by Zakharya David Shabbetai Segre
6539. Torino - Archivio Terracini 1499, p. 89-92, C, rubric: פירוש אנא האל הנקדש בקדושות שלשה.
Narbonne, commentary by Meir Meili of Narbonne[171]
6540. London - British Library Add. 19778, f. 36a, C, rubric: ליום שלישי.
North Africa, commentary by Yehuda Toledano
6541. New York - Jewish Theological Seminary Ms. 4300, f. 16a-19a, C.
Yemen Africa, commentary by Samḥun b. Salomo Ḥaloah
6542. Jerusalem - Makhon ben Zvi 2808, f. 58a, C.

---

[170] Edited by Prins, תשלום אבודרהם, p. 78.
[171] Edited by Sofer, ספר המכתם, p. 154-155.

אנא הבורא בורא כל במאמרו, סליחה

Yemen, commentary by Isaac b. Abraham Wanneh
6543. Chicago-Spertus College of Judaica D 2, 2, f. 247a, M, no incipit.
6544. Jerusalem - Sassoon 1158, p. 426, M, no incipit.
6545. London - British Library Or. 11122, f. 220b, M, no incipit.

אנא הבורא עולמו בימים ששה (א 6271), הושענא

Carpentras
6546. New York - Jewish Theological Seminary Ms. 1609, f. 99a-99b, C, rubric: יום ו'.
6547. New York - Jewish Theological Seminary Ms. 1609, f. 100a-110b, C, no incipit.

haAri, commentary by Mose b. Hayyim Pesante
6548. New York - Columbia University X 893 J 558, f. 205b, M.
6549. New York - Jewish Theological Seminary Ms. 4696, f. 18a-19a, C.

haAri, commentary by Simon b. Tsemaḥ Duran
6550. New York - Columbia University X 893 J 558, f. 205b, M.

Italia, commentary by Zakharya David Shabbetai Segre
6551. Torino - Archivio Terracini 1499, p. 125-129, C, rubric: פירוש אנא בורא עולמו בימים ששה.

Narbonne, commentary by Meir Meili of Narbonne[172]
6552. London - British Library Add. 19778, f. 37a-37b, C, rubric: ליום ששי, no incipit.

North Africa, commentary by Simon b. Tsemaḥ Duran
6553. New York - Jewish Theological Seminary Ms. 4121, f. 46b-48a, C, rubric: ליום ששי.

North Africa, commentary by Yehuda Toledano
6554. New York - Jewish Theological Seminary Ms. 4300, f. 30a-33a, C.

Sepharad, commentary by Josef Garad
6555. Oxford - Bodleian Library Heb.e.10 (Neubauer 2746/1), f. 26a-26b, C, no incipit.

Yemen
6556. Chicago-Spertus College of Judaica D 10, f. 126b-127b, M, incipit שש.
6557. Jerusalem - Michael Krupp 3391, f. 9a-10a, M.
6558. Jerusalem - Musad haRav Kook 327, f. 87a-87b, M.
6559. Jerusalem - Musad haRav Kook 334, f. 90b, M.
6560. Jerusalem - Musad haRav Kook 335, f. 96a, M.
6561. Jerusalem - Musad haRav Kook 952, f. 17b-18b, M, rubric: ליום ששי, incipit שש.
6562. Jerusalem - Sassoon 902, p. 179-180, M, no incipit.

---

[172] Edited by Sofer, ספר המכתם, p. 159-160.

6563. New York - Alfred Moldovan HH, f. 17a-18a, M, rubric: ליום שביעי.
6564. New York - Jewish Theological Seminary Ms. 4488, f. 70a, M, no incipit.
6565. New York - Jewish Theological Seminary Ms. 9325, f. 80a-80b, M.
6566. New York - Public Library, Heb. Ms. 10, f. 59b, M, no incipit.
6567. Ramat Gan - Universitat Bar Ilan 62, f. 29b, G, margins damaged.

Yemen, commentary by Isaac b. Abraham Wanneh

6568. Jerusalem - Benayahu ת 261, f. 83b-84a, M, rubric: הושענא.
6569. Jerusalem - Benayahu ת 282, f. 76a-76b, M, rubric: הושענא, incipit שׁ.
6570. Jerusalem - Israel Museum 180/78, f. 19b-20b, M, rubric: הושענא.
6571. Jerusalem - Makhon Ben Zvi 1156 (Tubi 155), f. 73a-73b, M, rubric: הושענא.
6572. Jerusalem - Makhon Ben Zvi 1169 (Tubi 159), f. 64a, M, incipit שׁ.
6573. Jerusalem - Makhon Ben Zvi 1174 (Tubi 154), f. 86a-86b, M, rubric: הושענא.
6574. Jerusalem - Makhon ben Zvi 1186 (Tubi 205), f. 9a-9b, M, rubric: ליום ששי, incipit שׁ.
6575. Jerusalem - Michael Krupp 604, f. 94a-94b, M, rubric: הושענא.
6576. Jerusalem - Michael Krupp 1990, f. 102a, M, rubric: הושענא.
6577. Jerusalem - Musad haRav Kook 325, f. 108b-109a, M, rubric: הושענא.
6578. Jerusalem - Musad haRav Kook 325, f. 125a-125b, M, rubric: הושענא, incipit שׁ.
6579. Jerusalem - Musad haRav Kook 330, f. 69a-69b, M.
6580. Jerusalem - Sassoon 1158, p. 217, M, rubric: הושענא.
6581. Jerusalem - Sassoon 1174, p. 145-146, M, rubric: הושענא.
6582. Jerusalem - Schocken Institute 70028, f. 189b-190a, M, rubric: ענה בהושענא, very short.
6583. Jerusalem - Yehiel haLevi 4, f. 89a, G.
6584. London - British Library Or. 11122, f. 123a-123b, M, rubric: הושענא.
6585. Muenchen - Bayerische Staatsbibliothek, Cod. hebr. 472, f. 100b-101a, M, rubric: הושענא.
6586. Nahariya - Menahem and Saida Yaakob 284, f. 18a-19a, M, rubric: הושענא.
6587. New York - Jewish Theological Seminary Ms. 3013, f. 76b, M, rubric: הושענא.
6588. New York - Jewish Theological Seminary Ms. 3028, f. 249a-250b, C, rubric: ליום ששי.
6589. New York - Jewish Theological Seminary Ms. 3108, f. 81b-83a, C, rubric: ליום ששי.
6590. New York - Jewish Theological Seminary Ms. 3193, f. 167a-167b, M, rubric: הושענא.
6591. New York - Jewish Theological Seminary Ms. 3295, f. 92b-93a, M, rubric: הושענא.
6592. New York - Jewish Theological Seminary Ms. 4195, f. 28b-30a, M.

6593. New York - Public Library, Heb. Ms. 9, f. 74a-74b, M, rubric: הושענא.
6594. Paris - G. Epstein 23/57, f. 106b-107a, C, incipit שש.
6595. Philadelphia - University of Pennsylvania HB 2, f. 99a-99b, M, rubric: הושענא.
6596. Ramat Gan - Universitat Bar Ilan 703, f. 196b-197a, M, rubric: הושענא.
6597. San Francisco - California State Library, Sutro Branch MS 154 (Brinner 125), p. 25b-26a, M, incipit שש.
6598. Strasbourg - Bibliotheque Nationale et Universitaire 3965 (Landauer 39), p. 243-244, M, rubric: הושענא.

Yemen, commentary by Samḥun b. Salomo Ḥaloah
6599. Jerusalem - Makhon ben Zvi 2808, f. 127a-129a, C.
6600. Jerusalem - Makhon ben Zvi 2808, f. 129a-139b, C.

Yemen, commentary by Simon b. Tsemaḥ Duran
6601. Jerusalem - Michael Krupp 1758, f. 12b, M, rubric: פירוש.

Yemen, commentary by Yiḥya b. Josef Tsalaḥ
6602. Montreal - Elberg 203, f. 15b-16a, M.

אנא הבורא עולמו ביסודות ארבעה (א 6272), הושענא

Carpentras
6603. New York - Jewish Theological Seminary Ms. 1609, f. 98b, C, rubric: יום ד׳, no incipit.

haAri, commentary by Mose b. Hayyim Pesante
6604. New York - Columbia University X 893 J 558, f. 203b-204a, M.
6605. New York - Jewish Theological Seminary Ms. 4696, f. 16a, C, rubric: ליום רביעי.

Italia, commentary by Zakharya David Shabbetai Segre
6606. Torino - Archivio Terracini 1499, p. 102-105, C, rubric: פירוש אנא האל הבורא עולמו ביסודות ארבעה.

North Africa, commentary by Yehuda Toledano
6607. New York - Jewish Theological Seminary Ms. 4300, f. 21b-23a, C.

Yemen, commentary by Samḥun b. Salomo Ḥaloah
6608. Jerusalem - Makhon ben Zvi 2808, f. 79a-79b, C.

אנא הגואלנו על ידי אחים שלשה, הושענא

Yemen, commentary by Samḥun b. Salomo Ḥaloah
6609. Jerusalem - Makhon ben Zvi 2808, f. 63a-64a, C.

אנא הואל סלוח (א 6277), סליחה

Ashkenaz
6610. Berlin - Staatsbibliothek (Preussischer Kulturbesitz) Or. Qu. 798-799 (Steinschneider 177), I, f. 97b-98a, M.

6611. Jerusalem - Schocken Institute 24100 / Mahzor Nuremberg, f. 463a, M, short.
6612. Muenchen - Bayerische Staatsbibliothek, Cod. hebr. 346, f. 137a, C, rubric: אחרת, very short.
6613. New York - Jewish Theological Seminary Ms. 4466, f. 342b-344a, M.
6614. New York - Jewish Theological Seminary Ms. 8097, f. 83b, C.
6615. Oxford - Bodleian Library MS Mich. 543 (Neubauer 1212), f. 25a, C, commentator: Isaac b. Jacob (compiler), short.
6616. Oxford - Bodleian Library MS Opp. 172 (Neubauer 1211), f. 87a, C, no incipit.
6617. Oxford - Bodleian Library MS Opp. 681 (Neubauer 1213), f. 26a-26b, C.
6618. Padova - Biblioteca del Seminario Vescovile Cod. 218, f. 174a-174b, M.
6619. Vatican - Biblioteca Apostolica ebr. 308, f. 147b, C, commentator: David b. Mose (compiler), rubric: אתחיל סליחות שך נעילה בעזרת השם.
6620. Vatican - Biblioteca Apostolica ebr. 422/1, f. 24a, C, very short.
6621. Vatican - Biblioteca Apostolica ebr. 422/2, f. 38b, CG, no incipit, very short.

Ashkenaz, commentary by Abraham b. Azriel[173]
6622. Frankfurt a M - Stadt- und Universitaetsbibliothek Fol. 16 (Merzbacher 95), f. 108b, C, very short.

Tsarfat
6623. Oxford - Bodleian Library MS Bodl. Or. 109 (Neubauer 1209), f. 65b-66a, C, commentator: Aaron b. Hayyim haKohen (compiler).

אנא הושיענא בני עפר מי מנה (א 6280), אלעזר ברבי קליר?, זולת לסוכות

Ashkenaz
6624. Berlin - Staatsbibliothek (Preussischer Kulturbesitz) Or. Qu. 798-799 (Steinschneider 177), I, f. 190a, M.
6625. Braunschweig - Landesmuseum fuer Geschichte und Volkstum R 2386, vol. I, f. 121a, M.
6626. Hamburg - Staats- und Universitaetsbibliothek Cod. hebr. 62 (Steinschneider 154), f. 33a, C, rubric: זולת.
6627. Jerusalem - Schocken Institute 24100 / Mahzor Nuremberg, f. 475b, M, short.
6628. London - British Library Add. 18695 (Margoliouth 683), f. 110b-111a, T, Yiddish.
6629. London - British Library Or. 11318/1, f. 129b-130a, C.
6630. London - Montefiore Library 261, f. 65a, C, commentator: Eliezer b. Natan?, short.

---

[173] Edited by Urbach, ערוגת הבושם, vol. III, p. 560.

6631. Oxford - Bodleian Library MS Mich. 365 (Neubauer 1208), f. 94b, C, rubric: זולת, no incipit, short.

Romania

6632. London - London School of Jewish Studies. Asher I.Myers collection 9, f. 201a, M, rubric: זולת, short.

אנא החק זמן חרותינו ימים שבעה (א 6283), הושענא

Yemen

6633. Jerusalem - Musad haRav Kook 952, f. 26a-27b, M, rubric: הקפה ז' דוד.

Yemen, commentary by Isaac b. Abraham Wanneh

6634. Jerusalem - Israel Museum 180/78, f. 30b, M.
6635. Nahariya - Menahem and Saida Yaakob 284, f. 20a, M.
6636. New York - Jewish Theological Seminary Ms. 3108, f. 84b-86b, C.
6637. New York - Jewish Theological Seminary Ms. 4195, f. 32a-32b, M.
6638. Ramat Gan - Universitat Bar Ilan 703, f. 198a, M, rubric: הקפה שביעית.

Yemen, commentary by Samḥun b. Salomo Ḥaloah

6639. Jerusalem - Makhon ben Zvi 2808, f. 195a-196a, C.

Yemen, commentary by Yiḥya b. Josef Tsalaḥ

6640. Montreal - Elberg 203, f. 17b-18b, M, rubric: הקפה ז' דוד.

אנא המוליכנו במדבר בדגלים ארבע, הושענא

Yemen, commentary by Samḥun b. Salomo Ḥaloah

6641. Jerusalem - Makhon ben Zvi 2808, f. 85a-89b, C.

אנא המחבר לאפוד שמו ששה, הושענא

Yemen, commentary by Samḥun b. Salomo Ḥaloah

6642. Jerusalem - Makhon ben Zvi 2808, f. 139b-140a, C.

אנא המיוחד לכבודו שמות חמשה (א 6288), הושענא

Carpentras

6643. New York - Jewish Theological Seminary Ms. 1609, f. 99a, C, rubric: יום ה', no incipit.

haAri, commentary by Mose b. Hayyim Pesante

6644. New York - Columbia University X 893 J 558, f. 204b, M.
6645. New York - Jewish Theological Seminary Ms. 4696, f. 16b-17b, C, rubric: ליום חמשי.

haAri, commentary by Simon b. Tsemaḥ Duran

6646. New York - Columbia University X 893 J 558, f. 204b, M.

Italia, commentary by Zakharya David Shabbetai Segre

6647. Torino - Archivio Terracini 1499, p. 112-117, C, rubric: פירוש אנא המיחד לכבודו שמות חמישה.

Narbonne, commentary by Meir Meili of Narbonne[174]
6648. London - British Library Add. 19778, f. 36b-37a, C, rubric: ליום חמישי.
North Africa, commentary by Simon b. Tsemaḥ Duran
6649. New York - Jewish Theological Seminary Ms. 4121, f. 45a-46b, C, rubric: ליום חמישי.
North Africa, commentary by Yehuda Toledano
6650. New York - Jewish Theological Seminary Ms. 4300, f. 25a-27b, C.
Sepharad, commentary by Josef Garad
6651. Oxford - Bodleian Library Heb.e.10 (Neubauer 2746/1), f. 26a, C, no incipit.
Yemen
6652. Chicago-Spertus College of Judaica D 10, f. 126a-126b, M, incipit מיחד.
6653. Jerusalem - Benayahu ת 414, f. 88a, M, rubric: 'פ.
6654. Jerusalem - Michael Krupp 3391, f. 8b, M.
6655. Jerusalem - Musad haRav Kook 327, f. 86b, M.
6656. Jerusalem - Musad haRav Kook 334, f. 90a, M, no incipit, starts: פירוש אנא וכו'.
6657. Jerusalem - Musad haRav Kook 335, f. 95b, M.
6658. Jerusalem - Musad haRav Kook 952, f. 16a-17b, M, rubric: הושענא.
6659. Jerusalem - Sassoon 264, f. 95a-96a, M, no incipit.
6660. Jerusalem - Sassoon 902, p. 178-179, M, no incipit.
6661. New York - Alfred Moldovan HH, f. 16a-16b, M, rubric: הושענא.
6662. New York - Jewish Theological Seminary Ms. 4488, f. 69b-70a, M, no incipit.
6663. New York - Jewish Theological Seminary Ms. 9325, f. 79a-79b, M, no incipit.
6664. New York - Public Library, Heb. Ms. 10, f. 59a-59b, M, no incipit, margins damaged
6665. Ramat Gan - Universitat Bar Ilan 62, f. 29a, G, margins damaged.
6666. Ramat Gan - Universitat Bar Ilan 63, f. 22a, G, margins damaged.
Yemen, commentary by Isaac b. Abraham Wanneh
6667. Chicago-Spertus College of Judaica D 1, f. 197a, M, rubric: פירוש.
6668. Jerusalem - Benayahu ת 261, f. 82b-83a, M, rubric: הושענא.
6669. Jerusalem - Benayahu ת 282, f. 75b-76a, M, no incipit.
6670. Jerusalem - Israel Museum 180/78, f. 18b-19a, M, rubric: הושענא.
6671. Jerusalem - Makhon Ben Zvi 1156 (Tubi 155), f. 73a, M, rubric: הושענא.
6672. Jerusalem - Makhon Ben Zvi 1169 (Tubi 159), f. 63b, M.
6673. Jerusalem - Makhon Ben Zvi 1174 (Tubi 154), f. 85a-85b, M, rubric: הושענא.
6674. Jerusalem - Makhon ben Zvi 1186 (Tubi 205), f. 8b, M, incipit שמות.

---

[174] Edited by Sofer, ספר המכתם, p. 157-159.

6675. Jerusalem - Michael Krupp 604, f. 94a, M, rubric: הושענא.
6676. Jerusalem - Michael Krupp 1990, f. 101a-101b, M, rubric: הושענא.
6677. Jerusalem - Musad haRav Kook 325, f. 124a-124b, M, rubric: הושענא, no incipit.
6678. Jerusalem - Musad haRav Kook 330, f. 68b-69a, M.
6679. Jerusalem - Musad haRav Kook 347, f. 59a, M, no incipit.
6680. Jerusalem - Sassoon 1158, p. 216, M, rubric: הושענא.
6681. Jerusalem - Sassoon 1174, p. 145, M, rubric: הושענא.
6682. Jerusalem - Schocken Institute 70028, f. 189a-189b, M, rubric: הושענא.
6683. Jerusalem - Yehiel haLevi 4, f. 88b, G.
6684. London - British Library Or. 11122, f. 122b, M, rubric: הושענא.
6685. Manchester - John Rylands University Library, Ms. Gaster 5, f. 151b, M, rubric: הושענא.
6686. Muenchen - Bayerische Staatsbibliothek, Cod. hebr. 472, f. 100a-100b, M, rubric: הושענא.
6687. Nahariya - Menahem and Saida Yaakob 284, f. 16b-17a, M.
6688. New York - Jewish Theological Seminary Ms. 3013, f. 76a, M, rubric: הושענא.
6689. New York - Jewish Theological Seminary Ms. 3028, f. 248a-249a, C, rubric: ליום חמישי.
6690. New York - Jewish Theological Seminary Ms. 3108, f. 80a-81b, C, rubric: ליום חמישי.
6691. New York - Jewish Theological Seminary Ms. 3193, f. 166a-166b, M, rubric: הוש'.
6692. New York - Jewish Theological Seminary Ms. 3295, f. 92a, M, rubric: הושענא.
6693. New York - Jewish Theological Seminary Ms. 4195, f. 25a-26a, M, incipit שמות.
6694. New York - Public Library, Heb. Ms. 9, f. 73b, M, rubric: הושענא, no incipit.
6695. Oxford - Bodleian Library MS Opp. Add. fol. 58 (Neubauer 2498), f. 143b-144a, M, rubric: הושענא.
6696. Paris - G. Epstein 23/57, f. 105a-106a, C.
6697. Philadelphia - University of Pennsylvania HB 2, f. 98b, M, rubric: הושענא.
6698. Ramat Gan - Universitat Bar Ilan 703, f. 196a, M, rubric: הושענא.
6699. San Francisco - California State Library, Sutro Branch MS 154 (Brinner 125), f. 25a-25b, M.
6700. San Francisco - California State Library, Sutro Branch MS 154 (Brinner 125), f. 108b-109b, C, rubric: ליום חמישי.
6701. Strasbourg - Bibliotheque Nationale et Universitaire 3965 (Landauer 39), p. 241-242, M, rubric: הושענא.

Yemen, commentary by Samḥun b. Salomo Ḥaloah
6702. Jerusalem - Makhon ben Zvi 2808, f. 104a-105a, C.
6703. Jerusalem - Makhon ben Zvi 2808, f. 105a-114a, C.
Yemen, commentary by Simon b. Tsemaḥ Duran
6704. Jerusalem - Michael Krupp 1758, f. 11a, M.
Yemen, commentary by Yiḥya b. Josef Tsalaḥ
6705. Montreal - Elberg 203, f. 14a-14b, M.

אנא המנחילנו דת ספרים חמשה, הושענא

Yemen
6706. Jerusalem - Musad haRav Kook 952, f. 24a-26a, M, rubric: הקפה ששית פינחס.
Yemen, commentary by Samḥun b. Salomo Ḥaloah
6707. Jerusalem - Makhon ben Zvi 2808, f. 115a-115b, C.
Yemen, commentary by Yiḥya b. Josef Tsalaḥ
6708. Montreal - Elberg 203, f. 16b, M.

אנא המנחילנו שבת לימים שבעה (א 6289), הושענא

Yemen, commentary by Isaac b. Abraham Wanneh
6709. Jerusalem - Musad haRav Kook 325, f. 109b, M, no incipit.
6710. New York - Jewish Theological Seminary Ms. 3108, f. 84b, C, short.
6711. Ramat Gan - Universitat Bar Ilan 703, f. 198a, M, rubric: הקפה ששית.

אנא המקדים לעולם דברים שבעה (א 6290), הושענא

Carpentras
6712. New York - Jewish Theological Seminary Ms. 1609, f. 99b-100a, C, rubric: להושענא רבא, no incipit.
haAri, commentary by Mose b. Hayyim Pesante
6713. New York - Jewish Theological Seminary Ms. 4696, f. 22b-23a, C, rubric: הקפה שביעית.
Italia, commentary by Zakharya David Shabbetai Segre
6714. Torino - Archivio Terracini 1499, p. 207-210, C, rubric: פירוש אנא המקדים לעולם דברים שבעה.
Narbonne, commentary by Meir Meili of Narbonne[175]
6715. London - British Library Add. 19778, f. 38a, C, rubric: הושענא רבה.
North Africa
6716. Jerusalem - Benayahu ז 27, f. 125b-126a, M.
North Africa, commentary by Yehuda Toledano
6717. New York - Jewish Theological Seminary Ms. 4300, f. 50b-53b, C, rubric: הקפה שביעית דוד.

---

[175] Edited by Sofer, ספר המכתם, p. 161.

Sepharad, commentary by David b. Josef Abudarham?

6718. Holon - Yehuda Nahum 278, f. 24a-24b, FC, rubric: להושענה רבה.

Yemen

6719. Jerusalem - Musad haRav Kook 325, f. 101b, M, rubric: פירוש מהדפוסין, short.

6720. Jerusalem - Musad haRav Kook 327, f. 88a, M.

6721. Jerusalem - Musad haRav Kook 334, f. 95a, M.

6722. Jerusalem - Musad haRav Kook 335, f. 96b-97a, M.

6723. Jerusalem - Musad haRav Kook 952, f. 19a-20a, M, rubric: הושענא רבה.

6724. Jerusalem - Sassoon 902, p. 180-181, M.

6725. New York - Alfred Moldovan HH, f. 18b, M, rubric: הקפה א'.

6726. New York - Jewish Theological Seminary Ms. 4488, f. 70b-71a, M.

6727. New York - Jewish Theological Seminary Ms. 9325, f. 80b-81a, M.

6728. New York - Public Library, Heb. Ms. 10, f. 60a-60b, M, no incipit, margins damaged.

6729. Ramat Gan - Universitat Bar Ilan 62, f. 29b-30a, G, margins damaged.

Yemen, commentary by Isaac b. Abraham Wanneh

6730. Jerusalem - Benayahu ת 261, f. 84b, M, rubric: הושענא.

6731. Jerusalem - Benayahu ת 282, f. 76b-77a, M, rubric: הושענא.

6732. Jerusalem - Israel Museum 180/78, f. 22b, M, rubric: הושענא.

6733. Jerusalem - Makhon b. Zvi 1168 (Tubi 157), f. 25b, M, margins damaged.

6734. Jerusalem - Makhon Ben Zvi 1156 (Tubi 155), f. 73b, 77a, M, rubric: הושענא, leafs bound in wrong order.

6735. Jerusalem - Makhon Ben Zvi 1169 (Tubi 159), f. 64b-65a, M.

6736. Jerusalem - Makhon Ben Zvi 1174 (Tubi 154), f. 87a, M, rubric: הושענא.

6737. Jerusalem - Makhon ben Zvi 1186 (Tubi 205), f. 10a, M, incipit דברים.

6738. Jerusalem - Michael Krupp 604, f. 95a-95b, M, rubric: הושענא.

6739. Jerusalem - Michael Krupp 1990, f. 102b-103a, M, rubric: הושענא.

6740. Jerusalem - Musad haRav Kook 325, f. 110a-111a, M, rubric: הושע'.

6741. Jerusalem - Musad haRav Kook 325, f. 126a-126b, M, rubric: הושענא.

6742. Jerusalem - Musad haRav Kook 330, f. 69b, M.

6743. Jerusalem - Musad haRav Kook 347, f. 60a-60b, M.

6744. Jerusalem - Sassoon 1158, p. 217-218, M, rubric: הושענא.

6745. Jerusalem - Sassoon 1174, p. 147, M, rubric: הושענא.

6746. Jerusalem - Schocken Institute 70028, f. 190a-190b, M, rubric: ליום שביעי.

6747. Jerusalem - Yehiel haLevi 4, f. 89b-90a, G.

6748. London - British Library Or. 11122, f. 123b, M, rubric: הושענא.

6749. London - British Library Or. 11121, f. 135a, C, rubric: הושענא.

6750. Muenchen - Bayerische Staatsbibliothek, Cod. hebr. 472, f. 101b-102a, M, rubric: הושענא.
6751. Nahariya - Menahem and Saida Yaakob 284, f. 4b, M, rubric: חידושין, incipit דברים.
6752. New York - Jewish Theological Seminary Ms. 3013, f. 79a, M, rubric: הושענא.
6753. New York - Jewish Theological Seminary Ms. 3193, f. 168a-169a, M, rubric: הושע'.
6754. New York - Jewish Theological Seminary Ms. 3295, f. 93b-94a, M, rubric: הושענא.
6755. New York - Jewish Theological Seminary Ms. 4195, f. 4b-5a, M, rubric: הקפה ראשונה אברהם.
6756. New York - Public Library, Heb. Ms. 9, f. 74b-75a, M, no incipit.
6757. Oxford - Bodleian Library MS Opp. Add. fol. 58 (Neubauer 2498), f. 144b-145a, M, rubric: הושענא.
6758. Oxford - Bodleian Library MS Opp. Add. fol. 58 (Neubauer 2498), f. 145a-145b, M, rubric: ליום שביעי.
6759. Paris - G. Epstein 23/57, f. 107b, C, rubric: פי' ההקפות להושענא רבא.
6760. Ramat Gan - Universitat Bar Ilan 703, f. 197b, M, rubric: פירוש ההקפות של א'.
6761. San Francisco - California State Library, Sutro Branch MS 154 (Brinner 125), f. 26a-26b, M, no incipit.
6762. Strasbourg - Bibliotheque Nationale et Universitaire 3965 (Landauer 39), p. 245-246, M, rubric: הושענא.

Yemen, commentary by Samḥun b. Salomo Ḥaloah
6763. Jerusalem - Makhon ben Zvi 2808, f. 181a-183a, C.

Yemen, commentary by Yiḥya b. Josef Tsalaḥ
6764. Montreal - Elberg 203, f. 5b-6a, M.

אנא המשמיענו תורה על ידי רועים שנים, הושענא

Yemen, commentary by Samḥun b. Salomo Ḥaloah
6765. Jerusalem - Makhon ben Zvi 2808, f. 43a-44b, C.

אנא הנשא והעיר נפלאות (א 6292), משה לוי, סליחה

Yemen
6766. Jerusalem - Benayahu ת 414, f. 128a, M.
6767. Jerusalem - Sassoon 902, p. 426, M.
6768. New York - Jewish Theological Seminary Ms. 3052, f. 30b-31a, M, rubric: אל מלך.

Yemen, commentary by Isaac b. Abraham Wanneh
6769. Chicago-Spertus College of Judaica D 2, 2, f. 208b-209a, M, no incipit.
6770. Jerusalem - Benayahu ת 261, f. 139a-139b, M, rubric: אל מלך.

6771. Jerusalem - Benayahu ת 282, f. 122b-123b, M, rubric: אל מלך.
6772. Jerusalem - Makhon Ben Zvi 1156 (Tubi 155), f. 121a-121b, M, rubric: אל מלך.
6773. Jerusalem - Makhon Ben Zvi 1174 (Tubi 154), f. 126a, M.
6774. Jerusalem - Michael Krupp 604, f. 153a-154a (153b empty), M, rubric: אל מלך.
6775. Jerusalem - Musad haRav Kook 325, f. 183a, M, rubric: אל מלך.
6776. Jerusalem - Sassoon 1158, p. 202, M, rubric: אל מלך סים' משה, no incipit.
6777. Jerusalem - Yehiel haLevi 4, f. 158a, G.
6778. London - British Library Or. 11122, f. 189a, M, rubric: אל מלך.
6779. Manchester - John Rylands University Library, Ms. Gaster 5, f. 197b-198a, M.
6780. Muenchen - Bayerische Staatsbibliothek, Cod. hebr. 472, f. 165b-166a, M, rubric: אל מלך.
6781. New York - Jewish Theological Seminary Ms. 3013, f. 122b, M, rubric: אל מלך.
6782. New York - Jewish Theological Seminary Ms. 3294, f. 10b, C.
6783. New York - Public Library, Heb. Ms. 9, f. 113b, M.
6784. Strasbourg - Bibliotheque Nationale et Universitaire 3965 (Landauer 39), p. 380, M, rubric: אל מלך.

אנא הפודינו על יד שביעי לרועים שבעה (א 6293), הושענא

Yemen
6785. Jerusalem - Musad haRav Kook 952, f. 23b-24a, M, rubric: הקפה ה' אהרן.

Yemen, commentary by Isaac b. Abraham Wanneh
6786. Jerusalem - Israel Museum 180/78, f. 28a, M.
6787. Jerusalem - Makhon ben Zvi 1186 (Tubi 205), f. 12a, M, incipit לרועים.
6788. Nahariya - Menahem and Saida Yaakob 284, f. 17a, M, rubric: הקפה, incipit לרועים.
6789. Paris - G. Epstein 23/57, f. 109b-110a, C, rubric: פי' ההקפה.
6790. Ramat Gan - Universitat Bar Ilan 703, f. 198a, M, rubric: הקפה חמישית.

Yemen, commentary by Yiḥya b. Josef Tsalaḥ
6791. Montreal - Elberg 203, f. 14b-15a, M.

אנא השם בכסאו חיות ארבע (א 6297), הושענא

Carpentras
6792. New York - Jewish Theological Seminary Ms. 1609, f. 100a, C, no incipit.

Narbonne, commentary by Meir Meili of Narbonne[176]
6793. London - British Library Add. 19778, f. 36a-36b, C, rubric: ליום רביעי.
North Africa, commentary by Simon b. Tsemaḥ Duran
6794. New York - Jewish Theological Seminary Ms. 4121, f. 44a-45a, C, rubric: ליום רביעי.
Sepharad, commentary by Josef Garad
6795. Oxford - Bodleian Library Heb.e.10 (Neubauer 2746/1), f. 26a, C, no incipit.
Yemen
6796. Chicago-Spertus College of Judaica D 10, f. 125a-125b, M, no incipit.
6797. Jerusalem - Benayahu ת 414, f. 87a-87b, M, rubric: פי'.
6798. Jerusalem - Michael Krupp 3391, f. 6a, M.
6799. Jerusalem - Michael Krupp 3391, f. 7a, M, no incipit.
6800. Jerusalem - Musad haRav Kook 327, f. 80b, M, short.
6801. Jerusalem - Musad haRav Kook 334, f. 89a, M, no incipit.
6802. Jerusalem - Musad haRav Kook 335, f. 94b, M.
6803. Jerusalem - Musad haRav Kook 952, f. 12b-13a, M, rubric: הושענא.
6804. Jerusalem - Sassoon 264, f. 94b-95a, M, no incipit.
6805. Jerusalem - Sassoon 902, p. 176-177, M, no incipit.
6806. New York - Alfred Moldovan HH, f. 9a-10a, M, rubric: הושענא.
6807. New York - Alfred Moldovan HH, f. 12b-13b, M, rubric: הושענא, no incipit.
6808. New York - Jewish Theological Seminary Ms. 4488, f. 68b-77a, M, no incipit.
6809. New York - Jewish Theological Seminary Ms. 9325, f. 77a, M.
6810. New York - Public Library, Heb. Ms. 10, f. 58b, M, no incipit, margins damaged.
6811. Ramat Gan - Universitat Bar Ilan 62, f. 28b, G, margins damaged.
6812. Ramat Gan - Universitat Bar Ilan 63, f. 21b-22a, G, margins damaged.
Yemen, commentary by Isaac b. Abraham Wanneh
6813. Chicago-Spertus College of Judaica D 1, f. 196a, M.
6814. Jerusalem - Benayahu ת 261, f. 81b-82a, M.
6815. Jerusalem - Benayahu ת 282, f. 75a, M, rubric: הושענא.
6816. Jerusalem - Israel Museum 180/78, f. 14a-15b, M, rubric: הושענא.
6817. Jerusalem - Makhon Ben Zvi 1156 (Tubi 155), f. 72a-72b, M, rubric: הושענא.
6818. Jerusalem - Makhon b. Zvi 1168 (Tubi 157), f. 24b, M, margins damaged.
6819. Jerusalem - Makhon Ben Zvi 1169 (Tubi 159), f. 63a, M, short.
6820. Jerusalem - Makhon Ben Zvi 1174 (Tubi 154), f. 84a, M, rubric: הושענא.

---

[176] Edited by Sofer, ספר המכתם, p. 156.

6821. Jerusalem - Makhon ben Zvi 1186 (Tubi 205), f. 6a-6b, M, rubric: הושענא, incipit חיות.
6822. Jerusalem - Michael Krupp 604, f. 92b-93a, M, rubric: הושענא.
6823. Jerusalem - Michael Krupp 1990, f. 100a, M, rubric: הושענא.
6824. Jerusalem - Musad haRav Kook 325, f. 105a-105b, M, rubric: הושענא.
6825. Jerusalem - Musad haRav Kook 325, f. 122b-123a, M, rubric: הושענא, no incipit, very short.
6826. Jerusalem - Musad haRav Kook 330, f. 68a, M.
6827. Jerusalem - Musad haRav Kook 347, f. 58a-58b, M.
6828. Jerusalem - Sassoon 1158, p. 214, M, rubric: הושענא.
6829. Jerusalem - Sassoon 1174, p. 143, M, rubric: הושענא.
6830. Jerusalem - Schocken Institute 70028, f. 188b, M, rubric: הושענא.
6831. Jerusalem - Yehiel haLevi 4, f. 88a, M, no incipit, very short.
6832. London - British Library Or. 11122, f. 121b-122a, M, rubric: הושענא.
6833. London - British Library Or. 11121, f. 132b, C, no incipit.
6834. Manchester - John Rylands University Library, Ms. Gaster 5, f. 148b-149a, M, rubric: הושענא.
6835. Muenchen - Bayerische Staatsbibliothek, Cod. hebr. 472, f. 99a-99b, M, rubric: הושענא.
6836. Nahariya - Menahem and Saida Yaakob 284, f. 13a-13b, M, rubric: הושענא, incipit חיות.
6837. New York - Jewish Theological Seminary Ms. 3013, f. 74b-75a, M, rubric: הושענא.
6838. New York - Jewish Theological Seminary Ms. 3028, f. 246b-248a, C, rubric: ליום רביעי.
6839. New York - Jewish Theological Seminary Ms. 3108, f. 79a-80a, C, rubric: ליום רביעי.
6840. New York - Jewish Theological Seminary Ms. 3193, f. 163a-163b, M, rubric: הושע'.
6841. New York - Jewish Theological Seminary Ms. 3295, f. 90a-90b, M, rubric: הושענא, incipit חיות.
6842. New York - Jewish Theological Seminary Ms. 4195, f. 18b-20b, M, incipit חיות.
6843. New York - Public Library, Heb. Ms. 9, f. 72a-72b, M, rubric: הושענא, no incipit.
6844. Oxford - Bodleian Library MS Opp. Add. fol. 58 (Neubauer 2498), f. 142a, M, rubric: הושענא.
6845. Paris - G. Epstein 23/57, f. 103a-103b, C.
6846. Philadelphia - University of Pennsylvania HB 2, f. 98a, M, rubric: הושענא.
6847. Ramat Gan - Universitat Bar Ilan 703, f. 194b-195a, M, rubric: הושענא.
6848. San Francisco - California State Library, Sutro Branch MS 154 (Brinner 125), f. 108a-108b, C, rubric: ליום רביעי.

6849. Strasbourg - Bibliotheque Nationale et Universitaire 3965 (Landauer 39), p. 237-238, M,rubric: הושענא.

Yemen, commentary by Samḥun b. Salomo Ḥaloah

6850. Jerusalem - Makhon ben Zvi 2808, f. 80a-84b, C.

Yemen, commentary by Simon b. Tsemaḥ Duran

6851. Jerusalem - Michael Krupp 1758, f. 9b-10b, M.

Yemen, commentary by Yiḥya b. Josef Tsalaḥ

6852. Montreal - Elberg 203, f. 8a-8b, M.

6853. Montreal - Elberg 203, f. 11a-11b, M, no incipit.

אנא השם הנכבד (א 6301), סליחה

Ashkenaz

6854. Berlin - Staatsbibliothek (Preussischer Kulturbesitz) Or. Qu. 798-799 (Steinschneider 177), I, f. 143b-144a, M.

6855. Muenchen - Bayerische Staatsbibliothek, Cod. hebr. 346, f. 136b-137a, C, rubric: אחרת, short.

6856. Oxford - Bodleian Library MS Mich. 543 (Neubauer 1212), f. 24b-25a, C, commentator: Isaac b. Jacob (compiler), rubric: ועתה אתחיל לכתו' הסליח' מיום כיפור ואתחיל באנא.

6857. Oxford - Bodleian Library MS Opp. 172 (Neubauer 1211), f. 55b-56a, C.

6858. Oxford - Bodleian Library MS Opp. 681 (Neubauer 1213), f. 23a, C,.

6859. Padova - Biblioteca del Seminario Vescovile Cod. 218, f. 172a-173a, M.

6860. Vatican - Bibliotcca Apostolica ebr. 422/1, f. 24a, C, very short.

Ashkenaz, commentary by Abraham b. Azriel[177]

6861. Frankfurt a M - Stadt- und Universitaetsbibliothek Fol. 16 (Merzbacher 95), f. 105b, C.

Tsarfat

6862. Oxford - Bodleian Library MS Bodl. Or. 109 (Neubauer 1209), f. 66a, C, commentator: Aaron b. Hayyim haKohen (compiler).

אנא השם סלח חטאתי תחילה ואחרכך חטאת עמך, סליחה

Ashkenaz

6863. Muenchen - Bayerische Staatsbibliothek, Cod. hebr. 346, f. 145a, C.

אנא השקיפה וראה מלך רם וגואל (א 6303), בנימין ב"ר זרח, זולת

Ashkenaz

6864. Muenchen - Bayerische Staatsbibliothek, Cod. hebr. 346, f. 138b-139a, C, rubric: אחרת.

---

[177] Edited by Urbach, ערוגת הבושם, vol. III, p. 550-551.

6865. Parma - Biblioteca Palatina Cod. Parm. 3205 (de Rossi 655), f. 149a-150a, C.

Ashkenaz, commentary by Abraham b. Azriel[178]

6866. Frankfurt a M - Stadt- und Universitaetsbibliothek Fol. 16 (Merzbacher 95), f. 105a, C, lacks introductory anecdote found in Ms Vatican and Ed. Urbach.

6867. Vatican - Biblioteca Apostolica ebr. 301,1, f. 16b-17b, C.

אנא זכור אב הבטחתו לרשת ארץ עמים שבעה (א 6306), הושענא

Yemen

6868. Chicago-Spertus College of Judaica D 10, f. 130b, M.
6869. Jerusalem - Musad haRav Kook 952, f. 20b-21a, M, rubric: פירוש.
6870. New York - Alfred Moldovan HH, f. 19b, M, rubric: הקפה ב', short.

Yemen, commentary by Isaac b. Abraham Wanneh

6871. Jerusalem - Israel Museum 180/78, f. 23b, M, rubric: הקפה, short.
6872. Jerusalem - Makhon ben Zvi 1186 (Tubi 205), f. 10b, M, incipit עממים, short.
6873. Jerusalem - Musad haRav Kook 325, f. 103a, M, rubric: פירוש.
6874. Nahariya - Menahem and Saida Yaakob 284, f. 7b, M, rubric: חידושין.
6875. New York - Jewish Theological Seminary Ms. 4195, f. 10a, M.
6876. Paris - G. Epstein 23/57, f. 108b, C, short.
6877. Ramat Gan - Universitat Bar Ilan 703, f. 197b, M, rubric: הקפה שנית, short.

Yemen, commentary by Samḥun b. Salomo Ḥaloah

6878. Jerusalem - Makhon ben Zvi 2808, f. 183a-194b, C.

Yemen, commentary by Yiḥya b. Josef Tsalaḥ

6879. Montreal - Elberg 203, f. 6a-6b, M, short.

אנא זכור אב ירש את הארץ (א 6309), הושענא

Carpentras

6880. New York - Jewish Theological Seminary Ms. 1609, f. 98a, C, kabbalistic, no incipit.

haAri, commentary by Mose b. Hayyim Pesante

6881. New York - Columbia University X 893 J 558, f. 199b-200a, M, very short.
6882. New York - Jewish Theological Seminary Ms. 4696, f. 10b, C, very short.

haAri, commentary by Simon b. Tsemaḥ Duran

6883. New York - Columbia University X 893 J 558, f. 199b-200a, M, very short.

---

[178] Edited by Urbach, ערוגת הבושם, vol. I, p. 104-109.

Yemen

6884. Chicago-Spertus College of Judaica D 10, f. 120b-121a, M, no incipit.
6885. Jerusalem - Musad haRav Kook 952, f. 4a-4b, M, incipit אב.

Yemen, commentary by Isaac b. Abraham Wanneh

6886. Jerusalem - Benayahu ת 282, f. 73a, M, rubric: הושענא, begins תבנה.
6887. Jerusalem - Israel Museum 180/78, f. 4b-5a, M, no incipit.
6888. Jerusalem - Makhon ben Zvi 1186 (Tubi 205), f. 2a, M, incipit תבנה.
6889. Paris - G. Epstein 23/57, f. 97b, C

Yemen, commentary by Samḥun b. Salomo Ḥaloah

6890. Jerusalem - Makhon ben Zvi 2808, f. 13a-17a, C.

אנא זכור יחיד בחרת בו לקץ נסים (6308 א), הושענא

Yemen

6891. Chicago-Spertus College of Judaica D 10, f. 132a, M, rubric: פירוש, no incipit.
6892. Jerusalem - Michael Krupp 3391, f. 12b, M, rubric: פירוש.
6893. Jerusalem - Musad haRav Kook 952, f. 21a-22b, M, rubric: הקפה שלישית יעקב.
6894. New York - Alfred Moldovan HH, f. 21a-21b, M, rubric: הקפה ג'.

Yemen, commentary by Isaac b. Abraham Wanneh

6895. Jerusalem - Israel Museum 180/78, f. 25a-25b, M, rubric: הושענא.
6896. Jerusalem - Makhon ben Zvi 1186 (Tubi 205), f. 11a-11b, M, incipit לקץ.
6897. Jerusalem - Musad haRav Kook 325, f. 104a, M, rubric: פירוש.
6898. Nahariya - Menaḥem and Saida Yaakob 284, f. 10a-10b, M, incipit לקץ.
6899. New York - Jewish Theological Seminary Ms. 4195, f. 14a-14b, M.
6900. Paris - G. Epstein 23/57, f. 108b-109a, C, rubric: פי' הקפה שלישית.
6901. Ramat Gan - Universitat Bar Ilan 703, f. 197b, M, rubric: הקפה ג' יעקב.

Yemen, commentary by Yiḥya b. Josef Tsalaḥ

6902. Montreal - Elberg 203, f. 8b-9a, M.

אנא זכור לאברהם ליצחק ולישראל (6310 א), אלעזר, סליחה

Ashkenaz

6903. Berlin - Staatsbibliothek (Preussischer Kulturbesitz) Or. Qu. 798-799 (Steinschneider 177), I, f. 170b-171a, M.
6904. Muenchen - Bayerische Staatsbibliothek, Cod. hebr. 346, f. 139a, C, rubric: אחרת.
6905. Vatican - Biblioteca Apostolica ebr. 422/1, f. 26b, C.
6906. Vatican - Biblioteca Apostolica ebr. 422/1, f. 31a, C, very short.
6907. Vatican - Biblioteca Apostolica ebr. 422/2, f. 40a, CG, no incipit, very short.

Ashkenaz, commentary by Abraham b. Azriel[179]
6908. Frankfurt a M - Stadt- und Universitaetsbibliothek Fol. 16 (Merzbacher 95), f. 104b-105a, C.

Tsarfat
6909. Oxford - Bodleian Library MS Bodl. Or. 109 (Neubauer 1209), f. 66b-67a, C, commentator: Aaron b. Hayyim haKohen (compiler).

אנא זכור תם המשתחוה אפים ארצה שבעה (א 6312), הושענא

Yemen
6910. Jerusalem - Musad haRav Kook 952, f. 22b-23b, M, rubric: 'הקפה ד משה.

Yemen, commentary by Isaac b. Abraham Wanneh
6911. Jerusalem - Musad haRav Kook 325, f. 106a, M, rubric: חדושין.
6912. Nahariya - Menahem and Saida Yaakob 284, f. 13b, M, inicpit צרפתו.
6913. Paris - G. Epstein 23/57, f. 109a, C, rubric: 'פי הקפה.
6914. Ramat Gan - Universitat Bar Ilan 703, f. 197b, M, rubric: 'הקפה ד משה.

Yemen, commentary by Yiḥya b. Josef Tsalaḥ
6915. Montreal - Elberg 203, f. 11b-12a, M.

אנא חטא העם הזה חטאה גדולה (א 6317), אליה ב"ר שמעיה, סליחה

Ashkenaz
6916. Cambridge - University Library Dd. 2.30, f. 32a-32b, G.
6917. Jerusalem - Schocken Institute 24100 / Mahzor Nuremberg, f. 395b-396a, M.
6918. Muenchen - Bayerische Staatsbibliothek, Cod. hebr. 346, f. 119b, C.
6919. Oxford - Bodleian Library MS Opp. 172 (Neubauer 1211), f. 55a-55b, C.
6920. Oxford - Bodleian Library MS Opp. 681 (Neubauer 1213), f. 23b-24b, C.
6921. Padova - Biblioteca del Seminario Vescovile Cod. 218, f. 173b-174a, M.
6922. Vatican - Biblioteca Apostolica ebr. 308, f. 109b-110a, C, commentator: David b. Mose (compiler).

Ashkenaz, commentary by Abraham b. Azriel[180]
6923. Frankfurt a M - Stadt- und Universitaetsbibliothek Fol. 16 (Merzbacher 95), f. 105a-105b, C.

Asti, Fossano, Moncalvo
6924. New Haven - Yale University, Beinecke Rare Book and MS Library, MS Heb. 52, f. 120a, M.

---

[179] Edited by Urbach, ערוגת הבושם, vol. III, p. 547-548.
[180] Edited by Urbach, ערוגת הבושם, vol. III, p. 549-550.

Tsarfat
6925. Oxford - Bodleian Library MS Bodl. Or. 109 (Neubauer 1209), f. 66a-66b, C, commentator: Aaron b. Hayyim haKohen (compiler).

אנא חיש נא ישעי (א 6318), יוסף בן יצחק קמחי, הושענא

haAri, commentary by Mose b. Hayyim Pesante
6926. New York - Columbia University X 893 J 558, f. 207b, M.
6927. New York - Jewish Theological Seminary Ms. 4696, f. 20b, C.

North Africa, commentary by Simon b. Tsemaḥ Duran
6928. New York - Jewish Theological Seminary Ms. 4121, f. 48a, C, no incipit.

North Africa, commentary by Yehuda Toledano
6929. New York - Jewish Theological Seminary Ms. 4300, f. 38b-39a, C.

Yemen, commentary by Isaac b. Abraham Wanneh
6930. Jerusalem - Makhon Ben Zvi 1156 (Tubi 155), f. 77b, M, no incipit.
6931. Jerusalem - Makhon Ben Zvi 1174 (Tubi 154), f. 88a, M, no incipit.
6932. Jerusalem - Musad haRav Kook 325, f. 127b, M, no incipit.
6933. Jerusalem - Sassoon 1158, p. 219, M, no incipit.
6934. Muenchen - Bayerische Staatsbibliothek, Cod. hebr. 472, f. 102b, M, no incipit.
6935. New York - Jewish Theological Seminary Ms. 3028, f. 250b, C, no incipit.
6936. New York - Jewish Theological Seminary Ms. 3108, f. 83a, C, no incipit.
6937. New York - Jewish Theological Seminary Ms. 3193, f. 169b, M, no incipit.
6938. New York - Jewish Theological Seminary Ms. 3295, f. 94b, M, no incipit.
6939. Strasbourg - Bibliotheque Nationale et Universitaire 3965 (Landauer 39), p. 248, M, no incipit.

Yemen, commentary by Samḥun b. Salomo Ḥaloah
6940. Jerusalem - Makhon ben Zvi 2808, f. 164b-166b, C.

Yemen, commentary by Simon b. Tsemaḥ Duran
6941. Jerusalem - Michael Krupp 1758, f. 21a, M, rubric: פירוש.

אנא יוצרי דורשני וכימי עולם חפשני (א 6322), יוסף אבן אביתור, הושענא

Carpentras
6942. New York - Jewish Theological Seminary Ms. 1609, f. 98a-98b, C, kabbalistic, rubric: 'יום ב', no incipit.

North Africa, commentary by Yehuda Toledano
6943. New York - Jewish Theological Seminary Ms. 4300, f. 14a-14b, C.

Yemen, commentary by Samḥun b. Salomo Ḥaloah
6944. Jerusalem - Makhon ben Zvi 2808, f. 51a-52a, C.

אנא יוצרי וקדושי שעה לחשי ורחשי ומחה (א 6323), יוסף אבן אביתור, הושענא
haAri, commentary by Mose b. Hayyim Pesante
6945. New York - Columbia University X 893 J 558, f. 205a, M, incipit מחה.
6946. New York - Jewish Theological Seminary Ms. 4696, f. 17b-18a, C, incipit מחה.
haAri, commentary by Simon b. Tsemaḥ Duran
6947. New York - Columbia University X 893 J 558, f. 205a, M, incipit מחה.
North Africa, commentary by Yehuda Toledano
6948. New York - Jewish Theological Seminary Ms. 4300, f. 28b, C.
Yemen, commentary by Samḥun b. Salomo Ḥaloah
6949. Jerusalem - Makhon ben Zvi 2808, f. 120b-122a, C.

אנא יסד יסוד מקדשי (א 6327), יוסף אבן אביתור, הושענא
haAri, commentary by Mose b. Hayyim Pesante
6950. New York - Columbia University X 893 J 558, f. 203a, M.
North Africa
6951. Jerusalem - Benayahu ז 27, f. 67a, M, no incipit.
North Africa, commentary by Yehuda Toledano
6952. New York - Jewish Theological Seminary Ms. 4300, f. 20a-20b, C, no incipit.
Yemen, commentary by Samḥun b. Salomo Ḥaloah
6953. Jerusalem - Makhon ben Zvi 2808, f. 71a-72b, C.

אנא יערב לך שועי בלולבי (א 6328), יוסף אבן אביתור, הושענא
Carpentras
6954. New York - Jewish Theological Seminary Ms. 1609, f. 98b, C, no incipit.
haAri, commentary by Mose b. Hayyim Pesante
6955. New York - Columbia University X 893 J 558, f. 204a, M.
6956. New York - Jewish Theological Seminary Ms. 4696, f. 16a-16b, C.
North Africa, commentary by Yehuda Toledano
6957. New York - Jewish Theological Seminary Ms. 4300, f. 24a-24b, C.
Yemen, commentary by Samḥun b. Salomo Ḥaloah
6958. Jerusalem - Makhon ben Zvi 2808, f. 96a-98a, C.

אנא ישר מערכי והישר מהלכי (א 6329), יוסף אבן אביתור, הושענא
haAri, commentary by Mose b. Hayyim Pesante
6959. New York - Columbia University X 893 J 558, f. 206a-206b, M, incipit הישר.
6960. New York - Jewish Theological Seminary Ms. 4696, f. 19b, C, incipit הישר.

North Africa, commentary by Yehuda Toledano
6961. New York - Jewish Theological Seminary Ms. 4300, f. 34a-34b, C, incipit הישר.
Yemen, commentary by Samḥun b. Salomo Ḥaloah
6962. Jerusalem - Makhon ben Zvi 2808, f. 145a-145b, C, incipit הישר.

אנא ישר עם בא בהושענא רבה לסלסלך בחבה (א 6330), הושענא
haAri, commentary by Mose b. Hayyim Pesante
6963. New York - Jewish Theological Seminary Ms. 4696, f. 23b, C.
North Africa
6964. Jerusalem - Benayahu ת 27, f. 127b-128a, M.
North Africa, commentary by Yehuda Toledano
6965. New York - Jewish Theological Seminary Ms. 4300, f. 55a-56a, C.
Yemen, commentary by Samḥun b. Salomo Ḥaloah
6966. Jerusalem - Makhon ben Zvi 2808, f. 198b-202b, C.

אנא כעב זדוני תמחהו (א 6332), משה אבן עזרא, סליחה
Yemen
6967. Jerusalem - Benayahu ת 88, f. 113b, M.
6968. New York - Jewish Theological Seminary Ms. 3193, f. 117a, M.
Yemen, commentary by Isaac b. Abraham Wanneh
6969. Chicago-Spertus College of Judaica D 2, 2, f. 179a, M.
6970. Jerusalem - Makhon Ben Zvi 1174 (Tubi 154), f. 99a-99b, M.
6971. London - British Library Or. 11122, f. 155b, M.
6972. Manchester - John Rylands University Library, Ms. Gaster 5, f. 173b, M.
6973. Philadelphia - University of Pennsylvania HB 2, f. 114a, M.

אנא מועד עת פלא פחד, סליחה
Ashkenaz
6974. Muenchen - Bayerische Staatsbibliothek, Cod. hebr. 346, f. 145a, C.

אנא מלך מלא רחמים (א 6340), יצחק ב"ר יקר, סליחה
Ashkenaz, commentary by Abraham b. Azriel[181]
6975. Frankfurt a M - Stadt- und Universitaetsbibliothek Fol. 16 (Merzbacher 95), f. 110a, C.

אנא משה רחימה ספרא דמלכה רמה (א 6346), לשמחת תורה
Yemen
6976. Jerusalem - Benayahu ת 283, f. 99b-100a.
6977. Jerusalem - Michael Krupp 1758, f. 25a-26a, M.

---

[181] Edited by Urbach, ערוגת הבושם, vol. III, p. 569.

6978. Jerusalem - Michael Krupp 3391, f. 18a, M.
6979. New York - Alfred Moldovan HH, f. 30a-31a.
6980. New York - Jewish Theological Seminary Ms. 3193, f. 170a-170b, M.
6981. New York - Jewish Theological Seminary Ms. 3295, f. 95b, M.
6982. New York - Jewish Theological Seminary Ms. 4488, f. 72a, M, very short.

Yemen, commentary by Isaac b. Abraham Wanneh?
6983. Jerusalem - Makhon Ben Zvi 1156 (Tubi 155), f. 78a, M, margin damaged.
6984. Manchester - John Rylands University Library, Ms. Gaster 5, f. 154b-155a, M.
6985. Muenchen - Bayerische Staatsbibliothek, Cod. hebr. 472, f. 103b, M, margin damaged.
6986. Nahariya - Menahem and Saida Yaakob 284, f. 22b-23b, M.
6987. New York - Jewish Theological Seminary Ms. 3013, f. 80b, M.
6988. New York - Jewish Theological Seminary Ms. 4195, f. 39a-42b, M.

Yemen, commentary by Yiḥya b. Josef Tsalaḥ
6989. Montreal - Elberg 203, f. 32a-33b, M.

אנא סגל סגלתך וקבץ קהלתך, הושענא

Yemen, commentary by Samḥun b. Salomo Ḥaloah
6990. Jerusalem - Makhon ben Zvi 2808, f. 146a-147a, C.

אנא עוררה אהבתך הישנה (א 6353), שלמה, סליחה

Ashkenaz
6991. Jerusalem - Schocken Institute 24100 / Mahzor Nuremberg, f. 250b, M.
6992. Muenchen - Bayerische Staatsbibliothek, Cod. hebr. 346, f. 150a, C.
6993. Vatican - Biblioteca Apostolica ebr. 308, f. 12a, C, commentator: David b. Mose (compiler).
6994. Vatican - Biblioteca Apostolica ebr. 308, f. 163a, C, commentator: David b. Mose (compiler), short.

אנא רחום אל תן ברשענו ביטה בחגיגנו ושענו (א 6363), הושענא

Italia, commentary by Yehoshua Segri
6995. Moscow - Russian State Library, Ms. Guenzburg 533, f. 52b-54a, C, rubric: לימוד כא.

אנא תרב עליצותיך (א 6373), זולת

Ashkenaz
6996. New York - Jewish Theological Seminary Ms. 4466, f. 444a-444b, M.
6997. Oxford - Bodleian Library MS Opp. 172 (Neubauer 1211), f. 91a, C, rubric: זולת.

6998. Parma - Biblioteca Palatina Cod. Parm. 3507 (Perreau 27), f. 175b-176a, C.

אנגלי מרומא פתחון לי לניעול (א 6374), רשות לעשרת הדברות בארמית
Ashkenaz, commentary by Benjamin b. Abarahm Anaw
6999. Jerusalem - Musad haRav Kook 478, p. 7-9, C, rubric: אלפא ביתא ב.
7000. London - Beth Din & Beth Hamidrash 6,9, f. 152a-153a, C, rubric: אלפא ביטא.
7001. Warszaw - Zydowski Instytut Historyczny 838, f 3b-4a, C, rubric: אלפא ביטא.

אנוסה בעזרה בעמדי בצרה (א 6395), סעדיה, סליחה
Yemen
7002. Jerusalem - Benayahu ת 301, f. 61a, G.
7003. New York - Jewish Theological Seminary Ms. 3028, f. 70a, G.
7004. New York - Jewish Theological Seminary Ms. 3052, f. 79a, M, no incipit.
Yemen, commentary by Isaac b. Abraham Wanneh
7005. Chicago-Spertus College of Judaica D 2, 2, f. 236a-236b, M, no incipit.
7006. Jerusalem - Benayahu ת 261, f. 164a, M.
7007. Jerusalem - Benayahu ת 282, f. 139b, M.
7008. Jerusalem - Makhon Ben Zvi 1156 (Tubi 155), f. 137b, M, no incipit.
7009. Jerusalem - Makhon Ben Zvi 1174 (Tubi 154), f. 134b, M.
7010. Jerusalem - Michael Krupp 604, f. 174a, M.
7011. Jerusalem - Musad haRav Kook 325, f. 192b, M.
7012. Jerusalem - Sassoon 1158, p. 414, M, no incipit.
7013. Jerusalem - Sassoon 1174, p. 267, M, no incipit, short.
7014. London - British Library Or. 11122, f. 213a-213b, M, no incipit.
7015. Manchester - John Rylands University Library, Ms. Gaster 5, f. 221b, M.
7016. Muenchen - Bayerische Staatsbibliothek, Cod. hebr. 472, f. 191b, M.
7017. New York - Jewish Theological Seminary Ms. 3013, f. 131b, M, no incipit.
7018. New York - Jewish Theological Seminary Ms. 3294, f. 16a, C.
7019. New York - Public Library, Heb. Ms. 9, f. 128a, M, no incipit, begins גליתי.
7020. Strasbourg - Bibliotheque Nationale et Universitaire 3965 (Landauer 39), p. 405, M.

אנוסה לעזרה אמצא נגדי (א 6396), יוסי בן יוסי, שופרות, מוסף ראש השנה
Ashkenaz

7021. Berlin - Staatsbibliothek (Preussischer Kulturbesitz) Or. Qu. 798-799 (Steinschneider 177), I, f. 50a-53a, M.
7022. Braunschweig - Landesmuseum fuer Geschichte und Volkstum R 2386, vol. II, f. 121b, M.
7023. Budapest - Magyar tudomanyos akademia, MS. Kaufmann A 400, p. 295-299, C.
7024. Cambridge - University Library Or. 785, f. 78b-81a, G.
7025. Darmstadt - Hessisches Landes- und Hochschulbibliothek Cod. Or. 15, f. 59b-61b, M.
7026. Darmstadt - Hessisches Landes- und Hochschulbibliothek Cod. Or. 15, f. 64b-66b, M.
7027. Hamburg - Staats- und Universitaetsbibliothek Cod. hebr. 17/2 (Steinschneider 152), f. 125a-126b, C, rubric: סדר שופרות.
7028. Hamburg - Staats- und Universitaetsbibliothek Cod. hebr. 40b (Steinschneider 110), f. 64a-66b, G.
7029. Hamburg - Staats- und Universitaetsbibliothek Cod. hebr. 40c (Steinschneider 111), f. 159b-160b, G.
7030. Hamburg - Staats- und Universitaetsbibliothek Cod. hebr. 132 (Steinschneider 155), f. 28a-30a, C.
7031. Jerusalem - Jewish National and University Library Ms Heb 8° 3037, f. 80b-82b, M.
7032. Jerusalem - Schocken Institute 24100 / Mahzor Nuremberg, f. 350b-352a, M.
7033. London - British Library Or. 11318/1, f. 55a-58b, C.
7034. London - Montefiore Library 261, f. 22a-25a, C, commentator: Eliezer b. Natan?.
7035. Moscow - Russian State Library, Ms. Guenzburg 191, f. 68b-70b, M.
7036. Moscow - Russian State Library, Ms. Guenzburg 615, f. 76b-79a, C.
7037. Muenchen - Bayerische Staatsbibliothek, Cod. hebr. 86, f. 82b-84a, M.
7038. Muenchen - Bayerische Staatsbibliothek, Cod. hebr. 346, f. 43a-46a, C.
7039. Muenchen - Bayerische Staatsbibliothek, Cod. hebr. 393, f. 146b-148a, C.
7040. New York - Jewish Theological Seminary Ms. 4466, f. 274a-278a, M.
7041. New York - Jewish Theological Seminary Ms. 8097, f. 69a, C.
7042. Oxford - Bodleian Library MS Mich. 365 (Neubauer 1208), f. 59b-62b, C.
7043. Oxford - Bodleian Library MS Opp. 170 (Neubauer 1205), f. 154a-160a, C, commentator: Salomo b. Isaac (Rashi)?, rubric: היום הרת.
7044. Oxford - Bodleian Library MS Opp. 172 (Neubauer 1211), f. 28a-30a, C.

7045. Oxford - Bodleian Library MS Opp. 619 (Neubauer 2374), f. 91b-93b, M.
7046. Oxford - Bodleian Library MS Opp. 675 (Neubauer 1210), f. 65a-66b, C, no incipit.
7047. Paris - Bibliotheque Nationale heb. 653, f. 40a-40b, G.
7048. Parma - Biblioteca Palatina Cod. Parm. 3205 (de Rossi 655), f. 221a-222b, C.
7049. Parma - Biblioteca Palatina Cod. Parm. 3270 (de Rossi 1215), f. 71b-74a, M.
7050. Parma - Biblioteca Palatina Cod. Parm. 3507 (Perreau 27), f. 140a-142b, C.
7051. Vatican - Biblioteca Apostolica ebr. 308, f. 86a-89b, C, commentator: David b. Mose (compiler).
7052. Zurich - Zentralbibliothek Heid. 139, f. 72a-72b, C, no incipit, additional marginal notes.

Asti, Fossano, Moncalvo

7053. New Haven - Yale University, Beinecke Rare Book and MS Library, MS Heb. 52, f. 77a-78b, M.

Tsarfat

7054. London - British Library Add. 11639 (Margoliouth 1056), f. 716b-717b, M.
7055. London - British Library Or. 8682, f. 49a-50a, Gl.
7056. London - David Sofer 5, f. 127a-128a, C.
7057. Oxford - Bodleian Library MS Bodl. Or. 109 (Neubauer 1209), f. 5b-8a, C, commentator: Aaron b. Hayyim haKohen (compiler).
7058. Oxford - Bodleian Library MS Laud. Or. 271 (Neubauer 1206), f. 161b-163b, C, commentator: Aaron b. Hayyim haKohen (compiler), rubric: שופרות.
7059. Oxford - Bodleian Library MS Opp. 171 (Neubauer 1207), f. 79a-80b, C.
7060. Parma - Biblioteca Palatina Cod. Parm. 1794 (de Rossi 1061), f. 103b-107a, M.
7061. Parma - Biblioteca Palatina Cod. Parm. 2125 (de Rossi 812), f. 36a-37a, C, rubric: שופרות.
7062. Parma - Biblioteca Palatina Cod. Parm. 3006 (de Rossi 654,1), f. 101a-102b, M.
7063. Vatican - Biblioteca Apostolica ebr. 306, f. 73a-75a, C.

אנוסה לעזרה פצתי עדיך (א 6398), אלעזר ב"ר יהודה מוורמייזא, סליחה

Ashkenaz

7064. Braunschweig - Landesmuseum fuer Geschichte und Volkstum R 2386, vol. II, f. 121b-123a, M.
7065. New York - Jewish Theological Seminary Ms. 8169 (Acc. 0016), f. 56a-58a, M.

7066. Oxford - Bodleian Library MS Mich. 543 (Neubauer 1212), f. 17a-17b, C, commentator: Isaac b. Jacob (compiler).
7067. Oxford - Bodleian Library MS Opp. 681 (Neubauer 1213), f. 38a, C, short.
7068. Vatican - Biblioteca Apostolica ebr. 422/1, f. 14a-14b, C.
Tsarfat
7069. Oxford - Bodleian Library MS Bodl. Or. 109 (Neubauer 1209), f. 79b-80a, C, commentator: Aaron b. Hayyim haKohen (compiler).

אנוסה עדיך לבקש רחמיך (א 6399), משה, סליחה
Yemen, commentary by Isaac b. Abraham Wanneh
7070. Chicago-Spertus College of Judaica D 2, 2, f. 246a, M, no incipit.
7071. Jerusalem - Sassoon 1158, p. 423-424, M, no incipit.
7072. London - British Library Or. 11122, f. 218b, M, no incipit.

אנוש איך יצדק פני יוצרו (א 6401), חלק ג׳, קדושתא למוסף יום כפור
Ashkenaz
7073. Parma - Biblioteca Palatina Cod. Parm. 3205 (de Rossi 655), f. 234a, C, incipit עד.

אנוש איך יתכפר (א 6403), תוכחה
Ashkenaz
7074. London - Montefiore Library 261, f. 63a, C, commentator: Eliezer b. Natan?, incipit מנויה, short.
7075. Vatican - Biblioteca Apostolica ebr. 308, f. 138b-139b, C, commentator: David b. Mose (compiler).

אנוש מה יזכה (א 6476), משולם ב״ר קלונימוס, חלק ג׳, קדושתא לשחרית יום כפור
Ashkenaz
7076. Berlin - Staatsbibliothek (Preussischer Kulturbesitz) Or. Qu. 798-799 (Steinschneider 177), I, f. 71b-72a, M.
7077. Braunschweig - Landesmuseum fuer Geschichte und Volkstum R 2386, vol. II, f. 184b-185a, M, no incipit.
7078. Budapest - Magyar tudomanyos akademia, MS. Kaufmann A 400, p. 306-308, C, incipit עד.
7079. Fulda - Hessische Landesbibliothek A 3 II, f. 122b-123a, C, commentator: Josef.
7080. Hamburg - Staats- und Universitaetsbibliothek Cod. hebr. 17/2 (Steinschneider 152), f. 150a-150b, C, rubric: תוכחה, incipit עד.
7081. Hamburg - Staats- und Universitaetsbibliothek Cod. hebr. 40b (Steinschneider 110), f. 90b-91a, G.
7082. Hamburg - Staats- und Universitaetsbibliothek Cod. hebr. 62 (Steinschneider 154), f. 2b-3a, C, rubric: תוכוחה.

7083. Jerusalem - Jewish National and University Library Ms Heb 8° 3037, f. 115a, M.
7084. Jerusalem - Schocken Institute 24100 / Mahzor Nuremberg, f. 375b, M.
7085. London - British Library Or. 11318/1, f. 70b-71b, C, no incipit.
7086. Moscow - Russian State Library, Ms. Guenzburg 615, f. 93a-93b, C, rubric: עד יום מותו תחכה לו וכו'.
7087. Ms JTS Mic. 4466, f. 303b-304a, M.
7088. Muenchen - Bayerische Staatsbibliothek, Cod. hebr. 393, f. 140a-140b, C, no incipit.
7089. Muenchen - Bayerische Staatsbibliothek, Cod. hebr. 86, f. 99b, M.
7090. New York - Jewish Theological Seminary Ms. 8097, f. 71a, C, additional glosses in the margins, incipit נפש.
7091. New York - Jewish Theological Seminary Ms. 8097, f. 82a, C.
7092. Oxford - Bodleian Library MS Mich. 365 (Neubauer 1208), f. 81a-81b, C, rubric: תוכיחה, incipit עד.
7093. Oxford - Bodleian Library MS Opp. 170 (Neubauer 1205), f. 165b-166a, C.
7094. Oxford - Bodleian Library MS Opp. 172 (Neubauer 1211), f. 36a-36b, C.
7095. Oxford - Bodleian Library MS Opp. 619 (Neubauer 2374), f. 138b-139b, M.
7096. Parma - Biblioteca Palatina Cod. Parm. 3271 (de Rossi 1216), f. 33b-34a, G.
7097. Vatican - Biblioteca Apostolica ebr. 308, f. 98(i)b 98(ii)a, C, commentator: David b. Mose (compiler).

Tsarfat
7098. Oxford - Bodleian Library MS Bodl. Or. 109 (Neubauer 1209), f. 18a-18b, C, commentator: Aaron b. Hayyim haKohen (compiler).
7099. Oxford - Bodleian Library MS Laud. Or. 271 (Neubauer 1206), f. 112a, C, commentator: Aaron b. Hayyim haKohen (compiler), rubric: תוכיחה פיזמונית, no incipit.

אנוש עד דכא תשב (א 6499), מאיר ב"ר יצחק, סליחה

Ashkenaz
7100. Cambridge - University Library Dd. 2.30, f. 53a-54a, G.
7101. Muenchen - Bayerische Staatsbibliothek, Cod. hebr. 346, f. 131a-132a, C.
7102. Muenchen - Bayerische Staatsbibliothek, Cod. hebr. 346, f. 164a-164b, C, short.
7103. Oxford - Bodleian Library MS Mich. 543 (Neubauer 1212), f. 34a-38a, C, commentator: Isaac b. Jacob (compiler).
7104. Oxford - Bodleian Library MS Opp. 681 (Neubauer 1213), f. 10b-15b, C.

7105. Parma - Biblioteca Palatina Cod. Parm. 3205 (de Rossi 655), f. 263b-265b, C.
7106. Vatican - Biblioteca Apostolica ebr. 422/1, f. 27b-28a, C.
7107. Vatican - Biblioteca Apostolica ebr. 422/1, f. 41a-41b, CG, no incipit. Ashkenaz, commentary by Abraham b. Azriel[182]
7108. Vatican - Biblioteca Apostolica ebr. 301,1, f. 149a-149b, C.
Ashkenaz, commentary by Elazar b. Yehuda of Worms
7109. Budapest - Magyar tudomanyos akademia, MS. Kaufmann A 400, p. 466-475, C, rubric: סליחה אחרת דר' מאיר שליח ציבור. בשוחר טוב מזמור תפילה למשה אנוש תשב עד דכא כנגד יחי ראובן וזהו בשביל שעשה תשוב.
7110. Budapest - Magyar tudomanyos akademia, MS. Kaufmann A 400, p. 495-503, C, rubric: פירוש מאילו ב' סליחות מאת מורי הר' אלעזר בן רבנא יהודא ז"ל ור' מאיר שליח ציבור יסדם.
7111. Hamburg - Staats- und Universitaetsbibliothek Cod. hebr. 17/2 (Steinschneider 152), f. 138b-141a, C, rubric: סליחה אחרת דר' מאיר שליח ציבור זצ"ל.
7112. Paris - Bibliotheque Nationale heb. 1408/22, f. 120a-123a, C, rubric: סליחה מהר' מאיר שליח ציבור בשוחר טוב במזמור תפילה למשה. תשב אנוש עד דכא כנגד ראובן שעשה תשובה.

אנושי לב כארי שועו עד בקר (א 6520), משה אבן עזרא, קדושתא למנחה יום כפור
Carpentras
7113. Cincinnati - Hebrew Union College 392, f. 101a, M, no incipit.
Carpentras, commentary by Josef b. Abraham of Montelitz
7114. New York Jewish Theological Seminary Ms. 4197, f. 234b, M.
7115. Paris - Ecole Rabbinique 32, f. 242a, M.
7116. Strasbourg - Bibliotheque Nationale et Universitaire 4081, f. 214b-215a, M.

אנחנו אשמנו במעשינו (א 6530), שמואל, סליחה
Ashkenaz
7117. Berlin - Staatsbibliothek (Preussischer Kulturbesitz) Or. Qu. 798-799 (Steinschneider 177), I, f. 99b, M.

אנחנו בני גלות דכאנו העוני והדלתות (א 6531), אברהם אבן עזרא, סליחה
Carpentras, commentary by Mordekhai b. Josef of Rocco Martino
7118. Cincinnati - Hebrew Union College 246/1, f. 56b-57a, C, rubric: פי' רהוטה אנחנו וכו'.

---

[182] Edited by Urbach, ערוגת הבושם, vol. III, p. 355-360.

אני אני המדבר (א 6652), אפרים ב"ר יצחק מרגנסבורג, סליחה

Ashkenaz
7119. Muenchen - Bayerische Staatsbibliothek, Cod. hebr. 346, f. 136b, C, rubric: אחרת.
7120. Oxford - Bodleian Library MS Opp. 172 (Neubauer 1211), f. 72a-73a, C.
7121. Oxford - Bodleian Library MS Opp. 681 (Neubauer 1213), f. 26b-27b, C.
7122. Padova - Biblioteca del Seminario Vescovile Cod. 218, f. 198b-199b, M.
7123. Vatican - Biblioteca Apostolica ebr. 308, f. 132a-133b, C, commentator: David b. Mose (compiler).

Ashkenaz, commentary by Abraham b. Azriel[183]
7124. Frankfurt a M - Stadt- und Universitaetsbibliothek Fol. 16 (Merzbacher 95), f. 106b, C.
7125. Vatican - Biblioteca Apostolica ebr. 301,1, f. 150b-151a, C.

Asti, Fossano, Moncalvo
7126. New Haven - Yale University, Beinecke Rare Book and MS Library, MS Heb. 52, f. 154b-155a, M, very ecclectic.

Tsarfat
7127. Oxford - Bodleian Library MS Bodl. Or. 109 (Neubauer 1209), f. 69b-70b, C, commentator: Aaron b. Hayyim haKohen (compiler).

אני אשאל שבח האל תחלה (א 6590), שלם שבזי

Yemen
7128. Cincinnati - Hebrew Union College 398, f. 171a-173a, M.

אני בינה שכנה מעונה ואמונה (א 6620), יצחק בן מרדכי קמחי, פתיחה לאזהרות

Carpentras
7129. New York - Jewish Theological Seminary Ms. 4268, f. 20b, C, rubric: פירוש הפתיחה.
7130. Parma - Biblioteca Palatina Cod. Parm. 3491, f. 15a-15b, M, rubric: פירוש.

Carpentras, commentary by Isaac b. Mordekhai Qimhi
7131. Marseille - Mlle. Odette Valabregue [1], f. 51b-52a, C, rubric: פירוש אזהרות של מנחם יום ראשון.
7132. Moscow - Russian State Library, Ms. Guenzburg 211, f. 57b-58a, M.
7133. Moscow - Russian State Library, Ms. Guenzburg 710, f. 70a-72a, M.

---

[183] Edited by Urbach, ערוגת הבושם, vol. III, p. 366-368.

אני ברוב חסדך אבא ביתך (א 6631), סליחה

Ashkenaz

7134. Moscow - Russian State Library, Ms. Guenzburg 190, f. 7b-8a, M.
7135. Oxford - Bodleian Library MS Mich. 543 (Neubauer 1212), f. 19b-20a, C, commentator: Isaac b. Jacob (compiler).
7136. Oxford - Bodleian Library MS Opp. 681 (Neubauer 1213), f. 10a-10b, C.
7137. Parma - Biblioteca Palatina Cod. Parm. 3205 (de Rossi 655), f. 284a, C.
7138. Vatican - Biblioteca Apostolica ebr. 422/1, f. 27a-27b, C, very short.
7139. Vatican - Biblioteca Apostolica ebr. 422/1, f. 41a, CG, no incipit.

Tsarfat

7140. London - David Sofer 5, f. 92b, C, very short.
7141. Oxford - Bodleian Library MS Bodl. Or. 109 (Neubauer 1209), f. 70b-71a, C, commentator: Aaron b. Hayyim haKohen (compiler).
7142. Oxford - Bodleian Library MS Laud. Or. 271 (Neubauer 1206), f. 129b, C, commentator: Aaron b. Hayyim haKohen (compiler).
7143. Parma - Biblioteca Palatina Cod. Parm. 3006 (de Rossi 654,1), f. 155b, M, very short.
7144. Vatican - Biblioteca Apostolica ebr. 306, f. 88b-89a, C.

Yemen

7145. Jerusalem - Benayahu ת 414, f. 125a, M, rubric: פירוש, .
7146. Jerusalem - Musad haRav Kook 334, f. 130a, M, page torn.
7147. Jerusalem - Sassoon 264, f. 149a, M, rubric: פירוש.
7148. New York - Jewish Theological Seminary Ms. 3028, f. 12a, M, short.
7149. New York - Jewish Theological Seminary Ms. 3108, f. 24a-24b, M, short.
7150. New York - Jewish Theological Seminary Ms. 4488, f. 105b, M, short.

Yemen, commentary by Isaac b. Abraham Wanneh

7151. Chicago-Spertus College of Judaica D 2, 2, f. 186b, M, rubric: פירוש הסליחות.
7152. Jerusalem - Benayahu ת 261, f. 124a, M, rubric: פירוש.
7153. Jerusalem - Benayahu ת 282, f. 109b, M, rubric: פירוש הסליחות.
7154. Jerusalem - Benayahu ת 301, f. 40b, M, rubric: חדושין.
7155. Jerusalem - Makhon Ben Zvi 1156 (Tubi 155), f. 107b, M, rubric: פירוש הסליחות.
7156. Jerusalem - Makhon Ben Zvi 1174 (Tubi 154), f. 106a, C, rubric: פירוש הסליחות.
7157. Jerusalem - Michael Krupp 604, f. 136a, M, rubric: פירוש הסליחות.
7158. Jerusalem - Musad haRav Kook 325, f. 155b, M, rubric: פירוש הסליחות.
7159. Jerusalem - Musad haRav Kook 347, f. 74b, M.
7160. Jerusalem - Sassoon 1158, p. 337, M, rubric: פירוש הסליחות.
7161. Jerusalem - Sassoon 1174, p. 207, M, rubric: פירוש הסליחות.

7162. London - British Library Or. 11122, f. 166b, M, rubric: פירוש הסליחות.
7163. Manchester - John Rylands University Library, Ms. Gaster 5, f. 181a-181b, M, rubric: פירוש הסליחות. להרב המחדש זלה"ה וז"ל.
7164. Muenchen - Bayerische Staatsbibliothek, Cod. hebr. 472, f. 145b, M, rubric: פירוש הסליחות.
7165. New York - Jewish Theological Seminary Ms. 3013, f. 107b, M, rubric: פרוש.
7166. New York - Jewish Theological Seminary Ms. 3294, f. 1b, C, rubric: אתחיל לכתוב פירוש הסליחות.
7167. New York - Public Library, Heb. Ms. 9, f. 102b, G .
7168. Philadelphia - University of Pennsylvania HB 2, f. 119a, M, rubric: פירוש הסליחות.

אני הגבר, קינה
Ashkenaz
7169. Budapest - Magyar tudomanyos akademia, MS. Kaufmann A 400, p. 185-187, C.

אני הגבר אקונן בליל זה במר ואתאונן (א 6641), קינה
Yemen, commentary by Isaac b. Abraham Wanneh
7170. Jerusalem - Sassoon 1158, p. 162, M, rubric: קינה סים' שלמה.
7171. London - British Library Or. 11122, f. 98a, M.

אני חומה ושדי כמגדלות (א 6688), יהודה ב"ר מנחם, יוצר לשבת הגדול
Roma
7172. Jerusalem - Jewish National and University Library Ms Heb 8° 4153, f. 157b, C, commentator: Daniel ben Salomo haRofe (compiler), rubric: פי' יוצר לשבת הגדול של פסח.
7173. Oxford - Bodleian Library MS Mich. 312,1 (Neubauer 2276,1), f. 23a, C, rubric: פי' יוצר לשבת הגדול של פסח.

אני יום אירא אליך (א 6698), שלמה הבבלי, סליחה
Ashkenaz
7174. Budapest - Magyar tudomanyos akademia, MS. Kaufmann A 400, p. 436-438, C, rubric: סליחה אחרת שלמונית.
7175. Cambridge - University Library Add. 858,1, f. 46a-47a, C, commentator: Elazar b. Yehuda of Worms?, incipit מעשה.
7176. Cambridge - University Library Dd. 2.30, f. 9b-10a, G.
7177. Hamburg - Staats- und Universitaetsbibliothek Cod. hebr. 17/2 (Steinschneider 152), f. 130b, C, rubric: אחרת שלמונית.
7178. Hamburg - Staats- und Universitaetsbibliothek Cod. hebr. 62 (Steinschneider 154), f. 30a-31a, C.

7179. Jerusalem - Schocken Institute 24100 / Mahzor Nuremberg, f. 240a, M.
7180. Moscow - Russian State Library, Ms. Guenzburg 190, f. 27b-28a, G.
7181. Moscow - Russian State Library, Ms. Guenzburg 615, f. 155b-156a, C, rubric: אל מלך.
7182. Muenchen - Bayerische Staatsbibliothek, Cod. hebr. 346, f. 128a, C, rubric: אחרת.
7183. Muenchen - Bayerische Staatsbibliothek, Cod. hebr. 346, f. 128b-129b, C.
7184. Oxford - Bodleian Library MS Mich. 543 (Neubauer 1212), f. 66b-67a, C, commentator: Isaac b. Jacob (compiler).
7185. Oxford - Bodleian Library MS Opp. 170 (Neubauer 1205), f. 224b-225a, C.
7186. Padova - Biblioteca del Seminario Vescovile Cod. 218, f. 63a-63b, M.
7187. Padova - Biblioteca del Seminario Vescovile Cod. 218, f. 63b, M, rubric: אחרת.
7188. Padova - Biblioteca del Seminario Vescovile Cod. 218, f. 240a-240b, M.
7189. Padova - Biblioteca del Seminario Vescovile Cod. 218, f. 240b-241a, M.
7190. Parma - Biblioteca Palatina Cod. Parm. 3205 (de Rossi 655), f. 254a-254b, C.
7191. Vatican - Biblioteca Apostolica ebr. 422/1, f. 27a, C.
7192. Vatican - Biblioteca Apostolica ebr. 422/1, f. 40b-41a, CG, no incipit.

Ashkenaz, commentary by Abraham b. Azriel[184]

7193. Vatican - Biblioteca Apostolica ebr. 301,1, f. 157a-157b, C, rubric: אחרת.

Tsarfat

7194. London - British Library Add. 11639 (Margoliouth 1056), f. 468b-469a, M.
7195. London - David Sofer 5, f. 89b-90b, C.
7196. Oxford - Bodleian Library MS Laud. Or. 271 (Neubauer 1206), f. 175b-176a, C, commentator: Aaron b. Hayyim haKohen (compiler).
7197. Oxford - Bodleian Library MS Opp. 171 (Neubauer 1207), f. 88a-88b, C, rubric: אחרת.
7198. Parma - Biblioteca Palatina Cod. Parm. 3007 (de Rossi 654,2), f. 63b-64a, M, partly censored.
7199. Vatican - Biblioteca Apostolica ebr. 306, f. 172a-173a, C.

אני מי מלך שמור, יצחק בן מרדכי קחמי, פתיחה לחלק ב' של אזהרות

Carpentras, commentary by Isaac b. Mordekhai Qimhi?

7200. Marseille - Mlle. Odette Valabregue [1], f. 72a, C, rubric: פי' האזהרות

---

[184] Edited by Urbach, ערוגת הבושם, vol. III, p. 412-414.

למנחם יום שני של שבועות.

7201. Moscow - Russian State Library, Ms. Guenzburg 211, f. 82b-83a, M.
7202. Moscow - Russian State Library, Ms. Guenzburg 710, f. 131a-132a, M.
7203. New York - Columbia University X 893 G 11, f. 24b, M.
7204. New York - Jewish Theological Seminary Ms. 4268, f. 49b, C.
7205. Parma - Biblioteca Palatina Cod. Parm. 3491, f. 39b-40a, M, rubric: פירוש הפתיחה.

אני עבדך בן אמתיך (א 6756), אפרים ב"ר יעקב מבון, סליחה

Ashkenaz

7206. Braunschweig - Landesmuseum fuer Geschichte und Volkstum R 2386, vol. II, f. 69b-70b, M.
7207. London - British Library Add. 18695 (Margoliouth 683), f. 166a-166b, T, Yiddish.
7208. Oxford - Bodleian Library MS Mich. 543 (Neubauer 1212), f. 20a, C, commentator: Isaac b. Jacob (compiler), only one marginal note.

אני שואל אשר יסד פני תבל, סליחה

Yemen

7209. New York - M. Lehmann 274, f. 125a, M, kabbalistic.

אנכי אחת דבר בקדשו (א 6793), יוסף ב"ר יעקב, מעריב לשבועות

Tsarfat

7210. Jerusalem - Schocken Institute 19623, f. 91a-91b, M, commentator: Yehuda b. Eliezer Zvi.
7211. London - David Sofer 5, f. 48b-49a, C, rubric: זה פירוש ממעריב של שבועות.
7212. Parma - Biblioteca Palatina Cod. Parm. 1902, f. 109b-112a, M.
7213. Parma - Biblioteca Palatina Cod. Parm. 3136 (de Rossi 405), f. 146b-147a, M.

אנכי בשם אל שדי (א 6804), אלעזר ברבי קליר, חלק ד', קדושתא לשבועות

Ashkenaz

7214. Berlin - Staatsbibliothek (Preussischer Kulturbesitz) Or. Qu. 798-799 (Steinschneider 177), II, f. 140a, M, inicpit אנכי.
7215. Braunschweig - Landesmuseum fuer Geschichte und Volkstum R 2386, vol. I, f. 97a, M, no incipit.
7216. Budapest - Magyar tudomanyos akademia, MS. Kaufmann A 400, p. 177, C, rubric: אל נא.
7217. Hamburg - Staats- und Universitaetsbibliothek Cod. hebr. 17/2 (Steinschneider 152), f. 86a, C.

7218. Jerusalem - Schocken Institute 24100 / Mahzor Nuremberg, f. 172a-172b, M.
7219. London - British Library Add. 18695 (Margoliouth 683), f. 85b-86a, T, Yiddish.
7220. London - British Library Add. 22431 (Margoliouth 662a), f. 56a, M.
7221. Moscow - Russian State Library, Ms. Guenzburg 615, f. 41b, C, incipit אל נא.
7222. Muenchen - Bayerische Staatsbibliothek, Cod. hebr. 88, f. 140a-140b, G.
7223. New York - Jewish Theological Seminary Ms. 4466, f. 167a, M, no incipit.
7224. Oxford - Bodleian Library MS Opp. 170 (Neubauer 1205), f. 87a, C.
7225. Paris - Bibliotheque Nationale heb. 709, f. 136a, C, no incipit.
7226. Parma - Biblioteca Palatina Cod. Parm. 2886 (de Rossi 585), f. 64b, M, later hand, margins cut.
7227. Parma - Biblioteca Palatina Cod. Parm. 3507 (Perreau 27), f. 88b-89a, C, no incipit.
7228. Parma - Biblioteca Palatina Cod. Parm. 3205 (de Rossi 655), f. 127b, C, no incipit.
7229. Zurich - Zentralbibliothek Heid. 139, f. 54b, C, no incipit, short, additional marginal notes.

אנכי גדול בנועדים גואלך (א 6805), זולת לשבועות
Ashkenaz
7230. Berlin Staatsbibliothek (Preussischer Kulturbesitz) Or. Qu. 798-799 (Steinschneider 177), II, f. 139a, M.
7231. Braunschweig - Landesmuseum fuer Geschichte und Volkstum R 2386, vol. 1, f. 96a, M.
7232. London - British Library Add. 22431 (Margoliouth 662a), f. 54a, M.

אנכי שמעת ונתאימו (א 6820), שמעון ב"ר יצחק, זולת לשבועות
Ashkenaz
7233. Berlin - Staatsbibliothek (Preussischer Kulturbesitz) Or. Qu. 798-799 (Steinschneider 177), II, f. 114b-115a, M.
7234. Braunschweig - Landesmuseum fuer Geschichte und Volkstum R 2386, vol. I, f. 72a, M.
7235. Budapest - Magyar tudomanyos akademia, MS. Kaufmann A 400, p. 153-154, C.
7236. Hamburg - Staats- und Universitaetsbibliothek Cod. hebr. 17/2 (Steinschneider 152), f. 82a, C.
7237. Jerusalem - Schocken Institute 24100 / Mahzor Nuremberg, f. 146a-146b, M, no incipit.

7238. London - British Library Add. 18695 (Margoliouth 683), f. 64b-65a, T, Yiddish, rubric: זולת.

7239. London - British Library Add. 18695 (Margoliouth 683), f. 84b-85a, T, Yiddish, rubric: דא היבט אן דש זולת.

7240. London - British Library Add. 22431 (Margoliouth 662a), f. 6b-7a, M.

7241. Muenchen - Bayerische Staatsbibliothek, Cod. hebr. 88, f. 115b, G.

7242. New York - Jewish Theological Seminary Ms. 4466, f. 124b-125a, M.

7243. Oxford - Bodleian Library MS Opp. 170 (Neubauer 1205), f. 86a-86b, C, rubric: זולת.

7244. Paris - Bibliotheque Nationale heb. 709, f. 120a-120b, C, rubric: זולת, incipit missing.

7245. Parma - Biblioteca Palatina Cod. Parm. 1002 (Ta 24), f. 176a, M.

7246. Parma - Biblioteca Palatina Cod. Parm. 3205 (de Rossi 655), f. 120a, C.

7247. Parma - Biblioteca Palatina Cod. Parm. 3507 (Perreau 27), f. 87b-88a, C.

7248. Zurich - Zentralbibliothek Heid. 139, f. 50a, C.

Tsarfat

7249. London - David Sofer 5, f. 50a-50b, C.

7250. Moscow - Russian State Library, Ms. Guenzburg 1665, f. 116b-117a, M.

7251. Parma - Biblioteca Palatina Cod. Parm. 3136 (de Rossi 405), f. 148a, M.

7252. Vatican - Biblioteca Apostolica ebr. 306, f. 226a-227a, C, rubric: זולת.

אנכי תכנתי עמודים (א 6821), דוד בן גדליה, זולת שבועות

Ashkenaz

7253. New York - Jewish Theological Seminary Ms. 4466, f. 165a-165b, M.

7254. Parma - Biblioteca Palatina Cod. Parm. 3205 (de Rossi 655), f. 127a, C, rubric: זולת.

אנסו אמונים בעלי אמונה, סליחה

Yemen, commentary by Isaac b. Abraham Wanneh

7255. Chicago-Spertus College of Judaica D 2, 2, f. 240a-241a, M, no incipit.

אנסיכה מלכי לפניו בהתהלכי (א 6823), אלעזר ברבי קליר, מלכויות

Ashkenaz

7256. Berlin - Staatsbibliothek (Preussischer Kulturbesitz) Or. Qu. 798-799 (Steinschneider 177), I, f. 22a-25b, M.

7257. Braunschweig - Landesmuseum fuer Geschichte und Volkstum R 2386, vol. II, f. 99a-100b, M.

7258. Budapest - Magyar tudomanyos akademia, MS. Kaufmann A 400, p. 273-276, C, rubric: סדר תקיעא.
7259. Darmstadt - Hessisches Landes- und Hochschulbibliothek Cod. Or. 15, f. 21b-23a, M.
7260. Hamburg - Staats- und Universitaetsbibliothek Cod. hebr. 12 (Steinschneider 102), f. 22a-23b, G.
7261. Hamburg - Staats- und Universitaetsbibliothek Cod. hebr. 17/2 (Steinschneider 152), f. 116b-118a, C, rubric: סדר תקועות דר׳ אלעזר.
7262. Hamburg - Staats- und Universitaetsbibliothek Cod. hebr. 40b (Steinschneider 110), f. 22a-24a, G.
7263. Hamburg - Staats- und Universitaetsbibliothek Cod. hebr. 40c (Steinschneider 111), f. 141b-142b, G.
7264. Hamburg - Staats- und Universitaetsbibliothek Cod. hebr. 132 (Steinschneider 155), f. 16b-18a, C.
7265. Jerusalem - Jewish National and University Library Ms Heb 8° 3037, f. 35a-37a, M.
7266. Jerusalem - Schocken Institute 15791/7, f. 65a-65b, C, kabbalistic.
7267. Jerusalem - Schocken Institute 24100 / Mahzor Nuremberg, f. 335a-336a, M.
7268. Koblenz - Staatsarchiv Abt. 701, Nr. 759,5,8, f. 1a-1b, FC, incomplete.
7269. London - British Library Or. 11318/1, f. 21a-25a, C.
7270. London - Montefiore Library 261, f. 31a-32b, C, commentator: Eliezer b. Natan?.
7271. Moscow - Russian State Library, Ms. Guenzburg 191, f. 20a-22a, M.
7272. Moscow - Russian State Library, Ms. Guenzburg 615, f. 79a-81a, C, rubric: סדר תקיעתא ליום ראשון.
7273. Moscow - Russian State Library, Ms. Guenzburg 1401/2, f. 19a-19b, C.
7274. Muenchen - Bayerische Staatsbibliothek, Cod. hebr. 86, f. 36b-39b, G.
7275. Muenchen - Bayerische Staatsbibliothek, Cod. hebr. 346, f. 21b-26a, C, rubric: תקיעתא קלירית.
7276. New York - Jewish Theological Seminary Ms. 4466, f. 233a-235a, M.
7277. New York - Jewish Theological Seminary Ms. 8097, f. 63a-63b, C, additional glosses in the margins.
7278. New York - Jewish Theological Seminary Ms. 8169 (Acc. 0016), f. 24b-26a, M.
7279. Oxford - Bodleian Library MS Mich. 365 (Neubauer 1208), f. 41b-42b, C, beginning missing.
7280. Oxford - Bodleian Library MS Opp. 170 (Neubauer 1205), f. 128a-131a, C, rubric: תקיעת.
7281. Oxford - Bodleian Library MS Opp. 172 (Neubauer 1211), f. 14b-15b, C.

7282. Oxford - Bodleian Library MS Opp. 619 (Neubauer 2374), f. 38a-40a, M.
7283. Oxford - Bodleian Library MS Opp. 675 (Neubauer 1210), f. 32a-34b, C, no incipit.
7284. Paris - Bibliotheque Nationale heb. 653, f. 20b-21b, G.
7285. Parma - Biblioteca Palatina Cod. Parm. 3205 (de Rossi 655), f. 212a-213b, C, rubric: סדר תקיעתא.
7286. Parma - Biblioteca Palatina Cod. Parm. 3270 (de Rossi 1215), f. 39b-41a, M.
7287. Parma - Biblioteca Palatina Cod. Parm. 3507 (Perreau 27), f. 124b-126a, C.
7288. Vatican - Biblioteca Apostolica ebr. 308, f. 59a-62a, C, commentator: David b. Mose (compiler).
7289. Vatican - Biblioteca Apostolica ebr. 422/1, f. 10b-11a, C.
7290. Zurich - Zentralbibliothek Heid. 139, f. 67a-68a, C, additional marginal notes.

Asti, Fossano, Moncalvo
7291. New Haven - Yale University, Beinecke Rare Book and MS Library, MS Heb. 52, f. 39b-41a, M.

Tsarfat
7292. London - British Library Add. 11639 (Margoliouth 1056), f. 711a-712b, M, rubric: תקיעתות.
7293. London - British Library Or. 8682, f. 27a-28a, GI.
7294. London - David Sofer 5, f. 116a-117a, C, rubric: תקיעתות.
7295. Oxford - Bodleian Library MS Laud. Or. 271 (Neubauer 1206), f. 149b-151a, C, commentator: Aaron b. Hayyim haKohen (compiler), rubric: אחל תקיעתות.
7296. Oxford - Bodleian Library MS Opp. 171 (Neubauer 1207), f. 69a-72a, C, rubric: תקיעתות קליריות.
7297. Paris - Bibliotheque Nationale heb. 445,9, f. 83a-85a, C.
7298. Parma - Biblioteca Palatina Cod. Parm. 2125 (de Rossi 812), f. 23a-25a, C.
7299. Parma - Biblioteca Palatina Cod. Parm. 3006 (de Rossi 654,1), f. 52a-53b, M.
7300. Vatican - Biblioteca Apostolica ebr. 306, f. 58b-61a, C.

אנעים זמירות ושירים אערוג, מעריב ליום כפור

Ashkenaz
7301. Braunschweig - Landesmuseum fuer Geschichte und Volkstum R 2386, vol. II, f. 177a-177b, M.

אנעים לקלס בעידוני (א 6825),יוסף ב"ר שמואל טוב עלם , יוצר ליום ח' של פסח

Tsarfat

7302. Parma - Biblioteca Palatina Cod. Parm. 3136 (de Rossi 405), f. 121b-122a, M.

אנקת מסלדיך תעל לפני כסא כבודך (א 6844), סילנו, סליחה

Ashkenaz

7303. Vatican - Biblioteca Apostolica ebr. 308, f. 151a, C, commentator: David b. Mose (compiler).
7304. Vatican - Biblioteca Apostolica ebr. 422/1, f. 32b, C, very short.

אנקתי תעלה למרומך (א 6848), סליחה

Ashkenaz

7305. Vatican - Biblioteca Apostolica ebr. 422/1, f. 31a, C, very short.
7306. Vatican - Biblioteca Apostolica ebr. 422/1, f. 42a, CG, very short.

אנשי אמונה אבדו באים בכח מעשיהם (א 6850), סליחה

Ashkenaz

7307. Braunschweig - Landesmuseum fuer Geschichte und Volkstum R 2386, vol. II, f. 40b, M, short.
7308. Muenchen - Bayerische Staatsbibliothek, Cod. hebr. 346, f. 145a, C, very short.
7309. Muenchen - Bayerische Staatsbibliothek, Cod. hebr. 346, f. 150b, C, short.
7310. Muenchen - Bayerische Staatsbibliothek, Cod. hebr. 346, f. 150b-151a, C, rubric: אחרת, short.
7311. Oxford - Bodleian Library MS Mich. 543 (Neubauer 1212), f. 12b, C, commentator: Isaac b. Jacob (compiler).
7312. Oxford - Bodleian Library MS Opp. 172 (Neubauer 1211), f. 82b, C.
7313. Oxford - Bodleian Library MS Opp. 681 (Neubauer 1213), f. 42b, C.
7314. Vatican - Biblioteca Apostolica ebr. 308/1, f. 9b, C, commentator: David b. Mose (compiler), short.
7315. Vatican - Biblioteca Apostolica ebr. 308, f. 142b, C, commentator: David b. Mose (compiler).
7316. Vatican - Biblioteca Apostolica ebr. 422/1, f. 26a, C.
7317. Vatican - Biblioteca Apostolica ebr. 422/2, f. 40a, CG, no incipit, very short.

Ashkenaz, commentary by Abraham b. Azriel[185]

7318. Frankfurt a M - Stadt- und Universitaetsbibliothek Fol. 16 (Merzbacher 95), f. 104a, C.

---

[185] Edited by Urbach, ערוגת הבושם, vol. III, p. 545-546.

Carpentras, commentary by Mordekhai b. Josef of Rocco Martino
7319. Cincinnati - Hebrew Union College 246/1, f. 86b-87a, C, rubric: פי׳ רהוטה אנשי אמנה, short.

Sepharad
7320. Jerusalem - Benayahu ז 25, f. 112b-113b, M, short.
7321. Jerusalem - Schocken Institute 70014, f. 60b, M.
7322. Skokie - Hebrew Theological College 3, f. 2.17b-18a, M.
7323. Skokie - Hebrew Theological College 3, f. 7b-8a, M.

Tsarfat
7324. Oxford - Bodleian Library MS Bodl. Or. 109 (Neubauer 1209), f. 46a-46b, C, commentator: Aaron b. Hayyim haKohen (compiler).

Yemen
7325. New York - Jewish Theological Seminary Ms. 3028, f. 94b, G.
7326. New York - Jewish Theological Seminary Ms. 3108, f. 9a, M, short.
7327. New York - Jewish Theological Seminary Ms. 3193, f. 117a-117b, M.
7328. New York - Jewish Theological Seminary Ms. 3193, f. 134a-134b, M, rubric: פי׳ י״ג סליחות.
7329. Ramat Gan - Universitat Bar Ilan 62, f. 35b, G.

Yemen, commentary by Isaac b. Abraham Wanneh
7330. Chicago-Spertus College of Judaica D 2, 2, f. 179a-179b, M.
7331. Jerusalem - Benayahu ת 282, f. 104b, M.
7332. Jerusalem - Sassoon 1158, p. 297, M.
7333. Jerusalem - Yehiel haLevi 4, f. 132a, M.
7334. London - British Library Or. 11122, f. 155b-156a, M.
7335. Manchester - John Rylands University Library, Ms. Gaster 5, f. 173b, M.
7336. New York - Jewish Theological Seminary Ms. 3013, f. 98b, M, very short.
7337. New York - Jewish Theological Seminary Ms. 3295, f. 101b, M, short.
7338. Strasbourg - Bibliotheque Nationale et Universitaire 3965 (Landauer 39), p. 305, M.

אנשי אמונה אבדו ואין איש עומד לפניך (א 6851), סליחה

Ashkenaz
7339. Muenchen - Bayerische Staatsbibliothek, Cod. hebr. 21, f. 244a-244b, M.

אנשי אמונה בתורת אל תדרוכו (א 6852), אהרן בן יוסף הרופא, פרשת בחקתי

Karaite, commentary by Berakha b. Josef haKohen
7340. New York - Jewish Theological Seminary Ms. 3367, f. 113b-117a, C, rubric: פרוש פרשת בחקתי.

אנשי אמנה עברו מרוב עונינו (א 6856), סליחה
Ashkenaz

7343. Oxford - Bodleian Library MS Mich. 543 (Neubauer 1212), f. 12b, C, commentator: Isaac b. Jacob (compiler).
7344. Oxford - Bodleian Library MS Opp. 681 (Neubauer 1213), f. 43a, C.

אנשי חסד הנושאים את הוד קולם (א 6865), משה אבן עזרא, סילוק, קדושתא לנעילה
Carpentras

7345. Cincinnati - Hebrew Union College 392, f. 116a, M, no incipit.
Carpentras, commentary by Josef b. Abraham of Montelitz
7346. Cincinnati - Hebrew Union College 291, f. 58b-59a, C, rubric: פי׳ פזמון אנשי חסד.
7347. Paris - Ecole Rabbinique 32, f. 277a-277b, M, no incipit.
7348. Strasbourg - Bibliotheque Nationale et Universitaire 4081, f. 247a-248a, M, no incipit.

אנשי משמר ואנשי מעמד (א 6878), מאיר ב״ר יצחק שליח ציבור, סליחה
Ashkenaz

7349. Berlin - Staatsbibliothek (Preussischer Kulturbesitz) Or. Qu. 798-799 (Steinschneider 177), I, f. 105a-106a, M.

אנת הוא אלהא דגלן קדמך עמיקתא, סליחה
Yemen, commentary by Isaac b. Abraham Wanneh

7350. Jerusalem - Makhon Ben Zvi 1174 (Tubi 154), f. 136b, M, short.
7351. New York - Jewish Theological Seminary Ms. 3013, f. 133a, M, short, no incipit.
7352. Strasbourg - Bibliotheque Nationale et Universitaire 3965 (Landauer 39), p. 409, M, short.

אסבח כאלקי מאדמת באקי (א 6893), שלם שבזי
Yemen

7353. Cincinnati - Hebrew Union College 398, f. 190b-192b, M.

אסבח כאלקי רב אל כלאייק (א 6894), שלם שבזי
Yemen

7354. Cincinnati - Hebrew Union College 398, f. 188b-190b, M.

אסדר לסעודתא בצפרא דשבתא (א 6898), יצחק לוריא, זמר לשבת
haAri, commentary by Jacob b. Raphael haLevi
7355. Cincinnati - Hebrew Union College 275, f. 3b-4a, 5a, C, rubric: 'פי מנחת יעקב על הזמר אסדר סעודתא לסעודה שניי' של שבת {בד' צא}, the commentary on the second part is written separately with the rubric על פי' החרוז שלפני מים אחרונים.

אסיר משחר עני רב (א 6925), יהודה הלוי, יוצר ליום א' של ראש השנה
Carpentras
7356. Cincinnati - Hebrew Union College 392, f. 23a, M, kabbalistic.
Carpentras, commentary by Eliyahu Carmi
7357. New York - Jewish Theological Seminary Ms. 3151, f. 36a, M.
Carpentras, commentary by Josef b. Abraham of Montelitz
7358. Cincinnati - Hebrew Union College 357, f. 42b, M.
7359. New York - Jewish Theological Seminary Ms. 4746, f. 8a-8b, M.
7360. Paris - Alliance Israelite Universelle H 422 A, f. 15b-16a, M.

אסיר תקותך אני והמוני, סליחה
Yemen, commentary by Isaac b. Abraham Wanneh
7361. Chicago-Spertus College of Judaica D 2, 2, f. 215b, M, no incipit.
7362. Jerusalem - Sassoon 1158, p. 368, M, no incipit.
7363. London - British Library Or. 11122, f. 184a, M, no incipit.

אסירי התקה חניטי חבצלת בנועם (א 6933), מנחם, זולת
Ashkenaz
7364. Budapest - Magyar tudomanyos akademia, MS. Kaufmann A 399, p. 445-446, C, rubric: זולתו.
7365. Oxford - Bodleian Library MS Can. Or. 82 (Neubauer 1148), f. 34a-34b, M.
7366. Parma - Biblioteca Palatina Cod. Parm. 3205 (de Rossi 655), f. 162a-162b, C, rubric: זולת.

אסירי תקותם בכלוא מעצבה (א 6936), משה אבן עזרא, אהבה
Carpentras
7367. Cincinnati - Hebrew Union College 392, f. 42a, M, no incipit.
Carpentras, commentary by Josef b. Abraham of Montelitz
7368. Cincinnati - Hebrew Union College 291, f. 17b-18a, C, rubric: 'פי אסירי תקותם וכו'.
7369. New York - Jewish Theological Seminary Ms. 4197, f. 97a-97b, M, no incipit.
7370. Paris - Ecole Rabbinique 32, f. 120a, M, no incipit.
7371. Strasbourg - Bibliotheque Nationale et Universitaire 4081, f. 97a, M, no incipit.

אסירים אשר בכושר (א 6937), אלעזר ברבי קליר, קדושתא ליום א' של פסח
Ashkenaz
7372. Braunschweig - Landesmuseum fuer Geschichte und Volkstum R 2386, vol. I, f. 36a, M.
7373. Berlin - Staatsbibliothek (Preussischer Kulturbesitz) Or. Qu. 798-799 (Steinschneider 177), II, f. 78b, M.
7374. Budapest - Magyar tudomanyos akademia, MS. Kaufmann A 384, f. 162a-162b, M.
7375. Budapest - Magyar tudomanyos akademia, MS. Kaufmann A 400, p. 130, C, rubric: קדושתא ליום שיני של פסח דר' אלעזר קליר.
7376. Hamburg - Staats- und Universitaetsbibliothek Cod. hebr. 17/2 (Steinschneider 152), f. 64b-65a, C, rubric: קדושתא ליום שיני דר' אלעזר.
7377. Jerusalem - Schocken Institute 24100 / Mahzor Nuremberg, f. 94a, M.
7378. London - British Library Add. 18695 (Margoliouth 683), f. 41a, T, Yiddish, rubric: קרובץ.
7379. Moscow - Russian State Library, Ms. Guenzburg 615, f. 22a-22b, C, rubric: קול רינה וישועה באהלי צדיקים. קרובץ.
7380. Muenchen - Bayerische Staatsbibliothek, Cod. hebr. 88, f. 72a-72b, G.
7381. Muenchen - Bayerische Staatsbibliothek, Cod. hebr. 393, f. 129b, C, no incipit.
7382. New York - Jewish Theological Seminary Ms. 4466, f. 73b, M.
7383. Paris - Bibliotheque Nationale heb. 709, f. 97b-98a, C.
7384. Parma - Biblioteca Palatina Cod. Parm. 1002 (Ta 24), f. 117b, M.
7385. Parma - Biblioteca Palatina Cod. Parm. 3205 (de Rossi 655), f. 101b 102a, C.
7386. Parma - Biblioteca Palatina Cod. Parm. 3507 (Perreau 27), f. 64b, C.
7387. Zurich - Zentralbibliothek Heid. 139, f. 37b, C, additional marginal notes.
Tsarfat
7388. London - British Library Add. 11639 (Margoliouth 1056), f. 293a, M.
7389. Moscow - Russian State Library, Ms. Guenzburg 1665, f. 71a, M, no incipit.
7390. Oxford - Bodleian Library MS Laud. Or. 271 (Neubauer 1206), f. 72b-73a, C, commentator: Aaron b. Hayyim haKohen (compiler), rubric: קרובי.

אסירים המקוים למלאך הבשורה (א 6939), אריה יהודה הירחי בן לוי, פזמון
Carpentras, commentary by Mordekhai b. Josef of Rocco Martino
7391. Cincinnati - Hebrew Union College 246/1, f. 30a-30b, C, rubric: פזמון אסירים המקום.

אסירים כיצאו ביד רמה (א 6940), זולת לשבת שקלים

Tsarfat
7392. London - David Sofer 5, f. 8a-8b, C.
7393. Moscow - Russian State Library, Ms. Guenzburg 1665, f. 12b-13b, M.
7394. Parma - Biblioteca Palatina Cod. Parm. 3136 (de Rossi 405), f. 20b-21b, M.
7395. Vatican - Biblioteca Apostolica ebr. 306, f. 156a-157a, C, no incipit.

אסלאד יא חורי אלגנאני, שלם שבזי

Yemen
7396. Cincinnati - Hebrew Union College 398, f. 48b-49b, M.

אסלאד יא עוהגי אלגזלאן, שלם שבזי

Yemen
7397. Cincinnati - Hebrew Union College 398, f. 50a-50b, M.
7398. New York - M. Lehmann 274, f. 68a-69b, M, kabbalistic.

אסלאד יא עוהגי זא צאח, שלמה בן אברהם

Yemen
7399. New York - M. Lehmann 274, f. 71a-72b, M, kabblistic.

אסלד לקורא הדורות (א 6943), בנימין ב"ר שמואל, חלק ז', קדושתא לראש השנה

Ashkenaz
7400. Moscow - Russian State Library, Ms. Guenzburg 191, f. 12b, M, short.
7401. New York - Jewish Theological Seminary Ms. 8169 (Acc. 0016), f. 47b, M.

Tsarfat
7402. London - David Sofer 5, f. 114b, C.
7403. Parma - Biblioteca Palatina Cod. Parm. 1794 (de Rossi 1061), f. 85a-85b, M.
7404. Parma - Biblioteca Palatina Cod. Parm. 3006 (de Rossi 654,1), f. 45b, M.

אספרה אל חוק אל צוה (א 6979), אברהם ב"ר חייא, קדושתא לשבת פרה

Carpentras, commentary by Mordekhai b. Josef of Rocco Martino
7405. Cincinnati - Hebrew Union College 246/1, f. 28a-28b, C, no incipit.
Sepharad, commentary by Josef Garad
7406. Oxford - Bodleian Library Heb.e.10 (Neubauer 2746/1), f. 11a, C, rubric: מגן.
7407. Oxford - Bodleian Library Heb.e.10 (Neubauer 2746/1), f. 19b, C, rubric: אספרה, no incipit, very short.

אספרה אל חוק (א 6980), אלעזר ברבי קליר, קרובה לפורים, פיוט הרכבה

Ashkenaz
7408. Berlin - Staatsbibliothek (Preussischer Kulturbesitz) Or. Qu. 798-799 (Steinschneider 177), II, f. 28b-29b, M.
7409. Budapest - Magyar tudomanyos akademia, MS. Kaufmann A 384, f. 68a-69a, M.
7410. Budapest - Magyar tudomanyos akademia, MS. Kaufmann A 400, p. 70-73, C.
7411. Hamburg - Staats- und Universitaetsbibliothek Cod. hebr. 17/2 (Steinschneider 152), f. 23b, C.
7412. Hamburg - Staats- und Universitaetsbibliothek Cod. hebr. 40c (Steinschneider 111), f. 16b-17a, G.
7413. Jerusalem - Schocken Institute 24100 / Mahzor Nuremberg, f. 50a-50b, M.
7414. Muenchen - Bayerische Staatsbibliothek, Cod. hebr. 88, f. 35a-35b, G.
7415. Muenchen - Bayerische Staatsbibliothek, Cod. hebr. 393, f. 98a-98b, C, no incipit.
7416. New York - Jewish Theological Seminary Ms. 4466, f. 1b-2b, M.
7417. Paris - Bibliotheque Nationale heb. 709, f. 30b-31b, C.
7418. Parma - Biblioteca Palatina Cod. Parm. 1002 (Ta 24), f. 48a-48b, M.
7419. Parma - Biblioteca Palatina Cod. Parm 3000 (de Rossi 378), f. 2a-2b, M, beginning missing.
7420. Parma - Biblioteca Palatina Cod. Parm. 3205 (de Rossi 655), f. 30b-31a, C.
7421. Parma - Biblioteca Palatina Cod. Parm. 3507 (Perreau 27), f. 24a-24b, C.
7422. Vatican - Biblioteca Apostolica ebr. 305,1, f. 35a-35b, C.
7423. Zurich - Zentralbibliothek Heid. 139, f. 2a-3a, C, additional marginal notes.

Tsarfat
7424. Moscow - Russian State Library, Ms. Guenzburg 1665, f. 23b-24a, M.
7425. Oxford - Bodleian Library MS Laud. Or. 271 (Neubauer 1206), f. 35b-36b, C, commentator: Aaron b. Hayyim haKohen (compiler).
7426. Oxford - Bodleian Library MS Opp. 171 (Neubauer 1207), f. 31a-31b, C.
7427. Parma - Biblioteca Palatina Cod. Parm. 3136 (de Rossi 405), f. 37a-37b, M.

אסתופף באולמך ישעי ואורי (א 6992), רשות למוסף ראש השנה

Ashkenaz
7428. Alessandria - Archivio di Stato Fr. ebr. 12, FC.
7429. Moscow - Russian State Library, Ms. Guenzburg 191, f. 8a, M.

Asti, Fossano, Moncalvo
7430. New Haven - Yale University, Beinecke Rare Book and MS Library, MS Heb. 52, f. 30a, M.

Tsarfat
7431. London - British Library Or. 8682, f. 18a, GI.
7432. London - David Sofer 5, f. 113a, C, rubric: רשות למוסף.
7433. Parma - Biblioteca Palatina Cod. Parm. 2125 (de Rossi 812), f. 31a-31b, C, rubric: רשות למוסף.
7434. Parma - Biblioteca Palatina Cod. Parm. 3006 (de Rossi 654,1), f. 41a, M, additional marginal notes.

אסתכל בעמך דגלא מניה יקריה, סליחה

Yemen
7435. Ramat Gan - Universitat Bar Ilan 62, f. 51b, G.

Yemen, commentary by Isaac b. Abraham Wanneh
7436. Chicago-Spertus College of Judaica D 2, 2, f. 236a, M, no incipit.
7437. Jerusalem - Makhon Ben Zvi 1174 (Tubi 154), f. 134b, M.
7438. Jerusalem - Musad haRav Kook 325, f. 192b, M.
7439. Jerusalem - Sassoon 1158, p. 413-414, M, no incipit.
7440. London - British Library Or. 11122, f. 213a, M, no incipit.
7441. New York - Jewish Theological Seminary Ms. 3013, f. 131a, M.
7442. New York - Jewish Theological Seminary Ms. 3294, f. 16a, C, incipit מרן.

אעורר טוב מחשבתי ואביע נלאותיך, סליחה

Yemen, commentary by Isaac b. Abraham Wanneh
7443. Chicago-Spertus College of Judaica D 2, 2, f. 218a-218b, M, no incipit.
7444. Jerusalem - Sassoon 1158, p. 378, M, no incipit.
7445. London - British Library Or. 11122, f. 189b, M, no incipit.

אעמוד במשמר מנעמי (א 7046), משה אבן עזרא, מאורה

Carpentras
7446. Cincinnati - Hebrew Union College 392, f. 41b-42a, M, no incipit.

Carpentras, commentary by Josef b. Abraham of Montelitz
7447. Cincinnati - Hebrew Union College 291, f. 17a-17b, C, rubric: פי' אעמוד מנעמי וכו'.
7448. New York - Jewish Theological Seminary Ms. 4197, f. 96a-96b, M, no incipit.
7449. Paris - Ecole Rabbinique 32, f. 119a-119b, M, no incipit.
7450. Strasbourg - Bibliotheque Nationale et Universitaire 4081, f. 96a-96b, M, rubric: אמר הצייד, no incipit.

אעניד לך תפארה והלל (א 7052), מעריב שמיני עצרת

Tsarfat

7451. London - David Sofer 5, f. 182b-183a, C, rubric: מעריב לליל שמיני עצרת.

אערוך ביום צומי רוב המוני, סליחה

Yemen

7452. New York - Jewish Theological Seminary Ms. 3028, f. 99b, G.
7453. New York - Jewish Theological Seminary Ms. 3193, f. 139a-139b, M.

Yemen, commentary by Isaac b. Abraham Wanneh

7454. London - British Library Or. 11122, f. 204b, M, no incipit.

אערוך לך ואצפה לקול קורא ומצפה, זולת לשבת זכור

Tsarfat

7455. London - David Sofer 5, f. 16a-16b, C, rubric: זולת.
7456. Parma - Biblioteca Palatina Cod. Parm. 3136 (de Rossi 405), f. 27a, M.
7457. Vatican - Biblioteca Apostolica ebr. 306, f. 160a-161a, C, no incipit.

אערוך מדברי דתי (א 7064), משה אבן עזרא, רשות לסדר עבודה

haAri

7458. New York - Columbia University X 893 J 558, f. 170b-171a, M, kabbalistic.

אערוך שועי בבית שועי גליתי בצום פשעי (א 7071), הושענא

Ashkenaz

7459. Berlin - Staatsbibliothek (Preussischer Kulturbesitz) Or. Qu. 361 (Steinschneider 51), f. 116a, M.
7460. Berlin - Staatsbibliothek (Preussischer Kulturbesitz) Or. Qu. 798-799 (Steinschneider 177), I, f. 203b, M, short.
7461. Budapest - Magyar tudomanyos akademia, MS. Kaufmann A 399, p. 299, C, short.
7462. Budapest - Magyar tudomanyos akademia, MS. Kaufmann A 400, p. 533-534, C.
7463. Cambridge - University Library Or. 790, f. 32b-33a, C, short.
7464. Frankfurt a M - Stadt- und Universitaetsbibliothek Oct. 227, f. 113b, M.
7465. Hamburg - Staats- und Universitaetsbibliothek Cod. hebr. 17/2 (Steinschneider 152), f. 166b, C, rubric: אחרת.
7466. Jerusalem - Schocken Institute 24100 / Mahzor Nuremberg, f. 493b, M.
7467. London - British Library Add. 18695 (Margoliouth 683), f. 148b-149a, T, Yiddish.

7468. London - British Library Add. 22431 (Margoliouth 662a), f. 118b, M.
7469. London - British Library Add. 27208 (Margolioth 654), f. 267b, M.
7470. London - British Library Add. 27556, f. 127a, M.
7471. Moscow - Russian State Library, Ms. Guenzburg 615, f. 128b, C, very short.
7472. New York - Jewish Theological Seminary Ms. 4466, f. 478a, M, short.
7473. Oxford - Bodleian Library MS Can. Or. 1 (Neubauer 1104), f. 24b-25a, M.
7474. Oxford - Bodleian Library MS Mich. 573 (Neubauer 1099), f. 18b, M.
7475. Oxford - Bodleian Library MS Opp 160 (Neubauer 1204), f. 233b-234a, C, commentator: Elazar b. Yehuda of Worms.[186]
7476. Oxford - Bodleian Library MS Opp. 170 (Neubauer 1205), f. 201a, C.
7477. Parma - Biblioteca Palatina Cod. Parm. 2895, p. 209-210, M, short.
7478. Parma - Biblioteca Palatina Cod. Parm. 3057.9 (de Rossi 1033), f. 92b, C.
7479. Parma - Biblioteca Palatina Cod. Parm. 3205 (de Rossi 655), f. 250a, C.
7480. Uppsala - Universitetsbibliotek O.Heb.22, f. 109a, M.
7481. Vatican - Biblioteca Apostolica ebr. 305,1, f. 43b, C, no incipit.
7482. Vatican - Biblioteca Apostolica ebr. 308, f. 156b, C, commentator: David b. Mose (compiler).
7483. Verona - Seminario Maggiore 34, f. 169a-169b, M, very short.

Ashkenaz, commentary by Eliezer b. Natan

7484. Hamburg - Staats- und Universitaetsbibliothek Cod. hebr. 61 (Steinschneider 153), f. 22b, C, short.
7485. London - Montefiore Library 261, f. 86b, C.
7486. Paris - Bibliotheque Nationale heb. 327/2, f. 38b, C, short.
7487. Warszaw - Uniwersytet, Inst. Orientalistyczny 258, f. 196a, C, short.

Italia

7488. Moscow - Russian State Library, Ms. Guenzburg 1594, f. 24a, C, no incipit.
7489. Torino - Archivio Terracini 1499, p. 48-49, C, commentator: Zakharya David Shabbetai Segre, rubric: פירוש להושענא אערוך שועי, very short.

Romania

7490. London - London School of Jewish Studies. Asher I.Myers collection 9, f. 211a, M, short.
7491. Roma - Collegio Rabbinico Italiano 110, f. 9b, M, short.
7492. Vatican - Biblioteca Apostolica ebr. 285/30, f. 234b, C, short.

Tsarfat

7493. Cambridge - University Library Add. 561.1, f. 114a, M, short.

---

[186] Edited by Katzenellenbogen, פירוש ההושענות, p. 25-27.

7494. Jerusalem - Schocken Institute 19623, f. 124b-125a, M, commentator: Yehuda b. Eliezer Zvi, short.
7495. London - British Library Or. 2735 (Margoliouth 663), f. 146a, M, short.
7496. London - David Sofer 5, f. 192a, C, very short.
7497. Moscow - Russian State Library, Ms. Guenzburg 1665, f. 181b, M.
7498. Parma - Biblioteca Palatina Cod. Parm. 1264, f. 96b, M.
7499. Parma - Biblioteca Palatina Cod. Parm. 1902, f. 176a-176b, M.
7500. Vatican - Biblioteca Apostolica ebr. 306, f. 122b, C, very short.

אערוץ ביום צומי רוב המוני (א 7085), סעדיה גאון, סליחה
Yemen, commentary by Isaac b. Abraham Wanneh
7501. Chicago-Spertus College of Judaica D 2, 2, f. 228a, M, no incipit.
7502. Jerusalem - Sassoon 1158, p. 315, M, no incipit.

אף אורח משפטיך אדני קוינוך (א 7090), אלעזר ברבי קליר, חלק ג', קדושתא למוסף ראש השנה
Ashkenaz
7503. Berlin - Staatsbibliothek (Preussischer Kulturbesitz) Or. Qu. 798-799 (Steinschneider 177), I, f. 15a-16a, M.
7504. Braunschweig - Landesmuseum fuer Geschichte und Volkstum R 2386, vol. II, f. 92b, M.
7505. Budapest - Magyar tudomanyos akademia, MS. Kaufmann A 400, p. 261-262, C.
7506. Darmstadt - Hessisches Landes- und Hochschulbibliothek Cod. Or. 15, f. 14a-14b, M.
7507. Hamburg - Staats- und Universitaetsbibliothek Cod. hebr. 12 (Steinschneider 102), f. 14a-14b, G.
7508. Hamburg - Staats- und Universitaetsbibliothek Cod. hebr. 17/2 (Steinschneider 152), f. 111a-111b, C.
7509. Hamburg - Staats- und Universitaetsbibliothek Cod. hebr. 40b (Steinschneider 110), f. 14b-15a, G.
7510. Hamburg - Staats- und Universitaetsbibliothek Cod. hebr. 40c (Steinschneider 111), f. 136b-137a, G.
7511. Hamburg - Staats- und Universitaetsbibliothek Cod. hebr. 132 (Steinschneider 155), f. 11b-12a, C.
7512. Hamburg - Staats- und Universitaetsbibliothek Cod. hebr. 139 (Steinschneider 115), f. 28b, G.
7513. Hamburg - Staats- und Universitaetsbibliothek Cod. hebr. 225, f. 226b-227a, G.
7514. Jerusalem - Jewish National and University Library Ms Heb 8° 3037, f. 25b-26b, M.

7515. Jerusalem - Schocken Institute 24100 / Mahzor Nuremberg, f. 330a-330b, M.
7516. London - British Library Or. 11318/1, f. 14b-15a, C.
7517. London - Montefiore Library 261, f. 7a-8a, C, commentator: Eliezer b. Natan?.
7518. Moscow - Russian State Library, Ms. Guenzburg 191, f. 9b-10b, M.
7519. Moscow - Russian State Library, Ms. Guenzburg 615, f. 65b-66a, C.
7520. Moscow - Russian State Library, Ms. Guenzburg 1401/2, f. 17b-18a, C.
7521. Muenchen - Bayerische Staatsbibliothek, Cod. hebr. 86, f. 21a-22a, M.
7522. Muenchen - Bayerische Staatsbibliothek, Cod. hebr. 346, f. 9b-11a, C.
7523. Muenchen - Bayerische Staatsbibliothek, Cod. hebr. 422, f. 77a, G.
7524. New York - Jewish Theological Seminary Ms. 4466, f. 222a-222b, M.
7525. New York - Jewish Theological Seminary Ms. 8097, f. 61a, C, additional glosses in the margins.
7526. New York - Jewish Theological Seminary Ms. 8169 (Acc. 0016), f. 15b-16a, M.
7527. Oxford - Bodleian Library MS Opp. 170 (Neubauer 1205), f. 116b-118a, C.
7528. Oxford - Bodleian Library MS Opp. 172 (Neubauer 1211), f. 9b, C.
7529. Oxford - Bodleian Library MS Opp. 619 (Neubauer 2374), f. 27a-27b, M.
7530. Oxford - Bodleian Library MS Opp. 675 (Neubauer 1210), f. 22a-23a, C, no incipit.
7531. Paris - Bibliotheque Nationale heb. 653, f. 14b, G.
7532. Parma - Biblioteca Palatina Cod. Parm. 3270 (de Rossi 1215), f. 29b-30a, M.
7533. Parma - Biblioteca Palatina Cod. Parm. 3507 (Perreau 27), f. 117a-118a, C, no incipit.
7534. Salzburg - Universitsetsbibliothek M II 342, f. 2a, FM.
7535. Vatican - Biblioteca Apostolica ebr. 308, f. 46b-47a, C, commentator: David b. Mose (compiler).
7536. Vatican - Biblioteca Apostolica ebr. 422/1, f. 9b, C.
7537. Zurich - Zentralbibliothek Heid. 139, f. 61a-61b, C, additional marginal notes.

Asti, Fossano, Moncalvo
7538. New Haven - Yale University, Beinecke Rare Book and MS Library, MS Heb. 52, f. 31b, M.

Tsarfat
7539. London - British Library Or. 8682, f. 19a-19b, 20b, GI.
7540. London - David Sofer 5, f. 113b-114a, C.
7541. Paris - Bibliotheque Nationale heb. 445,9, f. 72a-72b, C.

7542. Parma - Biblioteca Palatina Cod. Parm. 2125 (de Rossi 812), f. 15b-16a, C.

7543. Parma - Biblioteca Palatina Cod. Parm. 3006 (de Rossi 654,1), f. 43a-43b, M.

אף ברי אותה שם שר מטר (א 7091), אלעזר ברבי קליר, תפלת גשם
Ashkenaz

7544. Berlin - Staatsbibliothek (Preussischer Kulturbesitz) Or. Qu. 798-799 (Steinschneider 177), I, f. 213b, M.

7545. Braunschweig - Landesmuseum fuer Geschichte und Volkstum R 2386, vol. I, f. 152b, M.

7546. Budapest - Magyar tudomanyos akademia, MS. Kaufmann A 400, p. 394, C.

7547. Fulda - Hessische Landesbibliothek A 3 II, f. 137b-138a, C, commentator: Josef, rubric: גשם למוסף.

7548. Hamburg - Staats- und Universitaetsbibliothek Cod. hebr. 17/2 (Steinschneider 152), f. 169a-169b, C, rubric: ליום שמיני למוסף אומרין זה גשם קלירי.

7549. Hamburg - Staats- und Universitaetsbibliothek Cod. hebr. 62 (Steinschneider 154), f. 44a, C, rubric: גשם.

7550. Hamburg - Staats- und Universitaetsbibliothek Cod. hebr. 132 (Steinschneider 155), f. 57b-58a, C.

7551. Hamburg - Staats- und Universitaetsbibliothek Cod. hebr. 139 (Steinschneider 115), f. 179b-180a, G.

7552. Jerusalem - Jewish National and University Library Ms Heb 8° 3037, f. 287a, M.

7553. Jerusalem - Schocken Institute 24100 / Mahzor Nuremberg, f. 498b, M.

7554. London - British Library Add. 18695 (Margoliouth 683), f. 126b, T, Yiddish.

7555. London - British Library Add. 22431 (Margoliouth 662a), f. 134b-135a, M.

7556. London - British Library Or. 11318/1, f. 139a-139b, C, rubric: למוסף.

7557. London - Montefiore Library 261, f. 73a, C, commentator: Eliezer b. Natan?.

7558. Moscow - Russian State Library, Ms. Guenzburg 615, f. 116b-117a, C, rubric: גשם ליום שמיני.

7559. New York - Jewish Theological Seminary Ms. 4466, f. 457b-458a, M.

7560. Oxford - Bodleian Library MS Mich. 365 (Neubauer 1208), f. 106a-106b, C, rubric: לגשם קלירי.

7561. Oxford - Bodleian Library MS Opp. 170 (Neubauer 1205), f. 189a-189b, C, rubric: גשם ליום אחרון.

7562. Parma - Biblioteca Palatina Cod. Parm. 3205 (de Rossi 655), f. 242b-243a, C.

7563. Parma - Biblioteca Palatina Cod. Parm. 3507 (Perreau 27), f. 180a-181b, C.
7564. Vatican - Biblioteca Apostolica ebr. 305,1, f. 45a-45b, C, rubric: פירושי גשם.
7565. Vatican - Biblioteca Apostolica ebr. 422/1, f. 22b, C.
7566. Zurich - Zentralbibliothek Heid. 139, f. 94a-94b, C, additional marginal notes.

Romania
7567. London - London School of Jewish Studies. Asher I.Myers collection 9, f. 235b, M.
7568. New York - Jewish Theological Seminary Ms. 4823, f. 9b-10a, FM.
7569. New York - Jewish Theological Seminary Ms. 4823, f. 12b, FG.
7570. Vatican - Biblioteca Apostolica ebr. 320, f. 464b, M.
7571. Vatican - Biblioteca Apostolica ebr. 320, f. 568a-575a, C, commentator: Salomo b. Isaac?, rubric: פירוש מוסף לשאילת מטר לרבי שלמה הצרפתי.

Tsarfat
7572. London - British Library Add. 11639 (Margoliouth 1056), f. 662b, M, rubric: וזהו הגשם.
7573. London - David Sofer 5, f. 184b-185a, C.
7574. Moscow - Russian State Library, Ms. Guenzburg 1665, f. 190b, M.
7575. Oxford - Bodleian Library MS Laud. Or. 271 (Neubauer 1206), f. 98b-99a, C, commentator: Aaron b. Hayyim haKohen (compiler).
7576. Oxford - Bodleian Library MS Opp. 171 (Neubauer 1207), f. 154a-155b, C, rubric: ואתחיל הגשם.
7577. Parma - Biblioteca Palatina Cod. Parm. 1264, f. 121b-122a, M.
7578. Vatican - Biblioteca Apostolica ebr. 306, f. 113b, C, rubric: למוסף גשם.

אף לפי בגולה ברוב עינוי ותלאה (א 7097), אמתי ב"ר שפטיה, זולת

Ashkenaz
7579. Oxford - Bodleian Library MS Can. Or. 82 (Neubauer 1148), f. 22a, M, short.
7580. Oxford - Bodleian Library MS Opp. 169 (Neubauer 1151), f. 9b, M.
7581. Parma - Biblioteca Palatina Cod. Parm. 3205 (de Rossi 655), f. 147b-148a, C.

Ashkenaz, commentary by Abraham b. Azriel[187]
7582. Vatican - Biblioteca Apostolica ebr. 301,1, f. 12a, C, rubric: זולת.

---

[187] Edited by Urbach, ערוגת הבושם, vol. I, p. 76-78.

אפאר למלכי בקודש (א 7102), למנחה יום כפור

Ashkenaz
7583. Fulda - Hessische Landesbibliothek A 3 II, f. 128b, C, commentator: Josef, rubric: מי כאן ואילך לא שמעתי מי יסד, very short.
7584. Hamburg - Staats- und Universitaetsbibliothek Cod. hebr. 132 (Steinschneider 155), f. 49b, C, very short, incipit הומים.
7585. London - British Library Or. 11318/1, f. 124a-124b, C.
7586. London - Montefiore Library 261, f. 64a, C, commentator: Eliezer b. Natan?, very short.
7587. Muenchen - Bayerische Staatsbibliothek, Cod. hebr. 21, f. 240b, M.
7588. Oxford - Bodleian Library MS Mich. 365 (Neubauer 1208), f. 93b, C, rubric: מכאן ואילך לא שמעתי מי יסד, very short.
7589. Oxford - Bodleian Library MS Opp. 170 (Neubauer 1205), f. 181a, C, short.
7590. Oxford - Bodleian Library MS Opp. 172 (Neubauer 1211), f. 82a, C, very short.
7591. Parma - Biblioteca Palatina Cod. Parm. 3205 (de Rossi 655), f. 237b, C, short.
7592. Vatican - Biblioteca Apostolica ebr. 308, f. 140a-140b, C, commentator: David b. Mose (compiler).
7593. Vatican - Biblioteca Apostolica ebr. 422/1, f. 19b, C, very short.

Tsarfat
7594. London - David Sofer 5, f. 165b, margin, C, very short.
7595. Oxford - Bodleian Library MS Laud. Or. 271 (Neubauer 1206), f. 118b, C, commentator: Aaron b. Hayyim haKohen (compiler), rubric: ומכאן ואילך לא שמעתי מי יסד, no incipit, short.
7596. Parma - Biblioteca Palatina Cod. Parm. 3006 (de Rossi 654,1), f. 220b, M.

אפד מאז לשפט היום בחון מעשה כל יום (א 7106), אלעזר ברבי קליר, קדושתא למוסף ראש שנה

Ashkenaz
7597. Berlin - Staatsbibliothek (Preussischer Kulturbesitz) Or. Qu. 798-799 (Steinschneider 177), I, f. 13b-14b, M.
7598. Braunschweig - Landesmuseum fuer Geschichte und Volkstum R 2386, vol. II, f. 91b-92a, M.
7599. Budapest - Magyar tudomanyos akademia, MS. Kaufmann A 400, p. 255-259, C, rubric: קדושתא למוסף דר' אלעזר.
7600. Darmstadt - Hessisches Landes- und Hochschulbibliothek Cod. Or. 15, f. 13a, M.
7601. Hamburg - Staats- und Universitaetsbibliothek Cod. hebr. 12 (Steinschneider 102), f. 13a-13b, G.

7602. Hamburg - Staats- und Universitaetsbibliothek Cod. hebr. 17/2 (Steinschneider 152), f. 109a-110a, C, rubric: קדושתא למוסף דר' אלעזר.
7603. Hamburg - Staats- und Universitaetsbibliothek Cod. hebr. 40b (Steinschneider 110), f. 14a, G.
7604. Hamburg - Staats- und Universitaetsbibliothek Cod. hebr. 40c (Steinschneider 111), f. 136a-136b, G.
7605. Hamburg - Staats- und Universitaetsbibliothek Cod. hebr. 62 (Steinschneider 154), f. 29b-30a, C.
7606. Hamburg - Staats- und Universitaetsbibliothek Cod. hebr. 132 (Steinschneider 155), f. 10a-10b, C, rubric: למוסף.
7607. Hamburg - Staats- und Universitaetsbibliothek Cod. hebr. 139 (Steinschneider 115), f. 27b, G.
7608. Hamburg - Staats- und Universitaetsbibliothek Cod. hebr. 225, f. 224b-225b, G.
7609. Jerusalem - Jewish National and University Library Ms Heb 8° 3037, f. 24a-25a, M.
7610. Jerusalem - Schocken Institute 24100 / Mahzor Nuremberg, f. 329b-330a, M.
7611. London - British Library Or. 11318/1, f. 14a-14b, C.
7612. London - Montefiore Library 261, f. 4b-6a, C, commentator: Eliezer b. Natan?, rubric: למוסף. ברוך אתה הר'א'כ' עי' שיש לסיים כל הברכה עד באהבה ואחרכך מתחיל מסוד כי אין לשנות המטבע שטבעו חכמים בברכות.
7613. Moscow - Russian State Library, Ms. Guenzburg 191, f. 8b-9a, M.
7614. Moscow - Russian State Library, Ms. Guenzburg 615, f. 63a-65a, C, rubric: מוסף.
7615. Moscow - Russian State Library, Ms. Guenzburg 1401 /2, f. 17a-17b, C.
7616. Muenchen - Bayerische Staatsbibliothek, Cod. hebr. 86, f. 19a-19b, G.
7617. Muenchen - Bayerische Staatsbibliothek, Cod. hebr. 346, f. 8a-9a, C, rubric: למוסף.
7618. New York - Jewish Theological Seminary Ms. 4466, f. 220b-221a, M.
7619. New York - Jewish Theological Seminary Ms. 8097, f. 60b, C, additional glosses in the margins.
7620. New York - Jewish Theological Seminary Ms. 8169 (Acc. 0016), f. 14b-15a, M.
7621. Oxford - Bodleian Library MS Opp. 170 (Neubauer 1205), f. 114a-116a, C, rubric: למוסף אכסף.
7622. Oxford - Bodleian Library MS Opp. 172 (Neubauer 1211), f. 8b-9a, C.
7623. Oxford - Bodleian Library MS Opp. 619 (Neubauer 2374), f. 26a-26b, M.
7624. Oxford - Bodleian Library MS Opp. 675 (Neubauer 1210), f. 21a-21b, C, rubric: ואתחיל משל מוסף, no incipit.

7625. Paris - Bibliotheque Nationale heb. 653, f. 13b-14a, G.
7626. Parma - Biblioteca Palatina Cod. Parm. 3270 (de Rossi 1215), f. 28b, M.
7627. Parma - Biblioteca Palatina Cod. Parm. 3507 (Perreau 27), f. 116a-116b, C.
7628. Salzburg - Universitsetsbibliothek M II 342, f. 1b, FM, no incipit, end missing.
7629. Vatican - Bibliotheca Apostolica ebr. 298/1, f. 13a-14a, C, no incipit.
7630. Vatican - Bibliotheca Apostolica ebr. 308, f. 45a-45b, C, commentator: David b. Mose (compiler), rubric: תפילת מוסף ה' בעזר' אתחיל.
7631. Vatican - Bibliotheca Apostolica ebr. 422/1, f. 9a, C.
7632. Zurich - Zentralbibliothek Heid. 139, f. 60a-60b, C, rubric: למוסף, additional marginal notes.
7633. Zurich - Zentralbibliothek Heid. 139, f. 102a, C, commentator: Elazar b. Yehuda of Worms, rubric: מוסף, short, esoteric.

Asti, Fossano, Moncalvo

7634. New Haven - Yale University, Beinecke Rare Book and MS Library, MS Heb. 52, f. 30b, M.

Tsarfat

7635. London - British Library Or. 8682, f. 18b, GI.
7636. London - David Sofer 5, f. 113a-113b, C.
7637. Ms London British Museum 1056, f. 710a-710b, M, rubric: מוסף.
7638. Oxford - Bodleian Library MS Laud. Or. 271 (Neubauer 1206), f. 143b-145a, C, commentator: Aaron b. Hayyim haKohen (compiler).
7639. Oxford - Bodleian Library MS Opp. 171 (Neubauer 1207), f. 63b-65a, C, rubric: ואתחיל משל מוסף.
7640. Paris - Bibliotheque Nationale heb. 445,9, f. 70b-71a, C, no incipit.
7641. Parma - Biblioteca Palatina Cod. Parm. 2125 (de Rossi 812), f. 14a-14b, C, rubric: מוסף יום ראשון דר"ה.
7642. Parma - Biblioteca Palatina Cod. Parm. 3006 (de Rossi 654,1), f. 41b-42a, M.
7643. Vatican - Biblioteca Apostolica ebr. 306, f. 52b-54a, C.

אפודי שש לאל שונא שש אומרים קדוש (א 7109), קדושה לשחרית יום כפור

haAri

7644. Harvard University 067, f. 48b-52a, M, lexical explanations in Hebrew and Ladino.

North Africa, commentary by David b. Josef Abudarham

7645. New York - Jewish Theological Seminary Ms. 5426, f. 62b-63b, M, rubric: ובכן נקדישך.

Sepharad

7646. Jerusalem - Benayahu ז 25, f. 86a-87a, M.
7647. Jerusalem - Schocken Institute 70014, f. 43b-44b, M.

Sepharad, commentary by David b. Josef Abudarham[188]
7648. Budapest - Magyar tudomanyos akademia, MS. Kaufmann A 405/2, p. 182-183, C, rubric: למחר משכימין ובכן נקדישך.
7649. Cincinnati - Hebrew Union College 490, f. 2a-2b, C.
7650. New York - Columbia X893 Ab 93, f. 3a-3b, C, rubric: למחר ובכן נקדישך מלך.
7651. New York - Jewish Theological Seminary Ms. 3011, f. 2b-3a, C, rubric: קדושה ובכן נקדישך מלך.

אפוני אימיו בטל חיים לטללה (א 7114), אליעזר ב"ר נתן, יוצר לברית מילה
Ashkenaz
7652. Berlin - Staatsbibliothek (Preussischer Kulturbesitz) Or. Qu. 798-799 (Steinschneider 177), I, f. 256a-257b, M.
7653. Budapest - Magyar tudomanyos akademia, MS. Kaufmann A 399, p. 395-396, C, rubric: יוצר לשבת וברית מילה.
7654. Cambridge - University Library Add. 504,1, f. 63a-66a, C, rubric: לברית מילה כשאירע לבוא בשבת יוצר זה והר' אליעזר ב'ר' נתן יסדו וחקוק בו וגם האופן.
7655. Lund - Universitetsbibliothek Ms. L.O. 2, f. 108b-110a, M.
7656. Muenchen - Bayerische Staatsbibliothek, Cod. hebr. 393,9, f. 180a-191b, C.
7657. Oxford - Bodleian Library MS Can. Or. 82 (Neubauer 1148), f. 68b-70a, M.

אפחד במעשי אדאג בכל עת (א 7117), יוסי בן יוסי, זכרונות
Ashkenaz
7658. Berlin - Staatsbibliothek (Preussischer Kulturbesitz) Or. Qu. 798-799 (Steinschneider 177), I, 47b-50a, M.
7659. Braunschweig - Landesmuseum fuer Geschichte und Volkstum R 2386, vol. II, f. 120a-121a, M.
7660. Budapest - Magyar tudomanyos akademia, MS. Kaufmann A 400, p. 292-295, C.
7661. Cambridge - University Library Or. 785, f. 76a-77b, G.
7662. Darmstadt - Hessisches Landes- und Hochschulbibliothek Cod. Or. 15, f. 57a-59b, M.
7663. Darmstadt - Hessisches Landes- und Hochschulbibliothek Cod. Or. 15, f. 62a-64a, M, ecclectic.
7664. Hamburg - Staats- und Universitaetsbibliothek Cod. hebr. 17/2 (Steinschneider 152), f. 124a-125a, C, rubric: סדר זכרונות.
7665. Hamburg - Staats- und Universitaetsbibliothek Cod. hebr. 40b (Steinschneider 110), f. 61a-63b, G.

---
[188] Edited by Prins, תשלום אבודרהם, p. 8-14.

7666. Hamburg - Staats- und Universitaetsbibliothek Cod. hebr. 40c (Steinschneider 111), f. 158a-159a, G.
7667. Hamburg - Staats- und Universitaetsbibliothek Cod. hebr. 132 (Steinschneider 155), f. 27a-28a, C.
7668. Jerusalem - Jewish National and University Library Ms Heb 8° 3037, f. 78a-79b, M.
7669. Jerusalem - Schocken Institute 24100 / Mahzor Nuremberg , f. 349b-350a, M.
7670. London - British Library Or. 11318/1, f. 51b-55a, C.
7671. London - Montefiore Library 261, f. 21a-22a, C, commentator: Eliezer b. Natan?.
7672. Moscow - Russian State Library, Ms. Guenzburg 191, f. 65a-67a, M.
7673. Moscow - Russian State Library, Ms. Guenzburg 615, f. 74a-76b, C.
7674. Muenchen - Bayerische Staatsbibliothek, Cod. hebr. 86, f. 80b-82a, M, partly ecclectic.
7675. Muenchen - Bayerische Staatsbibliothek, Cod. hebr. 346 , f. 40b-43a, C.
7676. Muenchen - Bayerische Staatsbibliothek, Cod. hebr. 393 , f. 144b-146b, C, no incipit.
7677. New York - Jewish Theological Seminary Ms. 4466, f. 270b-273b, M.
7678. New York - Jewish Theological Seminary Ms. 8097, f. 68a-69a, C.
7679. New York - Jewish Theological Seminary Ms. 8169 (Acc. 0016), f. 54a-55a, M.
7680. New York - Jewish Theological Seminary Ms. 8753, FC, only first line.
7681. Oxford - Bodleian Library MS Mich. 365 (Neubauer 1208), f. 57a-59b, C.
7682. Oxford - Bodleian Library MS Opp. 170 (Neubauer 1205), f. 149b-154a, C, commentator: Salomo b. Isaac (Rashi)?, rubric: זכרונות .
7683. Oxford - Bodleian Library MS Opp. 172 (Neubauer 1211), f. 27a-28a, C.
7684. Oxford - Bodleian Library MS Opp. 619 (Neubauer 2374), f. 89a-91a, M.
7685. Oxford - Bodleian Library MS Opp. 675 (Neubauer 1210), f. 63b-65a, C, no incipit.
7686. Paris - Bibliotheque Nationale heb. 653, f. 38b-39a, G.
7687. Parma - Biblioteca Palatina Cod. Parm. 3205 (de Rossi 655), f. 220a-221a, C.
7688. Parma - Biblioteca Palatina Cod. Parm. 3270 (de Rossi 1215), f. 68b-70b, M.
7689. Parma - Biblioteca Palatina Cod. Parm. 3507 (Perreau 27), f. 138a-140a, C.
7690. Vatican - Biblioteca Apostolica ebr. 308, f. 83b-86a, C, commentator: David b. Mose (compiler).

7691. Vatican - Biblioteca Apostolica ebr. 422/1, f. 14a, C.
7692. Zurich - Zentralbibliothek Heid. 139, f. 72a, C, no incipit, additional marginal notes.
7693. Zurich - Zentralbibliothek Heid. 139, f. 103b, C, commentator: Elazar b. Yehuda of Worms, no incipit.

Asti, Fossano, Moncalvo
7694. New Haven - Yale University, Beinecke Rare Book and MS Library, MS Heb. 52, f. 75a-76b, M.

Tsarfat
7695. London - British Library Add. 11639 (Margoliouth 1056), f. 715b-716b, M.
7696. London - British Library Or. 8682, f. 47b-48b, GI.
7697. London - David Sofer 5, f. 126a-127a, C.
7698. Oxford - Bodleian Library MS Bodl. Or. 109 (Neubauer 1209), f. 3b-5b, C, commentator: Aaron b. Hayyim haKohen (compiler).
7699. Oxford - Bodleian Library MS Laud. Or. 271 (Neubauer 1206), f. 159b-161b, C, commentator: Aaron b. Hayyim haKohen (compiler), rubric: זכרונות .
7700. Oxford - Bodleian Library MS Opp. 171 (Neubauer 1207), f. 77b-79a, C.
7701. Parma - Biblioteca Palatina Cod. Parm. 1794 (de Rossi 1061), f. 100b-103b, M.
7702. Parma - Biblioteca Palatina Cod. Parm. 2125 (de Rossi 812), f. 35b-36a, C.
7703. Parma Biblioteca Palatina Cod. Parm. 3006 (de Rossi 654,1), f. 98b 100b, M.
7704. Vatican - Biblioteca Apostolica ebr. 306, f. 72a-73a, C.

אפילו כל נימי בפומי מיחלפן (א 7126), פיוט באמרית לשבועות

Tsarfat
7705. Parma - Biblioteca Palatina Cod. Parm. 1902, f. 138b-139a, M.

אפיק מען מעטר ביום המנטר (א 7128), אלעזר ברבי קליר, רשות לגשם

Ashkenaz
7706. Berlin - Staatsbibliothek (Preussischer Kulturbesitz) Or. Qu. 798-799 (Steinschneider 177), I, f. 213b-214b, M.
7707. Braunschweig - Landesmuseum fuer Geschichte und Volkstum R 2386, vol. I, f. 152b-153a, M.
7708. Budapest - Magyar tudomanyos akademia, MS. Kaufmann A 400, p. 394-397, C.
7709. Fulda - Hessische Landesbibliothek A 3 II, f. 138a-140b, C, commentator: Josef.

7710. Hamburg - Staats- und Universitaetsbibliothek Cod. hebr. 17/2 (Steinschneider 152), f. 169b-170a, C.
7711. Hamburg - Staats- und Universitaetsbibliothek Cod. hebr. 62 (Steinschneider 154), f. 44a-45b, C, no incipit.
7712. Hamburg - Staats- und Universitaetsbibliothek Cod. hebr. 132 (Steinschneider 155), f. 58a-60b, C.
7713. Hamburg - Staats- und Universitaetsbibliothek Cod. hebr. 139 (Steinschneider 115), f. 180a-180b, G.
7714. Jerusalem - Jewish National and University Library Ms Heb 8° 3037, f. 287a-288a, M.
7715. Jerusalem - Schocken Institute 24100 / Mahzor Nuremberg , f. 498b-499b, M.
7716. London - British Library Add. 18695 (Margoliouth 683), f. 126b-128a, T, Yiddish, rubric: דש זגט קהל.
7717. London - British Library Add. 22431 (Margoliouth 662a), f. 135a-136a, M.
7718. London - British Library Or. 11318/1, f. 139b-141b, C.
7719. London - Montefiore Library 261, f. 73a-74a, C, commentator: Eliezer b. Natan?.
7720. Moscow - Russian State Library, Ms. Guenzburg 615 , f. 117a-118b, C.
7721. New York - Jewish Theological Seminary Ms. 4466, f. 458a-459a, M.
7722. Oxford - Bodleian Library MS Mich. 365 (Neubauer 1208) , f. 106b-107b, C.
7723. Oxford - Bodleian Library MS Opp. 170 (Neubauer 1205), f. 189b-191a, C.
7724. Parma - Biblioteca Palatina Cod. Parm. 3205 (de Rossi 655), f. 243a-244a, C.
7725. Vatican - Biblioteca Apostolica ebr. 305,1, f. 45b-46b, C, no incipit.
7726. Vatican - Biblioteca Apostolica ebr. 422/1, f. 22b-23a, C.
7727. Zurich - Zentralbibliothek Heid. 139, f. 94b-95b, C, additional marginal notes.

Romania

7728. London - London School of Jewish Studies. Asher I.Myers collection 9, f. 235b-236b, M, the manuscript breaks off in this commentary.
7729. New York - Jewish Theological Seminary Ms. 4823, f. 10a-10b, FM.
7730. New York - Jewish Theological Seminary Ms. 4823, f. 12b-13a, FG.
7731. Vatican - Biblioteca Apostolica ebr. 320, f. 464b-465b, M.

Tsarfat

7732. London - British Library Add. 11639 (Margoliouth 1056), f. 662b-663b, M.
7733. London - David Sofer 5, f. 185a-185b, C, rubric: במוסף יואם׳ זה קרובה מגשם ואחר קדושה יואם׳ הכל.

7734. Moscow - Russian State Library, Ms. Guenzburg 1665, f. 190b-191b, M.
7735. Oxford - Bodleian Library MS Laud. Or. 271 (Neubauer 1206), f. 99a-100a, C, commentator: Aaron b. Hayyim haKohen (compiler).
7736. Parma - Biblioteca Palatina Cod. Parm. 1264, f. 122a-122b, M.
7737. Vatican - Biblioteca Apostolica ebr. 306, f. 113b-115a, C.

אפיק רנן ושירים (א 7129), משולם ב"ר קלונימוס, יוצר ליום ב' של פסח
Ashkenaz

7738. Berlin - Staatsbibliothek (Preussischer Kulturbesitz) Or. Qu. 798-799 (Steinschneider 177), II, f. 74b-76a, M.
7739. Braunschweig - Landesmuseum fuer Geschichte und Volkstum R 2386, vol. I, f. 33a-34b, M.
7740. Budapest - Magyar tudomanyos akademia, MS. Kaufmann A 384, f. 154a-157b, M.
7741. Budapest - Magyar tudomanyos akademia, MS. Kaufmann A 400, p. 122-129, C, rubric: יוצר ליום שיני המקום יעזרנו.
7742. Erlangen - Universitaetsbibliothek 2601 (Roth 67), f. 87b-88a, M.
7743. Friedberg - Stadtbibliothek und Stadtarchiv Fragm. Hebr. 20, f. 1a-1b, FC, incomplete.
7744. Hamburg - Staats- und Universitaetsbibliothek Cod. hebr. 17/2 (Steinschneider 152), f. 62b-64a, C, rubric: יוצר ליום שיני מרבי משולם בן רבינו קלונימוס זצ"ל.
7745. Jerusalem - Schocken Institute 24100 / Mahzor Nuremberg, f. 91a-92b, M.
7746. London - British Library Add. 18695 (Margoliouth 683), f. 36a-38b, T, Yiddish, rubric: יוצר צום אנדרן טג בון פסח.
7747. Moscow - Russian State Library, Ms. Guenzburg 615, f. 17a-20a, C, rubric: יוצר ליום שיני יסוד רבינו משלם.
7748. Muenchen - Bayerische Staatsbibliothek, Cod. hebr. 393, f. 127a-127b, C, no incipit.
7749. Muenchen - Bayerische Staatsbibliothek, Cod. hebr. 88, f. 68a-69b, G.
7750. New York - Jewish Theological Seminary Ms. 4466, f. 67b-70a, M.
7751. Oxford - Bodleian Library MS Opp. 170 (Neubauer 1205), f. 69b-73a, C, rubric: יוצר ליום שיני.
7752. Paris - Bibliotheque Nationale heb. 709, f. 90b-95a, C, rubric: יוצר מיום שיני של פסח.
7753. Parma - Biblioteca Palatina Cod. Parm. 1002 (Ta 24), f. 112b-114a, M.
7754. Parma - Biblioteca Palatina Cod. Parm. 3507 (Perreau 27), f. 60b-63a, C.
7755. Parma - Biblioteca Palatina Cod. Parm. 3205 (de Rossi 655), f. 89a-95b, C.

7756. Zurich - Zentralbibliothek Heid. 139, f. 34a-36a, C, additional marginal notes.

Tsarfat

7757. Moscow - Russian State Library, Ms. Guenzburg 1665, f. 67b-69a, M.
7758. Oxford - Bodleian Library MS Laud. Or. 271 (Neubauer 1206), f. 71a-72a, C, commentator: Aaron b. Hayyim haKohen (compiler), rubric: יוצר ליום שיני.
7759. Parma - Biblioteca Palatina Cod. Parm. 3136 (de Rossi 405), f. 99b-100b, M, lower part of f. 100 missing.

אפך השב (א 7132), שלמה ב"ר יצחק, סליחה

Tsarfat

7760. Vatican - Biblioteca Apostolica ebr. 306, f. 204b-205a, C.

אפס הוד כבודה נאלמה דברכית (א 7144), אליה ב"ר שמעיה, סליחה

Ashkenaz

7761. Braunschweig - Landesmuseum fuer Geschichte und Volkstum R 2386, vol. II, f. 142a-142b, M.
7762. Budapest - Magyar tudomanyos akademia, MS. Kaufmann A 400, p. 516, C.
7763. Moscow - Russian State Library, Ms. Guenzburg 190, f. 14b-15a, G.
7764. Muenchen - Bayerische Staatsbibliothek, Cod. hebr. 346, f. 163b, C, short.
7765. Oxford - Bodleian Library MS Mich. 543 (Neubauer 1212), f. 72b-73a, C, commentator: Isaac b. Jacob (compiler).
7766. Padova - Biblioteca del Seminario Vescovile Cod. 218, f. 74a, M.
7767. Padova - Biblioteca del Seminario Vescovile Cod. 218, f. 74a-75a, M, rubric: אחרת.
7768. Parma - Biblioteca Palatina Cod. Parm. 3205 (de Rossi 655), f. 269b, C.
7769. Vatican - Biblioteca Apostolica ebr. 422/1, f. 30b-31a, C.
7770. Vatican - Biblioteca Apostolica ebr. 422/1, f. 44a, CG, no incipit.

Ashkenaz, commentary by Abraham b. Azriel[189]

7771. Vatican - Biblioteca Apostolica ebr. 301,1, f. 161b, C, rubric: אחרת.

Tsarfat

7772. London - British Library Add. 11639 (Margoliouth 1056), f. 470a-470b, M.
7773. London - David Sofer 5, f. 84b-85a, C.
7774. Oxford - Bodleian Library MS Laud. Or. 271 (Neubauer 1206), f. 124a-124b, C, commentator: Aaron b. Hayyim haKohen (compiler).

---

[189] Edited by Urbach, ערוגת הבושם, vol. III, p. 437-438.

7775. Oxford - Bodleian Library MS Opp. 171 (Neubauer 1207), f. 110a-110b, C, rubric: אחרת.
7776. Parma - Biblioteca Palatina Cod. Parm. 3006 (de Rossi 654,1), f. 117b-118a, M.
7777. Vatican - Biblioteca Apostolica ebr. 306, f. 193a-193b, C.

אפס זבח ועולה במה נמצא לפניך מחילה (א 7145), זבדיה, סליחה

Ashkenaz
7778. Cambridge - University Library Dd. 2.30, f. 30b, G.
7779. Muenchen - Bayerische Staatsbibliothek, Cod. hebr. 21, f. 242a, M.
7780. Muenchen - Bayerische Staatsbibliothek, Cod. hebr. 346, f. 143a, C, rubric: אחרת, very short.
7781. Oxford - Bodleian Library MS Opp. 172 (Neubauer 1211), f. 83a, C, short.
7782. Vatican - Biblioteca Apostolica ebr. 308, f. 141b, C, commentator: David b. Mose (compiler).

Ashkenaz, commentary by Abraham b. Azriel[190]
7783. Frankfurt a M - Stadt- und Universitaetsbibliothek Fol. 16 (Merzbacher 95), f. 108a, C, very short.

אפס חיסר המזבח, סליחה

Tsarfat
7784. Oxford - Bodleian Library MS Bodl. Or. 109 (Neubauer 1209), f. 72a-72b, C, commentator: Aaron b. Hayyim haKohen (compiler).

אפס מזיח מחבב ומכפר (א 7148), שמעון ב"ר יצחק, סליחה

Ashkenaz
7785. Berlin - Staatsbibliothek (Preussischer Kulturbesitz) Or. Qu. 798-799 (Steinschneider 177), I, f. 166a-166b, M.
7786. Muenchen - Bayerische Staatsbibliothek, Cod. hebr. 346, f. 145a, C, short.
7787. New York - Jewish Theological Seminary Ms. 4466, f. 397b-398a, M.
7788. Oxford - Bodleian Library MS Mich. 543 (Neubauer 1212), f. 28b-29a, C, commentator: Isaac b. Jacob (compiler), very short.
7789. Oxford - Bodleian Library MS Opp. 172 (Neubauer 1211), f. 87a, C, very short.
7790. Oxford - Bodleian Library MS Opp. 619 (Neubauer 2374), f. 259a-259b, M.
7791. Oxford - Bodleian Library MS Opp. 681 (Neubauer 1213), f. 22a-22b, C.

---

[190] Edited by Urbach, ערוגת הבושם, vol. III, p. 560.

7792. Padova - Biblioteca del Seminario Vescovile Cod. 218, f. 177b-178b, M.
7793. Parma - Bibliotheca Palatina Cod. Parm. 3205 (de Rossi 655), f. 287b-288a, C.
7794. Vatican - Biblioteca Apostolica ebr. 308, f. 142a, C, commentator: David b. Mose (compiler).
7795. Vatican - Biblioteca Apostolica ebr. 422/1, f. 24b, C, very short.
7796. Vatican - Biblioteca Apostolica ebr. 422/2, f. 39b, CG, no incipit, very short.

Ashkenaz, commentary by Abraham b. Azriel[191]

7797. Frankfurt a M - Stadt- und Universitaetsbibliothek Fol. 16 (Merzbacher 95), f. 108a, C.
7798. Vatican - Biblioteca Apostolica ebr. 301,1, f. 143a-143b, C, rubric: אחרת.

Tsarfat
7799. London - David Sofer 5, f. 166a-166b, C, rubric: זה פירוש הסליחות של מנחה של יום הכפורים.
7800. Parma - Bibliotheca Palatina Cod. Parm. 3007 (de Rossi 654,2), f. 68a, M.

אפסו אמונים בעלי אמונה, סליחה

Yemen
7801. New York - Jewish Theological Seminary Ms. 3109, f. 23a-23b, G.
7802. New York - Jewish Theological Seminary Ms. 3028, f. 90a-90b, G.

אפסו אשים ובטלו קרבנות (א 7154), סליחה

Ashkenaz
7803. Berlin - Staatsbibliothek (Preussischer Kulturbesitz) Or. Qu. 798-799 (Steinschneider 177), I, f. 166b-167a, M.
7804. Braunschweig - Landesmuseum fuer Geschichte und Volkstum R 2386, vol. II, f. 243a, M, very short.
7805. Jerusalem - Schocken Institute 24100 / Mahzor Nuremberg, f. 448a, M.
7806. Moscow - Russian State Library, Ms. Guenzburg 190, f. 15b-16a, G.
7807. Muenchen - Bayerische Staatsbibliothek, Cod. hebr. 21, f. 241b-242a, M.
7808. Muenchen - Bayerische Staatsbibliothek, Cod. hebr. 346, f. 120a, C, rubric: למנחה, very short.
7809. New York - Jewish Theological Seminary Ms. 8097, f. 85b, C.
7810. Oxford - Bodleian Library MS Mich. 543 (Neubauer 1212), f. 25b, C, commentator: Isaac b. Jacob (compiler), short.

---

[191] Edited by Urbach, ערוגת הבושם, vol. III, p. 318.

7811. Oxford - Bodleian Library MS Opp. 172 (Neubauer 1211), f. 83a, C, short.
7812. Oxford - Bodleian Library MS Opp. 619 (Neubauer 2374), f. 258a-258b, M.
7813. Oxford - Bodleian Library MS Opp. 681 (Neubauer 1213), f. 29b-30a, C.
7814. Padova - Biblioteca del Seminario Vescovile Cod. 218, f. 193a-193b, M.
7815. Parma - Biblioteca Palatina Cod. Parm. 3205 (de Rossi 655), f. 258b, C, short.
7816. Vatican - Biblioteca Apostolica ebr. 308, f. 141b, C, commentator: David b. Mose (compiler).
7817. Vatican - Biblioteca Apostolica ebr. 422/1, f. 24b, C, very short.
7818. Vatican - Biblioteca Apostolica ebr. 422/2, f. 39b, CG, no incipit, very short.

Ashkenaz, commentary by Abraham b. Azriel[192]

7819. Frankfurt a M - Stadt- und Universitaetsbibliothek Fol. 16 (Merzbacher 95), f. 107b, C, rubric: למנחה.

Asti, Fossano, Moncalvo

7820. New Haven - Yale University, Beinecke Rare Book and MS Library, MS Heb. 52, f. 152a, M.

Romania

7821. Vatican - Biblioteca Apostolica ebr. 320, f. 397a, M.

Tsarfat

7822. London - David Sofer 5, f. 143b, C, rubric: אחרת.
7823. Oxford - Bodleian Library MS Bodl. Or. 109 (Neubauer 1209), f. 72b-73a, C, commentator: Aaron b. Hayyim haKohen (compiler), short.
7824. Oxford - Bodleian Library MS Bodl. Or. 109 (Neubauer 1209), f. 74b-75b, C, commentator: Aaron b. Hayyim haKohen (compiler), marginal note at beginning: והוצרכתי לכתוב זה הסליחה לפעם שנית בעל כרחי כי הוא משונה ורגזן גי׳.
7825. Parma - Biblioteca Palatina Cod. Parm. 1794 (de Rossi 1061), f. 17b-18a, M.
7826. Parma - Biblioteca Palatina Cod. Parm. 2890 (de Rossi 856), f. 96b, M.
7827. Parma - Biblioteca Palatina Cod. Parm. 3006 (de Rossi 654,1), f. 162a, M.
7828. Vatican - Biblioteca Apostolica ebr. 306, f. 88b, C.

---

[192] Edited by Urbach, ערוגת הבושם, vol. III, p. 558.

אפסו בעוני עצי המערכה, סליחה

Yemen, commentary by Isaac b. Abraham Wanneh

7829. Chicago-Spertus College of Judaica D 2, 2, f. 241a-241b, M, no incipit.
7830. Jerusalem - Sassoon 1158, p. 415-416, M, no incipit.
7831. Jerusalem - Sassoon 1158, p. 420-421, M, no incipit.
7832. London - British Library Or. 11122, f. 214b, M, no incipit.
7833. London - British Library Or. 11122, f. 217b-218a, M, no incipit.

אפסי ארץ בדברו הקים (א 7155), משולם ב"ר קלונימוס, חלק י"ג, קדושתא לשחרית יום כפור

Ashkenaz

7834. Berlin - Staatsbibliothek (Preussischer Kulturbesitz) Or. Qu. 798-799 (Steinschneider 177), I, f. 77b-78a, M.
7835. Braunschweig - Landesmuseum fuer Geschichte und Volkstum R 2386, vol. II, f. 190b, M.
7836. Budapest - Magyar tudomanyos akademia, MS. Kaufmann A 400, p. 315, C.
7837. Hamburg - Staats- und Universitaetsbibliothek Cod. hebr. 62 (Steinschneider 154), f. 4b-5a, C, short.
7838. Hamburg - Staats- und Universitaetsbibliothek Cod. hebr. 132 (Steinschneider 155), f. 34b, C, short.
7839. Jerusalem - Jewish National and University Library Ms Heb 8° 3037, f. 122a, M, very short.
7840. Jerusalem - Schocken Institute 24100 / Mahzor Nuremberg, f. 379a-379b, M, short.
7841. London - British Library Or. 11318/1, f. 75a-75b, C, short.
7842. London - Montefiore Library 261, f. 44a, C, commentator: Eliezer b. Natan?, short.
7843. Moscow - Russian State Library, Ms. Guenzburg 191, f. 90b, M.
7844. Muenchen - Bayerische Staatsbibliothek, Cod. hebr. 346, f. 53b, C, short.
7845. Muenchen - Bayerische Staatsbibliothek, Cod. hebr. 393, f. 142a, C, no incipit, very short.
7846. New York - Jewish Theological Seminary Ms. 4466, f. 312b-313a, M.
7847. New York - Jewish Theological Seminary Ms. 8097, f. 72a, C.
7848. Oxford - Bodleian Library MS Opp. 172 (Neubauer 1211), f. 39a, C, short.
7849. Parma - Biblioteca Palatina Cod. Parm. 2890 (de Rossi 856), f. 29b, M.
7850. Parma - Biblioteca Palatina Cod. Parm. 3271 (de Rossi 1216), f. 41a-41b, G.

7851. Vatican - Biblioteca Apostolica ebr. 308, f. 101a, C, commentator: David b. Mose (compiler).
7852. Vatican - Biblioteca Apostolica ebr. 422/1, f. 15b, C, very short.
Asti, Fossano, Moncalvo
7853. New Haven - Yale University, Beinecke Rare Book and MS Library, MS Heb. 52, f. 106b-107a, M.
Romania
7854. Vatican - Biblioteca Apostolica ebr. 320, f. 285a-285b, M.
Tsarfat
7855. Bern - Burgerbibliothek A 409, f. 84a, G.
7856. London - David Sofer 5, f. 138a-138b, C.
7857. Oxford - Bodleian Library MS Bodl. Or. 109 (Neubauer 1209), f. 20b, C, commentator: Aaron b. Hayyim haKohen (compiler), short.
7858. Parma - Biblioteca Palatina Cod. Parm. 1794 (de Rossi 1061), f. 124a-124b, M.
7859. Parma - Biblioteca Palatina Cod. Parm. 3006 (de Rossi 654,1), f. 143a-143b, M.

אפפוני מים עד נפש (א 7162), אמתי ב"ר שפטיה, סליחה

Ashkenaz
7860. Vatican - Biblioteca Apostolica ebr. 422/1, f. 45a, CG, no incipit.
Ashkenaz, commentary by Abraham b. Azriel[193]
7861. Vatican - Biblioteca Apostolica ebr. 301,1, f. 141b, C.

אפתח נא שפתי ואענה ברון (א 7199), מתתיה בן יצחק, פיוט להוצאת התורה

Italia, commentary by Zakharya David Shabbetai Segre
7862. Torino - Archivio Terracini 1499, p. 21-23, C, rubric: פירוש אפתח נא שפתי.

אפתח שיר בשפתי ולשון לבי תרון (א 7220), מרדכי בן יהודה דאטו, לפתיחת הארון

Italia, commentary by Mordekhai b. Yehuda Dato
7863. Moscow - Russian State Library, Ms. Guenzburg 249, f. 248a-249b, C.
7864. Moscow - Russian State Library, Ms. Guenzburg 674, f. 55b-57b, C.

אפתח שפתי בניגונותי אל תוך ביתיך (א 7223), אברהם אבן עזרא, סליחה

Yemen
7865. Jerusalem - Benayahu ת 301, f. 49b, G.
7866. Jerusalem - Sassoon 902, p. 418, M, very short.
Yemen, commentary by Isaac b. Abraham Wanneh
7867. Chicago-Spertus College of Judaica D 2, 2, f. 212a, M, no incipit.

---

[193] Edited by Urbach, ערוגת הבושם, vol. III, p. 308-309.

7868. Jerusalem - Sassoon 1158, p. 353, M, rubric: סים׳ אברהם, no incipit.

אפתחה שיר בשדי מחסי (א 7238), שלם שבזי
Yemen
7869. Cincinnati - Hebrew Union College 398, f. 21a-22a, M.

אפתחה שערי רנני (א 7240), יהודה הלוי, מיכמוכה לפסח, בתימן: סליחה
Yemen
7870. Jerusalem - Benayahu ת 414, f. 132a, M.
7871. Jerusalem - Sassoon 902, p. 384, M.
7872. New York - Jewish Theological Seminary Ms. 3052, f. 49b-50b, M, rubric: אל מלך.
7873. New York - Jewish Theological Seminary Ms. 3109, f. 76a, 77b, M. Yemen, commentary by Isaac b. Abraham Wanneh
7874. Jerusalem - Benayahu ת 282, f. 128b, M, rubric: אל מלך.
7875. Jerusalem - Benayahu ת 261, f. 145a, M, rubric: אל מלך.
7876. Jerusalem - Makhon Ben Zvi 1156 (Tubi 155), f. 127b-128a, M, rubric: אל מלך.
7877. Jerusalem - Makhon Ben Zvi 1174 (Tubi 154), f. 111a, M, rubric: אל מלך.
7878. Jerusalem - Michael Krupp 604, f. 162a, M, rubric: אל מלך.
7879. Jerusalem - Musad haRav Kook 325, f. 162a, M.
7880. Jerusalem - Sassoon 1158, p. 386, M, no incipit.
7881. Jerusalem - Sassoon 1174, p. 246, M, no incipit.
7882. Jerusalem - Yehiel haLevi 4, f. 143a-143b, G.
7883. London - British Library Or. 11122, f. 194b-195a, M, rubric: אל מלך.
7884. Manchester - John Rylands University Library, Ms. Gaster 5, f. 183b-184a, M.
7885. Muenchen - Bayerische Staatsbibliothek, Cod. hebr. 472, f. 175b, 177a, M, rubric: אל מלך.
7886. New York - Jewish Theological Seminary Ms. 3013, f. 111a, M, rubric: אל מלך, incipit רנני.
7887. New York - Jewish Theological Seminary Ms. 3294, f. 5a, C.
7888. New York - Public Library, Heb. Ms. 9, f. 120a, M.
7889. Philadelphia - University of Pennsylvania HB 2, f. 123b-124a, M, rubric: אל מלך, incipit רנני.
7890. Strasbourg - Bibliotheque Nationale et Universitaire 3965 (Landauer 39), p. 338, M, rubric: אל מלך.

אץ קוצץ בן קוצץ (א 7242), אלעזר ברבי קליר, חלק ה׳, קדושתא לשבת זכור
Ashkenaz
7891. Berlin - Staatsbibliothek (Preussischer Kulturbesitz) Or. Qu. 798-799 (Steinschneider 177), II, f. 22a-22b, M.

7892. Budapest - Magyar tudomanyos akademia, MS. Kaufmann A 384 , f. 54b-55b, M.
7893. Budapest - Magyar tudomanyos akademia, MS. Kaufmann A 400 , p. 39-42, C.
7894. Cambridge - University Library, Taylor Schechter Collection Misc. 33/3, f. 22a-22b, G.
7895. Erlangen - Universitaetsbibliothek 2601 (Roth 67), f. 35b, M.
7896. Hamburg - Staats- und Universitaetsbibliothek Cod. hebr. 17/2 (Steinschneider 152), f. 18b-19a, C.
7897. Jerusalem - Schocken Institute 24100 / Mahzor Nuremberg, f. 42b-43a, M.
7898. Muenchen - Bayerische Staatsbibliothek, Cod. hebr. 88, f. 25a-25b, G.
7899. Muenchen - Bayerische Staatsbibliothek, Cod. hebr. 393 , f. 91a-91b, C, no incipit.
7900. Oxford - Bodleian Library MS Opp. 170 (Neubauer 1205), f. 12a-13a, C.
7901. Paris - Bibliotheque Nationale heb. 709, f. 21b-22b, C.
7902. Parma - Biblioteca Palatina Cod. Parm. 1002 (Ta 24), f. 36b-37a, M.
7903. Parma - Biblioteca Palatina Cod. Parm. 3205 (de Rossi 655) , f. 21a-21b, C.
7904. Parma - Biblioteca Palatina Cod. Parm. 3507 (Perreau 27), f. 15b-16b, C, no incipit.
7905. Vatican - Biblioteca Apostolica ebr. 305,1, f. 14a-15a, C.

Tsarfat

7906. London - British Library Add. 11639 (Margoliouth 1056), f. 268b-269a, M.
7907. London - David Sofer 5, f. 20b-21b, C.
7908. Moscow - Russian State Library, Ms. Guenzburg 1665, f. 18b-19a, M.
7909. Oxford - Bodleian Library MS Laud. Or. 271 (Neubauer 1206), f. 21a-23b, C, commentator: Aaron b. Hayyim haKohen (compiler).
7910. Oxford - Bodleian Library MS Opp. 171 (Neubauer 1207), f. 17a-17b, C.
7911. Parma - Biblioteca Palatina Cod. Parm. 3136 (de Rossi 405) , f. 32a-32b, M.
7912. Vatican - Biblioteca Apostolica ebr. 306, f. 163b-165a, C, no incipit.

אצולה לפנים בכסא ערבות (א 7247), אברהם אבן עזרא, לשמחת תורה
Yemen, commentary by Yiḥya b. Josef Tsalaḥ
7913. Montreal - Elberg 203, f. 29a, M.

אצולים מפרך סונים (א 7255), משה בן קלונימוס, חלק ו', קדושתא לפסח

Ashkenaz

7914. Berlin - Staatsbibliothek (Preussischer Kulturbesitz) Or. Qu. 798-799 (Steinschneider 177), II, f. 93b-97a, M.
7915. Braunschweig - Landesmuseum fuer Geschichte und Volkstum R 2386, vol. I, 62b-64b, M.
7916. Budapest - Magyar tudomanyos akademia, MS. Kaufmann A 384, f. 205b-210b, M.
7917. Budapest - Magyar tudomanyos akademia, MS. Kaufmann A 400, p. 141-145, C, rubric: סדר.
7918. Erlangen - Universitaetsbibliothek 2601 (Roth 67), f. 118a, M.
7919. Hamburg - Staats- und Universitaetsbibliothek Cod. hebr. 17/2 (Steinschneider 152), f. 68a-69a, C, rubric: סדר.
7920. Jerusalem - Schocken Institute 24100 / Mahzor Nuremberg, f. 123b-126a, M.
7921. London - British Library Add. 18695 (Margoliouth 683), f. 60a-61a, T, Yiddish, begins in stanza 14.
7922. Moscow - Russian State Library, Ms. Guenzburg 615, f. 26a-27b, C, rubric: סדר.
7923. Muenchen - Bayerische Staatsbibliothek, Cod. hebr. 88, f. 84a-88a, G.
7924. Muenchen - Bayerische Staatsbibliothek, Cod. hebr. 393, f. 135b-136b, C.
7925. New York - Jewish Theological Seminary Ms. 4466, f. 111b-117a, M, party ecclectic.
7926. Oxford - Bodleian Library MS Opp. 170 (Neubauer 1205), f. 77a-78b, C.
7927. Paris - Bibliotheque Nationale heb. 709, f. 103b-105b, C, rubric: סדר.
7928. Parma - Biblioteca Palatina Cod. Parm. 1002 (Ta 24), f. 141a-143a, 144b-145a, M.
7929. Parma - Biblioteca Palatina Cod. Parm. 3507 (Perreau 27), f. 74b-77a, C.
7930. Parma - Biblioteca Palatina Cod. Parm. 3205 (de Rossi 655), f. 109b-110b, C, rubric: סדר.
7931. Zurich - Zentralbibliothek Heid. 139, f. 46b-47a, C, additional marginal notes.

Tsarfat

7932. London - David Sofer 5, f. 42b-44a, C, additional glosses.
7933. Moscow - Russian State Library, Ms. Guenzburg 1665, f. 91b-94b, M.
7934. Oxford - Bodleian Library MS Laud. Or. 271 (Neubauer 1206), f. 81b-83a, C, commentator: Aaron b. Hayyim haKohen (compiler).

אצולת אומן בצירוף זקוקה (א 7256), אלעזר ברבי קליר, קדושתא לשבת פרה

Ashkenaz

7935. Berlin - Staatsbibliothek (Preussischer Kulturbesitz) Or. Qu. 798-799 (Steinschneider 177), II, f. 32b, M.
7936. Budapest - Magyar tudomanyos akademia, MS. Kaufmann A 384, f. 76b, M.
7937. Erlangen - Universitaetsbibliothek 2601 (Roth 67), f. 45a, M.
7938. Hamburg - Staats- und Universitaetsbibliothek Cod. hebr. 17/2 (Steinschneider 152), f. 24a-25a, C, rubric: לפרה אדומה.
7939. Jerusalem - Schocken Institute 24100 / Mahzor Nuremberg, f. 61a, M.
7940. London - British Library Add. 11639 (Margoliouth 1056), f. 274b, M.
7941. Muenchen - Bayerische Staatsbibliothek, Cod. hebr. 88, f. 38a, G.
7942. Muenchen - Bayerische Staatsbibliothek, Cod. hebr. 393, f. 100b-101a, C, no incipit.
7943. New York - Jewish Theological Seminary Ms. 4466, f. 7b-8a, M.
7944. Oxford - Bodleian Library MS Opp. 170 (Neubauer 1205), f. 28b-29a, C, rubric: קרובה.
7945. Paris - Bibliotheque Nationale heb. 709, f. 35a-35b, C, rubric: קרובה לפרה אדומה.
7946. Parma - Biblioteca Palatina Cod. Parm. 1002 (Ta 24), f. 55a, M.
7947. Parma - Biblioteca Palatina Cod. Parm 3000 (de Rossi 378), f. 13b-14a, M.
7948. Parma - Biblioteca Palatina Cod. Parm. 3205 (de Rossi 655), f. 32b-33a, C.
7949. Parma - Biblioteca Palatina Cod. Parm. 3507 (Perreau 27), f. 27a-27b, C, rubric: קרוביץ.
7950. Vatican - Biblioteca Apostolica ebr. 305,1, f. 20a, C.
7951. Zurich - Zentralbibliothek Heid. 139, f. 4b-5a, C, additional marginal notes.

Tsarfat

7952. Moscow - Russian State Library, Ms. Guenzburg 1665, f. 34a, M.
7953. Oxford - Bodleian Library MS Laud. Or. 271 (Neubauer 1206), f. 38b-39b, C, commentator: Aaron b. Hayyim haKohen (compiler), rubric: קדושתא לפרש׳ פרה.
7954. Oxford - Bodleian Library MS Opp. 171 (Neubauer 1207), f. 35b-36a, C, rubric: קרובה קלירית.
7955. Parma - Biblioteca Palatina Cod. Parm. 3136 (de Rossi 405), f. 47b-48b, M.
7956. Vatican - Biblioteca Apostolica ebr. 306, f. 148b-149a, C.

אצורה ומופרשה (א 7260), אלעזר ברבי קליר, חלק ה׳, קדושתא לשבת פרה
Ashkenaz
7957. Berlin - Staatsbibliothek (Preussischer Kulturbesitz) Or. Qu. 798-799 (Steinschneider 177), II, f. 33b-34a, M.
7958. Budapest - Magyar tudomanyos akademia, MS. Kaufmann A 384 , f. 77b-78a, M.
7959. Erlangen - Universitaetsbibliothek 2601 (Roth 67), f. 46a, M.
7960. Hamburg - Staats- und Universitaetsbibliothek Cod. hebr. 17/2 (Steinschneider 152), f. 25b, C.
7961. Jerusalem - Schocken Institute 24100 / Mahzor Nuremberg, f. 61b-62a, M.
7962. Muenchen - Bayerische Staatsbibliothek, Cod. hebr. 88, f. 39a, G.
7963. Muenchen - Bayerische Staatsbibliothek, Cod. hebr. 393 , f. 101b, C, no incipit.
7964. New York - Jewish Theological Seminary Ms. 4466, f. 9b-10a, M.
7965. Oxford - Bodleian Library MS Opp. 170 (Neubauer 1205), f. 30a-30b, C.
7966. Paris - Bibliotheque Nationale heb. 709, f. 36b-37a, C.
7967. Parma - Biblioteca Palatina Cod. Parm. 1002 (Ta 24), f. 56a-56b, M.
7968. Parma - Biblioteca Palatina Cod. Parm 3000 (de Rossi 378), f. 15b-16a, M.
7969. Parma - Biblioteca Palatina Cod. Parm. 3205 (de Rossi 655) , f. 34a-34b, C, no incipit.
7970. Parma - Biblioteca Palatina Cod. Parm. 3507 (Perreau 27), f. 28a-28b, C,
7971. Vatican - Biblioteca Apostolica ebr. 305,1, f. 21a-21b, C, no incipit.
7972. Zurich - Zentralbibliothek Heid. 139, f. 5b-6a, C, no incipit, additional marginal notes.
Tsarfat
7973. London - British Library Add. 11639 (Margoliouth 1056), f. 275a-275b, M.
7974. London - David Sofer 5, f. 28a-28b, C.
7975. Moscow - Russian State Library, Ms. Guenzburg 1665, f. 34b-35a, M.
7976. Oxford - Bodleian Library MS Laud. Or. 271 (Neubauer 1206), f. 39b-40b, C, commentator: Aaron b. Hayyim haKohen (compiler).
7977. Oxford - Bodleian Library MS Opp. 171 (Neubauer 1207), f. 37b-38a, C.
7978. Parma - Biblioteca Palatina Cod. Parm. 3136 (de Rossi 405) , f. 49a-49b, M.
7979. Vatican - Biblioteca Apostolica ebr. 306, f. 150a-150b, C.

אצורי מקרב יעי חיות (א 7261), אלעזר ברבי קליר, חלק ז׳, קדושתא לשמיני עצרת
Tsarfat
7980. Oxford - Bodleian Library MS Opp. 171 (Neubauer 1207), f. 163a-163b, C.

אצילי מריעי נכד שעיר (א 7268), אלעזר ברבי קליר, חלק ג׳, קדושתא לשבת זכור
Ashkenaz
7981. Berlin - Staatsbibliothek (Preussischer Kulturbesitz) Or. Qu. 798-799 (Steinschneider 177), II, f. 21a-21b, M.
7982. Budapest - Magyar tudomanyos akademia, MS. Kaufmann A 384, f. 53b-54a, M.
7983. Cambridge - University Library, Taylor Schechter Collection Misc. 33/3, f. 21a-21b, G.
7984. Hamburg - Staats- und Universitaetsbibliothek Cod. hebr. 17/2 (Steinschneider 152), f. 18a-18b, C.
7985. Jerusalem - Schocken Institute 24100 / Mahzor Nuremberg, f. 42a, M.
7986. Muenchen - Bayerische Staatsbibliothek, Cod. hebr. 88, f. 24b, G.
7987. Muenchen - Bayerische Staatsbibliothek, Cod. hebr. 393, f. 90b-91a, C, no incipit.
7988. Paris - Bibliotheque Nationale heb. 709, f. 20a-20b, C, beginning of commentary crossed out.
7989. Parma - Biblioteca Palatina Cod. Parm. 1002 (Ta 24), f. 36a, M.
7990. Parma - Biblioteca Palatina Cod. Parm. 3205 (de Rossi 655), f. 20a-20b, C.
7991. Parma - Biblioteca Palatina Cod. Parm. 3507 (Perreau 27), f. 14a 15a, C, no incipit.
7992. Vatican - Biblioteca Apostolica ebr. 305,1, f. 13a-13b, C.
Tsarfat
7993. London - British Library Add. 11639 (Margoliouth 1056), f. 268a-268b, M.
7994. London - David Sofer 5, f. 19b-20b, C.
7995. Moscow - Russian State Library, Ms. Guenzburg 1665, f. 18a-18b, M.
7996. Oxford - Bodleian Library MS Laud. Or. 271 (Neubauer 1206), f. 19a-20b, C, commentator: Aaron b. Hayyim haKohen (compiler).
7997. Oxford - Bodleian Library MS Opp. 171 (Neubauer 1207), f. 16a-16b, C.
7998. Parma - Biblioteca Palatina Cod. Parm. 3136 (de Rossi 405), f. 31b, M.
7999. Vatican - Biblioteca Apostolica ebr. 306, f. 162b-163a, C, no incipit.

אציליי עם עולי גולה (א 7269), אלעזר ברבי קליר, חלק ו', קדושתא לשבת פרה
Ashkenaz
8000. Berlin - Staatsbibliothek (Preussischer Kulturbesitz) Or. Qu. 798-799 (Steinschneider 177), II, f. 34b-35a, M.
8001. Hamburg - Staats- und Universitaetsbibliothek Cod. hebr. 225, f. 41a-42a, G.
8002. Zurich - Zentralbibliothek Heid. 139, f. 7a-7b, C, additional marginal notes.

אציתו למימרי הדברין רברבנין ומלכוון (א 7278), פיוט בארמית לשבועות
Ashkenaz
8003. Oxford - Bodleian Library MS Can. Or. 1 (Neubauer 1104), f. 127a-127b, M, commentator: Mose, rubric: פירו' של דברות אילו פרשם הר' משה.
Tsarfat
8004. London - David Sofer 5, f. 56a-56b, C.

אקדמות מילין ושריות שותין (א 7314), מאיר ב"ר יצחק, לשבועות
Ashkenaz
8005. Amsterdam - Universiteitsbibliotheek MS Rosenthal 190/2, f. 1a-9b, M, Yiddish, commentator: Samuel b. David of Siena, commentary named ספר ליקוטי שמואל, rubric: פירוש נאה על אקדמות בלשון אשכנז.
8006. New York - Jewish Theological Seminary Ms. 8097, f. 88a-89b, C.
8007. Parma - Biblioteca Palatina Cod. Parm. 3205 (de Rossi 655), f. 179a-180a, C.
8008. Berlin - Staatsbibliothek (Preussischer Kulturbesitz) Or. Qu. 798-799 (Steinschneider 177), II, f. 153a-155a, M.
8009. Braunschweig - Landesmuseum fuer Geschichte und Volkstum R 2386, vol. I, f. 82b-84b, M.
8010. Budapest - Magyar tudomanyos akademia, MS. Kaufmann A 400, p. 543-546, C, rubric: פירוש הדיברות.
8011. Erlangen - Universitaetsbibliothek 2601 (Roth 67), f. 163a-164a, M.
8012. Hamburg - Staats- und Universitaetsbibliothek Cod. hebr. 17/2 (Steinschneider 152), f. 71a-72a, C.
8013. Krakow - Biblioteka Jagiellonska Fr. 629, f. 1b, FC, rubric: ובכן ולך תעלה קדושה, only beginning.
8014. London - British Library Add. 22431 (Margoliouth 662a), f. 24b-28a, M.
8015. Lund - Universitetsbibliothek Ms. L.O. 2, f. 102a-105a, M.
8016. New York - Jewish Theological Seminary Ms. 4466, f. 182a-185a, M.
8017. Oxford - Bodleian Library MS Opp. 170 (Neubauer 1205), f. 93a-94(ii)a, C.
8018. Paris - Bibliotheque Nationale heb. 709, f. 132b-135b, C.

אקוה חסדך שוכן מעונים שלח ישעך לעם קדש נדודים (א 7332), שלם שבזי
Yemen
8019. Cincinnati - Hebrew Union College 398, f. 173b-175a, M.

אקום להודות לך אלהי כל עוד בי נשמתי (א 7341), משה אבן עזרא, רשות לסדר עבודה
Carpentras
8020. Cincinnati - Hebrew Union College 392, f. 23a-23b, M.
Carpentras, commentary by Josef b. Abraham of Montelitz
8021. Cincinnati - Hebrew Union College 291, f. 11a-11b, C, rubric: פי׳ אקום להודות לך.
8022. New York - Jewish Theological Seminary Ms. 4197, f. 50b-51a, M.
8023. Paris - Ecole Rabbinique 32, f. 73b-74a, M.
8024. Strasbourg - Bibliotheque Nationale et Universitaire 4081, f. 53b-54a, M.

אקחה בראשון לאחרון (א 7368), אלעזר ברבי קליר, סילוק, קדושתא ליום א׳ של סוכות
Ashkenaz
8025. Berlin - Staatsbibliothek (Preussischer Kulturbesitz) Or. Qu. 798-799 (Steinschneider 177), I, f. 199b-200b, M, margins cut.
8026. Braunschweig - Landesmuseum fuer Geschichte und Volkstum R 2386, vol. I, f. 123b-124b, M.
8027. Budapest - Magyar tudomanyos akademia, MS. Kaufmann A 400, p. 370-372, C, rubric: סילוק.
8028. Fulda - Hessische Landesbibliothek A 3 II, f. 136b-137b, C, commentator: Josef, rubric: סילוק.
8029. Hamburg - Staats- und Universitaetsbibliothek Cod. hebr. 17/2 (Steinschneider 152), f. 164b-165b, C, rubric: סילוק.
8030. Hamburg - Staats- und Universitaetsbibliothek Cod. hebr. 62 (Steinschneider 154), f. 35a-36a, C, rubric: סילוק.
8031. Hamburg - Staats- und Universitaetsbibliothek Cod. hebr. 132 (Steinschneider 155), f. 56b-57a, C.
8032. Jerusalem - Jewish National and University Library Ms Heb 8° 3037, f. 238b-239a, M.
8033. Jerusalem - Schocken Institute 24100 / Mahzor Nuremberg, f. 477a-477b, M.
8034. London - British Library Add. 18695 (Margoliouth 683), f. 113a-114b, T, Yiddish, rubric: טן זגט קהל.
8035. London - British Library Add. 22431 (Margoliouth 662a), f. 103a-104a, M.
8036. London - British Library Or. 11318/1, f. 131b-132b, C, rubric: ובכן ויהי בשלם סוכו אז הייתה חניית סוכו וסילוק.

8037. London - Montefiore Library 261, f. 68a-69a, C, commentator: Eliezer b. Natan?.
8038. Moscow - Russian State Library, Ms. Guenzburg 615, f. 116a-116b, C, rubric: סילוק.
8039. New York - Jewish Theological Seminary Ms. 4466, f. 440b-441b, M.
8040. Oxford - Bodleian Library MS Mich. 365 (Neubauer 1208), f. 98b-100a, C, rubric: סילוק.
8041. Oxford - Bodleian Library MS Opp. 170 (Neubauer 1205), f. 188b-189a, C, rubric: סילוק.
8042. Oxford - Bodleian Library MS Opp. 172 (Neubauer 1211), f. 90b-91a, C, rubric: סילוק.
8043. Parma - Biblioteca Palatina Cod. Parm. 3205 (de Rossi 655), f. 242a-242b, C, no incipit.
8044. Parma - Biblioteca Palatina Cod. Parm. 3507 (Perreau 27), f. 175a-175b, C.
8045. Vatican - Biblioteca Apostolica ebr. 305,1, f. 39b-40a, C, rubric: סילוק.
8046. Vatican - Biblioteca Apostolica ebr. 422/1, f. 21b-22a, C.
8047. Zurich - Zentralbibliothek Heid. 139, f. 93b, C, no incipit, additional marginal notes.

Romania

8048. London - London School of Jewish Studies. Asher I.Myers collection 9, f. 203a-203b, M, ecclectic.

Tsarfat

8049. Oxford - Bodleian Library MS Laud. Or. 271 (Neubauer 1206), f. 98a-98b, C, commentator: Aaron b. Hayyim haKohen (compiler).
8050. Parma - Biblioteca Palatina Cod. Parm. 1264, f. 29a-30a, M.

אקחה פרי עץ הדר (א 7370), אלעזר ברבי קליר, חלק ה׳, קדושתא ליום א׳ של סוכות

Ashkenaz

8051. Berlin - Staatsbibliothek (Preussischer Kulturbesitz) Or. Qu. 798-799 (Steinschneider 177), I, f. 199a-199b, M.
8052. Braunschweig - Landesmuseum fuer Geschichte und Volkstum R 2386, vol. I, f. 123a-123b, M, no incipit.
8053. Hamburg - Staats- und Universitaetsbibliothek Cod. hebr. 62 (Steinschneider 154), f. 34a-35a, C, incipit אנובב.
8054. Hamburg - Staats- und Universitaetsbibliothek Cod. hebr. 132 (Steinschneider 155), f. 56a-56b, C, incipit שגיא.
8055. Jerusalem - Jewish National and University Library Ms Heb 8° 3037, f. 237a-237b, M.
8056. Jerusalem - Schocken Institute 24100 / Mahzor Nuremberg, f. 476b-477a, M.
8057. Krakow - Biblioteka Jagiellonska Fr. 629, f. 1a, FC, only end.

8058. London - British Library Add. 18695 (Margoliouth 683), f. 112a-113a, T, Yiddish, 1st incipit אנובב, 2nd incipit שגיא, 3rd incipit אקחה.
8059. London - British Library Add. 22431 (Margoliouth 662a), f. 102a-102b, M.
8060. London - British Library Or. 11318/1, f. 131a-131b, C, 1st incipit שגיא, 2nd incipit אקחה.
8061. London - Montefiore Library 261, f. 66b-67b, C, commentator: Eliezer b. Natan?.
8062. Moscow - Russian State Library, Ms. Guenzburg 615, f. 115b-116a, C, incipit שגיא כח.
8063. New York - Jewish Theological Seminary Ms. 4466, f. 439b, M, incipit יופי.
8064. Oxford - Bodleian Library MS Mich. 365 (Neubauer 1208), f. 96b-97b, C, 1st incipit אנובב, 2nd incipit סגיא, 3rd incipit אקחה.
8065. Oxford - Bodleian Library MS Opp. 170 (Neubauer 1205), f. 188a-188b, C, rubric: סילוק.
8066. Oxford - Bodleian Library MS Opp. 172 (Neubauer 1211), f. 90a-90b, C.
8067. Parma - Biblioteca Palatina Cod. Parm. 3205 (de Rossi 655), f. 242a, C, no incipit.
8068. Parma - Biblioteca Palatina Cod. Parm. 3507 (Perreau 27), f. 174a-174b, C, incipit שגיא כח.
8069. Vatican - Biblioteca Apostolica ebr. 422/1, f. 21b, C, incipit אנובב.
8070. Vatican - Biblioteca Apostolica ebr. 305,1, f. 39b, C, no incipit, begins סגיא.
8071. Zurich - Zentralbibliothek Heid. 139, f. 93a-93b, C, no incipit, additional marginal notes.

Romania
8072. London - London School of Jewish Studies. Asher I.Myers collection 9, f. 202b, M, rubric: סילוק.
8073. Vatican - Biblioteca Apostolica ebr. 320, f. 431b, M.

Tsarfat
8074. London - David Sofer 5, f. 179b, C.
8075. Moscow - Russian State Library, Ms. Guenzburg 1665, f. 170b, M.
8076. Oxford - Bodleian Library MS Laud. Or. 271 (Neubauer 1206), f. 97b-98a, C, commentator: Aaron b. Hayyim haKohen (compiler), no incipit.
8077. Parma - Biblioteca Palatina Cod. Parm. 1264, f. 28a, M.

אקף יא צבי אלבר (א 7372), שלם שבזי

Yemen
8078. Cincinnati - Hebrew Union College 398, f. 47a-48a, M.

אקרא אל אלהים קולי (א +7373), שלמה, סליחה

Ashkenaz

8079. Oxford - Bodleian Library MS Opp. 681 (Neubauer 1213), f. 68b, C, short.
8080. Vatican - Biblioteca Apostolica ebr. 308, f. 14b, C, commentator: David b. Mose (compiler).
8081. Vatican - Biblioteca Apostolica ebr. 422/1, f. 29b, C, short.
8082. Vatican - Biblioteca Apostolica ebr. 422/1, f. 42b, CG, no incipit, short.

אקשטה כסל וקרב (א 7419), אלעזר ברבי קליר, למוסף שמיני עצרת

Ashkenaz

8083. Berlin - Staatsbibliothek (Preussischer Kulturbesitz) Or. Qu. 798-799 (Steinschneider 177), I, f. 214b-216b, M.
8084. Braunschweig - Landesmuseum fuer Geschichte und Volkstum R 2386, vol. I, f. 153a-154b, M.
8085. Budapest - Magyar tudomanyos akademia, MS. Kaufmann A 400, p. 397-401, C.
8086. Fulda - Hessische Landesbibliothek A 3 II, f. 140b-144b, C, commentator: Josef.
8087. Hamburg - Staats- und Universitaetsbibliothek Cod. hebr. 17/2 (Steinschneider 152), f. 170a-172b, C.
8088. Hamburg - Staats- und Universitaetsbibliothek Cod. hebr. 62 (Steinschneider 154), f. 45b-47b, C, no incipit.
8089. Hamburg - Staats- und Universitaetsbibliothek Cod. hebr. 132 (Steinschneider 155), f. 60b-64a, C.
8090. Jerusalem - Jewish National and University Library Ms Heb 8° 3037, f. 288a-290b, M, no incipit.
8091. Jerusalem - Schocken Institute 24100 / Mahzor Nuremberg, f. 499b-501a, M.
8092. London - British Library Add. 18695 (Margoliouth 683), f. 128a-129a, T, Yiddish.
8093. London - British Library Add. 22431 (Margoliouth 662a), f. 136a-137b, M.
8094. London - British Library Or. 11318/1, f. 141b-144b, C.
8095. London - Montefiore Library 261, f. 74a-77a, C, commentator: Eliezer b. Natan?.
8096. Moscow - Russian State Library, Ms. Guenzburg 615, f. 118b-122b, C.
8097. New York - Jewish Theological Seminary Ms. 4466, f. 459b-462a, M.
8098. Oxford - Bodleian Library MS Mich. 365 (Neubauer 1208), f. 107b-109b, C.

8099. Oxford - Bodleian Library MS Opp. 170 (Neubauer 1205), f. 191a-193b, C.
8100. Parma - Biblioteca Palatina Cod. Parm. 3205 (de Rossi 655), f. 244a-245a, C.
8101. Parma - Biblioteca Palatina Cod. Parm. 3507 (Perreau 27), f. 181b-185a, C, no incipit.
8102. Vatican - Biblioteca Apostolica ebr. 305,1, f. 46b-47b, C, no incipit.
8103. Vatican - Biblioteca Apostolica ebr. 422/1, f. 23a, C.
8104. Zurich - Zentralbibliothek Heid. 139, f. 95b-97b, C, additional marginal notes.

Romania
8105. New York - Jewish Theological Seminary Ms. 4823, f. 13b-14a, FG.
8106. Vatican - Biblioteca Apostolica ebr. 320, f. 465b-467b, M.

Tsarfat
8107. London - British Library Add. 11639 (Margoliouth 1056), f. 663b-665b, M.
8108. London - David Sofer 5, f. 185b-187a, C.
8109. Moscow - Russian State Library, Ms. Guenzburg 1665, f. 191b-193b, M.
8110. Oxford - Bodleian Library MS Laud. Or. 271 (Neubauer 1206), f. 100a-101b, C, commentator: Aaron b. Hayyim haKohen (compiler).
8111. Oxford - Bodleian Library MS Opp. 171 (Neubauer 1207), f. 155b-157a, C.
8112. Parma - Biblioteca Palatina Cod. Parm. 1264, f. 123a-125a, M.
8113. Vatican - Biblioteca Apostolica ebr. 306, f. 115a-117a, C.

אראלי הוד פוצחים הלולו (א 7448), אליה ברבי מרדכי, חלק ד', קדושתא למנחה יום כפור

Ashkenaz
8114. Berlin - Staatsbibliothek (Preussischer Kulturbesitz) Or. Qu. 798-799 (Steinschneider 177), I, f. 162a-162b, M.
8115. Braunschweig - Landesmuseum fuer Geschichte und Volkstum R 2386, vol. II, f. 255a, M.
8116. Cambridge - University Library Or. 785, f. 205b-206a, G.
8117. Fulda - Hessische Landesbibliothek A 3 II, f. 128b, C, commentator: Josef, incipit מיכאל, very short.
8118. Hamburg - Staats- und Universitaetsbibliothek Cod. hebr. 62 (Steinschneider 154), f. 22b, C, incipit מיכאל, short.
8119. Hamburg - Staats- und Universitaetsbibliothek Cod. hebr. 132 (Steinschneider 155), f. 49b-50a, C, very short.
8120. London - British Library Or. 11318/1, f. 124b, C, short.
8121. London - Montefiore Library 261, f. 64a, C, commentator: Eliezer b. Natan?.

8122. Muenchen - Bayerische Staatsbibliothek, Cod. hebr. 21, f. 240b-241a, M.
8123. New York - Jewish Theological Seminary Ms. 4466, f. 415a-415b, M, incipit מיכאל and אראלי.
8124. Oxford - Bodleian Library MS Mich. 365 (Neubauer 1208), f. 93b, C, incipit מיכאל, very short.
8125. Oxford - Bodleian Library MS Opp. 170 (Neubauer 1205), f. 181a, C, short.
8126. Oxford - Bodleian Library MS Opp. 172 (Neubauer 1211), f. 82a-82b, C, short.
8127. Oxford - Bodleian Library MS Opp. 619 (Neubauer 2374), f. 255b, M, very short.
8128. Parma - Biblioteca Palatina Cod. Parm. 3205 (de Rossi 655), f. 237b, C, incipit מיכאל, short.
8129. Parma - Biblioteca Palatina Cod. Parm. 3507 (Perreau 27), f. 172a, C, short.
8130. Vatican - Biblioteca Apostolica ebr. 308, f. 140b, C, commentator: David b. Mose (compiler), short.
8131. Vatican - Biblioteca Apostolica ebr. 422/1, f. 19b, C, very short, incipit מיכאל.
8132. Zurich - Zentralbibliothek Heid. 139, f. 89a, C, no incipit, very short, additional marginal notes.

Tsarfat

8133. London - David Sofer 5, f. 172a-172b, C, rubric: קדושה אחרת. והוא יאמר מִיכָאֵל הימין מהלל, begins במנחה של יום הכפורים.
8134. Oxford - Bodleian Library MS Bodl. Or. 109 (Neubauer 1209), f. 42a, C, commentator: Aaron b. Hayyim haKohen (compiler), rubric: אין זה הפיוט שאומרים במדין' זו, incipit מיכאל, short.

אראלי מעלה אומרים הה אלהינו (א 7450), פתיחה

Sepharad

8135. Skokie - Hebrew Theological College 3, f. 2.18b, M.

Yemen, commentary by Isaac b. Abraham Wanneh

8136. Jerusalem - Yehiel haLevi 4, f. 133a, M.

אראלי מרומים בשיר ושבח קמים (א 7451), סליחה

Yemen

8137. Jerusalem - Benayahu ת 88, f. 126b, M.
8138. New York - Jewish Theological Seminary Ms. 3052, f. 99b, M.

Yemen, commentary by Isaac b. Abraham Wanneh

8139. Chicago-Spertus College of Judaica D 2, 2, f. 246b, M, no incipit.
8140. Jerusalem - Makhon Ben Zvi 1156 (Tubi 155), f. 144b, M, no incipit.
8141. Jerusalem - Makhon Ben Zvi 1174 (Tubi 154), f. 140b, M.

HEBREW LITURGICAL POETRY 463

8142. Jerusalem - Sassoon 1158, p. 425, M, no incipit.
8143. Jerusalem - Sassoon 1174, p. 282, M, rubric: פירוש.
8144. London - British Library Or. 11122, f. 219b-220a, M, no incipit.
8145. Muenchen - Bayerische Staatsbibliothek, Cod. hebr. 472, f. 202b, M.
8146. New York - Jewish Theological Seminary Ms. 3013, f. 136a, M.
8147. New York - Jewish Theological Seminary Ms. 3294, f. 19a, C.
8148. New York - Public Library, Heb. Ms. 9, f. 133b, M.

אראלים בשם תם ממליכים (א 7453), אליה ברבי מרדכי, חלק ג', קדושתא למנחה יום כפור

Ashkenaz

8149. Berlin - Staatsbibliothek (Preussischer Kulturbesitz) Or. Qu. 798-799 (Steinschneider 177), I, f. 161b-162a, M, short.
8150. Braunschweig - Landesmuseum fuer Geschichte und Volkstum R 2386, vol. II, f. 254b, M.
8151. Fulda - Hessische Landesbibliothek A 3 II, f. 128a, C, commentator: Josef.
8152. Hamburg - Staats- und Universitaetsbibliothek Cod. hebr. 17/2 (Steinschneider 152), f. 161a, C.
8153. Hamburg - Staats- und Universitaetsbibliothek Cod. hebr. 62 (Steinschneider 154), f. 22a-22b, C, short.
8154. Hamburg - Staats- und Universitaetsbibliothek Cod. hebr. 132 (Steinschneider 155), f. 49b, C, short, no incipit.
8155. Jerusalem - Jewish National and University Library Ms Heb 8° 3037, f. 215a-215b, M.
8156. Jerusalem - Schocken Institute 24100 / Mahzor Nuremberg, f. 443b-444a, M, short.
8157. London - British Library Or. 11318/1, f. 122b-123a, C.
8158. London - Montefiore Library 261, f. 63b, C, commentator: Eliezer b. Natan?, short.
8159. Moscow - Russian State Library, Ms. Guenzburg 191, f. 145a, M.
8160. Moscow - Russian State Library, Ms. Guenzburg 615, f. 108a, C.
8161. Muenchen - Bayerische Staatsbibliothek, Cod. hebr. 21, f. 240a, M.
8162. Muenchen - Bayerische Staatsbibliothek, Cod. hebr. 346, f. 87a-87b, C, short.
8163. New York - Jewish Theological Seminary Ms. 4466, f. 413b-414a, M.
8164. Oxford - Bodleian Library MS Mich. 365 (Neubauer 1208), f. 93a, C, no incipit.
8165. Oxford - Bodleian Library MS Opp. 170 (Neubauer 1205), f. 181a, C.
8166. Oxford - Bodleian Library MS Opp. 172 (Neubauer 1211), f. 82a, C, short.
8167. Oxford - Bodleian Library MS Opp. 619 (Neubauer 2374), f. 255a, M.

8168. Parma - Biblioteca Palatina Cod. Parm. 3205 (de Rossi 655), f. 237a, C, no incipit, short.

8169. Parma - Biblioteca Palatina Cod. Parm. 3270 (de Rossi 1215), f. 213a-213b, M.

8170. Vatican - Biblioteca Apostolica ebr. 308, f. 139b-140a, C, commentator: David b. Mose (compiler), short.

8171. Vatican - Biblioteca Apostolica ebr. 422/1, f. 19b, C, very short.

8172. Zurich - Zentralbibliothek Heid. 139, f. 88b, C, no incipit, very short, additional marginal notes.

Asti, Fossano, Moncalvo

8173. New Haven - Yale University, Beinecke Rare Book and MS Library, MS Heb. 52, f. 161a, M.

Tsarfat

8174. London - David Sofer 5, f. 165a-165b, C.

8175. Oxford - Bodleian Library MS Laud. Or. 271 (Neubauer 1206), f. 118a, C, commentator: Aaron b. Hayyim haKohen (compiler), short.

8176. Parma - Biblioteca Palatina Cod. Parm. 3006 (de Rossi 654,1), f. 219b-220a, M.

אראלים וחשמלים יתנו שיר לשם האל (א 7456), יוסף זבארה, אופן

Ashkenaz

8177. Oxford - Bodleian Library MS Opp. 169 (Neubauer 1151), f. 15b, M, short.

Ashkenaz, commentary by Abraham b. Azriel[194]

8178. Vatican - Biblioteca Apostolica ebr. 301,1, f. 6b-7b, C, rubric: אופן.

אראלים ומלאכים מקדישים ומברכים (א 7458), אמתי ב"ר שפטיה, אופן לשמיני עצרת

Ashkenaz

8179. Jerusalem - Schocken Institute 24100 / Mahzor Nuremberg, f. 498a, M.

8180. Muenchen - Bayerische Staatsbibliothek, Cod. hebr. 69, f. 76b-77b, M.

Ashkenaz, commentry by Abraham b. Azriel[195]

8181. Frankfurt a M - Stadt- und Universitaetsbibliothek Fol. 16 (Merzbacher 95), f. 90b-92a, C, rubric: אופן של ר' אמיתי ב"ר שפטיה ושניהם היו בעלי השם.

8182. Vatican - Biblioteca Apostolica ebr. 301,1, f. 77a-77b, C, rubric: אופן של ר' אמיתי בר שפטיה.

---

[194] Edited by Urbach, ערוגת הבושם, vol. I, p. 43-47.
[195] Edited by Urbach, ערוגת הבושם, vol. II, pp.181-187.

Tsarfat

8183. Parma - Biblioteca Palatina Cod. Parm. 1264, f. 110a-110b, M.

ארבעה מלכיות אכלו המוני (א 7469), לראש השנה

Ashkenaz

8184. Jerusalem - Schocken Institute 24100 / Mahzor Nuremberg, f. 246a, M, marginal notes by later hand only.

ארבע מלכוית אנושים, סליחה

Tsarfat

8185. Vatican - Biblioteca Apostolica ebr. 306, f. 203a, C.

ארד בתואר מכון, ליום כפור

Ashkenaz

8186. Parma - Biblioteca Palatina Cod. Parm. 3507 (Perreau 27), f. 172a-172b, C.

ארומם אלהי אבי ואלי (א 7505), שמואל ב"ר קלונימוס?, שיר היהוד ליום ד'

Ashkenaz

8187. Braunschweig - Landesmuseum fuer Geschichte und Volkstum R 2386, vol. II, f. 171a-173a, M, no incipit.

8188. Frankfurt a M - Stadt- und Universitaetsbibliothek Oct. 121/1 (Merzbacher 105), f. 16a-20b, C, no incipit.

8189. Paris - Alliance Israelite Universelle H 133 A, f. 12a-14a, M.

Romania

8190. Vatican - Biblioteca Apostolica ebr. 274, f. 176b-179b, C, kabbalistic, no incipit.

Sepharad

8191. Brussels - Bibliotheque Royale de Belgique 4781, f. 180a-180b, C, no incipit.

ארוממך אל חי אספרה שמך לאחי (א 7530), מאיר ב"ר יצחק, יוצר לשבת נחמו

Ashkenaz

8192. Berlin - Staatsbibliothek (Preussischer Kulturbesitz) Or. Qu. 798-799 (Steinschneider 177), I, f. 249a-253a, M.

8193. Budapest - Magyar tudomanyos akademia, MS. Kaufmann A 399, p. 425-429, C, rubric: יוצר שבת נחמו.

8194. Budapest - Magyar tudomanyos akademia, MS. Kaufmann A 399, p. 437-439, C.

8195. Cambridge - University Library Add. 504,1, f. 43b-47b, C, rubric: לנחמו ר' מאיר ש'ץ'.

8196. Frankfurt a M - Stadt- und Universitaetsbibliothek Oct. 227, f. 163a-164a, M.

8197. Lund - Universitetsbibliothek Ms. L.O. 2, f. 105b-107a, M.
8198. Muenchen - Bayerische Staatsbibliothek, Cod. hebr. 393,9, f. 165b-169a, C, rubric: לשבת נחמו.
8199. New York - Jewish Theological Seminary Ms. 4824, f. 2b, FM.
8200. Oxford - Bodleian Library MS Can. Or. 82 (Neubauer 1148), f. 27a-30b, M.
8201. Oxford - Bodleian Library MS Mich. 365 (Neubauer 1208), f. 28a-31a, C, rubric: יוצר לנחמו.
8202. Oxford - Bodleian Library MS Opp. 170 (Neubauer 1205), f. 246a-248a, C.
8203. Parma - Biblioteca Palatina Cod. Parm. 2895, p. 403-405, M, margins cut, text damaged.
8204. Parma - Biblioteca Palatina Cod. Parm. 3205 (de Rossi 655), f. 155b-158b, C, rubric: פירוש ליוצר שליח ציבור לשבת נחמו.
8205. Vatican - Biblioteca Apostolica ebr. 318, f. 115a-116b, GI.

Ashkenaz, commentary by Abraham b. Azriel[196]

8206. Frankfurt a M - Stadt- und Universitaetsbibliothek Fol. 16 (Merzbacher 95), f. 4b-5b, C, rubric: יוצר אחר לנחמו.
8207. Vatican - Biblioteca Apostolica ebr. 301,1, f. 39a-40a, C, rubric: יוצר.

Ashkenaz, commentary by Eliezer b. Natan

8208. Hamburg - Staats- und Universitaetsbibliothek Cod. hebr. 61 (Steinschneider 153), f. 35a-37b, C, rubric: זה היוצר שייך לשבת נחמו.
8209. Parma - Biblioteca Palatina Cod. Parm. 3057.12 (de Rossi 1033/10), f. 137b-142a, C, rubric: יוצר לשבת נחמו.
8210. Warszaw - Uniwersytet, Inst. Orientalistyczny 258, f. 187a-188b, C, rubric: יוצר לשבת של נחמו.

Tsarfat

8211. Oxford - Bodleian Library MS Laud. Or. 271 (Neubauer 1206), f. 187a-188b, C, commentator: Aaron b. Hayyim haKohen (compiler).

ארוממך חזקי וחלקי (א 7543), שלמה אבן גבירול, רשות לסדר עבודה

haAri

8212. New York - Columbia University X 893 J 558, f. 170b, M, kabbalistic.

Sepharad

8213. Jerusalem - Benayahu ז 25, f. 142b-143b, M.
8214. Jerusalem - Sassoon 1216, p. 33-36, M, commentator: Mose Nigrin.
8215. Jerusalem - Schocken Institute 70014, f. 75a-75b, M.

Sepharad, commentary by David b. Josef Abudarham[197]

8216. Budapest - Magyar tudomanyos akademia, MS. Kaufmann A 405/2, p. 215-216, C, rubric: רשות לסדר עבודה לר' שלמה ן' גיבירול.

---

[196] Edited by Urbach, ערוגת הבושם, vol. I, p. 238-244.
[197] Edited by Prins, תשלום אבודרהם, p. 34-36.

8217. Cincinnati - Hebrew Union College 490, f. 7a, C.
8218. New York - Columbia X893 Ab 93, f. 15a-15b, C, rubric: רשות לסדר עבודה.
8219. New York - Jewish Theological Seminary Ms. 3011, f. 10b-11a, C, rubric: רשות לסדר עבודה, no incipit.

Sepharad, commentary by Yehoshua Raphael b. Israel Benvenisti (עבודה תמה)
8220. Jerusalem - Benayahu ע 41, f. 1a-5a, M.
8221. New York - Columbia University X 893 J 724, f. 4a-5a, M.

Yemen
8222. New York - Jewish Theological Seminary Ms. 9325, f. 44b-45a, G.

ארוממך נצח בעוז וברננים (א 7549), יוסף ב"ר שמואל טוב עלם, חלק ד', קדושתא לשבועות

Tsarfat
8223. London - David Sofer 5, f. 68a-68b, C, incipit אל נא.
8224. Moscow - Russian State Library, Ms. Guenzburg 1665, f. 142a-142b, M, inicipit אל נא.
8225. Parma - Biblioteca Palatina Cod. Parm. 3136 (de Rossi 405), f. 170a, M, incipit אל נא.

ארוסת אמונה ארוסת צדק ומשפט (א 7556), יהודה בן מנחם, זולת לשבת הגדול

Roma
8226. Jerusalem - Jewish National and University Library Ms Heb 8° 4153, f. 157b, C, commentator: Daniel ben Salomo haRofe (compiler), very short.
8227. Oxford - Bodleian Library MS Mich. 312,1 (Neubauer 2276,1), f. 23a, C, rubric: פי' יוצר אחר לזה, very short.

ארחות אראלים יקדישו ברדתו בסיני (א 7569), אופן לשבועות

Ashkenaz
8228. London - British Library Add. 22431 (Margoliouth 662a), f. 52a-52b, M.

ארחותיך למדני עמך תמים עד אהיה (א 7572), אברהם אבן עזרא, פזמון

Sepharad, commentary by David b. Josef Abudarham[198]
8229. Budapest - Magyar tudomanyos akademia, MS. Kaufmann A 405/2, p. 195, C.
8230. Holon - Yehuda Nahum 278, f. 9a, FC, rubric: פזמון, incomplete.
8231. New York - Columbia X893 Ab 93, f. 8a-8b, C, rubric: פזמון.

---

[198] Edited by Prins, תשלום אבודרהם, p. 83-84.

ארחץ בנקיון כפות (א 7577), אלעזר ברבי קליר, קדושתא ליום ב' של סוכות

Ashkenaz

8232. Berlin - Staatsbibliothek (Preussischer Kulturbesitz) Or. Qu. 798-799 (Steinschneider 177), I, f. 190b-191a, M.
8233. Braunschweig - Landesmuseum fuer Geschichte und Volkstum R 2386, vol. I, f. 133b-134b, M.
8234. Budapest - Magyar tudomanyos akademia, MS. Kaufmann A 400, p. 372-373, C, rubric: ליום שיני.
8235. Cambridge - University Library Or. 785, f. 130a-130b, G.
8236. Fulda - Hessische Landesbibliothek A 3 II, f. 129b-130b, C, commentator: Josef, rubric: אתחיל קרובץ של סכות ליום ראשון.
8237. Hamburg - Staats- und Universitaetsbibliothek Cod. hebr. 17/2 (Steinschneider 152), f. 161b-162b, C, rubric: קדושתא ליום ראשון של סוכות דר' אלעזר קליר.
8238. Hamburg - Staats- und Universitaetsbibliothek Cod. hebr. 62 (Steinschneider 154), f. 36b-37b, C, rubric: קדושת'.
8239. Hamburg - Staats- und Universitaetsbibliothek Cod. hebr. 132 (Steinschneider 155), f. 51a-51b, C.
8240. Jerusalem - Jewish National and University Library Ms Heb 8° 3037, f. 253b-254a, M.
8241. Jerusalem - Schocken Institute 24100 / Mahzor Nuremberg, f. 480b-481a, M.
8242. London - British Library Add. 18695 (Margoliouth 683), f. 116b-117a, T, Yiddish, rubric: קרובץ.
8243. London - British Library Add. 22431 (Margoliouth 662a), f. 90b, M
8244. London - British Library Or. 11318/1, f. 133a-134a, C.
8245. London - Montefiore Library 261, f. 69b-70a, C, commentator: Eliezer b. Natan?.
8246. Moscow - Russian State Library, Ms. Guenzburg 615, f. 110a-110b, C, rubric: ליום ראשון של סוכות.
8247. New York - Jewish Theological Seminary Ms. 4826, f. 2a, FM, only end of commentary.
8248. New York - Jewish Theological Seminary Ms. 4466, f. 444b-445b, M.
8249. Oxford - Bodleian Library MS Mich. 365 (Neubauer 1208), f. 100b-101a, C, rubric: קרובה.
8250. Oxford - Bodleian Library MS Opp. 170 (Neubauer 1205), f. 182b-183b, C, rubric: קרובה עלייה . בעזר דר בשמי' . והא לך קרובוץ דחגא מטלייא.
8251. Oxford - Bodleian Library MS Opp. 172 (Neubauer 1211), f. 91a, C, rubric: קדושתין, the manuscript breaks off after a few lines.
8252. Parma - Biblioteca Palatina Cod. Parm. 3205 (de Rossi 655), f. 238b-239a, C.
8253. Parma - Biblioteca Palatina Cod. Parm. 3507 (Perreau 27), f. 176a-176b, C.
8254. Vatican - Biblioteca Apostolica ebr. 305,1, f. 40b, C.

8255. Vatican - Biblioteca Apostolica ebr. 422/1, f. 20a-20b, C.
8256. Zurich - Zentralbibliothek Heid. 139, f. 89b-90a, C, additional marginal notes.

Romania

8257. London - London School of Jewish Studies. Asher I.Myers collection 9, f. 218b-219a, M.
8258. Vatican - Biblioteca Apostolica ebr. 320, f. 429a-430a, M.

Tsarfat

8259. London - David Sofer 5, f. 181b, C.
8260. Moscow - Russian State Library, Ms. Guenzburg 1665, f. 162b, M.
8261. Oxford - Bodleian Library MS Laud. Or. 271 (Neubauer 1206), f. 94a-94b, C, commentator: Aaron b. Hayyim haKohen (compiler).
8262. Oxford - Bodleian Library MS Opp. 171 (Neubauer 1207), f. 145a, C.
8263. Parma - Biblioteca Palatina Cod. Parm. 1264, f. 54b-55a, M.

אריא וגנבי טובא מרעי ותונבי (א 7584), פיוט בארמית לשבועות

Ashkenaz

8264. Cambridge - University Library Add. 394,1 (Reif SCR 461), f. 60a-61a, C.
8265. Oxford - Bodleian Library MS Can. Or. 1 (Neubauer 1104), f. 125a-127a, M.
8266. Parma - Biblioteca Palatina Cod. Parm. 3205 (de Rossi 655), f. 184a-185a, C.

Tsarfat

8267. London - David Sofer 5, f. 64a-65a, C.
8268. Moscow - Russian State Library, Ms. Guenzburg 1665, f. 127a-127b, M.
8269. New York - Jewish Theological Seminary Ms. 4460, f. 63b-64b, M, pages damaged.
8270. London - British Library Add. 11639 (Margoliouth 1056), f. 683a-683b, M.
8271. London - British Library Or. 2735 (Margoliouth 663), f. 29a-31a, M.
8272. Parma - Biblioteca Palatina Cod. Parm. 3136 (de Rossi 405), f. 160b-161a, M.

אריאל בהיותו על מכונו ומוסדו (א 7585), אליעזר ב"ר נתן, סליחה

Ashkenaz

8273. Braunschweig - Landesmuseum fuer Geschichte und Volkstum R 2386, vol. II, f. 246a, M, very short.

Asti, Fossano, Moncalvo

8274. New Haven - Yale University, Beinecke Rare Book and MS Library, MS Heb. 52, f. 152b, M.

אריד בשיחי בשיחי לגוחי (א 7589), יצחק ב"ר יקר, סליחה

Ashkenaz

8275. Braunschweig - Landesmuseum fuer Geschichte und Volkstum R 2386, vol. II, 50b-51a, M.
8276. Oxford - Bodleian Library MS Mich. 543 (Neubauer 1212), f. 85b-86a, C, commentator: Isaac b. Jacob (compiler).
8277. Padova - Biblioteca del Seminario Vescovile Cod. 218, f. 82b-83a, M.

אריד בשיחי ואהימה (א 7591), יוסף בן סולי, סליחה

North Africa, commentary by David b. Josef Abudarham

8278. New York - Jewish Theological Seminary Ms. 5426, f. 62b, M.

Sepharad, commentary by David b. Josef Abudarham[199]

8279. Budapest - Magyar tudomanyos akademia, MS. Kaufmann A 405/2, p. 182, C.
8280. Cincinnati - Hebrew Union College 490, f. 2a, C.

Yemen, commentary by Isaac b. Abraham Wanneh

8281. Chicago-Spertus College of Judaica D 2, 2, f. 218b, M, no incipit.
8282. Jerusalem - Sassoon 1158, p. 381-382, M, no incipit.
8283. London - British Library Or. 11122, f. 191a, M, no incipit.
8284. New York - Columbia X893 Ab 93, f. 3a, C.

אריד בשיחי ויחרד לבי (א 7594), שלמה ברבי שמשון, רשות לקדושתא לראש השנה

Ashkenaz

8285. Berlin - Staatsbibliothek (Preussischer Kulturbesitz) Or. Qu. 798-799 (Steinschneider 177), I, f. 5a-5b, M.

אריה ביער דמיתי (א 7598), אליה ב"ר שמעיה, סליחה

Ashkenaz

8286. Cambridge - University Library Dd. 2.30, f. 12a-12b, G.
8287. Oxford - Bodleian Library MS Mich. 543 (Neubauer 1212), f. 50a-50b, C, commentator: Isaac b. Jacob (compiler).
8288. Oxford - Bodleian Library MS Opp. 681 (Neubauer 1213), f. 18a-18b, C.
8289. Padova - Biblioteca del Seminario Vescovile Cod. 218, f. 79b-80a, M.
8290. Vatican - Biblioteca Apostolica ebr. 422/1, f. 26a, C, very short.
8291. Vatican - Biblioteca Apostolica ebr. 422/2, f. 39b-40a, CG, no incipit.

Ashkenaz, commentary by Abraham b. Azriel[200]

8292. Vatican - Biblioteca Apostolica ebr. 301,1, f. 149b, C.

---

[199] Edited by Prins, תשלום אבודרהם, p. 33-34.
[200] Edited by Urbach, ערוגת הבושם, vol. III, p. 360-361.

אריות הדיחו ישראל שה פזורה (א 7608), סליחה

Ashkenaz

8293. Oxford - Bodleian Library MS Mich. 543 (Neubauer 1212), f. 49a-49b, C, commentator: Isaac b. Jacob (compiler).

8294. Oxford - Bodleian Library MS Opp. 681 (Neubauer 1213), f. 43a-43b, C.

אריות הדיחו פזורה (א 7609), יוסף ב"ר שמואל טוב עלם, זולת

Ashkenaz

8295. Budapest - Magyar tudomanyos akademia, MS. Kaufmann A 399, p. 422, C, rubric: זולת.

8296. Cambridge - University Library Add. 504,1, f. 43a-43b, C, rubric: ר' יוסף ב"ר' שמואל נ'ע' זצ"ל וחתום בו לסוף הזולת.

8297. Cambridge - University Library Dd. 2.30, f. 29b-30a, G.

8298. Frankfurt a M - Stadt- und Universitaetsbibliothek Oct. 227, f. 162a-162b, M.

8299. Hamburg - Staats- und Universitaetsbibliothek Cod. hebr. 62 (Steinschneider 154), f. 27b, C, rubric: זולת.

8300. Jerusalem - Schocken Institute 24100 / Mahzor Nuremberg, f. 134a-134b, M.

8301. Jerusalem - Schocken Institute 24100 / Mahzor Nuremberg, f. 246b, M, marginal notes by later hand only.

8302. Muenchen - Bayerische Staatsbibliothek, Cod. hebr. 393,9, f. 198b-199a, C.

8303. New York - Jewish Theological Seminary Ms. 4824, f. 4b, FM, only beginning.

8304. Oxford - Bodleian Library MS Opp. 169 (Neubauer 1151), f. 18a-19a, M.

8305. Parma - Biblioteca Palatina Cod. Parm. 3205 (de Rossi 655), f. 154b-155b, C.

Ashkenaz, commentary by Abraham b. Azriel[201]

8306. Vatican - Biblioteca Apostolica ebr. 301,1, f. 12b-13a, C, rubric: זולת.

Tsarfat

8307. London - British Library Add. 11639 (Margoliouth 1056), f. 672b, M, rubric: זולת, short.

8308. Moscow - Russian State Library, Ms. Guenzburg 1665, f. 38a-39a, M.

8309. Parma - Biblioteca Palatina Cod. Parm. 3136 (de Rossi 405), f. 58a-58b, M.

8310. Vatican - Biblioteca Apostolica ebr. 306, f. 148a-148b, C.

---

[201] Edited by Urbach, ערוגת הבושם, vol. I, p. 79-84.

ארך הזמן וגדלה הצרה (א 7636), משה בן אהרן, סליחה

Ashkenaz

8311. Vatican - Biblioteca Apostolica ebr. 422/1, f. 30b, C.
8312. Vatican - Biblioteca Apostolica ebr. 422/1, f. 42a, CG, no incipit.

ארכו הימים ודבר כל חזון (א 7641), שמעון ב"ר יצחק, סליחה

Ashkenaz

8313. Braunschweig - Landesmuseum fuer Geschichte und Volkstum R 2386, vol. II, f. 54a-54b, M.
8314. Cambridge - University Library Dd. 2.30, f. 10a-11a, G.
8315. Jerusalem - Schocken Institute 24100 / Mahzor Nuremberg, f. 247a, M, marginal notes by later hand only.
8316. Muenchen - Bayerische Staatsbibliothek, Cod. hebr. 346, f. 162a-162b, C.
8317. Oxford - Bodleian Library MS Mich. 543 (Neubauer 1212), f. 45b-47b, C, commentator: Isaac b. Jacob (compiler).
8318. Padova - Biblioteca del Seminario Vescovile Cod. 218, f. 68b-70a, M.
8319. Parma - Bibliotheca Palatina Cod. Parm. 3205 (de Rossi 655), f. 287b, C.

Ashkenaz, commentary by Abraham b. Azriel[202]

8320. Vatican - Biblioteca Apostolica ebr. 301,1, f. 148a-148b, C, rubric: אחרת.

ארכין יי שמיא לסיני (א 7648), פיוט בארמית לשבועות

Ashkenaz

8321. Berlin - Staatsbibliothek (Preussischer Kulturbesitz) Or. Qu. 798-799 (Steinschneider 177), II, f. 155a-155b, M.
8322. Hamburg - Staats- und Universitaetsbibliothek Cod. hebr. 17/2 (Steinschneider 152), f. 74a, C.
8323. Jerusalem - Schocken Institute 24100 / Mahzor Nuremberg, f. 154a-154b, M, short.
8324. Muenchen - Bayerische Staatsbibliothek, Cod. hebr. 21, f. 76b-77a, M.
8325. Muenchen - Bayerische Staatsbibliothek, Cod. hebr. 393, f. 149b-150a, C, rubric: אתחיל פי' מתרגו' ירושלמי אחר פיוטי דשבועות.
8326. Oxford - Bodleian Library MS Opp. 170 (Neubauer 1205), f. 94(ii)a, C, short.
8327. Parma - Biblioteca Palatina Cod. Parm. 3205 (de Rossi 655), f. 180a-180b, C.

---

[202] Edited by Urbach, ערוגת הבושם, vol. III, p. 350-353.

Ashkenaz, commentary by Benjamin b. Abraham Anaw
- 8328. London - Beth Din & Beth Hamidrash 6,9, f. 148a-152a, C, rubric: אלפביטא.
- 8329. Jerusalem - Musad haRav Kook 478, p. 1-7, C, rubric: אלפא ביתא א.
- 8330. Warszaw - Zydowski Instytut Historyczny 838, f. 1a-3a, C, rubric: אלפאביטא.

ארכן וקצר לא יחדל וימנען (א 7650), אליה ב"ר שמעיה, סליחה

Ashkenaz
- 8331. Braunschweig - Landesmuseum fuer Geschichte und Volkstum R 2386, vol. II, f. 57a, M.
- 8332. Budapest - Magyar tudomanyos akademia, MS. Kaufmann A 400, p. 512-514, C, rubric: אחרת.
- 8333. Cambridge - University Library Dd. 2.30, f. 34b-35a, G.
- 8334. Hamburg - Staats- und Universitaetsbibliothek Cod. hebr. 17/2 (Steinschneider 152), f. 146b-147a, C, rubric: סליחה.
- 8335. Moscow - Russian State Library, Ms. Guenzburg 190, f. 32a-32b, G.
- 8336. Moscow - Russian State Library, Ms. Guenzburg 615, f. 160a-161a, C, rubric: אל מלך.
- 8337. Oxford - Bodleian Library MS Mich. 543 (Neubauer 1212), f. 51b-52b, C, commentator: Isaac b. Jacob (compiler).
- 8338. Oxford - Bodleian Library MS Opp. 170 (Neubauer 1205), f. 229a-230a, C.
- 8339. Oxford - Bodleian Library MS Opp. 681 (Neubauer 1213), f. 15b-17a, C.
- 8340. Padova - Biblioteca del Seminario Vescovile Cod. 218, f. 137a-137b, M.
- 8341. Parma - Biblioteca Palatina Cod. Parm. 3205 (de Rossi 655), f. 277a-278a, C.

Ashkenaz, commentary by Abraham b. Azriel[203]
- 8342. Vatican - Biblioteca Apostolica ebr. 301,1, f. 161b-162a, C, rubric: אחרת.

Tsarfat
- 8343. London - British Library Add. 11639 (Margoliouth 1056), f. 472b-474b, M.
- 8344. London - David Sofer 5, f. 87b-88a, C.
- 8345. Oxford - Bodleian Library MS Laud. Or. 271 (Neubauer 1206), f. 124b-125a, C, commentator: Aaron b. Hayyim haKohen (compiler).
- 8346. Oxford - Bodleian Library MS Opp. 171 (Neubauer 1207), f. 111b-112b, C, rubric: אחרת.
- 8347. Parma - Biblioteca Palatina Cod. Parm. 3007 (de Rossi 654,2), f. 75b-76a, M.

---

[203] Edited by Urbach, ערוגת הבושם, vol. III, p. 438-441.

8348. Vatican - Biblioteca Apostolica ebr. 306, f. 175b-176b, C.

ארמון כשבתו על משפטו (א 7652), יוסף ב"ר שמואל טוב עלם, חלק ו', קדושתא לפסח
Tsarfat
8349. Parma - Biblioteca Palatina Cod. Parm. 3136 (de Rossi 405), f. 91b-92a, M.

ארנן חסדך לבקר (א 7657), יוסף ב"ר שמואל טוב עלם, יוצר לשבת הגדול
Ashkenaz
8350. Budapest - Magyar tudomanyos akademia, MS. Kaufmann A 399, p. 444-445, C, rubric: יוצר לרביעי של נחמו.
8351. Cambridge - University Library Add. 504,1, f. 53b-54b, C, rubric: ר' יוסף ב'ר' שמואל ט'ע' יסד זה וחקוק בחרוזה יוקר ספרירו.
8352. Oxford - Bodleian Library MS Can. Or. 82 (Neubauer 1148), f. 36a-37b, M.
8353. Parma - Biblioteca Palatina Cod. Parm 3000 (de Rossi 378), f. 24a-25a, C.
8354. Parma - Biblioteca Palatina Cod. Parm. 3205 (de Rossi 655), f. 163b-165a, C.

Tsarfat
8355. London - British Library Add. 11639 (Margoliouth 1056), f. 672b, M.
8356. London - David Sofer 5, f. 36b-38a, C, rubric: יוצר לשבת הגדול, additional glosses.
8357. Moscow - Russian State Library, Ms. Guenzburg 1665, f. 43a-43b, M.
8358. Parma - Biblioteca Palatina Cod. Parm. 3136 (de Rossi 405), f. 57a-58a, M.

ארעא ורקיעא ודי בהון ושבומו, פיוט בארמית
Ashkenaz, commentary by Benjamin b. Abraham Anaw
8359. Jerusalem - Musad haRav Kook 478, p. 40-47, C, rubric: אלפא ביתא ז.
8360. London - Beth Din & Beth Hamidrash 6,9, f. 172b-176b, C, rubric: אלפא ביט.

ארעא רקדא שמיא זמרו (א 7669), מאיר ב"ר יצחק, פיוט בארמית לשבועות
Ashkenaz
8361. Berlin - Staatsbibliothek (Preussischer Kulturbesitz) Or. Qu. 798-799 (Steinschneider 177), II, f. 155b-156b, M.
8362. Cambridge - University Library Add. 394,1 (Reif SCR 461), f. 56a-58a, C, rubric: פרוש של דברות.
8363. Hamburg - Staats- und Universitaetsbibliothek Cod. hebr. 17/2 (Steinschneider 152), f. 74a-74b, C.
8364. Jerusalem - Schocken Institute 24100 / Mahzor Nuremberg, f. 154b-155a, M.

8365. Moscow - Russian State Library, Ms. Guenzburg 206, f. 88b-89a, M.
8366. Muenchen - Bayerische Staatsbibliothek, Cod. hebr. 21, f. 77b-79a, M.
8367. Muenchen - Bayerische Staatsbibliothek, Cod. hebr. 393, f. 150a-151a, C.
8368. Oxford - Bodleian Library MS Can. Or. 1 (Neubauer 1104), f. 106a-110a, M.
8369. Oxford - Bodleian Library MS Opp. 170 (Neubauer 1205), f. 94(ii)a-95a, C.
8370. Parma - Biblioteca Palatina Cod. Parm. 3205 (de Rossi 655), f. 180b-182b, C.

Ashkenaz, commentary by Benjamin b. Abraham Anaw
8371. Jerusalem - Musad haRav Kook 478, p. 9-19, C, rubric: אלפא ביתא ג.
8372. London - Beth Din & Beth Hamidrash 6,9, f. 153a-160a, C, rubric: אלפא בימ'.
8373. Warszaw - Zydowski Instytut Historyczny 838, f. 4a-8b, C, rubric: אלפא ביטא.

Carpentras
8374. Marseille - Mlle. Odette Valabregue [1], f. 71b-72a, C, rubric: פירוש ארעא רקדא.
8375. Moscow - Russian State Library, Ms. Guenzburg 710, f. 128b-130a, M.

Tsarfat
8376. Cambridge - University Library Add. 561.1, f. 76a-76b, MT, Hebrew.
8377. Jerusalem - Schocken Institute 19623, f. 177a-178a, M, commentator: Yehuda b. Eliezer Zvi.
8378. London - British Library Add. 11639 (Margoliouth 1056), f. 675a-676a, M.
8379. London - British Library Or. 2735 (Margoliouth 663), f. 20b-22b, M.
8380. London - David Sofer 5, f. 56a-58b, C, rubric: זה פירו' מן הדברות.
8381. Moscow - Russian State Library, Ms. Guenzburg 1665, f. 125b-126b, M.
8382. New York - Jewish Theological Seminary Ms. 4460, f. 60b-61a, M, pages damaged.
8383. Parma - Biblioteca Palatina Cod. Parm. 1902, f. 139a-141a, M.
8384. Parma - Biblioteca Palatina Cod. Parm. 2574, f. 116b-117a, G, commentator: Simḥa b. Samuel, cp. Mahzor Vitry.
8385. Parma - Biblioteca Palatina Cod. Parm. 3136 (de Rossi 405), f. 156b-158a, M.

ארעד ואפחד (א 7671), משה בן שמואל בן אבשלום, רשות

Ashkenaz
8386. New York - Jewish Theological Seminary Rab. 1077/4 (Acc. 02505), f. 21a, FC.

8387. Torino - Archivio Terracini 1492, f. 9b, M.
Romania
8388. Vatican - Biblioteca Apostolica ebr. 320, f. 315a-316b, M.
Tsarfat
8389. London - British Library Add. 11639 (Margoliouth 1056), f. 708a, M, short.
8390. London - British Library Or. 8682, f. 9a-9b, G.
8391. London - David Sofer 5, f. 108a, C, rubric: רשות.
8392. Manchester - John Rylands University Library, Ms. Gaster 733, f. 80a, C, rubric: רשות, commentary block in Mahzor, manuscript damaged.
8393. Oxford - Bodleian Library MS Opp. 171 (Neubauer 1207), f. 54a-54b, C, rubric: רשות.
8394. Parma - Biblioteca Palatina Cod. Parm. 2890 (de Rossi 856), f. 68b, M.
8395. Parma - Biblioteca Palatina Cod. Parm. 3006 (de Rossi 654,1), f. 23a-23b, M.

ארץ התמוטטה והתפוררה (א 7682), יהודה הלוי, סילוק

Sepharad
8396. Jerusalem - Benayahu ז 25, f. 138a-139b, M.
8397. Jerusalem - Sassoon 1216, p. 28-30, M, commentator: Mose Nigrin.
8398. Jerusalem - Schocken Institute 70014, f. 72b-73b, M.
Sepharad, commentary by David b. Josef Abudarham[204]
8399. Budapest - Magyar tudomanyos akademia, MS. Kaufmann A 405/2, p. 214-215, C, rubric: סילוק לר' יהודה הלוי ז"ל.
8400. Cincinnati - Hebrew Union College 490, f. 7a, C.
8401. New York - Columbia X893 Ab 93, f. 14b-15a, C, rubric: ובכך ולך תעלה קדושה כי אתה אלהינו.

ארץ מטה ורעשה (א 7694), אלעזר ברבי קליר, קדושתא לשבועות

Ashkenaz
8402. Berlin - Staatsbibliothek (Preussischer Kulturbesitz) Or. Qu. 798-799 (Steinschneider 177), II, f. 139a-139b, M.
8403. Braunschweig - Landesmuseum fuer Geschichte und Volkstum R 2386, vol. I, f. 96b, M.
8404. Budapest - Magyar tudomanyos akademia, MS. Kaufmann A 400, p. 176, C.
8405. Hamburg - Staats- und Universitaetsbibliothek Cod. hebr. 17/2 (Steinschneider 152), f. 85b, C.

---

[204] Edited by Prins, תשלום אבודרהם, p. 31-32.

8406. Jerusalem - Schocken Institute 24100 / Mahzor Nuremberg, f. 171b, M.
8407. London - British Library Add. 18695 (Margoliouth 683), f. 85a-85b, T, Yiddish.
8408. London - British Library Add. 22431 (Margoliouth 662a), f. 55a, M.
8409. Moscow - Russian State Library, Ms. Guenzburg 615, f. 40b-41a, C, rubric: קדושתא.
8410. New York - Jewish Theological Seminary Ms. 4466, f. 165b-166a, M.
8411. Oxford - Bodleian Library MS Opp. 170 (Neubauer 1205), f. 86b, C, short.
8412. Paris - Bibliotheque Nationale heb. 709, f. 136a, C.
8413. Parma - Biblioteca Palatina Cod. Parm. 1002 (Ta 24), f. 204a, M, short.
8414. Parma - Biblioteca Palatina Cod. Parm. 2886 (de Rossi 585), f. 63a-63b, M, later hand, margins cut.
8415. Parma - Biblioteca Palatina Cod. Parm. 3205 (de Rossi 655), f. 127a, C.
8416. Parma - Biblioteca Palatina Cod. Parm. 3507 (Perreau 27), f. 88a, C.
8417. Zurich - Zentralbibliothek Heid. 139, f. 54a, C, short.

Tsarfat
8418. Oxford - Bodleian Library MS Laud. Or. 271 (Neubauer 1206), f. 87a-87b, C, commentator: Aaron b. Hayyim haKohen (compiler), rubric: קדושתא ליום שיני, short, ecclectic.

ארקא ורקיעא ודיבהון ושב ימי (א 7708), פיוט בארמית לשבועות

Ashkenaz
8419. Berlin - Staatsbibliothek (Preussischer Kulturbesitz) Or. Qu. 798-799 (Steinschneider 177), II, f. 161b-162b, M.
8420. Cambridge - University Library Add. 394,1 (Reif SCR 461), f. 61b-62a, C.
8421. Jerusalem - Schocken Institute 24100 / Mahzor Nuremberg, f. 161a-162a, M.
8422. Moscow - Russian State Library, Ms. Guenzburg 206, f. 90a-90b, M.
8423. Muenchen - Bayerische Staatsbibliothek, Cod. hebr. 21, f. 83a-84a, M.
8424. Muenchen - Bayerische Staatsbibliothek, Cod. hebr. 393, f. 152a-152b, C, no incipit.
8425. Oxford - Bodleian Library MS Can. Or. 1 (Neubauer 1104), f. 114a-116a, M.
8426. Oxford - Bodleian Library MS Opp. 170 (Neubauer 1205), f. 98a-98b, C.
8427. Parma - Biblioteca Palatina Cod. Parm. 3205 (de Rossi 655), f. 183b-184a, C.

Tsarfat

8428. Cambridge - University Library Add. 561.1, f. 80a-80b, MT, Hebrew.
8429. Jerusalem - Schocken Institute 19623, f. 182b-183b, M, commentator: Yehuda b. Eliezer Zvi.
8430. London - British Library Add. 11639 (Margoliouth 1056), f. 677b-678b, M.
8431. London - British Library Or. 2735 (Margoliouth 663), f. 31b-33a, M.
8432. London - David Sofer 5, f. 61b-62b, C.
8433. Moscow - Russian State Library, Ms. Guenzburg 1665, f. 128a, M.
8434. New York - Jewish Theological Seminary Ms. 4460, f. 64b-65a, M, pages damaged.
8435. Parma - Biblioteca Palatina Cod. Parm. 1902, f. 146a-147b, M.
8436. Parma - Biblioteca Palatina Cod. Parm. 2574, f. 120a-120b, G, commentator: Simḥa b. Samuel, cp. Mahzor Vitry.
8437. Parma - Biblioteca Palatina Cod. Parm. 3136 (de Rossi 405), f. 161b-162a, M.

ארשה בראש רחשון (א 7709), אלעזר ברבי קליר, למוסף יום א' של פסח

Ashkenaz

8438. Berlin - Staatsbibliothek (Preussischer Kulturbesitz) Or. Qu. 798-799 (Steinschneider 177), II, f. 64b-65a, M.
8439. Braunschweig - Landesmuseum fuer Geschichte und Volkstum R 2386, vol. I, f. 24a-24b, M.
8440. Budapest - Magyar tudomanyos akademia, MS. Kaufmann A 384, f. 138a 139a, M.
8441. Budapest - Magyar tudomanyos akademia, MS. Kaufmann A 400, p. 382-383, C.
8442. Hamburg - Staats- und Universitaetsbibliothek Cod. hebr. 225, f. 68b-70a, G.
8443. Jerusalem - Schocken Institute 24100 / Mahzor Nuremberg, f. 83b-84a, M.
8444. Koblenz - Staatsarchiv Abt. 701, Nr. 759,5,7, f. 1a, FC, only end.
8445. London - British Library Add. 18695 (Margoliouth 683), f. 26a-27a, T, Yiddish.
8446. Moscow - Russian State Library, Ms. Guenzburg 615, f. 9b-11a, C.
8447. Muenchen - Bayerische Staatsbibliothek, Cod. hebr. 88, f. 61b-63b, G.
8448. Muenchen - Bayerische Staatsbibliothek, Cod. hebr. 393, f. 126a-127a, C, no incipit.
8449. New York - Jewish Theological Seminary Ms. 4466, f. 57b-58b, M.
8450. Oxford - Bodleian Library MS Opp. 170 (Neubauer 1205), f. 62a-63b, C, rubric: רשות.
8451. Paris - Bibliotheque Nationale heb. 709, f. 76a-78a, C.
8452. Parma - Biblioteca Palatina Cod. Parm. 1002 (Ta 24), f. 97b-98a, M.

8453. Parma - Biblioteca Palatina Cod. Parm. 3205 (de Rossi 655), f. 84a-85a, C.
8454. Parma - Biblioteca Palatina Cod. Parm. 3507 (Perreau 27), f. 50b-52a, C.
8455. Zurich - Zentralbibliothek Heid. 139, f. 29a-29b, C, additional marginal notes.

Romania

8456. Cambridge - University Library Add. 377,3, f. 55b-56b, C.

Tsarfat

8457. Moscow - Russian State Library, Ms. Guenzburg 1665, f. 61a-61b, M.
8458. Parma - Biblioteca Palatina Cod. Parm. 3136 (de Rossi 405), f. 83b-84b, M.
8459. Vatican - Biblioteca Apostolica ebr. 306, f. 141a-142a, C, no incipit.

אש אוכלה הוא

Ashkenaz

8460. Muenchen - Bayerische Staatsbibliothek, Cod. hebr. 43, f. 17b-21a, C, no incipit.

אש תוקד בקרבי בהעלותי על לבי (א 7736), יהודה הלוי, קינה

Ashkenaz

8461. Berlin - Staatsbibliothek (Preussischer Kulturbesitz) Or. Qu. 798-799 (Steinschneider 177), II, f. 207b-208b, M.

Carpentras, commentary by Mordekhai b. Josef of Rocco Martino

8462. Cincinnati - Hebrew Union College 246/1, f. 68a-68b, C, rubric: פי׳ קינה אש תוקד בקרבי.

Yemen

8463. Ramat Gan - Universitat Bar Ilan 62, f. 20b-21a, G.

Yemen, commentary by Isaac b. Abraham Wanneh

8464. Jerusalem - Sassoon 1158, p. 167, M, rubric: קינה סים׳ אבג״ד חרוז בחרוז וסים׳ סנאתי ממץ׳.

אשא דעי בצדק (א 7745), למוסף יום א׳ של ראש השנה

Ashkenaz

8465. Berlin - Staatsbibliothek (Preussischer Kulturbesitz) Or. Qu. 798-799 (Steinschneider 177), I, f. 28b-32a, M.
8466. Bologna - Archivio di Stato MS Ebr. 353, f. 4a, FC, incomplete.
8467. Budapest - Magyar tudomanyos akademia, MS. Kaufmann A 400, p. 282-286, C.
8468. Hamburg - Staats- und Universitaetsbibliothek Cod. hebr. 17/2 (Steinschneider 152), f. 120a-121b, C, rubric: סדר שופרות.
8469. Hamburg - Staats- und Universitaetsbibliothek Cod. hebr. 40b (Steinschneider 110), f. 29b-32b, G.

8470. Hamburg - Staats- und Universitaetsbibliothek Cod. hebr. 40c (Steinschneider 111), f. 144a-145a, G.
8471. Hamburg - Staats- und Universitaetsbibliothek Cod. hebr. 132 (Steinschneider 155), f. 20b-22b, C.
8472. Jerusalem - Jewish National and University Library Ms Heb 8° 3037, f. 40b-42a, M.
8473. Jerusalem - Schocken Institute 24100 / Mahzor Nuremberg, f. 337b-339a, M.
8474. London - British Library Or. 11318/1, f. 32a-37a, C.
8475. London - Montefiore Library 261, f. 35b-37b, C, commentator: Eliezer b. Natan?.
8476. Moscow - Russian State Library, Ms. Guenzburg 191, f. 26a-28a, M.
8477. Muenchen - Bayerische Staatsbibliothek, Cod. hebr. 346, f. 30b-34b, C.
8478. New York - Jewish Theological Seminary Ms. 4466, f. 240b-243b, M.
8479. New York - Jewish Theological Seminary Ms. 8097, f. 64(ii)a-64(ii)b, C, additional glosses in the margins.
8480. New York - Jewish Theological Seminary Ms. 8169 (Acc. 0016), f. 28b-30a, M.
8481. Oxford - Bodleian Library MS Mich. 365 (Neubauer 1208), f. 45b-48b, C.
8482. Oxford - Bodleian Library MS Opp. 170 (Neubauer 1205), f. 138a-142b, C.
8483. Oxford - Bodleian Library MS Opp. 172 (Neubauer 1211), f. 17a-19a, C.
8484. Oxford - Bodleian Library MS Opp. 619 (Neubauer 2374), f. 43a-45a, M.
8485. Oxford - Bodleian Library MS Opp. 675 (Neubauer 1210), f. 40b-42b, C, no incipit.
8486. Paris - Bibliotheque Nationale heb. 653, f. 25a-25b, G.
8487. Parma - Biblioteca Palatina Cod. Parm. 3205 (de Rossi 655), f. 215a-216a, C.
8488. Parma - Biblioteca Palatina Cod. Parm. 3270 (de Rossi 1215), f. 45b-47b, M.
8489. Parma - Biblioteca Palatina Cod. Parm. 3507 (Perreau 27), f. 128a-130a, C.
8490. Vatican - Biblioteca Apostolica ebr. 308, f. 69a-72a, C, commentator: David b. Mose (compiler).
8491. Vatican - Biblioteca Apostolica ebr. 422/1, f. 11b-12a, C.
8492. Zurich - Zentralbibliothek Heid. 139, f. 69a-70a, C, no incipit, additional marginal notes.
8493. Zurich - Zentralbibliothek Heid. 139, f. 102b-103a, C, commentator: Elazar b. Yehuda of Worms.

Asti, Fossano, Moncalvo
8494. New Haven - Yale University, Beinecke Rare Book and MS Library, MS Heb. 52, f. 44a-45a, M.

Tsarfat
8495. London - British Library Add. 11639 (Margoliouth 1056), f. 713b-714b, M.
8496. London - British Library Or. 8682, f. 30b-31b, GI.
8497. London - David Sofer 5, f. 118a-119a, C.
8498. Oxford - Bodleian Library MS Opp. 171 (Neubauer 1207), f. 72a-75a, C.
8499. Oxford - Bodleian Library MS Opp. 171 (Neubauer 1207), f. 75a-77a, C.
8500. Paris - Bibliotheque Nationale heb. 445,9, f. 88a-89b, C.
8501. Parma - Biblioteca Palatina Cod. Parm. 2125 (de Rossi 812), f. 26b-28b, C.
8502. Parma - Biblioteca Palatina Cod. Parm. 3006 (de Rossi 654,1), f. 56b-58b, M.
8503. Vatican - Biblioteca Apostolica ebr. 306, f. 63b-65b, C.

אשא דעי למרחק אזכרה ימי עולמיי (א 7750), אברהם הכהן, חלק ה, מעריב לשבועות

Ashkenaz
8504. Lund - Universitetsbibliothek Ms. L.O. 2, f. 67b-68a, M.

Tsarfat
8505. Oxford - Bodleian Library MS Laud. Or. 271 (Neubauer 1206), f. 183a-183b, C, commentator: Aaron b. Hayyim haKohen (compiler), rubric: מעריב ביכור לשבועות.

אשא דעי למרחק (א 7753), אלעזר ברבי קליר, חלק ד', קדושתא למוסף יום כפור

Ashkenaz
8506. Berlin - Staatsbibliothek (Preussischer Kulturbesitz) Or. Qu. 798-799 (Steinschneider 177), I, f. 117b-118b, M.
8507. Braunschweig - Landesmuseum fuer Geschichte und Volkstum R 2386, vol. II, f. 103b-105a, M.
8508. Braunschweig - Landesmuseum fuer Geschichte und Volkstum R 2386, vol. II, f. 225a-226a, M.
8509. Budapest - Magyar tudomanyos akademia, MS. Kaufmann A 400, p. 353-354, C.
8510. Cambridge - University Library Add. 394,1 (Reif SCR 461), f. 69a-69b, C.
8511. Cambridge - University Library Add. 394,2.3, f. 1b, C.
8512. Darmstadt - Hessisches Landes- und Hochschulbibliothek Cod. Or. 15, f. 27a-29a, M.

8513. Fulda - Hessische Landesbibliothek A 3 II, f. 123a-123b, C, commentator: Josef.
8514. Hamburg - Staats- und Universitaetsbibliothek Cod. hebr. 17/2 (Steinschneider 152), f. 158a, C.
8515. Hamburg - Staats- und Universitaetsbibliothek Cod. hebr. 40c (Steinschneider 111), f. 212a-212b, G.
8516. Hamburg - Staats- und Universitaetsbibliothek Cod. hebr. 132 (Steinschneider 155), f. 44a-44b, C.
8517. Jerusalem - Jewish National and University Library Ms Heb 8° 3037, f. 176b-177a, M.
8518. Jerusalem - Schocken Institute 24100 / Mahzor Nuremberg, f. 409b-410a, M.
8519. London - British Library Or. 11318/1, f. 101a-102a, C.
8520. London - Montefiore Library 261, f. 54b-55a, C, commentator: Eliezer b. Natan?.
8521. Moscow - Russian State Library, Ms. Guenzburg 191, f. 116a-116b, M.
8522. Moscow - Russian State Library, Ms. Guenzburg 615, f. 83b-85b, C.
8523. Moscow - Russian State Library, Ms. Guenzburg 615, f. 103a-103b, C.
8524. Muenchen - Bayerische Staatsbibliothek, Cod. hebr. 86, f. 46a-48a, G.
8525. Muenchen - Bayerische Staatsbibliothek, Cod. hebr. 346, f. 76a-77a, C, no incipit.
8526. New York - Jewish Theological Seminary Ms. 4466, f. 368a-369a, M.
8527. New York - Jewish Theological Seminary Ms. 8169 (Acc. 0016), f. 90b-91a, M.
8528. Oxford - Bodleian Library MS Mich. 365 (Neubauer 1208), f. 81b-82b, C.
8529. Oxford - Bodleian Library MS Opp. 170 (Neubauer 1205), f. 175b, C.
8530. Oxford - Bodleian Library MS Opp. 172 (Neubauer 1211), f. 60b, C.
8531. Oxford - Bodleian Library MS Opp. 619 (Neubauer 2374), f. 204a-204b, M.
8532. Paris - Bibliotheque Nationale heb. 653, f. 87a-87b, G.
8533. Parma - Biblioteca Palatina Cod. Parm. 3205 (de Rossi 655), f. 117a-117b, C, rubric: אחר.
8534. Parma - Biblioteca Palatina Cod. Parm. 3205 (de Rossi 655), f. 234b, C.
8535. Parma - Biblioteca Palatina Cod. Parm. 3270 (de Rossi 1215), f. 166a-166b, M.
8536. Parma - Biblioteca Palatina Cod. Parm. 3271 (de Rossi 1216), f. 104a-105a, G.
8537. Parma - Biblioteca Palatina Cod. Parm. 3507 (Perreau 27), f. 162b-163a, C.

8538. Vatican - Biblioteca Apostolica ebr. 308, f. 117b-118a, C, commentator: David b. Mose (compiler).
8539. Vatican - Biblioteca Apostolica ebr. 422/1, f. 18a, C, inicpit נחשב.
8540. Zurich - Zentralbibliothek Heid. 139, f. 83b-84a, C.

Asti, Fossano, Moncalvo

8541. New Haven - Yale University, Beinecke Rare Book and MS Library, MS Heb. 52, f. 134a-134b, M.

Roma

8542. Berlin - Staatsbibliothek (Preussischer Kulturbesitz) Or. Oct. 3567, f. 6b-7a, FC.
8543. Berlin - Staatsbibliothek (Preussischer Kulturbesitz) Or. Oct. 3567, f. 7a, FC, rubric: פירוש אחר.
8544. Jerusalem - Jewish National and University Library Ms Heb 8° 4153, f. 140a, C, commentator: Daniel ben Salomo haRofe (compiler), no incipit.
8545. New York - Jewish Theological Seminary Ms. 1639, f. 26b, C, commentator: Salomo b. Samuel Rofe.

Romania

8546. Oxford - Bodleian Library MS Mich. 312,1 (Neubauer 2276,1), f. 7a-7b, C, no incipit.
8547. Vatican - Biblioteca Apostolica ebr. 320, f. 318b, M, no incipit.

Tsarfat

8548. London - British Library Or. 8682, f. 82b-83a, GI.
8549. London - David Sofer 5, f. 151a, C.
8550. Oxford - Bodleian Library MS Bodl. Or. 109 (Neubauer 1209), f. 30b-31b, C, commentator: Aaron b. Hayyim haKohen (compiler), incipit נחשב.
8551. Oxford - Bodleian Library MS Laud. Or. 271 (Neubauer 1206), f. 115a, C, commentator: Aaron b. Hayyim haKohen (compiler), rubric: פיזמון.
8552. Oxford - Bodleian Library MS Laud. Or. 271 (Neubauer 1206), f. 153b-155a, C, commentator: Aaron b. Hayyim haKohen (compiler).
8553. Oxford - Bodleian Library MS Opp. 171 (Neubauer 1207), f. 118a-118b, C, rubric: פיזמון, incipit נחשב.
8554. Parma - Biblioteca Palatina Cod. Parm. 1794 (de Rossi 1061), f. 160a-162a, M.
8555. Parma - Biblioteca Palatina Cod. Parm. 2890 (de Rossi 856), f. 71a-71b, M.
8556. Parma - Biblioteca Palatina Cod. Parm. 3006 (de Rossi 654,1), f. 179b-180a, M.
8557. Vatican - Biblioteca Apostolica ebr. 306, f. 104a-105a, C, no incipit.

אשא כנפי שחר תהלות ישראל משחר (א 7757), מאיר ב"ר יצחק סליחה
Ashkenaz
8558. Oxford - Bodleian Library MS Mich. 543 (Neubauer 1212), f. 44a-44b, C, commentator: Isaac b. Jacob (compiler).
8559. Oxford - Bodleian Library MS Opp. 681 (Neubauer 1213), f. 40a-40b, C.
8560. Vatican - Biblioteca Apostolica ebr. 308, f. 14a, C, commentator: David b. Mose (compiler).

אשא עיני אל אדון האדונים בצום ובכי ותפלה ותחנונים, סליחה
Yemen, commentary by Isaac b. Abraham Wanneh
8561. Chicago-Spertus College of Judaica D 2, 2, f. 247b, M, no incipit.
8562. Jerusalem - Sassoon 1158, p. 426, M, no incipit.
8563. London - British Library Or. 11122, f. 220b, M, no incipit.

אשא עיני אל צודק, סליחה
Yemen, commentary by Isaac b. Abraham Wanneh
8564. Jerusalem - Sassoon 1158, p. 430, M, no incipit.
8565. London - British Library Or. 11122, f. 224a-224b, M, no incipit.

אשא עיני אל רם ונשא, סליחה
Yemen
8566. Jerusalem - Benayahu ת 414, f. 165b, M, no incipit.
8567. New York - Jewish Theological Seminary Ms. 3052, f. 81a-81b, M, no incipit.
8568. Ramat Gan - Universitat Bar Ilan 62, f. 53a, G.
Yemen, commentary by Isaac b. Abraham Wanneh
8569. Chicago-Spertus College of Judaica D 2, 2, f. 237a, M, no incipit.
8570. Jerusalem - Benayahu ת 261, f. 164b, M.
8571. Jerusalem - Benayahu ת 282, f. 140a-140b, M.
8572. Jerusalem - Makhon Ben Zvi 1156 (Tubi 155), f. 137b-138a, M, no incipit.
8573. Jerusalem - Makhon Ben Zvi 1174 (Tubi 154), f. 135b, M.
8574. Jerusalem - Michael Krupp 604, f. 174b-175a, M, no incipit.
8575. Jerusalem - Musad haRav Kook 325, f. 193b, M.
8576. Jerusalem - Sassoon 1158, p. 415, M, no incipit.
8577. Jerusalem - Sassoon 1174, p. 268-269, M, no incipit.
8578. London - British Library Or. 11122, f. 214a, M, no incipit.
8579. Manchester - John Rylands University Library, Ms. Gaster 5, f. 222b, M, incipit מחסה.
8580. Muenchen - Bayerische Staatsbibliothek, Cod. hebr. 472, f. 192b, M.
8581. New York - Jewish Theological Seminary Ms. 3013, f. 132a, M.
8582. New York - Jewish Theological Seminary Ms. 3294, f. 16b, C.

8583. New York - Public Library, Heb. Ms. 9, f. 128b, M, no incipit.
8584. Strasbourg - Bibliotheque Nationale et Universitaire 3965 (Landauer 39), p. 407, M.

אשא עינים אקוד על אפים (א 7772), בן כתיר משה, סליחה

Yemen
8585. New York - Jewish Theological Seminary Ms. 3028, f. 79b, G.
8586. New York - Jewish Theological Seminary Ms. 3109, f. 12a-12b, G.
Yemen, commentary by Isaac b. Abraham Wanneh
8587. Jerusalem - Sassoon 1158, p. 431, M, no incipit.
8588. London - British Library Or. 11122, f. 224b-225a, M, no incipit.

אשא עיני על ההרים באתי לחלותך בקוחת דברים, סליחה

Yemen
8589. New York - Jewish Theological Seminary Ms. 3052, f. 86a, M.
Yemen, commentary by Isaac b. Abraham Wanneh
8590. Chicago-Spertus College of Judaica D 2, 2, f. 238b, M, no incipit.
8591. Jerusalem - Benayahu ת 261, f. 166a, M, short.
8592. Jerusalem - Benayahu ת 282, f. 142a, M.
8593. Jerusalem - Makhon Ben Zvi 1156 (Tubi 155), f. 139b, M, no incipit.
8594. Jerusalem - Makhon Ben Zvi 1174 (Tubi 154), f. 138a, M, short.
8595. Jerusalem - Michael Krupp 604, f. 176b, M.
8596. Jerusalem - Musad haRav Kook 325, f. 195b, M, short.
8597. Jerusalem - Sassoon 1158, p. 417, M, no incipit.
8598. London - British Library Or. 11122, f. 215b-216a, M, short.
8599. Manchester - John Rylands University Library, Ms. Gaster 5, f. 224b-225a, M.
8600. Muenchen - Bayerische Staatsbibliothek, Cod. hebr. 472, f. 195a, M, short.
8601. New York - Jewish Theological Seminary Ms. 3294, f. 17b-18a, C.
8602. Strasbourg - Bibliotheque Nationale et Universitaire 3965 (Landauer 39), p. 413, M, short.

אשאלה אלהי יגאל שבויים (א 7788), שלם שבזי

Yemen
8603. Cincinnati - Hebrew Union College 398, f. 11a-12b, M.

אשוב אל ביתי אדרוש עדתי כי גר הייתי בארץ נוכריה (א 7838), סליחה

Yemen, commentary by Isaac b. Abraham Wanneh
8604. Chicago-Spertus College of Judaica D 2, 2, f. 245a, M, no incipit.
8605. London - British Library Or. 11122, f. 223a, M, no incipit.

אשובה אל אישי הראשון (א 7839), שמואל בן משה, סליחה
Ashkenaz
8606. Oxford - Bodleian Library MS Mich. 543 (Neubauer 1212), f. 83a-84b, bottom margin, C, commentator: Isaac b. Jacob (compiler).

אשוחח נפלאותיך צור עולמים (א 7844), משולם ב"ר קלונימוס, סדר עבודה
Ashkenaz
8607. Jerusalem - Schocken Institute 24100 / Mahzor Nuremberg, f. 419a-419b, M, marginal notes and interlinear glosses by later hand only.
8608. London - British Library Or. 11318/1, f. 159b-173b, C.
8609. Oxford - Bodleian Library MS Opp. 172 (Neubauer 1211), f. 63b-69a, C.
8610. Parma - Biblioteca Palatina Cod. Parm. 3507 (Perreau 27), f. 166b-169a, C.
8611. Vatican - Biblioteca Apostolica ebr. 308, f. 119a-128a, C, commentator: David b. Mose (compiler), rubric: כאן סדר של מוסף.

אשורו צרף והפליא פעלו (א 7853), מנחם, חלק ב', קדושתא לשחרית ראש השנה
Carpentras
8612. Cincinnati - Hebrew Union College 429/1, f. 23a-23b, M, no incipit.
Carpentras, commentary by Josef b. Abraham of Montelitz
8613. Cincinnati - Hebrew Union College 357, f. 100b-101b, M.
8614. New York - Jewish Theological Seminary Ms. 4746, f. 33b-34a, M.
8615. Paris - Ecole Rabbinique 31, f. 139b-140a, M.

אשחר אל אל כל שנות (א 7880), מנחם ב"ר מכיר, יוצר לשבת שובה
Ashkenaz
8616. Jerusalem - Schocken Institute 24100 / Mahzor Nuremberg, f. 357a-358a, M.
8617. London - Montefiore Library 261, f. 82b-83a, C, commentator: Eliezer b. Natan?, rubric: יוצר לעשרת ימי תשובה.
8618. Muenchen - Bayerische Staatsbibliothek, Cod. hebr. 69, f. 69a-70a, M.
8619. Muenchen - Bayerische Staatsbibliothek, Cod. hebr. 88, f. 207b-209a, G.
Ashkenaz, commentary by Abraham b. Azriel[205]
8620. Frankfurt a M - Stadt- und Universitaetsbibliothek Fol. 16 (Merzbacher 95), f. 37b-46b, C, rubric: יוצר לשובה.
8621. Vatican - Biblioteca Apostolica ebr. 301,1, f. 64a-70a, C.

---

[205] Edited by Urbach, ערוגת הבושם, vol. II, p. 94-133.

HEBREW LITURGICAL POETRY

אשחר תשועתך נוצר חסידיך (א 7888), סעדיה, סליחה

Yemen
8622. New York - Jewish Theological Seminary Ms. 3028, f. 96a-97a, G.
8623. New York - Jewish Theological Seminary Ms. 3193, f. 136a-137a, M, no incipit.

Yemen, commentary by Isaac b. Abraham Wanneh
8624. Chicago-Spertus College of Judaica D 2, 2, f. 226b-227a, M, no incipit.
8625. Jerusalem - Sassoon 1158, p. 312-313, M, no incipit.
8626. London - British Library Or. 11122, f. 203a-203b, M, no incipit.

אשיחה בדברי נפלאותיך (א 7899), אמתי ב"ר שפטיה, יוצר

Ashkenaz
8627. Budapest - Magyar tudomanyos akademia, MS. Kaufmann A 399, p. 440-443, C, rubric: יוצר לשיני של נחמו.
8628. Cambridge - University Library Add. 504,1, f. 50a-52b, C.
8629. Oxford - Bodleian Library MS Can. Or. 82 (Neubauer 1148), f. 32b-33b, M, rubric: יוצר לשבת שיני אחר נח'.
8630. Parma - Biblioteca Palatina Cod. Parm. 3205 (de Rossi 655), f. 160b-162a, C.

אשירה ואזמרה לאלהי בעודי (א 8004), שמואל ב"ר קלונימוס?, שיר היחוד ליום א'

Ashkenaz
8631. Braunschweig - Landesmuseum fuer Geschichte und Volkstum R 2386, vol. II, f. 167b-168b, M.
8632. Frankfurt a M - Stadt- und Universitaetsbibliothek Oct. 121/1 (Merzbacher 105), f. 3a-4b, C.
8633. Moscow - Russian State Library, Ms. Guenzburg 1401/2, f. 10b-11a, C.
8634. Paris - Alliance Israelite Universelle H 133 A, f. 3b-5a, M.

Romania
8635. Vatican - Biblioteca Apostolica ebr. 274, f. 167b-169a, M, kabbalistic, additional glosses.

Sepharad
8636. Brussels - Bibliotheque Royale de Belgique 4781, f. 177b-178b, C.

אשישת שלוחתו בקטב תלה (א 8068), יוצר לשבת בראשית

Ashkenaz
8637. Berlin - Staatsbibliothek (Preussischer Kulturbesitz) Or. Qu. 798-799 (Steinschneider 177), I, f. 233a-234a, M.
8638. Budapest - Magyar tudomanyos akademia, MS. Kaufmann A 399, p. 317-322, C, rubric: פייוט לאל אדון.

8639. Moscow - Russian State Library, Ms. Guenzburg 615, f. 132a-134b, C, rubric: פיוט דר' שלמ' הבבלי לשבת בראשית.
8640. Oxford - Bodleian Library MS Can. Or. 82 (Neubauer 1148), f. 2b-3a, M.
8641. Parma - Biblioteca Palatina Cod. Parm. 3057.12 (de Rossi 1033/10), f. 148b-150a, C, commentator: Eliezer b. Natan?.
8642. Parma - Biblioteca Palatina Cod. Parm. 3205 (de Rossi 655), f. 130b-132a, C.

Romania
8643. Vatican - Biblioteca Apostolica ebr. 320, f. 556b-557b, M.

Tsarfat
8644. London - British Library Add. 11639 (Margoliouth 1056), f. 670b-672a, M.
8645. London - British Library Or. 2735 (Margoliouth 663), f. 168a-170a, M.
8646. Moscow - Russian State Library, Ms. Guenzburg 1665, f. 205a-205b, M.

אשכל אווי תאות כל נפש (א 8069), שבעתא לשבת שקלים

Ashkenaz
8647. Berlin - Staatsbibliothek (Preussischer Kulturbesitz) Or. Qu. 798-799 (Steinschneider 177), II, f. 17b-19a, M.
8648. Budapest - Magyar tudomanyos akademia, MS. Kaufmann A 384, f. 44b-46b, M, rubric: שבעתא.
8649. Budapest - Magyar tudomanyos akademia, MS. Kaufmann A 400, p. 25-29, C, rubric: שבעתא.
8650. Cambridge - University Library Add. 504,1, f. 9a-11a, C.
8651. Erlangen - Universitaetsbibliothek 2601 (Roth 67), f. 31b-32b, M.
8652. Hamburg - Staats- und Universitaetsbibliothek Cod. hebr. 17/2 (Steinschneider 152), f. 16a-17a, C, rubric: שבעתא.
8653. Jerusalem - Schocken Institute 24100 / Mahzor Nuremberg, f. 37a-38a (f. 37 missing), M.
8654. Muenchen - Bayerische Staatsbibliothek, Cod. hebr. 88, f. 18a-19a, G.
8655. Muenchen - Bayerische Staatsbibliothek, Cod. hebr. 393, f. 88a-88b, C, no incipit.
8656. Oxford - Bodleian Library MS Opp. 170 (Neubauer 1205), f. 7a-9a, C, rubric: שבעתא.
8657. Paris - Bibliotheque Nationale heb. 709, f. 14b-16b, C, rubric: שבעתא.
8658. Parma - Biblioteca Palatina Cod. Parm. 1002 (Ta 24), f. 28b-31a, M.
8659. Parma - Biblioteca Palatina Cod. Parm. 3205 (de Rossi 655), f. 17b-18a, C, rubric: שבעתא.
8660. Parma - Biblioteca Palatina Cod. Parm. 3205 (de Rossi 655), f. 45b-46a, C.

8661. Parma - Biblioteca Palatina Cod. Parm. 3507 (Perreau 27), f. 10b-11b, C, rubric: שבעתא, no incipit.

8662. Vatican - Biblioteca Apostolica ebr. 305,1, f. 9a-10b, C, rubric: שבעתא.

Tsarfat

8663. Oxford - Bodleian Library MS Laud. Or. 271 (Neubauer 1206), f. 15b-17a, C, commentator: Aaron b. Hayyim haKohen (compiler).

8664. Oxford - Bodleian Library MS Opp. 171 (Neubauer 1207), f. 12b-13b, C, rubric: אתחיל השבעתא.

אשל צדק היום בארבעה תפלות (א 8079), אברהם אבן עזרא, קדושתא לנעילה

Sepharad, commentary by David b. Josef Abudarham[206]

8665. Budapest - Magyar tudomanyos akademia, MS. Kaufmann A 405/2, p. 259, C, rubric: מגן.

8666. Holon - Yehuda Nahum 278, f. 1b, FC, short.

8667. New York - Columbia X893 Ab 93, f. 32b, C, rubric: מגן לר' אברהם ן' עזרא ז"ל.

אשלש תפלות החוק למלאות (א 8084), אברהם אבן עזרא, קדושתא למנחה ליום כפור

Sepharad, commentary by David b. Josef Abudarham[207]

8668. Budapest - Magyar tudomanyos akademia, MS. Kaufmann A 405/2, p. 253, C, rubric: מגן לר' אברהרם ן' עזרא ז"ל.

8669. New York - Columbia X893 Ab 93, f. 30b-31a, C, rubric: מגן לר' אברהרם ן' עזרא ז"ל.

אשם וזע מזדוניהו (א 8086), אברהם אבן עזרא, סליחה

Yemen

8670. Jerusalem - Benayahu ת 414, f. 129b, M, very short.

אשמחה בדודי אמרה (א 8093), לשמחת תורה

Yemen

8671. Jerusalem - Michael Krupp 1758, f. 27a, M.

8672. New York - Jewish Theological Seminary Ms. 3193, f. 170b, M, no incipit.

Yemen, commentary by Isaac b. Abraham Wanneh?

8673. Jerusalem - Makhon Ben Zvi 1156 (Tubi 155), f. 78b, M, margins damaged.

8674. Nahariya - Menahem and Saida Yaakob 284, f. 25a, M, very short.

8675. New York - Jewish Theological Seminary Ms. 4195, f. 45a-46b, M.

---

[206] Edited by Prins, תשלום אבודרהם, p. 140.
[207] Edited by Prins, תשלום אבודרהם, p. 126-127.

אשמנו אבל אנחנו אשמים בקרב העמים, ודוי

Yemen, commentary by Yiḥya b. Josef Tsalaḥ
8676. Montreal - Elberg 203, f. 34b-35a, M, very short.

אשמנו אבל אנחנו אשמים בקרב העמים, ודוי

Yemen, commentary by Isaac b. Abraham Wanneh
8677. Chicago-Spertus College of Judaica D 2, 2, f. 180b, M.

אשמנו באומר ובפועל (א 8112), בחיי בר יוסף הדיין, ודוי

Yemen, commentary by Isaac b. Abraham Wanneh
8678. Chicago-Spertus College of Judaica D 2, 2, f. 180a, M.

אשמנו וחטאתנו נרשם וכל איש ממנו אשום אשם (א* 2151), ודוי

Yemen, commentary by Isaac b. Abraham Wanneh
8679. Chicago-Spertus College of Judaica D 2, 2, f. 180a-180b, M.

אשמנו מכל עם בושנו מכל גוי (א 8115), סליחה

Ashkenaz
8680. Braunschweig - Landesmuseum fuer Geschichte und Volkstum R 2386, vol. II, f. 44b, M.
8681. London - British Library Add. 18695 (Margoliouth 683), f. 169a-169b, T, Yiddish.

North Africa, commentary by David b. Josef Abudarham?
8682. New York - Jewish Theological Seminary Ms. 5426, f. 60b, M.

Sepharad
8683. Jerusalem - Benayahu ז 25, f. 100a-100b, M.
8684. Skokie - Hebrew Theological College 3, f. 2.23a, M.
8685. Skokie - Hebrew Theological College 3, f. 9a, M.

Yemen
8686. New York - Jewish Theological Seminary Ms. 3193, f. 118a-119a, M.

Yemen, commentary by Isaac b. Abraham Wanneh
8687. Chicago-Spertus College of Judaica D 2, 2, f. 180a, M.
8688. Jerusalem - Yehiel haLevi 4, f. 132b, M.
8689. London - British Library Or. 11122, f. 156a-156b, M.

אשמעה ברכה לאום המבורכה (א 8119), יוצר לשמיני עצרת

Tsarfat
8690. London - David Sofer 5, f. 190b, C, rubric: זה פירוש מיוצר של שמיני עצרת מסוכות, very short.

אשמתי ולבי למחשבי, ודוי

Sepharad
8691. Jerusalem - Benayahu ז 25, f. 96b-97b, M, no incipit.
8692. Jerusalem - Schocken Institute 70014, f. 51a, M.

אשמתי עד לשמים גדלה בגדתי (א 8135), אליה ב"ר שמעיה, סליחה

Ashkenaz
8693. Oxford - Bodleian Library MS Opp. 681 (Neubauer 1213), f. 38a-38b, C.
8694. Vatican - Biblioteca Apostolica ebr. 422/1, f. 43b, CG, no incipit.

Ashkenaz, commentary by Abraham b. Azriel[208]
8695. Vatican - Biblioteca Apostolica ebr. 301,1, f. 148b, C.

אשמתינו כי רבה בית מקדשינו לחרבה (א 8140), שלמה הבבלי, סליחה

Ashkenaz
8696. Budapest - Magyar tudomanyos akademia, MS. Kaufmann A 400, p. 506-507, C, rubric: פיזמון אחר.
8697. Moscow - Russian State Library, Ms. Guenzburg 190, f. 108a-108b, G.
8698. Oxford - Bodleian Library MS Mich. 543 (Neubauer 1212), f. 77a-77b, C, commentator: Isaac b. Jacob (compiler).
8699. Parma - Biblioteca Palatina Cod. Parm. 3205 (de Rossi 655), f. 271b-272a, C.

Tsarfat
8700. London - British Library Add. 11639 (Margoliouth 1056), f. 484a-485a, M.
8701. London - David Sofer 5, f. 163b-164a, C, rubric: זכרונות.
8702. Oxford - Bodleian Library MS Laud. Or. 271 (Neubauer 1206), f. 174a-174b, C, commentator: Aaron b. Hayyim haKohen (compiler).
8703. Oxford - Bodleian Library MS Opp. 171 (Neubauer 1207), f. 103b-104a, C, rubric: אחרת.
8704. Parma - Biblioteca Palatina Cod. Parm. 2890 (de Rossi 856), f. 8b-9a, M.
8705. Parma - Biblioteca Palatina Cod. Parm. 3006 (de Rossi 654,1), f. 230b-231a, M.
8706. Parma - Biblioteca Palatina Cod. Parm. 3007 (de Rossi 654,2), f. 6b, M.
8707. Vatican - Biblioteca Apostolica ebr. 306, f. 184b-185b, C.

אשנבי שחקים נראים כנרתקים (א 8141), אמתי ב"ר שפטיה, אופן לשמחת תורה

Ashkenaz
8708. Berlin - Staatsbibliothek (Preussischer Kulturbesitz) Or. Qu. 798-799 (Steinschneider 177), I, f. 202b-203a, M.
8709. Jerusalem - Schocken Institute 24100 / Mahzor Nuremberg, f. 506b-507a, M.

---

[208] Edited by Urbach, ערוגת הבושם, vol. III, p. 353.

8710. London - Montefiore Library 261, f. 82a, C, commentator: Eliezer b. Natan?, rubric: אופן.

8711. Muenchen - Bayerische Staatsbibliothek, Cod. hebr. 69, f. 76a-76b, M.

Ashkenaz, commentary by Abraham b. Azriel[209]

8712. Frankfurt a M - Stadt- und Universitaetsbibliothek Fol. 16 (Merzbacher 95), f. 83a-83b, C.

8713. Vatican - Biblioteca Apostolica ebr. 301,1, f. 79a, C, rubric: אופן.

Tsarfat

8714. Parma - Biblioteca Palatina Cod. Parm. 1264, f. 137a, M.

אשפוך כמים מי דמעות ואלבש פחד וזעות (א 8148), שאול כספי, לעצירת גשמים

Sepharad, commentary by David b. Josef Abudarham[210]

8715. Budapest - Magyar tudomanyos akademia, MS. Kaufmann A 405/2, p. 211-212, C, rubric: מסתאג׳יב כי שומע אל אביונים יי.

8716. New York - Columbia X893 Ab 93, f. 13(ii)b-14a, C, rubric: מסתאג׳יב כי שומע אל אביונים יי.

8717. New York - Jewish Theological Seminary Ms. 3011, f. 21a, C, rubric: מסתאג׳יב. כי שומע אל אביונים יי.

אשפוך כים מי דמעות והיתה רק זועות (א 8149), אליה כרמי, סליחה

Carpentras, commentary by Mordekhai b. Josef of Rocco Martino

8718. Cincinnati - Hebrew Union College 246/1, f. 73a-73b, C, rubric: פי׳ קינה אשפוך כים עם הנחמה.

אשפוך לפניך שיחי בטחוני, סליחה

Yemen

8719. New York - Jewish Theological Seminary Ms. 3052, f. 89a, M.

Yemen, commentary by Isaac b. Abraham Wanneh

8720. Chicago-Spertus College of Judaica D 2, 2, f. 240a, M, no incipit.

8721. Jerusalem - Makhon Ben Zvi 1174 (Tubi 154), f. 140b, M.

8722. Jerusalem - Musad haRav Kook 325, f. 196b, M.

8723. Jerusalem - Sassoon 1158, p. 420, M, no incipit.

8724. London - British Library Or. 11122, f. 217a-217b, M, no incipit.

8725. Muenchen - Bayerische Staatsbibliothek, Cod. hebr. 472, f. 196b, M.

8726. New York - Jewish Theological Seminary Ms. 3013, f. 135b-136a, M, no incipit.

8727. New York - Jewish Theological Seminary Ms. 3294, f. 19a, C.

---

[209] Edited by Urbach, ערוגת הבושם, vol. II, p. 194-195.
[210] Edited by Prins, תשלום אבודרהם, p. 146-148.

8728. Strasbourg - Bibliotheque Nationale et Universitaire 3965 (Landauer 39), p. 419, M.

אשפוך שיחי לפניך צורי (א 8157), גרשום ב"ר יהודה מאור הגולה, סליחה

Ashkenaz

8729. Berlin - Staatsbibliothek (Preussischer Kulturbesitz) Or. Qu. 798-799 (Steinschneider 177), I, f. 168a-168b, M.
8730. Braunschweig - Landesmuseum fuer Geschichte und Volkstum R 2386, vol. II, f. 67a, M.
8731. Klosterneuburg - Stiftsbibliothek St. Augustini 271, FC, incomplete.
8732. London - British Library Add. 18695 (Margoliouth 683), f. 162a-162b, T, Yiddish.
8733. Muenchen - Bayerische Staatsbibliothek, Cod. hebr. 346, f. 145b, C, rubric: אחרת, short.
8734. New York - Jewish Theological Seminary Ms. 4466, f. 399a, M.
8735. New York - Jewish Theological Seminary Ms. 8097, f. 82b, C.
8736. Oxford - Bodleian Library MS Mich. 543 (Neubauer 1212), f. 18b-19a, C, commentator: Isaac b. Jacob (compiler).
8737. Oxford - Bodleian Library MS Opp. 172 (Neubauer 1211), f. 84b-85a, C.
8738. Oxford - Bodleian Library MS Opp. 619 (Neubauer 2374), f. 230b-231b, M.
8739. Oxford - Bodleian Library MS Opp. 681 (Neubauer 1213), f. 5b-6a, C.
8740. Padova - Biblioteca del Seminario Vescovile Cod. 218, f. 100a-101a, M.
8741. Padova - Biblioteca del Seminario Vescovile Cod. 218, f. 178b-180a, M.
8742. Vatican - Biblioteca Apostolica ebr. 308, f. 142a-142b, C, commentator: David b. Mose (compiler).
8743. Vatican - Biblioteca Apostolica ebr. 422/1, f. 24a-24b, C, short.
8744. Vatican - Biblioteca Apostolica ebr. 422/2, f. 38b, CG, no incipit, very short.

Ashkenaz, commentary by Abraham b. Azriel[211]

8745. Frankfurt a M - Stadt- und Universitaetsbibliothek Fol. 16 (Merzbacher 95), f. 104a-104b, C.

Asti, Fossano, Moncalvo

8746. New Haven - Yale University, Beinecke Rare Book and MS Library, MS Heb. 52, f. 122b-123a, M, ecclectic.

Tsarfat

8747. London - David Sofer 5, f. 144a-145a, C.

---

[211] Edited by Urbach, ערוגת הבושם, vol. III, p. 546.

8748. Oxford - Bodleian Library MS Bodl. Or. 109 (Neubauer 1209), f. 80a-80b, C, commentator: Aaron b. Hayyim haKohen (compiler).
8749. Parma - Biblioteca Palatina Cod. Parm. 1794 (de Rossi 1061), f. 22b-24a, M.
8750. Parma - Biblioteca Palatina Cod. Parm. 2890 (de Rossi 856), f. 99a-100a, M.
8751. Parma - Biblioteca Palatina Cod. Parm. 3006 (de Rossi 654,1), f. 201a-201b, M.
8752. Vatican - Biblioteca Apostolica ebr. 306, f. 96a-96b, C.

אשר אומץ תהילתיך באילי שחק (א 8175), משולם ב"ר קלונימוס, חלק י"א, קדושתא לשחרית יום כפור

Ashkenaz
8753. Berlin - Staatsbibliothek (Preussischer Kulturbesitz) Or. Qu. 798-799 (Steinschneider 177), I, f. 77a-77b, M.
8754. Braunschweig - Landesmuseum fuer Geschichte und Volkstum R 2386, vol. II, f. 190a, M.
8755. Budapest - Magyar tudomanyos akademia, MS. Kaufmann A 400, p. 314-315, C, incipit באילי.
8756. Hamburg - Staats- und Universitaetsbibliothek Cod. hebr. 17/2 (Steinschneider 152), f. 151a, C.
8757. Hamburg - Staats- und Universitaetsbibliothek Cod. hebr. 62 (Steinschneider 154), f. 4a, C, short.
8758. Hamburg - Staats- und Universitaetsbibliothek Cod. hebr. 132 (Steinschneider 155), f. 34a-34b, C.
8759. Jerusalem - Jewish National and University Library Ms Heb 8° 3037, f. 121b, M, very short.
8760. Jerusalem - Schocken Institute 24100 / Mahzor Nuremberg, f. 378b, M, short.
8761. London - British Library Or. 11318/1, f. 74b-75a, C, short.
8762. London - Montefiore Library 261, f. 43b-44a, C, commentator: Eliezer b. Natan?.
8763. Moscow - Russian State Library, Ms. Guenzburg 191, f. 90a, M, short.
8764. Muenchen - Bayerische Staatsbibliothek, Cod. hebr. 346, f. 53a, C, short.
8765. Muenchen - Bayerische Staatsbibliothek, Cod. hebr. 393, f. 142a, C, no incipit, very short.
8766. New York - Jewish Theological Seminary Ms. 4466, f. 312a, M.
8767. New York - Jewish Theological Seminary Ms. 8097, f. 72a, C.
8768. New York - Jewish Theological Seminary Ms. 8169 (Acc. 0016), f. 70b-71a, M.
8769. Oxford - Bodleian Library MS Mich. 365 (Neubauer 1208), f. 69a-69b, C, short.

8770. Oxford - Bodleian Library MS Opp. 172 (Neubauer 1211), f. 38b-39a, C, incipit missing, short.
8771. Parma - Biblioteca Palatina Cod. Parm. 3205 (de Rossi 655), f. 227b, C, short.
8772. Parma - Biblioteca Palatina Cod. Parm. 3271 (de Rossi 1216), f. 40b, G.
8773. Parma - Biblioteca Palatina Cod. Parm. 3507 (Perreau 27), f. 147a, C.
8774. Vatican - Biblioteca Apostolica ebr. 308, f. 100b, C, commentator: David b. Mose (compiler).
8775. Vatican - Biblioteca Apostolica ebr. 422/1, f. 15b, C, very short.

Asti, Fossano, Moncalvo

8776. New Haven - Yale University, Beinecke Rare Book and MS Library, MS Heb. 52, f. 106a, M.

Romania

8777. Vatican - Biblioteca Apostolica ebr. 320, f. 284b-285a, M.

Tsarfat

8778. London - British Library Or. 8682, f. 68b-69b, G.
8779. London - David Sofer 5, f. 138a, C.
8780. London - David Sofer 5, f. 138a, C, second commentary on margin.
8781. Oxford - Bodleian Library MS Bodl. Or. 109 (Neubauer 1209), f. 20a, C, commentator: Aaron b. Hayyim haKohen (compiler), short.
8782. Parma - Biblioteca Palatina Cod. Parm. 1794 (de Rossi 1061), f. 123a-123b, M.
8783. Parma - Biblioteca Palatina Cod. Parm. 2890 (de Rossi 856), f. 29a, M, short.
8784. Parma - Biblioteca Palatina Cod. Parm. 3006 (de Rossi 654,1), f. 142b, M.
8785. Vatican - Biblioteca Apostolica ebr. 306, f. 77a-77b, C.

אשר אימתיך באראלי אומן (א 8178), יניי?, חלק ח׳, קדושתא למוסף יום כפור

Ashkenaz

8786. Berlin - Staatsbibliothek (Preussischer Kulturbesitz) Or. Qu. 798-799 (Steinschneider 177), I, f. 120a-120b, M.
8787. Braunschweig - Landesmuseum fuer Geschichte und Volkstum R 2386, vol. II, f. 227a-227b, M.
8788. Cambridge - University Library Add. 394,1 (Reif SCR 461), f. 70a, C.
8789. Hamburg - Staats- und Universitaetsbibliothek Cod. hebr. 40c (Steinschneider 111), f. 215a-215b, G.
8790. Hamburg - Staats- und Universitaetsbibliothek Cod. hebr. 132 (Steinschneider 155), f. 44b-45a, C.
8791. Jerusalem - Jewish National and University Library Ms Heb 8° 3037, f. 179b-180a, M.
8792. Jerusalem - Schocken Institute 24100 / Mahzor Nuremberg, f. 411a-411b, M.

8793. London - British Library Or. 11318/1, f. 104a-104b, C.
8794. London - Montefiore Library 261, f. 56a, C, commentator: Eliezer b. Natan?.
8795. Moscow - Russian State Library, Ms. Guenzburg 191, f. 118b-119b, M.
8796. Muenchen - Bayerische Staatsbibliothek, Cod. hebr. 346, f. 78a, C, short.
8797. Muenchen - Bayerische Staatsbibliothek, Cod. hebr. 393, f. 148b-149a, C, no incipit.
8798. New York - Jewish Theological Seminary Ms. 4466, f. 371b-372b, M.
8799. New York - Jewish Theological Seminary Ms. 8097, f. 78b, C, short.
8800. New York - Jewish Theological Seminary Ms. 8169 (Acc. 0016), f. 94b-95b, M.
8801. Oxford - Bodleian Library MS Opp. 172 (Neubauer 1211), f. 60b-61a, C, short.
8802. Parma - Biblioteca Palatina Cod. Parm. 3271 (de Rossi 1216), f. 107a-107b, G.
8803. Parma - Biblioteca Palatina Cod. Parm. 3507 (Perreau 27), f. 163b-164a, C.
8804. Vatican - Biblioteca Apostolica ebr. 308, f. 118a, C, commentator: David b. Mose (compiler), short.
8805. Zurich - Zentralbibliothek Heid. 139, f. 84a, C.

Asti, Fossano, Moncalvo
8806. New Haven - Yale University, Beinecke Rare Book and MS Library, MS Heb. 52, f. 135b-136a, M.

Roma
8807. Berlin - Staatsbibliothek (Preussischer Kulturbesitz) Or. Oct. 3567, f. 7b, FC, short.
8808. Berlin - Staatsbibliothek (Preussischer Kulturbesitz) Or. Oct. 3567, f. 7b-8a, FC, rubric: פירוש אחר על אשר אימתך.
8809. Jerusalem - Jewish National and University Library Ms Heb 8° 4153, f. 140b, C, commentator: Daniel ben Salomo haRofe (compiler), short.
8810. New York - Jewish Theological Seminary Ms. 1639, f. 27a, C, commentator: Salomo b. Samuel Rofe.
8811. Oxford - Bodleian Library MS Mich. 312,1 (Neubauer 2276,1), f. 7b, C, short.

Romania
8812. Vatican - Biblioteca Apostolica ebr. 320, f. 321b-322a, M.

Tsarfat
8813. London - British Library Or. 8682, f. 84a, GI.
8814. London - David Sofer 5, f. 151b, C.
8815. Oxford - Bodleian Library MS Bodl. Or. 109 (Neubauer 1209), f. 31b-32a, C, commentator: Aaron b. Hayyim haKohen (compiler).

8816. Oxford - Bodleian Library MS Laud. Or. 271 (Neubauer 1206), f. 115b, C, commentator: Aaron b. Hayyim haKohen (compiler).
8817. Parma - Biblioteca Palatina Cod. Parm. 1794 (de Rossi 1061), f. 170a-171b, M.
8818. Parma - Biblioteca Palatina Cod. Parm. 2890 (de Rossi 856), f. 74b-75a, M.
8819. Parma - Biblioteca Palatina Cod. Parm. 3006 (de Rossi 654,1), f. 181a-181b, M.

אשר בגלל אבות בנים גידל (א 8188), לשמחת תורה

Ashkenaz
8820. Berlin - Staatsbibliothek (Preussischer Kulturbesitz) Or. Qu. 798-799 (Steinschneider 177), I, f. 229b-230b, M.
8821. Jerusalem - Schocken Institute 24100 / Mahzor Nuremberg, f. 512a, M.
8822. London - British Library Add. 18695 (Margoliouth 683), f. 140a-140b, T, Yiddish.
8823. Lund - Universitetsbibliothek Ms. L.O. 2, f. 94a, M, short.

Yemen
8824. Jerusalem - Michael Krupp 1758, f. 24a, M, short.
8825. New York - Jewish Theological Seminary Ms. 3193, f. 169b-170a, M, rubric: פירוש אשר בגלל.

Yemen, commentary by Isaac b. Abraham Wanneh
8826. Jerusalem - Makhon Ben Zvi 1156 (Tubi 155), f. 78a, M, short.
8827. Manchester - John Rylands University Library, Ms. Gaster 5, f. 154a-154b, M, short.
8828. Muenchen - Bayerische Staatsbibliothek, Cod. hebr. 472, f. 103a, M, short.
8829. Nahariya - Menahem and Saida Yaakob 284, f. 22a, M, short.
8830. New York - Jewish Theological Seminary Ms. 4195, f. 34b-38b, M, short.

Yemen, commentary by Yiḥya b. Josef Tsalaḥ
8831. Montreal - Elberg 203, f. 29a-31b, M, short.

אשר יסד ארקים ותלם על בלימה (א 8259), יהודה הלוי?, סליחה

Yemen
8832. Jerusalem - Sassoon 902, p. 437, M.

Yemen, commentary by Isaac b. Abraham Wanneh
8833. Chicago-Spertus College of Judaica D 2, 2, f. 189b-190a, M, no incipit.
8834. Jerusalem - Sassoon 1158, p. 356, M, rubric: אל מלך.
8835. Jerusalem - Yehiel haLevi 4, f. 166a, G.
8836. London - British Library Or. 11122, f. 176b-177a, M, no incipit.

אשר לו ים החרבה וכל מושב ומצבה (א 8299), סליחה

Tsarfat

8837. London - David Sofer 5, f. 92a, C.
8838. London - David Sofer 5, f. 147a-147b, C, rubric: פזמון.
8839. Parma - Biblioteca Palatina Cod. Parm. 3006 (de Rossi 654,1), f. 200b, M.
8840. Vatican - Biblioteca Apostolica ebr. 306, f. 185b, C.

Yemen

8841. Jerusalem - Sassoon 902, p. 414, M.

Yemen, commentary by Isaac b. Abraham Wanneh

8842. Chicago-Spertus College of Judaica D 2, 2, f. 193b-194a, M.
8843. Jerusalem - Sassoon 1158, p. 358, M, no incipit.
8844. Jerusalem - Yehiel haLevi 4, f. 165b, G.
8845. London - British Library Or. 11122, f. 178a-178b, M.

אשר מי יעשה כמעשיך וכגבורתיך (א 8307), שמעון ב"ר יצחק, סילוק, קדושתא לראש השנה

Ashkenaz

8846. Berlin - Staatsbibliothek (Preussischer Kulturbesitz) Or. Qu. 798-799 (Steinschneider 177), I, f. 41b-44b, M, ecclectic.
8847. Braunschweig - Landesmuseum fuer Geschichte und Volkstum R 2386, vol. II, f. 115a-117a, M.
8848. Darmstadt - Hessisches Landes- und Hochschulbibliothek Cod. Or. 15, f. 40a-42b, M, ecclectic.
8849. Darmstadt - Hessisches Landes- und Hochschulbibliothek Cod. Or. 15, f. 41a-44a, M, ecclectic.
8850. Hamburg - Staats- und Universitaetsbibliothek Cod. hebr. 17/2 (Steinschneider 152), f. 122b, C, rubric: סילוק.
8851. Hamburg - Staats- und Universitaetsbibliothek Cod. hebr. 132 (Steinschneider 155), f. 26a, C, short.
8852. Hamburg - Staats- und Universitaetsbibliothek Cod. hebr. 225, f. 265a, 269b-270a, G.
8853. Jerusalem - Jewish National and University Library Ms Heb 8° 3037, f. 62b-63a, M, very ecclectic.
8854. Jerusalem - Schocken Institute 24100 / Mahzor Nuremberg, f. 345b-347a, M, ecclectic.
8855. London - British Library Or. 11318/1, f. 45b-46a, C, rubric: זה הסילוק.
8856. London - Montefiore Library 261, f. 30a-30b, C, commentator: Eliezer b. Natan?.
8857. Moscow - Russian State Library, Ms. Guenzburg 191, f. 41b, 42b-43a, 44a-45a, M, very short, ecclectic.
8858. Moscow - Russian State Library, Ms. Guenzburg 615, f. 87b, C, rubric: סילוק.

8859. Muenchen - Bayerische Staatsbibliothek, Cod. hebr. 86, f. 74a-78a, G.
8860. Muenchen - Bayerische Staatsbibliothek, Cod. hebr. 346, f. 37b, C.
8861. New York - Jewish Theological Seminary Ms. 8097, f. 67a-67b, C.
8862. New York - Jewish Theological Seminary Ms. 8169 (Acc. 0016), f. 41a-42a, G.
8863. Oxford - Bodleian Library MS Mich. 365 (Neubauer 1208), f. 52a, C.
8864. Oxford - Bodleian Library MS Opp. 170 (Neubauer 1205), f. 144b, C, rubric: סילוק, short.
8865. Oxford - Bodleian Library MS Opp. 172 (Neubauer 1211), f. 24b-25a, C.
8866. Oxford - Bodleian Library MS Opp. 619 (Neubauer 2374), f. 67a-70b, M, ecclectic.
8867. Parma - Biblioteca Palatina Cod. Parm. 3507 (Perreau 27), f. 134a-134b, C, rubric: סילוק.
8868. Vatican - Biblioteca Apostolica ebr. 308, f. 79b-80b, C, commentator: David b. Mose (compiler).
8869. Vatican - Biblioteca Apostolica ebr. 422/1, f. 13b, C, rubric: סילוק.
8870. Zurich - Zentralbibliothek Heid. 139, f. 71a, C, no incipit, ecclectic, additional marginal notes.
8871. Zurich - Zentralbibliothek Heid. 139, f. 103a-103b, C, commentator: Elazar b. Yehuda of Worms, rubric: בסילוק, no incipit.

Asti, Fossano, Moncalvo
8872. New Haven - Yale University, Beinecke Rare Book and MS Library, MS Heb. 52, f. 57a-59b, M.

Tsarfat
8873. London - British Library Or. 8682, f. 40b-41a, Gl.
8874. London - David Sofer 5, f. 121b-122a, C, rubric: סילוק.
8875. Oxford - Bodleian Library MS Opp. 171 (Neubauer 1207), f. 68a-68b, C, rubric: סילוק, incipit מזור מכס יגהה.
8876. Parma - Biblioteca Palatina Cod. Parm. 2125 (de Rossi 812), f. 30b, C, rubric: סילוק.
8877. Parma - Biblioteca Palatina Cod. Parm. 3006 (de Rossi 654,1), f. 74b-75b, M.
8878. Vatican - Biblioteca Apostolica ebr. 306, f. 68b, C.

אשרי העם שלו ככה (א 8400), משה בן שמואל בן אבשלום, יוצר לשמחת תורה

Ashkenaz
8879. Berlin - Staatsbibliothek (Preussischer Kulturbesitz) Or. Qu. 361 (Steinschneider 51), f. 129a-130b, M.
8880. Berlin - Staatsbibliothek (Preussischer Kulturbesitz) Or. Qu. 798-799 (Steinschneider 177), I, f. 223b-226a, M.
8881. Braunschweig - Landesmuseum fuer Geschichte und Volkstum R 2386, vol. I, f. 160b-161b, M.

8882. Budapest - Magyar tudomanyos akademia, MS. Kaufmann A 399 , p. 310-312, C.
8883. Budapest - Magyar tudomanyos akademia, MS. Kaufmann A 400 , p. 411-417, C, rubric: יוצר לשמחת תורה.
8884. Frankfurt a M - Stadt- und Universitaetsbibliothek Oct. 227 , f. 136a-136b, M.
8885. Fulda - Hessische Landesbibliothek A 3 II, f. 147b, C, commentator: Josef, manuscript breaks off in this commentary.
8886. Hamburg - Staats- und Universitaetsbibliothek Cod. hebr. 132 (Steinschneider 155), f. 70a-71b, C, manuscript breaks off in this commentary.
8887. Jerusalem - Jewish National and University Library Ms Heb 8° 3037, f. 297b-301a, M.
8888. Jerusalem - Schocken Institute 24100 / Mahzor Nuremberg , f. 506a-506b, M.
8889. London - British Library Add. 18695 (Margoliouth 683), f. 133b-134b, T, Yiddish, rubric: דש יאשט דש יוצר בון שמחת תורה.
8890. London - British Library Add. 22431 (Margoliouth 662a), f. 149a-151a, M.
8891. London - British Library Add. 27556, f. 136b-138a, M.
8892. Lund - Universitetsbibliothek Ms. L.O. 2, f. 90a-91b, M.
8893. New York - Jewish Theological Seminary Ms. 4466, f. 469a-471b, M.
8894. Parma - Biblioteca Palatina Cod. Parm. 2895, p. 419-423, M, margins cut, text damaged.
8895. Parma - Biblioteca Palatina Cod. Parm. 3205 (de Rossi 655), f. 248a 249a, C.
8896. Parma - Biblioteca Palatina Cod. Parm. 3507 (Perreau 27), f. 188a-189b, C, commentator: Josef Qara, rubric: פירוש זה פירש רבי יוסף בר שמעו' איש חמודות בטוהר ובכשרון לפני רבי קלונימוס מן רומי.
8897. Vatican - Biblioteca Apostolica ebr. 305,1, f. 50b-52a, C, rubric: יוצר של שמחת תורה.

Ashkenaz, commentary by Eliezer b. Natan
8898. London - Montefiore Library 261, f. 80b-82a, C.
8899. Warszaw - Uniwersytet, Inst. Orientalistyczny 258 , f. 191b-194a, C, rubric: יוצר לשמחת תורה.

Tsarfat
8900. Oxford - Bodleian Library MS Laud. Or. 271 (Neubauer 1206), f. 192b-193b, C, commentator: Aaron b. Hayyim haKohen (compiler).
8901. Parma - Biblioteca Palatina Cod. Parm. 1264, f. 135a-136a, M.

אשרי כל חוסי בך (א 8406), אלעזר ברבי קילר, זולת לשבת פרה

Ashkenaz
8902. Berlin - Staatsbibliothek (Preussischer Kulturbesitz) Or. Qu. 798-799 (Steinschneider 177), II, f. 32a, M.

8903. Budapest - Magyar tudomanyos akademia, MS. Kaufmann A 384, f. 75b, M, short.
8904. Jerusalem - Schocken Institute 24100 / Mahzor Nuremberg, f. 60b, M, short.
8905. Muenchen - Bayerische Staatsbibliothek, Cod. hebr. 88, f. 37b, G.
8906. Oxford - Bodleian Library MS Opp. 170 (Neubauer 1205), f. 28b, C, short.
8907. Paris - Bibliotheque Nationale heb. 709, f. 35a, C, rubric: זולת, short.
8908. Parma - Biblioteca Palatina Cod. Parm. 3205 (de Rossi 655), f. 58a, C, short.
8909. Parma - Biblioteca Palatina Cod. Parm. 3507 (Perreau 27), f. 27a, C, rubric: זולת לפר' אדום', short.
8910. Zurich - Zentralbibliothek Heid. 139, f. 4b, C, very short, additional marginal notes.

אשרי עין ראתה אהלנו (א 8421), הוספה לסדר עבודה
Ashkenaz
8911. Braunschweig - Landesmuseum fuer Geschichte und Volkstum R 2386, vol. II, f. 238b, M, very short.
8912. Cambridge - University Library Or. 785, f. 187b-188a, G.
8913. Jerusalem - Jewish National and University Library Ms Heb 8° 3037, f. 195b, M, very short.
8914. London - Montefiore Library 261, f. 61b, C, commentator: Eliezer b. Natan?.
8915. Vatican Biblioteca Apostolica ebr. 308, f. 128a-128b, C, commentator: David b. Mose (compiler).

אשרי עין ראתה ארץ צבי וגוי אחד (א 8427), אברהם אבן עזרא, הוספה לסדר עבודה
Sepharad
8916. Jerusalem - Benayahu ז 25, f. 173b-174a, M.
8917. Jerusalem - Sassoon 1216, p. 156-158, M, commentator: Mose Nigrin.
8918. Jerusalem - Schocken Institute 70014, f. 86a, G.
Sepharad, commentary by David b. Josef Abudarham[212]
8919. Budapest - Magyar tudomanyos akademia, MS. Kaufmann A 405/2, p. 238, C, rubric: פזמון לר' אברהם ן' עזרא ז"ל.
8920. Cincinnati - Hebrew Union College 490, f. 13b-14a, C.
8921. New York - Columbia X893 Ab 93, f. 24b-25a, C, rubric: פזמון לר' אברהם ן' עזרא ז"ל.
8922. New York - Jewish Theological Seminary Ms. 3011, f. 19b, C.

---

[212] Edited by Prins, תשלום אבודרהם, p. 69-70.

אשרי עין ראתה הלא למשמע, הוספה לסדר עבודה

Carpentras

8923. Cincinnati - Hebrew Union College 392, f. 73a-73b, M, no incipit.

Carpentras, commentary by Josef b. Abraham of Montelitz

8924. Cincinnati - Hebrew Union College 291, f. 43a, C, rubric: פי' פזמון אשרי עין וכו'.

8925. New York - Jewish Theological Seminary Ms. 4197, f. 172a-172b, M, no incipit.

8926. Paris - Ecole Rabbinique 32, f. 182b, M, no incipit.

8927. Strasbourg - Bibliotheque Nationale et Universitaire 4081, f. 160a-160b, M, no incipit.

אשרי עין ראתה כהן בהוד ועטרת (א 8430), יהודה הלוי, פזמון

Sepharad

8928. Jerusalem - Sassoon 1216, p. 154-156, M, commentator: Mose Nigrin.

Sepharad, commentary by David b. Josef Abudarham[213]

8929. Budapest - Magyar tudomanyos akademia, MS. Kaufmann A 405/2, p. 238-239, C, rubric: פזמון לר' יהודה הלוי ז"ל.

8930. Cincinnati - Hebrew Union College 490, f. 14a, C.

8931. New York - Columbia X893 Ab 93, f. 25a, C, rubric: פזמון לר' יהודה הלוי ז"ל.

8932. New York - Jewish Theological Seminary Ms. 3011, f. 19b-20a, C.

אשרי עין ואוזן שושנת השרון (א 8434), שלמה אבן גבירול, הוספה לסדר עבודה

Sepharad

8933. Jerusalem - Benayahu ז 25, f. 171b-172a, .

8934. Jerusalem - Sassoon 1216, p. 152-153, M, commentator: Mose Nigrin.

Sepharad, commentary by David b. Josef Abudarham[214]

8935. Budapest - Magyar tudomanyos akademia, MS. Kaufmann A 405/2, p. 237, C, rubric: פזמון.

8936. Cincinnati - Hebrew Union College 490, f. 13b, C.

8937. New York - Columbia X893 Ab 93, f. 24b, C, rubric: פזמון.

8938. New York - Jewish Theological Seminary Ms. 3011, f. 19a-19b, C.

אשריך אום קדוש בהקדישך השם (א 8443), מנחם בן אביתר, אופן שמחת תורה

Ashkenaz

8939. Berlin - Staatsbibliothek (Preussischer Kulturbesitz) Or. Qu. 361 (Steinschneider 51), f. 131a-131b, M.

---

[213] Edited by Prins, תשלום אבודרהם, p. 70-72.
[214] Edited by Prins, תשלום אבודרהם, p. 68-69.

8940. Berlin - Staatsbibliothek (Preussischer Kulturbesitz) Or. Qu. 798-799 (Steinschneider 177), I, f. 226b, M.
8941. London - British Library Add. 18695 (Margoliouth 683), f. 135b, T, Yiddish.
8942. London - British Library Add. 22431 (Margoliouth 662a), f. 152a-152b, M.
8943. Lund - Universitetsbibliothek Ms. L.O. 2, f. 92a, M.
8944. Warszaw - Uniwersytet, Inst. Orientalistyczny 258, f. 194b-195a, C, commentator: Eliezer b. Natan, rubric: אופן.
8945. Zurich - Zentralbibliothek Heid. 139, f. 103b, C, commentator: Elazar b. Yehuda of Worms, rubric: שמחה תורה, no incipit, short, commentary breaks off here.

אשריך הר העברים על ההרים הגבוהים (א 8446), אברהם אבן עזרא, לשמחת תורה
Romania
8946. Vatican - Biblioteca Apostolica ebr. 285/30, f. 237b-238a, C.
Tsarfat
8947. London - British Library Or. 2735 (Margoliouth 663), f. 163b, M, ecclectic.

אשריך ישראל מי כמוך אשר כל סתום לא עממוך (א 8453), לשמחת תורה
Ashkenaz
8948. Berlin - Staatsbibliothek (Preussischer Kulturbesitz) Or. Qu. 361 (Steinschneider 51), f. 130b-131a, M.
8949. Budapest - Magyar tudomanyos akademia, MS. Kaufmann A 399, p. 312, C.
8950. London - British Library Add. 18695 (Margoliouth 683), f. 135a, T, Yiddish.
8951. London - British Library Add. 22431 (Margoliouth 662a), f. 151b, M.
8952. London - British Library Add. 27556, f. 138a-138b, M.
8953. Lund - Universitetsbibliothek Ms. L.O. 2, f. 91b-92a, M.
8954. New York - Jewish Theological Seminary Ms. 4466, f. 471b-472b, M.
8955. Warszaw - Uniwersytet, Inst. Orientalistyczny 258, f. 194b, C, commentator: Eliezer b. Natan.

אשריך ישראל מי כמוך עם סגולתו (א 8454), אליעזר ב"ר נתן, מעריב לשבועות
Ashkenaz
8956. Berlin - Staatsbibliothek (Preussischer Kulturbesitz) Or. Qu. 798-799 (Steinschneider 177), I, f. 226a-226b, M.
8957. Braunschweig - Landesmuseum fuer Geschichte und Volkstum R 2386, vol. I, f. 93b-94a, M.
8958. Budapest - Magyar tudomanyos akademia, MS. Kaufmann A 399, p. 228-232, C.

8959. Jerusalem - Schocken Institute 24100 / Mahzor Nuremberg, f. 169b-170b, M.
8960. London - British Library Add. 18695 (Margoliouth 683), f. 81a-83b, T, Yiddish.
8961. New York - Jewish Theological Seminary Ms. 4466, f. 159b-161b, M.
8962. Parma - Biblioteca Palatina Cod. Parm. 2895, p. 343-346, M, margins cut, text damaged.
8963. Parma - Biblioteca Palatina Cod. Parm. 3205 (de Rossi 655), f. 116b-117a, C.

אשת נעורים האהובה אשר ארסת (א 8470), אלחנן ב"ר יצחק, סליחה
Ashkenaz

8964. Hamburg - Staats- und Universitaetsbibliothek Cod. hebr. 17/2 (Steinschneider 152), f. 145b, C, rubric: אחרת.
8965. Muenchen - Bayerische Staatsbibliothek, Cod. hebr. 346, f. 143a, C, rubric: אחרת, short.
8966. Oxford - Bodleian Library MS Mich. 543 (Neubauer 1212), f. 5a, C, commentator: Isaac b. Jacob (compiler), short.
8967. Padova - Biblioteca del Seminario Vescovile Cod. 218, f. 135b, M, short.

Ashkenaz, commentary by Abraham b. Azriel[215]

8968. Frankfurt a M - Stadt- und Universitaetsbibliothek Fol. 16 (Merzbacher 95), f. 103b-104a, C, short.
8969. Vatican - Biblioteca Apostolica ebr. 301,1, f. 169a, C, short.

אשתחוה אל היכל קדשך (א 8476), סליחה
Tsarfat

8970. London - David Sofer 5, f. 83b-84a, C.
8971. London - David Sofer 5, f. 161a-161b, C, rubric: סליחה.
8972. Parma - Biblioteca Palatina Cod. Parm. 3006 (de Rossi 654,1), f. 112b, M.
8973. Parma - Biblioteca Palatina Cod. Parm. 3006 (de Rossi 654,1), f. 113a, M, rubric: פי' אחר מאשתחוה.
8974. Vatican - Biblioteca Apostolica ebr. 306, f. 205a-205b, C.

את יי בהמצאו לדורשו קידמתי (א 8496), אליה ב"ר שמעיה, סליחה
Ashkenaz

8975. Braunschweig - Landesmuseum fuer Geschichte und Volkstum R 2386, vol. II, f. 129b, M.
8976. Budapest - Magyar tudomanyos akademia, MS. Kaufmann A 400, p. 488, C, rubric: אחרת. זה מתפללין ביום צום גדליה.

---

[215] Edited by Urbach, ערוגת הבושם, vol. III, p. 491.

8977. Cambridge - University Library Add. 394,1 (Reif SCR 461), f. 96a, C, short.
8978. Cambridge - University Library Dd. 2.30, f. 11b-12a, G.
8979. Jerusalem - Schocken Institute 24100 / Mahzor Nuremberg, f. 266b, M, short.
8980. Moscow - Russian State Library, Ms. Guenzburg 190, f. 28b, G.
8981. Moscow - Russian State Library, Ms. Guenzburg 615, f. 159a-159b, C, rubric: אל מלך.
8982. Muenchen - Bayerische Staatsbibliothek, Cod. hebr. 346, f. 121a-121b, C.
8983. Muenchen - Bayerische Staatsbibliothek, Cod. hebr. 346, f. 127a, C.
8984. Oxford - Bodleian Library MS Mich. 543 (Neubauer 1212), f. 70b-71a, C, commentator: Isaac b. Jacob (compiler).
8985. Oxford - Bodleian Library MS Opp. 170 (Neubauer 1205), f. 228a-228b, C.
8986. Oxford - Bodleian Library MS Opp. 681 (Neubauer 1213), f. 9a-10a, C.
8987. Padova - Biblioteca del Seminario Vescovile Cod. 218, f. 126b-127a, M.
8988. Parma - Biblioteca Palatina Cod. Parm. 3205 (de Rossi 655), f. 268b, C.
8989. Vatican - Biblioteca Apostolica ebr. 308, f. 22a-22b, C, commentator: David b. Mose (compiler).
8990. Vatican - Biblioteca Apostolica ebr. 422/1, f. 29a, C.
8991. Vatican - Biblioteca Apostolica ebr. 422/1, f. 43b, CG, no incipit.

Ashkenaz, commentary by Abraham b. Azriel[216]

8992. Frankfurt a M - Stadt- und Universitaetsbibliothek Fol. 16 (Merzbacher 95), f. 112a-112b, C.
8993. Vatican - Biblioteca Apostolica ebr. 301,1, f. 160a-160b, C, rubric: אחרת.

Tsarfat

8994. London - British Library Add. 11639 (Margoliouth 1056), f. 469b, M, very short.
8995. London - David Sofer 5, f. 92a, C.
8996. Oxford - Bodleian Library MS Laud. Or. 271 (Neubauer 1206), f. 171a-171b, C, commentator: Aaron b. Hayyim haKohen (compiler).
8997. Oxford - Bodleian Library MS Opp. 171 (Neubauer 1207), f. 103a, C, rubric: אחרת.
8998. Parma - Biblioteca Palatina Cod. Parm. 2125 (de Rossi 812), f. 56b, C, rubric: סליחות ועקידות.
8999. Parma - Biblioteca Palatina Cod. Parm. 3007 (de Rossi 654,2), f. 80a-80b, M.

---

[216] Edited by Urbach, ערוגת הבושם, vol. III, p. 428-430.

9000. Vatican - Biblioteca Apostolica ebr. 306, f. 194a-194b, C.

את אשר חטאתי (א 8505), אליה, סליחה

Ashkenaz

9001. Vatican - Biblioteca Apostolica ebr. 308, f. 12b, C, commentator: David b. Mose (compiler).

את בין עצי עדן הדס פורח (א 8507), יהודה הלוי, מיוחס לשלם שבזי

Yemen

9002. Cincinnati - Hebrew Union College 398, f. 194a-195a, M.

את גומל מערבות לחייבים טובות (א 8511), אהרן, סליחה

Yemen

9003. Jerusalem - Sassoon 902, p. 410, M.
9004. New York - Jewish Theological Seminary Ms. 3052, f. 56a-58b (f. 57b empty), M, rubric: אל מלך.

Yemen, commentary by Isaac b. Abraham Wanneh

9005. Chicago-Spertus College of Judaica D 2, 2, f. 230a-230b, M, no incipit.
9006. Jerusalem - Benayahu ת 261, f. 158b-159a, M, rubric: אל מלך.
9007. Jerusalem - Benayahu ת 282, f. 130a-130b, M, rubric: אל מלך.
9008. Jerusalem - Makhon Ben Zvi 1156 (Tubi 155), f. 129b-130a, M, rubric: אל מלך.
9009. Jerusalem - Makhon Ben Zvi 1174 (Tubi 154), f. 129b, M.
9010. Jerusalem - Michael Krupp 604, f. 86a, M, rubric: אל מלך.
9011. Jerusalem - Musad haRav Kook 325, f. 187a, M, rubric: אל מלך.
9012. Jerusalem - Musad haRav Kook 330, f. 116b, G.
9013. Jerusalem - Musad haRav Kook 347, f. 88a, G.
9014. Jerusalem - Sassoon 1158, p. 202-203, M, rubric: סים׳ אהרן חבר.
9015. Jerusalem - Sassoon 1174, p. 250-251, M, no incipit.
9016. London - British Library Or. 11122, f. 206b, M, no incipit.
9017. Manchester - John Rylands University Library, Ms. Gaster 5, f. 210b, M.
9018. Muenchen - Bayerische Staatsbibliothek, Cod. hebr. 472, f. 179a-180a, M, rubric: אל מלך.
9019. New York - Jewish Theological Seminary Ms. 3013, f. 126b, M, rubric: אל מלך.
9020. New York - Jewish Theological Seminary Ms. 3294, f. 13b, C.
9021. New York - Public Library, Heb. Ms. 9, f. 121b-122a, M.
9022. Strasbourg - Bibliotheque Nationale et Universitaire 3965 (Landauer 39), p. 390, M, rubric: אל מלך.

את הברית ואת החסד (א 8517), מאיר ב"ר יצחק, סליחה

Ashkenaz
9023. Berlin - Staatsbibliothek (Preussischer Kulturbesitz) Or. Qu. 798-799 (Steinschneider 177), I, f. 167a-167b, M.
9024. Cambridge - University Library Dd. 2.30, f. 17a-18a, G.
9025. Jerusalem - Schocken Institute 24100 / Mahzor Nuremberg, f. 437a, M.
9026. Muenchen - Bayerische Staatsbibliothek, Cod. hebr. 346, f. 123b, C, rubric: עקידה למוסף דיום הכיפורים, short.
9027. New York - Jewish Theological Seminary Ms. 4466, f. 401b-402b, M.
9028. New York - Jewish Theological Seminary Ms. 8097, f. 86b-87a, C.
9029. Oxford - Bodleian Library MS Mich. 543 (Neubauer 1212), f. 27a-28b, C, commentator: Isaac b. Jacob (compiler), rubric: עקידה.
9030. Oxford - Bodleian Library MS Opp. 172 (Neubauer 1211), f. 88b-89a, C, rubric: עקידה.
9031. Oxford - Bodleian Library MS Opp. 619 (Neubauer 2374), f. 267a-268a, M.
9032. Oxford - Bodleian Library MS Opp. 681 (Neubauer 1213), f. 69b-70b, C.
9033. Parma - Biblioteca Palatina Cod. Parm. 3205 (de Rossi 655), f. 279a-279b, C.
9034. Vatican - Biblioteca Apostolica ebr. 308, f. 149b-150b, C, commentator: David b. Mose (compiler).
9035. Vatican - Biblioteca Apostolica ebr. 422/1, f. 25a, C, short.
9036. Vatican - Biblioteca Apostolica ebr. 422/2, f. 39b, CG, no incipit, very short.

Ashkenaz, commentary by Abraham b. Azriel[217]
9037. Frankfurt a M - Stadt- und Universitaetsbibliothek Fol. 16 (Merzbacher 95), f. 108b-109a, C.

Tsarfat
9038. Oxford - Bodleian Library MS Laud. Or. 271 (Neubauer 1206), f. 125b-126a, C, commentator: Aaron b. Hayyim haKohen (compiler).

את הברית ואת השבועה (א 8518), אליעזר ב"ר נתן, סליחה

Tsarfat
9039. London - David Sofer 5, f. 173b-174a, C, rubric: סליחה.
9040. Parma - Biblioteca Palatina Cod. Parm. 3007 (de Rossi 654,2), f. 80b-81a, M.

---

[217] Edited by Urbach, ערוגת הבושם, vol. III, p. 561-564.

את הוא אלהא דגלו קדמך עמיקתא, סליחה

Yemen
9041. New York - Jewish Theological Seminary Ms. 3052, f. 82b, M, no incipit.

Yemen, commentary by Isaac b. Abraham Wanneh
9042. Chicago-Spertus College of Judaica D 2, 2, f. 237b, M, no incipit.
9043. Jerusalem - Benayahu ת 282, f. 140b, M, no incipit, very short.
9044. Jerusalem - Makhon Ben Zvi 1156 (Tubi 155), f. 138b, M, no incipit.
9045. Jerusalem - Sassoon 1158, p. 416-417, M, no incipit.
9046. London - British Library Or. 11122, f. 214b, M, no incipit.
9047. New York - Jewish Theological Seminary Ms. 3294, f. 17a, C.

את הוא אלהא דשרי ברום רקיעיא, סליחה

Yemen, commentary by Isaac b. Abraham Wanneh
9048. Jerusalem - Benayahu ת 261, f. 164a, M.
9049. Jerusalem - Makhon Ben Zvi 1156 (Tubi 155), f. 137a, M, no incipit.
9050. Jerusalem - Makhon Ben Zvi 1174 (Tubi 154), f. 135a, M.
9051. Jerusalem - Sassoon 1174, p. 267, M, no incipit.
9052. New York - Jewish Theological Seminary Ms. 3294, f. 16b, C.
9053. New York - Public Library, Heb. Ms. 9, f. 127b, M.
9054. Strasbourg - Bibliotheque Nationale et Universitaire 3965 (Landauer 39), p. 405, M.

את הקול קול יעקב נוהם (א 8520), קלונימוס ב"ר יהודה, סליחה

Ashkenaz
9055. Berlin - Staatsbibliothek (Preussischer Kulturbesitz) Or. Qu. 798-799 (Steinschneider 177), I, f. 145a-145b, M.
9056. London - British Library Add. 18695 (Margoliouth 683), f. 165a-165b, T, Yiddish.
9057. Muenchen - Bayerische Staatsbibliothek, Cod. hebr. 346, f. 123b, C, short.
9058. New York - Jewish Theological Seminary Ms. 8097, f. 86a-86b, C.
9059. Oxford - Bodleian Library MS Mich. 543 (Neubauer 1212), f. 22a-23a, C, commentator: Isaac b. Jacob (compiler), rubric: גם הסליח' זו נוסדה על גזירו' רעות.
9060. Oxford - Bodleian Library MS Opp. 681 (Neubauer 1213), f. 6b, C, short.
9061. Vatican - Biblioteca Apostolica ebr. 422/1, f. 25a, C, short.
9062. Vatican - Biblioteca Apostolica ebr. 422/2, f. 39b, C, no incipit, short.

Tsarfat
9063. Oxford - Bodleian Library MS Bodl. Or. 109 (Neubauer 1209), f. 85a-86b, C, commentator: Aaron b. Hayyim haKohen (compiler), manuscript breaks off in this commentary.

את השם הנכבד והנורא (א 8522), יוסף ב"ר שמואל טוב עלם, קדושתא לפסח

Tsarfat

9064. Parma - Biblioteca Palatina Cod. Parm. 3136 (de Rossi 405), f. 108b-109a, M.

את השם הנכבד נאה להתילותיו (א 8523), מאיר ב"ר יצחק, יוצר לשבת וחול המועד סוכות

Ashkenaz

9065. Berlin - Staatsbibliothek (Preussischer Kulturbesitz) Or. Qu. 798-799 (Steinschneider 177), I, f. 200b-202a, M, margins cut.
9066. Braunschweig - Landesmuseum fuer Geschichte und Volkstum R 2386, vol. I, f. 141b-142b, M.
9067. Budapest - Magyar tudomanyos akademia, MS. Kaufmann A 399, p. 446-448, C, rubric: יוצר דחולו של מועד.
9068. Budapest - Magyar tudomanyos akademia, MS. Kaufmann A 399, p. 450-453, C, rubric: יוצר לשבת לחולו של מועד לוסוכות. ושלומי במים רבים בבריכות.
9069. Cambridge - University Library Add. 504,1, f. 56b-61b, C, rubric: יוצר לחול המועד דסוכות מרבי' מאיר ב'ר' יצחק ש'צ' וחקוק לסוף.
9070. Frankfurt a M - Stadt- und Universitaetsbibliothek Oct. 227, f. 166b-168b, M.
9071. Jerusalem - Schocken Institute 24100 / Mahzor Nuremberg, f. 472a-473a, M.
9072. London - British Library Add. 18695 (Margoliouth 683), f. 142b-147a, T, Yiddish, rubric: דא וויל איך אן היבן צו שרייבן דש יוצר בון שבת בון חול המועד בון צוכות.
9073. London - British Library Add. 22431 (Margoliouth 662a), f. 105a-106b, M.
9074. Lund - Universitetsbibliothek Ms. L.O. 2, f. 112a-114a, M.
9075. Muenchen - Bayerische Staatsbibliothek, Cod. hebr. 69, f. 72a-73b, M.
9076. Muenchen - Bayerische Staatsbibliothek, Cod. hebr. 393, f. 217b-223a, C, rubric: יוצר לשבת של סוכות.
9077. New York - Jewish Theological Seminary Ms. 4466, f. 452b-455a, M.
9078. Oxford - Bodleian Library MS Can. Or. 82 (Neubauer 1148), f. 41a-44a, M.
9079. Oxford - Bodleian Library MS Mich. 365 (Neubauer 1208), f. 32b-35a, C.
9080. Parma - Biblioteca Palatina Cod. Parm. 2895, p. 414-417, M, margins cut, text damaged.
9081. Vatican - Biblioteca Apostolica ebr. 318, f. 125b-127b, GI.
9082. Vatican - Biblioteca Apostolica ebr. 422/1, f. 22a-22b, C, rubric: יוצר לשבת של חולו המועד.

Ashkenaz, commentary by Abraham b. Azriel[218]
9083. Frankfurt a M - Stadt- und Universitaetsbibliothek Fol. 16 (Merzbacher 95), f. 79a-83a, C, rubric: יוצר.
9084. Vatican - Biblioteca Apostolica ebr. 301,1, f. 73a, C, rubric: יוצר.

Ashkenaz, commentary by Eliezer b. Natan
9085. Parma - Biblioteca Palatina Cod. Parm. 3057.12 (de Rossi 1033/10), f. 133b-137b, C, rubric: יוצר לחולו של מועד.
9086. London - Montefiore Library 261, f. 84a-85a, C, rubric: יוצר בין יום כיפור לסוכות.
9087. Hamburg - Staats- und Universitaetsbibliothek Cod. hebr. 61 (Steinschneider 153), f. 41a-43b, C, rubric: יוצר לחולו של מועד מסוכות.
9088. Warszaw - Uniwersytet, Inst. Orientalistyczny 258, f. 189a-191b, C, rubric: יוצר לחולו של מועד דסוכות.

את חטאי נוכח פני שמתי (א 8532), משה אבן עזרא, חלק ז', קדושתא לשחרית יום כפור
Carpentras, commentary by Josef b. Abraham of Montelitz
9089. Cincinnati - Hebrew Union College 291, f. 26b, C, rubric: פי' פזמון עסתריוטא.
9090. New York - Jewish Theological Seminary Ms. 4197, f. 116a-117b, M.
9091. Paris - Ecole Rabbinique 32, f. 135a-136a, M.
9092. Strasbourg - Bibliotheque Nationale et Universitaire 4081, f. 112a-113a, M.

את חיל יום פקודה (א 8533), אלעזר ברבי קליר, קדושתא לראש השנה
Ashkenaz
9093. Berlin - Staatsbibliothek (Preussischer Kulturbesitz) Or. Qu. 798-799 (Steinschneider 177), I, f. 5b-6a, M.
9094. Braunschweig - Landesmuseum fuer Geschichte und Volkstum R 2386, vol. II, f. 80b, M.
9095. Budapest - Magyar tudomanyos akademia, MS. Kaufmann A 400, p. 243-247, C.
9096. Cambridge - University Library Or. 785, f. 18a-19a, Gl.
9097. Darmstadt - Hessisches Landes- und Hochschulbibliothek Cod. Or. 15, f. 5b-6a, M.
9098. Hamburg - Staats- und Universitaetsbibliothek Cod. hebr. 12 (Steinschneider 102), f. 5a-5b, G.
9099. Hamburg - Staats- und Universitaetsbibliothek Cod. hebr. 17/2 (Steinschneider 152), f. 105b-106b, C.
9100. Hamburg - Staats- und Universitaetsbibliothek Cod. hebr. 40b (Steinschneider 110), f. 5b-6a, G.

---

[218] Edited by Urbach, ערוגת הבושם, vol. II, p. 153-181.

9101. Hamburg - Staats- und Universitaetsbibliothek Cod. hebr. 40c (Steinschneider 111), f. 132a-132b, G.
9102. Hamburg - Staats- und Universitaetsbibliothek Cod. hebr. 132 (Steinschneider 155), f. 3b-4b, C.
9103. Hamburg - Staats- und Universitaetsbibliothek Cod. hebr. 139 (Steinschneider 115), f. 20a-20b, G.
9104. Hamburg - Staats- und Universitaetsbibliothek Cod. hebr. 225, f. 216b-217b, G.
9105. Jerusalem - Jewish National and University Library Ms Heb 8° 3037, f. 7b-8a, M.
9106. Jerusalem - Schocken Institute 24100 / Mahzor Nuremberg, f. 323b-324a, M.
9107. Linz - Oberoesterreichische Landesbibliothek 570, f. 1a-1b, FM, incomplete.
9108. Moscow - Russian State Library, Ms. Guenzburg 363, f. 124b-125a, C, esoteric.
9109. Moscow - Russian State Library, Ms. Guenzburg 615, f. 54b-56a, C.
9110. Moscow - Russian State Library, Ms. Guenzburg 1401/2, f. 16a, C.
9111. Muenchen - Bayerische Staatsbibliothek, Cod. hebr. 422, f. 72b, G.
9112. New York - Jewish Theological Seminary Ms. 4466, f. 209b-210a, M.
9113. New York - Jewish Theological Seminary Ms. 8097, f. 58a-58b, C, additional glosses.
9114. New York - Jewish Theological Seminary Ms. 8169 (Acc. 0016), f. 3b-4a, M.
9115. New York - Jewish Theological Seminary Rab. 1077/4 (Acc. 02505), f. 21a-21b, FC, no incipit.
9116. Oxford - Bodleian Library MS Opp. 170 (Neubauer 1205), f. 101b-103b, C, rubric: אופן.
9117. Oxford - Bodleian Library MS Opp. 172 (Neubauer 1211), f. 2a-3a, C.
9118. Oxford - Bodleian Library MS Opp. 619 (Neubauer 2374), f. 9b-10b, M.
9119. Oxford - Bodleian Library MS Opp. 675 (Neubauer 1210), f. 13a-14a, C, no incipit.
9120. Paris - Bibliotheque Nationale heb. 653, f. 9a, G.
9121. Parma - Biblioteca Palatina Cod. Parm. 2404 (de Rossi 1104), f. 125b-126a, M, copied from printed edition Saloniki 1550 (Benjamin b. Meir Levi).
9122. Parma - Biblioteca Palatina Cod. Parm. 3205 (de Rossi 655), f. 203b-204a, C, rubric: קרבה.
9123. Parma - Biblioteca Palatina Cod. Parm. 3270 (de Rossi 1215), f. 19b, M.
9124. Parma - Biblioteca Palatina Cod. Parm. 3507 (Perreau 27), f. 108a-109b, C.

9125. Vatican - Bibliotheca Apostolica ebr. 298/1, f. 5b-8a, C, no incipit.
9126. Vatican - Biblioteca Apostolica ebr. 308, f. 27a-29a, C, commentator: David b. Mose (compiler).
9127. Vatican - Biblioteca Apostolica ebr. 308, f. 26a-27a, C, commentator: David b. Mose (compiler).
9128. Vatican - Biblioteca Apostolica ebr. 422/1, f. 7a-7b, C.
9129. Zurich - Zentralbibliothek Heid. 139, f. 56b-57a, C, additional marginal notes.
9130. Zurich - Zentralbibliothek Heid. 139, f. 101b-102a, C, commentator: Elazar b. Yehuda of Worms, esoteric.

Asti, Fossano, Moncalvo
9131. New Haven - Yale University, Beinecke Rare Book and MS Library, MS Heb. 52, f. 18a, M.

Romania
9132. Vatican - Biblioteca Apostolica ebr. 320, f. 147b-148a, M.

Tsarfat
9133. London - British Library Add. 11639 (Margoliouth 1056), f. 708a-708b, M.
9134. London - British Library Or. 8682, f. 9b, GI.
9135. London - David Sofer 5, f. 108a-108b, C.
9136. Manchester - John Rylands University Library, Ms. Gaster 733, f. 80a-80b, C, commentary block in Mahzor, manuscript damaged.
9137. Oxford - Bodleian Library MS Laud. Or. 271 (Neubauer 1206), f. 139a-140a, C, commentator: Aaron b. Hayyim haKohen (compiler).
9138. Oxford - Bodleian Library MS Opp. 171 (Neubauer 1207), f. 54b-56a, C.
9139. Paris - Bibliotheque Nationale heb. 445,9, f. 62a-62b, C.
9140. Parma - Biblioteca Palatina Cod. Parm. 1794 (de Rossi 1061), f. 55a-57a, M.
9141. Parma - Biblioteca Palatina Cod. Parm. 2125 (de Rossi 812), f. 5a-6b, C.
9142. Parma - Biblioteca Palatina Cod. Parm. 3006 (de Rossi 654,1), f. 23b-24a, M.
9143. Vatican - Biblioteca Apostolica ebr. 306, f. 46b-47b, C, rubric: קרובה.

את יום השמיני (א 8541), יצחק, מעריב שמיני עצרת

Ashkenaz
9144. Berlin - Staatsbibliothek (Preussischer Kulturbesitz) Or. Qu. 798-799 (Steinschneider 177), I, 195a-196b, M.
9145. London - British Library Add. 18695 (Margoliouth 683), f. 132b-133a, T, Yiddish.

Tsarfat
9146. London - David Sofer 5, f. 190b, C, rubric: מעריב ליל שמיני עצרת של סוכות.

את יום כפרה מחילה והתרה (א 8542), סליחה

Ashkenaz
9147. Berlin - Staatsbibliothek (Preussischer Kulturbesitz) Or. Qu. 798-799 (Steinschneider 177), I, f. 174a-174b, M.

את יום פדותם (א 8543), יהודה ב"ר מנחם, יוצר לשבת נחמו

Roma
9148. Jerusalem - Jewish National and University Library Ms Heb 8° 4153, f. 165b, C, commentator: Daniel ben Salomo haRofe (compiler), rubric: פי' יוצר לשבת נחמו, incipit בעוליה.
9149. Oxford - Bodleian Library MS Mich. 312,1 (Neubauer 2276,1), f. 29a, C, rubric: פי' יוצר של נחמו, incipit בעוליה.

את מלחמות יי בהנקמו לי (א 8567), יהודה הלוי, קדושתא לשבת זכור

Sepharad, commentary by Josef Garad
9150. Oxford - Bodleian Library Heb.e.10 (Neubauer 2746/1), f. 7b, C, rubric: מגן.
9151. Oxford - Bodleian Library Heb.e.10 (Neubauer 2746/1), f. 18a, C, rubric: את מלחמות, no incipit, short.

את נוי חטאתי השמימה, קינה

Ashkenaz
9152. Berlin - Staatsbibliothek (Preussischer Kulturbesitz) Or. Qu. 798-799 (Steinschneider 177), II, f. 207a-207b, M.

את נתיבי רעיון (א 8573), יהודה הלוי, סליחה

Yemen
9153. Jerusalem - Sassoon 264, f. 158a, M.
9154. Jerusalem - Sassoon 902, p. 390-391, M.
9155. New York - Jewish Theological Seminary Ms. 3052, f. 53a-53b, M, rubric: אל מלך.

Yemen, commentary by Isaac b. Abraham Wanneh
9156. Chicago-Spertus College of Judaica D 2, 2, f. 221b-222b, M, no incipit.
9157. Jerusalem - Benayahu ת 261, f. 146a, M, rubric: אל מלך, short.
9158. Jerusalem - Benayahu ת 282, f. 129b-130a, M, rubric: אל מלך.
9159. Jerusalem - Makhon Ben Zvi 1174 (Tubi 154), f. 112b, M, rubric: אל מלך.
9160. Jerusalem - Michael Krupp 604, f. 163a, M, rubric: אל מלך.
9161. Jerusalem - Musad haRav Kook 325, f. 163b, M.
9162. Jerusalem - Sassoon 1158, p. 395-396, M, no incipit.
9163. Jerusalem - Sassoon 1174, p. 248, M, no incipit.
9164. Jerusalem - Yehiel haLevi 4, f. 145a, G.

9165. London - British Library Or. 11122, f. 199b-200a, M, rubric: אל מלך.
9166. Manchester - John Rylands University Library, Ms. Gaster 5, f. 185b-186a, M.
9167. Muenchen - Bayerische Staatsbibliothek, Cod. hebr. 472, f. 178a-178b, M, rubric: אל מלך.
9168. New York - Jewish Theological Seminary Ms. 3013, f. 112a, M, rubric: אל מלך, very short.
9169. New York - Jewish Theological Seminary Ms. 3109, f. 82b, M, rubric: פירוש.
9170. New York - Jewish Theological Seminary Ms. 3294, f. 6a, C.
9171. Philadelphia - University of Pennsylvania HB 2, f. 125a, M, rubric: אל מלך.
9172. Strasbourg - Bibliotheque Nationale et Universitaire 3965 (Landauer 39), p. 341-342, M, rubric: אל מלך.

את עניך יי אבקש כעני על פתח נוקש, ודוי

Romania
9173. Vatican - Biblioteca Apostolica ebr. 320, f. 220b, M.

את פני מבין ויודע דין דל (א 8583), מאיר ב"ר יצחק, סליחה

Ashkenaz
9174. Cambridge - University Library Dd. 2.30, f. 24a-24b, G.
9175. Jerusalem - Schocken Institute 24100 / Mahzor Nuremberg, f. 244a, M, marginal notes by later hand only.
9176. Muenchen Bayerische Staatsbibliothek, Cod. hebr. 346, f. 124a, C.
9177. Muenchen - Bayerische Staatsbibliothek, Cod. hebr. 346, f. 133b, C, rubric: אחרת, short.
9178. Muenchen - Bayerische Staatsbibliothek, Cod. hebr. 346, f. 164b, C, very short.
9179. Oxford - Bodleian Library MS Opp. 681 (Neubauer 1213), f. 40b-41a, C.
9180. Vatican - Biblioteca Apostolica ebr. 422/2, f. 40a, CG, no incipit.

Ashkenaz, commentary by Abraham b. Azriel[219]
9181. Frankfurt a M - Stadt- und Universitaetsbibliothek Fol. 16 (Merzbacher 95), f. 109b, C.
9182. Vatican - Biblioteca Apostolica ebr. 301,1, f. 145a, C, rubric: אחרת.

את צום השביעי (א 8593), מנחם ב"ר יעקב, סליחה

Ashkenaz
9183. Oxford - Bodleian Library MS Mich. 543 (Neubauer 1212), f. 33b-34a, C, commentator: Isaac b. Jacob (compiler).

---

[219] Edited by Urbach, ערוגת הבושם, vol. III, p. 328-320, 565-567.

9184. Oxford - Bodleian Library MS Opp. 681 (Neubauer 1213), f. 9a, C.
9185. Padova - Biblioteca del Seminario Vescovile Cod. 218, f. 118b-119a, M.
9186. Parma - Bibliotheca Palatina Cod. Parm. 3205 (de Rossi 655), f. 288a, C.

את צועדי, אזהרות לשבת הגדול
Sepharad, commentary by Josef Garad
9187. Oxford - Bodleian Library Heb.e.10 (Neubauer 2746/1), f. 22a-23a, C, rubric: אזהרות לשבת הגדול. את צועדי, no incipit.

אתא בקר וגם לילה (א 8618), יוסף ב"ר יעקב, סילוק, קדושתא לנעילה
Tsarfat
9188. London - David Sofer 5, f. 171b, margin, C.

אתאנו לחלות פניך (א 8627), סליחה
Sepharad
9189. Skokie - Hebrew Theological College 3, f. 19b-20a, G.
Yemen
9190. New York - Jewish Theological Seminary Ms. 3193, f. 125a-125b, M, no incipit, short.
Yemen, commentary by Isaac b. Abraham Wanneh
9191. Chicago-Spertus College of Judaica D 2, 2, f. 184b, M, no incipit.
9192. Jerusalem - Musad haRav Kook 330, f. 91b, G.
9193. London - British Library Or. 11122, f. 160b, M, no incipit.

אתאנו לך יוצר רוחות (א 8630), סליחה
Ashkenaz
9194. Oxford - Bodleian Library MS Opp. 681 (Neubauer 1213), f. 34b-35a, C, rubric: לשבעה עשר בתמוז.
9195. Padova - Biblioteca del Seminario Vescovile Cod. 218, f. 256b, M, very short.
9196. Vatican - Biblioteca Apostolica ebr. 422/1, f. 45a, CG, no incipit, very short.
9197. Vatican - Biblioteca Apostolica ebr. 422/2, f. 40a, CG, no incipit.
Ashkenaz, commentary by Abraham b. Azriel[220]
9198. Vatican - Biblioteca Apostolica ebr. 301,1, f. 141b, C, rubric: סליחות לי"ז בתמוז.

---

[220] Edited by Urbach, ערוגת הבושם, vol. III, p. 307-308.

אתאנו על שמך יי עשה למען שמך (א 8641), סליחה
Yemen, commentary by Isaac b. Abraham Wanneh
9199. Chicago-Spertus College of Judaica D 2, 2, f. 232a-232b, M, no incipit.

אתאנו על שמך אדיר במרומך שליט בעולמך, סליחה
Yemen
9200. New York - Jewish Theological Seminary Ms. 3028, f. 80a-80b, G.
Yemen, commentary by Isaac b. Abraham Wanneh
9201. Chicago-Spertus College of Judaica D 2, 2, f. 245b-246a, M, no incipit.

אתה אדון כל הנמצאות (א 8646), משה אבן עזרא
Sepharad, commentary by David b. Josef Abudarham[221]
9202. Budapest - Magyar tudomanyos akademia, MS. Kaufmann A 405/2, p. 247, C, rubric: מסתאג'יב לר' משה ן' עזרא ז"ל.
9203. New York - Columbia X893 Ab 93, f. 28b, C, rubric: מסתג'יב לר' משה ן' עזרא ז"ל.

אתה יי אבינו, סליחה
Ashkenaz
9204. Parma - Biblioteca Palatina Cod. Parm. 3205 (de Rossi 655), f. 270b, C.

אתה אהבת עמך בעבורם רדת ממרומך (א 8660), זולת לשבת שקלים
Ashkenaz
9205. Berlin - Staatsbibliothek (Preussischer Kulturbesitz) Or. Qu. 798-799 (Steinschneider 177), II, f. 12b, M, short.
9206. Budapest - Magyar tudomanyos akademia, MS. Kaufmann A 384, f. 36b, M, rubric: זולת.
9207. Cambridge - University Library Add. 504,1, f. 1a-1b, C, rubric: זולת.
9208. Erlangen - Universitaetsbibliothek 2601 (Roth 67), f. 26b-27a, M, rubric: זולת.
9209. Jerusalem - Schocken Institute 24100 / Mahzor Nuremberg, f. 34a, M, short.
9210. Muenchen - Bayerische Staatsbibliothek, Cod. hebr. 393, f. 84b, C.
9211. Oxford - Bodleian Library MS Opp. 170 (Neubauer 1205), f. 3a, C, rubric: זולת.
9212. Paris - Bibliotheque Nationale heb. 709, f. 3a-3b, C, rubric: זולת.
9213. Parma - Biblioteca Palatina Cod. Parm. 1002 (Ta 24), f. 22b, M, rubric: זולת.

---

[221] Edited by Prins, תשלום אבודרהם, p. 153-155.

9214. Parma - Biblioteca Palatina Cod. Parm. 3205 (de Rossi 655), f. 10b, C, rubric: זולת זולת זולת, incipit ומתמידים.
9215. Parma - Biblioteca Palatina Cod. Parm. 3507 (Perreau 27), f. 2a, C, rubric: זולת.

Tsarfat
9216. Oxford - Bodleian Library MS Laud. Or. 271 (Neubauer 1206), f. 6a, C, commentator: Aaron b. Hayyim haKohen (compiler), very short.

אתה אל לכל ראש מתנשא (א 8668), אהרן בן ויסף הרופא, פרשת בראשית

Karaite, commentary by Berakha b. Josef haKohen
9217. New York - Jewish Theological Seminary Ms. 3367, f. 13a-19a, C, rubric: ומעתה אחל פרוש הפיוטים.
9218. St. Petersburg - Inst. of Oriental Studies of the Russian Academy B 431, f. 13a-16b, C, rubric: ומעתה אחל פירוש הפיוטים בע"ה הנותן לנו חקים ומשפטים. פירוש של פיוטי לפרשיות התורה. פיוט לפרשת בראשית.
9219. St. Petersburg - Russian National Library, Evr. IV 50, f. 10a-13b, C, rubric: בראשית.

אתה אל מתנשא ויושב בכסא ממלכה (א 8672), אהרן בן יוסף הרופא, פרשת אתם נצבים

Karaite, commentary by Berakha b. Josef haKohen
9220. New York - Jewish Theological Seminary Ms. 3367, f. 154a-157a, C, rubric: פרוש פרשת אתם נצבים.
9221. St. Petersburg - Inst. of Oriental Studies of the Russian Academy B 431, f. 104b-106b, C, rubric: פרשת אתם נצבים.
9222. St. Petersburg - Inst. of Oriental Studies of the Russian Academy B 483, f. 16b-17b, C, rubric: פרשת אתם נצבים.
9223. St. Petersburg - Inst. of Oriental Studies of the Russian Academy B 483, f. 18a, C.
9224. St. Petersburg - Russian National Library, Evr. IV 50, f. 121b-124b, C, rubric: אתם נצבים.

אתה אלהי האלהים אשר אליו נועד (א 8679), משה אבן עזרא, סילוק, קדושתא למוסף יום כפור

Carpentras
9225. Cincinnati - Hebrew Union College 392, f. 93b-95a, M, no incipit.

Carpentras, commentary by Josef b. Abraham of Montelitz
9226. Cincinnati - Hebrew Union College 291, f. 51b-52a, C, rubric: פי' אתה הוא וכו'.
9227. New York - Jewish Theological Seminary Ms. 4197, f. 153a-153b, M, no incipit.
9228. Paris - Ecole Rabbinique 32, f. 216a-216b, M, no incipit.

9229. Strasbourg - Bibliotheque Nationale et Universitaire 4081, f. 190a-190b, M, no incipit.

אתה אלהים וזולתך אין עוד (א 8688), משולם ב"ר קלונימוס, זולת
Ashkenaz

9230. Frankfurt a M - Stadt- und Universitaetsbibliothek Oct. 227, f. 158b-159b, M.
9231. Hamburg - Staats- und Universitaetsbibliothek Cod. hebr. 239a (Steinschneider 130), f. 20a-21a, G.
9232. Lund - Universitetsbibliothek Ms. L.O. 2, f. 95a-96a, M.
9233. Muenchen - Bayerische Staatsbibliothek, Cod. hebr. 393,9, f. 197b-198a, C, rubric: זולת.
9234. Oxford - Bodleian Library MS Can. Or. 82 (Neubauer 1148), f. 23a-24a, M.
9235. Parma - Biblioteca Palatina Cod. Parm. 3205 (de Rossi 655), f. 144a-144b, C.

אתה אלהים וזולתך אין צור בלעדיך (א 8693), יוסף
Ashkenaz

9236. Cambridge - University Library Add. 504,1, f. 40b-41a, C, rubric: משלם יסד זה וחתום לסוף.

אתה אלוה נהיית אתה אל רם נעלית, סליחה
Yemen, commentary by Isaac b. Abraham Wanneh

9237. Chicago-Spertus College of Judaica D 2, 2, f. 221a-221b, M, no incipit.
9238. Jerusalem - Michael Krupp 604, f. 166b, M, rubric: אל מלך.
9239. Jerusalem - Sassoon 1158, p. 394-395, M, no incipit.
9240. London - British Library Or. 11122, f. 199a, M, no incipit.

אתה אמרתה הטב איטיב עמך (א 8700), קינה
Ashkenaz

9241. Berlin - Staatsbibliothek (Preussischer Kulturbesitz) Or. Qu. 798-799 (Steinschneider 177), II, f. 191b-192a, M.
9242. Budapest - Magyar tudomanyos akademia, MS. Kaufmann A 400, p. 229-230, C, rubric: אחרת.
9243. Hamburg - Staats- und Universitaetsbibliothek Cod. hebr. 17/2 (Steinschneider 152), f. 100a, C.
9244. Jerusalem - Schocken Institute 24100 / Mahzor Nuremberg, f. 208a, M.
9245. Muenchen - Bayerische Staatsbibliothek, Cod. hebr. 88, f. 179a, G, ecclectic.

9246. Parma - Biblioteca Palatina Cod. Parm. 3205 (de Rossi 655), f. 197a, C, rubric: אחרת.
9247. Vatican - Biblioteca Apostolica ebr. 312, f. 51a-51b, G.
9248. Vatican - Biblioteca Apostolica ebr. 318, f. 236b-237b, GI.

Ashkenaz, commentary by Abraham b. Azriel[222]
9249. Vatican - Biblioteca Apostolica ebr. 301,1, f. 137a, C, rubric: אחרת, short.

אתה האל עושה פלא בכל דור ודור (א 8736), שמואל, סליחה

Ashkenaz
9250. Oxford - Bodleian Library MS Opp. 681 (Neubauer 1213), f. 33b-34a, C, short.
9251. Padova - Biblioteca del Seminario Vescovile Cod. 218, f. 251a-251b, M.
9252. Parma - Biblioteca Palatina Cod. Parm. 3205 (de Rossi 655), f. 284a-284b, C.

אתה האל עושה פלאות (א 8742), שמעון ב"ר יצחק, סליחה

Ashkenaz
9253. Klosterneuburg - Stiftsbibliothek St. Augustini 271, FC, incomplete.
9254. Oxford - Bodleian Library MS Opp. 681 (Neubauer 1213), f. 33b, C, rubric: לתענית אסתר, short.
9255. Padova - Biblioteca del Seminario Vescovile Cod. 218, f. 250a-250b, M.
9256. Vatican - Bibliotcca Apostolica cbr. 422/1, f. 44b, CG, no incipit.

Ashkenaz, commentary by Abraham b. Azriel[223]
9257. Vatican - Biblioteca Apostolica ebr. 301,1, f. 141a-141b, C.

אתה הארת יומם ולילה לפני מחני (א 8745), יוצר לפסח

Ashkenaz
9258. Berlin - Staatsbibliothek (Preussischer Kulturbesitz) Or. Qu. 798-799 (Steinschneider 177), II, f. 99b-101a, M.
9259. Braunschweig - Landesmuseum fuer Geschichte und Volkstum R 2386, vol. I, f. 58a-59b, M.
9260. Budapest - Magyar tudomanyos akademia, MS. Kaufmann A 384, f. 228a-229b, M.
9261. Cambridge - University Library Add. 394,1 (Reif SCR 461), f. 55a-55b, C, rubric: יוצר לשביעי של פסח.
9262. Muenchen - Bayerische Staatsbibliothek, Cod. hebr. 88, f. 92b-93b, G.

---

[222] Edited by Urbach, ערוגת הבושם, vol. III, p. 280.
[223] Edited by Urbach, ערוגת הבושם, vol. III, p. 306-307.

9263. Muenchen - Bayerische Staatsbibliothek, Cod. hebr. 393 , f. 134a, C, rubric: ליום שיני מהאחרוני׳, short.

9264. New York - Jewish Theological Seminary Ms. 4663, f. 5a-6a, FM, beginning missing.

9265. Paris - Bibliotheque Nationale heb. 709, f. 106b-107b, C, rubric: יוצר ליום אחרון.

9266. Parma - Biblioteca Palatina Cod. Parm. 1002 (Ta 24), f. 153a, 154a, M.

9267. Parma - Biblioteca Palatina Cod. Parm. 3507 (Perreau 27), f. 77b-78a, C.

Italia

9268. Parma - Biblioteca Palatin Cod. Parm. 2248 (de Rossi 149/2), f. 21b-23a, C, rubric: ביאור אתה היארת.

Roma

9269. New York - Jewish Theological Seminary Ms. 1639, f. 21b-23a, C, commentator: Salomo b. Samuel Rofe, rubric: ביאור אתה היארתה.

Tsarfat

9270. London - David Sofer 5, f. 39b-40b, C, rubric: זה פירוש מקרובוץ של יום שביעי של פסח, additional glosses.

9271. Moscow - Russian State Library, Ms. Guenzburg 1665, f. 87a-88a, M.

9272. Parma - Biblioteca Palatina Cod. Parm. 3136 (de Rossi 405), f. 107a-108a, M.

9273. Vatican - Biblioteca Apostolica ebr. 306, f. 216a-216b, C, rubric: יוצר לשביעי של פסח.

אתה הוא אלהינו בשמים ובארץ (א 8770), אלעזר ברבי קליר, חלק ד', קדושתא לראש השנה

Ashkenaz

9274. Berlin - Staatsbibliothek (Preussischer Kulturbesitz) Or. Qu. 798-799 (Steinschneider 177), I, f. 15b, M, rubric: אל נא.

9275. Moscow - Russian State Library, Ms. Guenzburg 191, f. 116a, M, short.

Tsarfat

9276. London - British Library Or. 8682, f. 19b, GI.

9277. Parma - Biblioteca Palatina Cod. Parm. 3006 (de Rossi 654,1), f. 25b-26a, M.

9278. Parma - Biblioteca Palatina Cod. Parm. 3006 (de Rossi 654,1), f. 138a, M, rubric: אל נא.

אתה הוא מקדם גר צדק הראשון, סליחה

Ashkenaz

9279. Oxford - Bodleian Library MS Opp. 681 (Neubauer 1213), f. 41b-42a, C.

אתה הנחלתה תורה לעמך (א 8788), אזהרות

Ashkenaz

9280. Berlin - Staatsbibliothek (Preussischer Kulturbesitz) Or. Qu. 798-799 (Steinschneider 177), II, f. 128a-135b, M.
9281. Braunschweig - Landesmuseum fuer Geschichte und Volkstum R 2386, vol. I, f. 86a-91a, M.
9282. Budapest - Magyar tudomanyos akademia, MS. Kaufmann A 400, p. 173-175, C, rubric: ואומרים אזהרות המומתות אזהרת דרבנן דמתיבתא.
9283. Hamburg - Staats- und Universitaetsbibliothek Cod. hebr. 17/2 (Steinschneider 152), f. 74b-75a, C, commentator: Ephraim b. Jacob of Bonn, rubric: זה פירשת של הרב׳ אפרים מבונא זצ״ל.
9284. Jerusalem - Schocken Institute 24100 / Mahzor Nuremberg, f. 164b-166a, 168a, M.
9285. London - British Library Add. 18695 (Margoliouth 683), f. 72b-77b, T, Yiddish, rubric: צו מוסף זגט מן דש דא צילט מן די תרי״ג מצות.
9286. London - British Library Add. 22431 (Margoliouth 662a), f. 33a-41a, M.
9287. Moscow - Russian State Library, Ms. Guenzburg 615, f. 36b-39b, C.
9288. New York - Jewish Theological Seminary Ms. 4466, f. 145a-152a, 153b, 154b, M.
9289. Oxford - Bodleian Library MS Opp. 170 (Neubauer 1205), f. 89a-93a, C, rubric: פירושי אזהרות.
9290. Paris - Bibliotheque Nationale heb. 709, f. 125a-132b, C.
9291. Parma - Biblioteca Palatina Cod. Parm. 1002 (Ta 24), f. 189b-192a, 193b-194a, M.
9292. Parma - Biblioteca Palatina Cod. Parm. 3205 (de Rossi 655), f. 121b-126b, C.
9293. Vatican - Biblioteca Apostolica ebr. 308, f. 151a, C, commentator: David b. Mose (compiler).
9294. Zurich - Zentralbibliothek Heid. 139, f. 51b-54a, C, additional marginal notes.

Tsarfat

9295. Oxford - Bodleian Library MS Laud. Or. 271 (Neubauer 1206), f. 88b-93b, C, commentator: Aaron b. Hayyim haKohen (compiler), rubric: אזהרות.

אתה הקדוש צור לבבי וחלקי, סליחה

Tsarfat

9296. Oxford - Bodleian Library MS Bodl. Or. 109 (Neubauer 1209), f. 81b-82b, C, commentator: Aaron b. Hayyim haKohen (compiler).

אתה חי וקיים שתה לכל עת וזמן (א 8799), אהרן בן יוסף הרופא, יוצר פרשת נח

Karaite, commentary by Berakha b. Josef haKohen

9297. New York - Jewish Theological Seminary Ms. 3367, f. 10a-12a, C.
9298. St. Petersburg - Inst. of Oriental Studies of the Russian Academy B 431, f. 11a-13a, C.

אתה חלקי וצור לבבי (א 8800), אליה ב"ר שמעיה, סליחה

Ashkenaz

9299. Cambridge - University Library Dd. 2.30, f. 66a-67a, G.
9300. Moscow - Russian State Library, Ms. Guenzburg 190, f. 41b-42b, G.
9301. Oxford - Bodleian Library MS Opp. 681 (Neubauer 1213), f. 67b-68b, C.
9302. Padova - Biblioteca del Seminario Vescovile Cod. 218, f. 139a-139b, M.
9303. Padova - Biblioteca del Seminario Vescovile Cod. 218, f. 139b-140a, M.

Tsarfat

9304. London - David Sofer 5, f. 101b, C.
9305. Parma - Biblioteca Palatina Cod. Parm. 1794 (de Rossi 1061), f. 36b-37b, M.
9306. Parma - Biblioteca Palatina Cod. Parm. 3006 (de Rossi 654,1), f. 115a-116a, M.
9307. Vatican - Biblioteca Apostolica ebr. 306, f. 97a-97b, C.

אתה כוננת לזרע אמוניך (א 8813), אהרן בן יוסף הרופא, פרשת משפטים

Karaite, commentary by Berakha b. Josef haKohen

9308. New York - Jewish Theological Seminary Ms. 3367, f. 76b-80a, C, rubric: פירוש פרשת המשפטים.
9309. St. Petersburg - Inst. of Oriental Studies of the Russian Academy B 431, f. 55a-57b, C, rubric: פרשת משפטים.
9310. St. Petersburg - Russian National Library, Evr. IV 50, f. 56a-58b, C, rubric: משפטים.

אתה כוננת משרים ועתרת יום פקודתך (א 8814), יהודה הלוי, רשות, קדושתא ליום א' של ראש השנה

Carpentras, commentary by Eliyahu Carmi

9311. New York - Jewish Theological Seminary Ms. 3151, f. 45b-46a, M.

Carpentras, commentary by Josef b. Abraham of Montelitz

9312. Cincinnati - Hebrew Union College 357, f. 52a-52b, M.
9313. New York - Jewish Theological Seminary Ms. 4746, f. 10b-11a, M.
9314. Paris - Alliance Israelite Universelle H 422 A, f. 29b-30a, M.
9315. Paris - Ecole Rabbinique 31, f. 98a-98b, M.

אתה כוננת עולם ברוב חסד (א 8815), יוסי בן יוסי, סדר עבודה

Ashkenaz

9316. Jerusalem - Schocken Institute 24100 / Mahzor Nuremberg, f. 364a-371 (f. 364 and 371 missing), M.

9317. Moscow - Russian State Library, Ms. Guenzburg 191, f. 133a-139b, M.

9318. New York - Jewish Theological Seminary Ms. 8169 (Acc. 0016), f. 106b-113b, M.

Asti, Fossano, Moncalvo

9319. New Haven - Yale University, Beinecke Rare Book and MS Library, MS Heb. 52, f. 144b-149b, M, very ecclectic.

haAri

9320. New York - Columbia University X 893 J 558, f. 171a-176a, M, kabbalistic.

9321. New York - Columbia University X 893 J 558, f. 171a-175a, M, kabbalistic, second commentary on the margins.

Roma

9322. Jerusalem - Jewish National and University Library Ms Heb 8° 4153, f. 140b-141a, C, commentator: Daniel ben Salomo haRofe (compiler), rubric: בסדר עבורה, no incipit.

9323. Oxford - Bodleian Library MS Mich. 312,1 (Neubauer 2276,1), f. 8b-9a, C, rubric: בסדר עבורה, no incipit.

Romania

9324. Vatican - Biblioteca Apostolica ebr. 320, f. 329b-336a, M.

Sepharad, commentary by Yehoshua Raphael b. Israel Benvenisti (עבודה תמה)

9325. New York - Columbia University X 893 J 724, f. 5b-10b, M.

Tsarfat

9326. London - British Library Add. 11639 (Margoliouth 1056), f. 722b-732a, M, rubric: רהיטים.

9327. London - David Sofer 5, f. 156a-159b, C.

9328. Oxford - Bodleian Library MS Opp. 171 (Neubauer 1207), f. 139b-144b, C, rubric: ואתחיל פירוש זה.

9329. Parma - Biblioteca Palatina Cod. Parm. 1794 (de Rossi 1061), f. 192b-206b, M.

9330. Parma - Biblioteca Palatina Cod. Parm. 2890 (de Rossi 856), f. 88a-94b, 96a, M.

9331. Parma - Biblioteca Palatina Cod. Parm. 3006 (de Rossi 654,1), f. 192b-198a, M.[224]

9332. Vatican - Biblioteca Apostolica ebr. 306, f. 105b-111b, C, rubric: סדר עבודה.

---

[224] Edited by Adler in פרקי שירה, p. 9-45.

אתה כוננת עולם מראש יסדת תבל והכל פעלת (א 8816), סדר עבודה

North Africa

9333. Jerusalem - Yehoshua Yakobovitz 2, f. 1b-8b, M, rubric: פירוש סדר עבודה הנדפס בפנים דף׳ לא עב׳.

North Africa, commentary by David b. Josef Abudarham

9334. New York - Jewish Theological Seminary Ms. 5426, f. 31a-47a, C, rubric: פירוש סדר עבודת יוה״כ מרהב בעל חמדת ימים עה״ו בע״ד.

Sepharad

9335. Jerusalem - Benayahu ז 25, f. 144b-168b, M.

9336. Jerusalem - Sassoon 1216, p. 36-151, M, commentator: Mose Nigrin, rubric: פירוש סדר עבודה.

9337. Jerusalem - Schocken Institute 70014, f. 76a-83a, M.

9338. London - Montefiore Library 50, f. 67a-82b, C, commentator: Josef b. Josef Ibn Naḥmiash, rubric: פירוש סדר עבודה לר׳ יוסף בן נחמיאש תלמיד הר׳ אשר זצ״ל, includes introduction.

Sepharad, commentary by David b. Josef Abudarham[225]

9339. Budapest - Magyar tudomanyos akademia, MS. Kaufmann A 405/2, p. 216-236, C, rubric: סדר עבודה לר׳ יוסף כהן גדול בן יוסי כהן גדול ז״ל.

9340. Cincinnati - Hebrew Union College 490, f. 7b-13b, C, includes introduction.

9341. Holon - Yehuda Nahum 278, f. 10a-12b, 14a-15b, 18a-18b, FC, only parts.

9342. New York - Columbia X893 Ab 93, f. 15b-24a, C, rubric: פי׳ סדר עבודה, includes introduction.

9343. New York - Jewish Theological Seminary Ms. 3011, f. 11a-19a, C, includes introduction.

Sepharad, commentary by Yehoshua Raphael b. Israel Benvenisti (עבודה תמה)

9344. Jerusalem - Benayahu ע 41, f. 5b-68b, M, includes introduction.

Yemen

9345. New York - Jewish Theological Seminary Ms. 9325, f. 46b-48b, G.

אתה לבדך יוצר כל הוא (א 8817), שיר היחוד ליום ו׳

Ashkenaz

9346. Braunschweig - Landesmuseum fuer Geschichte und Volkstum R 2386, vol. II, f. 175a-176a, M, no incipit.

9347. Frankfurt a M - Stadt- und Universitaetsbibliothek Oct. 121/1 (Merzbacher 105), f. 24a-25b, C, rubric: יום ו׳, additional marginal glosses.

9348. Moscow - Russian State Library, Ms. Guenzburg 1401/2, f. 11b-12a, C, beginning missing, pagination faulty.

---

[225] Edited by Prins, תשלום אבודרהם, p. 37-67.

9349. Vatican - Biblioteca Apostolica ebr. 274, f. 182b-184b, C, kabbalistic, no incipit.

אתה מבין סרעפי לב (א 8819), למוסף יום כפור

Ashkenaz
9350. New York - Jewish Theological Seminary Ms. 8097, f. 77a-77b, C.
9351. Vatican - Biblioteca Apostolica ebr. 422/1, f. 17b, C, rubric: סליחות.
Tsarfat
9352. Oxford - Bodleian Library MS Bodl. Or. 109 (Neubauer 1209), f. 28b-29a, C, commentator: Aaron b. Hayyim haKohen (compiler).

אתה מבין תעלומות (א 8820), אליה, סליחה

Ashkenaz
9353. Berlin - Staatsbibliothek (Preussischer Kulturbesitz) Or. Qu. 798-799 (Steinschneider 177), I, f. 63a-64a, M.
9354. Berlin - Staatsbibliothek (Preussischer Kulturbesitz) Or. Qu. 798-799 (Steinschneider 177), I, f. 108b-109a, M.

אתה מלא רחמים (א 8821), זולת לשבת זכור

Ashkenaz
9355. Cambridge - University Library Add. 504,1, f. 11b, C, short.
9356. Muenchen - Bayerische Staatsbibliothek, Cod. hebr. 88, f. 23b, G.
9357. Muenchen - Bayerische Staatsbibliothek, Cod. hebr. 393, f. 89a-89b, C, no incipit.
9358. Parma - Biblioteca Palatina Cod. Parm. 1002 (Ta 24), f. 34a, M, very short.
9359. Parma - Biblioteca Palatina Cod. Parm. 3507 (Perreau 27), f. 12a, C, rubric: זולת, no incipit, short.

אתה מקדם אלהינו אדונינו (א 8824), גרשום ב"ר יהודה מאור הגולה, סליחה

Ashkenaz
9360. Braunschweig - Landesmuseum fuer Geschichte und Volkstum R 2386, vol. II, f. 48b-49a, M.
9361. Cambridge - University Library Dd. 2.30, 19a-20b, G.
9362. Oxford - Bodleian Library MS Mich. 543 (Neubauer 1212), f. 44b-45b, C, commentator: Isaac b. Jacob (compiler), rubric: סליחה.
9363. Padova - Biblioteca del Seminario Vescovile Cod. 218, f. 77b-79a, M.
Tsarfat
9364. London - David Sofer 5, f. 101a, C.
9365. Parma - Biblioteca Palatina Cod. Parm. 3007 (de Rossi 654,2), f. 83a-83b, M.

אתה נאמן ביתי אל תורא אני עזרתיך (א 8827), אהרן בן יוסף הרופא, פרשת בוא אל פרעה

Karaite, commentary by Berakha b. Josef haKohen
9366. New York - Jewish Theological Seminary Ms. 3367, f. 68b-71a, C, rubric: פרוש פרשת בא אל פרעה.
9367. St. Petersburg - Inst. of Oriental Studies of the Russian Academy B 431, f. 50a-52a, C, rubric: בוא אל פרעה.
9368. St. Petersburg - Russian National Library, Evr. IV 50, f. 49a-51a, C, rubric: בוא אל פרעה.

אתה עדינה, זולת

Ashkenaz
9369. Budapest - Magyar tudomanyos akademia, MS. Kaufmann A 399, p. 448, C, rubric: זולת.

אתה צוית צדק עדותך (א 8839), יוסף ב"ר שמואל טוב עלם, חלק ד', קדושתא לפסח

Tsarfat
9370. Parma - Biblioteca Palatina Cod. Parm. 3136 (de Rossi 405), f. 90b-91a, M, incipit אל נא.

אתה קדוש ונורא עוז התאזרת (א 8845), אהרן בן יוסף הרופא, פרשת שמיני

Karaite, commentary by Berakha b. Josef haKohen
9371. New York - Jewish Theological Seminary Ms. 3367, f. 98b-100b, C, rubric: פרשת שמיני.
9372. St. Petersburg - Inst. of Oriental Studies of the Russian Academy B 431, f. 69a-70a, C, rubric: פרשת שמיני.
9373. St. Petersburg - Russian National Library, Evr. IV 50, f. 74a-75b, C, rubric: פ' שמיני.

אתה קדוש יושב תהלות בני איתן (א 8849), אהרן בן יוסף הרופא, פרשת ראה

Karaite, commentary by Berakha b. Josef haKohen
9374. New York - Jewish Theological Seminary Ms. 3367, f. 145b-147a, C, rubric: פרוש פרשת ראה.
9375. St. Petersburg - Inst. of Oriental Studies of the Russian Academy B 431, f. 98a-99a, C, rubric: פרשת ראה.
9376. St. Petersburg - Russian National Library, Evr. IV 50, f. 113b-115a, C, rubric: ראה.

אתה קדוש פועל גבורות (א 8852), אהרן בן יוסף הרופא, פרשת תולדות יצחק

Karaite, commentary by Berakha b. Josef haKohen
9377. New York - Jewish Theological Seminary Ms. 3367, f. 36b-40a, C, rubric: פרוש פרשת תולדות יצחק.

9378. St. Petersburg - Inst. of Oriental Studies of the Russian Academy B 431, f. 28a-30a, C, rubric: פרשת תולדות יצחק.
9379. St. Petersburg - Russian National Library, Evr. IV 50 , f. 27b-30a, C, rubric: פ' תולדות יצחק.

אתו מצות וחוקים (א 8866), אלעזר ברבי קליר, חלק ז', קדושתא לשבועות
Ashkenaz
9380. Berlin - Staatsbibliothek (Preussischer Kulturbesitz) Or. Qu. 798-799 (Steinschneider 177), II, f. 145a-148b, M.
9381. Braunschweig - Landesmuseum fuer Geschichte und Volkstum R 2386, vol. I, f. 100b-103a, M.
9382. Hamburg - Staats- und Universitaetsbibliothek Cod. hebr. 17/2 (Steinschneider 152), f. 87b-88b, C.
9383. Jerusalem - Schocken Institute 24100 / Mahzor Nuremberg , f. 175b-176a, M.
9384. London - British Library Add. 18695 (Margoliouth 683) , f. 90a-94a, T, Yiddish.
9385. London - British Library Add. 22431 (Margoliouth 662a), f. 61b-67b, M.
9386. Muenchen - Bayerische Staatsbibliothek, Cod. hebr. 88, f. 143b-146b, G.
9387. New York - Jewish Theological Seminary Ms. 4466, f. 173a-175a, 177a, M, partly ecclectic.
9388. Paris - Bibliotheque Nationale heb. 709, f. 137a-139a, C.
9389. Parma - Biblioteca Palatina Cod. Parm. 1002 (Ta 24) , f. 209a, 210a, 211a, 212a, M, ecclectic.
9390. Parma - Biblioteca Palatina Cod. Parm. 2886 (de Rossi 585), f. 70b-78b, M, later hand, margins cut.
9391. Parma - Biblioteca Palatina Cod. Parm. 3002 (de Rossi 407), f. 179a-179b, M, leaf from printed Mahzor bound into Ms.
9392. Parma - Biblioteca Palatina Cod. Parm. 3205 (de Rossi 655), f. 128a-128b, C, rubric: סדר.
9393. Parma - Biblioteca Palatina Cod. Parm. 3507 (Perreau 27), f. 92a-95a, C, rubric: סדר.
9394. Zurich - Zentralbibliothek Heid. 139, f. 55a, C, additional marginal notes.
Tsarfat
9395. Oxford - Bodleian Library MS Laud. Or. 271 (Neubauer 1206), f. 87b-88b, C, commentator: Aaron b. Hayyim haKohen (compiler), rubric: סדר.

אתחנן אל אמך אדיר במרומים, סליחה

Yemen, commentary by Isaac b. Abraham Wanneh
9396. London - British Library Or. 11122, f. 223b, M, no incipit.

אתחנן בבקשה בדברי מורשה, סליחה

Yemen, commentary by Isaac b. Abraham Wanneh
9397. Chicago-Spertus College of Judaica D 2, 2, f. 245a-245b, M, no incipit.
9398. London - British Library Or. 11122, f. 223a, M, no incipit.

אתי מלבנון כלה (א 8891), בנימין ב"ר זרח, יוצר לשבת הגדול

Ashkenaz
9399. Berlin - Staatsbibliothek (Preussischer Kulturbesitz) Or. Qu. 798-799 (Steinschneider 177), II, f. 45a-46a, M.
9400. Erlangen - Universitaetsbibliothek 2601 (Roth 67), f. 56a, G.
9401. Hamburg - Staats- und Universitaetsbibliothek Cod. hebr. 17/2 (Steinschneider 152), f. 30b, C, commentator: Ephraim b. Jacob of Bonn, rubric: לשבת הגדול פי' ר' אפרי' מבונא זצ"ל.
9402. Jerusalem - Schocken Institute 24100 / Mahzor Nuremberg, f. 69b, M, short.
9403. London - British Library Add. 18695 (Margoliouth 683), f. 8b-9b, T, Yiddish, rubric: יוצר שבת הגדול.
9404. Muenchen - Bayerische Staatsbibliothek, Cod. hebr. 88, f. 47a-48a, G.
9405. Muenchen - Bayerische Staatsbibliothek, Cod. hebr. 393, f. 106b-107b, C, rubric: לשבת הגדול, no incipit.
9406. New York - Jewish Theological Seminary Ms. 4466, f. 29b-32b, M.
9407. Parma - Biblioteca Palatina Cod. Parm. 3205 (de Rossi 655), f. 45a, C, rubric: לשבת הגדול.
9408. Parma - Biblioteca Palatina Cod. Parm. 3507 (Perreau 27), f. 33a, C, rubric: יוצר שבת הגדול.
9409. Zurich - Zentralbibliothek Heid. 139, f. 12b-13a, C, additional marginal notes.

אתיו אמונים בפחד (א 8893), יהודה הלוי, סליחה

Yemen
9410. Jerusalem - Sassoon 264, f. 161b, M.
9411. New York - Jewish Theological Seminary Ms. 3052, f. 41a-42b, M, rubric: אל מלך.
9412. Ramat Gan - Universitat Bar Ilan 62, f. 40a, G, margins damaged.

Yemen, commentary by Isaac b. Abraham Wanneh
9413. Chicago-Spertus College of Judaica D 2, 2, f. 211a-211b, M, no incipit.
9414. Jerusalem - Benayahu ת 282, f. 125b-126a, M, rubric: אל מלך.

9415. Jerusalem - Makhon Ben Zvi 1156 (Tubi 155), f. 124b-125a, M, rubric: אל מלך.
9416. Jerusalem - Makhon Ben Zvi 1174 (Tubi 154), f. 107b-108a, M, rubric: אל מלך.
9417. Jerusalem - Michael Krupp 604, f. 158b-159a, M, rubric: אל מלך.
9418. Jerusalem - Musad haRav Kook 325, f. 157b, M.
9419. Jerusalem - Sassoon 1158, p. 184, M, rubric: סליחות סים׳ אבג״ד.
9420. Jerusalem - Sassoon 1174, p. 239-240, M, no incipit.
9421. London - British Library Or. 11122, f. 194b, M, rubric: אל מלך.
9422. Manchester - John Rylands University Library, Ms. Gaster 5, f. 182a, M.
9423. Muenchen - Bayerische Staatsbibliothek, Cod. hebr. 472, f. 171b-172a, M, rubric: אל מלך.
9424. New York - Jewish Theological Seminary Ms. 3013, f. 108b, M, rubric: אל מלך, very short.
9425. New York - Jewish Theological Seminary Ms. 3109, f. 118b-119a, M, rubric: אל מלך.
9426. New York - Jewish Theological Seminary Ms. 3294, f. 3a, C.
9427. New York - Public Library, Heb. Ms. 9, f. 116b-117a, M.
9428. Philadelphia - University of Pennsylvania HB 2, f. 120b, M, rubric: אל מלך.
9429. Strasbourg - Bibliotheque Nationale et Universitaire 3965 (Landauer 39), p. 329-330, M, rubric: אל מלך.

אתיית עת דודים כגעה (א 8904), אלעזר ברבי קליר, קדושתא לשבת החדש
Ashkenaz

9430. Berlin - Staatsbibliothek (Preussischer Kulturbesitz) Or. Qu. 798-799 (Steinschneider 177), II, f. 39b-40a, M.
9431. Budapest - Magyar tudomanyos akademia, MS. Kaufmann A 384, f. 89a, M.
9432. Hamburg - Staats- und Universitaetsbibliothek Cod. hebr. 17/2 (Steinschneider 152), f. 27b-28a, C, rubric: קדושתא.
9433. Jerusalem - Schocken Institute 24100 / Mahzor Nuremberg, f. 64b-65a, M.
9434. London - British Library Add. 18695 (Margoliouth 683), f. 2a-2b, T, Yiddish, rubric: קרובץ.
9435. Muenchen - Bayerische Staatsbibliothek, Cod. hebr. 88, f. 43a-43b, G.
9436. Muenchen - Bayerische Staatsbibliothek, Cod. hebr. 393, f. 103b, C, no incipit.
9437. New York - Jewish Theological Seminary Ms. 4466, f. 19a-19b, M.
9438. Oxford - Bodleian Library MS Opp. 170 (Neubauer 1205), f. 33a-33b, C, rubric: פרשת החודש.

9439. Paris - Bibliotheque Nationale heb. 709 , f. 39a-39b, C, rubric: קרובה לפרשת החודש.
9440. Parma - Biblioteca Palatina Cod. Parm. 1002 (Ta 24), f. 67a, M.
9441. Parma - Biblioteca Palatina Cod. Parm 3000 (de Rossi 378), f. 19b-20a, M.
9442. Parma - Biblioteca Palatina Cod. Parm. 3205 (de Rossi 655) , f. 37b-38a, C.
9443. Parma - Biblioteca Palatina Cod. Parm. 3507 (Perreau 27), f. 29b-30a, C.
9444. Vatican - Biblioteca Apostolica ebr. 305,1, f. 24b-25a, C, rubric: פרשת החודש.
9445. Zurich - Zentralbibliothek Heid. 139, f. 8b-9a, C, additional marginal notes.

Tsarfat

9446. London - British Library Add. 11639 (Margoliouth 1056), f. 276b, M.
9447. London - David Sofer 5, f. 29b-30b, C, rubric: זה פרש' של פירוש של פרשת החדש.
9448. Moscow - Russian State Library, Ms. Guenzburg 1665, f. 39a-39b, M.
9449. Oxford - Bodleian Library MS Laud. Or. 271 (Neubauer 1206), f. 45a-46b, C, commentator: Aaron b. Hayyim haKohen (compiler), rubric: אתחיל פרשת החדש קדושתא.
9450. Parma - Biblioteca Palatina Cod. Parm. 3136 (de Rossi 405) , f. 53a-53b, M.
9451. Vatican - Biblioteca Apostolica ebr. 306, f. 152b, C.

אתיתי לחננך בלב קרוע (א 8906), שמעון ב"ר יצחק, רשות, קדושתא לראש השנה

Ashkenaz

9452. Berlin - Staatsbibliothek (Preussischer Kulturbesitz) Or. Qu. 798-799 (Steinschneider 177), f. 34a-34b, M.
9453. Braunschweig - Landesmuseum fuer Geschichte und Volkstum R 2386, vol. II, f. 110a-110b, M.
9454. Darmstadt - Hessisches Landes- und Hochschulbibliothek Cod. Or. 15, f. 33a-33b, M.
9455. Hamburg - Staats- und Universitaetsbibliothek Cod. hebr. 17/2 (Steinschneider 152), f. 121b, C, rubric: תחילות והראת לתלה מאורות ליום שיני דרבינו שמעון זצ"ל . רשות.
9456. Hamburg - Staats- und Universitaetsbibliothek Cod. hebr. 40c (Steinschneider 111), f. 146a-146b, G.
9457. Hamburg - Staats- und Universitaetsbibliothek Cod. hebr. 132 (Steinschneider 155), f. 23b, C.
9458. Jerusalem - Jewish National and University Library Ms Heb 8° 3037, f. 51a, M, short.

9459. Jerusalem - Schocken Institute 24100 / Mahzor Nuremberg , f. 340b-341a, M.
9460. London - British Library Or. 11318/1, f. 39a-39b, C.
9461. London - Montefiore Library 261 , f. 27a-27b, C, commentator: Eliezer b. Natan?.
9462. Moscow - Russian State Library, Ms. Guenzburg 191, f. 33b-34a, M.
9463. Moscow - Russian State Library, Ms. Guenzburg 615, f. 86a, C, short.
9464. Muenchen - Bayerische Staatsbibliothek, Cod. hebr. 86, f. 60b-61a, G.
9465. Muenchen - Bayerische Staatsbibliothek, Cod. hebr. 346, f. 35b, C, no incipit.
9466. New York - Jewish Theological Seminary Ms. 4466, f. 249a, M, short.
9467. New York - Jewish Theological Seminary Ms. 8097, f. 65a, C, short.
9468. New York - Jewish Theological Seminary Ms. 8169 (Acc. 0016), f. 32b, M.
9469. Oxford - Bodleian Library MS Mich. 365 (Neubauer 1208), f. 49b, C.
9470. Oxford - Bodleian Library MS Opp. 170 (Neubauer 1205), f. 143b, C, very short.
9471. Oxford - Bodleian Library MS Opp. 172 (Neubauer 1211), f. 20a-20b, C.
9472. Oxford - Bodleian Library MS Opp. 619 (Neubauer 2374), f. 57a-57b, M, short.
9473. Oxford - Bodleian Library MS Opp. 675 (Neubauer 1210), f. 49a-49b, C, no incipit.
9474. Parma - Biblioteca Palatina Cod. Parm. 3205 (de Rossi 655), f. 217a, C, short.
9475. Parma - Biblioteca Palatina Cod. Parm. 3507 (Perreau 27), f. 131b, C, rubric: רשות.
9476. Vatican - Biblioteca Apostolica ebr. 308, f. 74a-74b, C, commentator: David b. Mose (compiler).
9477. Vatican - Biblioteca Apostolica ebr. 422/1, f. 12b, C, very short.
9478. Zurich - Zentralbibliothek Heid. 139, f. 70b, C, short, additional marginal notes.

Asti, Fossano, Moncalvo
9479. New Haven - Yale University, Beinecke Rare Book and MS Library, MS Heb. 52, f. 52a, M.

Romania
9480. Vatican - Biblioteca Apostolica ebr. 320, f. 179a-179b, M.

Tsarfat
9481. London - British Library Or. 8682, f. 35a-35b, Gl.
9482. London - David Sofer 5, f. 119b, C, rubric: רשות, short.

9483. Oxford - Bodleian Library MS Laud. Or. 271 (Neubauer 1206), f. 156b, C, commentator: Aaron b. Hayyim haKohen (compiler), rubric: אחל קדושתא.
9484. Oxford - Bodleian Library MS Opp. 171 (Neubauer 1207), f. 67a, C, rubric: א"ה קרובה שמעונית, short.
9485. Parma - Biblioteca Palatina Cod. Parm. 2125 (de Rossi 812), f. 29b, C, rubric: רשות ליוצר, short.
9486. Parma - Biblioteca Palatina Cod. Parm. 3006 (de Rossi 654,1), f. 68a, M.
9487. Vatican - Biblioteca Apostolica ebr. 306, f. 66a, C.

אתיתי מתחנן מבקר עד ערב (א 8908), משה אבן עזרא, חלק ג', קדושתא למנחה יום כפור

Carpentras
9488. Cincinnati - Hebrew Union College 392, f. 102a, M, no incipit.
Carpentras, commentary by Josef b. Abraham of Montelitz
9489. New York - Jewish Theological Seminary Ms. 4197, f. 236b, M, no incipit.
9490. Paris - Ecole Rabbinique 32, f. 243b-244a, M, no incipit.
9491. Strasbourg - Bibliotheque Nationale et Universitaire 4081, f. 216a-216b, M, no incipit.

אתן לפועלי צדק (א 8942), שמעון ב"ר יצחק, חלק ו', קדושתא לראש השנה

Ashkenaz
9492. Berlin - Staatsbibliothek (Preussischer Kulturbesitz) Or. Qu. 798-799 (Steinschneider 177), I, f. 38b-39a, M.
9493. Bologna - Archivio di Stato MS Ebr. 353, f. 3-4, FC, only beginning.
9494. Braunschweig - Landesmuseum fuer Geschichte und Volkstum R 2386, vol. II, f. 112b, M.
9495. Cambridge - University Library Or. 785, f. 62b-63a, G.
9496. Darmstadt - Hessisches Landes- und Hochschulbibliothek Cod. Or. 15, f. 37a-37b, M.
9497. Hamburg - Staats- und Universitaetsbibliothek Cod. hebr. 225, f. 258a-259a, G.
9498. Jerusalem - Schocken Institute 24100 / Mahzor Nuremberg, f. 343a, M.
9499. London - British Library Or. 11318/1, f. 42a-42b, C.
9500. London - Montefiore Library 261, f. 29a, C, commentator: Eliezer b. Natan?.
9501. Moscow - Russian State Library, Ms. Guenzburg 191, f. 39b-40a, M.
9502. Muenchen - Bayerische Staatsbibliothek, Cod. hebr. 21, f. 180a, M.
9503. Muenchen - Bayerische Staatsbibliothek, Cod. hebr. 86, f. 68b-69b, G.

9504. Muenchen - Bayerische Staatsbibliothek, Cod. hebr. 346, f. 36a-36b, C.
9505. New York - Jewish Theological Seminary Ms. 4466, f. 254b-255a, M.
9506. New York - Jewish Theological Seminary Ms. 8169 (Acc. 0016), 38b, M.
9507. Oxford - Bodleian Library MS Mich. 365 (Neubauer 1208), f. 50b-51a, C, rubric: פזמון.
9508. Oxford - Bodleian Library MS Opp. 172 (Neubauer 1211), f. 22b-23a, C.
9509. Oxford - Bodleian Library MS Opp. 619 (Neubauer 2374), f. 62a-63a, M.
9510. Oxford - Bodleian Library MS Opp. 675 (Neubauer 1210), f. 52a-52b, C, no incipit.
9511. Paris - Bibliotheque Nationale heb. 653, f. 30b-31a, G.
9512. Parma - Biblioteca Palatina Cod. Parm. 3205 (de Rossi 655), f. 217b, C.
9513. Parma - Biblioteca Palatina Cod. Parm. 3270 (de Rossi 1215), f. 57b, M.
9514. Parma - Biblioteca Palatina Cod. Parm. 3507 (Perreau 27), f. 133a, C.
9515. Vatican - Biblioteca Apostolica ebr. 308, f. 77b, C, commentator: David b. Mose (compiler).
9516. Vatican - Biblioteca Apostolica ebr. 422/1, f. 13a, C.
9517. Zurich - Zentralbibliothek Heid. 139, f. 71a, C, no incipit, short, additional marginal notes.

Asti, Fossano, Moncalvo
9518. New Haven - Yale University, Beinecke Rare Book and MS Library, MS Heb. 52, f. 55b, M.

Tsarfat
9519. London - British Library Or. 8682, f. 38b-39a, GI.
9520. London - David Sofer 5, f. 121a, C.
9521. Oxford - Bodleian Library MS Laud. Or. 271 (Neubauer 1206), f. 157b, C, commentator: Aaron b. Hayyim haKohen (compiler), rubric: ישפוט, no incipit.
9522. Parma - Biblioteca Palatina Cod. Parm. 3006 (de Rossi 654,1), f. 72b-73a, M.

אתן תהלה לאל המהולל (8958 א), רשות לסדר עבודה

Ashkenaz
9523. Moscow - Russian State Library, Ms. Guenzburg 191, f. 131b-133a, M.
9524. New York - Jewish Theological Seminary Ms. 8169 (Acc. 0016), f. 105b-106a, M.
9525. Oxford - Bodleian Library MS Can. Or. 82 (Neubauer 1148), f. 16a-16b, M.

9526. Parma - Biblioteca Palatina Cod. Parm. 3205 (de Rossi 655), f. 140a-141a, C, rubric: זולת לוישע.

Asti, Fossano, Moncalvo

9527. New Haven - Yale University, Beinecke Rare Book and MS Library, MS Heb. 52, f. 143b, M.

Tsarfat

9528. London - British Library Or. 8682, f. 90a-90b, GI.
9529. London - David Sofer 5, f. 155a-156a, C.
9530. Parma - Biblioteca Palatina Cod. Parm. 1794 (de Rossi 1061), f. 189b-192a, M.
9531. Parma - Biblioteca Palatina Cod. Parm. 2890 (de Rossi 856), f. 86b-87b, M.
9532. Parma - Biblioteca Palatina Cod. Parm. 3006 (de Rossi 654,1), f. 192a-192b, M.

אתנה צדקות (א 8964), אהרן, מעריב לפסח

Romania

9533. Vatican - Biblioteca Apostolica ebr. 285/30, f. 231a-231b, C, rubric: מעריב אחר לליל שני, very short.

Tsarfat

9534. London - British Library Or. 2735 (Margoliouth 663), f. 101a-102a, M.

אתנו מתודים שעריך נקדים חשכינו בשרינו מחילה, סליחה

Yemen, commentary by Isaac b. Abraham Wannch

9535. Chicago-Spertus College of Judaica D 2, 2, f. 243b, M, no incipit.
9536. London - British Library Or. 11122, f. 221b, M, no incipit.

אתני שבחיה דחי עלמא דהוא הוה והוי והוא עתיד למהוה (א 8967), לחתן

Ashkenaz

9537. Budapest - Magyar tudomanyos akademia, MS. Kaufmann A 399, p. 378-379, C.
9538. Frankfurt a M - Stadt- und Universitaetsbibliothek Oct. 227, f. 150b-151a, M.
9539. Muenchen - Bayerische Staatsbibliothek, Cod. hebr. 393,9, f. 188a-188b, C, no incipit.
9540. Oxford - Bodleian Library MS Can. Or. 82 (Neubauer 1148), f. 53b-54a, M.
9541. Parma - Biblioteca Palatina Cod. Parm. 2895, p. 459-460, M, margins cut, text damaged.

אתפלל אתודה אתחנן ואקוה, סליחה

Yemen, commentary by Isaac b. Abraham Wanneh
9542. Chicago-Spertus College of Judaica D 2, 2, f. 246a, M, no incipit.
9543. Jerusalem - Sassoon 1158, p. 423, M, no incipit.
9544. London - British Library Or. 11122, f. 218b, M, no incipit.

אתפללה אל במקהלות, סליחה

Ashkenaz
9545. Vatican - Biblioteca Apostolica ebr. 308, f. 149a-149b, C, commentator: David b. Mose (compiler).

באנו ליחד שם האל היום בהלל ושבחה (ב 58), הושענא

Yemen
9546. Jerusalem - Benayahu ת 414, f. 90a, M, rubric: פ'.
Yemen, commentary Samḥun b. Salomo Ḥaloah
9547. Jerusalem - Makhon ben Zvi 2808, f. 168a-169a, C.

בארק במיקש אלחמא, ישראל

Yemen
9548. New York - M. Lehmann 274, f. 74a-74b, M, kabbalistic.

באשמורת הבוקר קראתיך אל מהלל (ב 70), יצחק גיאת, סליחה

Ashkenaz
9549. Moscow - Russian State Library, Ms. Guenzburg 190, f. 61b-62a, G.
9550. Oxford - Bodleian Library MS Mich. 543 (Neubauer 1212), f. 10a-10b, C, commentator: Isaac b. Jacob (compiler).
9551. Oxford - Bodleian Library MS Opp. 681 (Neubauer 1213), f. 81b-82a, C.
9552. Padova - Biblioteca del Seminario Vescovile Cod. 218, f. 143a-143b, M.
9553. Parma - Bibliotheca Palatina Cod. Parm. 3205 (de Rossi 655), f. 287a, C.
9554. Vatican - Biblioteca Apostolica ebr. 308/1, f. 11a, C, commentator: David b. Mose (compiler).
9555. Vatican - Biblioteca Apostolica ebr. 422/1, f. 31b, C.
9556. Vatican - Biblioteca Apostolica ebr. 422/1, f. 45b, CG, no incipit, short.
Ashkenaz, commentary by Abraham b. Azriel[226]
9557. Vatican - Biblioteca Apostolica ebr. 301,1, f. 139a, C, , rubric: אתחיל פזמונים, short.
9558. Vatican - Biblioteca Apostolica ebr. 301,1, f. 170b, C.

---

[226] Edited by Urbach, ערוגת הבושם, vol. III, p. 292, 498.

Tsarfat

9559. London - David Sofer 5, f. 92b-93a, C.
9560. Parma - Biblioteca Palatina Cod. Parm. 2890 (de Rossi 856), f. 50b-51a, M.
9561. Parma - Biblioteca Palatina Cod. Parm. 3007 (de Rossi 654,2), f. 115b-116a, M.
9562. Vatican - Biblioteca Apostolica ebr. 306, f. 206a-206b, C.

באשמורת הלילה קרית מועדינו, סליחה

Tsarfat

9563. Vatican - Biblioteca Apostolica ebr. 306, f. 207b-208a, C, short.

באתי לחלותך ברשיון עמותיך (ב 81), בנימין ב"ר שמואל, חלק ו', קדושתא למוסף ראש השנה

Ashkenaz

9564. New York - Jewish Theological Seminary Ms. 8169 (Acc. 0016), f. 46b-47a, M.

Tsarfat

9565. London - British Library Add. 11639 (Margoliouth 1056), f. 710b-711a, M, incipit הסכת, very short.
9566. London - British Library Or. 8682, f. 11a-11b, GI.
9567. London - David Sofer 5, f. 109b-110a, C, incipit הסכת.
9568. Parma - Biblioteca Palatina Cod. Parm. 3006 (de Rossi 654,1), f. 26b-27a, M, inicpit הסכת.
9569. Parma - Biblioteca Palatina Cod. Parm. 3006 (de Rossi 654,1), f. 72a-72b, M, incipit הסכת.

בבכי יונת אלם תתן קולה (ב 113), משה אבן עזרא, חלק ב', קדושתא לנעילה

Carpentras

9570. Cincinnati - Hebrew Union College 392, f. 115a, M, no incipit.

Carpentras, commentary by Josef b. Abraham of Montelitz

9571. New York - Jewish Theological Seminary Ms. 4197, f. 267a-267b, M, no incipit.
9572. Paris - Ecole Rabbinique 32, f. 275a, M, no incipit.
9573. Strasbourg - Bibliotheque Nationale et Universitaire 4081, f. 245b, M, no incipit.

בדעתו אביעה חידות (ב 162), אלעזר ברבי קליר, תעלת טל

Ashkenaz

9574. Berlin - Staatsbibliothek (Preussischer Kulturbesitz) Or. Qu. 798-799 (Steinschneider 177), II, f. 64a-64b, M.
9575. Braunschweig - Landesmuseum fuer Geschichte und Volkstum R 2386, vol. I, f. 23b-24a, M.

9576. Budapest - Magyar tudomanyos akademia, MS. Kaufmann A 384 , f. 138a, M.
9577. Budapest - Magyar tudomanyos akademia, MS. Kaufmann A 400 , p. 107-109, C.
9578. Budapest - Magyar tudomanyos akademia, MS. Kaufmann A 400 , p. 381, C.
9579. Erlangen - Universitaetsbibliothek 2601 (Roth 67), f. 75b-76a, M.
9580. Hamburg - Staats- und Universitaetsbibliothek Cod. hebr. 17/2 (Steinschneider 152), f. 55b-56a, C, rubric: הטל.
9581. Hamburg - Staats- und Universitaetsbibliothek Cod. hebr. 225, f. 68b, G.
9582. Jerusalem - Schocken Institute 24100 / Mahzor Nuremberg, f. 83a, M.
9583. London - British Library Add. 18695 (Margoliouth 683), f. 26a, T, Yiddish, rubric: מוסף, short.
9584. Moscow - Russian State Library, Ms. Guenzburg 615, f. 9a-9b, C, rubric: טל וגבורותיו אתוה ואותותיו.
9585. Muenchen - Bayerische Staatsbibliothek, Cod. hebr. 88, f. 61b, G.
9586. Muenchen - Bayerische Staatsbibliothek, Cod. hebr. 393 , f. 126a, C, rubric: למוסף.
9587. New York - Jewish Theological Seminary Ms. 4466, f. 57a-57b, M.
9588. New York - M. Lehmann Fr. 9.5, FC.
9589. Oxford - Bodleian Library MS Opp. 170 (Neubauer 1205), f. 61a-62a, C, rubric: בגלל אבות תושיע אתוה את הטל.
9590. Paris - Bibliotheque Nationale heb. 709, f. 75a-76a, C, rubric: עזרת הטל למוסף.
9591. Parma - Biblioteca Palatina Cod. Parm. 1002 (Ta 24), f. 97a-97b, M.
9592. Parma - Biblioteca Palatina Cod. Parm 3000 (de Rossi 378), f. 57a-58b, M, beginning missing.
9593. Parma - Biblioteca Palatina Cod. Parm. 3205 (de Rossi 655) , f. 83b-84a, C.
9594. Parma - Biblioteca Palatina Cod. Parm. 3507 (Perreau 27), f. 50a-50b, C.
9595. Zurich - Zentralbibliothek Heid. 139 , f. 28b-29a, C, additional marginal notes.

Romania, commentary by Shabbetai b. Yeshayahu haKohen Bilbo
9596. Cambridge - University Library Add. 377,3, f. 55b, C, rubric: פי' מוסף של פסח, introductory poem.

Tsarfat
9597. London - British Library Add. 11639 (Margoliouth 1056), f. 656a-657a, M, rubric: וזה הוא הטל.
9598. Moscow - Russian State Library, Ms. Guenzburg 1665, f. 61a, M.
9599. Oxford - Bodleian Library MS Laud. Or. 271 (Neubauer 1206), f. 64a-64b, C, commentator: Aaron b. Hayyim haKohen (compiler).

9600. Parma - Biblioteca Palatina Cod. Parm. 3136 (de Rossi 405), f. 83b, M.
9601. Vatican - Biblioteca Apostolica ebr. 306, f. 141a, C, rubric: טל.

בדרך מצותך נרוצה אחרי, לחברה קדישה
Ashkenaz, commentary by Alexander Sander Faber
9602. New York - Jewish Theological Seminary Rab. 1853, f. 90b-91a, M.

בהנחל עליון גוים בהפרידו בני אדם [אתה הצבת גבולת עמים] (א 8790), אהרן בן יוסף הרופא, פרשת היחי יעקב
Karaite, commentary by Berakha b. Josef haKohen
9603. New York - Jewish Theological Seminary Ms. 3367, f. 59b-62b, C, rubric: פרוש פרש' ויחי יעקב.
9604. St. Petersburg - Inst. of Oriental Studies of the Russian Academy B 431, f. 41b-43b, C, rubric: פרשת ויחי יעקב, postscript מכאן חסר סוף הספר. וכן בראש הספר
9605. St. Petersburg - Russian National Library, Evr. IV 50, f. 43a-45b, C, rubric: ויחי יעקב.

בוירק ילמע ונבה אצואת אלחמאים, שלם שבזי
Yemen
9606. Cincinnati - Hebrew Union College 398, f. 76a-77b, M.

בוקר וערב שם אל להודות נעים (ב 265), אברהם אבן עזרא, חלק ב', קדושתא למנחה יום כפור
Carpentras, commentary by Mordekhai b. Josef of Rocco Martino
9607. Cincinnati - Hebrew Union College 246/1, f. 73b, C, rubric: פי' קינה בורא עד אנא.
Sepharad, commentary by David b. Josef Abudarham[226]
9608. New York - Columbia X893 Ab 93, f. 31a, C, rubric: מחיה.

בורא עד אנה יונתך במצודה (ב 275), בנימין, סליחה
Sepharad, commentary by David b. Josef Abudarham
9609. Budapest - Magyar tudomanyos akademia, MS. Kaufmann A 405/2, p. 253, C, rubric: מחיה.

בורא עולם במדת רחמים בחר בעמו להודיעם גדלו, סליחה
Yemen, commentary by Isaac b. Abraham Wanneh
9610. Chicago-Spertus College of Judaica D 2, 2, f. 233b-234b, M, no incipit.

---

[226] Edited by Prins, תשלום אבודרהם, p. 156-157.

9611. Jerusalem - Makhon Ben Zvi 1156 (Tubi 155), f. 135b, M, no incipit.

בזאת הנשקפה יביט מירוי עליות

Tsarfat
9612. Vatican - Biblioteca Apostolica ebr. 306, f. 58a-58b, C.

בזכות אהרון רון ירון עמך בואמרם הושענא (ב 291), הושענא

haAri, commentary by Mose b. Hayyim Pesante
9613. New York - Jewish Theological Seminary Ms. 4696, f. 22b, C, rubric: הקפה ששית.

Italia, commentary by Zakharya David Shabbetai Segre
9614. Torino - Archivio Terracini 1499, p. 186, C, rubric: פירוש בזכות אהרן, short.

North Africa
9615. Jerusalem - Benayahu ז 27, f. 121a, M.

North Africa, commentary by Yehuda Toledano
9616. New York - Jewish Theological Seminary Ms. 4300, f. 47b-49a, C, rubric: הקפה חמישית אהרן.

Yemen
9617. New York - Jewish Theological Seminary Ms. 9325, f. 84b, M, very short.

Yemen, commentary by Isaac b. Abraham Wanneh
9618. Nahariya - Menahem and Saida Yaakob 284, f. 17a-17b, M.
9619. New York - Jewish Theological Seminary Ms. 3108, f. 84b, C, rubric: בהקפה חמישית.
9620. New York - Jewish Theological Seminary Ms. 4195, f. 26b, M.

Yemen, commentary by Samḥun b. Salomo Ḥaloah
9621. Jerusalem - Makhon ben Zvi 2808, f. 176a-177b, C.

בזכרי על משגבי (ב 296), יהודה בן בלעם, סליחה

Yemen
9622. Jerusalem - Sassoon 902, p. 431, M, very short.
9623. New York - Jewish Theological Seminary Ms. 3052, f. 39b-40b, M, rubric: אל מלך.

Yemen, commentary by Isaac b. Abraham Wanneh
9624. Chicago-Spertus College of Judaica D 2, 2, f. 211a, M, no incipit.
9625. Jerusalem - Benayahu ת 261, f. 142b, M, rubric: אל מלך.
9626. Jerusalem - Benayahu ת 282, f. 125a-125b, M, rubric: אל מלך.
9627. Jerusalem - Makhon Ben Zvi 1156 (Tubi 155), f. 124a-124b, M, rubric: אל מלך.
9628. Jerusalem - Makhon Ben Zvi 1174 (Tubi 154), f. 130a, M.
9629. Jerusalem - Musad haRav Kook 325, f. 187b, M.
9630. Jerusalem - Sassoon 1174, p. 239, M, no incipit.

9631. London - British Library Or. 11122, f. 182a, M, no incipit.
9632. Manchester - John Rylands University Library, Ms. Gaster 5, f. 211a-211b, M.
9633. Muenchen - Bayerische Staatsbibliothek, Cod. hebr. 472, f. 170b-171a, M, rubric: אל מלך.
9634. New York - Jewish Theological Seminary Ms. 3013, f. 127a, M, rubric: אל מלך.
9635. New York - Jewish Theological Seminary Ms. 3109, f. 125b-126a, M, rubric: אל מלך.
9636. New York - Jewish Theological Seminary Ms. 3294, f. 14a, C.
9637. New York - Public Library, Heb. Ms. 9, f. 118a, M.
9638. Strasbourg - Bibliotheque Nationale et Universitaire 3965 (Landauer 39), p. 392, M, rubric: אל מלך.

בחדש העשירי (ב 316), שמואל בן יהודה בן נתנאל, קרובה לי' בטבת
Sepharad, commentary by Josef Garad
9639. Oxford - Bodleian Library Heb.e.10 (Neubauer 2746/1), f. 27a, C, rubric: עשרה בטבת, no incipit.

בחירי אל ראו כי יי נתן לכם השבת (ב 343), שלם שבזי
Yemen
9640. Cincinnati - Hebrew Union College 398, f. 82b-85b, M.

בחנת כל עבור בראש השנה
Roma
9641. Jerusalem - Jewish National and University Library Ms Heb 8° 4153, f. 138a, C, commentator: Daniel ben Salomo haRofe (compiler).

בטרם סערה על פני זרומים נשבה (ב 426), אלעזר ברבי קליר, חלק ב', קדושתא לשבת שובה
Tsarfat
9642. Oxford - Bodleian Library MS Opp. 171 (Neubauer 1207), f. 81a-81b, C.

ביום כפור אדונינו שוב מאשר, סליחה
Yemen, commentary by Isaac b. Abraham Wanneh
9643. Chicago-Spertus College of Judaica D 2, 2, f. 213b, M, no incipit.
9644. Jerusalem - Sassoon 1158, p. 365, M, rubric: ביום כפור סים' לוי.
9645. London - British Library Or. 11122, f. 182b-183a, M, no incipit.

ביום שבת אשבח לאל חי גואלי (ב 512), שלם שבזי
Yemen
9646. Cincinnati - Hebrew Union College 398, f. 75a-75b, M.

ביום שבת קדש השב עם סגולה אל המנוחה (ב 514), הושענא

haAri, commentary by Mose b. Hayyim Pesante
9647. New York - Jewish Theological Seminary Ms. 4696, f. 20b, C.

North Africa, commentary by Yehuda Toledano
9648. New York - Jewish Theological Seminary Ms. 4300, f. 38a, C.

Yemen
9649. Jerusalem - Sassoon 264, f. 97a-97b, M, no incipit.

Yemen, commentary by Isaac b. Abraham Wanneh
9650. Jerusalem - Benayahu ת 261, f. 85a, M, rubric: פירוש.
9651. Jerusalem - Benayahu ת 282, f. 78b, M.
9652. Jerusalem - Makhon Ben Zvi 1156 (Tubi 155), f. 77b, M, no incipit.
9653. Jerusalem - Makhon Ben Zvi 1174 (Tubi 154), f. 87b, M, no incipit.
9654. Jerusalem - Michael Krupp 604, f. 96a, M.
9655. Jerusalem - Musad haRav Kook 325, f. 111b, M, rubric: 'פי.
9656. Jerusalem - Musad haRav Kook 325, f. 127b, M, rubric: 'פרוש.
9657. Jerusalem - Sassoon 1158, p. 219, M, no incipit, starts חוזך.
9658. Jerusalem - Sassoon 1174, p. 148, M, rubric: פירוש, no incipit.
9659. London - British Library Or. 11122, f. 124b, M.
9660. Muenchen - Bayerische Staatsbibliothek, Cod. hebr. 472, f. 102b, M, no incipit.
9661. New York - Jewish Theological Seminary Ms. 3193, f. 169a-169b, M, no incipit.
9662. New York - Jewish Theological Seminary Ms. 3295, f. 94b, M, no incipit.
9663. Strasbourg - Bibliotheque Nationale et Universitaire 3965 (Landauer 39), p. 248, M, no incipit.

Yemen, commentary by Samḥun b. Salomo Ḥaloah
9664. Jerusalem - Makhon ben Zvi 2808, f. 163a-164a, C, repetition of commentary on f. 164a crossed out.

בין כסא לעשור (ב 535), אליעזר ב"ר שמואל, סליחה

Ashkenaz
9665. Vatican - Biblioteca Apostolica ebr. 308/1, f. 11b, C, commentator: David b. Mose (compiler).

בירח איתנים (ב 570), אלעזר ברבי קליר, חלק ה', קדושתא לשבת שובה

Tsarfat
9666. Oxford - Bodleian Library MS Opp. 171 (Neubauer 1207), f. 82a-82b, C, rubric: פזמון.

בך אגילה ואשמחה, אלעזר ברבי קליר, חלק ב', קדושתא ליום א' של סוכות
Ashkenaz
9667. Hamburg - Staats- und Universitaetsbibliothek Cod. hebr. 17/2 (Steinschneider 152), f. 164b, C.

בל תהי מצות סוכה בעיניך קלה (ב 674), אלעזר ברבי קליר, חלק ד', קדושתא ליום א' של סוכות
Ashkenaz
9668. Berlin - Staatsbibliothek (Preussischer Kulturbesitz) Or. Qu. 798-799 (Steinschneider 177), I, f. 192a, M.
9669. Braunschweig - Landesmuseum fuer Geschichte und Volkstum R 2386, vol. I, f. 135b, M, incipit אל.
9670. Budapest - Magyar tudomanyos akademia, MS. Kaufmann A 400, p. 377, C, incipit לבל.
9671. Fulda - Hessische Landesbibliothek A 3 II, f. 132b, C, commentator: Josef, incipit אל נא.
9672. Hamburg - Staats- und Universitaetsbibliothek Cod. hebr. 17/2 (Steinschneider 152), f. 163a, C.
9673. Hamburg - Staats- und Universitaetsbibliothek Cod. hebr. 62 (Steinschneider 154), f. 39b-40a, C, incipit אל נא.
9674. Hamburg - Staats- und Universitaetsbibliothek Cod. hebr. 132 (Steinschneider 155), f. 52b-53a, C, incipit כי.
9675. Jerusalem - Jewish National and University Library Ms Heb 8° 3037, f. 255a-255b, M, incipit אל.
9676. Jerusalem - Schocken Institute 24100 / Mahzor Nuremberg, f. 481b-482a, M.
9677. London - British Library Add. 18695 (Margoliouth 683), f. 118a-118b, T, Yiddish.
9678. London - British Library Add. 22431 (Margoliouth 662a), f. 92a, M.
9679. London - British Library Or. 11318/1, f. 135b-136a, C.
9680. London - Montefiore Library 261, f. 72a, C, commentator: Eliezer b. Natan?, incipit לבל.
9681. Moscow - Russian State Library, Ms. Guenzburg 615, f. 122b-113a, C, incipit אל נא.
9682. New York - Jewish Theological Seminary Ms. 4466, f. 447b, M, incipit כי כל.
9683. New York - Jewish Theological Seminary Ms. 4826, f. 3a-3b, FM, incipit אל נא, margins damaged.
9684. Oxford - Bodleian Library MS Mich. 365 (Neubauer 1208), f. 103b-104a, C, incipit אל נא.
9685. Oxford - Bodleian Library MS Opp. 170 (Neubauer 1205), f. 184b-185a, C, incipit אל נא.

9686. Parma - Biblioteca Palatina Cod. Parm. 3205 (de Rossi 655), f. 240b, C, incipit אל נא.
9687. Parma - Biblioteca Palatina Cod. Parm. 3507 (Perreau 27), f. 178b, C, no incipit.
9688. Vatican - Biblioteca Apostolica ebr. 305,1, f. 42a, C, no incipit.
9689. Vatican - Biblioteca Apostolica ebr. 422/1, f. 20b, C, incipit אל נא.
9690. Zurich - Zentralbibliothek Heid. 139, f. 91a, C, no incipit, additional marginal notes.

Romania
9691. London - London School of Jewish Studies. Asher I.Myers collection 9, f. 220a-220b, M, incipit לבל.
9692. Vatican - Biblioteca Apostolica ebr. 320, f. 432a, M.

Tsarfat
9693. London - David Sofer 5, f. 179a-179b, C, incipit אל נא.
9694. Moscow - Russian State Library, Ms. Guenzburg 1665, f. 163b, M, incipit אל נא.
9695. Oxford - Bodleian Library MS Laud. Or. 271 (Neubauer 1206), f. 96a, C, commentator: Aaron b. Hayyim haKohen (compiler), no incipit.
9696. Oxford - Bodleian Library MS Opp. 171 (Neubauer 1207), f. 146a-146b, C, rubric: אל נא.
9697. Parma - Biblioteca Palatina Cod. Parm. 1264, f. 56a, M.

בלבב בר מאד נשבר (ב 689), משה אבן עזרא, סליחה

Carpentras, commentary by Josef b. Abraham of Montelitz
9698. Cincinnati - Hebrew Union College 291, f. 9a-9b, C, rubric: פירוש סליחה בלבב בר וכו׳.
9699. New York - Jewish Theological Seminary Ms. 4197, f. 34b, M.
9700. New York - Jewish Theological Seminary Ms. 4197, f. 183b-184a, M.
9701. Paris - Ecole Rabbinique 32, f. 40a-40b, M.
9702. Strasbourg - Bibliotheque Nationale et Universitaire 4081, f. 34a, M.

בליל זה בראש השנה (ב 730), סליחה

Yemen
9703. Jerusalem - Musad haRav Kook 334, f. 132b, M, page damaged, short.
9704. New York - Jewish Theological Seminary Ms. 3028, f. 34b, G.
9705. New York - Jewish Theological Seminary Ms. 4488, f. 106b, G.

Yemen, commentary by Isaac b. Abraham Wanneh
9706. Chicago-Spertus College of Judaica D 2, 2, f. 205a, M, no incipit.
9707. Jerusalem - Benayahu ת 261, f. 142b-143a, M, rubric: אל מלך.
9708. Jerusalem - Benayahu ת 282, f. 125b, M, rubric: אל מלך.

9709. Jerusalem - Makhon Ben Zvi 1156 (Tubi 155), f. 124b, M, rubric: אל מלך.
9710. Jerusalem - Makhon Ben Zvi 1174 (Tubi 154), f. 107a, M, short.
9711. Jerusalem - Michael Krupp 604, f. 158b, M, rubric: אל מלך, short.
9712. Jerusalem - Musad haRav Kook 325, f. 157a, M.
9713. Jerusalem - Musad haRav Kook 347, f. 76b, G.
9714. Jerusalem - Sassoon 1158, p. 185, M.
9715. Jerusalem - Sassoon 1174, p. 239, M, no incipit, short.
9716. London - British Library Or. 11122, f. 178a, M, short.
9717. New York - Jewish Theological Seminary Ms. 3294, f. 3a, C.
9718. New York - Public Library, Heb. Ms. 9, f. 116b, M, very short.
9719. Strasbourg - Bibliotheque Nationale et Universitaire 3965 (Landauer 39), p. 329, M, rubric: אל מלך, short.

בליל זה יבכיון ויילילו בני בליל זה חרב קדשי (ב 721), אלעזר ברבי קליר, קינה

Carpentras, commentary by Mordekhai b. Josef of Rocco Martino

9720. Cincinnati - Hebrew Union College 246/1, f. 64b-65a, C, rubric: 'פי קינה בליל זה.

Yemen, commentary by Isaac b. Abraham Wanneh

9721. Jerusalem - Sassoon 1158, p. 160, M.
9722. London - British Library Or. 11122, f. 97a, M.

בליל זה יבכיון ויילילו בני (ב 723), קינה

Ashkenaz

9723. Jerusalem - Schocken Institute 24100 / Mahzor Nuremberg, f. 193a, M.
9724. Muenchen - Bayerische Staatsbibliothek, Cod. hebr. 88, f. 162a, G.

Ashkenaz, commentary by Abraham b. Azriel[227]

9725. Vatican - Biblioteca Apostolica ebr. 301,1, f. 137b, C, rubric: אחרת.

בליל עשור להתכפר (ב 728), משה אבן עזרא, סליחה

Carpentras, commentary by Josef b. Abraham of Montelitz

9726. Paris - Ecole Rabbinique 32, f. 18a, M.
9727. Strasbourg - Bibliotheque Nationale et Universitaire 4081, f. 17a, M.

Tsarfat

9728. London - David Sofer 5, f. 133b-134a, C.
9729. Parma - Biblioteca Palatina Cod. Parm. 3006 (de Rossi 654,1), f. 114b, M.

---

[227] Edited by Urbach, ערוגת הבושם, vol. III, p. 282-283.

בלשון אשר הזכרת לזוכריך (ב 741), אלעזר ברבי קליר, חלק ד׳, קדושתא לשבת זכור

Ashkenaz

9730. Berlin - Staatsbibliothek (Preussischer Kulturbesitz) Or. Qu. 798-799 (Steinschneider 177), II, f. 21b-22a, M, incipit אל נא.

9731. Budapest - Magyar tudomanyos akademia, MS. Kaufmann A 384, f. 54b, M.

9732. Budapest - Magyar tudomanyos akademia, MS. Kaufmann A 400, p. 38-39, C, rubric: ואתה קדוש אל נא.

9733. Cambridge - University Library, Taylor Schechter Collection Misc. 33/3, f. 22a, G.

9734. Hamburg - Staats- und Universitaetsbibliothek Cod. hebr. 17/2 (Steinschneider 152), f. 18b, C.

9735. Jerusalem - Schocken Institute 24100 / Mahzor Nuremberg, f. 42a-42b, M.

9736. Muenchen - Bayerische Staatsbibliothek, Cod. hebr. 88, f. 24b-25a, G.

9737. Muenchen - Bayerische Staatsbibliothek, Cod. hebr. 393, f. 91a, C, incipit אל נא.

9738. Oxford - Bodleian Library MS Opp. 170 (Neubauer 1205), f. 11a-12a, C, rubric: אל נא.

9739. Paris - Bibliotheque Nationale heb. 709, f. 20b-21b, C, incipit אל נא.

9740. Parma - Biblioteca Palatina Cod. Parm. 1002 (Ta 24), f. 36b, M, incipit אל נא.

9741. Parma - Biblioteca Palatina Cod. Parm. 3205 (de Rossi 655), f. 20b-21a, C, incipit אל נא.

9742. Parma - Biblioteca Palatina Cod. Parm. 3507 (Perreau 27), f. 15a-15b, C, no incipit.

9743. Vatican - Biblioteca Apostolica ebr. 305,1, f. 13b-14a, C.

Tsarfat

9744. London - British Library Add. 11639 (Margoliouth 1056), f. 268b, M, incipit אל נא, short.

9745. London - David Sofer 5, f. 20b, C, incipit אל נא.

9746. Moscow - Russian State Library, Ms. Guenzburg 1665, f. 18b, M.

9747. Oxford - Bodleian Library MS Laud. Or. 271 (Neubauer 1206), f. 20b-21a, C, commentator: Aaron b. Hayyim haKohen (compiler), rubric: ואתה קדוש.

9748. Oxford - Bodleian Library MS Opp. 171 (Neubauer 1207), f. 16b-17a, C, rubric: אל נא, incipit לזוכריך.

9749. Parma - Biblioteca Palatina Cod. Parm. 3136 (de Rossi 405), f. 31b-32a, M, incipit אל נא.

9750. Vatican - Biblioteca Apostolica ebr. 306, f. 163a-163b, C, no incipit.

בלשון אשר הללוך על הים גברים (ב 742), יוסף ב"ר שמואל טוב עלם, חלק ד',
קדושתא לפסח

Tsarfat

9751. Parma - Biblioteca Palatina Cod. Parm. 3136 (de Rossi 405), f. 109b-110a, M.

במאי פומא נפתח במאי לישנא נשכח (ב 746), סליחה

Yemen, commentary by Isaac b. Abraham Wanneh

9752. London - British Library Or. 11122, f. 223b-224a, M, no incipit.

במה נחשב חדלו לכם, סליחה

Ashkenaz

9753. Fulda - Hessische Landesbibliothek A 3 II, f. 129a, C, commentator: Josef.

Tsarfat

9754. Oxford - Bodleian Library MS Laud. Or. 271 (Neubauer 1206), f. 118b, C, commentator: Aaron b. Hayyim haKohen (compiler), no incipit.

במוצאי מנוחה קדמנוך תחלה (ב 779), סליחה

Ashkenaz

9755. Braunschweig - Landesmuseum fuer Geschichte und Volkstum R 2386, vol. II, f. 42b, C.

9756. Oxford - Bodleian Library MS Mich. 543 (Neubauer 1212), f. 8a-8b, C, commentator: Isaac b. Jacob (compiler), rubric: בשם שוכן מעונים אתחיל כתו' פיזמונים.

9757. Oxford - Bodleian Library MS Opp. 681 (Neubauer 1213), f. 76a, C, rubric: פזמונים.

9758. Padova - Biblioteca del Seminario Vescovile Cod. 218, f. 46b, M.

9759. Parma - Bibliotheca Palatina Cod. Parm. 3205 (de Rossi 655), f. 287a, C, rubric: פזמון.

9760. Vatican - Biblioteca Apostolica ebr. 422/1, f. 31a-31b, C, short.

9761. Vatican - Biblioteca Apostolica ebr. 422/1, f. 45b, CG, rubric: אתחיל פזמונים בעז' דר מעוני', no incipit, very short.

Ashkenaz, commentary by Abraham b. Azriel[228]

9762. Vatican - Biblioteca Apostolica ebr. 301,1, f. 139a, C.

Romania

9763. Vatican - Biblioteca Apostolica ebr. 320, f. 388a, M.

Tsarfat

9764. London - David Sofer 5, f. 102b, C.

---

[228] Edited by Urbach, ערוגת הבושם, vol. III, p. 293-294.

9765. Parma - Biblioteca Palatina Cod. Parm. 3007 (de Rossi 654,2), f. 115a-115b, M.
9766. Vatican - Biblioteca Apostolica ebr. 306, f. 208a, C.

במוצאי שבת תפלות תצמיח בבן בנך בכורך (ב 780), בקשה
Carpentras, commentary by Josef b. Abraham of Montelitz
9767. Cincinnati - Hebrew Union College 291, f. 57a, C, rubric: פי' במוצאי שבת.
9768. New York - Jewish Theological Seminary Ms. 4197, f. 255a-255b, M.
9769. Paris - Ecole Rabbinique 32, f. 265a, M.
9770. Strasbourg - Bibliotheque Nationale et Universitaire 4081, f. 236a-236b, M.

במרומי ערץ כסא שבתך (ב 818), יוסף אבן אביתור, למוסף יום כפור
Sepharad
9771. Jerusalem - Benayahu ז 25, f. 137a-138a, M, begins ובכן נקדישך מלך.
9772. Jerusalem - Sassoon 1216, p. 26-27, M, commentator: Mose Nigrin.
Sepharad, commentary by David b. Josef Abudarham[229]
9773. Budapest - Magyar tudomanyos akademia, MS. Kaufmann A 405/2, p. 214, C, rubric: ובכן נקדישך מלך.
9774. Cincinnati - Hebrew Union College 490, f. 7a, C.
9775. Holon - Yehuda Nahum 278, f. 6a-6b, FC, rubric: קדושה.
9776. New York - Columbia X893 Ab 93, f. 14b, C, rubric: מגן למוסף ובכן נקדישך מלך.
9777. New York - Jewish Theological Seminary Ms. 3011, f. 10a-10b, C.

במתי מספר חילינו פניך (ב 833), משולם, סליחה
Ashkenaz
9778. Muenchen - Bayerische Staatsbibliothek, Cod. hebr. 88, f. 31a-32a, G.
9779. Oxford - Bodleian Library MS Opp. 681 (Neubauer 1213), f. 86a, C, rubric: פזמון לתענית אסתר.
9780. Padova - Biblioteca del Seminario Vescovile Cod. 218, f. 254a-254b, M.
Ashkenaz, commentary by Abraham b. Azriel[230]
9781. Vatican - Biblioteca Apostolica ebr. 301,1, f. 139b-140a, C, rubric: אחר לפורים.

בן אדם בן אדם מה לך נרדם (ב 848), סליחה
Sepharad
9782. Skokie - Hebrew Theological College 3, f. 4b, G.

---

[229] Edited by Prins, תשלום אבודרהם, p. 30.
[230] Edited by Urbach, ערוגת הבושם, vol. III, p. 297.

Yemen
9783. Jerusalem - Sassoon 902, p. 358, M.
9784. New York - Jewish Theological Seminary Ms. 3193, f. 115a, M.
Yemen, commentary by Isaac b. Abraham Wanneh
9785. Jerusalem - Makhon Ben Zvi 1174 (Tubi 154), f. 98a, M.
9786. Jerusalem - Sassoon 1158, p. 291, M.
9787. London - British Library Or. 11122, f. 152b, M.
9788. Manchester - John Rylands University Library, Ms. Gaster 5, f. 171b-172a, M.
9789. Philadelphia - University of Pennsylvania HB 2, f. 113a, M.

בני היכלא דכסיפין (ב 956), יצחק לוירא, זמר לשבת
haAri, commentary by Jacob b. Raphael haLevi
9790. Cincinnati - Hebrew Union College 275, f. 4a-4b, C, rubric: פי׳ מ׳י על הזמר בני היכלא לסעודה שלישית של שבת {ד׳ קיא}.

בני תמימים משכימים (ב 1029), משה אבן עזרא, סליחה
Carpentras
9791. Cincinnati - Hebrew Union College 392, f. 34b, M, no incipit.
Carpentras, commentary by Josef b. Abraham of Montelitz
9792. New York - Jewish Theological Seminary Ms. 4197, f. 84a-84b, M, no incipit.
9793. Paris - Ecole Rabbinique 32, f. 106b-107a, M, no incipit.
9794. Strasbourg - Bibliotheque Nationale et Universitaire 4081, f. 83b-84a, M, no incipit.

בנשף קדמתי ואל בית אל עליתי (ב 1074), משה אבן עזרא, סליחה
Carpentras, commentary by Josef b. Abraham of Montelitz
9795. Cincinnati - Hebrew Union College 291, f. 56b-57a, C, rubric: פי׳ סדר נעילה.
9796. New York - Jewish Theological Seminary Ms. 4197, f. 253b-254a, M.
9797. Paris - Ecole Rabbinique 32, f. 262a-262b, M.
9798. Strasbourg - Bibliotheque Nationale et Universitaire 4081, f. 233a-233b, M.
Tsarfat
9799. Parma - Biblioteca Palatina Cod. Parm. 3006 (de Rossi 654,1), f. 247b, M.
Yemen
9800. Jerusalem - Sassoon 902, p. 410, M, very short.
9801. New York - Jewish Theological Seminary Ms. 3052, f. 56a, M, rubric: אל מלך.
Yemen, commentary by Isaac b. Abraham Wanneh
9802. Chicago-Spertus College of Judaica D 2, 2, f. 230a, M, no incipit.

9803. Jerusalem - Benayahu ת 261, f. 158b, M, rubric: אל מלך, very short.
9804. Jerusalem - Benayahu ת 282, f. 130a, M, rubric: אל מלך, very short.
9805. Jerusalem - Makhon Ben Zvi 1156 (Tubi 155), f. 129a-129b, M, rubric: אל מלך.
9806. Jerusalem - Makhon Ben Zvi 1174 (Tubi 154), f. 129a, M, very short.
9807. Jerusalem - Michael Krupp 604, f. 85b-86a, M, rubric: אל מלך, short.
9808. Jerusalem - Musad haRav Kook 325, f. 186b, M, rubric: אל מלך, very short.
9809. Jerusalem - Musad haRav Kook 330, f. 116b, G.
9810. Jerusalem - Musad haRav Kook 347, f. 87b, G.
9811. Jerusalem - Sassoon 1158, p. 201, M, short.
9812. London - British Library Or. 11122, f. 206a-206b, M, short.
9813. Manchester - John Rylands University Library, Ms. Gaster 5, f. 211a, M.
9814. Muenchen - Bayerische Staatsbibliothek, Cod. hebr. 472, f. 179a, M, rubric: אל מלך, very short.
9815. New York - Jewish Theological Seminary Ms. 3013, f. 126a, M, rubric: אל מלך, very short.
9816. New York - Jewish Theological Seminary Ms. 3294, f. 13b, C.
9817. New York - Public Library, Heb. Ms. 9, f. 121b, M, very short.
9818. Strasbourg - Bibliotheque Nationale et Universitaire 3965 (Landauer 39), p. 389, M, rubric: אל מלך, very short.

בעוד אדני אפדני וכל צבא רום נטעו (ב 1099), יצחק השנירי, פיוט לראש השנה

Carpentras
9819. Cincinnati - Hebrew Union College 429/1, f. 26a-26b, M, no incipit.

Carpentras, commentary by Josef b. Abraham of Montelitz
9820. Cincinnati - Hebrew Union College 357, f. 105b-106b, M, rubric: פירוש, no incipit.
9821. New York - Jewish Theological Seminary Ms. 4746, f. 37a-38a, M, no incipit.
9822. Paris - Alliance Israelite Universelle H 422 A, f. 85b-86b, M, no incipit.
9823. Paris - Ecole Rabbinique 31, f. 144b-145b, M, no incipit.

בעוד שדי עמדי בעלנו דודי (ב 1103), בנימין בן פשדו, סליחה

Ashkenaz
9824. Budapest - Magyar tudomanyos akademia, MS. Kaufmann A 400, p. 523, C, rubric: אחרת מר' בנימן בר פסדו.
9825. Muenchen - Bayerische Staatsbibliothek, Cod. hebr. 346, f. 118b, C.
9826. Oxford - Bodleian Library MS Mich. 543 (Neubauer 1212), f. 80b, C, commentator: Isaac b. Jacob (compiler), rubric: מכניסי' דר' בנימן בר פשדו.

9827. Oxford - Bodleian Library MS Opp. 170 (Neubauer 1205), f. 238b-239a, C.
9828. Oxford - Bodleian Library MS Opp. 170 (Neubauer 1205), f. 245a-245b, C.
9829. Parma - Biblioteca Palatina Cod. Parm. 3205 (de Rossi 655), f. 285a-285b, C.

Tsarfat

9830. Oxford - Bodleian Library MS Opp. 171 (Neubauer 1207), f. 90a-90b, C, rubric: מחומסי דר' בנימין בר פשדו.
9831. Vatican - Biblioteca Apostolica ebr. 306, f. 212b-213a, C.

בעשור לחדש ביום בו כפור עוני קחו עמכם (ב 1154), חנניה, סליחה

Yemen

9832. Jerusalem - Benayahu ת 301, f. 55b, G.
9833. Jerusalem - Benayahu ת 414, f. 146b, M.
9834. Jerusalem - Sassoon 902, p. 434, M.
9835. New York - Jewish Theological Seminary Ms. 3028, f. 32a, G.
9836. New York - Jewish Theological Seminary Ms. 3052, f. 30a-30b, M, rubric: אל מלך.

Yemen, commentary by Isaac b. Abraham Wanneh

9837. Chicago-Spertus College of Judaica D 2, 2, f. 200b, M, very short, no incipit.
9838. Jerusalem - Benayahu ת 261, f. 139a, M, rubric: אל מלך, short.
9839. Jerusalem - Benayahu ת 282, f. 122b, M, rubric: אל מלך.
9840. Jerusalem - Makhon Ben Zvi 1156 (Tubi 155), f. 120b-121a, M, rubric: אל מלך, short.
9841. Jerusalem - Makhon Ben Zvi 1174 (Tubi 154), f. 125b-126a, M.
9842. Jerusalem - Michael Krupp 604, f. 153a, M, rubric: אל מלך.
9843. Jerusalem - Musad haRav Kook 325, f. 182b, M, rubric: אל מלך, short.
9844. Jerusalem - Musad haRav Kook 330, f. 105b, G.
9845. Jerusalem - Sassoon 1158, p. 360-361, M, no incipit.
9846. London - British Library Or. 11122, f. 179b, M.
9847. New York - Jewish Theological Seminary Ms. 3013, f. 122a, M, rubric: אל מלך, short.
9848. New York - Jewish Theological Seminary Ms. 3294, f. 10b, C.
9849. New York - Public Library, Heb. Ms. 9, f. 113a, M.
9850. Strasbourg - Bibliotheque Nationale et Universitaire 3965 (Landauer 39), p. 379, M, rubric: אל מלך, short.

בעשר מכות פתרוסים הפרכת (ב 1157), אלעזר ברבי קליר, סילוק, קדושתא לפסח

Ashkenaz

9851. Berlin - Staatsbibliothek (Preussischer Kulturbesitz) Or. Qu. 798-799 (Steinschneider 177), II, f. 80b-82a, M.

9852. Braunschweig - Landesmuseum fuer Geschichte und Volkstum R 2386, vol. I, f. 38a-38b, M, short.
9853. Budapest - Magyar tudomanyos akademia, MS. Kaufmann A 384, f. 165a-166b, M.
9854. Budapest - Magyar tudomanyos akademia, MS. Kaufmann A 400, p. 133-135, C, rubric: סילוק, incipit וארכה.
9855. Hamburg - Staats- und Universitaetsbibliothek Cod. hebr. 17/2 (Steinschneider 152), f. 65b-66a, C, rubric: סילוק, incipit וארכה.
9856. Jerusalem - Schocken Institute 24100 / Mahzor Nuremberg, f. 96a-96b, M.
9857. London - British Library Add. 18695 (Margoliouth 683), f. 43b-44b, T, Yiddish, rubric: סילוק.
9858. Moscow - Russian State Library, Ms. Guenzburg 615, f. 23b-24a, C.
9859. Muenchen - Bayerische Staatsbibliothek, Cod. hebr. 88, f. 74a-75a, G.
9860. New York - Jewish Theological Seminary Ms. 4466, f. 77a-78a, M.
9861. Paris - Bibliotheque Nationale heb. 709, f. 99b-100a, C.
9862. Parma - Biblioteca Palatina Cod. Parm. 1002 (Ta 24), f. 119b-120b, M.
9863. Parma - Biblioteca Palatina Cod. Parm. 3205 (de Rossi 655), f. 102b-103b, C.
9864. Parma - Biblioteca Palatina Cod. Parm. 3507 (Perreau 27), f. 66a, C, rubric: סילוק.
9865. Zurich - Zentralbibliothek Heid. 139, f. 38b-39a, C, additional marginal notes.

Tsarfat

9866. Oxford - Bodleian Library MS Laud. Or. 271 (Neubauer 1206), f. 73b-74a, C, commentator: Aaron b. Hayyim haKohen (compiler).
9867. Oxford - Bodleian Library MS Opp. 171 (Neubauer 1207), f. 41b-42a, C, rubric: סילוק, incipit וארכה.

בעת רצון תחנתי לך צורי ורנתי (ב 1207), משה, סליחה

Yemen

9868. Jerusalem - Benayahu ת 88, f. 113a, M.
9869. New York - Jewish Theological Seminary Ms. 3193, f. 116b, M.

Yemen, commentary by Isaac b. Abraham Wanneh

9870. Chicago-Spertus College of Judaica D 2, 2, f. 178b, M.

בפרש שדי דרכי (ב 1253), דוד בר גדליה, סליוק לשבועות

Ashkenaz

9871. New York - Jewish Theological Seminary Ms. 4466, f. 163a, M, short.
9872. Parma - Biblioteca Palatina Cod. Parm. 3205 (de Rossi 655), f. 127a, C, short, incipit וועדו.

בצורה עצורה חריבה, יצחק הנקדן

Ashkenaz
9873. Oxford - Bodleian Library MS Can. Or. 70 (Neubauer 1147,7), f. 87a-87b, M, rubric: אחרת.

בר יוחאי נמשחת אשריך (ב 1340), שמעון לוי

Yemen
9874. Nahariya - Menahem and Saida Yaakob 187, f. 19b, M.
9875. New York - Public Library, Jewish Items 2, f. 3b, M, rubric: פירוש.

ברוב לשוני כוננת אלהי ותבחר, תפלת גשם

Yemen
9876. Chicago-Spertus College of Judaica D 10, f. 147b, M, rubric: פירוש, short.

ברוח נשברה הסתופפתי במקדשך (ב 1398), בנימין ב"ר שמואל, חלק ג', קדושתא לפסח

Ashkenaz
9877. Moscow - Russian State Library, Ms. Guenzburg 191, f. 50a-50b, M.
9878. New York - Jewish Theological Seminary Ms. 8169 (Acc. 0016), f. 45b-46a, M.

Tsarfat
9879. London - British Library Or. 8682, f. 44a-44b, GI.
9880. London - David Sofer 5, f. 123b-124a, C.
9881. Oxford - Bodleian Library MS Opp. 171 (Neubauer 1207), f. 69a, C.
9882. Parma - Biblioteca Palatina Cod. Parm. 1794 (de Rossi 1061), f. 83b-84a, M.
9883. Parma - Biblioteca Palatina Cod. Parm. 2125 (de Rossi 812), f. 32a-33a, C.
9884. Parma - Biblioteca Palatina Cod. Parm. 3006 (de Rossi 654,1), f. 87a, M.
9885. Vatican - Biblioteca Apostolica ebr. 306, f. 70a-70b, C, no incipit.

ברוך אל אשר אין תכלה למהללו (ב 1413), אהרן בן יוסף הרופא, פרשת במדבר

Karaite, commentary by Berakha b. Josef haKohen
9886. New York - Jewish Theological Seminary Ms. 3367, f. 117a-119a, C, rubric: ספר במדבר. פרשת במדבר.
9887. St. Petersburg - Inst. of Oriental Studies of the Russian Academy B 431, f. 80b-82a, C, rubric: ספר במדבר. פרשת במדבר.
9888. St. Petersburg - Russian National Library, Evr. IV 50, f. 90a-91b, C, rubric: פ' במדבר.

ברוך אשר קידש ידיד מבטן

Ashkenaz
9889. Muenchen - Bayerische Staatsbibliothek, Cod. hebr. 393, f. 194a-194b, C.

ברוך שמם כבוד מלכותו, אופן

Ashkenaz
9890. Budapest - Magyar tudomanyos akademia, MS. Kaufmann A 400, p. 302-303, C.

ברח דודי אל מכון לשבתך (ב 1689), משולם ב"ר קלונימוס, גאולה ליום ב' של פסח

Ashkenaz
9891. Berlin - Staatsbibliothek (Preussischer Kulturbesitz) Or. Qu. 798-799 (Steinschneider 177), II, f. 78a, M.
9892. Budapest - Magyar tudomanyos akademia, MS. Kaufmann A 384, f. 161b, M.
9893. Hamburg - Staats- und Universitaetsbibliothek Cod. hebr. 17/2 (Steinschneider 152), f. 35a-35b, C.
9894. Jerusalem - Schocken Institute 24100 / Mahzor Nuremberg, f. 94a, M.
9895. London - British Library Add. 18695 (Margoliouth 683), f. 40b, T, Yiddish, rubric: אורט? . דש זגט דער חזן איער שמונה עשרה.
9896. Moscow - Russian State Library, Ms. Guenzburg 615, f. 22a, C, rubric: גאולה.
9897. Muenchen - Bayerische Staatsbibliothek, Cod. hebr. 88, f. 72a, G.
9898. Muenchen - Bayerische Staatsbibliothek, Cod. hebr. 393, f. 129a-129b, C, no incipit.
9899. New York - Jewish Theological Seminary Ms. 4466, f. 73a, M.
9900. Oxford - Bodleian Library MS Opp. 170 (Neubauer 1205), f. 75a, C.
9901. Paris - Bibliotheque Nationale heb. 709, f. 97b, C.
9902. Parma - Biblioteca Palatina Cod. Parm. 1002 (Ta 24), f. 117a, M.
9903. Parma - Biblioteca Palatina Cod. Parm. 3205 (de Rossi 655), f. 100b-101b, C.
9904. Parma - Biblioteca Palatina Cod. Parm. 3507 (Perreau 27), f. 64a-64b, C.
9905. Zurich - Zentralbibliothek Heid. 139, f. 37a, C, additional marginal notes.

Tsarfat
9906. Oxford - Bodleian Library MS Laud. Or. 271 (Neubauer 1206), f. 72b, C, commentator: Aaron b. Hayyim haKohen (compiler), very short.

ברח דודי אל שאנן נוה (ב 1692), שמעון ב"ר יצחק, גאולה ליום ז' של פסח

Ashkenaz

9907. Berlin - Staatsbibliothek (Preussischer Kulturbesitz) Or. Qu. 798-799 (Steinschneider 177), II, f. 86a-86b, M.
9908. Budapest - Magyar tudomanyos akademia, MS. Kaufmann A 384, f. 181a-181b, M.
9909. London - British Library Add. 18695 (Margoliouth 683), f. 53b, T, Yiddish.
9910. Muenchen - Bayerische Staatsbibliothek, Cod. hebr. 88, f. 78a, G.
9911. Muenchen - Bayerische Staatsbibliothek, Cod. hebr. 393, f. 132a-132b, C, no incipit.
9912. New York - Jewish Theological Seminary Ms. 4466, f. 84b-85a, M.
9913. Paris - Bibliotheque Nationale heb. 709, f. 115b, C.
9914. Parma - Biblioteca Palatina Cod. Parm. 3205 (de Rossi 655), f. 106b-107a, C.
9915. Zurich - Zentralbibliothek Heid. 139, f. 40b, C, additional marginal notes.

Tsarfat

9916. Oxford - Bodleian Library MS Laud. Or. 271 (Neubauer 1206), f. 75b, C, commentator: Aaron b. Hayyim haKohen (compiler), very short.

ברח דודי עד שתחפץ אהבת כלולינו (ב 1695a), שלמה הבבלי, גאולה ליום א' של פסח

Ashkenaz

9917. Berlin - Staatsbibliothek (Preussischer Kulturbesitz) Or. Qu. 798-799 (Steinschneider 177), II, f. 63b, M, short.
9918. Braunschweig - Landesmuseum fuer Geschichte und Volkstum R 2386, vol. I, f. 22a, M.
9919. Budapest - Magyar tudomanyos akademia, MS. Kaufmann A 384, f. 131a, M.
9920. Hamburg - Staats- und Universitaetsbibliothek Cod. hebr. 225, f. 68a, G.
9921. Jerusalem - Schocken Institute 24100 / Mahzor Nuremberg, f. 83a, M.
9922. London - British Library Add. 18695 (Margoliouth 683), f. 25b-26a, T, Yiddish.
9923. Moscow - Russian State Library, Ms. Guenzburg 615, f. 8b-9a, C, rubric: גאולה מעולה.
9924. Muenchen - Bayerische Staatsbibliothek, Cod. hebr. 88, f. 61a-61b, G.
9925. Muenchen - Bayerische Staatsbibliothek, Cod. hebr. 393, f. 125b-126a, C, no incipit.
9926. New York - Jewish Theological Seminary Ms. 4466, f. 56b-57a, M.

9927. Paris - Bibliotheque Nationale heb. 709, f. 75a, C.
9928. Parma - Biblioteca Palatina Cod. Parm. 3205 (de Rossi 655), f. 83b, C.
9929. Parma - Biblioteca Palatina Cod. Parm. 3507 (Perreau 27), f. 49b-50a, C.
9930. Zurich - Zentralbibliothek Heid. 139, f. 28b, C, no incipit.

Italia
9931. Parma - Biblioteca Palatin Cod. Parm. 2248 (de Rossi 149/2), f. 37b, C.

Tsarfat
9932. Moscow - Russian State Library, Ms. Guenzburg 1665, f. 57b, M.
9933. Vatican - Biblioteca Apostolica ebr. 306, f. 140a, C, no incipit.

בריק אלימן ישעל (ב 1714), שלם שבזי

Yemen
9934. Cincinnati - Hebrew Union College 398, f. 81a, M.
9935. New York - M. Lehmann 274, f. 78b-79a, M, kabbalistic.

ברית כרותה מלשכוח (ב 1717), בנימין ב"ר חייא, סליחה

Ashkenaz
9936. Jerusalem - Schocken Institute 24100 / Mahzor Nuremberg, f. 430b-431a, M.
9937. Muenchen - Bayerische Staatsbibliothek, Cod. hebr. 21, f. 232a-232b, M.
9938. Oxford - Bodleian Library MS Opp. 172 (Neubauer 1211), f. 74a-75a, C.
9939. Vatican - Biblioteca Apostolica ebr. 308, f. 113b, C, commentator: David b. Mose (compiler).
9940. Vatican - Biblioteca Apostolica ebr. 308, f. 161b-162b, C, commentator: David b. Mose (compiler).

Ashkenaz, commentary by Abraham b. Azriel[231]
9941. Frankfurt a M - Stadt- und Universitaetsbibliothek Fol. 16 (Merzbacher 95), f. 106b-107a, C
9942. Vatican - Biblioteca Apostolica ebr. 301,1, f. 138b-139a, C.

ברית נפקד אשר נעקד להעלות לפניך (ב 1718), הושענא

haAri, commentary by Mose b. Hayyim Pesante
9943. New York - Jewish Theological Seminary Ms. 4696, f. 21b, C, rubric: הקפה שנייה.

North Africa
9944. Jerusalem - Benayahu ז 27, f. 115a, M.

---

[231] Edited by Urbach, ערוגת הבושם, vol. III, p. 288-292.

North Africa, commentary by Yehuda Toledano
9945. New York - Jewish Theological Seminary Ms. 4300, f. 43a-44b, C, rubric: הקפה שנית יצחק.
North Africa, commentary by Simon b. Tsemaḥ Duran
9946. New York - Jewish Theological Seminary Ms. 4121, f. 48b, C, rubric: הקפה שנית ברית נפקד.

Yemen
9947. Jerusalem - Michael Krupp 3391, f. 11a, M.
9948. Jerusalem - Musad haRav Kook 952, f. 21a, M, rubric: הקפה שנית יצחק.
9949. New York - Jewish Theological Seminary Ms. 8767, p. 184, M.
9950. New York - Jewish Theological Seminary Ms. 9325, f. 81b-82b, M.
Yemen, commentary by Isaac b. Abraham Wanneh
9951. Jerusalem - Michael Krupp 1990, f. 98a, M, no incipit.
9952. Nahariya - Menahem and Saida Yaakob 284, f. 7b, M.
9953. New York - Jewish Theological Seminary Ms. 3108, f. 84a-84b, C, rubric: בהקפה שניה.
9954. New York - Jewish Theological Seminary Ms. 3295, f. 88b, M, rubric: חדושין.
9955. Philadelphia - University of Pennsylvania HB 2, f. 100b, M.
Yemen, commentary by Samḥun b. Salomo Ḥaloah
9956. Jerusalem - Makhon ben Zvi 2808, f. 172b-173b, C.
Yemen, commentary by Simon b. Tsemaḥ Duran
9957. Jerusalem - Michael Krupp 1758, f. 14b, M.
Yemen, commentary by Yiḥya b. Josef Tsalaḥ
9958. Montreal - Elberg 203, f. 6b, M, no incipit.

ברכו את יי המושל ראשי עולם וסופה (ב 1734), אהרן בן יוסף הרופא, פרשת צו את
Karaite, commentary by Berakha b. Josef haKohen
9959. New York - Jewish Theological Seminary Ms. 3367, f. 96b-98b, C, rubric: פירוש פרשת צו.
9960. St. Petersburg - Inst. of Oriental Studies of the Russian Academy B 431, f. 67b-69a, C, rubric: פרשת צו את.
9961. St. Petersburg - Russian National Library, Evr. IV 50, f. 72b-74a, C, rubric: פ׳ צו את.

ברכי אצולה מרוח הקדש (ב 1746), יהודה הלוי, פיוט למנחה יום כפור
Carpentras
9962. Cincinnati - Hebrew Union College 392, f. 2b-3b, M.
Carpentras, commentary by Josef b. Abraham of Montelitz
9963. Marseille - Mlle. Odette Valabregue [1], f. 87a, C, only the very end.
9964. New York - Jewish Theological Seminary Ms. 4197, f. 5a-7b, M.
9965. Paris - Ecole Rabbinique 32, f. 4b-7a, M.

9966. Strasbourg - Bibliotheque Nationale et Universitaire 4081, f. 4a-5b, M.

ברכי נפשי צור עושיבי גואל משחת חייבי, סליחה

Yemen, commentary by Isaac b. Abraham Wanneh
9967. Chicago-Spertus College of Judaica D 2, 2, f. 202b-203a, M, no incipit.
9968. Jerusalem - Michael Krupp 604, f. 154b-155a, M, rubric: אל מלך.
9969. Jerusalem - Sassoon 1158, p. 370, M, no incipit.
9970. London - British Library Or. 11122, f. 184b-185a, M, rubric: אל מלך.

בשם יי אל עולם בשם יי אדמות ומרומות (ב 1842), יהודה הלוי, סליחה

Yemen
9971. Jerusalem - Sassoon 902, p. 439, M.
Yemen, commentary by Isaac b. Abraham Wanneh
9972. Chicago-Spertus College of Judaica D 2, 2, f. 219b-220a, M, no incipit.
9973. Jerusalem - Michael Krupp 604, f. 166a-166b, M, rubric: אל מלך.
9974. Jerusalem - Sassoon 1158, p. 393-394, M, no incipit.
9975. London - British Library Or. 11122, f. 198b-199a, M, no incipit.

בשם אלהי אברהם אפתחה ובפחד יצחק אשוח (ב 1856), סליחה

Yemen
9976. Jerusalem - Benayahu ת 88, f. 106b, M.
9977. Jerusalem - Benayahu ת 301, f. 40b, G.
9978. Jerusalem - Benayahu ת 414, f. 125a, M, very short.
9979. Jerusalem - Sassoon 902, p. 375-377, M.
9980. New York - Jewish Theological Seminary Ms. 3028, f. 12b, M, very short.
9981. New York - Jewish Theological Seminary Ms. 3052, f. 1a-2a, M.
9982. New York - Jewish Theological Seminary Ms. 3108, f. 25a, M, short.
9983. New York - Jewish Theological Seminary Ms. 4488, f. 105b, M, very short.
9984. Ramat Gan - Universitat Bar Ilan 62, f. 39a, G.
Yemen, commentary by Isaac b. Abraham Wanneh
9985. Chicago-Spertus College of Judaica D 2, 2, f. 186b, M.
9986. Jerusalem - Benayahu ת 261, f. 124a-124b, M.
9987. Jerusalem - Benayahu ת 282, f. 109b, M, no incipit.
9988. Jerusalem - Makhon Ben Zvi 1156 (Tubi 155), f. 107b, M, no incipit.
9989. Jerusalem - Makhon Ben Zvi 1174 (Tubi 154), f. 106a, C.
9990. Jerusalem - Michael Krupp 604, f. 136a, M.
9991. Jerusalem - Musad haRav Kook 325, f. 155b, M.
9992. Jerusalem - Musad haRav Kook 330, f. 93b, G.

9993. Jerusalem - Sassoon 1158, p. 327, M, no incipit.
9994. Jerusalem - Sassoon 1174, p. 207, M.
9995. London - British Library Or. 11122, f. 166b, M.
9996. Muenchen - Bayerische Staatsbibliothek, Cod. hebr. 472, f. 145b-146a, M, no incipit.
9997. New York - Jewish Theological Seminary Ms. 3013, f. 107b, M, no incipit.
9998. New York - Jewish Theological Seminary Ms. 3294, f. 1b-2a, C, no incipit.
9999. New York - Public Library, Heb. Ms. 9, f. 102b-103a, M.
10000. Philadelphia - University of Pennsylvania HB 2, f. 119a, M.

בת עמי תייליל ביגוניה (ב 1935), קינה
Yemen, commentary by Isaac b. Abraham Wanneh
10001. Jerusalem - Sassoon 1158, p. 169, M.
10002. London - British Library Or. 11122, f. 101b, M.

בת ציון שמעתי ממררת אמריה (ב 1939), קינה
Yemen
10003. Ramat Gan - Universitat Bar Ilan 62, f. 21b, G, margin damaged.
Yemen, commentary by Isaac b. Abraham Wanneh
10004. Jerusalem - Sassoon 1158, p. 174, M, rubric: קינה סים׳ הלוי כי הראשונה סים׳ יהודה.
10005. London - British Library Or. 11122, f. 104a, M.

בתולת בת יהודה (ב 1965), בנימין ב״ר זרח, סליחה
Ashkenaz
10006. Oxford - Bodleian Library MS Mich. 543 (Neubauer 1212), f. 48b-49a, C, commentator: Isaac b. Jacob (compiler).
10007. Oxford - Bodleian Library MS Opp. 681 (Neubauer 1213), f. 32a-32b, C.
10008. Vatican - Biblioteca Apostolica ebr. 422/1, f. 42a, CG, no incipit, very short.

גאלנו גואל ישראל נאמן בדבריו, אהרן בן יוסף הרופא, פרשת שמות
Karaite, commentary by Berakha b. Josef haKohen
10009. New York - Jewish Theological Seminary Ms. 3367, f. 64a-66a, C, incomplete, beginning missing.
10010. St. Petersburg - Inst. of Oriental Studies of the Russian Academy B 431, f. 47b-48b, C, rubric: ספר טוב טעם. פרשת שמות.
10011. St. Petersburg - Russian National Library, Evr. IV 50, f. 46a-47a, C, incomplete, beginning missing.

גבקי שמים לך כסא כבוד (ג 15), חייא בן אל דאודי, פזמון

Sepharad, commentary by David b. Josef Abudarham[232]

10012. Budapest - Magyar tudomanyos akademia, MS. Kaufmann A 405/2 , p. 252, C, rubric: למנחה פזמון לקדושה.
10013. New York - Columbia X893 Ab 93, f. 30b, C, rubric: פזמון לקדושה.

גדאל אלבר בלש טרני, שלם שבזי

Yemen
10014. Cincinnati - Hebrew Union College 398, f. 88a-88b, M.

גדול עוני ולחטוא הוספתי (ג 96), גרשום ב"ר יהודה מאור הגולה, סליחה

Ashkenaz
10015. Oxford - Bodleian Library MS Mich. 543 (Neubauer 1212), f. 85a-85b, C, commentator: Isaac b. Jacob (compiler).
10016. Padova - Biblioteca del Seminario Vescovile Cod. 218, f. 133b-134a, M.
10017. Padova - Biblioteca del Seminario Vescovile Cod. 218, f. 236b-237b, M.
10018. Vatican - Biblioteca Apostolica ebr. 422/1, f. 33a, C.

גליא עמך דכחיש לן חילן, סליחה

Yemen, commentary by Isaac b. Abraham Wanneh
10019. London - British Library Or. 11122, f. 223b, M, no incipit.

גן נעול איוה שוכן תרשישים (ג 176), משולם ב"ר קלונימוס, אופן ליום ב' של פסח

Ashkenaz
10020. Berlin - Staatsbibliothek (Preussischer Kulturbesitz) Or. Qu. 798-799 (Steinschneider 177), II, f. 76b-77a, M.
10021. Budapest - Magyar tudomanyos akademia, MS. Kaufmann A 384 , f. 158b-159a, M.
10022. Jerusalem - Schocken Institute 24100 / Mahzor Nuremberg, f. 93a, M.
10023. London - British Library Add. 18695 (Margoliouth 683) , f. 39a-39b, T, Yiddish, rubric: אופן.
10024. Moscow - Russian State Library, Ms. Guenzburg 615 , f. 20b-21a, C, rubric: אופן.
10025. Muenchen - Bayerische Staatsbibliothek, Cod. hebr. 88, f. 70a-70b, G.
10026. Paris - Bibliotheque Nationale heb. 709, f. 95b-96a, C, rubric: אופן.
10027. Parma - Biblioteca Palatina Cod. Parm. 1002 (Ta 24), f. 1114b, M, short.

---

[232] Edited by Prins, תשלום אבודרהם, p. 125-126.

10028. Parma - Biblioteca Palatina Cod. Parm. 3205 (de Rossi 655), f. 97a-98b, C.

10029. Parma - Biblioteca Palatina Cod. Parm. 3507 (Perreau 27), f. 63a-63b, C.

10030. Zurich - Zentralbibliothek Heid. 139, f. 36b, C, additional marginal notes.

גרוני ניחר זועק חמס (ג 192), גרשום ב"ר יהודה מאור הגולה, סליחה

Ashkenaz

10031. Budapest - Magyar tudomanyos akademia, MS. Kaufmann A 400, p. 525-526, C, rubric: פירוש תחנון מרבנא גרשם לי"ז בתמוז.

10032. Muenchen - Bayerische Staatsbibliothek, Cod. hebr. 346, f. 133b-134b, C, no incipit.

10033. Oxford - Bodleian Library MS Mich. 543 (Neubauer 1212), f. 82a-82b, C, commentator: Isaac b. Jacob (compiler), rubric: מחי ומסי.

10034. Oxford - Bodleian Library MS Opp. 170 (Neubauer 1205), f. 239a-239b, C.

10035. Padova - Biblioteca del Seminario Vescovile Cod. 218, f. 262b-263a, M.

10036. Parma - Biblioteca Palatina Cod. Parm. 3205 (de Rossi 655), f. 271a-271b, C.

10037. Vatican - Biblioteca Apostolica ebr. 422/1, f. 34b-35a, C.

Ashkenaz, commentary by Abraham b. Azriel[233]

10038. Vatican - Biblioteca Apostolica ebr. 301,1, f. 163b-164a, C, rubric: אחר.

Tsarfat

10039. London - David Sofer 5, f. 93a-93b, C.

10040. London - David Sofer 5, f. 162a-162b, C, rubric: פזמון.

10041. Oxford - Bodleian Library MS Laud. Or. 271 (Neubauer 1206), f. 173a-173b, C, commentator: Aaron b. Hayyim haKohen (compiler).

10042. Oxford - Bodleian Library MS Opp. 171 (Neubauer 1207), f. 113a-113b, C, rubric: אחרת.

10043. Parma - Biblioteca Palatina Cod. Parm. 3007 (de Rossi 654,2), f. 117b-118a, M.

10044. Vatican - Biblioteca Apostolica ebr. 306, f. 200a-200b, C.

גרושים מבית תענוגיהם (ג 194), יצחק גיאת?, קינה

Yemen, commentary by Isaac b. Abraham Wanneh

10045. Jerusalem - Sassoon 1158, p. 166, M.

10046. London - British Library Or. 11122, f. 100b, M.

---

[233] Edited by Urbach, ערוגת הבושם, vol. III, p. 451-453.

דאיתקרי חוסיו יחיש נסיו, סליחה

Yemen

10047. New York - Jewish Theological Seminary Ms. 3052, f. 88a, M.

Yemen, commentary by Isaac b. Abraham Wanneh

10048. Chicago-Spertus College of Judaica D 2, 2, f. 239b, M, no incipit.

10049. Jerusalem - Benayahu ת 261, f. 166b, M, very short.

10050. Jerusalem - Benayahu ת 282, f. 142b, M, very short.

10051. Jerusalem - Makhon Ben Zvi 1156 (Tubi 155), f. 140a, M, no incipit.

10052. Jerusalem - Sassoon 1158, p. 419, M, no incipit.

10053. Jerusalem - Sassoon 1174, p. 272, M, no incipit, very short.

10054. London - British Library Or. 11122, f. 216b, M, no incipit.

10055. Muenchen - Bayerische Staatsbibliothek, Cod. hebr. 472, f. 196a, M, very short.

10056. New York - Jewish Theological Seminary Ms. 3013, f. 135a, M, no incipit, very short.

10057. New York - Jewish Theological Seminary Ms. 3294, f. 18b, C.

10058. Strasbourg - Bibliotheque Nationale et Universitaire 3965 (Landauer 39), p. 416, M, very short.

דבר ויקרא ארץ דלה אבירך ממצרים, הושענא

Yemen, commentary by Samḥun b. Salomo Ḥaloah

10059. Jerusalem - Makhon ben Zvi 2808, f. 92a-96a, C.

דברי שיר יחידה דברי שבחי את אלהים יוצרי (ד 53), שלם שבזי

Yemen

10060. Cincinnati - Hebrew Union College 398, f. 89b-90b, M.

דודי שליט בכל מפעל (ד 166), שמעון ב"ר יצחק, אופן ליום ז' של פסח

Ashkenaz

10061. Berlin - Staatsbibliothek (Preussischer Kulturbesitz) Or. Qu. 798-799 (Steinschneider 177), II, f. 84b-85a, M.

10062. Budapest - Magyar tudomanyos akademia, MS. Kaufmann A 384, f. 178a-178b, M.

10063. Hamburg - Staats- und Universitaetsbibliothek Cod. hebr. 17/2 (Steinschneider 152), f. 67a, C.

10064. London - British Library Add. 18695 (Margoliouth 683), f. 52a-52b, T, Yiddish, rubric: אופן.

10065. Muenchen - Bayerische Staatsbibliothek, Cod. hebr. 88, f. 77b, G.

10066. Paris - Bibliotheque Nationale heb. 709, f. 115a, C.

10067. Parma - Biblioteca Palatina Cod. Parm. 3205 (de Rossi 655), f. 105b-106a, C, rubric: אופן.

10068. Parma - Biblioteca Palatina Cod. Parm. 3507 (Perreau 27), f. 69b-70a, C.

Tsarfat

10069. London - David Sofer 5, f. 38a-38b, C, additional glosses.
10070. Moscow - Russian State Library, Ms. Guenzburg 1665, f. 78a-78b, M, no incipit.
10071. Oxford - Bodleian Library MS Laud. Or. 271 (Neubauer 1206), f. 75a, C, commentator: Aaron b. Hayyim haKohen (compiler).

דומה אלהים עמך לקדש, סליחה

Yemen, commentary by Isaac b. Abraham Wanneh
10072. London - British Library Or. 11122, f. 180b, M, no incipit.

דוק וחוג רעשו ותשכון עליו עננה (ד 192), דוד בן אלעזר בקודה?, קינה

Yemen, commentary by Isaac b. Abraham Wanneh
10073. Jerusalem - Sassoon 1158, p. 164, M.
10074. London - British Library Or. 11122, f. 99a-99b, M.
10075. London - British Library Or. 11122, f. 99b-100a, M.

דיברא קדמאה כד הוה נפיק, תרגום, דיבור ראשון

Ashkenaz
10076. Parma - Biblioteca Palatina Cod. Parm. 3205 (de Rossi 655), f. 180b, C.

דלתיך הלילה לשבי חטא הותרו (ד 260), דוד בן אלעזר בקודה?., סליחה

Yemen
10077. Jerusalem - Benayahu ת 301, f. 56a, G.
10078. Jerusalem - Sassoon 902, p. 412, M, very short.
10079. New York - Jewish Theological Seminary Ms. 3028, f. 48b, G.
10080. New York - Jewish Theological Seminary Ms. 3052, f. 58b-59a, M, rubric: אל מלך.

Yemen, commentary by Isaac b. Abraham Wanneh
10081. Chicago-Spertus College of Judaica D 2, 2, f. 230b, M, no incipit.
10082. Jerusalem - Benayahu ת 261, f. 159a, M, rubric: אל מלך.
10083. Jerusalem - Benayahu ת 282, f. 130b-131a, M, rubric: אל מלך.
10084. Jerusalem - Makhon Ben Zvi 1156 (Tubi 155), f. 130a, M, rubric: אל מלך.
10085. Jerusalem - Makhon Ben Zvi 1174 (Tubi 154), f. 129b, M.
10086. Jerusalem - Michael Krupp 604, f. 86a-86b, M, rubric: אל מלך.
10087. Jerusalem - Musad haRav Kook 325, f. 187a-187b, M, rubric: אל מלך.
10088. Jerusalem - Musad haRav Kook 330, f. 116a, G.
10089. Jerusalem - Musad haRav Kook 347, f. 88a, G.
10090. Jerusalem - Sassoon 1174, p. 251, M, no incipit.
10091. Jerusalem - Yehiel haLevi 4, f. 170a, G.
10092. London - British Library Or. 11122, f. 207a, M, no incipit.

10093. Manchester - John Rylands University Library, Ms. Gaster 5, f. 210b-211a, M.
10094. Muenchen - Bayerische Staatsbibliothek, Cod. hebr. 472, f. 180a-180b, M, rubric: אל מלך.
10095. New York - Jewish Theological Seminary Ms. 3013, f. 126b, M, rubric: אל מלך.
10096. New York - Jewish Theological Seminary Ms. 3109, f. 111b-112a, M, rubric: אל מלך, no incipit.
10097. New York - Jewish Theological Seminary Ms. 3294, f. 13b-14a, C.
10098. New York - Public Library, Heb. Ms. 9, f. 122a, M.
10099. Strasbourg - Bibliotheque Nationale et Universitaire 3965 (Landauer 39), p. 391, M, rubric: אל מלך.

דעני לעניי ענינן דעני לעשיקי ענינן (ד 327), פתיחה לסליחה

Yemen

10100. Jerusalem - Benayahu ת 88, f. 120b, M.
10101. New York - Jewish Theological Seminary Ms. 3193, f. 123a, M, no incipit.

Yemen, commentary by Isaac b. Abraham Wanneh

10102. Chicago-Spertus College of Judaica D 2, 2, f. 182a-182b, M.

דרכיך וחוקיך הביניני וחניני, סליחה

Yemen

10103. New York - Jewish Theological Seminary Ms. 3109, f. 91a, M.

Yemen, commentary by Isaac b. Abraham Wanneh

10104. New York - Jewish Theological Seminary Ms. 3109, f. 91a-91b, M, rubric: אל מלך.

דרכי שבעה רועים זכור לעם שנדכאו (ד 364), דניאל, סליחה

Yemen

10105. New York - Jewish Theological Seminary Ms. 3052, f. 59b, M, rubric: אל מלך.

Yemen, commentary by Isaac b. Abraham Wanneh

10106. Chicago-Spertus College of Judaica D 2, 2, f. 230b, M, no incipit.
10107. Jerusalem - Benayahu ת 261, f. 159a, M, rubric: אל מלך.
10108. Jerusalem - Benayahu ת 282, f. 131a, M, rubric: אל מלך.
10109. Jerusalem - Makhon Ben Zvi 1156 (Tubi 155), f. 130a-130b, M, rubric: אל מלך.
10110. Jerusalem - Makhon Ben Zvi 1174 (Tubi 154), f 130a, M.
10111. Jerusalem - Michael Krupp 604, f. 86b, M, rubric: אל מלך.
10112. Jerusalem - Musad haRav Kook 325, f. 187b, M, rubric: אל מלך.
10113. Jerusalem - Sassoon 1158, p. 203, M, rubric: סים' דניאל.
10114. Jerusalem - Sassoon 1174, p. 251-252, M, no incipit.

10115. London - British Library Or. 11122, f. 206b, M, rubric: אל מלך.
10116. New York - Jewish Theological Seminary Ms. 3013, f. 127a, M, rubric: אל מלך, very short.
10117. New York - Jewish Theological Seminary Ms. 3109, f. 126b, M.
10118. New York - Jewish Theological Seminary Ms. 3294, f. 14a, C.
10119. New York - Public Library, Heb. Ms. 9, f. 122b, M, short.
10120. Strasbourg - Bibliotheque Nationale et Universitaire 3965 (Landauer 39), p. 392, M, rubric: אל מלך.

דרכך היטיבי ושמעי את ניבי (ד 368), דניאל, סליחה
Yemen
10121. New York - Jewish Theological Seminary Ms. 3052, f. 86a-86b, M.
Yemen, commentary by Isaac b. Abraham Wanneh
10122. Chicago-Spertus College of Judaica D 2, 2, f. 238b-239a, M, no incipit.
10123. Jerusalem - Benayahu ת 261, f. 166a, M, short.
10124. Jerusalem - Benayahu ת 282, f. 142a, M.
10125. Jerusalem - Makhon Ben Zvi 1156 (Tubi 155), f. 139b, M, no incipit.
10126. Jerusalem - Makhon Ben Zvi 1174 (Tubi 154), f. 138a, M.
10127. Jerusalem - Michael Krupp 604, f. 176b, M, no incipit.
10128. Jerusalem - Sassoon 1158, p. 417, M, no incipit.
10129. Jerusalem - Sassoon 1174, p. 271, M, no incipit.
10130. London - British Library Or. 11122, f. 216a, M, no incipit.
10131. Manchester - John Rylands University Library, Ms. Gaster 5, f. 225a, M.
10132. Muenchen - Bayerische Staatsbibliothek, Cod. hebr. 472, f. 195a, M.
10133. New York - Jewish Theological Seminary Ms. 3013, f. 134b, M, short, no incipit.
10134. New York - Jewish Theological Seminary Ms. 3294, f. 18a, C.
10135. New York - Public Library, Heb. Ms. 9, f. 131a, M, no incipit.
10136. Strasbourg - Bibliotheque Nationale et Universitaire 3965 (Landauer 39), p. 414, M.

הא בעיני עבדיא אדם רבונהון, סליחה
Yemen, commentary by Isaac b. Abraham Wanneh
10137. Chicago-Spertus College of Judaica D 2, 2, f. 246b, M, no incipit, short.
10138. Jerusalem - Sassoon 1158, p. 425, M, no incipit.
10139. London - British Library Or. 11122, f. 219b, M, no incipit.

האדיר בשמי עליות (ה 14), משולם ב"ר קלונימוס, יוצר ליום כפור

Ashkenaz

10140. Berlin - Staatsbibliothek (Preussischer Kulturbesitz) Or. Qu. 798-799 (Steinschneider 177), I, f. 88b-89a, M, rubric: רחיטים.
10141. Braunschweig - Landesmuseum fuer Geschichte und Volkstum R 2386, vol II, f. 201a-201b, M.
10142. Budapest - Magyar tudomanyos akademia, MS. Kaufmann A 400, p. 338, C, short.
10143. Hamburg - Staats- und Universitaetsbibliothek Cod. hebr. 62 (Steinschneider 154), f. 10a-10b, C, rubric: רהיטים.
10144. Hamburg - Staats- und Universitaetsbibliothek Cod. hebr. 132 (Steinschneider 155), f. 38a, C, short.
10145. Jerusalem - Jewish National and University Library Ms Heb 8° 3037, f. 136a, M, short.
10146. Jerusalem - Schocken Institute 24100 / Mahzor Nuremberg, f. 386a, M, short.
10147. London - British Library Or. 11318/1, f. 85a-85b, C, rubric: אילו הרהיטים, short.
10148. London - Montefiore Library 261, f. 49, C, commentator: Eliezer b. Natan?, short.
10149. Moscow - Russian State Library, Ms. Guenzburg 191, f. 102a, M, short.
10150. Muenchen - Bayerische Staatsbibliothek, Cod. hebr. 346, f. 60a-60b, C.
10151. New York - Jewish Theological Seminary Ms. 4466, f. 329b-330a, M, short.
10152. New York - Jewish Theological Seminary Ms. 8097, f. 74b, C, short.
10153. New York - Jewish Theological Seminary Ms. 8169 (Acc. 0016), f. 82b-83a, M.
10154. Oxford - Bodleian Library MS Mich. 365 (Neubauer 1208), f. 79a-79b, C.
10155. Oxford - Bodleian Library MS Opp. 619 (Neubauer 2374), f. 164b, M, short.
10156. Oxford - Bodleian Library MS Opp. 172 (Neubauer 1211), f. 47a, C, short.
10157. Parma - Biblioteca Palatina Cod. Parm. 3205 (de Rossi 655), f. 227a, C.
10158. Parma - Biblioteca Palatina Cod. Parm. 3271 (de Rossi 1216), f. 55a, G.
10159. Parma - Biblioteca Palatina Cod. Parm. 3507 (Perreau 27), f. 159b, C, short.
10160. Vatican - Biblioteca Apostolica ebr. 308, f. 108b-102(ii)a, C, commentator: David b. Mose (compiler).
10161. Vatican - Biblioteca Apostolica ebr. 422/1, f. 16b, C, short.

Ashkenaz, commentary by Abraham b. Azriel[234]

10162. Vatican - Biblioteca Apostolica ebr. 301,1, f. 170b, C, rubric: רהיטין, short.

Asti, Fossano, Moncalvo

10163. New Haven - Yale University, Beinecke Rare Book and MS Library, MS Heb. 52, f. 115a, M.

Romania

10164. Vatican - Biblioteca Apostolica ebr. 320, f. 396a, M.

Tsarfat

10165. London - British Library Or. 8682, f. 75b, GI.

10166. London - David Sofer 5, f. 140b-141a, C, rubric: רהיטים.

10167. Oxford - Bodleian Library MS Bodl. Or. 109 (Neubauer 1209), f. 25b, C, commentator: Aaron b. Hayyim haKohen (compiler), short.

10168. Parma - Biblioteca Palatina Cod. Parm. 1794 (de Rossi 1061), f. 147a, M.

10169. Parma - Biblioteca Palatina Cod. Parm. 2890 (de Rossi 856), f. 40a, M.

10170. Parma - Biblioteca Palatina Cod. Parm. 3006 (de Rossi 654,1), f. 151b-152a, M.

10171. Parma - Biblioteca Palatina Cod. Parm. 3006 (de Rossi 654,1), f. 187b, M.

10172. Vatican - Biblioteca Apostolica ebr. 306, f. 81a-81b, C, rubric: רהיטים.

האדרת האמונה לחי עולמים (ה 16), חלק ט"ז, קדושתא לשחרית יום כפור

Ashkenaz

10173. Berlin - Staatsbibliothek (Preussischer Kulturbesitz) Or. Qu. 798-799 (Steinschneider 177), I, f. 78b-79b, M.

10174. Braunschweig - Landesmuseum fuer Geschichte und Volkstum R 2386, vol. II, f. 191b-192b, M, no incipit.

10175. Budapest - Magyar tudomanyos akademia, MS. Kaufmann A 400, p. 316-319, C.

10176. Cambridge - University Library Add. 394,1 (Reif SCR 461), f. 67b-68a, C.

10177. Hamburg - Staats- und Universitaetsbibliothek Cod. hebr. 17/2 (Steinschneider 152), f. 151b-152b, C.

10178. Hamburg - Staats- und Universitaetsbibliothek Cod. hebr. 40b (Steinschneider 110), f. 97a, G.

10179. Hamburg - Staats- und Universitaetsbibliothek Cod. hebr. 62 (Steinschneider 154), f. 5a-6b, C.

10180. Hamburg - Staats- und Universitaetsbibliothek Cod. hebr. 132 (Steinschneider 155), f. 34b-35b, C.

---

[234] Edited by Urbach, ערוגת הבושם, vol. III, p. 499.

10181. Jerusalem - Jewish National and University Library Ms Heb 8° 3037, f. 123b-124a, M.
10182. Jerusalem - Schocken Institute 24100 / Mahzor Nuremberg , f. 379b-380a, M.
10183. London - British Library Or. 11318/1, f. 75b-77a, C.
10184. London - Montefiore Library 261 , f. 44a-45b, C, commentator: Eliezer b. Natan?.
10185. Moscow - Russian State Library, Ms. Guenzburg 191, f. 91b-92a, M.
10186. Moscow - Russian State Library, Ms. Guenzburg 615, f. 94a-95b, C.
10187. Muenchen - Bayerische Staatsbibliothek, Cod. hebr. 346 , f. 59b-60a, C, rubric: שכחתי לכתוב שם.
10188. Muenchen - Bayerische Staatsbibliothek, Cod. hebr. 393, f. 142b-143a, C.
10189. New York - Jewish Theological Seminary Ms. 4466, f. 313b-315a, M.
10190. New York - Jewish Theological Seminary Ms. 8097, f. 72b, C, very short.
10191. New York - Jewish Theological Seminary Ms. 8169 (Acc. 0016), f. 72a-72b, M.
10192. Oxford - Bodleian Library MS Opp. 170 (Neubauer 1205), f. 166b-168a, C.
10193. Oxford - Bodleian Library MS Opp. 172 (Neubauer 1211), f. 39a-41a, C.
10194. Oxford - Bodleian Library MS Opp. 498 (Neubauer 1930), f. 22b-29a, C, commentator: Naftali Hirsh Trebitsh (compiler).
10195. Oxford - Bodleian Library MS Opp. 525,18 (Neubauer 1598/18), f. 103a, C, only end.
10196. Oxford - Bodleian Library MS Opp. 619 (Neubauer 2374), f. 149b-150a, M.
10197. Paris - Bibliotheque Nationale heb. 653, f. 60a, G.
10198. Parma - Biblioteca Palatina Cod. Parm. 3205 (de Rossi 655), f. 227b-228b, C.
10199. Parma - Biblioteca Palatina Cod. Parm. 3271 (de Rossi 1216), f. 42a-42b, G.
10200. Parma - Biblioteca Palatina Cod. Parm. 3507 (Perreau 27), f. 147b-151b, C, rubric: פי' מן האדרת האמונה.
10201. Vatican - Biblioteca Apostolica ebr. 308, f. 101a-103a (two leafs numbered 102), C, commentator: David b. Mose (compiler).
10202. Vatican - Biblioteca Apostolica ebr. 422/1, f. 15b, C, very short.
10203. Zurich - Zentralbibliothek Heid. 139, f. 77a, C, additional marginal notes.

Ashkenaz, commentary by Abraham b. Azriel[235]

10204. Vatican - Biblioteca Apostolica ebr. 301,1, f. 167a-168a, C.

---

[235] Edited by Urbach, ערוגת הבושם, vol. III, p. 477-484.

Ashkenaz, commentary by Elazar b. Yehuda of Worms[236]

10205. Cambridge - University Library Add. 858,1, f. 13b-14b, C, rubric: ובכן נאדרך חי עולמים.

10206. Muenchen - Bayerische Staatsbibliothek, Cod. hebr. 346, f. 98a-105a, C, rubric: פריש׳ רבי אלעזר מוורמש.

10207. Muenchen - Bayerische Staatsbibliothek, Cod. hebr. 393,9, f. 195b-196b, C.

10208. Oxford - Bodleian Library MS Opp. 498 (Neubauer 1930), f. 22a-22b, M.

10209. Oxford - Bodleian Library MS Opp. 525,18 (Neubauer 1598/18), f. 103a, C, no incipit.

10210. Oxford - Bodleian Library MS Opp. 696/13 (Neubauer 2253), f. 244a-250a, C.

10211. Vatican - Biblioteca Apostolica ebr. 228/10, f. 105a-112a, C, rubric: זה פירוש של אדרת. לכבוד השם יתע׳ ולתפארת.

Asti, Fossano, Moncalvo

10212. New Haven - Yale University, Beinecke Rare Book and MS Library, MS Heb. 52, f. 107b, M.

Italia, commentary Ḥat Hazzan of Padova

10213. London - Hirschler - Dzialowski (bookdealers), f. 26b-27b, G.

10214. Milano - Ambrosiana X 230 Sup., f. 17a-17b, M.

10215. Moscow - Russian State Library, Ms. Guenzburg 522, f. 56a-57b, G.

10216. New York - Jewish Theological Seminary Ms. 4392, f. 28b-29b, G.

Romania

10217. Vatican - Biblioteca Apostolica ebr. 320, f. 286a-286b, M.

Sepharad

10218. Jerusalem - Benayahu ז 25, f. 65a-65b, M.

Tsarfat

10219. Bern - Burgerbibliothek A 409, f. 84b-85a, G.

10220. London - British Library Or. 8682, f. 69b, GI.

10221. London - David Sofer 5, f. 138b, C.

10222. London - David Sofer 5, f. 176b-177b, C, rubric: פירוש אחר האדרת והאמונה. והוא ימצא לעיל ביו׳ הכיפורי׳.

10223. Oxford - Bodleian Library MS Bodl. Or. 109 (Neubauer 1209), f. 20b-21b, C, commentator: Aaron b. Hayyim haKohen (compiler).

10224. Oxford - Bodleian Library MS Laud. Or. 271 (Neubauer 1206), f. 105b-106b, C, commentator: Aaron b. Hayyim haKohen (compiler), rubric: עמי עשו: של צום כיפור.

10225. Oxford - Bodleian Library MS Laud. Or. 271 (Neubauer 1206), f. 113b, C, commentator: Aaron b. Hayyim haKohen (compiler), very short.

---

[236] On these commentaries cp. J. Dan, פירושי 'האדרת והאמונה' של חסידי אשכנז, *Tarbiz*, 50, 1981, pp. 396-404.

10226. Parma - Biblioteca Palatina Cod. Parm. 1794 (de Rossi 1061), f. 126b-127b, M.
10227. Parma - Biblioteca Palatina Cod. Parm. 2890 (de Rossi 856), f. 30b, M.
10228. Parma - Biblioteca Palatina Cod. Parm. 3006 (de Rossi 654,1), f. 143b, M.
10229. Parma - Biblioteca Palatina Cod. Parm. 3006 (de Rossi 654,1), f. 143b-144b, M.
10230. Vatican - Biblioteca Apostolica ebr. 306, f. 77b, C.

האוחז ביד מדת משפט (ה 19)

Ashkenaz

10231. Berlin - Staatsbibliothek (Preussischer Kulturbesitz) Or. Qu. 798-799 (Steinschneider 177), I, f. 125a-125b, M.
10232. Braunschweig - Landesmuseum fuer Geschichte und Volkstum R 2386, vol. II, f. 97b-98a, M.
10233. Cambridge - University Library Add. 394,1 (Reif SCR 461), f. 66a-66b, C, incipit missing.
10234. Darmstadt - Hessisches Landes- und Hochschulbibliothek Cod. Or. 15, f. 19a-20a, M.
10235. Darmstadt - Hessisches Landes- und Hochschulbibliothek Cod. Or. 25/55, f. 110a, C, esoteric.
10236. Hamburg - Staats- und Universitaetsbibliothek Cod. hebr. 12 (Steinschneider 102), f. 19b-20a, G.
10237. Hamburg - Staats- und Universitaetsbibliothek Cod. hebr. 17/2 (Steinschneider 152), f. 116a-116b, C, rubric: יוחנן ר׳ יסד וזה.
10238. Hamburg - Staats- und Universitaetsbibliothek Cod. hebr. 40b (Steinschneider 110), f. 20b, G.
10239. Hamburg - Staats- und Universitaetsbibliothek Cod. hebr. 40c (Steinschneider 111), f. 140b-141a, G.
10240. Hamburg - Staats- und Universitaetsbibliothek Cod. hebr. 132 (Steinschneider 155), f. 16b, C.
10241. Jerusalem - Jewish National and University Library Ms Heb 8° 3037, f. 32b-33a, M, rubric: ר׳ יוחנן יסד האוחז ביד מדת מידד וכל מידה שמזכיר להק׳ נותן שבח מעין אותה מידה בכל פסוק ופסוק.
10242. Jerusalem - Schocken Institute 15791/7, f. 62a-65a, C, kabbalistic.
10243. Jerusalem - Schocken Institute 24100 / Mahzor Nuremberg, f. 333b-334a, M.
10244. Jerusalem - Schocken Institute 24100 / Mahzor Nuremberg, f. 415a-415b, M.
10245. London - British Library Or. 11318/1, f. 20a-21a, C.
10246. London - Montefiore Library 261, f. 14a-15a, C, commentator: Eliezer b. Natan?.

10247. Moscow - Russian State Library, Ms. Guenzburg 1401/2, f. 18b-19a, C.
10248. Moscow - Russian State Library, Ms. Guenzburg 191, f. 4b-5a, M.
10249. Moscow - Russian State Library, Ms. Guenzburg 191, f. 45a-45b, M.
10250. Moscow - Russian State Library, Ms. Guenzburg 615, f. 71a-71b, C.
10251. Muenchen - Bayerische Staatsbibliothek, Cod. hebr. 86, f. 31b-32b, G.
10252. Muenchen - Bayerische Staatsbibliothek, Cod. hebr. 346, f. 20b-21b, C.
10253. New York - Jewish Theological Seminary Ms. 4466, f. 230a-230b, M.
10254. New York - Jewish Theological Seminary Ms. 8097, f. 63a, C, additional glosses, short.
10255. New York - Jewish Theological Seminary Ms. 8169 (Acc. 0016), f. 22b-23a, M, additional glosses.
10256. Oxford - Bodleian Library MS Mich. 365 (Neubauer 1208), f. 87a, C, short.
10257. Oxford - Bodleian Library MS Mich. 365 (Neubauer 1208), f. 91b, C.
10258. Oxford - Bodleian Library MS Opp. 170 (Neubauer 1205), f. 127a-128a, C.
10259. Oxford - Bodleian Library MS Opp. 172 (Neubauer 1211), f. 13a-13b, C.
10260. Oxford - Bodleian Library MS Opp. 525,18 (Neubauer 1598/18), f. 103a-104a, C, mainly gematriyot.
10261. Oxford - Bodleian Library MS Opp. 619 (Neubauer 2374), f. 35b-36a, M.
10262. Oxford - Bodleian Library MS Opp. 675 (Neubauer 1210), f. 29a-30a, C, no incipit.
10263. Paris - Bibliotheque Nationale heb. 653, f. 19a, G.
10264. Parma - Biblioteca Palatina Cod. Parm. 3205 (de Rossi 655), f. 211b, C.
10265. Parma - Biblioteca Palatina Cod. Parm. 3270 (de Rossi 1215), f. 36a-37a, M.
10266. Parma - Biblioteca Palatina Cod. Parm. 3270 (de Rossi 1215), f. 176b-177a, M.
10267. Parma - Biblioteca Palatina Cod. Parm. 3507 (Perreau 27), f. 123a, C.
10268. Vatican - Biblioteca Apostolica ebr. 308, f. 55a-56a, C, commentator: David b. Mose (compiler).
10269. Vatican - Biblioteca Apostolica ebr. 308, f. 56a-56b, C, commentator: David b. Mose (compiler), rubric: פ"א.
10270. Vatican - Bibliotheca Apostolica ebr. 298/1, f. 12b-13a, C, no incipit.
10271. Vatican - Bibliotheca Apostolica ebr. 422/1, f. 10b, C, very short.
10272. Zurich - Zentralbibliothek Heid. 139, f. 65b-66b (inserted leafs), C, additional marginal notes.

Ashkenaz, commentary by Elazar b. Yehuda of Worms

10273. Cambridge - University Library Add. 858,2, f. 15a-16b, C.

10274. Firenze - Biblioteca Medicea Laurentiana Plut. 44.13/6, f. 92a-92b, C, rubric: שימושים על דרך הקבלה על האוחז ביד מידת משפט.

10275. Muenchen - Bayerische Staatsbibliothek, Cod. hebr. 92/12, f. 26b-27a, C.

10276. Oxford - Bodleian Library MS Opp. 498 (Neubauer 1930), f. 19a-21a, M.

10277. Oxford - Bodleian Library MS Opp. 525,18 (Neubauer 1598/18), f. 103a-104a, C.

10278. Parma - Biblioteca Palatina Cod. Parm. 2430.14 (de Rossi 1138/15), f. 79a-81a, C.

10279. Zurich - Zentralbibliothek Heid. 139, f. 102b, C, no incipit, very short.

Asti, Fossano, Moncalvo

10280. New Haven - Yale University, Beinecke Rare Book and MS Library, MS Heb. 52, f. 60b, M.

10281. New Haven - Yale University, Beinecke Rare Book and MS Library, MS Heb. 52, f. 71a-71b, M, incipit missing.

10282. New Haven - Yale University, Beinecke Rare Book and MS Library, MS Heb. 52, f. 114b-115a, M.

10283. New Haven - Yale University, Beinecke Rare Book and MS Library, MS Heb. 52, f. 140b-141a, M.

10284. New Haven - Yale University, Beinecke Rare Book and MS Library, MS Hcb. 52, f. 163a-163b, M.

10285. New Haven - Yale University, Beinecke Rare Book and MS Library, MS Heb. 52, f. 177a, M.

Italia, commentary by Ḥat Hazzan of Padova

10286. Milano - Ambrosiana X 230 Sup., f. 11a, M.

10287. Moscow - Russian State Library, Ms. Guenzburg 522, f. 28b-30a, G.

10288. London - Hirschler - Dzialowski (bookdealers), f. 14b-15a, G.

10289. New York - Jewish Theological Seminary Ms. 4392, f. 17b-18a, M.

Roma

10290. Parma - Biblioteca Palatina Cod. Parm. 2224 (de Rossi 1028), f. 149a, M.

Romania

10291. Vatican - Biblioteca Apostolica ebr. 320, f. 156b-157a, G.

10292. Vatican - Biblioteca Apostolica ebr. 320, f. 295b-296a, M.

Tsarfat

10293. London - British Library Add. 11639 (Margoliouth 1056), f. 711a, M, very short.

10294. London - British Library Or. 8682, f. 87b, GI.

10295. London - David Sofer 5, f. 112b-113a, C.

10296. Oxford - Bodleian Library MS Laud. Or. 271 (Neubauer 1206), f. 149a-149b, C, commentator: Aaron b. Hayyim haKohen (compiler).
10297. Oxford - Bodleian Library MS Opp. 171 (Neubauer 1207), f. 63a-63b, C, rubric: סליק פירוש זה של יוצר.
10298. Paris - Bibliotheque Nationale heb. 445,9, f. 80b-82a, C, incipit missing.
10299. Parma - Biblioteca Palatina Cod. Parm. 1794 (de Rossi 1061), f. 73a-75b, M.
10300. Parma - Biblioteca Palatina Cod. Parm. 2125 (de Rossi 812), f. 13b, C.
10301. Parma - Biblioteca Palatina Cod. Parm. 3006 (de Rossi 654,1), f. 31b-32a, M.
10302. Parma - Biblioteca Palatina Cod. Parm. 3006 (de Rossi 654,1), f. 151a-151b, M.
10303. Vatican - Biblioteca Apostolica ebr. 306, f. 42b, C.

האומר אחטא ואשובה (ה 23), אלעזר ברבי קליר, חלק ד', קדושתא לשבת שובה
Tsarfat
10304. Oxford - Bodleian Library MS Opp. 171 (Neubauer 1207), f. 81b-82a, C, rubric: פזמון.

האומרים אחד אומרים יי אלהינו (ה 25), אלעזר ברבי קליר, חלק י"ז, קדושתא למוסף יום כפור
Ashkenaz
10305. Berlin - Staatsbibliothek (Preussischer Kulturbesitz) Or. Qu. 798-799 (Steinschneider 177), I, f. 125b-126a, M.
10306. Budapest - Magyar tudomanyos akademia, MS. Kaufmann A 400, p. 365-366, C.
10307. New York - Jewish Theological Seminary Ms. 4466, f. 381a-381b, M, incipit הגרורים.
10308. Vatican - Biblioteca Apostolica ebr. 422/1, f. 18b, C.
Tsarfat
10309. Oxford - Bodleian Library MS Bodl. Or. 109 (Neubauer 1209), f. 35b, C, commentator: Aaron b. Hayyim haKohen (compiler), very short.
10310. Oxford - Bodleian Library MS Bodl. Or. 109 (Neubauer 1209), f. 44b, C, commentator: Aaron b. Hayyim haKohen (compiler), short.

האזורים באהב אומרים יי אלהינו (ה 27), משולם ב"ר קלונימוס, יוצר ליום כפור
Ashkenaz
10311. Jerusalem - Jewish National and University Library Ms Heb 8° 3037, f. 143b, M, partly deleted.
10312. London - British Library Or. 11318/1, f. 95b-96a, C.

האזינו אבירים בני אלים (ה 28), מנחם ב"ר מכיר, אופן לשבת שובה

Ashkenaz

10313. Jerusalem - Schocken Institute 24100 / Mahzor Nuremberg, f. 473a, M.

10314. London - Montefiore Library 261, f. 83a-83b, C, commentator: Eliezer b. Natan?, rubric: אופן.

Ashkenaz, commentary by Abraham b. Azriel[237]

10315. Frankfurt a M - Stadt- und Universitaetsbibliothek Fol. 16 (Merzbacher 95), f. 45b-46b, C, rubric: אופן.

10316. Vatican - Biblioteca Apostolica ebr. 301,1, f. 70a-71a, C, rubric: אופן האזינו דר' מנחם.

האחד בעולמו ואין שני לא (ה 34), אלעזר ברבי קליר, חלק י"ד, קדושתא למוסף יום כפור

Ashkenaz

10317. Budapest - Magyar tudomanyos akademia, MS. Kaufmann A 400, p. 364-365, C, commentator: Ephraim b. Jacob of Bonn?, postscript אפרים.

10318. Jerusalem - Jewish National and University Library Ms Heb 8° 3037, f. 188a, M.

10319. London - British Library Or. 11318/1, f. 108a-108b, C.

10320. New York - Jewish Theological Seminary Ms. 4466, f. 380b-381a, M.

Tsarfat

10321. Oxford - Bodleian Library MS Bodl. Or. 109 (Neubauer 1209), f. 35b, C, commentator: Aaron b. Hayyım haKohen (compiler), short.

10322. Oxford - Bodleian Library MS Bodl. Or. 109 (Neubauer 1209), f. 44a-44b, C, commentator: Aaron b. Hayyım haKohen (compiler), short.

האל הנקרא ממערב וממזרח (ה 61), משה אבן עזרא, סילוק, קדושתא לשחרית יום כפור

Carpentras

10323. Cincinnati - Hebrew Union College 392, f. 60a-61b, M, no incipit.

Carpentras, commentary by Josef b. Abraham of Montelitz

10324. Cincinnati - Hebrew Union College 291, f. 34a-35b, C, rubric: פי' ובכן וכו'.

10325. New York - Jewish Theological Seminary Ms. 4197, f. 64a-67a, M.

10326. Paris - Ecole Rabbinique 32, f. 150b-153a, M, no incipit.

10327. Strasbourg - Bibliotheque Nationale et Universitaire 4081, f. 127a-130a, M, no incipit.

---

[237] Edited by Urbach, ערוגת הבושם, vol. II, p. 133-139.

הָאֵל הַתְּהִלָּה אֵל בְּלִימָה תֵּבֵל (ה 69), משה אבן עזרא, פזמון

Carpentras
10328. Cincinnati - Hebrew Union College 392, f. 53b-54b, M, no incipit.

Carpentras, commentary by Josef b. Abraham of Montelitz
10329. Cincinnati - Hebrew Union College 291, f. 28b-29a, C, rubric: פי׳ עזמון האל התולה וכו׳.
10330. New York - Jewish Theological Seminary Ms. 4197, f. 122a-122b, M, no incipit.
10331. Paris - Ecole Rabbinique 32, f. 139b-140b, M, no incipit.
10332. Strasbourg - Bibliotheque Nationale et Universitaire 4081, f. 116b-117a, M, no incipit.

Sepharad, commentary by David b. Josef Abudarham[238]
10333. Budapest - Magyar tudomanyos akademia, MS. Kaufmann A 405/2, p. 203, C, rubric: פזמון.
10334. New York - Columbia X893 Ab 93, f. 11a-11b, C, rubric: פזמון.

הָאֵל לְמוֹשָׁעוֹת עִם נוֹשַׁע בְּיָי (ה 73), הושענא

Yemen, commentary by Samḥun b. Salomo Ḥaloah
10335. Jerusalem - Makhon ben Zvi 2808, f. 238b-241a, C.

הָאֵימָן כפי שחקים (ה 94a), משולם ב״ר קלונימוס, חלק מן הרהיטים, קדושתא לשחרית יום כפור

Ashkenaz
10336. Berlin - Staatsbibliothek (Preussischer Kulturbesitz) Or. Qu. 798-799 (Steinschneider 177), I, f. 89a-89b, M.
10337. Braunschweig - Landesmuseum fuer Geschichte und Volkstum R 2386, vol. II, f. 201b-202a, M.
10338. Budapest - Magyar tudomanyos akademia, MS. Kaufmann A 400, p. 338-340, C.
10339. Fulda - Hessische Landesbibliothek A 3 II, f. 116a-116b, C, commentator: Josef, only end.
10340. Hamburg - Staats- und Universitaetsbibliothek Cod. hebr. 62 (Steinschneider 154), f. 10b, C, short.
10341. Jerusalem - Jewish National and University Library Ms Heb 8° 3037, f. 136b-137a, M.
10342. Jerusalem - Schocken Institute 24100 / Mahzor Nuremberg, f. 386b, M.
10343. London - British Library Or. 11318/1, f. 85b-86a, C.
10344. London - Montefiore Library 261, f. 49a-49b, C, commentator: Eliezer b. Natan?.

---

[238] Edited by Prins, תשלום אבודרהם, p. 97-98.

10345. Moscow - Russian State Library, Ms. Guenzburg 191 , f. 102b-103a, M.
10346. Muenchen - Bayerische Staatsbibliothek, Cod. hebr. 86, f. 126b-127a, G, ecclectic.
10347. Muenchen - Bayerische Staatsbibliothek, Cod. hebr. 346 , f. 60b-61a, C, no incipit, short.
10348. New York - Jewish Theological Seminary Ms. 4466, f. 330b-331a, M.
10349. New York - Jewish Theological Seminary Ms. 8097, f. 74b-75a, C.
10350. Oxford - Bodleian Library MS Mich. 365 (Neubauer 1208), f. 79b-80a, C.
10351. Oxford - Bodleian Library MS Opp. 172 (Neubauer 1211), f. 47b, C.
10352. Oxford - Bodleian Library MS Opp. 619 (Neubauer 2374), f. 165b, M.
10353. Parma - Biblioteca Palatina Cod. Parm. 3205 (de Rossi 655), f. 227b, C.
10354. Parma - Biblioteca Palatina Cod. Parm. 3271 (de Rossi 1216), f. 56a, G.
10355. Parma - Biblioteca Palatina Cod. Parm. 3507 (Perreau 27), f. 160a, C.
10356. Vatican - Biblioteca Apostolica ebr. 308, f. 102(ii)b, C, commentator: David b. Mose (compiler).
10357. Vatican - Biblioteca Apostolica ebr. 422/1, f. 16b, C, very short.
10358. Zurich - Zentralbibliothek Heid. 139, f. 78b, C, short, additional marginal notes.

Ashkenaz, commentary by Abraham b. Azriel[239]

10359. Vatican - Biblioteca Apostolica ebr. 301,1, f. 170b, C.

Asti, Fossano, Moncalvo

10360. New Haven - Yale University, Beinecke Rare Book and MS Library, MS Heb. 52, f. 115b-116a, M.

Romania

10361. Vatican - Biblioteca Apostolica ebr. 320, f. 386b, M.

Tsarfat

10362. London - David Sofer 5, f. 141a-142a, C.
10363. Oxford - Bodleian Library MS Bodl. Or. 109 (Neubauer 1209), f. 25b-26a, C, commentator: Aaron b. Hayyim haKohen (compiler).
10364. Oxford - Bodleian Library MS Laud. Or. 271 (Neubauer 1206), f. 135b, C, commentator: Aaron b. Hayyim haKohen (compiler).
10365. Parma - Biblioteca Palatina Cod. Parm. 2890 (de Rossi 856), f. 40a, M.
10366. Parma - Biblioteca Palatina Cod. Parm. 3006 (de Rossi 654,1), f. 152a-152b, M.
10367. Vatican - Biblioteca Apostolica ebr. 306, f. 81b, C.

---

[239] Edited by Urbach, ערוגת הבושם, vol. III, p. 500-501.

האת אלקלם יא צאפי אלדאת (ה 112), שלם שבזי
Yemen
10368. Cincinnati - Hebrew Union College 398, f. 91a-95a, M.

הבט משמים וראה מזבול קדשך, קינה
North Africa, commentary by Yehuda Toledano
10369. New York - Jewish Theological Seminary Rab. 949, f. 127b-129b, C.

הגוים אימים זמזומים קדר ואדומים (ה 178), פיוט אחרי הקדושה, שחרית יום כפור, כלל כמה חלקים
Ashkenaz
10370. Berlin - Staatsbibliothek (Preussischer Kulturbesitz) Or. Qu. 798-799 (Steinschneider 177), I, f. 94b-95a, M.
10371. Braunschweig - Landesmuseum fuer Geschichte und Volkstum R 2386, vol. II, f. 205a-206b, M.
10372. Fulda - Hessische Landesbibliothek A 3 II, f. 120b-121a, C, commentator: Josef.
10373. Hamburg - Staats- und Universitaetsbibliothek Cod. hebr. 62 (Steinschneider 154), f. 15a-16a, C.
10374. Hamburg - Staats- und Universitaetsbibliothek Cod. hebr. 132 (Steinschneider 155), f. 41b-42b, C.
10375. Jerusalem - Jewish National and University Library Ms Heb 8° 3037, f. 142a-142b, M.
10376. Jerusalem - Schocken Institute 24100 / Mahzor Nuremberg, f. 391a-391b, M.
10377. London - British Library Or. 11318/1, f. 93b-94b, C.
10378. London - Montefiore Library 261, f. 52b-53a, C, commentator: Eliezer b. Natan?.
10379. Moscow - Russian State Library, Ms. Guenzburg 615, f. 100b-101b, C.
10380. Muenchen - Bayerische Staatsbibliothek, Cod. hebr. 86, f. 134b-135b, G.
10381. New York - Jewish Theological Seminary Ms. 4466, f. 337b-338b, M, partly censored.
10382. New York - Jewish Theological Seminary Ms. 8097, f. 76a-76b, C.
10383. Oxford - Bodleian Library MS Mich. 365 (Neubauer 1208), f. 78a-78b, C.
10384. Oxford - Bodleian Library MS Opp. 170 (Neubauer 1205), f. 172b-173b, C.
10385. Oxford - Bodleian Library MS Opp. 172 (Neubauer 1211), f. 52a-52b, C.
10386. Oxford - Bodleian Library MS Opp. 619 (Neubauer 2374), f. 170a, M, only ובכל תוקף יאמן.

10387. Parma - Biblioteca Palatina Cod. Parm. 3205 (de Rossi 655), f. 232a-232b, C.
10388. Parma - Biblioteca Palatina Cod. Parm. 3271 (de Rossi 1216), f. 58b-60a, G.
10389. Parma - Biblioteca Palatina Cod. Parm. 3271 (de Rossi 1216), f. 62b-63b, G.
10390. Parma - Biblioteca Palatina Cod. Parm. 3507 (Perreau 27), f. 158b-159b, C.
10391. Vatican - Biblioteca Apostolica ebr. 306, f. 86b-97a, C.
10392. Vatican - Biblioteca Apostolica ebr. 308, f. 106(ii)b-107(ii)a, C, commentator: David b. Mose (compiler).
10393. Vatican - Biblioteca Apostolica ebr. 422/1, f. 17a-17b, C.
10394. Zurich - Zentralbibliothek Heid. 139, f. 81a-81b, C, additional marginal notes.

Ashkenaz, commentary by Abraham b. Azriel[240]

10395. Vatican - Biblioteca Apostolica ebr. 301,1, f. 173a-173b, C.

Tsarfat

10396. London - British Library Add. 11639 (Margoliouth 1056), f. 722a-722b, M.
10397. London - David Sofer 5, f. 166a, C, almost completely deleted.
10398. Oxford - Bodleian Library MS Bodl. Or. 109 (Neubauer 1209), f. 27(iv)a-27(iv)b, C, commentator: Aaron b. Hayyim haKohen (compiler).
10399. Oxford - Bodleian Library MS Laud. Or. 271 (Neubauer 1206), f. 110a-110b, C, commentator: Aaron b. Hayyim haKohen (compiler).

הגוים אפס והוהו נגדך חשובים (ה 179), פיוט אחרי הקדושה, שחרית יום כפור, כלל כמה חלקים

Ashkenaz

10400. Berlin - Staatsbibliothek (Preussischer Kulturbesitz) Or. Qu. 798-799 (Steinschneider 177), I, f. 91b-93a, M.
10401. Braunschweig - Landesmuseum fuer Geschichte und Volkstum R 2386, vol. II, f. 203b-204b, M.
10402. Fulda - Hessische Landesbibliothek A 3 II, f. 118a-119b, C, commentator: Josef.
10403. Hamburg - Staats- und Universitaetsbibliothek Cod. hebr. 40b (Steinschneider 110), f. 111b-112b, G.
10404. Hamburg - Staats- und Universitaetsbibliothek Cod. hebr. 62 (Steinschneider 154), f. 12b-13b, C.
10405. Hamburg - Staats- und Universitaetsbibliothek Cod. hebr. 132 (Steinschneider 155), f. 39b-40a, C.

---

[240] Edited by Urbach, ערוגת הבושם, vol. III, p. 515-516.

10406. Jerusalem - Jewish National and University Library Ms Heb 8° 3037, f. 138b-139b, M, first part censored.
10407. Jerusalem - Schocken Institute 24100 / Mahzor Nuremberg, f. 388a-389a, M.
10408. London - British Library Or. 11318/1, f. 88b-90a, C.
10409. London - Montefiore Library 261, f. 50b-51b, C, commentator: Eliezer b. Natan?.
10410. Moscow - Russian State Library, Ms. Guenzburg 191, f. 105b-106b, M, first part missing (deleted by censor?).
10411. Moscow - Russian State Library, Ms. Guenzburg 615, f. 97b-99a, C, partly censored.
10412. Muenchen - Bayerische Staatsbibliothek, Cod. hebr. 86, f. 129b-131b, G, ecclectic.
10413. Muenchen - Bayerische Staatsbibliothek, Cod. hebr. 346, f. 63b-65a, C, no incipit.
10414. Muenchen - Bayerische Staatsbibliothek, Cod. hebr. 346, f. 70a-70b, C, rubric: הגוים אפס ותוהו רהיטין לא פירש ופשוט הוא, only 2nd part.
10415. New York - Jewish Theological Seminary Ms. 4466, f. 333a-335a, M, partly censored.
10416. New York - Jewish Theological Seminary Ms. 8097, f. 75b, C.
10417. Oxford - Bodleian Library MS Mich. 365 (Neubauer 1208), f. 75b-76b, C.
10418. Oxford - Bodleian Library MS Opp. 170 (Neubauer 1205), f. 169b-171a, C.
10419. Oxford - Bodleian Library MS Opp. 172 (Neubauer 1211), f. 49a-50a, C.
10420. Parma - Biblioteca Palatina Cod. Parm. 3205 (de Rossi 655), f. 230a-231a, C.
10421. Parma - Biblioteca Palatina Cod. Parm. 3507 (Perreau 27), f. 156a-157a, C.
10422. Vatican - Biblioteca Apostolica ebr. 308, f. 104(ii)a-105(ii)a, C, commentator: David b. Mose (compiler).
10423. Vatican - Biblioteca Apostolica ebr. 422/1, f. 17a, C.
10424. Zurich - Zentralbibliothek Heid. 139, f. 79b-80a, C, additional marginal notes.

Ashkenaz, commentary by Abraham b. Azriel[241]

10425. Vatican - Biblioteca Apostolica ebr. 301,1, f. 171b-172a, C.

Asti, Fossano, Moncalvo

10426. New Haven - Yale University, Beinecke Rare Book and MS Library, MS Heb. 52, f. 118a, M, only 2nd part.

---

[241] Edited by Urbach, ערוגת הבושם, vol. III, p. 505-509.

Tsarfat
10427. London - British Library Add. 11639 (Margoliouth 1056), f. 721b-722a, M.
10428. London - David Sofer 5, f. 142a-142b, C.
10429. London - David Sofer 5, f. 154a-154b, C, rubric: רהיטים, only 2nd part.
10430. Oxford - Bodleian Library MS Bodl. Or. 109 (Neubauer 1209), f. 27(i)a-27(ii)b, C, commentator: Aaron b. Hayyim haKohen (compiler).
10431. Oxford - Bodleian Library MS Laud. Or. 271 (Neubauer 1206), f. 107b-108b, C, commentator: Aaron b. Hayyim haKohen (compiler).
10432. Parma - Biblioteca Palatina Cod. Parm. 1794 (de Rossi 1061), f. 153a-153b, M, only 2nd part.
10433. Parma - Biblioteca Palatina Cod. Parm. 1794 (de Rossi 1061), f. 183b, M, only 2nd part.
10434. Parma - Biblioteca Palatina Cod. Parm. 3006 (de Rossi 654,1), f. 188a-189a, M.
10435. Vatican - Biblioteca Apostolica ebr. 306, f. 83b-84b, C, incipit אפס.

הגיגנו דבורינו, סליחה

Ashkenaz
10436. Muenchen - Bayerische Staatsbibliothek, Cod. hebr. 346, f. 87a, C.

הדרך ועזוז ידך מלא עולם יחז יחד (ה 198), משה זכות, להושענא רבה
Italia, commentary by Zakharya David Shabbetai Segre
10437. Torino - Archivio Terracini 1499, p. 157-158, C, rubric: פירוש הדרך ועזוז ידך.

ההרים והגבעות יפצחו לפניכם רנה, לשמחת תורה
Yemen, commentary by Yiḥya b. Josef Tsalaḥ
10438. Montreal - Elberg 203, f. 39b-40a, M.

הוא אלהים חיים ומלך עולם, יצחק ב"ר יהודה, סליחה
Yemen, commentary by Isaac b. Abraham Wanneh
10439. Chicago-Spertus College of Judaica D 2, 2, f. 220b-221a, M, no incipit.
10440. Jerusalem - Michael Krupp 604, f. 165b-166a, M, rubric: אל מלך.
10441. Jerusalem - Sassoon 1158, p. 374, M, no incipit.
10442. London - British Library Or. 11122, f. 187a-187b, M, no incipit.

הוא נקרא ראש וראשון (ה+ 258), אלעזר ברבי קליר, סילוק, קדושתא לשבת החדש
Ashkenaz

10443. Berlin - Staatsbibliothek (Preussischer Kulturbesitz) Or. Qu. 798-799 (Steinschneider 177), II, f. 42a-43b, M.

10444. Budapest - Magyar tudomanyos akademia, MS. Kaufmann A 384, f. 92a-93b, M.

10445. Erlangen - Universitaetsbibliothek 2601 (Roth 67), f. 52a, M.

10446. Hamburg - Staats- und Universitaetsbibliothek Cod. hebr. 17/2 (Steinschneider 152), f. 29a-29b, C, rubric: סילוק.

10447. Jerusalem - Schocken Institute 24100 / Mahzor Nuremberg, f. 66b-67a, M.

10448. London - British Library Add. 18695 (Margoliouth 683), f. 5b-7a, T, Yiddish.

10449. Muenchen - Bayerische Staatsbibliothek, Cod. hebr. 88, f. 45a-46a, G.

10450. Muenchen - Bayerische Staatsbibliothek, Cod. hebr. 393, f. 105a-105b, C, no incipit.

10451. New York - Jewish Theological Seminary Ms. 4466, f. 23a-25a, M.

10452. Oxford - Bodleian Library MS Opp. 170 (Neubauer 1205), f. 35b-36b, C, rubric: סילוק.

10453. Paris - Bibliotheque Nationale heb. 709, f. 42a-43a, C, rubric: סילוק.

10454. Parma - Biblioteca Palatina Cod. Parm. 1002 (Ta 24), f. 69b-70a, M.

10455. Parma - Biblioteca Palatina Cod. Parm. 3205 (de Rossi 655), f. 43b-45a, C, rubric: סילוק.

10456. Parma - Biblioteca Palatina Cod. Parm. 3507 (Perreau 27), f. 31b-32a, C, rubric: סילוק.

10457. Vatican - Biblioteca Apostolica ebr. 305,1, f. 27a-29a, C, rubric: סילוק.

Tsarfat

10458. Oxford - Bodleian Library MS Laud. Or. 271 (Neubauer 1206), f. 48a-49a, C, commentator: Aaron b. Hayyim haKohen (compiler), rubric: סילוק.

הוד יוצרנו ועצמו אסם גבורות מצפניו (ה 262), משה זכות, להושענא רבה
Italia, commentary by Zakharya David Shabbetai Segre

10459. Torino - Archivio Terracini 1499, p. 215-219, C, rubric: פירוש הוד יוצרנו ועצמו.

הורית דרך תשוב לבת השובבה (ה+ 352), בנימין ב"ר זרח, פתיחה לסליחה
Ashkenaz

10460. Braunschweig - Landesmuseum fuer Geschichte und Volkstum R 2386, vol. II, f. 128a-128b, M.

10461. Muenchen - Bayerische Staatsbibliothek, Cod. hebr. 346, f. 150b, C, rubric: אחרת.

10462. Oxford - Bodleian Library MS Mich. 543 (Neubauer 1212), f. 38a, C, commentator: Isaac b. Jacob (compiler), rubric: פיזמון.
10463. Oxford - Bodleian Library MS Opp. 681 (Neubauer 1213), f. 78b-79a, C.
10464. Padova - Biblioteca del Seminario Vescovile Cod. 218, f. 123a-124a, M.
10465. Vatican - Biblioteca Apostolica ebr. 422/1, f. 32a, C.

Ashkenaz, commentary by Abraham b. Azriel[242]

10466. Vatican - Biblioteca Apostolica ebr. 301,1, f. 139b, C, rubric: אחר.
10467. Vatican - Biblioteca Apostolica ebr. 301,1, f. 170a, C.

Tsarfat

10468. London - David Sofer 5, f. 102b-103a, C.
10469. Parma - Biblioteca Palatina Cod. Parm. 3007 (de Rossi 654,2), f. 119a-119b, M.

הושענא מארוד וארפד ואכד ואלופיהם (ה 362), סעדיה גאון, הושענא

Yemen

10470. Chicago-Spertus College of Judaica D 10, f. 122b-123a, M, incipit מארוד.
10471. Jerusalem - Michael Krupp 3391, f. 5a, M.
10472. Jerusalem - Musad haRav Kook 334, f. 87b, M, rubric: פירוש.
10473. Jerusalem - Musad haRav Kook 952, f. 7b-8a, M, rubric: ליום שלישי.
10474. Jerusalem - Sassoon 264, f. 93a, M, no incipit.
10475. Jerusalem - Sassoon 902, p. 174, M, rubric: ליום ג׳, very short.
10476. New York - Alfred Moldovan HH, f. 8a 8b, M, rubric: ליום ג׳.
10477. New York - Jewish Theological Seminary Ms. 4488, f. 67b, M.
10478. New York - Jewish Theological Seminary Ms. 9325, f. 73b, M.
10479. New York - Public Library, Heb. Ms. 10, f. 57b, M, no incipit.
10480. Ramat Gan - Universitat Bar Ilan 62, f. 28a, G, margins damaged.

Yemen, commentary by Isaac b. Abraham Wanneh

10481. Chicago-Spertus College of Judaica D 1, f. 194b-195a, M.
10482. Jerusalem - Benayahu ת 261, f. 80b, M, rubric: ליום שלישי.
10483. Jerusalem - Benayahu ת 282, f. 74a, M, rubric: ליום שלישי.
10484. Jerusalem - Israel Museum 180/78, f. 8b-9b, M, rubric: ליום שלישי.
10485. Jerusalem - Makhon Ben Zvi 1156 (Tubi 155), f. 71a-71b, M, rubric: ליום שלישי.
10486. Jerusalem - Makhon Ben Zvi 1169 (Tubi 159), f. 61b-62a, M, very short.
10487. Jerusalem - Makhon Ben Zvi 1174 (Tubi 154), f. 82b, M, rubric: ליום שלישי.
10488. Jerusalem - Makhon ben Zvi 1186 (Tubi 205), f. 4a, M, rubric: ליום שלישי, incipit מארוד.

---

[242] Edited by Urbach, ערוגת הבושם, vol. III, p. 295-297, 496.

10489. Jerusalem - Michael Krupp 604, f. 91a, M, rubric: ליום שלישי.
10490. Jerusalem - Michael Krupp 1990, f. 98b, M, margins damaged.
10491. Jerusalem - Musad haRav Kook 325, f. 103a-103b, M, rubric: חידושין.
10492. Jerusalem - Musad haRav Kook 325, f. 120b-121a, M, rubric: ליום ג'.
10493. Jerusalem - Musad haRav Kook 330, f. 67a, M.
10494. Jerusalem - Musad haRav Kook 347, f. 57a, M.
10495. Jerusalem - Sassoon 1158, p. 213, M, rubric: ליום שלישי.
10496. Jerusalem - Sassoon 1174, p. 141, M, rubric: ליום שלישי.
10497. Jerusalem - Schocken Institute 70028, f. 186b-187a, M, rubric: ליום שלישי.
10498. Jerusalem - Yehiel haLevi 4, f. 86b, M.
10499. London - British Library Or. 11121, f. 131b, C, rubric: ליום שלישי.
10500. London - British Library Or. 11122, f. 121a, M, rubric: ליום שלישי.
10501. Manchester - John Rylands University Library, Ms. Gaster 5, f. 146b, M, rubric: ליום שלישי.
10502. Muenchen - Bayerische Staatsbibliothek, Cod. hebr. 472, f. 97b-98a, M, rubric: ליום שלישי.
10503. Nahariya - Menahem and Saida Yaakob 284, f. 8b-9a, M.
10504. New York - Jewish Theological Seminary Ms. 3013, f. 73b, M, rubric: ליום שלישי, margins damaged.
10505. New York - Jewish Theological Seminary Ms. 3193, f. 160b, M, rubric: ליום שלישי.
10506. New York - Jewish Theological Seminary Ms. 3295, f. 88b, M.
10507. New York - Jewish Theological Seminary Ms. 4195, f. 11b-12a, M.
10508. New York - Public Library, Heb. Ms. 9, f. 71a, M, rubric: ליום ג'.
10509. Oxford - Bodleian Library MS Opp. Add. fol. 58 (Neubauer 2498), f. 140a-140b, M, rubric: ליום שלישי.
10510. Paris - G. Epstein 23/57, f. 99a-100a, C, rubric: ליום שלישי.
10511. Philadelphia - University of Pennsylvania HB 2, f. 97a, M, rubric: ליום ג'.
10512. Ramat Gan - Universitat Bar Ilan 703, f. 193a, M, rubric: ליום שלישי.
10513. Strasbourg - Bibliotheque Nationale et Universitaire 3965 (Landauer 39), p. 234, M, rubric: ליום ג'.

Yemen, commentary by Simon b. Tsemaḥ Duran
10514. Jerusalem - Michael Krupp 1758, f. 6a-6b, M, rubric: פירוש.

Yemen, commentary by Yiḥya b. Josef Tsalaḥ
10515. Montreal - Elberg 203, f. 7a, M.

החדש הזה לכם לשמור (ה +368), אלעזר ברבי קליר, חלק ד', קדושתא לשבת החדש Ashkenaz
10516. London - British Library Add. 18695 (Margoliouth 683), f. 3b, T, Yiddish, incipits החדש and דורש.

החרשים שמעו מפי נוראות (ה 379), משה אבן עזרא, פזמון

Carpentras
10517. Cincinnati - Hebrew Union College 392, f. 51b-53b, M, no incipit.

Carpentras, commentary by Josef b. Abraham of Montelitz
10518. Cincinnati - Hebrew Union College 291, f. 26b-28b, C, rubric: ובכן פי׳ אזכור וכו׳.
10519. New York - Jewish Theological Seminary Ms. 4197, f. 118b-121b, M, no incipit.
10520. Paris - Ecole Rabbinique 32, f. 136b-139b, M, no incipit.
10521. Strasbourg - Bibliotheque Nationale et Universitaire 4081, f. 113b-116a, M, no incipit.

Sepharad, commentary by David b. Josef Abudarham[243]
10522. Budapest - Magyar tudomanyos akademia, MS. Kaufmann A 405/2, p. 200-202, C, rubric: פזמון. ובכן אזכור מעללי תבל כי כלמעשינו הבל.
10523. Cincinnati - Hebrew Union College 490, f. 6a-7a, C.
10524. Holon - Yehuda Nahum 278, f. 2a-2b, FC, rubric: פזמון.
10525. New York - Columbia X893 Ab 93, f. 10b-11a, C, rubric: ובכן. פזמון אזכור מעללי תבל כי כלמעשינו הבל.
10526. New York - Jewish Theological Seminary Ms. 3011, f. 9b-10a, C, rubric: פזמון.

הטה אלהי אזנך ושמע לתפלצת מנאצת (ה 392), אלעזר ברבי קליר, קינה

Ashkenaz
10527. Berlin - Staatsbibliothek (Preussischer Kulturbesitz) Or. Qu. 798-799 (Steinschneider 177), II, f. 193a-193b, M.
10528. Budapest - Magyar tudomanyos akademia, MS. Kaufmann A 400, p. 230-231, C, rubric: אחרת.
10529. Hamburg - Staats- und Universitaetsbibliothek Cod. hebr. 17/2 (Steinschneider 152), f. 100b, C.
10530. Jerusalem - Schocken Institute 24100 / Mahzor Nuremberg, f. 209a, M.
10531. Muenchen - Bayerische Staatsbibliothek, Cod. hebr. 88, f. 178b-179a, G, ecclectic.
10532. Parma - Biblioteca Palatina Cod. Parm. 3205 (de Rossi 655), f. 197a-197b, C, rubric: אחרת.
10533. Vatican - Biblioteca Apostolica ebr. 312, f. 52a-52b, G.

Ashkenaz, commentary by Abraham b. Azriel[244]
10534. Vatican - Biblioteca Apostolica ebr. 301,1, f. 137a, C, rubric: אחרת, very short.

---

[243] Edited by Prins, תשלום אבודרהם, p. 93-97.
[244] Edited by Urbach, ערוגת הבושם, vol. III, p. 281.

היום הרת עולם (ה 468)

Ashkenaz

10535. Berlin - Staatsbibliothek (Preussischer Kulturbesitz) Or. Qu. 798-799 (Steinschneider 177), I, f. 47a, M.
10536. Budapest - Magyar tudomanyos akademia, MS. Kaufmann A 400 , p. 272-276, C.
10537. Cambridge - University Library Or. 785, f. 44b, G.
10538. Darmstadt - Hessisches Landes- und Hochschulbibliothek Cod. Or. 15, f. 23b-24a, M.
10539. Hamburg - Staats- und Universitaetsbibliothek Cod. hebr. 17/2 (Steinschneider 152), f. 118a, C.
10540. Jerusalem - Schocken Institute 24100 / Mahzor Nuremberg , f. 336b, M.
10541. London - British Library Or. 11318/1, f. 25a-26a, C, commentator: Ephraim b. Jacob of Bonn.
10542. London - Montefiore Library 261 , f. 20b-21a, C, commentator: Eliezer b. Natan?.
10543. Lund - Universitetsbibliothek Ms. L.O. 2, f. 78a, M, short.
10544. Moscow - Russian State Library, Ms. Guenzburg 1401/2, f. 19b, C, manuscripts ends in the middle of the commentary.
10545. Moscow - Russian State Library, Ms. Guenzburg 482/3, f. 36a, M.
10546. Oxford - Bodleian Library MS Opp. 170 (Neubauer 1205), f. 114a, C.
10547. Oxford - Bodleian Library MS Opp. 170 (Neubauer 1205), f. 131a-132b, C, rubric: ותוקעין קשרק.
10548. Oxford - Bodleian Library MS Opp. 170 (Neubauer 1205), f. 162a, C, commentator: Aaron b. Mordekhai (compiler), rubric: של פי' אני אכתו' היום הרת עולם פי' אחר.
10549. Oxford - Bodleian Library MS Opp. 675 (Neubauer 1210), f. 35b, C, no incipit.
10550. Oxford - Bodleian Library MS Opp. 675 (Neubauer 1210), f. 47a-47b, C, rubric: ותוקעין קשרק.
10551. Parma - Biblioteca Palatina Cod. Parm. 3205 (de Rossi 655), f. 218a, C.
10552. Vatican - Biblioteca Apostolica ebr. 422/1, f. 14b, C, ecclectic.
10553. Verona - Seminario Maggiore 34, f. 255a, M.

Ashkenaz, commentary by Abraham b. Azriel[245]

10554. Frankfurt a M - Stadt- und Universitaetsbibliothek Fol. 16 (Merzbacher 95), f. 111a, C, very short.
10555. Vatican - Biblioteca Apostolica ebr. 301,1, f. 166b, C, very short.
10556. Vatican - Biblioteca Apostolica ebr. 301,1, f. 168a, C.

---

[245] Edited by Urbach, ערוגת הבושם, vol. III, p. 474 and 484-485.

Tsarfat
10557. Oxford - Bodleian Library MS Bodl. Or. 109 (Neubauer 1209), f. 8a, C, commentator: Aaron b. Hayyim haKohen (compiler), short.
10558. Oxford - Bodleian Library MS Laud. Or. 271 (Neubauer 1206), f. 151a, C, commentator: Aaron b. Hayyim haKohen (compiler), short.

היום מלכי מקדם פועל ישועות (ה 489), מרדכי בן שבתי, סליחה

Ashkenaz
10559. Jerusalem - Schocken Institute 24100 / Mahzor Nuremberg, f. 436a-436b, M, short.
10560. Muenchen - Bayerische Staatsbibliothek, Cod. hebr. 346, f. 138a, C, rubric: אחרת, short.
10561. Oxford - Bodleian Library MS Opp. 172 (Neubauer 1211), f. 78b, C, incipit מלכי.
10562. Vatican - Biblioteca Apostolica ebr. 308, f. 135a, C, commentator: David b. Mose (compiler).

Ashkenaz, commentary by Abraham b. Azriel[246]
10563. Frankfurt a M - Stadt- und Universitaetsbibliothek Fol. 16 (Merzbacher 95), f. 107b, C, incipit מלכי.

היטיבה יי לטובים, אלעזר ברבי קליר, חלק ד', קדושתא לשמיני עצרת

Tsarfat
10564. London - David Sofer 5, f. 184a, C, incipit אל נא.
10565. Oxford - Bodleian Library MS Opp. 171 (Neubauer 1207), f. 162a, C, incipit משלמי.

היך שפירתא בכולא (ה 520), קינה

North Africa
10566. Palo Alto L.U. Berman [2]/2, 77a-79a, M.

היכל יי ומקדש הדומו גלה כבודו ונפזר עמו (ה 522), יהודה הלוי, סליחה

Yemen, commentary by Isaac b. Abraham Wanneh
10567. Chicago-Spertus College of Judaica D 2, 2, f. 200b, M, no incipit.
10568. Jerusalem - Sassoon 1158, p. 360, M, no incipit.

הילילו הה ליום כי קצף עלינו איום (ה 532), אלעזר ברבי קליר, קינה

Ashkenaz
10569. Berlin - Staatsbibliothek (Preussischer Kulturbesitz) Or. Qu. 798-799 (Steinschneider 177), II, f. 203b, M.
10570. Budapest - Magyar tudomanyos akademia, MS. Kaufmann A 400, p. 206-207, C, rubric: אחרת.

---

[246] Edited by Urbach, ערוגת הבושם, vol. III, p. 557-558.

10571. Hamburg - Staats- und Universitaetsbibliothek Cod. hebr. 17/2 (Steinschneider 152), f. 94b, C.

10572. Jerusalem - Schocken Institute 24100 / Mahzor Nuremberg, f. 218b, M.

10573. Parma - Biblioteca Palatina Cod. Parm. 3205 (de Rossi 655), f. 197b, C, rubric: אחרת.

10574. Vatican - Biblioteca Apostolica ebr. 312, f. 44b, G.

Ashkenaz, commentary by Abraham b. Azriel[247]

10575. Vatican - Biblioteca Apostolica ebr. 301,1, f. 137b, C, rubric: אחרת.

הלא אמרית ליך כנישתא דישראל (ה 624), סליחה

Roma

10576. Berlin - Staatsbibliothek (Preussischer Kulturbesitz) Or. Oct. 3567, f. 3b, FC.

המבדיל בין קדש לחול חטאתינו ימחול (ה 741), יצחק, למוצאי שבת

Carpentras, commentary by Josef b. Abraham of Montelitz

10577. New York - Jewish Theological Seminary Ms. 4197, f. 258a, M.

10578. Paris - Ecole Rabbinique 32, f. 267a, M.

10579. Strasbourg - Bibliotheque Nationale et Universitaire 4081, f. 237a, M.

Yemen, commentary by Isaac b. Abraham Wanneh

10580. Jerusalem - Makhon Ben Zvi 1169 (Tubi 159), f. 27b, G.

המית קוראיך לשוחרך שיחר, הושענא

Yemen, commentary by Samḥun b. Salomo Ḥaloah

10581. Jerusalem - Makhon ben Zvi 2808, f. 67a-68a, C.

המלך יי רום ותחת קונה (ה 765), יהודה, סליחה

Yemen, commentary by Isaac b. Abraham Wanneh

10582. Jerusalem - Sassoon 1158, p. 191-193, M.

המלך שיר נדבות (ה 775), שלמה, רשות

Ashkenaz

10583. Berlin - Staatsbibliothek (Preussischer Kulturbesitz) Or. Qu. 798-799 (Steinschneider 177), I, f. 262b, M.

---

[247] Edited by Urbach, ערוגת הבושם, vol. III, p. 282.

הן לא קצרה יד אל מהושיע אתכם (ה 824), משה אבן עזרא, סליחה
Sepharad, commentary by David b. Josef Abudarham[248]

10584. Budapest - Magyar tudomanyos akademia, MS. Kaufmann A 405/2, p. 251, C.

הנקדש באלפי אלפים (ה 920), משולם ב"ר קלונימוס, חלק כ"א, קדושתא לשחרית יום כפור

Ashkenaz

10585. Berlin - Staatsbibliothek (Preussischer Kulturbesitz) Or. Qu. 798-799 (Steinschneider 177), I, f. 80b, M.

10586. Braunschweig - Landesmuseum fuer Geschichte und Volkstum R 2386, f. 193a, M.

10587. Budapest - Magyar tudomanyos akademia, MS. Kaufmann A 400, p. 320, C.

10588. Hamburg - Staats- und Universitaetsbibliothek Cod. hebr. 17/2 (Steinschneider 152), f. 152b, C.

10589. Hamburg - Staats- und Universitaetsbibliothek Cod. hebr. 62 (Steinschneider 154), f. 7a, C, short.

10590. Jerusalem - Jewish National and University Library Ms Heb 8° 3037, f. 125a, M, short.

10591. Jerusalem - Schocken Institute 24100 / Mahzor Nuremberg, f. 380b-381a, M, very short.

10592. London - British Library Or. 11318/1, f. 77b, C, very short, no incipit.

10593. London - Montefiore Library 261, f. 45b-46a, C, commentator: Eliezer b. Natan?.

10594. Moscow - Russian State Library, Ms. Guenzburg 191, f. 92b, M.

10595. New York - Jewish Theological Seminary Ms. 4466, f. 317a, M, short.

10596. New York - Jewish Theological Seminary Ms. 8097, f. 72b, C, very short.

10597. New York - Jewish Theological Seminary Ms. 8169 (Acc. 0016), f. 73a, M.

10598. Oxford - Bodleian Library MS Opp. 172 (Neubauer 1211), f. 41b, C, short.

10599. Oxford - Bodleian Library MS Opp. 619 (Neubauer 2374), f. 152b, M, short.

10600. Parma - Biblioteca Palatina Cod. Parm. 3271 (de Rossi 1216), f. 44a, G.

10601. Vatican - Biblioteca Apostolica ebr. 308, f. 103b, C, commentator: David b. Mose (compiler), short.

---

[248] Edited by Prins, תשלום אבודרהם, p. 122-123.

Asti, Fossano, Moncalvo
10602. New Haven - Yale University, Beinecke Rare Book and MS Library, MS Heb. 52, f. 108b-109a, M.

Romania
10603. Vatican - Biblioteca Apostolica ebr. 320, f. 287a-287b, M.

Tsarfat
10604. Bern - Burgerbibliothek A 409, f. 86a-86b, G.
10605. London - British Library Or. 8682, f. 70b, Gl.
10606. London - David Sofer 5, f. 138b-139a, C.
10607. Oxford - Bodleian Library MS Bodl. Or. 109 (Neubauer 1209), f. 22a, C, commentator: Aaron b. Hayyim haKohen (compiler), short.
10608. Parma - Biblioteca Palatina Cod. Parm. 1794 (de Rossi 1061), f. 128a-128b, M.
10609. Parma - Biblioteca Palatina Cod. Parm. 2890 (de Rossi 856), f. 31a, M.
10610. Vatican - Biblioteca Apostolica ebr. 306, f. 77b-78a, C.

הנקרא לאב זרע ונפנה לסור ממוקשי רע, חלק ב׳, קדושתא לנעילה

Ashkenaz
10611. Cambridge - University Library Add. 394,1 (Reif SCR 461), f. 73a, C, short.
10612. Vatican - Biblioteca Apostolica ebr. 308, f. 147a, C, commentator: David b. Mose (compiler).
10613. Zurich - Zentralbibliothek Heid. 139, f. 89a, C, no incipit, very short, additional marginal notes.

הסכת ושמע ישראל (ה 939), בנימין ב״ר שמואל, לשחרית ראש השנה

Tsarfat
10614. Manchester - John Rylands University Library, Ms. Gaster 733, f. 81b, C, commentary block in Mahzor, manuscript damaged.
10615. Vatican - Biblioteca Apostolica ebr. 306, f. 68a, C.

הרבינו לפשוע ובקש ציר בעדינו (ה 1040), סליחה

Yemen, commentary by Isaac b. Abraham Wanneh
10616. Chicago-Spertus College of Judaica D 2, 2, f. 229a-229b, M, no incipit.
10617. Jerusalem - Sassoon 1158, p. 317-318, M, no incipit.
10618. London - British Library Or. 11122, f. 205b, M, no incipit.

השכם והערב לצורי מניתי (ה +1125), אברהם אבן עזרא, משלש
Sepharad, commentary by David b. Josef Abudarham[249]
10619. Budapest - Magyar tudomanyos akademia, MS. Kaufmann A 405/2, p. 253-254, C, rubric: משלש.
10620. Holon - Yehuda Nahum 278, f. 4a-4b, FC, rubric: משלש.
10621. New York - Columbia X893 Ab 93, f. 31a, C, rubric: משלש.

השפילו שבו והעמיקו שפל (ה 1158), קינה
Carpentras, commentary by Mordekhai b. Josef of Rocco Martino
10622. Cincinnati - Hebrew Union College 246/1, f. 63a-64b, C, rubric: פי' קינה השפילו שבו וכו'.

השקיפה ממעון קדשך (ה 1162), אלעזר ברבי קליר, סילוק, קדושתא לשמיני עצרת
Tsarfat[250]
10623. Oxford - Bodleian Library MS Opp. 171 (Neubauer 1207), f. 152a-154a, C, rubric: סילוק.

התבוננו ונדעה כי נלכה ונסעה (ה 1189), משה אבן עזרא, חלק י', קדושתא לשחרית יום כפור
Carpentras, commentary by Josef b. Abraham of Montelitz
10624. Cincinnati - Hebrew Union College 291, f. 29a-29b, C, rubric: פי' תוכחה התבוננו וכו'.
10625. New York - Jewish Theological Seminary Ms. 4197, f. 123a-124a, M.
10626. Paris - Ecole Rabbinique 32, f. 140b-141b, M.
10627. Strasbourg - Bibliotheque Nationale et Universitaire 4081, f. 117a-118a, M.

התיכן מתחת זרועות עולם (ה 1226), משלום ב"ר קלונימוס, פיוט לאחרי הקדושה, שחרית יום כפור
Ashkenaz
10628. Berlin - Staatsbibliothek (Preussischer Kulturbesitz) Or. Qu. 798-799 (Steinschneider 177), I, f. 89a, M.
10629. Braunschweig - Landesmuseum fuer Geschichte und Volkstum R 2386, vol. II, f. 201b, M, no incipit.
10630. Budapest - Magyar tudomanyos akademia, MS. Kaufmann A 400, p. 338, C, short.
10631. Hamburg - Staats- und Universitaetsbibliothek Cod. hebr. 62 (Steinschneider 154), f. 10b, C, short.
10632. Hamburg - Staats- und Universitaetsbibliothek Cod. hebr. 132 (Steinschneider 155), f. 38a-38b, C, short, no incipit.

---

[249] Edited by Prins, תשלום אבודרהם, p. 158.
[250] An edition of this commentary is being prepared by E. Hollender.

10633. Jerusalem - Jewish National and University Library Ms Heb 8° 3037, f. 136a-136b, M.
10634. Jerusalem - Schocken Institute 24100 / Mahzor Nuremberg, f. 386a-386b, M, short.
10635. London - British Library Or. 11318/1, f. 85b, C.
10636. London - Montefiore Library 261, f. 49a, C, commentator: Eliezer b. Natan?, short.
10637. Moscow - Russian State Library, Ms. Guenzburg 191, f. 102a-102b, M.
10638. Muenchen - Bayerische Staatsbibliothek, Cod. hebr. 346, f. 60b, C, short.
10639. New York - Jewish Theological Seminary Ms. 4466, f. 330a-330b, M.
10640. New York - Jewish Theological Seminary Ms. 8097, f. 74b, C, short.
10641. New York - Jewish Theological Seminary Ms. 8169 (Acc. 0016), f. 102a-102b, M.
10642. Oxford - Bodleian Library MS Mich. 365 (Neubauer 1208), f. 79b, C, short.
10643. Oxford - Bodleian Library MS Opp. 172 (Neubauer 1211), f. 47a-47b, C.
10644. Oxford - Bodleian Library MS Opp. 619 (Neubauer 2374), f. 165a, M.
10645. Parma - Biblioteca Palatina Cod. Parm. 3205 (de Rossi 655), f. 227a-227b, C.
10646. Parma - Biblioteca Palatina Cod. Parm. 3271 (de Rossi 1216), f. 55a-55b, G.
10647. Parma - Biblioteca Palatina Cod. Parm. 3507 (Perreau 27), f. 159b-160a, C, short.
10648. Vatican - Biblioteca Apostolica ebr. 308, f. 102(ii)a, C, commentator: David b. Mose (compiler).
10649. Vatican - Biblioteca Apostolica ebr. 422/1, f. 16b, C, very short.
10650. Zurich - Zentralbibliothek Heid. 139, f. 78b, C, short, additional marginal notes.

Ashkenaz, commentary by Abraham b. Azriel[251]
10651. Vatican - Biblioteca Apostolica ebr. 301,1, f. 170b, C, short, incipit התוכן.

Asti, Fossano, Moncalvo
10652. New Haven - Yale University, Beinecke Rare Book and MS Library, MS Heb. 52, f. 115a-115b, M.

Romania
10653. Vatican - Biblioteca Apostolica ebr. 320, f. 396a-396b, M.

Tsarfat
10654. London - David Sofer 5, f. 141a, C.

---

[251] Edited by Urbach, ערוגת הבושם, vol. III, p. 499-500.

10655. Oxford - Bodleian Library MS Bodl. Or. 109 (Neubauer 1209), f. 25b, C, commentator: Aaron b. Hayyim haKohen (compiler), short.
10656. Oxford - Bodleian Library MS Laud. Or. 271 (Neubauer 1206), f. 135b, C, commentator: Aaron b. Hayyim haKohen (compiler).
10657. Parma - Biblioteca Palatina Cod. Parm. 1794 (de Rossi 1061), f. 147b-149a, M.
10658. Parma - Biblioteca Palatina Cod. Parm. 2890 (de Rossi 856), f. 40b, M.
10659. Parma - Biblioteca Palatina Cod. Parm. 3006 (de Rossi 654,1), f. 32a-32b, M.
10660. Parma - Biblioteca Palatina Cod. Parm. 3006 (de Rossi 654,1), f. 152a, M.
10661. Vatican - Biblioteca Apostolica ebr. 306, f. 81b-82a, C.

התעוררו תמהים ראות מבלי מחזה (ה 1248), משה אבן עזרא, אופן

Carpentras

10662. Cincinnati - Hebrew Union College 392, f. 40b-41a, M, no incipit.

Carpentras, commentary by Josef b. Abraham of Montelitz

10663. New York - Jewish Theological Seminary Ms. 4197, f. 94b-96a, M, no incipit.
10664. Paris - Ecole Rabbinique 32, f. 118a-119a, M, no incipit.
10665. Strasbourg - Bibliotheque Nationale et Universitaire 4081, f. 94b-95b, M, no incipit.

ואהיה שכונה בחביון עוז (ו+ 14), שמעון ב"ר יצחק, סילוק היוצר לשבועות

Ashkenaz

10666. Berlin - Staatsbibliothek (Preussischer Kulturbesitz) Or. Qu. 798-799 (Steinschneider 177), II, f. 114a, M.
10667. Braunschweig - Landesmuseum fuer Geschichte und Volkstum R 2386, vol. I, f. 70b, M, incipit שעשוע.
10668. Budapest - Magyar tudomanyos akademia, MS. Kaufmann A 400, p. 151-153, C.
10669. Hamburg - Staats- und Universitaetsbibliothek Cod. hebr. 17/2 (Steinschneider 152), f. 70b-71a, C.
10670. Jerusalem - Schocken Institute 24100 / Mahzor Nuremberg, f. 145b-146a, M.
10671. London - British Library Add. 18695 (Margoliouth 683), f. 64a, T, Yiddish.
10672. London - British Library Add. 22431 (Margoliouth 662a), f. 4a-4b, M.
10673. Moscow - Russian State Library, Ms. Guenzburg 615, f. 46a-47a, C, commentator: Elazar b. Yehuda of Worms.
10674. Muenchen - Bayerische Staatsbibliothek, Cod. hebr. 88, f. 115a, G.

10675. New York - Jewish Theological Seminary Ms. 4466, f. 123a-123b, M.
10676. Oxford - Bodleian Library MS Opp. 170 (Neubauer 1205), f. 85a-85b, C.
10677. Paris - Bibliotheque Nationale heb. 709, f. 119a-119b, C.
10678. Parma - Biblioteca Palatina Cod. Parm. 1002 (Ta 24), f. 174b, M.
10679. Parma - Biblioteca Palatina Cod. Parm. 3205 (de Rossi 655), f. 119a-119b, C.
10680. Parma - Biblioteca Palatina Cod. Parm. 3507 (Perreau 27), f. 87a, C.
10681. Zurich - Zentralbibliothek Heid. 139, f. 49a-49b, C, additional marginal notes.

Tsarfat

10682. London - David Sofer 5, f. 50a, C.
10683. Moscow - Russian State Library, Ms. Guenzburg 1665, f. 115b-116a, M.
10684. Oxford - Bodleian Library MS Laud. Or. 271 (Neubauer 1206), f. 85a-85b, C, commentator: Aaron b. Hayyim haKohen (compiler).
10685. Parma - Biblioteca Palatina Cod. Parm. 3136 (de Rossi 405), f. 148a, M.
10686. Vatican - Biblioteca Apostolica ebr. 306, f. 225a-225b, C, no incipit.

ואיזו תהלה כפי גדלך (ו 17), אלעזר ברבי קליר, חלק י"ב, קדושתא למוסף יום כפור

Ashkenaz

10687. Braunschweig - Landesmuseum fuer Geschichte und Volkstum R 2386, vol. II, f. 231b, M, short.
10688. Budapest - Magyar tudomanyos akademia, MS. Kaufmann A 400, p. 363-364, C, rubric: רהיטים, incipit קדם.
10689. New York - Jewish Theological Seminary Ms. 4466, f. 379b-380a, M.

Tsarfat

10690. Oxford - Bodleian Library MS Bodl. Or. 109 (Neubauer 1209), f. 35b, C, commentator: Aaron b. Hayyim haKohen (compiler), very short.
10691. Oxford - Bodleian Library MS Bodl. Or. 109 (Neubauer 1209), f. 44a, C, commentator: Aaron b. Hayyim haKohen (compiler), very short.

ואני עבדך בן אמתך (ו 61), שמואל ב"ר קלונימוס?, שיר היחוד ליום ב'

Ashkenaz

10692. Braunschweig - Landesmuseum fuer Geschichte und Volkstum R 2386, vol. II, f. 168b-169b, M, no incipit.
10693. Frankfurt a M - Stadt- und Universitaetsbibliothek Oct. 121/1 (Merzbacher 105), f. 4b-10a, C, no incipit.

Romania

10694. Vatican - Biblioteca Apostolica ebr. 274, f. 169a-172a, M, kabbalistic, no incipit, addditional glosses.

Sepharad
10695. Brussels - Bibliotheque Royale de Belgique 4781, f. 179a, C, no incipit.

וארץ אשפיל ואפיל תחנתי (ו 69), שלמה אבן גבירול, קדושתא לשחרית יום כפור
Sepharad, commentary by David b. Josef Abudarham[252]
10696. Budapest - Magyar tudomanyos akademia, MS. Kaufmann A 405/2, p. 187-188, C, rubric: מגן לר' שלמה ן' גבירול ז"ל.
10697. Cincinnati - Hebrew Union College 490, f. 3b-4a, C.
10698. New York - Columbia X893 Ab 93, f. 5a-5b, C, rubric: מגן לר' שלמה ן' היבירול ז"ל.
10699. New York - Jewish Theological Seminary Ms. 3011, f. 4a-4b, C, rubric: מגן' וידוי לרעיו נקים ואתרי אום'.

וארץ שפלה רומי וגדל שברי (ו 71), שמעיה בן דוד, קרובה לי' בטבת
Carpentras, commentary by Mordekhai b. Josef of Rocco Martino
10700. Cincinnati - Hebrew Union College 246/1, f. 84b-86b, C, rubric: פי' וארץ שפל וכו'.

וארץ שפל רומי ונקלה כבודי (ו 72), שלמה בן יהודה, קרובה לשחרית בט' באב
Yemen, commentary by Isaac b. Abraham Wanneh
10701. Jerusalem - Sassoon 1158, p. 164, 165, M, rubric: תקון לשחרית תשעה באב.
10702. London - British Library Or. 11122, f. 99a, M.

וארץ שפל רומי יום דמה צר להכניעי (ו 73), שמואל בן יהודה, קרובה לי"ז בתמוז
Carpentras, commentary by Mordekhai b. Josef of Rocco Martino
10703. Cincinnati - Hebrew Union College 246/1, f. 53a-55a, C.

ואתה אזון קול מפאריך (ו 81), אלעזר ברבי קליר, חלק ט', קדושתא למוסף ראש השנה
Ashkenaz
10704. Berlin - Staatsbibliothek (Preussischer Kulturbesitz) Or. Qu. 798-799 (Steinschneider 177), I, f. 20a-21b, M.
10705. Braunschweig - Landesmuseum fuer Geschichte und Volkstum R 2386, vol. II, f. 96b-97a, M.
10706. Budapest - Magyar tudomanyos akademia, MS. Kaufmann A 400, p. 271-272, addition on p. 273, C.
10707. Darmstadt - Hessisches Landes- und Hochschulbibliothek Cod. Or. 15, f. 18a-19a, M.
10708. Hamburg - Staats- und Universitaetsbibliothek Cod. hebr. 12 (Steinschneider 102), f. 18b, G.

---

[252] Edited by Prins, תשלום אבודרהם, p. 14-17.

10709. Hamburg - Staats- und Universitaetsbibliothek Cod. hebr. 17/2 (Steinschneider 152), f. 115a-116a, C.
10710. Hamburg - Staats- und Universitaetsbibliothek Cod. hebr. 40b (Steinschneider 110), f. 19a-19b, G.
10711. Hamburg - Staats- und Universitaetsbibliothek Cod. hebr. 40c (Steinschneider 111), f. 139b-140a, G.
10712. Hamburg - Staats- und Universitaetsbibliothek Cod. hebr. 132 (Steinschneider 155), f. 15b-16b, C.
10713. Jerusalem - Jewish National and University Library Ms Heb 8° 3037, f. 31a-32a, M.
10714. Jerusalem - Schocken Institute 24100 / Mahzor Nuremberg, f. 333a, M.
10715. London - British Library Or. 11318/1, f. 18b-19a, C.
10716. London - Montefiore Library 261, f. 12b-14a, C, commentator: Eliezer b. Natan?.
10717. Moscow - Russian State Library, Ms. Guenzburg 615, f. 70a-71a, C.
10718. Muenchen - Bayerische Staatsbibliothek, Cod. hebr. 86, f. 29a-30a, M.
10719. Muenchen - Bayerische Staatsbibliothek, Cod. hebr. 346, f. 18a-19a, C.
10720. New York - Jewish Theological Seminary Ms. 4466, f. 228b-229a, M.
10721. New York - Jewish Theological Seminary Ms. 8097, f. 62b-63a, C, additional glosses in the margin.
10722. Oxford - Bodleian Library MS Opp. 170 (Neubauer 1205), f. 125a-127a, C.
10723. Oxford - Bodleian Library MS Opp. 172 (Neubauer 1211), f. 12b, C, no incipit.
10724. Oxford - Bodleian Library MS Opp. 619 (Neubauer 2374), f. 33b-34a, M.
10725. Oxford - Bodleian Library MS Opp. 675 (Neubauer 1210), f. 28a-28b, C, no incipit.
10726. Oxford - Bodleian Library MS Opp. 675 (Neubauer 1210), f. 61a-61b, C, no incipit, only on line נפש רוח נשמה.
10727. Paris - Bibliotheque Nationale heb. 653, f. 18a-18b, G.
10728. Parma - Biblioteca Palatina Cod. Parm. 3205 (de Rossi 655), f. 210b-211a, C.
10729. Parma - Biblioteca Palatina Cod. Parm. 3270 (de Rossi 1215), f. 35a-35b, M.
10730. Parma - Biblioteca Palatina Cod. Parm. 3507 (Perreau 27), f. 122a-122b, C, no incipit.
10731. Vatican - Biblioteca Apostolica ebr. 308, f. 53a-54a, C, commentator: David b. Mose (compiler).
10732. Vatican - Biblioteca Apostolica ebr. 422/1, f. 10b, C.

Tsarfat

10733. London - David Sofer 5, f. 125b, C, rubric: זה פירוש מן ואתה אזון.

10734. Paris - Bibliotheque Nationale heb. 445,9, f. 78b-79b, C.

10735. Parma - Biblioteca Palatina Cod. Parm. 2125 (de Rossi 812), f. 21a-23a, C.

ואתה קדוש, סליחה

Ashkenaz

10736. London - British Library Add. 18695 (Margoliouth 683), f. 167a, T, Yiddish.

ובכל תוקף יאמן עוז (ו+ 104), פיוט לאחרי הקדושה, לשחרית יום כפור

Asti, Fossano, Moncalvo

10737. New Haven - Yale University, Beinecke Rare Book and MS Library, MS Heb. 52, f. 163b-164a, M.

Tsarfat

10738. Parma - Biblioteca Palatina Cod. Parm. 2125 (de Rossi 812), f. 42b-43a, C.

10739. Parma - Biblioteca Palatina Cod. Parm. 2890 (de Rossi 856), f. 123b-124a, M.

10740. Parma - Biblioteca Palatina Cod. Parm. 3006 (de Rossi 654,1), f. 242a, M.

ובכן אין לפניך לילה והכל לפניך יום, יניי, סילוק, קדושלא לפסח

Ashkenaz

10741. Berlin - Staatsbibliothek (Preussischer Kulturbesitz) Or. Qu. 798-799 (Steinschneider 177), II, f. 52a, M.

10742. Budapest - Magyar tudomanyos akademia, MS. Kaufmann A 384, f. 110b, M.

10743. Hamburg - Staats- und Universitaetsbibliothek Cod. hebr. 225, f. 55b-57a, G.

10744. London - British Library Add. 18695 (Margoliouth 683), f. 13a, T, Yiddish, rubric: סילוק.

ובכן ולך הכל יכתירו עליונים

Ashkenaz

10745. Budapest - Magyar tudomanyos akademia, MS. Kaufmann A 400, p. 355, C.

ובכן מה נהדר כהן גדול בצאתו בשלום מן הקדש (כ 15), יוסף אבן אביתור, פיוט לאחרי סדר עבודה

Sepharad

10746. Jerusalem - Schocken Institute 70014, f. 85a, M.

Sepharad, commentary by David b. Josef Abudarham[253]

10747. Budapest - Magyar tudomanyos akademia, MS. Kaufmann A 405/2, p. 237, C.

10748. New York - Columbia X893 Ab 93, f. 24a-24b, C.

ובכן מי לא יראך מלך הגוים (ו 114), קלונימוס מלוקא?, לשחרית יום כפור

Ashkenaz

10749. Hamburg - Staats- und Universitaetsbibliothek Cod. hebr. 132 (Steinschneider 155), f. 39a, C, no incipit.

Tsarfat

10750. Oxford - Bodleian Library MS Opp. 171 (Neubauer 1207), f. 117a-118a, C, incipit מי לאל.

וחיות אשר הנה מרובעות לכסא (ו 189), אלעזר ברבי קליר, חלק ז', קדושתא למוסף ראש השנה

Ashkenaz

10751. Berlin - Staatsbibliothek (Preussischer Kulturbesitz) Or. Qu. 798-799 (Steinschneider 177), I, f. 18a-20a, M, rubric: אופן.

10752. Braunschweig - Landesmuseum fuer Geschichte und Volkstum R 2386, vol. II, f. 95a-96a, M.

10753. Budapest - Magyar tudomanyos akademia, MS. Kaufmann A 400, p. 267, C.

10754. Cambridge - University Library Add. 858,1, f. 10b-13b, C, commentator: Elazar b. Yehuda of Worms?, rubric: "סוד החיות אשר הנה כג.

10755. Darmstadt - Hessisches Landes- und Hochschulbibliothek Cod. Or. 15, f. 16b, M.

10756. Hamburg - Staats- und Universitaetsbibliothek Cod. hebr. 12 (Steinschneider 102), f. 17a-18b, G.

10757. Hamburg - Staats- und Universitaetsbibliothek Cod. hebr. 17/2 (Steinschneider 152), f. 113b-115a, C, rubric: קדושה דר' אלעזר.

10758. Hamburg - Staats- und Universitaetsbibliothek Cod. hebr. 40b (Steinschneider 110), f. 18a-19a, G.

10759. Hamburg - Staats- und Universitaetsbibliothek Cod. hebr. 40c (Steinschneider 111), f. 138b-139b, G.

10760. Hamburg - Staats- und Universitaetsbibliothek Cod. hebr. 132 (Steinschneider 155), f. 13b-14b, C.

10761. Hamburg - Staats- und Universitaetsbibliothek Cod. hebr. 139 (Steinschneider 115), f. 31b-32b, G.

10762. Jerusalem - Jewish National and University Library Ms Heb 8° 3037, f. 29b-30b, M.

---

[253] Edited by Prins, תשלום אבודרהם, p. 67.

10763. Jerusalem - Schocken Institute 24100 / Mahzor Nuremberg , f. 331b-333a, M.
10764. London - British Library Or. 11318/1, f. 17a-18b, C.
10765. London - Montefiore Library 261 , f. 10b-11b, C, commentator: Eliezer b. Natan?.
10766. Moscow - Russian State Library, Ms. Guenzburg 191, f. 15b-17a, M.
10767. Moscow - Russian State Library, Ms. Guenzburg 1401/2, f. 18b, C, very short.
10768. Moscow - Russian State Library, Ms. Guenzburg 191, f. 57a, M.
10769. Muenchen - Bayerische Staatsbibliothek, Cod. hebr. 86, f. 27a-27b, M.
10770. Muenchen - Bayerische Staatsbibliothek, Cod. hebr. 346 , f. 13b-18a (count without f. 16-17), C.
10771. New York - Jewish Theological Seminary Ms. 4466, f. 226b-227b, M.
10772. New York - Jewish Theological Seminary Ms. 8097, f. 62a-62b, C.
10773. New York - Jewish Theological Seminary Ms. 8169 (Acc. 0016), f. 21a-22a, M.
10774. Oxford - Bodleian Library MS Opp. 12 (Neubauer 1029), f. 217a, G, one gloss only.
10775. Oxford - Bodleian Library MS Opp. 170 (Neubauer 1205), f. 121b-123b, C.
10776. Oxford - Bodleian Library MS Opp. 172 (Neubauer 1211), f. 11b-12a, C, no incipit.
10777. Oxford - Bodleian Library MS Opp. 619 (Neubauer 2374), f. 31b-32b, M.
10778. Oxford - Bodleian Library MS Opp. 675 (Neubauer 1210), f. 25b-26b, C, no incipit.
10779. Paris - Bibliotheque Nationale heb. 653, f. 17a-18a, G.
10780. Parma - Biblioteca Palatina Cod. Parm. 3270 (de Rossi 1215), f. 33a-34b, M.
10781. Parma - Biblioteca Palatina Cod. Parm. 3507 (Perreau 27), f. 120a-121a, C.
10782. Vatican - Biblioteca Apostolica ebr. 308, f. 51a-52a, C, commentator: David b. Mose (compiler).
10783. Vatican - Biblioteca Apostolica ebr. 422/1, f. 10a-10b, C.
10784. Zurich - Zentralbibliothek Heid. 139, f. 62b, 64a-64b, 67a (inserted leafes are counted in Ms), C, additional marginal notes.

Asti, Fossano, Moncalvo
10785. New Haven - Yale University, Beinecke Rare Book and MS Library, MS Heb. 52, f. 36a-36b, M, no incipit.
10786. New Haven - Yale University, Beinecke Rare Book and MS Library, MS Heb. 52, f. 69b-70a, M.

Tsarfat

10787. London - British Library Add. 11639 (Margoliouth 1056), f. 711a, M, rubric: אופן למוסף.

10788. London - British Library Or. 8682, f. 23b, GI.

10789. London - David Sofer 5, f. 115b-116a, C.

10790. Oxford - Bodleian Library MS Laud. Or. 271 (Neubauer 1206), f. 146b-149a, C, commentator: Aaron b. Hayyim haKohen (compiler).

10791. Paris - Bibliotheque Nationale heb. 445,9, f. 75(ii)b-77b, C.

10792. Parma - Biblioteca Palatina Cod. Parm. 2125 (de Rossi 812), f. 19b-20b, C.

10793. Parma - Biblioteca Palatina Cod. Parm. 3006 (de Rossi 654,1), f. 48a-49a, M.

10794. Vatican - Biblioteca Apostolica ebr. 306, f. 54b-55b, C.

וחיות בוערות בכס רם לויות (ו 190), בנימין ב"ר שמואל, קדושה

Tsarfat

10795. London - David Sofer 5, f. 165b, C, rubric: קדושות.

10796. Parma - Biblioteca Palatina Cod. Parm. 3006 (de Rossi 654,1), f. 240b-241a, M.

וחיות בוערות מראיהן כגחלי אש (ו 191), בנימין ב'' שמואל, קדושה ליום א' של ראש השנה

Ashkenaz

10797. Jerusalem - Schocken Institute 24100 / Mahzor Nuremberg, f. 327b-328a, M.

10798. London - British Library Or. 11318/1, f. 156b-158a, C.

10799. London - Montefiore Library 261, f. 3a-3b, C, commentator: Eliezer b. Natan?.

10800. London - Montefiore Library 261, f. 3b-4a, C, commentator: Eliezer b. Natan?, rubric: במטבע אחר.

10801. Moscow - Russian State Library, Ms. Guenzburg 615, f. 68a-69a, C.

10802. New York - Jewish Theological Seminary Ms. 2269/5, f. 43a-43b, FC.

10803. New York - Jewish Theological Seminary Ms. 8169 (Acc. 0016), f. 119a, C.

10804. Oxford - Bodleian Library MS Opp. 172 (Neubauer 1211), f. 6b-7a, C.

10805. Oxford - Bodleian Library MS Opp. 675 (Neubauer 1210), f. 19a-21a, C, no incipit.

10806. Oxford - Bodleian Library MS Opp. 675 (Neubauer 1210), f. 60b-61a, C, no incipit.

10807. Parma - Biblioteca Palatina Cod. Parm. 3205 (de Rossi 655), f. 209b-210a, C.

10808. Salzburg - Universitaetsbibliothek M II 342, f. 1a-1b, FM.
10809. Vatican - Biblioteca Apostolica ebr. 308, f. 38b-39b, C, commentator: David b. Mose (compiler).

Tsarfat

10810. London - David Sofer 5, f. 39a-39b, C.
10811. Oxford - Bodleian Library MS Opp. 171 (Neubauer 1207), f. 60b-63a, C, rubric: אופן.
10812. Paris - Bibliotheque Nationale heb. 445,9, f. 68b-69b, C.
10813. Vatican - Biblioteca Apostolica ebr. 306, f. 58a, C.

ויאהב אומן יתומת הגן (ו 197), אלעזר ברבי קליר, קרובה לפורים

Ashkenaz

10814. Berlin - Staatsbibliothek (Preussischer Kulturbesitz) Or. Qu. 798-799 (Steinschneider 177), II, f. 25a-26b, M.
10815. Budapest - Magyar tudomanyos akademia, MS. Kaufmann A 384, f. 63a-65b, M.
10816. Budapest - Magyar tudomanyos akademia, MS. Kaufmann A 400, p. 52-59, C, rubric: י״ח ברכות של פורי׳.
10817. Erlangen - Universitaetsbibliothek 2601 (Roth 67), f. 38a-40a, M.
10818. Hamburg - Staats- und Universitaetsbibliothek Cod. hebr. 17/2 (Steinschneider 152), f. 21b-22a, C, rubric: לפורים.
10819. Hamburg - Staats- und Universitaetsbibliothek Cod. hebr. 40c (Steinschneider 111), f. 13b-14b, G.
10820. Jerusalem - Schocken Institute 24100 / Mahzor Nuremberg, f. 47b-48b, M.
10821. Muenchen - Bayerische Staatsbibliothek, Cod. hebr. 88, f. 32b-33b, G.
10822. Muenchen - Bayerische Staatsbibliothek, Cod. hebr. 393, f. 93a-94b, C, rubric: קרובץ של פורים, no incipit.
10823. Oxford - Bodleian Library MS Opp. 170 (Neubauer 1205), f. 16a-19b, C, rubric: אתחיל פירוש לקרובוץ של פורים.
10824. Paris - Bibliotheque Nationale heb. 709, f. 24b-27a, C, rubric: בשם משפיל ומרים אתחיל י״ח של פורים.
10825. Parma - Biblioteca Palatina Cod. Parm. 1002 (Ta 24), f. 43b-46a, M.
10826. Parma - Biblioteca Palatina Cod. Parm. 3205 (de Rossi 655), f. 27a-29a, C, rubric: לפורים.
10827. Parma - Biblioteca Palatina Cod. Parm. 3507 (Perreau 27), f. 19b-21b, C, rubric: לפורים, no incipit.
10828. Vatican - Biblioteca Apostolica ebr. 305,1, f. 29a-31b, C, rubric: בשם שוכן רום אוירים אתווה י״ח דפורים.

Tsarfat

10829. London - British Library Add. 11639 (Margoliouth 1056), f. 271b-272b, M.

10830. London - David Sofer 5, f. 24a-25a, C, rubric: פירוש קרובוץ הפורים, additional glosses.
10831. Moscow - Russian State Library, Ms. Guenzburg 1665, f. 20b-22a, M.
10832. Oxford - Bodleian Library MS Laud. Or. 271 (Neubauer 1206), f. 27b-30b, C, commentator: Aaron b. Hayyim haKohen (compiler).
10833. Oxford - Bodleian Library MS Opp. 171 (Neubauer 1207), f. 24b-26b, C, rubric: קרובה ליום פורים.
10834. Parma - Biblioteca Palatina Cod. Parm. 3136 (de Rossi 405), f. 34b-35b, M.

ויאמן אומר גולה אזנים (ו 198), פיוט ליום כפור

Carpentras
10835. Cincinnati - Hebrew Union College 392, f. 90b-91b, M, no incipit.
Carpentras, commentary by Josef b. Abraham of Montelitz
10836. Cincinnati - Hebrew Union College 291, f. 48b-49b, C, rubric: פי' פזמון ויאמן אומר וכו'.
10837. New York - Jewish Theological Seminary Ms. 4197, f. 204a-205b, M, no incipit.
10838. Paris - Ecole Rabbinique 32, f. 211b-212b, M, no incipit.
10839. Strasbourg - Bibliotheque Nationale et Universitaire 4081, f. 186b-187a, M, no incipit.

ויאתיו כל לעבדך (ו 201), פיוט לראש השנה ויום כפור

Ashkenaz
10840. London - Montefiore Library 261, f. 15a, C, commentator: Eliezer b. Natan?, short.
10841. Oxford - Bodleian Library MS Opp. 172 (Neubauer 1211), 13b-14a, C.
10842. Oxford - Bodleian Library MS Opp. 675 (Neubauer 1210), f. 30b, C, no incipit.
10843. Parma - Biblioteca Palatina Cod. Parm. 3507 (Perreau 27), f. 123a-123b, C.
10844. Zurich - Zentralbibliothek Heid. 139, f. 102b, C, commentator: Elazar b. Yehuda of Worms, no incipit, very short.

Tsarfat
10845. London - David Sofer 5, f. 113a, C.
10846. Parma - Biblioteca Palatina Cod. Parm. 3006 (de Rossi 654,1), f. 32b, M.

ויבא ארז ראש קצינים (ו 202), אלעזר ברבי קליר, שבעתא לשבת קודם שבת זכור

Ashkenaz
10847. Budapest - Magyar tudomanyos akademia, MS. Kaufmann A 400, p. 51-52, C.

10848. Hamburg - Staats- und Universitaetsbibliothek Cod. hebr. 17/2 (Steinschneider 152), f. 21a, C, rubric: שבעתא.
10849. Oxford - Bodleian Library MS Opp. 170 (Neubauer 1205), f. 15a-16a, C, rubric: שבעתא.
10850. Parma - Biblioteca Palatina Cod. Parm. 3205 (de Rossi 655), f. 26a-26b, C, rubric: שבעתא.
10851. Parma - Biblioteca Palatina Cod. Parm. 3507 (Perreau 27), f. 18b-19b, C, rubric: שבעתא.
10852. Vatican - Biblioteca Apostolica ebr. 305,1, f. 19a-20a, C.

Tsarfat

10853. Oxford - Bodleian Library MS Laud. Or. 271 (Neubauer 1206), f. 27a-27b, C, commentator: Aaron b. Hayyim haKohen (compiler), rubric: שבעתא.
10854. Oxford - Bodleian Library MS Opp. 171 (Neubauer 1207), f. 23a-24b, C, rubric: שבעתא.

ויבן אומן אומנות אבות (ו 205), מאיר ב"ר יצחק, שבעתא למוסף שבת זכור

Ashkenaz

10855. Parma - Biblioteca Palatina Cod. Parm. 3205 (de Rossi 655), f. 26b-27a, C, rubric: שבעתא.

Tsarfat

10856. Oxford - Bodleian Library MS Laud. Or. 271 (Neubauer 1206), f. 25a-26b, C, commentator: Aaron b. Hayyim haKohen (compiler), rubric: שבעתא.

ויושע אדון איומה מכף מעני (ו 229), יוסף ב"ר שמואל טוב עלם, מעריב ליום ז' של פסח

Tsarfat

10857. London - David Sofer 5, f. 44a-44b, C, rubric: פירוש ממעריב ליל שמיני עצרת.
10858. Parma - Biblioteca Palatina Cod. Parm. 3136 (de Rossi 405), f. 106a-106b, M.

ויושע יי אום למושעות (ו 231), יוסף בר יעקב קלעי, מעריב ליום ז' של פסח

Ashkenaz

10859. Jerusalem - Schocken Institute 24100 / Mahzor Nuremberg, f. 105b-106a, M.

Tsarfat

10860. London - David Sofer 5, f. 39b, C, rubric: וזה פירוש ממעריב של יום אחרון של פסח.
10861. Parma - Biblioteca Palatina Cod. Parm. 3136 (de Rossi 405), f. 121a-121b, M.

ויושע אור ישראל (ו 239), מאיר ב"ר יצחק, יוצר ליום ז' של פסח
Ashkenaz
10862. Hamburg - Staats- und Universitaetsbibliothek Cod. hebr. 17/2 (Steinschneider 152), f. 41b-43a, C.
10863. Jerusalem - Schocken Institute 24100 / Mahzor Nuremberg, f. 131a-132a, M.
10864. New York - Jewish Theological Seminary Ms. 4466, f. 103a-106b, M.
10865. Oxford - Bodleian Library MS Opp. 169 (Neubauer 1151), f. 13b-15a, M.
10866. Parma - Biblioteca Palatina Cod. Parm. 3205 (de Rossi 655), f. 111a-114a, C, rubric: יוצר ליום אחרון של פסח.
10867. Zurich - Zentralbibliothek Heid. 139, f. 44b-45b, C, additional marginal notes.

Ashkenaz, commentary by Abraham b. Azriel[254]
10868. Vatican - Biblioteca Apostolica ebr. 301,1, f. 1a-6b, C, introductory paragraph before this commentary.
Tsarfat
10869. Oxford - Bodleian Library MS Laud. Or. 271 (Neubauer 1206), f. 79b-80a, C, commentator: Ephraim b. Jacob of Bonn?, Aaron b. Hayyim haKohen (compiler), rubric: ליום אחרון.

ויושע איום אום אני חומה (ו 240), יוסף ב"ר שמואל טוב עלם, חלק ח', קדושתא לפסח
Tsarfat
10870. Parma - Biblioteca Palatina Cod. Parm. 3136 (de Rossi 405), f. 111b-114a, M.

ויושע שושני פרח (ו 245), שמעון ב"ר יצחק, יוצר ליום ז' של פסח
Ashkenaz
10871. Berlin - Staatsbibliothek (Preussischer Kulturbesitz) Or. Qu. 798-799 (Steinschneider 177), II, f. 88b-89a, M.
10872. Braunschweig - Landesmuseum fuer Geschichte und Volkstum R 2386, vol. I, f. 48a-49a, M.
10873. Budapest - Magyar tudomanyos akademia, MS. Kaufmann A 384, f. 197a-198a, M.
10874. Hamburg - Staats- und Universitaetsbibliothek Cod. hebr. 17/2 (Steinschneider 152), f. 37a-37b, C, rubric: לשביעי של פסח.
10875. Jerusalem - Schocken Institute 24100 / Mahzor Nuremberg, f. 107a-107b, M.
10876. London - British Library Add. 18695 (Margoliouth 683), f. 46b-47b, T, Yiddish, rubric: יוצר צו שביעי בון פסח.

---

[254] Edited by Urbach, ערוגת הבושם, vol. I, p. 1-43.

10877. Moscow - Russian State Library, Ms. Guenzburg 615 , f. 24a-24b, C, rubric: יוצר שמעוני ליום שביעי של פסח.
10878. Muenchen - Bayerische Staatsbibliothek, Cod. hebr. 88, f. 80a-80b, G.
10879. Muenchen - Bayerische Staatsbibliothek, Cod. hebr. 393 , f. 132b-133a, C, rubric: ליו' שבעי של פסח.
10880. New York - Jewish Theological Seminary Ms. 4466, f. 85b-86b, M.
10881. Oxford - Bodleian Library MS Opp. 170 (Neubauer 1205), f. 75a-76a, C, rubric: קרובה ליום אחרון.
10882. Paris - Bibliotheque Nationale heb. 709, f. 100a-101a, C.
10883. Parma - Biblioteca Palatina Cod. Parm. 1002 (Ta 24), f. 135b-136a, M.
10884. Parma - Biblioteca Palatina Cod. Parm. 3205 (de Rossi 655), f. 107a-107b, C.
10885. Parma - Biblioteca Palatina Cod. Parm. 3507 (Perreau 27), f. 70b-71b, C.
10886. Zurich - Zentralbibliothek Heid. 139, f. 40b-41a, C, rubric: לשביעי של פסח.

Tsarfat

10887. London - David Sofer 5, f. 44b-45a, C, rubric: פירוש מיוצר של שמיני של פסח.
10888. Moscow - Russian State Library, Ms. Guenzburg 1665, f. 103a-103b, M.
10889. Oxford - Bodleian Library MS Laud. Or. 271 (Neubauer 1206), f. 75b-76a, C, commentator: Ephraim b. Jacob of Bonn?, Aaron b. Hayyim haKohen (compiler), rubric: יוצר זה ליום אחרו' של ראשון מימי פסח.

וירד אביר יעקב נורא עלילה (ו 257), יוסף ב"ר שמואל טוב עלם, מעריב לשבועות

Ashkenaz

10890. Berlin - Staatsbibliothek (Preussischer Kulturbesitz) Or. Qu. 798-799 (Steinschneider 177), II, f. 111b-112b, M.
10891. Braunschweig - Landesmuseum fuer Geschichte und Volkstum R 2386, vol. I, f. 68b-69a, M.
10892. Budapest - Magyar tudomanyos akademia, MS. Kaufmann A 399 , p. 221-222, C, rubric: מעריב של ליל שבועות דרבינו יוסף עלם טוב.
10893. Jerusalem - Schocken Institute 24100 / Mahzor Nuremberg, f. 169a-169b, M.
10894. London - British Library Add. 18695 (Margoliouth 683) , f. 62a-62b, T, Yiddish, rubric: מעריב די ערשט נכט בון שבועות.
10895. Lund - Universitetsbibliothek Ms. L.O. 2, f. 67a, M.
10896. Paris - Bibliotheque Nationale heb. 709, f. 116a-116b, C.
10897. Parma - Biblioteca Palatina Cod. Parm. 2895, p. 332-336, M.

10898. Warszaw - Uniwersytet, Inst. Orientalistyczny 258 , f. 208a-209b, C, commentator: Eliezer b. Natan, rubric: מעריב דרבי יוצף טוב עלם בר שמואל לליל ראשון של שבועות.

Tsarfat

10899. Jerusalem - Schocken Institute 19623, f. 92a-92b, M, commentator: Yehuda b. Eliezer Zvi, ecclectic.
10900. London - David Sofer 5, f. 66b-67a, C.
10901. Vatican - Biblioteca Apostolica ebr. 306, f. 221a-221b, C, rubric: מעריב.

וירד אביר לבאר קשות ורכות (ו 258), יוסף ב"ר שמואל טוב עלם, חלק ח', קדושתלא לשבועות

Tsarfat

10902. London - David Sofer 5, f. 70a-71a, C.
10903. Moscow - Russian State Library, Ms. Guenzburg 1665, f. 146a-148a, 149a, M.
10904. Parma - Biblioteca Palatina Cod. Parm. 3136 (de Rossi 405), f. 174b-177a, M.

וכל העם רואים (ו 288), שמעון ב"ר יצחק, סילוק, קדושתא לשבועות

Ashkenaz

10905. Berlin - Staatsbibliothek (Preussischer Kulturbesitz) Or. Qu. 798-799 (Steinschneider 177), II, f. 126b-128a, M.
10906. Braunschweig - Landesmuseum fuer Geschichte und Volkstum R 2386, vol. I, f. 81a-82a, M.
10907. Budapest - Magyar tudomanyos akademia, MS. Kaufmann A 400 , p. 169-173, C, rubric: סילוק, short.
10908. London - British Library Add. 18695 (Margoliouth 683) , f. 72a-72b, T, Yiddish, rubric: סילוק.
10909. London - British Library Add. 22431 (Margoliouth 662a), f. 20b-22a, M.
10910. Moscow - Russian State Library, Ms. Guenzburg 615, f. 36b, C, rubric: סילוק, incipit הנראה.
10911. New York - Jewish Theological Seminary Ms. 4466, f. 144b, M.
10912. Parma - Biblioteca Palatina Cod. Parm. 1002 (Ta 24), f. 186a, M.
10913. Parma - Biblioteca Palatina Cod. Parm. 3205 (de Rossi 655), f. 121b, C, no incipit.
10914. Parma - Biblioteca Palatina Cod. Parm. 3507 (Perreau 27), f. 104b-105b, C, rubric: סילוק.
10915. Zurich - Zentralbibliothek Heid. 139, f. 51b, C, very short, additional marginal notes.

Tsarfat

10916. Oxford - Bodleian Library MS Laud. Or. 271 (Neubauer 1206), f. 87a, C, commentator: Aaron b. Hayyim haKohen (compiler), no incipit, very short.

ונתנה תוקף (ו 451), סילוק, קדושתא למוסף ראש השנה

Ashkenaz

10917. Berlin - Staatsbibliothek (Preussischer Kulturbesitz) Or. Qu. 798-799 (Steinschneider 177), I, f. 17b-18a, M.
10918. Braunschweig - Landesmuseum fuer Geschichte und Volkstum R 2386, vol. II, f. 94a-94b, M.
10919. Budapest - Magyar tudomanyos akademia, MS. Kaufmann A 400, p. 265-267, C.
10920. Cambridge - University Library Add. 394,1 (Reif SCR 461), f. 66a, C, rubric: סילוק.
10921. Cambridge - University Library Add. 394,1 (Reif SCR 461), f. 81b-82a, C, rubric: סילוק.
10922. Darmstadt - Hessisches Landes- und Hochschulbibliothek Cod. Or. 15, f. 16a, M.
10923. Hamburg - Staats- und Universitaetsbibliothek Cod. hebr. 17/2 (Steinschneider 152), f. 113a-113b, C, rubric: סילוק דר׳ אמנון.
10924. Hamburg - Staats- und Universitaetsbibliothek Cod. hebr. 40c (Steinschneider 111), f. 138b, G.
10925. Hamburg - Staats- und Universitaetsbibliothek Cod. hebr. 132 (Steinschneider 155), f. 13a-13b, C.
10926. Jerusalem - Jewish National and University Library Ms Heb 8° 3037, f. 28b-29a, M.
10927. Jerusalem - Schocken Institute 24100 / Mahzor Nuremberg, f. 331b, M.
10928. Jerusalem - Schocken Institute 24100 / Mahzor Nuremberg, f. 413b, M.
10929. London - British Library Or. 11318/1, f. 16a-16b, C.
10930. London - Montefiore Library 261, f. 9b-10b, C, commentator: Eliezer b. Natan?.
10931. Moscow - Russian State Library, Ms. Guenzburg 191, f. 15a-15b, M.
10932. Moscow - Russian State Library, Ms. Guenzburg 363, f. 124a-124b, 125b-126a, C, esoteric.
10933. Moscow - Russian State Library, Ms. Guenzburg 615, f. 68a, C, rubric: סילוק.
10934. Moscow - Russian State Library, Ms. Guenzburg 1401/2, f. 18b, C.
10935. Muenchen - Bayerische Staatsbibliothek, Cod. hebr. 86, f. 25b-26a, G.
10936. Muenchen - Bayerische Staatsbibliothek, Cod. hebr. 346, f. 13b, C, short.

10937. Muenchen - Bayerische Staatsbibliothek, Cod. hebr. 346 , f. 89b-90b, C.
10938. New York - Jewish Theological Seminary Ms. 4466, f. 225a-226a, M.
10939. New York - Jewish Theological Seminary Ms. 8097 , f. 62a, C, additional glosses in the margin.
10940. New York - Jewish Theological Seminary Ms. 8169 (Acc. 0016), f. 20a-21a, M.
10941. Oxford - Bodleian Library MS Opp. 170 (Neubauer 1205), f. 120b-121b, C.
10942. Oxford - Bodleian Library MS Opp. 172 (Neubauer 1211), f. 11a-11b, C, no incipit.
10943. Oxford - Bodleian Library MS Opp. 619 (Neubauer 2374), f. 30b-31a, M.
10944. Oxford - Bodleian Library MS Opp. 675 (Neubauer 1210), f. 24b-25b, C, no incipit.
10945. Paris - Bibliotheque Nationale heb. 653, f. 16b, G.
10946. Parma - Biblioteca Palatina Cod. Parm. 3270 (de Rossi 1215), f. 32a-33a, M.
10947. Parma - Biblioteca Palatina Cod. Parm. 3205 (de Rossi 655), f. 207b-208b, C.
10948. Parma - Biblioteca Palatina Cod. Parm. 3507 (Perreau 27), f. 119b-120a, C.
10949. Vatican - Biblioteca Apostolica ebr. 308, f. 50a-51a, C, commentator: David b. Mose (compiler).
10950. Vatican - Biblioteca Apostolica ebr. 422/1, f. 10a, C, very short.
10951. Zurich - Zentralbibliothek Heid. 139, f. 62b, C, very short, additional marginal notes.
10952. Zurich - Zentralbibliothek Heid. 139, f. 102b, C, commentator: Elazar b. Yehuda of Worms, rubric: בקדושה, one line only.

Asti, Fossano, Moncalvo

10953. New Haven - Yale University, Beinecke Rare Book and MS Library, MS Heb. 52, f. 35b, M.
10954. New Haven - Yale University, Beinecke Rare Book and MS Library, MS Heb. 52, f. 69a, M.

Roma

10955. Jerusalem - Jewish National and University Library Ms Heb 8° 4153, f. 135a-135b, C, commentator: Daniel ben Salomo haRofe (compiler), rubric: פי׳ ונתנה תוקף.
10956. Oxford - Bodleian Library MS Mich. 312,1 (Neubauer 2276,1), f. 3b-4b, C, rubric: פי׳ קדושה גדולה היא ונתנה תוקף.

Tsarfat

10957. London - David Sofer 5, f. 115a-115b, C.
10958. Oxford - Bodleian Library MS Laud. Or. 271 (Neubauer 1206), f. 146a-146b, C, commentator: Aaron b. Hayyim haKohen (compiler).

10959. Paris - Bibliotheque Nationale heb. 445,9, f. 75(i)b-75(ii)b, C.
10960. Parma - Biblioteca Palatina Cod. Parm. 2125 (de Rossi 812), f. 18a-19b, C.
10961. Parma - Biblioteca Palatina Cod. Parm. 3006 (de Rossi 654,1), f. 47b-48a, M.
10962. Vatican - Biblioteca Apostolica ebr. 306, f. 54a-54b, C.

ועמך תלואים בתשובה להתיחד (ו 468), אלעזר ברבי קליר, חלק ח׳, קדושתא למוסף ראש השנה

Ashkenaz

10963. Budapest - Magyar tudomanyos akademia, MS. Kaufmann A 400, p. 269-271, C.
10964. Darmstadt - Hessisches Landes- und Hochschulbibliothek Cod. Or. 15, f. 17a-17b, M.
10965. Hamburg - Staats- und Universitaetsbibliothek Cod. hebr. 132 (Steinschneider 155), f. 14b-15a, C.
10966. Jerusalem - Jewish National and University Library Ms Heb 8° 3037, f. 30b-31a, M.
10967. London - Montefiore Library 261, f. 11b-12b, C, commentator: Eliezer b. Natan?.
10968. Moscow - Russian State Library, Ms. Guenzburg 615, f. 69a-70a, C.
10969. Muenchen - Bayerische Staatsbibliothek, Cod. hebr. 86, f. 28a-28b, M, additional glosses.
10970. New York - Jewish Theological Seminary Ms. 4466, f. 227b-228b, M.
10971. New York - Jewish Theological Seminary Ms. 8097, f. 62b, C, additional glosses in the margins.
10972. Oxford - Bodleian Library MS Opp. 170 (Neubauer 1205), f. 123b-125a, C.
10973. Oxford - Bodleian Library MS Opp. 172 (Neubauer 1211), f. 12a-12b, C, no incipit.
10974. Oxford - Bodleian Library MS Opp. 619 (Neubauer 2374), f. 32b-33b, M.
10975. Oxford - Bodleian Library MS Opp. 675 (Neubauer 1210), f. 26b-28a, C.
10976. Oxford - Bodleian Library MS Opp. 675 (Neubauer 1210), f. 61a, C, no incipit.
10977. Parma - Biblioteca Palatina Cod. Parm. 3205 (de Rossi 655), f. 210a-210b, C.
10978. Parma - Biblioteca Palatina Cod. Parm. 3507 (Perreau 27), f. 121a-122a, C.
10979. Vatican - Biblioteca Apostolica ebr. 308, f. 52a-53a, C, commentator: David b. Mose (compiler).
10980. Vatican - Biblioteca Apostolica ebr. 422/1, f. 10b, C, very short.

Asti, Fossano, Moncalvo

10981. New Haven - Yale University, Beinecke Rare Book and MS Library, MS Heb. 52, f. 36b-37a, M, no incipit.

10982. New Haven - Yale University, Beinecke Rare Book and MS Library, MS Heb. 52, f. 70a-70b, M.

Tsarfat

10983. Paris - Bibliotheque Nationale heb. 445,9, f. 77b-78b, C, incipit missing.

10984. Parma - Biblioteca Palatina Cod. Parm. 2125 (de Rossi 812), f. 20b-21a, C.

10985. Parma - Biblioteca Palatina Cod. Parm. 3006 (de Rossi 654,1), f. 49a-49b, M.

וערב לפניך כמו קרבן מוספין

Carpentras, commentary by Josef b. Abraham of Montelitz

10986. New York - Jewish Theological Seminary Ms. 4197, f. 179a, M.

ועתה בנים שירו למלך (ו 477), שמעון ב"ר יצחק, אופן לשבועות

Ashkenaz

10987. Berlin - Staatsbibliothek (Preussischer Kulturbesitz) Or. Qu. 798-799 (Steinschneider 177), II, f. 114b, M.

10988. Braunschweig - Landesmuseum fuer Geschichte und Volkstum R 2386, vol. I, f. 71a, M.

10989. Budapest - Magyar tudomanyos akademia, MS. Kaufmann A 400, p. 153, C.

10990. Hamburg - Staats- und Universitaetsbibliothek Cod. hebr. 17/2 (Steinschneider 152), f. 71a, C, rubric: אופן.

10991. Jerusalem - Schocken Institute 24100 / Mahzor Nuremberg, f. 146a, M, short, no incipit.

10992. London - British Library Add. 18695 (Margoliouth 683), f. 64a-64b, T, Yiddish, rubric: אופן.

10993. London - British Library Add. 22431 (Margoliouth 662a), f. 5a-5b, M.

10994. Moscow - Russian State Library, Ms. Guenzburg 615, f. 47a-49a, C, commentator: Elazar b. Yehuda of Worms.

10995. Muenchen - Bayerische Staatsbibliothek, Cod. hebr. 88, f. 115a-115b, G.

10996. New York - Jewish Theological Seminary Ms. 4466, f. 123b-124b, M, short.

10997. Oxford - Bodleian Library MS Opp. 170 (Neubauer 1205), f. 85b-86a, C, rubric: אופן.

10998. Paris - Bibliotheque Nationale heb. 709, f. 119b-120a, C.

10999. Parma - Biblioteca Palatina Cod. Parm. 1002 (Ta 24), f. 175a-175b, M.

11000. Parma - Biblioteca Palatina Cod. Parm. 3205 (de Rossi 655), f. 119b-120a, C.

11001. Parma - Biblioteca Palatina Cod. Parm. 3507 (Perreau 27), f. 87a-87b, C, no incipit.

11002. Zurich - Zentralbibliothek Heid. 139, f. 49b, C, additional marginal notes.

Tsarfat

11003. London - David Sofer 5, f. 50a, C.

11004. Moscow - Russian State Library, Ms. Guenzburg 1665, f. 116a-116b, M, no incipit.

11005. Oxford - Bodleian Library MS Laud. Or. 271 (Neubauer 1206), f. 85b, C, commentator: Aaron b. Hayyim haKohen (compiler), rubric: אופן.

11006. Vatican - Biblioteca Apostolica ebr. 306, f. 225b-226a, C, rubric: אופן.

ועתה יי אבינו ... שבטי שעשוע, סליחה

Tsarfat

11007. Vatican - Biblioteca Apostolica ebr. 306, f. 173b-174a, C.

ותוקעין שלישים קולות וזה סדרן וכוונתן, לראש השנה

Yemen

11008. Jerusalem - Michael Krupp 2807, f. 2a-4a, M.

ותיק ישר המהלך התם (ו 532), משה זכות, להושענא רבה

Italia, commentary by Zakharya David Shabbetai Segre

11009. Torino - Archivio Terracini 1499, p. 168-170, C, rubric: פירוש ותיק ישר.

זאבי ערב וכל דוב אורב (ז 2), זרחיה הלוי ב"ר יצחק גירונדי, קינה

Carpentras, commentary by Mordekhai b. Josef of Rocco Martino

11010. Cincinnati - Hebrew Union College 246/1, f. 74b-76a, C, rubric: פי' קינה זאבי ערב.

Yemen, commentary by Isaac b. Abraham Wanneh

11011. Jerusalem - Sassoon 1158, p. 171, M.

11012. London - British Library Or. 11122, f. 102b-103a, M.

זאת הוקשת מאד (ז *2)

Ashkenaz

11013. Hamburg - Staats- und Universitaetsbibliothek Cod. hebr. 17/2 (Steinschneider 152), f. 43a-44a, C, rubric: לשבת תקנו.

זבוד זה זבד טוב (ז 15), יצחק בן זרחיה גירונדי, חלק ו', קדושתא לשבת שקלים
Carpentras, commentary by Mordekhai b. Josef of Rocco Martino
11014. Cincinnati - Hebrew Union College 246, f. 10a-11a, C, rubric: פי'
פזמון זבוד זה זבד טוב.
Sepharad, commentary by Josef Garad
11015. Oxford - Bodleian Library Heb.e.10 (Neubauer 2746/1), f. 4b, C, rubric: פזמון.

זולתך אדונים בעלונו (ז 82), קלונימוס ב"ר יהודה, זולת
Ashkenaz
11016. Budapest - Magyar tudomanyos akademia, MS. Kaufmann A 399, p. 424, C, rubric: זולת.
11017. Cambridge - University Library Add. 504,1, f. 41a-41b, C.
11018. Lund - Universitetsbibliothek Ms. L.O. 2, f. 98b-99b, M.
11019. Parma - Biblioteca Palatina Cod. Parm. 3205 (de Rossi 655), f. 148a-149a, C, incipit אדונים.
Tsarfat
11020. Oxford - Bodleian Library MS Laud. Or. 271 (Neubauer 1206), f. 185b-186a, C, commentator: Aaron b. Hayyim haKohen (compiler).

זועק בקראו גרונו נחר (ז 84), זרחיה הלוי ב"ר יצחק גירונדי, סליחה
Carpentras
11021. Cincinnati - Hebrew Union College 392, f. 10a-11a, M.
Carpentras, commentary by Josef b. Abraham of Montelitz
11022. Cincinnati - Hebrew Union College 291, f. 6a-6b, C, rubric: פי' זועק בקראו וכו'.
11023. New York - Jewish Theological Seminary Ms. 4197, f. 23a-24a, M.
11024. Paris - Ecole Rabbinique 32, f. 26a-27b, M.
11025. Strasbourg - Bibliotheque Nationale et Universitaire 4081, f. 24a-26a, M.

זיו כבודך תמוץ (ז 85), יצחק בן זרחיה גירונדי, חלק ה', קדושתא לשבת שקלים
Carpentras, commentary by Mordekhai b. Josef of Rocco Martino
11026. Cincinnati - Hebrew Union College 246, f. 9b-10a, C, rubric: פי' מחיה דו כבודך תמוץ.
Sepharad, commentary by Josef Garad
11027. Oxford - Bodleian Library Heb.e.10 (Neubauer 2746/1), f. 4a, C, rubric: משלש.

זך הכיר תמים דעים (ז 88), זרחיה הלוי ב"ר יצחק גירונדי, זולת לראש השנה
Carpentras
11028. Cincinnati - Hebrew Union College 429/1, f. 20a-21b, M, no incipit.

Carpentras, commentary by Josef b. Abraham of Montelitz
11029. Cincinnati - Hebrew Union College 357, f. 97a-98b, M, rubric: פירוש.
11030. New York - Jewish Theological Seminary Ms. 4746, f. 30b-31b, M.
11031. Paris - Alliance Israelite Universelle H 422 A, f. 77b-79a, M.
11032. Paris - Ecole Rabbinique 31, f. 136a-137a, M.

זכור יי מה היה לנו, סדר רחמים
Yemen, commentary by Isaac b. Abraham Wanneh
11033. Jerusalem - Makhon Ben Zvi 1156 (Tubi 155), f. 134b-135b, M, no incipit.
11034. Muenchen - Bayerische Staatsbibliothek, Cod. hebr. 472, f. 187a-188b, M.
11035. New York - Jewish Theological Seminary Ms. 3294, f. 15a-15b, C.

זכור יי מה היה לנו הביטה וראה את חרפתינו זכור יי (ז 97), אברהם, קינה
Yemen, commentary by Isaac b. Abraham Wanneh
11036. Jerusalem - Musad haRav Kook 325, f. 189b-190a, M.

זכור יי מה היה לנו אוי הביטה וראה את חרפתנו אוי מה היה לנו. אקונן בכל שנה ודמעתי אתמיד (ז 98), קינה
North Africa, commentary by Yehuda Toledano
11037. New York - Jewish Theological Seminary Rab. 949, f. 123b-127b, C.
Yemen
11038. New York - Jewish Theological Seminary Ms. 3052, f. 70b-74a, M.
Yemen, commentary by Isaac b. Abraham Wanneh
11039. Chicago-Spertus College of Judaica D 2, 2, f. 232b-233a, M.
11040. Jerusalem - Sassoon 1158, p. 160, M, rubric: חידושין.
11041. Jerusalem - Sassoon 1158, p. 175-176, M.
11042. London - British Library Or. 11122, f. 105a, M.
11043. London - British Library Or. 11122, f. 97a, M, rubric: חידושין.

זכור איכה אנו (ז 108), אלעזר ברבי קליר, קרובה לט' באב
Romania
11044. New York - Jewish Theological Seminary Ms. 4362, f. 1a-6a, C, Ginzburg attributed this commentary to Tobia b. Eliezer.[255]

זכור איש אשר הגויע (ז 109), אלעזר ברבי קליר, חלק ה', קדושתא לשבת זכור
Ashkenaz
11045. Berlin - Staatsbibliothek (Preussischer Kulturbesitz) Or. Qu. 798-799 (Steinschneider 177), II, f. 22b-23a, M.

---

[255] Edited by L. Ginzberg, in מדרש לקח טוב על הקרובה הקלירית זכר איכה אנו. גנזי שכטר ספר א: קטעי מדרש ואגדה, New York, Jewish Theological Seminary, 1928, pp. 246-297.

11046. Budapest - Magyar tudomanyos akademia, MS. Kaufmann A 384 , f. 55b-56a, M.
11047. Budapest - Magyar tudomanyos akademia, MS. Kaufmann A 400 , p. 42-46, C.
11048. Cambridge - University Library, Taylor Schechter Collection Misc. 33/3, f. 22b-23b, G.
11049. Hamburg - Staats- und Universitaetsbibliothek Cod. hebr. 17/2 (Steinschneider 152), f. 19a-20a, C.
11050. Jerusalem - Schocken Institute 24100 / Mahzor Nuremberg, f. 43a, M.
11051. Muenchen - Bayerische Staatsbibliothek, Cod. hebr. 88, f. 25b-26a, G.
11052. Muenchen - Bayerische Staatsbibliothek, Cod. hebr. 393 , f. 91b-92a, C, no incipit.
11053. Oxford - Bodleian Library MS Opp. 170 (Neubauer 1205), f. 13a-14a, C, incipit אשר.
11054. Paris - Bibliotheque Nationale heb. 709, f. 22b-23b, C.
11055. Parma - Biblioteca Palatina Cod. Parm. 1002 (Ta 24), f. 37a-37b, M.
11056. Parma - Biblioteca Palatina Cod. Parm. 3205 (de Rossi 655), f. 21b-24a, C.
11057. Parma - Biblioteca Palatina Cod. Parm. 3507 (Perreau 27), f. 16b-17b, C, no incipit.
11058. Vatican - Biblioteca Apostolica ebr. 305,1, f. 15a-17a, M.

Tsarfat

11059. London - British Library Add. 11639 (Margoliouth 1056), f. 269a-271a, M.
11060. London - David Sofer 5, f. 21b-24a, C.
11061. Moscow - Russian State Library, Ms. Guenzburg 1665, f. 19b-20a, M.
11062. Oxford - Bodleian Library MS Opp. 171 (Neubauer 1207), f. 17b-21b, C, rubric: פזמון.
11063. Parma - Biblioteca Palatina Cod. Parm. 3136 (de Rossi 405), f. 32b-34a, M.

זכור את אשר עשה צר פנים (ז 111), אלעזר ברבי קליר, קינה

Ashkenaz

11064. Berlin - Staatsbibliothek (Preussischer Kulturbesitz) Or. Qu. 798-799 (Steinschneider 177), II, f. 19a-20a, M.
11065. Berlin - Staatsbibliothek (Preussischer Kulturbesitz) Or. Qu. 798-799 (Steinschneider 177), II, f. 191a-191b, M.
11066. Budapest - Magyar tudomanyos akademia, MS. Kaufmann A 400, p. 225-228, C, rubric: אחרת.
11067. Hamburg - Staats- und Universitaetsbibliothek Cod. hebr. 17/2 (Steinschneider 152), f. 99a-99b, C.
11068. Jerusalem - Schocken Institute 24100 / Mahzor Nuremberg, f. 40a, M, short.

11069. Jerusalem - Schocken Institute 24100 / Mahzor Nuremberg, f. 200a-200b, M.
11070. Oxford - Bodleian Library MS Can. Or. 70 (Neubauer 1147,8), f. 123b-125a, M, incipit זכור אשר עש צר.
11071. Parma - Biblioteca Palatina Cod. Parm. 3205 (de Rossi 655), f. 196a-196b, C, rubric: אחרת.
11072. Vatican - Biblioteca Apostolica ebr. 312, f. 50a-50b, G.
11073. Vatican - Biblioteca Apostolica ebr. 318, f. 239a240a, GI.
Ashkenaz, commentary by Abraham b. Azriel[256]
11074. Vatican - Biblioteca Apostolica ebr. 301,1, f. 136b, C, rubric: אחרת.

זכור את אשר עשה ויהי לבו ולמשיסה (ז 112), אלעזר ברבי קילר, יוצר לשבת זכור
Ashkenaz
11075. Budapest - Magyar tudomanyos akademia, MS. Kaufmann A 384, f. 49a-50a, M.
11076. Cambridge - University Library Add. 394,1 (Reif SCR 461), f. 42b-43a, C, rubric: יוזר לפרשת זכור.
11077. Cambridge - University Library Add. 504,1, f. 11a-11b, C, rubric: לפרשה שנייה.
11078. Erlangen - Universitaetsbibliothek 2601 (Roth 67), f. 33a, M, very short.
11079. Muenchen - Bayerische Staatsbibliothek, Cod. hebr. 88, f. 22a-23a, G.
11080. Muenchen - Bayerische Staatsbibliothek, Cod. hebr. 393, f. 89a, C, rubric: פרשת זכור.
11081. Parma - Biblioteca Palatina Cod. Parm. 1002 (Ta 24), f. 31b-32a, M, short.
11082. Parma - Biblioteca Palatina Cod. Parm. 3205 (de Rossi 655), f. 57a-57b, C, rubric: אתחיל יוצר לפרשת זכור ולא מצאתי לעיל.
11083. Parma - Biblioteca Palatina Cod. Parm. 3269, f. 15a-15b, G, later hand.
11084. Parma - Biblioteca Palatina Cod. Parm. 3507 (Perreau 27), f. 12a, C, rubric: קרוביץ לפרשה זכור, no incipit.
11085. Vatican - Biblioteca Apostolica ebr. 305,1, f. 10b-11a, C, rubric: יוצר.
Italia
11086. Parma - Biblioteca Palatin Cod. Parm. 2248 (de Rossi 149/2), f. 18b-19a, C, rubric: ביאור יוצר פרשת זכור.
Roma
11087. Jerusalem - Jewish National and University Library Ms Heb 8° 4153, f. 156b, C, commentator: Daniel ben Salomo haRofe (compiler), rubric: פי' יוצר דזכור, additional glosses.
11088. New York - Jewish Theological Seminary Ms. 1639, f. 16b-17b, C, commentator: Salomo b. Samuel Rofe, rubric: ביאור יוצר פרשת זכור.

---

[256] Edited by Urbach, ערוגת הבושם, vol. III, p. 275-276.

11089. Oxford - Bodleian Library MS Mich. 312,1 (Neubauer 2276,1), f. 22a-22b, C, rubric: פי׳ יוצר דפרש׳ זכור.
Tsarfat
11090. London - David Sofer 5, f. 16a, C, rubric: יוצר לפרשת זכור.
11091. Moscow - Russian State Library, Ms. Guenzburg 1665, f. 16a-17b, M.
11092. Parma - Biblioteca Palatina Cod. Parm. 3136 (de Rossi 405), f. 26a-26b, M.
11093. Vatican - Biblioteca Apostolica ebr. 306, f. 159b-160a, C, rubric: לפרשת זכור.

זכור ברית אברהם ועקדת יצחק והשב שבות אהלי יעקב (ז 115+), הקדמה
Ashkenaz
11094. Berlin - Staatsbibliothek (Preussischer Kulturbesitz) Or. Qu. 798-799 (Steinschneider 177), I, f. 183a, M.
11095. Oxford - Bodleian Library MS Opp. 681 (Neubauer 1213), f. 78a-78b, C.
11096. Vatican - Biblioteca Apostolica ebr. 422/1, f. 31b-32a, C.

זכור ברית ... אדמתי לכליון וחרץ, סליחה
Tsarfat
11097. Vatican - Biblioteca Apostolica ebr. 306, f. 209b-210a, C.

זכור סגן אשר נגן עלי עשור וגם נבל (ז 132), הושענא
haAri, commentary by Mose b. Hayyim Pesante
11098. New York - Jewish Theological Seminary Ms. 4696, f. 23a-23b, C, incipit סגן.
Italia, commentary by Zakharya David Shabbetai Segre
11099. Torino - Archivio Terracini 1499, p. 222-223, C, rubric: פירוש זכור סגן, incipit סגן.
North Africa
11100. Jerusalem - Benayahu ז 27, f. 126a, M, incipit סגן.
11101. Jerusalem - Michael Krupp 3391, f. 17b, M, covers only part of piyyut.
North Africa, commentary by Yehuda Toledano
11102. New York - Jewish Theological Seminary Ms. 4300, f. 53b-55a, C.
Yemen, commentary by Samḥun b. Salomo Ḥaloah
11103. Jerusalem - Makhon ben Zvi 2808, f. 196b-198a, C, incipit סגן.

זכות אם יפעל בעודנו
Ashkenaz
11104. Berlin - Staatsbibliothek (Preussischer Kulturbesitz) Or. Qu. 798-799 (Steinschneider 177), I, f. 178b, M, short.

זכות משה אל תנשה חתום במדת הנצח (ז 138), סעדיה גאון, הושענא

haAri, commentary by Mose b. Hayyim Pesante
11105. New York - Jewish Theological Seminary Ms. 4696, f. 22a-22b, C, rubric: הקפה חמישית.

Italia, commentary by Zakharya David Shabbetai Segre
11106. Torino - Archivio Terracini 1499, p. 180, C, rubric: פירוש זכות משה, short.

North Africa, commentary by Yehuda Toledano
11107. New York - Jewish Theological Seminary Ms. 4300, f. 46b-47b, C, rubric: הקפה רביעית משה.

Yemen
11108. New York - Jewish Theological Seminary Ms. 9325, f. 83b-84b, M.

Yemen, commentary by Isaac b. Abraham Wanneh
11109. Jerusalem - Musad haRav Kook 325, f. 107b-108a, M, rubric: חידושין.
11110. Nahariya - Menahem and Saida Yaakob 284, f. 13b, M.

Yemen, commentary by Samḥun b. Salomo Ḥaloah
11111. Jerusalem - Makhon ben Zvi 2808, f. 175a-176a, C.

זכות נשמר וברית שמר במדת היסוד (ג 139), הושענא

haAri, commentary by Mose b. Hayyim Pesante
11112. New York - Jewish Theological Seminary Ms. 4696, f. 21b-22a, C, rubric: הקפה רביעית.

Italia, commentary by Zakharya David Shabbetai Segre
11113. Torino - Archivio Terracini 1499, p. 198-200, C, rubric: פירוש זכות נשמר.

Yemen, commentary by Isaac b. Abraham Wanneh
11114. New York - Jewish Theological Seminary Ms. 3108, f. 84b, C, rubric: בהקפה רביעית.

Yemen, commentary by Samḥun b. Salomo Ḥaloah
11115. Jerusalem - Makhon ben Zvi 2808, f. 177b-180a, C.

זכות פינחס המיומס למדת צדיק (ז 140), הושענא

North Africa
11116. Jerusalem - Benayahu ז 27, f. 123b, M, no incipit.

North Africa, commentary by Yehuda Toledano
11117. New York - Jewish Theological Seminary Ms. 4300, f. 49a-50b, C, rubric: הקפה ששית פינחס.

זכר עשה לחבל נחלתו (ז +145), חלק מן הפיוט אסיר משחר את פני רבו

Carpentras, commentary by Eliyahu Carmi
11118. New York - Jewish Theological Seminary Ms. 3151, f. 36b, M.

Carpentras, commentary by Josef b. Abraham of Montelitz
11119. Paris - Alliance Israelite Universelle H 422 A, f. 16a, M.

זכר פורים לא יעבור (ז 146), זרחיה הלוי ב"ר יצחק גירונדי, לפורים
Sepharad, commentary by Josef Garad

11120. Oxford - Bodleian Library Heb.e.10 (Neubauer 2746/1), f. 19a, C, rubric: זכר פורים, no incipit.

זכר תחילת כל מעש (ז 149), אלעזר ברבי קליר, זכרונות למוסף ראש השנה
Ashkenaz

11121. Berlin - Staatsbibliothek (Preussischer Kulturbesitz) Or. Qu. 798-799 (Steinschneider 177), I, f. 25b-28b, M.
11122. Braunschweig - Landesmuseum fuer Geschichte und Volkstum R 2386, vol. II, f. 101b-103a, M.
11123. Budapest - Magyar tudomanyos akademia, MS. Kaufmann A 400, p. 277-282, C.
11124. Cambridge - University Library Or. 785, f. 45a-47a, G.
11125. Darmstadt - Hessisches Landes- und Hochschulbibliothek Cod. Or. 15, f. 25a-26b, M.
11126. Hamburg - Staats- und Universitaetsbibliothek Cod. hebr. 17/2 (Steinschneider 152), f. 118a-120a, C, rubric: זכר זכרונות.
11127. Hamburg - Staats- und Universitaetsbibliothek Cod. hebr. 40b (Steinschneider 110), f. 25a-28a, G.
11128. Hamburg - Staats- und Universitaetsbibliothek Cod. hebr. 40c (Steinschneider 111), f. 143a-143b, G.
11129. Hamburg - Staats- und Universitaetsbibliothek Cod. hebr. 132 (Steinschneider 155), f. 18a-20b, C.
11130. Jerusalem - Jewish National and University Library Ms Heb 8° 3037, f. 37b-40a, M.
11131. Jerusalem - Schocken Institute 24100 / Mahzor Nuremberg, f. 336b-337a, M.
11132. Koblenz - Staatsarchiv Abt. 701, Nr. 759,5,8, f. 1b-2b, FC, incomplete.
11133. London - British Library Or. 11318/1, f. 26a-32a, C.
11134. London - Montefiore Library 261, f. 32b-35b, C, commentator: Eliezer b. Natan?.
11135. Modena - Archivio di Stato 27, FM, incomplete.
11136. Moscow - Russian State Library, Ms. Guenzburg 191, f. 23a-25a, M.
11137. Moscow - Russian State Library, Ms. Guenzburg 615, f. 81a-83b, C, rubric: היום הרת.
11138. Muenchen - Bayerische Staatsbibliothek, Cod. hebr. 86, f. 41b-44b, G.
11139. Muenchen - Bayerische Staatsbibliothek, Cod. hebr. 346, f. 26a-30b, C.
11140. New York - Jewish Theological Seminary Ms. 4466, f. 236b-239a, M.

11141. New York - Jewish Theological Seminary Ms. 8097, f. 63b-64(ii)a, C, additional glosses in the margins.
11142. New York - Jewish Theological Seminary Ms. 8169 (Acc. 0016), f. 26b-28a, M.
11143. Oxford - Bodleian Library MS Mich. 365 (Neubauer 1208), f. 42b-45b, C.
11144. Oxford - Bodleian Library MS Opp. 170 (Neubauer 1205), f. 132b-138a, C.
11145. Oxford - Bodleian Library MS Opp. 172 (Neubauer 1211), f. 15b-17a, C.
11146. Oxford - Bodleian Library MS Opp. 619 (Neubauer 2374), f. 40b-42b, M.
11147. Oxford - Bodleian Library MS Opp. 675 (Neubauer 1210), f. 35b-38a, C, no incipit.
11148. Paris - Bibliotheque Nationale heb. 653, f. 21b-23b, G.
11149. Parma - Biblioteca Palatina Cod. Parm. 3205 (de Rossi 655), f. 213b-215a, C.
11150. Parma - Biblioteca Palatina Cod. Parm. 3270 (de Rossi 1215), f. 43a-44b, M.
11151. Parma - Biblioteca Palatina Cod. Parm. 3507 (Perreau 27), f. 126a-128a, C, no incipit.
11152. Vatican - Biblioteca Apostolica ebr. 308, f. 64a-67b, C, commentator: David b. Mose (compiler).
11153. Vatican - Biblioteca Apostolica ebr. 422/1, f. 11a-11b, C.
11154. Zurich - Zentralbibliothek Heid. 139 , f. 68a-69a, C, additional marginal notes.
11155. Zurich - Zentralbibliothek Heid. 139, f. 102b, C, commentator: Elazar b. Yehuda of Worms, short.

Asti, Fossano, Moncalvo

11156. New Haven - Yale University, Beinecke Rare Book and MS Library, MS Heb. 52, f. 41b-42a, M.

Tsarfat

11157. London - British Library Add. 11639 (Margoliouth 1056), f. 712b-713b, M, rubric: נשלמו מלכיות וזה שופרות זכרונות.
11158. London - British Library Or. 8682, f. 28b-29b, GI.
11159. London - David Sofer 5, f. 117a-118a, C.
11160. Oxford - Bodleian Library MS Laud. Or. 271 (Neubauer 1206), f. 151a-153b, C, commentator: Aaron b. Hayyim haKohen (compiler).
11161. Paris - Bibliotheque Nationale heb. 445,9, f. 85b-88a, C.
11162. Parma - Biblioteca Palatina Cod. Parm. 2125 (de Rossi 812), f. 25a-26b, C.
11163. Parma - Biblioteca Palatina Cod. Parm. 3006 (de Rossi 654,1), f. 54a-56a, M.
11164. Vatican - Biblioteca Apostolica ebr. 306, f. 61a-63b, C.

זכרון ועל כל מה עדותם, לפורים

Sepharad, commentary by Josef Garad

11165. Oxford - Bodleian Library Heb.e.10 (Neubauer 2746/1), f. 9a-10a, C, rubric: פזמון לפורים.

11166. Oxford - Bodleian Library Heb.e.10 (Neubauer 2746/1), f. 19a, C, rubric: זכרון, no incipit.

זכרנו לחיים (ז 164)

Ashkenaz

11167. Budapest - Magyar tudomanyos akademia, MS. Kaufmann A 399, p. 165, C.

11168. London - Montefiore Library 261, f. 6a, C, commentator: Eliezer b. Natan?.

11169. Lund - Universitetsbibliothek Ms. L.O. 2, f. 75b, M.

11170. Oxford - Bodleian Library MS Opp. 170 (Neubauer 1205), f. 111a, C, short.

Italia

11171. Moscow - Russian State Library, Ms. Guenzburg 134,8, f. 80a, C.

Sepharad

11172. Jerusalem - Benayahu ז 25, f. 187a, M.

Tsarfat

11173. Jerusalem - Schocken Institute 19623, f. 107b, M, commentator: Yehuda b. Eliezer Zvi.

11174. London - British Library Or. 2735 (Margoliouth 663), f. 110a-110b, M.

זמן הבלי ימי סבלי (ז 205), משה אבן עזרא, סליחה

Carpentras

11175. Cincinnati - Hebrew Union College 392, f. 78b-79a, M, no incipit.

Carpentras, commentary by Josef b. Abraham of Montelitz

11176. Cincinnati - Hebrew Union College 291, f. 43b-44b, C, rubric: פי' סליחה זמן הבלי וכו'.

11177. New York - Jewish Theological Seminary Ms. 4197, f. 181b-182b, M, no incipit.

11178. Paris - Ecole Rabbinique 32, f. 191b-192a, M, no incipit.

11179. Strasbourg - Bibliotheque Nationale et Universitaire 4081, f. 168a-169a, M.

Yemen

11180. New York - Jewish Theological Seminary Ms. 3052, f. 33a-35b, M, rubric: אל מלך.

Yemen, commentary by Isaac b. Abraham Wanneh

11181. Chicago-Spertus College of Judaica D 2, 2, f. 208a-208b, M, no incipit.

11182. Jerusalem - Makhon Ben Zvi 1156 (Tubi 155), f. 122a-122b, M, rubric: אל מלך.
11183. Jerusalem - Makhon Ben Zvi 1174 (Tubi 154), f. 127a-127b, M.
11184. Jerusalem - Michael Krupp 604, f. 155a-156a, M.
11185. Jerusalem - Musad haRav Kook 325, f. 184a-184b, M.
11186. Jerusalem - Sassoon 1158, p. 376-377, M, no incipit.
11187. Jerusalem - Sassoon 1174, p. 235-237, M, no incipit.
11188. London - British Library Or. 11122, f. 188b-189a, M, no incipit.
11189. Muenchen - Bayerische Staatsbibliothek, Cod. hebr. 472, f. 167a-168b, M, rubric: אל מלך.
11190. New York - Jewish Theological Seminary Ms. 3013, f. 123a-123b, M, rubric: אל מלך.
11191. New York - Jewish Theological Seminary Ms. 3109, f. 123a-124a, M, rubric: אל מלך.
11192. New York - Jewish Theological Seminary Ms. 3294, f. 11b-12a, C.
11193. Strasbourg - Bibliotheque Nationale et Universitaire 3965 (Landauer 39), p. 384-385, M, rubric: אל מלך.

חג האסיף תקופת השנה (ח 31), אליעזר ב"ר שמשון, מעריב ליום ב' של סוכות

Ashkenaz
11194. London - British Library Add. 18695 (Margoliouth 683), f. 114b, T, Yiddish.

חד גדיא (ח 39), זמר לפסח

Ashkenaz
11195. Oxford - Bodleian Library MS Opp. 521/1 (Neubauer 1936), f. 1a-5b, C, kabbalistic.

Azerbeidjan
11196. St. Petersburg - Russian National Library Evr. IV 148, f. 34b-35b, C, rubric: פירוש על חד גדיא.

Italia
11197. Jerusalem - Benayahu צ 155, f. 19b-25a, C, kabbalistic, first introduction, then commentary, allegoric.
11198. Leeds - Brotherton Library, MS Roth 711/6, f. 40b-42b, C, commentator: Mose Nahman, rubric: הקדמה על פירוש חד גדיא / פירוש על חד גדיא, first introduction, then commentary, allegoric.

חדו חדו רבנן שמתה תורה תמימה (ח 40), פיוט בארמית לשמחת תורה

Yemen
11199. Jerusalem - Michael Krupp 1758, f. 26b-27a, M.
11200. Jerusalem - Michael Krupp 3391, f. 18b-19b, M.
11201. New York - Alfred Moldovan HH, f. 32b, M.
11202. New York - Jewish Theological Seminary Ms. 4488, f. 72a-72b, G.

Yemen, commentary by Isaac b. Abraham Wanneh?
11203. Jerusalem - Makhon Ben Zvi 1156 (Tubi 155), f. 78b, M, margins damaged.
11204. Manchester - John Rylands University Library, Ms. Gaster 5, f. 155b, M.
11205. Muenchen - Bayerische Staatsbibliothek, Cod. hebr. 472, f. 104a, M, margins damaged.
11206. Nahariya - Menahem and Saida Yaakob 284, f. 24a-24b, M.
11207. New York - Jewish Theological Seminary Ms. 4195, f. 43b-45a, M.
Yemen, commentary by Yiḥya b. Josef Tsalaḥ
11208. Montreal - Elberg 203, f. 34a-34b, M.

חולחל פתרוס אורחותם בעבטם (ח 81), יוסף ב"ר שמואל טוב עלם, חלק ב' קדושתא לפסח

Tsarfat
11209. Parma - Biblioteca Palatina Cod. Parm. 3136 (de Rossi 405), f. 109a-109b, M.

חוללים כל מעייני, יצחק הנקדן

Ashkenaz
11210. Oxford - Bodleian Library MS Can. Or. 70 (Neubauer 1147,7), f. 92a-93a, M, rubric: אחרת.

חוללת בראת מחללת

Carpentras, commentary by Eliyahu Carmi
11211. Marseille - Mlle. Odette Valabregue [1], f. 34a, C.

חון שוטחים אליך כפים חנון רחום יי ארך אפים, הושענא

Yemen, commentary by Samḥun b. Salomo Ḥaloah
11212. Jerusalem - Makhon ben Zvi 2808, f. 68a-70b, C.

חוקר הכל וסוקר ומבין (ח 126), יצחק, סליחה

Ashkenaz
11213. Moscow - Russian State Library, Ms. Guenzburg 190, f. 21a-21b, G.
11214. Vatican - Biblioteca Apostolica ebr. 308/1, f. 11b, C, commentator: David b. Mose (compiler).
Ashkenaz, cmmentary by Abraham b. Azriel[257]
11215. Vatican - Biblioteca Apostolica ebr. 301,1, f. 170a-170b, C.
Tsarfat
11216. London - David Sofer 5, f. 103a, C.

---

[257] Edited by Urbach, ערוגת הבושם, vol. III, p. 497-498.

11217. Parma - Biblioteca Palatina Cod. Parm. 1794 (de Rossi 1061), f. 20a-20b, M.
11218. Parma - Biblioteca Palatina Cod. Parm. 2890 (de Rossi 856), f. 51a, M.
11219. Parma - Biblioteca Palatina Cod. Parm. 3007 (de Rossi 654,2), f. 123a-123b, M.
11220. Vatican - Biblioteca Apostolica ebr. 306, f. 206b, C.

חזיון קדושים עשרה

Ashkenaz
11221. Oxford - Bodleian Library MS Mich. 365 (Neubauer 1208), f. 14a-14b, C, no incipit.

חי אני תמים דעים (ה 213), משה אבן עזרא, חלק ד', קדושתא למוסף יום כפור

Carpentras
11222. Cincinnati - Hebrew Union College 392, f. 88b-89b, M, no incipit.
Carpentras, commentary by Josef b. Abraham of Montelitz
11223. New York - Jewish Theological Seminary Ms. 4197, f. 201a-202a, M.
11224. Paris - Ecole Rabbinique 32, f. 209a-210a, M.
11225. Strasbourg - Bibliotheque Nationale et Universitaire 4081, f. 183b-185a, M.

חיים ארוכים תכתבנו נטוע בלי לעקור (ה 247), סליחה

Ashkenaz
11226. Muenchen - Bayerische Staatsbibliothek, Cod. hebr. 346, f. 148b, C, rubric: אחרת.
11227. Vatican - Biblioteca Apostolica ebr. 308, f. 16a-17a, C, commentator: David b. Mose (compiler).
11228. Vatican - Biblioteca Apostolica ebr. 308, f. 163b, C, commentator: David b. Mose (compiler).
Ashkenaz, commentary by Abraham b. Azriel[258]
11229. Frankfurt a M - Stadt- und Universitaetsbibliothek Fol. 16 (Merzbacher 95), f. 107b, C.

חכמי תום דרך המאחלים (ה +315), פיוט אחרי הקדושה לשחרית יום כפור

Ashkenaz
11230. Muenchen - Bayerische Staatsbibliothek, Cod. hebr. 346, f. 67a-68b, C, no incipit.
Ashkenaz, commentary by Abraham b. Azriel[259]
11231. Vatican - Biblioteca Apostolica ebr. 301,1, f. 173a, C.

---

[258] Edited by Urbach, ערוגת הבושם, vol. III, p. 557.
[259] Edited by Urbach, ערוגת הבושם, vol. III, p. 514-515.

Tsarfat

11232. London - David Sofer 5, f. 165b-166a, C, rubric: רהיטים.

11233. Parma - Biblioteca Palatina Cod. Parm. 1794 (de Rossi 1061), f. 187a-188a, M, no incipit.

11234. Parma - Biblioteca Palatina Cod. Parm. 3006 (de Rossi 654,1), f. 223b, M.

חנון ורחום יי על עם כבודו גלה (ח 398), יוסף, סליחה לתענית אסתר

Carpentras, commentary by Mordekhai b. Josef of Rocco Martino

11235. Cincinnati - Hebrew Union College 246/1, f. 91b-92a, C, rubric: פי׳ סליחה חנון ורחום.

חננו יי חננו (ח 414), שלמה הבבלי, סליחה

Ashkenaz

11236. Budapest - Magyar tudomanyos akademia, MS. Kaufmann A 400, p. 433-435, C, rubric: פיזמון שלמונית.

11237. Forli - Archivio di Stato 4, FC, incomplete.

11238. Hamburg - Staats- und Universitaetsbibliothek Cod. hebr. 17/2 (Steinschneider 152), f. 129b-130a, C, rubric: פזמון שלמוני.

11239. Jerusalem - Schocken Institute 24100 / Mahzor Nuremberg, f. 306b, M.

11240. Moscow - Russian State Library, Ms. Guenzburg 615, f. 166b, C, end missing.

11241. Oxford - Bodleian Library MS Mich. 543 (Neubauer 1212), f. 75b-76a, C, commentator: Isaac b. Jacob (compiler).

11242. Oxford - Bodleian Library MS Opp. 170 (Neubauer 1205), f. 236a-237a, C.

11243. Oxford - Bodleian Library MS Opp. 681 (Neubauer 1213), f. 76a-77a, C.

11244. Padova - Biblioteca del Seminario Vescovile Cod. 218, f. 76a-76b, M.

11245. Padova - Biblioteca del Seminario Vescovile Cod. 218, f. 76b-77a, M, rubric: אחרת.

11246. Parma - Biblioteca Palatina Cod. Parm. 3205 (de Rossi 655), f. 278a-278b, C.

11247. Vatican - Biblioteca Apostolica ebr. 422/1, f. 32a, C.

Ashkenaz, commentary by Abraham b. Azriel[260]

11248. Vatican - Biblioteca Apostolica ebr. 301,1, f. 163a-163b, C, rubric: אחר.

---

[260] Edited by Urbach, ערוגת הבושם, vol. III, p. 448-451.

חנניה מישאל ועזריה אודעו שמיה דקודשא (ח 421), רשות לדבור שני

Ashkenaz

11249. Berlin - Staatsbibliothek (Preussischer Kulturbesitz) Or. Qu. 798-799 (Steinschneider 177), II, f. 157b-158b, M.

11250. Cambridge - University Library Add. 394,1 (Reif SCR 461), f. 58a-59a, C.

11251. Hamburg - Staats- und Universitaetsbibliothek Cod. hebr. 17/2 (Steinschneider 152), f. 72a-72b, C, incipit ננסא.

11252. Jerusalem - Schocken Institute 24100 / Mahzor Nuremberg, f. 156a-156b, M, rubric: אחרת, short.

11253. Moscow - Russian State Library, Ms. Guenzburg 206, f. 89a-89b, M.

11254. Muenchen - Bayerische Staatsbibliothek, Cod. hebr. 393, f. 151b-152a, C, rubric: אחרת, no incipit.

11255. New York - Jewish Theological Seminary Ms. 4466, f. 185b-186a, M.

11256. Oxford - Bodleian Library MS Can. Or. 1 (Neubauer 1104), f. 110b-111b, M.

11257. Oxford - Bodleian Library MS Opp. 170 (Neubauer 1205), f. 95b, C, rubric: אחרת, short.

11258. Parma - Biblioteca Palatina Cod. Parm. 3205 (de Rossi 655), f. 183a-183b, C.

Tsarfat

11259. Cambridge - University Library Add. 561.1, f. 76b-77b, MT, Hebrew.

11260. Jerusalem - Schocken Institute 19623, f. 178b-179b, M, commentator: Yehuda b. Eliezer Zvi, rubric: אחרת, short.

11261. London - British Library Add. 11639 (Margoliouth 1056), f. 676a-676b, M.

11262. London - British Library Or. 2735 (Margoliouth 663), f. 23a-24b, M.

11263. London - David Sofer 5, f. 59a-60b, C.

11264. Moscow - Russian State Library, Ms. Guenzburg 1665, f. 126b, M.

11265. New York - Jewish Theological Seminary Ms. 4460, f. 61a-62a, M, pages damaged.

11266. Parma - Biblioteca Palatina Cod. Parm. 1902, f. 141a-142b, M.

11267. Parma - Biblioteca Palatina Cod. Parm. 2574, f. 117a-118a, G, commentator: Simḥa b. Samuel, cp. Mahzor Vitry.

11268. Parma - Biblioteca Palatina Cod. Parm. 3136 (de Rossi 405), f. 158b-159b, M.

חסדי יי אזכיר תהלות יי (ח 432), שמעון ב"ר יצחק, סילוק, קדושתא לפסח

Ashkenaz

11269. Berlin - Staatsbibliothek (Preussischer Kulturbesitz) Or. Qu. 798-799 (Steinschneider 177), II, f. 108b-111a, M.

11270. Braunschweig - Landesmuseum fuer Geschichte und Volkstum R 2386, vol. I, f. 54b-55b, M, short.

11271. Budapest - Magyar tudomanyos akademia, MS. Kaufmann A 384, f. 242b-245a, M, ecclectic.
11272. Erlangen - Universitaetsbibliothek 2601 (Roth 67), f. 139a, M, ecclectic.
11273. Hamburg - Staats- und Universitaetsbibliothek Cod. hebr. 17/2 (Steinschneider 152), f. 40b-41b, C, commentator: Ephraim b. Jacob of Bonn.
11274. Jerusalem - Schocken Institute 24100 / Mahzor Nuremberg, f. 114a-115b, M, very ecclectic.
11275. New York - Jewish Theological Seminary Ms. 4466, f. 98b-102b, M, very ecclectic.
11276. Parma - Biblioteca Palatina Cod. Parm. 3205 (de Rossi 655), f. 115b, C, rubric: סילוק.
11277. Parma - Biblioteca Palatina Cod. Parm. 3507 (Perreau 27), f. 84b-85b, C.
11278. Zurich - Zentralbibliothek Heid. 139, f. 44b, C, very short, additional marginal notes.

Tsarfat
11279. Oxford - Bodleian Library MS Laud. Or. 271 (Neubauer 1206), f. 78a, C, commentator: Ephraim b. Jacob of Bonn (mainly), Aaron b. Hayyim haKohen (compiler), rubric: סילוק.

חסדך יי בל תמיש (ח 457), סליחה

Tsarfat
11280. London - David Sofer 5, f. 173b, C, rubric: פזמון.
11281. Parma - Biblioteca Palatina Cod. Parm. 3006 (de Rossi 654,1), f. 246b-247a, M.

חקור תש"ת הראשון לעורר

Yemen
11282. Jerusalem - Michael Krupp 2807, f. 1a-1b, M.

חרדו רעיני כי אלהי משפט (ח 512), אברהם אבן עזרא

Carpentras
11283. Cincinnati - Hebrew Union College 392, f. 59b, M, no incipit.
11284. Cincinnati - Hebrew Union College 429/1, f. 11a-11b, M, no incipit.

Carpentras, commentary by Josef b. Abraham of Montelitz
11285. Cincinnati - Hebrew Union College 291, f. 33b-34a, C, rubric: פי' פזמון חרדו רעיוני.
11286. Cincinnati - Hebrew Union College 357, f. 60a-61a, M, rubric: פירוש, no incipit.
11287. New York - Jewish Theological Seminary Ms. 4197, f. 136b-137a, M, no incipit.

11288. New York - Jewish Theological Seminary Ms. 4746, f. 17a-17b, M, no incipit.
11289. Paris - Ecole Rabbinique 31, f. 106a-106b, M, no incipit.
11290. Paris - Ecole Rabbinique 32, f. 149a-150a, M, no incipit.
11291. Strasbourg - Bibliotheque Nationale et Universitaire 4081, f. 126a-126b, M, rubric: אמר הצייד, no incipit.

חרדים לבית תפלתם (ה 516), משה אבן עזרא, חלק ה', קדושתא לשחרית יום כפור
Carpentras
11292. Cincinnati - Hebrew Union College 392, f. 58a-58b, M, no incipit.
Carpentras, commentary by Josef b. Abraham of Montelitz
11293. New York - Jewish Theological Seminary Ms. 4197, f. 131a-131b, M, no incipit.
11294. Paris - Ecole Rabbinique 32, f. 147a-147b, M, no incipit.
11295. Strasbourg - Bibliotheque Nationale et Universitaire 4081, f. 123b-124a, M, no incipit.
Sepharad, commentary by David b. Josef Abudarham[261]
11296. Budapest - Magyar tudomanyos akademia, MS. Kaufmann A 405/2, p. 206, C, rubric: פזמון.
11297. New York - Columbia X893 Ab 93, f. 12b, C, rubric: פזמון.
11298. New York - Jewish Theological Seminary Ms. 3011, f. 20a-20b, C, rubric: פזמון.

חרדתי ופחדתי מתגברת ידיך (ה 517), סליחה
Yemen, commentary by Isaac b. Abraham Wanneh
11299. Chicago-Spertus College of Judaica D 2, 2, f. 193b, M, no incipit.
11300. Jerusalem - Sassoon 1158, p. 358, M.
11301. London - British Library Or. 11122, f. 178a, M.

חרדתי ופחדתי מתגרות, חסדאי, סליחה
Ashkenaz
11302. Moscow - Russian State Library, Ms. Guenzburg 190, f. 61a-61b, G.
Tsarfat
11303. London - David Sofer 5, f. 169b, C, rubric: פזמון.
11304. Parma - Biblioteca Palatina Cod. Parm. 3007 (de Rossi 654,2), f. 123b-124a, M.
11305. Vatican - Biblioteca Apostolica ebr. 306, f. 211b-212a, C.

---

[261] Edited by Prins, תשלום אבודרהם, p. 25-26.

טבע זיו תארה, אלעזר ברבי קליר, חלק ג׳, קדושתא לנעילה

Ashkenaz

11306. Vatican - Biblioteca Apostolica ebr. 308, f. 147a-147b, C, commentator: David b. Mose (compiler).

11307. Zurich - Zentralbibliothek Heid. 139, f. 89a, C, very short, no incipit, additional marginal notes.

טהור עינים בצוותו (ט +21), אברהם בר חיים, חלק ג׳, קדושתא לפרשת פרה

Carpentras, commentary by Mordekhai b. Josef of Rocco Martino

11308. Cincinnati - Hebrew Union College 246/1, f. 29a-30a, C, rubric: פי׳ מחיה טהור עינים.

Sepharad, commentary by Josef Garad

11309. Oxford - Bodleian Library Heb.e.10 (Neubauer 2746/1), f. 11b, C, rubric: מחיה.

11310. Oxford - Bodleian Library Heb.e.10 (Neubauer 2746/1), f. 19b, C, rubric: טהור עינים, no incipit.

טוב במלאכת המשכן צוה לתמימים (ט ++33), מאיר הכהן, חלק ב׳, ברכת מזון לשבת נישוין

Ashkenaz

11311. Parma - Biblioteca Palatina Cod. Parm. 3205 (de Rossi 655), f. 173a-173b, C.

טורף אריה בדי גוריו (ט 102), יוסף ב״ר שמואל טוב עלם, חלק ה׳, קדושתא לפסח

Tsarfat

11312. Parma - Biblioteca Palatina Cod. Parm. 3136 (de Rossi 405), f. 91a-91b, M.

טיר אלגון יבאת יחדי, שלם שבזי

Yemen

11313. Cincinnati - Hebrew Union College 398, f. 95a-98b, M.

יא זון אזהאר אלמששאמים, שלם שבזי

Yemen

11314. Cincinnati - Hebrew Union College 398, f. 101b-104b, M.

11315. New York - M. Lehmann 274, f. 43a-43b, M, kabbalistic.

יא טאיר אלבאן ורתת פי קלבי אשגאן ... שיר הממונה גנת אגוז (י 15), שלם שבזי

Yemen

11316. Cincinnati - Hebrew Union College 398, f. 113b-115a, M.

יא מחיי אלנפוס סלם עלא גסמי (י 6), שלם שבזי

Yemen
11317. Cincinnati - Hebrew Union College 398, f. 111a-112a, M.

יא צאח לא תגבט, שלם שבזי

Yemen
11318. Cincinnati - Hebrew Union College 398, f. 104b-106a, M.

יאתה שדי לך ברכה ותהלה

Ashkenaz
11319. Berlin - Staatsbibliothek (Preussischer Kulturbesitz) Or. Qu. 798-799 (Steinschneider 177), I, f. 262b, M.

יאתה שדי לך קדושה וגדולה

Tsarfat
11320. London - British Library Or. 2735 (Margoliouth 663), f. 183a-183b, M, margins cut.

יאתה תהלה ועוז לבקודש נאדר (י 75), פיוט אחרי הקדושה לשחרית יום כפור, כלל כמה חלקים

Ashkenaz
11321. Berlin - Staatsbibliothek (Preussischer Kulturbesitz) Or. Qu. 798-799 (Steinschneider 177), I, f. 93a-94b, M.
11322. Braunschweig - Landesmuseum fuer Geschichte und Volkstum R 2386, vol. II, f. 204b-205a, C.
11323. Fulda - Hessische Landesbibliothek A 3 II, f. 119b-120b, C, commentator: Josef.
11324. Hamburg - Staats- und Universitaetsbibliothek Cod. hebr. 40b (Steinschneider 110), f. 114a-114b, G.
11325. Hamburg - Staats- und Universitaetsbibliothek Cod. hebr. 62 (Steinschneider 154), f. 13b-15a, C.
11326. Hamburg - Staats- und Universitaetsbibliothek Cod. hebr. 132 (Steinschneider 155), f. 40a-41b, C.
11327. Jerusalem - Jewish National and University Library Ms Heb 8° 3037, f. 139b-141b, M.
11328. Jerusalem - Schocken Institute 24100 / Mahzor Nuremberg, f. 389b-391a, M.
11329. London - British Library Or. 11318/1, f. 90a-93a, C.
11330. London - Montefiore Library 261, f. 51b-52b, C, commentator: Eliezer b. Natan?.
11331. Moscow - Russian State Library, Ms. Guenzburg 191, f. 106b-107a, M.

11332. Moscow - Russian State Library, Ms. Guenzburg 191, f. 126b-127a, M, only the parts כי אדוקי אש באימה יאכדוך and בכל און אוסיף.
11333. Moscow - Russian State Library, Ms. Guenzburg 615, f. 99a-100b, C.
11334. Muenchen - Bayerische Staatsbibliothek, Cod. hebr. 86, f. 131b-134a, G.
11335. Muenchen - Bayerische Staatsbibliothek, Cod. hebr. 346, f. 65a-67a, C, no incipit.
11336. Muenchen - Bayerische Staatsbibliothek, Cod. hebr. 346, f. 70b-71a, C, no incipit.
11337. New York - Jewish Theological Seminary Ms. 4466, f. 335a-337b, M.
11338. New York - Jewish Theological Seminary Ms. 8097, f. 76a, C.
11339. New York - Jewish Theological Seminary Ms. 8169 (Acc. 0016), f. 102b-104a, M.
11340. Oxford - Bodleian Library MS Mich. 365 (Neubauer 1208), f. 76b-78a, C.
11341. Oxford - Bodleian Library MS Opp. 170 (Neubauer 1205), f. 171a-173b, C.
11342. Oxford - Bodleian Library MS Opp. 172 (Neubauer 1211), f. 50a-52a, C.
11343. Oxford - Bodleian Library MS Opp. 525,18 (Neubauer 1598/18), f. 104a, C, only some parts, only gematriot.
11344. Oxford - Bodleian Library MS Opp. 619 (Neubauer 2374), f. 168b-169b, M.
11345. Parma - Biblioteca Palatina Cod. Parm. 3205 (de Rossi 655), f. 231a-232a, C.
11346. Parma - Biblioteca Palatina Cod. Parm. 3271 (de Rossi 1216), f. 60a-62a, G.
11347. Parma - Biblioteca Palatina Cod. Parm. 3507 (Perreau 27), f. 157a-158b, C.
11348. Vatican - Biblioteca Apostolica ebr. 308, f. 105(ii)a-106(ii)b, C, commentator: David b. Mose (compiler).
11349. Vatican - Biblioteca Apostolica ebr. 422/1, f. 17a, C.
11350. Zurich - Zentralbibliothek Heid. 139, f. 80a-81a, C, additional marginal notes.

Ashkenaz, commentary by Abraham b. Azriel[262]

11351. Vatican - Biblioteca Apostolica ebr. 301,1, f. 172a-173a, C.

Asti, Fossano, Moncalvo

11352. New Haven - Yale University, Beinecke Rare Book and MS Library, MS Heb. 52, f. 141a-142a, M.

Tsarfat

11353. London - British Library Add. 11639 (Margoliouth 1056), f. 722a, M.
11354. London - British Library Or. 8682, f. 88a-88b, GI.

---

[262] Edited by Urbach, ערוגת הבושם, vol. III, p. 509-514.

11355. London - David Sofer 5, f. 154b-155a, C.
11356. Oxford - Bodleian Library MS Bodl. Or. 109 (Neubauer 1209), f. 27(ii)b-27(iv)a, C, commentator: Aaron b. Hayyim haKohen (compiler).
11357. Oxford - Bodleian Library MS Laud. Or. 271 (Neubauer 1206), f. 108b-110a, C, commentator: Aaron b. Hayyim haKohen (compiler).
11358. Paris - Bibliotheque Nationale heb. 653, f. 72a, G.
11359. Parma - Biblioteca Palatina Cod. Parm. 1794 (de Rossi 1061), f. 184b-187a, M.
11360. Parma - Biblioteca Palatina Cod. Parm. 2125 (de Rossi 812), f. 41a-42b, C.
11361. Parma - Biblioteca Palatina Cod. Parm. 2890 (de Rossi 856), f. 82a-83b, M.
11362. Parma - Biblioteca Palatina Cod. Parm. 3006 (de Rossi 654,1), f. 189a-189b, M.
11363. Parma - Biblioteca Palatina Cod. Parm. 3006 (de Rossi 654,1), f. 222b-223b, M, only from כי אדוקי.
11364. Vatican - Biblioteca Apostolica ebr. 306, f. 84b-86b, C.

יבאונו חסדיך צורי שוכן שחק (י 109), יצחק בר יהודה, חלק ה', קדושתא לשחרית ראש השנה

Carpentras
11365. Cincinnati - Hebrew Union College 429/1, f. 23b, M, no incipit, very short.

Carpentras, commentary by Josef b. Abraham of Montelitz
11366. Cincinnati - Hebrew Union College 357, f. 102a-102b, M, rubric: פירוש.
11367. New York - Jewish Theological Seminary Ms. 4746, f. 34a-34b, M.
11368. Paris - Alliance Israelite Universelle H 422 A, f. 82a-82b, M.
11369. Paris - Ecole Rabbinique 31, f. 140b-141a, M.

יבושר עם לא אלמן בהגלות קץ נטמן (י 137), יהודה הלוי, זולת, בתימן: סליחה

Yemen
11370. Jerusalem - Musad haRav Kook 334, f. 138a, M.
11371. Jerusalem - Sassoon 902, p. 411, M.
11372. New York - Jewish Theological Seminary Ms. 3028, f. 31a, G.
11373. Ramat Gan - Universitat Bar Ilan 62, f. 47b, G, margins damaged.

Yemen, commentary by Isaac b. Abraham Wanneh
11374. Chicago-Spertus College of Judaica D 2, 2, f. 198a, M.
11375. Jerusalem - Benayahu ת 261, f. 136a, M, rubric: אל מלך.
11376. Jerusalem - Benayahu ת 282, f. 120a-120b, M, rubric: אל מלך.
11377. Jerusalem - Makhon Ben Zvi 1156 (Tubi 155), f. 118a, M, rubric: אל מלך.

11378. Jerusalem - Makhon Ben Zvi 1174 (Tubi 154), f. 123a, M.
11379. Jerusalem - Michael Krupp 604, f. 148b-149a, M, rubric: אל מלך.
11380. Jerusalem - Musad haRav Kook 325, f. 178b, M, rubric: אל מלך.
11381. Jerusalem - Musad haRav Kook 330, f. 107a, G.
11382. Jerusalem - Musad haRav Kook 347, f. 84b, G.
11383. Jerusalem - Sassoon 1158, p. 348, M, no incipit.
11384. Jerusalem - Sassoon 1174, p. 228, M, no incipit.
11385. Jerusalem - Yehiel haLevi 4, f. 153a, G.
11386. Manchester - John Rylands University Library, Ms. Gaster 5, f. 195a, M.
11387. Muenchen - Bayerische Staatsbibliothek, Cod. hebr. 472, f. 161a-161b, M, rubric: אל מלך.
11388. New York - Jewish Theological Seminary Ms. 3013, f. 119b-120a, M, rubric: אל מלך.
11389. New York - Public Library, Heb. Ms. 9, f. 116a, M.
11390. Philadelphia - University of Pennsylvania HB 2, f. 131b, M.
11391. Strasbourg - Bibliotheque Nationale et Universitaire 3965 (Landauer 39), p. 371, M, rubric: אל מלך.

יבשו אלי וספו אלי (י 181), יהודה הלוי
Sepharad, commentary by Josef Garad
11392. Oxford - Bodleian Library Heb.e.10 (Neubauer 2746/1), f. 27a, C, rubric: שבת איכה, no incipit.

יגורתי מפני שמיח קווה (י 235?), יצחק רן קפרון, חליחה
Yemen
11393. New York - Jewish Theological Seminary Ms. 3028, f. 83a, G.
11394. New York - Jewish Theological Seminary Ms. 3052, f. 88b-89a, M.
Yemen, commentary by Isaac b. Abraham Wanneh
11395. Chicago-Spertus College of Judaica D 2, 2, f. 239b-240a, M, no incipit.
11396. Jerusalem - Benayahu ת 261, f. 167a, M.
11397. Jerusalem - Benayahu ת 282, f. 143a, M.
11398. Jerusalem - Makhon Ben Zvi 1156 (Tubi 155), f. 140b, M, no incipit.
11399. Jerusalem - Makhon Ben Zvi 1174 (Tubi 154), f. 140a, M.
11400. Jerusalem - Michael Krupp 604, f. 178a, M, short.
11401. Jerusalem - Musad haRav Kook 325, f. 196a, M, short.
11402. Jerusalem - Sassoon 1158, p. 420, M, no incipit.
11403. Jerusalem - Sassoon 1174, p. 272-273, M, no incipit.
11404. London - British Library Or. 11122, f. 217a, M, no incipit.
11405. Muenchen - Bayerische Staatsbibliothek, Cod. hebr. 472, f. 196b, M.
11406. New York - Jewish Theological Seminary Ms. 3013, f. 135b, M, no incipit.

11407. New York - Jewish Theological Seminary Ms. 3294, f. 19a, C.
11408. New York - Public Library, Heb. Ms. 9, f. 132a-132b, M, no incipit.
11409. Strasbourg - Bibliotheque Nationale et Universitaire 3965 (Landauer 39), p. 418, M.

יגלה צור ישועתו לעם מפחדו נדהם (י 261), יצחק בר יהודה, פזמון לראש השנה
Carpentras, commentary by Josef b. Abraham of Montelitz
11410. Cincinnati - Hebrew Union College 357, f. 100a-100b, M, rubric: פירוש.
11411. New York - Jewish Theological Seminary Ms. 4746, f. 32b-33a, M.
11412. Paris - Alliance Israelite Universelle H 422 A, f. 80a-81b, M.
11413. Paris - Ecole Rabbinique 31, f. 138b-139a, M.

יד תתיר לבן מעתיר (י 302), יצחק גיאת, חלק ח', קדושתא לשחרית יום כפור
Sepharad, commentary by David b. Josef Abudarham
11414. Budapest - Magyar tudomanyos akademia, MS. Kaufmann A 405/2, p. 210-211, C, rubric: פזמון.
11415. New York - Columbia X893 Ab 93, f. 13(ii)a-13(ii)b, C, rubric: פזמון.

ידועי שם בבור נשם (י 335), יעקב, אופן לפסח
Ashkenaz
11416. Jerusalem - Schocken Institute 24100 / Mahzor Nuremberg, f. 121a, M.
11417. Oxford - Bodleian Library MS Opp. 169 (Neubauer 1151), f. 12b-13a, M.
Ashkenaz, commentary by Abraham b. Azriel[263]
11418. Frankfurt a M - Stadt- und Universitaetsbibliothek Fol. 16 (Merzbacher 95), f. 64b-65b, C, rubric: אופן.
11419. Vatican - Biblioteca Apostolica ebr. 301,1, f. 98b-99b, C, rubric: אופן.

ידוץ חתנא עם כלתא בסגיאות טבבתא (י 337), יוסף, לחתן
Tsarfat
11420. London - British Library Or. 2735 (Margoliouth 663), f. 177a-177b, M, margins cut.

ידי דלים נחשלים (י 351), יהודה הלוי, רשות או אופן, בתימון: סליחה
Carpentras
11421. Cincinnati - Hebrew Union College 392, f. 93a, M, no incipit.
11422. Cincinnati - Hebrew Union College 429/1, f. 27a, M, no incipit, short.

---

[263] Edited by Urbach, ערוגת הבושם, vol. III, p. 25-32.

Carpentras, commentary by Josef b. Abraham of Montelitz
11423. Cincinnati - Hebrew Union College 291, f. 50b-51b, C, rubric: 'פי פזמון ידי דלים.
11424. Cincinnati - Hebrew Union College 357, f. 106b-107b, M, no incipit, short.
11425. New York - Jewish Theological Seminary Ms. 4197, f. 207b-208b, M, no incipit.
11426. New York - Jewish Theological Seminary Ms. 4746, f. 38a-39a, M, no incipit, short.
11427. Paris - Alliance Israelite Universelle H 422 A, f. 87a-87b, M, no incipit, short.
11428. Paris - Ecole Rabbinique 31, f. 145b-146b, M, no incipit, short.
11429. Paris - Ecole Rabbinique 32, f. 214b-215b, M, no incipit.
11430. Strasbourg - Bibliotheque Nationale et Universitaire 4081, f. 189a-189b, M, no incipit.

Sepharad
11431. Skokie - Hebrew Theological College 3, f. 83b-84a, M.

Yemen
11432. Jerusalem - Benayahu ת 414, f. 141a, M.
11433. Jerusalem - Musad haRav Kook 334, f. 144a-144b, M.
11434. Jerusalem - Sassoon 264, f. 152b, M.
11435. Jerusalem - Sassoon 902, p. 399, M.
11436. New York - Jewish Theological Seminary Ms. 3028, f. 15b, M, very short, Arabic.
11437. New York - Jewish Theological Seminary Ms. 3052, f. 8b-9b, M, rubric: אל מלך.
11438. Ramat Gan - Universitat Bar Ilan 62, f. 41b, G, margins damaged.

Yemen, commentary by Isaac b. Abraham Wanneh
11439. Chicago-Spertus College of Judaica D 2, 2, f. 193a-193b, M.
11440. Jerusalem - Benayahu ת 261, f. 128a-128b, M, rubric: אל מלך.
11441. Jerusalem - Benayahu ת 282, f. 113a-113b, M, no incipit.
11442. Jerusalem - Makhon Ben Zvi 1156 (Tubi 155), f. 110b-111a, M, rubric: אל מלך.
11443. Jerusalem - Makhon Ben Zvi 1174 (Tubi 154), f. 116b-117a, M.
11444. Jerusalem - Michael Krupp 604, f. 140a-140b, M, rubric: אל מלך.
11445. Jerusalem - Musad haRav Kook 325, f. 169a-169b, M, rubric: אל מלך.
11446. Jerusalem - Musad haRav Kook 330, f. 100b, G.
11447. Jerusalem - Sassoon 1158, p. 187-188, M, rubric: סים' יהודה. אל מלך.
11448. Jerusalem - Sassoon 1174, p. 214-215, M, rubric: אל מלך.
11449. Jerusalem - Yehiel haLevi 4, f. 142a, G.
11450. London - British Library Or. 11122, f. 169a-169b, M, rubric: אל מלך.
11451. London - British Library Or. 11122, f. 171a-171b, M, rubric: אל מלך.
11452. Manchester - John Rylands University Library, Ms. Gaster 5, f. 189b-190a, M.

11453. New York - Jewish Theological Seminary Ms. 3013, f. 115b, M, rubric: אל מלך.
11454. New York - Jewish Theological Seminary Ms. 3109, f. 87a-87b, M, rubric: אל מלך.
11455. New York - Public Library, Heb. Ms. 9, f. 107b, M, rubric: אל מלך.
11456. Strasbourg - Bibliotheque Nationale et Universitaire 3965 (Landauer 39), p. 353, M, rubric: אל מלך.

ידי צרי ניחתה בי, סליחה

Yemen, commentary by Isaac b. Abraham Wanneh
11457. Chicago-Spertus College of Judaica D 2, 2, f. 215b, M, no incipit.
11458. Jerusalem - Sassoon 1158, p. 367-368, M, no incipit.
11459. London - British Library Or. 11122, f. 183b-184a, M, rubric: אל מלך.

ידיד עליון שמע הגיון (י 425), יהודה, אהבה לפרשת עקב

Ashkenaz
11460. Jerusalem - Schocken Institute 24100 / Mahzor Nuremberg, f. 222b-223a, M.
11461. Muenchen - Bayerische Staatsbibliothek, Cod. hebr. 69, f. 63a-64a, M.

Ashkenaz, commentary by Abraham b. Azriel[264]
11462. Frankfurt a M - Stadt- und Universitaetsbibliothek Fol. 16 (Merzbacher 95), f. 25a-26b, C, rubric: לפרשת והיה עקב.
11463. Vatican - Biblioteca Apostolica ebr. 301,1, f. 55a-63b, C, rubric: לפרשה והיה עקב.

Yemen, commentary by Isaac b. Abraham Wanneh
11464. Chicago-Spertus College of Judaica D 2, 2, f. 191b-192a, M, no incipit.
11465. Jerusalem - Sassoon 1158, p. 341-342, M, rubric: אל מלך.
11466. Jerusalem - Yehiel haLevi 4, f. 153b, G.
11467. New York - Jewish Theological Seminary Ms. 3013, f. 125a, M, rubric: אל מלך.
11468. New York - Jewish Theological Seminary Ms. 3109, f. 124a-125a, C, rubric: וזה פירוש ידי עליון שמע הגיון.

ידידי השכחת חנותך בבין שדי (י 499), יהודה הלוי, רשות לנשמת

Carpentras, commentary by Mordekhai b. Josef of Rocco Martino
11469. Cincinnati - Hebrew Union College 246, f. 15a-15b, C, rubric: פי' ידידי השבחת וכו'.

---

[264] Edited by Urbach, ערוגת הבושם, vol. II, p. 36-89.

ידידי ום וקטלמוס קח בידך, שלם שבזי

Yemen
11470. Cincinnati - Hebrew Union College 398, f. 198b-199a, M.

ידידיך מאמש חין ותפלה סדרו (י 571), יהודה הלוי, סליחה לנעילה

Sepharad, commentary by David b. Josef Abudarham[265]

11471. Budapest - Magyar tudomanyos akademia, MS. Kaufmann A 405/2, p. 259, C, rubric: פזמון.
11472. New York - Columbia X893 Ab 93, f. 33a, C, rubric: פזמון.

Yemen
11473. Jerusalem - Benayahu ת 301, f. 56a, G.
11474. Jerusalem - Sassoon 902, p. 409, M, short.
11475. New York - Jewish Theological Seminary Ms. 3028, f. 30a, G.
11476. New York - Jewish Theological Seminary Ms. 3052, f. 55a-56a, M, rubric: אל מלך.
11477. Ramat Gan - Universitat Bar Ilan 62, f. 47b, G.

Yemen, commentary by Isaac b. Abraham Wanneh
11478. Chicago-Spertus College of Judaica D 2, 2, f. 229b-230a, M, no incipit.
11479. Jerusalem - Benayahu ת 261, f. 158a-158b, M, rubric: לתפלת נעילה.
11480. Jerusalem - Benayahu ת 282, f. 130a, M, rubric: אל מלך.
11481. Jerusalem - Makhon Ben Zvi 1156 (Tubi 155), f. 129a, M, rubric: אל מלך.
11482. Jerusalem - Makhon Ben Zvi 1174 (Tubi 154), f. 128b-129a, M.
11483. Jerusalem - Michael Krupp 604, f. 85a, M.
11484. Jerusalem - Musad haRav Kook 325, f. 186a, M.
11485. Jerusalem - Sassoon 1158, p. 201, M, rubric: סים' יהודה, very short.
11486. Jerusalem - Sassoon 1174, p. 249-250, M, rubric: לתפלת נעילה.
11487. Jerusalem - Yehiel haLevi 4, f. 169b, G.
11488. London - British Library Or. 11122, f. 206a, M, rubric: ענין נעילה.
11489. Manchester - John Rylands University Library, Ms. Gaster 5, f. 210a, M, rubric: פירוש.
11490. Muenchen - Bayerische Staatsbibliothek, Cod. hebr. 472, f. 178b-179a, M, rubric: אל מלך. לתפלת נעילה.
11491. New York - Jewish Theological Seminary Ms. 3013, f. 126a, M, rubric: אל מלך.
11492. New York - Jewish Theological Seminary Ms. 3294, f. 13a, C.
11493. New York - Public Library, Heb. Ms. 9, f. 121a, M.
11494. Strasbourg - Bibliotheque Nationale et Universitaire 3965 (Landauer 39), p. 388-389, M, rubric: אל מלך.

---

[265] Edited by Prins, תשלום אבודרהם, p. 140-141.

ידידים כיצאו בכושרות (י 583), יוסף ב"ר שמואל טוב עלם, חלק ה', קדושתא לפסח
Tsarfat
11495. Parma - Biblioteca Palatina Cod. Parm. 3136 (de Rossi 405), f. 110a-110b, M.

ידידים לבית אל חשו (י 585), משה אבן עזרא, סליחה
Carpentras, commentary by Josef b. Abraham of Montelitz
11496. Cincinnati - Hebrew Union College 291, f. 13a-13b, C, rubric: פי' סליחה לשבת ידידים לבית אל.
11497. New York - Jewish Theological Seminary Ms. 4197, f. 73b-74a, M.
11498. Paris - Ecole Rabbinique 32, f. 95b-96a, M.
11499. Paris - Ecole Rabbinique 32, f. 116a-116b, M.
11500. Strasbourg - Bibliotheque Nationale et Universitaire 4081, f. 92b-93a, M.

ידיכם קדש תשאו צבאים להלל כבראו (י 606), יצחק, סליחה
Yemen
11501. Jerusalem - Sassoon 902, p. 416, M.
11502. Ramat Gan - Universitat Bar Ilan 62, f. 47a, G, margins damaged.
Yemen, commentary by Isaac b. Abraham Wanneh
11503. Chicago-Spertus College of Judaica D 2, 2, f. 199a-199b, M, no incipit.
11504. Jerusalem - Michael Krupp 604, f. 150b, M, page damaged at beginning of commentary.
11505. Jerusalem - Sassoon 1158, p. 373, M, no incipit.
11506. London - British Library Or. 11122, f. 186b, M, no incipit.

ידך נשאת לעם שמך (י 624), יצחק בן זרחיה גירונדי, חלק ג', קדושתא לשבת שקלים
Carpentras, commentary by Mordekhai b. Josef of Rocco Martino
11507. Cincinnati - Hebrew Union College 246, f. 8b-9a, C, rubric: פי' מחיה ידך נשאת וכו'.
Sepharad, commentary by Josef Garad
11508. Oxford - Bodleian Library Heb.e.10 (Neubauer 2746/1), f. 3a-3b, C.

ידך תחיש לשא (י 628), יצחק גיאת, פזמון לשבת שקלים
Carpentras, commentary by Mordekhai b. Josef of Rocco Martino
11509. Cincinnati - Hebrew Union College 246, f. 13a-14a, C, rubric: פי' ידך תחיש וכו'.
Sepharad, commentary by Josef Garad
11510. Oxford - Bodleian Library Heb.e.10 (Neubauer 2746/1), f. 5b, C, rubric: פזמון.
11511. Oxford - Bodleian Library Heb.e.10 (Neubauer 2746/1), f. 17b, C, rubric: ידך תחיש, no incipit.

Tsarfat

11512. London - David Sofer 5, f. 11b, C.

11513. London - David Sofer 5, f. 12a, C.

ידענו אלהים עונותינו (י 650), משה אבן עזרא, פזמון

Sepharad, commentary by David b. Josef Abudarham[266]

11514. Budapest - Magyar tudomanyos akademia, MS. Kaufmann A 405/2, p. 248, C, rubric: פזמון, short.

11515. New York - Columbia X893 Ab 93, f. 28b-29a, C, rubric: פזמון, short.

ידעתיך ידידות כל סגולה (י 664), יצחק גיאת, רשות לנשמת

Ashkenaz

11516. Oxford - Bodleian Library MS Can. Or. 70 (Neubauer 1147,7), f. 82a-82b, M, rubric: אחרת.

יה אור מסות אור בראו (י 690), יצחק בן זרחיה גירונדי, חלק ב', קדושתא לשבת ההדש

Carpentras, commentary by Mordekhai b. Josef of Rocco Martino

11517. Cincinnati - Hebrew Union College 246/1, f. 39b-41a, C, rubric: פזמון יה אור מסות אור בראו.

Sepharad, commentary by Josef Garad

11518. Oxford - Bodleian Library Heb.e.10 (Neubauer 2746/1), f. 13b-14a, C, rubric: פזמון.

יה איום זכור היום ברית שבעת (י 696), סליחה

Ashkenaz

11519. Moscow - Russian State Library, Ms. Guenzburg 190, f. 106b-107a, G.

Carpentras

11520. Cincinnati - Hebrew Union College 392, f. 32a-32b, M.

Carpentras, commentary by Josef b. Abraham of Montelitz

11521. Cincinnati - Hebrew Union College 291, f. 14a-15a, C, rubric: פי' סליחה יה איום וכו'.

11522. New York - Jewish Theological Seminary Ms. 4197, f. 80a-81a, M.

11523. Paris - Ecole Rabbinique 32, f. 102b-103b, M.

11524. Strasbourg - Bibliotheque Nationale et Universitaire 4081, f. 79b-80b, M.

haAri, commentary by Mose b. Hayyim Pesante

11525. New York - Jewish Theological Seminary Ms. 4696, f. 21b, C, rubric: הקפה ראשונה.

---

[266] Edited by Prins, תשלום אבודרהם, p. 156.

Italia, commentary by Zakharya David Shabbetai Segre
11526. Torino - Archivio Terracini 1499, p. 151, C, rubric: פירוש יה הטוב יה איום.
North Africa, commentary by Simon b. Tsemaḥ Duran?
11527. New York - Jewish Theological Seminary Ms. 4121, f. 48b, C, rubric: הושענא רבא. הקפה ראשונה יה איום וכו׳, incipit שבעת.
North Africa, commentary by Yehuda Toledano
11528. New York - Jewish Theological Seminary Ms. 4300, f. 40a-42b, C, rubric: הקפה ראשונה אברהם.
Sepharad, commentary by David b. Josef Abudarham[267]
11529. Budapest - Magyar tudomanyos akademia, MS. Kaufmann A 405/2, p. 207, C, rubric: פזמון.
11530. Cincinnati - Hebrew Union College 490, f. 14a-14b, C.
11531. New York - Columbia X893 Ab 93, f. 13a, C, rubric: פז.
Tsarfat
11532. London - David Sofer 5, f. 163a-163b, C, rubric: פזמון.
11533. Parma - Biblioteca Palatina Cod. Parm. 3006 (de Rossi 654,1), f. 202a, M.
11534. Vatican - Biblioteca Apostolica ebr. 306, f. 205b-206a, C.
Yemen
11535. New York - Jewish Theological Seminary Ms. 8767, p. 182, M, short.
Yemen, commentary by Isaac b. Abraham Wanneh
11536. Chicago-Spertus College of Judaica D 2, 2, f. 200a-200b, M.
11537. Jerusalem - Michael Krupp 604, f. 164a, M, rubric: אל מלך.
11538. Jerusalem - Michael Krupp 1990, f. 97a, M, end missing.
11539. Jerusalem - Sassoon 1158, p. 357, M, no incipit.
11540. Jerusalem - Yehiel haLevi 4, f. 155a, G.
11541. London - British Library Or. 11122, f. 177a-177b, M.
11542. Nahariya - Menahem and Saida Yaakob 284, f. 4b, M, incipit ברית.
11543. New York - Jewish Theological Seminary Ms. 3028, f. 251b, C, rubric: בהקפה ראשונה, end missing?.
11544. New York - Jewish Theological Seminary Ms. 3108, f. 84a, C, rubric: בהקפה ראשונה.
11545. New York - Jewish Theological Seminary Ms. 4195, f. 5a-6a, M, incipit שבעת.
11546. New York - Jewish Theological Seminary Ms. 3295, f. 87b, M, rubric: חדושין.
11547. Philadelphia - University of Pennsylvania HB 2, f. 100a, M.
11548. Ramat Gan - Universitat Bar Ilan 703, f. 191b, M, rubric: חידושין.
Yemen, commentary by Samḥun b. Salomo Ḥaloah
11549. Jerusalem - Makhon ben Zvi 2808, f. 171a-172a, C.

---

[267] Edited by Prins, תשלום אבודרהם, p. 26-27.

Yemen, commentary by Simon b. Tsemaḥ Duran

11550. Jerusalem - Michael Krupp 1758, f. 13b, M, rubric: פירוש, incipit שבעת.

יה אנא אמצאך מקומך נעלה ונעלם (י 770), יהודה הלוי, אופן, בתימן: סליחה

Tsarfat

11551. London - British Library Or. 2735 (Margoliouth 663), f. 184a-184b, M, margins cut.

Yemen

11552. Jerusalem - Sassoon 902, p. 308, M.

Yemen, commentary by Isaac b. Abraham Wanneh

11553. Chicago-Spertus College of Judaica D 2, 2, f. 187b, M, rubric: אל מלך, short.

11554. Jerusalem - Benayahu ת 261, f. 126b-127a, M, rubric: אל מלך.

11555. Jerusalem - Makhon Ben Zvi 1156 (Tubi 155), f. 109b, M, rubric: אל מלך, short.

11556. Jerusalem - Michael Krupp 604, f. 138b, M, rubric: אל מלך, very short.

11557. Jerusalem - Musad haRav Kook 325, f. 168b, M, rubric: אל מלך.

11558. Jerusalem - Sassoon 1158, p. 338, M, no incipit.

11559. London - British Library Or. 11122, f. 167b, M, short.

11560. Manchester - John Rylands University Library, Ms. Gaster 5, f. 189a, M.

11561. Muenchen - Bayerische Staatsbibliothek, Cod. hebr. 472, f. 148b, M, rubric: אל מלך, very short.

11562. Muenchen - Bayerische Staatsbibliothek, Cod. hebr. 472, f. 150b-151a, M, rubric: אל מלך.

11563. New York - Jewish Theological Seminary Ms. 3013, f. 115a, M, rubric: אל מלך, short.

11564. New York - Jewish Theological Seminary Ms. 3109, f. 86b, M, rubric: פירו'.

11565. New York - Jewish Theological Seminary Ms. 3294, f. 8b, C.

11566. New York - Public Library, Heb. Ms. 9, f. 105b, M.

11567. Philadelphia - University of Pennsylvania HB 2, f. 127b-128a, M, rubric: אל מלך, very short.

11568. Strasbourg - Bibliotheque Nationale et Universitaire 3965 (Landauer 39), p. 351, M, rubric: אל מלך, very short.

יה אשר אשפוך לפניו כשי שיחי (י 779), משה אבן עזרא, פזמון

Sepharad, commentary by David b. Josef Abudarham[268]

11569. Budapest - Magyar tudomanyos akademia, MS. Kaufmann A 405/2, p. 253, C.

יה ברדתו מגבוהים, יוסף ב"ר שמואל טוב עלם, חלק ב', קדושתא לשבועות

Tsarfat

11570. London - David Sofer 5, f. 68b, C.

11571. Parma - Biblioteca Palatina Cod. Parm. 3136 (de Rossi 405), f. 170a-170b, M.

יה ברדתי מגבוהים אדר ענים בהים (י 804), יוסף ב"ר שמואל טוב עלם, חלק ה', קדושתא לשבועות

Tsarfat

11572. Moscow - Russian State Library, Ms. Guenzburg 1665, f. 142b-143a, M, no incipit.

יה בשר שר צבאיך אתה שלום וביתך (י 806), יהושפט הגר, לחתן

Tsarfat

11573. London - British Library Or. 2735 (Margoliouth 663), f. 178b-179a, M, margins cut.

יה הטוב ומקור החיים מזהיר אור מנוגה נגדו (י 836), משה זכות, להושענא רבה

Italia, commentary by Zakharya David Shabbetai Segre

11574. Torino - Archivio Terracini 1499, p. 149, C, rubric: פירוש יה הטוב.

יה כגיבור על הים נראה, יצחק הנקדן

Ashkenaz

11575. Oxford - Bodleian Library MS Can. Or. 70 (Neubauer 1147,7), f. 100b-102a, M, rubric: אחרת.

יה להלל ביום וליל גדולתך עזריני (י 927), יצחק גיאת, סליחה

Yemen

11576. Jerusalem - Benayahu ת 301, f. 54a, G.

11577. Jerusalem - Sassoon 902, p. 429, M.

11578. New York - Jewish Theological Seminary Ms. 3028, f. 46a, G.

Yemen, commentary by Isaac b. Abraham Wanneh

11579. Chicago-Spertus College of Judaica D 2, 2, f. 197b, M, no incipit.

11580. Jerusalem - Sassoon 1158, p. 372, M, no incipit.

---

[268] Edited by Prins, תשלום אבודרהם, p. 127-128.

11581. London - British Library Or. 11122, f. 186a, M, rubric: אל מלך.

יה למתי צפנת חזיון (י 948), יהודה הלוי, סליחה

Ashkenaz
11582. Cambridge - University Library Add. 394,1 (Reif SCR 461), f. 96b-97a, C.

Roma
11583. Berlin - Staatsbibliothek (Preussischer Kulturbesitz) Or. Oct. 3567, f. 1a, FC.

Sepharad, commentary by David b. Josef Abudarham[269]
11584. Budapest - Magyar tudomanyos akademia, MS. Kaufmann A 405/2, p. 245, C, rubric: פזמון.
11585. New York - Columbia X893 Ab 93, f. 27b-28a, C, rubric: פזמון.
11586. New York - Jewish Theological Seminary Ms. 3011, f. 21b, C, rubric: פזמון, the manuscript breaks off after a few lines.

Tsarfat
11587. Vatican - Biblioteca Apostolica ebr. 306, f. 208b-209a, C.

Yemen
11588. Jerusalem - Benayahu ת 414, f. 139b, M.
11589. Jerusalem - Sassoon 902, p. 398, M.
11590. New York - Jewish Theological Seminary Ms. 3052, f. 5a-6b, M, rubric: אל מלך.
11591. Ramat Gan - Universitat Bar Ilan 62, f. 41a, G, margins damaged.

Yemen, commentary by Isaac b. Abraham Wanneh
11592. Chicago-Spertus College of Judaica D 2, 2, f. 189b, M.
11593. Jerusalem - Benayahu ת 261, f. 126b, M, rubric: אל מלך.
11594. Jerusalem - Benayahu ת 282, f. 111b-112a, M.
11595. Jerusalem - Makhon Ben Zvi 1156 (Tubi 155), f. 109a-109b, M, rubric: אל מלך.
11596. Jerusalem - Makhon Ben Zvi 1174 (Tubi 154), f. 114b, M, rubric: אל מלך.
11597. Jerusalem - Michael Krupp 604, f. 138b, M, rubric: אל מלך.
11598. Jerusalem - Musad haRav Kook 325, f. 166b, M, rubric: אל מלך.
11599. Jerusalem - Sassoon 1158, p. 340-341, M, rubric: אל מלך.
11600. Jerusalem - Sassoon 1174, p. 211, M.
11601. Jerusalem - Yehiel haLevi 4, f. 147a, G.
11602. London - British Library Or. 11122, f. 169a, M.
11603. Manchester - John Rylands University Library, Ms. Gaster 5, f. 187b, M.
11604. Muenchen - Bayerische Staatsbibliothek, Cod. hebr. 472, f. 148a-148b, M, rubric: אל מלך.

---

[269] Edited by Prins, תשלום אבודרהם, p. 142-143.

11605. New York - Jewish Theological Seminary Ms. 3013, f. 113b, M, rubric: אל מלך, incipit למתי.
11606. New York - Jewish Theological Seminary Ms. 3109, f. 86a, M, rubric: אל מלך.
11607. New York - Jewish Theological Seminary Ms. 3294, f. 7b, C.
11608. New York - Public Library, Heb. Ms. 9, f. 105b, M.
11609. Philadelphia - University of Pennsylvania HB 2, f. 126b-127a, M, rubric: אל מלך, incipit למתי.
11610. Strasbourg - Bibliotheque Nationale et Universitaire 3965 (Landauer 39), p. 347, M, rubric: אל מלך.

יה לשועת מתענה מיחל כפוריך (י 955), יצחק בן זרחיה גירונדי, סליחה

Carpentras

11611. Cincinnati - Hebrew Union College 392, f. 11b, M.

Carpentras, commentary by Josef b. Abraham of Montelitz

11612. Cincinnati - Hebrew Union College 291, f. 6b-7a, C, rubric: פי' סליחה יה לשועת וכו'.
11613. New York - Jewish Theological Seminary Ms. 4197, f. 25a, M.
11614. Paris - Ecole Rabbinique 32, f. 28b-29a, M.
11615. Strasbourg - Bibliotheque Nationale et Universitaire 4081, f. 26b-27a, M.

יה מלאך שמך בקרבו (י 971), יהודה הלוי, סליחה

Yemen

11616. Jerusalem - Bcnayahu ת 301, f. 44a, M.
11617. Jerusalem - Benayahu ת 414, f. 137b, M, very short.
11618. Jerusalem - Sassoon 902, p. 399-400, M.
11619. New York - Jewish Theological Seminary Ms. 3028, f. 20a, G, Arabic.
11620. New York - Jewish Theological Seminary Ms. 3052, f. 7a-7b, M, rubric: אל מלך.
11621. Ramat Gan - Universitat Bar Ilan 62, f. 41b, G, margins damaged.

Yemen, commentary by Isaac b. Abraham Wanneh

11622. Chicago-Spertus College of Judaica D 2, 2, f. 192b, M.
11623. Jerusalem - Benayahu ת 261, f. 127a, M, rubric: אל מלך.
11624. Jerusalem - Benayahu ת 282, f. 112a-112b, M, page torn.
11625. Jerusalem - Makhon Ben Zvi 1156 (Tubi 155), f. 110a, M, rubric: אל מלך.
11626. Jerusalem - Makhon Ben Zvi 1174 (Tubi 154), f. 116a-116b, M.
11627. Jerusalem - Michael Krupp 604, f. 139a-139b, M, rubric: אל מלך.
11628. Jerusalem - Musad haRav Kook 325, f. 168b-169a, M, rubric: אל מלך.
11629. Jerusalem - Musad haRav Kook 330, f. 100b, G.
11630. Jerusalem - Sassoon 1158, p. 345, M, no incipit.

11631. Jerusalem - Sassoon 1174, p. 212, M.
11632. Jerusalem - Yehiel haLevi 4, f. 151a, G.
11633. London - British Library Or. 11122, f. 171a, M.
11634. Manchester - John Rylands University Library, Ms. Gaster 5, f. 189a-189b, M.
11635. Muenchen - Bayerische Staatsbibliothek, Cod. hebr. 472, f. 149b-150a, M, rubric: אל מלך.
11636. New York - Jewish Theological Seminary Ms. 3013, f. 115a, M, rubric: אל מלך.
11637. New York - Jewish Theological Seminary Ms. 3294, f. 8b-9a, C.
11638. New York - Public Library, Heb. Ms. 9, f. 107a, M.
11639. Philadelphia - University of Pennsylvania HB 2, f. 128a, M, rubric: אל מלך.
11640. Strasbourg - Bibliotheque Nationale et Universitaire 3965 (Landauer 39), p. 352, M, rubric: אל מלך.

יה מפתיין אלעלם ואלדין, שלם שבזי

Yemen

11641. New York - M. Lehmann 274, f. 64a-65b, M, kabbalistic.

יה מתי תשבור קרן מצעירה (י 1005), ישוע בן יעקב, סליחה

Yemen

11642. New York - Jewish Theological Seminary Ms. 3028, f. 77a-77b, G.
11643. New York - Jewish Theological Seminary Ms. 3052, f. 86b-87b, M.

Yemen, commentary by Isaac b. Abraham Wanneh

11644. Chicago-Spertus College of Judaica D 2, 2, f. 239a, M, no incipit.
11645. Jerusalem - Makhon Ben Zvi 1156 (Tubi 155), f. 139b-140a, M, no incipit.
11646. Jerusalem - Makhon Ben Zvi 1174 (Tubi 154), f. 139a, M.
11647. Jerusalem - Michael Krupp 604, f. 177a, M.
11648. Jerusalem - Sassoon 1158, p. 418, M, no incipit.
11649. Jerusalem - Sassoon 1174, p. 271-272, M, no incipit.
11650. London - British Library Or. 11122, f. 216a-216b, M, no incipit.
11651. Manchester - John Rylands University Library, Ms. Gaster 5, f. 225a, M.
11652. Muenchen - Bayerische Staatsbibliothek, Cod. hebr. 472, f. 195b-196a, M.
11653. New York - Jewish Theological Seminary Ms. 3013, f. 134b-135a, M.
11654. New York - Jewish Theological Seminary Ms. 3294, f. 18a-18b, C.
11655. New York - Public Library, Heb. Ms. 9, f. 131b-132a, M, no incipit.
11656. Strasbourg - Bibliotheque Nationale et Universitaire 3965 (Landauer 39), p. 415, M.

יה צור מחסי עז מגדל (י 1061), יצחק הנקדן, לקדיש

Ashkenaz
11657. Oxford - Bodleian Library MS Can. Or. 70 (Neubauer 1147,7), f. 98a-98b, M, rubric: אחרת.

יה שמך ארוממך (י 1143), יהודה הלוי, רשות לקדיש, בתימן: סליחה

Carpentras
11658. Cincinnati - Hebrew Union College 429/1, f. 4a-5a, M, no incipit.
Carpentras, commentary by Eliyahu Carmi
11659. New York - Jewish Theological Seminary Ms. 3151, f. 35a-35b, M, no incipit.
Carpentras, commentary by Josef b. Abraham of Montelitz
11660. Cincinnati - Hebrew Union College 357, f. 41a-42a, M, rubric: פירוש, no incipit.
11661. New York - Jewish Theological Seminary Ms. 4746, f. 7a-8a, M, no incipit.
11662. Paris - Alliance Israelite Universelle H 422 A, f. 14a-15a, M, no incipit.
11663. Paris - Ecole Rabbinique 31, f. 85b-86b, M, no incipit.
Italia, commentary by Zakharya David Shabbetai Segre
11664. Torino - Archivio Terracini 1499, p. 16-18, C, rubric: פירוש יה שמך.
Sepharad
11665. Skokie - Hebrew Theological College 3, f. 84a-85a, M.
Yemen
11666. New York - Jewish Theological Seminary Ms. 3109, f. 87b, M.
Yemen, commentary by Isaac b. Abraham Wanneh
11667. Chicago-Spertus College of Judaica D 2, 2, f. 190a-190b, M, no incipit.
11668. Jerusalem - Makhon Ben Zvi 1156 (Tubi 155), f. 109b, M, rubric: אל מלך.
11669. Jerusalem - Makhon Ben Zvi 1174 (Tubi 154), f. 124a-124b, M.
11670. Jerusalem - Michael Krupp 604, f. 138b-139a, M, rubric: אל מלך.
11671. Jerusalem - Musad haRav Kook 325, f. 180b-181a, M, rubric: אל מלך.
11672. Jerusalem - Sassoon 1158, p. 343, M, no incipit.
11673. Jerusalem - Sassoon 1174, p. 211-212, M.
11674. London - British Library Or. 11122, f. 170a, M.
11675. Manchester - John Rylands University Library, Ms. Gaster 5, f. 196a, M.
11676. Muenchen - Bayerische Staatsbibliothek, Cod. hebr. 472, f. 148b-149a, M, rubric: אל מלך, incipit מסך.
11677. New York - Jewish Theological Seminary Ms. 3013, f. 121a, M, rubric: אל מלך.

11678. New York - Jewish Theological Seminary Ms. 3109, f. 88a-88b, M, rubric: אל מלך.
11679. New York - Jewish Theological Seminary Ms. 3294, f. 9a-9b, C.
11680. New York - Public Library, Heb. Ms. 9, f. 106a, M.
11681. Philadelphia - University of Pennsylvania HB 2, f. 132b, M.
11682. Strasbourg - Bibliotheque Nationale et Universitaire 3965 (Landauer 39), p. 375-376, M, rubric: אל מלך.

יה שעה שופכי שיחה (י 1154), משה אבן עזרא, חלק ה', קדושתא למנחה יום כפור
Carpentras
11683. Cincinnati - Hebrew Union College 392, f. 102b-103b, M, no incipit.
Carpentras, commentary by Josef b. Abraham of Montelitz
11684. Cincinnati - Hebrew Union College 291, f. 53b-56b, C, rubric: פי' ובכן אזכור וכו'.
11685. New York - Jewish Theological Seminary Ms. 4197, f. 238b-240a, M, no incipit.
11686. Paris - Ecole Rabbinique 32, f. 245b-247a, M, no incipit.
11687. Strasbourg - Bibliotheque Nationale et Universitaire 4081, f. 218a-219b, M, no incipit.
Sepharad, commentary by David b. Josef Abudarham[270]
11688. Budapest - Magyar tudomanyos akademia, MS. Kaufmann A 405/2, p. 256, C, rubric: ובכן אזכור צדקת שלשה שופכי שיחה ונעתור להם במנחה לר' משה ן' עזרא ז"ל.
11689. Holon - Yehuda Nahum 278, f. 16a, FC, incomplete.

יהודה וישראל דעו מר לי (י 1192), יהודה בר דוד אבן יחייא, קינה
Carpentras, commentary by Mordekhai b. Josef of Rocco Martino
11690. Cincinnati - Hebrew Union College 246/1, f. 77a-78a, C, rubric: פי' קינה יאודה וישראל.
Yemen, commentary by Isaac b. Abraham Wanneh
11691. Jerusalem - Sassoon 1158, p. 170, M.

יהודים קמו בכל דור, סליחה
Yemen, commentary by Isaac b. Abraham Wanneh
11692. Jerusalem - Sassoon 1158, p. 238-239, M.

יהיו נא אמרי פי לפניך ערבים (י 1466), סליחה
Carpentras, commentary by Josef b. Abraham of Montelitz
11693. Strasbourg - Bibliotheque Nationale et Universitaire 4081, f. 235b, M.

---

[270] Edited by Prins, תשלום אבודרהם, p. 131-133.

HEBREW LITURGICAL POETRY

יודעי דעת אלהיכם (י 1565), יצחק בן זרחיה גירונדי, חלק ד', קדושתא לשבת החדש
Carpentras, commentary by Mordekhai b. Josef of Rocco Martino
11694. Cincinnati - Hebrew Union College 246/1, f. 42b-43a, C, rubric: 'פי פזמון יודעי דעת אלקיכם.
Sepharad, commentary by Josef Garad
11695. Oxford - Bodleian Library Heb.e.10 (Neubauer 2746/1), f. 14b, C, rubric: פזמון.
11696. Oxford - Bodleian Library Heb.e.10 (Neubauer 2746/1), f. 21b, C, rubric: יודעי דעת, no incipit, very short.

יודעי הפיצוני ימי עוני (י 1567), יהודה הלוי, אהבה, בתימן: סליחה
Yemen
11697. Jerusalem - Sassoon 902, p. 404, M.
11698. New York - Jewish Theological Seminary Ms. 3052, f. 25b-26a, M, rubric: אל מלך.
Yemen, commentary by Isaac b. Abraham Wanneh
11699. Chicago-Spertus College of Judaica D 2, 2, f. 205b, M, no incipit.
11700. Jerusalem - Benayahu ת 261, f. 136b-137a, M, rubric: אל מלך.
11701. Jerusalem - Makhon Ben Zvi 1174 (Tubi 154), f. 121b-122a, M.
11702. Jerusalem - Michael Krupp 604, f. 150a-150b, M, rubric: אל מלך.
11703. Jerusalem - Musad haRav Kook 325, f. 177a, M, rubric: אל מלך.
11704. Jerusalem - Musad haRav Kook 330, f. 106b, G.
11705. Jerusalem - Musad haRav Kook 347, f. 86a, G.
11706. Jerusalem - Sassoon 1158, p. 351-352, M, no incipit.
11707. Jerusalem - Sassoon 1174, p. 229-230, M, no incipit.
11708. London - British Library Or. 11122, f. 174b-175a, M, rubric: אל מלך.
11709. Manchester - John Rylands University Library, Ms. Gaster 5, f. 194a-194b, M.
11710. Muenchen - Bayerische Staatsbibliothek, Cod. hebr. 472, f. 162a-162b, M, rubric: אל מלך.
11711. New York - Jewish Theological Seminary Ms. 3013, f. 118b-119a, M, rubric: אל מלך.
11712. Philadelphia - University of Pennsylvania HB 2, f. 131a, M.
11713. Strasbourg - Bibliotheque Nationale et Universitaire 3965 (Landauer 39), p. 368-369, M, rubric: אל מלך.

יודעי יגוני יספו באש לבי כידוד (י 1569), יהודה הלוי, זולת, בתימן: סליחה
Yemen
11714. New York - Jewish Theological Seminary Ms. 3052, f. 27b-28a, M, rubric: אל מלך.
Yemen, commentary by Isaac b. Abraham Wanneh
11715. Chicago-Spertus College of Judaica D 2, 2, f. 196b-197a, M, no incipit.

11716. Jerusalem - Benayahu ת 261, f. 137b-138a, M, rubric: אל מלך.
11717. Jerusalem - Benayahu ת 282, f. 121a-121b, M, rubric: אל מלך, no incipit.
11718. Jerusalem - Makhon Ben Zvi 1156 (Tubi 155), f. 118b-119a, M, rubric: אל מלך.
11719. Jerusalem - Makhon Ben Zvi 1156 (Tubi 155), f. 120a, M, rubric: אל מלך.
11720. Jerusalem - Makhon Ben Zvi 1174 (Tubi 154), f. 122b, M.
11721. Jerusalem - Michael Krupp 604, f. 151a-151b, M, rubric: אל מלך, no incipit.
11722. Jerusalem - Musad haRav Kook 325, f. 178a, M, rubric: אל מלך.
11723. Jerusalem - Musad haRav Kook 330, f. 115b, G.
11724. Jerusalem - Sassoon 1158, p. 347-348, M, rubric: אל מלך.
11725. Jerusalem - Sassoon 1174, p. 231, M, no incipit.
11726. London - British Library Or. 11122, f. 172b-173a, M, no incipit.
11727. Manchester - John Rylands University Library, Ms. Gaster 5, f. 195a, M.
11728. Muenchen - Bayerische Staatsbibliothek, Cod. hebr. 472, f. 163b-164a, M, rubric: אל מלך.
11729. New York - Jewish Theological Seminary Ms. 3013, f. 119b, M, rubric: אל מלך.
11730. Philadelphia - University of Pennsylvania HB 2, f. 131b, M.
11731. Strasbourg - Bibliotheque Nationale et Universitaire 3965 (Landauer 39), p. 371, M, rubric: אל מלך.

יום אויבי ענה בי, קינה
Yemen, commentary by Isaac b. Abraham Wanneh
11732. Jerusalem - Sassoon 1158, p. 172, M.

יום אכפי הכבדתי ויכפלו עוני (י 1605), יהודה הלוי, קינה
Yemen, commentary by Isaac b. Abraham Wanneh
11733. Jerusalem - Sassoon 1158, p. 173, M.
11734. London - British Library Or. 11122, f. 103b-104a, M.

יום אעטוף כשואל בינה הגיוני (י 1611), יהודה הלוי, סליחה
Sepharad, commentary by David b. Josef Abudarham[271]
11735. Budapest - Magyar tudomanyos akademia, MS. Kaufmann A 405/2, p. 251, C, rubric: פזמון, short.
11736. New York - Columbia X893 Ab 93, f. 30a, C, rubric: פזמון, short.

---
[271] Edited by Prins, תשלום אבודרהם, p. 157-158.

יום אשר אשמינו יוצלל (י 1624), יוחנן הכהן, סליחה

Ashkenaz
11737. Berlin - Staatsbibliothek (Preussischer Kulturbesitz) Or. Qu. 798-799 (Steinschneider 177), I, f. 111a-112a, M.
11738. Cambridge - University Library Or. 785, f. 153b-154b, G.

יום אשר הוחק לכפרתינו (י 1625), למנחה יום כפור

Ashkenaz
11739. Berlin - Staatsbibliothek (Preussischer Kulturbesitz) Or. Qu. 798-799 (Steinschneider 177), I, f. 177a-178a, M, ecclectic.

יום אתא לכפר פשעי ישנה (י 1628), אלעזר ברבי קליר?, למוסף יום כפור

Ashkenaz
11740. Berlin - Staatsbibliothek (Preussischer Kulturbesitz) Or. Qu. 798-799 (Steinschneider 177), I, f. 155b-156b, M, ecclectic.
11741. Cambridge - University Library Or. 785, f. 198b-199b, G.
11742. London - Montefiore Library 261, f. 63a, C, commentator: Eliezer b. Natan?, short.

יום באתם להלות פני אל רמים (י 1633), יצחק כנזי, סליחה

Carpentras, commentary by Mordekhai b. Josef of Rocco Martino
11743. Cincinnati - Hebrew Union College 246/1, f. 82b-83a, C, rubric: פי' סליחה יום באתם.
Yemen
11744. Jerusalem - Benayahu ת 301, f. 54b, G.
11745. Jerusalem - Sassoon 902, p. 440, M.
11746. New York - Jewish Theological Seminary Ms. 3028, f. 44a, G.
Yemen, commentary by Isaac b. Abraham Wanneh
11747. Chicago-Spertus College of Judaica D 2, 2, f. 197a-197b, M.
11748. Jerusalem - Sassoon 1158, p. 373, M, no incipit.
11749. Jerusalem - Yehiel haLevi 4, f. 168b, G.
11750. London - British Library Or. 11122, f. 186a, M, no incipit.

יום הודו וכבודו ונחת ידו (י 1665), יעקב ב"ר מאיר, מאורה לשבת שני של חנוכה

Ashkenaz
11751. Jerusalem - Schocken Institute 24100 / Mahzor Nuremberg, f. 358a-358b, M.
11752. Muenchen - Bayerische Staatsbibliothek, Cod. hebr. 69, f. 70b-71a, M.

Ashkenaz, commentary by Abraham b. Azriel[272]
11753. Frankfurt a M - Stadt- und Universitaetsbibliothek Fol. 16 (Merzbacher 95), f. 49b, C.

יום השבת כוכב דרוך (י 1692), יהודה
Yemen
11754. Cincinnati - Hebrew Union College 398, f. 112a-113b, M.

יום זה הואל והדרש לשואל (י 1720), יצחק גיאת, חלק ו', קדושתא למנחה יום כפור
Sepharad, commentary by David b. Josef Abudarham[273]
11755. Budapest - Magyar tudomanyos akademia, MS. Kaufmann A 405/2, p. 258, C, rubric: מסתג׳יב. ובכן ויהי בעלות המנחה, short.
11756. New York - Columbia X893 Ab 93, f. 32b, C, rubric: מסתג׳יב. ובכן ויהי מעלות המנחה.

יום זה הוריד לבן שריד (י 1721), יצחק בן ראובן אלברגוני, רשות לאזהרות
North Africa, commentary by Amram b. Elqayim
11757. Jerusalem - Musad haRav Kook 1129, f. 2b-4a, M, rubric: פזמון סי׳ יצחק.
11758. New York - Jewish Theological Seminary Ms. 3183, f. 3a-5a, M.

יום זה למרום שאו בלב (י 1729), בלעם, סליחה
Yemen, commentary by Isaac b. Abraham Wanneh
11759. Chicago-Spertus College of Judaica D 2, 2, f. 203a, M, no incipit.
11760. Jerusalem - Michael Krupp 604, f. 155a, M, rubric: אל מלך.
11761. London - British Library Or. 11122, f. 184b, M, rubric: אל מלך.

יום זה מאז הכנתו (י +1731), יהודה הלוי, חלק מן הפיוט איר משחר את פני רבו
Carpentras
11762. Cincinnati - Hebrew Union College 429/1, f. 5a-5b, M, no incipit.
Carpentras, commentary by Eliyahu Carmi
11763. New York - Jewish Theological Seminary Ms. 3151, f. 36b, M.
Carpentras, commentary by Josef b. Abraham of Montelitz
11764. Cincinnati - Hebrew Union College 357, f. 42b-43a, M.
11765. New York - Jewish Theological Seminary Ms. 4746, f. 8b, M.
11766. Paris - Alliance Israelite Universelle H 422 A, f. 16a, M.

יום יום ידרושון לך למעז, סליחה
Tsarfat
11767. London - David Sofer 5, f. 145b, C.

---

[272] Edited by Urbach, ערוגת הבושם, vol. III, p. 531-532.
[273] Edited by Prins, תשלום אבודרהם, p. 139-140.

11768. London - David Sofer 5, f. 160a-160b, C, rubric: פזמון.
11769. Parma - Biblioteca Palatina Cod. Parm. 2890 (de Rossi 856), f. 103b-104a, M.
11770. Parma - Biblioteca Palatina Cod. Parm. 3006 (de Rossi 654,1), f. 163b-164a, M.

יום יום יחידתי הוי הודרת (י 1779), יואב, סליחה

Yemen
11771. Jerusalem - Sassoon 902, p. 431, M.
Yemen, commentary by Isaac b. Abraham Wanneh
11772. Chicago-Spertus College of Judaica D 2, 2, f. 214b-215a, M, no incipit.
11773. Jerusalem - Sassoon 1158, p. 366-367, M, no incipit.
11774. London - British Library Or. 11122, f. 183b, M, no incipit.

יום יעלה נקראה לאלהים בנדבה (י 1797), יוסף, סליחה

Roma
11775. Jerusalem - Jewish National and University Library Ms Heb 8° 4153, f. 136a-136b, C, commentator: Daniel ben Salomo haRofe (compiler), rubric: בסליחות צום העשור בערבית, only from פתוך תאותך, short.
11776. Oxford - Bodleian Library MS Mich. 312,1 (Neubauer 2276,1), f. 5a, C, rubric: בסליחות יום כפור בערבית, only from פתוך תאותיך, short.

יום יצאה כלת עדנים (י 1800), זרחיה הלוי ב"ר יצחק גירונדי, לשבועות

Sepharad, commentary by Natan b. Isaac
11777. London - British Library Add. 19787 (Margoliouth 697), f. 114a-120a, C, rubric: פי' יום יצאתה שעשה ר' נתן בר יצחק ז"ל.

יום ישבתי להודות כחשי (י 1803), יעקב בר אברהם, סליחה

Yemen, commentary by Isaac b. Abraham Wanneh
11778. Jerusalem - Makhon Ben Zvi 1174 (Tubi 154), f. 138b, M, short.
11779. London - British Library Or. 11122, f. 216a, M, no incipit.
11780. New York - Jewish Theological Seminary Ms. 3294, f. 18a, C.
11781. New York - Public Library, Heb. Ms. 9, f. 131b, M, no incipit.

יום כפורים זה הוכן לברר ולקשטה (י 1806), יצחק, סליחה

Tsarfat
11782. London - David Sofer 5, f. 93b-94a, C.
11783. Parma - Biblioteca Palatina Cod. Parm. 1794 (de Rossi 1061), f. 13a-14a, M.
11784. Parma - Biblioteca Palatina Cod. Parm. 2890 (de Rossi 856), f. 52a-52b, M.

11785. Parma - Biblioteca Palatina Cod. Parm. 3006 (de Rossi 654,1), f. 200a, M.

11786. Vatican - Biblioteca Apostolica ebr. 306, f. 214a, C.

יום לבי סבותי חזות איה טובתי (י 1810), יצחק גיאת, סליחה

Yemen

11787. Jerusalem - Benayahu ת 301, f. 54a, G, no incipit.

11788. Jerusalem - Sassoon 902, p. 428, M, very short.

11789. New York - Jewish Theological Seminary Ms. 3028, f. 45a, G.

Yemen, commentary by Isaac b. Abraham Wanneh

11790. Chicago-Spertus College of Judaica D 2, 2, f. 213a-213b, M, no incipit.

11791. Jerusalem - Sassoon 1158, p. 365, M, rubric: יום לבי סים' גיאת.

11792. London - British Library Or. 11122, f. 182b, M, no incipit.

יום להטיב תקרא מי זה יכלה טובך (י 1812), יהודה הלוי, סליחה

Sepharad, commentary by David b. Josef Abudarham[274]

11793. Budapest - Magyar tudomanyos akademia, MS. Kaufmann A 405/2, p. 248, C, rubric: פזמון, short.

11794. New York - Columbia X893 Ab 93, f. 29a, C, rubric: פזמון, short.

Yemen

11795. Jerusalem - Sassoon 264, f. 151a, M.

11796. Jerusalem - Sassoon 902, p. 389, M.

11797. New York - Jewish Theological Seminary Ms. 3052, f. 9b, M, rubric: אל מלך.

11798. Ramat Gan - Universitat Bar Ilan 62, f. 42a, G, margins damaged.

Yemen, commentary by Isaac b. Abraham Wanneh

11799. Chicago-Spertus College of Judaica D 2, 2, f. 194a, M.

11800. Jerusalem - Benayahu ת 261, f. 128b, M, rubric: אל מלך.

11801. Jerusalem - Benayahu ת 282, f. 113b, M, rubric: אל מלך, no incipit.

11802. Jerusalem - Makhon Ben Zvi 1156 (Tubi 155), f. 111a, M, rubric: אל מלך.

11803. Jerusalem - Makhon Ben Zvi 1174 (Tubi 154), f. 113b, M, rubric: אל מלך.

11804. Jerusalem - Michael Krupp 604, f. 140b-141a, M, rubric: אל מלך.

11805. Jerusalem - Musad haRav Kook 325, f. 164b-165a, M.

11806. Jerusalem - Sassoon 1158, p. 345, M, no incipit.

11807. Jerusalem - Sassoon 1174, p. 215, M, no incipit.

11808. Jerusalem - Yehiel haLevi 4, f. 149a, G.

11809. London - British Library Or. 11122, f. 171b, M, rubric: אל מלך.

---

[274] Edited by Prins, תשלום אבודרהם, p. 117-118.

11810. Manchester - John Rylands University Library, Ms. Gaster 5, f. 186b, M.
11811. Muenchen - Bayerische Staatsbibliothek, Cod. hebr. 472, f. 151a-151b, M, rubric: אל מלך.
11812. New York - Jewish Theological Seminary Ms. 3013, f. 112b, M, rubric: אל מלך.
11813. New York - Jewish Theological Seminary Ms. 3294, f. 6b, C.
11814. New York - Public Library, Heb. Ms. 9, f. 107b-108a, M.
11815. Strasbourg - Bibliotheque Nationale et Universitaire 3965 (Landauer 39), p. 343-344, M, rubric: אל מלך.

יום ליבשה נהפכו מצולים (י 1814), יהודה הלוי, גאולה, בתימן: סליחה
Ashkenaz
11816. Hamburg - Staats- und Universitaetsbibliothek Cod. hebr. 62 (Steinschneider 154), f. 28a-28b, C, rubric: גאולה למילה.
11817. Jerusalem - Schocken Institute 24100 / Mahzor Nuremberg, f. 30a, M. Ashkenaz, commentary by Abraham b. Azriel[275]
11818. Vatican - Biblioteca Apostolica ebr. 301,1, f. 10b-11a, C.
Yemen, commentary by Isaac b. Abraham Wanneh
11819. Chicago-Spertus College of Judaica D 2, 2, f. 246b, M, no incipit.
11820. Jerusalem - Sassoon 1158, p. 425, M, no incipit.
11821. London - British Library Or. 11122, f. 220a, M, no incipit.

יום לריב תעמוד ולדין עמים (י 1831), לוי אלתבאן, פזמון, בתימן: סליחה
Yemen, commentary by Isaac b. Abraham Wanneh
11822. Chicago-Spertus College of Judaica D 2, 2, f. 214a, M, no incipit.
11823. Jerusalem - Sassoon 1158, p. 362, M, no incipit.
11824. London - British Library Or. 11122, f. 180b, M, no incipit.

יום מימים הוחס (י 1837), אלעזר ברבי קליר, חלק ב', קדושתא למוסף יום כפור
Ashkenaz
11825. Berlin - Staatsbibliothek (Preussischer Kulturbesitz) Or. Qu. 798-799 (Steinschneider 177), I, f. 116a-116b, M.
11826. Braunschweig - Landesmuseum fuer Geschichte und Volkstum R 2386, vol. II, f. 224b, M.
11827. Budapest - Magyar tudomanyos akademia, MS. Kaufmann A 400, p. 353, C.
11828. Cambridge - University Library Add. 394,1 (Reif SCR 461), f. 68b-69a, C.
11829. Cambridge - University Library Add. 394,2.3, f. 1b, C.

---

[275] Edited by Urbach, ערוגת הבושם, vol. I, p. 66-71.

11830. Fulda - Hessische Landesbibliothek A 3 II, f. 122a-122b, C, commentator: Josef.
11831. Hamburg - Staats- und Universitaetsbibliothek Cod. hebr. 17/2 (Steinschneider 152), f. 157b, C.
11832. Hamburg - Staats- und Universitaetsbibliothek Cod. hebr. 40c (Steinschneider 111), f. 211b, G.
11833. Hamburg - Staats- und Universitaetsbibliothek Cod. hebr. 132 (Steinschneider 155), f. 43b, C.
11834. Jerusalem - Jewish National and University Library Ms Heb 8° 3037, f. 174b-175b, M.
11835. Jerusalem - Schocken Institute 24100 / Mahzor Nuremberg, f. 409a, M.
11836. London - British Library Or. 11318/1, f. 99a-100a, C, no incipit.
11837. London - Montefiore Library 261, f. 54a-54b, C, commentator: Eliezer b. Natan?.
11838. Moscow - Russian State Library, Ms. Guenzburg 191, f. 114a-115a, M.
11839. Moscow - Russian State Library, Ms. Guenzburg 615, f. 102b-103a, C.
11840. Muenchen - Bayerische Staatsbibliothek, Cod. hebr. 21, f. 218a, M.
11841. Muenchen - Bayerische Staatsbibliothek, Cod. hebr. 346, f. 74a-75b, C, no incipit.
11842. New York - Jewish Theological Seminary Ms. 4466, f. 366a-366b, M.
11843. New York - Jewish Theological Seminary Ms. 8097, f. 77b-78a, C.
11844. New York - Jewish Theological Seminary Ms. 8169 (Acc. 0016), f. 89a-89b, M.
11845. Oxford - Bodleian Library MS Mich. 365 (Neubauer 1208), f. 80b-81a, C.
11846. Oxford - Bodleian Library MS Opp. 170 (Neubauer 1205), f. 174b-175a, C.
11847. Oxford - Bodleian Library MS Opp. 172 (Neubauer 1211), f. 59b-60a, C.
11848. Oxford - Bodleian Library MS Opp. 619 (Neubauer 2374), f. 202a-203a, M.
11849. Paris - Bibliotheque Nationale heb. 653, f. 86b, G.
11850. Parma - Biblioteca Palatina Cod. Parm. 3270 (de Rossi 1215), f. 164b-165a, M.
11851. Parma - Biblioteca Palatina Cod. Parm. 3271 (de Rossi 1216), f. 102b-103b, G.
11852. Parma - Biblioteca Palatina Cod. Parm. 3205 (de Rossi 655), f. 233b-234a, C, no incipit.
11853. Parma - Biblioteca Palatina Cod. Parm. 3507 (Perreau 27), f. 161b-162a, C, no incipit.

11854. Vatican - Biblioteca Apostolica ebr. 308, f. 116b-117a, C, commentator: David b. Mose (compiler).
11855. Vatican - Biblioteca Apostolica ebr. 422/1, f. 18a, C, short.
11856. Zurich - Zentralbibliothek Heid. 139, f. 82b-83a, C, additional marginal notes.

Asti, Fossano, Moncalvo

11857. New Haven - Yale University, Beinecke Rare Book and MS Library, MS Heb. 52, f. 133a, M.

Roma

11858. Berlin - Staatsbibliothek (Preussischer Kulturbesitz) Or. Oct. 3567, f. 5b-6a, FC.
11859. Jerusalem - Jewish National and University Library Ms Heb 8° 4153, f. 139a-139b, C, commentator: Daniel ben Salomo haRofe (compiler), no incipit.
11860. New York - Jewish Theological Seminary Ms. 1639, f. 25b-26a, C, commentator: Salomo b. Samuel Rofe.
11861. Oxford - Bodleian Library MS Mich. 312,1 (Neubauer 2276,1), f. 6a-6b, C.

Romania

11862. Vatican - Biblioteca Apostolica ebr. 320, f. 316b, 317b, M.

Tsarfat

11863. London - British Library Or. 8682, f. 81b, GI.
11864. London - David Sofer 5, f. 150a-150b, C.
11865. Oxford - Bodleian Library MS Bodl. Or. 109 (Neubauer 1209), f. 29b-30b, C, commentator: Aaron b. Hayyim haKohen (compiler).
11866. Oxford - Bodleian Library MS Laud. Or. 271 (Neubauer 1206), f. 114b, C, commentator: Aaron b. Hayyim haKohen (compiler), no incipit.
11867. Parma - Biblioteca Palatina Cod. Parm. 1794 (de Rossi 1061), f. 156b-158a, M.
11868. Parma - Biblioteca Palatina Cod. Parm. 2890 (de Rossi 856), f. 69b, M.
11869. Parma - Biblioteca Palatina Cod. Parm. 3006 (de Rossi 654,1), f. 178a-178b, M.
11870. Vatican - Biblioteca Apostolica ebr. 306, f. 103a-103b, C.

יום נלחמו בי (י 1861), אברהם אבן עזרא, קינה

Carpentras, commentary by Mordekhai b. Josef of Rocco Martino

11871. Cincinnati - Hebrew Union College 246/1, f. 76b-77a, C, rubric: פי׳ קינה יום נלמחו בי.

יום נעקד יצחק לקרבן עולת, סליחה

Yemen, commentary by Isaac b. Abraham Wanneh
11872. Chicago-Spertus College of Judaica D 2, 2, f. 216b-217a, M, no incipit.
11873. London - British Library Or. 11122, f. 193b-194a, M, no incipit.
11874. Manchester - John Rylands University Library, Ms. Gaster 5, f. 200b, M.
11875. Philadelphia - University of Pennsylvania HB 2, f. 121b, M, rubric: אל מלך, incipit כאבר.

יום ערום אעמוד מצדקתי (י 1875), יצחק גיאת, חלק ב', קדושתא לשחרית יום כפור

Sepharad, commentary by David b. Josef Abudarham[276]
11876. Budapest - Magyar tudomanyos akademia, MS. Kaufmann A 405/2, p. 206-207, C, rubric: פזמון.
11877. New York - Columbia X893 Ab 93, f. 13a, C, rubric: פזמון.
Yemen
11878. Jerusalem - Sassoon 902, p. 429, M.
Yemen, commentary by Isaac b. Abraham Wanneh
11879. Chicago-Spertus College of Judaica D 2, 2, f. 198b, M, no incipit.
11880. Jerusalem - Michael Krupp 604, f. 150a, M, rubric: אל מלך.
11881. Jerusalem - Sassoon 1158, p. 361-362, M, no incipit.

יום פוריה יומא דנן בר לפגר ממלתיה (י 1888), יצחק גיאת, פיוט לפורים

Carpentras, commentary by Mordekhai b. Josef of Rocco Martino
11882. Cincinnati - Hebrew Union College 246/1, f. 27a-27b, C, rubric: פי' ליום פוריא.
Sepharad, commentary by Josef Garad
11883. Oxford - Bodleian Library Heb.e.10 (Neubauer 2746/1), f. 10b, C, rubric: שלום לפורים.
11884. Oxford - Bodleian Library Heb.e.10 (Neubauer 2746/1), f. 18b, C, rubric: בתפלת פורים. יום פוריא, no incipit.

יום צדו צעדי ונטתה למוט רגלי (י 1895), יצחק גיאת, חלק ד', קדושתא לשחרית יום כפור

Carpentras
11885. Cincinnati - Hebrew Union College 392, f. 47a-47b, M, no incipit.
Carpentras, commentary by Josef b. Abraham of Montelitz
11886. Cincinnati - Hebrew Union College 291, f. 23a-23b, C, rubric: פי' פזמון יום צדו.
11887. New York - Jewish Theological Seminary Ms. 4197, f. 108a-108b, M, no incipit.

---

[276] Edited by Prins, תשלום אבודרהם, p. 100-101.

11888. Paris - Ecole Rabbinique 32, f. 128b-129b, M, no incipit.
11889. Strasbourg - Bibliotheque Nationale et Universitaire 4081, f. 105b-106b, M, no incipit.

Sepharad, commentary by David b. Josef Abudarham[277]

11890. Budapest - Magyar tudomanyos akademia, MS. Kaufmann A 405/2, p. 192-193, C, rubric: פזמון.
11891. Cincinnati - Hebrew Union College 490, f. 5a, C.
11892. New York - Columbia X893 Ab 93, f. 7a-7b, C, rubric: פזמון.
11893. New York - Jewish Theological Seminary Ms. 3011, f. 6a-6b, C, rubric: פזמון.

יום צעקו שבים (י 1898), יצחק גיאת, חלק ו׳, קדושתא לשחרית יום כפור, בתימן: סליחה
Carpentras

11894. Cincinnati - Hebrew Union College 392, f. 48b-49a, M, no incipit.

Carpentras, commentary by Josef b. Abraham of Montelitz

11895. Cincinnati - Hebrew Union College 291, f. 25a-25b, C, rubric: פי׳ פזמון יום צעקו וכו׳.
11896. New York - Jewish Theological Seminary Ms. 4197, f. 112a, M, no incipit.
11897. Paris - Ecole Rabbinique 32, f. 132a, M, no incipit.
11898. Strasbourg - Bibliotheque Nationale et Universitaire 4081, f. 109a-109b, M, no incipit.

Sepharad, commentary by David b. Josef Abudarham[278]

11899. Budapest - Magyar tudomanyos akademia, MS. Kaufmann A 405/2, p. 194-195, C, rubric: פזמון.
11900. Cincinnati - Hebrew Union College 490, f. 5b-6a, C.
11901. Holon - Yehuda Nahum 278, f. 4b, FC, rubric: פזמון, only beginning.
11902. New York - Jewish Theological Seminary Ms. 3011, f. 7a-7b, C, rubric: פזמון.

Yemen, commentary by Isaac b. Abraham Wanneh

11903. Chicago-Spertus College of Judaica D 2, 2, f. 218b-219a, M, no incipit.
11904. Jerusalem - Sassoon 1158, p. 370, M, no incipit.
11905. London - British Library Or. 11122, f. 185a, M, rubric: אל מלך.

יום צעקי מאישון במעמדי הראשון (י 1899), יצחק גיאת, סליחה
Yemen, commentary by Isaac b. Abraham Wanneh

11906. Chicago-Spertus College of Judaica D 2, 2, f. 197b, M.
11907. Jerusalem - Michael Krupp 604, f. 151a, M, rubric: אל מלך.
11908. Jerusalem - Sassoon 1158, p. 360, M, no incipit.

---

[277] Edited by Prins, תשלום אבודרהם, p. 81-82.
[278] Edited by Prins, תשלום אבודרהם, p. 82-83.

11909. Jerusalem - Yehiel haLevi 4, f. 171a, G.
11910. London - British Library Or. 11122, f. 179a-179b, M.

יום שבת וכפורים איש באחיו דבקו (י 1932), יצחק גיאת, סליחה

Tsarfat
11911. London - David Sofer 5, f. 175b-176a, C, rubric: אחר.
11912. Parma - Biblioteca Palatina Cod. Parm. 3007 (de Rossi 654,2), f. 156b-157a, M.

יום שבת תשמח מאד נפשי (י 1939), שלם שבזי

Yemen
11913. Cincinnati - Hebrew Union College 398, f. 99b-101b, M, long.

יום שבתון אין לשכוח זכרו כריח ניחוח (י 1940), יהודה, זמר לשבת

Yemen
11914. Cincinnati - Hebrew Union College 398, f. 106b, M.

יומם ולילה אבכה (י 1984), יהודה בן יעקב, קינה

Carpentras, commentary by Mordekhai b. Josef of Rocco Martino
11915. Cincinnati - Hebrew Union College 246/1, f. 74a, C, rubric: פי' קינה יומם ולילה.

יומם ולילה אפיל תחנוני (י 1985), יצחק, סליחה

Yemen, commentary by Isaac b. Abraham Wanneh
11916. Chicago-Spertus College of Judaica D 2, 2, f. 214a-214b, M, no incipit.
11917. Jerusalem - Sassoon 1158, p. 366, M, rubric: אל מלך.
11918. London - British Library Or. 11122, f. 183a, M, no incipit.

יומם עינינו תלויות (י 1997), יצחק בן מאיר, סליחה

Ashkenaz
11919. Budapest - Magyar tudomanyos akademia, MS. Kaufmann A 400, p. 526-527, C, rubric: אחרת.
11920. Cambridge - University Library Add. 394,1 (Reif SCR 461), f. 97b, C.
11921. Moscow - Russian State Library, Ms. Guenzburg 190, f. 16a-16b, G.
11922. Oxford - Bodleian Library MS Mich. 543 (Neubauer 1212), f. 76b-77a, C, commentator: Isaac b. Jacob (compiler).

Roma
11923. Berlin - Staatsbibliothek (Preussischer Kulturbesitz) Or. Oct. 3567, f. 3a, FC.

Tsarfat
11924. London - David Sofer 5, f. 94a, C.

11925. Oxford - Bodleian Library MS Laud. Or. 271 (Neubauer 1206), f. 173b-174a, C, commentator: Aaron b. Hayyim haKohen (compiler).
11926. Oxford - Bodleian Library MS Opp. 171 (Neubauer 1207), f. 113b, C, rubric: אחרת.

Yemen, commentary by Isaac b. Abraham Wanneh
11927. Chicago-Spertus College of Judaica D 2, 2, f. 197a, M.
11928. Jerusalem - Sassoon 1158, p. 359, M, no incipit.
11929. London - British Library Or. 11122, f. 179a, M.

יונה בצלמון בהשליגה (י 2004), יצחק בן זרחיה גירונדי, קדושתא לשבת שקלים

Carpentras, commentary by Mordekhai b. Josef of Rocco Martino
11930. Cincinnati - Hebrew Union College 246, f. 5a-7b, C, rubric: פי' לפרשת שקלים.

Sepharad, commentary by Josef Garad
11931. Oxford - Bodleian Library Heb.e.10 (Neubauer 2746/1) , f. 1a-2b, C, rubric: פרשת שקלים.
11932. Oxford - Bodleian Library Heb.e.10 (Neubauer 2746/1), f. 17a, C, rubric: פרשת שקלים. יונה בצלמון, no incipit.

יונה הבלועה שוחרת מצפר (י 2009), יצחק השנירי, לראש השנה

Carpentras
11933. Cincinnati - Hebrew Union College 429/1, f. 14a-15a, M, no incipit.

Carpentras, commentary by Josef b. Abraham of Montelitz
11934. Cincinnati - Hebrew Union College 357 , f. 69b, M, rubric: פירוש, no incipit.
11935. New York - Jewish Theological Seminary Ms. 4746, f. 22a, M, no incipit.
11936. Paris - Alliance Israelite Universelle H 422 A, f. 41b-45a, M, no incipit.
11937. Paris - Ecole Rabbinique 31, f. 114b-115a, M, no incipit.

יונה זמיריך הרבי (י 2016), משה אבן עזרא, סליחה

Yemen
11938. Jerusalem - Sassoon 902, p. 427, M, very short.
11939. New York - Jewish Theological Seminary Ms. 3028, f. 42b, G.
11940. New York - Jewish Theological Seminary Ms. 3052 , f. 31b-32b, M, rubric: אל מלך.

Yemen, commentary by Isaac b. Abraham Wanneh
11941. Chicago-Spertus College of Judaica D 2, 2, f. 209a-209b, M, no incipit.
11942. Jerusalem - Benayahu ת 261, f. 139b-140a, M, rubric: אל מלך.
11943. Jerusalem - Benayahu ת 282, f. 123a-123b, M, rubric: אל מלך.

11944. Jerusalem - Makhon Ben Zvi 1156 (Tubi 155), f. 121b-122a, M, rubric: אל מלך.
11945. Jerusalem - Makhon Ben Zvi 1174 (Tubi 154), f. 126b, M.
11946. Jerusalem - Michael Krupp 604, f. 154a-154b, M, rubric: אל מלך.
11947. Jerusalem - Musad haRav Kook 325, f. 183a-183b, M, rubric: אל מלך.
11948. Jerusalem - Sassoon 1158, p. 377-378, M, no incipit.
11949. Jerusalem - Sassoon 1174, p. 234-235, M, no incipit.
11950. Jerusalem - Yehiel haLevi 4, f. 67b, G.
11951. London - British Library Or. 11122, f. 189a-189b, M, rubric: אל מלך.
11952. Manchester - John Rylands University Library, Ms. Gaster 5, f. 198a, M.
11953. Muenchen - Bayerische Staatsbibliothek, Cod. hebr. 472, f. 166a-167a, M, rubric: אל מלך.
11954. New York - Jewish Theological Seminary Ms. 3013, f. 122b, M, rubric: אל מלך.
11955. New York - Jewish Theological Seminary Ms. 3294, f. 10b-11a, C.
11956. Strasbourg - Bibliotheque Nationale et Universitaire 3965 (Landauer 39), p. 381, M, rubric: אל מלך.

יונה מה לך מקוננת תרבי (י 2039), יהודה, קינה
Yemen, commentary by Isaac b. Abraham Wanneh
11957. Jerusalem - Sassoon 1158, p. 173, M.
11958. London - British Library Or. 11122, f. 103b, M.

יונה מה תהגי ומה תהמי (י 2040), יהודה הלוי, אהבה לסוכות, בתימן: סליחה
Yemen
11959. Cincinnati - Hebrew Union College 199, f. 76b, G, one gloss only.
11960. Jerusalem - Benayahu ת 414, f. 136b, M.
11961. Jerusalem - Musad haRav Kook 334, f. 142a, M.
11962. Jerusalem - Sassoon 264, f. 151b, M.
11963. Jerusalem - Sassoon 902, p. 377, M, no incipit.
Yemen, commentary by Isaac b. Abraham Wanneh
11964. Chicago-Spertus College of Judaica D 2, 2, f. 217b-218a, M, no incipit.
11965. Jerusalem - Makhon b. Zvi 1168 (Tubi 157), f. 18a, M, margins damaged.
11966. Jerusalem - Musad haRav Kook 330, f. 99a, G.
11967. Jerusalem - Musad haRav Kook 347, f. 78a, G.
11968. Jerusalem - Sassoon 1158, p. 352, M, no incipit.
11969. Jerusalem - Yehiel haLevi 4, f. 143b-144b, G.
11970. London - British Library Or. 11122, f. 175a-175b, M, no incipit.
11971. New York - Jewish Theological Seminary Ms. 3294, f. 8b, C.

יונה נודדת מקנך (י 2050), ישוע קשלארי, סליחה

Yemen
11972. New York - Jewish Theological Seminary Ms. 3052, f. 79a-79b, M, no incipit.

Yemen, commentary by Isaac b. Abraham Wanneh
11973. Chicago-Spertus College of Judaica D 2, 2, f. 236b, M, no incipit.
11974. Jerusalem - Benayahu ת 282, f. 139b, M.
11975. Jerusalem - Makhon Ben Zvi 1156 (Tubi 155), f. 137a-137b, M, no incipit.
11976. Jerusalem - Makhon Ben Zvi 1174 (Tubi 154), f. 135a, M.
11977. Jerusalem - Michael Krupp 604, f. 174a, M.
11978. Jerusalem - Musad haRav Kook 325, f. 192b-193a, M.
11979. Jerusalem - Sassoon 1158, p. 414, M, no incipit.
11980. Jerusalem - Sassoon 1174, p. 267-268, M, no incipit.
11981. Manchester - John Rylands University Library, Ms. Gaster 5, f. 221b-222a, M.
11982. Muenchen - Bayerische Staatsbibliothek, Cod. hebr. 472, f. 191b, M.
11983. New York - Jewish Theological Seminary Ms. 3013, f. 131b, M, no incipit.
11984. New York - Jewish Theological Seminary Ms. 3294, f. 16b, C.
11985. New York - Public Library, Heb. Ms. 9, f. 128a, M, no incipit.
11986. Strasbourg - Bibliotheque Nationale et Universitaire 3965 (Landauer 39), p. 405, M.

יונה נשאתה על כנפי נשרים (י 2056), יהודה הלוי, גאולה, בתימן: סליחה

Ashkenaz
11987. Budapest - Magyar tudomanyos akademia, MS. Kaufmann A 399, p. 362-363, C, rubric: אחר.

Yemen
11988. Cincinnati - Hebrew Union College 199, f. 79b, G.
11989. Jerusalem - Benayahu ת 414, f. 139b, M.
11990. Jerusalem - Musad haRav Kook 334, f. 134b, M.
11991. Jerusalem - Sassoon 264, f. 151a, M.
11992. Jerusalem - Sassoon 902, p. 382, M.
11993. New York - Jewish Theological Seminary Ms. 3052, f. 11b-13a, M, rubric: אל מלך.
11994. New York - Jewish Theological Seminary Ms. 3109, f. 75b, M.
11995. Ramat Gan - Universitat BarIlan 62, f. 43a, G, margins damaged.

Yemen, commentary by Isaac b. Abraham Wanneh
11996. Chicago-Spertus College of Judaica D 2, 2, f. 196a-196b, M, no incipit.
11997. Jerusalem - Benayahu ת 261, f. 129b-130b, M, rubric: אל מלך.

11998. Jerusalem - Benayahu ת 282, f. 114b-115b, M, rubric: אל מלך, no incipit.
11999. Jerusalem - Makhon Ben Zvi 1156 (Tubi 155), f. 112b-113a, M, rubric: אל מלך.
12000. Jerusalem - Makhon Ben Zvi 1174 (Tubi 154), f. 114a-114b, M, rubric: אל מלך.
12001. Jerusalem - Michael Krupp 604, f. 142a-143a, M, rubric: אל מלך.
12002. Jerusalem - Musad haRav Kook 325, f. 166a, M, rubric: אל מלך.
12003. Jerusalem - Musad haRav Kook 330, f. 96a, G.
12004. Jerusalem - Musad haRav Kook 347, f. 77b, G.
12005. Jerusalem - Sassoon 1158, p. 346-347, M, no incipit.
12006. Jerusalem - Sassoon 1174, p. 217-218, M, rubric: אל מלך.
12007. Jerusalem - Yehiel haLevi 4, f. 148a, G.
12008. London - British Library Or. 11122, f. 172a, M, rubric: אל מלך, no incipit.
12009. Manchester - John Rylands University Library, Ms. Gaster 5, f. 187a-187b, M.
12010. Muenchen - Bayerische Staatsbibliothek, Cod. hebr. 472, f. 153a-153b, M, rubric: אל מלך.
12011. New York - Jewish Theological Seminary Ms. 3013, f. 113a-113b, M, rubric: אל מלך.
12012. New York - Jewish Theological Seminary Ms. 3294, f. 6b-7a, C.
12013. New York - Public Library, Heb. Ms. 9, f. 109b, M.
12014. Philadelphia - University of Pennsylvania HB 2, f. 126b, M, rubric: אל מלך.
12015. Strasbourg - Bibliotheque Nationale et Universitaire 3965 (Landauer 39), p. 346-347, M, rubric: אל מלך.

יונה פותה יקושת כל מעבר (י 2063), יהודה הלוי, סליחה

Yemen
12016. Jerusalem - Benayahu ת 414, f. 136a, M.
12017. Jerusalem - Sassoon 264, f. 150a, M.
12018. Jerusalem - Sassoon 902, p. 388, M.
12019. New York - Jewish Theological Seminary Ms. 3052, f. 22a-23a, M, rubric: אל מלך.
12020. New York - Jewish Theological Seminary Ms. 3109, f. 80a, M.
12021. Ramat Gan - Universitat Bar Ilan 62, f. 44b, G, margin damaged.

Yemen, commentary by Isaac b. Abraham Wanneh
12022. Chicago-Spertus College of Judaica D 2, 2, f. 204b, M, no incipit.
12023. Jerusalem - Benayahu ת 261, f. 134b-135a, M, rubric: אל מלך.
12024. Jerusalem - Benayahu ת 282, f. 119a-119b, M, rubric: אל מלך.
12025. Jerusalem - Makhon Ben Zvi 1156 (Tubi 155), f. 116b-117a, M, rubric: אל מלך.

12026. Jerusalem - Makhon Ben Zvi 1174 (Tubi 154), f. 109a, M, rubric: אל מלך.
12027. Jerusalem - Michael Krupp 604, f. 147a-147b, M, rubric: אל מלך.
12028. Jerusalem - Musad haRav Kook 325, f. 160b, M.
12029. Jerusalem - Musad haRav Kook 330, f. 95a-95b, G.
12030. Jerusalem - Musad haRav Kook 347, f. 76b, G.
12031. Jerusalem - Sassoon 1158, p. 350, M, no incipit.
12032. Jerusalem - Sassoon 1174, p. 225-226, M, no incipit.
12033. Jerusalem - Yehiel haLevi 4, f. 150a, G.
12034. Manchester - John Rylands University Library, Ms. Gaster 5, f. 182a-182b, M.
12035. Muenchen - Bayerische Staatsbibliothek, Cod. hebr. 472, f. 159a-159b, M, rubric: אל מלך.
12036. New York - Jewish Theological Seminary Ms. 3013, f. 109a-109b, M, rubric: אל מלך.
12037. New York - Jewish Theological Seminary Ms. 3294, f. 4a-4b, C.
12038. New York - Public Library, Heb. Ms. 9, f. 117b-118a, M.
12039. Philadelphia - University of Pennsylvania HB 2, f. 122a-122b, M, rubric: אל מלך.
12040. Strasbourg - Bibliotheque Nationale et Universitaire 3965 (Landauer 39), p. 333-334, M, rubric: אל מלך.

יונות הושתו שכם בארץ ערבה ושוחה (י 2085), יהודה הלוי, סליחה

Yemen
12041. Jerusalem - Sassoon 902, p. 392-393, M.
12042. New York - Jewish Theological Seminary Ms. 3028, f. 13b, M, short.
12043. New York - Jewish Theological Seminary Ms. 3052, f. 11a-11b, M, rubric: אל מלך.
12044. New York - Jewish Theological Seminary Ms. 3109, f. 83b-84a, M.
12045. Ramat Gan - Universitat Bar Ilan 62, f. 43a, G, margins damaged.

Yemen, commentary by Isaac b. Abraham Wanneh
12046. Chicago-Spertus College of Judaica D 2, 2, f. 194a-194b, M.
12047. Jerusalem - Benayahu ת 261, f. 129b, M, rubric: אל מלך.
12048. Jerusalem - Benayahu ת 282, f. 114b, M, rubric: אל מלך, no incipit.
12049. Jerusalem - Makhon Ben Zvi 1156 (Tubi 155), f. 112a-112b, M, rubric: אל מלך.
12050. Jerusalem - Makhon Ben Zvi 1174 (Tubi 154), f. 113b, M, rubric: אל מלך.
12051. Jerusalem - Michael Krupp 604, f. 142a, M, rubric: אל מלך.
12052. Jerusalem - Musad haRav Kook 325, f. 165b, M, rubric: אל מלך.
12053. Jerusalem - Musad haRav Kook 347, f. 78a, G.
12054. Jerusalem - Sassoon 1158, p. 345-346, M, no incipit.
12055. Jerusalem - Sassoon 1174, p. 217, M, no incipit.
12056. Jerusalem - Yehiel haLevi 4, f. 148b, G.

12057. London - British Library Or. 11122, f. 172a, M, rubric: אל מלך.
12058. Manchester - John Rylands University Library, Ms. Gaster 5, f. 187a, M.
12059. Muenchen - Bayerische Staatsbibliothek, Cod. hebr. 472, f. 152b-153a, M, rubric: אל מלך.
12060. New York - Jewish Theological Seminary Ms. 3013, f. 113a, M, rubric: אל מלך.
12061. New York - Jewish Theological Seminary Ms. 3109, f. 84a, M, rubric: אל מלך.
12062. New York - Jewish Theological Seminary Ms. 3294, f. 6b, C.
12063. New York - Public Library, Heb. Ms. 9, f. 109a, M.
12064. Philadelphia - University of Pennsylvania HB 2, f. 126a, M, rubric: אל מלך.
12065. Strasbourg - Bibliotheque Nationale et Universitaire 3965 (Landauer 39), p. 345, M, rubric: אל מלך.

יוני גאיות הומות בפחדן גלה מחמדן (י 2086), יהודה הלוי, סליחה

Yemen
12066. Jerusalem - Musad haRav Kook 334, f. 136a, M.
12067. Jerusalem - Sassoon 264, f. 157b, M.
12068. Jerusalem - Sassoon 902, p. 393, M.
12069. New York - Jewish Theological Seminary Ms. 3028, f. 14a, M, very short, Arabic.
12070. New York - Jewish Theological Seminary Ms. 3052, f. 13a-14a, M, rubric: אל מלך.
12071. New York - Jewish Theological Seminary Ms. 3109, f. 84b-85a, M.
12072. Ramat Gan - Universitat Bar Ilan 62, f. 42b-43a, G, margins damaged.

Yemen, commentary by Isaac b. Abraham Wanneh
12073. Chicago-Spertus College of Judaica D 2, 2, f. 194b-195a, M.
12074. Jerusalem - Benayahu ת 261, f. 130b-131a, M, rubric: אל מלך.
12075. Jerusalem - Benayahu ת 282, f. 115b-116a, M, rubric: אל מלך.
12076. Jerusalem - Makhon Ben Zvi 1156 (Tubi 155), f. 113a-113b, M, rubric: אל מלך.
12077. Jerusalem - Makhon Ben Zvi 1174 (Tubi 154), f. 115a-115b, M, rubric: יוני גאיות.
12078. Jerusalem - Michael Krupp 604, f. 143a-143b, M, rubric: אל מלך.
12079. Jerusalem - Musad haRav Kook 325, f. 167b, M, rubric: אל מלך.
12080. Jerusalem - Musad haRav Kook 330, f. 99b, M.
12081. Jerusalem - Musad haRav Kook 347, f. 79a, M.
12082. Jerusalem - Sassoon 1158, p. 346, M, no incipit.
12083. Jerusalem - Sassoon 1174, p. 218-219, M, rubric: אל מלך.
12084. Manchester - John Rylands University Library, Ms. Gaster 5, f. 188a-188b, M.

12085. Muenchen - Bayerische Staatsbibliothek, Cod. hebr. 472, f. 153b-154b, M, rubric: אל מלך.
12086. New York - Jewish Theological Seminary Ms. 3013, f. 114a-114b, M, rubric: אל מלך.
12087. New York - Jewish Theological Seminary Ms. 3109, f. 85a-85b, M, rubric: אל מלך.
12088. New York - Jewish Theological Seminary Ms. 3294, f. 8a, M.
12089. New York - Public Library, Heb. Ms. 9, f. 110a, M.
12090. Philadelphia - University of Pennsylvania HB 2, f. 127b, M, rubric: אל מלך.
12091. Strasbourg - Bibliotheque Nationale et Universitaire 3965 (Landauer 39), p. 349-350, M, rubric: אל מלך.

יונת אלם התעוררי (י 2096), יוסף ב"ר שמואל טוב עלם, לשבועות
Tsarfat
12092. Parma - Biblioteca Palatina Cod. Parm. 3136 (de Rossi 405), f. 171b-172a, M.

יונת אלם קץ ישועה, סליחה
Yemen, commentary by Isaac b. Abraham Wanneh
12093. Jerusalem - Sassoon 1158, p. 431, M, no incipit.
12094. London - British Library Or. 11122, f. 225a, M, no incipit.

יוסד ארץ על מכוניה, יצחק הנקדן
Ashkenaz
12095. Oxford - Bodleian Library MS Can. Or. 70 (Neubauer 1147,7), f. 83b-85a, M, rubric: אחרת.

יוסיף לקנות מקנה (י 2154), יצחק בן זרחיה גירונדי, חלק ד' קדושתא לשבת שקלים
Carpentras, commentary by Mordekhai b. Josef of Rocco Martino
12096. Cincinnati - Hebrew Union College 246, f. 9a-9b, C, rubric: פי' פזמון יוסיף לקנות וכו'.
Sepharad, commentary by Josef Garad
12097. Oxford - Bodleian Library Heb.e.10 (Neubauer 2746/1), f. 3b-4a, C, rubric: פזמון.

יוסיף שנית ידו אלהי צבאות (י 2160), יצחק בן זרחיה גירונדי, חלק ה,' קדושתא לשבת החדש
Carpentras, commentary by Mordekhai b. Josef of Rocco Martino
12098. Cincinnati - Hebrew Union College 246/1, f. 43a-43b, C, rubric: פי' משלש יוסיף שנית ידו.

Sepharad, commentary by Josef Garad
12099. Oxford - Bodleian Library Heb.e.10 (Neubauer 2746/1), f. 14b, C, rubric: משלש.

יוסף תקיף יצירה כדתבעתיה מרתיהה (י 2161), פיוט בארמית לשבועות

Ashkenaz
12100. Berlin - Staatsbibliothek (Preussischer Kulturbesitz) Or. Qu. 798-799 (Steinschneider 177), II, f. 164b-165a, M.
12101. Cambridge - University Library Add. 394,1 (Reif SCR 461), f. 63a-64a, C.
12102. Jerusalem - Schocken Institute 24100 / Mahzor Nuremberg, f. 163b-164a, M.
12103. Muenchen - Bayerische Staatsbibliothek, Cod. hebr. 21, f. 86a-86b, M.
12104. Muenchen - Bayerische Staatsbibliothek, Cod. hebr. 393, f. 153a, C, no incipit.
12105. Oxford - Bodleian Library MS Can. Or. 1 (Neubauer 1104), f. 118b-120a, M.
12106. Oxford - Bodleian Library MS Opp. 170 (Neubauer 1205), f. 98b-99a, C.
12107. Parma - Biblioteca Palatina Cod. Parm. 3205 (de Rossi 655), f. 186a-186b, C.

Tsarfat
12108. Cambridge - University Library Add. 561.1, f. 82a-83a, MT, Hebrew.
12109. London - British Library Add. 11639 (Margoliouth 1056), f. 681a-682a, M.
12110. London - British Library Or. 2735 (Margoliouth 663), f. 37b-38b, M.
12111. London - David Sofer 5, f. 63b-64a, C.
12112. Moscow - Russian State Library, Ms. Guenzburg 1665, f. 129a, M.
12113. New York - Jewish Theological Seminary Ms. 4460, f. 66a-66b, M, pages damaged.
12114. Parma - Biblioteca Palatina Cod. Parm. 1902, f. 149b-150b, M.
12115. Parma - Biblioteca Palatina Cod. Parm. 2574, f. 130a, G, commentator: Simḥa b. Samuel, cp. Mahzor Vitry.
12116. Parma - Biblioteca Palatina Cod. Parm. 3136 (de Rossi 405), f. 163a-164a, M.

יוספים שנית לעמוד במשמרת תחלתם (י 2162), פזמון ליום כפור, תימן ובבקרפנטרס: סליחה

Carpentras
12117. Cincinnati - Hebrew Union College 392, f. 75b, M, no incipit.

Carpentras, commentary by Josef b. Abraham of Montelitz
12118. Cincinnati - Hebrew Union College 291, f. 43a-43b, C, rubric: 'פי סליחה יוסיפים וכו'.
12119. New York - Jewish Theological Seminary Ms. 4197, f. 178a-178b, M, no incipit.
12120. Paris - Ecole Rabbinique 32, f. 186b, M, no incipit.
12121. Strasbourg - Bibliotheque Nationale et Universitaire 4081, f. 163b-164a, M, no incipit.

Sepharad, commentary by David b. Josef Abudarham[279]
12122. Budapest - Magyar tudomanyos akademia, MS. Kaufmann A 405/2, p. 241, C, rubric: פזמון.
12123. New York - Columbia X893 Ab 93, f. 26a, C, rubric: פזמון.

Yemen
12124. Jerusalem - Benayahu ת 414, f. 129a, M.

יועץ וחכם חרשים, יצחק הנקדן

Ashkenaz
12125. Oxford - Bodleian Library MS Can. Or. 70 (Neubauer 1147,7), f. 82b-83a, M, rubric: אחרת.

יוצק יום יום לחשו (י 2183), יצחק בן זרחיה גירונדי, חלק ו', קדושתא לשבת החדש

Sepharad, commentary Josef Garad
12126. Oxford - Bodleian Library Heb.e.10 (Neubauer 2746/1), f. 14b-15a, C, rubric: פזמון, no incipit.
12127. Oxford - Bodleian Library Heb.e.10 (Neubauer 2746/1), f. 21b, C, rubric: יוצק יום, no incipit, very short.

יוצר הארץ ועושה (י 2195), יוסף ב"ר שמואל טוב עלם, סליחה

Tsarfat
12128. London - David Sofer 5, f. 104a, C.

יוצרי אתה וצורי, סליחה

Carpentras, commentary by Eliyahu Carmi
12129. Marseille - Mlle. Odette Valabregue [1], f. 33b, C, no incipit.

יוצר מרומות ונגהם ישר לב עקוב (י 2223), יצחק בן זרחיה גירונדי, פזמון לראש השנה

Carpentras
12130. Cincinnati - Hebrew Union College 429/1, f. 24b-25a, M, no incipit.
Carpentras, commentary by Josef b. Abraham of Montelitz
12131. Cincinnati - Hebrew Union College 357, f. 104a, M, rubric: פירוש.

---

[279] Edited by Prins, תשלום אבודרהם, p. 76.

12132. New York - Jewish Theological Seminary Ms. 4746, f. 36a, M.
12133. Paris - Alliance Israelite Universelle H 422 A, f. 83b-84a, M.
12134. Paris - Ecole Rabbinique 31, f. 142b-143a, M.

יוצר נגוהים (י 2224), יצחק בן זרחיה גירונדי, לשבת שקלים
Carpentras, commentary by Mordekhai b. Josef of Rocco Martino
12135. Cincinnati - Hebrew Union College 246, f. 14b, C, rubric: פי' תוכחה מי אתה וכו'.

יושב בגובהי ממרומים (י 2278), יוסף, סליחה
Ashkenaz
12136. Braunschweig - Landesmuseum fuer Geschichte und Volkstum R 2386, vol. II, f. 47b-48a, M.
12137. Budapest - Magyar tudomanyos akademia, MS. Kaufmann A 400, p. 511-512, C, rubric: חטאנו אחרת מרבנא יוסף.
12138. Moscow - Russian State Library, Ms. Guenzburg 190, f. 114a-114b, G.
12139. Oxford - Bodleian Library MS Mich. 543 (Neubauer 1212), f. 83a, C, commentator: Isaac b. Jacob (compiler).
12140. Oxford - Bodleian Library MS Opp. 170 (Neubauer 1205), f. 239b-240(i)a, C.
12141. Oxford - Bodleian Library MS Opp. 681 (Neubauer 1213), f. 87a-87b, C, rubric: חטאנו צורינו סלח לנו יוצרינו.
12142. Padova - Biblioteca del Seminario Vescovile Cod. 218, f. 47b-48b, M.
12143. Padova - Biblioteca del Seminario Vescovile Cod. 218, f. 231a-231b, M.
12144. Padova - Biblioteca del Seminario Vescovile Cod. 218, f. 255a-255b, M.
12145. Parma - Biblioteca Palatina Cod. Parm. 3205 (de Rossi 655), f. 276a-276b, C.
Tsarfat
12146. Parma - Biblioteca Palatina Cod. Parm. 3006 (de Rossi 654,1), f. 231b, M.
12147. London - David Sofer 5, f. 93b, C.
12148. Oxford - Bodleian Library MS Laud. Or. 271 (Neubauer 1206), f. 128a-128b, C, commentator: Aaron b. Hayyim haKohen (compiler), rubric: דר' אליה בר' שמעיה. חטאנו.
12149. Oxford - Bodleian Library MS Opp. 171 (Neubauer 1207), f. 114b-115a, C, rubric: אחרת.
12150. Parma - Biblioteca Palatina Cod. Parm. 2890 (de Rossi 856), f. 108a-108b, M.
12151. Parma - Biblioteca Palatina Cod. Parm. 3007 (de Rossi 654,2), f. 11a-11b, M.

12152. Vatican - Biblioteca Apostolica ebr. 306, f. 177b-178a, C.

יושב בשמים ומביט עד קצה מים, סליחה

Yemen

12153. New York - Jewish Theological Seminary Ms. 3052, f. 82b-83a, M. Yemen, commentary by Isaac b. Abraham Wanneh
12154. Chicago-Spertus College of Judaica D 2, 2, f. 237b, M, no incipit.
12155. Jerusalem - Benayahu ת 261, f. 165a, M, very short.
12156. Jerusalem - Benayahu ת 282, f. 140b, M, very short.
12157. Jerusalem - Makhon Ben Zvi 1156 (Tubi 155), f. 138b, M, no incipit.
12158. Jerusalem - Michael Krupp 604, f. 175b, M, short.
12159. Jerusalem - Sassoon 1174, p. 269, M, no incipit, short.
12160. London - British Library Or. 11122, f. 214b, M, no incipit, short.
12161. Manchester - John Rylands University Library, Ms. Gaster 5, f. 223b, M, no incipit, short.
12162. Muenchen - Bayerische Staatsbibliothek, Cod. hebr. 472, f. 193a-193b, M, short.
12163. New York - Jewish Theological Seminary Ms. 3013, f. 133a, M, short, no incipit.
12164. New York - Jewish Theological Seminary Ms. 3294, f. 17a, C.
12165. New York - Public Library, Heb. Ms. 9, f. 129a, M, no incipit.
12166. Strasbourg - Bibliotheque Nationale et Universitaire 3965 (Landauer 39), p. 409, M, short.

יושבי ביתיך מעת לעת, יוסף ב"ר יעקב, חלק ג', קדושתא לנעילה

Tsarfat

12167. Parma - Biblioteca Palatina Cod. Parm. 3006 (de Rossi 654,1), f. 240a, M.

יושב משמים מפשעיהו (י 2323), יצחק, סליחה

Tsarfat

12168. London - David Sofer 5, f. 175a-175b, C, rubric: פזמון.
12169. Parma - Biblioteca Palatina Cod. Parm. 3006 (de Rossi 654,1), f. 246a-246b, M.
12170. Vatican - Biblioteca Apostolica ebr. 306, f. 206b-207a, C.

יושב נסתר עליון, סליחה

Ashkenaz

12171. Vatican - Biblioteca Apostolica ebr. 308/1, f. 11a, C, commentator: David b. Mose (compiler).

יושב על כסא רחמים מתנהג בחסידות מחול עון, סליחה

Yemen
12172. Jerusalem - Benayahu ת 88, f. 148a, M.
12173. Jerusalem - Benayahu ת 301, f. 41a, G.
12174. Jerusalem - Benayahu ת 414, f. 125b, M, rubric: 'פ.
12175. Jerusalem - Musad haRav Kook 334, f. 130b, M, page torn.
12176. New York - Jewish Theological Seminary Ms. 3052, f. 2a-2b, M, rubric: האל מלך.
12177. New York - Jewish Theological Seminary Ms. 3108, f. 25a-25b, M, short.
12178. New York - Jewish Theological Seminary Ms. 4488, f. 106a, M.

Yemen, commentary by Isaac b. Abraham Wanneh
12179. Chicago-Spertus College of Judaica D 2, 2, f. 186b-187a, M, rubric: האל מלך.
12180. Jerusalem - Benayahu ת 261, f. 124b, M, rubric: האל מלך.
12181. Jerusalem - Benayahu ת 282, f. 109b-110a, M, rubric: אל מלך.
12182. Jerusalem - Makhon Ben Zvi 1156 (Tubi 155), f. 107b, M, rubric: אל מלך.
12183. Jerusalem - Makhon Ben Zvi 1174 (Tubi 154), f. 106a, C, rubric: אל מלך.
12184. Jerusalem - Michael Krupp 604, f. 136a-136b, M, rubric: אל מלך.
12185. Jerusalem - Musad haRav Kook 325, f. 155b-156a, M, rubric: אל מלך וגו'.
12186. Jerusalem - Musad haRav Kook 330, f. 87a, M.
12187. Jerusalem - Musad haRav Kook 330, f. 93b, G.
12188. Jerusalem - Musad haRav Kook 347, f. 75a, M.
12189. Jerusalem - Sassoon 1158, p. 337-338, M, rubric: אל מלך.
12190. Jerusalem - Sassoon 1174, p. 207-208, M, rubric: אל מלך.
12191. Jerusalem - Yehiel haLevi 4, f. 131a, M.
12192. Jerusalem - Yehiel haLevi 4, f. 139a, G.
12193. London - British Library Or. 11122, f. 166b-167a, M, rubric: האל מלך.
12194. Manchester - John Rylands University Library, Ms. Gaster 5, f. 181b, M, rubric: אל מלך.
12195. Muenchen - Bayerische Staatsbibliothek, Cod. hebr. 472, f. 146a, M, rubric: אל מלך.
12196. New York - Jewish Theological Seminary Ms. 3013, f. 107b, M, rubric: אל מלך.
12197. New York - Jewish Theological Seminary Ms. 3294, f. 2a, C, rubric: אל מלך.
12198. New York - Public Library, Heb. Ms. 9, f. 193a, M, rubric: פירוש.
12199. Philadelphia - University of Pennsylvania HB 2, f. 119b, M, rubric: אל מלך.
12200. Strasbourg - Bibliotheque Nationale et Universitaire 3965 (Landauer 39), p. 328, M, rubric: אל מלך.

יושב עננה שיר חדש ענה ולתקות ואחרית

Italia, commentary by Isaac b. Mordekhai Qimhi
12201. New York - Columbia University X 893 G 11, f. 9b-10a, M, rubric: אמר רבי יצחק בן מרדכי נע.

יושב קדם איום ונורא יום זה תאמץ (י 2335), יוסף, הושענא

haAri, commentary by Mose b. Hayyim Pesante
12202. New York - Jewish Theological Seminary Ms. 4696, f. 25a, C, incipit ונופף.
North Africa
12203. Jerusalem - Benayahu ז 27, f. 131b, M, incipit ונופף.
Yemen, commentary by Samḥun b. Salomo Ḥaloah
12204. Jerusalem - Makhon ben Zvi 2808, f. 237a-238a, C.

יושב תהלות מאין תחלות עורה והגלה (י 2361), יהודה הלוי, חלק ז׳, קדושתא לשבת זכור

Carpentras, commentary by Mordekhai b. Josef of Rocco Martino
12205. Cincinnati - Hebrew Union College 246, f. 14b, C, rubric: פי׳ פזמון לקדושה.

יושעון קהליך העומדים בבית יי בלילות (י 2393), יצחק, סליחה

Yemen
12206. Ramat Gan - Universitat Bar Ilan 62, f. 44b, G, margins damaged.
Yemen, commentary by Isaac b. Abraham Wanneh
12207. Chicago-Spertus College of Judaica D 2, 2, f. 199b, M, no incipit.
12208. Jerusalem - Sassoon 1158, p. 371, M, no incipit.
12209. London - British Library Or. 11122, f. 185b, M, no incipit.

יזם אגגי לחלק שולל (י 2421), יהודה הלוי, חלק ד׳, קדושתא לשבת זכור

Carpentras, commentary by Mordekhai b. Josef of Rocco Martino
12210. Cincinnati - Hebrew Union College 246/1, f. 22b-23a, C, rubric: פי׳ פזמון יזם אגגי וכו׳.
Sepharad, commentary by Josef Garad
12211. Oxford - Bodleian Library Heb.e.10 (Neubauer 2746/1), f. 8a, C, rubric: פזמון.

יחביאינו צל ידו (י 2428), יצחק בן שמואל, סליחה

Ashkenaz
12212. Jerusalem - Schocken Institute 24100 / Mahzor Nuremberg, f. 470b, M, short.
12213. Oxford - Bodleian Library MS Mich. 543 (Neubauer 1212), f. 11a, C, commentator: Isaac b. Jacob (compiler).

12214. Vatican - Biblioteca Apostolica ebr. 308/1, f. 11a, C, commentator: David b. Mose (compiler).
Ashkenaz, commentary by Abraham b. Azriel[280]
12215. Vatican - Biblioteca Apostolica ebr. 301,1, f. 170a, C.

יחדו נא יחדו נא וחדו נא כל איש בטוב רחשו (י 2457), יהודה הלוי, אופן
Tsarfat
12216. London - British Library Or. 2735 (Margoliouth 663), f. 183b-184a, M, margins cut.

יחדיו לב נשלם לעבד לבורא, יוספיה, פיוט לברכו
Ashkenaz
12217. Budapest - Magyar tudomanyos akademia, MS. Kaufmann A 399, p. 360-361, C, rubric: פיוט לברכו מר' יוספיה.
12218. Oxford - Bodleian Library MS Can. Or. 82 (Neubauer 1148), f. 46b-47a, M, short.

יחו לשון חזות אישון (י 2474), יהודה הלוי, אופן, בתימן: סליחה
Ashkenaz
12219. Jerusalem - Schocken Institute 24100 / Mahzor Nuremberg, f. 8b-9a, M.
Ashkenaz, commentary by Abraham b. Azriel[281]
12220. Frankfurt a M - Stadt- und Universitaetsbibliothek Fol. 16 (Merzbacher 95), f. 48b-49b, C, rubric: אופן יחו לשון.
12221. Frankfurt a M - Stadt- und Universitaetsbibliothek Fol. 16 (Merzbacher 95), f. 50(i)a-50(ii)b, C.
12222. Vatican - Biblioteca Apostolica ebr. 301,1, f. 77b-79a, C, rubric: אופן דר' יהוד' הקשטלי.
Tsarfat
12223. Parma - Biblioteca Palatina Cod. Parm. 1264, f. 73a-73b, M.
Yemen
12224. Jerusalem - Sassoon 902, p. 408, M.
12225. New York - Jewish Theological Seminary Ms. 3052, f. 6b-7a, M, rubric: אל מלך.
Yemen, commentary by Isaac b. Abraham Wanneh
12226. Chicago-Spertus College of Judaica D 2, 2, f. 192a-192b, M, no incipit.
12227. Jerusalem - Benayahu ת 261, f. 127a, M, rubric: אל מלך.
12228. Jerusalem - Benayahu ת 282, f. 112a, M, no incipit.

---

[280] Edited by Urbach, ערוגת הבושם, vol. III, p. 496-497.
[281] Edited by Urbach, ערוגת הבושם, vol. II, p. 187-194.

12229. Jerusalem - Makhon Ben Zvi 1156 (Tubi 155), f. 109b-110a, M, rubric: אל מלך.
12230. Jerusalem - Makhon Ben Zvi 1174 (Tubi 154), f. 124b-125a, M.
12231. Jerusalem - Michael Krupp 604, f. 139a, M, rubric: אל מלך.
12232. Jerusalem - Musad haRav Kook 325, f. 181b, M, rubric: אל מלך.
12233. Jerusalem - Musad haRav Kook 347, f. 85a-85b, G.
12234. Jerusalem - Sassoon 1158, p. 344-345, M, rubric: אל מלך.
12235. Jerusalem - Sassoon 1174, p. 212, M, no incipit.
12236. Jerusalem - Yehiel haLevi 4, f. 146a-147b, G.
12237. London - British Library Or. 11122, f. 171a, M.
12238. Manchester - John Rylands University Library, Ms. Gaster 5, f 196a-196b, M.
12239. Muenchen - Bayerische Staatsbibliothek, Cod. hebr. 472, f. 149a-149b, M, rubric: אל מלך.
12240. New York - Jewish Theological Seminary Ms. 3013, f. 121b, M, rubric: אל מלך.
12241. New York - Jewish Theological Seminary Ms. 3294, f. 9b-10a, C.
12242. New York - Public Library, Heb. Ms. 9, f. 106b, M.
12243. Philadelphia - University of Pennsylvania HB 2, f. 133a, M.
12244. Strasbourg - Bibliotheque Nationale et Universitaire 3965 (Landauer 39), p. 376-377, M, rubric: אל מלך.

יחיד באחד יוצא משנים (י 2503), יוסף בן יהודה, פיוט לברכו

Ashkenaz
12245. New York - Jewish Theological Seminary Ms. 2577, f. 40a-41b, M.
Carpentras
12246. Parma - Biblioteca Palatina Cod. Parm. 3175, f. 40a-40b, M.

יחיד ויושר ענני סתרי אתה ומגיני

Carpentras, commentary by Josef b. Abraham of Montelitz
12247. Cincinnati - Hebrew Union College 357, f. 96a-96b, M.

יחיד ערץ יסוד ארץ (י 2600), יעקב, אופן

Ashkenaz
12248. London - Montefiore Library 261, f. 85a, C, commentator: Eliezer b. Natan?, rubric: אופן.
Ashkenaz, commentary by Abraham b. Azriel[282]
12249. Vatican - Biblioteca Apostolica ebr. 301,1, f. 79a-79b, C, rubric: אופן.

---

[282] Edited by Urbach, ערוגת הבושם, vol. II, p. 196-199.

יחידה עקבך כרוך (י 2638), יצחק בן זרחיה גירונדי, תוכחה

Ashkenaz
12250. Cambridge - University Library Add. 394,1 (Reif SCR 461), f. 97a-97b, C.
12251. Moscow - Russian State Library, Ms. Guenzburg 190, f. 89b-91a, G.

Roma
12252. Berlin - Staatsbibliothek (Preussischer Kulturbesitz) Or. Oct. 3567, f. 2a, FC, rubric: פירוש הסליחה.

Tsarfat
12253. London - David Sofer 5, f. 103a-104a, C.
12254. Parma - Biblioteca Palatina Cod. Parm. 3006 (de Rossi 654,1), f. 162b-163b, M.
12255. Vatican - Biblioteca Apostolica ebr. 306, f. 213a-213b, C.

יחידתי התאכחי והתאנכי בכל יום תמיד, סליחה

Yemen, commentary by Isaac b. Abraham Wanneh
12256. Chicago-Spertus College of Judaica D 2, 2, f. 214b, M, no incipit.
12257. Jerusalem - Sassoon 1158, p. 366, M, rubric: אל מלך.
12258. London - British Library Or. 11122, f. 183a-183b, M, rubric: אל מלך.

יחידתי מחולת מחנים סגולה חפצי בה, אהבה

Ashkenaz, commentary by Abraham b. Azriel[283]
12259. Frankfurt a M - Stadt- und Universitaetsbibliothek Fol. 16 (Merzbacher 95), f. 67a-70a, C, rubric: אהבה.
12260. Vatican - Biblioteca Apostolica ebr. 301,1, f. 7b-9b, C, rubric: אהבה.

יחיל לבי בקרבי והומה למואב בנהי יסעיר (י 2695), קינה

Carpentras, commentary by Mordekhai b. Josef of Rocco Martino
12261. Cincinnati - Hebrew Union College 246/1, f. 63a, C, rubric: פי' קינה קודם והוא רחום.

יחיל לבי וכצל היו יצורי (י 2697), יוסף, סליחה

Carpentras, commentary by Mordekhai b. Josef of Rocco Martino
12262. Cincinnati - Hebrew Union College 246/1, f. 60a-62a, C, rubric: פי' רהוטה יחיל לבי וכו'.

יחלת עבדיך בחזיוני כתביהם (י 2721), יצחק גיאת, סליחה לתענית אסתר

Yemen, commentary by Isaac b. Abraham Wanneh
12263. Jerusalem - Sassoon 1158, p. 238, M.

---

[283] Edited by Urbach, ערוגת הבושם, vol. I, p. 47-62.

יין כי יתאדם למצוה הוא מוקדם

Tsarfat

12264. Parma - Biblioteca Palatina Cod. Parm. 3136 (de Rossi 405), f. 62a-63b, M.

12265. Vatican - Biblioteca Apostolica ebr. 306, f. 166b-168a, C, no incipit.

ילוד יעקב יצעק לאל שוכן גבוהים (י 2855), יהודה הלוי, סליחה

Yemen

12266. Jerusalem - Benayahu ת 301, f. 44b, G.
12267. Jerusalem - Benayahu ת 414, f. 142b, M.
12268. Jerusalem - Musad haRav Kook 334, f. 147a, M.
12269. Jerusalem - Sassoon 264, f. 153a, M.
12270. Jerusalem - Sassoon 902, p. 401-402, M.
12271. New York - Jewish Theological Seminary Ms. 3028, f. 16a-16b, M, Arabic.
12272. New York - Jewish Theological Seminary Ms. 3052, f. 21a-22a, M, rubric: אל מלך.
12273. New York - Jewish Theological Seminary Ms. 3109, f. 94b-95a, M.
12274. Ramat Gan - Universitat Bar Ilan 62, f. 42a, G.

Yemen, commentary by Isaac b. Abraham Wanneh

12275. Chicago-Spertus College of Judaica D 2, 2, f. 202a-202b, M, no incipit.
12276. Jerusalem - Benayahu ת 261, f. 133b-134b, M, rubric: אל מלך.
12277. Jerusalem - Benayahu ת 282, f. 118b-119a, M, rubric: אל מלך.
12278. Jerusalem - Makhon Ben Zvi 1156 (Tubi 155), f. 116a-116b, M, rubric: אל מלך.
12279. Jerusalem - Makhon Ben Zvi 1174 (Tubi 154), f. 120a-120b, M.
12280. Jerusalem - Michael Krupp 604, f. 146b-147a, M, rubric: אל מלך.
12281. Jerusalem - Musad haRav Kook 325, f. 174a, M, rubric: אל מלך.
12282. Jerusalem - Musad haRav Kook 330, f. 101b, G.
12283. Jerusalem - Sassoon 1158, p. 349, M, no incipit.
12284. Jerusalem - Sassoon 1174, p. 224-225, M, no incipit.
12285. Jerusalem - Yehiel haLevi 4, f. 146b, G.
12286. London - British Library Or. 11122, f. 173a-173b, M, rubric: אל מלך.
12287. Manchester - John Rylands University Library, Ms. Gaster 5, f. 192a-192b, M.
12288. Muenchen - Bayerische Staatsbibliothek, Cod. hebr. 472, f. 158b-159a, M, rubric: אל מלך.
12289. New York - Jewish Theological Seminary Ms. 3013, f. 117b, M, rubric: אל מלך.
12290. New York - Jewish Theological Seminary Ms. 3109, f. 94b-95a, M, rubric: אל מלך.
12291. New York - Public Library, Heb. Ms. 9, f. 117b, M.

12292. Philadelphia - University of Pennsylvania HB 2, f. 130a, M.
12293. Strasbourg - Bibliotheque Nationale et Universitaire 3965 (Landauer 39), p. 362-363, M, rubric: אל מלך.

ימי האדם צבא (י 2904), אברהם אבן עזרא
Carpentras
12294. Cincinnati - Hebrew Union College 392, f. 87b-88b, M, no incipit.
Carpentras, commentary by Josef b. Abraham of Montelitz
12295. Cincinnati - Hebrew Union College 291, f. 46a-48b, C, rubric: פי' תוכחה ימי האדם צבא.
12296. New York - Jewish Theological Seminary Ms. 4197, f. 199b-200b, M, no incipit.
12297. Paris - Ecole Rabbinique 32, f. 207b-208b, M, no incipit.
12298. Strasbourg - Bibliotheque Nationale et Universitaire 4081, f. 182b-183b, M, no incipit.

ימי חדות מעוזכם בניסן (א 2910), יצחק גיאת, לשבת פרה
Ashkenaz
12299. Parma - Biblioteca Palatina Cod. Parm 3000 (de Rossi 378), f. 23a, C, incipit ומעוזכם.
Carpentras, commentary by Mordekhai b. Josef of Rocco Martino
12300. Cincinnati - Hebrew Union College 246/1, f. 43b-44a, C, rubric: פי' ימי חרות מעוזכם.
Sepharad, commentary by Josef Garad
12301. Oxford Bodleian Library Heb.c.10 (Neubauer 2746/1), f. 21b, C, rubric: ימי חדות, no incipit.
Tsarfat
12302. Parma - Biblioteca Palatina Cod. Parm. 3136 (de Rossi 405), f. 56a, M.

ימי חרפי זכרתים (א 2918), יהודה הלוי, אהבה, בתימן: סליחה
Yemen
12303. Jerusalem - Sassoon 902, p. 407, M.
12304. New York - Jewish Theological Seminary Ms. 3052, f. 27a-27b, M, rubric: אל מלך.
Yemen, commentary by Isaac b. Abraham Wanneh
12305. Chicago-Spertus College of Judaica D 2, 2, f. 196b, M, no incipit, very short.
12306. Jerusalem - Benayahu ת 261, f. 137b, M, rubric: אל מלך.
12307. Jerusalem - Makhon Ben Zvi 1156 (Tubi 155), f. 119b-120a, M, rubric: אל מלך.
12308. Jerusalem - Makhon Ben Zvi 1174 (Tubi 154), f. 122b, M.
12309. Jerusalem - Michael Krupp 604, f. 151a, M, rubric: אל מלך.

12310. Jerusalem - Musad haRav Kook 325, f. 178a, M, rubric: אל מלך.
12311. Jerusalem - Sassoon 1158, p. 347, M, no incipit.
12312. Jerusalem - Sassoon 1174, p. 231, M, no incipit.
12313. Jerusalem - Yehiel haLevi 4, f. 152b, G.
12314. London - British Library Or. 11122, f. 172b, M.
12315. Manchester - John Rylands University Library, Ms. Gaster 5, f. 194b-195a, M.
12316. Muenchen - Bayerische Staatsbibliothek, Cod. hebr. 472, f. 163b, M, rubric: אל מלך.
12317. New York - Jewish Theological Seminary Ms. 3013, f. 119b, M, rubric: אל מלך, short.
12318. New York - Jewish Theological Seminary Ms. 3109, f. 94a, M, rubric: אל מלך, no incipit, very short.
12319. Philadelphia - University of Pennsylvania HB 2, f. 131b, M.
12320. Strasbourg - Bibliotheque Nationale et Universitaire 3965 (Landauer 39), p. 370, M, rubric: אל מלך.

ימי פרישה וזמן קדושה (א 2936), יצחק בן זרחיה גירונדי, חלק ז', קדושתא לשבת שקלים
Carpentras, commentary by Mordekhai b. Josef of Rocco Martino
12321. Cincinnati - Hebrew Union College 246, f. 11a-13a, C, rubric: פי' קיקלר ימי פרישה.
Sepharad, commentary by Josef Garad
12322. Oxford - Bodleian Library Heb.e.10 (Neubauer 2746/1), f. 4b-5b, C, rubric: קיקלר.
12323. Oxford - Bodleian Library Heb.e.10 (Neubauer 2746/1), f. 17a-17b, C, rubric: ימי פרישה, no incipit.

ימינך נושא עונו כל, סליחה
Yemen
12324. Jerusalem - Sassoon 902, p. 432, M.
12325. New York - Jewish Theological Seminary Ms. 3052, f. 7b-8b, M, rubric: אל מלך.
Yemen, commentary by Isaac b. Abraham Wanneh
12326. Jerusalem - Yehiel haLevi 4, f. 150a-150b, G.

ימינך נושא עוני פשוטה לקבל תשובה (א 2983), יהודה הלוי, סליחה
Sepharad, commentary by David b. Josef Abudarham[284]
12327. Budapest - Magyar tudomanyos akademia, MS. Kaufmann A 405/2, p. 208-209, C, rubric: פזמון.
12328. New York - Columbia X893 Ab 93, f. 13a-13b, C, rubric: פזמון.

---

[284] Edited by Prins, תשלום אבודרהם, p. 102-104.

Yemen, commentary by Isaac b. Abraham Wanneh
12329. Chicago-Spertus College of Judaica D 2, 2, f. 190b-191b, M, no incipit.
12330. Jerusalem - Benayahu ת 261, f. 127b-128a, M, rubric: אל מלך.
12331. Jerusalem - Benayahu ת 282, f. 112b-113a, M, no incipit, page torn.
12332. Jerusalem - Makhon Ben Zvi 1156 (Tubi 155), f. 110a-110b, M, rubric: אל מלך.
12333. Jerusalem - Makhon Ben Zvi 1174 (Tubi 154), f. 123b-124a, M.
12334. Jerusalem - Michael Krupp 604, f. 139b-140a, M, rubric: אל מלך.
12335. Jerusalem - Musad haRav Kook 325, f. 179b-180a, M, rubric: אל מלך.
12336. Jerusalem - Musad haRav Kook 330, f. 102a, G.
12337. Jerusalem - Sassoon 1158, p. 343-344, M, no incipit.
12338. Jerusalem - Sassoon 1174, p. 212-214, M, rubric: אל מלך.
12339. London - British Library Or. 11122, f. 170a-171a, M, rubric: אל מלך.
12340. Manchester - John Rylands University Library, Ms. Gaster 5, f. 195b-196a, M.
12341. Muenchen - Bayerische Staatsbibliothek, Cod. hebr. 472, f. 150a-150b, M, rubric: אל מלך.
12342. New York - Jewish Theological Seminary Ms. 3013, f. 120b, M, rubric: אל מלך.
12343. Philadelphia - University of Pennsylvania HB 2, f. 132a-132b, M, rubric: אל מלך.
12344. Strasbourg - Bibliotheque Nationale et Universitaire 3965 (Landauer 39), p. 373-374, M, rubric: אל מלך.

יסוד הכל אשר אין לו תחלה (א 3071), יוסף בן יצחק קמחי, פיוט למגילה
Carpentras, commentary by Mordekhai b. Josef of Rocco Martino
12345. Cincinnati - Hebrew Union College 246/1, f. 26a-26b, C, rubric: פי׳ לליל פורים. פי׳ יסוד הכל וכו׳.

יסוד טעם סתרי (א 3082), יצחק גיאת, פזמון לשבת פרה
Carpentras, commentary by Mordekhai b. Josef of Rocco Martino
12346. Cincinnati - Hebrew Union College 246/1, f. 32a-32b, C, rubric: פי׳ פזמון יסוד טעם וכו׳.
Sepharad, commentary by Josef Garad
12347. Oxford - Bodleian Library Heb.e.10 (Neubauer 2746/1), f. 12a, C, rubric: פזמון.
12348. Oxford - Bodleian Library Heb.e.10 (Neubauer 2746/1), f. 20a, C, rubric: יסוד טעם, no incipit.
Tsarfat
12349. London - David Sofer 5, f. 29b, C.
12350. Parma - Biblioteca Palatina Cod. Parm. 3136 (de Rossi 405), f. 50a-51a, M.

יסוד כל הסודות ועמוד העדות, יצחק בן מרדכי קמחי, אזהרות

Carpentras, commentary by Isaac b. Mordekhai Qimhi?
12351. Marseille - Mlle. Odette Valabregue [1], f. 52a-57b, 72a-80b, C.
12352. Moscow - Russian State Library, Ms. Guenzburg 710, f. 72a-87a, 132a-156b, M.
12353. New York - Jewish Theological Seminary Ms. 4268, f. 20b-29b, 49b-62b, M.
12354. Parma - Biblioteca Palatina Cod. Parm. 3491, f. 15b-28b, 40a-62a, M.
Italia, commentary by Isaac b. Mordekhai Qimhi?
12355. Moscow - Russian State Library, Ms. Guenzburg 211, f. 58a-71a, 83a-105b, M.
12356. New York - Columbia University X 893 G 11, f. 11a-23a, 25a-45a, M.

יסף יגון יוספים אומץ באל עליון (י 3101), יהודה לוי, מאורה, בתימן: סליחה

Yemen
12357. Jerusalem - Sassoon 902, p. 403, M.
12358. New York - Jewish Theological Seminary Ms. 3028, f. 18b, G, Arabic.
12359. New York - Jewish Theological Seminary Ms. 3052, f. 24b-25b, M.
Yemen, commentary by Isaac b. Abraham Wanneh
12360. Chicago-Spertus College of Judaica D 2, 2, f. 205a-205b, M, no incipit.
12361. Jerusalem - Benayahu ת 261, f. 136a-136b, M, rubric: אל מלך.
12362. Jerusalem - Benayahu ת 282, f. 120b-121a, M, rubric: אל מלך, no incipit.
12363. Jerusalem - Makhon Ben Zvi 1156 (Tubi 155), f. 118b, M, no incipit.
12364. Jerusalem - Makhon Ben Zvi 1174 (Tubi 154), f. 121b, M.
12365. Jerusalem - Michael Krupp 604, f. 149a-149b, M, rubric: אל מלך.
12366. Jerusalem - Musad haRav Kook 325, f. 176b, M, rubric: אל מלך.
12367. Jerusalem - Musad haRav Kook 330, f. 106a-106b, G.
12368. Jerusalem - Musad haRav Kook 347, f. 85a, G.
12369. Jerusalem - Sassoon 1158, p. 351, M, no incipit.
12370. Jerusalem - Yehiel haLevi 4, f. 152a, G.
12371. London - British Library Or. 11122, f. 174b, M.
12372. Manchester - John Rylands University Library, Ms. Gaster 5, f. 193b-194a, M.
12373. Muenchen - Bayerische Staatsbibliothek, Cod. hebr. 472, f. 161b-162a, M, rubric: אל מלך.
12374. New York - Jewish Theological Seminary Ms. 3013, f. 118b, M, rubric: אל מלך.
12375. Philadelphia - University of Pennsylvania HB 2, f. 131a, M.

12376. Strasbourg - Bibliotheque Nationale et Universitaire 3965 (Landauer 39), p. 367-368, M, rubric: אל מלך.

יספת אלהים לנחלתך (י 3107), יצחק גיאת, פזמון
Sepharad, commentary by David b. Josef Abudarham[285]
12377. Budapest - Magyar tudomanyos akademia, MS. Kaufmann A 405/2, p. 242-243, C, rubric: פזמון לר׳ יצחק גיאת ז״ל.
12378. New York - Columbia X893 Ab 93, f. 26b, C, rubric: פזמון לר׳ יצחק ן׳ גיאת ז״ל.

יעזוב רשע נתיבו ויכניע רום לבבו (י 3136), סליחה
Tsarfat
12379. London - David Sofer 5, f. 104a, C.
12380. Parma - Biblioteca Palatina Cod. Parm. 3007 (de Rossi 654,2), f. 131b, M.

Yemen, commentary by Isaac b. Abraham Wanneh
12381. Chicago-Spertus College of Judaica D 2, 2, f. 200b, M.
12382. Jerusalem - Michael Krupp 604, f. 164a-164b, M, rubric: אל מלך.
12383. Jerusalem - Sassoon 1158, p. 357-358, M, no incipit.
12384. London - British Library Or. 11122, f. 177b-178a, M.

יעירוני רעיוני וסוד לבי (י 3155), יהודה הלוי, תחנון
Yemen
12385. Jerusalem - Benayahu ת 88, f. 107b, M.
12386. Jerusalem - Sassoon 902, p. 358-359, M, no incipit.
12387. New York - Jewish Theological Seminary Ms. 3028, f. 19a, G, Arabic.
12388. New York - Jewish Theological Seminary Ms. 3052, f. 10a, M, rubric: אל מלך.
12389. New York - Jewish Theological Seminary Ms. 3193, f. 113b-114a, M.
12390. Ramat Gan - Universitat Bar Ilan 62, f. 47a, G, margins damaged.

Yemen, commentary by Isaac b. Abraham Wanneh
12391. Chicago-Spertus College of Judaica D 2, 2, f. 188a, M, rubric: אל מלך, very short.
12392. Jerusalem - Benayahu ת 261, f. 128b-129a, M, rubric: אל מלך.
12393. Jerusalem - Benayahu ת 282, f. 113b, M, rubric: אל מלך, very short.
12394. Jerusalem - Makhon Ben Zvi 1156 (Tubi 155), f. 111a-111b, M, rubric: אל מלך.
12395. Jerusalem - Musad haRav Kook 325, f. 175a, M, rubric: אל מלך.
12396. Jerusalem - Musad haRav Kook 330, f. 106a, G.
12397. Jerusalem - Musad haRav Kook 347, f. 83a, G.

---

[285] Edited by Prins, תשלום אבודרהם, p. 146.

12398. Jerusalem - Sassoon 1158, p. 291-292, M, rubric: אל מלך.
12399. Jerusalem - Sassoon 1174, p. 215, M, no incipit.
12400. Jerusalem - Yehiel haLevi 4, f. 145b, G.
12401. London - British Library Or. 11122, f. 153a, M, rubric: אל מלך.
12402. Muenchen - Bayerische Staatsbibliothek, Cod. hebr. 472, f. 151b, M, rubric: אל מלך.
12403. Philadelphia - University of Pennsylvania HB 2, f. 113a-113b, M.
12404. Strasbourg - Bibliotheque Nationale et Universitaire 3965 (Landauer 39), p. 364-365, M, rubric: אל מלך.

יעלה תחנננו מערב (י 3181), סליחה

Ashkenaz

12405. Braunschweig - Landesmuseum fuer Geschichte und Volkstum R 2386, vol. II, f. 158b, M.
12406. London - Montefiore Library 261, f. 38a-38b, C, commentator: Eliezer b. Natan?.
12407. Muenchen - Bayerische Staatsbibliothek, Cod. hebr. 346, f. 145b, C, rubric: אחרת.
12408. Parma - Biblioteca Palatina Cod. Parm. 3270 (de Rossi 1215), f. 81a, M.

Ashkenaz, commentary by Abraham b. Azriel[286]

12409. Frankfurt a M - Stadt- und Universitaetsbibliothek Fol. 16 (Merzbacher 95), f. 105b, C.

יעלו לאלף ולרבבה (י 3184), יהודה הלוי, סליחה

Yemen

12410. Jerusalem - Benayahu ת 414, f. 126a, M.
12411. Jerusalem - Musad haRav Kook 334, f. 131a, M, page damaged.
12412. New York - Jewish Theological Seminary Ms. 3052, f. 2b-3b, M, rubric: אל מלך.
12413. New York - Jewish Theological Seminary Ms. 4488, f. 107a, G.
12414. Ramat Gan - Universitat Bar Ilan 62, f. 39b, G.

Yemen, commentary by Isaac b. Abraham Wanneh

12415. Chicago-Spertus College of Judaica D 2, 2, f. 187a-187b, M.
12416. Jerusalem - Benayahu ת 261, f. 124b-125a, M, rubric: אל מלך.
12417. Jerusalem - Benayahu ת 282, f. 110a-110b, M, no incipit.
12418. Jerusalem - Makhon Ben Zvi 1156 (Tubi 155), f. 108a, M, rubric: אל מלך.
12419. Jerusalem - Makhon Ben Zvi 1174 (Tubi 154), f. 106b-107a, M, rubric: אל מלך.
12420. Jerusalem - Michael Krupp 604, f. 136b-137a, M, rubric: אל מלך.

---

[286] Edited by Urbach, ערוגת הבושם, vol. III, p. 551.

12421. Jerusalem - Musad haRav Kook 325, f. 156b, M, rubric: אל מלך.
12422. Jerusalem - Musad haRav Kook 347, f. 75b, G.
12423. Jerusalem - Sassoon 1158, p. 187, M.
12424. Jerusalem - Sassoon 1174, p. 208-209, M.
12425. London - British Library Or. 11122, f. 167a-167b, M.
12426. Muenchen - Bayerische Staatsbibliothek, Cod. hebr. 472, f. 146b-147a, M, rubric: אל מלך.
12427. New York - Jewish Theological Seminary Ms. 3013, f. 108a, M, rubric: אל מלך.
12428. New York - Jewish Theological Seminary Ms. 3294, f. 2b, C, no incipit.
12429. New York - Public Library, Heb. Ms. 9, f. 103b, M.
12430. Philadelphia - University of Pennsylvania HB 2, f. 120a, M, rubric: אל מלך.

יענה את מהלל יוצרו (י 3233), יהודה הלוי, אופן
Tsarfat
12431. London - British Library Or. 2735 (Margoliouth 663), f. 185a, M, incipit שלשו from Petiḥa, margins cut.

יענה בבור אבות לבן מחטא מזוהם (י 3234), פזמון, בתימן: סליחה
Carpentras
12432. Cincinnati - Hebrew Union College 392, f. 45b, M, no incipit.
Carpentras, commentary by Josef b. Abraham of Montelitz
12433. Cincinnati - Hebrew Union College 291, f. 21b-22a, C, rubric: פי׳ פזמון יענה.
12434. New York - Jewish Theological Seminary Ms. 4197, f. 104b, M, no incipit.
12435. Paris - Ecole Rabbinique 32, f. 126a-126b, M, no incipit.
12436. Strasbourg - Bibliotheque Nationale et Universitaire 4081, f. 103a, M, rubric: אמר הצייד, no incipit.
Sepharad, commentary by David b. Josef Abudarham[287]
12437. Budapest - Magyar tudomanyos akademia, MS. Kaufmann A 405/2, p. 190-191, C, rubric: פזמון.
12438. Cincinnati - Hebrew Union College 490, f. 4b, C.
12439. Holon - Yehuda Nahum 278, f. 13a, FC, rubric: פזמון, incomplete.
12440. New York - Columbia X893 Ab 93, f. 6b, C, rubric: פזמון.
Yemen
12441. Jerusalem - Benayahu ת 414, f. 128a, M.

---

[287] Edited by Prins, תשלום אבודרהם, p. 20.

יעץ הצר תחבולות (י 3249), יהודה הלוי, חלק ב', קדושתא לשבת זכור

Carpentras, commentary by Mordekhai b. Josef of Rocco Martino
12442. Cincinnati - Hebrew Union College 246/1, f. 22a, C, rubric: פי' פזמון יעץ הצר וכו'.

Sepharad, commentary by Josef Garad
12443. Oxford - Bodleian Library Heb.e.10 (Neubauer 2746/1), f. 7b-8a, C, rubric: פזמון.

יערב לך חין ערבנו (י 3267), יחיאל, סליחה

Tsarfat
12444. London - David Sofer 5, f. 146a-146b, C.
12445. Parma - Biblioteca Palatina Cod. Parm. 2890 (de Rossi 856), f. 133a-133b, M.

יערב לפניך כמו קרבן מוספים (י 3274), יוסף, סליחה

Carpentras
12446. Cincinnati - Hebrew Union College 392, f. 76b, M, no incipit, very short.

Carpentras, commentary by Josef b. Abraham of Montelitz
12447. Strasbourg - Bibliotheque Nationale et Universitaire 4081, f. 165a, M, no incipit, very short.

Tsarfat
12448. London - David Sofer 5, f. 167b, C, rubric: פזמון.

יערב מיעוט דמי (י 3277), יוסף, סליחה

Tsarfat
12449. London - David Sofer 5, f. 160b-161a, C, rubric: פזמון.
12450. Parma - Biblioteca Palatina Cod. Parm. 2890 (de Rossi 856), f. 129a, M.
12451. Parma - Biblioteca Palatina Cod. Parm. 3006 (de Rossi 654,1), f. 161a-161b, M.

יפה נוף אנופף בחזיון העודה (י 3348), יוסף אבן אביתור, הושענא

Italia, commentary by Zakharya David Shabbetai Segre
12452. Torino - Archivio Terracini 1499, p. 250-251, C, rubric: פירוש קול מבשר.

North Africa
12453. Jerusalem - Benayahu ז 27, f. 132b-133a, M.

Yemen, commentary by Samḥun b. Salomo Ḥaloah
12454. Jerusalem - Makhon ben Zvi 2808, f. 241a-243a, C.

יפה צביה ראת עיני למולי הלכה, שלם שבזי
Yemen
12455. Cincinnati - Hebrew Union College 398, f. 106b-107b, M.

יפתח ארץ לישע (י 3466), אלעזר ברבי קליר, גשם
Ashkenaz
12456. Berlin - Staatsbibliothek (Preussischer Kulturbesitz) Or. Qu. 798-799 (Steinschneider 177), I, f. 217a-221a, M.
12457. London - British Library Or. 11318/1, f. 146a-152b, C.
12458. Braunschweig - Landesmuseum fuer Geschichte und Volkstum R 2386, vol. I, f. 155b-157a, M.
12459. Budapest - Magyar tudomanyos akademia, MS. Kaufmann A 400, p. 403-411, C.
12460. Fulda - Hessische Landesbibliothek A 3 II, f. 146a-147a, C, commentator: Josef.
12461. Fulda - Hessische Landesbibliothek A 3 II, f. 147a-147b, C, commentator: Josef.
12462. Hamburg - Staats- und Universitaetsbibliothek Cod. hebr. 17/2 (Steinschneider 152), f. 173b-176b, C, rubric: פירוש הסדר.
12463. Hamburg - Staats- und Universitaetsbibliothek Cod. hebr. 132 (Steinschneider 155), f. 66a-70a, C.
12464. Jerusalem - Jewish National and University Library Ms Heb 8° 3037, f. 291a-294b, M.
12465. Jerusalem - Schocken Institute 24100 / Mahzor Nuremberg, f. 502a-504a, M.
12466. London - British Library Add. 18695 (Margoliouth 683), f. 129b-131b, T, Yiddish.
12467. London - British Library Add. 22431 (Margoliouth 662a), f. 139a-143b, M.
12468. London - Montefiore Library 261, f. 78a-80b, C, commentator: Eliezer b. Natan?.
12469. Moscow - Russian State Library, Ms. Guenzburg 615, f. 123b-128a, C.
12470. New York - Jewish Theological Seminary Ms. 4466, f. 463b-468a, M.
12471. Oxford - Bodleian Library MS Mich. 365 (Neubauer 1208), f. 110b-111b, C.
12472. Oxford - Bodleian Library MS Opp. 170 (Neubauer 1205), f. 195a-199b, C.
12473. Parma - Biblioteca Palatina Cod. Parm. 3205 (de Rossi 655), f. 245b-248a, C.
12474. Vatican - Biblioteca Apostolica ebr. 305,1, f. 48a-50b, C, no incipit.
12475. Zurich - Zentralbibliothek Heid. 139, f. 98a-100a, C, additional marginal notes.

Romania

12476. New York - Jewish Theological Seminary Ms. 4823, f. 14b-15b, FG.

12477. Vatican - Biblioteca Apostolica ebr. 320, f. 575a-580b, C, no incipit.

Tsarfat

12478. London - British Library Add. 11639 (Margoliouth 1056), f. 666b-670b, M.

12479. London - David Sofer 5, f. 188a-190b, C.

12480. Moscow - Russian State Library, Ms. Guenzburg 1665, f. 194b-196b, M.

12481. Oxford - Bodleian Library MS Laud. Or. 271 (Neubauer 1206), f. 102a-105a, C, commentator: Aaron b. Hayyim haKohen (compiler).

12482. Parma - Biblioteca Palatina Cod. Parm. 1264, f. 126a-129a, M.

12483. Vatican - Biblioteca Apostolica ebr. 306, f. 118a-121a, C.

12484. Vatican - Biblioteca Apostolica ebr. 320, f. 468b-471a, M.

יצאת לישע עמך כפושים ביד מושל (י 3486), יוסף ב"ר שמואל טוב עלם, חלק ג', קדושתא לפסח

Tsarfat

12485. Parma - Biblioteca Palatina Cod. Parm. 3136 (de Rossi 405), f. 90b, M.

יצאת לישע רעיה (י 3488), יצחק בן זרחיה גירונדי, חלק ג', קדושתא לשבת החדש
Carpentras, commentary by Mordekhai b. Josef of Rocco Martino

12486. Cincinnati - Hebrew Union College 246/1, f. 41a-42b, C, rubric: פי' מחיה יצאת לישע וכו'.

Sepharad, commentary by Josef Garad

12487. Oxford - Bodleian Library Heb.e.10 (Neubauer 2746/1), f. 14a-14b, C, rubric: מחיה.

12488. Oxford - Bodleian Library Heb.e.10 (Neubauer 2746/1), f. 21a-21b, C, rubric: יצאת לישע, no incipit.

יצבתי עמודים באבני פז (י 3491), יצחק גיאת, סליחה

Yemen, commentary by Isaac b. Abraham Wanneh

12489. Chicago-Spertus College of Judaica D 2, 2, f. 213a, M, no incipit.

12490. Jerusalem - Sassoon 1158, p. 374, M, no incipit.

12491. London - British Library Or. 11122, f. 187b, M, no incipit.

יצו אל ממרומו (י 3493), משה אבן עזרא, פזמון

Sepharad, commentary by David b. Josef Abudarham[288]

12492. Budapest - Magyar tudomanyos akademia, MS. Kaufmann A 405/2, p. 213-214, C, rubric: פזמון.

---

[288] Edited by Prins, תשלום אבודרהם, p. 153.

12493. New York - Columbia X893 Ab 93, f. 14b, C, rubric: פזמון.
12494. New York - Jewish Theological Seminary Ms. 3011, f. 21b, C, rubric: פזמון.

יצו האל לדל שואל (י 3497), יהודה הלוי, סליחה
Sepharad, commentary by David b. Josef Abudarham[289]
12495. Budapest - Magyar tudomanyos akademia, MS. Kaufmann A 405/2, p. 209, C, rubric: פזמון.
12496. Cincinnati - Hebrew Union College 490, f. 14b, C.
12497. New York - Columbia X893 Ab 93, f. 13b-13(ii)a, C, rubric: פזמון.
12498. New York - Jewish Theological Seminary Ms. 3011, f. 20b, C.
Yemen
12499. Jerusalem - Musad haRav Kook 334, f. 146b, M.
12500. Jerusalem - Sassoon 902, p. 396, M.
12501. New York - Jewish Theological Seminary Ms. 3052, f. 4a-5a, M, rubric: אל מלך.
12502. New York - Jewish Theological Seminary Ms. 3109, f. 91b, M.
Yemen, commentary by Isaac b. Abraham Wanneh
12503. Chicago-Spertus College of Judaica D 2, 2, f. 188b-189b, M, no incipit.
12504. Jerusalem - Benayahu ת 261, f. 125b-126b, M, rubric: אל מלך.
12505. Jerusalem - Benayahu ת 282, f. 111a-111b, M, no incipit.
12506. Jerusalem - Makhon Ben Zvi 1156 (Tubi 155), f. 108b-109a, M, rubric: אל מלך.
12507. Jerusalem - Makhon Ben Zvi 1174 (Tubi 154), f. 119a-119b, M.
12508. Jerusalem - Michael Krupp 604, f. 137b-138b, M, rubric: אל מלך.
12509. Jerusalem - Musad haRav Kook 325, f. 172b-173b, M, rubric: אל מלך.
12510. Jerusalem - Musad haRav Kook 330, f. 101a, G.
12511. Jerusalem - Musad haRav Kook 347, f. 84a, G.
12512. Jerusalem - Sassoon 1158, p. 342-343, M, no incipit.
12513. Jerusalem - Sassoon 1174, p. 210-211, M.
12514. Jerusalem - Yehiel haLevi 4, f. 150b, G.
12515. London - British Library Or. 11122, f. 169b-170a, M, no incipit.
12516. Manchester - John Rylands University Library, Ms. Gaster 5, f. 191b-192a, M.
12517. Muenchen - Bayerische Staatsbibliothek, Cod. hebr. 472, f. 147b-148a, M, rubric: אל מלך.
12518. New York - Jewish Theological Seminary Ms. 3013, f. 117a, M, rubric: אל מלך, incipit המון.
12519. New York - Jewish Theological Seminary Ms. 3109, f. 92a, M, rubric: אל מלך.
12520. New York - Public Library, Heb. Ms. 9, f. 104b-105a, M.

---

[289] Edited by Prins, תשלום אבודרהם, p. 27-29.

HEBREW LITURGICAL POETRY

12521. Philadelphia - University of Pennsylvania HB 2, f. 129b, M, incipit המון.

12522. Strasbourg - Bibliotheque Nationale et Universitaire 3965 (Landauer 39), p. 360-361, M, rubric: אל מלך.

יצורים וצפון חבם כחומר בימינך (י 3517), יהודה הלוי, סליחה

Yemen

12523. Jerusalem - Sassoon 902, p. 402, M.

12524. New York - Jewish Theological Seminary Ms. 3052, f. 23a-23b, M, rubric: אל מלך.

12525. Ramat Gan - Universitat Bar Ilan 62, f. 42a, G, margins damaged.

Yemen, commentary by Isaac b. Abraham Wanneh

12526. Chicago-Spertus College of Judaica D 2, 2, f. 202a, M, no incipit.

12527. Jerusalem - Benayahu ת 261, f. 135a, M, rubric: אל מלך.

12528. Jerusalem - Benayahu ת 282, f. 119b, M, rubric: אל מלך.

12529. Jerusalem - Makhon Ben Zvi 1156 (Tubi 155), f. 117a-117b, M, rubric: אל מלך.

12530. Jerusalem - Michael Krupp 604, f. 147b-148a, M, rubric: אל מלך.

12531. Jerusalem - Musad haRav Kook 325, f. 174b, M, rubric: אל מלך.

12532. Jerusalem - Musad haRav Kook 330, f. 101b-102a, G.

12533. Jerusalem - Musad haRav Kook 347, f. 83a, G.

12534. Jerusalem - Sassoon 1158, p. 348-349, M, no incipit.

12535. Jerusalem - Sassoon 1174, p. 226, M, no incipit.

12536. Jerusalem - Yehiel haLevi 4, f. 147b, G.

12537. Manchester - John Rylands University Library, Ms. Gaster 5, f. 192b-193a, M.

12538. Muenchen - Bayerische Staatsbibliothek, Cod. hebr. 472, f. 160a, M, rubric: אל מלך.

12539. New York - Jewish Theological Seminary Ms. 3013, f. 117b, M, rubric: אל מלך.

12540. New York - Jewish Theological Seminary Ms. 3109, f. 95b, M, rubric: אל מלך, no incipit.

12541. New York - Public Library, Heb. Ms. 9, f. 115b, M.

12542. Philadelphia - University of Pennsylvania HB 2, f. 130a, M.

12543. Strasbourg - Bibliotheque Nationale et Universitaire 3965 (Landauer 39), p. 363-364, M, rubric: אל מלך.

יצלח מלכי, יצחק הנקדן

Ashkenaz

12544. Oxford - Bodleian Library MS Can. Or. 70 (Neubauer 1147,7), f. 102b-103a, M, rubric: אחרת.

יצרי ויצורי ממך היו (י ++3563), יהודה הלוי, לפסח
Carpentras, commentary by Josef b. Abraham of Montelitz
12545. Cincinnati - Hebrew Union College 357, f. 93a-93b, M, rubric: פירוש.
12546. New York - Jewish Theological Seminary Ms. 4746, f. 27b, M.
12547. Paris - Alliance Israelite Universelle H 422 A, f. 63a-63b, M.
12548. Paris - Ecole Rabbinique 31, f. 132b-133a, M.

יצרי ראשית צרי (י 3566), יהודה הלוי, סליחה
Carpentras, commentary by Eliyahu Carmi
12549. Marseille - Mlle. Odette Valabregue [1], f. 31b-33a, C.
12550. New York - Jewish Theological Seminary Ms. 3151, f. 48b-49a, M.
Carpentras, commentary by Josef b. Abraham of Montelitz
12551. Cincinnati - Hebrew Union College 357, f. 55a-55b, M, rubric: פירוש.
12552. New York - Jewish Theological Seminary Ms. 4746, f. 13a-13b, M.
12553. Paris - Alliance Israelite Universelle H 422 A, f. 32b-33b, M.
12554. Paris - Ecole Rabbinique 31, f. 101a-102a, M.
Sepharad, commentary by David b. Josef Abudarham[290]
12555. Budapest - Magyar tudomanyos akademia, MS. Kaufmann A 405/2, p. 250, C, rubric: פזמון.
12556. New York - Columbia X893 Ab 93, f. 30a, C, rubric: פזמון.
Tsarfat
12557. London - David Sofer 5, f. 168b-169a, C, rubric: פזמון.
12558. Parma - Biblioteca Palatina Cod. Parm. 3007 (de Rossi 654,2), f. 133b, M.
12559. Vatican Biblioteca Apostolica ebr. 306, f. 215a-215b, C.
Yemen
12560. Jerusalem - Sassoon 264, f. 150b, G.
12561. Jerusalem - Sassoon 902, p. 388-389, M.
12562. New York - Jewish Theological Seminary Ms. 3052, f. 10a-10b, M, rubric: אל מלך.
12563. New York - Jewish Theological Seminary Ms. 3109, f. 80b, M.
12564. Ramat Gan - Universitat Bar Ilan 62, f. 42a-42b, G, margins damaged.
Yemen, commentary by Isaac b. Abraham Wanneh
12565. Chicago-Spertus College of Judaica D 2, 2, f. 188b, M, rubric: אל מלך.
12566. Jerusalem - Benayahu ת 261, f. 129a-129b, M, rubric: אל מלך.
12567. Jerusalem - Makhon Ben Zvi 1156 (Tubi 155), f. 111b-112a, M, rubric: אל מלך.
12568. Jerusalem - Makhon Ben Zvi 1174 (Tubi 154), f. 113a, M, rubric: אל מלך.
12569. Jerusalem - Michael Krupp 604, f. 141b, M, rubric: אל מלך.

---

[290] Edited by Prins, תשלום אבודרהם, p. 121-122.

12570. Jerusalem - Musad haRav Kook 325, f. 164a-164b, M.
12571. Jerusalem - Musad haRav Kook 330, f. 95b, G.
12572. Jerusalem - Musad haRav Kook 347, f. 77a-77b, G.
12573. Jerusalem - Sassoon 1158, p. 339-340, M, rubric: אל מלך.
12574. Jerusalem - Sassoon 1174, p. 216, M, rubric: אל מלך.
12575. Jerusalem - Yehiel haLevi 4, f. 148b, G.
12576. London - British Library Or. 11122, f. 168a-168b, M, rubric: אל מלך.
12577. Manchester - John Rylands University Library, Ms. Gaster 5, f. 186a-186b, M.
12578. Muenchen - Bayerische Staatsbibliothek, Cod. hebr. 472, f. 152a, M, rubric: אל מלך.
12579. New York - Jewish Theological Seminary Ms. 3013, f. 112b, M, rubric: אל מלך.
12580. New York - Jewish Theological Seminary Ms. 3294, f. 6a-6b, C.
12581. New York - Public Library, Heb. Ms. 9, f. 108a-108b, M.
12582. Philadelphia - University of Pennsylvania HB 2, f. 125b-126a, M, rubric: אל מלך.
12583. Strasbourg - Bibliotheque Nationale et Universitaire 3965 (Landauer 39), p. 343, M, rubric: אל מלך.

יקדישון ביום שלש שרפי אש נשקה (י 3577), יהודה הלוי, סליחה

Yemen

12584. Jerusalem - Sassoon 902, p. 413, M.

Yemen, commentary by Isaac b. Abraham Wanneh

12585. Chicago-Spertus College of Judaica D 2, 2, f. 203a, M, no incipit.
12586. Jerusalem - Benayahu ת 261, f. 138a-138b, M, rubric: אל מלך.
12587. Jerusalem - Benayahu ת 282, f. 121b-122a, M, rubric: אל מלך, no incipit.
12588. Jerusalem - Makhon Ben Zvi 1156 (Tubi 155), f. 120b, M, rubric: אל מלך.
12589. Jerusalem - Makhon Ben Zvi 1174 (Tubi 154), f. 125a-125b, M.
12590. Jerusalem - Michael Krupp 604, f. 152a-152b, M, rubric: אל מלך.
12591. Jerusalem - Musad haRav Kook 325, f. 181b-182a, M, rubric: אל מלך.
12592. Jerusalem - Sassoon 1158, p. 349, M, rubric: אל מלך.
12593. Jerusalem - Sassoon 1174, p. 231-232, M, no incipit.
12594. London - British Library Or. 11122, f. 173b, M.
12595. Manchester - John Rylands University Library, Ms. Gaster 5, f. 196b-197a, M.
12596. Muenchen - Bayerische Staatsbibliothek, Cod. hebr. 472, f. 164b-165a, M, rubric: אל מלך.
12597. New York - Jewish Theological Seminary Ms. 3013, f. 121b-122a, M, rubric: אל מלך.
12598. New York - Jewish Theological Seminary Ms. 3294, f. 10a, C.
12599. Philadelphia - University of Pennsylvania HB 2, f. 133a-133b, M.

12600. Strasbourg - Bibliotheque Nationale et Universitaire 3965 (Landauer 39), p. 377-378, M, rubric: אל מלך.

יקדש בכוס ישועות ושמחה (י 3579), ישראל איסרלין, לפסח

Italia

12601. Paris - Alliance Israelite Universelle H 10 A/11, f. 117a-125a, C, additional glosses.

יקול אב שמעון מנאמי שרד, שלם שבזי

Yemen

12602. Cincinnati - Hebrew Union College 398, f. 107b-111a, M, very long.

יקול אלמשתואי אללאגב, שלם שבזי

Yemen

12603. New York - M. Lehmann 274, f. 139b, M, kabbalistic.

יקוש בעוניו (י 3608), יצחק, גאולה

Ashkenaz

12604. Jerusalem - Schocken Institute 24100 / Mahzor Nuremberg, f. 139b-140a, M.

Ashkenaz, commentary by Abraham b. Azriel[291]

12605. Vatican - Biblioteca Apostolica ebr. 301,1, f. 19b, C, rubric: גאולה.

יקירים אדירים משרתי אל בהדומו (י 3620), יהודה הלוי, סליחה

Yemen

12606. Jerusalem - Benayahu ת 301, f. 47b, G.
12607. Jerusalem - Benayahu ת 414, f. 137a, M, short.
12608. Jerusalem - Sassoon 902, p. 395, M.
12609. New York - Jewish Theological Seminary Ms. 3052, f. 15a, M, rubric: אל מלך.
12610. New York - Jewish Theological Seminary Ms. 3109, f. 92b, M.

Yemen, commentary by Isaac b. Abraham Wanneh

12611. Chicago-Spertus College of Judaica D 2, 2, f. 193a, M.
12612. Jerusalem - Benayahu ת 261, f. 131a-132b, M, rubric: אל מלך.
12613. Jerusalem - Benayahu ת 282, f. 116b, M, rubric: אל מלך.
12614. Jerusalem - Makhon Ben Zvi 1156 (Tubi 155), f. 114a-114b, M, rubric: אל מלך.
12615. Jerusalem - Makhon Ben Zvi 1174 (Tubi 154), f. 117a-117b, M.
12616. Jerusalem - Michael Krupp 604, f. 144a, M, rubric: אל מלך.
12617. Jerusalem - Musad haRav Kook 325, f. 170a, M, rubric: אל מלך.
12618. Jerusalem - Musad haRav Kook 347, f. 86a, G.

---

[291] Edited by Urbach, ערוגת הבושם, vol. I, p. 120-122.

12619. Jerusalem - Sassoon 1158, p. 340, M, no incipit.
12620. Jerusalem - Sassoon 1174, p. 220, M, no incipit.
12621. Jerusalem - Yehiel haLevi 4, f. 148a, G.
12622. London - British Library Or. 11122, f. 168a, M, rubric: אל מלך.
12623. Manchester - John Rylands University Library, Ms. Gaster 5, f. 190a-190b, M.
12624. Muenchen - Bayerische Staatsbibliothek, Cod. hebr. 472, f. 155a, M, rubric: אל מלך.
12625. New York - Jewish Theological Seminary Ms. 3109, f. 92b, M, rubric: אל מלך.
12626. New York - Public Library, Heb. Ms. 9, f. 110b, M.
12627. Philadelphia - University of Pennsylvania HB 2, f. 128b, M.
12628. Strasbourg - Bibliotheque Nationale et Universitaire 3965 (Landauer 39), p. 355, M, rubric: אל מלך.

יקר אדון הנפלאות לא שבעה עין לראות (י 3628), יהודה הלוי, אופן

Tsarfat
12629. London - British Library Or. 2735 (Margoliouth 663), f. 182b-183a, M, margins cut.

יקר גדלו כבודו מלא עולם ופינותיה (י 3630), יהודה ב"ר קלונימוס, אופן

Ashkenaz, commentary by Abraham b. Azriel (compiler)[292]
12630. Vatican - Biblioteca Apostolica ebr. 301,1, f. 21b-23a, C, commentator: Elazar. b. Yehuda of Worms, rubric: אופן דרבנא יהוד' בר' קלונימוס ופי' הר' אלע' בנו.

יקר יום השבת תגדיל בברית שלום (י 3640), יהודה הלוי, למוצאי שבת

Yemen
12631. Cincinnati - Hebrew Union College 398, f. 98b-99a, M.

יראי יי הללוהו כל זרע יעקב כבדוהו (י 3759), יהודה הלוי, סילוק, קדושתא לראש השנה, בתימן: סליחה

Carpentras
12632. Cincinnati - Hebrew Union College 429/1, f. 12a-13a, M, no incipit.
Carpentras, commentary by Josef b. Abraham of Montelitz
12633. Cincinnati - Hebrew Union College 357, f. 61a-63b, M.
12634. New York - Jewish Theological Seminary Ms. 4746, f. 18a-19b, M.
12635. Paris - Alliance Israelite Universelle H 422 A, f. 23b-25b, M.
12636. Paris - Ecole Rabbinique 31, f. 107a-109a, M.

---

[292] Edited by Urbach, ערוגת הבושם, vol. I, p. 136-144.

Yemen, commentary by Isaac b. Abraham Wanneh

12637. Chicago-Spertus College of Judaica D 2, 2, f. 215a-215b, M, no incipit.

12638. Jerusalem - Sassoon 1158, p. 186, M, no incipit.

12639. London - British Library Or. 11122, f. 181a, M, no incipit.

יראיו בתום מנחה (י 3768), יצחק גיאת, פזמון לשבת זכור

Carpentras, commentary by Mordekhai b. Josef of Rocco Martino

12640. Cincinnati - Hebrew Union College 246/1, f. 23a-23b, C, rubric: פי׳ פזמון יראיו בתום מנחה וכו׳.

Sepharad, commentary by Josef Garad

12641. Oxford - Bodleian Library Heb.e.10 (Neubauer 2746/1), f. 8b, C, rubric: פזמון.

12642. Oxford - Bodleian Library Heb.e.10 (Neubauer 2746/1), f. 18a-18b, C, rubric: יריאו בתום, no incipit.

Tsarfat

12643. Parma - Biblioteca Palatina Cod. Parm. 3136 (de Rossi 405), f. 34a, M.

יראים מבקשי פניך יודעי חביון צמניך (י 3773), יוסף ב״ר שמואל טוב עלם, לראש השנה

Ashkenaz

12644. Moscow - Russian State Library, Ms. Guenzburg 191, f. 51a-52a, M.

12645. Torino - Archivio Terracini 1492, f. 33b, M.

יראך אדון פועל למענך פעלת (י +3776), משולם ב״ר קלונימוס, פיוט לאחרי הקדושה

Ashkenaz

12646. Hamburg - Staats- und Universitaetsbibliothek Cod. hebr. 132 (Steinschneider 155), f. 39a-39b, C.

12647. Muenchen - Bayerische Staatsbibliothek, Cod. hebr. 346, f. 69b-70a, C, no incipit.

12648. New York - Jewish Theological Seminary Ms. 8169 (Acc. 0016), f. 83b-84a, M.

Tsarfat

12649. Oxford - Bodleian Library MS Laud. Or. 271 (Neubauer 1206), f. 107a-107b, C, commentator: Aaron b. Hayyim haKohen (compiler).

12650. Parma - Biblioteca Palatina Cod. Parm. 1794 (de Rossi 1061), f. 150b-151a, M.

יראתי בפצותי שיח להשחיל (י 3787), יקותיאל בר משה, רשות

Ashkenaz

12651. Jerusalem - Schocken Institute 24100 / Mahzor Nuremberg, f. 323a, M.

12652. Muenchen - Bayerische Staatsbibliothek, Cod. hebr. 346, f. 144b, C.
12653. Parma - Biblioteca Palatina Cod. Parm. 3507 (Perreau 27), f. 108a, C.
12654. Vatican - Biblioteca Apostolica ebr. 308, f. 26a, C, commentator: David b. Mose (compiler).
12655. Zurich - Zentralbibliothek Heid. 139, f. 63a (extra leaf bound into volume), C, rubric: זה שייך לעיל קודם את חיל.

Tsarfat

12656. Paris - Bibliotheque Nationale heb. 445,9, f. 61b-62a, C.

ירד צוה אז מענה (י 3799), יצחק בן זרחיה גירונדי, חלק ב', קדושתא לשבת שקלים

Carpentras, commentary by Mordekhai b. Josef of Rocco Martino

12657. Cincinnati - Hebrew Union College 246, f. 7b-8b, C, rubric: פזמון ירד צוה וכו', no incipit.

Sepharad, commentary by Josef Garad

12658. Oxford - Bodleian Library Heb.e.10 (Neubauer 2746/1), f. 2b-3a, C.
12659. Oxford - Bodleian Library Heb.e.10 (Neubauer 2746/1), f. 17a, C, rubric: ירד צוה, no incipit.

ירדו שמי כבדי היה לי עליהם (י 3803), יהודה הלוי, סליחה

Yemen

12660. Jerusalem - Sassoon 902, p. 411, M.
12661. New York - Jewish Theological Seminary Ms. 3052, f. 26a-27a, M, rubric: אל מלך.
12662. New York - Jewish Theological Seminary Ms. 3109, f. 93a, M.

Yemen, commentary by Isaac b. Abraham Wanneh

12663. Chicago-Spertus College of Judaica D 2, 2, f. 206a-206b, M, no incipit.
12664. Jerusalem - Benayahu ת 261, f. 137a-137b, M, rubric: אל מלך.
12665. Jerusalem - Makhon Ben Zvi 1156 (Tubi 155), f. 119a-119b, M, rubric: אל מלך.
12666. Jerusalem - Makhon Ben Zvi 1174 (Tubi 154), f. 122a, M.
12667. Jerusalem - Michael Krupp 604, f. 150b-151a, M, rubric: אל מלך, no incipit.
12668. Jerusalem - Musad haRav Kook 325, f. 177b, M, rubric: אל מלך.
12669. Jerusalem - Sassoon 1158, p. 352, M, rubric: אל מלך.
12670. Jerusalem - Sassoon 1174, p. 230-231, M, no incipit.
12671. Jerusalem - Yehiel haLevi 4, f. 152a-152b, G.
12672. London - British Library Or. 11122, f. 175a, M, rubric: אל מלך.
12673. Manchester - John Rylands University Library, Ms. Gaster 5, f. 194b, M.
12674. Muenchen - Bayerische Staatsbibliothek, Cod. hebr. 472, f. 162b-163b, M, rubric: אל מלך.

12675. New York - Jewish Theological Seminary Ms. 3013, f. 119a-119b, M, rubric: אל מלך.
12676. New York - Jewish Theological Seminary Ms. 3109, f. 93a-94a, M, rubric: אל מלך.
12677. Philadelphia - University of Pennsylvania HB 2, f. 131a, M.
12678. Strasbourg - Bibliotheque Nationale et Universitaire 3965 (Landauer 39), p. 369-370, M, rubric: אל מלך.

ירדת להציל עמך להודיעם ארח (י 3806), יוסף ב"ר שמואל טוב עלם, חלק ה', קדושתלא שבת הגדול

Ashkenaz
12679. Jerusalem - Schocken Institute 24100 / Mahzor Nuremberg, f. 72b, M.
12680. Muenchen - Bayerische Staatsbibliothek, Cod. hebr. 88, f. 50b-51a, G.
12681. Parma - Biblioteca Palatina Cod. Parm 3000 (de Rossi 378), f. 28b-29a, M.
12682. Parma - Biblioteca Palatina Cod. Parm. 3507 (Perreau 27), f. 34a-34b, M, no incipit.

Tsarfat
12683. London - British Library Add. 11639 (Margoliouth 1056), f. 673a, M, incipit יוצאת.
12684. Moscow - Russian State Library, Ms. Guenzburg 1665, f. 46a, M.
12685. Parma - Biblioteca Palatina Cod. Parm. 3136 (de Rossi 405), f. 59b-60a, M.

ירדתי לתחתיות ואבד נצכי (י 3807), יוסף בן סולי, סליחה

Yemen, commentary by Isaac b. Abraham Wanneh
12686. Jerusalem - Sassoon 1158, p. 164, M.
12687. London - British Library Or. 11122, f. 99a, M.

ירומם כל מחולל, יצחק הנקדן

Ashkenaz
12688. Oxford - Bodleian Library MS Can. Or. 70 (Neubauer 1147,7), f. 81b-82a, M.

ירום נופל ונשוף אפל (י 3831), יצחק הנקדן

Ashkenaz
12689. Oxford - Bodleian Library MS Can. Or. 70 (Neubauer 1147,7), f. 103a-104a, M, rubric: אחרת.

ירושלים האנחי ודמעך ציון הסכי (י 3856), יהודה הלוי, סליחה

Yemen
12690. Jerusalem - Sassoon 902, p. 384, M.

12691. New York - Jewish Theological Seminary Ms. 3052, f. 10a, M, no incipit.
12692. New York - Jewish Theological Seminary Ms. 3109, f. 78a, M.
12693. Ramat Gan - Universitat Bar Ilan 62, f. 42b, G, margins damaged.

Yemen, commentary by Isaac b. Abraham Wanneh

12694. Chicago-Spertus College of Judaica D 2, 2, f. 188b, M, rubric: אל מלך, no incipit.
12695. Jerusalem - Benayahu ת 261, f. 129a, M, rubric: אל מלך.
12696. Jerusalem - Benayahu ת 282, f. 113b-114a, M, rubric: אל מלך, no incipit.
12697. Jerusalem - Makhon Ben Zvi 1156 (Tubi 155), f. 111b, M, rubric: אל מלך.
12698. Jerusalem - Makhon Ben Zvi 1174 (Tubi 154), f. 112b-113a, M, rubric: אל מלך.
12699. Jerusalem - Michael Krupp 604, f. 141a, M, rubric: אל מלך.
12700. Jerusalem - Musad haRav Kook 325, f. 164a, M.
12701. Jerusalem - Musad haRav Kook 330, f. 95b, G.
12702. Jerusalem - Musad haRav Kook 347, f. 76b-77a, G.
12703. Jerusalem - Sassoon 1158, p. 339, M, rubric: אל מלך.
12704. Jerusalem - Sassoon 1174, p. 215-216, M, no incipit.
12705. London - British Library Or. 11122, f. 168a, M, rubric: אל מלך, short.
12706. Manchester - John Rylands University Library, Ms. Gaster 5, f. 186a, M.
12707. Muenchen - Bayerische Staatsbibliothek, Cod. hebr. 472, f. 151b-152a, M, rubric: אל מלך.
12708. New York - Jewish Theological Seminary Ms. 3013, f. 112a, M, rubric: אל מלך, very short.
12709. New York - Jewish Theological Seminary Ms. 3294, f. 6a, C.
12710. New York - Public Library, Heb. Ms. 9, f. 108a, M.
12711. Philadelphia - University of Pennsylvania HB 2, f. 125b, M, no incipit.
12712. Strasbourg - Bibliotheque Nationale et Universitaire 3965 (Landauer 39), p. 342, M, rubric: אל מלך.

ירושלים למוגיך הקשי (י 3861), יהודה הלוי, סליחה

Yemen
12713. Jerusalem - Benayahu ת 301, f. 45b, G.
12714. Jerusalem - Benayahu ת 414, f. 143a, M.
12715. Jerusalem - Sassoon 902, p. 407, M, no incipit.
12716. New York - Jewish Theological Seminary Ms. 3028, f. 19b, G, Arabic.
12717. New York - Jewish Theological Seminary Ms. 3052, f. 23b-24a, M, rubric: אל מלך.
12718. Ramat Gan - Universitat Bar Ilan 62, f. 42b, G, margins damaged.

Yemen, commentary by Isaac b. Abraham Wanneh

12719. Chicago-Spertus College of Judaica D 2, 2, f. 204b-205a, M, no incipit.
12720. Jerusalem - Benayahu ת 261, f. 135a-135b, M, rubric: אל מלך.
12721. Jerusalem - Benayahu ת 282, f. 119b-120a, M, rubric: אל מלך.
12722. Jerusalem - Makhon Ben Zvi 1156 (Tubi 155), f. 117b, M, rubric: אל מלך.
12723. Jerusalem - Makhon Ben Zvi 1174 (Tubi 154), f. 120b, M.
12724. Jerusalem - Michael Krupp 604, f. 148a-148b, M, rubric: אל מלך.
12725. Jerusalem - Musad haRav Kook 325, f. 175a-175b, M, rubric: אל מלך.
12726. Jerusalem - Musad haRav Kook 347, f. 83b, G.
12727. Jerusalem - Sassoon 1158, p. 350-351, M, rubric: אל מלך, no incipit.
12728. Jerusalem - Sassoon 1174, p. 226-227, M, no incipit.
12729. Jerusalem - Yehiel haLevi 4, f. 151b, G.
12730. London - British Library Or. 11122, f. 174a-174b, M, no incipit.
12731. Manchester - John Rylands University Library, Ms. Gaster 5, f. 193a, M.
12732. Muenchen - Bayerische Staatsbibliothek, Cod. hebr. 472, f. 160a-160b, M, rubric: אל מלך.
12733. New York - Jewish Theological Seminary Ms. 3013, f. 118a, M, rubric: אל מלך.
12734. New York - Public Library, Heb. Ms. 9, f. 115b, M, no incipit.
12735. Philadelphia - University of Pennsylvania HB 2, f. 130b, M.
12736. Strasbourg - Bibliotheque Nationale et Universitaire 3965 (Landauer 39), p. 365, M, rubric: אֶל מֶלֶךְ.

ירח למועדים בעשותך בתרץ (י 3871), יצחק בן זרחיה גירונדי, קדושתא לשבת החדש
Carpentras, commentary by Mordekhai b. Josef of Rocco Martino

12737. Cincinnati - Hebrew Union College 246/1, f. 35a-39b, C, rubric: פי' לפרשת החדש. פי' ירח למועדים וכו'.

Sepharad, commentary by Josef Garad

12738. Oxford - Bodleian Library Heb.e.10 (Neubauer 2746/1), f. 13a-13b, C, rubric: מגן.
12739. Oxford - Bodleian Library Heb.e.10 (Neubauer 2746/1), f. 20b-21a, C, rubric: פרשת החדש. ירח למועדים, no incipit.

יריעות שלמה איך בתוך אהלי קדר שניתם (י 3897), יהודה הלוי, מאורה, בקרפנטרס: קינה
Carpentras, commentary by Mordekhai b. Josef of Rocco Martino

12740. Cincinnati - Hebrew Union College 246/1, f. 76a-76b, C, rubric: פי' קינה יריעות שלמה.

ירצה לפניך מעמד השחר (י 3912), יצחק בן זרחיה גירונדי, סליחה

Carpentras, commentary by Josef b. Abraham of Montelitz
12741. Cincinnati - Hebrew Union College 291, f. 13b-14a, C, rubric: 'פי סליחה ירצה לפניך.
12742. New York - Jewish Theological Seminary Ms. 4197, f. 77a-77b, C.
12743. Paris - Ecole Rabbinique 32, f. 99a-99b, M.
12744. Strasbourg - Bibliotheque Nationale et Universitaire 4081, f. 76b-77a, C.

ירצה עם אביון (י 3917), יצחק גיאת, סליחה

Ashkenaz
12745. Cambridge - University Library Add. 394,1 (Reif SCR 461), f. 97a, C, very short.

Carpentras
12746. Cincinnati - Hebrew Union College 392, f. 9a-9b, M.

Carpentras, commentary by Josef b. Abraham of Montelitz
12747. Cincinnati - Hebrew Union College 291, f. 5b-6a, C, rubric: ירצה 'פי עם אביון וכו'.
12748. New York - Jewish Theological Seminary Ms. 4197, f. 21b, M.
12749. Paris - Ecole Rabbinique 32, f. 24a-24b, M.
12750. Strasbourg - Bibliotheque Nationale et Universitaire 4081, f. 22b, M.

Roma
12751. Berlin - Staatsbibliothek (Preussischer Kulturbesitz) Or. Oct. 3567, f. 1a, FC.

Sepharad
12752. Skokie - Hebrew Theological College 3, f. 2.14b-15a, M.

Tsarfat
12753. London - David Sofer 5, f. 134a, C.
12754. Parma - Biblioteca Palatina Cod. Parm. 1794 (de Rossi 1061), f. 6a-6b, M.
12755. Parma - Biblioteca Palatina Cod. Parm. 3006 (de Rossi 654,1), f. 113a-113b, M.
12756. Vatican - Biblioteca Apostolica ebr. 306, f. 208a, C, short.

ירצה צום עמך (י 3920), יצחק בן אביגדור, סליחה

Ashkenaz
12757. Braunschweig - Landesmuseum fuer Geschichte und Volkstum R 2386, vol. II, f. 151a, M.
12758. Oxford - Bodleian Library MS Mich. 543 (Neubauer 1212), f. 11a-11b, C, commentator: Isaac b. Jacob (compiler).
12759. Oxford - Bodleian Library MS Opp. 681 (Neubauer 1213), f. 77a-77b, C.

12760. Padova - Biblioteca del Seminario Vescovile Cod. 218, f. 108a, M, short.
12761. Vatican - Biblioteca Apostolica ebr. 422/1, f. 32a, C, short.

Ashkenaz, commentary by Abraham b. Azriel[293]

12762. Vatican - Biblioteca Apostolica ebr. 301,1, f. 170a, C.

Carpentras

12763. Cincinnati - Hebrew Union College 392, f. 33a, M.

Carpentras, commentary by Josef b. Abraham of Montelitz

12764. Cincinnati - Hebrew Union College 291, f. 15a-17a (f. 16 skipped in numbering), C, rubric: פי' סליחה ירצה צום עמך וכו'.
12765. New York - Jewish Theological Seminary Ms. 4197, f. 82a-82b, M.
12766. Paris - Ecole Rabbinique 32, f. 104b-105a, M.
12767. Strasbourg - Bibliotheque Nationale et Universitaire 4081, f. 81b-82a, M.

Tsarfat

12768. London - David Sofer 5, f. 174b-175a, C, rubric: אחר.
12769. Parma - Biblioteca Palatina Cod. Parm. 3006 (de Rossi 654,1), f. 247b-289a, M.

ירצה צור אין כערכו (י 3921), יהודה הלוי, פזמון למגן לראש השנה

Carpentras

12770. Cincinnati - Hebrew Union College 429/1, f. 7a-8a, M, no incipit.

Carpentras, commentary by Eliyahu Carmi

12771. New York - Jewish Theological Seminary Ms. 3151, f. 46b, M.

Carpentras, commentary by Josef b. Abraham of Montelitz

12772. Cincinnati - Hebrew Union College 357, f. 53a-53b, M, rubric: פירוש.
12773. New York - Jewish Theological Seminary Ms. 4746, f. 11a-12a, M.
12774. Paris - Alliance Israelite Universelle H 422 A, f. 30a-31a, M.
12775. Paris - Ecole Rabbinique 31, f. 99a-99b, M.

Tsarfat

12776. London - David Sofer 5, f. 104a-104b, C.

ירצה שוע קהל נועדו (י 3923), ישוע בן יעקב, סליחה

Yemen

12777. New York - Jewish Theological Seminary Ms. 3052, f. 88b, M.

Yemen, commentary by Isaac b. Abraham Wanneh

12778. Chicago-Spertus College of Judaica D 2, 2, f. 239b, M, no incipit.
12779. Jerusalem - Benayahu ת 261, f. 167a, M, short.
12780. Jerusalem - Benayahu ת 282, f. 143a, M.
12781. Jerusalem - Makhon Ben Zvi 1156 (Tubi 155), f. 140b, M, no incipit.
12782. Jerusalem - Makhon Ben Zvi 1174 (Tubi 154), f. 140a, M, short.

---

[293] Edited by Urbach, ערוגת הבושם, vol. III, p. 495.

12783. Jerusalem - Michael Krupp 604, f. 178a, M.
12784. Jerusalem - Musad haRav Kook 325, f. 196a, M, very short.
12785. Jerusalem - Sassoon 1158, p. 419, M, no incipit.
12786. Jerusalem - Sassoon 1174, p. 272, M, no incipit, short.
12787. London - British Library Or. 11122, f. 217a, M, no incipit.
12788. Muenchen - Bayerische Staatsbibliothek, Cod. hebr. 472, f. 196a-196b, M, short.
12789. New York - Jewish Theological Seminary Ms. 3013, f. 135b, M, no incipit, short.
12790. New York - Jewish Theological Seminary Ms. 3294, f. 19a, C.
12791. New York - Public Library, Heb. Ms. 9, f. 132a, M, no incipit.
12792. Strasbourg - Bibliotheque Nationale et Universitaire 3965 (Landauer 39), p. 418, M, short.

ישבחונך בכל מפלל (י 3980), יצחק ב"ר אברהם, יוצר לשבת בראשית

Romania

12793. Vatican - Biblioteca Apostolica ebr. 320, f. 555a-556a, M.

Tsarfat

12794. London - British Library Or. 2735 (Margoliouth 663), f. 164b-166a, M.
12795. London - David Sofer 5, f. 190b-191a, C, rubric: זה פירוש מיוצר משבת בראשית.
12796. Moscow - Russian State Library, Ms. Guenzburg 1665, f. 204a-204b, M.

ישובון עמך לבצרון (י 4002), יוסף ב"ר שמואל טוב עלם, לראש השנה

Tsarfat

12797. London - David Sofer 5, f. 114b, C.
12798. London - David Sofer 5, f. 120b, C, short.
12799. Parma - Biblioteca Palatina Cod. Parm. 3006 (de Rossi 654,1), f. 88b-89a, M, additional commentary in the margins.

ישמח חתן ושושביניו על ארץ יהי ברוכים (י 4086), זמר לחתן

Ashkenaz

12800. Parma - Biblioteca Palatina Cod. Parm. 3205 (de Rossi 655), f. 174b-175b, C.

ישמיענו סלחתי יושב בסתר עליון (י 4116), שלמה בר שמואל בר יואל, סליחה

Ashkenaz

12801. Jerusalem - Schocken Institute 24100 / Mahzor Nuremberg, f. 420a-470b, M, short.

Ashkenaz, commentary by Abraham b. Azriel[294]

12802. Vatican - Biblioteca Apostolica ebr. 301,1, f. 169b, C, rubric: פיזמונים.

ישמע לאדום כשמע מצרים יחילו (י +4123), יניי, חלק ג, קדושתא לשבת הגדול
Ashkenaz

12803. Budapest - Magyar tudomanyos akademia, MS. Kaufmann A 384, f. 109a, M.
12804. London - British Library Add. 18695 (Margoliouth 683), f. 11b, T, Yiddish.
12805. Berlin - Staatsbibliothek (Preussischer Kulturbesitz) Or. Qu. 798-799 (Steinschneider 177), II, f. 48a, M.
12806. Hamburg - Staats- und Universitaetsbibliothek Cod. hebr. 17/2 (Steinschneider 152), f. 31a-31b, C.
12807. Paris - Bibliotheque Nationale heb. 709, f. 44b, C, incipit בתכלית.

ישמעיני אלהים בקראי לנגדו (י 4130), יוסף, סליחה
Yemen

12808. Jerusalem - Benayahu ת 414, f. 143b, M.
12809. Jerusalem - Sassoon 902, p. 406, M.
12810. New York - Jewish Theological Seminary Ms. 3028, f. 17b-18a, G, Arabic.
12811. New York - Jewish Theological Seminary Ms. 3052, f. 24a-24b, M, rubric: אל מלך.
12812. Ramat Gan - Universitat Bar Ilan 62, f. 43a-43b, G, margins damaged.

Yemen, commentary by Isaac b. Abraham Wanneh

12813. Chicago-Spertus College of Judaica D 2, 2, f. 203b, M, no incipit.
12814. Jerusalem - Benayahu ת 261, f. 135b-136a, M, rubric: אל מלך.
12815. Jerusalem - Benayahu ת 282, f. 120a, M, rubric: אל מלך.
12816. Jerusalem - Makhon Ben Zvi 1156 (Tubi 155), f. 117b-118a, M, rubric: אל מלך.
12817. Jerusalem - Makhon Ben Zvi 1174 (Tubi 154), f. 120b-121a, M.
12818. Jerusalem - Michael Krupp 604, f. 148b, M, rubric: אל מלך.
12819. Jerusalem - Musad haRav Kook 325, f. 175b-176a, M, rubric: אל מלך.
12820. Jerusalem - Sassoon 1158, p. 364, M, rubric: אל מלך. חידושין.
12821. Jerusalem - Sassoon 1174, p. 227-228, M, no incipit.
12822. Jerusalem - Yehiel haLevi 4, f. 151b, G.
12823. London - British Library Or. 11122, f. 181b, M.
12824. Manchester - John Rylands University Library, Ms. Gaster 5, f. 193a-193b, M.

---

[294] Edited by Urbach, ערוגת הבושם, vol. III, p. 492-493.

12825. Muenchen - Bayerische Staatsbibliothek, Cod. hebr. 472, f. 160b-161a, M, rubric: אל מלך.
12826. New York - Jewish Theological Seminary Ms. 3013, f. 118a, M, rubric: אל מלך, incipit פוצחי.
12827. Philadelphia - University of Pennsylvania HB 2, f. 130b, M, incipit פוצחי.
12828. Strasbourg - Bibliotheque Nationale et Universitaire 3965 (Landauer 39), p. 366, M, rubric: אל מלך.

ישן אל תרדם וזעוב התלהלהיך (י 4132), יהודה הלוי, סליחה

Yemen
12829. Jerusalem - Benayahu ת 88, f. 107a, M.
12830. Jerusalem - Benayahu ת 414, f. 114a, M.
12831. Jerusalem - Sassoon 902, p. 357, M.
12832. New York - Jewish Theological Seminary Ms. 3052, f. 11a, M, rubric: אל מלך.
12833. New York - Jewish Theological Seminary Ms. 3109, f. 83a, M.
12834. New York - Jewish Theological Seminary Ms. 3193, f. 113a-113b, M.
12835. Ramat Gan - Universitat Bar Ilan 62, f. 44b, G.

Yemen, commentary by Isaac b. Abraham Wanneh
12836. Chicago-Spertus College of Judaica D 2, 2, f. 176a-176b, M.
12837. Jerusalem - Benayahu ת 261, f. 129b, M, rubric: אל מלך.
12838. Jerusalem - Benayahu ת 282, f. 114a-114b, M, rubric: אל מלך.
12839. Jerusalem - Makhon Ben Zvi 1156 (Tubi 155), f. 112a, M, rubric: אל מלך.
12840. Jerusalem - Makhon Ben Zvi 1174 (Tubi 154), f. 97b, M, rubric: בתולעת יעקב, no incipit.
12841. Jerusalem - Musad haRav Kook 325, f. 165a, M.
12842. Jerusalem - Musad haRav Kook 330, f. 96a, G.
12843. Jerusalem - Sassoon 1158, p. 291, M.
12844. Jerusalem - Sassoon 1174, p. 216-217, M, rubric: אל מלך.
12845. Jerusalem - Yehiel haLevi 4, f. 145b, G.
12846. London - British Library Or. 11122, f. 152b, M.
12847. London - British Library Or. 11122, f. 168a, M, very short.
12848. Manchester - John Rylands University Library, Ms. Gaster 5, f. 171a-171b, M.
12849. Muenchen - Bayerische Staatsbibliothek, Cod. hebr. 472, f. 152b, M, rubric: אל מלך.
12850. New York - Jewish Theological Seminary Ms. 3109, f. 83a, M.
12851. New York - Jewish Theological Seminary Ms. 3294, f. 6b, C.
12852. Philadelphia - University of Pennsylvania HB 2, f. 113a, M.
12853. Strasbourg - Bibliotheque Nationale et Universitaire 3965 (Landauer 39), p. 301, M.

12854. Strasbourg - Bibliotheque Nationale et Universitaire 3965 (Landauer 39), p. 344, M, rubric: אל מלך.

ישנה בחיק ילדות (י 4146), יהודה הלוי, רשות

Carpentras
12855. Cincinnati - Hebrew Union College 429/1, f. 17a, M, no incipit.
Carpentras, commentary by Josef b. Abraham of Montelitz
12856. Cincinnati - Hebrew Union College 357, f. 90b, M, rubric: פירוש.
12857. New York - Jewish Theological Seminary Ms. 4746, f. 26a, M.
12858. Paris - Alliance Israelite Universelle H 422 A, f. 60b-61a, M.
12859. Paris - Ecole Rabbinique 31, f. 137a, M.

ישעי וכבודי משגבי ומנוסי (י 4175), יוסף ב"ר שמואל טוב עלם, חלק ג', קדושתא לשבת הגדול

Ashkenaz
12860. Jerusalem - Schocken Institute 24100 / Mahzor Nuremberg, f. 72b, M, no incipit.
12861. Muenchen - Bayerische Staatsbibliothek, Cod. hebr. 88, f. 50a, G.
12862. Parma - Biblioteca Palatina Cod. Parm 3000 (de Rossi 378), f. 27b-28a, C, no incipit.
12863. Parma - Biblioteca Palatina Cod. Parm. 3507 (Perreau 27), f. 33b, C, no incipit.

Tsarfat
12864. London - British Library Add. 11639 (Margoliouth 1056), f. 672b-673a, M, no incipit.
12865. Moscow - Russian State Library, Ms. Guenzburg 1665, f. 45b, M, no incipit.
12866. Parma - Biblioteca Palatina Cod. Parm. 3136 (de Rossi 405), f. 59a-59b, M.

ישעך הראה יה האל גדול דעה (י 4186), יוסף בן יצחק קמחי, הושענא

Yemen, commentary by Samḥun b. Salomo Ḥaloah
12867. Jerusalem - Makhon ben Zvi 2808, f. 101b-103b, C.

ישעך יזכירו עם בך יכתירו (י 4188), יהודה הלוי, קדיש לשבת חנוכה, בתימן: סליחה

Yemen
12868. Jerusalem - Benayahu ת 414, f. 144a, M.
12869. Jerusalem - Sassoon 902, p. 402-403, M.
12870. New York - Jewish Theological Seminary Ms. 3028, f. 17a, G, Arabic.
12871. New York - Jewish Theological Seminary Ms. 3052, f. 24b, M, rubric: אל מלך.

Yemen, commentary by Isaac b. Abraham Wanneh

12872. Chicago-Spertus College of Judaica D 2, 2, f. 198b, M, no incipit.
12873. Jerusalem - Benayahu ת 261, f. 136a, M, rubric: אל מלך.
12874. Jerusalem - Benayahu ת 282, f. 120b, M, rubric: אל מלך, no incipit.
12875. Jerusalem - Makhon Ben Zvi 1156 (Tubi 155), f. 118a, M, rubric: אל מלך.
12876. Jerusalem - Makhon Ben Zvi 1174 (Tubi 154), f. 121a-121b, M.
12877. Jerusalem - Michael Krupp 604, f. 149a, M, rubric: אל מלך.
12878. Jerusalem - Musad haRav Kook 325, f. 176a, M, rubric: אל מלך.
12879. Jerusalem - Sassoon 1158, p. 348, M, no incipit.
12880. Jerusalem - Sassoon 1174, p. 228-229, M, no incipit.
12881. Jerusalem - Yehiel haLevi 4, f. 152a, G.
12882. Manchester - John Rylands University Library, Ms. Gaster 5, f. 193b, M.
12883. Muenchen - Bayerische Staatsbibliothek, Cod. hebr. 472, f. 161b, M, rubric: אל מלך.
12884. New York - Jewish Theological Seminary Ms. 3013, f. 118b, M, rubric: אל מלך.
12885. New York - Jewish Theological Seminary Ms. 3109, f. 96a, M, rubric: אל מלך, no incipit.
12886. New York - Public Library, Heb. Ms. 9, f. 116a, M.
12887. Philadelphia - University of Pennsylvania HB 2, f. 130b-131a, M.
12888. Strasbourg - Bibliotheque Nationale et Universitaire 3965 (Landauer 39), p. 367, M, rubric: אל מלך.

ישפוט תבל בצדק

Tsarfat

12889. Vatican - Biblioteca Apostolica ebr. 306, f. 67b, C.

ישראל בחירי אל ילדי איתניך (י 4216), יצחק כנזי, סליחה

Yemen

12890. Jerusalem - Sassoon 902, p. 436, M.

Yemen, commentary by Isaac b. Abraham Wanneh

12891. Chicago-Spertus College of Judaica D 2, 2, f. 190b, M, rubric: אל מלך.
12892. Jerusalem - Sassoon 1158, p. 354-355, M, no incipit.
12893. London - British Library Or. 11122, f. 176a-176b, M, rubric: אל מלך.

ישראל בחירי אל עבדיך ועדיך (י 4217), יהודה הלוי, רשות לקדיש, בתימן: סליחה

Yemen

12894. Jerusalem - Benayahu ת 414, f. 137a, M.
12895. Jerusalem - Sassoon 902, p. 395, M, very short.
12896. New York - Jewish Theological Seminary Ms. 3052, f. 3b, M, rubric: אל מלך.

Yemen, commentary by Isaac b. Abraham Wanneh
12897. Chicago-Spertus College of Judaica D 2, 2, f. 187b-188a, M, rubric: אל מלך.
12898. Jerusalem - Benayahu ת 261, f. 125a-125b, M, rubric: אל מלך.
12899. Jerusalem - Makhon Ben Zvi 1156 (Tubi 155), f. 108b, M, rubric: אל מלך.
12900. Jerusalem - Makhon Ben Zvi 1174 (Tubi 154), f. 117a, M.
12901. Jerusalem - Michael Krupp 604, f. 137a-137b, M, rubric: אל מלך.
12902. Jerusalem - Musad haRav Kook 325, f. 169b-170a, M, rubric: אל מלך.
12903. Jerusalem - Musad haRav Kook 330, f. 100b, G.
12904. Jerusalem - Sassoon 1158, p. 338, M, no incipit.
12905. Jerusalem - Sassoon 1174, p. 209, M, rubric: אל מלך.
12906. London - British Library Or. 11122, f. 167b, M, rubric: אל מלך.
12907. Manchester - John Rylands University Library, Ms. Gaster 5, f. 190a, M.
12908. Muenchen - Bayerische Staatsbibliothek, Cod. hebr. 472, f. 147a, M, rubric: אל מלך.
12909. New York - Jewish Theological Seminary Ms. 3013, f. 115b, M, rubric: אל מלך.
12910. New York - Public Library, Heb. Ms. 9, f. 104a, M.
12911. Philadelphia - University of Pennsylvania HB 2, f. 128a-128b, M, rubric: אל מלך.
12912. Strasbourg - Bibliotheque Nationale et Universitaire 3965 (Landauer 39), p. 354, M, rubric: אל מלך.

ישראל נושע ביי תשועת עולמים (י 4234), שפטיה בר אמתי, סליחה
Ashkenaz
12913. Braunschweig - Landesmuseum fuer Geschichte und Volkstum R 2386, vol. II, f. 50a-50b, M.
12914. Jerusalem - Schocken Institute 24100 / Mahzor Nuremberg, f. 470b-471a, M.
12915. Oxford - Bodleian Library MS Mich. 543 (Neubauer 1212), f. 8b-9a, C, commentator: Isaac b. Jacob (compiler).
12916. Padova - Biblioteca del Seminario Vescovile Cod. 218, f. 241a, M.
12917. Vatican - Biblioteca Apostolica ebr. 422/1, f. 32a, C, very short.
Ashkenaz, commentary by Abraham b. Azriel[295]
12918. Vatican - Biblioteca Apostolica ebr. 301,1, f. 139b, C, rubric: אחר.

---

[295] Edited by Urbach, ערוגת הבושם, vol. III, p. 294-295.

ישראל עבדיך לפניך נאספים (י 4236), פזמון ליום כפור

Carpentras
12919. Cincinnati - Hebrew Union College 392, f. 77b, M, no incipit, very short.

Carpentras, commentary by Josef b. Abraham of Montelitz
12920. Cincinnati - Hebrew Union College 291, f. 43b, C, rubric: פי' סליחה ישראל וכו'.
12921. New York - Jewish Theological Seminary Ms. 4197, f. 180b, M, no incipit, very short.
12922. Paris - Ecole Rabbinique 32, f. 190a, M, no incipit, very short.
12923. Strasbourg - Bibliotheque Nationale et Universitaire 4081, f. 166b, M.

Sepharad
12924. Jerusalem - Benayahu ז 25, f. 186a-186b, M.

Sepharad, commentary by David b. Josef Abudarham[296]
12925. Budapest - Magyar tudomanyos akademia, MS. Kaufmann A 405/2, p. 244, C, rubric: פזמון, short.
12926. Cincinnati - Hebrew Union College 490, f. 14b, C, short.
12927. New York - Columbia X893 Ab 93, f. 27b, C, rubric: פזמון, short.
12928. New York - Jewish Theological Seminary Ms. 3011, f. 21b, C, rubric: פזמון, short.

Yemen
12929. Jerusalem - Benayahu ת 414, f. 129a, M, short.

ישראל עבדיך שופכים שיחם ורחשם, סליחה

Yemen
12930. New York - Jewish Theological Seminary Ms. 3052, f. 28a, M, rubric: אל מלך.

Yemen, commentary by Isaac b. Abraham Wanneh
12931. Chicago-Spertus College of Judaica D 2, 2, f. 198b, M, no incipit.
12932. Jerusalem - Michael Krupp 604, f. 151b, M, rubric: אל מלך.
12933. Jerusalem - Sassoon 1158, p. 372-373, M, no incipit.
12934. London - British Library Or. 11122, f. 186b, M, rubric: אל מלך.

ישראל עלובים טרודיה, סליחה

Ashkenaz
12935. Muenchen - Bayerische Staatsbibliothek, Cod. hebr. 346, f. 164a, C, short.

ישראל עם קדוש יגל וישמח לבו (י 4239), סליחה

Yemen
12936. Jerusalem - Sassoon 902, p. 436-437, M.

---

[296] Edited by Prins, תשלום אבודרהם, p. 113-114.

Yemen, commentary by Isaac b. Abraham Wanneh
12937. Chicago-Spertus College of Judaica D 2, 2, f. 210b, M, no incipit.
12938. Jerusalem - Michael Krupp 604, f. 143b, M, rubric: אל מלך.
12939. Jerusalem - Sassoon 1158, p. 184-185, M, rubric: אל מלך.
12940. Jerusalem - Yehiel haLevi 4, f. 156a, G.
12941. London - British Library Or. 11122, f. 182a, M, rubric: אל מלך.

ישראל עמך תחינה עורכים (י 4248), יצחק בן מאיר, סליחה
Ashkenaz
12942. Moscow - Russian State Library, Ms. Guenzburg 190, f. 43b, G.
12943. Oxford - Bodleian Library MS Mich. 543 (Neubauer 1212), f. 48a-48b, C, commentator: Isaac b. Jacob (compiler).
12944. Padova - Biblioteca del Seminario Vescovile Cod. 218, f. 60b-61a, M.
12945. Padova - Biblioteca del Seminario Vescovile Cod. 218, f. 61a-61b, M, rubric: אחר.
12946. Padova - Biblioteca del Seminario Vescovile Cod. 218, f. 234b, M.
12947. Padova - Biblioteca del Seminario Vescovile Cod. 218, f. 235a, M.
12948. Parma - Biblioteca Palatina Cod. Parm. 3205 (de Rossi 655), f. 286b, C.
12949. Vatican - Biblioteca Apostolica ebr. 308/1, f. 10a, C, commentator: David b. Mose (compiler).
12950. Vatican - Biblioteca Apostolica ebr. 422/1, f. 26a, C, one line only.
12951. Vatican - Biblioteca Apostolica ebr. 422/2, f. 40a, CG, no incipit, very short.
Ashkenaz, commentary by Abraham b. Azriel[297]
12952. Vatican - Biblioteca Apostolica ebr. 301,1, f. 143a, C.

ישראל עמך תפילה יוסף, סליחה
Tsarfat
12953. London - David Sofer 5, f. 160b, C, rubric: סליחה.

ישרים וכנים הליכי הדרך (י 4263), משה זכות, להושענא רבה
Italia, commentary by Zakharya David Shabbetai Segre
12954. Torino - Archivio Terracini 1499, p. 176-178, C, rubric: פירוש ישרים וכנים הליכי הדרך.

ישרים שלשה ערכו לך תחנה ובמנחת הערב, סליחה
Tsarfat
12955. London - David Sofer 5, f. 167a-167b, C, rubric: פזמון.

---

[297] Edited by Urbach, ערוגת הבושם, vol. III, p. 317.

12956. Parma - Biblioteca Palatina Cod. Parm. 3007 (de Rossi 654,2), f. 137b-138a, M.

ישתחוו להדרת קדש הר אריאל (י* 378), יהודה הלוי, סליחה, גם: משתחוים להדרת

Carpentras

12957. Cincinnati - Hebrew Union College 392, f. 6b, M.

Carpentras, commentary by Josef b. Abraham of Montelitz

12958. Cincinnati - Hebrew Union College 291, f. 4a-4b, C, rubric: פי׳ סליחה ישראל משתחוים וכו׳.

12959. New York - Jewish Theological Seminary Ms. 4197, f. 18a-18b, M.

12960. Paris - Ecole Rabbinique 32, f. 19b-20a, M.

12961. Strasbourg - Bibliotheque Nationale et Universitaire 4081, f. 18b-19a, M.

North Africa, commentary by David b. Josef Abudarham

12962. New York - Jewish Theological Seminary Ms. 5426, f. 62a, M.

Sepharad, commentary by David b. Josef Abudarham[298]

12963. Budapest - Magyar tudomanyos akademia, MS. Kaufmann A 405/2, p. 180-181, C, rubric: פזמון.

12964. Cincinnati - Hebrew Union College 490, f. 1b-2a, C, rubric: פזמון.

12965. Holon - Yehuda Nahum 278, f. 6b, FC, only beginning.

12966. New York - Columbia X893 Ab 93, f. 2b, C, rubric: פזמון.

12967. New York - Jewish Theological Seminary Ms. 3011, f. 2a-2b, C.

Yemen

12968. Jerusalem - Sassoon 902, p. 397, M.

12969. New York - Jewish Theological Seminary Ms. 3052, f. 20b-21a, M, rubric: אל מלך.

12970. Ramat Gan - Universitat Bar Ilan 62, f. 41a, G.

Yemen, commentary by Isaac b. Abraham Wanneh

12971. Chicago-Spertus College of Judaica D 2, 2, f. 195b-196a, M, no incipit.

12972. Jerusalem - Benayahu ת 261, f. 133b, M, rubric: אל מלך.

12973. Jerusalem - Benayahu ת 282, f. 118b, M, rubric: אל מלך.

12974. Jerusalem - Makhon Ben Zvi 1156 (Tubi 155), f. 116a, M, rubric: אל מלך.

12975. Jerusalem - Makhon Ben Zvi 1174 (Tubi 154), f. 118b-119a, M.

12976. Jerusalem - Musad haRav Kook 325, f. 172a, M, rubric: אל מלך.

12977. Jerusalem - Sassoon 1158, p. 371, M, no incipit.

12978. Jerusalem - Sassoon 1174, p. 224, M, rubric: אל מלך, no incipit.

12979. London - British Library Or. 11122, f. 185a-185b, M, no incipit.

12980. Manchester - John Rylands University Library, Ms. Gaster 5, f. 191b, M.

---

[298] Edited by Prins, תשלום אבודרהם, p. 7-8.

12981. Muenchen - Bayerische Staatsbibliothek, Cod. hebr. 472, f. 158a-158b, M, rubric: אל מלך.
12982. New York - Jewish Theological Seminary Ms. 3013, f. 116b, M.
12983. New York - Jewish Theological Seminary Ms. 3109, f. 89b, M, rubric: אל מלך.
12984. New York - Public Library, Heb. Ms. 9, f. 117a, M.
12985. Philadelphia - University of Pennsylvania HB 2, f. 129a-129b, M.
12986. Strasbourg - Bibliotheque Nationale et Universitaire 3965 (Landauer 39), p. 359, M, rubric: אל מלך.

יתגדל אל עליון השם ליראיו עינו (י 4318), אהרן בן יוסף הרופא, פרשת פנחס
Karaite, commentary by Berakha b. Josef haKohen

12987. New York - Jewish Theological Seminary Ms. 3367, f. 133a-134b, C, rubric: פרוש פרשת פינחס.
12988. St. Petersburg - Inst. of Oriental Studies of the Russian Academy B 431, f. 90b-91b, C, rubric: פרשת פינחס.
12989. St. Petersburg - Inst. of Oriental Studies of the Russian Academy B 483, f. 8b-9b, C, rubric: פרשת פינחס.
12990. St. Petersburg - Russian National Library, Evr. IV 50, f. 103a-105b, C, rubric: פינחס.

יתומים היינו בארץ נכרייה (י 4328), קינה
Yemen, commentary by Isaac b. Abraham Wanneh

12991. Jerusalem - Sassoon 1158, p. 170-171, M.
12992. London - British Library Or. 11122, f. 102a-102b, M.

כאהל הנמתח בדרי מעלה (כ 6), הוספה לעבודה
Ashkenaz

12993. Berlin - Staatsbibliothek (Preussischer Kulturbesitz) Or. Qu. 798-799 (Steinschneider 177), I, f. 133a-134a, M.
12994. Braunschweig - Landesmuseum fuer Geschichte und Volkstum R 2386, vol. II, f. 238a, M.
12995. Jerusalem - Jewish National and University Library Ms Heb 8° 3037, f. 195a-195b, M.

כאחלמה קבוע (כ 15), יוסף אבן אביתור, הוספה לעבודה
Sepharad, commentary by David b. Josef Abudarham

12996. Cincinnati - Hebrew Union College 490, f. 13b, C.
12997. New York - Jewish Theological Seminary Ms. 3011, f. 19a, C.

כבודו אהל כהיום ברחמים מלך (כ 61), אלעזר ברבי קליר, אופן לראש השנה

Ashkenaz

12998. Berlin - Staatsbibliothek (Preussischer Kulturbesitz) Or. Qu. 798-799 (Steinschneider 177), I, f. 3a-3b, M.
12999. Braunschweig - Landesmuseum fuer Geschichte und Volkstum R 2386, vol. II, f. 79a-79b, M.
13000. Cambridge - University Library Add. 394,1 (Reif SCR 461), f. 65b-66a, C.
13001. Cambridge - University Library Or. 785, f. 15b-16a, G.
13002. Darmstadt - Hessisches Landes- und Hochschulbibliothek Cod. Or. 15, f. 3a-3b, M.
13003. Hamburg - Staats- und Universitaetsbibliothek Cod. hebr. 12 (Steinschneider 102), f. 3a-3b, G.
13004. Hamburg - Staats- und Universitaetsbibliothek Cod. hebr. 17/2 (Steinschneider 152), f. 104b-105a, C.
13005. Hamburg - Staats- und Universitaetsbibliothek Cod. hebr. 40c (Steinschneider 111), f. 132a, G.
13006. Hamburg - Staats- und Universitaetsbibliothek Cod. hebr. 132 (Steinschneider 155), f. 3a-3b, C.
13007. Hamburg - Staats- und Universitaetsbibliothek Cod. hebr. 225, f. 216a-216b, G.
13008. Jerusalem - Jewish National and University Library Ms Heb 8° 3037, f. 3b-4a, M.
13009. Jerusalem - Schocken Institute 24100 / Mahzor Nuremberg, f. 322a-322b, M.
13010. London - British Library Or. 11318/1, f. 9b-10b, C.
13011. Moscow - Russian State Library, Ms. Guenzburg 1401/2, f. 15b-16a, C.
13012. Moscow - Russian State Library, Ms. Guenzburg 191, f. 33a-33b, M.
13013. Moscow - Russian State Library, Ms. Guenzburg 615, f. 54a-54b, C.
13014. Muenchen - Bayerische Staatsbibliothek, Cod. hebr. 86, f. 5a-5b, G.
13015. New York - Jewish Theological Seminary Ms. 4466, f. 208b-209b, M.
13016. New York - Jewish Theological Seminary Ms. 8097, f. 58a, C, additional glosses.
13017. New York - Jewish Theological Seminary Ms. 8169 (Acc. 0016), f. 2a-3a, M.
13018. New York - Jewish Theological Seminary Rab. 1077/4 (Acc. 02505), f. 21a, FC.
13019. Oxford - Bodleian Library MS Opp. 12 (Neubauer 1029), f. 205a, G, one gloss only.
13020. Oxford - Bodleian Library MS Opp. 172 (Neubauer 1211), f. 1b-2a, C.
13021. Oxford - Bodleian Library MS Opp. 619 (Neubauer 2374), f. 8a, M.

13022. Oxford - Bodleian Library MS Opp. 675 (Neubauer 1210), f. 9b-13a, C.
13023. Paris - Bibliotheque Nationale heb. 653, f. 8b-9a, G.
13024. Parma - Biblioteca Palatina Cod. Parm. 2404 (de Rossi 1104), f. 125a, M, copied from printed edition Saloniki 1550 (Benyamin b. Meir Levi).
13025. Parma - Biblioteca Palatina Cod. Parm. 3205 (de Rossi 655), f. 203a-203b, C, rubric: אופן ליוצר.
13026. Parma - Biblioteca Palatina Cod. Parm. 3270 (de Rossi 1215), f. 17b-18a, M.
13027. Parma - Biblioteca Palatina Cod. Parm. 3507 (Perreau 27), f. 107b-108a, C.
13028. Vatican - Bibliotheca Apostolica ebr. 298/1, f. 4b-5b, C, no incipit.
13029. Vatican - Bibliotheca Apostolica ebr. 308, f. 25a-25b, C, commentator: David b. Mose (compiler), rubric: הא לך האופן.
13030. Vatican - Bibliotheca Apostolica ebr. 308, f. 25b-26a, C, commentator: David b. Mose (compiler), rubric: פ"א.
13031. Vatican - Bibliotheca Apostolica ebr. 422/1, f. 7a, C, rubric: אופן.
13032. Zurich - Zentralbibliothek Heid. 139, f. 56b, C, short, additional marginal notes.

Asti, Fossano, Moncalvo

13033. New Haven - Yale University, Beinecke Rare Book and MS Library, MS Heb. 52, f. 16b, M.
13034. New Haven - Yale University, Beinecke Rare Book and MS Library, MS Heb. 52, f. 50b-51a, M.

Roma

13035. Jerusalem - Jewish National and University Library Ms Heb 8° 4153, f. 134a-134b, C, commentator: Daniel ben Salomo haRofe (compiler), rubric: אופן.
13036. Oxford - Bodleian Library MS Mich. 312,1 (Neubauer 2276,1), f. 3a-3b, C, incipit אופן.

Romania

13037. Vatican - Biblioteca Apostolica ebr. 320, f. 146a-146b, M.

Tsarfat

13038. London - British Library Add. 11639 (Margoliouth 1056), f. 708a, M.
13039. London - British Library Or. 8682, f. 4a, GI.
13040. London - David Sofer 5, f. 107b-108a, C, rubric: אופן.
13041. Manchester - John Rylands University Library, Ms. Gaster 733, f. 80a, C, commentary block in Mahzor, manuscript damaged.
13042. Oxford - Bodleian Library MS Laud. Or. 271 (Neubauer 1206), f. 138b-139a, C, commentator: Aaron b. Hayyim haKohen (compiler), rubric: אופן.
13043. Oxford - Bodleian Library MS Opp. 171 (Neubauer 1207), f. 53b, C, rubric: אופן.

13044. Paris - Bibliotheque Nationale heb. 445,9, f. 61a-61b, C.
13045. Parma - Biblioteca Palatina Cod. Parm. 1794 (de Rossi 1061), f. 53b-54b, M.
13046. Parma - Biblioteca Palatina Cod. Parm. 2125 (de Rossi 812), f. 4b-5a, C.
13047. Parma - Biblioteca Palatina Cod. Parm. 3006 (de Rossi 654,1), f. 19b-20a, M.
13048. Parma - Biblioteca Palatina Cod. Parm. 3006 (de Rossi 654,1), f. 66a-66b, M.
13049. Vatican - Biblioteca Apostolica ebr. 306, f. 46b, C.

כבודו אור יזריח במקדש קדש גיה נרות נחזה (כ 64), אופן לשבת ראשון של חנוכה
Ashkenaz
13050. Budapest - Magyar tudomanyos akademia, MS. Kaufmann A 399, p. 405, C, rubric: אופן של חנוכה.
13051. Oxford - Bodleian Library MS Can. Or. 82 (Neubauer 1148), f. 13a, M, very short.
13052. Parma - Biblioteca Palatina Cod. Parm. 3205 (de Rossi 655), f. 139b-140a, C, rubric: אופן.

כבודו אות בריבו אות (כ 66), מאיר ב"ר יצחק, אופן
Ashkenaz
13053. Jerusalem - Schocken Institute 24100 / Mahzor Nuremberg, f. 185a-185b, M.
13054. Muenchen - Bayerische Staatsbibliothek, Cod. hebr. 69, f. 56b-57a, M.
Ashkenaz, commentary by Abraham b. Azriel[299]
13055. Vatican - Biblioteca Apostolica ebr. 301,1, f. 32a-35b, C, rubric: אופן דר' מאיר שליח ציבור מאבלי ציון, אע"פ שאין בו סימן, קבלה היא שהוא פיוטו.

כבודו אפוד להנשא (כ 71), משה סופר, אופן לחתן
Ashkenaz
13056. Jerusalem - Schocken Institute 24100 / Mahzor Nuremberg, f. 224a-224b, M.
13057. Muenchen - Bayerische Staatsbibliothek, Cod. hebr. 69, f. 79b-80b, M.
Ashkenaz, commentary by Abraham b. Azriel[300]
13058. Frankfurt a M - Stadt- und Universitaetsbibliothek Fol. 16 (Merzbacher 95), f. 77b-79b, C, rubric: אופן.

---

[299] Edited by Urbach, ערוגת הבושם, vol. I, p. 197-217.
[300] Edited by Urbach, ערוגת הבושם, vol. III, p. 122-132.

13059. Vatican - Biblioteca Apostolica ebr. 301,1, f. 113b-115a, C, rubric: אופן.

כבודו אראלים מספרים בועד (כ 72), מנחם, קדושה למנחה יום כפור
Ashkenaz
13060. Fulda - Hessische Landesbibliothek A 3 II, f. 128b-129a, C, commentator: Josef.
13061. Oxford - Bodleian Library MS Opp. 170 (Neubauer 1205), f. 181b-182a, C, rubric: קדושתא.
Tsarfat
13062. Oxford - Bodleian Library MS Laud. Or. 271 (Neubauer 1206), f. 118b, C, commentator: Aaron b. Hayyim haKohen (compiler), no incipit, very short.

כהושעת אב המון השליך עליך יהב (כ 108), הושענא
Ashkenaz
13063. Berlin - Staatsbibliothek (Preussischer Kulturbesitz) Or. Qu. 798-799 (Steinschneider 177), I, f. 206b-207b, M.
13064. Budapest - Magyar tudomanyos akademia, MS. Kaufmann A 399, p. 309-310, C.
13065. Cambridge - University Library Add. 394,1 (Reif SCR 461), f. 75a-75b, C, rubric: הושענא.
13066. Frankfurt a M - Stadt- und Universitaetsbibliothek Oct. 227, f. 114b, M.
13067. London - British Library Add. 18695 (Margoliouth 683), f. 153a-153b, T, Yiddish.
13068. London - British Library Add. 22431 (Margoliouth 662a), f. 117b, M.
13069. London - British Library Add. 27208 (Margolioth 654), f. 284b-285b, M.
13070. London - British Library Add. 27556, f. 131a-131b, M.
13071. Lund - Universitetsbibliothek Ms. L.O. 2, f. 87a, M, two commentaries on the same page.
13072. New York - Jewish Theological Seminary Ms. 4466, f. 486a-486b, M.
13073. Parma - Biblioteca Palatina Cod. Parm. 2895, p. 213-214, M.
13074. Parma - Biblioteca Palatina Cod. Parm. 3057.9 (de Rossi 1033), f. 95a-95b, C.
13075. Parma - Biblioteca Palatina Cod. Parm. 3205 (de Rossi 655), f. 250b-251a, C.
13076. Vatican - Biblioteca Apostolica ebr. 308, f. 157b-158a, C, commentator: David b. Mose (compiler), incipit אב.
Italia, commentary by Zakharya David Shabbetai Segre
13077. Torino - Archivio Terracini 1499, p. 140-144, C, rubric: פירוש כהושעת אב המון.

Romania
13078. Vatican - Biblioteca Apostolica ebr. 285/30, f. 232a-232b, C.
Tsarfat
13079. Cambridge - University Library Add. 561.1, f. 113a-113b, M.
13080. Jerusalem - Schocken Institute 19623, f. 123a-123b, M, commentator: Yehuda b. Eliezer Zvi.
13081. London - British Library Or. 2735 (Margoliouth 663), f. 140b-141a, M.
13082. Moscow - Russian State Library, Ms. Guenzburg 1665, f. 182b-183a, M.
13083. Parma - Biblioteca Palatina Cod. Parm. 1902, f. 173b-174b, M.

כהושעת אלים בלוד עמך בצאת לישע עמך (כ 110), הושענא

Ashkenaz
13084. Berlin - Staatsbibliothek (Preussischer Kulturbesitz) Or. Qu. 798-799 (Steinschneider 177), I, f. 207b, M.
13085. Budapest - Magyar tudomanyos akademia, MS. Kaufmann A 399, p. 302-303, C.
13086. Cambridge - University Library Add. 394,1 (Reif SCR 461), f. 75b-76a, C, rubric: הושענא.
13087. Frankfurt a M - Stadt- und Universitaetsbibliothek Oct. 227, f. 114b-115b, M.
13088. Jerusalem - Schocken Institute 24100 / Mahzor Nuremberg, f. 494a-494b, M.
13089. London - British Library Add. 18695 (Margoliouth 683), f. 152a-152b, T, Yiddish.
13090. London - British Library Add. 22431 (Margoliouth 662a), f. 123a, M.
13091. London - British Library Add. 27208 (Margolioth 654), f. 271b, M.
13092. London - British Library Add. 27208 (Margolioth 654), f. 272a, M, rubric: פי' אחר.
13093. New York - Jewish Theological Seminary Ms. 4466, f. 480a, M, incipit אלים.
13094. Oxford - Bodleian Library MS Mich. 573 (Neubauer 1099), f. 20b-21a, M.
13095. Oxford - Bodleian Library MS Opp 160 (Neubauer 1204), f. 238b-240a, C, commentator: Elazar b. Yehuda of Worms.[301]
13096. Parma - Biblioteca Palatina Cod. Parm. 2895, p. 220-221, M.
13097. Parma - Biblioteca Palatina Cod. Parm. 3057.9 (de Rossi 1033), f. 94b-95a, C.
13098. Parma - Biblioteca Palatina Cod. Parm. 3205 (de Rossi 655), f. 250a-250b, C.
13099. Uppsala - Universitetsbibliotek O.Heb.22, f. 112b-113a, M.

---

[301] Edited by Katzenellenbogen, פירוש ההושענות, p. 43-48.

13100. Vatican - Biblioteca Apostolica ebr. 305,1, f. 44a, C, no incipit.
13101. Vatican - Biblioteca Apostolica ebr. 308, f. 157b, C, commentator: David b. Mose (compiler), incipit אלים.

Ashkenaz, commentary by Eliezer b. Natan
13102. London - Montefiore Library 261, f. 89a-89b, C.
13103. Paris - Bibliotheque Nationale heb. 327/2, f. 43a-44a, C.

Italia
13104. Moscow - Russian State Library, Ms. Guenzburg 1594, f. 24b, C, no incipit.
13105. Moscow - Russian State Library, Ms. Guenzburg 533, f. 37b-39b, C, commentator: Yehoshua Segre, rubric: לימוד ט"ו.

Italia, commentary by Zakharya David Shabbetai Segre
13106. Torino - Archivio Terracini 1499, p. 57-65, C, rubric: הקדמה לפירוש (60). פירוש כהושעת אלים בלוד עמך (57) כהושעת אלים בלוד עמך.

Roma
13107. Jerusalem - Jewish National and University Library Ms Heb 8° 4153, f. 143a-143b, C, commentator: Daniel ben Salomo haRofe (compiler).
13108. Oxford - Bodleian Library MS Mich. 312,1 (Neubauer 2276,1), f. 11a-11b, C.

Romania
13109. London - London School of Jewish Studies. Asher I.Myers collection 9, f. 211b, M.
13110. Roma - Collegio Rabbinico Italiano 110, f. 3b-4a, M.
13111. Vatican - Biblioteca Apostolica ebr. 285/30, f. 231b-232a, C.
13112. Vatican - Biblioteca Apostolica ebr. 320, f. 447a-447b, M.

Tsarfat
13113. Cambridge - University Library Add. 561.1, f. 113b, M, incipit אלי' בלוד.
13114. Jerusalem - Schocken Institute 19623, f. 123b-124a, M, commentator: Yehuda b. Eliezer Zvi.
13115. London - British Library Or. 2735 (Margoliouth 663), f. 139a-140a, M.
13116. Moscow - Russian State Library, Ms. Guenzburg 1665, f. 182b, M.
13117. New York - Jewish Theological Seminary Ms. 4460, f. 81a, G.
13118. Parma - Biblioteca Palatina Cod. Parm. 1264, f. 97b-98a, M.
13119. Parma - Biblioteca Palatina Cod. Parm. 1902, f. 173a-173b, M.

כהושעת טמון גומא לשדים צמא (כ 113), יוסף ב"ר שמואל טוב עלם, הושענא

Tsarfat
13120. Jerusalem - Schocken Institute 19623, f. 124a-124b, M, commentator: Yehuda b. Eliezer Zvi.
13121. London - British Library Or. 2735 (Margoliouth 663), f. 142a, M, ecclectic.
13122. London - David Sofer 5, f. 192a, C.

כהושעת יגיעי נשם ומוכי גו וגשם (כ 114), יוסף אבן אביתור, הושענא

Carpentras
13123. New York - Jewish Theological Seminary Ms. 1609, f. 98b, C, kabbalistic, no incipit.

haAri, commentary by Mose b. Hayyim Pesante
13124. New York - Columbia University X 893 J 558, f. 202a-202b, M.

Narbonne, commentary by Meir Meili of Narbonne[302]
13125. London - British Library Add. 19778, f. 35b-36a, C, no incipit.

North Africa, commentary by Yehuda Toledano
13126. New York - Jewish Theological Seminary Ms. 4300, f. 14b-16a, C.

Yemen, commentary by Samḥun b. Salomo Ḥaloah
13127. Jerusalem - Makhon ben Zvi 2808, f. 52a-54b, C.

כהושעת ידידים מכף מעבידים (כ 116), יוסף אבן אביתור, הושענא

Carpentras
13128. New York - Jewish Theological Seminary Ms. 1609, f. 98b, C, kabbalistic, no incipit.

haAri, commentary by Mose b. Hayyim Pesante
13129. New York - Columbia University X 893 J 558, f. 203a-203b, M.
13130. New York - Jewish Theological Seminary Ms. 4696, f. 23b-24a, C, no incipit.

North Africa
13131. Jerusalem - Benayahu ז 27, f. 128b, M, no incipit.

North Africa, commentary by Yehuda Toledano
13132. New York - Jewish Theological Seminary Ms. 4300, f. 20b-21b, C, no incipit.
13133. New York - Jewish Theological Seminary Ms. 4300, f. 56a-57a, C.

Yemen, commentary by Samḥun b. Salomo Ḥaloah
13134. Jerusalem - Makhon ben Zvi 2808, f. 72b-75b, C, no incipit.
13135. Jerusalem - Makhon ben Zvi 2808, f. 202b-207b, C, no incipit.

כהושעת ידידים מכף מעבידים (כ 117), יוסף אבן אביתור, הושענא

Narbonne, commentary by Meir Meili of Narbonne[303]
13136. London - British Library Add. 19778, f. 36a, C, no incipit.

כהושעת יהודה ואפרים מיד מלך מצרים (כ 118), יצחק, הושענא

Narbonne, commentary by Meir Meili of Narbonne[304]
13137. London - British Library Add. 19778, f. 37b-38a, C, no incipit.

---

[302] Edited by Sofer, ספר המכתם, p. 153.
[303] Edited by Sofer, ספר המכתם, p. 155.
[304] Edited by Sofer, ספר המכתם, p. 162-163.

כהושעת יוצאי חנס במופת ונס (כ 119), הושענא
Narbonne, commentary by Meir Meili of Narbonne[305]
13138. London - British Library Add. 19778, f. 36a, C, no incipit, very short.
Yemen, commentary by Samḥun b. Salomo Ḥaloah
13139. Jerusalem - Makhon ben Zvi 2808, f. 55a-56a, C.

כהושעת יוצאי פתרוס ורעצת ערוץ (כ 120), יוסף אבן אביתור, הושענא
haAri, commentary by Mose b. Hayyim Pesante
13140. New York - Columbia University X 893 J 558, f. 207b-208a, M.
13141. New York - Jewish Theological Seminary Ms. 4696, f. 20b-21a, C.
North Africa, commentary by Simon b. Tsemaḥ Duran
13142. New York - Jewish Theological Seminary Ms. 4121, f. 48a, C, no incipit.
North Africa, commentary by Yehuda Toledano
13143. New York - Jewish Theological Seminary Ms. 4300, f. 39a-39b, C.
Yemen, commentary by Isaac b. Abraham Wanneh
13144. Jerusalem - Benayahu ת 261, f. 85b, M, rubric: חידושין, no incipit.
13145. Jerusalem - Benayahu ת 282, f. 78b, M, no incipit.
13146. Jerusalem - Makhon Ben Zvi 1156 (Tubi 155), f. 77b, M, no incipit.
13147. Jerusalem - Makhon Ben Zvi 1174 (Tubi 154), f. 88a, M, no incipit.
13148. Jerusalem - Musad haRav Kook 325, f. 127b, M, no incipit.
13149. Jerusalem - Sassoon 1158, p. 219-220, M, no incipit.
13150. Jerusalem - Sassoon 1174, p. 149, M, rubric: פירוש, no incipit.
13151. New York - Jewish Theological Seminary Ms. 3028, f. 250b, C, no incipit.
13152. New York - Jewish Theological Seminary Ms. 3108, f. 83a, C, no incipit.
13153. New York - Jewish Theological Seminary Ms. 3193, f. 169b, M.
13154. New York - Jewish Theological Seminary Ms. 3295, f. 94b, M.
13155. Strasbourg - Bibliotheque Nationale et Universitaire 3965 (Landauer 39), p. 248-249, M, no incipit.
Yemen, commentary by Samḥun b. Salomo Ḥaloah
13156. Jerusalem - Makhon ben Zvi 2808, f. 166b-168a, C.
Yemen, commentary by Simon b. Tsemaḥ Duran
13157. Jerusalem - Michael Krupp 1758, f. 21a-21b, M, rubric: פירוש, no incipit.

כהושעת יחילי תור מארץ כפתור (כ 121), יוסף אבן אביתור, הושענא
Narbonne, commentary by Meir Meili of Narbonne[306]
13158. London - British Library Add. 19778, f. 37b, C, no incipit.

---

[305] Edited by Sofer, ספר המכתם, p. 154.
[306] Edited by Sofer, ספר המכתם, p. 161.

Yemen, commentary by Samḥun b. Salomo Ḥaloah
13159. Jerusalem - Makhon ben Zvi 2808, f. 148b-149b, C.

כהושעת ילידי אהב מאור הלהב (כ 122), יוסף אבן אביתור, הושענא
haAri, commentary by Mose b. Hayyim Pesante
13160. New York - Columbia University X 893 J 558, f. 206a-206b, M.
13161. New York - Jewish Theological Seminary Ms. 4696, f. 19b, C.
Narbonne, commentary by Meir Meili of Narbonne[307]
13162. London - British Library Add. 19778, f. 37b, C, no incipit.
North Africa, commentary by Yehuda Toledano
13163. New York - Jewish Theological Seminary Ms. 4300, f. 34b-36a, C.
Yemen, commentary by Samḥun b. Salomo Ḥaloah
13164. Jerusalem - Makhon ben Zvi 2808, f. 147a-148b, C.

כהושעת יפה נוף ממכלא מוף (כ 123), יוסף אבן אביתור, הושענא
Narbonne, commentary by Meir Meili of Narbonne[308]
13165. London - British Library Add. 19778, f. 36a, C, no incipit, very short.

כהושעת יקושי מלבן מרמסת התבן (כ 124), יוסף אבן אביתור, הושענא
haAri, commentary by Mose b. Hayyim Pesante
13166. New York - Columbia University X 893 J 558, f. 205a-205b, M.
Narbonne, commentary by Meir Meili of Narbonne[309]
13167. London - British Library Add. 19778, f. 37a, C, no incipit.
North Africa, commentary by Yehuda Toledano
13168. New York - Jewish Theological Seminary Ms. 4300, f. 29a-30a, C.
Yemen, commentary by Samḥun b. Salomo Ḥaloah
13169. Jerusalem - Makhon ben Zvi 2808, f. 122a-124b, C.

כהושעת יקיר משוד מקרקר קיר (כ 125), יוסף אבן אביתור, הושענא
haAri, commentary by Mose b. Hayyim Pesante
13170. New York - Columbia University X 893 J 558, f. 204a-204b, M.
Narbonne, commentary by Meir Meili of Narbonne[310]
13171. London - British Library Add. 19778, f. 36b, C, no incipit.
North African, commentary by Yehuda Toledano
13172. New York - Jewish Theological Seminary Ms. 4300, f. 24b-25a, C.
Yemen, commentary by Samḥun b. Salomo Ḥaloah
13173. Jerusalem - Makhon ben Zvi 2808, f. 98a-101b, C.

---

[307] Edited by Sofer, ספר המכתם, p. 160-161.
[308] Edited by Sofer, ספר המכתם, p. 155.
[309] Edited by Sofer, ספר המכתם, p. 159.
[310] Edited by Sofer, ספר המכתם, p. 156-157.

כהושעת ירויי היאור בעוזך הנאור (כ 126), יוסף אבן אביתור, הושענא

Carpentras

13174. New York - Jewish Theological Seminary Ms. 1609, f. 98a, C, kabblistic, no incipit.

haAri, commentary by Mose b. Hayyim Pesante

13175. New York - Columbia University X 893 J 558, f. 200b-201a, M.

13176. New York - Jewish Theological Seminary Ms. 4696, f. 11a-11b, C.

haAri, commentary by Simon b. Tsemaḥ Duran

13177. New York - Columbia University X 893 J 558, f. 200b-201a, M.

Narbonne, commentary by Meir Meili of Narbonne[311]

13178. London - British Library Add. 19778, f. 35a-36a, C, no incipit.

North Africa, commentary by Yehuda Toledano

13179. New York - Jewish Theological Seminary Ms. 4300, f. 9b-10b, C.

Yemen, commentary by commentator: Samḥun b. Salomo Ḥaloah

13180. Jerusalem - Makhon ben Zvi 2808, f. 25b-30a, C.

כהושעת מאז עדתך כן הושיעה את עמך, הושענא

Yemen, commentary by Samḥun b. Salomo Ḥaloah

13181. Jerusalem - Makhon ben Zvi 2808, f. 30a, C.

כי אם שם אדיר (כ ++182), אופן, הוספה לאילי שחק עומדים

Ashkenaz

13182. Berlin - Staatsbibliothek (Preussischer Kulturbesitz) Or. Qu. 798-799 (Steinschneider 177), I, f. 54(i)a-54(i)b, M.

13183. Braunschweig - Landesmuseum fuer Geschichte und Volkstum R 2386, vol. II, f. 124b, M.

13184. Oxford - Bodleian Library MS Can. Or. 82 (Neubauer 1148), f. 39a-40a, M.

13185. Oxford - Bodleian Library MS Mich. 365 (Neubauer 1208), f. 9a-9b, C.

13186. Parma - Biblioteca Palatina Cod. Parm. 2895, p. 411-412, M, rubric: אופן, margins cut, text damaged.

13187. Parma - Biblioteca Palatina Cod. Parm. 3205 (de Rossi 655), f. 167a-167b, C, rubric: פירוש האופן.

כי אקח מועד לבא לקץ (כ 189), אלעזר ברבי קליר, סילוק, קדושתא ליום א' של סוכות

Ashkenaz

13188. Berlin - Staatsbibliothek (Preussischer Kulturbesitz) Or. Qu. 798-799 (Steinschneider 177), I, f. 193b-195b, M.

13189. Braunschweig - Landesmuseum fuer Geschichte und Volkstum R 2386, vol. I, f. 136b-138a, M.

---

[311] Edited by Sofer, ספר המכתם, p. 151-152.

13190. Budapest - Magyar tudomanyos akademia, MS. Kaufmann A 400, p. 379-381, C, rubric: סילוק.
13191. Fulda - Hessische Landesbibliothek A 3 II, f. 134b-135b, C, commentator: Josef.
13192. Hamburg - Staats- und Universitaetsbibliothek Cod. hebr. 17/2 (Steinschneider 152), f. 164a, C.
13193. Hamburg - Staats- und Universitaetsbibliothek Cod. hebr. 62 (Steinschneider 154), f. 41a-44a, C, rubric: סילוק.
13194. Hamburg - Staats- und Universitaetsbibliothek Cod. hebr. 132 (Steinschneider 155), f. 54b-55a, C, rubric: סילוק, no incipit.
13195. Jerusalem - Jewish National and University Library Ms Heb 8° 3037, f. 256b-259a, M.
13196. Jerusalem - Schocken Institute 24100 / Mahzor Nuremberg, f. 482b-484a, M.
13197. London - British Library Add. 18695 (Margoliouth 683), f. 120a-122b, T, Yiddish, rubric: טן זגט קהל דען סילוק.
13198. London - British Library Add. 22431 (Margoliouth 662a), f. 93b-95a, 96a, M.
13199. London - British Library Or. 11318/1, f. 137b-139a, C.
13200. London - Montefiore Library 261, f. 72b-73a, C, commentator: Eliezer b. Natan?.
13201. Moscow - Russian State Library, Ms. Guenzburg 615, f. 114a-115a, C, rubric: סילוק.
13202. New York - Jewish Theological Seminary Ms. 4466, f. 449b-451b, M.
13203. Oxford - Bodleian Library MS Mich. 365 (Neubauer 1208), f. 105b-106a, C.
13204. Oxford - Bodleian Library MS Opp. 170 (Neubauer 1205), f. 186a-187a, C, rubric: סילוק.
13205. Parma - Biblioteca Palatina Cod. Parm. 3205 (de Rossi 655), f. 241b, C, no incipit.
13206. Parma - Biblioteca Palatina Cod. Parm. 3507 (Perreau 27), f. 179b-180a, C, no incipit.
13207. Vatican - Biblioteca Apostolica ebr. 305,1, f. 42b-43a, C, rubric: סילוק.
13208. Zurich - Zentralbibliothek Heid. 139, f. 92a-92b, C, no incipit, additional marginal notes.
Romania
13209. London - London School of Jewish Studies. Asher I.Myers collection 9, f. 221b-222a, M, rubric: סלוק.
Tsarfat
13210. Oxford - Bodleian Library MS Laud. Or. 271 (Neubauer 1206), f. 97a-97b, C, commentator: Aaron b. Hayyim haKohen (compiler), rubric: סילוק.

13211. Oxford - Bodleian Library MS Opp. 171 (Neubauer 1207), f. 147b-149a, C, rubric: סילוק.
13212. Parma - Biblioteca Palatina Cod. Parm. 1264, f. 57b-58b, 59b, M.

כי אשמרה שבת (כ 194), שלם שבזי
Yemen
13213. Cincinnati - Hebrew Union College 398, f. 86a-87b, M.

כי אתה אל עולם (כ 195), יצחק בן זרחיה גירונדי, סילוק, קדושתא לשבת החדש
Carpentras, commentary by Mordekhai b. Josef of Rocco Martino
13214. Cincinnati - Hebrew Union College 246/1, f. 44a-44b, C, rubric: פי׳ פזמון לקדושה.
Sepharad, commentary by Josef Garad
13215. Oxford - Bodleian Library Heb.e.10 (Neubauer 2746/1), f. 15a, C, rubric: סלוק.

כי בשמחה תצאו ובשלום תובלון (א 1389), לשמחת תורה
Yemen
13216. New York - Jewish Theological Seminary Ms. 3295, f. 96b, M, short.
Yemen, commentary by Isaac b. Abraham Wanneh?
13217. Jerusalem - Makhon Ben Zvi 1156 (Tubi 155), f. 79a, M.
13218. Manchester - John Rylands University Library, Ms. Gaster 5, f. 156a, M.
13219. Muenchen - Bayerische Staatsbibliothek, Cod. hebr. 472, f. 105a, M.
13220. New York - Jewish Theological Seminary Ms. 3013, f. 82a, M, short.
13221. New York - Jewish Theological Seminary Ms. 4195, f. 49b-50b, M.

כי הנה כחומר ביד היוצר (כ 203), פיוט לליל כפור
Ashkenaz
13222. Braunschweig - Landesmuseum fuer Geschichte und Volkstum R 2386, vol. II, f. 145b, M.
13223. Jerusalem - Schocken Institute 24100 / Mahzor Nuremberg, f. 358(ii)b, M, very short.
13224. Oxford - Bodleian Library MS Mich. 543 (Neubauer 1212), f. 11b-12a, C, commentator: Isaac b. Jacob (compiler).
13225. Oxford - Bodleian Library MS Opp. 172 (Neubauer 1211), f. 32a, C.
13226. Oxford - Bodleian Library MS Opp. 681 (Neubauer 1213), f. 85b-86a, C.
13227. Padova - Biblioteca del Seminario Vescovile Cod. 218, f. 164b-165a, M.
13228. Vatican - Biblioteca Apostolica ebr. 422/1, f. 32a-32b, C.

Ashkenaz, commentary by Abraham b. Azriel[312]
13229. Frankfurt a M - Stadt- und Universitaetsbibliothek Fol. 16 (Merzbacher 95), f. 105b-106a, C.
13230. Vatican - Biblioteca Apostolica ebr. 301,1, f. 169b, C.

כי הנה כחומר כל אומן, סליחה

Ashkenaz
13231. Vatican - Biblioteca Apostolica ebr. 308, f. 92b-93a, C, commentator: David b. Mose (compiler).

כי לו נאה כי לו יאה אדיר במלוכה (כ 215)

Ashkenaz
13232. Cincinnati - Hebrew Union College 436, f. 74a-74b, G.

כי לפניך לילה, יניי, סילוק, קדושתא לפסח

Ashkenaz
13233. Oxford - Bodleian Library MS Opp. 170 (Neubauer 1205), f. 38a-38b, C, rubric: סילוק.

כי מקדישיך כערכך קדשת (כ 218), הוספה לקדושה של מוסף ראש השנה

Ashkenaz
13234. Berlin - Staatsbibliothek (Preussischer Kulturbesitz) Or. Qu. 798-799 (Steinschneider 177), f. 163b, M.
13235. Budapest - Magyar tudomanyos akademia, MS. Kaufmann A 400, p. 338, C, short.
13236. London - British Library Or. 11318/1, f. 84b-85a, C.
13237. Oxford - Bodleian Library MS Mich. 365 (Neubauer 1208), f. 86a, C, short.
13238. Oxford - Bodleian Library MS Opp. 619 (Neubauer 2374), f. 35a, M.
13239. Oxford - Bodleian Library MS Opp. 675 (Neubauer 1210), f. 29a, C, no incipit.
13240. Paris - Bibliotheque Nationale heb. 653, f. 18b, G.
13241. Zurich - Zentralbibliothek Heid. 139, f. 65b, C.
Tsarfat
13242. London - British Library Add. 11639 (Margoliouth 1056), f. 710a, M, short.
13243. London - David Sofer 5, f. 112b, C.
13244. Paris - Bibliotheque Nationale heb. 445,9, f. 80a-80b, C.
13245. Parma - Biblioteca Palatina Cod. Parm. 3006 (de Rossi 654,1), f. 31a, M.

---

[312] Edited by Urbach, ערוגת הבושם, vol. III, p. 493, 552-553.

13246. Parma - Biblioteca Palatina Cod. Parm. 3006 (de Rossi 654,1), f. 151a, M.
13247. Vatican - Biblioteca Apostolica ebr. 306, f. 52a-52b, C.

כי על רחמיך הרבים אנו בטוחים (כ 219), סליחה
Ashkenaz
13248. Berlin - Staatsbibliothek (Preussischer Kulturbesitz) Or. Qu. 798-799 (Steinschneider 177), I, f. 56b-57a, M.
Yemen, commentary by Isaac b. Abraham Wanneh
13249. Chicago-Spertus College of Judaica D 2, 2, f. 225b-226a, M, rubric: חידושין לשחרית כפור.
13250. Jerusalem - Sassoon 1158, p. 311, M, rubric: חידושין.
13251. London - British Library Or. 11122, f. 202b, M, no incipit.

כי רכובו בערבות (כ 223), אליה ברבי מרדכי, סילוק, קדושתא למנחה יום כפור
Ashkenaz
13252. Berlin - Staatsbibliothek (Preussischer Kulturbesitz) Or. Qu. 798-799 (Steinschneider 177), I, f. 162b-163a, M.
13253. Braunschweig - Landesmuseum fuer Geschichte und Volkstum R 2386, vol. II, f. 255b, M.
13254. Fulda - Hessische Landesbibliothek A 3 II, f. 128b, C, commentator: Josef, short.
13255. Hamburg - Staats- und Universitaetsbibliothek Cod. hebr. 17/2 (Steinschneider 152), f. 161a, C, rubric: סילוק.
13256. Hamburg - Staats- und Universitaetsbibliothek Cod. hebr. 62 (Steinschneider 154), f. 22b, C, incipit ערבות.
13257. Jerusalem - Jewish National and University Library Ms Heb 8° 3037, f. 217b, M.
13258. Jerusalem - Schocken Institute 24100 / Mahzor Nuremberg, f. 445a-445b, M.
13259. London - British Library Or. 11318/1, f. 124b-125a, C, rubric: סילוק.
13260. London - Montefiore Library 261, f. 64a-64b, C, commentator: Eliezer b. Natan?.
13261. Muenchen - Bayerische Staatsbibliothek, Cod. hebr. 346, f. 87b-88a, C, no incipit.
13262. New York - Jewish Theological Seminary Ms. 4466, f. 416a, M.
13263. Oxford - Bodleian Library MS Mich. 365 (Neubauer 1208), f. 93b, C, rubric: סילוק, incipit ערבות.
13264. Oxford - Bodleian Library MS Opp. 170 (Neubauer 1205), f. 181a-181b, C, incipit ערבות.
13265. Oxford - Bodleian Library MS Opp. 172 (Neubauer 1211), f. 82b, C, rubric: סילוק.

13266. Parma - Biblioteca Palatina Cod. Parm. 3205 (de Rossi 655), f. 237b-238a, C, incipit לרוכב.

13267. Vatican - Biblioteca Apostolica ebr. 308, f. 140b-141a, C, commentator: David b. Mose (compiler).

13268. Vatican - Biblioteca Apostolica ebr. 422/1, f. 19b, C.

Asti, Fossano, Moncalvo

13269. New Haven - Yale University, Beinecke Rare Book and MS Library, MS Heb. 52, f. 162a, M.

Tsarfat

13270. London - David Sofer 5, f. 165b, C, rubric: סילוק, incipit ערבות.

13271. Oxford - Bodleian Library MS Bodl. Or. 109 (Neubauer 1209), f. 42a-42b, C, commentator: Aaron b. Hayyim haKohen (compiler), rubric: סילוק.

13272. Oxford - Bodleian Library MS Laud. Or. 271 (Neubauer 1206), f. 118b, C, commentator: Aaron b. Hayyim haKohen (compiler), no incipit, very short.

13273. Parma - Biblioteca Palatina Cod. Parm. 3006 (de Rossi 654,1), f. 221a, M, incipit ערבות.

כי שבת היום ליי את יום השביעי ברך וקידש, סליחה

Yemen, commentary by Isaac b. Abraham Wanneh

13274. Chicago-Spertus College of Judaica D 2, 2, f. 210b-211a, M, no incipit.

13275. Jerusalem - Michael Krupp 604, f. 163b-164a, M, no incipit.

13276. Jerusalem - Sassoon 1158, p. 382, M, no incipit.

13277. London - British Library Or. 11122, f. 191a-191b, M, rubric: אל מלך.

כל אשר עלה במחשבה (כ 280), משה אבן עזרא, חלק יא, קדושתא לשחרית יום כפור

Carpentras

13278. Cincinnati - Hebrew Union College 392, f. 54b-55a, M, no incipit.

13279. Cincinnati - Hebrew Union College 429/1, f. 18a-18b, M, no incipit.

Carpentras, commentary by Josef b. Abraham of Montelitz

13280. Cincinnati - Hebrew Union College 291, f. 29b-30b, C, rubric: פי' ובכן כל עצמותי תאמרנה.

13281. New York - Jewish Theological Seminary Ms. 4197, f. 124a-125b, M.

13282. Paris - Ecole Rabbinique 32, f. 141b-142b, M.

13283. Strasbourg - Bibliotheque Nationale et Universitaire 4081, f. 118b-119b, M.

כל ברואי מעלה ומטה (כ 282), שלמה, בקשה

Italia

13284. Oxford - Bodleian Library Heb.e.20 (Neubauer 2748), f. 1a-2b, M.

כל המיחלים לישע צורכם (כ 302), משה אבן עזרא, פזמון ליום כפור

Sepharad, commentary by David b. Josef Abudarham

13285. Holon - Yehuda Nahum 278, f. 1b, FC, rubric: פזמון.

13286. New York - Columbia X893 Ab 93, f. 33a, C, rubric: פזמון.

כל מעשה יי מאד נורא הוא (כ 354), משה אבן עזרא, חלק, קדושתא לשחרית יום כפור

Carpentras

13287. Cincinnati - Hebrew Union College 392, f. 55b, M, no incipit.

Carpentras, commentary by Josef b. Abraham of Montelitz

13288. Cincinnati - Hebrew Union College 291, f. 30b-31a, C, rubric: פי׳ עזמון כל מעשה ה׳.

13289. New York - Jewish Theological Seminary Ms. 4197, f. 125b-126b, M, no incipit.

13290. Paris - Ecole Rabbinique 32, f. 143a-143b, M, no incipit.

13291. Strasbourg - Bibliotheque Nationale et Universitaire 4081, f. 120a-120b, M, no incipit.

Sepharad, commentary by David b. Josef Abudarham[313]

13292. Budapest - Magyar tudomanyos akademia, MS. Kaufmann A 405/2, p. 203, C, rubric: פזמון לר׳ משה ן׳ עזרא ז״ל.

13293. New York - Columbia X893 Ab 93, f. 11b, C, rubric: פזמון לר׳ משה ן׳ עזרא ז״ל.

Yemen, commentary by Isaac b. Abraham Wanneh

13294. Chicago-Spertus College of Judaica D 2, 2, f. 215b, M, no incipit, short.

13295. London British Library Or. 11122, f. 188a, M, no incipit.

כל עבודת כהן גדול, סדר עבודה?

Tsarfat

13296. London - British Library Add. 11639 (Margoliouth 1056), f. 732a-733a, M, rubric: וזה סדר עבודתו.

כל עצמותי תאמרנה יי מי כמוך (כ 376), אברהם אבן עזרא, בתימן: סליחה

Yemen

13297. New York - Jewish Theological Seminary Ms. 3028, f. 54b, G.

13298. New York - Jewish Theological Seminary Ms. 3109, f. 118a, G.

כל שנאני שחק (כ 393), שמעון ב״ר יצחק, חלק ז׳, קדושתא לראש השנה

Ashkenaz

13299. Berlin - Staatsbibliothek (Preussischer Kulturbesitz) Or. Qu. 798-799 (Steinschneider 177), I, f. 41a-41b, M.

---

[313] Edited by Prins, תשלום אבודרהם, p. 98-99.

13300. Braunschweig - Landesmuseum fuer Geschichte und Volkstum R 2386, vol. II, f. 114b-115a, M.
13301. Darmstadt - Hessisches Landes- und Hochschulbibliothek Cod. Or. 15, f. 39b-40a, M, ecclectic.
13302. Darmstadt - Hessisches Landes- und Hochschulbibliothek Cod. Or. 15, f. 40b-41a, M, ecclectic.
13303. Hamburg - Staats- und Universitaetsbibliothek Cod. hebr. 132 (Steinschneider 155), f. 25b-26a, C, short.
13304. London - British Library Or. 11318/1, f. 45a-45b, C.
13305. London - Montefiore Library 261, f. 30a, C, commentator: Eliezer b. Natan?, short.
13306. Muenchen - Bayerische Staatsbibliothek, Cod. hebr. 21, f. 181b-182a, M.
13307. Muenchen - Bayerische Staatsbibliothek, Cod. hebr. 86, f. 73a-73b, Gl.
13308. Muenchen - Bayerische Staatsbibliothek, Cod. hebr. 346, f. 37b, C, no incipit.
13309. New York - Jewish Theological Seminary Ms. 8097, f. 67a, C.
13310. New York - Jewish Theological Seminary Ms. 8169 (Acc. 0016), f. 40a-40b, M, ecclectic.
13311. Oxford - Bodleian Library MS Mich. 365 (Neubauer 1208), f. 52a, C, no incipit, short.
13312. Oxford - Bodleian Library MS Opp. 172 (Neubauer 1211), f. 24a-25a, C, short.
13313. Oxford - Bodleian Library MS Opp. 619 (Neubauer 2374), f. 65b-66b, M.
13314. Parma - Biblioteca Palatina Cod. Parm. 3507 (Perreau 27), f. 134a, C, no incipit, short.
13315. Vatican - Biblioteca Apostolica ebr. 308, f. 79b, C, commentator: David b. Mose (compiler).
13316. Vatican - Biblioteca Apostolica ebr. 422/1, f. 13b, C, ecclectic.

Asti, Fossano, Moncalvo
13317. New Haven - Yale University, Beinecke Rare Book and MS Library, MS Heb. 52, f. 34b-35a, M.

Tsarfat
13318. London - British Library Or. 8682, f. 21b-22a, Gl.
13319. London - David Sofer 5, f. 121b, C.
13320. Parma - Biblioteca Palatina Cod. Parm. 1794 (de Rossi 1061), f. 86b-88a, M.
13321. Parma - Biblioteca Palatina Cod. Parm. 3006 (de Rossi 654,1), f. 73b-74a, M.

כמפעלי צור גואלי אלי (כ 472), סליחה

Yemen
13322. Jerusalem - Sassoon 902, p. 433, M, very short.
13323. New York - Jewish Theological Seminary Ms. 3052, f. 30a, M, rubric: אל מלך.

Yemen, commentary by Isaac b. Abraham Wanneh
13324. Jerusalem - Benayahu ת 261, f. 138b-139a, M, rubric: אל מלך.
13325. Jerusalem - Benayahu ת 282, f. 122a, M, rubric: אל מלך.
13326. Jerusalem - Makhon Ben Zvi 1156 (Tubi 155), f. 120b, M, rubric: אל מלך, very short.
13327. Jerusalem - Makhon Ben Zvi 1174 (Tubi 154), f. 125b, M, very short.
13328. Jerusalem - Michael Krupp 604, f. 152b, M, rubric: אל מלך.
13329. Jerusalem - Musad haRav Kook 325, f. 182a, M, rubric: אל מלך.
13330. Jerusalem - Sassoon 1158, p. 361, M, rubric: אל מלך.
13331. Jerusalem - Sassoon 1174, p. 232, M, no incipit.
13332. London - British Library Or. 11122, f. 179b, M, rubric: אל מלך.
13333. Manchester - John Rylands University Library, Ms. Gaster 5, f. 197a, M.
13334. Muenchen - Bayerische Staatsbibliothek, Cod. hebr. 472, f. 165a, M, rubric: אל מלך, very short.
13335. New York - Jewish Theological Seminary Ms. 3013, f. 122a, M, rubric: אל מלך, very short.
13336. New York - Jewish Theological Seminary Ms. 3109, f. 112b, M, rubric: אל מלך.
13337. New York - Jewish Theological Seminary Ms. 3294, f. 10a-10b, C.
13338. Strasbourg - Bibliotheque Nationale et Universitaire 3965 (Landauer 39), p. 378, M, rubric: אל מלך, very short.

כמראה השמש באדר וזוהר (כ 473), משה אבן עזרא, חלק ד' סדר עבודה

Carpentras
13339. Cincinnati - Hebrew Union College 392, f. 72b-73a, M, no incipit.

Carpentras, commentary by Josef b. Abraham of Montelitz
13340. Cincinnati - Hebrew Union College 291, f. 42a-42b, C, rubric: פי' פזמון ובכן מה נהדר.
13341. New York - Jewish Theological Seminary Ms. 4197, f. 171a-171b, M, no incipit.
13342. Paris - Ecole Rabbinique 32, f. 181b-182a, M, no incipit.
13343. Strasbourg - Bibliotheque Nationale et Universitaire 4081, f. 159a-159b, M, no incipit.

כנסת ישראל זעקת בקולה (כ 486), אליה ב"ר שמעיה, תחנה

Roma
13344. Parma - Biblioteca Palatina Cod. Parm. 2577 (de Rossi 310), f. 201b, G.

כרם המר נטע שעשועים (כ+ 537), יוסף ב"ר שמואל טוב עלם, חלק ד', קדושתא לשבת הגדול

Ashkenaz
13345. Jerusalem - Schocken Institute 24100 / Mahzor Nuremberg, f. 72b, M, very short.
13346. Muenchen - Bayerische Staatsbibliothek, Cod. hebr. 88, f. 50a-50b, G.
13347. Parma - Biblioteca Palatina Cod. Parm 3000 (de Rossi 378), f. 28a-28b, M.
13348. Parma - Biblioteca Palatina Cod. Parm. 3507 (Perreau 27), f. 33b-34a, C, no incipit.

Tsarfat
13349. London - British Library Add. 11639 (Margoliouth 1056), f. 673a, M, incipit אל נא.
13350. Moscow - Russian State Library, Ms. Guenzburg 1665, f. 45b-46a, M, incipit אל נא.
13351. Parma - Biblioteca Palatina Cod. Parm. 3136 (de Rossi 405), f. 59b, M, incipit אל נא.

כתועים ואין לבקש (כ 574), הוספה לסדר עבודה

Ashkenaz
13352. Berlin - Staatsbibliothek (Preussischer Kulturbesitz) Or. Qu. 798-799 (Steinschneider 177), I, f. 135b-136a, M.
13353. London - Montefiore Library 261, f. 62a, C, commentator: Eliezer b. Natan?, very short.
13354. Oxford - Bodleian Library MS Opp. 172 (Neubauer 1211), f. 69a, C, short.

כתר מלוכה, אלעזר ברבי קליר, חלק יג עד יט, קרובה לפורים

Ashkenaz
13355. Berlin - Staatsbibliothek (Preussischer Kulturbesitz) Or. Qu. 798-799 (Steinschneider 177), II, f. 30a-31a, M, leaf damaged.
13356. Budapest - Magyar tudomanyos akademia, MS. Kaufmann A 384, f. 69b-71b, M.
13357. Budapest - Magyar tudomanyos akademia, MS. Kaufmann A 400, p. 75-79, C.
13358. Hamburg - Staats- und Universitaetsbibliothek Cod. hebr. 17/2 (Steinschneider 152), f. 24a, C.

13359. Hamburg - Staats- und Universitaetsbibliothek Cod. hebr. 40c (Steinschneider 111), f. 17a, G.
13360. Jerusalem - Schocken Institute 24100 / Mahzor Nuremberg, f. 51a-52a, M.
13361. Muenchen - Bayerische Staatsbibliothek, Cod. hebr. 88, f. 36a-37a, G.
13362. Muenchen - Bayerische Staatsbibliothek, Cod. hebr. 393, f. 99b-100a, C.
13363. New York - Jewish Theological Seminary Ms. 4466, f. 4a-5b, M.
13364. Oxford - Bodleian Library MS Opp. 170 (Neubauer 1205), f. 26a-27a, C.
13365. Paris - Bibliotheque Nationale heb. 709, f. 32b-33a, C.
13366. Parma - Biblioteca Palatina Cod. Parm. 1002 (Ta 24), f. 49a-50b, M.
13367. Parma - Biblioteca Palatina Cod. Parm 3000 (de Rossi 378), f. 3a-3b, M.
13368. Parma - Biblioteca Palatina Cod. Parm. 3205 (de Rossi 655), f. 31b-32b, C.
13369. Parma - Biblioteca Palatina Cod. Parm. 3507 (Perreau 27), f. 25a-26a, C.
13370. Vatican - Biblioteca Apostolica ebr. 305,1, f. 36b-37a, C.
13371. Zurich - Zentralbibliothek Heid. 139, f. 3b-4a, C, additional marginal notes.

Tsarfat
13372. London - British Library Add. 11639 (Margoliouth 1056), f. 274a, M.
13373. London - David Sofer 5, f. 27b-28a, C.
13374. Moscow - Russian State Library, Ms. Guenzburg 1665, f. 24b 25b, M.
13375. Oxford - Bodleian Library MS Laud. Or. 271 (Neubauer 1206), f. 37b-38b, C, commentator: Aaron b. Hayyim haKohen (compiler).
13376. Oxford - Bodleian Library MS Opp. 171 (Neubauer 1207), f. 32b-33b, C.
13377. Parma - Biblioteca Palatina Cod. Parm. 3136 (de Rossi 405), f. 38a-39a, M.

כתר מלכות (כ 581), שלמה אבן גבירול

Persia
13378. New York - Jewish Theological Seminary Ms. 1393, f. 36a-72b, T, Persian, rubric: בשם אל עוזר דלים אתחיל לכתוב תפסיר כתר מלכות.
13379. St. Petersburg - Inst. of Oriental Studies of the Russian Academy A 133, f. 4a-35a, T, Persian.

Sepharad
13380. Jerusalem - Benayahu ו 25, f. 1b-27a, M.
13381. Jerusalem - Benayahu ו 26, f. 5b-26b, M.
13382. Jerusalem - Makhon Ben Zvi 921, f. 1a-6a, FC, incomplete, chapters 4-14.

13383. Jerusalem - Schocken Institute 70014, f. 17a-29a, M.
13384. St. Petersburg - Inst. of Oriental Studies of the Russian Academy A 33, f. 1b-22a, M.

Yemen

13385. Jerusalem - Makhon Ben Zvi 4509, f. 1a-87a, T, Arabic, complete Tafsir.

Yemen, commentary by Isaac b. Abraham Wanneh

13386. Jerusalem - Sassoon 1158, p. 319-327, M, rubric: כתר מלכות. חידושין.
13387. London - British Library Or. 11122, f. 162a-165b, M, rubric: חידושין. כתר מלכות.

לא אדע נפשי, סליחה

Carpentras, commentary by Mordekhai b. Josef of Rocco Martino

13388. Cincinnati - Hebrew Union College 246/1, f. 84a, C, rubric: פי' התחנה.

לא ארמון על משפטו (א 3048), סליחה

Ashkenaz

13389. London - Montefiore Library 261, f. 61b-62a, C, commentator: Eliezer b. Natan?.

לאט האל בעם נדכה ומכאובים (ל 144), יהודה הלוי, סליחה

Yemen

13390. Jerusalem - Benayahu ת 414, f. 142a, M.
13391. Jerusalem - Musad haRav Kook 334, f. 147a, M.
13392. Jerusalem - Sassoon 902, p. 396, M.
13393. New York - Jewish Theological Seminary Ms. 3052, f. 20a-20b, M, rubric: אל מלך.
13394. New York - Jewish Theological Seminary Ms. 3109, f. 88b, M.
13395. Ramat Gan - Universitat Bar Ilan 62, f. 41a, G, margins damaged.

Yemen, commentary by Isaac b. Abraham Wanneh

13396. Chicago-Spertus College of Judaica D 2, 2, f. 195b, M.
13397. Jerusalem - Benayahu ת 261, f. 133a-133b, M, rubric: אל מלך.
13398. Jerusalem - Benayahu ת 282, f. 118a-118b, M, rubric: אל מלך.
13399. Jerusalem - Makhon Ben Zvi 1156 (Tubi 155), f. 115b-116a, M, rubric: אל מלך.
13400. Jerusalem - Makhon Ben Zvi 1174 (Tubi 154), f. 119b-120a, M.
13401. Jerusalem - Musad haRav Kook 325, f. 173b, M, rubric: אל מלך.
13402. Jerusalem - Musad haRav Kook 330, f. 105b, G.
13403. Jerusalem - Musad haRav Kook 347, f. 84a-84b, G.
13404. Jerusalem - Sassoon 1158, p. 302-303, M.
13405. Jerusalem - Sassoon 1174, p. 223-224, M, rubric: אל מלך.
13406. Jerusalem - Yehiel haLevi 4, f. 146a, G.
13407. London - British Library Or. 11122, f. 178b-179a, M, rubric: אל מלך.

13408. Manchester - John Rylands University Library, Ms. Gaster 5, f. 192a, M.
13409. Muenchen - Bayerische Staatsbibliothek, Cod. hebr. 472, f. 157b-158a, M, rubric: אל מלך.
13410. New York - Jewish Theological Seminary Ms. 3013, f. 117a, M, rubric: אל מלך.
13411. New York - Jewish Theological Seminary Ms. 3109 , f. 89a, M, rubric: אל מלך.
13412. New York - Public Library, Heb. Ms. 9, f. 111b, M.
13413. Philadelphia - University of Pennsylvania HB 2, f. 129b-130a, M.
13414. Strasbourg - Bibliotheque Nationale et Universitaire 3965 (Landauer 39), p. 361-362, M, rubric: אל מלך.

לאיש כמוני רשעי וצדקתי לבן אדם (ל 162), לוי אלתבאן, סליחה
Yemen
13415. Jerusalem - Sassoon 902, p. 415, M.
13416. Ramat Gan - Universitat Bar Ilan 62, f. 43b, G, margins damaged.
Yemen, commentary by Isaac b. Abraham Wanneh
13417. Chicago-Spertus College of Judaica D 2, 2, f. 195b, M.
13418. Jerusalem - Michael Krupp 604, f. 146b, M, rubric: אל מלך.
13419. Jerusalem - Sassoon 1158, p. 358-359, M, rubric: אל מלך.
13420. Jerusalem - Yehiel haLevi 4, f. 169a, G.
13421. London - British Library Or. 11122, f. 178b, M.

לאל סודר בדין /נ̇וו ̇ ̇בו ̇י̇ו̇ת ביום דין, לו אש ו̇שנה
Tsarfat
13422. London - David Sofer 5, f. 121b, C.
13423. Parma - Biblioteca Palatina Cod. Parm. 3006 (de Rossi 654,1), f. 74b, M.

לאל עולם נתנה שיר וביעה תהלתו (ל 215), מרדכי בן יהודה דאטו, שיר לקבלת שבת
Italia
13424. Oxford - Bodleian Library Heb.e.20 (Neubauer 2748), f. 4a-11b, M.

לאל עורך דין (ל 216), אלעזר ברבי קליר, חלק ז, קדושתא לראש השנה
Ashkenaz
13425. Berlin - Staatsbibliothek (Preussischer Kulturbesitz) Or. Qu. 798-799 (Steinschneider 177), I, f. 8b-9a, M.
13426. Braunschweig - Landesmuseum fuer Geschichte und Volkstum R 2386, vol. II, f. 83a, M.
13427. Darmstadt - Hessisches Landes- und Hochschulbibliothek Cod. Or. 15, f. 8b, M.

13428. Hamburg - Staats- und Universitaetsbibliothek Cod. hebr. 12 (Steinschneider 102), f. 7b-8a, G.
13429. Hamburg - Staats- und Universitaetsbibliothek Cod. hebr. 40c (Steinschneider 111), f. 134a, G.
13430. Hamburg - Staats- und Universitaetsbibliothek Cod. hebr. 132 (Steinschneider 155), f. 8a, C, very short.
13431. Jerusalem - Jewish National and University Library Ms Heb 8° 3037, f. 11a, M.
13432. Jerusalem - Schocken Institute 15791/7, f. 60b-61b, C, no incipit, kabbalistic.
13433. Jerusalem - Schocken Institute 24100 / Mahzor Nuremberg , f. 325b-326a, M.
13434. Jerusalem - Schocken Institute 24100 / Mahzor Nuremberg , f. 344b-345a, M.
13435. London - British Library Or. 11318/1, f. 12b, C, very short.
13436. Moscow - Russian State Library, Ms. Guenzburg 191, f. 1b-2a, M, manuscript damaged.
13437. Moscow - Russian State Library, Ms. Guenzburg 615, f. 59b-60a, C.
13438. Muenchen - Bayerische Staatsbibliothek, Cod. hebr. 86, f. 6a, G.
13439. Muenchen - Bayerische Staatsbibliothek, Cod. hebr. 346, f. 5a-5b, C.
13440. New York - Jewish Theological Seminary Ms. 4466, f. 213b-214a, M.
13441. Oxford - Bodleian Library MS Opp. 170 (Neubauer 1205), f. 107b-108a, C.
13442. Oxford - Bodleian Library MS Opp. 172 (Neubauer 1211) , f. 5a-5b, C.
13443. Oxford - Bodleian Library MS Opp. 619 (Neubauer 2374), f. 13b-14a, M.
13444. Oxford - Bodleian Library MS Opp. 675 (Neubauer 1210), f. 17b-18a, C, no incipit.
13445. Parma - Biblioteca Palatina Cod. Parm. 3205 (de Rossi 655), f. 206a, C.
13446. Parma - Biblioteca Palatina Cod. Parm. 3270 (de Rossi 1215), f. 22b, M.
13447. Parma - Biblioteca Palatina Cod. Parm. 3507 (Perreau 27), f. 113b-114a, C.
13448. Vatican - Bibliotheca Apostolica ebr. 298/1, f. 10b-11a, C, no incipit.
13449. Vatican - Bibliotheca Apostolica ebr. 298/1, f. 11a-12b, C, no incipit.
13450. Vatican - Biblioteca Apostolica ebr. 308, f. 35a-36a, C, commentator: David b. Mose (compiler).
13451. Zurich - Zentralbibliothek Heid. 139, f. 102a, C, commentator: Elazar b. Yehuda of Worms, no incipit, short.

Asti, Fossano, Moncalvo
13452. New Haven - Yale University, Beinecke Rare Book and MS Library, MS Heb. 52, f. 21b, M.

Tsarfat

13453. London - David Sofer 5, f. 111a-111b, C.

13454. Oxford - Bodleian Library MS Laud. Or. 271 (Neubauer 1206), f. 141b-142a, C, commentator: Aaron b. Hayyim haKohen (compiler).

13455. Paris - Bibliotheque Nationale heb. 445,9, f. 66b, C.

13456. Parma - Biblioteca Palatina Cod. Parm. 2125 (de Rossi 812), f. 11b-12a, C, page damaged.

13457. Parma - Biblioteca Palatina Cod. Parm. 3006 (de Rossi 654,1), f. 28a, M.

13458. Vatican - Biblioteca Apostolica ebr. 320, f. 153b, M.

לב אדם בואו יורגז, סליחה

Ashkenaz, commentary by Abraham b. Azriel[314]

13459. Frankfurt a M - Stadt- und Universitaetsbibliothek Fol. 16 (Merzbacher 95), f. 103b, C, very short.

13460. Vatican - Biblioteca Apostolica ebr. 301,1, f. 169a, C, very short.

לב ונפש נשפוך כמים (ל+ 243), סליחה

Ashkenaz

13461. Oxford - Bodleian Library MS Mich. 543 (Neubauer 1212), f. 5a, C, commentator: Isaac b. Jacob (compiler).

13462. Padova - Biblioteca del Seminario Vescovile Cod. 218, f. 126a, M, short.

לבבי יחשקה עפרה לשכלי החלי (ל 285), שלם שבזי

Yemen

13463. Cincinnati - Hebrew Union College 398, f. 116a-118b, M.

לבי ובשרי ירננו אל אל חי, לחתן?

Tsarfat

13464. London - British Library Or. 2735 (Margoliouth 663), f. 180a-180b, M, very ecclectic.

לבי יחיל בקרבי מיגורי יום קפדה (ל 356), לוי אלתבאן, סליחה

Yemen

13465. Jerusalem - Sassoon 902, p. 430, M.

Yemen, commentary by Isaac b. Abraham Wanneh

13466. Chicago-Spertus College of Judaica D 2, 2, f. 213b-214a, M, no incipit.

13467. Jerusalem - Sassoon 1158, p. 365-366, M, rubric: אל מלך, no incipit.

---

[314] Edited by Urbach, ערוגת הבושם, vol. III, p. 490.

13468. London - British Library Or. 11122, f. 183a, M, no incipit.

לבעל התפארת (ל 447), בנימין ב"ר זרח, אופן

Ashkenaz
13469. Berlin - Staatsbibliothek (Preussischer Kulturbesitz) Or. Qu. 361 (Steinschneider 51), f. 159b-160a, M, no incipit.
13470. Berlin - Staatsbibliothek (Preussischer Kulturbesitz) Or. Qu. 798-799 (Steinschneider 177), I, f. 234a-234b, M.
13471. Budapest - Magyar tudomanyos akademia, MS. Kaufmann A 399, p. 322, C, rubric: אופן דרבינו בנימן.
13472. Cambridge - University Library Add. 504,1, f. 28a, C, rubric: בנימין יסד זה כך חתום באות שנייה, very short.
13473. Jerusalem - Schocken Institute 24100 / Mahzor Nuremberg, f. 68b, M, short.
13474. Lund - Universitetsbibliothek Ms. L.O. 2, f. 118b-119a, M.
13475. Oxford - Bodleian Library MS Mich. 365 (Neubauer 1208), f. 21a, C, rubric: אופן.
13476. Oxford - Bodleian Library MS Opp. 169 (Neubauer 1151), f. 10b, M.
13477. Parma - Biblioteca Palatina Cod. Parm. 2895, p. 371-372, M, rubric: אופן.
13478. Parma - Biblioteca Palatina Cod. Parm. 3205 (de Rossi 655), f. 133b-134a, C.

Ashkenaz, commentary by Abraham b. Azriel[315]
13479. Frankfurt a M - Stadt- und Universitaetsbibliothek Fol. 16 (Merzbacher 95), f. 93b, C, rubric: אופן דרבינו בנימן הגדול.

Tsarfat
13480. London - British Library Add. 11639 (Margoliouth 1056), f. 674b, M.
13481. Vatican - Biblioteca Apostolica ebr. 306, f. 148a, C.

להודות באתי על חטא סתרי (ל 508), משה אבן עזרא, תחנון

Tsarfat
13482. London - David Sofer 5, f. 162b, C, rubric: פזמון.
13483. Parma - Biblioteca Palatina Cod. Parm. 3007 (de Rossi 654,2), f. 139a-139b, M.

Yemen
13484. New York - Jewish Theological Seminary Ms. 3052, f. 79b-80a, M, no incipit.

Yemen, commentary by Isaac b. Abraham Wanneh
13485. Chicago-Spertus College of Judaica D 2, 2, f. 236b, M, no incipit.
13486. Jerusalem - Benayahu ת 261, f. 164a-164b, M.
13487. Jerusalem - Benayahu ת 282, f. 139b-140a, M.

---

[315] Edited by Urbach, ערוגת הבושם, vol. III, p. 534-535.

13488. Jerusalem - Makhon Ben Zvi 1156 (Tubi 155), f. 137b, M, no incipit.
13489. Jerusalem - Michael Krupp 604, f. 174a-174b, M.
13490. Jerusalem - Musad haRav Kook 325, f. 193a, M.
13491. Jerusalem - Sassoon 1158, p. 414, M, no incipit.
13492. Jerusalem - Sassoon 1174, p. 268, M, no incipit.
13493. London - British Library Or. 11122, f. 213b, M, no incipit.
13494. Manchester - John Rylands University Library, Ms. Gaster 5, f. 222a, M, incipit מרן.
13495. Muenchen - Bayerische Staatsbibliothek, Cod. hebr. 472, f. 191b-192a, M.
13496. New York - Jewish Theological Seminary Ms. 3013, f. 131b-132a, M.
13497. New York - Jewish Theological Seminary Ms. 3294, f. 16b, C.
13498. Strasbourg - Bibliotheque Nationale et Universitaire 3965 (Landauer 39), p. 406, M.

לוכד חכמים בערמה (ל 589), יהודה הלוי, חלק ה' קדושתא לשבת זכור
Carpentras, commentary by Mordekhai b. Josef of Rocco Martino
13499. Cincinnati - Hebrew Union College 246/1, f. 23a, C, rubric: פי' משלש לוכד חכמים וכו'.

Sepharad, commentary by Josef Garad
13500. Oxford - Bodleian Library Heb.e.10 (Neubauer 2746/1), f. 8a-8b, C, rubric: משלש.

לו תאזין מציאת כופר
Tsarfat
13501. Oxford - Bodleian Library MS Laud. Or. 271 (Neubauer 1206), f. 170b, C, commentator: Aaron b. Hayyim haKohen (compiler), short.
13502. Oxford - Bodleian Library MS Opp. 171 (Neubauer 1207), f. 95a, C, rubric: אחרת.

לידך בני עולם מצפים (ל 689), יצחק גיאת, חלק י', קדושתא לשחרית יום כפור
Sepharad, commentary by David b. Josef Abudarham[316]
13503. Budapest - Magyar tudomanyos akademia, MS. Kaufmann A 405/2, p. 207-208, C, rubric: פזמון.
13504. Budapest - Magyar tudomanyos akademia, MS. Kaufmann A 405/2, p. 210, C, rubric: פזמון.
13505. New York - Columbia X893 Ab 93, f. 13a, C, rubric: פזמון.
13506. New York - Columbia X893 Ab 93, f. 13(ii)a, C, rubric: פזמון, reference to commentary in the same manuscript.

---

[316] Edited by Prins, תשלום אבודרהם, p. 101-102.

ליום קדושה וכבוד האל יזכור זבוד, ליום כפור

Carpentras

13507. Cincinnati - Hebrew Union College 392, f. 15b, M, very short.

ליל בו נוי שודד בו כלה חרון וזעם (ל 709), פתיחה לאיכה

Ashkenaz

13508. London - British Library Add. 18695 (Margoliouth 683) , f. 97a-97b, T, Yiddish, rubric: דש זיין די קינות די מן זגט צו נכט.

לילי זכרון עמדתי מרעיד, סליחה

Yemen

13509. New York - Jewish Theological Seminary Ms. 3028, f. 85b, G.
13510. New York - Jewish Theological Seminary Ms. 3052, f. 83b, M.

Yemen, commentary by Isaac b. Abraham Wanneh

13511. Chicago-Spertus College of Judaica D 2, 2, f. 237b, M, no incipit.
13512. Jerusalem - Benayahu ת 261, f. 165a-165b, M.
13513. Jerusalem - Benayahu ת 282, f. 141a, M.
13514. Jerusalem - Makhon Ben Zvi 1156 (Tubi 155), f. 138b, M, no incipit.
13515. Jerusalem - Makhon Ben Zvi 1174 (Tubi 154), f. 137a, M.
13516. Jerusalem - Michael Krupp 604, f. 175b, M.
13517. Jerusalem - Sassoon 1174, p. 269-270, M, no incipit.
13518. London - British Library Or. 11122, f. 215a, M, no incipit.
13519. Manchester - John Rylands University Library, Ms. Gaster 5, f. 227a, M.
13520. Muenchen - Bayerische Staatsbibliothek, Cod. hebr. 472, f. 193b, M.
13521. New York - Jewish Theological Seminary Ms. 3013, f. 133b, M.
13522. New York - Jewish Theological Seminary Ms. 3294, f. 17a, C.
13523. New York - Public Library, Heb. Ms. 9, f. 130a, M, no incipit.
13524. Strasbourg - Bibliotheque Nationale et Universitaire 3965 (Landauer 39), p. 411, M.

ליל שימורים אור ישראל קדוש (ל 724), מאיר ב"ר יצחק, מעריב ליום ב של פסח

Ashkenaz

13525. Berlin - Staatsbibliothek (Preussischer Kulturbesitz) Or. Qu. 361 (Steinschneider 51), f. 134b-137a, M, no incipit.
13526. Berlin - Staatsbibliothek (Preussischer Kulturbesitz) Or. Qu. 798-799 (Steinschneider 177), II, f. 72a-73b, M.
13527. Braunschweig - Landesmuseum fuer Geschichte und Volkstum R 2386, vol. I, f. 31a, M.
13528. Budapest - Magyar tudomanyos akademia, MS. Kaufmann A 384 , f. 148a-151b, M.
13529. Budapest - Magyar tudomanyos akademia, MS. Kaufmann A 399 , p. 199-208, C, rubric: מעריב של ליל שיני של פסח דר' נהוראי.

13530. Cincinnati - Hebrew Union College 436, f. 127a-129a, G.
13531. Erlangen - Universitaetsbibliothek 2601 (Roth 67), f. 83b-84a, M.
13532. Frankfurt a M - Stadt- und Universitaetsbibliothek Oct. 227, f. 122b-124a, M.
13533. Hamburg - Staats- und Universitaetsbibliothek Cod. hebr. 17/2 (Steinschneider 152), f. 33b-35a, C, commentator: Ephraim b. Jacob of Bonn, rubric: אפרים. מעריב לליל שיני.
13534. Hamburg - Staats- und Universitaetsbibliothek Cod. hebr. 225, f. 78a-82a, G.
13535. Jerusalem - Schocken Institute 24100 / Mahzor Nuremberg, f. 88b-89b, M.
13536. London - British Library Add. 18695 (Margoliouth 683), f. 32a-34a, T, Yiddish, rubric: מעריב צו דער אנדרן נכט.
13537. Lund - Universitetsbibliothek Ms. L.O. 2, f. 62b-63b, M.
13538. Moscow - Russian State Library, Ms. Guenzburg 615, f. 173a-176b, C, rubric: מעריב ליל שיני.
13539. Muenchen - Bayerische Staatsbibliothek, Cod. hebr. 393,9, f. 205a-212a, C, rubric: ליל שימורים ליל שיני.
13540. New York - Jewish Theological Seminary Ms. 4466, f. 194b-198b, M.
13541. Oxford - Bodleian Library MS Can. Or. 1 (Neubauer 1104), f. 48b, 57a-63b, M, rubric: אתחיל מעריב דליל שיני. המריב עשה לר׳ נהוראי, interrupted by pages from different ms.
13542. Parma - Biblioteca Palatina Cod. Parm. 2895, p. 311-317, M, margins cut, text damaged.
13543. Parma - Biblioteca Palatina Cod. Parm. 3205 (de Rossi 655), f. 59b-63b, C.
13544. Parma - Biblioteca Palatina Cod. Parm. 3507 (Perreau 27), f. 56b-59b, C.

Ashkenaz, commentary by Abraham b. Azriel[317]

13545. Vatican - Biblioteca Apostolica ebr. 301,1, f. 152a-153a, C, rubric: אחר.

Ashkenaz, commentary by Eliezer b. Natan

13546. Hamburg - Staats- und Universitaetsbibliothek Cod. hebr. 61 (Steinschneider 153), f. 44a-45b, C.
13547. Warszaw - Uniwersytet, Inst. Orientalistyczny 258, f. 201b-206a, C, rubric: מעריב לליל שיני.

Tsarfat

13548. London - British Library Or. 2735 (Margoliouth 663), f. 80a, M, very short.

---

[317] Edited by Urbach, ערוגת הבושם, vol. III, p. 377-384.

ליל שימורים אור עולמו נגלה (ל 725), יוסף ב"ר יעקב, מעריב ליום ב' של פסח
Ashkenaz
13549. Moscow - Russian State Library, Ms. Guenzburg 206, f. 68a-68b, M, incipit אור עולמו.
Romania
13550. Vatican - Biblioteca Apostolica ebr. 285/30, f. 228a-228b, C, rubric: ליל שיני.
Tsarfat
13551. Parma - Biblioteca Palatina Cod. Parm. 3136 (de Rossi 405), f. 88a, M.

ליל שימורים אותו אל חצה (ל 726), מאיר ב"ר יצחק, מעריב ליום א' של פסח
Ashkenaz
13552. Berlin - Staatsbibliothek (Preussischer Kulturbesitz) Or. Qu. 361 (Steinschneider 51), f. 132b-133b, M.
13553. Berlin - Staatsbibliothek (Preussischer Kulturbesitz) Or. Qu. 798-799 (Steinschneider 177), II, f. 52b-54b, M.
13554. Budapest - Magyar tudomanyos akademia, MS. Kaufmann A 384, f. 116a-118a, M.
13555. Budapest - Magyar tudomanyos akademia, MS. Kaufmann A 399, p. 190-195, C.
13556. Erlangen - Universitaetsbibliothek 2601 (Roth 67), f. 61b-62a, M.
13557. Frankfurt a M - Stadt- und Universitaetsbibliothek Oct. 227, f. 120b-122b, M.
13558. Hamburg - Staats- und Universitaetsbibliothek Cod. hebr. 17/2 (Steinschneider 152), f. 33a-33b, C, rubric: פי' למעריב.
13559. Jerusalem - Schocken Institute 24100 / Mahzor Nuremberg, f. 76b-77a, M.
13560. London - British Library Add. 18695 (Margoliouth 683), f. 17a-18a, T, Yiddish.
13561. London - British Library Add. 27556, f. 185b-189b, M.
13562. Lund - Universitetsbibliothek Ms. L.O. 2, f. 61a-62a, M.
13563. Moscow - Russian State Library, Ms. Guenzburg 615, f. 167a-170b, C.
13564. Muenchen - Bayerische Staatsbibliothek, Cod. hebr. 88, f. 56b-57b, G.
13565. Muenchen - Bayerische Staatsbibliothek, Cod. hebr. 393,9, f. 199b-201b, C.
13566. New York - Jewish Theological Seminary Ms. 4466, f. 191b-193a, M.
13567. Oxford - Bodleian Library MS Can. Or. 1 (Neubauer 1104), f. 41a-46a, M.
13568. Oxford - Bodleian Library MS Opp. 170 (Neubauer 1205), f. 38b-39b, C, rubric: מעריב לליל ראשון של פסח.

13569. Parma - Biblioteca Palatina Cod. Parm. 2895, p. 303-308, G.
13570. Parma - Biblioteca Palatina Cod. Parm. 3205 (de Rossi 655), f. 58a-58b, C.
13571. Parma - Biblioteca Palatina Cod. Parm. 3507 (Perreau 27), f. 35b-37b, C.

Ashkenaz, commentary by Abraham b. Azriel[318]

13572. Vatican - Biblioteca Apostolica ebr. 301,1, f. 151a-152a, C, rubric: אתחיל מעריבים.

Ashkenaz, commentary by Eliezer b. Natan

13573. Hamburg - Staats- und Universitaetsbibliothek Cod. hebr. 61 (Steinschneider 153), f. 43b-44a, C, rubric: ואתחיל לכתוב מעריבים.
13574. Warszaw - Uniwersytet, Inst. Orientalistyczny 258, f. 199b-200a, C, rubric: ואתחיל פירוש של מעריבים בעזרת פושט ידו לשבים.

Romania

13575. Vatican - Biblioteca Apostolica ebr. 285/30, f. 227a-228a, C.

Tsarfat

13576. Jerusalem - Schocken Institute 19623, f. 86a-87a, M, commentator: Yehuda b. Eliezer Zvi.
13577. London - British Library Or. 2735 (Margoliouth 663), f. 79a-80a, M.
13578. Moscow - Russian State Library, Ms. Guenzburg 1665, f. 50a, M.
13579. Oxford - Bodleian Library MS Laud. Or. 271 (Neubauer 1206), f. 51b-52a, C, commentator: Aaron b. Hayyim haKohen (compiler), rubric: מעריב לליל ראשון פסח.
13580. Parma - Biblioteca Palatina Cod. Parm. 1902, f. 104a-105a, M.
13581. Parma - Biblioteca Palatina Cod. Parm. 3136 (de Rossi 405), f. 68b-76a, M

לישע עמך בחצי ליל יצאת (ל ++748), יניי, חלק ד', קדושתא לפסח

Ashkenaz

13582. Berlin - Staatsbibliothek (Preussischer Kulturbesitz) Or. Qu. 798-799 (Steinschneider 177), II, f. 48a-48b, M.
13583. Budapest - Magyar tudomanyos akademia, MS. Kaufmann A 384, f. 109a, M.
13584. London - British Library Add. 18695 (Margoliouth 683), f. 11b-12a, T, Yiddish.
13585. Paris - Bibliotheque Nationale heb. 709, f. 44b, C, incipit אל נא.

לך יי הגדולה אורות (א 2003), קלונימוס ב"ר יהודה, יוצר לחתן

Ashkenaz

13586. Budapest - Magyar tudomanyos akademia, MS. Kaufmann A 399, p. 379-388, C, rubric: יוצר לחתן מרבנא קלונימוס.

---

[318] Edited by Urbach, ערוגת הבושם, vol. III, p. 369-376.

13587. Parma - Biblioteca Palatina Cod. Parm. 3205 (de Rossi 655), f. 176b-177a, C, rubric: יוצר לחתן.

לך יי הצדקה באותות אשר הפלאתה (ל 765), אלעזר ברבי קליר, קינה
Ashkenaz
13588. Berlin - Staatsbibliothek (Preussischer Kulturbesitz) Or. Qu. 798-799 (Steinschneider 177), II, f. 192b-193a, M.
13589. Budapest - Magyar tudomanyos akademia, MS. Kaufmann A 400, p. 230, , rubric: אחרת.
13590. Hamburg - Staats- und Universitaetsbibliothek Cod. hebr. 17/2 (Steinschneider 152), f. 100a-100b, C.
13591. Jerusalem - Schocken Institute 24100 / Mahzor Nuremberg, f. 208b, M.
13592. Parma - Biblioteca Palatina Cod. Parm. 3205 (de Rossi 655), f. 197a, C, rubric: אחרת.
13593. Vatican - Biblioteca Apostolica ebr. 312, f. 51b-52a, G.
13594. Vatican - Biblioteca Apostolica ebr. 318, f. 237b-239a, GI.
Ashkenaz, commentary by Abraham b. Azriel[319]
13595. Frankfurt a M - Stadt- und Universitaetsbibliothek Fol. 16 (Merzbacher 95), f. 108a-108b, C.
13596. Vatican - Biblioteca Apostolica ebr. 301,1, f. 137b, C, rubric: אחרת.

לך יי הצדקה ולנו בושת הפנים מה נתאונן (ל 771), סליחה
Ashkenaz
13597. Moscow - Russian State Library, Ms. Guenzburg 615, f. 164a-164b, C, rubric: פיזמונים.
13598. Muenchen - Bayerische Staatsbibliothek, Cod. hebr. 346, f. 154b-155a, C.
13599. Oxford - Bodleian Library MS Mich. 543 (Neubauer 1212), f. 4a, C, commentator: Isaac b. Jacob (compiler).
13600. Padova - Biblioteca del Seminario Vescovile Cod. 218, f. 38b, M.

לך יי הצדקה תלבושת (ל 782), שלמה הבבלי, סליחה
Ashkenaz
13601. Berlin - Staatsbibliothek (Preussischer Kulturbesitz) Or. Qu. 798-799 (Steinschneider 177), I, f. 183a-183b, M.
13602. Braunschweig - Landesmuseum fuer Geschichte und Volkstum R 2386, vol. II, f. 60b, M.
13603. Budapest - Magyar tudomanyos akademia, MS. Kaufmann A 400, p. 464-466, C, rubric: פיזמון שלמונית.

---

[319] Edited by Urbach, ערוגת הבושם, vol. III, p. 284.

13604. Hamburg - Staats- und Universitaetsbibliothek Cod. hebr. 17/2 (Steinschneider 152), f. 138a-138b, C, rubric: פזמון שלמונית.
13605. Jerusalem - Schocken Institute 24100 / Mahzor Nuremberg, f. 456a-456b, M.
13606. Muenchen - Bayerische Staatsbibliothek, Cod. hebr. 346, f. 123a-123b, C.
13607. Oxford - Bodleian Library MS Mich. 543 (Neubauer 1212), f. 74b-75b, C, commentator: Isaac b. Jacob (compiler).
13608. Oxford - Bodleian Library MS Opp. 170 (Neubauer 1205), f. 233a-234a, C, rubric: בשם דר במעונים . אכתוב פי' פיזמון'.
13609. Oxford - Bodleian Library MS Opp. 172 (Neubauer 1211), f. 85b-86a, C, rubric: פזמון.
13610. Oxford - Bodleian Library MS Opp. 681 (Neubauer 1213), f. 79a-81b, C.
13611. Padova - Biblioteca del Seminario Vescovile Cod. 218, f. 153a-154a, M, rubric: אל מלך.
13612. Padova - Biblioteca del Seminario Vescovile Cod. 218, f. 217b-219a, M.
13613. Parma - Biblioteca Palatina Cod. Parm. 3205 (de Rossi 655), f. 255a-256a, C.
13614. Vatican - Biblioteca Apostolica ebr. 308/1, f. 2b-3a, C, commentator: David b. Mose (compiler), additional glosses.
13615. Vatican - Biblioteca Apostolica ebr. 308, f. 136b-138a, C, commentator: David b. Mose (compiler).

Ashkenaz, commentary by Abraham b. Azriel[320]

13616. Vatican - Biblioteca Apostolica ebr. 301,1, f. 162b-163a, C, rubric: אחר.

Asti, Fossano, Moncalvo

13617. New Haven - Yale University, Beinecke Rare Book and MS Library, MS Heb. 52, f. 169b-170a, M.

Tsarfat

13618. London - British Library Add. 11639 (Margoliouth 1056), f. 482b-484a, M.
13619. London - David Sofer 5, f. 94a-95b, C, rubric: סליחה.
13620. Oxford - Bodleian Library MS Laud. Or. 271 (Neubauer 1206), f. 166a-166b, C, commentator: Aaron b. Hayyim haKohen (compiler), rubric: פיזמון.
13621. Oxford - Bodleian Library MS Laud. Or. 271 (Neubauer 1206), f. 176b-177a, C, commentator: Aaron b. Hayyim haKohen (compiler).
13622. Oxford - Bodleian Library MS Opp. 171 (Neubauer 1207), f. 108b-109b, C, rubric: אחרת.

---

[320] Edited by Urbach, ערוגת הבושם, vol. III, p. 444-448.

HEBREW LITURGICAL POETRY   739

13623. Parma - Biblioteca Palatina Cod. Parm. 3007 (de Rossi 654,2), f. 138a-139a, M.
13624. Vatican - Biblioteca Apostolica ebr. 306, f. 178a-180a, C.

לך אדר נאה מכל פה (ל +783), פיוט לאחרי הקדושה, שחרית יום כפור
Tsarfat
13625. Parma - Biblioteca Palatina Cod. Parm. 2890 (de Rossi 856), f. 81b-82a, M.

לך אלי תשוקתי בך חשקי ואהבתי (ל 809), אברהם אבן עזרא
Sepharad
13626. Skokie - Hebrew Theological College 3, f. 88a-90b, M, internal count skips some pages between the last and this commentary.

לך אלים אלפי אלפים (ל 810), בנימין ב"ר זרח, אופן לשבת וראש חדש
Ashkenaz
13627. Berlin - Staatsbibliothek (Preussischer Kulturbesitz) Or. Qu. 361 (Steinschneider 51), f. 163b, M, no incipit.
13628. Berlin - Staatsbibliothek (Preussischer Kulturbesitz) Or. Qu. 798-799 (Steinschneider 177), I, f. 241b-242a, M.
13629. Hamburg - Staats- und Universitaetsbibliothek Cod. hebr. 239a (Steinschneider 130), f. 7b-8a, G.
13630. Oxford - Bodleian Library MS Can. Or. 82 (Neubauer 1148), f. 7a-7b, M, short.
13631. Oxford Bodleian Library MS Mich. 365 (Neubauer 1208), f. 24a, C, rubric: אופן לשבת וראש חדש.
13632. Parma - Biblioteca Palatina Cod. Parm. 2895, p. 439, M.
13633. Parma - Biblioteca Palatina Cod. Parm. 3205 (de Rossi 655), f. 135b-136a, C, rubric: אופן.
13634. Uppsala - Universitetsbibliotek O.Heb.22, f. 133a-133b, M.
13635. Vatican - Biblioteca Apostolica ebr. 318, f. 113b, Gl.
Ashkenaz, commentary by Abraham b. Azriel[321]
13636. Frankfurt a M - Stadt- und Universitaetsbibliothek Fol. 16 (Merzbacher 95), f. 93b, C, rubric: אופן.
13637. Vatican - Biblioteca Apostolica ebr. 301,1, f. 107a-107b, C, rubric: אופן אחר.
Ashkenaz, commentary by Eliezer b. Natan
13638. Hamburg - Staats- und Universitaetsbibliothek Cod. hebr. 61 (Steinschneider 153), f. 32a-32b, C, rubric: אופן לשבת וראש חדש.
13639. Parma - Biblioteca Palatina Cod. Parm. 3057.12 (de Rossi 1033/10), f. 125b-128a, C, rubric: אופן.

---

[321] Edited by Urbach, ערוגת הבושם, vol. III, p. 80-82.

13640. Warszaw - Uniwersytet, Inst. Orientalistyczny 258 , f. 182a-182b, C, rubric: אופן.

לך יאדיר כל יציר (ל 843), אלעזר ברבי קליר, חלק יב׳, קדושתא למוסף יום כפור
Ashkenaz
13641. Budapest - Magyar tudomanyos akademia, MS. Kaufmann A 400 , p. 364, C, incipit תאציר.
13642. New York - Jewish Theological Seminary Ms. 4466, f. 380a-380b, M, incipit יאדיר.
Tsarfat
13643. Oxford - Bodleian Library MS Bodl. Or. 109 (Neubauer 1209), f. 35b, C, commentator: Aaron b. Hayyim haKohen (compiler), very short.
13644. Oxford - Bodleian Library MS Bodl. Or. 109 (Neubauer 1209), f. 44a, C, commentator: Aaron b. Hayyim haKohen (compiler), very short.

לך יהגה חכנו הט לנו אזניך (ל 846), פזמון
Carpentras, commentary by Josef b. Abraham of Montelitz
13645. New York - Jewish Theological Seminary Ms. 4746, f. 20a, M.

לך יהמה לבי ותלכה רוחי (ל 847), פזמון
Carpentras, commentary by Josef b. Abraham of Montelitz
13646. Cincinnati - Hebrew Union College 357, f. 65a, M, rubric: פירוש.
13647. New York - Jewish Theological Seminary Ms. 4746, f. 21a, M.
13648. Paris - Alliance Israelite Universelle H 422 A, f. 39b, M.
13649. Paris - Ecole Rabbinique 31, f. 111a, M.

לך עיני צופיות פנה בי משמיך (ל 875), לוי אלתבאן, סליחה
Yemen
13650. Jerusalem - Sassoon 902, p. 430, M.
Yemen, commentary by Isaac b. Abraham Wanneh
13651. Chicago-Spertus College of Judaica D 2, 2, f. 215a, M, no incipit.
13652. Jerusalem - Sassoon 1158, p. 363, M, rubric: אל מלך.
13653. London - British Library Or. 11122, f. 181a, M, no incipit.

לכה דודי לקראת כלה (ל 928), שלמה אלקביץ, פיוט לקבלת שבת
North Africa
13654. Jerusalem - Benayahu ק 165, f. 144a-147b, C, no incipit, kabbalistic.
Yemen
13655. Jerusalem - Benayahu ת 282, f. 15b-17b, M, begins אמר המדפיס.
13656. Jerusalem - Makhon Ben Zvi 1156 (Tubi 155), f. 14b, M, begins אמר המדפיס.
13657. Jerusalem - Makhon Ben Zvi 1174 (Tubi 154), f. 30b, M, begins אמר המדפיס.

13658. Jerusalem - Michael Krupp 604, f. 18a, M, begins אמר המדפיס.
13659. Jerusalem - Musad haRav Kook 325, f. 27a-28b, M, begins אמר המדפיס.
13660. Jerusalem - Sassoon 1158, p. 49-50, M, begins אמר המדפיס.
13661. Jerusalem - Sassoon 1174, p. 29-30, M, begins אמר המדפיס.
13662. Manchester - John Rylands University Library, Ms. Gaster 5, f. 38a-38b, M, begins אמר המדפיס.
13663. Muenchen - Bayerische Staatsbibliothek, Cod. hebr. 472, f. 20a-20b, M, begins אמר המדפיס.
13664. Nahariya - Menahem and Saida Yaakob 187, f. 19a, M, begins אמר המדפיס, shorter than usual.
13665. New York - Jewish Theological Seminary Ms. 3013, f. 16b, M, begins אמר המדפיס.
13666. New York - Public Library, Heb. Ms. 9, f. 16a, M, begins אמר המדפיס.
13667. New York - Public Library, Jewish Items 2, f. 3a-3b, M, begins אמר המדפיס.
13668. Oxford - Bodleian Library MS Opp. Add. fol. 58 (Neubauer 2498), f. 28b-29a, M, rubric: לך דודי, begins אמר המדפיס.
13669. Strasbourg - Bibliotheque Nationale et Universitaire 3965 (Landauer 39), p. 62-63, M, begins אמר המדפיס.

לכו נטל ענינו הנפשות נאנחות, סליחה
Yemen, commentary by Isaac b. Abraham Wanneh
13670. London - British Library Or. 11122, f. 184b, M, no incipit.

לכם בני ציון הכואבים (ל 997), יהודה הלוי, אהבה, בתימן: סליחה
Yemen
13671. Jerusalem - Benayahu ת 414, f. 140b, M.
13672. Jerusalem - Sassoon 902, p. 388, M, no incipit.
13673. New York - Jewish Theological Seminary Ms. 3052, f. 14a-14b, M, rubric: אל מלך.
Yemen, commentary by Isaac b. Abraham Wanneh
13674. Chicago-Spertus College of Judaica D 2, 2, f. 192b-193a, M, no incipit.
13675. Jerusalem - Benayahu ת 261, f. 131a, M, no incipit.
13676. Jerusalem - Benayahu ת 282, f. 116a, M, rubric: אל מלך, no incipit.
13677. Jerusalem - Makhon Ben Zvi 1156 (Tubi 155), f. 114a, M, no incipit.
13678. Jerusalem - Makhon Ben Zvi 1174 (Tubi 154), f. 115b-116a, M, no incipit.
13679. Jerusalem - Michael Krupp 604, f. 143b-144a, M, rubric: אל מלך.
13680. Jerusalem - Musad haRav Kook 325, f. 168a, M, rubric: אל מלך, no incipit.
13681. Jerusalem - Musad haRav Kook 330, f. 100a, G.

13682. Jerusalem - Musad haRav Kook 347, f. 79b, G.
13683. Jerusalem - Sassoon 1158, p. 340, M, no incipit.
13684. Jerusalem - Sassoon 1174, p. 219, M, rubric: אל מלך, no incipit.
13685. Jerusalem - Yehiel haLevi 4, f. 149b, G.
13686. London - British Library Or. 11122, f. 168b-169a, M, no incipit.
13687. Manchester - John Rylands University Library, Ms. Gaster 5, f. 188b-189a, M.
13688. Muenchen - Bayerische Staatsbibliothek, Cod. hebr. 472, f. 154b, M, rubric: אל מלך.
13689. New York - Jewish Theological Seminary Ms. 3013, f. 114b, M, rubric: אל מלך.
13690. New York - Jewish Theological Seminary Ms. 3294, f. 8b, C.
13691. New York - Public Library, Heb. Ms. 9, f. 110a-110b, M.
13692. Strasbourg - Bibliotheque Nationale et Universitaire 3965 (Landauer 39), f. 350, M, rubric: אל מלך.

למבצע על רפתא כזית׳ וכביעותא (ל +1010), יצחק לוריא
hAri, commentary by Jacob b. Raphael haLevi
13693. Cincinnati - Hebrew Union College 275, f. 2a, M, kabbalistic, rubric: פי׳ מנחת יעקב, copied from printed book.

למה אמרו הגוים איה נא אלהיהם למה יאמרו הגוים איה צור חסין בו, סליחה
Yemen, commentary by Isaac b. Abraham Wanneh
13694. Jerusalem - Musad haRav Kook 325, f. 190a, M, short.

למודך וגם ידידך ישראל לך מקורא (ל 1073), הושענא
haAri, commentary by Mose b. Hayyim Pesante
13695. New York - Jewish Theological Seminary Ms. 4696, f. 21b, C, rubric: הקפה שלישית.
North Africa
13696. Jerusalem - Benayahu ז 27, f. 117a, M.
North Africa, commentary by Simon b. Tsemaḥ Duran
13697. New York - Jewish Theological Seminary Ms. 4121, f. 48b, C, rubric: הקפה שלישית למודך.
North Africa, commentary by Yehuda Toledano
13698. New York - Jewish Theological Seminary Ms. 4300, f. 44b-46b, C, rubric: הקפה שלישית יעקב.
Yemen
13699. New York - Jewish Theological Seminary Ms. 8767, p. 185, M.
13700. New York - Jewish Theological Seminary Ms. 9325, f. 82b-83a, M, short.
Yemen, commentary by Isaac b. Abraham Wanneh
13701. Jerusalem - Michael Krupp 1990, f. 99a, M, no incipit.

13702. Nahariya - Menahem and Saida Yaakob 284, f. 10b, M.
13703. New York - Jewish Theological Seminary Ms. 3295, f. 89a, M.
13704. Philadelphia - University of Pennsylvania HB 2, f. 100b, M.
Yemen, commentary by Samhun b. Salomo Haloah
13705. Jerusalem - Makhon ben Zvi 2808, f. 173b-175a, C.

למען אב אומץ ממוצאי עלילה (א 3869), יוסף בן יצחק קמחי, הושענא

haAri, commentary by Mose b. Hayyim Pesante
13706. New York - Jewish Theological Seminary Ms. 4696, f. 24a-24b, C.
Yemen, commentary by Samhun b. Salomo Haloah
13707. Jerusalem - Makhon ben Zvi 2808, f. 222b-225a, C

למען אב אץ לבא ביחוד השם (ל 1125), הושענא

haAri, commentary by Mose b. Hayyim Pesante
13708. New York - Columbia University X 893 J 558, f. 205b-206a, M.
13709. New York - Jewish Theological Seminary Ms. 4696, f. 19a-19b, C.
haAri, commentary by Simon b. Tsemah Duran
13710. New York - Columbia University X 893 J 558, f. 205b-206a, M.
North Africa
13711. Jerusalem - Benayahu ז 27, f. 130b, M.
North Africa, commentary by Yehuda Toledano
13712. New York - Jewish Theological Seminary Ms. 4300, f. 33a-34a, C.
Yemen, commentary by Samhun b. Salomo Haloah
13713. Jerusalem - Makhon ben Zvi 2808, f. 140a-145a, C.

למען אב בן שלוש שנים, הושענא

Romania
13714. Vatican - Biblioteca Apostolica ebr. 285/30, f. 233a, C, incipit אב.
Tsarfat
13715. London - British Library Or. 2735 (Margoliouth 663), f. 142b-143a, M, incipit אב.
13716. London - David Sofer 5, f. 191b, C, incipit אב.

למען אב השכים ושני נעריו קח, הושענא

Tsarfat
13717. London - David Sofer 5, f. 192a, C.

למען אב ידעך מבין מנאצים (ל 1132), סעדיה גאון, הושענא

Yemen
13718. Chicago-Spertus College of Judaica D 10, f. 124a-125a, M, incipit ברודים.
13719. Cincinnati - Hebrew Union College 199, f. 45b, G, one gloss only.
13720. Jerusalem - Michael Krupp 3391, f. 6a-6b, M, incipit ברודים.

13721. Jerusalem - Musad haRav Kook 327, f. 80a, M.
13722. Jerusalem - Musad haRav Kook 334, f. 88b, M.
13723. Jerusalem - Musad haRav Kook 335, f. 94a, M.
13724. Jerusalem - Musad haRav Kook 952, f. 9b-11a, M, rubric: ליום רביעי.
13725. Jerusalem - Sassoon 264, f. 93b-94a, M, no incipit.
13726. Jerusalem - Sassoon 902, p. 175, M, no incipit.
13727. New York - Alfred Moldovan HH, f. 10a-11b, M, rubric: 'ליום ד, incipit ברודים.
13728. New York - Jewish Theological Seminary Ms. 4488, f. 68a-68b, M.
13729. New York - Jewish Theological Seminary Ms. 9325, f. 75a-76a, M, rubric: 'ליום ד.
13730. New York - Public Library, Heb. Ms. 10, f. 58a-58b, M, no incipit, margins damaged.
13731. Ramat Gan - Universitat Bar Ilan 62, f. 28b, G, margins damaged.
13732. Ramat Gan - Universitat Bar Ilan 63, f. 21b, G, margins damaged.

Yemen, commentary by Isaac b. Abraham Wanneh

13733. Chicago-Spertus College of Judaica D 1, f. 195b, M.
13734. Jerusalem - Benayahu ת 261, f. 81a-81b, M, rubric: ליום רביעי.
13735. Jerusalem - Benayahu ת 282, f. 74b, M, rubric: ליום רביעי.
13736. Jerusalem - Israel Museum 180/78, f. 11b-13a, M, rubric: ליום רביעי.
13737. Jerusalem - Makhon Ben Zvi 1156 (Tubi 155), f. 71b-72a, M, rubric: ליום רביעי.
13738. Jerusalem - Makhon Ben Zvi 1169 (Tubi 159), f. 62b, M.
13739. Jerusalem - Makhon Ben Zvi 1174 (Tubi 154), f. 83a-83b, M, rubric: ליום רביעי.
13740. Jerusalem - Makhon ben Zvi 1186 (Tubi 205), f. 5a-5b, M, incipit אב.
13741. Jerusalem - Michael Krupp 604, f. 91b-92a, M, rubric: ליום רביעי.
13742. Jerusalem - Michael Krupp 1990, f. 99b, M, rubric: ליום רביעי.
13743. Jerusalem - Musad haRav Kook 325, f. 104b-105a, M, rubric: ליום רביעי.
13744. Jerusalem - Musad haRav Kook 325, f. 121b-122a, M, rubric: 'ליום ד.
13745. Jerusalem - Musad haRav Kook 330, f. 67b, M.
13746. Jerusalem - Musad haRav Kook 347, f. 57b-58a, M, no incipit.
13747. Jerusalem - Sassoon 1158, p. 213-214, M, rubric: ליום רביעי.
13748. Jerusalem - Sassoon 1174, p. 142, M, rubric: ליום רביעי.
13749. Jerusalem - Schocken Institute 70028, f. 187b-188a, M, rubric: ליום רביעי.
13750. Jerusalem - Yehiel haLevi 4, f. 87b, M.
13751. London - British Library Or. 11122, f. 121a-121b, M, rubric: ליום רביעי.
13752. London - British Library Or. 11121, f. 131b-132a, C, rubric: ליום רביעי.
13753. Manchester - John Rylands University Library, Ms. Gaster 5, f. 147b-148a, M, rubric: ליום רביעי.

13754. Muenchen - Bayerische Staatsbibliothek, Cod. hebr. 472, f. 98b, M, rubric: ליום רביעי.
13755. Nahariya - Menahem and Saida Yaakob 284, f. 11b-12a, M, incipit אב.
13756. New York - Jewish Theological Seminary Ms. 3013, f. 74a, M, rubric: ליום ד'.
13757. New York - Jewish Theological Seminary Ms. 3193, f. 161b-162b, M, rubric: ליום רביעי.
13758. New York - Jewish Theological Seminary Ms. 3295, f. 89b-90a, M, rubric: ליום רביעי. חדושין.
13759. New York - Jewish Theological Seminary Ms. 4195, f. 15b-17a, M.
13760. New York - Public Library, Heb. Ms. 9, f. 71b, M, rubric: ליום ד'.
13761. Oxford - Bodleian Library MS Opp. Add. fol. 58 (Neubauer 2498), f. 141a-141b, M, rubric: ליום רביעי.
13762. Paris - G. Epstein 23/57, f. 101a-102a, C, rubric: ליום רביעי.
13763. Philadelphia - University of Pennsylvania HB 2, f. 97b, M, rubric: ליום ד'.
13764. Ramat Gan - Universitat Bar Ilan 703, f. 194a, M, rubric: ליום רביעי.
13765. Strasbourg - Bibliotheque Nationale et Universitaire 3965 (Landauer 39), p. 236-237, M, rubric: ליום ד'.

Yemen, commentary by Simon b. Tsemaḥ Duran
13766. Jerusalem - Michael Krupp 1758, f. 8a-9a, M, rubric: פירוש.

Yemen, commentary by Yiḥya b. Josef Tsalaḥ
13767. Montreal - Elberg 203, f. 9b-10a, M, rubric: ליום רביעי, incipit ברודים.

למען אב נם יוקח נא (ל 1136), סעדיה גאון, הושענא

Yemen
13768. Jerusalem - Sassoon 902, p. 179, M, no incipit, very short.
13769. New York - Jewish Theological Seminary Ms. 4488, f. 70a, M.
13770. New York - Public Library, Heb. Ms. 10, f. 59b, M, no incipit, margins damaged.
13771. Ramat Gan - Universitat Bar Ilan 62, f. 29a, G, margins damaged.

Yemen, commentary by Isaac b. Abraham Wanneh
13772. Chicago-Spertus College of Judaica D 1, f. 197b, M, rubric: פ'.
13773. Jerusalem - Benayahu ת 261, f. 83a-83b, M, rubric: ליום ששי.
13774. Jerusalem - Benayahu ת 282, f. 76a, M, rubric: ליום ששי.
13775. Jerusalem - Makhon Ben Zvi 1156 (Tubi 155), f. 73a, M, rubric: ליום ששי.
13776. Jerusalem - Makhon Ben Zvi 1174 (Tubi 154), f. 85b-86a, M, rubric: ליום ששי.
13777. Jerusalem - Michael Krupp 604, f. 94a, M, rubric: ליום ששי.
13778. Jerusalem - Michael Krupp 1990, f. 101b, M, rubric: חדושין.
13779. Jerusalem - Musad haRav Kook 325, f. 108a-108b, M, rubric: ליום ששי, very short.

13780. Jerusalem - Musad haRav Kook 325, f. 124b-125a, M, rubric: ליום ו'.
13781. Jerusalem - Musad haRav Kook 330, f. 69a, M, very short.
13782. Jerusalem - Musad haRav Kook 347, f. 59a, M, no incipit.
13783. Jerusalem - Sassoon 1158, p. 216-217, M, rubric: ליום ששי.
13784. Jerusalem - Sassoon 1174, p. 145, M, rubric: ליום ששי.
13785. Jerusalem - Schocken Institute 70028, f. 189b, M, rubric: ליום ששי.
13786. London - British Library Or. 11122, f. 123a, M, rubric: ליום ששי.
13787. London - British Library Or. 11121, f. 134a-134b, C, rubric: ליום ששי.
13788. Muenchen - Bayerische Staatsbibliothek, Cod. hebr. 472, f. 100b, M, rubric: ליום ששי.
13789. New York - Jewish Theological Seminary Ms. 3013, f. 76a-76b, M, rubric: ליום ששי.
13790. New York - Jewish Theological Seminary Ms. 3193, f. 166b-167a, M, rubric: ליום ששי.
13791. New York - Jewish Theological Seminary Ms. 3295, f. 92b, M, rubric: ליום ששי.
13792. New York - Public Library, Heb. Ms. 9, f. 73b-74b, M, rubric: ליום ששי.
13793. Oxford - Bodleian Library MS Opp. Add. fol. 58 (Neubauer 2498), f. 144a, M, rubric: ליום ששי.
13794. Philadelphia - University of Pennsylvania HB 2, f. 98b-99a, M, rubric: ליום ששי.
13795. Ramat Gan - Universitat Bar Ilan 703, f. 196a-196b, M, rubric: ליום ששי.
13796. Strasbourg - Bibliotheque Nationale et Universitaire 3965 (Landauer 39), p. 242-243, M, rubric: ליום ו'.

Yemen, commentary by commentator: Samḥun b. Salomo Ḥaloah
13797. Jerusalem - Makhon ben Zvi 2808, f. 225a-229a, C.

Yemen, commentary by Yiḥya b. Josef Tsalaḥ
13798. Montreal - Elberg 203, f. 15a, M, rubric: ליום ששי.

למען אב נפקד ויבחן ככלות (ל 1139), יוסף, הושענא

haAri, commentary by Mose b. Hayyim Pesante
13799. New York - Jewish Theological Seminary Ms. 4696, f. 24b-25a, C, incipit אב.

Yemen, commentary by Samḥun b. Salomo Ḥaloah
13800. Jerusalem - Makhon ben Zvi 2808, f. 229a-236b, C, incipit אב.

למען אב עקד בן למען בן בירך גביר (ל 1141), סעדיה גאון, הושענא

Yemen
13801. Chicago-Spertus College of Judaica D 10, f. 121a-121b, M, incipit דגלים.
13802. Jerusalem - Musad haRav Kook 334, f. 86b-87a, M.

13803. Jerusalem - Musad haRav Kook 952, f. 5a-5b, M, rubric: פירוש.
13804. Jerusalem - Sassoon 264, f. 92a-92b, M, no incipit.
13805. New York - Alfred Moldovan HH, f. 5a-6a, M, rubric: ליום שני.
13806. New York - Jewish Theological Seminary Ms. 4488, f. 65b-66a, M.
13807. New York - Jewish Theological Seminary Ms. 4488, f. 67a, M.
13808. New York - Jewish Theological Seminary Ms. 9325, f. 71b, M.
13809. New York - Public Library, Heb. Ms. 10, f. 57a, M, no incipit.
13810. Ramat Gan - Universitat Bar Ilan 62, f. 27b, G, margin damaged.

Yemen, commentary by Isaac b. Abraham Wanneh

13811. Chicago-Spertus College of Judaica D 1, f. 194a, M, rubric: ליום שני.
13812. Jerusalem - Benayahu ת 261, f. 80a, M, rubric: ליום שני.
13813. Jerusalem - Benayahu ת 282, f. 73a-73b, M, rubric: ליום שני.
13814. Jerusalem - Israel Museum 180/78, f. 5b-6b, M, rubric: ליום שני.
13815. Jerusalem - Makhon Ben Zvi 1156 (Tubi 155), f. 71a, M, rubric: ליום שני.
13816. Jerusalem - Makhon Ben Zvi 1174 (Tubi 154), f. 81b-82a, M, rubric: ליום שני.
13817. Jerusalem - Makhon ben Zvi 1186 (Tubi 205), f. 2b, M, rubric: ליום שני, incipit אב.
13818. Jerusalem - Michael Krupp 604, f. 90b, M, rubric: ליום שני.
13819. Jerusalem - Michael Krupp 1990, f. 97a, M, rubric: ליום שני.
13820. Jerusalem - Musad haRav Kook 325, f. 101b-102a, M, rubric: חידושין.
13821. Jerusalem - Musad haRav Kook 325, f. 119b-120a, M, rubric: ליום שני.
13822. Jerusalem - Musad haRav Kook 330, f. 66a-66b, M.
13823. Jerusalem - Musad haRav Kook 347, f. 56b, M.
13824. Jerusalem - Sassoon 1158, p. 212, M, rubric: ליום שני.
13825. Jerusalem - Sassoon 1174, p. 140, M, rubric: ליום שני.
13826. Jerusalem - Schocken Institute 70028, f. 186a, M, rubric: ליום שני, no incipit.
13827. Jerusalem - Yehiel haLevi 4, f. 86a, M.
13828. London - British Library Or. 11121, f. 131a, C, rubric: ליום שני.
13829. London - British Library Or. 11122, f. 120b, M, rubric: ליום שני, page damaged.
13830. Manchester - John Rylands University Library, Ms. Gaster 5, f. 145b-146a, M, rubric: ליום שני.
13831. Muenchen - Bayerische Staatsbibliothek, Cod. hebr. 472, f. 97a, M, rubric: ליום שני.
13832. Nahariya - Menahem and Saida Yaakob 284, f. 5b-6a, M.
13833. New York - Jewish Theological Seminary Ms. 3013, f. 72b-73a, M, rubric: ליום שני.
13834. New York - Jewish Theological Seminary Ms. 3193, f. 159b-160a, M, rubric: ליום שני.
13835. New York - Jewish Theological Seminary Ms. 3295, f. 87b-88a, M, rubric: חדושין.

13836. New York - Jewish Theological Seminary Ms. 4195, f. 7a-7b, M, rubric: ליום שני.
13837. New York - Public Library, Heb. Ms. 9, f. 70a-70b, M, rubric: ליום שני.
13838. Oxford - Bodleian Library MS Opp. Add. fol. 58 (Neubauer 2498), f. 139a, M.
13839. Paris - G. Epstein 23/57, f. 97b-98a, C.
13840. Philadelphia - University of Pennsylvania HB 2, f. 96b, M, rubric: ליום שני.
13841. Ramat Gan - Universitat Bar Ilan 703, f. 192a, M, rubric: ליום שני.
13842. Strasbourg - Bibliotheque Nationale et Universitaire 3965 (Landauer 39), p. 232, M, rubric: ליום ב'.

Yemen, commentary by Simon b. Tsemaḥ Duran
13843. Jerusalem - Michael Krupp 1758, f. 4a-5a, M, rubric: פירוש.

Yemen, commentary by Yiḥya b. Josef Tsalaḥ
13844. Montreal - Elberg 203, f. 3b, M.

למען אברהם האהוב שכליל מקדשך החרוב (ל 1143), סעדיה גאון, הושענא
Yemen
13845. New York - Jewish Theological Seminary Ms. 4488, f. 70b, M, two leafs bound wrongly into the Hoshaanot.
13846. New York - Public Library, Heb. Ms. 10, f. 60a, M, no incipit, margins damaged.

Yemen, commentary by Isaac b. Abraham Wanneh
13847. Jerusalem - Benayahu ת 261, f. 84a, M, rubric: ליום שביעי.
13848. Jerusalem - Benayahu ת 282, f. 76b, M, rubric: ליום שביעי.
13849. Jerusalem - Makhon Ben Zvi 1156 (Tubi 155), f. 73b, M, rubric: ליום שביעי.
13850. Jerusalem - Makhon b. Zvi 1168 (Tubi 157), f. 25b, M, margins damaged.
13851. Jerusalem - Makhon Ben Zvi 1174 (Tubi 154), f. 86b, M, rubric: ליום 'ז.
13852. Jerusalem - Michael Krupp 604, f. 94b-95a, M, rubric: ליום שביעי.
13853. Jerusalem - Michael Krupp 1990, f. 102b, M, rubric: ליום שביעי.
13854. Jerusalem - Musad haRav Kook 325, f. 109b-110a, M, rubric: ליום שביעי.
13855. Jerusalem - Musad haRav Kook 325, f. 125b-126a, M, rubric: ליום שביעי.
13856. Jerusalem - Sassoon 1158, p. 217, M, rubric: ליום שביעי.
13857. Jerusalem - Sassoon 1174, p. 146-147, M, rubric: ליום שביעי.
13858. London - British Library Or. 11122, f. 123b, M, rubric: ליום שביעי, short.
13859. Muenchen - Bayerische Staatsbibliothek, Cod. hebr. 472, f. 101b, M, rubric: ליום שביעי.

13860. New York - Jewish Theological Seminary Ms. 3013, f. 76b, 79a, M, rubric: ליום ז'.
13861. New York - Jewish Theological Seminary Ms. 3193, f. 167b-168a, M, rubric: ליום שביעי, short.
13862. New York - Jewish Theological Seminary Ms. 3295, f. 93b, M, rubric: ליום שביעי.
13863. New York - Public Library, Heb. Ms. 9, f. 74b, M, rubric: ליום ז'.
13864. Ramat Gan - Universitat Bar Ilan 703, f. 197a, M, rubric: ליום שביעי, short.
13865. Strasbourg - Bibliotheque Nationale et Universitaire 3965 (Landauer 39), p. 244-245, M, rubric: ליום ז'.

למען אומץ בן שלש (ל 1147), הושענא
Romania
13866. Vatican - Biblioteca Apostolica ebr. 285/30, f. 233a-233b, C, incipit אומץ.
Tsarfat
13867. Cambridge - University Library Add. 561.1, f. 112a-113a, M.
13868. London - British Library Or. 2735 (Margoliouth 663), f. 143b-144a, M, incipit אומץ.
13869. London - David Sofer 5, f. 191b, C, incipit אומץ.
13870. Moscow - Russian State Library, Ms. Guenzburg 1665, f. 181b, M, incipit אומץ.

למען אזרחי הנשלך בכבשן אש, הושענא
Romania
13871. Vatican - Biblioteca Apostolica ebr. 285/30, f. 234a-234b, C.
Tsarfat
13872. London - British Library Or. 2735 (Margoliouth 663), f. 145a-145b, M.

למען איתן הנזרק בלהב (ל 1149), הושענא
Ashkenaz
13873. Berlin - Staatsbibliothek (Preussischer Kulturbesitz) Or. Qu. 361 (Steinschneider 51), f. 118b-119a, M.
13874. Berlin - Staatsbibliothek (Preussischer Kulturbesitz) Or. Qu. 798-799 (Steinschneider 177), I, f. 205b-206a, M.
13875. Budapest - Magyar tudomanyos akademia, MS. Kaufmann A 399, p. 301-302, C.
13876. Budapest - Magyar tudomanyos akademia, MS. Kaufmann A 400, p. 534-535, C.
13877. Cambridge - University Library Or. 790, f. 33a-33b, C.

13878. Cremona - Archivio di Stato 68, f. 1a-1b, FC, commentator: Ephraim b. Jacob of Bonn.
13879. Hamburg - Staats- und Universitaetsbibliothek Cod. hebr. 17/2 (Steinschneider 152), f. 166b-167a, C, rubric: אחרת.
13880. Jerusalem - Schocken Institute 24100 / Mahzor Nuremberg, f. 494a, M.
13881. London - British Library Add. 18695 (Margoliouth 683), f. 151a-151b, T, Yiddish.
13882. London - British Library Add. 22431 (Margoliouth 662a), f. 122a, M.
13883. London - British Library Add. 27208 (Margolioth 654), f. 269b-270a, M.
13884. London - British Library Add. 27556, f. 129b-130b, M.
13885. Lund - Universitetsbibliothek Ms. L.O. 2, f. 87a-87b, M.
13886. Moscow - Russian State Library, Ms. Guenzburg 615, f. 130a-130b, C, rubric: אחרת.
13887. New York - Jewish Theological Seminary Ms. 4416, f. 13b-14a, M.
13888. New York - Jewish Theological Seminary Ms. 4466, f. 478(ii)b-479a, M.
13889. Oxford - Bodleian Library MS Can. Or. 1 (Neubauer 1104), f. 28a-29a, M.
13890. Oxford - Bodleian Library MS Mich. 573 (Neubauer 1099), f. 19b, M.
13891. Oxford - Bodleian Library MS Opp 160 (Neubauer 1204), f. 237b, C, commentator: Elazar b. Yehuda of Worms.[322]
13892. Oxford - Bodleian Library MS Opp. 170 (Neubauer 1205), f. 202a-202b, C.
13893. Parma - Biblioteca Palatina Cod. Parm. 2895, p. 217-218, M.
13894. Parma - Biblioteca Palatina Cod. Parm. 3057.9 (de Rossi 1033), f. 93a-94a, C.
13895. Parma - Biblioteca Palatina Cod. Parm. 3205 (de Rossi 655), f. 251a, C.
13896. Uppsala - Universitetsbibliotek O.Heb.22, f. 111b-112a, M, no incipit.
13897. Vatican - Biblioteca Apostolica ebr. 305,1, f. 43b-44a, C, no incipit.
13898. Vatican - Biblioteca Apostolica ebr. 308, f. 156b-157a, C, commentator: David b. Mose (compiler).
13899. Vatican - Biblioteca Apostolica ebr. 318, f. 199b, GI.
13900. Verona - Seminario Maggiore 34, f. 172a-172b, M, margins partly damaged.

Ashkenaz, commentary by Eliezer b. Natan
13901. Hamburg - Staats- und Universitaetsbibliothek Cod. hebr. 61 (Steinschneider 153), f. 23b-24a, C.
13902. London - Montefiore Library 261, f. 86b-87a, C.

---

[322] Edited by Katzenellenbogen, פירוש ההושענות, p. 38-40.

13903. Paris - Bibliotheque Nationale heb. 327/2, f. 39a-39b, C.
Italia
13904. Moscow - Russian State Library, Ms. Guenzburg 1594, f. 24b, C, no incipit.
Italia, commentary by Zakharya David Shabbetai Segre
13905. Torino - Archivio Terracini 1499, p. 190-193, C, rubric: פירוש למען איתן הנזרק בלהב אש.
Roma
13906. Oxford - Bodleian Library MS Mich. 312,1 (Neubauer 2276,1), f. 10a, C, very short.
Romania
13907. Vatican - Biblioteca Apostolica ebr. 285/30, f. 233b-234a, C.
Tsarfat
13908. London - British Library Or. 2735 (Margoliouth 663), f. 144b, M.
13909. London - David Sofer 5, f. 191b, C.
13910. Parma - Biblioteca Palatina Cod. Parm. 1264, f. 97a-97b, M.
13911. Vatican - Biblioteca Apostolica ebr. 306, f. 123a-123b, C.

למען אלהינו הושע נא, הושענא

Ashkenaz
13912. Budapest - Magyar tudomanyos akademia, MS. Kaufmann A 399, p. 297, C, rubric: הושענות, very short.
13913. Budapest - Magyar tudomanyos akademia, MS. Kaufmann A 400, p. 530-531, C, rubric: בשם שוכן מעונות אחרט פירושי הושענות.
Ashkenaz, commentary by Eliezer b. Natan
13914. London - Montefiore Library 261, f. 85a, C.
13915. Paris - Bibliotheque Nationale heb. 327/2, f. 42b, C, rubric: שכחתי לכתוב זה הפירוש ושייך לעיל לאחר המתחיל הושען', very short.
haAri, commentary by Mose b. Hayyim Pesante
13916. New York - Jewish Theological Seminary Ms. 4696, f. 8a-8b, C.

למען אמתך למען בריתך (ל 1151), הושענא

Ashkenaz
13917. Berlin - Staatsbibliothek (Preussischer Kulturbesitz) Or. Qu. 361 (Steinschneider 51), f. 114a-114b, M.
13918. Budapest - Magyar tudomanyos akademia, MS. Kaufmann A 399, p. 297, C, very short.
13919. Cambridge - University Library Or. 790, f. 31a, C.
13920. Hamburg - Staats- und Universitaetsbibliothek Cod. hebr. 17/2 (Steinschneider 152), f. 165b, C, very short.
13921. Jerusalem - Schocken Institute 24100 / Mahzor Nuremberg, f. 493a, M.

13922. London - British Library Add. 18695 (Margoliouth 683), f. 148b, T, Yiddish.
13923. London - British Library Add. 22431 (Margoliouth 662a), f. 118a, M.
13924. Lund - Universitetsbibliothek Ms. L.O. 2, f. 85b, M.
13925. Moscow - Russian State Library, Ms. Guenzburg 615, f. 128a-128b, C, rubric: הושענות.
13926. Oxford - Bodleian Library MS Can. Or. 1 (Neubauer 1104), f. 24b, M.
13927. Oxford - Bodleian Library MS Opp. 170 (Neubauer 1205), f. 199b, C, very short.
13928. Parma - Biblioteca Palatina Cod. Parm. 2895, p. 209, M, very short.
13929. Parma - Biblioteca Palatina Cod. Parm. 2895, p. 215, M, very short.
13930. Parma - Biblioteca Palatina Cod. Parm. 3057.9 (de Rossi 1033), f. 90b-91a, C, rubric: ובשם שוכן מעונות אתחיל פירוש הושענות.
13931. Parma - Biblioteca Palatina Cod. Parm. 3205 (de Rossi 655), f. 249a, C, very short.
13932. Uppsala - Universitetsbibliotek O.Heb.22, f. 111a, M.

Ashkenaz, commentary by Eliezer b. Natan
13933. Hamburg - Staats- und Universitaetsbibliothek Cod. hebr. 61 (Steinschneider 153), f. 22a, C, rubric: פירוש מהושענות.
13934. Paris - Bibliotheque Nationale heb. 327/2, f. 42b-43a, C.

Italia
13935. Moscow - Russian State Library, Ms. Guenzburg 1594, f. 24a, C, no incipit.
13936. Moscow - Russian State Library, Ms. Guenzburg 533, f. 8b-12b, C, rubric: לימוד ח, commentator: Yehoshua Segre, no incipit.

Romania
13937. Roma - Collegio Rabbinico Italiano 110, f. 1b-2a, M.

Sepharad
13938. Skokie - Hebrew Theological College 3, f. 20a, M.

Tsarfat
13939. Vatican - Biblioteca Apostolica ebr. 306, f. 123a, C.

למען ישן כטבור עולם, הושענא

North Africa
13940. Jerusalem - Benayahu ז 27, f. 131a-131b, M.

למען תמים בדורותיו הנמלט ברוב צדקתיו (ל 1159), אלעזר ברבי קליר, הושענא

Ashkenaz
13941. Berlin - Staatsbibliothek (Preussischer Kulturbesitz) Or. Qu. 361 (Steinschneider 51), f. 121a-122b, M.
13942. Berlin - Staatsbibliothek (Preussischer Kulturbesitz) Or. Qu. 798-799 (Steinschneider 177), I, f. 208b-210a, M.

13943. Budapest - Magyar tudomanyos akademia, MS. Kaufmann A 399 , p. 304-306, C.
13944. Budapest - Magyar tudomanyos akademia, MS. Kaufmann A 400 , p. 537-540, C.
13945. Cambridge - University Library Add. 394,1 (Reif SCR 461) , f. 76b-78a, C, rubric: הושענא.
13946. Cambridge - University Library Or. 790, f. 35a-36b, C.
13947. Frankfurt a M - Stadt- und Universitaetsbibliothek Oct. 227 , f. 116a-117a, M.
13948. Hamburg - Staats- und Universitaetsbibliothek Cod. hebr. 17/2 (Steinschneider 152), f. 167b-168b, C.
13949. Jerusalem - Schocken Institute 24100 / Mahzor Nuremberg , f. 495a-496a, M.
13950. London - British Library Add. 18695 (Margoliouth 683), f. 154b-156a, T, Yiddish.
13951. London - British Library Add. 22431 (Margoliouth 662a), f. 124b-126a, M.
13952. London - British Library Add. 27208 (Margolioth 654), f. 275a-279b, M.
13953. London - British Library Add. 27556, f. 132b-134b, M.
13954. Lund - Universitetsbibliothek Ms. L.O. 2, f. 88b-89a, M.
13955. Moscow - Russian State Library, Ms. Guenzburg 615 , f. 129a-130a, C.
13956. New York - Jewish Theological Seminary Ms. 4416 , f. 14b, M, only beginning.
13957. New York - Jewish Theological Seminary Ms. 4466, f. 481b-483b, M.
13958. Oxford - Bodleian Library MS Can. Or. 1 (Neubauer 1104), f. 30a-33b, M.
13959. Oxford - Bodleian Library MS Mich. 573 (Neubauer 1099), f. 22a-23b, M.
13960. Oxford - Bodleian Library MS Opp 160 (Neubauer 1204), f. 243a-246a, C, commentator: Elazar b. Yehuda of Worms.[323]
13961. Oxford - Bodleian Library MS Opp. 170 (Neubauer 1205), f. 203a-205b, C.
13962. Parma - Biblioteca Palatina Cod. Parm. 2895, p. 224-227, M.
13963. Parma - Biblioteca Palatina Cod. Parm. 3057.9 (de Rossi 1033), f. 97a-99b, C, rubric: הושענא.
13964. Parma - Biblioteca Palatina Cod. Parm. 3205 (de Rossi 655), f. 251a-252b, C.
13965. Uppsala - Universitetsbibliotek O.Heb.22 , f. 114a-114b, M, no incipit.
13966. Vatican - Biblioteca Apostolica ebr. 305,1, f. 44b-45a, C, no incipit.

---

[323] Edited by Katzenellenbogen, פירוש ההושענות, p. 56-63.

13967. Vatican - Biblioteca Apostolica ebr. 308, f. 158b-160b, C, commentator: David b. Mose (compiler).
13968. Verona - Seminario Maggiore 34, f. 170b-171a, M, margins damaged.

Ashkenaz, commentary by Eliezer b. Natan
13969. Hamburg - Staats- und Universitaetsbibliothek Cod. hebr. 61 (Steinschneider 153), f. 24b-26a, C.
13970. London - Montefiore Library 261, f. 87b-89a, C.
13971. Paris - Bibliotheque Nationale heb. 327/2, f. 40b-42b, C.

Italia
13972. Moscow - Russian State Library, Ms. Guenzburg 1594, f. 25a-25b, C, no incipit.
13973. Moscow - Russian State Library, Ms. Guenzburg 533, f. 39b-45a, C, commentator Yehoshua Segre, rubric: לימוד י"ו.

Italia, commentary by Zakharya David Shabbetai Segre
13974. Torino - Archivio Terracini 1499, p. 238-240, C, rubric: פירוש למען תמים בדורותיו.

Roma
13975. Jerusalem - Jewish National and University Library Ms Heb 8° 4153, f. 143b-145a, C, commentator: Daniel ben Salomo haRofe (compiler).
13976. Oxford - Bodleian Library MS Mich. 312,1 (Neubauer 2276,1), f. 11b-13a, C.

Romania
13977. London - London School of Jewish Studies. Asher I.Myers collection 9, f. 212a-213b, M.
13978. Roma - Collegio Rabbinico Italiano 110, f. 17a, M.
13979. Vatican - Biblioteca Apostolica ebr. 285/30, f. 236a-237a, C, incipit תמים.
13980. Vatican - Biblioteca Apostolica ebr. 320, f. 448a-449b, M.

Tsarfat
13981. Cambridge - University Library Add. 561.1, f. 115b-116b, M.
13982. Jerusalem - Schocken Institute 19623, f. 127b-128b, M, commentator: Yehuda b. Eliezer Zvi.
13983. London - British Library Or. 2735 (Margoliouth 663), f. 151a-153a, M, incipit תמים.
13984. London - David Sofer 5, f. 193a, C.
13985. Moscow - Russian State Library, Ms. Guenzburg 1665, f. 183b-184a, M.
13986. Parma - Biblioteca Palatina Cod. Parm. 1264, f. 98b-100b, M.
13987. Parma - Biblioteca Palatina Cod. Parm. 1902, f. 181a-184a, M.
13988. Vatican - Biblioteca Apostolica ebr. 306, f. 123b-126a, C.

למען תקיף אלהי קדם מעונה (ל 1175), סעדיה גאון, הושענא

Yemen
13989. Chicago-Spertus College of Judaica D 10, f. 125b, M, no incipit.

13990. Jerusalem - Michael Krupp 3391, f. 7b, M, no incipit.
13991. Jerusalem - Musad haRav Kook 334, f. 89b, M, no incipit.
13992. Jerusalem - Musad haRav Kook 952, f. 13b-14a, M, rubric: פירוש.
13993. Jerusalem - Sassoon 902, p. 177, M, rubric: ליום חמישי.
13994. New York - Alfred Moldovan HH, f. 13b-14b, M, rubric: לים חמישי, no incipit.
13995. New York - Jewish Theological Seminary Ms. 4488, f. 69a, M.
13996. New York - Jewish Theological Seminary Ms. 9325, f. 77b-78a, M.
13997. New York - Public Library, Heb. Ms. 10, f. 58b-59a, M, no incipit.
13998. Ramat Gan - Universitat Bar Ilan 62, f. 29a, G, margins damaged.

Yemen, commentary by Isaac b. Abraham Wanneh
13999. Chicago-Spertus College of Judaica D 1, f. 196b, M.
14000. Jerusalem - Benayahu ת 261, f. 82a, M, rubric: ליום חמישי.
14001. Jerusalem - Benayahu ת 282, f. 75a, M, rubric: ליום חמישי.
14002. Jerusalem - Israel Museum 180/78, f. 15b-16b, M, rubric: ליום ה.
14003. Jerusalem - Makhon Ben Zvi 1156 (Tubi 155), f. 72b, M, rubric: יום חמישי.
14004. Jerusalem - Makhon Ben Zvi 1169 (Tubi 159), f. 63a, M.
14005. Jerusalem - Makhon Ben Zvi 1174 (Tubi 154), f. 84a-84b, M, rubric: יום ה'.
14006. Jerusalem - Makhon ben Zvi 1186 (Tubi 205), f. 6b-7a, M, rubric: ליום חמישי.
14007. Jerusalem - Michael Krupp 604, f. 93a, M, rubric: ליום חמישי.
14008. Jerusalem - Michael Krupp 1990, f. 100a-100b, M, rubric: ליום חמישי.
14009. Jerusalem - Musad haRav Kook 325, f. 106a-106b, M, rubric: ליום חמישי.
14010. Jerusalem - Musad haRav Kook 325, f. 123a, M, rubric: ליום ה'.
14011. Jerusalem - Musad haRav Kook 330, f. 68a, M.
14012. Jerusalem - Musad haRav Kook 347, f. 58b, M.
14013. Jerusalem - Sassoon 1158, p. 215, M, rubric: יום חמישי.
14014. Jerusalem - Sassoon 1174, p. 143-144, M, rubric: ליום חמישי.
14015. Jerusalem - Schocken Institute 70028, f. 188b-189a, M, rubric: ליום חמישי.
14016. London - British Library Or. 11121, f. 132b-133a, C, rubric: ליום חמישי.
14017. London - British Library Or. 11122, f. 122a, M, rubric: ליום חמישי.
14018. Manchester - John Rylands University Library, Ms. Gaster 5, f. 149a-150a, M, rubric: ליום ה'.
14019. Muenchen - Bayerische Staatsbibliothek, Cod. hebr. 472, f. 99b, M, rubric: ליום חמישי.
14020. Nahariya - Menahem and Saida Yaakob 284, f. 14b-15b, M.
14021. New York - Jewish Theological Seminary Ms. 3013, f. 75a-75b, M, rubric: ליום חמישי.

14022. New York - Jewish Theological Seminary Ms. 3193, f. 164a-164b, M, rubric: ליום חמישי.
14023. New York - Jewish Theological Seminary Ms. 3295, f. 90b-91a, M, rubric: ליום חמישי.
14024. New York - Jewish Theological Seminary Ms. 4195, f. 21b-22b, M.
14025. New York - Public Library, Heb. Ms. 9, f. 72b-73a, M, rubric: ליום ה'.
14026. Oxford - Bodleian Library MS Opp. Add. fol. 58 (Neubauer 2498), f. 142a-142b, M, rubric: ליום חמישי.
14027. Paris - G. Epstein 23/57, f. 103b-104a, C, rubric: ליום חמישי.
14028. Philadelphia - University of Pennsylvania HB 2, f. 98a, M, rubric: ליום ה'.
14029. Ramat Gan - Universitat Bar Ilan 703, f. 195a, M, rubric: ליום חמישי.
14030. Strasbourg - Bibliotheque Nationale et Universitaire 3965 (Landauer 39), p. 238-239, M, rubric: ליום ה'.

Yemen, commentary by Yiḥya b. Josef Tsalaḥ
14031. Montreal - Elberg 203, f. 12b, M, no incipit.

למענך אדיר באדירים למענך בורא רוח (ל 1161), סעדיה גאון, הושענא

haAri, commentary by Mose b. Hayyim Pesante
14032. New York - Columbia University X 893 J 558, f. 199b, M.
14033. New York - Jewish Theological Seminary Ms. 4696, f. 8b-10a, C.

haAri, commentary by Simon b. Tsemaḥ Duran
14034. New York - Columbia University X 893 J 558, f. 199b, M.

Italia, commentary by Zakharya David Shabbetai Segre
14035. Torino - Archivio Terracini 1499, p. 42-46, C, rubric: פירוש הושענא למענך אדיר אדירים.

North-Africa
14036. Jerusalem - Benayahu ז 27, f. 52b-54a, M.

Yemen
14037. Jerusalem - Benayahu ת 88, f. 27b, M.
14038. Jerusalem - Benayahu ת 283, f. 97a, M, short.
14039. Jerusalem - Michael Krupp 3391, f. 2a, M.
14040. Jerusalem - Musad haRav Kook 335, f. 91a-92a, M.
14041. Jerusalem - Musad haRav Kook 952, f. 1b-2b, M.
14042. Jerusalem - Sassoon 264, f. 91a-92b, M, rubric: פירוש.
14043. Jerusalem - Sassoon 902, p. 169-170, M.
14044. New York - Alfred Moldovan HH, f. 2a-3b, M.
14045. New York - Jewish Theological Seminary Ms. 9325, f. 69a-69b, M.
14046. New York - Public Library, Heb. Ms. 10, f. 56a, M, rubric: פירוש השענון, margin damaged.
14047. Ramat Gan - Universitat Bar Ilan 62, f. 27a, G, margin damaged.

Yemen, commentary by Isaac b. Abraham Wanneh
14048. Chicago-Spertus College of Judaica D 1, f. 193a, M, rubric: פירוש השענון.

14049. Jerusalem - Benayahu ת 261, f. 79a-79b, M, rubric: פירושי ההושענות. ליום ראשון.
14050. Jerusalem - Benayahu ת 282, f. 72b-73a, M, rubric: פי' ההושענות.
14051. Jerusalem - Israel Museum 180/78, f. 2a-3b, M, rubric: ליום א'.
14052. Jerusalem - Makhon Ben Zvi 1156 (Tubi 155), f. 70b, M, rubric: פירוש ההושענות.
14053. Jerusalem - Makhon Ben Zvi 1169 (Tubi 159), f. 60b, M, very short.
14054. Jerusalem - Makhon Ben Zvi 1174 (Tubi 154), f. 80b-81a, M, rubric: ליום ראשן.
14055. Jerusalem - Makhon ben Zvi 1186 (Tubi 205), f. 1a-1b, M, rubric: חדושי מה"ריו.
14056. Jerusalem - Michael Krupp 604, f. 90a, M, rubric: פי' ההושענות. ליום ראשון.
14057. Jerusalem - Michael Krupp 1990, f. 96a-96b, M, rubric: הושענות ליום ראשון.
14058. Jerusalem - Musad haRav Kook 325, f. 100a-101a, M, rubric: פירוש ההושענות.
14059. Jerusalem - Musad haRav Kook 325, f. 118b-119a, M, rubric: חידושין, very short.
14060. Jerusalem - Musad haRav Kook 330, f. 65b, M, rubric: פירוש השענון.
14061. Jerusalem - Musad haRav Kook 347, f. 55b, M.
14062. Jerusalem - Sassoon 1158, p. 211, M, rubric: פירוש ליום ראשון.
14063. Jerusalem - Sassoon 1174, p. 139, M, rubric: פירוש ההושענות.
14064. Jerusalem - Schocken Institute 70028, f. 185a-185b, M.
14065. Jerusalem - Yehiel haLevi 4, f. 85a, M, rubric: פירוש השענון.
14066. London - British Library Or. 11121, f. 130b, C.
14067. London - British Library Or. 11122, f. 120a, M, rubric: פי' ההושענות. ליום ראשון.
14068. Manchester - John Rylands University Library, Ms. Gaster 5, f. 144b-145a, M, rubric: ליום ראשון.
14069. Muenchen - Bayerische Staatsbibliothek, Cod. hebr. 472, f. 96b, M, rubric: פירוש.
14070. Nahariya - Menahem and Saida Yaakob 284, f. 2a-2b, M, rubric: פירוש.
14071. New York - Jewish Theological Seminary Ms. 3013, f. 72a-72b, M, rubric: ליום ראשון.
14072. New York - Jewish Theological Seminary Ms. 3193, f. 159a-159b, M, rubric: ליום ראשון.
14073. New York - Jewish Theological Seminary Ms. 4195, f. 1a-2b, M, rubric: חידושין למהר"יו ז"ל.
14074. New York - Public Library, Heb. Ms. 9, f. 69b-70a, M, rubric: פי' ההושענות ליום ראשון.
14075. Oxford - Bodleian Library MS Opp. Add. fol. 58 (Neubauer 2498), f. 137b-138b, M, rubric: פירוש.

14076. Paris - G. Epstein 23/57, f. 96a-96b, C, rubric: חדושים מהר״ר יצחק ונה ז״ל.
14077. Philadelphia - University of Pennsylvania HB 2, f. 95b-96a, M, rubric: ליום ראשון.
14078. Ramat Gan - Universitat Bar Ilan 703, f. 190b-191a, M, rubric: ׳פי׳ הושענות של יום א׳.
14079. San Francisco - California State Library, Sutro Branch MS 154 (Brinner 125), f. 106a-106b, C, rubric: פירוש הושענות לסכות.
14080. Strasbourg - Bibliotheque Nationale et Universitaire 3965 (Landauer 39), p 229-230, M, rubric: ליום ראשון.

Yemen, commentary by Samḥun b. Salomo Ḥaloah
14081. Jerusalem - Makhon ben Zvi 2808, f. 10a-11a, C.

Yemen, commentary by Simon b. Tsemaḥ Duran
14082. Jerusalem - Michael Krupp 1758, f. 2a, M.

Yemen, commentary by Yiḥya b. Josef Tsalaḥ
14083. Montreal - Elberg 203, f. 1a-1b, M, rubric: עץ חיים.

למענך אלהי רצה עם לך שחר (ל 1170), דוד בן בקודה, פזמון ליום כפור haAri
14084. Harvard University 067, f. 96b, 97b, C.

Sepharad
14085. Jerusalem - Benayahu ז 25, f. 107b-108a, M, lexical explanations in Hebrew and Ladino.

Sepharad, commentary by David b. Josef Abudarham[324]
14086. Budapest - Magyar tudomanyos akademia, MS Kaufmann A 405/2, p. 188, C, rubric: פזמון לר׳ דוד בן בקודה ז״ל.
14087. Cincinnati - Hebrew Union College 490, f. 4a, M, rubric: פזמון לר׳ דוד בן פקודא ז״ל.
14088. Holon - Yehuda Nahum 278, f. 8a-8b, FC, only lower half of leaf extant, rubric: פזמון.
14089. New York - Columbia X893 Ab 93, f. 5b, C, rubric: פזמון לר׳ דוד בן בקודה ז״ל.
14090. New York - Jewish Theological Seminary Ms. 3011, f. 4b-5a, C, rubric: פזמון.

למשפט כונן כסאו (ל 1190), יהודה הלוי, חלק ג׳, קדושתא לראש השנה
Carpentras
14091. Cincinnati - Hebrew Union College 429/1, f. 9a, M, no incipit.

Carpentras, commentary by Josef b. Abraham of Montelitz
14092. Cincinnati - Hebrew Union College 357, f. 56a-56b, M, rubric: פירוש.
14093. New York - Jewish Theological Seminary Ms. 4746, f. 14a, M.

---

[324] Edited by Prins, תשלום אבודרהם, p. 80-81.

14094. Paris - Alliance Israelite Universelle H 422 A, f. 33b-34a, M, no incipit.
14095. Paris - Ecole Rabbinique 31, f. 102b, M, no incipit.

למתודה חטאתיו ומבין תגרת קמיו (ל 1191), משה אבן עזרא, סליחה
Sepharad, commentary by David b. Josef Abudarham[325]
14096. Budapest - Magyar tudomanyos akademia, MS. Kaufmann A 405/2, p. 209, C, rubric: פזמון.
14097. New York - Columbia X893 Ab 93, f. 13(ii)a, C, rubric: פזמון.
14098. New York - Jewish Theological Seminary Ms. 3011, f. 20b-21a, C, rubric: פזמון.
Yemen
14099. Jerusalem - Benayahu ת 414, f. 122a, M.
14100. Jerusalem - Sassoon 902, p. 369, M.
14101. New York - Jewish Theological Seminary Ms. 3193, f. 123a-123b, M.
Yemen, commentary by Isaac b. Abraham Wanneh
14102. Chicago-Spertus College of Judaica D 2, 2, f. 183a, M.
14103. Jerusalem - Musad haRav Kook 330, f. 90b, G.
14104. Jerusalem - Sassoon 1158, p. 303, M.
14105. Manchester - John Rylands University Library, Ms. Gaster 5, f. 177b-178a, M.

לעינינו עשקו עמלנו ממושך ומורט ממנו (ל +1253), סליחה
Yemen
14106. Jerusalem - Benayahu ת 414, f. 119b, M.
14107. New York - Jewish Theological Seminary Ms. 3193, f. 120b, M.
Yemen, commentary by Isaac b. Abraham Wanneh
14108. Chicago-Spertus College of Judaica D 2, 2, f. 180b-181a, M.
14109. New York - Jewish Theological Seminary Ms. 3013, f. 99a, M.

לעמו ישראל יצו שדי סליחה (ל 1260), יצחק בן שמואל הלוי, סליחה
Carpentras
14110. Cincinnati - Hebrew Union College 392, f. 15a, M.
Carpentras, commentary by Josef b. Abraham of Montelitz
14111. Cincinnati - Hebrew Union College 291, f. 8b-9a, C, rubric: פירוש סליחה לשבת יצו שדי וכו'.
14112. New York - Jewish Theological Seminary Ms. 4197, f. 30a-30b, M.
14113. Paris - Ecole Rabbinique 32, f. 35a-35b, M.
14114. Strasbourg - Bibliotheque Nationale et Universitaire 4081, f. 41a-42b, M.

---

[325] Edited by Prins, תשלום אבודרהם, p. 29.

לפני המלך אשפוך את עתירתי (ל 1300), משה אבן עזרא, סליחה

Yemen

14115. Jerusalem - Sassoon 902, p. 443, M.
14116. New York - Jewish Theological Seminary Ms. 3109, f. 73a, M.

Yemen, commentary by Isaac b. Abraham Wanneh

14117. Chicago-Spertus College of Judaica D 2, 2, f. 223a, M, no incipit.
14118. Jerusalem - Sassoon 1158, p. 376, M, rubric: סימן למשה, no incipit.
14119. London - British Library Or. 11122, f. 188a, M, no incipit.

לקראת שבת אצא בחבה (ל 1370), דוד

Yemen

14120. Cincinnati - Hebrew Union College 398, f. 115b-116a, M.

לשכינה עלתה ויללה כי רבתה אללי לי אויה לי (ל 1448), קינה

Yemen, commentary by Isaac b. Abraham Wanneh

14121. Jerusalem - Sassoon 1158, p. 172, M, no incipit.
14122. London - British Library Or. 11122, f. 103a, M, no incipit.

מאהב ויחיד לאמו (מ+ 37), אליה ברבי מרדכי, חלק ב', קדושתא למנחה יום כפור

Ashkenaz

14123. Berlin - Staatsbibliothek (Preussischer Kulturbesitz) Or. Qu. 798-799 (Steinschneider 177), I, f. 161a-161b, M.
14124. Braunschweig - Landesmuseum fuer Geschichte und Volkstum R 2386, vol. II, f. 254a-254b, M
14125. Fulda - Hessische Landesbibliothek A 3 II, f. 127b-128a, C, commentator: Josef.
14126. Hamburg - Staats- und Universitaetsbibliothek Cod. hebr. 17/2 (Steinschneider 152), f. 160b-161a, C.
14127. Hamburg - Staats- und Universitaetsbibliothek Cod. hebr. 62 (Steinschneider 154), f. 22a, C, short.
14128. Hamburg - Staats- und Universitaetsbibliothek Cod. hebr. 132 (Steinschneider 155), f. 49b, C, short, no incipit.
14129. Jerusalem - Jewish National and University Library Ms Heb 8° 3037, f. 214b-215a, M.
14130. Jerusalem - Schocken Institute 24100 / Mahzor Nuremberg, f. 443b, M, short.
14131. London - British Library Or. 11318/1, f. 122a-122b, C.
14132. London - Montefiore Library 261, f. 63b, C, commentator: Eliezer b. Natan?, short.
14133. Moscow - Russian State Library, Ms. Guenzburg 191, f. 144b, M.
14134. Moscow - Russian State Library, Ms. Guenzburg 615, f. 108a, C, no incipit.
14135. Muenchen - Bayerische Staatsbibliothek, Cod. hebr. 21, f. 239b, M.

14136. Muenchen - Bayerische Staatsbibliothek, Cod. hebr. 346, f. 87a, C, short.
14137. New York - Jewish Theological Seminary Ms. 4466, f. 413a-413b, M.
14138. New York - Jewish Theological Seminary Ms. 8169 (Acc. 0016), f. 114b-115a, M.
14139. Oxford - Bodleian Library MS Mich. 365 (Neubauer 1208), f. 92b-93a, C, no incipit.
14140. Oxford - Bodleian Library MS Opp. 170 (Neubauer 1205), f. 180b-181a, C.
14141. Oxford - Bodleian Library MS Opp. 172 (Neubauer 1211), f. 82a, C, short.
14142. Oxford - Bodleian Library MS Opp. 619 (Neubauer 2374), f. 254b, M.
14143. Parma - Biblioteca Palatina Cod. Parm. 3205 (de Rossi 655), f. 237a, C, no incipit, short.
14144. Parma - Biblioteca Palatina Cod. Parm. 3507 (Perreau 27), f. 172a, C, no incipit.
14145. Vatican - Biblioteca Apostolica ebr. 308, f. 139b, C, commentator: David b. Mose (compiler), short.
14146. Vatican - Biblioteca Apostolica ebr. 422/1, f. 19b, C, very short.
14147. Zurich - Zentralbibliothek Heid. 139, f. 88b, C, no incipit, very short, additional marginal notes.

Asti, Fossano, Moncalvo
14148. New Haven - Yale University, Beinecke Rare Book and MS Library, MS Heb. 52, f. 161a, M.

Tsarfat
14149. London - David Sofer 5, f. 165a, C.
14150. Oxford - Bodleian Library MS Laud. Or. 271 (Neubauer 1206), f. 118a, C, commentator: Aaron b. Hayyim haKohen (compiler), no incipit, short.
14151. Parma - Biblioteca Palatina Cod. Parm. 3006 (de Rossi 654,1), f. 219a-219b, M.

מאין כמוך באמצך שמים ושמי שמים (מ +76), פיוט לאחרי הקדושה, שחרית יום כפור

Ashkenaz
14152. Muenchen - Bayerische Staatsbibliothek, Cod. hebr. 86, f. 136b-137a, G.
14153. Muenchen - Bayerische Staatsbibliothek, Cod. hebr. 346, f. 68b-69a, C, no incipit.

Asti, Fossano, Moncalvo
14154. New Haven - Yale University, Beinecke Rare Book and MS Library, MS Heb. 52, f. 164a, M.

מאין סוף נפשי תעירני (מ 78), שלם שבזי

Yemen
14155. Cincinnati - Hebrew Union College 398, f. 135a-136a, M.

מאלמי מגדים ארבעה (מ +93), אלעזר ברבי קליר, חלק ב', קדושתא ליום ב' של סוכות

Ashkenaz
14156. Berlin - Staatsbibliothek (Preussischer Kulturbesitz) Or. Qu. 798-799 (Steinschneider 177), I, f. 198a-198b, M.
14157. Braunschweig - Landesmuseum fuer Geschichte und Volkstum R 2386, vol. I, f. 122a, M.
14158. Budapest - Magyar tudomanyos akademia, MS. Kaufmann A 400, p. 369, C, no incipit, short.
14159. Hamburg - Staats- und Universitaetsbibliothek Cod. hebr. 62 (Steinschneider 154), f. 33b, C, no incipit, short.
14160. Hamburg - Staats- und Universitaetsbibliothek Cod. hebr. 132 (Steinschneider 155), f. 55b-56a, C.
14161. Jerusalem - Jewish National and University Library Ms Heb 8° 3037, f. 236a-236b, M.
14162. Jerusalem - Schocken Institute 24100 / Mahzor Nuremberg, f. 476a, M.
14163. London - British Library Add. 18695 (Margoliouth 683), f. 111b, T, Yiddish.
14164. London - British Library Add. 22431 (Margoliouth 662a), f. 101a-101b, M.
14165. London - British Library Or. 11318/1, f. 130b, C, short, no incipit.
14166. London - Montefiore Library 261, f. 65b-66a, C, commentator: Eliezer b. Natan?.
14167. Moscow - Russian State Library, Ms. Guenzburg 615, f. 115b, C, no incipit.
14168. Oxford - Bodleian Library MS Mich. 365 (Neubauer 1208), f. 95a-95b, C.
14169. Oxford - Bodleian Library MS Opp. 172 (Neubauer 1211), f. 90a, C, very short.
14170. Parma - Biblioteca Palatina Cod. Parm. 3507 (Perreau 27), f. 174a, C, no incipit.
14171. Vatican - Biblioteca Apostolica ebr. 305,1, f. 39a, C, no incipit.
14172. Vatican - Biblioteca Apostolica ebr. 422/1, f. 21b, C, very short.
14173. Zurich - Zentralbibliothek Heid. 139, f. 93a, C, no incipit, additional marginal notes.

Romania
14174. London - London School of Jewish Studies. Asher I.Myers collection 9, f. 201b, M.
14175. Vatican - Biblioteca Apostolica ebr. 320, f. 411a-411b, M.

Tsarfat

14176. London - David Sofer 5, f. 179a, C.
14177. Oxford - Bodleian Library MS Laud. Or. 271 (Neubauer 1206), f. 97b, C, commentator: Aaron b. Hayyim haKohen (compiler), no incipit, short.
14178. Parma - Biblioteca Palatina Cod. Parm. 1264, f. 27a-27b, M.

מארם ומאדום וממואב ומאלופיהם (מ 121), הושענא

Carpentras

14179. New York - Jewish Theological Seminary Ms. 1609, f. 99b, C, rubric: ליום שבת, no incipit.

מארץ שפלנו (מ 122), משה אבן עזרא, קדושתא לשחרית יום כפור

Carpentras

14180. Cincinnati - Hebrew Union College 392, f. 43a-44b, M, no incipit.

Carpentras, commentary by Josef b. Abraham of Montelitz

14181. Cincinnati - Hebrew Union College 291, f. 19a-20a, C, rubric: פי' מארץ שפלנו וכו'.
14182. New York - Jewish Theological Seminary Ms. 4197, f. 99b-102a, M, no incipit.
14183. Paris - Ecole Rabbinique 32, f. 122a-124a, M, no incipit.
14184. Strasbourg - Bibliotheque Nationale et Universitaire 4081, f. 99a-100b, M, no incipit.

מאתך תהילתי שומע עתירה ושועה (מ 131), מרדכי בן שבתי, סליחה

Ashkenaz

14185. Jerusalem - Schocken Institute 24100 / Mahzor Nuremberg , f. 465b-466a, M.
14186. Muenchen - Bayerische Staatsbibliothek, Cod. hebr. 346 , f. 145a-145b, C, rubric: אחרת.
14187. Oxford - Bodleian Library MS Opp. 172 (Neubauer 1211), f. 88b, C.
14188. Vatican - Biblioteca Apostolica ebr. 308, f. 149a, C, commentator: David b. Mose (compiler).

Ashkenaz, commentary by Abraham b. Azriel[326]

14189. Frankfurt a M - Stadt- und Universitaetsbibliothek Fol. 16 (Merzbacher 95), f. 104a, C.

מבורך רחמנא מהשנא עידנה (מ 137), בנימין הכהן, לשמחת תורה

Yemen, commentary by Yiḥya b. Josef Tsalaḥ

14190. Montreal - Elberg 203, f. 37b-38a, M.

---

[326] Edited by Urbach, ערוגת הבושם, vol. III, p. 544.

מבין שגיאות

Ashkenaz
14191. Budapest - Magyar tudomanyos akademia, MS. Kaufmann A 400 , p. 354, C.

מבית מלוני קמתי בצוקי ולבית אדוני באתי בחוקי (מ 170), משה אבן עזרא, סליחה

Yemen
14192. Jerusalem - Sassoon 902, p. 373, M.
14193. New York - Jewish Theological Seminary Ms. 3108, f. 20b, M, short.
14194. New York - Jewish Theological Seminary Ms. 3193, f. 127a, M, no incipit.

Yemen, commentary by Isaac b. Abraham Wanneh
14195. Chicago-Spertus College of Judaica D 1, f. 229b-230a, M, rubric: 'פ.
14196. Chicago-Spertus College of Judaica D 2, 2, f. 185b, M, rubric: מבית מלוני פירוש.
14197. Jerusalem - Musad haRav Kook 330, f. 93a, M.
14198. Jerusalem - Musad haRav Kook 347, f. 74a, G.
14199. Jerusalem - Sassoon 1158, p. 310, M, no incipit.
14200. Jerusalem - Yehiel haLevi 4, f. 137b, M.
14201. Manchester - John Rylands University Library, Ms. Gaster 5, f. 180a, M, short.
14202. New York - Jewish Theological Seminary Ms. 3013, f. 102b, M, short.

מגדל עוז שם יי להנצל (מ 198+), יהודה הלוי, חלק ב, קדושתא לשחרית יום כפור

Carpentras, commentary by Josef b. Abraham of Montelitz
14203. Cincinnati - Hebrew Union College 357, f. 53b-54a, M.
14204. New York - Jewish Theological Seminary Ms. 4746, f. 12a, M.
14205. Paris - Alliance Israelite Universelle H 422 A, f. 31a-31b, M.
14206. Paris - Ecole Rabbinique 31, f. 100a, M.

מגלות לבי מאד חרד (מ 214), שלם שבזי

Yemen
14207. Cincinnati - Hebrew Union College 398, f. 123b-127a, M, long.

מדי שנה קינה בליל זה מזומנה (מ 256), קינה

Yemen, commentary by Isaac b. Abraham Wanneh
14208. Jerusalem - Sassoon 1158, p. 160, M.
14209. London - British Library Or. 11122, f. 97a, M.

מדמי הלבבות וחלבי הכליות (מ 263), משה אבן עזרא, חלק, קדושתא לשחרית יום
כפור, בתימן: סליחה

Carpentras

14210. Cincinnati - Hebrew Union College 392, f. 50b-51b, M, no incipit.

Carpentras, commentary by Josef b. Abraham of Montelitz

14211. Cincinnati - Hebrew Union College 291, f. 26a-26b, C, rubric: פי' מדמי הלבבות וכו'.

14212. New York - Jewish Theological Seminary Ms. 4197, f. 115a-115b, M.

14213. Paris - Ecole Rabbinique 32, f. 134b, M, no incipit.

14214. Strasbourg - Bibliotheque Nationale et Universitaire 4081, f. 111b-112a, M, no incipit.

Sepharad, commentary by David b. Josef Abudarham[327]

14215. Budapest - Magyar tudomanyos akademia, MS. Kaufmann A 405/2, p. 197, C, rubric: פזמון.

14216. Cincinnati - Hebrew Union College 490, f. 6a, C.

14217. Holon - Yehuda Nahum 278, f. 9b, FC, rubric: פזמון, only beginning.

14218. New York - Columbia X893 Ab 93, f. 9a, C, rubric: פזמון.

14219. New York - Jewish Theological Seminary Ms. 3011, f. 8a, C, rubric: פזמון.

Yemen

14220. Jerusalem - Sassoon 902, p. 427, M, very short.

14221. New York - Jewish Theological Seminary Ms. 3052, f. 32b, M, rubric: אל מלך.

Yemen, commentary by Isaac b. Abraham Wanneh

14222. Chicago-Spertus College of Judaica D 2, 2, f. 201a, M.

14223. Jerusalem - Benayahu ת 261, f. 140a, M, rubric: אל מלך, short.

14224. Jerusalem - Makhon Ben Zvi 1156 (Tubi 155), f. 122a, M, rubric: אל מלך, short.

14225. Jerusalem - Makhon Ben Zvi 1174 (Tubi 154), f. 126b, M, short.

14226. Jerusalem - Michael Krupp 604, f. 155a, M, rubric: אל מלך.

14227. Jerusalem - Musad haRav Kook 325, f. 183b, M, rubric: אל מלך, short.

14228. Jerusalem - Sassoon 1158, p. 375, M, short, no incipit.

14229. Jerusalem - Sassoon 1174, p. 235, M, short, no incipit.

14230. London - British Library Or. 11122, f. 187b-188a, M, short.

14231. Manchester - John Rylands University Library, Ms. Gaster 5, f. 198a-198b, M, short.

14232. Muenchen - Bayerische Staatsbibliothek, Cod. hebr. 472, f. 167a, M, rubric: אל מלך, short.

14233. New York - Jewish Theological Seminary Ms. 3013, f. 123a, M, rubric: אל מלך.

14234. New York - Jewish Theological Seminary Ms. 3294, f. 11a, C.

14235. New York - Public Library, Heb. Ms. 9, f. 113b, M, short.

---

[327] Edited by Prins, תשלום אבודרהם, p. 86-87.

14236. Strasbourg - Bibliotheque Nationale et Universitaire 3965 (Landauer 39), p. 382, M, rubric: אל מלך, short.

מה אילו פלאי נסיך (מ +280), אלעזר ברבי קליר, חלק ב', קדושתא לפסח

Ashkenaz

14237. Berlin - Staatsbibliothek (Preussischer Kulturbesitz) Or. Qu. 798-799 (Steinschneider 177), II, f. 78b-79a, M.
14238. Braunschweig - Landesmuseum fuer Geschichte und Volkstum R 2386, vol. I, f. 36b, M.
14239. Budapest - Magyar tudomanyos akademia, MS. Kaufmann A 384, f. 162b-163a, M.
14240. Budapest - Magyar tudomanyos akademia, MS. Kaufmann A 400, p. 130-131, C, no incipit.
14241. Hamburg - Staats- und Universitaetsbibliothek Cod. hebr. 17/2 (Steinschneider 152), f. 64b-65a, C.
14242. Jerusalem - Schocken Institute 24100 / Mahzor Nuremberg, f. 94a-94b, M.
14243. London - British Library Add. 18695 (Margoliouth 683), f. 41a-41b, T, Yiddish.
14244. Moscow - Russian State Library, Ms. Guenzburg 615, f. 22b, C.
14245. Muenchen - Bayerische Staatsbibliothek, Cod. hebr. 88, f. 72b, G.
14246. Muenchen - Bayerische Staatsbibliothek, Cod. hebr. 393, f. 129b-130a, C, no incipit.
14247. New York - Jewish Theological Seminary Ms. 4466, f. 74a, M, very short.
14248. Paris - Bibliotheque Nationale heb. 709, f. 98a, C, no incipit.
14249. Parma - Biblioteca Palatina Cod. Parm. 1002 (Ta 24), f. 118a, M.
14250. Parma - Biblioteca Palatina Cod. Parm. 3205 (de Rossi 655), f. 102a, C.
14251. Parma - Biblioteca Palatina Cod. Parm. 3507 (Perreau 27), f. 64b, C, no incipit.
14252. Zurich - Zentralbibliothek Heid. 139, f. 37b, C, no incipit, additional marginal notes.

Tsarfat

14253. London - British Library Add. 11639 (Margoliouth 1056), f. 293a, M.
14254. Moscow - Russian State Library, Ms. Guenzburg 1665, f. 71a-71b, M, no incipit.

מה טוב ומה נעים חברת בני תורה (מ 336), שלם שבזי

Yemen

14255. Cincinnati - Hebrew Union College 398, f. 133a-134b, M.

מה יקרה שבת ומה כבודה (מ 402), דוד בן יוסף

Yemen
14256. Cincinnati - Hebrew Union College 398, f. 121b-123a, M.

מה יתרון לאדם בעמלו ובכבודו (מ 412), יהודה הלוי, תוכחה

Yemen
14257. Jerusalem - Benayahu ת 301, f. 42b, M, rubric: 'פ.
14258. Jerusalem - Sassoon 902, p. 401, M, no incipit.
Yemen, commentary by Isaac b. Abraham Wanneh
14259. Chicago-Spertus College of Judaica D 2, 2, f. 201b-202a, M, no incipit.
14260. Jerusalem - Benayahu ת 261, f. 132b-133a, M, rubric: אל מלך.
14261. Jerusalem - Benayahu ת 282, f. 117b-118a, M, rubric: אל מלך, no incipit.
14262. Jerusalem - Makhon Ben Zvi 1156 (Tubi 155), f. 115b, M, rubric: אל מלך.
14263. Jerusalem - Makhon Ben Zvi 1174 (Tubi 154), f. 118b, M.
14264. Jerusalem - Michael Krupp 604, f. 145b-146a, M, rubric: אל מלך.
14265. Jerusalem - Musad haRav Kook 325, f. 171b-172a, M, rubric: אל מלך.
14266. Jerusalem - Musad haRav Kook 330, f. 103b, G.
14267. Jerusalem - Musad haRav Kook 347, f. 80a, G.
14268. Jerusalem - Sassoon 1158, p. 364-365, M, no incipit.
14269. Jerusalem - Yehiel haLevi 4, f. 153a, G.
14270. London - British Library Or. 11122, f. 182a-182b, M, no incipit.
14271. Manchester - John Rylands University Library, Ms. Gaster 5, f. 191a, M.
14272. Muenchen - Bayerische Staatsbibliothek, Cod. hebr. 472, f. 156b-157b, M, rubric: אל מלך.
14273. New York - Jewish Theological Seminary Ms. 3013, f. 116b, M, rubric: אל מלך.
14274. New York - Jewish Theological Seminary Ms. 3109, f. 90b-91a, M, rubric: אל מלך, no incipit.
14275. Philadelphia - University of Pennsylvania HB 2, f. 129a, M.
14276. Strasbourg - Bibliotheque Nationale et Universitaire 3965 (Landauer 39), p. 358, M, rubric: אל מלך.

מה לי ללכת אחרי ההבל, סליחה

Yemen, commentary by Isaac b. Abraham Wanneh
14277. Jerusalem - Sassoon 1158, p. 429-430, M, no incipit.
14278. London - British Library Or. 11122, f. 224a, M, no incipit.

מה מועיל רשע בעליו (מ 520), משה בן קלונימוס, חלק ד', קדושתא ליום ח' של פסח
Ashkenaz
14279. Berlin - Staatsbibliothek (Preussischer Kulturbesitz) Or. Qu. 798-799 (Steinschneider 177), II, f. 92a-93a, M.
14280. Budapest - Magyar tudomanyos akademia, MS. Kaufmann A 384, f. 204a-205a, M.
14281. Budapest - Magyar tudomanyos akademia, MS. Kaufmann A 400, p. 138-141, C, no incipit.
14282. Hamburg - Staats- und Universitaetsbibliothek Cod. hebr. 17/2 (Steinschneider 152), f. 67a-68a, C, no incipit.
14283. Jerusalem - Schocken Institute 24100 / Mahzor Nuremberg, f. 123a-123b, M.
14284. Moscow - Russian State Library, Ms. Guenzburg 615, f. 25a-26a, C.
14285. Muenchen - Bayerische Staatsbibliothek, Cod. hebr. 88, f. 83b-84a, G.
14286. Muenchen - Bayerische Staatsbibliothek, Cod. hebr. 393, f. 135a-135b, C, no incipit.
14287. New York - Jewish Theological Seminary Ms. 4466, f. 110a-111b, M, incipit שלישלים.
14288. Oxford - Bodleian Library MS Opp. 170 (Neubauer 1205), f. 76b-77a, C, no incipit.
14289. Paris - Bibliotheque Nationale heb. 709, f. 102b-103b, C, no incipit.
14290. Parma - Biblioteca Palatina Cod. Parm. 1002 (Ta 24), f. 141a, M, incipit חכם.
14291. Parma - Biblioteca Palatina Cod. Parm. 3205 (de Rossi 655), f. 109a-109b, C, incipit חכם.
14292. Parma - Biblioteca Palatina Cod. Parm. 3507 (Perreau 27), f. 73b-74b, C, no incipit.
14293. Zurich - Zentralbibliothek Heid. 139, f. 46a-46b, C, no incipit, additional marginal notes.
Tsarfat
14294. London - David Sofer 5, f. 42a-42b, C, incipit חכם, additional glosses.
14295. Moscow - Russian State Library, Ms. Guenzburg 1665, f. 90b-91b, M, no incipit.
14296. Oxford - Bodleian Library MS Laud. Or. 271 (Neubauer 1206), f. 81a-81b, C, commentator: Aaron b. Hayyim haKohen (compiler).
14297. Vatican - Biblioteca Apostolica ebr. 306, f. 218a-219a, C, no incipit.

מה נאמר לפניך יי אלהינו מה נדבר ומה נצטדק, סליחה
Yemen, commentary by Isaac b. Abraham Wanneh
14298. Chicago-Spertus College of Judaica D 2, 2, f. 231b-232a, M, no incipit.

מה נדבר ומה נצטדק (מ 536), סליחה

Ashkenaz

14299. Muenchen - Bayerische Staatsbibliothek, Cod. hebr. 346 , f. 154a, C, short.

מה רבו פלאיך ועצמו מוראיך (מ 611), יצחק גיאת, חלק ח', קדושתא לשחרית יום כפור, בתימן: סליחה

Yemen, commentary by Isaac b. Abraham Wanneh

14300. Chicago-Spertus College of Judaica D 2, 2, f. 198a-198b, M, no incipit.
14301. Jerusalem - Michael Krupp 604, f. 149b-150a, M.
14302. Jerusalem - Sassoon 1158, p. 372, M, no incipit.
14303. London - British Library Or. 11122, f. 186a-186b, M, rubric: אל מלך.

מהדר חתן וכלה זרחו נפשי ושכלי (מ 655), שלם שבזי

Yemen

14304. Cincinnati - Hebrew Union College 398, f. 127a-129a, M.

מורה חטאים סלול להתהלך (מ 804), משולם ב"ר קלונימוס, חלק ה', קדושתא לשחרית יום כפור

Ashkenaz

14305. Berlin - Staatsbibliothek (Preussischer Kulturbesitz) Or. Qu. 798-799 (Steinschneider 177), I, f. 73a-73b, M.
14306. Braunschweig - Landesmuseum fuer Geschichte und Volkstum R 2386, vol. II, f. 185b-186b, M, no incipit.
14307. Budapest - Magyar tudomanyos akademia, MS. Kaufmann A 400 , p. 310-311, C.
14308. Cambridge - University Library Or. 785, f. 114a-115a, G.
14309. Hamburg - Staats- und Universitaetsbibliothek Cod. hebr. 17/2 (Steinschneider 152), f. 151a, C, incipit אנא.
14310. Hamburg - Staats- und Universitaetsbibliothek Cod. hebr. 62 (Steinschneider 154), f. 3b, C.
14311. Hamburg - Staats- und Universitaetsbibliothek Cod. hebr. 132 (Steinschneider 155), f. 33a-33b, C.
14312. Jerusalem - Jewish National and University Library Ms Heb 8° 3037, f. 116b-117a, M.
14313. Jerusalem - Schocken Institute 24100 / Mahzor Nuremberg , f. 376a-376b, M.
14314. London - British Library Or. 11318/1, f. 72a-73a, C.
14315. London - Montefiore Library 261, f. 43a, C, commentator: Eliezer b. Natan?.
14316. Moscow - Russian State Library, Ms. Guenzburg 191, f. 85a-86a, M.

14317. Muenchen - Bayerische Staatsbibliothek, Cod. hebr. 86, f. 101a-102a, G.
14318. Muenchen - Bayerische Staatsbibliothek, Cod. hebr. 346, f. 52b, C.
14319. Muenchen - Bayerische Staatsbibliothek, Cod. hebr. 393, f. 141a-141b, C, no incipit.
14320. New York - Jewish Theological Seminary Ms. 4466, f. 305b-306b, M.
14321. New York - Jewish Theological Seminary Ms. 8097, f. 71b, C.
14322. New York - Jewish Theological Seminary Ms. 8169 (Acc. 0016), f. 66b-67a, M.
14323. Oxford - Bodleian Library MS Mich. 365 (Neubauer 1208), f. 68b-69a, C.
14324. Oxford - Bodleian Library MS Opp. 172 (Neubauer 1211), f. 37b, C.
14325. Oxford - Bodleian Library MS Opp. 619 (Neubauer 2374), f. 140b-141b, M.
14326. Paris - Bibliotheque Nationale heb. 653, f. 55a-55b, G.
14327. Parma - Biblioteca Palatina Cod. Parm. 3205 (de Rossi 655), f. 225a-225b, C, incipit אגא.
14328. Parma - Biblioteca Palatina Cod. Parm. 3271 (de Rossi 1216), f. 35a-36a, G.
14329. Parma - Biblioteca Palatina Cod. Parm. 3507 (Perreau 27), f. 146b-147a, C.
14330. Vatican - Biblioteca Apostolica ebr. 308, f. 98(ii)b-99a, C, commentator: David b. Mose (compiler).
14331. Vatican - Biblioteca Apostolica ebr. 422/1, f. 15a, C, short.
14332. Zurich - Zentralbibliothek Heid. 139, f. 76a, C, additional marginal notes.

Asti, Fossano, Moncalvo
14333. New Haven - Yale University, Beinecke Rare Book and MS Library, MS Heb. 52, f. 102b-103b, M.

Romania
14334. Vatican - Biblioteca Apostolica ebr. 320, f. 279b-280b, M.

Tsarfat
14335. Bern - Burgerbibliothek A 409, f. 79a-79b, G.
14336. London - British Library Or. 8682, f. 66a-66b, GI.
14337. London - David Sofer 5, f. 137a, C.
14338. Oxford - Bodleian Library MS Bodl. Or. 109 (Neubauer 1209), f. 19a, C, commentator: Aaron b. Hayyim haKohen (compiler), incipit אגא.
14339. Oxford - Bodleian Library MS Laud. Or. 271 (Neubauer 1206), f. 112b, C, commentator: Aaron b. Hayyim haKohen (compiler), no incipit.
14340. Parma - Biblioteca Palatina Cod. Parm. 1794 (de Rossi 1061), f. 114b-116a, M.
14341. Parma - Biblioteca Palatina Cod. Parm. 2125 (de Rossi 812), f. 39a-39b, C.

14342. Parma - Biblioteca Palatina Cod. Parm. 2890 (de Rossi 856), f. 25a, M.
14343. Parma - Biblioteca Palatina Cod. Parm. 3006 (de Rossi 654,1), f. 138b-139a, M.
14344. Vatican - Biblioteca Apostolica ebr. 306, f. 76a-76b, C, incipit אנא סלח נא.

מושך חסד ליודעיו וצדקה (מ 828), מאיר ב"ר יצחק, לחתן תורה

Tsarfat
14345. London - British Library Or. 2735 (Margoliouth 663), f. 159a, M, ecclectic.

מושכי עול עונים מסבול (מ 829), משה אבן עזרא, חלק ד', קדושתא למנחה יום כפור

Sepharad, commentary by David b. Josef Abudarham[328]
14346. Budapest - Magyar tudomanyos akademia, MS. Kaufmann A 405/2, p. 255, C, rubric: פזמון, short.
14347. New York - Columbia X893 Ab 93, f. 31b, C, rubric: פזמון, short.

מותמם בטבע שמנה, אלעזר ברבי קליר, חלק ב', קדושתא לשמיני עצרת

Romania
14348. Vatican - Biblioteca Apostolica ebr. 320, f. 459b, M.
Tsarfat
14349. Moscow - Russian State Library, Ms. Guenzburg 1665, f. 187a, M.

מזמרת שירתי הבאתי מנחתי (מ 901), משה אבן עזרא, תוכחה

Sepharad, commentary by David b. Josef Abudarham[329]
14350. Budapest - Magyar tudomanyos akademia, MS. Kaufmann A 405/2, p. 255, C, rubric: פזמון.
14351. New York - Columbia X893 Ab 93, f. 31b, C, rubric: פזמון.

מחוללת מהוללת (מ 921), משה ב"ר יצחק, יוצר ליום ח' של פסח

Ashkenaz, commentary by Abraham b. Azriel[330]
14352. Frankfurt a M - Stadt- und Universitaetsbibliothek Fol. 16 (Merzbacher 95), f. 65b-67a, C, rubric: אופן ליום טוב אחרון של פסח.
14353. Vatican - Biblioteca Apostolica ebr. 301,1, f. 97b-98b, C, rubric: אופן דפסח.

---

[328] Edited by Prins, תשלום אבודרהם, p. 131.
[329] Edited by Prins, תשלום אבודרהם, p. 129-131.
[330] Edited by Urbach, ערוגת הבושם, vol. III, p. 18-25.

מחי ומסי ממית ומחיה (מ 927), תחנונים

Ashkenaz

14354. Braunschweig - Landesmuseum fuer Geschichte und Volkstum R 2386, vol. II, f. 45a, M.

14355. Budapest - Magyar tudomanyos akademia, MS. Kaufmann A 400 , p. 528, C, rubric: אחרת.

14356. London - British Library Add. 18695 (Margoliouth 683) , f. 170b, T, Yiddish.

14357. Oxford - Bodleian Library MS Mich. 543 (Neubauer 1212), f. 4a-4b, C, commentator: Isaac b. Jacob (compiler).

14358. Padova - Biblioteca del Seminario Vescovile Cod. 218, f. 53b, M.

14359. Vatican - Biblioteca Apostolica ebr. 308, f. 20b-21a, C, commentator: David b. Mose (compiler).

14360. Vatican - Biblioteca Apostolica ebr. 422/1, f. 35a, C.

Sepharad

14361. Skokie - Hebrew Theological College 3, f. 20b, M.

Tsarfat

14362. London - David Sofer 5, f. 128, C, rubric: ערב יום כפורים שחר' לאחר כל הסליחות יאמר חרוזי כולו ואחר יאמ' זה.

14363. Oxford - Bodleian Library MS Opp. 171 (Neubauer 1207), f. 88b, C, rubric: אחרת.

14364. Parma - Biblioteca Palatina Cod. Parm. 3007 (de Rossi 654,2), f. 18a, M.

14365. Vatican - Biblioteca Apostolica ebr. 306, f. 213b-214a, C.

Yemen

14366. New York - Jewish Theological Seminary Ms. 3052, f. 81b-82a, M.

14367. New York - Jewish Theological Seminary Ms. 3108, f. 18b, M, short.

14368. New York - Jewish Theological Seminary Ms. 3193, f. 125b-126a, M, no incipit.

Yemen, commentary by Isaac b. Abraham Wanneh

14369. Chicago-Spertus College of Judaica D 2, 2, f. 184b, M, no incipit.

14370. Chicago-Spertus College of Judaica D 2, 2, f. 237a, M, no incipit.

14371. Jerusalem - Benayahu ת 261, f. 164b-165a, M.

14372. Jerusalem - Makhon Ben Zvi 1156 (Tubi 155), f. 138a, M, no incipit.

14373. Jerusalem - Makhon Ben Zvi 1174 (Tubi 154), f. 136a, M.

14374. Jerusalem - Michael Krupp 604, f. 175a, M, no incipit.

14375. Jerusalem - Musad haRav Kook 325, f. 194a, M.

14376. Jerusalem - Sassoon 1158, p. 415, M, no incipit.

14377. London - British Library Or. 11122, f. 214a, M, no incipit.

14378. Manchester - John Rylands University Library, Ms. Gaster 5, f. 222b-223a, M.

14379. Muenchen - Bayerische Staatsbibliothek, Cod. hebr. 472, f. 192b-193a, M.

מטא מיא עד נחירי, סליחה

Yemen, commentary by Isaac b. Abraham Wanneh
14383. Jerusalem - Makhon Ben Zvi 1156 (Tubi 155), f. 135b, M, no incipit.

מי אדיר אפסך (מ 981), פיוט לאחרי הקדושה לשחרית יום כפור

Ashkenaz
14384. Berlin - Staatsbibliothek (Preussischer Kulturbesitz) Or. Qu. 798-799 (Steinschneider 177), I, f. 89b-91b, M.
14385. Braunschweig - Landesmuseum fuer Geschichte und Volkstum R 2386, vol. II, f. 202a-203a, M.
14386. Budapest - Magyar tudomanyos akademia, MS. Kaufmann A 400, p. 340-350, C, rubric: רהיטי דרבינו משלם מן לוקא.
14387. Fulda - Hessische Landesbibliothek A 3 II, f. 116b-118a, C, commentator: Josef.
14388. Hamburg - Staats- und Universitaetsbibliothek Cod. hebr. 17/2 (Steinschneider 152), f. 153a-157a, C, rubric: ובכן רהיטים דרבינו קלונימוס הזק. מי לא יראך מלך הגיום כי לך יאתה כי בכל חכמיהגיום ובכל מלכותם מאין כמוך.
14389. Hamburg - Staats- und Universitaetsbibliothek Cod. hebr. 40b (Steinschneider 110), f. 110a-111a, G.
14390. Hamburg - Staats- und Universitaetsbibliothek Cod. hebr. 62 (Steinschneider 154), f. 10b-12a, C.
14391. Jerusalem - Jewish National and University Library Ms Heb 8° 3037, f. 137a-138a, M.
14392. Jerusalem - Schocken Institute 24100 / Mahzor Nuremberg, f. 386b-388a, M.
14393. London - British Library Or. 11318/1, f. 86a-88b, C.
14394. London - Montefiore Library 261, f. 49b-50b, C, commentator: Eliezer b. Natan?, rubric: רהיטי דרבינו משלם מן לוקא.
14395. Moscow - Russian State Library, Ms. Guenzburg 191, f. 103a-104b, M.
14396. Moscow - Russian State Library, Ms. Guenzburg 615, f. 96a-97b, C.
14397. Muenchen - Bayerische Staatsbibliothek, Cod. hebr. 86, f. 127a-128a, G, ecclectic.
14398. Muenchen - Bayerische Staatsbibliothek, Cod. hebr. 346, f. 61a-63a, C, no incipit.
14399. Muenchen - Bayerische Staatsbibliothek, Cod. hebr. 346, f. 69a-69b, C, rubric: מפרישה אחרת, no incipit.

14400. New York - Jewish Theological Seminary Ms. 4466, f. 331a-332b, M.
14401. New York - Jewish Theological Seminary Ms. 8097, f. 75a-75b, C.
14402. New York - Jewish Theological Seminary Ms. 8169 (Acc. 0016), f. 83a-83b, M.
14403. Oxford - Bodleian Library MS Mich. 365 (Neubauer 1208), f. 74a-75b, C.
14404. Oxford - Bodleian Library MS Opp. 170 (Neubauer 1205), f. 168a-169b, C.
14405. Oxford - Bodleian Library MS Opp. 172 (Neubauer 1211), f. 47b-49a, C.
14406. Oxford - Bodleian Library MS Opp. 619 (Neubauer 2374), f. 166a-167a, M.
14407. Parma - Biblioteca Palatina Cod. Parm. 3205 (de Rossi 655), f. 229a-230a, C.
14408. Parma - Biblioteca Palatina Cod. Parm. 3271 (de Rossi 1216), f. 56b-58a, G.
14409. Parma - Biblioteca Palatina Cod. Parm. 3507 (Perreau 27), f. 154b-156a, C.
14410. Vatican - Biblioteca Apostolica ebr. 308, f. 102(ii)b-103(ii)a, C, commentator: David b. Mose (compiler).
14411. Vatican - Biblioteca Apostolica ebr. 422/1, f. 16b-17a, C.
14412. Zurich - Zentralbibliothek Heid. 139, f. 78b-79b, C.

Ashkenaz, commentary by Abraham b. Azriel[331]

14413. Vatican - Biblioteca Apostolica ebr. 301,1, f. 171a-171b, C.

Asti, Fossano, Moncalvo

14414. New Haven - Yale University, Beinecke Rare Book and MS Library, MS Heb. 52, f. 116a-117a, M.

Tsarfat

14415. London - British Library Add. 11639 (Margoliouth 1056), f. 721b, M, rubric: מרהיטים.
14416. London - David Sofer 5, f. 141b-142a, C.
14417. Oxford - Bodleian Library MS Bodl. Or. 109 (Neubauer 1209), f. 26a-27a, C, commentator: Aaron b. Hayyim haKohen (compiler).
14418. Oxford - Bodleian Library MS Laud. Or. 271 (Neubauer 1206), f. 106b-107a, C, commentator: Aaron b. Hayyim haKohen (compiler), no incipit.
14419. Oxford - Bodleian Library MS Opp. 171 (Neubauer 1207), f. 118a-119a, C, rubric: רהיטים דר׳ משולם ליום כיפור אחר קדוש יוצר.
14420. Oxford - Bodleian Library MS Opp. 171 (Neubauer 1207), f. 119a-125a, C, rubric: ועתה אתחיל נינוקי מרהיטי ר׳ משולם.
14421. Parma - Biblioteca Palatina Cod. Parm. 1794 (de Rossi 1061), f. 149a-150a, M.

---

[331] Edited by Urbach, ערוגת הבושם, vol. III, p. 501-504.

14422. Parma - Biblioteca Palatina Cod. Parm. 2890 (de Rossi 856), f. 41a-42a, M.
14423. Parma - Biblioteca Palatina Cod. Parm. 3006 (de Rossi 654,1), f. 152b-153b, M.
14424. Vatican - Biblioteca Apostolica ebr. 306, f. 82a-83a, C.

מי אדר והוד עליו הועלם (מ 983), יוצר לשבת בראשית

Ashkenaz

14425. Budapest - Magyar tudomanyos akademia, MS. Kaufmann A 399, p. 316-317, C, rubric: פייוט לאל אדון.
14426. Cambridge - University Library Add. 504,1, f. 27b-28a, C.
14427. Hamburg - Staats- und Universitaetsbibliothek Cod. hebr. 62 (Steinschneider 154), f. 27a-27b, C, rubric: אזכה לעושר ולברכה משוכן נפרכה פירוש דפיוט מי אדר.
14428. Oxford - Bodleian Library MS Can. Or. 82 (Neubauer 1148), f. 3a-3b, M.
14429. Oxford - Bodleian Library MS Mich. 365 (Neubauer 1208), f. 26a, C.
14430. Parma - Biblioteca Palatina Cod. Parm. 3205 (de Rossi 655), f. 130a-130b, C.

Ashkenaz, commentary by Abraham b. Azriel[332]

14431. Vatican - Biblioteca Apostolica ebr. 301,1, f. 81a, C, rubric: כל עצמותי תאמרנה ה' מי כמוך.

מי אל כמוך נושא עון, סליחה

Ashkenaz

14432. Parma - Bibliotheca Palatina Cod. Parm. 3205 (de Rossi 655), f. 286b, C.

מי אל נסתר מפני נראה (מ 989), משה אבן עזרא, חלק יד, קדושתא לשחרית יום כפור

Carpentras

14433. Cincinnati - Hebrew Union College 392, f. 57a-57b, M, no incipit.

Carpentras, commentary by Josef b. Abraham of Montelitz

14434. New York - Jewish Theological Seminary Ms. 4197, f. 129b-130b, M, no incipit.
14435. Paris - Ecole Rabbinique 32, f. 145b-146b, M, no incipit.
14436. Strasbourg - Bibliotheque Nationale et Universitaire 4081, f. 122b-123a, M, no incipit.

---

[332] Edited by Urbach, ערוגת הבושם, vol. II, p. 208-209.

מי יוכל לשער כל הפקודים אשר בחבל (מ+ 1087), אלעזר ברבי קליר, חלק ד', קדושתא לשבת שקלים

Ashkenaz
14437. Berlin - Staatsbibliothek (Preussischer Kulturbesitz) Or. Qu. 798-799 (Steinschneider 177), II, f. 14a-14b, M, no incipit.
14438. Budapest - Magyar tudomanyos akademia, MS. Kaufmann A 384, f. 38b, M.
14439. Budapest - Magyar tudomanyos akademia, MS. Kaufmann A 400, p. 7-8, C.
14440. Cambridge - University Library Add. 504,1, f. 4a-5a, C, incipit אל.
14441. Hamburg - Staats- und Universitaetsbibliothek Cod. hebr. 17/2 (Steinschneider 152), f. 12a-13a, C.
14442. Jerusalem - Schocken Institute 24100 / Mahzor Nuremberg, f. 35a-35b, M.
14443. Muenchen - Bayerische Staatsbibliothek, Cod. hebr. 88, f. 15b-16a, G.
14444. Muenchen - Bayerische Staatsbibliothek, Cod. hebr. 393, f. 85b-86a, C, no incipit.
14445. Oxford - Bodleian Library MS Opp. 170 (Neubauer 1205), f. 5a, C.
14446. Paris - Bibliotheque Nationale heb. 709, f. 6a-6b, C, incipit אל נא.
14447. Parma - Biblioteca Palatina Cod. Parm. 1002 (Ta 24), f. 24b, M, incipit אל נא.
14448. Parma - Biblioteca Palatina Cod. Parm. 3205 (de Rossi 655), f. 13a, C, incipit אל נא.
14449. Parma - Biblioteca Palatina Cod. Parm. 3507 (Perreau 27), f. 4a-4b, C, no incipit.
14450. Vatican - Biblioteca Apostolica ebr. 305,1, f. 4a-4b, C, no incipit.

Tsarfat
14451. London - British Library Add. 11639 (Margoliouth 1056), f. 265a, M, incipit אל נא.
14452. London - David Sofer 5, f. 10b-11a, C, incipit אל נא.
14453. Moscow - Russian State Library, Ms. Guenzburg 1665, f. 14b, M, incipit אל נא, short.
14454. Oxford - Bodleian Library MS Opp. 171 (Neubauer 1207), f. 7a-7b, C, incipit אל נא.
14455. Parma - Biblioteca Palatina Cod. Parm. 3136 (de Rossi 405), f. 23a-23b, M, incipit אל נא.
14456. Vatican - Biblioteca Apostolica ebr. 306, f. 159b, C, no incipit.

מי ימלל גבורות חיליך (מ 1095), אלעזר ברבי קליר, חלק טו', קדושתא למוסף יום כפור

Ashkenaz
14457. Cambridge - University Library Add. 394,1 (Reif SCR 461), f. 71a-72a, C.

14458. Moscow - Russian State Library, Ms. Guenzburg 191, f. 121a-123b, M.

Tsarfat

14459. London - David Sofer 5, f. 152b-153a, C, rubric: סילוק.
14460. Parma - Biblioteca Palatina Cod. Parm. 3006 (de Rossi 654,1), f. 183b-185a, M.

מי יערוך אליך מענה (מ 1110), אלעזר ברבי קליר, סילוק, קדושתא למוסף יום כפור

Ashkenaz

14461. Berlin - Staatsbibliothek (Preussischer Kulturbesitz) Or. Qu. 798-799 (Steinschneider 177), f. 123a-124a, M.
14462. Braunschweig - Landesmuseum fuer Geschichte und Volkstum R 2386, vol. II, f. 229a-230a, M, short.
14463. Budapest - Magyar tudomanyos akademia, MS. Kaufmann A 400, p. 359-360, C.
14464. Cambridge - University Library Add. 394,1 (Reif SCR 461), f. 70b, C, rubric: סילוק.
14465. London - British Library Or. 11318/1, f. 105a-105b, C.
14466. New York - Jewish Theological Seminary Ms. 8097, f. 79a, C.
14467. New York - Jewish Theological Seminary Ms. 8169 (Acc. 0016), f. 117a-118b, C.
14468. Oxford - Bodleian Library MS Mich. 365 (Neubauer 1208), f. 84a, C, rubric: סילוק, no incipit.
14469. Vatican - Biblioteca Apostolica ebr. 422/1, f. 18a-18b, C, rubric: סילוק.

Roma

14470. Berlin - Staatsbibliothek (Preussischer Kulturbesitz) Or. Oct. 3567, f. 8b, FC, rubric: סלוק.

Tsarfat

14471. Oxford - Bodleian Library MS Bodl. Or. 109 (Neubauer 1209), f. 32b-33a, C, commentator: Aaron b. Hayyim haKohen (compiler), rubric: סילוק.
14472. Parma - Biblioteca Palatina Cod. Parm. 2890 (de Rossi 856), f. 121a, M.

מי יתן ראשי מים ועיני מקור נוזלי (מ 1122), קלונימוס ב"ר יהודה, קינה

Ashkenaz

14473. Berlin - Staatsbibliothek (Preussischer Kulturbesitz) Or. Qu. 798-799 (Steinschneider 177), II, f. 201a-202a, M.

מי יתנה תוקף תהלתך (מ 1129), משולם ב"ר קלונימוס, חלק כד', קדושתא לשחרית יום כפור

Ashkenaz

14474. Berlin - Staatsbibliothek (Preussischer Kulturbesitz) Or. Qu. 798-799 (Steinschneider 177), I, f. 82b-86a, M.
14475. Braunschweig - Landesmuseum fuer Geschichte und Volkstum R 2386, vol. II, f. 195a-199a, M.
14476. Budapest - Magyar tudomanyos akademia, MS. Kaufmann A 400, p. 325-332, C.
14477. Hamburg - Staats- und Universitaetsbibliothek Cod. hebr. 17/2 (Steinschneider 152), f. 153a, C.
14478. Hamburg - Staats- und Universitaetsbibliothek Cod. hebr. 62 (Steinschneider 154), f. 7a-9a, C.
14479. Hamburg - Staats- und Universitaetsbibliothek Cod. hebr. 132 (Steinschneider 155), f. 36a-37b, C, incipit יתנה.
14480. Jerusalem - Jewish National and University Library Ms Heb 8° 3037, f. 126b-132b, M.
14481. Jerusalem - Schocken Institute 24100 / Mahzor Nuremberg, f. 382a-384b, M.
14482. London - British Library Or. 11318/1, f. 79b-83a, C.
14483. London - Montefiore Library 261, f. 46a-48a, C, commentator: Eliezer b. Natan?.
14484. Moscow - Russian State Library, Ms. Guenzburg 191, f. 94b-99b, M.
14485. Muenchen - Bayerische Staatsbibliothek, Cod. hebr. 346, f. 55a-57b, C.
14486. New York - Jewish Theological Seminary Ms. 4466, f. 319b-326a, M.
14487. New York - Jewish Theological Seminary Ms. 8169 (Acc. 0016), f. 75a-82a, M.
14488. Oxford - Bodleian Library MS Mich. 365 (Neubauer 1208), f. 70b-72b, C, rubric: סילוק.
14489. Oxford - Bodleian Library MS Opp. 172 (Neubauer 1211), f. 43a-45b, C.
14490. Oxford - Bodleian Library MS Opp. 619 (Neubauer 2374), f. 155a-160b, M.
14491. Parma - Biblioteca Palatina Cod. Parm. 3205 (de Rossi 655), f. 226b, C, incipit ומי.
14492. Parma - Biblioteca Palatina Cod. Parm. 3271 (de Rossi 1216), f. 46b-51b, G.
14493. Parma - Biblioteca Palatina Cod. Parm. 3507 (Perreau 27), f. 152a-153b, C.
14494. Vatican - Biblioteca Apostolica ebr. 308, f. 104b-107a, C, commentator: David b. Mose (compiler).
14495. Vatican - Biblioteca Apostolica ebr. 422/1, f. 16a, C.

14496. Zurich - Zentralbibliothek Heid. 139, f. 77b-78a, C, additional marginal notes.

Asti, Fossano, Moncalvo

14497. New Haven - Yale University, Beinecke Rare Book and MS Library, MS Heb. 52, f. 110b-113b, M.

Romania

14498. Vatican - Biblioteca Apostolica ebr. 320, f. 289b-295a, M.

Tsarfat

14499. Bern - Burgerbibliothek A 409, f. 88a-91b, G.
14500. London - British Library Or. 8682, f. 72a-74b, GI.
14501. London - David Sofer 5, f. 139b-140b, C, rubric: סילוק.
14502. Oxford - Bodleian Library MS Bodl. Or. 109 (Neubauer 1209), f. 22b-24a, C, commentator: Aaron b. Hayyim haKohen (compiler).
14503. Oxford - Bodleian Library MS Laud. Or. 271 (Neubauer 1206), f. 113b, C, commentator: Aaron b. Hayyim haKohen (compiler), rubric: סילוק, only on end of piyyut.
14504. Parma - Biblioteca Palatina Cod. Parm. 2890 (de Rossi 856), f. 33b, 34b, 36a-37a, M.
14505. Parma - Biblioteca Palatina Cod. Parm. 3006 (de Rossi 654,1), f. 146a-149a, M.
14506. Vatican - Biblioteca Apostolica ebr. 306, f. 78b-80b, C.

מי יתני ליקח תורתיך, לשחרית יום כפור

Tsarfat

14507. Parma - Biblioteca Palatina Cod. Parm. 1794 (de Rossi 1061), f. 133a-134a, M.

מי יתנני עבד אלוה עושני (מ 1135), יהודה הלוי, מחרך

Carpentras

14508. Cincinnati - Hebrew Union College 429/1, f. 3a-4a, M.

Carpentras, commentary by Eliyahu Carmi

14509. Cincinnati - Hebrew Union College 357, f. 38a, M, rubric: תנא ר' אליהו.
14510. New York - Jewish Theological Seminary Ms. 3151, f. 32a, M.
14511. Paris - Ecole Rabbinique 31, f. 82a, M.

Carpentras, commentary by Josef b. Abraham of Montelitz

14512. Cincinnati - Hebrew Union College 357, f. 37b-38a, M.
14513. New York - Jewish Theological Seminary Ms. 4746, f. 5b-6a, M.
14514. Paris - Alliance Israelite Universelle H 422 A, f. 10b-11a, M.
14515. Paris - Ecole Rabbinique 31, f. 81b-82a, M.

מי כיי אבי עדני מצותיו השביענו (מ 1136), אהרן בן יוסף הרופא, פרשת כי תצא

Karaite, commentary by Berakha b. Josef haKohen

14516. New York - Jewish Theological Seminary Ms. 3367, f. 150a-152a, C, rubric: פרוש פרשת כי תצא.

14517. St. Petersburg - Inst. of Oriental Studies of the Russian Academy B 431, f. 101a-103a, C, rubric: פרשת כי תצא.

14518. St. Petersburg - Inst. of Oriental Studies of the Russian Academy B 483, f. 15a-16a, C, rubric: פרשת כי תצא.

14519. St. Petersburg - Russian National Library, Evr. IV 50, f. 117b-119b, C, rubric: כי תצא.

מי כיי אלהינו המגביהי לשבת (מ 1137), אהרן בן יוסף הרופא, פרשת בשלח

Karaite, commentary by Berakha b. Josef haKohen

14520. New York - Jewish Theological Seminary Ms. 3367, f. 71b-73b, C, rubric: פרוש פרשת בשלח.

14521. St. Petersburg - Inst. of Oriental Studies of the Russian Academy B 431, f. 52a-53b, C, rubric: פרשת בשלח.

14522. St. Petersburg - Russian National Library, Evr. IV 50, f. 51b-53a, C, rubric: בשלח.

מי כיי אשר לא יכילו גוים זעמו (מ 1139), אהרן בן יוסף הרופא, פרשת בלק

Karaite, commentary by Berakha b. Josef haKohen

14523. New York - Jewish Theological Seminary Ms. 3367, f. 130a-133a, C, rubric: פרוש פרשת בלק.

14524. St. Petersburg - Inst. of Oriental Studies of the Russian Academy B 431, f. 88b-90b, C, rubric: פרשת בלק.

14525. St. Petersburg - Inst. of Oriental Studies of the Russian Academy B 483, f. 6b-8b, C, rubric: פרשת בלק.

14526. St. Petersburg - Russian National Library, Evr. IV 50, f. 100b-103a, C, rubric: בלק.

מי כמוך אדיר במרומים (מ 1144), משולם ב״ר קלונימוס, חלק יד׳, קדושתא לשחרית יום כפור

Ashkenaz

14527. Berlin - Staatsbibliothek (Preussischer Kulturbesitz) Or. Qu. 798-799 (Steinschneider 177), I, f. 78a, M.

14528. Braunschweig - Landesmuseum fuer Geschichte und Volkstum R 2386, vol. II, f. 191a, M, no incipit.

14529. Budapest - Magyar tudomanyos akademia, MS. Kaufmann A 400, p. 315-316, C, incipit אדיר, short.

14530. Hamburg - Staats- und Universitaetsbibliothek Cod. hebr. 132 (Steinschneider 155), f. 38b, C, no incipit.

14531. Hamburg - Staats- und Universitaetsbibliothek Cod. hebr. 62 (Steinschneider 154), f. 5a, C, very short.
14532. Jerusalem - Jewish National and University Library Ms Heb 8° 3037, f. 122b, M, very short.
14533. Jerusalem - Schocken Institute 24100 / Mahzor Nuremberg, f. 379b, M, very short.
14534. London - British Library Or. 11318/1, f. 75b, , very short.
14535. London - Montefiore Library 261, f. 44a, C, commentator: Eliezer b. Natan?, short, incipit אדיר.
14536. Moscow - Russian State Library, Ms. Guenzburg 191, f. 91a, G.
14537. Muenchen - Bayerische Staatsbibliothek, Cod. hebr. 393, f. 142a, C, no incipit, very short.
14538. New York - Jewish Theological Seminary Ms. 8097, f. 72a, C.
14539. Oxford - Bodleian Library MS Opp. 172 (Neubauer 1211), f. 39a, C, very short.
14540. Parma - Biblioteca Palatina Cod. Parm. 3271 (de Rossi 1216), f. 41b, G.
14541. Parma - Biblioteca Palatina Cod. Parm. 3271 (de Rossi 1216), f. 41b-42a, G.
14542. Vatican - Biblioteca Apostolica ebr. 308, f. 101a, C, commentator: David b. Mose (compiler).
14543. Vatican - Biblioteca Apostolica ebr. 422/1, f. 15b, C, very short.

Asti, Fossano, Moncalvo

14544. New Haven - Yale University, Beinecke Rare Book and MS Library, MS Hcb. 52, f. 107a, M.

Romania

14545. Vatican - Biblioteca Apostolica ebr. 320, f. 285b, M.

Tsarfat

14546. Bern - Burgerbibliothek A 409, f. 84a-84b, G.
14547. London - David Sofer 5, f. 138b, C, incipit אין.
14548. London - David Sofer 5, f. 138b, C, second commentary on margin.
14549. Oxford - Bodleian Library MS Bodl. Or. 109 (Neubauer 1209), f. 20b, C, commentator: Aaron b. Hayyim haKohen (compiler), very short.

מי כמוך אדיר ונורא אלהי עולם (מ 1146), אהרן בן יוסף הרופא, פרשת האזינו
Karaite, commentary by Berakha b. Josef haKohen

14550. New York - Jewish Theological Seminary Ms. 3367, f. 157a-159b, C, rubric: פרוש פרשת האזינו.
14551. St. Petersburg - Inst. of Oriental Studies of the Russian Academy B 431, f. 106b-108b, C, rubric: פרשת האזינו.
14552. St. Petersburg - Inst. of Oriental Studies of the Russian Academy B 483, f. 18a-20a, C, rubric: פרשת האזינו.
14553. St. Petersburg - Russian National Library, Evr. IV 50, f. 124b-127a, C, rubric: האזינו.

מי כמוך את מועדי יי אליכם ארקא בחירי אל, לשבת הגדול

Corfu

14554. New York - Jewish Theological Seminary Ms. 4821, f. 4a, G.

מי כמוך דעה מורה (מ 1173), שמואל ב"ר קלונימוס?, שיר היחוד ליום ה'

Ashkenaz

14555. Braunschweig - Landesmuseum fuer Geschichte und Volkstum R 2386, vol. II, f. 173b-175a, M, no incipit.

14556. Frankfurt a M - Stadt- und Universitaetsbibliothek Oct. 121/1 (Merzbacher 105), f. 20b-24a, C, rubric: יום חמישי, additional glosses in the margins.

14557. Paris - Alliance Israelite Universelle H 133 A, f. 17a-18a, M.

Romania

14558. Vatican - Biblioteca Apostolica ebr. 274, f. 179b-182b, C, kabbalistic, no incipit.

Sepharad

14559. Brussels - Bibliotheque Royale de Belgique 4781, f. 180b-181a, C, no incipit.

מי כמוך יחיד הנסתר מאישון (מ 1177), יהודה הלוי, סליחה

Yemen

14560. Jerusalem - Benayahu ת 414, f. 135a, M.

14561. New York - Jewish Theological Seminary Ms. 3028, f. 29a-29b, G.

Yemen, commentary by Isaac b. Abraham Wanneh

14562. Chicago-Spertus College of Judaica D 2, 2, f. 206b-207b, M, no incipit.

14563. Jerusalem - Michael Krupp 604, f. 159b-160b, M.

14564. Jerusalem - Sassoon 1158, p. 386-389, M, no incipit.

14565. Jerusalem - Yehiel haLevi 4, f. 156a-158a, G.

14566. London - British Library Or. 11122, f. 195a-196a, M, no incipit.

מי כמוך ממליך כל מלך כל מלך חולף ובוטל מלכותו, סליחה

Yemen

14567. Jerusalem - Sassoon 902, p. 415, M.

Yemen, commentary by Isaac b. Abraham Wanneh

14568. Chicago-Spertus College of Judaica D 2, 2, f. 201a-201b, M, no incipit.

14569. Jerusalem - Sassoon 1158, p. 389-390, M, no incipit.

14570. London - British Library Or. 11122, f. 196a-196b, M, no incipit.

מי לא יראך מלך, אלעזר ברבי קליר, סילוק, קדושתא למוסף יום כפור
Tsarfat[333]
14571. Oxford - Bodleian Library MS Opp. 171 (Neubauer 1207), f. 65a-66b, C, rubric: סילוק.

מי נשקני ואני גולה וסר (מ 1229), שלם שבזי
Yemen
14572. Cincinnati - Hebrew Union College 398, f. 211b, M.

מי נשקני מנשיקות אהבה (מ 1239), שלם שבזי
Yemen
14573. Cincinnati - Hebrew Union College 398, f. 209a-211a, M.

מי שענה לאברהם אבינו מבהר המוריה הוא יעננו (מ 1278), סליחה
Ashkenaz
14574. London - British Library Add. 18695 (Margoliouth 683), f. 170a-170b, T, Yiddish.

מי תמים יעיר לבבו (מ 1283), משה אבן עזרא, חלק יג', קדושתא לשחרית יום כפור
Carpentras
14575. Cincinnati - Hebrew Union College 392, f. 56a-57a, M, no incipit.
Carpentras, commentary by Josef b. Abraham of Montelitz
14576. Cincinnati - Hebrew Union College 291, f. 31a-33a, C, rubric: פי' פזמון מי תמים וכו'.
14577. New York - Jewish Theological Seminary Ms. 4197, f. 126b-128b, M, no incipit.
14578. Paris - Ecole Rabbinique 32, f. 143b-145a, M, no incipit.
14579. Strasbourg - Bibliotheque Nationale et Universitaire 4081, f. 121a-122a, M, no incipit.

מיוחד באהיה אשר אהיה הוא היה והוא הוה והוא יהיה (מ 1309), סליחה
Yemen
14580. New York - Jewish Theological Seminary Ms. 3193, f. 121a, M.
14581. New York - Public Library, Heb. Ms. 10, f. 72b, M, no incipit.
Yemen, commentary by Isaac b. Abraham Wanneh
14582. Jerusalem - Musad haRav Kook 330, f. 88b, M.
14583. Jerusalem - Musad haRav Kook 347, f. 70a, M.
14584. Jerusalem - Yehiel haLevi 4, f. 133a, M, no incipit.
14585. London - Valmadonna Trust 13, f. 89b, M.

---

[333] To be edited by J. Yahalom and B. Leffler in Sefer Mirsky.

מיחדים שם האל היום בשירה ערוכה (מ 1339), משה, הושענא

Yemen, commentary by Samḥun b. Salomo Ḥaloah

14586. Jerusalem - Makhon ben Zvi 2808, f. 76a-78b, C.

מים רבים שמתה נתיבה (מ 1364), שמעון ב"ר יצחק, סילוק הזולת לפסח

Ashkenaz

14587. Berlin - Staatsbibliothek (Preussischer Kulturbesitz) Or. Qu. 798-799 (Steinschneider 177), II, f. 85b-86a, M, no incipit.

14588. Budapest - Magyar tudomanyos akademia, MS. Kaufmann A 384 , f. 180b, M.

14589. London - British Library Add. 18695 (Margoliouth 683), f. 53a, T, Yiddish.

14590. Muenchen - Bayerische Staatsbibliothek, Cod. hebr. 88, f. 78a, G.

14591. Parma - Biblioteca Palatina Cod. Parm. 3205 (de Rossi 655), f. 106b, C.

14592. Parma - Biblioteca Palatina Cod. Parm. 3507 (Perreau 27), f. 70b, C, short, no incipit.

Tsarfat

14593. London - David Sofer 5, f. 39a, C, additional glosses.

14594. Moscow - Russian State Library, Ms. Guenzburg 1665, f. 79b, M, short.

14595. Parma - Biblioteca Palatina Cod. Parm. 3136 (de Rossi 405), f. 106a, M, short.

מים רבים תללת ערימות, משולם ב"ר קלונימוס, סילוק הזולת לפסח

Ashkenaz

14596. Berlin - Staatsbibliothek (Preussischer Kulturbesitz) Or. Qu. 798-799 (Steinschneider 177), II, f. 77b-78a, M.

מישך שדרך ועבר נגו (מ +1376), מאיר ב"ר יצחק, פיוט בארמית לשבועות

Ashkenaz

14597. Berlin - Staatsbibliothek (Preussischer Kulturbesitz) Or. Qu. 798-799 (Steinschneider 177), II, f. 158b-159b, M.

14598. Cambridge - University Library Add. 394,1 (Reif SCR 461), f. 59a-60a, C, rubric: ר' מאיר שליח ציבור גמר אלפא ביתא על פי האגדה.

14599. Jerusalem - Schocken Institute 24100 / Mahzor Nuremberg , f. 156b-160a, M, pagination skips 157-158.

14600. Moscow - Russian State Library, Ms. Guenzburg 206 , f. 89b, M, no incipit.

14601. Muenchen - Bayerische Staatsbibliothek, Cod. hebr. 21, f. 81a-81b, M.

14602. New York - Jewish Theological Seminary Ms. 4466, f. 186b-188a, M.

14603. Oxford - Bodleian Library MS Can. Or. 1 (Neubauer 1104), f. 111b-113a, M.
14604. Oxford - Bodleian Library MS Can. Or. 1 (Neubauer 1104), f. 123a-125a, M, rubric: פירוש ממשך שדרך מר' מאיר שליח ציבו' והראשון שכתבתי אינו שוה כלל.
14605. Oxford - Bodleian Library MS Opp. 170 (Neubauer 1205), f. 95b-97a, C.
14606. Parma - Biblioteca Palatina Cod. Parm. 3205 (de Rossi 655), f. 182b-183a, C.

Tsarfat
14607. Cambridge - University Library Add. 561.1, f. 77b-78b, MT, Hebrew.
14608. Jerusalem - Schocken Institute 19623, f. 179b-181a, M, commentator: Yehuda b. Eliezer Zvi.
14609. London - British Library Add. 11639 (Margoliouth 1056), f. 676b-677b, M.
14610. London - British Library Or. 2735 (Margoliouth 663), f. 25a-26b, M.
14611. London - David Sofer 5, f. 60b-61a, C.
14612. New York - Jewish Theological Seminary Ms. 4460, f. 62a-62b, M, pages damaged.
14613. Parma - Biblioteca Palatina Cod. Parm. 1902, f. 142b-144b, M.
14614. Parma - Biblioteca Palatina Cod. Parm. 2574, f. 118a-118b, G, commentator: Simḥa b. Samuel, cp. Mahzor Vitry.

מכל המון רומי שלהבת, סליחה

Ashkenaz
14615. Vatican - Biblioteca Apostolica ebr. 308, f. 113b-114b, C, commentator: David b. Mose (compiler).

מכניסי רחמים הכניסו רחמינו לפני בעל הרחמים (מ 1419), סליחה

Ashkenaz
14616. Braunschweig - Landesmuseum fuer Geschichte und Volkstum R 2386, vol. II, f. 45a-45b, M.
14617. Hamburg - Staats- und Universitaetsbibliothek Cod. hebr. 17/2 (Steinschneider 152), f. 145a-145b, C.
14618. London - British Library Add. 18695 (Margoliouth 683), f. 171b-172a, T, Yiddish.
14619. Padova - Biblioteca del Seminario Vescovile Cod. 218, f. 53b, M, short.
14620. Vatican - Biblioteca Apostolica ebr. 308, f. 21a, C, commentator: David b. Mose (compiler).

Tsarfat
14621. London - David Sofer 5, f. 130b, C.

14622. Parma - Biblioteca Palatina Cod. Parm. 3007 (de Rossi 654,2), f. 20b, M, short.

Yemen

14623. Ramat Gan - Universitat Bar Ilan 62, f. 53a, G.

Yemen, commentary by Isaac b. Abraham Wanneh

14624. Chicago-Spertus College of Judaica D 2, 2, f. 230b, M, no incipit.

14625. Jerusalem - Sassoon 1158, p. 203, M, no incipit.

מכנף הארץ זמירות שמעו אזננו (מ +1420), יהודה הלוי, חלק ג', קדושתא לשבת זכור
Carpentras, commentary by Mordekhai b. Josef of Rocco Martino

14626. Cincinnati - Hebrew Union College 246/1, f. 22b, C, rubric: פי' מחיה מכנף הארץ וכו'.

Sepharad, commentary by Josef Garad

14627. Oxford - Bodleian Library Heb.e.10 (Neubauer 2746/1), f. 8a, C, rubric: מחייה.

14628. Oxford - Bodleian Library Heb.e.10 (Neubauer 2746/1), f. 18a, C, rubric: מכנף הארץ, very short, no incipit.

מלא כל הארץ כבוד מלכותו (מ 1441), משה בן שמואל בן אבשלום, אופן לחתן
Tsarfat

14629. London - British Library Or. 2735 (Margoliouth 663), f. 173b-174a, M, margins partly damaged.

מלא רחמים ונושא עון חון על אשמים מצאם עון (מ 1454), שלמה, סליחה
Tsarfat

14630. Parma - Biblioteca Palatina Cod. Parm. 3136 (de Rossi 405), f. 90a-90b, M.

Yemen

14631. Jerusalem - Sassoon 902, p. 442, M, very short.

Yemen, commentary by Isaac b. Abraham Wanneh

14632. Chicago-Spertus College of Judaica D 2, 2, f. 210a, M, no incipit.

14633. Jerusalem - Sassoon 1158, p. 380, M, rubric: סימן שלמה, no incipit.

14634. London - British Library Or. 11122, f. 190a, M, no incipit.

מלאכי צבאות בעלצון (מ 1476), מנחם ב"ר מכיר, אופן
Ashkenaz

14635. Jerusalem - Schocken Institute 24100 / Mahzor Nuremberg, f. 39a-39b, M, rubric: וזה האופן.

Ashkenaz, commentary by Abraham b. Azriel[334]

14636. Frankfurt a M - Stadt- und Universitaetsbibliothek Fol. 16 (Merzbacher 95), f. 61b-62a, C, rubric: אופן.

---

[334] Edited by Urbach, ערוגת הבושם, vol. III, p. 1-5.

14637. Vatican - Biblioteca Apostolica ebr. 301,1, f. 95a-95b, C, rubric: אופן.

מלאכי רחמים משרתי עליון (מ 1478), שמואל כהן, סליחה

Ashkenaz

14638. Braunschweig - Landesmuseum fuer Geschichte und Volkstum R 2386, vol. II, f. 47a-47b, M.
14639. Oxford - Bodleian Library MS Mich. 543 (Neubauer 1212), f. 8b, C, commentator: Isaac b. Jacob (compiler).
14640. Oxford - Bodleian Library MS Opp. 681 (Neubauer 1213), f. 75b-76a, C.
14641. Padova - Biblioteca del Seminario Vescovile Cod. 218, f. 70b, M.
14642. Vatican - Biblioteca Apostolica ebr. 308/1, f. 11b-12a, C, commentator: David b. Mose (compiler).
14643. Vatican - Biblioteca Apostolica ebr. 422/1, f. 31b, C.
14644. Vatican - Biblioteca Apostolica ebr. 422/1, f. 45b, CG, no incipit.

מלאכים מרופפים (מ+ 1480), לנעילה

Ashkenaz

14645. Oxford - Bodleian Library MS Opp. 170 (Neubauer 1205), f. 182a-182b, C, short.

Tsarfat

14646. London - David Sofer 5, f. 172a, C, rubric: קדושה.
14647. Oxford - Bodleian Library MS Bodl. Or. 109 (Neubauer 1209), f. 43a, C, commentator: Aaron b. Hayyim haKohen (compiler), short.

מלוש בצק עד חומצתו (מ 1494), יוסף ב"ר שמואל טוב עלם, חלק ב', קדושתא לפסח

Tsarfat

14648. Parma - Biblioteca Palatina Cod. Parm. 3136 (de Rossi 405), f. 90a-90b, M.

מלך אזור גבורה (מ 1529), אלעזר ברבי קליר, יוצר לראש השנה

Ashkenaz

14649. Berlin - Staatsbibliothek (Preussischer Kulturbesitz) Or. Qu. 798-799 (Steinschneider 177), I, f. 1b-2b, M.
14650. Braunschweig - Landesmuseum fuer Geschichte und Volkstum R 2386, vol. II, f. 77b-78a, M.
14651. Budapest - Magyar tudomanyos akademia, MS. Kaufmann A 400, p. 239-242, C, rubric: קדושתא לראש השנה דר' אלעזר.
14652. Cambridge - University Library Add. 394,1 (Reif SCR 461), f. 65a-65b, C, rubric: קרובץ של ראש השנה.
14653. Darmstadt - Hessisches Landes- und Hochschulbibliothek Cod. Or. 15, f. 1b-2a, M.

14654. Hamburg - Staats- und Universitaetsbibliothek Cod. hebr. 12 (Steinschneider 102), f. 2a-2b, G.
14655. Hamburg - Staats- und Universitaetsbibliothek Cod. hebr. 17/2 (Steinschneider 152), f. 103a-104b, C, rubric: פי' יוצר של יום ראשון של ראש השנה.
14656. Hamburg - Staats- und Universitaetsbibliothek Cod. hebr. 40b (Steinschneider 110), f. 1b-2a, G.
14657. Hamburg - Staats- und Universitaetsbibliothek Cod. hebr. 40c (Steinschneider 111), f. 131b-132a, G.
14658. Hamburg - Staats- und Universitaetsbibliothek Cod. hebr. 62 (Steinschneider 154), f. 24a-25b, C.
14659. Hamburg - Staats- und Universitaetsbibliothek Cod. hebr. 132 (Steinschneider 155), f. 1b-3a, C.
14660. Jerusalem - Jewish National and University Library Ms Heb 8° 3037, f. 1b-2b, M.
14661. Jerusalem - Schocken Institute 15791/7, f. 56b-59a, C.
14662. Jerusalem - Schocken Institute 24100 / Mahzor Nuremberg, f. 321b-322a, M.
14663. London - British Library Or. 11318/1, f. 9a-9b, C.
14664. Moscow - Russian State Library, Ms. Guenzburg 1401/2, f. 15b, C.
14665. Moscow - Russian State Library, Ms. Guenzburg 191, f. 30b, M.
14666. Moscow - Russian State Library, Ms. Guenzburg 615, f. 52b-54a, C.
14667. Muenchen - Bayerische Staatsbibliothek, Cod. hebr. 86, f. 2b-4a, G.
14668. New York - Jewish Theological Seminary Ms. 4466, f. 207a-208a, M.
14669. New York - Jewish Theological Seminary Ms. 8097, f. 57b, C, incipit missing, additional glosses.
14670. New York - Jewish Theological Seminary Ms. 8169 (Acc. 0016), f. 1b-2a, M.
14671. New York - Jewish Theological Seminary Rab. 1077/4 (Acc. 02505), f. 21a, FC.
14672. Oxford - Bodleian Library MS Opp. 170 (Neubauer 1205), f. 101a-101b, C, rubric: בשם אל דר במעונה אכתוב פיר' של ראש השנה.
14673. Oxford - Bodleian Library MS Opp. 172 (Neubauer 1211), f. 1a-1b, C.
14674. Oxford - Bodleian Library MS Opp. 619 (Neubauer 2374), f. 5b-7a, M.
14675. Oxford - Bodleian Library MS Opp. 675 (Neubauer 1210), f. 7a-9b, C, no incipit.
14676. Parma - Biblioteca Palatina Cod. Parm. 2404 (de Rossi 1104), f. 124b-125a, M, copied from printed edition Saloniki 1550 (Benyamin b. Meir Levi).
14677. Parma - Biblioteca Palatina Cod. Parm. 3205 (de Rossi 655), f. 203a, C, rubric: יוצר לראש השנה.
14678. Parma - Biblioteca Palatina Cod. Parm. 3266, f. 60b, C.

14679. Parma - Biblioteca Palatina Cod. Parm. 3507 (Perreau 27), f. 107a-107b, C.
14680. Vatican - Bibliotheca Apostolica ebr. 298/1, f. 1a-4b, C.
14681. Vatican - Biblioteca Apostolica ebr. 308, f. 23a-25a, C, commentator: David b. Mose (compiler), rubric: אתחיל יוצר מראש השנה בעזרת שוכן מעונה.
14682. Vatican - Biblioteca Apostolica ebr. 422/1, f. 7a, C.
14683. Zurich - Zentralbibliothek Heid. 139, f. 56a-56b, C, additional marginal notes.
14684. Zurich - Zentralbibliothek Heid. 139, f. 101b, C, commentator: Elazar b. Yehuda of Worms, short, esoteric.

Asti, Fossano, Moncalvo

14685. New Haven - Yale University, Beinecke Rare Book and MS Library, MS Heb. 52, f. 15a-15b, M.

Roma

14686. Jerusalem - Jewish National and University Library Ms Heb 8° 4153, f. 132a-134a, C, commentator: Daniel ben Salomo haRofe (compiler), rubric: בנים האל הוא הסבה הראשונה אתחיל לכתו' פי' יוצר ראש השנה.
14687. Oxford - Bodleian Library MS Mich. 312,1 (Neubauer 2276,1), f. 1a-3a, C.

Romania

14688. Vatican - Biblioteca Apostolica ebr. 320, f. 144b-145b, M.

Tsarfat

14689. London - British Library Add. 11639 (Margoliouth 1056), f. 708a, M.
14690. London - British Library Or. 8682, f. 5b-6a, Gl.
14691. London - David Sofer 5, f. 107a-107b, C, rubric: יוצר.
14692. Manchester - John Rylands University Library, Ms. Gaster 733, f. 79b-80a, C, commentary block in Mahzor, manuscript damaged.
14693. Oxford - Bodleian Library MS Laud. Or. 271 (Neubauer 1206), f. 138b, C, commentator: Aaron b. Hayyim haKohen (compiler).
14694. Oxford - Bodleian Library MS Opp. 171 (Neubauer 1207), f. 53a-53b, C.
14695. Paris - Bibliotheque Nationale heb. 445,9, f. 59b-61a, C.
14696. Parma - Biblioteca Palatina Cod. Parm. 1794 (de Rossi 1061), f. 52a-53b, M.
14697. Parma - Biblioteca Palatina Cod. Parm. 2125 (de Rossi 812), f. 2b-4b, C.
14698. Parma - Biblioteca Palatina Cod. Parm. 3006 (de Rossi 654,1), f. 18a-19a, M.
14699. Vatican - Biblioteca Apostolica ebr. 306, f. 46a-46b, C.

מלך אחד יהיה אל העמים (מ 1531), סליחה

Ashkenaz

14700. Vatican - Biblioteca Apostolica ebr. 308, f. 17a-18a, C, commentator: David b. Mose (compiler).

מלך אמון מאמרך מרחוק מצב (מ 1543), שמעון ב"ר יצחק, יוצר לראש השנה

Ashkenaz

14701. Berlin - Staatsbibliothek (Preussischer Kulturbesitz) Or. Qu. 798-799 (Steinschneider 177), I, f. 32b-34a, M.
14702. Bologna - Archivio di Stato MS Ebr. 353, f. 1, FC, incomplete, only beginning.
14703. Braunschweig - Landesmuseum fuer Geschichte und Volkstum R 2386, vol. II, f. 107b-108b, M.
14704. Darmstadt - Hessisches Landes- und Hochschulbibliothek Cod. Or. 15, f. 31a-32b, M.
14705. Hamburg - Staats- und Universitaetsbibliothek Cod. hebr. 40c (Steinschneider 111), f. 145a-146a, G.
14706. Hamburg - Staats- und Universitaetsbibliothek Cod. hebr. 62 (Steinschneider 154), f. 25b-27a, C, rubric: יוצר ליום שיני דראש השנה.
14707. Hamburg - Staats- und Universitaetsbibliothek Cod. hebr. 132 (Steinschneider 155), f. 22b-23b, C.
14708. Jerusalem - Jewish National and University Library Ms Heb 8° 3037, f. 45b-46b, M.
14709. Jerusalem - Schocken Institute 24100 / Mahzor Nuremberg, f. 339b-340b, M.
14710. London - British Library Or. 11318/1, f. 37a-39a, C.
14711. London - Montefiore Library 261, f. 26a-27a, C, commentator: Eliezer b. Natan?, rubric: יוצר ליום שיני.
14712. Modena - Archivio di Stato 27, FM.
14713. Moscow - Russian State Library, Ms. Guenzburg 191, f. 32a-33a, M.
14714. Muenchen - Bayerische Staatsbibliothek, Cod. hebr. 86, f. 54a-56a, G.
14715. Muenchen - Bayerische Staatsbibliothek, Cod. hebr. 346, f. 34b-35b, C, rubric: ליום שיני.
14716. New York - Jewish Theological Seminary Ms. 4466, f. 246a-248a, M.
14717. New York - Jewish Theological Seminary Ms. 8097, f. 64(ii)b-65a, C, additional glosses in the margins.
14718. New York - Jewish Theological Seminary Ms. 8169 (Acc. 0016), f. 31a-32a, M.
14719. Oxford - Bodleian Library MS Mich. 365 (Neubauer 1208), f. 48b-49b, C, rubric: יוצר ליום שיני.
14720. Oxford - Bodleian Library MS Opp. 170 (Neubauer 1205), f. 143a-143b, C, rubric: יוצר ליום שיני דרבא שמעון הגדול.

14721. Oxford - Bodleian Library MS Opp. 172 (Neubauer 1211), f. 19a-20a, C.
14722. Oxford - Bodleian Library MS Opp. 619 (Neubauer 2374), f. 53a-54b, M.
14723. Oxford - Bodleian Library MS Opp. 675 (Neubauer 1210), f. 47b-49a, C, no incipit.
14724. Paris - Bibliotheque Nationale heb. 653, f. 27a-27b, G.
14725. Parma - Biblioteca Palatina Cod. Parm. 3205 (de Rossi 655), f. 216b-217a, C.
14726. Parma - Biblioteca Palatina Cod. Parm. 3507 (Perreau 27), f. 130a-130b, C, rubric: ליום שיני.
14727. Vatican - Biblioteca Apostolica ebr. 308, f. 73a-74a, C, commentator: David b. Mose (compiler), rubric: זה יוצר ליום שיני.
14728. Vatican - Biblioteca Apostolica ebr. 422/1, f. 12a-12b, C, rubric: ליום שיני של ראש השנה.
14729. Zurich - Zentralbibliothek Heid. 139, f. 70a-70b, C, rubric: יוצר ליום שני של ר"ה, incipit אמון, additional marginal notes.
14730. Zurich - Zentralbibliothek Heid. 139, f. 103a, C, commentator: Elazar b. Yehuda of Worms, very short.

Asti, Fossano, Moncalvo
14731. New Haven - Yale University, Beinecke Rare Book and MS Library, MS Heb. 52, f. 49a-50a, M.

Romania
14732. Vatican - Biblioteca Apostolica ebr. 320, f. 177b-179a, M.

Tsarfat
14733. London - British Library Or. 8682, f. 34a-35a, GI.
14734. London - David Sofer 5, f. 119a-119b, C, rubric: יוצר ליום שיני.
14735. Oxford - Bodleian Library MS Laud. Or. 271 (Neubauer 1206), f. 155a-156b, C, commentator: Aaron b. Hayyim haKohen (compiler), rubric: אחל יוצר ליום שיני.
14736. Oxford - Bodleian Library MS Opp. 171 (Neubauer 1207), f. 66b-67a, C, rubric: ואתחיל יוצר ליום שיני.
14737. Parma - Biblioteca Palatina Cod. Parm. 2125 (de Rossi 812), f. 28b-29a, C.
14738. Parma - Biblioteca Palatina Cod. Parm. 3006 (de Rossi 654,1), f. 64b-65b, M, additional commentary on the margins.
14739. Vatican - Biblioteca Apostolica ebr. 306, f. 65b-66a, C, rubric: ליום שני.

מלך אמיץ כח ורב עלילה (מ 1545), יוסף ב"ר שמואל טוב עלם, מעריב לראש השנה

Tsarfat
14740. London - David Sofer 5, f. 119a, C, rubric: מעריב לליל שיני.

מלך אשר דמותו מעין כל יצורים (מ 1550), יוסף אבן אביתור, יוצר לראש השנה Carpentras

14741. Cincinnati - Hebrew Union College 429/1, f. 19b, M.
Carpentras, commentary by Josef b. Abraham of Montelitz
14742. Cincinnati - Hebrew Union College 357, f. 96a, M, rubric: פירוש.
14743. New York - Jewish Theological Seminary Ms. 4746, f. 29b-30a, M.
14744. Paris - Alliance Israelite Universelle H 422 A, f. 66b-67a, M.
14745. Paris - Ecole Rabbinique 31, f. 134b-135b, M.

מלך במשפט יעמיד ארץ (מ 1572), אלעזר ברבי קליר, סילוק, קדושתא לראש השנה Ashkenaz

14746. Berlin - Staatsbibliothek (Preussischer Kulturbesitz) Or. Qu. 798-799 (Steinschneider 177), I, f. 9a-11a, M.
14747. Braunschweig - Landesmuseum fuer Geschichte und Volkstum R 2386, vol. II, f. 83b-85a, M.
14748. Budapest - Magyar tudomanyos akademia, MS. Kaufmann A 400, p. 254-255, C, rubric: סילוק, incipit ענוי הארץ, ecclectic.
14749. Darmstadt - Hessisches Landes- und Hochschulbibliothek Cod. Or. 15, f. 9a-10a, M.
14750. Hamburg - Staats- und Universitaetsbibliothek Cod. hebr. 12 (Steinschneider 102), f. 8a-9a, G.
14751. Hamburg - Staats- und Universitaetsbibliothek Cod. hebr. 17/2 (Steinschneider 152), f. 109a, C, rubric: סילוק, incipit ענוי הארץ, ecclectic.
14752. Hamburg - Staats- und Universitaetsbibliothek Cod. hebr. 40c (Steinschneider 111), f. 134b-136a, G.
14753. Hamburg - Staats- und Universitaetsbibliothek Cod. hebr. 132 (Steinschneider 155), f. 8a-10a, C.
14754. Hamburg - Staats- und Universitaetsbibliothek Cod. hebr. 225, f. 223a-223b, G.
14755. Jerusalem - Jewish National and University Library Ms Heb 8° 3037, f. 11b-13b, M.
14756. Jerusalem - Schocken Institute 24100 / Mahzor Nuremberg, f. 326a-327a, M.
14757. London - British Library Or. 11318/1, f. 13a-13b, C.
14758. London - Montefiore Library 261, f. 1a-3a, C, commentator: Eliezer b. Natan?.
14759. Moscow - Russian State Library, Ms. Guenzburg 191, f. 2a-4a, M, manuscript damaged.
14760. Moscow - Russian State Library, Ms. Guenzburg 615, f. 60a-62b, C, rubric: סילוק.
14761. Moscow - Russian State Library, Ms. Guenzburg 1401 /2, f. 16b-17a, C.
14762. Muenchen - Bayerische Staatsbibliothek, Cod. hebr. 86, f. 6b-9a, G.

14763. Muenchen - Bayerische Staatsbibliothek, Cod. hebr. 346, f. 5b-8a, C.
14764. New York - Jewish Theological Seminary Ms. 4466, f. 214b-217b, M.
14765. New York - Jewish Theological Seminary Ms. 8097, f. 60a-60b, C, rubric: סילוק מלך במשפט.
14766. New York - Jewish Theological Seminary Ms. 8169 (Acc. 0016), f. 9a-10b, M, pages damaged.
14767. Oxford - Bodleian Library MS Opp. 170 (Neubauer 1205), f. 108a-111a, C.
14768. Oxford - Bodleian Library MS Opp. 172 (Neubauer 1211) , f. 5b-6b, C.
14769. Oxford - Bodleian Library MS Opp. 619 (Neubauer 2374), f. 14a-16b, M.
14770. Oxford - Bodleian Library MS Opp. 675 (Neubauer 1210), f. 18a-19a, C, no incipit.
14771. Paris - Bibliotheque Nationale heb. 653, f. 11b-12b, G.
14772. Parma - Biblioteca Palatina Cod. Parm. 3205 (de Rossi 655), f. 206a, C, rubric: סילוק.
14773. Parma - Biblioteca Palatina Cod. Parm. 3507 (Perreau 27), f. 114a-116a, C, rubric: סילוק.
14774. Salzburg - Universitaetsbibliothek M II 342, f. 1a, FM, only end.
14775. Vatican - Biblioteca Apostolica ebr. 308, f. 36a-38b, C, commentator: David b. Mose (compiler).
14776. Vatican - Biblioteca Apostolica ebr. 422/1, f. 8b-9a, C, rubric: סילוק.
14777. Zurich - Zentralbibliothek Heid. 139, f. 102a, C, commentator: Elazar b. Yehuda of Worms, rubric: בסילוק, no incipit, short, esoteric.

Asti, Fossano, Moncalvo
14778. New Haven - Yale University, Beinecke Rare Book and MS Library, MS Heb. 52, f. 22a-23a, M.

Tsarfat
14779. London - British Library Add. 11639 (Margoliouth 1056), f. 709b, M.
14780. London - British Library Or. 8682, f. 13b-14a, GI.
14781. London - David Sofer 5, f. 111b-112b, C.
14782. Oxford - Bodleian Library MS Laud. Or. 271 (Neubauer 1206), f. 142a-143b, C, commentator: Aaron b. Hayyim haKohen (compiler), rubric: סילוק.
14783. Oxford - Bodleian Library MS Opp. 171 (Neubauer 1207), f. 59b-60b, 84a-84b, C, rubric: סילוק.
14784. Paris - Bibliotheque Nationale heb. 445,9, f. 66b-68b, C.
14785. Parma - Biblioteca Palatina Cod. Parm. 1794 (de Rossi 1061), f. 67a-72a, M.
14786. Parma - Biblioteca Palatina Cod. Parm. 2125 (de Rossi 812) , f. 12a-13b, C.
14787. Parma - Biblioteca Palatina Cod. Parm. 3006 (de Rossi 654,1), f. 28b-30b, M.

14788. Vatican - Biblioteca Apostolica ebr. 306, f. 50b-52a, C.
14789. Vatican - Biblioteca Apostolica ebr. 320, f. 153b-156a, M.

מלך דר בנהורה עוטה כשמלה אורה, לראש השנה

Ashkenaz

14790. Hamburg - Staats- und Universitaetsbibliothek Cod. hebr. 225, f. 214b-215b, G.

מלך כל מלך יושב במרום משגבו (מ 1598), יצחק

Carpentras

14791. Cincinnati - Hebrew Union College 429/1, f. 25a-26a, M, no incipit.

Carpentras, commentary by Josef b. Abraham of Montelitz

14792. Cincinnati - Hebrew Union College 357, f. 104b-105a, M, no incipit.
14793. New York - Jewish Theological Seminary Ms. 4746, f. 36b-37a, M, no incipit.
14794. Paris - Alliance Israelite Universelle H 422 A, f. 84b-85a, M, no incipit.
14795. Paris - Ecole Rabbinique 31, f. 143a-144a, M, no incipit.

מלך כתרו גבה (מ 1602), מרדכי בן יהודה דאטו, ראשות לקדיש

Italia, commentary by Mordekhai b. Yehuda Dato

14796. Moscow - Russian State Library, Ms. Guenzburg 249, f. 242b-247b, C.
14797. Moscow - Russian State Library, Ms. Guenzburg 674, f. 41a-55a, C.

מלך מכל מרומם ומתנשא (מ 1611), משה אבן עזרא, חלק ו', קדושתא לשחרית יום כפור

Sepharad, commentary by David b. Josef Abudarham[335]

14798. Budapest - Magyar tudomanyos akademia, MS. Kaufmann A 405/2, p. 204, C, rubric: פזמון.
14799. New York - Columbia X893 Ab 93, f. 12a, C, rubric: פזמון.

מלך מלכים רם על רמים (מ1621), משה בן שמואל בן אבשלום, סליחה

Ashkenaz

14800. Oxford - Bodleian Library MS Mich. 543 (Neubauer 1212), f. 81a-81b, bottom margin, C, commentator: Isaac b. Jacob (compiler).
14801. Padova - Biblioteca del Seminario Vescovile Cod. 218, f. 134b-135a, M.

---

[335] Edited by Prins, תשלום אבודרהם, p. 93.

Tsarfat
14802. Oxford - Bodleian Library MS Bodl. Or. 109 (Neubauer 1209), f. 46b-47a, C, commentator: Aaron b. Hayyim haKohen (compiler).

מלך עליון אל דר במרום (מ 1653), אלעזר ברבי קליר, חלק ג', קדושתא למוסף ראש השנה

Ashkenaz
14803. Berlin - Staatsbibliothek (Preussischer Kulturbesitz) Or. Qu. 798-799 (Steinschneider 177), I, f. 17a-17b, M.
14804. Braunschweig - Landesmuseum fuer Geschichte und Volkstum R 2386, vol. II, f. 94a, M.
14805. Darmstadt - Hessisches Landes- und Hochschulbibliothek Cod. Or. 15, f. 15b, M.
14806. Hamburg - Staats- und Universitaetsbibliothek Cod. hebr. 132 (Steinschneider 155), f. 13a, C, short.
14807. London - British Library Or. 11318/1, f. 16a, C, very short.
14808. Muenchen - Bayerische Staatsbibliothek, Cod. hebr. 86, f. 24a-25a, G, ecclectic.
14809. New York - Jewish Theological Seminary Ms. 4466, f. 224b-225a, M.
14810. New York - Jewish Theological Seminary Ms. 8097, f. 62a, C.
14811. Oxford - Bodleian Library MS Opp. 172 (Neubauer 1211), f. 10b-11a, C.
14812. Oxford - Bodleian Library MS Opp. 619 (Neubauer 2374), f. 29a, M.
14813. Oxford - Bodleian Library MS Opp. 675 (Neubauer 1210), f. 24a-24b, C, no incipit.
14814. Vatican - Biblioteca Apostolica ebr. 308, f. 49b, C, commentator: David b. Mose (compiler).
14815. Vatican - Biblioteca Apostolica ebr. 422/1, f. 10a, C, short.
14816. Zurich - Zentralbibliothek Heid. 139, f. 102b, C, commentator: Elazar b. Yehuda of Worms, no incipit, short, esoteric.

Asti, Fossano, Moncalvo
14817. New Haven - Yale University, Beinecke Rare Book and MS Library, MS Heb. 52, f. 20b-21b, M.

Carpentras
14818. Cincinnati - Hebrew Union College 429/1, f. 9b-10b, M, no incipit.

Carpentras, commentary by Josef b. Abraham of Montelitz
14819. Cincinnati - Hebrew Union College 357, f. 57a-59a, M.
14820. New York - Jewish Theological Seminary Ms. 4746, f. 15a-16a, M.
14821. Paris - Alliance Israelite Universelle H 422 A, f. 34b-36a, M.
14822. Paris - Ecole Rabbinique 31, f. 103b-105a, M.

Romania
14823. Vatican - Biblioteca Apostolica ebr. 320, f. 152a-152b, M.

Tsarfat
14824. London - David Sofer 5, f. 111a, C.

14825. Paris - Bibliotheque Nationale heb. 445,9, f. 75(i)a-75(i)b, C.
14826. Parma - Biblioteca Palatina Cod. Parm. 1794 (de Rossi 1061), f. 64b-65a, M.
14827. Parma - Biblioteca Palatina Cod. Parm. 2125 (de Rossi 812), f. 17b-18a, C.
14828. Parma - Biblioteca Palatina Cod. Parm. 3006 (de Rossi 654,1), f. 27b, M, incipit אל דר.
14829. Vatican - Biblioteca Apostolica ebr. 306, f. 50a-50b, C.

מלך עליון אמיץ בכח, לראש השנה
Tsarfat
14830. London - David Sofer 5, f. 124b, C.
14831. Parma - Biblioteca Palatina Cod. Parm. 3006 (de Rossi 654,1), f. 46a-46b, M.

מלך עליון אמיץ מנושא (מ 1654), שמעון ב"ר יצחק, חלק ז', קדושתא לראש השנה
Ashkenaz
14832. Berlin - Staatsbibliothek (Preussischer Kulturbesitz) Or. Qu. 798-799 (Steinschneider 177), I, f. 40a-41a, M.
14833. Braunschweig - Landesmuseum fuer Geschichte und Volkstum R 2386, vol. II, f. 113b-114a, M.
14834. Cambridge - University Library Or. 785, f. 64b-65b, G, ecclectic.
14835. Darmstadt - Hessisches Landes- und Hochschulbibliothek Cod. Or. 15, f. 38b-39a, M.
14836. Darmstadt - Hessisches Landes- und Hochschulbibliothek Cod. Or. 15, f. 39a-40a, M, ecclectic.
14837. Hamburg - Staats- und Universitaetsbibliothek Cod. hebr. 17/2 (Steinschneider 152), f. 122a-122b, C.
14838. Hamburg - Staats- und Universitaetsbibliothek Cod. hebr. 40b (Steinschneider 110), f. 44a-44b, G.
14839. Hamburg - Staats- und Universitaetsbibliothek Cod. hebr. 40c (Steinschneider 111), f. 151b-152a, G.
14840. Hamburg - Staats- und Universitaetsbibliothek Cod. hebr. 132 (Steinschneider 155), f. 25b, C, incipit אמרותיך.
14841. Hamburg - Staats- und Universitaetsbibliothek Cod. hebr. 225, f. 261b-264a, G.
14842. Jerusalem - Jewish National and University Library Ms Heb 8° 3037, f. 57b-58a, M.
14843. Jerusalem - Schocken Institute 24100 / Mahzor Nuremberg, f. 344a-344b, M.
14844. London - British Library Or. 11318/1, f. 44a-45a, C.
14845. London - Montefiore Library 261, f. 30a, C, commentator: Eliezer b. Natan?.

14846. Moscow - Russian State Library, Ms. Guenzburg 191, f. 13a-14a, M.
14847. Moscow - Russian State Library, Ms. Guenzburg 615, f. 87a-87b, C.
14848. Muenchen - Bayerische Staatsbibliothek, Cod. hebr. 21, f. 181a-181b, M.
14849. Muenchen - Bayerische Staatsbibliothek, Cod. hebr. 86, f. 71b-72b, G.
14850. Muenchen - Bayerische Staatsbibliothek, Cod. hebr. 346 , f. 37a-37b, C.
14851. New York - Jewish Theological Seminary Ms. 4466, f. 257a-257b, M, ecclectic.
14852. New York - Jewish Theological Seminary Ms. 8097, f. 67a, C.
14853. New York - Jewish Theological Seminary Ms. 8169 (Acc. 0016), f. 39a-39b, M.
14854. Oxford - Bodleian Library MS Mich. 365 (Neubauer 1208), f. 50b, C.
14855. Oxford - Bodleian Library MS Opp. 170 (Neubauer 1205), f. 144a-144b, C.
14856. Oxford - Bodleian Library MS Opp. 172 (Neubauer 1211), f. 23b-24a, C.
14857. Oxford - Bodleian Library MS Opp. 619 (Neubauer 2374), f. 64a-65b, M.
14858. Oxford - Bodleian Library MS Opp. 675 (Neubauer 1210), f. 53b, C, no incipit.
14859. Paris - Bibliotheque Nationale heb. 653, f. 32b, G.
14860. Parma - Biblioteca Palatina Cod. Parm. 3270 (de Rossi 1215), f. 59a-59b, M.
14861. Parma - Biblioteca Palatina Cod. Parm. 3507 (Perreau 27), f. 133a, C.
14862. Vatican - Biblioteca Apostolica ebr. 308, f. 79a-79b, C, commentator: David b. Mose (compiler).
14863. Vatican - Biblioteca Apostolica ebr. 422/1, f. 13a, C.
14864. Zurich - Zentralbibliothek Heid. 139, f. 103a, C, commentator: Elazar b. Yehuda of Worms, no incipit, very short.
14865. Zurich - Zentralbibliothek Heid. 139, f. 70b (margin), C.

Asti, Fossano, Moncalvo
14866. New Haven - Yale University, Beinecke Rare Book and MS Library, MS Heb. 52, f. 56a-56b, M.

Romania
14867. Vatican - Biblioteca Apostolica ebr. 320, f. 184b-185a, M.

Tsarfat
14868. London - British Library Or. 8682, f. 39a-39b, Gl.
14869. London - David Sofer 5, f. 121a-121b, C, incipit אמיץ.
14870. Manchester - John Rylands University Library, Ms. Gaster 733, f. 81b, C, commentary block in Mahzor, manuscript damaged.

14871. Oxford - Bodleian Library MS Laud. Or. 271 (Neubauer 1206), f. 157b, C, commentator: Aaron b. Hayyim haKohen (compiler), rubric: מלך עליון, short.
14872. Oxford - Bodleian Library MS Opp. 171 (Neubauer 1207), f. 68a, C, rubric: מלך עליון, incipit נישא ונושא.
14873. Parma - Biblioteca Palatina Cod. Parm. 2125 (de Rossi 812), f. 30a-30b, C.
14874. Parma - Biblioteca Palatina Cod. Parm. 3006 (de Rossi 654,1), f. 73a-73b, M, incipit אמיץ.
14875. Vatican - Biblioteca Apostolica ebr. 306, f. 68a-68b, C.

מלך עליון ארתכי תרשישים (מ 1655), יהודה
Ashkenaz
14876. Moscow - Russian State Library, Ms. Guenzburg 191, f. 40a-40b, M.
14877. Torino - Archivio Terracini 1492, f. 22a, M.
Tsarfat
14878. London - David Sofer 5, f. 114b-115a, C.
14879. Parma - Biblioteca Palatina Cod. Parm. 3006 (de Rossi 654,1), f. 89b, M.
14880. Vatican - Biblioteca Apostolica ebr. 306, f. 56a, C.

מלך עלמין דגלגלוהי שביבין דינורין, סליחה
Yemen
14881. New York - Jewish Theological Seminary Ms. 3052, f. 78b-79a, M, rubric: מלך עלמין.
Yemen, commentary by Isaac b. Abraham Wanneh
14882. Chicago-Spertus College of Judaica D 2, 2, f. 236a, M.
14883. Jerusalem - Benayahu ת 261, f. 164a, M, rubric: מלך עלמין.
14884. Jerusalem - Benayahu ת 282, f. 139b, M, rubric: מלך עלמין.
14885. Jerusalem - Makhon Ben Zvi 1156 (Tubi 155), f. 137b, M, no incipit.
14886. Jerusalem - Makhon Ben Zvi 1174 (Tubi 154), f. 134b, M.
14887. Jerusalem - Michael Krupp 604, f. 174a, M.
14888. Jerusalem - Sassoon 1158, p. 413, M, no incipit.
14889. Jerusalem - Sassoon 1174, p. 267, M, no incipit, short.
14890. London - British Library Or. 11122, f. 212b-213a, M, rubric: מרן.
14891. Muenchen - Bayerische Staatsbibliothek, Cod. hebr. 472, f. 191a, M.
14892. New York - Jewish Theological Seminary Ms. 3013, f. 131b, M, no incipit.
14893. New York - Jewish Theological Seminary Ms. 3294, f. 16a, C, incipit מרן.
14894. Strasbourg - Bibliotheque Nationale et Universitaire 3965 (Landauer 39), p. 404, M, rubric: מלך עלמין.

מלך תר כל סתרי גנזים (מ 1682), פיוט לאחרי הקדושה לשחרית יום כפור, כלל חלקים

Ashkenaz

14895. Braunschweig - Landesmuseum fuer Geschichte und Volkstum R 2386, vol. II, f. 203a-203b, M.
14896. Fulda - Hessische Landesbibliothek A 3 II, f. 118a, C, commentator: Josef.
14897. Hamburg - Staats- und Universitaetsbibliothek Cod. hebr. 40b (Steinschneider 110), f. 111a-111b, G.
14898. Hamburg - Staats- und Universitaetsbibliothek Cod. hebr. 62 (Steinschneider 154), f. 12a-12b, C.
14899. Jerusalem - Schocken Institute 24100 / Mahzor Nuremberg, f. 388a, M.
14900. London - British Library Or. 11318/1, f. 88b, C.
14901. London - Montefiore Library 261, f. 50b, C, commentator: Eliezer b. Natan?.
14902. Moscow - Russian State Library, Ms. Guenzburg 191, f. 104b-105a, M.
14903. Moscow - Russian State Library, Ms. Guenzburg 615, f. 97b, C.
14904. Muenchen - Bayerische Staatsbibliothek, Cod. hebr. 346, f. 63a-63b, C, no incipit.
14905. New York - Jewish Theological Seminary Ms. 4466, f. 332b-333a, M.
14906. New York - Jewish Theological Seminary Ms. 8097, f. 75b, C, short.
14907. New York - Jewish Theological Seminary Ms. 8169 (Acc. 0016), f. 84a-85a, M.
14908. Oxford - Bodleian Library MS Mich. 365 (Neubauer 1208), f. 75b, C.
14909. Oxford - Bodleian Library MS Opp. 170 (Neubauer 1205), f. 169b, C.
14910. Oxford - Bodleian Library MS Opp. 172 (Neubauer 1211), f. 49a, C.
14911. Oxford - Bodleian Library MS Opp. 619 (Neubauer 2374), f. 167b-168a, M.
14912. Parma - Biblioteca Palatina Cod. Parm. 3205 (de Rossi 655), f. 230a, C.
14913. Parma - Biblioteca Palatina Cod. Parm. 3507 (Perreau 27), f. 156a, C.
14914. Vatican - Biblioteca Apostolica ebr. 308, f. 103(ii)b-104(ii)a, C, commentator: David b. Mose (compiler).
14915. Vatican - Biblioteca Apostolica ebr. 422/1, f. 17a, C.
14916. Zurich - Zentralbibliothek Heid. 139, f. 79b, C, very short, additional marginal notes.

Ashkenaz, commentary by Abraham b. Azriel[336]

14917. Vatican - Biblioteca Apostolica ebr. 301,1, f. 171b, C.

Asti, Fossano, Moncalvo

14918. New Haven - Yale University, Beinecke Rare Book and MS Library, MS Heb. 52, f. 117a-117b, M.

---

[336] Edited by Urbach, ערוגת הבושם, vol. III, p. 504-505.

Tsarfat

14919. London - British Library Add. 11639 (Margoliouth 1056), f. 721b, M, very short.
14920. London - David Sofer 5, f. 141a, C, incipit תר.
14921. Oxford - Bodleian Library MS Bodl. Or. 109 (Neubauer 1209), f. 27a, C, commentator: Aaron b. Hayyim haKohen (compiler).
14922. Oxford - Bodleian Library MS Laud. Or. 271 (Neubauer 1206), f. 107b, C, commentator: Aaron b. Hayyim haKohen (compiler).
14923. Parma - Biblioteca Palatina Cod. Parm. 1794 (de Rossi 1061), f. 151b-153a, M.
14924. Parma - Biblioteca Palatina Cod. Parm. 2890 (de Rossi 856), f. 42a-42b, M, second part censored.
14925. Parma - Biblioteca Palatina Cod. Parm. 3006 (de Rossi 654,1), f. 187b-188a, M.
14926. Vatican - Biblioteca Apostolica ebr. 306, f. 83a-83b, C, incipit תר.

מלכותו בקהל עדתי (מ +1687), אופן
Tsarfat

14927. Parma - Biblioteca Palatina Cod. Parm. 3006 (de Rossi 654,1), f. 131a-131b, M.
14928. Vatican - Biblioteca Apostolica ebr. 306, f. 75a-75b, C.

מלכותם באבדך עובדי פסילי נסכים (מ 1692), פיוט לאחרי הקדושה, שחרית יום כפור
Ashkenaz

14929. Berlin - Staatsbibliothek (Preussischer Kulturbesitz) Or. Qu. 798-799 (Steinschneider 177), I, f. 95a-96a, M.
14930. Braunschweig - Landesmuseum fuer Geschichte und Volkstum R 2386, vol. II, f. 206b-207b, M.
14931. Fulda - Hessische Landesbibliothek A 3 II, f. 121a-121b, C, commentator: Josef.
14932. Hamburg - Staats- und Universitaetsbibliothek Cod. hebr. 62 (Steinschneider 154), f. 16a-16b, C.
14933. Hamburg - Staats- und Universitaetsbibliothek Cod. hebr. 132 (Steinschneider 155), f. 42b-43a, C.
14934. Jerusalem - Jewish National and University Library Ms Heb 8° 3037, f. 142b-143b, M.
14935. Jerusalem - Schocken Institute 24100 / Mahzor Nuremberg, f. 391b-392b, M.
14936. London - British Library Or. 11318/1, f. 94b-95b, C.
14937. London - Montefiore Library 261, f. 53a-53b, C, commentator: Eliezer b. Natan?.
14938. Moscow - Russian State Library, Ms. Guenzburg 615, f. 101b-102a, C.

14939. New York - Jewish Theological Seminary Ms. 4466, f. 338b-339b, M.
14940. New York - Jewish Theological Seminary Ms. 8097, f. 76b-77a, C.
14941. Oxford - Bodleian Library MS Mich. 365 (Neubauer 1208), f. 78b-79a, C.
14942. Oxford - Bodleian Library MS Opp. 170 (Neubauer 1205), f. 173b-174a, C.
14943. Oxford - Bodleian Library MS Opp. 172 (Neubauer 1211), f. 52b-53a, C.
14944. Oxford - Bodleian Library MS Opp. 619 (Neubauer 2374), f. 170b-171a, M.
14945. Parma - Biblioteca Palatina Cod. Parm. 3205 (de Rossi 655), f. 232b-233a, C.
14946. Parma - Biblioteca Palatina Cod. Parm. 3271 (de Rossi 1216), f. 63b-65a, G.
14947. Vatican - Biblioteca Apostolica ebr. 308, f. 107(ii)a-107(ii)b, C, commentator: David b. Mose (compiler).
14948. Vatican - Biblioteca Apostolica ebr. 422/1, f. 17b, C.
14949. Zurich - Zentralbibliothek Heid. 139, f. 81b-82a, C, additional marginal notes.

Ashkenaz, commentary by Abraham b. Azriel[337]
14950. Vatican - Biblioteca Apostolica ebr. 301,1, f. 173b, C.

Tsarfat
14951. London - British Library Add. 11639 (Margoliouth 1056), f. 722b, M.
14952. London - David Sofer 5, f. 172b-173a, C, rubric: רהיטים.
14953. Oxford - Bodleian Library MS Bodl. Or. 109 (Neubauer 1209), f. 27(iv)b-28a, C, commentator: Aaron b. Hayyim haKohen (compiler).
14954. Oxford - Bodleian Library MS Laud. Or. 271 (Neubauer 1206), f. 110b, C, commentator: Aaron b. Hayyim haKohen (compiler).
14955. Parma - Biblioteca Palatina Cod. Parm. 2125 (de Rossi 812), f. 43a-43b, C.
14956. Parma - Biblioteca Palatina Cod. Parm. 2890 (de Rossi 856), f. 124a-124b, M.
14957. Parma - Biblioteca Palatina Cod. Parm. 3006 (de Rossi 654,1), f. 242b-243b, M.
14958. Vatican - Biblioteca Apostolica ebr. 306, f. 87a-88a, C.

ממסגר אסיר בצאת לחופש (מ +1769), יוסף ב״ר שמואל טוב עלם, חלק ב׳, קדושתא לשבת הגדול

Ashkenaz
14959. Muenchen - Bayerische Staatsbibliothek, Cod. hebr. 88, f. 49b-50a, G.

---
[337] Edited by Urbach, ערוגת הבושם, vol. III, p. 516-518.

14960. Parma - Biblioteca Palatina Cod. Parm 3000 (de Rossi 378), f. 27a-27b, C, no incipit.
14961. Parma - Biblioteca Palatina Cod. Parm. 3507 (Perreau 27), f. 33b, C, no incipit.

Tsarfat
14962. London - British Library Add. 11639 (Margoliouth 1056), f. 672b, M, no incipit.
14963. Moscow - Russian State Library, Ms. Guenzburg 1665, f. 45b, M, no incipit.
14964. Parma - Biblioteca Palatina Cod. Parm. 3136 (de Rossi 405), f. 59a, M.

ממיצר צעקתי מחמת מציק כופשי (מ 1780), משה בר נתן, סליחה
Tsarfat
14965. London - David Sofer 5, f. 104b, C.
14966. Parma - Biblioteca Palatina Cod. Parm. 3007 (de Rossi 654,2), f. 143a-144a, M.

ממעון בהמוני, סליחה
Ashkenaz
14967. Oxford - Bodleian Library MS Opp. 172 (Neubauer 1211), f. 88b, C, very short.

ממעמקים קראתיך יי אדיר מטה עליות רקע (מ +1805), סליחה
Yemen
14968. Jerusalem - Benayahu ת 414, f. 154a, M.
Yemen, commentary by Isaac b. Abraham Wanneh
14969. Chicago-Spertus College of Judaica D 2, 2, f. 220a-220b, M, no incipit.
14970. Jerusalem - Michael Krupp 604, f. 165a-165b, M, rubric: אל מלך, no incipit.
14971. Jerusalem - Sassoon 1158, p. 383-384, M, no incipit.
14972. London - British Library Or. 11122, f. 191b-192a, M, no incipit.

ממקומו מופיע כל ענין (מ 1813), אהרן בן יוסף הרופא, פרשת היהי מקץ
Karaite, commentary by Berakha b. Josef haKohen
14973. New York - Jewish Theological Seminary Ms. 3367, f. 53a-56a, C, rubric: פרוש פרשת ויהי קץ.
14974. St. Petersburg - Inst. of Oriental Studies of the Russian Academy B 431, f. 37b-39b, C, rubric: פרשת מקץ.
14975. St. Petersburg - Russian National Library, Evr. IV 50, f. 39a-41a, C, rubric: היהי מקץ.

ממרה חקה גזר (מ +1816), אלעזר ברבי קליר, חלק ב', קדושתא לשבת פרה

Ashkenaz
14976. Berlin - Staatsbibliothek (Preussischer Kulturbesitz) Or. Qu. 798-799 (Steinschneider 177), II, f. 32b-33a, M.
14977. Budapest - Magyar tudomanyos akademia, MS. Kaufmann A 384, f. 77a, M.
14978. Jerusalem - Schocken Institute 24100 / Mahzor Nuremberg, f. 61a-61b, M.
14979. Muenchen - Bayerische Staatsbibliothek, Cod. hebr. 88, f. 38a-38b, G.
14980. Muenchen - Bayerische Staatsbibliothek, Cod. hebr. 393, f. 101a, C, no incipit.
14981. New York - Jewish Theological Seminary Ms. 4466, f. 8a-8b, M.
14982. Oxford - Bodleian Library MS Opp. 170 (Neubauer 1205), f. 29a-29b, C.
14983. Paris - Bibliotheque Nationale heb. 709, f. 35b-36a, C.
14984. Parma - Biblioteca Palatina Cod. Parm. 1002 (Ta 24), f. 55b, M.
14985. Parma - Biblioteca Palatina Cod. Parm 3000 (de Rossi 378), f. 14a-14b, M, no incipit.
14986. Parma - Biblioteca Palatina Cod. Parm. 3205 (de Rossi 655), f. 33a-33b, C, no incipit.
14987. Parma - Biblioteca Palatina Cod. Parm. 3507 (Perreau 27), f. 27b, C.
14988. Vatican - Biblioteca Apostolica ebr. 305,1, f. 20a-20b, C, no incipit.
14989. Zurich - Zentralbibliothek Heid. 139, f. 5a-5b, C, no incipit, additional marginal notes.

Tsarfat
14990. London - British Library Add. 11639 (Margoliouth 1056), f. 274b-275a, M.
14991. Moscow - Russian State Library, Ms. Guenzburg 1665, f. 34a, M, no incipit.
14992. Oxford - Bodleian Library MS Opp. 171 (Neubauer 1207), f. 36a-36b, C.
14993. Parma - Biblioteca Palatina Cod. Parm. 3136 (de Rossi 405), f. 48b, M.
14994. Vatican - Biblioteca Apostolica ebr. 306, f. 149a-149b, C, no incipit.

ממרום לבן ערום (מ 1820), משה אבן עזרא, חלק יז', קדושתא לשחרית יום כפור

Carpentras
14995. Cincinnati - Hebrew Union College 392, f. 59a, M, no incipit.

Carpentras, commentary by Josef b. Abraham of Montelitz
14996. Cincinnati - Hebrew Union College 291, f. 33a-33b, C, rubric: 'פי פזמון ממרום וכו'.

14997. New York - Jewish Theological Seminary Ms. 4197, f. 132b-133a, M, no incipit.
14998. Paris - Ecole Rabbinique 32, f. 148b-149a, M, no incipit.
14999. Strasbourg - Bibliotheque Nationale et Universitaire 4081, f. 125a-125b, M, rubric: אמר הצייד, no incipit.

מן ההר למעוניו (מ +1838), אלעזר ברבי קליר, חלק ב', קדושתא לשבועות
Ashkenaz
15000. Berlin - Staatsbibliothek (Preussischer Kulturbesitz) Or. Qu. 798-799 (Steinschneider 177), II, f. 139b-140a, M.
15001. Braunschweig - Landesmuseum fuer Geschichte und Volkstum R 2386, vol. I, f. 96b, M, incipit קרא.
15002. Budapest - Magyar tudomanyos akademia, MS. Kaufmann A 400, p. 176, C, no incipit.
15003. Hamburg - Staats- und Universitaetsbibliothek Cod. hebr. 17/2 (Steinschneider 152), f. 86b, C, no incipit.
15004. Jerusalem - Schocken Institute 24100 / Mahzor Nuremberg, f. 171b-172a, M.
15005. London - British Library Add. 18695 (Margoliouth 683), f. 85b, T, Yiddish.
15006. London - British Library Add. 22431 (Margoliouth 662a), f. 55b, M.
15007. Moscow - Russian State Library, Ms. Guenzburg 615, f. 41a, C, no incipit.
15008. New York - Jewish Theological Seminary Ms. 4466, f. 166a, M, no incipit.
15009. Oxford - Bodleian Library MS Opp. 170 (Neubauer 1205), f. 86b, C, no incipit.
15010. Paris - Bibliotheque Nationale heb. 709, f. 136a, C, no incipit.
15011. Parma - Biblioteca Palatina Cod. Parm. 1002 (Ta 24), f. 204b, M, no incipit, short.
15012. Parma - Biblioteca Palatina Cod. Parm. 2886 (de Rossi 585), f. 63b-64a, M, later hand, margins cut.
15013. Parma - Biblioteca Palatina Cod. Parm. 3205 (de Rossi 655), f. 127a-127b, C, no incipit.
15014. Parma - Biblioteca Palatina Cod. Parm. 3507 (Perreau 27), f. 88a-88b, C, no incipit.
15015. Zurich - Zentralbibliothek Heid. 139, f. 54a-54b, C, no incipit, short.

מנויה וגמורה בסוד חכמי תורה, סליחה
Ashkenaz
15016. Hamburg - Staats- und Universitaetsbibliothek Cod. hebr. 62 (Steinschneider 154), f. 31a-31b, C.

Tsarfat
15017. London - David Sofer 5, f. 104b-105a, C.
15018. Parma - Biblioteca Palatina Cod. Parm. 3007 (de Rossi 654,2), f. 142b-143a, M, ecclectic.

מנום הקיצו אמוני מושכי בחבלי שוא עוני (מ +1873), משה אבן עזרא
Carpentras, commentary by Josef b. Abraham of Montelitz
15019. Paris - Ecole Rabbinique 32, f. 155b, M.

מנומם בעת קומם להמליכך (מ 1875), משה אבן עזרא, פזמון לראש השנה
Yemen
15020. Jerusalem - Sassoon 902, p. 434, M.
Yemen, commentary by Isaac b. Abraham Wanneh
15021. Jerusalem - Sassoon 1158, p. 186, M.
15022. London - British Library Or. 11122, f. 178a, M.

מסאן באלרצא ואלעאפייה (מ 1917), שלם שבזי
Yemen
15023. Cincinnati - Hebrew Union College 398, f. 130b-131a, M.

מעביר יום ומביא לילהם, יוסף ב"ר יעקב, חלק ב', קדושתא לנעילה
Tsarfat
15024. London - David Sofer 5, f. 171b, C.
15025. Parma - Biblioteca Palatina Cod. Parm. 3006 (de Rossi 654,1), f. 239b-240a, M.

מעון אדיר מאז ראשון נסתר (מ 1963), שלמה אבן גבירול, סליחה
Yemen
15026. New York - Jewish Theological Seminary Ms. 3028, f. 38a-38b, G.

מעונה אלהי קדם בך בטחתי (מ 1980), מרדכי בן שבתי, סליחה
Ashkenaz
15027. Oxford - Bodleian Library MS Opp. 172 (Neubauer 1211), f. 57b, C, short.
15028. Vatican - Biblioteca Apostolica ebr. 308, f. 134b, C, commentator: David b. Mose (compiler), short.
Ashkenaz, commentary by Abraham b. Azriel[338]
15029. Frankfurt a M - Stadt- und Universitaetsbibliothek Fol. 16 (Merzbacher 95), f. 108a, C, very short.

---

[338] Edited by Urbach, ערוגת הבושם, vol. III, p. 560.

מעוני שמים שחקים יזבולך מלאים (מ 1987), מנחם ב"ר יעקב, קינה
Ashkenaz
15030. Berlin - Staatsbibliothek (Preussischer Kulturbesitz) Or. Qu. 798-799 (Steinschneider 177), II, f. 206b-207a, M.

מעלות השחר בקראו גרונו נוחר, פזמון
Sepharad, commentary by David b. Josef Abudarham
15031. New York - Columbia X893 Ab 93, f. 32b-33a, C, rubric: פזמון.

מעלות השחר קראתיך הרב עננני אל (מ 2029), אברהם אבן עזרא, פזמון למנחה יום כפור
Sepharad, commentary by David b. Josef Abudarham[339]
15032. Budapest - Magyar tudomanyos akademia, MS. Kaufmann A 405/2, p. 254, C, rubric: פזמון.
15033. Budapest - Magyar tudomanyos akademia, MS. Kaufmann A 405/2, p. 259, C, rubric: פזמון.
15034. New York - Columbia X893 Ab 93, f. 31a, C, rubric: פזמון.

מעשה שמרתי במופי (מ 2053), משה אבן עזרא, חלק ה', קדושתא לשחרית יום כפור
Carpentras
15035. Cincinnati - Hebrew Union College 392, f. 49a-50b, M, no incipit.
Carpentras, commentary by Josef b. Abraham of Montelitz
15036. Cincinnati - Hebrew Union College 291, f. 25b-26a, C, rubric: פי' ובכן אלמדני צור דתיך.
15037. New York - Jewish Theological Seminary Ms. 4197, f. 112b-115a, M.
15038. Paris - Ecole Rabbinique 32, f. 132b-134a, M.
15039. Strasbourg - Bibliotheque Nationale et Universitaire 4081, f. 109b-111b, M.

מעשרה מאמרות (מ 2060), אלעזר ברבי קליר, סילוק, קדושתא לשבת שובה
Tsarfat
15040. Oxford - Bodleian Library MS Opp. 171 (Neubauer 1207), f. 82b-84a, C, rubric: סילוק.

מעתיק פלוסים (מ +2067), אלעזר ברבי קליר, חלק ב', קדושתא לשבת שקלים
Ashkenaz
15041. Berlin - Staatsbibliothek (Preussischer Kulturbesitz) Or. Qu. 798-799 (Steinschneider 177), II, f. 13a-13b, M.
15042. Budapest - Magyar tudomanyos akademia, MS. Kaufmann A 384, f. 37b-38a, M.

---

[339] Edited by Prins, תשלום אבודרהם, p. 159.

15043. Budapest - Magyar tudomanyos akademia, MS. Kaufmann A 400 , p. 6-7, C.
15044. Cambridge - University Library Add. 504,1, f. 2b-3a, C, no incipit.
15045. Erlangen - Universitaetsbibliothek 2601 (Roth 67), f. 27a-27b, M.
15046. Hamburg - Staats- und Universitaetsbibliothek Cod. hebr. 225, f. 10b, G.
15047. Jerusalem - Schocken Institute 24100 / Mahzor Nuremberg, f. 34b-35a, M.
15048. Muenchen - Bayerische Staatsbibliothek, Cod. hebr. 88, f. 15a, G.
15049. Muenchen - Bayerische Staatsbibliothek, Cod. hebr. 393 , f. 84b-85a, C, no incipit.
15050. Oxford - Bodleian Library MS Opp. 170 (Neubauer 1205) , f. 4a-4b, C.
15051. Paris - Bibliotheque Nationale heb. 709, f. 4b-5a, C.
15052. Parma - Biblioteca Palatina Cod. Parm. 1002 (Ta 24), f. 23b-24a, M.
15053. Parma - Biblioteca Palatina Cod. Parm. 3205 (de Rossi 655) , f. 11b-12a, C.
15054. Parma - Biblioteca Palatina Cod. Parm. 3507 (Perreau 27), f. 2b-3a, C, no incipit.
15055. Vatican - Biblioteca Apostolica ebr. 305,1, f. 3a-3b, C, no incipit.

Tsarfat
15056. London - British Library Add. 11639 (Margoliouth 1056), f. 264a-264b, M.
15057. London - David Sofer 5, f. 9b-10a, C.
15058. Moscow - Russian State Library, Ms. Guenzburg 1665, f. 13b-14a, M.
15059. Oxford - Bodleian Library MS Opp. 171 (Neubauer 1207) , f. 5b-6b, C.
15060. Parma - Biblioteca Palatina Cod. Parm. 3136 (de Rossi 405) , f. 22a-22b, M, no incipit.
15061. Vatican - Biblioteca Apostolica ebr. 306, f. 157b-158a, C, no incipit.

מפלטי אלי צורי סתרי ומגיני (מ 2069), מרדכי בן שבתי, סליחה

Ashkenaz
15062. Jerusalem - Schocken Institute 24100 / Mahzor Nuremberg , f. 400b-401a, M.
15063. Muenchen - Bayerische Staatsbibliothek, Cod. hebr. 346 , f. 138b, C, rubric: אחרת, short.
15064. Oxford - Bodleian Library MS Mich. 543 (Neubauer 1212), f. 26a-26b, C, commentator: Isaac b. Jacob (compiler).
15065. Oxford - Bodleian Library MS Opp. 172 (Neubauer 1211), f. 57b-58a, C, rubric: עקידה.
15066. Oxford - Bodleian Library MS Opp. 681 (Neubauer 1213), f. 28a-29a, C.

15067. Padova - Biblioteca del Seminario Vescovile Cod. 218, f. 183b-184a, M, rubric: עקידה.
15068. Vatican - Biblioteca Apostolica ebr. 308, f. 112b-113b, C, commentator: David b. Mose (compiler).

Ashkenaz, commentary by Abraham b. Azriel[340]

15069. Frankfurt a M - Stadt- und Universitaetsbibliothek Fol. 16 (Merzbacher 95), f. 110b, C.

מפרי שפתיו זבח ומנחה (מ +2107), משה אבן עזרא, חלק ב', קדושתא למנחה יום כפור
Carpentras

15070. Cincinnati - Hebrew Union College 392, f. 101b-102a, M, no incipit.

Carpentras, commentary by Josef b. Abraham of Montelitz

15071. New York - Jewish Theological Seminary Ms. 4197, f. 235b-236b, M, no incipit.
15072. Paris - Ecole Rabbinique 32, f. 243a-243b, M, no incipit.
15073. Strasbourg - Bibliotheque Nationale et Universitaire 4081, f. 215b-216a, M, no incipit.

מצוקי רגב שתית וטרם מתיחת אהילת סיכוכו, חלק ד', קדושתא לסוכות
Tsarfat

15074. Moscow - Russian State Library, Ms. Guenzburg 1665, f. 170b, M, very short.

מצעק מעלות השחר (מ 2164), משה אבן עזרא, חלק ד', קדושתא לנעילה
Ashkenaz

15075. Jerusalem - Schocken Institute 24100 / Mahzor Nuremberg, f. 467a, M, very short.
15076. Muenchen - Bayerische Staatsbibliothek, Cod. hebr. 346, f. 149a-149b, C.
15077. Oxford - Bodleian Library MS Opp. 172 (Neubauer 1211), f. 88b, C, short.
15078. Vatican - Biblioteca Apostolica ebr. 308, f. 149b, C, commentator: David b. Mose (compiler).

Ashkenaz, commentary by Abraham b. Azriel[341]

15079. Frankfurt a M - Stadt- und Universitaetsbibliothek Fol. 16 (Merzbacher 95), f. 104a, C, rubric: אחרת.

Carpentras

15080. Cincinnati - Hebrew Union College 392, f. 115b, M, no incipit.

---

[340] Edited by Urbach, ערוגת הבושם, vol. III, p. 570-571.
[341] Edited by Urbach, ערוגת הבושם, vol. III, p. 543-544.

Carpentras, commentary by Josef b. Abraham of Montelitz
15081. Cincinnati - Hebrew Union College 291, f. 58b, C, rubric: פי' תוכחה מצעק וכו'.
15082. Paris - Ecole Rabbinique 32, f. 276a-276b, M, no incipit.
15083. Strasbourg - Bibliotheque Nationale et Universitaire 4081, f. 246b, M, no incipit.

Sepharad, commentary by David b. Josef Abudarham
15084. Holon - Yehuda Nahum 278, f. 1b, FC, rubric: פזמון, short.

Tsarfat
15085. London - David Sofer 5, f. 174b, C, rubric: אחר.
15086. Parma - Biblioteca Palatina Cod. Parm. 3006 (de Rossi 654,1), f. 248b, M.

מקדים וראש לקוראים זוכה (מ 2180), מאיר ב"ר יצחק, רשות לחתן בראשית

Tsarfat
15087. London - British Library Or. 2735 (Margoliouth 663), f. 160a, M.

מקוה ישראל יי מושיעו בעת צרה (מ 2198), שמעון ב"ר יצחק, סליחה

Ashkenaz
15088. Oxford - Bodleian Library MS Mich. 543 (Neubauer 1212), f. 82a-83a, bottom margin, C, commentator: Isaac b. Jacob (compiler).
15089. Vatican - Biblioteca Apostolica ebr. 422/1, f. 34b, C, short.

Tsarfat
15090. Oxford - Bodleian Library MS Bodl. Or. 109 (Neubauer 1209), f. 46b, C, commentator: Aaron b. Hayyim haKohen (compiler).

מקור דמעה אתן עיני וראשי למען מים (מ 2230), מרדכי בר יעקב, קינה

Carpentras, commentary by Mordekhai b. Josef of Rocco Martino
15091. Cincinnati - Hebrew Union College 246/1, f. 78a-78b, C, rubric: פי' קינה מקור דמעה.

מקור עיני על עוני יתהלך לעתותי (מ 2238), משה אבן עזרא, חלק יב', קדושתא לשחרית יום כפור, בתימן: סליחה

Sepharad, commentary by David b. Josef Abudarham[342]
15092. New York - Columbia X893 Ab 93, f. 11b-12a, C, rubric: פזמון.

Yemen
15093. Jerusalem - Benayahu ת 414, f. 129b, M, short.

Yemen, commentary by Isaac b. Abraham Wanneh
15094. Chicago-Spertus College of Judaica D 2, 2, f. 222b, M, no incipit.
15095. Jerusalem - Sassoon 1158, p. 378, M, no incipit.

---

[342] Edited by Prins, תשלום אבודרהם, p. 99-100.

15096. London - British Library Or. 11122, f. 189b, M, no incipit.

מקשיב שועם וזעקתם (מ ++2260)

Carpentras
15097. Cincinnati - Hebrew Union College 392, f. 23b-24a, M.

מראשית גוי קדוש היינו (מ 2291), קינה

Yemen, commentary by Isaac b. Abraham Wanneh
15098. Jerusalem - Sassoon 1158, p. 171, M.
15099. London - British Library Or. 11122, f. 102b, M.

מרום וקדוש שעה שעואת שבויים (מ 2336), משה אבן עזרא, חלק י, קדושתא לשחרית יום כפור, בתימן: סליחה

Carpentras
15100. Cincinnati - Hebrew Union College 392, f. 58b, M, no incipit.

Carpentras, commentary by Josef b. Abraham of Montelitz
15101. New York - Jewish Theological Seminary Ms. 4197, f. 131b, M, no incipit.
15102. Paris - Ecole Rabbinique 32, f. 147b-148a, M, no incipit.
15103. Strasbourg - Bibliotheque Nationale et Universitaire 4081, f. 124a-124b, M, no incipit.

Yemen, commentary by Isaac b. Abraham Wanneh
15104. Chicago-Spertus College of Judaica D 2, 2, f. 219b, M, no incipit.
15105. Jerusalem - Sassoon 1158, p. 376, M, no incipit.
15106. London - British Library Or. 11122, f. 188a-188b, M, rubric: אל מלך.

מרום נורא עלילותיה (מ 2356), מנחם, לראש השנה

Carpentras
15107. Cincinnati - Hebrew Union College 429/1, f. 15a, M, no incipit, very short.

Carpentras, commentary by Eliyahu Carmi
15108. Marseille - Mlle. Odette Valabregue [1], f. 33a-33b, C.

Carpentras, commentary by Josef b. Abraham of Montelitz
15109. Cincinnati - Hebrew Union College 357, f. 4a, M, rubric: פירוש.
15110. New York - Jewish Theological Seminary Ms. 4746, f. 23b, M.
15111. Paris - Ecole Rabbinique 31, f. 128a-128b, M.

מרום שוכן עד נערץ בקדושה (מ 2370), משה, הושענא

Yemen, commentary by Samḥun b. Salomo Ḥaloah
15112. Jerusalem - Makhon ben Zvi 2808, f. 124b-126b, C.

מרימי עול עגלה לחלאות (מ +2409), אלעזר ברבי קליר, חלק ב׳, קדושתא לשבת החדש
Ashkenaz
15113. Berlin - Staatsbibliothek (Preussischer Kulturbesitz) Or. Qu. 798-799 (Steinschneider 177), II, f. 40a, M.
15114. Budapest - Magyar tudomanyos akademia, MS. Kaufmann A 384, f. 89b, M.
15115. Erlangen - Universitaetsbibliothek 2601 (Roth 67), f. 50a, M.
15116. Jerusalem - Schocken Institute 24100 / Mahzor Nuremberg, f. 65a, M.
15117. London - British Library Add. 18695 (Margoliouth 683), f. 2b-3a, T, Yiddish.
15118. Muenchen - Bayerische Staatsbibliothek, Cod. hebr. 88, f. 43b, G.
15119. Muenchen - Bayerische Staatsbibliothek, Cod. hebr. 393, f. 103b-104a, C, no incipit.
15120. New York - Jewish Theological Seminary Ms. 4466, f. 20a, M.
15121. Oxford - Bodleian Library MS Opp. 170 (Neubauer 1205), f. 33b-34a, C.
15122. Paris - Bibliotheque Nationale heb. 709, f. 39b, C.
15123. Parma - Biblioteca Palatina Cod. Parm. 1002 (Ta 24), f. 67b, M.
15124. Parma - Biblioteca Palatina Cod. Parm 3000 (de Rossi 378), f. 20a-20b, M.
15125. Parma - Biblioteca Palatina Cod. Parm. 3205 (de Rossi 655), f. 38a-38b, C, no incipit.
15126. Parma - Biblioteca Palatina Cod. Parm. 3507 (Perreau 27), f. 30a-30b, C, no incipit.
15127. Vatican - Biblioteca Apostolica ebr. 305,1, f. 25a, C, no incipit.
15128. Zurich - Zentralbibliothek Heid. 139, f. 9a, C, additional marginal notes.
Tsarfat
15129. London - British Library Add. 11639 (Margoliouth 1056), f. 276b, M, short.
15130. London - David Sofer 5, f. 30b-31a, C.
15131. Moscow - Russian State Library, Ms. Guenzburg 1665, f. 39b, M, short, no incipit.
15132. Parma - Biblioteca Palatina Cod. Parm. 3136 (de Rossi 405), f. 53b, M.
15133. Vatican - Biblioteca Apostolica ebr. 306, f. 152b-153a, C, no incipit.

מרן דבשמיא לך מתחנין כעבדיא דמתחנין קדם מריה (מ 2425), סליחה
Ashkenaz
15134. London - British Library Add. 18695 (Margoliouth 683), f. 173a, T, Yiddish.
15135. Vatican - Biblioteca Apostolica ebr. 308, f. 21b, C, commentator: David b. Mose (compiler).

15136. Vatican - Biblioteca Apostolica ebr. 422/1, f. 35a, C, very short.
Roma
15137. Berlin - Staatsbibliothek (Preussischer Kulturbesitz) Or. Oct. 3567, f. 3a-3b, FC.
Sepharad
15138. Skokie - Hebrew Theological College 3, f. 20a, G.
Tsarfat
15139. London - David Sofer 5, f. 130b, C.
15140. Parma - Biblioteca Palatina Cod. Parm. 3007 (de Rossi 654,2), f. 21a, M, short.
Yemen
15141. Chicago-Spertus College of Judaica D 2, 2, f. 184b, G.
15142. New York - Jewish Theological Seminary Ms. 3052, f. 78b, M.
Yemen, commentary by Isaac b. Abraham Wanneh
15143. Jerusalem - Benayahu ת 282, f. 139b, M.

מרן דבשמיא מר עלי כלמרי, סליחה

Yemen
15144. New York - Jewish Theological Seminary Ms. 3052, f. 82a, M, no incipit.
15145. Ramat Gan - Universitat Bar Ilan 62, f. 51a, G.
Yemen, commentary by Isaac b. Abraham Wanneh
15146. Jerusalem - Benayahu ת 261, f. 165a, M, short.
15147. Jerusalem - Benayahu ת 282, f. 140b, M.
15148. Jerusalem - Makhon Ben Zvi 1156 (Tubi 155), f. 138a, M, no incipit.
15149. Jerusalem - Michael Krupp 604, f. 175a, M, very short.
15150. Jerusalem - Musad haRav Kook 325, f. 194a, M, short.
15151. Jerusalem - Sassoon 1158, p. 415, M, no incipit.
15152. London - British Library Or. 11122, f. 214a, M, no incipit.
15153. Muenchen - Bayerische Staatsbibliothek, Cod. hebr. 472, f. 193a, M, very short.
15154. New York - Jewish Theological Seminary Ms. 3294, f. 17a, C.
15155. Strasbourg - Bibliotheque Nationale et Universitaire 3965 (Landauer 39), p. 408, M, very short.

מרשות אל עליון קונה שמים וארץ (מ 2455), אליעזר ב"ר נתן, רשות לחתן

Ashkenaz
15156. Budapest - Magyar tudomanyos akademia, MS. Kaufmann A 399, p. 375, C, rubric: רשויות מרבינו אליעזר בר נתן זצ"ל.
15157. Budapest - Magyar tudomanyos akademia, MS. Kaufmann A 399, p. 392-395, C, rubric: אילו דרבינו אבן, incipit missing.
15158. Oxford - Bodleian Library MS Can. Or. 82 (Neubauer 1148), f. 66b-67b, M.

מרשות אלהי האלהים ואדוני האדונים (מ 2456), רשות לחתן בראשית

Ashkenaz

15159. Berlin - Staatsbibliothek (Preussischer Kulturbesitz) Or. Qu. 798-799 (Steinschneider 177), I, f. 229a-229b, M.
15160. London - British Library Add. 18695 (Margoliouth 683), f. 139a-140a, T, Yiddish.
15161. Lund - Universitetsbibliothek Ms. L.O. 2, f. 93b, M, very short.

מרשות אלהי קדם עוטה אור כשלמה (מ 2460), יצחק הלוי בר אלעזר, רשות לחתן

Ashkenaz

15162. Budapest - Magyar tudomanyos akademia, MS. Kaufmann A 399, p. 373-375, C.
15163. Budapest - Magyar tudomanyos akademia, MS. Kaufmann A 399, p. 375-378, C, rubric: מרבנא יצחק סגן הלוייה.

מרשות האל הגדול הגבויר והנורא (מ 2473), רשות לחתן תורה

Ashkenaz

15164. Berlin - Staatsbibliothek (Preussischer Kulturbesitz) Or. Qu. 798-799 (Steinschneider 177), I, f. 228a-228b, M.
15165. London - British Library Add. 18695 (Margoliouth 683), f. 138b-139a, T, Yiddish.

מרשות קונה שמים וארץ (מ 2570), קלונימוס ב"ר יהודה, רשות לחתן

Ashkenaz

15166. Budapest - Magyar tudomanyos akademia, MS. Kaufmann A 399, p. 388-392, C, rubric: דרבינו קלונימוס שיסד לך יי הגדולה.

מרשות שוכן עד (מ 2512), שמעון ב"ר יצחק, רשות לחתן

Ashkenaz

15167. Budapest - Magyar tudomanyos akademia, MS. Kaufmann A 399, p. 354-360, C, rubric: רשויות מרבנא שנעון הגדול.
15168. Jerusalem - Schocken Institute 24100 / Mahzor Nuremberg, f. 227a-227b, M.
15169. Muenchen - Bayerische Staatsbibliothek, Cod. hebr. 69, f. 81b, M.
15170. Muenchen - Bayerische Staatsbibliothek, Cod. hebr. 393,9, f. 185b-188a, C.
15171. Oxford - Bodleian Library MS Can. Or. 82 (Neubauer 1148), f. 51b-53a, M.

Tsarfat

15172. London - British Library Or. 2735 (Margoliouth 663), f. 175b-176b, M, margins partly damaged.

משאת כפי מנחת ערב רצה נא בכשר (מ 2519), מרדכי בן שבתי, סליחה
Ashkenaz
15173. Jerusalem - Schocken Institute 24100 / Mahzor Nuremberg, f. 455a, M.
15174. Muenchen - Bayerische Staatsbibliothek, Cod. hebr. 346, f. 138a, C, rubric: אחרת, short.
15175. Oxford - Bodleian Library MS Mich. 543 (Neubauer 1212), f. 32a-32b, C, commentator: Isaac b. Jacob (compiler).
15176. Oxford - Bodleian Library MS Opp. 172 (Neubauer 1211), f. 85a-85b, C, short.
15177. Oxford - Bodleian Library MS Opp. 681 (Neubauer 1213), f. 29a-29b, C.
15178. Padova - Biblioteca del Seminario Vescovile Cod. 218, f. 205a-206a, M.
15179. Vatican - Biblioteca Apostolica ebr. 308, f. 143a-143b, C, commentator: David b. Mose (compiler).

Ashkenaz, commentary by Abraham b. Azriel[343]
15180. Frankfurt a M - Stadt- und Universitaetsbibliothek Fol. 16 (Merzbacher 95), f. 107b, C.

משאת שיר וזמירות וצבי מחמד מלה (מ 2520), משה אבן עזרא, סליחה
Yemen
15181. Jerusalem - Sassoon 902, p. 426, M, short.
15182. New York - Jewish Theological Seminary Ms. 3028, f. 42a, G.
15183. New York - Jewish Theological Seminary Ms. 3052, f. 30b, M, rubric: אל מלך.

Yemen, commentary by Isaac b. Abraham Wanneh
15184. Chicago-Spertus College of Judaica D 2, 2, f. 200a, M.
15185. Jerusalem - Benayahu ת 261, f. 139a, M, rubric: אל מלך, short.
15186. Jerusalem - Benayahu ת 282, f. 122b, M, rubric: אל מלך.
15187. Jerusalem - Makhon Ben Zvi 1156 (Tubi 155), f. 121a, M, rubric: אל מלך, short.
15188. Jerusalem - Makhon Ben Zvi 1174 (Tubi 154), f. 126a, M, short.
15189. Jerusalem - Michael Krupp 604, f. 153a, M, rubric: אל מלך.
15190. Jerusalem - Musad haRav Kook 325, f. 192b, M, rubric: אל מלך, short.
15191. Jerusalem - Sassoon 1158, p. 374-375, M, no incipit.
15192. Jerusalem - Sassoon 1174, p. 233-234, M, no incipit.
15193. London - British Library Or. 11122, f. 187b, M, rubric: אל מלך, no incipit.
15194. Manchester - John Rylands University Library, Ms. Gaster 5, f. 197b, M.

---

[343] Edited by Urbach, ערוגת הבושם, vol. III, p. 558-559.

15195. Muenchen - Bayerische Staatsbibliothek, Cod. hebr. 472, f. 165b, M, rubric: אל מלך, short.
15196. New York - Jewish Theological Seminary Ms. 3013, f. 122b, M, rubric: אל מלך, short.
15197. New York - Jewish Theological Seminary Ms. 3294, f. 10b, C.
15198. New York - Public Library, Heb. Ms. 9, f. 113a, M, very short.
15199. Strasbourg - Bibliotheque Nationale et Universitaire 3965 (Landauer 39), p. 380, M, rubric: אל מלך, short.

משוך החן להשפיע אל הרסה (מ 2551), שלם שבזי
Yemen
15200. Cincinnati - Hebrew Union College 398, f. 212b-213a, M.

משוך נא חסדיך מרומם בעבדך (מ 2556), מנחם, אזהרות
Romania, commentary by Menahem b. Mose Tamar
15201. Leiden - Bibliotheek der Rijksuniversiteit Cod. Or. 4772, f. 9a-71a, M.

משוש חתן עלה עלי לבי (מ 2574), שלם שבזי
Yemen
15202. Cincinnati - Hebrew Union College 398, f. 119b-121a, M.

משמעך רהו אנשים ויתמהו (מ 2641), יצחק גיאת, תוכחה
Sepharad, commentary by David b. Josef Abudarham[344]
15203. Budapest - Magyar tudomanyos akademia, MS. Kaufmann A 405/2, p. 243, C, rubric: תוכחה לר' יצחק גיאת ז"ל.
15204. New York - Columbia X893 Ab 93, f. 27a, C, rubric: תוכחה לר' יצחק גיאת ז"ל. משמעך רהו.

משרתיו עומדים (מ 2672), מאיר ב"ר יצחק, אופן לשבת וראש חדש
Ashkenaz
15205. Berlin - Staatsbibliothek (Preussischer Kulturbesitz) Or. Qu. 361 (Steinschneider 51), f. 163b-164a, M, no incipit.
15206. Berlin - Staatsbibliothek (Preussischer Kulturbesitz) Or. Qu. 798-799 (Steinschneider 177), I, f. 242a-243a, M.
15207. Budapest - Magyar tudomanyos akademia, MS. Kaufmann A 399, p. 329, C, rubric: אופן.
15208. Jerusalem - Schocken Institute 24100 / Mahzor Nuremberg, f. 11a, M, short.
15209. Oxford - Bodleian Library MS Can. Or. 82 (Neubauer 1148), f. 8a, M.

---

[344] Edited by Prins, תשלום אבודרהם, p. 110-111.

15210. Parma - Biblioteca Palatina Cod. Parm. 3205 (de Rossi 655), f. 137b-138a, C, rubric: אופן.
15211. Uppsala - Universitetsbibliotek O.Heb.22 , f. 132b-133a, M, rubric: אופן אינו כדי לפרשם.

Ashkenaz, commentary by Abraham b. Azriel[345]

15212. Frankfurt a M - Stadt- und Universitaetsbibliothek Fol. 16 (Merzbacher 95), f. 83b, C.
15213. Vatican - Biblioteca Apostolica ebr. 301,1, f. 106b-107a, C, rubric: אופן.

Ashkenaz, commentary by Eliezer b. Natan

15214. Hamburg - Staats- und Universitaetsbibliothek Cod. hebr. 61 (Steinschneider 153), f. 32b-33b, C, rubric: אופן אחר דר' מאיר שליח ציבור ציר נאמן.
15215. Warszaw - Uniwersytet, Inst. Orientalistyczny 258 , f. 182b-183b, C, rubric: אופן אחר דר' מאיר ציר נאמן.

מתא יא רעבוב תבלג צמידך, שלם שבזי

Yemen
15216. Cincinnati - Hebrew Union College 398, f. 136b-139a, M.

מתי אבוא ואראה פני אלהים להקבילה (מ 2697), מנחם ב"ר יעקב, מעריב ליום ז' של פסח

Ashkenaz
15217. Budapest - Magyar tudomanyos akademia, MS. Kaufmann A 399 , p. 219 220, C.
15218. London - British Library Add. 18695 (Margoliouth 683) , f. 46a-46b, T, Yiddish.
15219. New York - Jewish Theological Seminary Ms. 4466, f. 203a-203b, M, only stanza 1-3.
15220. Parma - Biblioteca Palatina Cod. Parm. 2895 , p. 325-327, M, rubric: תוספת.

מתים בכל בית בנוף כנחנקו (מ+ 2774), יניי, חלק ב', קדושתא לפסח

Ashkenaz
15221. Berlin - Staatsbibliothek (Preussischer Kulturbesitz) Or. Qu. 798-799 (Steinschneider 177), II, f. 47b-48a, M, no incipit.
15222. Budapest - Magyar tudomanyos akademia, MS. Kaufmann A 384 , f. 108b, M.
15223. Erlangen - Universitaetsbibliothek 2601 (Roth 67), f. 58a, M, very short.

---

[345] Edited by Urbach, ערוגת הבושם, vol. III, p. 78-80.

15224. London - British Library Add. 18695 (Margoliouth 683), f. 11a-11b, T, Yiddish.
15225. Paris - Bibliotheque Nationale heb. 709, f. 44b, C, inicpit נאקות.

מתמם בטבע שמונה, אלעזר ברבי קליר, חלק ב', קדושתא לשמיני עצרת
Tsarfat
15226. London - David Sofer 5, f. 183b-184a, C.
15227. Oxford - Bodleian Library MS Opp. 171 (Neubauer 1207), f. 162a, C, no incipit.
15228. Vatican - Biblioteca Apostolica ebr. 306, f. 112b, C.

מתני אחזו חלחלה (מ 2780), משה בן בנימין, רשות לקדושתא למוסף יום כפור
Italia
15229. Parma - Biblioteca Palatin Cod. Parm. 2248 (de Rossi 149/2), f. 41a-42b, C, rubric: פירוש למתני אחזו חלחלה.
Roma
15230. Berlin - Staatsbibliothek (Preussischer Kulturbesitz) Or. Oct. 3567, f. 4b-5a, FC, rubric: ביאור מתני אחזו חלחלה.
15231. Jerusalem - Jewish National and University Library Ms Heb 8° 4153, f. 136b, C, commentator: Daniel ben Salomo haRofe (compiler), rubric: בשחרית.
15232. Oxford - Bodleian Library MS Mich. 312,1 (Neubauer 2276,1), f. 5a-5b, C, rubric: בשחרית כדתני אחזו יש זה הפי'.

נאור מקור חיים בף נפשי בטוחה (נ 50), אברהם אבן עזרא, פזמון ליום כפור
Carpentras
15233. Cincinnati - Hebrew Union College 392, f. 86b, M, no incipit.
Carpentras, commentary by Josef b. Abraham of Montelitz
15234. Cincinnati - Hebrew Union College 291, f. 45a-45b, C, rubric: פי' פזמון נאור וכו'.
15235. New York - Jewish Theological Seminary Ms. 4197, f. 197a-198a, M, no incipit.
15236. Paris - Ecole Rabbinique 32, f. 206a-206b, M, no incipit.
15237. Strasbourg - Bibliotheque Nationale et Universitaire 4081, f. 181a, M, no incipit.

נאמירך באימה (נ 57), משולם ב"ר קלונימוס, חלק יז', קדושתא לשחרית יום כפור
Ashkenaz
15238. Berlin - Staatsbibliothek (Preussischer Kulturbesitz) Or. Qu. 798-799 (Steinschneider 177), I, f. 79b, M, very short.
15239. Braunschweig - Landesmuseum fuer Geschichte und Volkstum R 2386, vol. II, f. 192b, M, no incipit.

15240. Budapest - Magyar tudomanyos akademia, MS. Kaufmann A 400, p. 319, C, short.
15241. Hamburg - Staats- und Universitaetsbibliothek Cod. hebr. 17/2 (Steinschneider 152), f. 152b, C.
15242. Hamburg - Staats- und Universitaetsbibliothek Cod. hebr. 62 (Steinschneider 154), f. 6b, C, very short.
15243. Hamburg - Staats- und Universitaetsbibliothek Cod. hebr. 132 (Steinschneider 155), f. 35b, C.
15244. Jerusalem - Jewish National and University Library Ms Heb 8° 3037, f. 124a, M, very short.
15245. Jerusalem - Schocken Institute 24100 / Mahzor Nuremberg, f. 380a, M, very short.
15246. London - British Library Or. 11318/1, f. 77a, C, very short.
15247. London - Montefiore Library 261, f. 45b, C, commentator: Eliezer b. Natan?, very short.
15248. Moscow - Russian State Library, Ms. Guenzburg 615, f. 95b-96a, C.
15249. Muenchen - Bayerische Staatsbibliothek, Cod. hebr. 393, f. 143a, C, no incipit, very short.
15250. New York - Jewish Theological Seminary Ms. 4466, f. 315a, M, short.
15251. New York - Jewish Theological Seminary Ms. 8097, f. 72b, C, very short.
15252. Oxford - Bodleian Library MS Opp. 170 (Neubauer 1205), f. 168a, C, rubric: דרך אחר להם.
15253. Oxford - Bodleian Library MS Opp. 172 (Neubauer 1211), f 41a-41b, C, short.
15254. Oxford - Bodleian Library MS Opp. 619 (Neubauer 2374), f. 150b, M, very short.
15255. Parma - Biblioteca Palatina Cod. Parm. 3205 (de Rossi 655), f. 228b, C, very short.
15256. Parma - Biblioteca Palatina Cod. Parm. 3271 (de Rossi 1216), f. 42b, G.
15257. Vatican - Biblioteca Apostolica ebr. 308, f. 103a, C, commentator: David b. Mose (compiler).
15258. Vatican - Biblioteca Apostolica ebr. 422/1, f. 15b, C, very short.

Asti, Fossano, Moncalvo
15259. New Haven - Yale University, Beinecke Rare Book and MS Library, MS Heb. 52, f. 108b, M.

Romania
15260. Vatican - Biblioteca Apostolica ebr. 320, f. 286b, M, very short.

Tsarfat
15261. Bern - Burgerbibliothek A 409, f. 85a, G.
15262. Oxford - Bodleian Library MS Bodl. Or. 109 (Neubauer 1209), f. 21b, C, commentator: Aaron b. Hayyim haKohen (compiler), very short.

15263. Oxford - Bodleian Library MS Laud. Or. 271 (Neubauer 1206), f. 106b, C, commentator: Aaron b. Hayyim haKohen (compiler), very short.
15264. Parma - Biblioteca Palatina Cod. Parm. 2890 (de Rossi 856), f. 31a, M, very short.

נאמן רוח מכסה, יצחק הנקדן

Ashkenaz
15265. Oxford - Bodleian Library MS Can. Or. 70 (Neubauer 1147,7), f. 93a-94a, M, rubric: אחרת.

נבעו בים רזיך, יצחק הנקדן

Ashkenaz
15266. Oxford - Bodleian Library MS Can. Or. 70 (Neubauer 1147,7), f. 98b-99b, M, rubric: אחרת.

נגידי זהיון קבוצי רגיון, יצחק הנקדן

Ashkenaz
15267. Oxford - Bodleian Library MS Can. Or. 70 (Neubauer 1147,7), f. 100a-100b, M, rubric: אחרת.

נוה האולם קומס ועלי בל נסתר ונעלם (נ ++207), יהודה הלוי

Carpentras, commentary by Eliyahu Carmi
15268. New York - Jewish Theological Seminary Ms. 3151, f. 45a, M, very short.

נוטי שחקים ואים אשר בם, יצחק הנקדן

Ashkenaz
15269. Oxford - Bodleian Library MS Can. Or. 70 (Neubauer 1147,7), f. 99b-100a, M, rubric: אחרת.

נורא מכל ואים הדרש לשועתי (נ 256), משה אבן עזרא, סליחה

Carpentras
15270. Cincinnati - Hebrew Union College 392, f. 29a, M.
Carpentras, commentary by Josef b. Abraham of Montelitz
15271. Cincinnati - Hebrew Union College 291, f. 12b-13a, C, rubric: פי׳ סליחה נורא מכל ואיום.
15272. New York - Jewish Theological Seminary Ms. 4197, f. 75a-75b, M.
15273. Paris - Ecole Rabbinique 32, f. 97b-98a, M.
15274. Strasbourg - Bibliotheque Nationale et Universitaire 4081, f. 75a-75b, M.

נחמד יום מימים, יצחק הנקדן

Ashkenaz

15275. Oxford - Bodleian Library MS Can. Or. 70 (Neubauer 1147,7), f. 102a-102b, M, rubric: אחרת.

נחמתי על זדוני (נ 291), משה אבן עזרא, תוכחה, חלק ד', קדושתא למנחה יום כפור

Carpentras

15276. Cincinnati - Hebrew Union College 392, f. 102b, M, no incipit.

Carpentras, commentary by Josef b. Abraham of Montelitz

15277. Cincinnati - Hebrew Union College 291, f. 53b, C, rubric: פי' תוכחה נחמתי על זדוני.

15278. New York - Jewish Theological Seminary Ms. 4197, f. 237b-238a, M, no incipit.

15279. Paris - Ecole Rabbinique 32, f. 244b-245a, M, no incipit.

15280. Strasbourg - Bibliotheque Nationale et Universitaire 4081, f. 217a-217b, M, no incipit.

נפלאו מני ספורות, יצחק הנקדן

Ashkenaz

15281. Oxford - Bodleian Library MS Can. Or. 70 (Neubauer 1147,7), f. 85b-86b, M, rubric: אחרת.

נפש יחידה איך בסור אל תצפני (נ 448), שלם שבזי

Yemen

15282. Cincinnati - Hebrew Union College 398, f. 213b-214a, M.

נפש כל חי תודך, יצחק הנקדן

Ashkenaz

15283. Oxford - Bodleian Library MS Can. Or. 70 (Neubauer 1147,7), f. 81a-81b, M.

נצב בעדת נאמני, יצחק הנקדן

Ashkenaz

15284. Oxford - Bodleian Library MS Can. Or. 70 (Neubauer 1147,7), f. 94a-95a, M, rubric: אחרת.

נשא על כל גבוהים, יצחק הנקדן

Ashkenaz

15285. Oxford - Bodleian Library MS Can. Or. 70 (Neubauer 1147,7), f. 86b, M, rubric: אחרת.

נשמת ידועי חלאים אנשי מכאובות (נ 714), יהודה הלוי, נשמת לשבת זכור
Carpentras, commentary by Mordekhai b. Josef of Rocco Martino
15286. Cincinnati - Hebrew Union College 246/1, f. 15b-16a, C, rubric: פי' נשמתים.

נשמת ידידי עליון שכני ציון (נ 718), יהודה הלוי, נשמת
Carpentras, commentary by Eliyahu Carmi
15287. Cincinnati - Hebrew Union College 357, f. 39a, M, rubric: תנא ר' אליהו.
15288. New York - Jewish Theological Seminary Ms. 3151, f. 33a, M.
15289. Paris - Ecole Rabbinique 31, f. 83a, M.
Carpentras, commentary by Josef b. Abraham of Montelitz
15290. Cincinnati - Hebrew Union College 357, f. 38b-39a, M, rubric: פירוש.
15291. New York - Jewish Theological Seminary Ms. 4746, f. 6a-6b, M.
15292. Paris - Alliance Israelite Universelle H 422 A, f. 11b, M.
15293. Paris - Ecole Rabbinique 31, f. 82b-83a, M.

נשמת יושבת נבדלת ומלתקוע תשבת (נ 739), נשמת
Carpentras, commentary by Josef b. Abraham of Montelitz
15294. Cincinnati - Hebrew Union College 357, f. 39a-39b, M.
15295. New York - Jewish Theological Seminary Ms. 4746, f. 6b-7a, M.
15296. Paris - Alliance Israelite Universelle H 422 A, f. 12a-12b, M, no incipit.
15297. Paris - Ecole Rabbinique 31, f. 83a-83b, M.

נשמת שאר יעקב אשר בעדות (נ 803), שלמה אבן גבירול, נשמת ליום ב' של ראש השנה
Carpentras
15298. Cincinnati - Hebrew Union College 429/1, f. 17b-18a, M, no incipit.
Carpentras, commentary by Josef b. Abraham of Montelitz
15299. Cincinnati - Hebrew Union College 357, f. 91b-92a, M, rubric: פירוש, no incipit.
15300. New York - Jewish Theological Seminary Ms. 4746, f. 27a, M, no incipit.
15301. Paris - Alliance Israelite Universelle H 422 A, f. 62a-62b, M, no incipit.
15302. Paris - Ecole Rabbinique 31, f. 131b-132a, M, no incipit.

סאלם יקול יא ודי קף ענדי (ס 2), שלם שבזי
Yemen
15303. Cincinnati - Hebrew Union College 398, f. 140b-144b, M.

סבאני עוהגי אלגזלאן (ס 5), שלם שבזי

Yemen

15304. Cincinnati - Hebrew Union College 398, f. 139b-140b, M.

סדר חטאתי וחטאת עדתי, סליחה

Yemen, commentary by Isaac b. Abraham Wanneh

15305. Jerusalem - Sassoon 1158, p. 429, M, no incipit.

סימן טוב סימן טוב סימן טוב יהיה לכל (ס 116), לשמחת תורה

Yemen

15306. Jerusalem - Michael Krupp 1758, f. 27a-27b, M, incipit אשכול.
15307. New York - Jewish Theological Seminary Ms. 3193, f. 170b-171a, M, incipit אשכול.
15308. New York - Jewish Theological Seminary Ms. 3295, f. 96a, M, short, incipit אשכול.
15309. New York - Jewish Theological Seminary Ms. 4488, f. 72b, G.

Yemen, commentary by Isaac b. Abraham Wanneh?

15310. Muenchen - Bayerische Staatsbibliothek, Cod. hebr. 472, f. 104b, M.
15311. Nahariya - Menahem and Saida Yaakob 284, f. 25a, M.
15312. New York - Jewish Theological Seminary Ms. 3013, f. 81b, M, short, incipit אשכול.
15313. New York - Jewish Theological Seminary Ms. 4195, f. 46b-49b, M.

Yemen, commentary by Yiḥya b. Josef Tsalaḥ

15314. Montreal - Elberg 203, f. 35a-37a, M.

סכה אזכירה מעללי נורא (ס 119), אליעזר ב"ר שמעון, מעריב סוכות

Ashkenaz

15315. Braunschweig - Landesmuseum fuer Geschichte und Volkstum R 2386, vol. I, f. 130a-130b, M.
15316. London - British Library Add. 18695 (Margoliouth 683), f. 114b-115b, T, Yiddish.

סלח ופשעים לאומיך, סליחה

Tsarfat

15317. London - David Sofer 5, f. 162b, C.

סלח נא אדומים כתולעת, סליחה

Ashkenaz

15318. Fulda - Hessische Landesbibliothek A 3 II, f. 129a, C, commentator: Josef.

Tsarfat

15319. Oxford - Bodleian Library MS Laud. Or. 271 (Neubauer 1206), f. 118b, C, commentator: Aaron b. Hayyim haKohen (compiler), no incipit.

סלעי ומצודתי ומפלטי מסבל (ס+ 161), יוסף ב"ר שמואל טוב עלם, חלק ג', קדושתא לפסח

Tsarfat

15320. Parma - Biblioteca Palatina Cod. Parm. 3136 (de Rossi 405), f. 109b, M.

סמיך וסעיד הני סך שמן דומה, סליחה

Yemen, commentary by Isaac b. Abraham Wanneh

15321. London - British Library Or. 11122, f. 223b, M, no incipit.

סמר גבי צור משגבי (ס 171), סולימן, סליחה

Yemen

15322. Jerusalem - Benayahu ת 414, f. 148b, M, no incipit.
15323. Jerusalem - Sassoon 902, p. 419, M.

Yemen, commentary by Isaac b. Abraham Wanneh

15324. Chicago-Spertus College of Judaica D 2, 2, f. 212a, M, no incipit.
15325. Jerusalem - Sassoon 1158, p. 364, M, no incipit.
15326. London - British Library Or. 11122, f. 182a, M, no incipit.

ספדי ואולילי ועדת יקותיאל (ס 200), קינה

Yemen, commentary by Isaac b. Abraham Wanneh

15327. London - British Library Or. 11122, f. 105b, M, no incipit.

ספו חסידים ופסו אמונים, סליחה

Yemen, commentary by Isaac b. Abraham Wanneh

15328. Chicago-Spertus College of Judaica D 2, 2, f. 240a, M, no incipit.
15329. Jerusalem - Benayahu ת 282, f. 143a, M.
15330. Jerusalem - Makhon Ben Zvi 1174 (Tubi 154), f. 140a, M.
15331. Jerusalem - Michael Krupp 604, f. 178a, M.
15332. Jerusalem - Musad haRav Kook 325, f. 196a, M, short.
15333. Jerusalem - Sassoon 1158, p. 420, M, no incipit.
15334. London - British Library Or. 11122, f. 217a, M, no incipit.
15335. New York - Jewish Theological Seminary Ms. 3013, f. 135b, M, no incipit, short.
15336. New York - Jewish Theological Seminary Ms. 3294, f. 19a, C.
15337. New York - Public Library, Heb. Ms. 9, f. 132b, M, no incipit.
15338. Strasbourg - Bibliotheque Nationale et Universitaire 3965 (Landauer 39), p. 418, M.

עבד לילו מדד ערבו (ע 9), משה אבן עזרא, סליחה

Ashkenaz
15339. Moscow - Russian State Library, Ms. Guenzburg 190, f. 64b, G.

Tsarfat
15340. London - David Sofer 5, f. 133a, C.
15341. Parma - Biblioteca Palatina Cod. Parm. 1794 (de Rossi 1061), f. 9a-9b, M.
15342. Parma - Biblioteca Palatina Cod. Parm. 3006 (de Rossi 654,1), f. 120b, M.
15343. Vatican - Biblioteca Apostolica ebr. 306, f. 209b, C.

עד לא מכון, למוסף יום כפור

Ashkenaz
15344. Oxford - Bodleian Library MS Mich. 365 (Neubauer 1208), f. 86a-87a, C.

עד לא מצוקי רגב (ע 72+), אלעזר ברבי קליר, חלק ד', קדושתא לסוכות

Ashkenaz
15345. Berlin - Staatsbibliothek (Preussischer Kulturbesitz) Or. Qu. 798-799 (Steinschneider 177), I, f. 198b, M.
15346. Budapest - Magyar tudomanyos akademia, MS. Kaufmann A 400, p. 370, C.
15347. Hamburg - Staats- und Universitaetsbibliothek Cod. hebr. 132 (Steinschneider 155), f. 56a, C.
15348. London - British Library Add. 18695 (Margoliouth 683), f. 112a, T, Yiddish, incipit אל נא.
15349. London - British Library Add. 22431 (Margoliouth 662a), f. 102a, M, incipit אל נא.
15350. London - British Library Or. 11318/1, f. 131a, C, incipit אל נא, short.
15351. Oxford - Bodleian Library MS Mich. 365 (Neubauer 1208), f. 96a-96b, C, incipit אל נא.
15352. Parma - Biblioteca Palatina Cod. Parm. 3507 (Perreau 27), f. 174a, C, no incipit.
15353. Vatican - Biblioteca Apostolica ebr. 305,1, f. 39b, C, no incipit.
15354. Vatican - Biblioteca Apostolica ebr. 422/1, f. 21b, C, incipit אל נא.
15355. Zurich - Zentralbibliothek Heid. 139, f. 93a, C, no incipit, very short, additional marginal notes.

Romania
15356. London - London School of Jewish Studies. Asher I.Myers collection 9, f. 202a, only one gloss.

Tsarfat

15357. Oxford - Bodleian Library MS Laud. Or. 271 (Neubauer 1206), f. 97b, C, commentator: Aaron b. Hayyim haKohen (compiler), no incipit.

עד מתי יי יום זה לעומתיך (ע 88), קינה

Yemen, commentary by Isaac b. Abraham Wanneh

15358. Jerusalem - Sassoon 1158, p. 165-166, M.
15359. London - British Library Or. 11122, f. 100a, M.

עובר על פשע לא חפץ ברשע (ע 137), משה, סליחה

Ashkenaz

15360. Budapest - Magyar tudomanyos akademia, MS. Kaufmann A 400, p. 528, C, rubric: אחרת.
15361. Oxford - Bodleian Library MS Mich. 543 (Neubauer 1212), f. 77b-78a, C, commentator: Isaac b. Jacob (compiler).

Tsarfat

15362. London - David Sofer 5, f. 95b, C.
15363. Oxford - Bodleian Library MS Laud. Or. 271 (Neubauer 1206), f. 174b, C, commentator: Aaron b. Hayyim haKohen (compiler), short.
15364. Oxford - Bodleian Library MS Opp. 171 (Neubauer 1207), f. 113b-114a, C, rubric: אחרת.
15365. Parma - Biblioteca Palatina Cod. Parm. 3007 (de Rossi 654,2), f. 145b-146a, M.

עובר על פשע ונושא חובה (ע 138), משה אבן עזרא, סליחה

Yemen, commentary by Isaac b. Abraham Wanneh

15366. Chicago-Spertus College of Judaica D 2, 2, f. 218a, M, no incipit.
15367. London - British Library Or. 11122, f. 185a, M, rubric: אל מלך.

עולמים שנים בראת עבור עמק להאר (ע +185), מאיר הכהן

Ashkenaz

15368. Parma - Biblioteca Palatina Cod. Parm. 3205 (de Rossi 655), f. 172a-172b, C.

עורה נא ימינך רמה (ע 239), יחיי אל דאודי, קינה

Yemen, commentary by Isaac b. Abraham Wanneh

15369. Jerusalem - Sassoon 1158, p. 163, M.
15370. London - British Library Or. 11122, f. 98b, M.

עורר חמלתיך לשארית המוני, סליחה

Yemen, commentary by Isaac b. Abraham Wanneh

15371. Chicago-Spertus College of Judaica D 2, 2, f. 215b-216a, M, no incipit.
15372. Jerusalem - Sassoon 1158, p. 368, M, no incipit.
15373. London - British Library Or. 11122, f. 184a, M, rubric: אל מלך.

עילה דוקיונו מעין מעלה

Ashkenaz

15374. Budapest - Magyar tudomanyos akademia, MS. Kaufmann A 399, p. 366-369, C.

עינינו לך תלינו אל תעאבנו (ע 410), אמתי, סליחה

Ashkenaz

15375. Vatican - Biblioteca Apostolica ebr. 422/1, f. 35a, C, very short.

על אהבתך אשתה גביעי (ע 424), יהודה הלוי, זמר לשבת

Yemen

15376. Cincinnati - Hebrew Union College 398, f. 144b-146b, M.

על אלה ועל אלה אני בוכיה עיני עיני יורדה מים (ע +431), קינה

Ashkenaz

15377. Berlin - Staatsbibliothek (Preussischer Kulturbesitz) Or. Qu. 798-799 (Steinschneider 177), II, f. 179a-180b, M.

על היכלי אבכה (ע 466), יהודה שמואל עבאס, קינה

Yemen, commentary by Isaac b. Abraham Wanneh

15378. Jerusalem - Sassoon 1158, p. 177, M.
15379. London - British Library Or. 11122, f. 105b, M, no incipit.

על הרי בשמים (ע +488), שלמה הבבלי, גאולה לפסח

Ashkenaz

15380. Berlin - Staatsbibliothek (Preussischer Kulturbesitz) Or. Qu. 798-799 (Steinschneider 177), II, f. 62b-63a, M.
15381. Braunschweig - Landesmuseum fuer Geschichte und Volkstum R 2386, vol. I, f. 21b, M.
15382. Budapest - Magyar tudomanyos akademia, MS. Kaufmann A 384, f. 130a-130b, M.
15383. Budapest - Magyar tudomanyos akademia, MS. Kaufmann A 400, p. 104-107, C.
15384. Cambridge - University Library Add. 394,1 (Reif SCR 461), f. 55a, C.

15385. Hamburg - Staats- und Universitaetsbibliothek Cod. hebr. 17/2 (Steinschneider 152), f. 55a-55b, C.
15386. Jerusalem - Schocken Institute 24100 / Mahzor Nuremberg, f. 82b-83a, M.
15387. London - British Library Add. 18695 (Margoliouth 683), f. 25a-25b, T, Yiddish.
15388. Moscow - Russian State Library, Ms. Guenzburg 615, f. 7a-8a, C.
15389. Muenchen - Bayerische Staatsbibliothek, Cod. hebr. 88, f. 61a, G.
15390. Muenchen - Bayerische Staatsbibliothek, Cod. hebr. 393, f. 125a-125b, C, no incipit.
15391. New York - Jewish Theological Seminary Ms. 4466, f. 55b-56b, M.
15392. Oxford - Bodleian Library MS Opp. 170 (Neubauer 1205), f. 59b-61a, C.
15393. Paris - Bibliotheque Nationale heb. 709, f. 74a-75a, C.
15394. Parma - Biblioteca Palatina Cod. Parm. 1002 (Ta 24), f. 93a-93b, M.
15395. Parma - Biblioteca Palatina Cod. Parm. 3205 (de Rossi 655), f. 83a-83b, C.
15396. Parma - Biblioteca Palatina Cod. Parm. 3507 (Perreau 27), f. 49a-49b, C.
15397. Zurich - Zentralbibliothek Heid. 139, f. 28a-28b, C, additional marginal notes.

Italia
15398. Parma - Biblioteca Palatin Cod. Parm. 2248 (de Rossi 149/2), f. 37a-37b, C.

Tsarfat
15399. London - British Library Add. 11639 (Margoliouth 1056), f. 290a-290b, M.
15400. Moscow - Russian State Library, Ms. Guenzburg 1665, f. 57a, M.
15401. Parma - Biblioteca Palatina Cod. Parm. 3136 (de Rossi 405), f. 81a, M.
15402. Vatican - Biblioteca Apostolica ebr. 306, f. 140a-141a, C, no incipit.

על זה היה דוה לבינו (ע 497), קינה
Yemen, commentary by Isaac b. Abraham Wanneh
15403. Jerusalem - Sassoon 1158, p. 160, M.
15404. London - British Library Or. 11122, f. 97a-97b, M.

על חטא שחטאנו לפניך באונס (ע 505), ודוי
Ashkenaz
15405. Berlin - Staatsbibliothek (Preussischer Kulturbesitz) Or. Qu. 798-799 (Steinschneider 177), I, f. 154b-155a, M.
15406. Berlin - Staatsbibliothek (Preussischer Kulturbesitz) Or. Qu. 798-799 (Steinschneider 177), I, f. 175b-176a, M.

Sepharad

15407. Jerusalem - Benayahu ז 25, f. 102a-102b, M, no incipit.

על יום חרבן היכל מקודש (ע 519), קינה
Yemen, commentary by Isaac b. Abraham Wanneh

15408. Jerusalem - Sassoon 1158, p. 161, M.

על ישראל אמונתו (ע 524), משולם ב"ר קלונימוס, חלק יב', קדושתא לשחרית יום כפור

Ashkenaz

15409. Berlin - Staatsbibliothek (Preussischer Kulturbesitz) Or. Qu. 798-799 (Steinschneider 177), I, f. 77b, M.
15410. Braunschweig - Landesmuseum fuer Geschichte und Volkstum R 2386, vol. II, f. 190a, M.
15411. Hamburg - Staats- und Universitaetsbibliothek Cod. hebr. 17/2 (Steinschneider 152), f. 151a-151b, C.
15412. Hamburg - Staats- und Universitaetsbibliothek Cod. hebr. 40b (Steinschneider 110), f. 95b-96a, G.
15413. Hamburg - Staats- und Universitaetsbibliothek Cod. hebr. 62 (Steinschneider 154), f. 4a-4b, C, short.
15414. Hamburg - Staats- und Universitaetsbibliothek Cod. hebr. 132 (Steinschneider 155), f. 34b, C, short.
15415. Jerusalem - Schocken Institute 24100 / Mahzor Nuremberg, f. 379a, M, short.
15416. London - British Library Or. 11318/1, f. 75a, C, short.
15417. London Montefiore Library 261, f. 44a, C, commentator. Eliezer b. Natan?, short.
15418. Moscow - Russian State Library, Ms. Guenzburg 191, f. 90a-90b, M.
15419. Moscow - Russian State Library, Ms. Guenzburg 615, f. 93b-94a, C.
15420. Muenchen - Bayerische Staatsbibliothek, Cod. hebr. 346, f. 53b, C.
15421. New York - Jewish Theological Seminary Ms. 4466, f. 312b, M.
15422. Oxford - Bodleian Library MS Mich. 365 (Neubauer 1208), f. 69b-70a, C, short.
15423. Oxford - Bodleian Library MS Opp. 170 (Neubauer 1205), f. 166a-166b, C.
15424. Oxford - Bodleian Library MS Opp. 172 (Neubauer 1211), f. 39a, C, no incipit, short.
15425. Oxford - Bodleian Library MS Opp. 619 (Neubauer 2374), f. 147b-148a, M.
15426. Parma - Biblioteca Palatina Cod. Parm. 3205 (de Rossi 655), f. 226a-226b, C.
15427. Parma - Biblioteca Palatina Cod. Parm. 3205 (de Rossi 655), f. 228b-229a, C.

15428. Parma - Biblioteca Palatina Cod. Parm. 3271 (de Rossi 1216), f. 40b-41a, G.
15429. Parma - Biblioteca Palatina Cod. Parm. 3507 (Perreau 27), f. 147b, C.
15430. Vatican - Biblioteca Apostolica ebr. 308, f. 100b, C, commentator: David b. Mose (compiler).

Asti, Fossano, Moncalvo
15431. New Haven - Yale University, Beinecke Rare Book and MS Library, MS Heb. 52, f. 106b, M.

Romania
15432. Vatican - Biblioteca Apostolica ebr. 320, f. 295a, M.

Tsarfat
15433. Bern - Burgerbibliothek A 409, f. 83b, G, short.
15434. London - David Sofer 5, f. 138a, C, written on the margin.
15435. Oxford - Bodleian Library MS Bodl. Or. 109 (Neubauer 1209), f. 20b, C, commentator: Aaron b. Hayyim haKohen (compiler), short.
15436. Oxford - Bodleian Library MS Laud. Or. 271 (Neubauer 1206), f. 135a-135b, C, commentator: Aaron b. Hayyim haKohen (compiler), rubric: שוב מצאתי רהיטים.
15437. Parma - Biblioteca Palatina Cod. Parm. 1794 (de Rossi 1061), f. 123b-124a, M.
15438. Parma - Biblioteca Palatina Cod. Parm. 2890 (de Rossi 856), f. 29a, M.
15439. Parma - Biblioteca Palatina Cod. Parm. 3006 (de Rossi 654,1), f. 142b-143a, M.
15440. Vatican - Biblioteca Apostolica ebr. 306, f. 77b, C.

על נהרות בבל אשכה יפעת אודותים (ע 578), יהודה הלוי, קינה
Yemen, commentary by Isaac b. Abraham Wanneh
15441. Jerusalem - Sassoon 1158, p. 172, M.
15442. London - British Library Or. 11122, f. 103a-103b, M.

על שבר בת עמי בשכבי ובקומי (ע 598), קינה
Carpentras, commentary by Mordekhai b. Josef of Rocco Martino
15443. Cincinnati - Hebrew Union College 246/1, f. 74b, C, rubric: פי' קינה על שבר בת עמי.

עלה עלה משה לראש הר סיני (ע 612), יצחק בן ראובן אלברגלוני, רשות לאזהרות
North Africa, commentary by Amram b. Elqayim
15444. Jerusalem - Musad haRav Kook 1129, f. 1a-2b, M, rubric: אתחיל לכתוב אזהרות לרבינו יצחק בר ראובן עם פי' רבי' עמרם בן אלקיים זצו"ל.
15445. New York - Jewish Theological Seminary Ms. 3183, f. 2a-3a, M.

North Africa, commentary by Mose Muati
15446. New York - Jewish Theological Seminary Benaim 130, f. 82a-82b, C.

עם יי השלחה היום לכם בשורה (ע 696), סליחה

Yemen

15447. Jerusalem - Sassoon 902, p. 410, M, very short.
15448. New York - Jewish Theological Seminary Ms. 3052 , f. 56a, M, rubric: אל מלך.

Yemen, commentary by Isaac b. Abraham Wanneh

15449. Chicago-Spertus College of Judaica D 2, 2, f. 230a, M, no incipit.
15450. Jerusalem - Benayahu ת 282, f. 130a, M, rubric: אל מלך, very short.
15451. Jerusalem - Makhon Ben Zvi 1156 (Tubi 155), f. 129a, M, rubric: אל מלך.
15452. Jerusalem - Makhon Ben Zvi 1174 (Tubi 154), f. 129a, M, very short.
15453. Jerusalem - Michael Krupp 604, f. 85b, M, rubric: אל מלך, very short.
15454. Jerusalem - Musad haRav Kook 325, f. 186b, M, rubric: אל מלך, very short.
15455. Jerusalem - Sassoon 1158, p. 202, M, short.
15456. Jerusalem - Sassoon 1174, p. 250, M, no incipit, short.
15457. Jerusalem - Yehiel haLevi 4, f. 169b, G.
15458. London - British Library Or. 11122, f. 206b, M, no incipit, short.
15459. Manchester - John Rylands University Library, Ms. Gaster 5, f. 210a, M.
15460. Muenchen - Bayerische Staatsbibliothek, Cod. hebr. 472, f. 179a, M, rubric: אל מלך, very short.
15461. New York - Jewish Theological Seminary Ms. 3013, f. 126a, M, rubric: אל מלך, very short.
15462. New York - Jewish Theological Seminary Ms. 3294, f. 13a-13b, C.
15463. Strasbourg - Bibliotheque Nationale et Universitaire 3965 (Landauer 39), p. 389, M, rubric: אל מלך, very short.

עם יי חזקו ונתחזקה (ע 698), אליה ב"ר שמעיה, סליחה

Ashkenaz

15464. Braunschweig - Landesmuseum fuer Geschichte und Volkstum R 2386, vol. II, f. 133a, M.
15465. Muenchen - Bayerische Staatsbibliothek, Cod. hebr. 346 , f. 146a, C, short.
15466. Oxford - Bodleian Library MS Mich. 543 (Neubauer 1212), f. 7b-8a, C, commentator: Isaac b. Jacob (compiler), rubric: בהרבה מקומות אום' פתיח' זו בבוקר לערב יום כיפור.
15467. Padova - Biblioteca del Seminario Vescovile Cod. 218, f. 116a-116b, M.

Ashkenaz, commentary by Abraham b. Azriel[346]
15468. Frankfurt a M - Stadt- und Universitaetsbibliothek Fol. 16 (Merzbacher 95), f. 103b, C.
15469. Vatican - Biblioteca Apostolica ebr. 301,1, f. 169a, C.

עמדי יחידתי עלי משמרת (ע 738), עבאסי, סליחה
Yemen, commentary by Isaac b. Abraham Wanneh
15470. Chicago-Spertus College of Judaica D 2, 2, f. 202b, M, no incipit.
15471. Jerusalem - Michael Krupp 604, f. 154b, M.
15472. Jerusalem - Sassoon 1158, p. 362, M, no incipit.
15473. London - British Library Or. 11122, f. 180b, M, rubric: אל מלך, no incipit.

ענה אחוזי ארבעת מינים תבנית ארבעתם מוונים (ע 790), סעדיה גאון, הושענא
Yemen
15474. Chicago-Spertus College of Judaica D 10, f. 123a-123b, M, incipit ארבעת.
15475. Jerusalem - Michael Krupp 3391, f. 5a-5b, M.
15476. Jerusalem - Musad haRav Kook 952, f. 8a-8b, M, rubric: ענה בהושענא.
15477. Jerusalem - Sassoon 264, f. 93a-93b, M, no incipit.
15478. New York - Alfred Moldovan HH, f. 8b-9a, M, rubric: עןʽבה.
15479. New York - Jewish Theological Seminary Ms. 4488, f. 68a, M, short.
15480. New York - Jewish Theological Seminary Ms. 9325, f. 74a-74b, M, short.
15481. New York - Public Library, Heb. Ms. 10, f. 57b, M, no incipit, margins damaged.
15482. Ramat Gan - Universitat Bar Ilan 63, f. 21a, G, margins damaged.
Yemen, commentary by Isaac b. Abraham Wanneh
15483. Chicago-Spertus College of Judaica D 1, f. 195a, M.
15484. Jerusalem - Benayahu ת 261, f. 80b-81a, M, rubric: ענה בהושענא.
15485. Jerusalem - Benayahu ת 282, f. 74a, M, rubric: ענה בהושענא.
15486. Jerusalem - Israel Museum 180/78, f. 9b-10a, M, rubric: ענה בהושענא.
15487. Jerusalem - Makhon Ben Zvi 1156 (Tubi 155), f. 71b, M, rubric: ענה בהושענא.
15488. Jerusalem - Makhon Ben Zvi 1174 (Tubi 154), f. 82b, M, rubric: עןʽ בהוʽ.
15489. Jerusalem - Makhon ben Zvi 1186 (Tubi 205), f. 4a, M, rubric: ענה בהושענא, incipit תבנית.
15490. Jerusalem - Michael Krupp 604, f. 91a-91b, M, rubric: ענה בההושענא.
15491. Jerusalem - Michael Krupp 1990, f. 98b, M, rubric: ענה בהושענא, no incipit, margins damaged.

---

[346] Edited by Urbach, ערוגת הבושם, vol. III, p. 490.

15492. Jerusalem - Musad haRav Kook 325, f. 103b-104a, M, rubric: ענה בהושענא.
15493. Jerusalem - Musad haRav Kook 325, f. 121a, M, rubric: 'ענ' בהו', very short.
15494. Jerusalem - Musad haRav Kook 330, f. 67a, M, page damaged.
15495. Jerusalem - Musad haRav Kook 347, f. 57b, M.
15496. Jerusalem - Sassoon 1158, p. 213, M, rubric: ענה בהושענא.
15497. Jerusalem - Sassoon 1174, p. 141, M, rubric: ענה בהושענא.
15498. Jerusalem - Schocken Institute 70028, f. 187a, M, rubric: ענה בהושענא.
15499. Jerusalem - Yehiel haLevi 4, f. 87a, M, very short.
15500. London - British Library Or. 11121, f. 131b, C, rubric: ענה בהושענא.
15501. London - British Library Or. 11122, f. 121a, M, rubric: ענה בהושענא.
15502. Manchester - John Rylands University Library, Ms. Gaster 5, f. 147a, M, rubric: ענה בהושענא.
15503. Muenchen - Bayerische Staatsbibliothek, Cod. hebr. 472, f. 98a, M, rubric: ענה בהושענא.
15504. Nahariya - Menahem and Saida Yaakob 284, f. 9a, M, rubric: ענה בהושענא.
15505. New York - Jewish Theological Seminary Ms. 3013, f. 73b, M, no incipit, margins damaged.
15506. New York - Jewish Theological Seminary Ms. 3193, f. 160b-161a, M, rubric: 'ען' בהוש'.
15507. New York - Jewish Theological Seminary Ms. 3295, f. 88b-89a, M, rubric: ענה בהושענא.
15508. New York - Jewish Theological Seminary Ms. 4195, f. 12b-13a, M, incipit תבנית.
15509. New York - Public Library, Heb. Ms. 9, f. 71a, M, rubric: ענה בהו'.
15510. Oxford - Bodleian Library MS Opp. Add. fol. 58 (Neubauer 2498), f. 140b-141a, M, rubric: ענה בהושענא.
15511. Paris - G. Epstein 23/57, f. 100a-100b, C, rubric: ענה בהושענא.
15512. Philadelphia - University of Pennsylvania HB 2, f. 97a-97b, M, rubric: ענה בהושענא.
15513. Ramat Gan - Universitat Bar Ilan 703, f. 193a, M, rubric: ענה בהושענא.
15514. Strasbourg - Bibliotheque Nationale et Universitaire 3965 (Landauer 39), p. 235, M, rubric: ענה בהו'.

Yemen, commentary by Simon b. Tsemaḥ Duran
15515. Jerusalem - Michael Krupp 1758, f. 6b-7a, M, rubric: פירוש.

Yemen, commentary by Yiḥya b. Josef Tsalaḥ
15516. Montreal - Elberg 203, f. 7b-8a, M.

ענה אומני חוקה נסוכה בהקימם מצות סוכה (ע 791), סעדיה גאון, הושענא
Yemen
15517. Chicago-Spertus College of Judaica D 10, f. 125a, M, no incipit.
15518. Jerusalem - Benayahu ת 414, f. 87a, M, rubric: 'פי, first word חלמה.

15519. Jerusalem - Michael Krupp 3391, f. 6b-7a, M, no incipit.
15520. Jerusalem - Musad haRav Kook 334, f. 88b-89a, M.
15521. Jerusalem - Musad haRav Kook 952, f. 11a-12b, M, rubric: ענה בהושענא.
15522. Jerusalem - Sassoon 264, f. 94a-94b, M, no incipit.
15523. Jerusalem - Sassoon 902, p. 175-176, M, no incipit.
15524. New York - Jewish Theological Seminary Ms. 4488, f. 68b, M, no incipit.
15525. New York - Jewish Theological Seminary Ms. 9325, f. 76a-76b, M.
15526. New York - Public Library, Heb. Ms. 10, f. 58b, M, no incipit.
15527. Ramat Gan - Universitat Bar Ilan 62, f. 28b, G, margins damaged.

Yemen, commentary by Isaac b. Abraham Wanneh

15528. Chicago-Spertus College of Judaica D 1, f. 196a, M.
15529. Jerusalem - Benayahu ת 261, f. 81b, M, rubric: ענה בהושענא.
15530. Jerusalem - Benayahu ת 282, f. 74b-75a, M, rubric: ענה בהושענא.
15531. Jerusalem - Israel Museum 180/78, f. 13a-14a, M, rubric: ענה בהושענא.
15532. Jerusalem - Makhon Ben Zvi 1156 (Tubi 155), f. 72a, M, rubric: ענה בהושענא.
15533. Jerusalem - Makhon Ben Zvi 1174 (Tubi 154), f. 83b-84a, M, rubric: ענה בהושענא.
15534. Jerusalem - Makhon ben Zvi 1186 (Tubi 205), f. 5b-6a, M, rubric: ענה הושענא, incipit אומני.
15535. Jerusalem - Michael Krupp 604, f. 92a-92b, M, rubric: ענה בהושענא.
15536. Jerusalem - Michael Krupp 1990, f. 99b-100a, M, rubric: ענה בהושענא.
15537. Jerusalem - Musad haRav Kook 325, f. 105a, M, rubric: ענה בהושענא.
15538. Jerusalem - Musad haRav Kook 325, f. 122a-122b, M, rubric: ענ' בהו'.
15539. Jerusalem - Musad haRav Kook 330, f. 67b-68a, M, no incipit.
15540. Jerusalem - Musad haRav Kook 347, f. 58a, M, no incipit.
15541. Jerusalem - Sassoon 1158, p. 214, M, rubric: ענה בהושע'.
15542. Jerusalem - Sassoon 1174, p. 142-143, M, rubric: ענה בהושענא.
15543. Jerusalem - Schocken Institute 70028, f. 188a, M, rubric: ענה בהושענא.
15544. Jerusalem - Yehiel haLevi 4, f. 87b-88a, M, rubric: ענה בהושענא.
15545. London - British Library Or. 11121, f. 132a-132b, C.
15546. London - British Library Or. 11122, f. 121b, M, rubric: ענה בהושענא.
15547. Manchester - John Rylands University Library, Ms. Gaster 5, f. 148a-148b, M, rubric: ענה בהושענא.
15548. Muenchen - Bayerische Staatsbibliothek, Cod. hebr. 472, f. 98b-99a, M, rubric: ענה בהושענא.
15549. Nahariya - Menahem and Saida Yaakob 284, f. 12a-13a, M, rubric: ענה הושענא.
15550. New York - Jewish Theological Seminary Ms. 3013, f. 74a-74b, M, no incipit.
15551. New York - Jewish Theological Seminary Ms. 3193, f. 162b-163a, M, rubric: ענה בהוש'.

15552. New York - Jewish Theological Seminary Ms. 3295 , f. 90a, M, rubric: ענה הושענא.
15553. New York - Jewish Theological Seminary Ms. 4195, f. 17a-18b, M, incipit אומני.
15554. New York - Public Library, Heb. Ms. 9, f. 72a, M, rubric: ענה בהושענא.
15555. Oxford - Bodleian Library MS Opp. Add. fol. 58 (Neubauer 2498), f. 141b-142a, M, rubric: ענה בהושענא.
15556. Paris - G. Epstein 23/57, f. 102a-103a, C.
15557. Philadelphia - University of Pennsylvania HB 2 , f. 97b-98a, M, rubric: ענה בהושענא.
15558. Ramat Gan - Universitat Bar Ilan 703 , f. 194a-194b, M, rubric: ענה בהושענא.
15559. Strasbourg - Bibliotheque Nationale et Universitaire 3965 (Landauer 39), p. 237, M, rubric: ענה בהו'.

Yemen, commentary by Yiḥya b. Josef Tsalaḥ

15560. Montreal - Elberg 203, f. 10a-11a, M, no incipit.

ענה איומה אמרתך לוקחת (ע 792), סעדיה גאון, הושענא

Yemen

15561. Chicago-Spertus College of Judaica D 10, f. 125b-126a, M, incipit איומה.
15562. Jerusalem - Michael Krupp 3391, f. 8a, M.
15563. Jerusalem - Musad haRav Kook 327, f. 86a, M, short.
15564. Jerusalem - Musad haRav Kook 334, f. 89b-90a, M, no incipit.
15565. Jerusalem - Musad haRav Kook 335, f. 95a, M.
15566. Jerusalem - Musad haRav Kook 952, f. 14a-16a, M, rubric: ענה בהושענא.
15567. Jerusalem - Sassoon 902, p. 177-178, M, no incipit.
15568. New York - Alfred Moldovan HH, f. 11b-12b, M, rubric: ענה בהושענא.
15569. New York - Alfred Moldovan HH, f. 14b-16a, M, rubric: ען'בה.
15570. New York - Jewish Theological Seminary Ms. 4488, f. 69a-69b, M, no incipit.
15571. New York - Jewish Theological Seminary Ms. 9325, f. 78a-79a, M.
15572. New York - Public Library, Heb. Ms. 10 , f. 59a, M, no incipit, margins damaged.
15573. Ramat Gan - Universitat Bar Ilan 62, f. 29a, G, margins damaged.
15574. Ramat Gan - Universitat Bar Ilan 63, f. 22a, G, margins damaged.

Yemen, commentary by Isaac b. Abraham Wanneh

15575. Chicago-Spertus College of Judaica D 1, f. 196b-197a, M.
15576. Jerusalem - Benayahu ת 261, f. 82a-82b, M, rubric: ענה בהושענא.
15577. Jerusalem - Benayahu ת 282, f. 75a-75b, M.
15578. Jerusalem - Israel Museum 180/78, f. 16b-18b, M, rubric: ענה בהושענא.
15579. Jerusalem - Makhon Ben Zvi 1156 (Tubi 155), f. 72b-73a, M, rubric: ענה בהושענא.

15580. Jerusalem - Makhon Ben Zvi 1169 (Tubi 159), f. 63b, M, short.
15581. Jerusalem - Makhon Ben Zvi 1174 (Tubi 154), f. 84b-85a, M, rubric: ענ' בהו'.
15582. Jerusalem - Makhon ben Zvi 1186 (Tubi 205), f. 7a-8b, M, rubric: ענה הושענא, incipit איומה.
15583. Jerusalem - Michael Krupp 604, f. 93a-94a, M, rubric: ענה בהושענא.
15584. Jerusalem - Michael Krupp 1990, f. 100b-101a, M, rubric: ענה בהושענא.
15585. Jerusalem - Musad haRav Kook 325, f. 106b-107a, M, rubric: ענה בהושענא.
15586. Jerusalem - Musad haRav Kook 325, f. 123b-124a, M, rubric: ענ' בהו'.
15587. Jerusalem - Musad haRav Kook 330, f. 68b, M.
15588. Jerusalem - Musad haRav Kook 347, f. 58b-59a, M, no incipit.
15589. Jerusalem - Sassoon 1158, p. 215-216, M, rubric: ענה בהושענא.
15590. Jerusalem - Sassoon 1174, p. 144-145, M, rubric: ענה בהושענא.
15591. Jerusalem - Yehiel haLevi 4, f. 88b, G.
15592. London - British Library Or. 11121, f. 133a-134a, C, rubric: ענה בהושענא.
15593. London - British Library Or. 11122, f. 122a-122b, M, rubric: ענה בהושענא.
15594. Manchester - John Rylands University Library, Ms. Gaster 5, f. 150a-151a, M, rubric: ענה בהושענא.
15595. Muenchen - Bayerische Staatsbibliothek, Cod. hebr. 472, f. 99b-100a, M, rubric: ענה בהושענא.
15596. Nahariya - Menahem and Saida Yaakob 284, f. 15b-16b, M, rubric: ענה הושענא.
15597. New York - Jewish Theological Seminary Ms. 3013, f. 75b-76a, M, rubric: ענה בהושענא.
15598. New York - Jewish Theological Seminary Ms. 3193, f. 164b-166a, M, rubric: ענה בהוש'.
15599. New York - Jewish Theological Seminary Ms. 3295, f. 91a-92a, M, rubric: ענה הושענא.
15600. New York - Jewish Theological Seminary Ms. 4195, f. 23a-25a, M, incipit איומה.
15601. New York - Public Library, Heb. Ms. 9, f. 73a-73b, M, no incipit.
15602. Oxford - Bodleian Library MS Opp. Add. fol. 58 (Neubauer 2498), f. 143a-143b, M, rubric: ענה בהושע נא.
15603. Paris - G. Epstein 23/57, f. 104a-105a, C.
15604. Philadelphia - University of Pennsylvania HB 2, f. 98a-98b, M, rubric: ענה בהושענא.
15605. Ramat Gan - Universitat Bar Ilan 703, f. 195a-196a, M, rubric: ענה בהושענא.
15606. San Francisco - California State Library, Sutro Branch MS 154 (Brinner 125), f. 25a, M.

15607. Strasbourg - Bibliotheque Nationale et Universitaire 3965 (Landauer 39), p. 239-241, M, rubric: 'ענ' בהו.

Yemen, commentary by Yiḥya b. Josef Tsalaḥ

15608. Montreal - Elberg 203, f. 12b-14a, M.

ענה איומה קוראה בתחנוני (ע 793), סעדיה גאון, הושענא

Yemen

15609. New York - Jewish Theological Seminary Ms. 4488, f. 70b, M, very short.

15610. New York - Public Library, Heb. Ms. 10, f. 60a, M, no incipit, margins damaged, very short.

Yemen, commentary by Isaac b. Abraham Wanneh

15611. Jerusalem - Benayahu ת 261, f. 84a-84b, M, rubric: ענה בהושענא.

15612. Jerusalem - Benayahu ת 282, f. 76b, M, rubric: ענה בהושענא.

15613. Jerusalem - Makhon Ben Zvi 1156 (Tubi 155), f. 73b, M, rubric: ענה בהושענא, very short.

15614. Jerusalem - Makhon Ben Zvi 1174 (Tubi 154), f. 86b, M, rubric: 'ענ' בהוש', very short.

15615. Jerusalem - Michael Krupp 604, f. 95a, M, rubric: ענה בהושענא.

15616. Jerusalem - Michael Krupp 1990, f. 102b, M, rubric: ענה בהושענא.

15617. Jerusalem - Musad haRav Kook 325, f. 110a, M, rubric: ענה בהושענא.

15618. Jerusalem - Musad haRav Kook 325, f. 126a, M, rubric: 'ענ' בהו.

15619. Jerusalem - Musad haRav Kook 347, f. 60a, M, short.

15620. Jerusalem - Sassoon 1158, p. 217, M, rubric: ענה בהושענא, very short.

15621. Jerusalem - Sassoon 1174, p 147, M, rubric: ענה הושענא.

15622. London - British Library Or. 11122, f. 123b, M, rubric: ענה בהושענא.

15623. Muenchen - Bayerische Staatsbibliothek, Cod. hebr. 472, f. 101b, M, rubric: ענה בהושענא.

15624. New York - Jewish Theological Seminary Ms. 3013, f. 79a, M, rubric: 'ענה בהו.

15625. New York - Jewish Theological Seminary Ms. 3193, f. 168a, M, rubric: 'ענה בהוש.

15626. New York - Jewish Theological Seminary Ms. 3295, f. 93b, M, rubric: ענה הושענא, short.

15627. New York - Public Library, Heb. Ms. 9, f. 74b, M, no incipit, very short.

15628. Ramat Gan - Universitat BarIlan 703, f. 197a-197b, M, rubric: ענה בהושענא.

15629. San Francisco - California State Library, Sutro Branch MS 154 (Brinner 125), f. 26a, M.

15630. Strasbourg - Bibliotheque Nationale et Universitaire 3965 (Landauer 39), p. 245, M, rubric: 'ענ' בהו.

ענה איומים בעוז ברוכים בברכת עוז (ע 794), סעדיה גאון, הושענא

Yemen

15631. Jerusalem - Sassoon 902, p. 179, M, no incipit, very short.
15632. New York - Jewish Theological Seminary Ms. 4488, f. 70a, M, no incipit, very short.
15633. New York - Public Library, Heb. Ms. 10, f. 59b, M, no incipit, very short.

Yemen, commentary by Isaac b. Abraham Wanneh

15634. Jerusalem - Benayahu ת 261, f. 83b, M, rubric: ענה בהושענא, short.
15635. Jerusalem - Benayahu ת 282, f. 76a, M, rubric: ענה בהושענא, very short.
15636. Jerusalem - Makhon Ben Zvi 1156 (Tubi 155), f. 73a, M, rubric: ענה בהושענא, very short.
15637. Jerusalem - Makhon Ben Zvi 1174 (Tubi 154), f. 86a, M, rubric: ענ' בהו', very short.
15638. Jerusalem - Michael Krupp 604, f. 94a, M, rubric: ענה בהושענא, very short.
15639. Jerusalem - Michael Krupp 1990, f. 101b-102a, M, rubric: ענה בהושענא, very short.
15640. Jerusalem - Musad haRav Kook 325, f. 108b, M, rubric: ענה בהושענא, short.
15641. Jerusalem - Musad haRav Kook 325, f. 125a, M, rubric: ענ' בהו', very short.
15642. Jerusalem - Musad haRav Kook 347, f. 59b, M, very short.
15643. Jerusalem - Sassoon 1158, p. 217, M, rubric: ענה בהו', very short.
15644. Jerusalem - Sassoon 1174, p. 145, M, no incipit, short.
15645. London - British Library Or. 11121, f. 134b, C.
15646. London - British Library Or. 11122, f. 123a, M, rubric: ענה בהושענא, very short.
15647. Muenchen - Bayerische Staatsbibliothek, Cod. hebr. 472, f. 100b, M, rubric: ענה בהושענא, very short.
15648. New York - Jewish Theological Seminary Ms. 3013, f. 76b, M, no incipit, very short.
15649. New York - Jewish Theological Seminary Ms. 3193, f. 167a, M, rubric: ענה בהוש', very short.
15650. New York - Jewish Theological Seminary Ms. 3295, f. 93b, M, rubric: ענה בהושענא, very short.
15651. New York - Public Library, Heb. Ms. 9, f. 74a, M, no incipit, very short.
15652. Oxford - Bodleian Library MS Opp. Add. fol. 58 (Neubauer 2498), f. 144a-144b, M, rubric: ענה בהושענא, very short.
15653. Philadelphia - University of Pennsylvania HB 2, f. 99a, M, rubric: ענה בהושענא, very short.

15654. Ramat Gan - Universitat Bar Ilan 703, f. 196b, M, rubric: ענה בהושענא, very short.

15655. Strasbourg - Bibliotheque Nationale et Universitaire 3965 (Landauer 39), p. 243, M, rubric: 'ענ' בהו, very short.

Yemen, commentary by Yihya b. Josef Tsalah

15656. Montreal - Elberg 203, f. 15b, M, no incipit, very short.

ענה אתוים בשמך דצים הבאים בסוכה ונרצים (ע 795), סעדיה גאון, הושענא

Yemen

15657. Chicago-Spertus College of Judaica D 10, f. 119b-120a, M.

15658. Jerusalem - Benayahu ת 88, f. 27b, M.

15659. Jerusalem - Michael Krupp 3391, f. 2b, M.

15660. Jerusalem - Musad haRav Kook 334, f. 86a, M.

15661. Jerusalem - Musad haRav Kook 952, f. 2b-3b, M, rubric: ענה בהושענא.

15662. Jerusalem - Sassoon 264, f. 91b, M, no incipit.

15663. Jerusalem - Sassoon 902, p. 170, M, no incipit, very short.

15664. New York - Alfred Moldovan HH, f. 3b, M, rubric: ענה בהושענא.

15665. New York - Jewish Theological Seminary Ms. 4488, f. 66a, M, no incipit.

15666. New York - Jewish Theological Seminary Ms. 9325, f. 69b-70a, M, no incipit.

15667. Ramat Gan - Universitat Bar Ilan 62, f. 27b, G, margin damaged.

Yemen, commentary by Isaac b. Abraham Wanneh

15668. Chicago-Spertus College of Judaica D 1, f. 193b, M.

15669. Jerusalem - Benayahu ת 261, f. 79b-80a, M, rubric: ענה בהושענא.

15670. Jerusalem - Benayahu ת 282, f. 73a, M, rubric: ענה בהושענא.

15671. Jerusalem - Israel Museum 180/78, f. 3b-4a, M, rubric: ענה בהושענא.

15672. Jerusalem - Makhon Ben Zvi 1156 (Tubi 155), f. 70b, M, rubric: ענה בהושענא.

15673. Jerusalem - Makhon Ben Zvi 1174 (Tubi 154), f. 81a, M, rubric: 'ענ' בהוש'.

15674. Jerusalem - Makhon ben Zvi 1186 (Tubi 205), f. 1b, M.

15675. Jerusalem - Michael Krupp 604, f. 90a-90b, M, rubric: ענה בהושענא.

15676. Jerusalem - Michael Krupp 1990, f. 96b-97a, M.

15677. Jerusalem - Musad haRav Kook 325, f. 101a, M, rubric: ענה בהושענא.

15678. Jerusalem - Musad haRav Kook 325, f. 119a, M, rubric: 'ענ' בהו.

15679. Jerusalem - Musad haRav Kook 330, f. 65b, M, no incipit, very short.

15680. Jerusalem - Sassoon 1158, p. 211, M, rubric: ענה בהושענא.

15681. Jerusalem - Sassoon 1174, p. 139-140, M, rubric: ענה בהושענא.

15682. Jerusalem - Yehiel haLevi 4, f. 85b, M.

15683. London - British Library Or. 11121, f. 130b-131a, C.

15684. London - British Library Or. 11122, f. 120a, M, rubric: ענה בהושענא.

15685. Manchester - John Rylands University Library, Ms. Gaster 5, f. 145a, M, rubric: ענה בהושענא.

15686. Muenchen - Bayerische Staatsbibliothek, Cod. hebr. 472, f. 96b, M, rubric: ענה בהושענא.
15687. Nahariya - Menahem and Saida Yaakob 284, f. 3a, M, rubric: ענה בהושענא.
15688. New York - Jewish Theological Seminary Ms. 3013, f. 72b, M, no incipit.
15689. New York - Jewish Theological Seminary Ms. 3193, f. 159b, M, rubric: ענה בהושענא.
15690. New York - Jewish Theological Seminary Ms. 4195, f. 2b-3b, M, rubric: ענה בהושענא.
15691. New York - Public Library, Heb. Ms. 9, f. 70a, M, rubric: ענה בהושענא.
15692. Oxford - Bodleian Library MS Opp. Add. fol. 58 (Neubauer 2498), f. 138b-139a, M, rubric: ענה הושענא.
15693. Paris - G. Epstein 23/57, f. 96b-97a, C.
15694. Philadelphia - University of Pennsylvania HB 2, f. 96a, M, rubric: ענה בהושענא.
15695. Ramat Gan - Universitat Bar Ilan 703, f. 191a, M, rubric: ענה בהושענא.
15696. Strasbourg - Bibliotheque Nationale et Universitaire 3965 (Landauer 39), p. 230-231, M, rubric: ענ' בהו'.

Yemen, commentary by Simon b. Tsemaḥ Duran

15697. Jerusalem - Michael Krupp 1758, f. 2b, M, rubric: פירוש.

Yemen, commentary by Yiḥya b. Josef Tsalaḥ

15698. Montreal - Elberg 203, f. 2a-2b, M.

ענה תואבי ישעך שוכן שחקים (ע 799), סעדיה גאון, הושענא

Yemen

15699. Chicago-Spertus College of Judaica D 10, f. 121b-122a, M, incipit בראשי.
15700. Jerusalem - Michael Krupp 3391, f. 4a, M.
15701. Jerusalem - Musad haRav Kook 334, f. 87a, M.
15702. Jerusalem - Musad haRav Kook 335, f. 93a, M.
15703. Jerusalem - Musad haRav Kook 952, f. 6a-7a, M, rubric: ענה בהושענא.
15704. Jerusalem - Sassoon 264, f. 92b, M, no incipit.
15705. Jerusalem - Sassoon 902, p. 171, M, no incipit.
15706. New York - Alfred Moldovan HH, f. 6a-7a, M, rubric: ענה בהושענא.
15707. New York - Jewish Theological Seminary Ms. 4488, f. 67a, M.
15708. New York - Jewish Theological Seminary Ms. 9325, f. 72a, M.
15709. New York - Public Library, Heb. Ms. 10, f. 57a, M, no incipit, margins damaged.
15710. Ramat Gan - Universitat Bar Ilan 62, f. 27b-28a, G, margins damaged.

Yemen, commentary by Isaac b. Abraham Wanneh

15711. Chicago-Spertus College of Judaica D 1, f. 194a-194b, M.
15712. Jerusalem - Benayahu ת 261, f. 80a-80b, M, rubric: ענה בהושענא.

15713. Jerusalem - Benayahu ת 282, f. 73b, M, rubric: ענה בהושענא, no incipit.
15714. Jerusalem - Israel Museum 180/78, f. 7a-7b, M, rubric: ענה בהושענא.
15715. Jerusalem - Makhon Ben Zvi 1156 (Tubi 155), f. 71a, M, rubric: ענה בהושענא.
15716. Jerusalem - Makhon Ben Zvi 1174 (Tubi 154), f. 82a, M, rubric: ענה בהוש׳.
15717. Jerusalem - Makhon ben Zvi 1186 (Tubi 205), f. 2b-3b, M, incipit תואבי.
15718. Jerusalem - Michael Krupp 604, f. 90b-91a, M, rubric: ענה בהושענא, no incipit.
15719. Jerusalem - Michael Krupp 1990, f. 97a-97b, M, rubric: ענה בהושענא.
15720. Jerusalem - Musad haRav Kook 325, f. 102a, M, rubric: ענה בהושענא.
15721. Jerusalem - Musad haRav Kook 325, f. 120a-120b, M, no incipit.
15722. Jerusalem - Musad haRav Kook 330, f. 66b, M, no incipit.
15723. Jerusalem - Musad haRav Kook 347, f. 56b, M.
15724. Jerusalem - Sassoon 1158, p. 212, M, rubric: ענה בהושענא.
15725. Jerusalem - Sassoon 1174, p. 140, M, rubric: ענה בהושענא.
15726. Jerusalem - Schocken Institute 70028, f. 186a-186b, M, rubric: ענה בהושענא, no incipit.
15727. Jerusalem - Yehiel haLevi 4, f. 86a, M.
15728. London - British Library Or. 11121, f. 131a-131b, C, rubric: ענה בהושענא, no incipit.
15729. London - British Library Or. 11122, f. 120b, M, rubric: ענה בהושענא, page damaged.
15730. Manchester - John Rylands University Library, Ms Gaster 5, f. 146a, M, rubric: ענה בהושענא.
15731. Muenchen - Bayerische Staatsbibliothek, Cod. hebr. 472, f. 97a-97b, M, rubric: ענה בהושענא, no incipit.
15732. Nahariya - Menahem and Saida Yaakob 284, f. 6a-7a, M, rubric: ענה בהושענא.
15733. New York - Jewish Theological Seminary Ms. 3013, f. 73a, M, no incipit.
15734. New York - Jewish Theological Seminary Ms. 3193, f. 160a, M, rubric: ענה בהוש׳, page damaged.
15735. New York - Jewish Theological Seminary Ms. 3295, f. 88a, M, rubric: ענה בהושענא.
15736. New York - Jewish Theological Seminary Ms. 4195, f. 7b-9a, M, incipit תואבי.
15737. New York - Public Library, Heb. Ms. 9, f. 70b, M, rubric: ענה בהו׳.
15738. Oxford - Bodleian Library MS Opp. Add. fol. 58 (Neubauer 2498), f. 139b-140a, M, rubric: ענה בהושענא, no incipit.
15739. Paris - G. Epstein 23/57, f. 98b-99a, C, no incipit.
15740. Philadelphia - University of Pennsylvania HB 2, f. 97a, M, rubric: ענה בהושענא, short.

15741. Ramat Gan - Universitat Bar Ilan 703, f. 192a, M, rubric: ענה בההושענא.
15742. Strasbourg - Bibliotheque Nationale et Universitaire 3965 (Landauer 39), p. 232-233, M, rubric: 'ענ' בהו, no incipit.
Yemen, commentary by Simon b. Tsemaḥ Duran
15743. Jerusalem - Michael Krupp 1758, f. 5a, M, no incipit.
Yemen, commentary by Yiḥya b. Josef Tsalaḥ
15744. Montreal - Elberg 203, f. 3b-4b, M, no incipit.

עננו אבינו עננו עננו בוראנו עננו (ע 830), סליחה

Ashkenaz
15745. London - British Library Add. 18695 (Margoliouth 683), f. 170a, T, Yiddish.

Sepharad
15746. Skokie - Hebrew Theological College 3, f. 12b, G.
15747. Skokie - Hebrew Theological College 3, f. 2.19a, M.

Yemen, commentary by Isaac b. Abraham Wanneh
15748. Chicago-Spertus College of Judaica D 2, 2, f. 181b, M.

ערב אשר עלה (ע +926), אלעזר ברבי קליר, חלק ד', קדושתא לפסח

Ashkenaz
15749. Berlin - Staatsbibliothek (Preussischer Kulturbesitz) Or. Qu. 798-799 (Steinschneider 177), II, f. 79b, M, incipit אל נא.
15750. Budapest - Magyar tudomanyos akademia, MS. Kaufmann A 384, f. 163b, M, incipit אל נא.
15751. Budapest - Magyar tudomanyos akademia, MS. Kaufmann A 400, p. 132, C, rubric: אל נא, no incipit.
15752. Hamburg - Staats- und Universitaetsbibliothek Cod. hebr. 17/2 (Steinschneider 152), f. 65a, C.
15753. Jerusalem - Schocken Institute 24100 / Mahzor Nuremberg, f. 94b, M, incipit אל נא.
15754. London - British Library Add. 18695 (Margoliouth 683), f. 42a, T, Yiddish, incipit אל נא.
15755. Moscow - Russian State Library, Ms. Guenzburg 615, f. 23a, C, incipit אל נא.
15756. Muenchen - Bayerische Staatsbibliothek, Cod. hebr. 88, f. 73a, G.
15757. Muenchen - Bayerische Staatsbibliothek, Cod. hebr. 393, f. 130a, C, incipit אל נא.
15758. New York - Jewish Theological Seminary Ms. 4466, f. 75a, M.
15759. Paris - Bibliotheque Nationale heb. 709, f. 98a, C.
15760. Parma - Biblioteca Palatina Cod. Parm. 1002 (Ta 24), f. 118b, M, incipit אל נא, short.

15761. Parma - Biblioteca Palatina Cod. Parm. 3205 (de Rossi 655), f. 102b, C, incipit אל נא.
15762. Parma - Biblioteca Palatina Cod. Parm. 3507 (Perreau 27), f. 65a, C.
15763. Zurich - Zentralbibliothek Heid. 139, f. 38a, C, no incipit, additional marginal notes.

Tsarfat

15764. London - British Library Add. 11639 (Margoliouth 1056), f. 293a-293b, M, incipit אל נא.
15765. Moscow - Russian State Library, Ms. Guenzburg 1665, f. 71b, M, incipit אל נא.
15766. Oxford - Bodleian Library MS Laud. Or. 271 (Neubauer 1206), f. 73a, C, commentator: Aaron b. Hayyim haKohen (compiler), short.
15767. Oxford - Bodleian Library MS Opp. 171 (Neubauer 1207), f. 41a-41b, C, incipit אל נא.

עשה ירח כבוד אלהים (ע 965), יצחק בן זרחיה גירונדי, סילוק, קדושתא לשבת החדש
Carpentras, commentary by Mordekhai b. Josef of Rocco Martino
15768. Cincinnati - Hebrew Union College 246/1, f. 44b-47b, C, rubric: פי' עשה ירח וכו', no incipit.

Sepharad, commentary by Josef Garad
15769. Oxford - Bodleian Library Heb.e.10 (Neubauer 2746/1), f. 15a-15b, C, no incipit.
15770. Oxford - Bodleian Library Heb.e.10 (Neubauer 2746/1), f. 21b-22a, C, rubric: סלוק, no incipit.

עשה למען מלאכיך המשרתים פניך (ע 971), סליחה
Yemen, commentary by Isaac b. Abraham Wanneh
15771. Chicago-Spertus College of Judaica D 2, 2, f. 181b-182a, M.

עת שערי צדק היום נפתחו, סליחה
Yemen, commentary by Isaac b. Abraham Wanneh
15772. Chicago-Spertus College of Judaica D 2, 2, f. 217a-217b, M, no incipit.
15773. Jerusalem - Sassoon 1158, p. 190-191, M, rubric: סים' סעדיה בן זכריה אלבדיחי, no incipit.
15774. London - British Library Or. 11122, f. 194a-194b, M, no incipit.

עת שערי רחמים להפתח (ע 1053), יהודה שמואל עבאס, עקידה
Carpentras
15775. Cincinnati - Hebrew Union College 429/1, f. 28b-29b, M, no incipit.
Carpentras, commentary by Josef b. Abraham of Montelitz
15776. Cincinnati - Hebrew Union College 357, f. 115b-117b, M, no incipit.

15777. Marseille - Mlle. Odette Valabregue [1], f. 101a, C, rubric: פירוש לסדר ראש השנה, no incipit.
15778. New York - Jewish Theological Seminary Ms. 4746, f. 42b-43a, M, no incipit.
15779. Paris - Alliance Israelite Universelle H 422 A, f. 91b-92b, M, no incipit.
15780. Paris - Ecole Rabbinique 31, f. 155b-157a, M, no incipit.

Sepharad, commentary by David b. Josef Abudarham[347]

15781. Budapest - Magyar tudomanyos akademia, MS. Kaufmann A 405/2, p. 256-257, C, rubric: פזמון.
15782. Budapest - Magyar tudomanyos akademia, MS. Kaufmann A 405/2, p. 257-258, C, rubric: פזמון.
15783. Cincinnati - Hebrew Union College 490, f. 14b-15a, C.
15784. Cincinnati - Hebrew Union College 490, f. 15a, C.
15785. Holon - Yehuda Nahum 278, f. 16a, FC, rubric: פזמון.
15786. New York - Columbia X893 Ab 93, f. 31b-32a, C, rubric: פזמון.
15787. New York - Columbia X893 Ab 93, f. 32a, C, rubric: פזמון.

Yemen

15788. Jerusalem - Benayahu ת 414, f. 127b, M, no incipit.
15789. Jerusalem - Sassoon 264, f. 160b, M.
15790. New York - Jewish Theological Seminary Ms. 1725, f. 1a-4a.
15791. New York - Jewish Theological Seminary Ms. 3052, f. 43a-47b, M, rubric: אל מלך.
15792. New York - Jewish Theological Seminary Ms. 4488, f. 106b, G.
15793. Ramat Gan Universitat Bar Ilan 62, f. 39b, G, margins damaged.

Yemen, commentary by Isaac b. Abraham Wanneh

15794. Chicago-Spertus College of Judaica D 2, 2, f. 216a-216b, M, no incipit.
15795. Jerusalem - Benayahu ת 261, f. 143b-144b, M, rubric: אל מלך.
15796. Jerusalem - Benayahu ת 282, f. 126b-127b, M, rubric: אל מלך.
15797. Jerusalem - Makhon Ben Zvi 1174 (Tubi 154), f. 108a-108b, M, rubric: אל מלך.
15798. Jerusalem - Musad haRav Kook 325, f. 158a-158b, 160a, M.
15799. Jerusalem - Musad haRav Kook 330, f. 94b-95a, G.
15800. Jerusalem - Musad haRav Kook 347, f. 76b, G.
15801. Jerusalem - Sassoon 1158, p. 188-190, M, no incipit.
15802. Jerusalem - Sassoon 1174, p. 240-243, M, no incipit.
15803. London - British Library Or. 11122, f. 193a-193b, M, rubric: אל מלך, no incipit.
15804. Manchester - John Rylands University Library, Ms. Gaster 5, f. 121b-122a, M, rubric: פירוש.

---

[347] Edited by Prins, תשלום אבודרהם, p. 133-135.

15805. Manchester - John Rylands University Library, Ms. Gaster 5, f. 200b-201b, M.
15806. Muenchen - Bayerische Staatsbibliothek, Cod. hebr. 472, f. 172b-174b, M, rubric: אל מלך.
15807. New York - Jewish Theological Seminary Ms. 3013, f. 109a, M, rubric: אל מלך.
15808. New York - Jewish Theological Seminary Ms. 3109, f. 70b-72a, M, rubric: אל מלך.
15809. New York - Jewish Theological Seminary Ms. 3294, f. 3a-4a, C.
15810. New York - Public Library, Heb. Ms. 9, f. 112b, M.
15811. Philadelphia - University of Pennsylvania HB 2, f. 120b-121b, M, rubric: אל מלך.
15812. Strasbourg - Bibliotheque Nationale et Universitaire 3965 (Landauer 39), p. 331-332, M, rubric: אל מלך.

עתר משמי קדש אל נאור בקדש, סליחה
Tsarfat
15813. London - David Sofer 5, f. 147a, C.
15814. Parma - Biblioteca Palatina Cod. Parm. 3007 (de Rossi 654,2), f. 120a-120b, M.

פדות שלח מראש (פ 17+), אברהם בר חיים, חלק ד', קדושתא לשבת פרה
Carpentras, commentary by Mordekhai b. Josef of Rocco Martino
15815. Cincinnati - Hebrew Union College 246/1, f. 30b-31b, C, rubric: פי' משלש כדות שלח מראש וכו'.
Sepharad, commentary by Josef Garad
15816. Oxford - Bodleian Library Heb.e.10 (Neubauer 2746/1), f. 11b-12a, C, rubric: משלש.
15817. Oxford - Bodleian Library Heb.e.10 (Neubauer 2746/1), f. 19b-20a, C, rubric: פדות שלח, no incipit.

פדם היום מדין, לראש השנה
Tsarfat
15818. Parma - Biblioteca Palatina Cod. Parm. 1794 (de Rossi 1061), f. 54b-55a, M.

פדע קמרי אלבאן (פ 46), שלם שבזי
Yemen
15819. Cincinnati - Hebrew Union College 398, f. 146b-147b, M.

פרה אמרה קשה מכל ניחוחי אשה (p 186), אלעזר ברבי קליר, שבעתא לשבת פרה
Ashkenaz
15820. Hamburg - Staats- und Universitaetsbibliothek Cod. hebr. 17/2 (Steinschneider 152), f. 27a, C, rubric: שבעתא.
15821. Oxford - Bodleian Library MS Opp. 170 (Neubauer 1205), f. 32b-33a, C, rubric: שבעתא.
15822. Parma - Biblioteca Palatina Cod. Parm. 3507 (Perreau 27), f. 29a-29b, C, rubric: שבעתא.
15823. Vatican - Biblioteca Apostolica ebr. 305,1, f. 24a-24b, C, rubric: שבעתא.

צאינה וראינה מלך ביופיו (צ 24), משולם ב"ר קלונימוס, סילוק היוצר לפסח
Ashkenaz
15824. Berlin - Staatsbibliothek (Preussischer Kulturbesitz) Or. Qu. 798-799 (Steinschneider 177), II, f. 76a-76b, M.
15825. Braunschweig - Landesmuseum fuer Geschichte und Volkstum R 2386, vol. I, f. 34b-35a, M.
15826. Budapest - Magyar tudomanyos akademia, MS. Kaufmann A 384, f. 157b-158a, M.
15827. Budapest - Magyar tudomanyos akademia, MS. Kaufmann A 400, p. 129-130, C.
15828. Hamburg - Staats- und Universitaetsbibliothek Cod. hebr. 17/2 (Steinschneider 152), f. 64b, C.
15829. Hamburg - Staats- und Universitaetsbibliothek Cod. hebr. 225, f. 87b, G.
15830. Jerusalem - Schocken Institute 24100 / Mahzor Nuremberg, f. 92b-93a, M.
15831. London - British Library Add. 18695 (Margoliouth 683), f. 38b, T, Yiddish.
15832. Moscow - Russian State Library, Ms. Guenzburg 615, f. 20a-20b, C.
15833. Muenchen - Bayrische Staatsbibliothek, Cod. hebr. 88, f. 69b-70a, G.
15834. Muenchen - Bayerische Staatsbibliothek, Cod. hebr. 393, f. 127b-128b, C, no incipit.
15835. New York - Jewish Theological Seminary Ms. 4466, f. 70b-71b, M.
15836. Oxford - Bodleian Library MS Opp. 170 (Neubauer 1205), f. 73a-74a, C.
15837. Paris - Bibliotheque Nationale heb. 709, f. 95a-95b, C.
15838. Parma - Biblioteca Palatina Cod. Parm. 1002 (Ta 24), f. 114a, M, short.
15839. Parma - Biblioteca Palatina Cod. Parm. 3205 (de Rossi 655), f. 95b-97a, C.
15840. Parma - Biblioteca Palatina Cod. Parm. 3507 (Perreau 27), f. 63a, C.

15841. Zurich - Zentralbibliothek Heid. 139, f. 36a-36b, C, additional marginal notes.

Tsarfat

15842. Moscow - Russian State Library, Ms. Guenzburg 1665, f. 69b-70a, M.
15843. Oxford - Bodleian Library MS Laud. Or. 271 (Neubauer 1206), f. 72a, C, commentator: Aaron b. Hayyim haKohen (compiler).
15844. Parma - Biblioteca Palatina Cod. Parm. 3136 (de Rossi 405), f. 100b-101a, M, lower part of f. 100 missing.

צאינה וראינה משכיל שיר (צ 25), שלמה הבבלי, סילוק היוצר לפסח

Ashkenaz

15845. Berlin - Staatsbibliothek (Preussischer Kulturbesitz) Or. Qu. 798-799 (Steinschneider 177), II, f. 58a-59a, M.
15846. Braunschweig - Landesmuseum fuer Geschichte und Volkstum R 2386, vol. I, f. 18a-19a, M.
15847. Budapest - Magyar tudomanyos akademia, MS. Kaufmann A 384, f. 123b-125b, M.
15848. Budapest - Magyar tudomanyos akademia, MS. Kaufmann A 400, p. 87-89, C, no incipit.
15849. Hamburg - Staats- und Universitaetsbibliothek Cod. hebr. 17/2 (Steinschneider 152), f. 51b-53a, C.
15850. Hamburg - Staats- und Universitaetsbibliothek Cod. hebr. 225, f. 63a-64a, G.
15851. Jerusalem - Schocken Institute 24100 / Mahzor Nuremberg, f. 80b-81a (leaf 80 missing), M
15852. London - British Library Add. 18695 (Margoliouth 683), f. 22a-23a, T, Yiddish.
15853. Moscow - Russian State Library, Ms. Guenzburg 615, f. 1a-3a, C, beginning missing.
15854. Muenchen - Bayerische Staatsbibliothek, Cod. hebr. 21, f. 25b-26a, M.
15855. Muenchen - Bayrische Staatsbibliothek Cod. hebr. 88, f. 59a-59b, G.
15856. Muenchen - Bayerische Staatsbibliothek, Cod. hebr. 393, f. 119a-121a, C.
15857. New York - Jewish Theological Seminary Ms. 4466, f. 50b-52a, M.
15858. Oxford - Bodleian Library MS Opp. 170 (Neubauer 1205), f. 52b-55a, C.
15859. Paris - Bibliotheque Nationale heb. 709, f. 67b-70a, C.
15860. Parma - Biblioteca Palatina Cod. Parm. 1002 (Ta 24), f. 89a-89b, M.
15861. Parma - Biblioteca Palatina Cod. Parm. 3205 (de Rossi 655), f. 75b-78b, C.
15862. Parma - Biblioteca Palatina Cod. Parm. 3507 (Perreau 27), f. 44b-46b, C.

15863. Zurich - Zentralbibliothek Heid. 139, f. 23b-25a, C, additional marginal notes.

Italia

15864. Parma - Biblioteca Palatin Cod. Parm. 2248 (de Rossi 149/2), f. 31a-33a, C.

Roma

15865. Parma - Biblioteca Palatina Cod. Parm. 3141 (de Rossi 767), f. 112a-113a, M.

Tsarfat

15866. London - British Library Add. 11639 (Margoliouth 1056), f. 288a-288b, M.
15867. Moscow - Russian State Library, Ms. Guenzburg 1665, f. 55a-56a, M.
15868. Oxford - Bodleian Library MS Laud. Or. 271 (Neubauer 1206), f. 56a-59a, C, commentator: Aaron b. Hayyim haKohen (compiler).
15869. Paris - Bibliotheque Nationale heb. 635, f. 50a-51b, M.
15870. Parma - Biblioteca Palatina Cod. Parm. 3136 (de Rossi 405), f. 78b-79b, M.
15871. Vatican - Biblioteca Apostolica ebr. 306, f. 133b-136a, C.

צאינה וראינה שור בעתטרה (צ 26), שמעון ב"'ר יצחק, סילוק היוצר לפסח

Ashkenaz

15872. Berlin - Staatsbibliothek (Preussischer Kulturbesitz) Or. Qu. 798-799 (Steinschneider 177), II, f. 83b-84a, M.
15873. Braunschweig - Landesmuseum fuer Geschichte und Volkstum R 2386, vol. I, f. 41b, M.
15874. Budapest - Magyar tudomanyos akademia, MS. Kaufmann A 384, f. 176b-177a, M.
15875. Hamburg - Staats- und Universitaetsbibliothek Cod. hebr. 17/2 (Steinschneider 152), f. 67a, C.
15876. London - British Library Add. 18695 (Margoliouth 683), f. 51b-52a, T, Yiddish.
15877. Muenchen - Bayerische Staatsbibliothek, Cod. hebr. 88, f. 77a, G.
15878. Muenchen - Bayerische Staatsbibliothek, Cod. hebr. 393, f. 132a, C, no incipit.
15879. New York - Jewish Theological Seminary Ms. 4466, f. 81b-83a, M.
15880. Paris - Bibliotheque Nationale heb. 709, f. 114b-115a, C.
15881. Parma - Biblioteca Palatina Cod. Parm. 1002 (Ta 24), f. 128a, M, incipit missing.
15882. Parma - Biblioteca Palatina Cod. Parm. 3205 (de Rossi 655), f. 105b, C.
15883. Parma - Biblioteca Palatina Cod. Parm. 3507 (Perreau 27), f. 69a-69b, C.
15884. Zurich - Zentralbibliothek Heid. 139, f. 40a-40b, C, additional marginal notes.

Tsarfat

15885. London - David Sofer 5, f. 38a, C, additional glosses.
15886. Moscow - Russian State Library, Ms. Guenzburg 1665, f. 77b-78a, M.
15887. Oxford - Bodleian Library MS Laud. Or. 271 (Neubauer 1206), f. 74b-75a, C, commentator: Aaron b. Hayyim haKohen (compiler), no incipit.
15888. Parma - Biblioteca Palatina Cod. Parm. 3136 (de Rossi 405), f. 105a-105b, M.

צדק כפרך תגדיל לעדה נבאה (צ 139)
Carpentras, commentary by Josef b. Abraham of Montelitz
15889. Paris - Ecole Rabbinique 32, f. 155a, M.

צדק לפועלי אתנה וחסדו (צ 140), משה אבן עזרא, סילוק, קדושתא למנחה יום כפור
Carpentras
15890. Cincinnati - Hebrew Union College 392, f. 104a, M, no incipit.
Carpentras, commentary by Josef b. Abraham of Montelitz
15891. Cincinnati - Hebrew Union College 291, f. 56b, C, rubric: פי׳ צדק וכו׳.
15892. New York - Jewish Theological Seminary Ms. 4197, f. 221b, M, no incipit.
15893. Paris - Ecole Rabbinique 32, f. 248b, M, no incipit.
15894. Strasbourg - Bibliotheque Nationale et Universitaire 4081, f. 220b-221a, M, no incipit.

צור ישעי ומושיעי אשר צופה נג׳ ו׳וה (צ 202), ט׳׳יחה
Carpentras, commentary by Mordekhai b. Josef of Rocco Martino
15895. Cincinnati - Hebrew Union College 246/1, f. 87a-88a, C, rubric: פי׳ סליחה צור ישעי.

צורי שעה שועי וקול מעני (צ 263), שלם שבזי
Yemen
15896. Cincinnati - Hebrew Union College 398, f. 147b-150a, M.

ציון הלא תשאלי (צ 292), יהודה הלוי, קינה
Ashkenaz
15897. Berlin - Staatsbibliothek (Preussischer Kulturbesitz) Or. Qu. 798-799 (Steinschneider 177), II, f. 208b-209b, M.
15898. Hamburg - Staats- und Universitaetsbibliothek Cod. hebr. 239a (Steinschneider 130), f. 161b-162b, G.
Carpentras, commentary by Mordekhai b. Josef of Rocco Martino
15899. Cincinnati - Hebrew Union College 246/1, f. 78b-80b, C, rubric: פי׳ נחמה ציון הלא תשאלי.

צעקה יוכבד בקול מר וקשה (צ 371), שלמה?, לשמחת תורה
North Africa, commentary by Mordekhai b. Mose
15900. New York - Jewish Theological Seminary Rab. 2027, f. 284b, C, rubric: אתחיל לכתוב פירוש פיוט צעקה יוכבד בלשון ג׳כלי סימן זכר סאשא מאטיה.

צפה בבת תמותה (צ 373), אלעזר ברבי קליר, חלק ג׳, קדושתא למוסף יום כפור
Ashkenaz
15901. Berlin - Staatsbibliothek (Preussischer Kulturbesitz) Or. Qu. 798-799 (Steinschneider 177), I, f. 116b-117b, M.
15902. Braunschweig - Landesmuseum fuer Geschichte und Volkstum R 2386, vol. II, f. 224b-225a, M.
15903. Budapest - Magyar tudomanyos akademia, MS. Kaufmann A 400, p. 352-353, C.
15904. Cambridge - University Library Add. 394,1 (Reif SCR 461), f. 69a, C.
15905. Cambridge - University Library Add. 394,2.3, f. 1b, C.
15906. Fulda - Hessische Landesbibliothek A 3 II, f. 123a, C, commentator: Josef.
15907. Hamburg - Staats- und Universitaetsbibliothek Cod. hebr. 17/2 (Steinschneider 152), f. 157b-158a, C.
15908. Hamburg - Staats- und Universitaetsbibliothek Cod. hebr. 40c (Steinschneider 111), f. 211b-212a, G.
15909. Hamburg - Staats- und Universitaetsbibliothek Cod. hebr. 132 (Steinschneider 155), f. 43b-44a, C, no incipit.
15910. Jerusalem - Jewish National and University Library Ms Heb 8° 3037, f. 175b-176a, M.
15911. Jerusalem - Schocken Institute 24100 / Mahzor Nuremberg, f. 409a-409b, M.
15912. London - British Library Or. 11318/1, f. 100a-101a, C.
15913. London - Montefiore Library 261, f. 54b, C, commentator: Eliezer b. Natan?.
15914. Moscow - Russian State Library, Ms. Guenzburg 191, f. 115a-115b, M.
15915. Moscow - Russian State Library, Ms. Guenzburg 615, f. 103a, C, short.
15916. Muenchen - Bayerische Staatsbibliothek, Cod. hebr. 21, f. 218b, M.
15917. Muenchen - Bayerische Staatsbibliothek, Cod. hebr. 346, f. 75b-76a, C.
15918. New York - Jewish Theological Seminary Ms. 4466, f. 367a-367b, M.
15919. New York - Jewish Theological Seminary Ms. 8097, f. 78a-78b, C.
15920. New York - Jewish Theological Seminary Ms. 8169 (Acc. 0016), f. 89b-90a, M.
15921. Oxford - Bodleian Library MS Mich. 365 (Neubauer 1208), f. 81b, C.

15922. Oxford - Bodleian Library MS Opp. 170 (Neubauer 1205), f. 175a-175b, C.
15923. Oxford - Bodleian Library MS Opp. 172 (Neubauer 1211), f. 60a-60b, C.
15924. Oxford - Bodleian Library MS Opp. 619 (Neubauer 2374), f. 203a-203b, M.
15925. Paris - Bibliotheque Nationale heb. 653, f. 87a, G.
15926. Parma - Biblioteca Palatina Cod. Parm. 3205 (de Rossi 655), f. 234a-234b, C.
15927. Parma - Biblioteca Palatina Cod. Parm. 3270 (de Rossi 1215), f. 165a-166a, M.
15928. Parma - Biblioteca Palatina Cod. Parm. 3271 (de Rossi 1216), f. 103b-104a, G.
15929. Parma - Biblioteca Palatina Cod. Parm. 3507 (Perreau 27), f. 162a-162b, C, no incipit.
15930. Vatican - Biblioteca Apostolica ebr. 308, f. 117a-117b, C, commentator: David b. Mose (compiler).
15931. Vatican - Biblioteca Apostolica ebr. 422/1, f. 18a, C, short.
15932. Zurich - Zentralbibliothek Heid. 139, f. 83a-83b, C, no incipit.

Asti, Fossano, Moncalvo
15933. New Haven - Yale University, Beinecke Rare Book and MS Library, MS Heb. 52, f. 133a-133b, M.

Roma
15934. Berlin - Staatsbibliothek (Preussischer Kulturbesitz) Or. Oct. 3567, f. 6a-6b, FC.
15935. Jerusalem - Jewish National and University Library Ms Heb 8° 4153, f. 139b-140a, C, commentator: Daniel ben Salomo haRofe (compiler).
15936. New York - Jewish Theological Seminary Ms. 1639, f. 26a, C, commentator: Salomo b. Samuel Rofe.
15937. Oxford - Bodleian Library MS Mich. 312,1 (Neubauer 2276,1), f. 6b-7a, C.

Tsarfat
15938. London - British Library Or. 8682, f. 82a, GI.
15939. London - David Sofer 5, f. 150b-151a, C.
15940. Oxford - Bodleian Library MS Bodl. Or. 109 (Neubauer 1209), f. 30b, C, commentator: Aaron b. Hayyim haKohen (compiler).
15941. Oxford - Bodleian Library MS Laud. Or. 271 (Neubauer 1206), f. 114b-115a, C, commentator: Aaron b. Hayyim haKohen (compiler), no incipit.
15942. Parma - Biblioteca Palatina Cod. Parm. 1794 (de Rossi 1061), f. 158b-159a, M.
15943. Parma - Biblioteca Palatina Cod. Parm. 2890 (de Rossi 856), f. 70a, M.

15944. Parma - Biblioteca Palatina Cod. Parm. 3006 (de Rossi 654,1), f. 179a, M.
15945. Vatican - Biblioteca Apostolica ebr. 306, f. 103b-104a, C.

קאל אב שמעון באלאקואל, שלם שבזי
Yemen
15946. Cincinnati - Hebrew Union College 398, f. 150a-151b, M, contains drawings of squares with 9 letters each.

קאל אבן משתא שית, שלם שבזי
Yemen
15947. Cincinnati - Hebrew Union College 398, f. 214b-217a, M.

קאל אלאדיב אללה אלאכבר, שלם שבזי
Yemen
15948. Cincinnati - Hebrew Union College 398, f. 151b-153b, M.

קדוש אדיר בעליתו (ק 20), יוצר ליום כפור
Ashkenaz
15949. Berlin - Staatsbibliothek (Preussischer Kulturbesitz) Or. Qu. 798-799 (Steinschneider 177), I, 69a, M, incipit אדיר.
15950. Braunschweig - Landesmuseum fuer Geschichte und Volkstum R 2386, vol. II, f. 180b-181a, M.
15951. Cambridge - University Library Add. 394,1 (Reif SCR 461), f. 67a, C.
15952. Hamburg - Staats- und Universitaetsbibliothek Cod. hebr. 40c (Steinschneider 111), f. 175a-175b, G.
15953. Hamburg - Staats- und Universitaetsbibliothek Cod. hebr. 62 (Steinschneider 154), f. 2a, C.
15954. Jerusalem - Jewish National and University Library Ms Heb 8° 3037, f. 108a-108b, M, incipit כבוד.
15955. Jerusalem - Schocken Institute 24100 / Mahzor Nuremberg, f. 373a-373b, M.
15956. Moscow - Russian State Library, Ms. Guenzburg 191, f. 81b-82a, M.
15957. Muenchen - Bayerische Staatsbibliothek, Cod. hebr. 346, f. 51a, C, rubric: אופן.
15958. New York - Jewish Theological Seminary Ms. 4466, f. 300b-301a, M.
15959. New York - Jewish Theological Seminary Ms. 8169 (Acc. 0016), f. 63b, M.
15960. Oxford - Bodleian Library MS Opp. 172 (Neubauer 1211), f. 34b-35a, C, incipit מלכותו.
15961. Oxford - Bodleian Library MS Opp. 619 (Neubauer 2374), f. 132a, M, short.

15962. Parma - Biblioteca Palatina Cod. Parm. 3205 (de Rossi 655), f. 224a-224b, C, incipit מלכותו.
15963. Vatican - Biblioteca Apostolica ebr. 308, f. 97a, C, commentator: David b. Mose (compiler).

Roma

15964. Berlin - Staatsbibliothek (Preussischer Kulturbesitz) Or. Oct. 3567, f. 4a, FC.

Romania

15965. Vatican - Biblioteca Apostolica ebr. 320, f. 271a, M.

Tsarfat

15966. London - David Sofer 5, f. 136a, C, incipit מלכותו, written on the margin.
15967. Oxford - Bodleian Library MS Bodl. Or. 109 (Neubauer 1209), f. 17a-17b, C, commentator: Aaron b. Hayyim haKohen (compiler).
15968. Oxford - Bodleian Library MS Laud. Or. 271 (Neubauer 1206), f. 111a, C, commentator: Aaron b. Hayyim haKohen (compiler), rubric: אופן, no incipit.
15969. Parma - Biblioteca Palatina Cod. Parm. 2890 (de Rossi 856), f. 19b, M.

קדוש הופיע מפארן (ק +25), אלעזר ברבי קליר, חלק ג', קדושתא לשבועות

Ashkenaz

15970. Berlin - Staatsbibliothek (Preussischer Kulturbesitz) Or. Qu. 798-799 (Steinschneider 177), II, f. 140a, M.
15971. Braunschweig - Landesmuseum fuer Geschichte und Volkstum R 2386, vol. I, f. 96b-97a, M, no incipit.
15972. Budapest - Magyar tudomanyos akademia, MS. Kaufmann A 400, p. 176-177, C, no incipit.
15973. Hamburg - Staats- und Universitaetsbibliothek Cod. hebr. 17/2 (Steinschneider 152), f. 85b, C, no incipit.
15974. Jerusalem - Schocken Institute 24100 / Mahzor Nuremberg, f. 172a, M.
15975. London - British Library Add. 18695 (Margoliouth 683), f. 85b, T, Yiddish.
15976. London - British Library Add. 22431 (Margoliouth 662a), f. 55b-56a, M.
15977. Moscow - Russian State Library, Ms. Guenzburg 615, f. 41a-41b, C, no incipit.
15978. Muenchen - Bayerische Staatsbibliothek, Cod. hebr. 88, f. 139b-140a, G.
15979. New York - Jewish Theological Seminary Ms. 4466, f. 166a, 167a, M, no incipit, very short.
15980. Oxford - Bodleian Library MS Opp. 170 (Neubauer 1205), f. 86b-87a, C, no incipit.

15981. Paris - Bibliotheque Nationale heb. 709, f. 136a, C, no incipit.
15982. Parma - Biblioteca Palatina Cod. Parm. 2886 (de Rossi 585), f. 64a-64b, M, later hand, margins cut.
15983. Parma - Biblioteca Palatina Cod. Parm. 3205 (de Rossi 655), f. 127b, C, no incipit.
15984. Parma - Biblioteca Palatina Cod. Parm. 3507 (Perreau 27), f. 88b, C, no incipit.
15985. Zurich - Zentralbibliothek Heid. 139, f. 54b, C, no incipit, short.

קהל איתנים נעצר בירח האיתנים (ק +55), אלעזר ברבי קליר, חלק ג', קדושתא לסוכות

Tsarfat
15986. London - David Sofer 5, f. 184a, C.
15987. Moscow - Russian State Library, Ms. Guenzburg 1665, f. 187a, M.
15988. Oxford - Bodleian Library MS Opp. 171 (Neubauer 1207), f. 162a-162b, C.
15989. Vatican - Biblioteca Apostolica ebr. 306, f. 112b-113a, C, no incipit.
15990. Vatican - Biblioteca Apostolica ebr. 320, f. 459b-460a, M.

קול דממה לשכן שמימה (ק 86), קלונימוס ב"ר יהודה, אופן לברית מילה

Ashkenaz
15991. Berlin - Staatsbibliothek (Preussischer Kulturbesitz) Or. Qu. 798-799 (Steinschneider 177), I, f. 260b-261a, M.

קול יללה אשמיעה (ק 97), קינה

Yemen, commentary by Isaac b. Abraham Wanneh
15992. Jerusalem - Sassoon 1158, p. 172, M.
15993. London - British Library Or. 11122, f. 103a, M.

קול שומרו וקול חתן מצאוני עוני לארץ אחרת, קינה

Yemen, commentary by Isaac b. Abraham Wanneh
15994. Jerusalem - Sassoon 1158, p. 171-172, M.

קול שופר הדרור קל מהרה יזומן (ק 121), סליחה

Carpentras, commentary by Josef b. Abraham of Montelitz
15995. New York - Jewish Theological Seminary Ms. 4746, f. 22b, M.
15996. Paris - Alliance Israelite Universelle H 422 A, f. 45a, M.
15997. Paris - Ecole Rabbinique 31, f. 115a-115b, M.

קולי למלך רב יכון בכליל מוקרב (ק 133), ליום כפור

Ashkenaz
15998. Berlin - Staatsbibliothek (Preussischer Kulturbesitz) Or. Qu. 798-799 (Steinschneider 177), I, f. 173a, M.

קוּמָה אֱלֹהִים עֶזְרָתָה. לִי וַעֲנֵה בְצָרָתָה (ק 177), אברהם אבן עזרא, זמר לפורים
Mizrah, commentary by Meir b. Mose Buchritz
15999. Jerusalem - Michael Krupp 2818, f. 2b-4a, M.

קוּמִי וְסִפְדִי תוֹרָה וְעָשׂוּ קִינוֹת זְכִירָה (ק 213), קינה
Yemen, commentary by Isaac b. Abraham Wanneh
16000. London - British Library Or. 11122, f. 105b, M, no incipit.

קוֹרְאֵי מְגִלָּה הֵם יְרַנְּנוּ אֵל אֵל (ק 242), אברהם אבן עזרא, פתיחה לשבת זכור
Carpentras, commentary by Mordekhai b. Josef of Rocco Martino
16001. Cincinnati - Hebrew Union College 246/1, f. 26b-27a, C, rubric: 'פי קוראי מגילה וכו'.
Mizrah, commentary by Meir b. Mose Buchritz
16002. Jerusalem - Michael Krupp 2818, f. 4b-5a, M.
Sepharad, commentary by Josef Garad
16003. Oxford - Bodleian Library Heb.e.10 (Neubauer 2746/1), f. 10a-10b, C, rubric: פזמון לאחר מקרא מגלה.
16004. Oxford - Bodleian Library Heb.e.10 (Neubauer 2746/1), f. 18b-19a, C, rubric: קוראי מגלה, no incipit.

קוֹשְׁטְ שְׁעִינַת עֵץ (ק +245), אלעזר ברבי קליר, חלק ג', קדושתא לסוכות
Ashkenaz
16005. Berlin - Staatsbibliothek (Preussischer Kulturbesitz) Or. Qu. 798-799 (Steinschneider 177), I, f. 198b, M.
16006. Braunschweig - Landesmuseum fuer Geschichte und Volkstum R 2386, vol. I, f. 122b-123a, M.
16007. Budapest - Magyar tudomanyos akademia, MS. Kaufmann A 400, p. 369-370, C, no incipit, short.
16008. Fulda - Hessische Landesbibliothek A 3 II, f. 136a-136b, C, commentator: Josef.
16009. Hamburg - Staats- und Universitaetsbibliothek Cod. hebr. 17/2 (Steinschneider 152), f. 164b, C.
16010. Hamburg - Staats- und Universitaetsbibliothek Cod. hebr. 62 (Steinschneider 154), f. 33b, C, no incipit.
16011. Hamburg - Staats- und Universitaetsbibliothek Cod. hebr. 132 (Steinschneider 155), f. 56a, C.
16012. Jerusalem - Jewish National and University Library Ms Heb 8° 3037, f. 236b, M, no incipit.
16013. Jerusalem - Schocken Institute 24100 / Mahzor Nuremberg, f. 476a-476b, M.
16014. London - British Library Add. 18695 (Margoliouth 683), f. 111b-112a, T, Yiddish.
16015. London - British Library Add. 22431 (Margoliouth 662a), f. 101b, M.

16016. London - British Library Or. 11318/1, f. 130b-131a, C, short.
16017. London - Montefiore Library 261, f. 66a-66b, C, commentator: Eliezer b. Natan?.
16018. Moscow - Russian State Library, Ms. Guenzburg 615, f. 115b, C.
16019. New York - Jewish Theological Seminary Ms. 4466, f. 438a-439a, M, ecclectic.
16020. Oxford - Bodleian Library MS Mich. 365 (Neubauer 1208), f. 95b-96a, C, no incipit.
16021. Oxford - Bodleian Library MS Opp. 170 (Neubauer 1205), f. 187b-188a, C.
16022. Oxford - Bodleian Library MS Opp. 172 (Neubauer 1211), f. 90a, C, short.
16023. Parma - Biblioteca Palatina Cod. Parm. 3205 (de Rossi 655), f. 242a, C, no incipit.
16024. Parma - Biblioteca Palatina Cod. Parm. 3507 (Perreau 27), f. 174a, C, no incipit.
16025. Vatican - Biblioteca Apostolica ebr. 305,1, f. 39a-39b, C, no incipit.
16026. Vatican - Biblioteca Apostolica ebr. 422/1, f. 21b, C, very short.
16027. Zurich - Zentralbibliothek Heid. 139, f. 93a, C, additional marginal notes.

Romania
16028. London - London School of Jewish Studies. Asher I.Myers collection 9, f. 202a, M.
16029. Vatican - Biblioteca Apostolica ebr. 320, f. 411b, M.

Tsarfat
16030. London - David Sofer 5, f. 179a, C.
16031. Oxford - Bodleian Library MS Laud. Or. 271 (Neubauer 1206), f. 97b, C, commentator: Aaron b. Hayyim haKohen (compiler), no incipit, short.
16032. Parma - Biblioteca Palatina Cod. Parm. 1264, f. 27b, M.

קיחת עלית עקד (ק +320), אלעזר ברבי קליר, חלק ג', קדושתא לשבת החדש

Ashkenaz
16033. Berlin - Staatsbibliothek (Preussischer Kulturbesitz) Or. Qu. 798-799 (Steinschneider 177), II, f. 40a-40b, M.
16034. Budapest - Magyar tudomanyos akademia, MS. Kaufmann A 384, f. 89b-90b, M.
16035. Erlangen - Universitaetsbibliothek 2601 (Roth 67), f. 50b, M, only on Ḥatima.
16036. Hamburg - Staats- und Universitaetsbibliothek Cod. hebr. 17/2 (Steinschneider 152), f. 28a, C.
16037. Jerusalem - Schocken Institute 24100 / Mahzor Nuremberg, f. 65a, M.
16038. London - British Library Add. 18695 (Margoliouth 683), f. 3a-3b, T, Yiddish.

16039. Muenchen - Bayerische Staatsbibliothek, Cod. hebr. 88, f. 43b-44a, G.
16040. Muenchen - Bayerische Staatsbibliothek, Cod. hebr. 393, f. 104a-104b, C, no incipit.
16041. New York - Jewish Theological Seminary Ms. 4466, f. 20b-21a, M.
16042. Oxford - Bodleian Library MS Opp. 170 (Neubauer 1205), f. 34a-34b, C.
16043. Paris - Bibliotheque Nationale heb. 709, f. 39b-40b, C.
16044. Parma - Biblioteca Palatina Cod. Parm. 1002 (Ta 24), f. 67b-68a, M.
16045. Parma - Biblioteca Palatina Cod. Parm 3000 (de Rossi 378), f. 20b-21a, M.
16046. Parma - Biblioteca Palatina Cod. Parm. 3205 (de Rossi 655), f. 38b-39a, C, no incipit.
16047. Parma - Biblioteca Palatina Cod. Parm. 3507 (Perreau 27), f. 30b, C.
16048. Vatican - Biblioteca Apostolica ebr. 305,1, f. 25a-25b, C, no incipit.
16049. Zurich - Zentralbibliothek Heid. 139, f. 9a-9b, C, additional marginal notes.

Tsarfat

16050. London - British Library Add. 11639 (Margoliouth 1056), f. 276b-277a, M.
16051. London - David Sofer 5, f. 31a-32a, C.
16052. Moscow - Russian State Library, Ms. Guenzburg 1665, f. 39b, M, no incipit.
16053. Parma - Biblioteca Palatina Cod. Parm. 3136 (de Rossi 405), f. 53b-54a, M.
16054. Vatican - Biblioteca Apostolica ebr. 306, f. 153a-153b, C, no incipit.

קמי קהליך (ק +336), אלעזר ברבי קליר, חלק ג', קדושתא לפסח

Ashkenaz

16055. Berlin - Staatsbibliothek (Preussischer Kulturbesitz) Or. Qu. 798-799 (Steinschneider 177), II, f. 79a, M.
16056. Budapest - Magyar tudomanyos akademia, MS. Kaufmann A 384, f. 163a, M.
16057. Budapest - Magyar tudomanyos akademia, MS. Kaufmann A 400, p. 131-132, C, no incipit.
16058. Hamburg - Staats- und Universitaetsbibliothek Cod. hebr. 17/2 (Steinschneider 152), f. 65a, C.
16059. Jerusalem - Schocken Institute 24100 / Mahzor Nuremberg, f. 94b, M.
16060. London - British Library Add. 18695 (Margoliouth 683), f. 41b, T, Yiddish.
16061. Moscow - Russian State Library, Ms. Guenzburg 615, f. 22b-23a, C.
16062. Muenchen - Bayerische Staatsbibliothek, Cod. hebr. 88, f. 72b, G.
16063. Muenchen - Bayerische Staatsbibliothek, Cod. hebr. 393, f. 130a, C, no incipit.

16064. New York - Jewish Theological Seminary Ms. 4466, f. 74b, M.
16065. Paris - Bibliotheque Nationale heb. 709, f. 98a, C, no incipit.
16066. Parma - Biblioteca Palatina Cod. Parm. 1002 (Ta 24), f. 118a, M, short.
16067. Parma - Biblioteca Palatina Cod. Parm. 3205 (de Rossi 655), f. 102a-102b, C.
16068. Parma - Biblioteca Palatina Cod. Parm. 3507 (Perreau 27), f. 64b-65a, C, no incipit.
16069. Zurich - Zentralbibliothek Heid. 139, f. 37b-38a, C, no incipit, additional marginal notes.

Tsarfat
16070. London - British Library Add. 11639 (Margoliouth 1056), f. 293a, M.
16071. Moscow - Russian State Library, Ms. Guenzburg 1665, f. 71b, M, no incipit.
16072. Oxford - Bodleian Library MS Opp. 171 (Neubauer 1207), f. 41a, C, beginning missing.

קמתי ותדד שנתי להיות כפרה (ק 343), יהודה, סליחה

Yemen
16073. Jerusalem - Benayahu ת 414, f. 116b, M.
16074. Jerusalem - Sassoon 264, f. 139a-139b, M.
16075. New York - Jewish Theological Seminary Ms. 3193, f. 115b-116a, M.

Yemen, commentary by Isaac b. Abraham Wanneh
16076. Chicago-Spertus College of Judaica D 2, 2, f. 178a-178b, M.
16077. Jerusalem - Musad haRav Kook 330, f. 86a-86b, M.
16078. Jerusalem - Musad haRav Kook 347, f. 67b, M.
16079. Jerusalem - Yehiel haLevi 4, f. 130a-130b, M.
16080. London - British Library Or. 11122, f. 154b, M.
16081. Manchester - John Rylands University Library, Ms. Gaster 5, f. 172b-173a, M.
16082. New York - Jewish Theological Seminary Ms. 3013, f. 95b, M, short.
16083. Philadelphia - University of Pennsylvania HB 2, f. 114a, M.

קפאון חוק (ק +++396), אלעזר ברבי קליר, חלק ג', קדושתא לשבת פרה

Ashkenaz
16084. Berlin - Staatsbibliothek (Preussischer Kulturbesitz) Or. Qu. 798-799 (Steinschneider 177), II, f. 33a, M.
16085. Budapest - Magyar tudomanyos akademia, MS. Kaufmann A 384, f. 77a-77b, M.
16086. Hamburg - Staats- und Universitaetsbibliothek Cod. hebr. 17/2 (Steinschneider 152), f. 25a, C.
16087. Jerusalem - Schocken Institute 24100 / Mahzor Nuremberg, f. 61b, M.
16088. Muenchen - Bayerische Staatsbibliothek, Cod. hebr. 88, f. 38b, G.

16089. Muenchen - Bayerische Staatsbibliothek, Cod. hebr. 393 , f. 101a, C, no incipit.
16090. New York - Jewish Theological Seminary Ms. 4466, f. 8b-9a, M.
16091. Oxford - Bodleian Library MS Opp. 170 (Neubauer 1205), f. 29b, C.
16092. Paris - Bibliotheque Nationale heb. 709, f. 36a-36b, C.
16093. Parma - Biblioteca Palatina Cod. Parm. 1002 (Ta 24), f. 55b, M.
16094. Parma - Biblioteca Palatina Cod. Parm. 3000 (de Rossi 378) , f. 14b-15a, M, no incipit.
16095. Parma - Biblioteca Palatina Cod. Parm. 3205 (de Rossi 655) , f. 33b-34a, C.
16096. Parma - Biblioteca Palatina Cod. Parm. 3507 (Perreau 27), f. 27b-28a, C.
16097. Vatican - Biblioteca Apostolica ebr. 305,1, f. 20b-21a, C, no incipit.
16098. Zurich - Zentralbibliothek Heid. 139, f. 5b, C.

Tsarfat

16099. London - British Library Add. 11639 (Margoliouth 1056), f. 275a, M.
16100. Moscow - Russian State Library, Ms. Guenzburg 1665, f. 34a-34b, M, no incipit.
16101. Oxford - Bodleian Library MS Laud. Or. 271 (Neubauer 1206), f. 39b, C, commentator: Aaron b. Hayyim haKohen (compiler).
16102. Oxford - Bodleian Library MS Opp. 171 (Neubauer 1207), f. 36b-37a, C.
16103. Parma - Biblioteca Palatina Cod. Parm. 3136 (de Rossi 405) , f. 48b-49a, M.
16104. Vatican - Biblioteca Apostolica ebr. 306, f. 149b, C, no incipit.

קצובה היא (ק ++398), אלעזר ברבי קליר, חלק ג', קדושתא לשבת שקלים

Ashkenaz

16105. Berlin - Staatsbibliothek (Preussischer Kulturbesitz) Or. Qu. 798-799 (Steinschneider 177), II, f. 13b-14a, M.
16106. Budapest - Magyar tudomanyos akademia, MS. Kaufmann A 384 , f. 38a-38b, M.
16107. Budapest - Magyar tudomanyos akademia, MS. Kaufmann A 400 , p. 4-5, C.
16108. Cambridge - University Library Add. 504,1, f. 3a-4a, C, no incipit.
16109. Jerusalem - Schocken Institute 24100 / Mahzor Nuremberg, f. 35a, M.
16110. Muenchen - Bayerische Staatsbibliothek, Cod. hebr. 88, f. 15b, G.
16111. Muenchen - Bayerische Staatsbibliothek, Cod. hebr. 393 , f. 85a-85b, C, no incipit.
16112. Oxford - Bodleian Library MS Opp. 170 (Neubauer 1205) , f. 4b-5a, C.
16113. Paris - Bibliotheque Nationale heb. 709, f. 5a-6a, C.
16114. Parma - Biblioteca Palatina Cod. Parm. 1002 (Ta 24), f. 24a, M.

16115. Parma - Biblioteca Palatina Cod. Parm. 3205 (de Rossi 655), f. 12a-13a, C.

16116. Parma - Biblioteca Palatina Cod. Parm. 3507 (Perreau 27), f. 3a-4a, C, no incipit.

16117. Vatican - Biblioteca Apostolica ebr. 305,1, f. 3b-4a, C, no incipit.

Tsarfat

16118. London - British Library Add. 11639 (Margoliouth 1056), f. 264b-265a, M.

16119. London - David Sofer 5, f. 10a-10b, C.

16120. Moscow - Russian State Library, Ms. Guenzburg 1665, f. 14a, M, no incipit.

16121. Oxford - Bodleian Library MS Opp. 171 (Neubauer 1207), f. 6b-7a, C.

16122. Parma - Biblioteca Palatina Cod. Parm. 3136 (de Rossi 405), f. 22b-23a, M.

16123. Vatican - Biblioteca Apostolica ebr. 306, f. 158a-158b, C, no incipit.

קצח סגולתך ובית נכותך (ק 399), פיוט אחרי אבינו מלכנו

Carpentras

16124. Cincinnati - Hebrew Union College 429/1, f. 28a-28b, M, no incipit.

Carpentras, commentary by Josef b. Abraham of Montelitz

16125. Cincinnati - Hebrew Union College 357, f. 112a-112b, M, no incipit.

16126. New York - Jewish Theological Seminary Ms. 4746, f. 41b, M, no incipit.

16127. Paris - Alliance Israelite Universelle H 422 A, f. 89a, M, no incipit.

16128. Paris - Ecole Rabbinique 31, f. 151a, M, no incipit.

קראתי מצרה למצא היום רוחה (ק 441), משה אבן עזרא, סליחה

Carpentras, commentary by Josef b. Abraham of Montelitz

16129. Cincinnati - Hebrew Union College 291, f. 52a-53a, C, rubric: פי׳ קראתי מצרה.

16130. New York - Jewish Theological Seminary Ms. 4197, f. 226a-226b, M.

16131. Strasbourg - Bibliotheque Nationale et Universitaire 4081, f. 206b, M.

Sepharad, commentary by David b. Josef Abudarham[348]

16132. Budapest - Magyar tudomanyos akademia, MS. Kaufmann A 405/2, p. 254-255, C, rubric: פזמון.

16133. New York - Columbia X893 Ab 93, f. 31a-31b, C, rubric: פזמון.

Tsarfat

16134. London - David Sofer 5, f. 167b, C, rubric: פזמון.

16135. Parma - Biblioteca Palatina Cod. Parm. 3007 (de Rossi 654,2), f. 146a-146b, M.

---

[348] Edited by Prins, תשלום אבודרהם, p. 129.

ראשו כתם פז (ר +234), שלמה הבבלי, אופן לפסח

Ashkenaz

16136. Berlin - Staatsbibliothek (Preussischer Kulturbesitz) Or. Qu. 798-799 (Steinschneider 177), II, 59b-60b, M.
16137. Braunschweig - Landesmuseum fuer Geschichte und Volkstum R 2386, vol. I, f. 19b, M.
16138. Budapest - Magyar tudomanyos akademia, MS. Kaufmann A 384, f. 126b-127a, M.
16139. Budapest - Magyar tudomanyos akademia, MS. Kaufmann A 400, p. 89-95, C.
16140. Cambridge - University Library Add. 394,1 (Reif SCR 461), f. 52a-52b, C, rubric: אופן.
16141. Hamburg - Staats- und Universitaetsbibliothek Cod. hebr. 17/2 (Steinschneider 152), f. 53a-53b, C, rubric: אופן.
16142. Hamburg - Staats- und Universitaetsbibliothek Cod. hebr. 225, f. 65a, G.
16143. Jerusalem - Schocken Institute 24100 / Mahzor Nuremberg, f. 81a-81b, M.
16144. London - British Library Add. 18695 (Margoliouth 683), f. 23a-23b, T, Yiddish.
16145. Moscow - Russian State Library, Ms. Guenzburg 615, f. 3a-4a, C, rubric: אופן.
16146. Muenchen - Bayerische Staatsbibliothek, Cod. hebr. 21, f. 26a-26b, M.
16147. Muenchen - Bayerische Staatsbibliothek, Cod. hebr. 88, f. 59b-60a, G.
16148. Muenchen - Bayerische Staatsbibliothek, Cod. hebr. 393, f. 121a-122a, C, rubric: אופן, incipit דודי.
16149. New York - Jewish Theological Seminary Ms. 4466, f. 52b-53a, M.
16150. Oxford - Bodleian Library MS Opp. 170 (Neubauer 1205), f. 55a-56b, C, rubric: אופן.
16151. Paris - Bibliotheque Nationale heb. 709, f. 70a-71b, C, rubric: אופן.
16152. Parma - Biblioteca Palatina Cod. Parm. 1002 (Ta 24), f. 90b-91a, M.
16153. Parma - Biblioteca Palatina Cod. Parm. 3205 (de Rossi 655), f. 78b-80a, C.
16154. Parma - Biblioteca Palatina Cod. Parm. 3507 (Perreau 27), f. 46b-47a, C.
16155. Zurich - Zentralbibliothek Heid. 139, f. 25a-25b, C, additional marginal notes.

Italia

16156. Parma - Biblioteca Palatin Cod. Parm. 2248 (de Rossi 149/2), f. 33b-34b, C, rubric: אופן.

Tsarfat

16157. London - British Library Add. 11639 (Margoliouth 1056), f. 288b-289a, M, rubric: אופן.

16158. Moscow - Russian State Library, Ms. Guenzburg 1665, f. 56a-56b, M.

16159. Oxford - Bodleian Library MS Laud. Or. 271 (Neubauer 1206), f. 59a-60a, C, commentator: Aaron b. Hayyim haKohen (compiler), rubric: אופן.

16160. Parma - Biblioteca Palatina Cod. Parm. 3136 (de Rossi 405), f. 79b-80a, M.

16161. Vatican - Biblioteca Apostolica ebr. 306, f. 136a-137a, C.

ראשון אמצת לפרח שושנים (ר 236), אלעזר ברבי קליר, שבעתא לשבת החדש

Ashkenaz

16162. Berlin - Staatsbibliothek (Preussischer Kulturbesitz) Or. Qu. 798-799 (Steinschneider 177), II, f. 43b-45a, M.

16163. Budapest - Magyar tudomanyos akademia, MS. Kaufmann A 384, f. 97a-100a, M.

16164. Erlangen - Universitaetsbibliothek 2601 (Roth 67), f. 53a-54b, M, ecclectic.

16165. Hamburg - Staats- und Universitaetsbibliothek Cod. hebr. 17/2 (Steinschneider 152), f. 29b-30a, C, rubric: שבעתא.

16166. Jerusalem - Schocken Institute 24100 / Mahzor Nuremberg, f. 67a-68a, M.

16167. London - British Library Add. 18695 (Margoliouth 683), f. 7a-8a, T, Yiddish, rubric: צו מוסף.

16168. Muenchen - Bayerische Staatsbibliothek, Cod. hebr. 88, f. 45a-47a, G.

16169. Muenchen - Bayerische Staatsbibliothek, Cod. hebr. 393, f. 105b-106b, C, rubric: שבעתא, no incipit.

16170. New York - Jewish Theological Seminary Ms. 4466, f. 25b-27a, M.

16171. Oxford - Bodleian Library MS Opp. 170 (Neubauer 1205), f. 36b-37b, C, rubric: שבעתא.

16172. Paris - Bibliotheque Nationale heb. 709, f. 43a-44a, C, rubric: שבעתא למוסף.

16173. Parma - Biblioteca Palatina Cod. Parm. 1002 (Ta 24), f. 71b-74a, M.

16174. Parma - Biblioteca Palatina Cod. Parm. 3205 (de Rossi 655), f. 45a-45b, C, rubric: שבעתא לפרש׳ החדש.

16175. Parma - Biblioteca Palatina Cod. Parm. 3507 (Perreau 27), f. 32a-32b, C, rubric: שבעתא.

16176. Zurich - Zentralbibliothek Heid. 139, f. 11a-12a, C, additional marginal notes.

Tsarfat

16177. Oxford - Bodleian Library MS Laud. Or. 271 (Neubauer 1206), f. 49a-49b, C, commentator: Aaron b. Hayyim haKohen (compiler), rubric: שבעתא.

ראשון הוא לתהליך התקופות (ר 237), לשבת החדש

Ashkenaz?
16178. Parma - Biblioteca Palatina Cod. Parm. 3205 (de Rossi 655), f. 43a-43b, C.

ראשון טלה ביכור ביד שכר שיכור (ר 239), דוד ב"ר ידידיה, לחתונה

Sepharad
16179. Vatican - Biblioteca Apostolica ebr. 232, f. 23a-44b, C.

רבונו של עולם בראותי בחורותי (ר 479), שמטוב בן ארדוטיאל בן יצחק, ודוי

Sepharad
16180. Jerusalem - Sassoon 1216, p. 162-168, M, commentator: Mose Nigrin.

רבות עשית וחשבת וספרת (ר +644), אלעזר ברבי קליר, חלק ד', קדושתא לשבת החדש

Ashkenaz
16181. Berlin - Staatsbibliothek (Preussischer Kulturbesitz) Or. Qu. 798-799 (Steinschneider 177), II, f. 41a, M, incipit אל נא.
16182. Budapest - Magyar tudomanyos akademia, MS. Kaufmann A 384, f. 90b, M, incipit אל נא.
16183. Hamburg - Staats- und Universitaetsbibliothek Cod. hebr. 17/2 (Steinschneider 152), f. 28a-28b, C.
16184. Jerusalem - Schocken Institute 24100 / Mahzor Nuremberg, f. 65b, M, incipit אל נא.
16185. London - British Library Add. 18695 (Margoliouth 683), f. 3b, T, Yiddish, incipit אל נא.
16186. Muenchen - Bayerische Staatsbibliothek, Cod. hebr. 88, f. 44a, G.
16187. Muenchen - Bayerische Staatsbibliothek, Cod. hebr. 393, f.104b, C, incipit אל נא.
16188. New York - Jewish Theological Seminary Ms. 4466, f. 21b, M, short.
16189. Oxford - Bodleian Library MS Opp. 170 (Neubauer 1205), f. 34b, C, incipit אל.
16190. Paris - Bibliotheque Nationale heb. 709, f. 40b, C, incipit אל נא.
16191. Parma - Biblioteca Palatina Cod. Parm. 1002 (Ta 24), f. 68a, M, incipit אל נא.
16192. Parma - Biblioteca Palatina Cod. Parm. 3000 (de Rossi 378), f. 21b, M, incipit אל נא.
16193. Parma - Biblioteca Palatina Cod. Parm. 3205 (de Rossi 655), f. 39a-40a, C, incipit אל נא.
16194. Parma - Biblioteca Palatina Cod. Parm. 3507 (Perreau 27), f. 30b, C.
16195. Vatican - Biblioteca Apostolica ebr. 305,1, f. 25b-26a, C, no incipit.

16196. Zurich - Zentralbibliothek Heid. 139, f. 9b, C, additional marginal notes.

Tsarfat

16197. London - David Sofer 5, f. 32a-33b, C, incipit אל נא.
16198. Moscow - Russian State Library, Ms. Guenzburg 1665, f. 40a, M, incipit אל נא.
16199. Oxford - Bodleian Library MS Laud. Or. 271 (Neubauer 1206), f. 46b-47a, C, commentator: Aaron b. Hayyim haKohen (compiler).
16200. Parma - Biblioteca Palatina Cod. Parm. 3136 (de Rossi 405), f. 54a, M, incipit אל נא.
16201. Vatican - Biblioteca Apostolica ebr. 306, f. 153b-154a, C, incipit אל נא.

רומה אלהים שמך לקדש (ר 735), סליחה

Yemen

16202. Jerusalem - Benayahu ת 414, f. 126b, M.
16203. Jerusalem - Sassoon 902, p. 412, M.
16204. New York - Jewish Theological Seminary Ms. 3052, f. 40b-41a, M, rubric: אל מלך.
16205. New York - Jewish Theological Seminary Ms. 4488, f. 107a, G.

Yemen, commentary by Isaac b. Abraham Wanneh

16206. Chicago-Spertus College of Judaica D 2, 2, f. 205a, M, no incipit.
16207. Jerusalem - Benayahu ת 261, f. 142b, M, rubric: אל מלך, short.
16208. Jerusalem - Benayahu ת 282, f. 125b, M, rubric: אל מלך.
16209. Jerusalem - Makhon Ben Zvi 1156 (Tubi 155), f. 124b, M, rubric: אל מלך.
16210. Jerusalem - Makhon Ben Zvi 1174 (Tubi 154), f. 107a, M, rubric: אל מלך.
16211. Jerusalem - Michael Krupp 604, f. 158a-158b, M, rubric: אל מלך.
16212. Jerusalem - Musad haRav Kook 325, f. 157a, M.
16213. Jerusalem - Musad haRav Kook 347, f. 75b, G.
16214. Jerusalem - Sassoon 1158, p. 185, M.
16215. Jerusalem - Sassoon 1174, p. 239, M, no incipit.
16216. Muenchen - Bayerische Staatsbibliothek, Cod. hebr. 472, f. 171a-171b, M, rubric: אל מלך.
16217. New York - Jewish Theological Seminary Ms. 3013, f. 108a, M, rubric: אל מלך.
16218. New York - Jewish Theological Seminary Ms. 3294, f. 2b-3a, C.
16219. New York - Public Library, Heb. Ms. 9, f. 116b, M.
16220. Philadelphia - University of Pennsylvania HB 2, f. 120a, M, rubric: אל מלך.
16221. Strasbourg - Bibliotheque Nationale et Universitaire 3965 (Landauer 39), p. 328, M, rubric: אל מלך.

רוממו אדיר ונורא (ר 741), משולם ב"ר קלונימוס, חלק יט', קדושתא לשחרית יום כפור
Ashkenaz
16222. Berlin - Staatsbibliothek (Preussischer Kulturbesitz) Or. Qu. 798-799 (Steinschneider 177), I, f. 80a, M.
16223. Budapest - Magyar tudomanyos akademia, MS. Kaufmann A 400, p. 319, C.
16224. Hamburg - Staats- und Universitaetsbibliothek Cod. hebr. 62 (Steinschneider 154), f. 6b, C, very short.
16225. Jerusalem - Jewish National and University Library Ms Heb 8° 3037, f. 124b, M, very short.
16226. Jerusalem - Schocken Institute 24100 / Mahzor Nuremberg, f. 380b, M, very short.
16227. London - Montefiore Library 261, f. 45b, C, commentator: Eliezer b. Natan?, very short.
16228. Oxford - Bodleian Library MS Opp. 172 (Neubauer 1211), f. 41b, C, short.
16229. Oxford - Bodleian Library MS Opp. 619 (Neubauer 2374), f. 151b, M, very short.
16230. Vatican - Biblioteca Apostolica ebr. 308, f. 103b, C, commentator: David b. Mose (compiler), very short.
Asti, Fossano, Moncalvo
16231. New Haven - Yale University, Beinecke Rare Book and MS Library, MS Heb. 52, f. 108a, M.
Tsarfat
16232. Oxford - Bodleian Library MS Bodl. Or. 109 (Neubauer 1209), f. 21b, C, commentator: Aaron b. Hayyim haKohen (compiler), very short.
16233. Parma - Biblioteca Palatina Cod. Parm. 2890 (de Rossi 856), f. 31a, M, very short.

רוממו אל מלך נאמן (ר 743), משולם ב"ר קלונימוס, חלק יח', קדושתא לשחרית יום כפור
Ashkenaz
16234. Berlin - Staatsbibliothek (Preussischer Kulturbesitz) Or. Qu. 798-799 (Steinschneider 177), I, f. 79b, M, short.
16235. Budapest - Magyar tudomanyos akademia, MS. Kaufmann A 400, p. 319, C, short.
16236. Hamburg - Staats- und Universitaetsbibliothek Cod. hebr. 17/2 (Steinschneider 152), f. 152b, C.
16237. Hamburg - Staats- und Universitaetsbibliothek Cod. hebr. 62 (Steinschneider 154), f. 6b, C, very short.
16238. Jerusalem - Jewish National and University Library Ms Heb 8° 3037, f. 124a, M, very short.
16239. London - British Library Or. 11318/1, f. 77a-77b, C, very short.

16240. London - Montefiore Library 261, f. 45b, C, commentator: Eliezer b. Natan?, very short.
16241. New York - Jewish Theological Seminary Ms. 8097, f. 72b, C, very short.
16242. Oxford - Bodleian Library MS Opp. 172 (Neubauer 1211), f. 41b, C, very short.
16243. Oxford - Bodleian Library MS Opp. 619 (Neubauer 2374), f. 151a, M, very short.
16244. Parma - Biblioteca Palatina Cod. Parm. 3271 (de Rossi 1216), f. 42b-43a, G.
16245. Vatican - Biblioteca Apostolica ebr. 308, f. 103a, C, commentator: David b. Mose (compiler), very short.

Asti, Fossano, Moncalvo
16246. New Haven - Yale University, Beinecke Rare Book and MS Library, MS Heb. 52, f. 108a, M.

Tsarfat
16247. London - British Library Or. 8682, f. 70a-70b, GI.
16248. Oxford - Bodleian Library MS Bodl. Or. 109 (Neubauer 1209), f. 21b, C, commentator: Aaron b. Hayyim haKohen (compiler), very short.

רוממו ידידים, לשחרית יום כפור

Ashkenaz
16249. Oxford - Bodleian Library MS Mich. 365 (Neubauer 1208), f. 70a, C.

רועה ישראל האזינה נוהג צאן (ר 762), סליחה

Ashkenaz
16250. Braunschweig - Landesmuseum fuer Geschichte und Volkstum R 2386, vol. II, f. 132a, M.
16251. Oxford - Bodleian Library MS Mich. 543 (Neubauer 1212), f. 9a, C, commentator: Isaac b. Jacob (compiler).
16252. Oxford - Bodleian Library MS Opp. 619 (Neubauer 2374), f. 241a, M, short.
16253. Oxford - Bodleian Library MS Opp. 681 (Neubauer 1213), f. 77a, C.
16254. Padova - Biblioteca del Seminario Vescovile Cod. 218, f. 81b-82a, M.
16255. Padova - Biblioteca del Seminario Vescovile Cod. 218, f. 235b-236a, M.
16256. Parma - Biblioteca Palatina Cod. Parm. 3205 (de Rossi 655), f. 271a, C.
16257. Vatican - Biblioteca Apostolica ebr. 422/1, f. 31b, C, short.

רחום וחנון חטאנו לפניך רחם עלינו אדון הסליחות בוחן הלבבות (ר 805), סליחה
Yemen
16258. Jerusalem - Benayahu ת 88, f. 119a, M.

Yemen, commentary by Isaac b. Abraham Wanneh
16259. Chicago-Spertus College of Judaica D 2, 2, f. 181b, M.

רחום כמאז כונן נסיך (ר 809), יוצר ליום ב' של ראש השנה

Carpentras
16260. Cincinnati - Hebrew Union College 429/1, f. 20a, M, no incipit, very short.

Carpentras, commentary by Josef b. Abraham of Montelitz
16261. Cincinnati - Hebrew Union College 357, f. 96b, M.
16262. Paris - Ecole Rabbinique 31, f. 135b, M.

רחמיך בקשנו ממך כי רבים רחמים עמך, סליחה

Yemen, commentary by Isaac b. Abraham Wanneh
16263. Chicago-Spertus College of Judaica D 2, 2, f. 184b, M, short.

רחמיך שאלתי וכלו לישעך עיני (ר 836), יהודה הלוי, סליחה

Yemen
16264. Jerusalem - Sassoon 902, p. 394, M.
16265. New York - Jewish Theological Seminary Ms. 3052, f. 16b-18a (f. 17b empty), M, rubric: אל מלך.
16266. New York - Jewish Theological Seminary Ms. 3109, f. 89b, M.

Yemen, commentary by Isaac b. Abraham Wanneh
16267. Chicago-Spertus College of Judaica D 2, 2, f. 197b-198a, M, no incipit.
16268. Jerusalem - Benayahu ת 261, f. 132a-132b, M, rubric: אל מלך.
16269. Jerusalem - Benayahu ת 282, f. 117a-117b, M, rubric: אל מלך, no incipit.
16270. Jerusalem - Makhon Ben Zvi 1156 (Tubi 155), f. 115a-115b, M, rubric: אל מלך.
16271. Jerusalem - Makhon Ben Zvi 1174 (Tubi 154), f. 118a, M.
16272. Jerusalem - Michael Krupp 604, f. 145a-145b, M, rubric: אל מלך.
16273. Jerusalem - Musad haRav Kook 325, f. 171a, M, rubric: אל מלך.
16274. Jerusalem - Musad haRav Kook 330, f. 103a, G.
16275. Jerusalem - Musad haRav Kook 347, f. 79b, G.
16276. Jerusalem - Sassoon 1158, p. 361, M, rubric: אל מלך.
16277. Jerusalem - Sassoon 1174, p. 221-222, M, no incipit.
16278. London - British Library Or. 11122, f. 179b-180a, M.
16279. London - British Library Or. 11122, f. 180a-180b, M, rubric: אל מלך.
16280. Manchester - John Rylands University Library, Ms. Gaster 5, f. 190b-191a, M.
16281. Muenchen - Bayerische Staatsbibliothek, Cod. hebr. 472, f. 156a-156b, M, rubric: אל מלך.

16282. New York - Jewish Theological Seminary Ms. 3013, f. 116a, M, rubric: אל מלך, incipit זהלתי.
16283. New York - Jewish Theological Seminary Ms. 3109, f. 90a, M, rubric: אל מלך.
16284. New York - Public Library, Heb. Ms. 9, f. 111b, M.
16285. Philadelphia - University of Pennsylvania HB 2, f. 129a, M, incipit זהלתי.
16286. Strasbourg - Bibliotheque Nationale et Universitaire 3965 (Landauer 39), p. 357, M, rubric: אל מלך.

רחמנא אדכר לן קיימיה דאברהם (ר 841), סליחה

Sepharad
16287. Skokie - Hebrew Theological College 3, f. 6b-7a, M.
16288. Skokie - Hebrew Theological College 3, f. 2.16b, M.
Yemen
16289. Jerusalem - Benayahu ת 88, f. 113b, M.
Yemen, commentary by Isaac b. Abraham Wanneh
16290. Jerusalem - Benayahu ת 88, f. 178b-179a, M.

רחמנא אתרצי לן רחמנא ברכתך איתי לן (ר 844), סליחה

Yemen
16291. New York - Jewish Theological Seminary Ms. 3052, f. 69a-70b, M.
Yemen, commentary by Isaac b. Abraham Wanneh
16292. Jerusalem - Makhon Ben Zvi 1156 (Tubi 155), f. 134a-134b, M, no incipit.
16293. Jerusalem - Makhon Ben Zvi 1174 (Tubi 154), f. 131b, M.
16294. Jerusalem - Musad haRav Kook 325, f. 189a, M.
16295. Muenchen - Bayerische Staatsbibliothek, Cod. hebr. 472, f. 186b-187a, M.
16296. New York - Jewish Theological Seminary Ms. 3013, f. 128a, M.
16297. New York - Jewish Theological Seminary Ms. 3294, f. 14b-15a, C.

רחמנא דעני לעניי ענינא (ר +845), סליחה

Ashkenaz
16298. London - British Library Add. 18695 (Margoliouth 683), f. 170b, T, Yiddish.
16299. Padova - Biblioteca del Seminario Vescovile Cod. 218, f. 53a, M.

רחמנא רחים על עמך ישראל דאנון קימין קמך בתחנונא וצלו (ר 854), סליחה

Yemen
16300. New York - Jewish Theological Seminary Ms. 3052, f. 78a-78b, M.
Yemen, commentary by Isaac b. Abraham Wanneh

16301. Chicago-Spertus College of Judaica D 2, 2, f. 233a-233b, M, no incipit.
16302. Chicago-Spertus College of Judaica D 2, 2, f. 235a-235b, M, no incipit.
16303. Chicago-Spertus College of Judaica D 2, 2, f. 235b, M, no incipit.
16304. Jerusalem - Benayahu ת 261, f. 163b-164a, M.
16305. Jerusalem - Benayahu ת 282, f. 139a-139b, M.
16306. Jerusalem - Michael Krupp 604, f. 173b-174a, M.
16307. Jerusalem - Yehiel haLevi 4, f. 180a, G.
16308. Muenchen - Bayerische Staatsbibliothek, Cod. hebr. 472, f. 190b-191a, M.
16309. New York - Jewish Theological Seminary Ms. 3013, f. 131a, M.
16310. Strasbourg - Bibliotheque Nationale et Universitaire 3965 (Landauer 39), p. 403, M.

רחמנא רחים על עמך ישראל רחמנא דאפיקתא יתהון בחילך (ר 855), סליחה
Yemen, commentary by Isaac b. Abraham Wanneh
16311. Chicago-Spertus College of Judaica D 2, 2, f. 234b-235a, M, no incipit.

רחמנא רחים על עמך ישראל דתלן לך עינין, סליחה
Yemen
16312. Jerusalem - Benayahu ת 414, f. 164a, M.

רכב תפארתו רעש בהגלותו (ר 886), דוד חווא רן גדליה, אופן לשבועות
Ashkenaz
16313. New York - Jewish Theological Seminary Ms. 4466, f. 163b-164b, M, ecclectic.
16314. Parma - Biblioteca Palatina Cod. Parm. 3205 (de Rossi 655), f. 127a, C, rubric: אופן, short, incipit תוכן.

רמאני עיטמוס מן פוק וכרה, שלם שבזי
Yemen
16315. Cincinnati - Hebrew Union College 398, f. 217a-218b, M.

רנתי לפניך צור תערב ותשפרק (ר 954), סליחה
Carpentras, commentary by Mordekhai b. Josef of Rocco Martino
16316. Cincinnati - Hebrew Union College 246/1, f. 81a-82a, C, rubric: פי' סליחה רינתי לפניך.

רעה בשבטך עם יקוה פדיום (ר 965), משה אבן עזרא, לראש השנה
Carpentras
16317. Cincinnati - Hebrew Union College 429/1, f. 17b, M, no incipit.

Carpentras, commentary by Josef b. Abraham of Montelitz

16318. Cincinnati - Hebrew Union College 357, f. 91a, M, rubric: פירוש, no incipit.
16319. New York - Jewish Theological Seminary Ms. 4746, f. 26b, M, no incipit.
16320. Paris - Alliance Israelite Universelle H 422 A, f. 61a-61b, M, no incipit.
16321. Paris - Ecole Rabbinique 31, f. 131a-131b, M, no incipit.

רצה רנת מתיחדים ותהיה למנחה חשובה (ר 1029), יהודה הלוי, סליחה
Yemen, commentary by Isaac b. Abraham Wanneh

16322. Chicago-Spertus College of Judaica D 2, 2, f. 218a, M, no incipit.
16323. Jerusalem - Sassoon 1158, p. 369, M, rubric: אל מלך, no incipit.
16324. London - British Library Or. 11122, f. 184b, M, no incipit.

שאגת אריה וקול שחל ולביא (ש 14), שאלתיאל בן לוי, גאולה
Ashkenaz

16325. Oxford - Bodleian Library MS Opp. 169 (Neubauer 1151), f. 20a, M, no incipit.

שאו מנחה משבחה ביום מנוחה התשירו (ש 33), מנחם ב"ר מכיר, אופן לשבת נחמו
Ashkenaz

16326. Berlin - Staatsbibliothek (Preussischer Kulturbesitz) Or. Qu. 798-799 (Steinschneider 177), I, f. 253a-254b, M.
16327. Budapest - Magyar tudomanyos akademia, MS. Kaufmann A 399, p. 429-432, C, rubric: אופן.
16328. Budapest - Magyar tudomanyos akademia, MS. Kaufmann A 399, p. 439-440, C, rubric: אופן שלו.
16329. Cambridge - University Library Add. 504,1, f. 47b-49a, C, rubric: אופן.
16330. Jerusalem - Schocken Institute 24100 / Mahzor Nuremberg, f. 220b-221a, M.
16331. Lund - Universitetsbibliothek Ms. L.O. 2, f. 107a-107b, M.
16332. Muenchen - Bayerische Staatsbibliothek, Cod. hebr. 69, f. 60b-61b, M.
16333. Muenchen - Bayerische Staatsbibliothek, Cod. hebr. 393,9, f. 169a-171b, C, rubric: אופן.
16334. Oxford - Bodleian Library MS Can. Or. 82 (Neubauer 1148), f. 31a-31b, M.
16335. Oxford - Bodleian Library MS Mich. 365 (Neubauer 1208), f. 31a-32a, C, rubric: אופן נחמו.
16336. Parma - Biblioteca Palatina Cod. Parm. 2895, p. 405-407, M, rubric: אופן.

16337. Parma - Biblioteca Palatina Cod. Parm. 3205 (de Rossi 655), f. 158b-159b, C, rubric: אופן.
16338. Vatican - Biblioteca Apostolica ebr. 318, f. 116b-117b, GI.
Ashkenaz, commentary by Abraham b. Azriel[349]
16339. Frankfurt a M - Stadt- und Universitaetsbibliothek Fol. 16 (Merzbacher 95), f. 13b-16b, C, rubric: אופן.
16340. Vatican - Biblioteca Apostolica ebr. 301,1, f. 46a-48b, C, rubric: אופן.
Ashkenaz, commentary by Eliezer b. Natan
16341. Hamburg - Staats- und Universitaetsbibliothek Cod. hebr. 61 (Steinschneider 153), f. 37b-38b, C, rubric: אופן משבת נחמו.
16342. Parma - Biblioteca Palatina Cod. Parm. 3057.12 (de Rossi 1033/10), f. 142a-143a, C, rubric: הכל יודוך אופן.

שאו נא עיניכם אל אלהיכם, סליחה
Yemen
16343. New York - Jewish Theological Seminary Ms. 3052, f. 83a, M, no incipit.
Yemen, commentary by Isaac b. Abraham Wanneh
16344. Chicago-Spertus College of Judaica D 2, 2, f. 237b, M, no incipit.
16345. Jerusalem - Benayahu ת 282, f. 140b-141a, M, no incipit.
16346. Jerusalem - Makhon Ben Zvi 1174 (Tubi 154), f. 136b, M.
16347. Jerusalem - Michael Krupp 604, f. 175b, M, no incipit.
16348. London - British Library Or. 11122, f. 214b-215a, M, no incipit.
16349. New York - Jewish Theological Seminary Ms. 3013, f. 133a, M, no incipit.
16350. New York - Jewish Theological Seminary Ms. 3294, f. 17a, C.
16351. Strasbourg - Bibliotheque Nationale et Universitaire 3965 (Landauer 39), p. 410, M.

שאי אל אל עיניך, סליחה
Tsarfat
16352. Vatican - Biblioteca Apostolica ebr. 306, f. 211b, C.

שאי קינה במגינה בת ציון ונודי (ש 65), שמואל, קינה
Yemen, commentary by Isaac b. Abraham Wanneh
16353. London - British Library Or. 11122, f. 100a-100b, M, no incipit.

שאלו שחקים ושיחו לאדמה (ש 98), שלמה אבן גבירול, אופן לשבת בראשית
Ashkenaz
16354. Jerusalem - Schocken Institute 24100 / Mahzor Nuremberg, f. 8b, M.

---
[349] Edited by Urbach, ערוגת הבושם, vol. I, p. 281-296.

Ashkenaz, commentary by Abarahm b. Azriel[350]
16355. Frankfurt a M - Stadt- und Universitaetsbibliothek Fol. 16 (Merzbacher 95), f. 52a-52b, C, rubric: אופן.
16356. Vatican - Biblioteca Apostolica ebr. 301,1, f. 81a-81b, C, rubric: אופן.
Tsarfat
16357. Parma - Biblioteca Palatina Cod. Parm. 1264, f. 164b, M.

שארית אום נעצבת לפניך נצבת (ש 150), שלמה אבן גבירול, סליחה
Carpentras, commentary by Mordekhai b. Josef of Rocco Martino
16358. Cincinnati - Hebrew Union College 246/1, f. 86a-86b, C, rubric: פי'
סליחה שארית אום.

שבוית מרום לקחה כהיום (ויקם עדות ביעקב) (ש 178), שמעון ב"ר יחק, חלק ה',
קדושתא לשבועות
Ashkenaz
16359. Berlin - Staatsbibliothek (Preussischer Kulturbesitz) Or. Qu. 798-799 (Steinschneider 177), II, f. 117b-118a, M, incipit ויקם.
16360. Braunschweig - Landesmuseum fuer Geschichte und Volkstum R 2386, vol. I, f. 74b-75b, M.
16361. Budapest - Magyar tudomanyos akademia, MS. Kaufmann A 400, p. 156, C, commentator: Ephraim b. Jacob of Bonn, short.
16362. Hamburg - Staats- und Universitaetsbibliothek Cod. hebr. 17/2 (Steinschneider 152), f. 82b, C.
16363. Jerusalem - Schocken Institute 24100 / Mahzor Nuremberg, f. 148a-148b, M.
16364. London - British Library Add. 18695 (Margoliouth 683), f. 66b-67a, T, Yiddish.
16365. London - British Library Add. 22431 (Margoliouth 662a), f. 10a-11a, M, no incipit.
16366. Moscow - Russian State Library, Ms. Guenzburg 615, f. 31b-32b, C, incipit ויקם.
16367. Muenchen - Bayerische Staatsbibliothek, Cod. hebr. 88, f. 117b-118a, G.
16368. New York - Jewish Theological Seminary Ms. 4466, f. 128b-129a, M, ecclectic, short.
16369. Paris - Bibliotheque Nationale heb. 709, f. 121b-122a, C.
16370. Parma - Biblioteca Palatina Cod. Parm. 1002 (Ta 24), f. 179a, M, very short.
16371. Parma - Biblioteca Palatina Cod. Parm. 3205 (de Rossi 655), f. 121a, C, incipit ויקם, short.

---

[350] Edited by Urbach, ערוגת הבושם, vol. II, p. 209-212.

16372. Parma - Biblioteca Palatina Cod. Parm. 3507 (Perreau 27), f. 98a-98b, C, incipit ויקם.

16373. Zurich - Zentralbibliothek Heid. 139, f. 50b, C, short, incipit ויקם.
Tsarfat

16374. London - David Sofer 5, f. 51a-51b, C, commentary on refrain in smaller script before commentary.

16375. Moscow - Russian State Library, Ms. Guenzburg 1665, f. 118b-119a, M.

16376. Parma - Biblioteca Palatina Cod. Parm. 3136 (de Rossi 405), f. 150a-151a, M, partly bleached.

16377. Vatican - Biblioteca Apostolica ebr. 306, f. 230a-230b, C, no incipit.

שבועה קבועה פנה נא אליה (ש 180), שלמה אבן גבירול, סליחה
Yemen

16378. Jerusalem - Sassoon 902, p. 422, M.

Yemen, commentary by Isaac b. Abraham Wanneh

16379. Chicago-Spertus College of Judaica D 2, 2, f. 213b, M, no incipit.

16380. Jerusalem - Sassoon 1158, p. 378-379, M, rubric: שלמה 'סים. אל מלך.

16381. London - British Library Or. 11122, f. 189b, M, no incipit.

שבח אומרים בני אמוני (ש 186), שלם שבזי
Yemen

16382. Cincinnati - Hebrew Union College 398, f. 156a-157b, M.

שׂרה אל חי אשר ברא לכל חי ומלכותו עדי נצח נצחים (ש 190), שלם שבזי
Yemen

16383. Cincinnati - Hebrew Union College 398, f. 219a-219b, M.

שבח מי יגמור ליוצר אור לאמֹר (ש 226), שמואל דוולין החזן, נשמת לחתן
Ashkenaz

16384. Oxford - Bodleian Library MS Can. Or. 82 (Neubauer 1148), f. 48b, M.

שבח נותנים כל צבא מרום לעלוֹ (ש 227), מרדכי, נשמת לשבת ברית מילה
Ashkenaz

16385. Oxford - Bodleian Library MS Can. Or. 70 (Neubauer 1147,7), f. 83a-83b, M, rubric: אחרת.

שבחי יגונך נפש הומיה, סליחה
Yemen, commentary by Isaac b. Abraham Wanneh

16386. Chicago-Spertus College of Judaica D 2, 2, f. 222b-223a, M, no incipit.

16387. Jerusalem - Sassoon 1158, p. 381, M, no incipit.

16388. London - British Library Or. 11122, f. 190b-191a, M, rubric: אל מלך.

שבט יהודה בדוחק ובצער (ש +260), שמעיה, סליחה

Sepharad
16389. Jerusalem - Benayahu ז 25, f. 187b-188a, M, no incipit.
Yemen
16390. Jerusalem - Benayahu ת 88, f. 112b, M.
Yemen, commentary by Isaac b. Abraham Wanneh
16391. Chicago-Spertus College of Judaica D 2, 2, f. 178b, M.

שבטי יה הוצאת לפדיום (ש 262), שמעון ב"ר יצחק, חלק ג', קדושתא לפסח

Ashkenaz
16392. Berlin - Staatsbibliothek (Preussischer Kulturbesitz) Or. Qu. 798-799 (Steinschneider 177), II, f. 102b-103a, M.
16393. Budapest - Magyar tudomanyos akademia, MS. Kaufmann A 384, f. 234b-235a, M.
16394. Erlangen - Universitaetsbibliothek 2601 (Roth 67), f. 133a, M.
16395. Hamburg - Staats- und Universitaetsbibliothek Cod. hebr. 17/2 (Steinschneider 152), f. 38b-39a, C, commentator: Ephraim b. Jacob of Bonn.
16396. Jerusalem - Schocken Institute 24100 / Mahzor Nuremberg, f. 109b, M, very short.
16397. London - British Library Add. 18695 (Margoliouth 683), f. 55b-56b, T, Yiddish.
16398. Muenchen - Bayerische Staatsbibliothek, Cod. hebr. 88, f. 95b-96a, G.
16399. New York - Jewish Theological Seminary Ms. 4466, f. 90a-90b, M.
16400. Paris - Bibliotheque Nationale heb. 709, f. 108a, C, no incipit.
16401. Parma - Biblioteca Palatina Cod. Parm. 1002 (Ta 24), f. 158a, M.
16402. Parma - Biblioteca Palatina Cod. Parm. 3205 (de Rossi 655), f. 114b, C, no incipit.
16403. Parma - Biblioteca Palatina Cod. Parm. 3507 (Perreau 27), f. 79a-79b, C, no incipit.
16404. Zurich - Zentralbibliothek Heid. 139, f. 42b, C, additional marginal notes.
Tsarfat
16405. London - David Sofer 5, f. 46a, C.
16406. Moscow - Russian State Library, Ms. Guenzburg 1665, f. 105b, M.
16407. Oxford - Bodleian Library MS Laud. Or. 271 (Neubauer 1206), f. 76b, C, commentator: Ephraim b. Jacob of Bonn (mainly), Aaron b. Hayyim haKohen (compiler).
16408. Parma - Biblioteca Palatina Cod. Parm. 3136 (de Rossi 405), f. 124a-124b, M.

שבטי שעשוע בכל מאוים (ש 265), שלמה הבבלי, סליחה

Ashkenaz

16409. Oxford - Bodleian Library MS Mich. 543 (Neubauer 1212), f. 76a-76b, C, commentator: Isaac b. Jacob (compiler).

Ashkenaz, commentary by Abraham b. Azriel[351]

16410. Frankfurt a M - Stadt- und Universitaetsbibliothek Fol. 16 (Merzbacher 95), f. 112b, C.

16411. Vatican - Biblioteca Apostolica ebr. 301,1, f. 147a-147b, C, rubric: אחרת.

Tsarfat

16412. London - British Library Add. 11639 (Margoliouth 1056), f. 476a-476b, M.

16413. London - David Sofer 5, f. 95b-96a, C.

16414. Oxford - Bodleian Library MS Laud. Or. 271 (Neubauer 1206), f. 128b, C, commentator: Aaron b. Hayyim haKohen (compiler).

16415. Parma - Biblioteca Palatina Cod. Parm. 3007 (de Rossi 654,2), f. 122a, M.

16416. Vatican - Biblioteca Apostolica ebr. 306, f. 207a-207b, C.

שבטי שעשוע כי יאיר, סליחה

Tsarfat

16417. Oxford - Bodleian Library MS Opp. 171 (Neubauer 1207), f. 97a-97b, C, rubric: אחרת.

שביבי שלהרוח החזורי להרוח (ש 271?), שמעון ב"ר יצחק, אופן לחתן

Ashkenaz

16418. Berlin - Staatsbibliothek (Preussischer Kulturbesitz) Or. Qu. 798-799 (Steinschneider 177), I, f. 264a-264b, M.

16419. Budapest - Magyar tudomanyos akademia, MS. Kaufmann A 399, p. 353, C, rubric: אופן לחתן.

16420. Lund - Universitetsbibliothek Ms. L.O. 2, f. 111a, M.

16421. Muenchen - Bayerische Staatsbibliothek, Cod. hebr. 393,9, f. 183b-184a, C, no incipit.

Ashkenaz, commentary by Abraham b. Azriel[352]

16422. Frankfurt a M - Stadt- und Universitaetsbibliothek Fol. 16 (Merzbacher 95), f. 94b-95b, C, rubric: אופן אחר.

---

[351] Edited by Urbach, ערוגת הבושם, vol. III, p. 342-344.
[352] Edited by Urbach, ערוגת הבושם, vol. III, p. 535-539.

שביה עניה בארץ נכריה (ש 273), שלמה אבן גבירול, גאולה
Ashkenaz
16423. Jerusalem - Schocken Institute 24100 / Mahzor Nuremberg , f. 133b, M.
16424. Oxford - Bodleian Library MS Opp. 169 (Neubauer 1151), f. 17a-17b, M.
Ashkenaz, commentary by Abraham b. Azriel[353]
16425. Vatican - Biblioteca Apostolica ebr. 301,1, f. 12a-12b, C, rubric: גאולה.

שבים אליך בכל לב שועתם (ש 275), סליחה
Sepharad
16426. Skokie - Hebrew Theological College 3, f. 5a, G.

שבעה שחקים לא יכלכלוך (ש 285), שלמה אבן גבירול, לקדיש
Ashkenaz
16427. Berlin - Staatsbibliothek (Preussischer Kulturbesitz) Or. Qu. 798-799 (Steinschneider 177), I, f. 262b, M.

שבעת ימים קודם ליום הכפורים (ש 287), סדר עבודה
Sepharad
16428. Oxford - Bodleian Library MS Reggio 63/3 (Neubauer 1081/3), f. 341a-374b, M, not next to the Seder Avoda, incomplete.

שבת הכסא אשר למעלה מנשא (ש 313), שמעון ב"ר יצחק, סליחה
Ashkenaz
16429. Budapest - Magyar tudomanyos akademia, MS. Kaufmann A 400, p. 528-529, C, rubric: פירוש תחנון אחר.
16430. Hamburg - Staats- und Universitaetsbibliothek Cod. hebr. 17/2 (Steinschneider 152), f. 145a, C.
16431. Muenchen - Bayerische Staatsbibliothek, Cod. hebr. 346, f. 118a, C.
16432. Oxford - Bodleian Library MS Mich. 543 (Neubauer 1212), f. 80a-80b, C, commentator: Isaac b. Jacob (compiler).
16433. Padova - Biblioteca del Seminario Vescovile Cod. 218, f. 145b, M, rubric: אחרת.
16434. Parma - Biblioteca Palatina Cod. Parm. 3205 (de Rossi 655), f. 284b, C, short.
16435. Vatican - Biblioteca Apostolica ebr. 422/1, f. 34b, C, short.
Tsarfat
16436. London - David Sofer 5, f. 96a-96b, C.

---

[353] Edited by Urbach, ערוגת הבושם, vol. I, p. 78-79.

16437. Oxford - Bodleian Library MS Opp. 171 (Neubauer 1207), f. 89b, C, rubric: אחרת.

שבת מנוחה היא לבני סגולה (ש 330), שלם שבזי
Yemen
16438. Cincinnati - Hebrew Union College 398, f. 154b-156a, M.

שבת מששי ורבו יגוני גבר שוסי ועצמו מוני (ש 336), שלמה אבן גבירול, תחנון
Yemen
16439. Jerusalem - Sassoon 902, p. 425, M.
Yemen, commentary by Isaac b. Abraham Wanneh
16440. Chicago-Spertus College of Judaica D 2, 2, f. 212b, M, no incpit.
16441. Chicago-Spertus College of Judaica D 2, 2, f. 246b-247a, M, no incipit.
16442. Jerusalem - Sassoon 1158, p. 380-381, M, no incpit.
16443. Jerusalem - Sassoon 1158, p. 425, M, no incipit.
16444. London - British Library Or. 11122, f. 190b, M, no incpit.
16445. London - British Library Or. 11122, f. 220a, M, no incipit.
16446. Manchester - John Rylands University Library, Ms. Gaster 5, f. 199b, M.

שבת סורו מני (ש 337), אלעזר ברבי קליר, מחלקה שניה, קרובה לט' באב
Ashkenaz
16447. Berlin - Staatsbibliothek (Preussischer Kulturbesitz) Or. Qu. 798-799 (Steinschneider 177), II, f. 185a-186a, M, later hand, margins cut.
16448. Budapest - Magyar tudomanyos akademia, MS. Kaufmann A 400, p. 200-205, C, rubric: סדר הקינה.
16449. Hamburg - Staats- und Universitaetsbibliothek Cod. hebr. 17/2 (Steinschneider 152), f. 93b-94b, C, rubric: פירוש הקינה.
16450. Hamburg - Staats- und Universitaetsbibliothek Cod. hebr. 233, f. 71a-71b, G.
16451. Jerusalem - Schocken Institute 24100 / Mahzor Nuremberg, f. 194b-195a, M.
16452. Muenchen - Bayerische Staatsbibliothek, Cod. hebr. 88, f. 163a-164b, G.
16453. Oxford - Bodleian Library MS Can. Or. 70 (Neubauer 1147,8), f. 111a-112b, M.
16454. Oxford - Bodleian Library MS Opp. 170 (Neubauer 1205), f. 266b-268a, C, rubric: ולפי שאין אומרין יותר בתפילה ולא סדר הפייט שיסד אאביך כי יום עד העי"ן . מתחיל כאן באלפא ביתא של קינות בסמ"ך ובזכור יי עד איכה ישן'.
16455. Parma - Biblioteca Palatina Cod. Parm. 2886 (de Rossi 585), f. 114b-115a, M, later hand, margins cut.
16456. Vatican - Biblioteca Apostolica ebr. 312, f. 43a-43b, G.

16457. Vatican - Biblioteca Apostolica ebr. 318, f. 225b-226b, GI. Ashkenaz, commentary by Abraham b. Azriel[354]

16458. Vatican - Biblioteca Apostolica ebr. 301,1, f. 133b-134a, C.

שבתי וראה תחת השמש (ש 348), שמעון ב"ר יצחק, חלק ז', קדושתא לראש השנה
Ashkenaz

16459. Berlin - Staatsbibliothek (Preussischer Kulturbesitz) Or. Qu. 798-799 (Steinschneider 177), I, f. 39a-40a, M.
16460. Bologna - Archivio di Stato MS Ebr. 353, f. 4, FC, incomplete, only beginning.
16461. Braunschweig - Landesmuseum fuer Geschichte und Volkstum R 2386, vol. II, f. 113a-113b, M.
16462. Darmstadt - Hessisches Landes- und Hochschulbibliothek Cod. Or. 15, f. 37b-38a, M.
16463. Hamburg - Staats- und Universitaetsbibliothek Cod. hebr. 40c (Steinschneider 111), f. 150b-151b, G.
16464. Hamburg - Staats- und Universitaetsbibliothek Cod. hebr. 132 (Steinschneider 155), f. 25a-25b, C.
16465. Hamburg - Staats- und Universitaetsbibliothek Cod. hebr. 225, f. 259a-261a, G.
16466. Jerusalem - Jewish National and University Library Ms Heb 8° 3037, f. 56a-57a, M.
16467. Jerusalem - Schocken Institute 24100 / Mahzor Nuremberg, f. 343b-344a, M.
16468. London - British Library Or. 11318/1, f. 43a-44a, C.
16469. London - Montefiore Library 261, f. 29a-30a, C, commentator: Eliezer b. Natan?.
16470. Moscow - Russian State Library, Ms. Guenzburg 191, f. 38a-39b, M.
16471. Muenchen - Bayerische Staatsbibliothek, Cod. hebr. 21, f. 180b-181a, M.
16472. Muenchen - Bayerische Staatsbibliothek, Cod. hebr. 86, f. 70a-71b, G.
16473. Muenchen - Bayerische Staatsbibliothek, Cod. hebr. 346, f. 36b-37a, C.
16474. Muenchen - Bayerische Staatsbibliothek, Cod. hebr. 346, f. 89a-89b, C, rubric: ליום שיני דראש השנה.
16475. New York - Jewish Theological Seminary Ms. 4466, f. 255a-256a, M.
16476. New York - Jewish Theological Seminary Ms. 8097, f. 66a-67a, C.
16477. Oxford - Bodleian Library MS Mich. 365 (Neubauer 1208), f. 51a-52a, C.
16478. Oxford - Bodleian Library MS Opp. 172 (Neubauer 1211), f. 23a-23b, C.

---

[354] Edited by Urbach, ערוגת הבושם, vol. III, p. 256-260.

16479. Oxford - Bodleian Library MS Opp. 619 (Neubauer 2374), f. 63a-64a, M.
16480. Oxford - Bodleian Library MS Opp. 675 (Neubauer 1210), f. 52b-53b, C, no incipit.
16481. Paris - Bibliotheque Nationale heb. 653, f. 31a-32a, G.
16482. Parma - Biblioteca Palatina Cod. Parm. 3205 (de Rossi 655), f. 217b-218a, C.
16483. Parma - Biblioteca Palatina Cod. Parm. 3270 (de Rossi 1215), f. 57b-58a, M.
16484. Parma - Biblioteca Palatina Cod. Parm. 3507 (Perreau 27), f. 133a-134a, C.
16485. Vatican - Biblioteca Apostolica ebr. 308, f. 77b-79a, C, commentator: David b. Mose (compiler).
16486. Vatican - Biblioteca Apostolica ebr. 422/1, f. 13a, C, incipit הן.
16487. Zurich - Zentralbibliothek Heid. 139, f. 103a, C, commentator: Elazar b. Yehuda of Worms, no incipit, very short.
Tsarfat
16488. London - David Sofer 5, f. 124a-124b, C.
16489. Oxford - Bodleian Library MS Laud. Or. 271 (Neubauer 1206), f. 157b, C, commentator: Aaron b. Hayyim haKohen (compiler), rubric: שבתי, no incipit.

שגאני בארך אלקבלה, שלם שבזי

Yemen
16490. Cincinnati - Hebrew Union College 398, f. 166a-167b, M.

שדודים נדודים לציון תקבץ (ש 358), שלמה אבן גבירול, גאולה

Ashkenaz
16491. Oxford - Bodleian Library MS Opp. 169 (Neubauer 1151), f. 19a-19b, M.
Ashkenaz, commentary by Abraham b. Azriel[355]
16492. Vatican - Biblioteca Apostolica ebr. 301,1, f. 19a, C, rubric: גאולה.
Yemen
16493. Jerusalem - Benayahu ת 301, f. 51b, G.
16494. Jerusalem - Sassoon 902, p. 425, M.
16495. New York - Jewish Theological Seminary Ms. 3028, f. 36b, G.
Yemen, commentary by Isaac b. Abraham Wanneh
16496. New York - Jewish Theological Seminary Ms. 3013, f. 125b, M, rubric: אל מלך.

---

[355] Edited by Urbach, ערוגת הבושם, vol. I, p. 117-118.

שה פזורה ישראל (ש 442), שמואל, סליחה
Yemen, commentary by Isaac b. Abraham Wanneh
16497. Philadelphia - University of Pennsylvania HB 2, f. 120a-120b, M, the piyyut is not written near the commentary, instead there is ביום זה בראש השנה שברנו לבבינו, which has no commentary.

שואף כמו עבר שאף ליד דבו (ש 461), שלמה אבן גבירול, רשות לנשמת
Carpentras
16498. Cincinnati - Hebrew Union College 429/1, f. 2b, M, no incipit.
Carpentras, commentary by Eliyahu Carmi
16499. Cincinnati - Hebrew Union College 357, f. 37a-37b, M, rubric: תנא ר' אליהו.
16500. New York - Jewish Theological Seminary Ms. 3151, f. 31b, M.
Carpentras, commentary by Josef b. Abraham of Montelitz
16501. Cincinnati - Hebrew Union College 357, f. 37a-37b, M.
16502. New York - Jewish Theological Seminary Ms. 4746, f. 5a-5b, M.
16503. Paris - Alliance Israelite Universelle H 422 A, f. 10a-10b, M.
16504. Paris - Ecole Rabbinique 31, f. 81a-81b, M.

שובה למעונך ושכון בבית מאויך (ש 500), הושענא
Yemen, commentary by Samḥun b. Salomo Ḥaloah
16505. Jerusalem - Makhon ben Zvi 2808, f. 30b-31a, C.

שובי נפשי למנוחיכי (ש 536), שמואל כהן, סליחה
Yemen
16506. Jerusalem - Benayahu ת 414, f. 136b, M.
16507. Jerusalem - Sassoon 902, p. 391, M, short.
16508. Jerusalem - Yehiel haLevi 4, f. 149a, G.
16509. New York - Jewish Theological Seminary Ms. 3052, f. 14b-15a, M, rubric: אל מלך.
Yemen, commentary by Isaac b. Abraham Wanneh
16510. Chicago-Spertus College of Judaica D 2, 2, f. 193a, M.
16511. Jerusalem - Benayahu ת 282, f. 116a-116b, M, rubric: אל מלך.
16512. Jerusalem - Makhon Ben Zvi 1156 (Tubi 155), f. 114a, M, rubric: אל מלך.
16513. Jerusalem - Makhon Ben Zvi 1174 (Tubi 154), f. 116a, M, no incipit.
16514. Jerusalem - Michael Krupp 604, f. 144a, M, rubric: אל מלך.
16515. Jerusalem - Musad haRav Kook 325, f. 168a, M, rubric: אל מלך.
16516. Jerusalem - Musad haRav Kook 330, f. 99a, G.
16517. Jerusalem - Musad haRav Kook 347, f. 78b, G.
16518. Jerusalem - Sassoon 1158, p. 340, M, no incipit.
16519. Jerusalem - Sassoon 1174, p. 219-220, M.
16520. London - British Library Or. 11122, f. 168b, M.

16521. Manchester - John Rylands University Library, Ms. Gaster 5, f. 189a, M.
16522. Muenchen - Bayerische Staatsbibliothek, Cod. hebr. 472, f. 154b-155a, M, rubric: אל מלך.
16523. New York - Jewish Theological Seminary Ms. 3013, f. 114b, M, rubric: אל מלך.
16524. New York - Jewish Theological Seminary Ms. 3109, f. 83a, M, rubric: פירוש.
16525. New York - Jewish Theological Seminary Ms. 3294, f. 8b, C.
16526. New York - Public Library, Heb. Ms. 9, f. 110b, M.
16527. Strasbourg - Bibliotheque Nationale et Universitaire 3965 (Landauer 39), p. 351, M, rubric: אל מלך.

שובי נפשי לקונך (ש 540), יוסף בן סולי, תוכחה
Sepharad, commentary by David b. Josef Abudarham[356]
16528. Budapest - Magyar tudomanyos akademia, MS. Kaufmann A 405/2, p. 243, C, rubric: תוכחה.
16529. New York - Columbia X893 Ab 93, f. 26b-27a, C, rubric: 'תוכחה לר יצחק גיאת ז"ל.

שוכני בתי חומר (ש 632), שלמה אבן גבירול, תוכחה
Sepharad, commentary by David b. Josef Abudarham[357]
16530. Budapest - Magyar tudomanyos akademia, MS. Kaufmann A 405/2, p. 258, C, rubric: תוכחה, short.
16531. Holon - Yehuda Nahum 278, f. 1b, FC, rubric: תוכחה, short.
16532. New York - Columbia X893 Ab 93, f. 32b, C, rubric: תוכחה, short.
Tsarfat
16533. London - David Sofer 5, f 105a, C.
16534. Parma - Biblioteca Palatina Cod. Parm. 3006 (de Rossi 654,1), f. 118b-119a, M.

שולחתי במלאכות (ש 641), שמעון ב"ר יצחק, חלק ג', קדושתא לראש השנה
Ashkenaz
16535. Berlin - Staatsbibliothek (Preussischer Kulturbesitz) Or. Qu. 798-799 (Steinschneider 177), I, f. 36a-37a, M.
16536. Braunschweig - Landesmuseum fuer Geschichte und Volkstum R 2386, vol. II, f. 111a-111b, M, no incipit.
16537. Darmstadt - Hessisches Landes- und Hochschulbibliothek Cod. Or. 15, f. 35a, M, ecclectic.

---

[356] Edited by Prins, תשלום אבודרהם, p. 109-110.
[357] Edited by Prins, תשלום אבודרהם, p. 137-138.

16538. Hamburg - Staats- und Universitaetsbibliothek Cod. hebr. 17/2 (Steinschneider 152), f. 122a, C.
16539. Hamburg - Staats- und Universitaetsbibliothek Cod. hebr. 40b (Steinschneider 110), f. 40b-41a, G.
16540. Hamburg - Staats- und Universitaetsbibliothek Cod. hebr. 40c (Steinschneider 111), f. 147b-148b, G.
16541. Hamburg - Staats- und Universitaetsbibliothek Cod. hebr. 132 (Steinschneider 155), f. 24a-24b, C, incipit במלאכות.
16542. Hamburg - Staats- und Universitaetsbibliothek Cod. hebr. 225, f. 253b-255a, G.
16543. Jerusalem - Jewish National and University Library Ms Heb 8° 3037, f. 53a-53b, M.
16544. Jerusalem - Schocken Institute 24100 / Mahzor Nuremberg, f. 341b-342a, M.
16545. London - British Library Or. 11318/1, f. 40b-41a, C.
16546. London - Montefiore Library 261, f. 28a, C, commentator: Eliezer b. Natan?.
16547. Moscow - Russian State Library, Ms. Guenzburg 191, f. 35b-36a, M.
16548. Moscow - Russian State Library, Ms. Guenzburg 615, f. 86a-86b, C, short.
16549. Muenchen - Bayerische Staatsbibliothek, Cod. hebr. 21, f. 179a-179b, M.
16550. Muenchen - Bayerische Staatsbibliothek, Cod. hebr. 86, f. 64a-65b, GI.
16551. Muenchen - Bayerische Staatsbibliothek, Cod. hebr. 346, f. 35b-36a, C.
16552. New York - Jewish Theological Seminary Ms. 4466, f. 251b, M, short.
16553. New York - Jewish Theological Seminary Ms. 8097, f. 65b, C.
16554. New York - Jewish Theological Seminary Ms. 8169 (Acc. 0016), f. 34b-35b, M.
16555. Oxford - Bodleian Library MS Mich. 365 (Neubauer 1208), f. 50a, C.
16556. Oxford - Bodleian Library MS Opp. 170 (Neubauer 1205), f. 143b-144a, C.
16557. Oxford - Bodleian Library MS Opp. 172 (Neubauer 1211), f. 21a-22a, C.
16558. Oxford - Bodleian Library MS Opp. 619 (Neubauer 2374), f. 59a-60a, M, short.
16559. Oxford - Bodleian Library MS Opp. 675 (Neubauer 1210), f. 50b-51a, C.
16560. Parma - Biblioteca Palatina Cod. Parm. 3205 (de Rossi 655), f. 217a, C, no incipit.
16561. Parma - Biblioteca Palatina Cod. Parm. 3507 (Perreau 27), f. 132a-132b, C, no incipit.

16562. Vatican - Biblioteca Apostolica ebr. 308, f. 75b-76a, C, commentator: David b. Mose (compiler).
16563. Vatican - Biblioteca Apostolica ebr. 422/1, f. 12b, C.
16564. Zurich - Zentralbibliothek Heid. 139, f. 70b-71a, C, no incipit, short, additional marginal notes.
16565. Zurich - Zentralbibliothek Heid. 139, f. 103a, C, commentator: Elazar b. Yehuda of Worms, no incipit, very short.

Asti, Fossano, Moncalvo

16566. New Haven - Yale University, Beinecke Rare Book and MS Library, MS Heb. 52, f. 53a-53b, M.

Romania

16567. Vatican - Biblioteca Apostolica ebr. 320, f. 181b-182a, M.

Tsarfat

16568. London - British Library Or. 8682, f. 36b-37a, GI.
16569. London - David Sofer 5, f. 120a-120b, C.
16570. Oxford - Bodleian Library MS Laud. Or. 271 (Neubauer 1206), f. 157a, C, commentator: Aaron b. Hayyim haKohen (compiler), no incipit.
16571. Oxford - Bodleian Library MS Opp. 171 (Neubauer 1207), f. 67b, C.
16572. Parma - Biblioteca Palatina Cod. Parm. 2125 (de Rossi 812), f. 30a, C, short.
16573. Parma - Biblioteca Palatina Cod. Parm. 3006 (de Rossi 654,1), f. 69b-70b, M, additional commentary on the margins.
16574. Vatican - Biblioteca Apostolica ebr. 306, f. 66b-67a, C, no incipit.

שולמית בלי מרמית למולך תפי לתחנה (ש 642), שלמה, סליחה

Yemen

16575. Jerusalem - Sassoon 902, p. 426, M.

Yemen, commentary by Isaac b. Abraham Wanneh

16576. Chicago-Spertus College of Judaica D 2, 2, f. 212b-213a, M, no incipit.
16577. Jerusalem - Sassoon 1158, p. 381, M, no incipit.
16578. London - British Library Or. 11122, f. 190b, M, no incipit.
16579. Manchester - John Rylands University Library, Ms. Gaster 5, f. 201b, M.

שולמית יספה שועה ותישר (ש 647), שלמה אבן גבירול, קדושתא למוסף יום כפור

Sepharad, commentary by David b. Josef Abudarham[358]

16580. Budapest - Magyar tudomanyos akademia, MS. Kaufmann A 405/2, p. 240-241, C, rubric: מגן לר' שלמה ן' גיבירול תנצב"ה.

---

[358] Edited by Prins, תשלום אבודרהם, p. 74-75.

16581. New York - Columbia X893 Ab 93, f. 25b-26a, C, rubric: מגן לר' שלמה ן' גיבירול ז"ל.

שוממתי ברוב יגוני (ש 665), שלמה אבן גבירול, תוכחה
Ashkenaz
16582. Jerusalem - Schocken Institute 24100 / Mahzor Nuremberg, f. 249b, M, one later marginal note only.
16583. Muenchen - Bayerische Staatsbibliothek, Cod. hebr. 346, f. 146b-147a, C, rubric: אחרת.
16584. Oxford - Bodleian Library MS Opp. 681 (Neubauer 1213), f. 67a-67b, C.
16585. Padova - Biblioteca del Seminario Vescovile Cod. 218, f. 150a-150b, M.
16586. Vatican - Biblioteca Apostolica ebr. 308, f. 14a-14b, C, commentator: David b. Mose (compiler).

Sepharad, commentary by David b. Josef Abudarham[359]
16587. Budapest - Magyar tudomanyos akademia, MS. Kaufmann A 405/2, p. 239-240, C, rubric: תוכחה לר' שלמה ן' גיבירול ז"ל.
16588. New York - Columbia X893 Ab 93, f. 25b, C, rubric: תוכחה לר' שלמה ן' גיבירול ז"ל.

שומע תפלה עדיך (ש 661), מאיר, סדר רחמים
Yemen
16589. New York - Jewish Theological Seminary Ms. 3052, f. 67b-69a, M, rubric: סדר הרחמים.

Yemen, commentary by Isaac b. Abraham Wanneh
16590. Chicago-Spertus College of Judaica D 2, 2, f. 231b, M, rubric: סדר הרחמים.
16591. Jerusalem - Benayahu ת 261, f. 159b-162a, M, rubric: סדר הרחמים.
16592. Jerusalem - Benayahu ת 282, f. 135a-137b, M, rubric: סדר הרחמים.
16593. Jerusalem - Makhon Ben Zvi 1156 (Tubi 155), f. 133b-134a, M, rubric: פירוש סדר רחמים.
16594. Jerusalem - Makhon Ben Zvi 1174 (Tubi 154), f. 130b, M.
16595. Jerusalem - Sassoon 1158, p. 403-413, M.
16596. Muenchen - Bayerische Staatsbibliothek, Cod. hebr. 472, f. 185b-186b, M, rubric: פירוש סדר רחמים.
16597. New York - Jewish Theological Seminary Ms. 3294, f. 14b, C, rubric: פירוש סדר רחמים.

---

[359] Edited by Prins, תשלום אבודרהם, p. 72-73.

שומר ישראל שמור שארית ישראל ואל יאבד ישראל (ש 673), סליחה
Yemen, commentary by Isaac b. Abraham Wanneh
16598. Chicago-Spertus College of Judaica D 2, 2, f. 185b, M, very short.
16599. Chicago-Spertus College of Judaica D 2, 2, f. 230b, M, no incipit.

שומרון קול חתן מצאוני עוני לארץ אחרת (ש 686), שלמה אבן גבירול, קינה
Ashkenaz
16600. Muenchen - Bayerische Staatsbibliothek, Cod. hebr. 88, f. 162a-163a, G, ecclectic.
Yemen, commentary by Isaac b. Abraham Wanneh
16601. London - British Library Or. 11122, f. 103a, M.

שופט כל ארץ ואותה במשפט (ש 712), שלמה, סליחה
Ashkenaz
16602. Berlin - Staatsbibliothek (Preussischer Kulturbesitz) Or. Qu. 798-799 (Steinschneider 177), I, f. 104a-104b, M.
16603. Cambridge - University Library Add. 394,1 (Reif SCR 461), f. 96b, C, very short.
16604. Jerusalem - Schocken Institute 24100 / Mahzor Nuremberg, f. 401a-401b, M.
16605. London - British Library Add. 18695 (Margoliouth 683), f. 166b-167a, T, Yiddish.
16606. Moscow - Russian State Library, Ms. Guenzburg 190, f. 61b, G.
16607. Muenchen - Bayerische Staatsbibliothek, Cod. hebr. 346, f. 143a-143b, C, rubric; אחרת
16608. New York - Jewish Theological Seminary Ms. 4466, f. 348a-348b, M.
16609. Oxford - Bodleian Library MS Mich. 543 (Neubauer 1212), f. 10b, C, commentator: Isaac b. Jacob (compiler), short.
16610. Oxford - Bodleian Library MS Opp. 172 (Neubauer 1211), f. 58a, C.
16611. Oxford - Bodleian Library MS Opp. 619 (Neubauer 2374), f. 185a-185b, M, short.
16612. Oxford - Bodleian Library MS Opp. 681 (Neubauer 1213), f. 77b-78a, C.
16613. Padova - Biblioteca del Seminario Vescovile Cod. 218, f. 108a-109a, M.
16614. Padova - Biblioteca del Seminario Vescovile Cod. 218, f. 185a-185b, M.
16615. Vatican - Biblioteca Apostolica ebr. 308, f. 115a, C, commentator: David b. Mose (compiler).
16616. Vatican - Biblioteca Apostolica ebr. 422/1, f. 31b, C, very short.

Ashkenaz, commentary by Abraham b. Azriel[360]

16617. Frankfurt a M - Stadt- und Universitaetsbibliothek Fol. 16 (Merzbacher 95), f. 106a, C.

16618. Vatican - Biblioteca Apostolica ebr. 301,1, f. 169b-170a, C.

Carpentras

16619. Cincinnati - Hebrew Union College 392, f. 28b, M.

North Africa, commentary by David b. Josef Abudarham

16620. New York - Jewish Theological Seminary Ms. 5426, f. 61a-61b, M.

Tsarfat

16621. London - David Sofer 5, f. 145a, C, rubric: פזמון.

16622. Parma - Biblioteca Palatina Cod. Parm. 2890 (de Rossi 856), f. 60a, M.

16623. Parma - Biblioteca Palatina Cod. Parm. 3006 (de Rossi 654,1), f. 157a-157b, M.

16624. Vatican - Biblioteca Apostolica ebr. 306, f. 208a, C, short.

Yemen

16625. Jerusalem - Sassoon 902, p. 422, M, short.

16626. New York - Jewish Theological Seminary Ms. 3052, f. 37b, M, rubric: אל מלך.

Yemen, commentary by Isaac b. Abraham Wanneh

16627. Chicago-Spertus College of Judaica D 2, 2, f. 203b-204a, M, no incipit.

16628. Jerusalem - Benayahu ת 261, f. 141b, M, rubric: אל מלך, short.

16629. Jerusalem - Benayahu ת 282, f. 124a-124b, M, rubric: אל מלך.

16630. Jerusalem - Makhon Ben Zvi 1156 (Tubi 155), f. 123b, M, rubric: אל מלך, short.

16631. Jerusalem - Makhon Ben Zvi 1174 (Tubi 154), f. 128a, M, short.

16632. Jerusalem - Michael Krupp 604, f. 157a, M, rubric: אל מלך, short.

16633. Jerusalem - Musad haRav Kook 325, f. 185a, M, rubric: אל מלך, short.

16634. Jerusalem - Sassoon 1158, p. 185, M, rubric: אל מלך.

16635. Jerusalem - Sassoon 1158, p. 379, M, no incipit.

16636. Jerusalem - Sassoon 1174, p. 237-238, M, no incipit.

16637. Jerusalem - Yehiel haLevi 4, f. 166b, G.

16638. London - British Library Or. 11122, f. 189b, M, rubric: אל מלך.

16639. Muenchen - Bayerische Staatsbibliothek, Cod. hebr. 472, f. 169b, M, rubric: אל מלך, short.

16640. New York - Jewish Theological Seminary Ms. 3013, f. 124a, M, rubric: אל מלך, short.

16641. New York - Jewish Theological Seminary Ms. 3294, f. 12b, C.

16642. New York - Public Library, Heb. Ms. 9, f. 114a, M, short.

---

[360] Edited by Urbach, ערוגת הבושם, vol. III, p. 494-495.

16643. Strasbourg - Bibliotheque Nationale et Universitaire 3965 (Landauer 39), p. 386, M, rubric: אל מלך, short.

שוקלי דמם (ש 723), שלמה, גאולה
Ashkenaz, commentary by Abraham b. Azriel[361]
16644. Frankfurt a M - Stadt- und Universitaetsbibliothek Fol. 16 (Merzbacher 95), f. 95b, C, rubric: גאולה.

שור אשר מאז עלי עופר (ש 727), אלעזר ברבי קליר, חלק ה', קדושתא לפסח
Ashkenaz
16645. Muenchen - Bayerische Staatsbibliothek, Cod. hebr. 88, f. 73b-74a, G.
16646. Parma - Biblioteca Palatina Cod. Parm. 3507 (Perreau 27), f. 65a-66a, C, additional incipit ואמרתם.

שושן עמק אוימה (ש 765), אלעזר ברבי קליר, קדושתא למוסף יום כפור
Ashkenaz
16647. Berlin - Staatsbibliothek (Preussischer Kulturbesitz) Or. Qu. 798-799 (Steinschneider 177), I, f. 115a-116a, M.
16648. Braunschweig - Landesmuseum fuer Geschichte und Volkstum R 2386, vol. II, f. 224a, M.
16649. Budapest - Magyar tudomanyos akademia, MS. Kaufmann A 400, p. 351-352, C.
16650. Cambridge - University Library Add. 394,1 (Reif SCR 461), f. 68a-68b, C.
16651. Cambridge - University Library Add. 394,2.3, f. 1a-1b, C.
16652. Fulda - Hessische Landesbibliothek A 3 II, f. 121b-122a, C, commentator: Josef, rubric: קרובה למוסף.
16653. Hamburg - Staats- und Universitaetsbibliothek Cod. hebr. 17/2 (Steinschneider 152), f. 157a-157b, C, rubric: למוסף יום הכיפורים דר' אלעזר.
16654. Hamburg - Staats- und Universitaetsbibliothek Cod. hebr. 40c (Steinschneider 111), f. 211a, G.
16655. Hamburg - Staats- und Universitaetsbibliothek Cod. hebr. 62 (Steinschneider 154), f. 16b, C, rubric: פסומל הבורק, end missing.
16656. Hamburg - Staats- und Universitaetsbibliothek Cod. hebr. 132 (Steinschneider 155), f. 43a-43b, C.
16657. Jerusalem - Jewish National and University Library Ms Heb 8° 3037, f. 174a-174b, M.
16658. Jerusalem - Schocken Institute 24100 / Mahzor Nuremberg, f. 408b-409a, M.
16659. London - British Library Or. 11318/1, f. 97b-99a, C.

---

[361] Edited by Urbach, ערוגת הבושם, vol. III, p. 539-541.

16660. London - Montefiore Library 261, f. 53b-54a, C, commentator: Eliezer b. Natan?, rubric: מוסף.
16661. Moscow - Russian State Library, Ms. Guenzburg 191, f. 113b-114a, M.
16662. Moscow - Russian State Library, Ms. Guenzburg 615, f. 102a-102b, C, rubric: למוסף.
16663. Muenchen - Bayerische Staatsbibliothek, Cod. hebr. 21, f. 218a, M.
16664. Muenchen - Bayerische Staatsbibliothek, Cod. hebr. 346, f. 73b-74a, C, rubric: מוסף.
16665. New York - Jewish Theological Seminary Ms. 4466, f. 365a-366a, M.
16666. New York - Jewish Theological Seminary Ms. 8097, f. 77b, C.
16667. New York - Jewish Theological Seminary Ms. 8169 (Acc. 0016), f. 88a-88b, M.
16668. Oxford - Bodleian Library MS Mich. 365 (Neubauer 1208), f. 80a-80b, C, rubric: למוסף.
16669. Oxford - Bodleian Library MS Opp. 170 (Neubauer 1205), f. 174a-174b, C, rubric: והא לך תפילת מוסף.
16670. Oxford - Bodleian Library MS Opp. 172 (Neubauer 1211), f. 59a-59b, C, rubric: למוסף.
16671. Oxford - Bodleian Library MS Opp. 619 (Neubauer 2374), f. 201a-201b, M.
16672. Paris - Bibliotheque Nationale heb. 653, f. 86a, G.
16673. Parma - Biblioteca Palatina Cod. Parm. 3205 (de Rossi 655), f. 233a-233b, C, rubric: למוסף.
16674. Parma - Biblioteca Palatina Cod. Parm. 3270 (de Rossi 1215), f. 164a-164b, M.
16675. Parma - Biblioteca Palatina Cod. Parm. 3271 (de Rossi 1216), f. 102a-102b, G.
16676. Parma - Biblioteca Palatina Cod. Parm. 3507 (Perreau 27), f. 161a-161b, C, rubric: למוסף.
16677. Vatican - Biblioteca Apostolica ebr. 308, f. 116b, C, commentator: David b. Mose (compiler), rubric: אתחיל לכתו׳ פירוש מתפילת מוסף.
16678. Vatican - Biblioteca Apostolica ebr. 422/1, f. 17b-18a, C, short.
16679. Zurich - Zentralbibliothek Heid. 139, f. 82a-82b, C, additional marginal notes.

Roma

16680. Berlin - Staatsbibliothek (Preussischer Kulturbesitz) Or. Oct. 3567, f. 5a-5b, FC.
16681. Jerusalem - Jewish National and University Library Ms Heb 8° 4153, f. 138b-139a, C, commentator: Daniel ben Salomo haRofe (compiler), rubric: פי׳ שושן עמק.
16682. New York - Jewish Theological Seminary Ms. 1639, f. 24b-25a, C, commentator: Salomo b. Samuel Rofe.

16683. Oxford - Bodleian Library MS Mich. 312,1 (Neubauer 2276,1), f. 5b-6a, C.

Romania

16684. Vatican - Biblioteca Apostolica ebr. 320, f. 315b-316a, M.

Tsarfat

16685. London - British Library Or. 8682, f. 81a-81b, GI.

16686. London - David Sofer 5, f. 150a, C, rubric: מוסף.

16687. Oxford - Bodleian Library MS Bodl. Or. 109 (Neubauer 1209), f. 29a-29b, C, commentator: Aaron b. Hayyim haKohen (compiler).

16688. Oxford - Bodleian Library MS Laud. Or. 271 (Neubauer 1206), f. 114a-114b, C, commentator: Aaron b. Hayyim haKohen (compiler), rubric: רשות לקדושתא.

16689. Oxford - Bodleian Library MS Opp. 171 (Neubauer 1207), f. 117a-118a, C.

16690. Parma - Biblioteca Palatina Cod. Parm. 1794 (de Rossi 1061), f. 155b-156b, M.

16691. Parma - Biblioteca Palatina Cod. Parm. 2890 (de Rossi 856), f. 68b-69a, M.

16692. Parma - Biblioteca Palatina Cod. Parm. 3006 (de Rossi 654,1), f. 177b-178a, M.

16693. Vatican - Biblioteca Apostolica ebr. 306, f. 102b-103a, C, rubric: סדר מוסף.

שושנת ורד בין חוחים גדוליה (ש 771), שמואל, פתיחה

Ashkenaz

16694. Muenchen - Bayerische Staatsbibliothek, Cod. hebr. 346, f. 149b, C, rubric: אחרת.

16695. Vatican - Biblioteca Apostolica ebr. 308/1, f. 3b-4a, C, commentator: David b. Mose (compiler).

Ashkenaz, commentary by Abraham b. Azriel[362]

16696. Frankfurt a M - Stadt- und Universitaetsbibliothek Fol. 16 (Merzbacher 95), f. 103a, C.

16697. Vatican - Biblioteca Apostolica ebr. 301,1, f. 169a, C.

שזופי פליטי אפופי עיטי (ש 775), שלמה אבן גבירול, חלק ב', קדושתא למנחה יום פכור

Sepharad, commentary by David b. Josef Abudarham[363]

16698. Budapest - Magyar tudomanyos akademia, MS. Kaufmann A 405/2, p. 248-250, C, rubric: מחיה לר' שלמה ן' גבירול ז"ל.

---

[362] Edited by Urbach, ערוגת הבושם, vol. III, p. 491-492.
[363] Edited by Prins, תשלום אבודרהם, p. 118-120.

16699. New York - Columbia X893 Ab 93, f. 29a-30a, C, rubric: 'מחיה לר
שלמה גיבירול ז"ל.

שחורה ונאוה כאהלי קדר (ש 793), שלמה אבן גבירול, גאולה, בתימן: סליחה
Yemen
16700. Jerusalem - Sassoon 902, p. 422-423, M.
16701. New York - Jewish Theological Seminary Ms. 3052, f. 37b-38b, M, rubric: אל מלך.
Yemen, commentary by Isaac b. Abraham Wanneh
16702. Chicago-Spertus College of Judaica D 2, 2, f. 210a, M, no incipit.
16703. Jerusalem - Benayahu ת 261, f. 141b-142a, M, rubric: אל מלך.
16704. Jerusalem - Benayahu ת 282, f. 124b, M, rubric: אל מלך.
16705. Jerusalem - Makhon Ben Zvi 1156 (Tubi 155), f. 123b-124a, M, rubric: אל מלך.
16706. Jerusalem - Makhon Ben Zvi 1174 (Tubi 154), f. 128a, M.
16707. Jerusalem - Michael Krupp 604, f. 157a-157b, M, rubric: אל מלך.
16708. Jerusalem - Musad haRav Kook 325, f. 185b, M, rubric: אל מלך.
16709. Jerusalem - Sassoon 1158, p. 379, M, no incipit.
16710. Jerusalem - Sassoon 1174, p. 238, M, no incipit.
16711. Jerusalem - Yehiel haLevi 4, f. 167a, G.
16712. London - British Library Or. 11122, f. 190a, M, no incipit.
16713. Manchester - John Rylands University Library, Ms. Gaster 5, f. 199b-200a, M.
16714. Muenchen - Bayerische Staatsbibliothek, Cod. hebr. 472, f. 169b-170a, M, rubric: אל מלך.
16715. New York - Jewish Theological Seminary Ms. 3013, f. 124a, M, rubric: אל מלך.
16716. New York - Jewish Theological Seminary Ms. 3294, f. 12b, C.
16717. New York - Public Library, Heb. Ms. 9, f. 114b, M.
16718. Strasbourg - Bibliotheque Nationale et Universitaire 3965 (Landauer 39), p. 386-387, M, rubric: אל מלך.

שחותי ונדכיתי ולבי זחל (ש 798), שלמה בן יהודה גיאת, סליחה
Carpentras, commentary by Mordekhai b. Josef of Rocco Martino
16719. Cincinnati - Hebrew Union College 246/1, f. 88a-89b, C, rubric: 'פי
רההוטה שחותי וכו'.

שחר קדמתי מדרך לא סרתי, סליחה
Tsarfat
16720. London - David Sofer 5, f. 174b, C, rubric: פזמון.

שחר קמתי להודות (ש 849), שלמה אבן גבירול, סליחה

Ashkenaz
16721. Braunschweig - Landesmuseum fuer Geschichte und Volkstum R 2386, vol. II, f. 140a, M.
16722. Cambridge - University Library Add. 394,1 (Reif SCR 461), f. 96b, C, short.
16723. Moscow - Russian State Library, Ms. Guenzburg 190, f. 62a-62b, G.
16724. Oxford - Bodleian Library MS Mich. 543 (Neubauer 1212), f. 9b-10a, C, commentator: Isaac b. Jacob (compiler), short.
16725. Oxford - Bodleian Library MS Opp. 681 (Neubauer 1213), f. 77a, C, short.
16726. Padova - Biblioteca del Seminario Vescovile Cod. 218, f. 132b, M, very short.
16727. Vatican - Biblioteca Apostolica ebr. 308/1, f. 11a-11b, C, commentator: David b. Mose (compiler).

Romania
16728. Vatican - Biblioteca Apostolica ebr. 320, f. 304a-304b, M, short.

Tsarfat
16729. London - David Sofer 5, f. 106a, C.
16730. Parma - Biblioteca Palatina Cod. Parm. 2890 (de Rossi 856), f. 49a-49b, M.
16731. Parma - Biblioteca Palatina Cod. Parm. 3006 (de Rossi 654,1), f. 158b, M.
16732. Vatican - Biblioteca Apostolica ebr. 306, f. 208b, C.

Yemen
16733. Jerusalem - Sassoon 902, p. 421, M, short.
16734. New York - Jewish Theological Seminary Ms. 3028, f. 35b, G.
16735. New York - Jewish Theological Seminary Ms. 3052, f. 37a-37b, M, rubric: אל מלך.

Yemen, commentary by Isaac b. Abraham Wanneh
16736. Chicago-Spertus College of Judaica D 2, 2, f. 203b, M, very short, no incipit.
16737. Jerusalem - Benayahu ת 261, f. 141b, M, rubric: אל מלך, short.
16738. Jerusalem - Benayahu ת 282, f. 124a, M, rubric: אל מלך, short.
16739. Jerusalem - Makhon Ben Zvi 1156 (Tubi 155), f. 123a-123b, M, rubric: אל מלך, short.
16740. Jerusalem - Makhon Ben Zvi 1174 (Tubi 154), f. 127b, M, short.
16741. Jerusalem - Michael Krupp 604, f. 157a, M, rubric: אל מלך, short.
16742. Jerusalem - Musad haRav Kook 325, f. 185a, M, rubric: אל מלך, short.
16743. Jerusalem - Sassoon 1158, p. 379, M, rubric: אל מלך.
16744. Jerusalem - Sassoon 1174, p. 237, M, short.
16745. London - British Library Or. 11122, f. 189b, M, rubric: אל מלך.
16746. Manchester - John Rylands University Library, Ms. Gaster 5, f. 199a-199b, M.

16747. Muenchen - Bayerische Staatsbibliothek, Cod. hebr. 472, f. 169b, M, rubric: אל מלך, short.
16748. New York - Jewish Theological Seminary Ms. 3013, f. 123b-124a, M, rubric: אל מלך, short.
16749. New York - Jewish Theological Seminary Ms. 3294, f. 12a, M.
16750. New York - Public Library, Heb. Ms. 9, f. 114a, M, short.
16751. Strasbourg - Bibliotheque Nationale et Universitaire 3965 (Landauer 39), p. 386, M, rubric: אל מלך, short.

שחרנוך בקשנוך יוצר הרים (ש 861), שמואל ב"ר אברהם, סליחה

Ashkenaz
16752. Hamburg - Staats- und Universitaetsbibliothek Cod. hebr. 17/2 (Steinschneider 152), f. 145b, C, rubric: אחרת.
16753. Klosterneuburg - Stiftsbibliothek St. Augustini 271, FC, incomplete.
16754. Muenchen - Bayerische Staatsbibliothek, Cod. hebr. 346, f. 119a, C, very short.
16755. Oxford - Bodleian Library MS Mich. 543 (Neubauer 1212), f. 5b, C, commentator: Isaac b. Jacob (compiler), short.
16756. Padova - Biblioteca del Seminario Vescovile Cod. 218, f. 146a, M, short.
16757. Vatican - Biblioteca Apostolica ebr. 308/1, f. 4a, C, commentator: David b. Mose (compiler).

Ashkenaz, commentary by Abraham b. Azriel[364]
16758. Frankfurt a M - Stadt- und Universitaetsbibliothek Fol. 16 (Merzbacher 95), f. 103a, C, short.
16759. Vatican - Biblioteca Apostolica ebr. 301,1, f. 169a, C, short.

שטפוני דמעותי ונגרו עלי עיני (ש 880), שמריה, סליחה

Yemen
16760. Jerusalem - Sassoon 902, p. 441, M.

Yemen, commentary by Isaac b. Abraham Wanneh
16761. Chicago-Spertus College of Judaica D 2, 2, f. 196a, M.
16762. Jerusalem - Michael Krupp 604, f. 146b, M, rubric: אל מלך.
16763. Jerusalem - Sassoon 1158, p. 359, M, no incipit.
16764. London - British Library Or. 11122, f. 179a, M.

שטר עלי בעדים (ש 881), שלמה אבן גבירול, תוכחה

Ashkenaz
16765. Oxford - Bodleian Library MS Opp. 681 (Neubauer 1213), f. 6b-7a, C.

---

[364] Edited by Urbach, ערוגת הבושם, vol. III, p. 491.

Carpentras
16766. Cincinnati - Hebrew Union College 392, f. 7a-8a, M.
Carpentras, commentary by Josef b. Abraham of Montelitz
16767. Cincinnati - Hebrew Union College 291, f. 4b-5b, C, rubric: פי' שטר עלי וכו'.
16768. Marseille - Mlle. Odette Valabregue [1], f. 101a, C, rubric: פירוש לסדר יום הכפורים לפיוט שטר עלי.
16769. New York - Jewish Theological Seminary Ms. 4197, f. 18b-20a, M.
16770. Paris - Ecole Rabbinique 32, f. 20b-22b, M.
16771. Strasbourg - Bibliotheque Nationale et Universitaire 4081, f. 19a-21a, M.

Sepharad, commentary by David b. Josef Abudarham[365]
16772. Budapest - Magyar tudomanyos akademia, MS. Kaufmann A 405/2, p. 178-180a, C, rubric: תוכחה.
16773. Cincinnati - Hebrew Union College 490, f. 1a-1b, C.
16774. New York - Columbia X893 Ab 93, f. 1b-2a, C.
16775. New York - Jewish Theological Seminary Ms. 3011, f. 1a-2a, C, rubric: תוכחה.

שירו ילדי אמוני שיר (ש 1039), משה אבן עזרא, סליחה

Yemen
16776. New York - Jewish Theological Seminary Ms. 3052, f. 35b-36a, M, rubric: אל מלך.
Yemen, commentary by Isaac b. Abraham Wanneh
16777. Chicago-Spertus College of Judaica D ?, 2, f. 203b, M.
16778. Jerusalem - Benayahu ת 261, f. 141a, M, rubric: אל מלך.
16779. Jerusalem - Benayahu ת 282, f. 123b-124a, M, rubric: אל מלך.
16780. Jerusalem - Makhon Ben Zvi 1156 (Tubi 155), f. 122b-123a, M, rubric: אל מלך.
16781. Jerusalem - Makhon Ben Zvi 1174 (Tubi 154), f. 127b, M.
16782. Jerusalem - Michael Krupp 604, f. 156b, M, rubric: אל מלך.
16783. Jerusalem - Musad haRav Kook 325, f. 184b-185a, M, rubric: אל מלך.
16784. Jerusalem - Sassoon 1158, p. 375, M.
16785. Jerusalem - Sassoon 1174, p. 237, M, no incipit.
16786. London - British Library Or. 11122, f. 188a, M.
16787. Manchester - John Rylands University Library, Ms. Gaster 5, f. 199a, M.
16788. Muenchen - Bayerische Staatsbibliothek, Cod. hebr. 472, f. 168b-169a, M, rubric: אל מלך.
16789. New York - Jewish Theological Seminary Ms. 3013, f. 123b, M, rubric: אל מלך, very short.

---

[365] Edited by Prins, תשלום אבודרהם, p. 4-7.

16790. Strasbourg - Bibliotheque Nationale et Universitaire 3965 (Landauer 39), p. 385, M, rubric: אל מלך.

שירו לאל הודו לשמו הנקדש בקדשה רבה (ש 1053), שמואל יצחק, רשות לנשמות
Italia, commentary by Zakharya David Shabbetai Segre
16791. Torino - Archivio Terracini 1499, p. 7-10, C, rubric: פירוש שירו לאל, no incipit.

שכולה אכולה למה תבכי (ש 1145), שלמה אבן גבירול, גאולה, בתימן: סליחה
Ashkenaz
16792. Muenchen - Bayerische Staatsbibliothek, Cod. hebr. 88, f. 107b, G.
Yemen
16793. Jerusalem - Sassoon 902, p. 424, M.
Yemen, commentary by Isaac b. Abraham Wanneh
16794. Chicago-Spertus College of Judaica D 2, 2, f. 212a-212b, M, no incipit.
16795. Jerusalem - Sassoon 1158, p. 380, M, no incipit.
16796. London - British Library Or. 11122, f. 190a, M, no incipit.
16797. New York - Jewish Theological Seminary Ms. 3013, f. 125b, M, rubric: אל מלך.
16798. New York - Jewish Theological Seminary Ms. 3294, f. 12a, C.

שכולה עכורה מה לך בוכה (ש 1156), שלמה אבן גבירול, סליחה
Yemen
16799. Jerusalem - Sassoon 902, p. 423, M, no incipit.
Yemen, commentary by Isaac b. Abraham Wanneh
16800. Chicago-Spertus College of Judaica D 2, 2, f. 212b, M, no incipit.
16801. Jerusalem - Sassoon 1158, p. 380, M, no incipit.
16802. London - British Library Or. 11122, f. 190b, M, no incipit.

שכורה ולא מיון השליכי תופיך (ש 1158), שלמה אבן גבירול, קינה
Yemen, commentary by Isaac b. Abraham Wanneh
16803. Jerusalem - Sassoon 1158, p. 168, M.
16804. London - British Library Or. 11122, f. 101b, M.

שכחי יגונך נפש הומיה (ש 1162), שלמה אבן גבירול, תוכחה
Sepharad, commentary by David b. Josef Abudarham[366]
16805. Budapest - Magyar tudomanyos akademia, MS. Kaufmann A 405/2, p. 258, C, rubric: תוכחה.
16806. Cincinnati - Hebrew Union College 490, f. 15a, C.
16807. Holon - Yehuda Nahum 278, f. 16b, FC, rubric: תוכחה, incomplete.

---

[366] Edited by Prins, תשלום אבודרהם, p. 136-137.

16808. New York - Columbia X893 Ab 93, f. 32a-32b, C, rubric: תוכחה.

שכינה צועקת בהרע שובו בנים אדלו הרע (ש 1167), יוסף, קינה
Yemen, commentary by Isaac b. Abraham Wanneh
16809. Jerusalem - Sassoon 1158, p. 164-165, M.

שכלי ונפשי יהמו בלילה (ש 1182), שלם שבזי
Yemen
16810. Cincinnati - Hebrew Union College 398, f. 160a-162a, M.

שלום לבוא שבת שלום ושמחה (ש 1212), שלם שבזי
Yemen
16811. Cincinnati - Hebrew Union College 398, f. 153b-154a, M.

שלום תשפוט לנו (ש 1292), סליחה
Ashkenaz
16812. Vatican - Biblioteca Apostolica ebr. 308, f. 18a-18b, C, commentator: David b. Mose (compiler).

שלומי עליון (ש 1309), שמואל, סליחה
Yemen
16813. Jerusalem - Benayahu ת 88, f. 148a, M.
16814. Ramat Gan - Universitat BarIlan 62, f. 39a, G, margins damaged.
Yemen, commentary by Isaac b. Abraham Wanneh
16815. Jerusalem - Makhon Ben Zvi 1156 (Tubi 155), f. 107b-108a, M.
16816. Jerusalem - Makhon Ben Zvi 1174 (Tubi 154), f. 106b, M.
16817. Jerusalem - Michael Krupp 604, f. 136b, M.
16818. Jerusalem - Musad haRav Kook 325, f. 156a, M.
16819. Manchester - John Rylands University Library, Ms. Gaster 5, f. 181b-182a, M.
16820. Muenchen - Bayerische Staatsbibliothek, Cod. hebr. 472, f. 146a-146b, C.
16821. New York - Jewish Theological Seminary Ms. 3013, f. 107b, M, rubric: אל מלך.
16822. New York - Jewish Theological Seminary Ms. 3294, f. 2a-2b, C.
16823. New York - Public Library, Heb. Ms. 9, f. 103b, M.
16824. Philadelphia - University of Pennsylvania HB 2, f. 119b, M.

שלח מבשר בביאה חוטר, סליחה

Ashkenaz, commentary by Abraham b. Azriel[367]

16825. Vatican - Biblioteca Apostolica ebr. 301,1, f. 19a-19b, C, rubric: גאולה.

שלמא לכון שארא דישראל, סליחה

Yemen

16826. New York - Jewish Theological Seminary Ms. 3052, f. 82a, M, no incipit.

Yemen, commentary by Isaac b. Abraham Wanneh

16827. Jerusalem - Benayahu ת 282, f. 140b, M.
16828. Jerusalem - Makhon Ben Zvi 1156 (Tubi 155), f. 138a, M, no incipit.
16829. Jerusalem - Makhon Ben Zvi 1174 (Tubi 154), f. 136a, M.
16830. Jerusalem - Michael Krupp 604, f. 175a, M.
16831. Jerusalem - Sassoon 1158, p. 415, M, no incipit.
16832. Jerusalem - Sassoon 1174, p. 269, M, no incipit.
16833. London - British Library Or. 11122, f. 214a, M, no incipit.
16834. Muenchen - Bayerische Staatsbibliothek, Cod. hebr. 472, f. 193a, M.
16835. New York - Jewish Theological Seminary Ms. 3294, f. 17a, C.
16836. New York - Public Library, Heb. Ms. 9, f. 129a, M.
16837. Strasbourg - Bibliotheque Nationale et Universitaire 3965 (Landauer 39), p. 408, M.

שלמו בחקותם מצות רם עאה (ש 1373), שלמה אבן גבירול, פזמון למצות עשה מאזהרות

Carpentras

16838. New York - Jewish Theological Seminary Ms. 4268, f. 18b-19a, M.

שלמים בחמתם (ש 1380), שמעון ב"ר יצחק, חלק ג', קדושתא לשבועות

Ashkenaz

16839. Berlin - Staatsbibliothek (Preussischer Kulturbesitz) Or. Qu. 798-799 (Steinschneider 177), II, f. 116a-117a, M.
16840. Braunschweig - Landesmuseum fuer Geschichte und Volkstum R 2386, vol. I, f. 73b-74a, M.
16841. Budapest - Magyar tudomanyos akademia, MS. Kaufmann A 400, p. 156, C, incipit ההרה.
16842. Hamburg - Staats- und Universitaetsbibliothek Cod. hebr. 17/2 (Steinschneider 152), f. 82a-82b, C.
16843. Jerusalem - Schocken Institute 24100 / Mahzor Nuremberg, f. 147b, M, incipit ההרה.

---

[367] Edited by Urbach, ערוגת הבושם, vol. I, p. 118-120.

16844. London - British Library Add. 18695 (Margoliouth 683), f. 65b-66a, T, Yiddish.
16845. London - British Library Add. 22431 (Margoliouth 662a), f. 8b-9b, M, no incipit.
16846. Moscow - Russian State Library, Ms. Guenzburg 615, f. 30a-31a, C.
16847. Muenchen - Bayerische Staatsbibliothek, Cod. hebr. 88, f. 116b-117a, G.
16848. New York - Jewish Theological Seminary Ms. 4466, f. 127a-127b, M.
16849. Paris - Bibliotheque Nationale heb. 709, f. 121a-121b, C.
16850. Parma - Biblioteca Palatina Cod. Parm. 1002 (Ta 24), f. 178a-178b, M.
16851. Parma - Biblioteca Palatina Cod. Parm. 3205 (de Rossi 655), f. 120b-121a, C, no incipit.
16852. Parma - Biblioteca Palatina Cod. Parm. 3507 (Perreau 27), f. 97a-97b, C.
16853. Zurich - Zentralbibliothek Heid. 139, f. 50b, C, additional marginal notes.

Tsarfat
16854. London - David Sofer 5, f. 51a, C.
16855. Moscow - Russian State Library, Ms. Guenzburg 1665, f. 117b-118a, M, no incipit.
16856. Parma - Biblioteca Palatina Cod. Parm. 3136 (de Rossi 405), f. 149a-149b, M.
16857. Vatican - Biblioteca Apostolica ebr. 306, f. 228a-229b, C, no incipit.

שלוש עשרה מידות (ש 1386), שלמה בר מנחם, סליחה

Ashkenaz
16858. Muenchen - Bayerische Staatsbibliothek, Cod. hebr. 346, f. 137a-137b, C, rubric: אחרת.
16859. Oxford - Bodleian Library MS Opp. 172 (Neubauer 1211), f. 57b, C.
16860. Vatican - Biblioteca Apostolica ebr. 308, f. 112a-112b, C, commentator: David b. Mose (compiler).

Ashkenaz, commentary by Abraham b. Azriel[368]
16861. Frankfurt a M - Stadt- und Universitaetsbibliothek Fol. 16 (Merzbacher 95), f. 104b, C.

שם אלהי צבאות איחד לאלהותו לא אכחד (ש 1426), שלמה אבן גבירול, סליחה
Ashkenaz, commentary by Abraham b. Azriel[369]
16862. Vatican - Biblioteca Apostolica ebr. 301,1, f. 81b-82a, C.

---

[368] Edited by Urbach, ערוגת הבושם, vol. III, p. 546-547.
[369] Edited by Urbach, ערוגת הבושם, vol. II, p. 212-215.

שם ודאי תורק שמן (ש 1435), שלמה, סליחה

Tsarfat

16863. Oxford - Bodleian Library MS Laud. Or. 271 (Neubauer 1206), f. 130b-131a, C, commentator: Aaron b. Hayyim haKohen (compiler).

שם ייחוד מלכי וצורו אזכיר אותו בחלומי (ש 1442), שלם שבזי

Yemen

16864. Cincinnati - Hebrew Union College 398, f. 168a-168b, M.

שמור לבי מענה (ש 1482), שלמה אבן גבירול, אזהרות

Carpentras

16865. New York - Jewish Theological Seminary Ms. 4268, f. 4a-18b, 30b-48a, M.

16866. Parma - Biblioteca Palatina Cod. Parm. 1923, f. 189a-189b, G, only beginning.

Carpentras, commentary by Isaac b. Mordekhai Qimhi

16867. Moscow - Russian State Library, Ms. Guenzburg 710, f. 44a-68a, 96b-128a, M, rubric: 'ביאור לרב מורינו יצחק בר' מרדכי על האזהרות מר' שלמה בן גאבאיירול עם ההשנות שהאיג עליו.

Carpentras, commentary by Mose b. Samuel Ibn Tibbon

16868. Marseille - Mlle. Odette Valabregue [1], f. 39a-51a, 57b-71b, C, rubric: פי' האזהרות של יום שני בשחרית (f. 57b), introduction only.

Carpentras, commentary by Simon b. Tsemaḥ Duran

16869. Parma - Biblioteca Palatina Cod. Parm. 3491, f. 6a-8a, 9a-12b, 29a-38b, M, short version.

Cochin

16870. Cambridge - University Library Oo. 6.71.6, f. 1a-3b, FC, rubric: ברוך נותן ליעף כח ולאין אונים עצמה ולבה בעזרת צור מחסה אתחיל פירוש מצות לא תעשה, only beginning of prohibition-part.

haAri, commentary by Mose b. Hayyim Pesante

16871. New York - Jewish Theological Seminary Ms. 4696, f. 37a-104a, M, end missing.

Italia

16872. Moscow - Russian State Library, Ms. Guenzburg 211, f. 49a-54b, 72b-81b, M.

16873. New York - Columbia University X 893 G 11, f. 2a-8b, M.

Italia, commentary by Mose b. Samuel Ibn Tibbon

16874. New York - Jewish Theological Seminary Ms. 1670, FC, incomplete, on binding of ספר האורה.

Mizrah, commentary by Simon b. Tsemaḥ Duran

16875. Hamburg - Staats- und Universitaetsbibliothek, Ms. Levy 111, f. 8a-110a, C, incomplete.

North Africa

16876. New York - Jewish Theological Seminary Benaim 68, f. 97b-106a, M, Ms burned and badly damaged.

16877. New York - Jewish Theological Seminary Ms. 3061, f. 82a-86a, 88b-96a, FG, printed pages bound together with Ms, incomplete.

16878. New York - Jewish Theological Seminary Ms. 4687, f. 1a-79a, M, rubric: אזהרות כרבי שלמה בן גבירול ז"ל, corrections in the text and on the margins.

North Africa, commentary by Ibn Shoshan

16879. Oxford - Bodleian Library MS Laud. Or. 106 (Neubauer 1178/1), f. 1a-93b, C.

North Africa, commentary by Isaac b. Todros

16880. Oxford - Bodleian Library MS Laud. Or. 106 (Neubauer 1178/1), f. 1a-93b, C.

16881. Paris - Bibliotheque Nationale heb. 842, f. 131a-160b, C, rubric: פירוש מצות עשה ומצות לא תעשה.

Roma

16882. Parma - Biblioteca Palatina Cod. Parm. 2736 (de Rossi 804), f. 121b-125a, G, ecclectic.

Romania

16883. London - British Library Or. 10105, f. 1a-22a, 24b-49b, C.

16884. London - Montefiore Library 419, f. 7b, FM.

16885. New York - Columbia University X 893.1 BE P 43, f. 110a-128b, T, Greek.

Romania, commentary by Mose b. Samuel Ibn Tibbon

16886. New York - Jewish Theological Seminary Ms. 4361, f. 1a-35a, M, beginning missing.

Sepharad

16887. London - British Library Add. 19787 (Margolioth 697), f. 1a-2b, C, only introduction.

16888. Paris - Alliance Israelite Universelle III B 1, f. 1a-10b, C, rubric: פירוש מצות עשה ומצות לא תעש', incomplete.

Sepharad, commentary by Isaac b. Salomo Ḥadab

16889. New York - Jewish Theological Seminary Lutzki 888, f. 61a-79a, C.

Sepharad, commentary by Isaac b. Todros of Barcelona

16890. Frankfurt a M - Stadt- und Universitaetsbibliothek Oct. 134, f. 93a-115b, M, rubric: פירוש אזהרות להחכם יצחק בן ר' טודרוס ז"ל. פירו' אזהרות לר' שלמה בן גבירול ז"ל.

16891. London - British Library Add. 19787 (Margolioth 697), f. 3a-63a, C, rubric: ע"ן שפי' אחר שלא מפי' שעשה ר' יצחק טודרוס ז"ל.

16892. London - Montefiore Library 263, f. 1a-54b (additional numbering of Vorlage: 150a-203b), C, kabbalistic, rubric: פירוש האזהרות.

16893. Paris - Bibliotheque Nationale heb. 273, f. 150a-203b, C, rubric: פירוש האזהרות אמ' הכות' ר' יצחק בן טודרוס נ"ע.

Sepharad, commentary by Josef Garad
16894. Oxford - Bodleian Library Heb.e.10 (Neubauer 2746/1), f. 23a-25b, C, rubric: אזהרות לשבועות, no incipit, additional rubric on f. 24a מצות לא תעשה.

Sepharad, commentary by Mose b. Samuel Ibn Tibbon
16895. Cambridge - Trinity College F 12 16, f. 19b-60b, C.
16896. London - Montefiore Library 297, f. 2a-49a, C, rubric: פירוש האזרות אשר חבר החכם ר׳ משה אבן תיבון ז״ש.
16897. Moscow - Russian State Library, Ms. Guenzburg 111, f. 181a-217b, C, rubric: פירוש האזרות אשר חבר החכם ר׳ משה אבן תיבון ז״ל, incomplete, end missing.
16898. Moscow - Russian State Library, Ms. Guenzburg 775, f. 292b-300b, C, kabbalistic, rubric: פירוש לאזהרות לר׳ שלמה ן׳ גבירול ז״ל, inclomplete, end missing.
16899. New York - Jewish Theological Seminary Rab. 1493, f. 48a-105b, C, rubric: בעזרת שוכן ערבות אכתוב פי׳ אזהרות שעשה ר׳ שמואל ז״ל בן תבון, end missing.
16900. Oxford - Bodleian Library Heb.e.13 (Cowley 2747/1), f. 3a-63a, C.

Sepharad, commentary by Raphael Salomo b. Jacob haKohen Prato, short version of זוהר הרקיע by Simon b. Tsemaḥ Duran
16901. London - British Library Or. 9951, f. 18b-47b, C, rubric: פירוש האזהרות בקצור.
16902. Wien - Oesterreichische Nationalbibliothek Cod hebr. 111/2, f. 81a-112b, C, rubric: פירוש האזהרות בקצור.

Sepharad, commentary by Simon b. Tsemaḥ Duran, זוהר הרקיע
16903. London - British Library Add. 19787 (Margolioth 697), f. 63a-99b, C, incomplete.
16904. London - British Library Or. 5066, f. 1a-100b, C, incomplete.
16905. Oxford - Bodleian Library MS Mich. 344 (Neubauer 1177), f. 7b-148b, C, rubric: בשם יי אל עולם אם׳ שמעון ב״ר צמח הק׳ זצ״ל.

Yemen
16906. Chicago-Spertus College of Judaica D 10, f. 42b-57a, M, rubric: פירוש.
16907. Jerusalem - Benayahu ת 88, f. 92b-105a, M.
16908. Jerusalem - Benayahu ת 261, f. 50a-51a, M.
16909. Jerusalem - Benayahu ת 282, f. 46b-47b, M, only on commandments.
16910. Jerusalem - Makhon Ben Zvi 1156 (Tubi 155), f. 42b-43b, M, only on commandments.
16911. Jerusalem - Makhon Ben Zvi 1174 (Tubi 154), f. 59b-61b, M, only on commandments.
16912. Jerusalem - Michael Krupp 604, f. 56a-57b, M, only on commandments.
16913. Jerusalem - Musad haRav Kook 325, f. 75a-76b, M.
16914. Jerusalem - Sassoon 264, f. 57b-62b, M.

16915. Jerusalem - Sassoon 1158, p. 120-127, M.
16916. Jerusalem - Sassoon 1174, p. 90-93, M, only on commandments.
16917. Manchester - John Rylands University Library, Ms. Gaster 4, f. 60a-65a, M.
16918. Manchester - John Rylands University Library, Ms. Gaster 5, f. 93a-95a, M, only on commandments.
16919. New York - Jewish Theological Seminary Ms. 3013, f. 50b-52b, G, only on commandments.
16920. New York - Jewish Theological Seminary Ms. 3193, f. 141b-143a, M, only on commandments.
16921. New York - Jewish Theological Seminary Ms. 4799, f. 10a-16b, M.
16922. New York - Jewish Theological Seminary Ms. 9325, f. 7a-22b, M, beginning missing, pages 1-6, 13 missing.
16923. Strasbourg - Bibliotheque Nationale et Universitaire 3965 (Landauer 39), p. 142-146, M, only on commandments.

Yemen, commentary by Isaac b. Abraham Wanneh?

16924. Chicago-Spertus College of Judaica D 1, f. 28a-29a, C, rubric: לאהזרות ופירו׳ מעט למצות עשה, does not cover the complete Azharot.
16925. Jerusalem - Michael Krupp 1990, f. 50a-55b, M.
16926. Jerusalem - Musad haRav Kook 347, f. 124a-128a, M.
16927. London - British Library Or. 11122, f. 80a-83b, M, manuscript burned and badly damaged.
16928. Muenchen - Bayerische Staatsbibliothek, Cod. hebr. 472, f. 62b-63b, M, only on commandments.
16929. New York - Jewish Theological Seminary Ms. 3295, f. 35b-40b, M.
16930. New York - Public Library, Heb. Ms. 9, f. 47b-50a, M, only on commandments.
16931. New York - Public Library, Jewish Items 2, f. 63b-64b, M, only on commandments.
16932. Philadelphia - University of Pennsylvania HB 2, f. 63a-64a, M, only on commandments.
16933. Ramat Gan - Universitat Bar Ilan 703, f. 54b-59a, M.

Yemen, commentary by Yiḥya b. Josef Tsalaḥ

16934. Montreal - Elberg 203, f. 19a-28b, M.

שמחו בשמחת תורה כי היא אורה כי מציון תצא תורה (ש 1551), לשמחת תורה
Yemen, commentary by Isaac b. Abraham Wanneh

16935. Manchester - John Rylands University Library, Ms. Gaster 5, f. 155a-155b, M, rubric: ליום עצרת.
16936. New York - Jewish Theological Seminary Ms. 4195, f. 42b-43b, M

Yemen, commentary by Yiḥya b. Josef Tsalaḥ

16937. Montreal - Elberg 203, f. 33b-34a, M.

שמחו בשמחת תורת משה (ש 1552), לשמחת תורה
Yemen, commentary by Isaac b. Abraham Wanneh
16938. New York - Jewish Theological Seminary Ms. 4195, f. 38b, M.
Yemen, commentary by Yiḥya b. Josef Tsalaḥ
16939. Montreal - Elberg 203, f. 31b, M.

שמיני אותותיו ומעשיו בספר כתובים (ש 1602), יוסף ב"ר נתן, מעריב לשמיני עצרת
Ashkenaz
16940. Berlin - Staatsbibliothek (Preussischer Kulturbesitz) Or. Qu. 798-799 (Steinschneider 177), I, f. 221b-223b, M.
16941. Braunschweig - Landesmuseum fuer Geschichte und Volkstum R 2386, vol. I, f. 146b-147a, M.
16942. Frankfurt a M - Stadt- und Universitaetsbibliothek Oct. 227, f. 133a-136a, M.
16943. London - British Library Add. 18695 (Margoliouth 683), f. 122b-124a, T, Yiddish, rubric: מעריב צו שמיני עצרת.
16944. Lund - Universitetsbibliothek Ms. L.O. 2, f. 70a-74b, M.
16945. Oxford - Bodleian Library MS Mich. 365 (Neubauer 1208), f. 9b-12b, C.
16946. Parma - Biblioteca Palatina Cod. Parm. 2342.17 (de Rossi 541,14), f. 256a-262a, C, rubric: עניין אחר.
16947. Parma - Biblioteca Palatina Cod. Parm. 2895, p. 356-359, M.

שמך נורא ביום נירא למגדל עוז, סליחה
Tsarfat
16948. London - David Sofer 5, f. 105a-105b, C.
16949. Parma - Biblioteca Palatina Cod. Parm. 3006 (de Rossi 654,1), f. 160a-160b, M.
16950. Vatican - Biblioteca Apostolica ebr. 306, f. 209a-209b, C.

שמם הר ציון בעונות אבותינו (ש 1630), שלמה אבן גבירול, פזמון
Sepharad
16951. Jerusalem - Sassoon 1216, p. 159-161, M, commentator: Mose Nigrin.
Sepharad, commentary by David b. Josef Abudarham[370]
16952. Budapest - Magyar tudomanyos akademia, MS. Kaufmann A 405/2, p. 239, C, rubric: פזמון.
16953. New York - Columbia X893 Ab 93, f. 25a-25b, C, rubric: פזמון לר' שלמה ן' גיבירול.

---

[370] Edited by Prins, תשלום אבודרהם, p. 72.

16954. New York - Jewish Theological Seminary Ms. 3011, f. 20a, C, rubric: פזמון.

שמעיאל השר משמיעם, אופן

Tsarfat
16955. Oxford - Bodleian Library MS Opp. 171 (Neubauer 1207), f. 44a, C, short.

שמע נא קהלי והקשיב לקולי (ש 1710), לברית מילה

Italia
16956. Leeds - Brotherton Library, MS Roth 60, f. 73a-192b, M.

שמע עליון, סליחה לי' בטבת

Ashkenaz
16957. Oxford - Bodleian Library MS Opp. 681 (Neubauer 1213), f. 86b-87a, C, rubric: פזמון לעשרה בטבת במדינת זכשן ומיישן.

שמע קולי אשר ישמע בקולות (ש 1738), האי גאון, בקשה

Sepharad
16958. Skokie - Hebrew Theological College 3, f. 90b-91a, M.

שמעתי מפאתי תימן קול ידיד קיים ברית נאמן (ש 1860), שלם שבזי, לברית מילה

Yemen
16959. Cincinnati - Hebrew Union College 398, f. 157b-159a, M.

שמעתי קול תוף וגם מחול (ש 1865), שלם שבזי, לברית מילה

Yemen
16960. Cincinnati - Hebrew Union College 398, f. 159a-159b, M.

שמש יודיע דעת וחשבון (ש 1908), יצחק בן זרחיה גירונדי, סילוק, קדושתא לשבת החדש

Carpentras, commentary by Mordekhai b. Josef of Rocco Martino
16961. Cincinnati - Hebrew Union College 246/1, f. 47b-49a, C, rubric: פי' ובכן שמש וכו', no incipit.

Sepharad, commentary by Josef Garad
16962. Oxford - Bodleian Library Heb.e.10 (Neubauer 2746/1), f. 15b-16a, C, no incipit.
16963. Oxford - Bodleian Library Heb.e.10 (Neubauer 2746/1), f. 22a, C, no incipit.

שנאננים שנאננים כניצוצים ילהבו (ש 1946), שלמה אבן גבירול, סליחה
haAri
16964. Harvard University 067, f. 125a-129b, M.
Sepharad
16965. Jerusalem - Benayahu ז 25, f. 62b-64b, M.
Yemen
16966. Jerusalem - Benayahu ת 414, f. 128b, M.

שנה שנה האל היוצר בראשית (ש 1950), יצחק השנירי, רשות לברכו
Carpentras, commentary by Josef b. Abraham of Montelitz
16967. Cincinnati - Hebrew Union College 357, f. 93b-95b (no leaf 94), M.
16968. New York - Jewish Theological Seminary Ms. 4746, f. 28b-29a, M.
16969. Paris - Alliance Israelite Universelle H 422 A, f. 65a-66a, M.
16970. Paris - Ecole Rabbinique 31, f. 133b-134a, M.

שנותינו ספו (ש 1952), שלמה אבן גבירול, גאולה, בתימן: סליחה
Ashkenaz, commentary by Abraham b. Azriel[371]
16971. Vatican - Biblioteca Apostolica ebr. 301,1, f. 18b-19a, C, rubric: גאולה.
Yemen
16972. Jerusalem - Benayahu ת 301, f. 51b, G.
16973. Jerusalem - Sassoon 902, p. 424, M.
16974. New York - Jewish Theological Seminary Ms. 3028, f. 36a, G.
16975. New York - Jewish Theological Seminary Ms. 3052, f. 39b, M, rubric: אל מלך.
Yemen, commentary by Isaac b. Abraham Wanneh
16976. Chicago-Spertus College of Judaica D 2, 2, f. 204a-204b, M, no incipit.
16977. Jerusalem - Benayahu ת 282, f. 125a, M, rubric: אל מלך.
16978. Jerusalem - Makhon Ben Zvi 1156 (Tubi 155), f. 124a, M, rubric: אל מלך.
16979. Jerusalem - Makhon Ben Zvi 1174 (Tubi 154), f. 128b, M.
16980. Jerusalem - Michael Krupp 604, f. 158a, M, rubric: אל מלך.
16981. Jerusalem - Musad haRav Kook 325, f. 186a, M.
16982. Jerusalem - Sassoon 1158, p. 379, M, no incipit.
16983. Jerusalem - Sassoon 1174, p. 239, M, no incipit.
16984. Jerusalem - Yehiel haLevi 4, f. 167a, G.
16985. London - British Library Or. 11122, f. 189b, M, rubric: אל מלך.
16986. Manchester - John Rylands University Library, Ms. Gaster 5, f. 200a-200b, M.
16987. Muenchen - Bayerische Staatsbibliothek, Cod. hebr. 472, f. 170b, M.

---

[371] Edited by Urbach, ערוגת הבושם, vol. I, p. 116-117.

16988. New York - Jewish Theological Seminary Ms. 3013, f. 124b, M, rubric: אל מלך.
16989. New York - Jewish Theological Seminary Ms. 3109, f. 65a-65b, M, rubric: אל מלך.
16990. New York - Jewish Theological Seminary Ms. 3294, f. 13a, C.
16991. New York - Public Library, Heb. Ms. 9, f. 114b-115a, M.
16992. Strasbourg - Bibliotheque Nationale et Universitaire 3965 (Landauer 39), p. 388, M.

שני זיתים נכרתים בגן נעול יצהירו (ש 1960), שלמה, זולת לשבת חנוכה
Ashkenaz

16993. Berlin - Staatsbibliothek (Preussischer Kulturbesitz) Or. Qu. 798-799 (Steinschneider 177), II, f. 5a-6a, M.
16994. Budapest - Magyar tudomanyos akademia, MS. Kaufmann A 384, f. 22b-23a, M.
16995. Budapest - Magyar tudomanyos akademia, MS. Kaufmann A 399, p. 406-407, C.
16996. Cambridge - University Library Add. 504,1, f. 20b-21b, C.
16997. Erlangen - Universitaetsbibliothek 2601 (Roth 67), f. 25a, M, short.
16998. Frankfurt a M - Stadt- und Universitaetsbibliothek Oct. 227, f. 145b-146a, M.
16999. Hamburg - Staats- und Universitaetsbibliothek Cod. hebr. 17/2 (Steinschneider 152), f. 8b, C.
17000. Jerusalem - Schocken Institute 24100 / Mahzor Nuremberg, f. 21a, M.
17001. Muenchen - Bayerische Staatsbibliothek, Cod. hebr. 88, f. 4a-5a, G.
17002. Oxford - Bodleian Library MS Can. Or. 82 (Neubauer 1148), f. 13b-14a, M.
17003. Oxford - Bodleian Library MS Mich. 365 (Neubauer 1208), f. 18a, C, short.
17004. Oxford - Bodleian Library MS Opp. 170 (Neubauer 1205), f. 275b, C.
17005. Parma - Biblioteca Palatina Cod. Parm. 1002 (Ta 24), f. 13b-14a, M.
17006. Parma - Biblioteca Palatina Cod. Parm. 2895, p. 381-382, M.
17007. Parma - Biblioteca Palatina Cod. Parm. 3205 (de Rossi 655), f. 5a-6a, C.
17008. Vatican - Biblioteca Apostolica ebr. 318, f. 215a-215b, Gl.

Ashkenaz, commentary by Abraham b. Azriel[372]

17009. Frankfurt a M - Stadt- und Universitaetsbibliothek Fol. 16 (Merzbacher 95), f. 36b-37b, C.
17010. Vatican - Biblioteca Apostolica ebr. 301,1, f. 63b-64a, C.

Tsarfat

17011. London - David Sofer 5, f. 4a-4b, C, rubric: מאורה.

---

[372] Edited by Urbach, ערוגת הבושם, vol. II, p. 89-94.

17012. Moscow - Russian State Library, Ms. Guenzburg 1665, f. 5b, M.

שני חיי ומאויי לריק ספו בחובותי (ש 1961), שלמה אבן גבירול, סליחה
Ashkenaz
17013. Moscow - Russian State Library, Ms. Guenzburg 190, f. 18b-19a, G.
Tsarfat
17014. London - David Sofer 5, f. 105b-106a, C.
17015. London - David Sofer 5, f. 166b, C, rubric: פזמון.
17016. Parma - Biblioteca Palatina Cod. Parm. 3007 (de Rossi 654,2), f. 152b-153a, M.
17017. Vatican - Biblioteca Apostolica ebr. 306, f. 205b, C.
Yemen
17018. Jerusalem - Sassoon 902, p. 421, M.
Yemen, commentary by Isaac b. Abraham Wanneh
17019. Chicago-Spertus College of Judaica D 2, 2, f. 213a, M, no incipit.
17020. Jerusalem - Sassoon 1158, p. 367, M, rubric: אל מלך.
17021. London - British Library Or. 11122, f. 183b, M, no incipit.

שני ימים מקויימים נועדו לעמוסים (ש 1962), שלמה אבן גבירול, פזמון לשבת וראש חדש
Carpentras
17022. Cincinnati - Hebrew Union College 429/1, f. 8a-9a, M, no incipit.
Carpentras, commentary by Eliyahu Carmi
17023. New York - Jewish Theological Seminary Ms. 3151, f. 47b-48a, M, no incipit.
Carpentras, commentary by Josef b. Abraham of Montelitz
17024. Cincinnati - Hebrew Union College 357, f. 54b, M, commentator: rubric: פירוש, no incipit.
17025. New York - Jewish Theological Seminary Ms. 4746, f. 12b, M, no incipit.
17026. Paris - Alliance Israelite Universelle H 422 A, f. 31b-32a, M, no incipit.
17027. Paris - Ecole Rabbinique 31, f. 100b-101a, M, no incipit.

שננו לשונם בני אונם (ש 1986), שמואל, אהבה לפרשת וירא
Ashkenaz
17028. Jerusalem - Schocken Institute 24100 / Mahzor Nuremberg, f. 17b-18a, M.
Ashkenaz, commentary by Abraham b. Azriel[373]
17029. Frankfurt a M - Stadt- und Universitaetsbibliothek Fol. 16 (Merzbacher 95), f. 92a-93a, C, rubric: אהבה לוירא.

---

[373] Edited by Urbach, ערוגת הבושם, vol. II, p. 228-232.

17030. Vatican - Biblioteca Apostolica ebr. 301,1, f. 84a-84b, C, rubric: לפרשת וירא.

Tsarfat

17031. Parma - Biblioteca Palatina Cod. Parm. 1264, f. 165b-166a, M.

שעה זכרון דתי כמעשה למעוז (ש 2001), שלמה אבן גבירול, פזמון ליום כפור
Sepharad, commentary by David b. Josef Abudarham[374]

17032. Budapest - Magyar tudomanyos akademia, MS. Kaufmann A 405/2, p. 195-197, C, rubric: ובכן למדתי דתך בזכרי עבודתיך.

שעה נאסר אשר נמסר (ש 2008), שלמה אבן גבירול, פזמון לי"ז תמוז
Ashkenaz

17033. Oxford - Bodleian Library MS Opp. 681 (Neubauer 1213), f. 86a-86b, C, rubric: פזמון לי"ז בתמוז.

17034. Padova - Biblioteca del Seminario Vescovile Cod. 218, f. 260b-261a, M.

17035. Vatican - Biblioteca Apostolica ebr. 422/1, f. 45a, CG, no incipit.

Carpentras, commentary by Mordekhai b. Josef of Rocco Martino

17036. Cincinnati - Hebrew Union College 246/1, f. 55a-56b, C, rubric: פי' סליחה שעה נאסר וכו'.

שעה עליון לחשי נערץ בקדושה היום לך בדרשי (ש 2012), הושענא
Yemen, commentary by Samḥun b. Salomo Ḥaloah

17037. Jerusalem - Makhon ben Zvi 2808, f. 150a-152a, C.

שעה קולי בהתעטפי (ש 2022), משה אבן עזרא, חלק ו', קדושתא למוסף יום כפור
Carpentras

17038. Cincinnati - Hebrew Union College 392, f. 91b-92b, M, no incipit.

Carpentras, commentary by Josef b. Abraham of Montelitz

17039. Cincinnati - Hebrew Union College 291, f. 49b-50b, C, rubric: פי' תוכחה שעה קולי וכו.

17040. New York - Jewish Theological Seminary Ms. 4197, f. 206a-207b, M, no incipit.

17041. Paris - Ecole Rabbinique 32, f. 213a-214b, M, no incipit.

17042. Strasbourg - Bibliotheque Nationale et Universitaire 4081, f. 187b-189a, M, no incipit.

Sepharad, commentary by David b. Josef Abudarham[375]

17043. Budapest - Magyar tudomanyos akademia, MS. Kaufmann A 405/2, p. 251-252, C, rubric: תוכחה.

---

[374] Edited by Prins, תשלום אבודרהם, p. 84-86.
[375] Edited by Prins, תשלום אבודרהם, p. 123-125.

17044. New York - Columbia X893 Ab 93, f. 30a-30b, C, rubric: תוכחה.

שעה שועתי בשקדי אלהי בית מעונך (ש 2030), שמואל, סליחה
Carpentras, commentary by Josef b. Abraham of Montelitz
17045. Paris - Ecole Rabbinique 32, f. 37b-38b, M.

שערי ארמון (ש 2064), שמעון ב"ר אבון, חלק ה', קדושתא לנעילה
Ashkenaz
17046. Berlin - Staatsbibliothek (Preussischer Kulturbesitz) Or. Qu. 798-799 (Steinschneider 177), I, f. 180b, M.
17047. Braunschweig - Landesmuseum fuer Geschichte und Volkstum R 2386, vol. II, f. 270a, M.
17048. Fulda - Hessische Landesbibliothek A 3 II, f. 129b, C, commentator: Josef, very short.
17049. Hamburg - Staats- und Universitaetsbibliothek Cod. hebr. 62 (Steinschneider 154), f. 23a-23b, C.
17050. London - British Library Or. 11318/1, f. 127a-127b, C, rubric: סילוק.
17051. London - Montefiore Library 261, f. 64b, C, commentator: Eliezer b. Natan?, very short.
17052. New York - Jewish Theological Seminary Ms. 4466, f. 426a, M.
17053. Oxford - Bodleian Library MS Mich. 365 (Neubauer 1208), f. 94a, C, short.
17054. Oxford - Bodleian Library MS Opp. 170 (Neubauer 1205), f. 182a, C, rubric: סילוק, very short.
17055. Oxford - Bodleian Library MS Opp. 172 (Neubauer 1211), f. 86b, C, short.
17056. Parma - Biblioteca Palatina Cod. Parm. 3205 (de Rossi 655), f. 238a, C, rubric: סילוק.
17057. Parma - Biblioteca Palatina Cod. Parm. 3270 (de Rossi 1215), f. 239a, M, rubric: סילוק.
17058. Vatican - Biblioteca Apostolica ebr. 308, f. 147b, C, commentator: David b. Mose (compiler).
17059. Vatican - Biblioteca Apostolica ebr. 422/1, f. 19b-20a, C, very short.
Tsarfat
17060. London - David Sofer 5, f. 172a, C, no incipit, very short.
17061. Oxford - Bodleian Library MS Bodl. Or. 109 (Neubauer 1209), f. 43a, C, commentator: Aaron b. Hayyim haKohen (compiler), short.
17062. Oxford - Bodleian Library MS Laud. Or. 271 (Neubauer 1206), f. 119a, C, commentator: Aaron b. Hayyim haKohen (compiler), no incipit.

שערי שמים בלולי אש ומים (ש 2076), שמעון ב"ר יצחק, סליחה
Ashkenaz
17063. Braunschweig - Landesmuseum fuer Geschichte und Volkstum R 2386, vol. II, f. 141a, M.
17064. Budapest - Magyar tudomanyos akademia, MS. Kaufmann A 400, p. 529, C, rubric: עוד אחר.
17065. Hamburg - Staats- und Universitaetsbibliothek Cod. hebr. 17/2 (Steinschneider 152), f. 144b-145a, C.
17066. Jerusalem - Schocken Institute 24100 / Mahzor Nuremberg, f. 312b, M, short.
17067. Muenchen - Bayerische Staatsbibliothek, Cod. hebr. 346, f. 118a-118b, C, short.
17068. Oxford - Bodleian Library MS Mich. 543 (Neubauer 1212), f. 79a-81a, bottom margin, C, commentator: Isaac b. Jacob (compiler).
17069. Padova - Biblioteca del Seminario Vescovile Cod. 218, f. 156a-156b, M.
17070. Parma - Biblioteca Palatina Cod. Parm. 3205 (de Rossi 655), f. 285a, C.
17071. Vatican - Biblioteca Apostolica ebr. 422/1, f. 34b, C, very short.
Tsarfat
17072. London - David Sofer 5, f. 106a, C, very short.
17073. Oxford - Bodleian Library MS Bodl. Or. 109 (Neubauer 1209), f. 47a-47b, C, commentator: Aaron b. Hayyim haKohen (compiler).
17074. Oxford - Bodleian Library MS Opp. 171 (Neubauer 1207), f. 89b-90a, C, rubric: עוד אחר.

שעשוע יום יום (ש 12087), שמעון ב"ר יצחק, חלק ו', קדושתא לשבועות
Ashkenaz
17075. Berlin - Staatsbibliothek (Preussischer Kulturbesitz) Or. Qu. 798-799 (Steinschneider 177), II, f. 118b-121a, M.
17076. Braunschweig - Landesmuseum fuer Geschichte und Volkstum R 2386, vol. I, f. 75b-77b, M.
17077. Budapest - Magyar tudomanyos akademia, MS. Kaufmann A 400, p. 157-159, C.
17078. Hamburg - Staats- und Universitaetsbibliothek Cod. hebr. 17/2 (Steinschneider 152), f. 82b-83b, C.
17079. Jerusalem - Schocken Institute 24100 / Mahzor Nuremberg, f. 148b-150b, M, ecclectic.
17080. London - British Library Add. 18695 (Margoliouth 683), f. 67a-69a, T, Yiddish.
17081. London - British Library Add. 22431 (Margoliouth 662a), f. 11b-14b, M.
17082. Moscow - Russian State Library, Ms. Guenzburg 615, f. 32b-34a, C.

17083. Muenchen - Bayerische Staatsbibliothek, Cod. hebr. 88, f. 118a-120a, G.
17084. New York - Jewish Theological Seminary Ms. 4466, f. 130a-130b, M, only beginning.
17085. Paris - Bibliotheque Nationale heb. 709, f. 122a-122b, C.
17086. Parma - Biblioteca Palatina Cod. Parm. 1002 (Ta 24), f. 180a, M, very short.
17087. Parma - Biblioteca Palatina Cod. Parm. 3205 (de Rossi 655), f. 121a, C, short.
17088. Parma - Biblioteca Palatina Cod. Parm. 3507 (Perreau 27), f. 98b-101a, C.
17089. Zurich - Zentralbibliothek Heid. 139, f. 50b-51a, C, additional marginal notes.

Tsarfat
17090. London - David Sofer 5, f. 51b-52b, C.
17091. Moscow - Russian State Library, Ms. Guenzburg 1665, f. 119a-121a, M.
17092. Oxford - Bodleian Library MS Laud. Or. 271 (Neubauer 1206), f. 86b, C, commentator: Aaron b. Hayyim haKohen (compiler), very short, ecclectic.
17093. Parma - Biblioteca Palatina Cod. Parm. 3136 (de Rossi 405), f. 151a-153a, M.
17094. Vatican - Biblioteca Apostolica ebr. 306, f. 230b-234b, C, no incipit.

שפל רוח שפל ברך וקומה (ש 2103), שלמה אבן גבירול, רשות לנשמת

Sepharad
17095. Skokie - Hebrew Theological College 3, f. 86a, M.

שרד מנאמי עוהגי אלחור (ש 2178), שלם שבזי

Yemen
17096. Cincinnati - Hebrew Union College 398, f. 162b-164b, M.

שרי קדש היום איש ברעהו (ש 2184), סליחה

Ashkenaz
17097. Berlin - Staatsbibliothek (Preussischer Kulturbesitz) Or. Qu. 798-799 (Steinschneider 177), I, f. 173a-174a, M.
17098. Oxford - Bodleian Library MS Mich. 543 (Neubauer 1212), f. 12a, C, commentator: Isaac b. Jacob (compiler), rubric: הפיזמון זה אום׳ כשיבוא יום כיפור על השבת, breaks off after 1.5 lines.
17099. Vatican - Biblioteca Apostolica ebr. 422/1, f. 32b, C.

Tsarfat
17100. London - David Sofer 5, f. 175b, C, rubric: פזמון.

17101. Parma - Biblioteca Palatina Cod. Parm. 3006 (de Rossi 654,1), f. 164b-165a, M.

שרידים נדודים לציון תקבץ, סליחה
Yemen, commentary by Isaac b. Abraham Wanneh
17102. New York - Jewish Theological Seminary Ms. 3109, f. 66a, M, no incpit.

שרקתי וקבצתי מסביב תאניה (ש 2212), שמואל, סליחה
Carpentras, commentary by Mordekhai b. Josef of Rocco Martino
17103. Cincinnati - Hebrew Union College 246/1, f. 57a-60a, C, rubric: פי' סליחה שרקתי וקבצתי וכו'.

שרש בנו ישי עד אן תהי נקבר (ש 2214), שלמה אבן גבירול, רשות לשבת וחול המועד פסח
Corfu
17104. New York - Jewish Theological Seminary Ms. 4821, f. 18b, M.

שש מאות נקראות בדת האל (ש 2232), שלמה אבן גבירול, אהבה, פרשת בשלח
Ashkenaz
17105. Jerusalem - Schocken Institute 24100 / Mahzor Nuremberg, f. 186b-187a, M.
17106. Muenchen - Bayerische Staatsbibliothek, Cod. hebr. 69, f. 58a-58b, M.

Ashkenaz, commentary by Abraham b. Azriel[376]
17107. Frankfurt a M - Stadt- und Universitaetsbibliothek Fol. 16 (Merzbacher 95), f. 93a-93b, C, rubric: לפרשת ציצית.
17108. Vatican - Biblioteca Apostolica ebr. 301,1, f. 127a-132b, C.

שתי פעמים מקוימים (ש 2274), שלמה בן יהודה, אהבה לשבת נחמו
Ashkenaz
17109. Jerusalem - Schocken Institute 24100 / Mahzor Nuremberg, f. 221b-222a, M.
17110. Muenchen - Bayerische Staatsbibliothek, Cod. hebr. 69, f. 61b-62a, M.

Ashkenaz, commentary by Abraham b. Azriel[377]
17111. Frankfurt a M - Stadt- und Universitaetsbibliothek Fol. 16 (Merzbacher 95), f. 18b, C, rubric: לאהבה.

---

[376] Edited by Urbach, ערוגת הבושם, vol. III, p. 206-249.
[377] Edited by Urbach, ערוגת הבושם, vol. II, p. 1-36.

17112. Vatican - Biblioteca Apostolica ebr. 301,1, f. 50a-54b, C, rubric: לאהבה.

שתיל עמיאל ושורשו (ש 2281), שלמה, סליחה
Yemen
17113. New York - Jewish Theological Seminary Ms. 3052, f. 38b-39b, M, rubric: אל מלך.
Yemen, commentary by Isaac b. Abraham Wanneh
17114. Chicago-Spertus College of Judaica D 2, 2, f. 210a, M, no incipit.
17115. Jerusalem - Benayahu ת 261, f. 142a-142b, M, rubric: אל מלך.
17116. Jerusalem - Benayahu ת 282, f. 124b-125a, M, rubric: אל מלך.
17117. Jerusalem - Makhon Ben Zvi 1156 (Tubi 155), f. 124a, M, rubric: אל מלך.
17118. Jerusalem - Makhon Ben Zvi 1174 (Tubi 154), f. 128b, M.
17119. Jerusalem - Michael Krupp 604, f. 158a, M, rubric: אל מלך.
17120. Jerusalem - Musad haRav Kook 325, f. 185b, M, rubric: אל מלך.
17121. Jerusalem - Sassoon 1158, p. 371-372, M, rubric: אל מלך.
17122. Jerusalem - Sassoon 1174, p. 238-239, M, no incipit.
17123. Jerusalem - Yehiel haLevi 4, f. 162a, G.
17124. London - British Library Or. 11122, f. 185b-186a, M, rubric: אל מלך.
17125. Muenchen - Bayerische Staatsbibliothek, Cod. hebr. 472, f. 170a-170b, M, rubric: אל מלך.
17126. New York - Jewish Theological Seminary Ms. 3013, f. 124a-124b, M, rubric: אל מלך.
17127. New York - Jewish Theological Seminary Ms. 3109, f. 67b, M, rubric: אל מלך.
17128. New York - Jewish Theological Seminary Ms. 3294, f. 12b-13a, C.
17129. New York - Public Library, Heb. Ms. 9, f. 114b, M.
17130. Strasbourg - Bibliotheque Nationale et Universitaire 3965 (Landauer 39), p. 387, M, rubric: אל מלך.

תא שמע מרי עלמא צלותא שפירא (ת 4), אפרים ב"ר יעקב מבון, סליחה
Ashkenaz
17131. Braunschweig - Landesmuseum fuer Geschichte und Volkstum R 2386, vol. II, f. 146b-148a, M, no incipit.
17132. Cambridge - University Library Add. 504,1, f. 71a-73a, C.
17133. Padova - Biblioteca del Seminario Vescovile Cod. 218, f. 167a-169b, M.
17134. Parma - Bibliotheca Palatina Cod. Parm. 3205 (de Rossi 655), f. 288b-289b, C.
17135. Vatican - Biblioteca Apostolica ebr. 422/1, f. 36a, C.
Italia
17136. Cincinnati - Hebrew Union College 559/2, f. 1a, MT, Hebrew.

תאבת יום זה מכל ימות השנה (ת 8), סליחה

Ashkenaz
17137. Muenchen - Bayerische Staatsbibliothek, Cod. hebr. 346 , f. 137b, C, rubric: אחרת, short.
17138. Oxford - Bodleian Library MS Mich. 543 (Neubauer 1212), f. 26b-27a, C, commentator: Isaac b. Jacob (compiler), rubric: תאבת זו 'הסליח'. מצא במחזור ובמנחה'.
17139. Oxford - Bodleian Library MS Opp. 172 (Neubauer 1211), f. 72a, C.
17140. Oxford - Bodleian Library MS Opp. 681 (Neubauer 1213), f. 44b-45a, C, short.
17141. Vatican - Biblioteca Apostolica ebr. 308, f. 148b-149a, C, commentator: David b. Mose (compiler).
17142. Vatican - Biblioteca Apostolica ebr. 422/1, f. 24a, C, very short.
17143. Vatican - Biblioteca Apostolica ebr. 422/2, f. 38b, CG, no incipit, very short.

Ashkenaz, commentary by Abraham b. Azriel[378]
17144. Frankfurt a M - Stadt- und Universitaetsbibliothek Fol. 16 (Merzbacher 95), f. 107a, C, short.

תאדי אלגניב מנבה ובאדר באלסלאם, שלם שבזי

Yemen
17145. Cincinnati - Hebrew Union College 398, f. 196b-197b, M.

תאות לב לא השגנו (ת 17), הוספה לעבודה

Ashkenaz
17146. Berlin - Staatsbibliothek (Preussischer Kulturbesitz) Or. Qu. 798-799 (Steinschneider 177), I, f. 135b, M, ecclectic.
17147. Braunschweig - Landesmuseum fuer Geschichte und Volkstum R 2386, vol. II, f. 239a-239b, M.
17148. London - Montefiore Library 261, f. 62a, C, commentator: Eliezer b. Natan?, very short.
17149. Muenchen - Bayerische Staatsbibliothek, Cod. hebr. 346 , f. 143b, C, rubric: אחרת רהוטות, short.
17150. Oxford - Bodleian Library MS Opp. 172 (Neubauer 1211), f. 69a, C.
17151. Vatican - Biblioteca Apostolica ebr. 308, f. 128b, C, commentator: David b. Mose (compiler).

Ashkenaz, commentary by Abraham b. Azriel[379]
17152. Vatican - Biblioteca Apostolica ebr. 301,1, f. 168b, C, short.

---

[378] Edited by Urbach, ערוגת הבושם, vol. III, p. 555.
[379] Edited by Urbach, ערוגת הבושם, vol. III, p. 489.

Tsarfat

17153. Oxford - Bodleian Library MS Bodl. Or. 109 (Neubauer 1209), f. 40a, C, commentator: Aaron b. Hayyim haKohen (compiler), short.

תאות נפש לשמך ולזכרך (ת 19), משולם ב"ר קלונימוס, חלק ב', קדושתא לשחרית יום כפור

Ashkenaz

17154. Berlin - Staatsbibliothek (Preussischer Kulturbesitz) Or. Qu. 798-799 (Steinschneider 177), I, f. 71a-71b, M.
17155. Braunschweig - Landesmuseum fuer Geschichte und Volkstum R 2386, vol. II, f. 184a-184b, M.
17156. Budapest - Magyar tudomanyos akademia, MS. Kaufmann A 400, p. 305-306, C.
17157. Hamburg - Staats- und Universitaetsbibliothek Cod. hebr. 17/2 (Steinschneider 152), f. 150b, C.
17158. Hamburg - Staats- und Universitaetsbibliothek Cod. hebr. 40b (Steinschneider 110), f. 90a, G.
17159. Hamburg - Staats- und Universitaetsbibliothek Cod. hebr. 132 (Steinschneider 155), f. 32b-33a, C.
17160. Jerusalem - Jewish National and University Library Ms Heb 8° 3037, f. 114a-114b, M.
17161. Jerusalem - Schocken Institute 24100 / Mahzor Nuremberg, f. 375a-375b, M.
17162. London - British Library Or. 11318/1, f. 70a-70b, C, no incipit.
17163. London - Montefiore Library 261, f. 42a-42b, C, commentator: Eliezer b. Natan?.
17164. Moscow - Russian State Library, Ms. Guenzburg 191, f. 83b-84a, M.
17165. Moscow - Russian State Library, Ms. Guenzburg 615, f. 92b-93a, C, no incipit.
17166. Muenchen - Bayerische Staatsbibliothek, Cod. hebr. 86, f. 98b-99a, G.
17167. Muenchen - Bayerische Staatsbibliothek, Cod. hebr. 346, f. 51b-52a, C.
17168. Muenchen - Bayerische Staatsbibliothek, Cod. hebr. 393, f. 139b-140a, C, no incipit.
17169. New York - Jewish Theological Seminary Ms. 4466, f. 303a-303b, M.
17170. New York - Jewish Theological Seminary Ms. 8097, f. 71a, C.
17171. New York - Jewish Theological Seminary Ms. 8169 (Acc. 0016), f. 65a-65b, M.
17172. Oxford - Bodleian Library MS Mich. 365 (Neubauer 1208), f. 68a-68b, C.
17173. Oxford - Bodleian Library MS Opp. 170 (Neubauer 1205), f. 165a-165b, C.

17174. Oxford - Bodleian Library MS Opp. 172 (Neubauer 1211), f. 35b-36a, C.
17175. Oxford - Bodleian Library MS Opp. 619 (Neubauer 2374), f. 138a-138b, M.
17176. Paris - Bibliotheque Nationale heb. 653, f. 54a, G.
17177. Parma - Biblioteca Palatina Cod. Parm. 3205 (de Rossi 655), f. 224b-225a, C, no incipit.
17178. Parma - Biblioteca Palatina Cod. Parm. 3271 (de Rossi 1216), f. 33a-33b, G.
17179. Parma - Biblioteca Palatina Cod. Parm. 3507 (Perreau 27), f. 146b, C, no incipit.
17180. Vatican - Biblioteca Apostolica ebr. 308, f. 98a-98b, C, commentator: David b. Mose (compiler).
17181. Vatican - Biblioteca Apostolica ebr. 422/1, f. 15a, C, short.
17182. Zurich - Zentralbibliothek Heid. 139, f. 75b-76a, C, additional marginal notes.

Asti, Fossano, Moncalvo
17183. New Haven - Yale University, Beinecke Rare Book and MS Library, MS Heb. 52, f. 101b-102a, M.

Romania
17184. Vatican - Biblioteca Apostolica ebr. 320, f. 277b-278a, M.

Tsarfat
17185. Bern - Burgerbibliothek A 409, f. 78a, G.
17186. London - British Library Or. 8682, f. 65a-65b, Gl.
17187. London - David Sofer 5, f. 136a-136b, C.
17188. Oxford - Bodleian Library MS Bodl. Or. 109 (Neubauer 1209), f. 18a, C, commentator: Aaron b. Hayyim haKohen (compiler).
17189. Oxford - Bodleian Library MS Laud. Or. 271 (Neubauer 1206), f. 111b-112a, C, commentator: Aaron b. Hayyim haKohen (compiler), no incipit.
17190. Parma - Biblioteca Palatina Cod. Parm. 1794 (de Rossi 1061), f. 111b-112a, M.
17191. Parma - Biblioteca Palatina Cod. Parm. 2125 (de Rossi 812), f. 38b-39a, C.
17192. Parma - Biblioteca Palatina Cod. Parm. 2890 (de Rossi 856), f. 23a, M.
17193. Parma - Biblioteca Palatina Cod. Parm. 3006 (de Rossi 654,1), f. 136b-137a, M.
17194. Vatican - Biblioteca Apostolica ebr. 306, f. 76a, C.

תאחר מיום זכרון חותם קריאה (ת 21), סעדיה גאון, סליחה

Yemen
17195. New York - Jewish Theological Seminary Ms. 3193, f. 135b-136a, M.

Yemen, commentary by Isaac b. Abraham Wanneh
17196. Chicago-Spertus College of Judaica D 2, 2, f. 226b, M, no incipit.
17197. Jerusalem - Sassoon 1158, p. 312, M, rubric: אל מלך.
17198. London - British Library Or. 11122, f. 203a, M, rubric: אל מלך.

תאלת זו כחפין (ת 23), אלעזר ברבי אלעזר, חלק ב', קדושתא לראש השנה
Ashkenaz
17199. Berlin - Staatsbibliothek (Preussischer Kulturbesitz) Or. Qu. 798-799 (Steinschneider 177), I, f. 6a-6b, M.
17200. Braunschweig - Landesmuseum fuer Geschichte und Volkstum R 2386, vol. II, f. 81a, M.
17201. Budapest - Magyar tudomanyos akademia, MS. Kaufmann A 400, p. 247-249, C, no incipit.
17202. Cambridge - University Library Or. 785, f. 19a, G.
17203. Darmstadt - Hessisches Landes- und Hochschulbibliothek Cod. Or. 15, f. 6a-6b, M.
17204. Hamburg - Staats- und Universitaetsbibliothek Cod. hebr. 12 (Steinschneider 102), f. 5b-6a, G.
17205. Hamburg - Staats- und Universitaetsbibliothek Cod. hebr. 17/2 (Steinschneider 152), f. 106b-107b, C.
17206. Hamburg - Staats- und Universitaetsbibliothek Cod. hebr. 40c (Steinschneider 111), f. 132b, G.
17207. Hamburg - Staats- und Universitaetsbibliothek Cod. hebr. 132 (Steinschneider 155), f. 4b-5b, C.
17208. Hamburg - Staats- und Universitaetsbibliothek Cod. hebr. 139 (Steinschneider 115), f. 20b-21a, G.
17209. Hamburg - Staats- und Universitaetsbibliothek Cod. hebr. 225, f. 217b-218b, G.
17210. Jerusalem - Jewish National and University Library Ms Heb 8° 3037, f. 8a-8b, M.
17211. Jerusalem - Schocken Institute 24100 / Mahzor Nuremberg, f. 324a, M.
17212. Moscow - Russian State Library, Ms. Guenzburg 615, f. 56a-57a, C.
17213. Moscow - Russian State Library, Ms. Guenzburg 1401/2, f. 16a, C.
17214. Muenchen - Bayerische Staatsbibliothek, Cod. hebr. 346, f. 1a-2b, C, beginning missing.
17215. Muenchen - Bayerische Staatsbibliothek, Cod. hebr. 422, f. 72b-73a, G.
17216. New York - Jewish Theological Seminary Ms. 4466, f. 210b-211b, M.
17217. New York - Jewish Theological Seminary Ms. 8097, f. 58b, C, additional glosses in the margins.
17218. New York - Jewish Theological Seminary Ms. 8169 (Acc. 0016), f. 4a-4b, M.

17219. New York - Jewish Theological Seminary Rab. 1077/4 (Acc. 02505), f. 21b, FC.
17220. Oxford - Bodleian Library MS Opp. 170 (Neubauer 1205), f. 103b-104b, C.
17221. Oxford - Bodleian Library MS Opp. 172 (Neubauer 1211), f. 3a-3b, C.
17222. Oxford - Bodleian Library MS Opp. 619 (Neubauer 2374), f. 10b-11a, M.
17223. Oxford - Bodleian Library MS Opp. 675 (Neubauer 1210), f. 14a-15a, C, no incipit.
17224. Paris - Bibliotheque Nationale heb. 653, f. 9b, G.
17225. Parma - Biblioteca Palatina Cod. Parm. 2404 (de Rossi 1104), f. 126a-126b, M, copied from printed edition Saloniki 1550 (Benyamin b. Meir Levi).
17226. Parma - Biblioteca Palatina Cod. Parm. 3205 (de Rossi 655), f. 204a-204b, C.
17227. Parma - Biblioteca Palatina Cod. Parm. 3270 (de Rossi 1215), f. 20a-20b, M.
17228. Parma - Biblioteca Palatina Cod. Parm. 3507 (Perreau 27), f. 109b-110b, C.
17229. Vatican - Biblioteca Apostolica ebr. 308, f. 29a-30b, C, commentator: David b. Mose (compiler), uses the old French Ḥatima מלך עליון ונורא.
17230. Vatican - Bibliotheca Apostolica ebr. 298/1, f. 8a-9a, C, no incipit.
17231. Vatican - Biblioteca Apostolica ebr. 422/1, f. 7b-8a, C.
17232. Zurich - Zentralbibliothek Heid. 139, f. 57a-58a, C, additional marginal notes.
17233. Zurich - Zentralbibliothek Heid. 139, f. 102a, C, commentator: Elazar b. Yehuda of Worms, no incipit, very short, esoteric.

Asti, Fossano, Moncalvo
17234. New Haven - Yale University, Beinecke Rare Book and MS Library, MS Heb. 52, f. 18b, M.

Romania
17235. Vatican - Biblioteca Apostolica ebr. 320, f. 148b, M.

Tsarfat
17236. London - British Library Add. 11639 (Margoliouth 1056), f. 708b-709a, M, no incipit.
17237. London - British Library Or. 8682, f. 10a, GI.
17238. London - David Sofer 5, f. 108b-109a, C.
17239. Manchester - John Rylands University Library, Ms. Gaster 733, f. 80b-81a, C, commentary block in Mahzor, manuscript damaged.
17240. Oxford - Bodleian Library MS Laud. Or. 271 (Neubauer 1206), f. 140a-140b, C, commentator: Aaron b. Hayyim haKohen (compiler).
17241. Oxford - Bodleian Library MS Opp. 171 (Neubauer 1207), f. 56a-56b, C.

17242. Paris - Bibliotheque Nationale heb. 445,9, f. 62b-63b, C, uses the old French Hatima מלך עליון ונורא.
17243. Parma - Biblioteca Palatina Cod. Parm. 1794 (de Rossi 1061), f. 57a-58a, M.
17244. Parma - Biblioteca Palatina Cod. Parm. 2125 (de Rossi 812), f. 6b-8a, C.
17245. Parma - Biblioteca Palatina Cod. Parm. 3006 (de Rossi 654,1), f. 24a-25a, M.
17246. Vatican - Biblioteca Apostolica ebr. 306, f. 47b-48a, C, no incipit.

תבא לפניך שועת חינון (ת 33), שלמה הבבלי, סליחה
Ashkenaz

17247. Bologna - Archivio di Stato MS Ebr. 253, f. 1b, FC.
17248. Braunschweig - Landesmuseum fuer Geschichte und Volkstum R 2386, vol. II, f. 41b-42a, M.
17249. Budapest - Magyar tudomanyos akademia, MS. Kaufmann A 400, p. 448-450, C, rubric: אחרת שלמונית.
17250. Hamburg - Staats- und Universitaetsbibliothek Cod. hebr. 17/2 (Steinschneider 152), f. 133b-134a, C, rubric: אחרת שלמונית.
17251. Jerusalem - Schocken Institute 24100 / Mahzor Nuremberg, f. 237b-238a, M.
17252. Moscow - Russian State Library, Ms. Guenzburg 190, f. 46b-47a, G.
17253. Moscow - Russian State Library, Ms. Guenzburg 615, f. 150b-151b, C, rubric: אל מלך.
17254. Muenchen - Bayerische Staatsbibliothek, Cod. hebr. 346, f. 135b-136a, C, rubric: אחרת.
17255. Muenchen - Bayerische Staatsbibliothek, Cod. hebr. 346, f. 163a-163b, C.
17256. Oxford - Bodleian Library MS Mich. 543 (Neubauer 1212), f. 58b-59b, C, commentator: Isaac b. Jacob (compiler).
17257. Oxford - Bodleian Library MS Opp. 170 (Neubauer 1205), f. 215a-216b, C.
17258. Padova - Biblioteca del Seminario Vescovile Cod. 218, f. 55a-56a, M.
17259. Padova - Biblioteca del Seminario Vescovile Cod. 218, f. 226b-227b, M.
17260. Parma - Biblioteca Palatina Cod. Parm. 3205 (de Rossi 655), f. 256b-257a, C.
17261. Vatican - Biblioteca Apostolica ebr. 308/1, f. 4a-4b, C, commentator: David b. Mose (compiler).
17262. Vatican - Biblioteca Apostolica ebr. 422/1, f. 1a-3a, C, rubric: אחרת.
17263. Vatican - Biblioteca Apostolica ebr. 422/1, f. 26a, C, very short.
17264. Vatican - Biblioteca Apostolica ebr. 422/2, f. 40a, CG, no incipit, very short.

Ashkenaz, commentary by Abraham b. Azriel[380]

17265. Frankfurt a M - Stadt- und Universitaetsbibliothek Fol. 16 (Merzbacher 95), f. 116a, C, manuscript martly damaged.

17266. Vatican - Biblioteca Apostolica ebr. 301,1, f. 147a, C.

Tsarfat

17267. London - British Library Add. 11639 (Margoliouth 1056), f. 467b-468b, M.

17268. London - David Sofer 5, f. 97b-98a, C.

17269. Oxford - Bodleian Library MS Laud. Or. 271 (Neubauer 1206), f. 177a-177b, C, commentator: Aaron b. Hayyim haKohen (compiler).

17270. Oxford - Bodleian Library MS Opp. 171 (Neubauer 1207), f. 92a-92b, C, rubric: אחרת.

17271. Parma - Biblioteca Palatina Cod. Parm. 3007 (de Rossi 654,2), f. 89a-90a, M.

17272. Vatican - Biblioteca Apostolica ebr. 306, f. 99a-100a, C.

תבר גיברי שמע קלא דתבירי, סליחה

Yemen, commentary by Isaac b. Abraham Wanneh

17273. Chicago-Spertus College of Judaica D 2, 2, f. 247a, M, no incipit.

17274. Jerusalem - Sassoon 1158, p. 426, M, no incipit.

17275. London - British Library Or. 11122, f. 220b, M, no incipit.

תגרת יד אסף (ת 89), סליחה

Ashkenaz

17276. Bologna - Archivio di Stato MS Ebr. 253, f. ?b, FC.

17277. Budapest - Magyar tudomanyos akademia, MS. Kaufmann A 400, p. 485-486, C, rubric: אחרת.

17278. Forli - Archivio di Stato 4, FC.

17279. Jerusalem - Schocken Institute 24100 / Mahzor Nuremberg, f. 280a, M.

17280. Moscow - Russian State Library, Ms. Guenzburg 615, f. 157a-157b, C, rubric: אל מלך.

17281. Muenchen - Bayerische Staatsbibliothek, Cod. hebr. 346, f. 162a, C.

17282. New York - Jewish Theological Seminary Ms. 8097, f. 85a, C.

17283. Oxford - Bodleian Library MS Mich. 543 (Neubauer 1212), f. 31b-32a, C, commentator: Isaac b. Jacob (compiler).

17284. Oxford - Bodleian Library MS Mich. 543 (Neubauer 1212), f. 72a-72b, C, commentator: Isaac b. Jacob (compiler).

17285. Oxford - Bodleian Library MS Opp. 170 (Neubauer 1205), f. 226a-226b, C.

---

[380] Edited by Urbach, ערוגת הבושם, vol. III, p. 341-343.

17286. Oxford - Bodleian Library MS Opp. 681 (Neubauer 1213), f. 23a-23b, C.

17287. Padova - Biblioteca del Seminario Vescovile Cod. 218, f. 175b-176b, M.

17288. Parma - Bibliotheca Palatina Cod. Parm. 3205 (de Rossi 655), f. 287b, C.

17289. Parma - Biblioteca Palatina Cod. Parm. 3271 (de Rossi 1216), f. 78a-78b, G.

17290. Vatican - Biblioteca Apostolica ebr. 422/1, f. 25b, C.

17291. Vatican - Biblioteca Apostolica ebr. 422/2, f. 39a, CG, no incipit, short.

Ashkenaz, commentary by Abraham b. Azriel[381]

17292. Vatican - Biblioteca Apostolica ebr. 301,1, f. 162b, C, rubric: אחל פזמונים לתפילה מתוקנים כצילצול פעמונים בתוך הרימונים.

Tsarfat

17293. London - David Sofer 5, f. 98b-99a, C.

17294. Oxford - Bodleian Library MS Bodl. Or. 109 (Neubauer 1209), f. 73b-74b, C, commentator: Aaron b. Hayyim haKohen (compiler).

17295. Oxford - Bodleian Library MS Bodl. Or. 109 (Neubauer 1209), f. 77a, C, commentator: Aaron b. Hayyim haKohen (compiler), breaks off at the end of the page.

17296. Oxford - Bodleian Library MS Laud. Or. 271 (Neubauer 1206), f. 173a, C, commentator: Aaron b. Hayyim haKohen (compiler).

17297. Oxford - Bodleian Library MS Opp. 171 (Neubauer 1207), f. 109b-110a, C, rubric: אחרת.

17298. Parma - Biblioteca Palatina Cod. Parm. 3007 (de Rossi 654,2), f. 147a, M.

תהום השוטף על ראשי צפה (ת 107), סעדיה גאון, סליחה

Yemen

17299. New York - Jewish Theological Seminary Ms. 3028, f. 97a-97b, G.

17300. New York - Jewish Theological Seminary Ms. 3193, f. 137a-137b, M.

Yemen, commentary by Isaac b. Abraham Wanneh

17301. Chicago-Spertus College of Judaica D 2, 2, f. 227a-227b, M, no incipit.

17302. Jerusalem - Sassoon 1158, p. 313-314, M, no incipit.

17303. London - British Library Or. 11122, f. 203b-204a, M, no incipit.

---

[381] Edited by Urbach, ערוגת הבושם, vol. III, p. 442-443.

תהלה רוממה לאל נותן חכמה (ש ++123), יצחק בן מרדכי קמחי, חתימה לאזהרות
Italia, commentary by Isaac b. Mordekhai Qimḥi?
17304. Moscow - Russian State Library, Ms. Guenzburg 211, f. 106b, M, rubric: פירוש החתימה, short.

תהילות כבודך אומצך מלא כל הארץ (ת 126), אלעזר ברבי קליר, חלק י, קדושתא למוסף ראש השנה

Ashkenaz
17305. Berlin - Staatsbibliothek (Preussischer Kulturbesitz) Or. Qu. 798-799 (Steinschneider 177), I, f. 21b-22a, M.
17306. Budapest - Magyar tudomanyos akademia, MS. Kaufmann A 400, p. 272-273, C.
17307. Hamburg - Staats- und Universitaetsbibliothek Cod. hebr. 40b (Steinschneider 110), f. 19b, G.
17308. Hamburg - Staats- und Universitaetsbibliothek Cod. hebr. 40c (Steinschneider 111), f. 140a-140b, G.
17309. Jerusalem - Schocken Institute 24100 / Mahzor Nuremberg, f. 333b, M.
17310. London - British Library Or. 11318/1, f. 19a-20a, C.
17311. Moscow - Russian State Library, Ms. Guenzburg 191, f. 17a-17b, M.
17312. Muenchen - Bayerische Staatsbibliothek, Cod. hebr. 86, f. 30a-31a, G.
17313. Muenchen - Bayerische Staatsbibliothek, Cod. hebr. 346, f. 19a-20b, C.
17314. New York - Jewish Theological Seminary Ms. 4466, f. 229a-229b, M.
17315. Oxford - Bodleian Library MS Opp. 172 (Neubauer 1211), f. 12b-13a, C.
17316. Oxford - Bodleian Library MS Opp. 619 (Neubauer 2374), f. 34b, M.
17317. Oxford - Bodleian Library MS Opp. 675 (Neubauer 1210), f. 28b-29a, C, no incipit.
17318. Paris - Bibliotheque Nationale heb. 653, f. 18b, G.
17319. Parma - Biblioteca Palatina Cod. Parm. 3205 (de Rossi 655), f. 211a-211b, C.
17320. Parma - Biblioteca Palatina Cod. Parm. 3270 (de Rossi 1215), f. 35b-36a, M.
17321. Parma - Biblioteca Palatina Cod. Parm. 3507 (Perreau 27), f. 122b-123a, C.
17322. Vatican - Biblioteca Apostolica ebr. 308, f. 54a-55a, C, commentator: David b. Mose (compiler).
17323. Vatican - Biblioteca Apostolica ebr. 422/1, f. 10b, C, very short.
17324. Zurich - Zentralbibliothek Heid. 139, f. 65a-65b (inserted leaf), C.

Asti, Fossano, Moncalvo
17325. New Haven - Yale University, Beinecke Rare Book and MS Library, MS Heb. 52, f. 37a-37b, M.

17326. New Haven - Yale University, Beinecke Rare Book and MS Library, MS Heb. 52, f. 70b-71a, M.

Tsarfat

17327. Oxford - Bodleian Library MS Laud. Or. 271 (Neubauer 1206), f. 149a, C, commentator: Aaron b. Hayyim haKohen (compiler).
17328. Paris - Bibliotheque Nationale heb. 445,9, f. 79b-80a, C.
17329. Parma - Biblioteca Palatina Cod. Parm. 2125 (de Rossi 812), f. 22b, C.
17330. Parma - Biblioteca Palatina Cod. Parm. 3006 (de Rossi 654,1), f. 49b, M.
17331. Vatican - Biblioteca Apostolica ebr. 306, f. 55b-56a, C.

תוחלת ישראל חסד לא נעזב (ת 150), שלמה הבבלי, סליחה

Ashkenaz

17332. Bologna - Archivio di Stato MS Ebr. 253, f. 2a, FC, incomplete, only end.
17333. Budapest - Magyar tudomanyos akademia, MS. Kaufmann A 400, p. 451-455, C, rubric: אחרת שלמונית.
17334. Cambridge - University Library Dd. 2.30, f. 57b-58b, G.
17335. Hamburg - Staats- und Universitaetsbibliothek Cod. hebr. 17/2 (Steinschneider 152), f. 134b-135b, C, rubric: אחרת שלמונית.
17336. Jerusalem - Schocken Institute 24100 / Mahzor Nuremberg, f. 276a-276b, M.
17337. Moscow - Russian State Library, Ms. Guenzburg 190, f. 45b-46a, G.
17338. Moscow - Russian State Library, Ms. Guenzburg 615, f. 139b-142a, C.
17339. Muenchen - Bayerische Staatsbibliothek, Cod. hebr. 346, f. 132a-133b, C, rubric: אחרת למנחה.
17340. Muenchen - Bayerische Staatsbibliothek, Cod. hebr. 346, f. 161a-161b, C.
17341. Oxford - Bodleian Library MS Mich. 543 (Neubauer 1212), f. 59b-61b, C, commentator: Isaac b. Jacob (compiler).
17342. Oxford - Bodleian Library MS Opp. 170 (Neubauer 1205), f. 217a-219a, C.
17343. Oxford - Bodleian Library MS Opp. 681 (Neubauer 1213), f. 52a-55a, C.
17344. Padova - Biblioteca del Seminario Vescovile Cod. 218, f. 162b-163b, M.
17345. Parma - Biblioteca Palatina Cod. Parm. 3205 (de Rossi 655), f. 261a-262a, C.
17346. Vatican - Biblioteca Apostolica ebr. 422/1, f. 4b-6a, C, rubric: אחרת.
17347. Vatican - Biblioteca Apostolica ebr. 422/1, f. 26b-27a, C.
17348. Vatican - Biblioteca Apostolica ebr. 422/1, f. 40b, CG, no incipit, short.

Ashkenaz, commentary by Abraham b. Azriel[382]

17349. Vatican - Biblioteca Apostolica ebr. 301,1, f. 159a-159b, C, rubric: אחרת.

Tsarfat

17350. London - British Library Add. 11639 (Margoliouth 1056), f. 464a-465b, M.

17351. London - David Sofer 5, f. 96b-97b, C.

17352. Oxford - Bodleian Library MS Laud. Or. 271 (Neubauer 1206), f. 164b-166a, C, commentator: Aaron b. Hayyim haKohen (compiler).

17353. Oxford - Bodleian Library MS Opp. 171 (Neubauer 1207), f. 99a-100b, C, rubric: אחרת.

17354. Parma - Biblioteca Palatina Cod. Parm. 2890 (de Rossi 856), f. 126a-127b, M.

17355. Parma - Biblioteca Palatina Cod. Parm. 3007 (de Rossi 654,2), f. 90b-92a, M.

17356. Vatican - Biblioteca Apostolica ebr. 306, f. 97b-99a, C.

תורה הקדושה התחנני (ת 180), שמעון ב"ר יצחק, סליחה

Ashkenaz

17357. Budapest - Magyar tudomanyos akademia, MS. Kaufmann A 400, p. 521-523, C, rubric: תחינה אחרת.

17358. Hamburg - Staats- und Universitaetsbibliothek Cod. hebr. 17/2 (Steinschneider 152), f. 144a-144b, C.

17359. Jerusalem - Schocken Institute 24100 / Mahzor Nuremberg, f. 313a-313b, M.

17360. Muenchen - Bayerische Staatsbibliothek, Cod. hebr. 346, f. 117b-118a, C.

17361. Oxford - Bodleian Library MS Mich. 543 (Neubauer 1212), f. 80b-81b, C, commentator: Isaac b. Jacob (compiler), rubric: מחי ומסי.

17362. Oxford - Bodleian Library MS Opp. 170 (Neubauer 1205), f. 237a-238a, C.

17363. Padova - Biblioteca del Seminario Vescovile Cod. 218, f. 125a-125b, M.

17364. Parma - Biblioteca Palatina Cod. Parm. 3205 (de Rossi 655), f. 284b-285a, C.

17365. Vatican - Biblioteca Apostolica ebr. 422/1, f. 34b, C.

Tsarfat

17366. Oxford - Bodleian Library MS Laud. Or. 271 (Neubauer 1206), f. 169b-170b, C, commentator: Aaron b. Hayyim haKohen (compiler).

17367. Oxford - Bodleian Library MS Opp. 171 (Neubauer 1207), f. 89a-89b, C, rubric: אחרת.

---

[382] Edited by Urbach, ערוגת הבושם, vol. III, p. 421-426.

17368. Parma - Biblioteca Palatina Cod. Parm. 3007 (de Rossi 654,2), f. 101b-102b, M.
17369. Vatican - Biblioteca Apostolica ebr. 306, f. 212a-212b, C.

תורה תמימה משיבה נפש (ת 190), יוסף ב"ר שמואל טוב עלם, חלק ב', קדושתא לשבועות

Tsarfat
17370. London - David Sofer 5, f. 68a, C.
17371. Moscow - Russian State Library, Ms. Guenzburg 1665, f. 141b, M, no incipit.
17372. Parma - Biblioteca Palatina Cod. Parm. 3136 (de Rossi 405), f. 169a-169b, M, no incipit.

תורתא דמרביא בטולי וברנני (ת+203), סליחה

Ashkenaz
17373. Budapest - Magyar tudomanyos akademia, MS. Kaufmann A 400, p. 527, C, rubric: אחרת.

Yemen
17374. New York - Jewish Theological Seminary Ms. 3052, f. 84b-85b, M.
17375. New York - Jewish Theological Seminary Ms. 3109, f. 26a-26b, M, no incipit.

Yemen, commentary by Isaac b. Abraham Wanneh
17376. Chicago-Spertus College of Judaica D 2, 2, f. 238a, M, no incipit.
17377. Jerusalem - Benayahu ת 261, f. 165b-166a, M, no incipit.
17378. Jerusalem - Benayahu ת 282, f. 141a-141b, M.
17379. Jerusalem - Makhon Ben Zvi 1156 (Tubi 155), f. 139a, M, no incipit.
17380. Jerusalem - Makhon Ben Zvi 1174 (Tubi 154), f. 137b, M.
17381. Jerusalem - Michael Krupp 604, f. 176a, M.
17382. Jerusalem - Musad haRav Kook 325, f. 195b, M.
17383. Jerusalem - Sassoon 1174, p. 270, M, no incipit.
17384. London - British Library Or. 11122, f. 215b, M, no incipit.
17385. Manchester - John Rylands University Library, Ms. Gaster 5, f. 224a-224b, M.
17386. Muenchen - Bayerische Staatsbibliothek, Cod. hebr. 472, f. 194a-194b, M.
17387. New York - Jewish Theological Seminary Ms. 3013, f. 133b-134a, M, no incipit.
17388. New York - Jewish Theological Seminary Ms. 3294, f. 17a-17b, C.
17389. New York - Public Library, Heb. Ms. 9, f. 130b-131a, M, no incipit.
17390. Strasbourg - Bibliotheque Nationale et Universitaire 3965 (Landauer 39), p. 412, M.

תחבולות עש רב עצה וגבורה (ת 211), משה בן קלונימוס, חלק ב', קדושתא לפסח
Ashkenaz
17391. Berlin - Staatsbibliothek (Preussischer Kulturbesitz) Or. Qu. 798-799 (Steinschneider 177), II, f. 90b-91a, M.
17392. Braunschweig - Landesmuseum fuer Geschichte und Volkstum R 2386, vol. I, f. 60b-61a, M.
17393. Budapest - Magyar tudomanyos akademia, MS. Kaufmann A 384, f. 202a-202b, M.
17394. Budapest - Magyar tudomanyos akademia, MS. Kaufmann A 400, p. 137-138, C.
17395. Hamburg - Staats- und Universitaetsbibliothek Cod. hebr. 17/2 (Steinschneider 152), f. 67a, C.
17396. Jerusalem - Schocken Institute 24100 / Mahzor Nuremberg, f. 121b, M, very short.
17397. Moscow - Russian State Library, Ms. Guenzburg 615, f. 25a, C, very short, no incipit.
17398. Muenchen - Bayerische Staatsbibliothek, Cod. hebr. 88, f. 82a-82b, G.
17399. Muenchen - Bayerische Staatsbibliothek, Cod. hebr. 393, f. 134b, C, no incipit.
17400. New York - Jewish Theological Seminary Ms. 4466, f. 107b, M, very short.
17401. Oxford - Bodleian Library MS Opp. 170 (Neubauer 1205), f. 76a, C, very short.
17402. Paris - Bibliotheque Nationale heb. 709, f. 102a, C, no incipit.
17403. Parma - Biblioteca Palatina Cod. Parm. 3205 (de Rossi 655), f. 108b, C, short, no incipit.
17404. Parma - Biblioteca Palatina Cod. Parm. 3507 (Perreau 27), f. 72b-73a, C, no incipit.
17405. Zurich - Zentralbibliothek Heid. 139, f. 45b-46a, C, no incipit, additional marginal notes.
Tsarfat
17406. London - David Sofer 5, f. 41a-41b, C, additional glosses.
17407. Moscow - Russian State Library, Ms. Guenzburg 1665, f. 89b, M.
17408. Vatican - Biblioteca Apostolica ebr. 306, f. 217a-217b, C, no incipit.

תחבושת אילמה למור (ת 212), בנימין ב"ר שמואל, חלק ב', קדושתא לראש השנה
Ashkenaz
17409. Moscow - Russian State Library, Ms. Guenzburg 191, f. 49b-50a, M.
17410. New York - Jewish Theological Seminary Ms. 8169 (Acc. 0016), f. 45a-45b, M.
Tsarfat
17411. London - British Library Or. 8682, f. 43b-44a, Gl.

17412. London - David Sofer 5, f. 123b, C, no incipit.
17413. Oxford - Bodleian Library MS Opp. 171 (Neubauer 1207), f. 69a, C.
17414. Parma - Biblioteca Palatina Cod. Parm. 1794 (de Rossi 1061), f. 82a-83a, M.
17415. Parma - Biblioteca Palatina Cod. Parm. 2125 (de Rossi 812), f. 32a, C.
17416. Parma - Biblioteca Palatina Cod. Parm. 3006 (de Rossi 654,1), f. 86b-87a, M.
17417. Vatican - Biblioteca Apostolica ebr. 306, f. 69b-70a, C, no incipit.

תחרות רוגז הניח ותזכור רחם (ת 229), אליה ב"ר שמעיה, סליחה
Ashkenaz
17418. Bologna - Archivio di Stato MS Ebr. 253, f. 1b, FC, only beginning.
17419. Budapest - Magyar tudomanyos akademia, MS. Kaufmann A 400, p. 484-485, C, rubric: אחרת והיא לתענית גזירה.
17420. Cambridge - University Library Dd. 2.30, f. 52a-53a, G.
17421. Jerusalem - Schocken Institute 24100 / Mahzor Nuremberg, f. 269b-270a, M.
17422. Moscow - Russian State Library, Ms. Guenzburg 190, f. 47b-48a, G.
17423. Moscow - Russian State Library, Ms. Guenzburg 615, f. 161a-161b, C, rubric: אל מלך.
17424. Muenchen - Bayerische Staatsbibliothek, Cod. hebr. 346, f. 134b-135a, C, rubric: אחרת.
17425. Muenchen - Bayerische Staatsbibliothek, Cod. hebr. 346, f. 162a, C.
17426. Oxford - Bodlcian Library MS Mich. 543 (Neubauer 1212), f. 71b-72a, C, commentator: Isaac b. Jacob (compiler).
17427. Oxford - Bodleian Library MS Opp. 170 (Neubauer 1205), f. 230a-230b, C.
17428. Oxford - Bodleian Library MS Opp. 681 (Neubauer 1213), f. 55a-56b, C.
17429. Padova - Biblioteca del Seminario Vescovile Cod. 218, f. 140b-141a, M.
17430. Padova - Biblioteca del Seminario Vescovile Cod. 218, f. 141a-141b, M.
17431. Parma - Biblioteca Palatina Cod. Parm. 3205 (de Rossi 655), f. 257b-258a, C.
Ashkenaz, commentary by Abraham b. Azriel[383]
17432. Frankfurt a M - Stadt- und Universitaetsbibliothek Fol. 16 (Merzbacher 95), f. 116a-116b, C.
17433. Vatican - Biblioteca Apostolica ebr. 301,1, f. 154b-155a, C.

---

[383] Edited by Urbach, ערוגת הבושם, vol. III, p. 395-397.

Tsarfat

17434. London - British Library Add. 11639 (Margoliouth 1056), f. 474b-475a, M.
17435. London - David Sofer 5, f. 176a-176b, C, rubric: סליחה.
17436. Oxford - Bodleian Library MS Laud. Or. 271 (Neubauer 1206), f. 172a-172b, C, commentator: Aaron b. Hayyim haKohen (compiler).
17437. Oxford - Bodleian Library MS Opp. 171 (Neubauer 1207), f. 92b-93a, C, rubric: אחרת דר' אליהו בר שמעיה.
17438. Parma - Biblioteca Palatina Cod. Parm. 1794 (de Rossi 1061), f. 18b-20a, M.
17439. Parma - Biblioteca Palatina Cod. Parm. 2125 (de Rossi 812), f. 56b-57b, C.
17440. Parma - Biblioteca Palatina Cod. Parm. 2890 (de Rossi 856), f. 52b-53b, M.
17441. Parma - Biblioteca Palatina Cod. Parm. 3006 (de Rossi 654,1), f. 203a-203b, M.
17442. Vatican - Biblioteca Apostolica ebr. 306, f. 89a-89b, C.

תחת אילת עופר בורך מושיע בטל (ת 231), אלעזר ברבי קליר, תפלת טל

Ashkenaz

17443. Berlin - Staatsbibliothek (Preussischer Kulturbesitz) Or. Qu. 798-799 (Steinschneider 177), II, f. 67a-67b, M.
17444. Braunschweig - Landesmuseum fuer Geschichte und Volkstum R 2386, vol. I, f. 26a-26b, M.
17445. Budapest - Magyar tudomanyos akademia, MS. Kaufmann A 384, f. 141a-142a, M.
17446. Budapest - Magyar tudomanyos akademia, MS. Kaufmann A 400, p. 115-118, C, no incipit.
17447. Budapest - Magyar tudomanyos akademia, MS. Kaufmann A 400, p. 388-390, C.
17448. Hamburg - Staats- und Universitaetsbibliothek Cod. hebr. 17/2 (Steinschneider 152), f. 58b-59b, C.
17449. Jerusalem - Schocken Institute 24100 / Mahzor Nuremberg, f. 85b-86a, M.
17450. London - British Library Add. 18695 (Margoliouth 683), f. 28b-29b, T, Yiddish.
17451. Moscow - Russian State Library, Ms. Guenzburg 615, f. 14a-15b, C.
17452. Muenchen - Bayerische Staatsbibliothek, Cod. hebr. 21, f. 29a, M.
17453. New York - Jewish Theological Seminary Ms. 4466, f. 61a-62b, M.
17454. Oxford - Bodleian Library MS Opp. 170 (Neubauer 1205), f. 66b-68a, C.
17455. Paris - Bibliotheque Nationale heb. 709, f. 82b-84b, C.
17456. Parma - Biblioteca Palatina Cod. Parm. 1002 (Ta 24), f. 99b-100b, M.

17457. Parma - Biblioteca Palatina Cod. Parm. 3000 (de Rossi 378), f. 62a-63a, M.
17458. Parma - Biblioteca Palatina Cod. Parm. 3205 (de Rossi 655), f. 87a-88a, C.
17459. Parma - Biblioteca Palatina Cod. Parm. 3507 (Perreau 27), f. 54a, C, no incipit.
17460. Zurich - Zentralbibliothek Heid. 139, f. 31a-31b, C, additional marginal notes.

Romania
17461. Cambridge - University Library Add. 377,3, f. 59a-60a, C.
17462. New York - Jewish Theological Seminary Ms. 4823, f. 1b, FM, only beginning.

Tsarfat
17463. London - British Library Add. 11639 (Margoliouth 1056), f. 659a-660a, M.
17464. Moscow - Russian State Library, Ms. Guenzburg 1665, f. 63a-64a, M.
17465. Oxford - Bodleian Library MS Laud. Or. 271 (Neubauer 1206), f. 66a-67a, C, commentator: Aaron b. Hayyim haKohen (compiler).
17466. Parma - Biblioteca Palatina Cod. Parm. 3136 (de Rossi 405), f. 85b-86a, M.
17467. Vatican - Biblioteca Apostolica ebr. 306, f. 144a-145b, C, no incipit.

תחת התפוח עוררת איומתך (ת 235), יצחק בן אליעזר, זולת לשבת חתן

Ashkenaz
17468. Budapest - Magyar tudomanyos akademia, MS. Kaufmann A 399, p. 370-373, C, rubric: זולת.

תכון תפלתי לאל ישועתי (ת 255), יעקב בן חיים, תפלת התמיד

Carpentras
17469. Cincinnati - Hebrew Union College 357, f. 151a-154b, M, rubric: פירוש שיידי טהרה.

תכנם לארץ וחוצות (ת 267), אלעזר ברבי קליר, למוסף שמיני עצרת

Ashkenaz
17470. Berlin - Staatsbibliothek (Preussischer Kulturbesitz) Or. Qu. 798-799 (Steinschneider 177), I, f. 216b-217a, M.
17471. Braunschweig - Landesmuseum fuer Geschichte und Volkstum R 2386, vol. I, f. 154b-155a, M.
17472. Budapest - Magyar tudomanyos akademia, MS. Kaufmann A 400, p. 401-403, C.
17473. Fulda - Hessische Landesbibliothek A 3 II, f. 144b-146a, C, commentator: Josef.

17474. Hamburg - Staats- und Universitaetsbibliothek Cod. hebr. 17/2 (Steinschneider 152), f. 172b-173b, C.
17475. Hamburg - Staats- und Universitaetsbibliothek Cod. hebr. 62 (Steinschneider 154), f. 47b-48b, C, no incipit, end missing.
17476. Hamburg - Staats- und Universitaetsbibliothek Cod. hebr. 132 (Steinschneider 155), f. 64a-66a, C.
17477. Jerusalem - Jewish National and University Library Ms Heb 8° 3037, f. 290b, M, short.
17478. Jerusalem - Schocken Institute 24100 / Mahzor Nuremberg, f. 501a-502a, M.
17479. London - British Library Add. 18695 (Margoliouth 683), f. 129a-129b, T, Yiddish.
17480. London - British Library Add. 22431 (Margoliouth 662a), f. 138a-138b, M.
17481. London - British Library Or. 11318/1, f. 144b-146a, C.
17482. London - Montefiore Library 261, f. 77a-78a, C, commentator: Eliezer b. Natan?.
17483. Moscow - Russian State Library, Ms. Guenzburg 615, f. 122b-123b, C.
17484. New York - Jewish Theological Seminary Ms. 4466, f. 462a-463a, M.
17485. Oxford - Bodleian Library MS Mich. 365 (Neubauer 1208), f. 109b-110b, C.
17486. Oxford - Bodleian Library MS Opp. 170 (Neubauer 1205), f. 193b-195a, C.
17487. Parma - Biblioteca Palatina Cod. Parm. 3205 (de Rossi 655), f. 245a-245b, C.
17488. Parma - Biblioteca Palatina Cod. Parm. 3507 (Perreau 27), f. 185a-188a, C.
17489. Vatican - Biblioteca Apostolica ebr. 305,1, f. 47b-48a, C, no incipit.
17490. Zurich - Zentralbibliothek Heid. 139, f. 97b-98a, C, additional marginal notes.

Romania
17491. New York - Jewish Theological Seminary Ms. 4823, f. 14a-14b, FM.
17492. Vatican - Biblioteca Apostolica ebr. 320, f. 467b-468b, M.

Tsarfat
17493. London - British Library Add. 11639 (Margoliouth 1056), f. 666a-666b, M.
17494. London - David Sofer 5, f. 187a-188a, C.
17495. Moscow - Russian State Library, Ms. Guenzburg 1665, f. 193b-194b, M.
17496. Oxford - Bodleian Library MS Laud. Or. 271 (Neubauer 1206), f. 101b-102a, C, commentator: Aaron b. Hayyim haKohen (compiler), no incipit.

17497. Oxford - Bodleian Library MS Opp. 171 (Neubauer 1207), f. 157a-161b, C.
17498. Parma - Biblioteca Palatina Cod. Parm. 1264, f. 125a-126a, M.
17499. Vatican - Biblioteca Apostolica ebr. 306, f. 117a-118a, C.

תם אהל צדק (ת 291), משה אבן עזרא, חלק ד', קדושתא לשחרית יום כפור

Carpentras
17500. Cincinnati - Hebrew Union College 392, f. 47b-48b, M, no incipit.
Carpentras, commentary by Josef b. Abraham of Montelitz
17501. Cincinnati - Hebrew Union College 291, f. 23b-25a, C, rubric: פי' תם אהל צדק וכו'.
17502. New York - Jewish Theological Seminary Ms. 4197, f. 109b-111a, M, no incipit.
17503. Paris - Ecole Rabbinique 32, f. 130a-131b, M, no incipit.
17504. Strasbourg - Bibliotheque Nationale et Universitaire 4081, f. 107a-108b, M, no incipit.

תמהים מחובם בשבתם וקימתם (ת 305), משה אבן עזרא, חלק ג', קדושתא למוסף יום כפור

Carpentras
17505. Cincinnati - Hebrew Union College 392, f. 87a, M.
Carpentras, commentary by Josef b. Abraham of Montelitz
17506. Cincinnati - Hebrew Union College 291, f. 45b-46a, C, rubric: פי' פזמון תמהים וכו'.
17507. New York - Jewish Theological Seminary Ms. 4197, f. 198b-199a, M.
17508. Paris - Ecole Rabbinique 32, f. 206b-207b, M.
17509. Strasbourg - Bibliotheque Nationale et Universitaire 4081, f. 181b-182a, M.

תמהנו מרעות תשש כחנו מצרות (ת 307), סליחה

Sepharad
17510. Jerusalem - Schocken Institute 70014, f. 61a, M.
17511. Skokie - Hebrew Theological College 3, f. 8b, M.
17512. Skokie - Hebrew Theological College 3, f. 2.18a, M.
Yemen
17513. Jerusalem - Sassoon 264, f. 143a, M, short.
17514. New York - Jewish Theological Seminary Ms. 3193, f. 117b, M.
Yemen, commentary by Isaac b. Abraham Wanneh
17515. Chicago-Spertus College of Judaica D 2, 2, f. 179b, M.
17516. Jerusalem - Sassoon 1158, p. 297-298, M.
17517. London - British Library Or. 11122, f. 156a, M.

תמו פסו עבודת בית עולמים (ת 311), מאיר ב"ר יצחק, סליחה

Ashkenaz

17518. Cambridge - University Library Dd. 2.30, f. 69a-69b, G.
17519. Muenchen - Bayerische Staatsbibliothek, Cod. hebr. 346, f. 124a, C, no incipit, very short.

תמוט לתמיד, סליחה

Ashkenaz

17520. Muenchen - Bayerische Staatsbibliothek, Cod. hebr. 346, f. 163b-164a, C, short.

תמור עבודת מזין שועת עני תאזין (ת 319), מאיר ב"ר יצחק, סליחה

Ashkenaz

17521. Jerusalem - Schocken Institute 24100 / Mahzor Nuremberg, f. 449a, M, short.
17522. Muenchen - Bayerische Staatsbibliothek, Cod. hebr. 346, f. 149b, C, rubric: אחרת, short.
17523. Oxford - Bodleian Library MS Opp. 172 (Neubauer 1211), f. 83a-83b, C.
17524. Oxford - Bodleian Library MS Opp. 681 (Neubauer 1213), f. 40a, C, short.
17525. Oxford - Bodleian Library MS Opp. 681 (Neubauer 1213), f. 73b, C, very short.
17526. Vatican - Biblioteca Apostolica ebr. 308, f. 142a, C, commentator: David b. Mose (compiler).

Ashkenaz, commentary by Abraham b. Azriel[384]

17527. Frankfurt a M - Stadt- und Universitaetsbibliothek Fol. 16 (Merzbacher 95), f. 107b, C, short.

Tsarfat

17528. London - David Sofer 5, f. 99a, C, very short.
17529. Parma - Biblioteca Palatina Cod. Parm. 3007 (de Rossi 654,2), f. 90b, M, very short.
17530. Vatican - Biblioteca Apostolica ebr. 306, f. 201b, C, very short.

תמיד קרוב לעמך נדרש (ת 326), נתנאל ב"ר יוסף, סדר התמיד

Ashkenaz

17531. Cambridge - University Library Add. 394,1 (Reif SCR 461), f. 87b-95b, C, rubric: תמיד לרבינו הרב ר' נתנאל.

---

[384] Edited by Urbach, ערוגת הבושם, vol. III, p. 558.

תמיד תתלונן בידך כל נפש (ת 327), משולם ב"ר קלונימוס, חלק כה', קדושתא לשחרית יום כפור

Ashkenaz

17532. Berlin - Staatsbibliothek (Preussischer Kulturbesitz) Or. Qu. 798-799 (Steinschneider 177), I, f. 87a-87b, M.
17533. Braunschweig - Landesmuseum fuer Geschichte und Volkstum R 2386, vol. II, f. 199b-200a, M, no incipit.
17534. Budapest - Magyar tudomanyos akademia, MS. Kaufmann A 400 , p. 335-336, C.
17535. Cambridge - University Library Add. 394,1 (Reif SCR 461), f. 72a-72b margin, C.
17536. Cambridge - University Library Add. 394,1 (Reif SCR 461), f. 72b, C.
17537. Jerusalem - Jewish National and University Library Ms Heb 8° 3037, f. 133b-134a, M, no incipit.
17538. Jerusalem - Schocken Institute 24100 / Mahzor Nuremberg , f. 385a, M.
17539. London - British Library Or. 11318/1, f. 83b-84b, C.
17540. London - Montefiore Library 261, f. 48b, C, commentator: Eliezer b. Natan?.
17541. Moscow - Russian State Library, Ms. Guenzburg 191 , f. 124a-124b, M.
17542. Muenchen - Bayerische Staatsbibliothek, Cod. hebr. 346 , f. 58b-59b, C.
17543. New York - Jewish Theological Seminary Ms. 4466, f. 327a-327b, M.
17544. New York - Jewish Theological Seminary Ms. 8169 (Acc. 0016), f. 100b, M.
17545. Oxford - Bodleian Library MS Mich. 365 (Neubauer 1208), f. 73b-74a, C.
17546. Oxford - Bodleian Library MS Opp. 172 (Neubauer 1211), f. 46a-46b, C.
17547. Parma - Biblioteca Palatina Cod. Parm. 3205 (de Rossi 655), f. 227a, C.
17548. Parma - Biblioteca Palatina Cod. Parm. 3271 (de Rossi 1216), f. 52b-53a, G.
17549. Parma - Biblioteca Palatina Cod. Parm. 3507 (Perreau 27), f. 154a-154b, C, no incipit.
17550. Vatican - Biblioteca Apostolica ebr. 308, f. 108a-108b, C, commentator: David b. Mose (compiler).
17551. Vatican - Biblioteca Apostolica ebr. 422/1, f. 16b, C, short.

Asti, Fossano, Moncalvo

17552. New Haven - Yale University, Beinecke Rare Book and MS Library, MS Heb. 52, f. 139b, M.

Roma

17553. Jerusalem - Jewish National and University Library Ms Heb 8° 4153, f. 140b, C, commentator: Daniel ben Salomo haRofe (compiler), no incipit, very short.
17554. Oxford - Bodleian Library MS Mich. 312,1 (Neubauer 2276,1), f. 8b, C, very short.

Tsarfat

17555. London - David Sofer 5, f. 153b-154a, C.
17556. Oxford - Bodleian Library MS Bodl. Or. 109 (Neubauer 1209), f. 24b-25a, C, commentator: Aaron b. Hayyim haKohen (compiler).
17557. Parma - Biblioteca Palatina Cod. Parm. 1794 (de Rossi 1061), f. 182a-182b, M.
17558. Parma - Biblioteca Palatina Cod. Parm. 2890 (de Rossi 856), f. 79b, M.
17559. Parma - Biblioteca Palatina Cod. Parm. 3006 (de Rossi 654,1), f. 185b-186a, M.

תמים פעלך גדול העצה (ת 332), שמעון ב"ר יצחק, חלק ב', קדושתא לראש השנה

Ashkenaz

17560. Berlin - Staatsbibliothek (Preussischer Kulturbesitz) Or. Qu. 798-799 (Steinschneider 177), I, f. 35b-36a, M.
17561. Braunschweig - Landesmuseum fuer Geschichte und Volkstum R 2386, vol. II, f. 110b-111a, M.
17562. Cambridge - University Library Or. 785, f. 59b-60a, G.
17563. Darmstadt - Hessisches Landes- und Hochschulbibliothek Cod. Or. 15, f. 34a-34b, M, short.
17564. Hamburg - Staats- und Universitaetsbibliothek Cod. hebr. 17/2 (Steinschneider 152), f. 122a, C.
17565. Hamburg - Staats- und Universitaetsbibliothek Cod. hebr. 40b (Steinschneider 110), f. 40a, G.
17566. Hamburg - Staats- und Universitaetsbibliothek Cod. hebr. 40c (Steinschneider 111), f. 147a, G.
17567. Hamburg - Staats- und Universitaetsbibliothek Cod. hebr. 132 (Steinschneider 155), f. 24a, C, incipit בו.
17568. Hamburg - Staats- und Universitaetsbibliothek Cod. hebr. 225, f. 252b-253a, G.
17569. Jerusalem - Jewish National and University Library Ms Heb 8° 3037, f. 52a-53a, M.
17570. Jerusalem - Schocken Institute 24100 / Mahzor Nuremberg, f. 341a-341b, M.
17571. London - British Library Or. 11318/1, f. 40a-40b, C.
17572. London - Montefiore Library 261, f. 27b-28a, C, commentator: Eliezer b. Natan?.
17573. Moscow - Russian State Library, Ms. Guenzburg 191, f. 35a-35b, M.

17574. Moscow - Russian State Library, Ms. Guenzburg 615, f. 86a, C, short.
17575. Muenchen - Bayerische Staatsbibliothek, Cod. hebr. 21, f. 178b-179a, M.
17576. Muenchen - Bayerische Staatsbibliothek, Cod. hebr. 86, f. 63a-64a, G.
17577. Muenchen - Bayerische Staatsbibliothek, Cod. hebr. 346, f. 35b, C.
17578. New York - Jewish Theological Seminary Ms. 4466, f. 250b-251a, M.
17579. New York - Jewish Theological Seminary Ms. 8097, f. 65a-65b, C.
17580. New York - Jewish Theological Seminary Ms. 8169 (Acc. 0016), f. 33b-34a, M.
17581. Oxford - Bodleian Library MS Mich. 365 (Neubauer 1208), f. 49b-50a, C.
17582. Oxford - Bodleian Library MS Opp. 170 (Neubauer 1205), f. 143b, C, short.
17583. Oxford - Bodleian Library MS Opp. 172 (Neubauer 1211), f. 20b-21a, C.
17584. Oxford - Bodleian Library MS Opp. 619 (Neubauer 2374), f. 58b-59a, M, short.
17585. Oxford - Bodleian Library MS Opp. 675 (Neubauer 1210), f. 50a-50b, C, no incipit.
17586. Parma - Biblioteca Palatina Cod. Parm. 3205 (de Rossi 655), f. 217a, C, no incipit, short.
17587. Parma - Biblioteca Palatina Cod. Parm. 3507 (Perreau 27), f. 132a, C, short, no incipit.
17588. Vatican - Biblioteca Apostolica ebr. 308, f. 75a-75b, C, commentator: David b. Mose (compiler).
17589. Vatican - Biblioteca Apostolica ebr. 422/1, f. 12b, C, short.
17590. Zurich - Zentralbibliothek Heid. 139, f. 70b, C, no incipit, short, additional marginal notes.

Asti, Fossano, Moncalvo

17591. New Haven - Yale University, Beinecke Rare Book and MS Library, MS Heb. 52, f. 52b-53a, M.

Romania

17592. Vatican - Biblioteca Apostolica ebr. 320, f. 180b-181b, M.

Tsarfat

17593. London - British Library Or. 8682, f. 36a-36b, Gl.
17594. London - David Sofer 5, f. 120a, C.
17595. Oxford - Bodleian Library MS Laud. Or. 271 (Neubauer 1206), f. 157a, C, commentator: Aaron b. Hayyim haKohen (compiler), no incipit.
17596. Oxford - Bodleian Library MS Opp. 171 (Neubauer 1207), f. 67a-67b, C, short.
17597. Parma - Biblioteca Palatina Cod. Parm. 2125 (de Rossi 812), f. 29b-30a, C, short.

17598. Parma - Biblioteca Palatina Cod. Parm. 3006 (de Rossi 654,1), f. 69a-69b, M, additonal commentary on the margins.
17599. Vatican - Biblioteca Apostolica ebr. 306, f. 66b, C, no incipit.

תמימי אורח חיל אזרו (ת 334), יצחק גיאת, חלק ג', קדושתא למוסף יום כפור
Sepharad, commentary by David b. Josef Abudarham[385]
17600. Budapest - Magyar tudomanyos akademia, MS. Kaufmann A 405/2, p. 246, C, rubric: משלש לר' יצחק גיאת.
17601. New York - Columbia X893 Ab 93, f. 28a-28b, C, rubric: משלש לר' יצחק ן' גיאת ז"ל.

תמימים בעודם בסין רפודים (ת 335), אלעזר ברבי קליר, חלק ב', קדושתא לשבת זכור
Ashkenaz
17602. Berlin - Staatsbibliothek (Preussischer Kulturbesitz) Or. Qu. 798-799 (Steinschneider 177), II, f. 20b-21a, M.
17603. Budapest - Magyar tudomanyos akademia, MS. Kaufmann A 384, f. 53a-53b, M.
17604. Cambridge - University Library Add. 504,1, f. 13a-14a, C, no incipit.
17605. Cambridge - University Library, Taylor Schechter Collection Misc. 33/3, f. 20b-21a, G.
17606. Erlangen - Universitaetsbibliothek 2601 (Roth 67), f. 34b, M, very short.
17607. Hamburg - Staats- und Universitaetsbibliothek Cod. hebr. 225, f. 22a-22b, G.
17608. Jerusalem - Schocken Institute 24100 / Mahzor Nuremberg, f. 41b, M.
17609. Muenchen - Bayerische Staatsbibliothek, Cod. hebr. 88, f. 24a-24b, G.
17610. Muenchen - Bayerische Staatsbibliothek, Cod. hebr. 393, f. 90a-90b, C, no incipit.
17611. Oxford - Bodleian Library MS Opp. 170 (Neubauer 1205), f. 10a-11a, C.
17612. Paris - Bibliotheque Nationale heb. 709, f. 18b-20a, C.
17613. Parma - Biblioteca Palatina Cod. Parm. 1002 (Ta 24), f. 35b-36a, M.
17614. Parma - Biblioteca Palatina Cod. Parm. 3205 (de Rossi 655), f. 19a-20a, C, no incipit.
17615. Parma - Biblioteca Palatina Cod. Parm. 3507 (Perreau 27), f. 13a-14a, C, no incipit.
17616. Vatican - Biblioteca Apostolica ebr. 305,1, f. 12a-13a, C.
Tsarfat
17617. London - British Library Add. 11639 (Margoliouth 1056), f. 267b-268a, M.

---

[385] Edited by Prins, תשלום אבודרהם, p. 116-117.

17618. London - David Sofer 5, f. 18b-19b, C.
17619. Moscow - Russian State Library, Ms. Guenzburg 1665, f. 18a, M.
17620. Oxford - Bodleian Library MS Opp. 171 (Neubauer 1207), f. 14b-16a, C, no incipit.
17621. Parma - Biblioteca Palatina Cod. Parm. 3136 (de Rossi 405), f. 31a-31b, M.
17622. Vatican - Biblioteca Apostolica ebr. 306, f. 162a-162b, C, no incipit.

תמימים כרשו ארץ נערץ (ת 336), אלעזר ברבי קליר, פיוט הרכבה לקרובה לפורים
Ashkenaz
17623. Berlin - Staatsbibliothek (Preussischer Kulturbesitz) Or. Qu. 798-799 (Steinschneider 177), II, f. 27b-28a, M.
17624. Budapest - Magyar tudomanyos akademia, MS. Kaufmann A 384, f. 66b-67b, M.
17625. Budapest - Magyar tudomanyos akademia, MS. Kaufmann A 400, p. 64-68, C, no incipit.
17626. Erlangen - Universitaetsbibliothek 2601 (Roth 67), f. 40b, M, no incipit.
17627. Hamburg - Staats- und Universitaetsbibliothek Cod. hebr. 17/2 (Steinschneider 152), f. 22b-23a, C.
17628. Jerusalem - Schocken Institute 24100 / Mahzor Nuremberg, f. 49b-50a, M.
17629. Muenchen - Bayerische Staatsbibliothek, Cod. hebr. 88, f. 34a-34b, G.
17630. Muenchen - Bayerische Staatsbibliothek, Cod. hebr. 393, f. 96a-97a, C, no incipit.
17631. Oxford - Bodleian Library MS Opp. 170 (Neubauer 1205), f. 21b-23a, C.
17632. Paris - Bibliotheque Nationale heb. 709, f. 28b-30a, C.
17633. Parma - Biblioteca Palatina Cod. Parm. 1002 (Ta 24), f. 46b-47b, M.
17634. Parma - Biblioteca Palatina Cod. Parm. 3205 (de Rossi 655), f. 29b-30a, C.
17635. Parma - Biblioteca Palatina Cod. Parm. 3507 (Perreau 27), f. 22b-23b, C.
17636. Vatican - Biblioteca Apostolica ebr. 305,1, f. 33a-34a, C.
17637. Zurich - Zentralbibliothek Heid. 139, f. 1a, C, only end of commentary, beginning of manuscript missing.
Tsarfat
17638. London - British Library Add. 11639 (Margoliouth 1056), f. 273a-273b, M.
17639. London - David Sofer 5, f. 26a-27b, C, additional glosses.
17640. Moscow - Russian State Library, Ms. Guenzburg 1665, f. 22b-23a, M.
17641. Oxford - Bodleian Library MS Laud. Or. 271 (Neubauer 1206), f. 32b-34b, C, commentator: Aaron b. Hayyim haKohen (compiler).

17642. Oxford - Bodleian Library MS Opp. 171 (Neubauer 1207), f. 28b-30a, C.
17643. Parma - Biblioteca Palatina Cod. Parm. 3136 (de Rossi 405), f. 36b, M, no incipit.

תמכו כבוד נחלי תעודה (ת 339), שמעון ב"ר יצחק, חלק ב', קדושתא לשבועות
Ashkenaz
17644. Berlin - Staatsbibliothek (Preussischer Kulturbesitz) Or. Qu. 798-799 (Steinschneider 177), II, f. 115b-116a, M.
17645. Braunschweig - Landesmuseum fuer Geschichte und Volkstum R 2386, vol. I, f. 73b, M.
17646. Budapest - Magyar tudomanyos akademia, MS. Kaufmann A 400, p. 155-156, C.
17647. Hamburg - Staats- und Universitaetsbibliothek Cod. hebr. 17/2 (Steinschneider 152), f. 82a, C, no incipit.
17648. Jerusalem - Schocken Institute 24100 / Mahzor Nuremberg, f. 147a, M.
17649. London - British Library Add. 18695 (Margoliouth 683), f. 65b, T, Yiddish.
17650. London - British Library Add. 22431 (Margoliouth 662a), f. 8a-8b, M.
17651. Moscow - Russian State Library, Ms. Guenzburg 615, f. 29b-30a, C, no incipit.
17652. Muenchen - Bayerische Staatsbibliothek, Cod. hebr. 88, f. 116a-116b, G.
17653. Paris - Bibliotheque Nationale heb. 709, f. 121a, C, no incipit.
17654. Parma - Biblioteca Palatina Cod. Parm. 1002 (Ta 24), f. 178a, M.
17655. Parma - Biblioteca Palatina Cod. Parm. 3205 (de Rossi 655), f. 120b, C, no incipit.
17656. Parma - Biblioteca Palatina Cod. Parm. 3507 (Perreau 27), f. 96b-97a, C, no incipit.
17657. Zurich - Zentralbibliothek Heid. 139, f. 50a-50b, C, additional marginal notes.
Tsarfat
17658. London - David Sofer 5, f. 50b-51a, C.
17659. Moscow - Russian State Library, Ms. Guenzburg 1665, f. 117a-117b, M, no incipit.
17660. Parma - Biblioteca Palatina Cod. Parm. 3136 (de Rossi 405), f. 149a, M, no incipit.
17661. Vatican - Biblioteca Apostolica ebr. 306, f. 227b-229a, C, no incipit.

תמרת סנסנה חסונה (ת 344), מאיר ב"ר יצחק, סליחה

Ashkenaz

17662. Cambridge - University Library Dd. 2.30, f. 22b-23b, G.
17663. Oxford - Bodleian Library MS Opp. 681 (Neubauer 1213), f. 38b-40a, C.

תומת צורים וחסדם (ת 345), בנימין ב"ר זרח, עקידה

Ashkenaz

17664. Berlin - Staatsbibliothek (Preussischer Kulturbesitz) Or. Qu. 798-799 (Steinschneider 177), I, f. 58a-58b, M.
17665. Jerusalem - Jewish National and University Library Ms Heb 8° 3037, f. 95b-96a, M.
17666. London - British Library Or. 11318/1, f. 64b, C.
17667. Moscow - Russian State Library, Ms. Guenzburg 190, f. 97a-97b, G.
17668. Muenchen - Bayerische Staatsbibliothek, Cod. hebr. 86, f. 89b, M.
17669. Muenchen - Bayerische Staatsbibliothek, Cod. hebr. 346, f. 140b-141a, C, rubric: אחרת.
17670. New York - Jewish Theological Seminary Ms. 8097, f. 70a, C.
17671. New York - M. Lehmann FR 17.4, FC, rubric: אחל עקידות, only beginning.
17672. Oxford - Bodleian Library MS Mich. 365 (Neubauer 1208), f. 63b-64a, C.
17673. Oxford - Bodleian Library MS Opp. 619 (Neubauer 2374), f. 111a-111b, M.
17674. Oxford - Bodleian Library MS Opp. 681 (Neubauer 1213), f. 71b-72a, C.
17675. Parma - Biblioteca Palatina Cod. Parm. 3205 (de Rossi 655), f. 278a, C.
17676. Vatican - Biblioteca Apostolica ebr. 422/1, f. 28a, C, short.

Ashkenaz, commentary by Abraham b. Azriel[386]

17677. Vatican - Biblioteca Apostolica ebr. 301,1, f. 144a-144b, C.

Tsarfat

17678. London - David Sofer 5, f. 162b-163a, C, rubric: עקידה.
17679. Oxford - Bodleian Library MS Bodl. Or. 109 (Neubauer 1209), f. 11b-12a, C, commentator: Aaron b. Hayyim haKohen (compiler), short.
17680. Parma - Biblioteca Palatina Cod. Parm. 1794 (de Rossi 1061), f. 24a-24b, M.
17681. Parma - Biblioteca Palatina Cod. Parm. 3006 (de Rossi 654,1), f. 205b-206a, M.

---

[386] Edited by Urbach, ערוגת הבושם, vol. III, p. 324.

17682. Vatican - Biblioteca Apostolica ebr. 306, f. 183a-183b, C.

תן לרצות ארצך שיתנו ברכה בריצה
Ashkenaz
17683. Hamburg - Staats- und Universitaetsbibliothek Cod. hebr. 225, f. 77b-78a, G.

תנות צרות לא נוכל (ת 401), הוספה לסדר עבודה
Ashkenaz
17684. Berlin - Staatsbibliothek (Preussischer Kulturbesitz) Or. Qu. 798-799 (Steinschneider 177), I, f. 135a-135b, M.
17685. London - Montefiore Library 261, f. 62a, C, commentator: Eliezer b. Natan?, very short.
17686. Muenchen - Bayerische Staatsbibliothek, Cod. hebr. 346, f. 143b, C, short.
17687. Oxford - Bodleian Library MS Opp. 172 (Neubauer 1211), f. 69a, C.
17688. Oxford - Bodleian Library MS Opp. 619 (Neubauer 2374), f. 223a-224a, M.
17689. Vatican - Biblioteca Apostolica ebr. 308, f. 128b, C, commentator: David b. Mose (compiler).
Ashkenaz, commentary by Abraham b. Azriel[387]
17690. Frankfurt a M - Stadt- und Universitaetsbibliothek Fol. 16 (Merzbacher 95), f. 106a, C, short.
17691. Vatican - Biblioteca Apostolica ebr. 301,1, f. 168b, C, short.
Romania
17692. Vatican - Biblioteca Apostolica ebr. 320, f. 307a, M, short.
Tsarfat
17693. London - David Sofer 5, f. 106b, C, very short.
17694. Oxford - Bodleian Library MS Bodl. Or. 109 (Neubauer 1209), f. 40a-40b, C, commentator: Aaron b. Hayyim haKohen (compiler), short.

תסתר לאלם תרשישים מרון (ת 410), אלעזר ברבי קליר, קינה
Ashkenaz
17695. Budapest - Magyar tudomanyos akademia, MS. Kaufmann A 400, p. 189-192, C.
17696. Hamburg - Staats- und Universitaetsbibliothek Cod. hebr. 17/2 (Steinschneider 152), f. 90b-91b, C, rubric: באב ט׳ לליל קינות פירוש.
17697. Hamburg - Staats- und Universitaetsbibliothek Cod. hebr. 233, f. 66a-67a, G.
17698. Jerusalem - Schocken Institute 24100 / Mahzor Nuremberg, f. 203a-203b, M.

---

[387] Edited by Urbach, ערוגת הבושם, vol. III, p. 488.

17699. London - British Library Add. 18695 (Margoliouth 683), f. 97b-98b, T, Yiddish, rubric: איין אנדרי קינה.
17700. Lund - Universitetsbibliothek Ms. L.O. 2, f. 123a-123b, M.
17701. Oxford - Bodleian Library MS Can. Or. 70 (Neubauer 1147,8), f. 105a-106b, M.
17702. Oxford - Bodleian Library MS Opp. 170 (Neubauer 1205), f. 255a-256a, C, rubric: אחרת.
17703. Parma - Biblioteca Palatina Cod. Parm. 3205 (de Rossi 655), f. 189a-189b, C, rubric: פירוש לקינות.
17704. Vatican - Biblioteca Apostolica ebr. 318, f. 217b-218b, GI.
Ashkenaz, commentary by Abraham b. Azriel[388]
17705. Vatican - Biblioteca Apostolica ebr. 301,1, f. 136b-137a, C, rubric: אחרת, incipit על חורבן.

תעה לבבי אחרי התוהו (ת 413), שלמה אבן גבירול
Carpentras
17706. Cincinnati - Hebrew Union College 429/1, f. 15b-16a, M, no incipit.
Carpentras, commentary by Josef b. Abraham of Montelitz
17707. Cincinnati - Hebrew Union College 357, f. 88a-89a, M, rubric: פירוש.
17708. New York - Jewish Theological Seminary Ms. 4746, f. 23b-24b, M.
17709. Paris - Alliance Israelite Universelle H 422 A, f. 58b-59b, M.
17710. Paris - Ecole Rabbinique 31, f. 128b-130a, M.

תעוב שמלות בשחת נטבל (ת 415), אליה, סליחה
Ashkenaz
17711. Oxford - Bodleian Library MS Mich. 543 (Neubauer 1212), f. 17b-18a, C, commentator: Isaac b. Jacob (compiler).
17712. Oxford - Bodleian Library MS Opp. 681 (Neubauer 1213), f. 44a, C, short.
17713. Parma - Bibliotheca Palatina Cod. Parm. 3205 (de Rossi 655), f. 287b, C.
17714. Vatican - Biblioteca Apostolica ebr. 422/1, f. 30a, C, short.
17715. Vatican - Biblioteca Apostolica ebr. 422/1, f. 44b, CG, no incipit.

תעינו מאחריך שגגנו ממצוותיך (ת 423), הוספה לסדר עבודה
Ashkenaz
17716. Berlin - Staatsbibliothek (Preussischer Kulturbesitz) Or. Qu. 798-799 (Steinschneider 177), I, f. 136b-137a, M, ecclectic.
17717. London - Montefiore Library 261, f. 62b, C, commentator: Eliezer b. Natan?, very short.

---

[388] Edited by Urbach, ערוגת הבושם, vol. III, p. 277-279.

17718. Muenchen - Bayerische Staatsbibliothek, Cod. hebr. 346 , f. 154a, C, very short.

17719. Oxford - Bodleian Library MS Opp. 172 (Neubauer 1211), f. 69b, C, very short.

תעיתי כשה אובד בקש (ת 424), סליחה

Yemen

17720. New York - Jewish Theological Seminary Ms. 3028, f. 87b, G.

תעלה תפלתינו למען שמך (ת 429), משה בן שמואל בן אבשלום, סליחה

Ashkenaz

17721. Berlin - Staatsbibliothek (Preussischer Kulturbesitz) Or. Qu. 798-799 (Steinschneider 177), I, f. 98b, M.

17722. Muenchen - Bayerische Staatsbibliothek, Cod. hebr. 346 , f. 120a, C, very short.

17723. Oxford - Bodleian Library MS Opp. 681 (Neubauer 1213), f. 30a, C, very short.

17724. Padova - Biblioteca del Seminario Vescovile Cod. 218, f. 203b-204a, M, short.

Ashkenaz, commentary by Abraham b. Azriel[389]

17725. Frankfurt a M - Stadt- und Universitaetsbibliothek Fol. 16 (Merzbacher 95), f. 108a, C, short.

תעלו ותעתרו מן השמים, סליחה

Yemen, commentary by Isaac b. Abraham Wanneh

17726. Jerusalem - Yehiel haLevi 4, f. 137b, M, no incipit, short.

תעלת צרי תרף וחובש למזור (ת 431), שלמה הבבלי, סליחה

Ashkenaz

17727. Budapest - Magyar tudomanyos akademia, MS. Kaufmann A 400 , p. 438-442, C, rubric: אחרת שלמונית.

17728. Cambridge - University Library Dd. 2.30, f. 60a-61a, G.

17729. Hamburg - Staats- und Universitaetsbibliothek Cod. hebr. 17/2 (Steinschneider 152), f. 131a-131b, C, rubric: אחרת שלמונית.

17730. Jerusalem - Schocken Institute 24100 / Mahzor Nuremberg , f. 464b-465a, M.

17731. Moscow - Russian State Library, Ms. Guenzburg 190, f. 44b-45b, G.

17732. Moscow - Russian State Library, Ms. Guenzburg 615 , f. 146b-149a, C.

17733. Muenchen - Bayerische Staatsbibliothek, Cod. hebr. 346 , f. 92b-93a, C, rubric: סליחה.

---

[389] Edited by Urbach, ערוגת הבושם, vol. III, p. 559.

17734. Muenchen - Bayerische Staatsbibliothek, Cod. hebr. 346, f. 141a-142b, C, rubric: אחרת.
17735. Muenchen - Bayerische Staatsbibliothek, Cod. hebr. 346, f. 161a, C.
17736. Oxford - Bodleian Library MS Mich. 543 (Neubauer 1212), f. 55b-58a, C, commentator: Isaac b. Jacob (compiler).
17737. Oxford - Bodleian Library MS Opp. 170 (Neubauer 1205), f. 211b-214a, C.
17738. Oxford - Bodleian Library MS Opp. 172 (Neubauer 1211), f. 87a-88a, C.
17739. Oxford - Bodleian Library MS Opp. 681 (Neubauer 1213), f. 56b-60a, C.
17740. Parma - Biblioteca Palatina Cod. Parm. 3205 (de Rossi 655), f. 259a-259b, C.
17741. Vatican - Biblioteca Apostolica ebr. 308, f. 146b-147a, C, commentator: David b. Mose (compiler).
17742. Vatican - Biblioteca Apostolica ebr. 308, f. 148a-148b, C, commentator: David b. Mose (compiler).
17743. Vatican - Biblioteca Apostolica ebr. 422/1, f. 26b, C.
17744. Vatican - Biblioteca Apostolica ebr. 422/2, f. 40a-40b, CG, no incipit, very short.

Ashkenaz, commentary by Abraham b. Azriel[390]

17745. Frankfurt a M - Stadt- und Universitaetsbibliothek Fol. 16 (Merzbacher 95), f. 108b, C.
17746. Frankfurt a M - Stadt- und Universitaetsbibliothek Fol. 16 (Merzbacher 95), f. 117a-117b, C, manuscript damaged, manuscript breaks off after f. 117.
17747. Vatican - Biblioteca Apostolica ebr. 301,1, f. 155a-155b, C, rubric: אחרת.

Tsarfat

17748. London - British Library Add. 11639 (Margoliouth 1056), f. 463a-464a, M.
17749. London - David Sofer 5, f. 169a-169b, C, rubric: סליחה.
17750. Oxford - Bodleian Library MS Laud. Or. 271 (Neubauer 1206), f. 119a-120a, C, commentator: Aaron b. Hayyim haKohen (compiler).
17751. Oxford - Bodleian Library MS Opp. 171 (Neubauer 1207), f. 94a-94b, C, rubric: אחרת.
17752. Parma - Biblioteca Palatina Cod. Parm. 3007 (de Rossi 654,2), f. 93b-95a, M.
17753. Vatican - Biblioteca Apostolica ebr. 306, f. 100a-101a, C.

---

[390] Edited by Urbach, ערוגת הבושם, vol. III, p. 398-402, 560-561.

תענה אמונים שופכי לב כמים (ת 437), סעדיה גאון, הושענא

Ashkenaz

17754. Berlin - Staatsbibliothek (Preussischer Kulturbesitz) Or. Qu. 798-799 (Steinschneider 177), I, f. 210a-211a, M.
17755. Budapest - Magyar tudomanyos akademia, MS. Kaufmann A 399 , p. 306-307, C.
17756. Budapest - Magyar tudomanyos akademia, MS. Kaufmann A 400 , p. 540-541, C.
17757. Cambridge - University Library Add. 394,1 (Reif SCR 461), f. 78a, C, rubric: הושענא.
17758. Frankfurt a M - Stadt- und Universitaetsbibliothek Oct. 227 , f. 117a, M.
17759. Hamburg - Staats- und Universitaetsbibliothek Cod. hebr. 17/2 (Steinschneider 152), f. 168b-169a, C.
17760. Jerusalem - Schocken Institute 24100 / Mahzor Nuremberg , f. 496a, M.
17761. London - British Library Add. 18695 (Margoliouth 683), f. 156a-156b, T, Yiddish.
17762. London - British Library Add. 22431 (Margoliouth 662a), f. 126a-126b, M.
17763. London - British Library Add. 27208 (Margolioth 654), f. 280a-281a, M.
17764. London - British Library Add. 27556, f. 134b-135a, M.
17765. Lund - Universitetsbibliothek Ms. L.O. 2, f. 89b, M.
17766. Lund - Universitetsbibliothek Ms. L.O. 2, f. 90b, M, short.
17767. Lund - Universitetsbibliothek Ms. L.O. 2, f. 91b, M, short.
17768. Moscow - Russian State Library, Ms. Guenzburg 615, f. 131a, C.
17769. New York - Jewish Theological Seminary Ms. 4466, f. 484a-484b, M.
17770. Oxford - Bodleian Library MS Can. Or. 1 (Neubauer 1104), f. 34a-35a, M.
17771. Oxford - Bodleian Library MS Mich. 573 (Neubauer 1099), f. 24a-24b, M.
17772. Oxford - Bodleian Library MS Opp 160 (Neubauer 1204), f. 246a-247b, C, commentator: Elazar b. Yehuda of Worms.[391]
17773. Oxford - Bodleian Library MS Opp. 170 (Neubauer 1205), f. 206a, C.
17774. Parma - Biblioteca Palatina Cod. Parm. 2895, p. 227-228, M.
17775. Parma - Biblioteca Palatina Cod. Parm. 3057.9 (de Rossi 1033), f. 96a-96b, C.
17776. Parma - Biblioteca Palatina Cod. Parm. 3205 (de Rossi 655), f. 252b-253a, C.
17777. Vatican - Biblioteca Apostolica ebr. 305,1, f. 45a, C, no incipit.

---

[391] Edited by Katzenellenbogen, פירוש ההושענות, p. 63-65.

17778. Vatican - Biblioteca Apostolica ebr. 308, f. 160b-161a, C, commentator: David b. Mose (compiler).
17779. Verona - Seminario Maggiore 34, f. 173a, M, margins partly damaged.

Ashkenaz, commentary by Eliezer b. Natan
17780. Hamburg - Staats- und Universitaetsbibliothek Cod. hebr. 61 (Steinschneider 153), f. 26a, C.
17781. London - Montefiore Library 261, f. 89a, C.
17782. Warszaw - Uniwersytet, Inst. Orientalistyczny 258, f. 198b-199a, C.

Italia
17783. Moscow - Russian State Library, Ms. Guenzburg 1594, f. 25b, C, no incipit.

Italia, commentary by Yehoshua Segre
17784. Moscow - Russian State Library, Ms. Guenzburg 533, f. 49a-51a, C, rubric: לימוד י"ט, no incipit.

Italia, commentary by Zakharya David Shabbetai Segre
17785. Torino - Archivio Terracini 1499, p. 243-244, C, rubric: פירוש תענה אמונים.

Roma
17786. Jerusalem - Jewish National and University Library Ms Heb 8° 4153, f. 145b-146a, C, commentator: Daniel ben Salomo haRofe (compiler).
17787. Oxford - Bodleian Library MS Mich. 312,1 (Neubauer 2276,1), f. 13a-13b, C.

Romania
17788. London - London School of Jewish Studies. Asher I.Myers collection 9, f. 215a, M.
17789. Vatican - Biblioteca Apostolica ebr. 285/30, f. 237a-237b, C.
17790. Vatican - Biblioteca Apostolica ebr. 320, f. 451b-452a, M.

Tsarfat
17791. Cambridge - University Library Add. 561.1, f. 116b-117a, M.
17792. Jerusalem - Schocken Institute 19623, f. 129a-129b, M, commentator: Yehuda b. Eliezer Zvi.
17793. London - British Library Or. 2735 (Margoliouth 663), f. 154a-154b, M.
17794. London - David Sofer 5, f. 193b, C.
17795. Moscow - Russian State Library, Ms. Guenzburg 1665, f. 184b, M.
17796. Parma - Biblioteca Palatina Cod. Parm. 1264, f. 100b-101a, M.
17797. Parma - Biblioteca Palatina Cod. Parm. 1902, f. 185a-185b, M.
17798. Vatican - Biblioteca Apostolica ebr. 306, f. 126a-126b, C.

תענו ותעתרו מן השמים בשר נא (ת 440), סליחה
Yemen, commentary by Isaac b. Abraham Wanneh
17799. London - British Library Or. 11122, f. 206a, M, rubric: אל מלך, short.

תענית ציבור קבוע צרכים (ת 442), מאיר ב"ר יצחק, סליחה

Ashkenaz

17800. Budapest - Magyar tudomanyos akademia, MS. Kaufmann A 400 , p. 503-505, C, commentator: Elazar b. Yehuda of Worms, rubric: סליחה דר' מאיר שליח ציבור.
17801. Cambridge - University Library Dd. 2.30, f. 23b-24a, G.
17802. Oxford - Bodleian Library MS Opp. 681 (Neubauer 1213), f. 36a-36b, C.
17803. Oxford - Bodleian Library MS Opp. 681 (Neubauer 1213), f. 36b-37a, C.
17804. Parma - Biblioteca Palatina Cod. Parm. 3205 (de Rossi 655), f. 280a-280b, C.
17805. Vatican - Biblioteca Apostolica ebr. 422/1, f. 26a-26b, C.
17806. Vatican - Biblioteca Apostolica ebr. 422/2 , f. 40a, CG, no incipit, short.

Tsarfat

17807. London - David Sofer 5, f. 99a, C.
17808. Oxford - Bodleian Library MS Laud. Or. 271 (Neubauer 1206), f. 130a-130b, C, commentator: Aaron b. Hayyim haKohen (compiler).
17809. Oxford - Bodleian Library MS Opp. 171 (Neubauer 1207), f. 114a-114b, C, rubric: אחרת.
17810. Parma - Biblioteca Palatina Cod. Parm. 3007 (de Rossi 654,2), f. 95a-95b, M.

תערב לפניך ותפלת המנחה (ת 445), סליחה

Carpentras, commentary by Josef b. Abraham of Montelitz

17811. New York - Jewish Theological Seminary Ms. 4197, f. 227a, M, very short.
17812. Paris - Ecole Rabbinique 32, f. 235a-235b, M, very short.
17813. Strasbourg - Bibliotheque Nationale et Universitaire 4081, f. 207b, M, very short.

תערוג אליך כאיל על אפיקים (ת 449), שלמה הבבלי, סליחה

Ashkenaz

17814. Budapest - Magyar tudomanyos akademia, MS. Kaufmann A 400 , p. 486-488, C, rubric: אחרת.
17815. Moscow - Russian State Library, Ms. Guenzburg 615 , f. 163a-163b, C, rubric: אל מלך.
17816. Muenchen - Bayerische Staatsbibliothek, Cod. hebr. 346 , f. 126a, C, rubric: אחרת.
17817. Oxford - Bodleian Library MS Mich. 543 (Neubauer 1212), f. 69a-69b, C, commentator: Isaac b. Jacob (compiler).

17818. Oxford - Bodleian Library MS Opp. 170 (Neubauer 1205), f. 232a-232b, C.
17819. Oxford - Bodleian Library MS Opp. 681 (Neubauer 1213), f. 19a-20b, C.
17820. Padova - Biblioteca del Seminario Vescovile Cod. 218, f. 149a-149b, M.
17821. Parma - Biblioteca Palatina Cod. Parm. 3205 (de Rossi 655), f. 269a-269b, C.
17822. Vatican - Biblioteca Apostolica ebr. 308/1, f. 7a-7b, C, commentator: David b. Mose (compiler).
17823. Vatican - Biblioteca Apostolica ebr. 422/1, f. 30a-30b, C.
17824. Vatican - Biblioteca Apostolica ebr. 422/1, f. 43b, CG, no incipit.

Ashkenaz, commentary by Abraham b. Azriel[392]

17825. Vatican - Biblioteca Apostolica ebr. 301,1, f. 161a-161b, C, rubric: אחרת.

Tsarfat

17826. London - British Library Add. 11639 (Margoliouth 1056), f. 472a-472b, M.
17827. London - David Sofer 5, f. 98a-98b, C.
17828. Oxford - Bodleian Library MS Laud. Or. 271 (Neubauer 1206), f. 124a, C, commentator: Aaron b. Hayyim haKohen (compiler).
17829. Oxford - Bodleian Library MS Laud. Or. 271 (Neubauer 1206), f. 125a, C, commentator: Aaron b. Hayyim haKohen (compiler).
17830. Oxford - Bodleian Library MS Opp. 171 (Neubauer 1207), f. 112b-113a, C, rubric: אחרת.
17831. Parma - Biblioteca Palatina Cod. Parm. 3007 (de Rossi 654,2), f. 95b-96a, M, partly censored.
17832. Vatican - Biblioteca Apostolica ebr. 306, f. 174b-175b, C.

תעשה כטוב באעיניך לאין למו מעשים, קינה

Yemen, commentary by Isaac b. Abraham Wanneh

17833. Jerusalem - Sassoon 1158, p. 181, M.
17834. London - British Library Or. 11122, f. 107a, M, no incipit.

תפלה לקדמך בקר (ת 471), שלמה ב"ר יצחק, סליחה

Ashkenaz

17835. Cambridge - University Library Dd. 2.30, f. 85a-86a, G.
17836. Hamburg - Staats- und Universitaetsbibliothek Cod. hebr. 62 (Steinschneider 154), f. 28b-29b, C.

Tsarfat

17837. London - David Sofer 5, f. 143b-144a, C.

---

[392] Edited by Urbach, ערוגת הבושם, vol. III, p. 435-437.

17838. Parma - Biblioteca Palatina Cod. Parm. 1794 (de Rossi 1061), f. 16a-17b, M.
17839. Parma - Biblioteca Palatina Cod. Parm. 3007 (de Rossi 654,2), f. 96a-97a, M.
17840. Vatican - Biblioteca Apostolica ebr. 306, f. 204a-204b, C.

תפלה תקח תחנה תבחר (ת 473), מאיר ב"ר יצחק, סליחה

Ashkenaz

17841. Braunschweig - Landesmuseum fuer Geschichte und Volkstum R 2386, vol. II, f. 73a-74a, M.
17842. Budapest - Magyar tudomanyos akademia, MS. Kaufmann A 400 , p. 517-521, C.
17843. Cambridge - University Library Add. 394,1 (Reif SCR 461) , f. 83b-87a, C, rubric: סדר עבודה בבלי.
17844. Hamburg - Staats- und Universitaetsbibliothek Cod. hebr. 17/2 (Steinschneider 152), f. 142b-144a, C.
17845. Hamburg - Staats- und Universitaetsbibliothek Cod. hebr. 40c (Steinschneider 111), f. 288a, G.
17846. Jerusalem - Schocken Institute 24100 / Mahzor Nuremberg , f. 265a-266a, M.
17847. Moscow - Russian State Library, Ms. Guenzburg 190, f. 49a-50a, G.
17848. Moscow - Russian State Library, Ms. Guenzburg 190 , f. 130b-132b, G.
17849. Moscow - Russian State Library, Ms. Guenzburg 615 , f. 135a-138a, C, commentator: Josef Qara (attr.), rubric: לערב ׀ אש השנח מר׳ מאיר מר׳, postscript: פי׳ סליק מר׳ יוסף קרא שליח ציבו׳׳ר.
17850. Muenchen - Bayerische Staatsbibliothek, Cod. hebr. 346 , f. 117a-117b, C.
17851. Oxford - Bodleian Library MS Mich. 543 (Neubauer 1212), f. 78a-80a, C, commentator: Isaac b. Jacob (compiler), rubric: אפרש תחנינם לשוכן מעונים למחי מסי.
17852. Oxford - Bodleian Library MS Opp. 170 (Neubauer 1205), f. 241a-244a, C.
17853. Oxford - Bodleian Library MS Opp. 170 (Neubauer 1205), f. 244a-245a, C, rubric: חסרת פיר׳ של תפילה תקח מדר׳ יוסף קרא שבח לאל גדול ונרא פירוש אחר של תפילה תקח.
17854. Padova - Biblioteca del Seminario Vescovile Cod. 218, f. 114a-116a, M.
17855. Parma - Biblioteca Palatina Cod. Parm. 3205 (de Rossi 655), f. 280b-284a, C.
17856. London - British Library Add. 18695 (Margoliouth 683), f. 170b-171b, T, Yiddish.
17857. Vatican - Biblioteca Apostolica ebr. 308, f. 18b-20b, C, commentator: David b. Mose (compiler).

17858. Vatican - Biblioteca Apostolica ebr. 422/1, f. 34a, C. Ashkenaz, commentary by Abraham b. Azriel[393]

17859. Vatican - Biblioteca Apostolica ebr. 301,1, f. 150a-150b, C. Italia

17860. Toronto - University of Toronto, MS Friedberg 3-014, p. 64-65, M. Tsarfat

17861. London - British Library Add. 11639 (Margoliouth 1056), f. 717b-721a, M, commentator: Jacob, rubric: ערב יום הפיפורים או לה, postscript: פירוש זה מר' יעקב. יום כיפור.

17862. London - David Sofer 5, f. 128a-130b, C.

17863. Oxford - Bodleian Library MS Laud. Or. 271 (Neubauer 1206), f. 179b-182b, C, commentator: Aaron b. Hayyim haKohen (compiler), rubric: דר' מאיר שליח ציבור זצק"ל.

17864. Oxford - Bodleian Library MS Opp. 171 (Neubauer 1207), f. 85a-88a, C.

17865. Parma - Biblioteca Palatina Cod. Parm. 2125 (de Rossi 812), f. 53b-56b, C.

17866. Parma - Biblioteca Palatina Cod. Parm. 2890 (de Rossi 856), f. 47a-48a, M.

17867. Parma - Biblioteca Palatina Cod. Parm. 3007 (de Rossi 654,2), f. 18b-20b, M.

17868. Parma - Biblioteca Palatina Cod. Parm. 3007 (de Rossi 654,2), f. 21b, M, page with commentary only, rubric: לקוטי תפלה תקח.

17869. Vatican - Biblioteca Apostolica ebr. 306, f. 185b-190b, C.

תפן במכון לכס שבת (ת 478), אלעזר ברבי קליר, חלק ב', קדושתא למוסף ראש השנה
Ashkenaz

17870. Berlin - Staatsbibliothek (Preussischer Kulturbesitz) Or. Qu. 798-799 (Steinschneider 177), I, f. 14b-15a, M.

17871. Braunschweig - Landesmuseum fuer Geschichte und Volkstum R 2386, vol. II, f. 92a, M.

17872. Budapest - Magyar tudomanyos akademia, MS. Kaufmann A 400, p. 259-261, C, no incipit.

17873. Darmstadt - Hessisches Landes- und Hochschulbibliothek Cod. Or. 15, f. 13b, M.

17874. Hamburg - Staats- und Universitaetsbibliothek Cod. hebr. 12 (Steinschneider 102), f. 13b-14a, G.

17875. Hamburg - Staats- und Universitaetsbibliothek Cod. hebr. 17/2 (Steinschneider 152), f. 110a-111a, C.

17876. Hamburg - Staats- und Universitaetsbibliothek Cod. hebr. 40b (Steinschneider 110), f. 14b, G.

---

[393] Edited by Urbach, ערוגת הבושם, vol. III, p. 361-364.

17877. Hamburg - Staats- und Universitaetsbibliothek Cod. hebr. 40c (Steinschneider 111), f. 136b, G.
17878. Hamburg - Staats- und Universitaetsbibliothek Cod. hebr. 132 (Steinschneider 155), f. 10b-11b, C.
17879. Hamburg - Staats- und Universitaetsbibliothek Cod. hebr. 139 (Steinschneider 115), f. 28a, G.
17880. Hamburg - Staats- und Universitaetsbibliothek Cod. hebr. 225, f. 225b-226b, G.
17881. Jerusalem - Jewish National and University Library Ms Heb 8° 3037, f. 25a-25b, M.
17882. Jerusalem - Schocken Institute 24100 / Mahzor Nuremberg, f. 330a, M.
17883. London - Montefiore Library 261, f. 6a-7a, C, commentator: Eliezer b. Natan?.
17884. Moscow - Russian State Library, Ms. Guenzburg 191, f. 9a-9b, M.
17885. Moscow - Russian State Library, Ms. Guenzburg 615, f. 65a-65b, C.
17886. Moscow - Russian State Library, Ms. Guenzburg 1401/2, f. 17b, C.
17887. Muenchen - Bayerische Staatsbibliothek, Cod. hebr. 86, f. 20a-21a, M.
17888. Muenchen - Bayerische Staatsbibliothek, Cod. hebr. 346, f. 9a-9b, C, no incipit.
17889. New York - Jewish Theological Seminary Ms. 4466, f. 221a-222a, M.
17890. New York - Jewish Theological Seminary Ms. 8097, f. 60b-61a, C.
17891. New York - Jewish Theological Seminary Ms. 8169 (Acc. 0016), f. 15a-15b, M.
17892. Oxford - Bodleian Library MS Opp. 170 (Neubauer 1205), f. 116a-116b, C, additional glosses.
17893. Oxford - Bodleian Library MS Opp. 172 (Neubauer 1211), f. 9a-9b, C.
17894. Oxford - Bodleian Library MS Opp. 619 (Neubauer 2374), f. 26b-27a, M.
17895. Oxford - Bodleian Library MS Opp. 675 (Neubauer 1210), f. 21b-22a, C, no incipit.
17896. Paris - Bibliotheque Nationale heb. 653, f. 14a, G.
17897. Parma - Biblioteca Palatina Cod. Parm. 3270 (de Rossi 1215), f. 29a-29b, M.
17898. Parma - Biblioteca Palatina Cod. Parm. 3507 (Perreau 27), f. 116b-117a, C, no incipit.
17899. Salzburg - Universitsetsbibliothek M II 342, f. 2a, FM, only end.
17900. Torino - Archivio Terracini 1492, f. 20b, M, very short.
17901. Vatican - Biblioteca Apostolica ebr. 308, f. 45b-46b, C, commentator: David b. Mose (compiler).
17902. Vatican - Biblioteca Apostolica ebr. 422/1, f. 9a-9b, C.

17903. Vatican - Bibliotheca Apostolica ebr. 298/1, f. 14a-14b, C, no incipit, end of fragment.
17904. Zurich - Zentralbibliothek Heid. 139, f. 60b-61a, C, additional marginal notes.

Asti, Fossano, Moncalvo

17905. New Haven - Yale University, Beinecke Rare Book and MS Library, MS Heb. 52, f. 31a, M.

Tsarfat

17906. London - British Library Or. 8682, f. 19a, Gl.
17907. London - David Sofer 5, f. 113b, C.
17908. Paris - Bibliotheque Nationale heb. 445,9, f. 71a-72a, C.
17909. Parma - Biblioteca Palatina Cod. Parm. 2125 (de Rossi 812), f. 15a-15b, C.
17910. Parma - Biblioteca Palatina Cod. Parm. 3006 (de Rossi 654,1), f. 42a-42b, M.

תפן בענוי ודוחק שכח חטא ועון תרחק (ת 479), זבדיה, סליחה

Ashkenaz

17911. Berlin - Staatsbibliothek (Preussischer Kulturbesitz) Or. Qu. 798-799 (Steinschneider 177), I, f. 170a-170b, M, ecclectic.
17912. Vatican - Biblioteca Apostolica ebr. 308, f. 14b, C, commentator: David b. Mose (compiler).

תפן להקשיב ממעונים שועת עם קראתם בנים (ת 480), סעדיה גאון, סליחה

Yemen

17913. New York - Jewish Theological Seminary Ms. 3028, f. 94b, G.
17914. New York - Jewish Theological Seminary Ms. 3193, f. 134b-135a, M, no incipit.

Yemen, commentary by Isaac b. Abraham Wanneh

17915. Chicago-Spertus College of Judaica D 2, 2, f. 226a, M, no incipit, short.
17916. Jerusalem - Sassoon 1158, p. 311, M, no incipit.
17917. London - British Library Or. 11122, f. 202b-203a, M, rubric: אל מלך, no incipit.

תקפו עלינו צרות (ת 505), הוספה לסדר עבודה

Ashkenaz

17918. Berlin - Staatsbibliothek (Preussischer Kulturbesitz) Or. Qu. 798-799 (Steinschneider 177), I, f. 134a-135a, M.
17919. Braunschweig - Landesmuseum fuer Geschichte und Volkstum R 2386, vol. II, f. 238b-239a, M.
17920. London - Montefiore Library 261, f. 62a, C, commentator: Eliezer b. Natan?.

17921. Muenchen - Bayerische Staatsbibliothek, Cod. hebr. 346, f. 143b-144a, C.
17922. Oxford - Bodleian Library MS Opp. 172 (Neubauer 1211), f. 69b-70a, C.
17923. Oxford - Bodleian Library MS Opp. 619 (Neubauer 2374), f. 222b-223a, M.

Ashkenaz, commentary by Abraham b. Azriel[394]

17924. Frankfurt a M - Stadt- und Universitaetsbibliothek Fol. 16 (Merzbacher 95), f. 106a, C.
17925. Vatican - Biblioteca Apostolica ebr. 301,1, f. 168b, C.

Tsarfat

17926. Oxford - Bodleian Library MS Bodl. Or. 109 (Neubauer 1209), f. 40b, C, commentator: Aaron b. Hayyim haKohen (compiler).

תקרב ותרצה ותבחר ערך תפלת השחר (ת 510), תוכחה

Carpentras

17927. Cincinnati - Hebrew Union College 392, f. 30b-31a, M.

Carpentras, commentary by Josef b. Abraham of Montelitz

17928. Cincinnati - Hebrew Union College 291, f. 14a, C, rubric: פי' תקרב ותרצה.
17929. New York - Jewish Theological Seminary Ms. 4197, f. 79a, M.
17930. Paris - Ecole Rabbinique 32, f. 100a-101a, M.
17931. Strasbourg - Bibliotheque Nationale et Universitaire 4081, f. 77b-78a, M.

תרגלת עמוסים (ת 519), שמעון ב"ר יצחק, חלק ב', קדושתא לפסח

Ashkenaz

17932. Berlin - Staatsbibliothek (Preussischer Kulturbesitz) Or. Qu. 798-799 (Steinschneider 177), II, f. 102a-102b, M.
17933. Braunschweig - Landesmuseum fuer Geschichte und Volkstum R 2386, vol. I, f. 50a-50b, M.
17934. Budapest - Magyar tudomanyos akademia, MS. Kaufmann A 384, f. 233b-234a, M.
17935. Hamburg - Staats- und Universitaetsbibliothek Cod. hebr. 17/2 (Steinschneider 152), f. 38a-38b, C.
17936. Jerusalem - Schocken Institute 24100 / Mahzor Nuremberg, f. 109a-109b, M, very short.
17937. London - British Library Add. 18695 (Margoliouth 683), f. 54a-55b, T, Yiddish, f. 54b-55a empty.
17938. Muenchen - Bayerische Staatsbibliothek, Cod. hebr. 88, f. 95a, G.
17939. New York - Jewish Theological Seminary Ms. 4466, f. 89a-89b, M.

---

[394] Edited by Urbach, ערוגת הבושם, vol. III, p. 488-489.

17940. Paris - Bibliotheque Nationale heb. 709, f. 108a, C, no incipit.
17941. Parma - Biblioteca Palatina Cod. Parm. 3205 (de Rossi 655), f. 114a-114b, C, no incipit.
17942. Parma - Biblioteca Palatina Cod. Parm. 3507 (Perreau 27), f. 78b-79a, C, no incipit.
17943. Zurich - Zentralbibliothek Heid. 139, f. 42a-42b, C.

Tsarfat

17944. London - David Sofer 5, f. 45b-46a, C, no incipit.
17945. Moscow - Russian State Library, Ms. Guenzburg 1665, f. 105a, M, no incipit.
17946. Oxford - Bodleian Library MS Laud. Or. 271 (Neubauer 1206), f. 76b, C, commentator: Ephraim b. Jacob of Bonn (mainly), Aaron b. Hayyim haKohen (compiler), no incipit.
17947. Parma - Biblioteca Palatina Cod. Parm. 3136 (de Rossi 405), f. 123b-124a, M, no incipit.

תשוב תרחמינו (ת 549), שלמה הבבלי, סליחה

Ashkenaz

17948. Budapest - Magyar tudomanyos akademia, MS. Kaufmann A 400, p. 488-489, C, rubric: אחרת.
17949. Jerusalem - Schocken Institute 24100 / Mahzor Nuremberg, f. 278a, M.
17950. Moscow - Russian State Library, Ms. Guenzburg 615, f. 163b-164a, C, rubric: אל מלך.
17951. Muenchen - Bayerische Staatsbibliothek, Cod. hebr. 346, f. 124b, C.
17952. Oxford - Bodleian Library MS Mich. 543 (Neubauer 1212), f. 69b-70a, C, commentator: Isaac b. Jacob (compiler).
17953. Oxford - Bodleian Library MS Opp. 170 (Neubauer 1205), f. 232b-233a, C.
17954. Oxford - Bodleian Library MS Opp. 681 (Neubauer 1213), f. 47a-47b, C, rubric: שלמוניות ושלישיות.
17955. Padova - Biblioteca del Seminario Vescovile Cod. 218, f. 121a-121b, M.
17956. Parma - Biblioteca Palatina Cod. Parm. 3205 (de Rossi 655), f. 267a, C.
17957. Vatican - Biblioteca Apostolica ebr. 308/1, f. 9a-9b, C, commentator: David b. Mose (compiler).
17958. Vatican - Biblioteca Apostolica ebr. 422/1, f. 6a, C, rubric: אחרת.
17959. Vatican - Biblioteca Apostolica ebr. 422/1, f. 29a, C.
17960. Vatican - Biblioteca Apostolica ebr. 422/1, f. 43a, CG, no incipit.

Ashkenaz, commentary by Abraham b. Azriel[395]

17961. Vatican - Biblioteca Apostolica ebr. 301,1, f. 160b-161a, C, rubric: אחרת.

Tsarfat

17962. London - British Library Add. 11639 (Margoliouth 1056), f. 475a-476a, M.
17963. London - David Sofer 5, f. 106a-106b, C.
17964. Oxford - Bodleian Library MS Laud. Or. 271 (Neubauer 1206), f. 123a-123b, C, commentator: Aaron b. Hayyim haKohen (compiler), rubric: דר׳ שלמה הבבלי.
17965. Oxford - Bodleian Library MS Opp. 171 (Neubauer 1207), f. 116a-116b, C, rubric: אחרת.
17966. Parma - Biblioteca Palatina Cod. Parm. 3007 (de Rossi 654,2), f. 97b-98a, M.
17967. Vatican - Biblioteca Apostolica ebr. 306, f. 192b-193a, C.

תשורת שי אלפים שבעים (ת 560), אלעזר ברבי קליר, חלק ב, קדושתא לסוכות

Ashkenaz

17968. Berlin - Staatsbibliothek (Preussischer Kulturbesitz) Or. Qu. 798-799 (Steinschneider 177), I, f. 191a-191b, M, no incipit.
17969. Braunschweig - Landesmuseum fuer Geschichte und Volkstum R 2386, vol. I, f. 134b-135a, M.
17970. Budapest - Magyar tudomanyos akademia, MS. Kaufmann A 400, p. 373-376, C, no incipit.
17971. Fulda - Hessische Landesbibliothek A 3 II, f. 130b-131b, C, commentator: Josef.
17972. Hamburg - Staats- und Universitaetsbibliothek Cod. hebr. 62 (Steinschneider 154), f. 37b-38b, C, no incipit.
17973. Hamburg - Staats- und Universitaetsbibliothek Cod. hebr. 132 (Steinschneider 155), f. 51b-52a, C, no incipit.
17974. Jerusalem - Jewish National and University Library Ms Heb 8° 3037, f. 354a-254b, M.
17975. Jerusalem - Schocken Institute 24100 / Mahzor Nuremberg, f. 481a, M.
17976. London - British Library Add. 18695 (Margoliouth 683), f. 117a-117b, T, Yiddish.
17977. London - British Library Add. 22431 (Margoliouth 662a), f. 91a-91b, M.
17978. London - British Library Or. 11318/1, f. 134a-134b, C.
17979. London - Montefiore Library 261, f. 70a-71a, C, commentator: Eliezer b. Natan?.

---

[395] Edited by Urbach, ערוגת הבושם, vol. III, p. 432-433.

17980. Moscow - Russian State Library, Ms. Guenzburg 615 , f. 110b-112a, C.
17981. New York - Jewish Theological Seminary Ms. 4466, f. 445b-446a, M.
17982. New York - Jewish Theological Seminary Ms. 4826, f. 2a-2b, FM.
17983. Oxford - Bodleian Library MS Mich. 365 (Neubauer 1208) , f. 101a-102b, C.
17984. Oxford - Bodleian Library MS Opp. 170 (Neubauer 1205), f. 183a-183b, C.
17985. Parma - Biblioteca Palatina Cod. Parm. 3205 (de Rossi 655), f. 239a-240a, C, no incipit.
17986. Parma - Biblioteca Palatina Cod. Parm. 3507 (Perreau 27), f. 176b-177b, C, no incipit.
17987. Vatican - Biblioteca Apostolica ebr. 305,1, f. 40b-41a, C, no incipit.
17988. Vatican - Biblioteca Apostolica ebr. 422/1, f. 20b, C.
17989. Zurich - Zentralbibliothek Heid. 139 , f. 90a-90b, C, no incipit, additional marginal notes.

Romania

17990. London - London School of Jewish Studies. Asher I.Myers collection 9, f. 219a-219b, M.
17991. Vatican - Biblioteca Apostolica ebr. 320, f. 430a-430b, M.

Tsarfat

17992. London - David Sofer 5, f. 181b-182a, C.
17993. Moscow - Russian State Library, Ms. Guenzburg 1665, f. 162b-163a, M.
17994. Oxford - Bodleian Library MS Laud. Or. 271 (Neubauer 1206), f. 94b-95b, C, commentator: Aaron b. Hayyim haKohen (compiler), no incipit.
17995. Oxford - Bodleian Library MS Opp. 171 (Neubauer 1207), f. 145b, C, no incipit.
17996. Parma - Biblioteca Palatina Cod. Parm. 1264, f. 55a-55b, M.

תתן אחרית לעמך (א 8343), סליחה

Ashkenaz

17997. Berlin - Staatsbibliothek (Preussischer Kulturbesitz) Or. Qu. 798-799 (Steinschneider 177), I, f. 137a, M.
17998. Hamburg - Staats- und Universitaetsbibliothek Cod. hebr. 62 (Steinschneider 154), f. 21a, C, short.
17999. London - Montefiore Library 261, f. 62b, C, commentator: Eliezer b. Natan?, very short.
18000. Muenchen - Bayerische Staatsbibliothek, Cod. hebr. 346 , f. 144a, C, short.
18001. Oxford - Bodleian Library MS Opp. 172 (Neubauer 1211), f. 69b, C, short.

18002. Vatican - Biblioteca Apostolica ebr. 308, f. 128b, C, commentator: David b. Mose (compiler).

Ashkenaz, commentary by Abraham b. Azriel[396]

18003. Vatican - Biblioteca Apostolica ebr. 301,1, f. 158b, C, short.

Tsarfat

18004. Oxford - Bodleian Library MS Bodl. Or. 109 (Neubauer 1209), f. 41a, C, commentator: Aaron b. Hayyim haKohen (compiler), short.

תתננו לשם ולתהלה (ת 594), אלעזר ברבי קליר, הושענא

Ashkenaz

18005. Berlin - Staatsbibliothek (Preussischer Kulturbesitz) Or. Qu. 798-799 (Steinschneider 177), I, f. 206a, M.

18006. Budapest - Magyar tudomanyos akademia, MS. Kaufmann A 399, p. 302, C.

18007. London - British Library Add. 18695 (Margoliouth 683), f. 151b-152a, T, Yiddish.

18008. London - British Library Add. 27208 (Margolioth 654), f. 270b, M, very short.

18009. Lund - Universitetsbibliothek Ms. L.O. 2, f. 87b, M.

18010. Oxford - Bodleian Library MS Opp 160 (Neubauer 1204), f. 237b-238b, C, commentator: Elazar b. Yehuda of Worms.[397]

18011. Parma - Biblioteca Palatina Cod. Parm. 2895, p. 219, M.

18012. Parma - Biblioteca Palatina Cod. Parm. 3057.9 (de Rossi 1033), f. 94a, C.

Italia, commentary by Zakharya David Shabbetai Segre

18013. Torino - Archivio Terracini 1499, p. 204-205, C, rubric: פירוש תתננו לשם ולתהלה, very short.

Tsarfat

18014. Jerusalem - Schocken Institute 19623, f. 126a, M, commentator: Yehuda b. Eliezer Zvi.

18015. London - David Sofer 5, f. 192b, C.

18016. Parma - Biblioteca Palatina Cod. Parm. 1902, f. 179a-179b, M, very short.

תתפרקון ושתיזבון (ת 597), הושענא

Yemen

18017. Jerusalem - Musad haRav Kook 952, f. 4b, M, very short.

18018. Jerusalem - Sassoon 264, f. 92a, M, no incipit, very short.

Yemen, commentary by Isaac b. Abraham Wanneh

18019. Jerusalem - Makhon ben Zvi 1186 (Tubi 205), f. 2a-2b, M, very short.

18020. Jerusalem - Sassoon 1158, p. 211-212, M, no incipit, short.

---

[396] Edited by Urbach, ערוגת הבושם, vol. III, p. 490.
[397] Edited by Katzenellenbogen, פירוש ההושענות, p. 40-43.

18021. Paris - G. Epstein 23/57, f. 97b, C, very short.

תתקבצו מלאכים זה אל זה, לשמחת תורה
Ashkenaz
18022. Berlin - Staatsbibliothek (Preussischer Kulturbesitz) Or. Qu. 798-799 (Steinschneider 177), I, f. 230b, M, short.
18023. Jerusalem - Schocken Institute 24100 / Mahzor Nuremberg, f. 512a-512b, M.
18024. London - British Library Add. 18695 (Margoliouth 683), f. 141b-142a, T, Yiddish.
18025. Lund - Universitetsbibliothek Ms. L.O. 2, f. 94b, M, short.

BIBLIOGRAPHY

CATALOGUES AND MANUSCRIPT DESCRIPTIONS

N. Allony, and E. Kupfer, רשימת תצלומי כתבי־יד העבריים במכון, Jerusalem, Mass, 1964.

Bibliothecae Apostolicae Vaticanae Codicum Manuscriptorum Catalogus, Partis Primae Tomus Primuus Complectens Codices Ebraicos et Samarinanos, S. E. Assemanus and J. S. Assemanus, Roma, 1756.

J. B. De-Rossi, *Mss. Codices Hebraici Biblioth. I.B. De-Rossi*, Parma, 1803.

R. Di Segni, Catalogue of the Manuscripts of the Library of the Collegio Rabbinico Italiano, Rome Italy, Ramat-Gan - Rome, 1990 (Special supplement to Alei Sefer).

L. Fuks, and R. Fuks-Mansfeld, *Hebrew and Judaic Manuscripts in Amsterdam Public Collections*, Vol. I, Rosenthaliana, Leiden, 1973.

H. Hirschfeld, *Descriptive Catalogue of the Hebrew Mss. of the Montefiore Library*, London, Macmillan and Co, 1904.

A. Luzzatto, *Hebraica Ambrosiana. I Catalogue of Undescribed Hebrew Manuscripts in the Ambrosiana Library. II Description of Decorated and Illuminated Hebrew Manuscripts in the Ambrosiana Library*, L. Mortara Ottolenghi (Part II), Milano, Edizioni il Polifoli, 1972.

G. Margoliouth, *Catalogue of the Hebrew and Samaritan Manuscripts in the British Museum*, London, Trustees of the British Museum, 1965.

A. Neubauer, *Catalogue of the Hebrew Manuscripts in the Bodlean Library*, Oxford, Clarendon Press, 1886.

——. *Catalogue of the Hebrew Manuscripts of the Jews' College London*, Oxford, 1886.

I. Perles, Bibliographische Mittheilungen aus München, *MGWJ*, XXV, 1876, p. 360-375.

P. Perreau, Hebräische Handschriften in Parma, *ZfHB*, 8, p. 26.

S. C. Reif, *Hebrew Manuscripts at Cambridge University Library. A description and introduction*, Cambridge, Cambridge University Press, [1997].

C. Roth, Catalogue of Manuscripts in the Roth Collection, in *Alexander Marx Jubilee Volume*, New York, JTSA, 1950, p. 503-535.

A. Z. Schwarz, *Die hebräischen Handschriften in Österreich (ausserhalb der Nationalbibliothek in Wien)*, Leipzig, Verlag Karl W. Hiersemann, 1931.

M. Steinschneider, *Catalogus Codicum Hebraeorum Bibliothecae Academiae Lugduno-Batavae*, Leiden, Brill, 1858.

——. *Catalog der hebräischen Handschriften in der Stadtbibliothek zu Hamburg und der sich anschliessenden anderen Sprachen*, Reprographischer Nachdruck der Ausgabe Hamburg 1878, H. Braun (foreword by), Hildesheim, Georg Olms Verlag, 1969.

——. Verzeichniss der Hebräischen Handschriften, in *Die Handschriftenverzeichnisse der Königlichen Bibliothek zu Berlin.*, Berlin, Königl. Akademie der Wissenschaften, 1878.

——. *Die Hebraeischen Handschriften der K. Hof- und Staatsbibliothek in Muenchen*, zweite, größtenteils umgearbeitete und erweiterte Auflage, München, 1895.

——. Verzeichniss der Hebräischen Handschriften. Zweite Abtheilung, in *Die Handschriftenverzeichnisse der Königlichen Bibliothek zu Berlin.*, Berlin, A. Asher & Co, 1897.

H. Striedl (ed), *Hebräische Handschriften. Teil 2*, E. Róth, Verzeichnis der orientalischen Handschriften in Deutschland. Bd. VI,2, Wiesbaden, Franz Steiner Verlag, 1965.

Y. Tubi, כתבי־היד התימניים במכון בן־צבי, Jerusalem, Yad Ben Zvi; Hebrew University, 1982.

M. Weinberg, Die hebräischen Handschriften der Landesbibliothek Fulda, *JJLG*, 22, 1929, p. 273-296.

M. Weisz, *Katalog der hebräischen Handschriften und Bücher in der Bibliothek des Professors Dr. David Kaufmann s.A.*, Frankfurt a.M., Kauffmann, 1906.

H. Zotenberg, *Catalogues des Manuscrits Hébreux et Samaritains de la Bibliothèque Impériale*, [1866].

EDITIONS OF PIYYUT-COMMENTARY

J. Adler, פירוש מחזור נירנברג לקרובה "אורח חיים מוסר תוכחת" לחג השבועות לרבי שמעון בן יצחק, *Sinai*, 83, 1978, p. 237-258.

——. *פרקי שירה*, in מגני, פירוש כתב־יד לעבודה ליום כיפור "אתה כוננת ברב חסד" ליוסי בן יוסי השירה והפיוט של קהילות ישראל, Ramat Gan, Bar Ilan University Press, (1990), p. 9-45.

L. Ginzberg, גנזי שכטר. ספר א: קטעי מדרש, in מדרש לקח טוב על הקרובה הקלירית זכר איכה אנו ואגדה, New York, Jewish Theological Seminary, 1928, p. 246-297.

A. M. Habermann, ספר קרובה, ידיעות המכון לחקר השירה העברית, 3, 1936, p. 91-132.

I. Han, קטעים מן הגניזה. באוסף, in קטע מן התרגום הערבי של אזהרות "אתה הנחלת תורה לעמך" קופמן בבודפסט, Budapest, 1949, p. 71-80.

M. L. Katzenellenbogen, פירוש "אתה הראת" ופיוטי שמחת תורה לרבי אלעזר מגרמייזא בעל הרוקח, *Sinai*, 123-124, 2000, p. 479-494.

——. ספר זכרון להגאון רבי שליה רפאל, in פירוש ההושענות לרבי אלעזר מגרמייזא [בעל הרוקח] ז"ל, J. E. h. Mobshovitz, Jerusalem, Musad haRav Kook, 1998, p. 23-70.

D. Kaufmann, Aus Abraham b. Asriels ערוגת הבושם, *MGWJ*, 31, 1882, p. 316-324; 360-370; 410-422; 564-566.

——, Aus der vatikanischen Handschrift von Abraham ben Asriel's Machsorcommentar, *Magazin für die Wissenschaft des Judenthums*, 13, 1886, p. 129-160.

E. Kupfer, פרוש אזהרות דרבנא אליהו הזקן בר מנחם ממנש, מאת חכם אחד מחוג בניו של רבנו חיים בר חננאל הכהן, קובץ על יד, *N.S.*, 11, 1989, p. 109-207.

Z. Malachi, and (ed), סדר עבודת יום הכפורים ליצחק אבן גיאת הספרדי, Lod, Habermann Institut, 1997.

S. A. Poznanski, פתרוני ר' מנחם בר חלבו, Warschau, 1904.

L. P. Prins (ed), ספר תשלום אבודרהם. והוא סדר עבודת יום הכפורים המיוחס ליוסי בן יוסי וגם פיוטים שונים של הפייטנים הגדולים עם פירוש גדול המפרשים רבינו דוד בר' יוסף בר' דוד אבודרהם, Berlin, Mekize Nirdamim, 1900.

E. Roth (ed), *Staats- und Universitätsbibliothek Hamburg Handschrift Hebr 17 (Steinschneider 152-153)*, Faksimile, Jerusalem, 1972.

S. J. Schachter, *The liturgical Commentary of Mahzor Ashkenaz (Jewish Theological Seminary of America Ms. # 4466)*, dissertation, New York, The Graduate School of the Jewish Theological Seminary of America, 1986.

M. Schmelzer, פירוש אלפביתין, פירוש על י"ג פיוטים ארמיים לר' בנימין בן אברהם מן הענוים, *Meḥqarim u-Meqorot*, *1*, 1978, p. 167-274.

A. Sofer (ed.), ספר המכתם, New York, 1959.

S.A. Stern, סדר ארוסין ונשואין, Bne Brak 1990, p. 50-56.

S. Stern, קובץ מעשי ידי גאונים קדמונים, על סדר עבודה לר"י בן אביתור, J. Rosenberg (ed.), Berlin, Friedländer'sche Buchdruckerei, 1896, p. 117-122.

E. E. Urbach (ed), ספר ערוגת הבושם. כולל פירושים לפיוטים, Jerusalem, Mekize Nirdamim, 1939.

——. מילואים ותיקונים לס' ערוגת הבושם ג' וד', *Qiryat Sefer*, *41*, 1966, p. 17-18.

——. ספר חיים שירמן. קובץ מחקרים in פירוש לסילוק הקלירי לפרשת שקלים 'אז ראית וספרת', S. Abramson and A. Mirsky, Jerusalem, Schocken Institute for Jewish Research, 1970, p. 1-26.

G. Zinner, ספר אוצר פסקי הראשונים, Brooklyn 1985.

LITERATURE ON PIYYUT-COMMENTARIES

W. Bacher, Der südarabische Siddur und Jaḥjā Sāliḥ's Commentar zu demselben, *JQR*, *14*, 1902, p. 581-621.

J. Dan, פירושי 'האדרת והאמונה' של חסידי אשכנז, *Tarbiẕ*, *50*, 1981, p. 396-404.

S. Emanuel, חשבון הלוח וחשבון הקץ: פולמוס יהודי-נוצרי בשנת 1100, *Zion*, *63*, 1998, p. 143-155.

M. Fruchtman, דקדוקי פיוט. עיונים בשיטה הדקדוקית-הפרשנית בימי-הביניים על פי 'ספר ערוגת הבושם' לר' אברהם בן עזריאל, Beer Sheva, Ben Gurion University of the Negev, 1999.

——. המפרש כעורך לשוני פיוטים בימי הביניים. עיון בפירוש של פיוט ב'ספר ערוגת הבושם' לרבי אברהם בן עזריאל, in קובץ מחקרים בספרות העברית לדורות. ספר ישראל לוין, Tel Aviv, Tel Aviv University, 1994, p. I, 277-287.

P. Ghayyat, ראשית פרשנות הפיוט בתימן: פרשנותו של רבי יצחק ונה לפיוטי הסליחות, MA Thesis, Haifa, University of Haifa, 2003.

H. Gross, Ein anonymer Handschriftlicher Kommentar zum Machsor, *Zeitschrift für hebräische Bibliographie*, *11*, 1907, p. 169-181.

A. Grossman, Exegesis of the *piyyut* in 11th century France, in *Rashi et la culture juive en France du Nord au moyen âge*, Paris, Peeters, 1997, p. 261-278.

——. פולמוס אנטי-נוצרי בפירושיו של ר' יוסף קרא למקרא ולפיוט, *WCJS*, *9B 1*, 1986, p. 71-78.

——. פירוש הפיוטים לר' אהרון בר' חיים הכהן, in מחקרים בתרבות ישראל מוגשים באורח חיים. לאהרון מירסקי, Lod, Habermann Institut, 1986, p. 451-468.

——. הרקע לצמיחת פרשנות הפיוט בגרמניה ובצרפת במאה הי"א, in ספר יובל לשלמה סימונסון, Tel Aviv, Tel Aviv University, 1993, p. 45-72.

——. שבחי ר' אלעזר בירבי קליר בפירוש הפיוטים של ר"י קרא, in כנסת עזרא. ספרות וחיים בבית הכנסת, Jerusalem, Yad Yitzhaq Ben Zvi, 1994, p. 293-308.

——. חכמי צרפת הראשונים, Jerusalem, Magnes, 1995.

E. Hollender, Die Fortschreibung der Aggada. Zur Verwendung rabbinischer Literatur im Pijjut-Kommentar, *Trumah*, *12*, 2003, p. 35-53.

——. Fauna and Flora in Medieval Piyyut-Commentary, *Zutot*, *2*, 2002, p. 65-70.

——. Compilatory Literature in the Middle Ages: Piyyut-Commentary, 29. AJS Conference conference presentation, Boston, 12, 1997.

——. Mittelalterliche hebräische Kompilationsliteratur am Beispiel aschkenasischer und französischer Pijjutkommentare, Habilitationsschrift, Duisburg, Gerhard-Mercator-Universität, 2000.

——. Narrative Exegesis in Ashkenas and Zarfat: The Case of Piyyut-Commentary, in *Jewish Studies at the Turn of the Twentieth Century*, Proceedings of the 6th EAJS Congress, Leiden, Brill, 1999, p. I, 429-435.

——. Hebräische Kommentare hebräischer liturgischer Poesie: Eine Taxonomie der wichtigsten Kommentarelemente, in *Der Kommentar in Antike und Mittelalter. Beiträge zu seiner Erforschung*, Leiden, Brill, 2002, p. 163-182.

——. Eine permanente Renaissance? Zum status (quaestionis) von Pijjut-Kommentar, in *An der Schwelle zur Moderne. Juden in der Renaissance*, Leiden, Brill, 2003, p. 25-50.

I. Levine, פירוש על המחזור המיוחס לראב"ן, *Tarbiẓ*, *29*, 1960, p. 162-175.

A. Mirsky, פירושי "המפרש" ללשון הפיוט, *Sinai*, *87*, 1980, p. 216-250.

——. ביקור על אברהם בן עזריאל. ספר ערוגת הבשם יו"ל עם הגהות והערות מאת א.א. אורבך. חלק ד: מבוא ומפתחות, *Qiryat Sefer*, *41*, 1966, p. 9-17.

——. ארשת, עכבות של השמטות, *5*, 1972, p. 131-135.

M. Schmelzer, "תא שמע" הזואר, מעשה ר' אמנון והסלוחה, *43*:38, 1964, p. 734.

I. M. Ta-Shma, על הפירוש לפיוטים הארמיים שבמחזור ויתרי, *Qiryat Sefer*, *57*, 1983, p. 701-708.

N. Weissenstern, מילון לערוגת הבושם, unpublished manuscript, Jerusalem.

M. Weisz, Ein Kommentar zu Nummer 10 des Kuntras ha-Pijutim, *MGWJ*, *41*, 1897, p. 145-155.

B. Ziemlich, *Das Machsor Nürnberg. Ein Beitrag zur Erforschung des Ritus und der Commentarliteratur des Deutschen Machsor*, Berlin, 1886.

L. Zunz, *Die Ritus des synagogalen Gottesdienstes, geschichtlich entwickelt*, Berlin, Louis Lamm, 1859.

RELATED LITERATURE

J. Assmann, Text und Kommentar. Einführung, in *Text und Kommentar*, Archäologie der literarischen Kommunikation IV, München, Fink, 1995, p. 9–33.

M. Banitt, דברי האקדמיה, חקר הגלוסארים המקראיים של יהודי צרפת בימי הביניים. שיטה ויישום הלאומית הישראלית למדעים, *2*, 1969, p. 135-149.

S. L. Boynton, *Glossed Hymns in Eleventh-Century Continental Hymnaries*, dissertation, Brandeis University, 1997.

I. Davidson, *Thesaurus of Medieval Hebrew Poetry.* אוצר השירה והפיוט, New York, Jewish Theological Seminary, 1924–1933, 4 Bde.

C. Epping-Jäger, *Die Inszenierung der Schrift. Der Literalisierungsprozeß und die Entstehungsgeschichte des Dramas*, Stuttgart, M. & P. Verlag für Wissenschaft und Forschung, 1996.

A. Epstein, החוקר, מדרש לכו נרננה ומדרש הרנינו, *1*, 1891, p. 65-70, 190-191.

Y. Fraenkel, מחזור שבועות לפי מנהגי בני אשכנז לכל ענפיהם, Jerusalem, Koren, 2000.

——. מחזור פסח לפי מנהגי בני אשכנז לכל ענפיהם, Jerusalem, Koren, 2003.

A. Geulla, מדרש אבכיר. מבואת ומובאות, master's thesis, Jerusalem, 1998.

D. Goldschmidt, *מחזור לימים הנוראים. לפי מנהגי בני אשכנז לכל ענפיהם*, Jerusalem, Koren, 1970.

——. *מחזור סוכות, שמיני עצרת ושמחת תורה. לפי מנהגי בני אשכנז לכל ענפיהם*, Y. Fraenkel (ed.), Jerusalem, Koren, 1981.

A. Grossman, *תרבות וחברה בתולדות ישראל בימי הביניים*, in *גלות וגאולה במשנתו של ר' יוסף קרא*, *קובץ מאמרים לזכרו של חיים הלל בן־ששון*, Jerusalem, The Historical Society of Israel / The Zalman Shazar Center, 1989, p. 269-301.

E. Hakohen, *קובץ על יד*, 'אמיתך וחסדך אל תרחק' קרובה י"ח ספק קילירית לפורים, N.S., 14, 1998, p. 1–40.

C. Heymann, La Liturgie de France du Nord d'apres les Manuscrits, in *Rashi et la culture juive en France du Nord au moyen âge*, Paris, Peeters, 1997, p. 279-285.

S. Horowitz (ed), *מחזור ויטרי לרבינו שמחה אחד מתלמידי רש"י ז"ל. עם תוספות הגהות תקונים ובאורים*, Berlin, Mekize Nirdamim, ²1905.

S. Japhet, The Nature and Distribution of Medieval Compilatory Commentaries in the Light of Rabbi Joseph Kara's Commentary on the Book of Job, in *The Midrashic Imagination. Jewish Exegesis, Thought, and History*, Albany, State University of New York Press, 1993, p. 97–130.

——. *ידיעון האיגוד העולמי למדעי*, כיווני מחקר והלכי רוח בחקר פרשנות ימי הביניים בצפון צרפת, *היהדות*, 25, 1985, p. 3-18.

——. *ספר היובל לרב מרדכי ברויאר. אסופת*, in פירוש החזקוני לתורה. דמותו שלל החיבור ולמטרתו, *מאמרים במדעי היהדות*, Jerusalem, Akademon, 1992, p. 91–111.

R. Langer, Kalir was a Tanna. Rabbenu Tam's Invocation of Antiquity in Defense of the Ashkenazi Payyetanic Tradition, *HUCA*, 67, 1997, p. 95-106.

——*To Worship God Properly. Tensions between Liturgical Customs and Halakha in Judaism*, Cincinnati, Hebrew Union College Press, 1998.

Y. Levin-Katz, *מפי הרבנית מאורליאש. נשים מפרשות פיוטים*, *Kolech*, 73, 2003, pp. 3-4.

H. Kreisel (ed.), Levi ben Avraham, *לוית חן. החלק השלישי מן המאמר הששי מעשה בראשית*, Jerusalem, World Union of Jewish Studies, 2004.

A. Mirsky, *ביקור על אברהם בן עזריאל. ספר ערוגת הבשם יו"ל עם הגהות והערות מאת א.א. אורבך*, *חלק ד: מבוא ומפתחות*, *Qiryat Sefer*, 41, 1966, p. 9-17.

L. Raspe, Jüdische Hagiographie im mittelalterlichen Aschkenas, forthcoming.

E. E. Urbach, *בעלי התוספות. תולדותיהם, חיבוריהם ושיטתם*, Jerusalem.

M. Zohari, *דברי משה הדרשן ופיוטי אלעזר הקלירי בפירושי רש"י*, Jerusalem, Karmel, 1995.

INDEX OF POETS

Aaron (אהרן), 4593-4598, 9003-9022, 9533-9534

Aaron b. Josef haRofe (אהרן בן יוסף הרופא), 288-290, 705-707, 867-870(?), 983-985, 1390-1396, 1968-1974, 2161-2162, 2459-2462, 2545-2548, 3203-3208, 3689-3691, 3725-3727, 3876-3878, 3906-3915, 3945-3947, 4108-4110, 4196-4198, 4293-4295, 4432-4437, 4439-4441, 4548-4550, 4601-4604, 4794-4797, 4804-4807, 5121-5123, 5256-5258, 5543-5546, 6079-6081, 6188-6190, 6196-6198, 7340-7342, 9217-9224, 9297-9298, 9308-9310, 9366-9368, 9371-9379, 9603-9605, 9886-9888, 9959-9961, 10009-10011, 12987-12990, 14516-14526, 14550-14553, 14973-14975

Abbasi (עבאסי), 15470-15473

Abraham (אברהם), 330-332, 1005-1009, 2173-2178, 5639-5640, 11036

Abraham b. Hayyim (אברהם בר חיים), 11308-11310, 15815-15817

Abraham b. Ḥiyya (אברהם ב"ר חייא), 4973-4977, 5333-5335, 7405-7407

Abraham b. Isaac haKohen (אברהם בן יצחק הכהן), 2400, 2405

Abraham b. Menahem (אברהם בן מנחם), 394-397

Abraham b. Yehuda haKohen (אברהם בן יהודה הכהן), 4929-4930

Abraham Gerondi (אברהם גירונדי), 3177-3186

Abraham haKohen (אברהם הכהן), 8504-8505

Abraham Ibn Ezra (אברהם אבן עזרא), 314-315, 1452-1453, 1472, 2963-2970, 3094-3095, 3098-3099, 3621-3622, 3809-3811, 4251-4258, 4371-4372, 4425-4431, 4449-4452, 4759-4763, 4769-4772, 4810-4819, 5324-5325, 5336-5353, 5433-5434, 5513-5516, 5561-5579, 5674, 5869-5870, 6024-6026, 6193-6195, 7118, 7865-7868, 7913, 8665-8670, 8916-8922, 8946-8947, 9607-9608, 10619-10621, 11283-11291, 11871, 12294-12298, 13297-13298, 13626, 15032-15034, 15233-15237, 15999, 16001-16004

Amitai (אמתי), 2973-2995, 15375

Amitai b. Shefatya (אמתי ב"ר שפטיה), 1449-1451, 5332, 5405-5412, 7579-7582, 7860-7861, 8179-8183, 8627-8630, 8708-8714

Arie Yehuda haYarḥi ben Levi (אריה יהודה הירחי בן לוי), 7391

Baḥya bar Josef haDayyan (בחיי בר יוסף הדיין), 8678

Baruch b. Samuel (ברוך בן שמואל), 3211

Ben Ketir Mose (בן כתיר משה), 8585-8588

Benjamin (בנימין), 9609

Benjamin b. Ḥiyya (בנימין ב"ר חייא), 9936-9942

Benjamin b. Pashdu (בנימין בן פשדו), 9824-9831

Benjamin b. Samuel (בנימין ב"ר שמואל), 515-525, 3331, 4111-4117, 7400-7404, 9564-9569, 9877-9885, 10614-10615, 10795-10813, 17409-17417

Benjamin b. Zeraḥ (בנימין ב"ר זרח), 316-321, 343-359, 527-533, 1425-1441, 1488-1492, 2180-2185, 2785-2787, 3212-3214, 3304-3305, 3423-3432, 4865-4871, 5007-5035, 5193-5197, 5599-5632, 5907-5915, 6235-6240, 9399-9409, 10006-10008, 10460-10469, 13469-13481, 13627-13640, 17664-17682

Benjamin haKohen (בנימין הכהן), 14190

Bileam (בלעם), 11759-11761

Daniel (דניאל), 10105-10136

David (דוד), 872-874, 14120

David b. Baquda (דוד בן בקודה), 14084-14090
David b. Elazar Baquda (דוד בן אלעזר בקודה), 911-912, 5547-5557, 5681-5684, 6531-6535, 10073-10075(?), 10077-10099(?)
David b. Gedalya (דוד בן גדליה), 6083-6084, 7253-7254, 9871-9872
David b. Josef (דוד בן יוסף), 14256
David b. Meshullam (דוד בן משולם), 4844-4864
David b. Samuel haLevi (דוד בר שמואל הלוי), 851-866
David b. Yedidya (דוד ב"ר ידידיה), 16179
David Manoa b. Gedalya (דוד מנוא בן גדליה) 16313-16314

Elazar (אלעזר), 6903-6909
Elazar b. Yehuda of Worms (אלעזר ב"ר יהודה מוורמייזא), 7064-7069
Elazar birabbi Qallir (אלעזר ברבי קליר), 1-86, 89-131, 141-170, 291-313, 398-446, 723-744, 987-1000, 1019-1020, 1024-1036, 1062-1099, 1114-1203, 1232-1248, 1342-1385, 1478-1486, 1541, 1653-1682, 1773-1802, 1976-1996, 1998-2036, 2044-2106, 2439-2458, 2527-2528, 2611-2630, 2640-2645, 2702-2784, 2793-2813, 2827-2843, 2940-2961, 3060-3080, 3159-3166, 3171-3176, 3256-3261, 3306, 3433-3487, 3490-3495, 3544-3563, 3734-3749, 3845-3874, 3994-3996, 4162-4188(?), 4192-4194, 4453-4481, 4487-4488, 4630, 4644-4662, 4694-4700, 4718, 4872-4889, 5067, 5198-5217, 5240-5255, 5261-5314, 5388-5404, 5517-5525, 5633-5634, 5723-5771, 5877-5905, 5916, 6001-6023, 6119-6138, 6293-6305, 6624-6632(?), 7214-7229, 7256-7300, 7372-7390, 7408-7427, 7503-7578, 7597-7643, 7706-7737, 7891-7912, 7935-8002, 8025-8077, 8083-8113, 8232-8263, 8402-8418, 8438-8459, 8506-8557, 9093-9143, 9274-9278, 9380-9395, 9430-9451, 9574-9601, 9642, 9666-9697, 9720-9722, 9730-9750, 9851-9867, 10304-10310, 10317-10322, 10443-10458, 10516, 10527-10534, 10564-10565, 10569-10575, 10623, 10687-10691, 10704-10735, 10751-10794, 10814-10834, 10847-10854, 10963-10985, 11044-11074, 11121-11164, 11306-11307, 11740-11742(?), 11825-11870, 12456-12484, 12998-13049, 13188-13212, 13355-13377, 13425-13458, 13588-13596, 13641-13644, 13941-13988, 14156-14178, 14237-14254, 14348-14349, 14437-14472, 14571, 14649-14699, 14746-14789, 14803-14829, 14976-14994, 15000-15015, 15040-15061, 15113-15133, 15226-15228, 15345-15357, 15749-15767, 15820-15823, 15901-15945, 15970-15990, 16005-16072, 16084-16123, 16162-16177, 16181-16201, 16447-16458, 16645-16693, 17199-17246, 17305-17331, 17443-17467, 17470-17499, 17602-17643, 17695-17705, 17870-17910, 17968-17996, 18005-18016
Elazar birabbi Qillir (אלעזר ברבי קילר), 1856-1876, 2409-2430, 8902-8910, 11075-11093
Elhanan b. Isaac (אלחנן ב"ר יצחק), 8964-8969
Eliezer b. Isaac haLevi (אליעזר ב"ר יצחק הלוי), 4752-4755
Eliezer b. Natan (אליעזר ב"ר נתן), 1389, 2311-2322, 2401-2404, 2922-2923, 4149-4158, 4216-4222, 4226, 4373-4377, 4918-4922, 7652-7657, 8273-8274, 8956-8963, 9039-9040, 15156-15158
Eliezer b. Samuel (אליעזר ב"ר שמואל), 9665
Eliezer b. Shimshon (אליעזר ב"ר שמשון), 11194, 15315-15316
Eliya (אליה), 340, 4229-4230, 4636, 9001, 9353-9354, 17711-17715
Eliya b. Menahem (אליה ב"ר מנחם), 6199-6207
Eliya b. Mordekhai (אליה ברבי מרדכי), 3948-3979, 8114-8134, 8149-8176, 13252-13273, 14123-14151

INDEX OF POETS

Eliya b. Shemaya (אליה ב"ר שמעיה), 225-231, 267-281, 608-628, 1811-1822, 3241-3246, 3499-3515, 3905, 4787-4790, 5218-5219, 5228-5234, 6916-6925, 7761-7777, 8286-8292, 8331-8348, 8693-8695, 8975-9000, 9299-9307, 13344, 15464-15469, 17418-17442

Eliya Carmi (אליה כרמי), 8718

Eliyahu (אליהו), 5235-5239

Eliyahu b. Tsadoq (אליהו בן צדוק), 3348-3349

Ephraim b. Isaac of Regensburg (אפרים ב"ר יצחק מרגנסבורג), 1001-1003, 2037, 2518, 4749-4751, 4764-4768, 4833-4834, 4964-4965, 5373-5383, 5675, 7119-7127

Ephraim b. Jacob of Bonn (אפרים ב"ר יעקב מבון), 2519-2521, 4972-4973, 7206-7208, 17131-17136

Ephraim b. Yaqar (אפרים ב"ר יקר), 3879-3882, 6975

Gershom b. Yehuda Meor haGola (גרשום ב"ר יהודה מאור הגולה), 234-248, 3281-3303, 5126-5128, 5803-5834, 8729-8752, 9360-9365, 10015-10018, 10031-10044

Hillel b. Jacob of Bonn (הלל ב"ר יעקב מבון), 5585-5587

Hai Gaon (האי גאון), 16958

Hananya (חנניה), 9832-9850

Hisdai (חסדאי), 11302-11305

Hiyya (חייא), 3812-3813

Hiyya b. al-Daudi (חייא בן אל דאודי), 10012-10013

Isaac (יצחק), 3004-3010, 5315-5320, 5588-5592(?), 5635-5639, 9144-9146, 10577-10580, 11213-11220, 11501-11506, 11782-11786, 11916-11918, 12168-12170, 12206-12209, 12604-12605, 13137, 14791-14795

Isaac b. Abraham (יצחק ב"ר אברהם), 12793-12796

Isaac b. Avigdor (יצחק בן אביגדור), 12757-12769

Isaac b. Eliezer (יצחק בן אליעזר), 3115-3117, 3202, 17468

Isaac b. Meir (יצחק בן מאיר), 4808-4809, 11919-11929, 12942-12952

Isaac b. Mordekhai Qimhi (יצחק בן מרדכי קמחי), 4693, 7129-7133, 7200-7205, 12351-12356, 17304

Isaac b. Qaprun (יצחק בן קפרון), 11393-11409

Isaac b. Ruben Al-Bargeloni (יצחק בן ראובן אלברגלוני), 3247-3255, 11757-11758, 15444-15446

Isaac b. Saadya (יצחק בן סעדיה), 3370-3378

Isaac b. Samuel (יצחק בן שמואל), 12212-12215

Isaac b. Samuel haLevi (יצחק בן שמואל הלוי), 14110-14114

Isaac b. Waliq (יצחק בר ואליק) [Isaac Giat?], 4366-4370

Isaac b. Yaqar (יצחק ב"ר יקר), 8275-8277

Isaac b. Yehuda (יצחק ב"ר יהודה), 10439-10442, 11365-11369, 11410-11413

Isaac b. Zerahya Gerondi (יצחק בן זרחיה גירונדי), 2298, 11014-11015, 11026-11027, 11507-11508, 11517-11518, 11611-11615, 11694-11696, 11930-11932, 12096-12099, 12126-12127, 12130-12135, 12250-12255, 12321-12323, 12486-12488, 12657-12659, 12737-12739, 12741-12744, 13214-13215, 15768-15770, 16961-16963

Isaac Giat (יצחק גיאת), 506-507, 4199, 4970-4971, 9549-9562, 10045-10046(?), 11414-11415, 11509-11513, 11516, 11576-11581, 11755-11756, 11787-11792, 11876-11912, 12263, 12299-12302, 12346-12350, 12377-12378, 12489-12491, 12640-12643, 12745-12756, 13503-13506, 14300-14303, 15203-15204, 17600-17601

Isaac haKohen heHaver (יצחק הכהן החבר), 588-607

Isaac haLevi b. Elazar (יצחק הלוי בר אלעזר), 15162-15163

Isaac haNaqdan (יצחק הנקדן), 2962, 4345, 4821, 4827, 4831, 9873, 11210, 11575, 11657, 12095, 12125, 12544, 12688-

12689, 15265-15267, 15269, 15275, 15281, 15283-15285
Isaac haSeniri (יצחק השנירי), 224, 4832, 6187, 9819-9823, 11933-11937, 16967-16970
Isaac Kanazi (יצחק כנזי), 11743-11750, 12890-12893
Isaac Luria (יצחק לוריא), 3041, 7355, 9790, 13693
Israel Isserlin (ישראל איסרלין), 12601

Jacob (יעקב), 883-908, 11416-11419, 12248-12249
Jacob b. Abraham (יעקב בר אברהם), 11778-11781
Jacob b. Ḥizqiya (יעקב ב"ר חזקיה), 526
Jacob b. Hayyim (יעקב בן חיים), 17469
Jacob b. Meir (יעקב ב"ר מאיר), 11751-11753
Josef (יוסף), 514, 758-760, 1975, 2133-2158, 4296-4314, 9236, 11235, 11420, 11775-11776, 12136-12152, 12202-12204, 12262, 12446-12451, 12808-12828, 13799-13800, 16809
Josef b. Isaac (יוסף ב"ר יצחק), 708-722
Josef b. Isaac Qimḥi (יוסף בן יצחק קמחי), 6926-6941, 12345, 12867, 13706-13707
Josef b. Jacob (יוסף ב"ר יעקב), 1447-1448, 7210-7213, 9188, 12167, 13549-13551, 15024-15025
Josef b. Jacob Qalay (יוסף בר יעקב קלעי), 10859-10861
Josef b. Natan (יוסף ב"ר נתן), 1565-1567, 4824, 16940-16947
Josef b. Salomo of Carcasonne (יוסף ב"ר שלמה), 1591-1625
Josef b. Samuel Tov Elem (יוסף ב"ר שמואל טוב עלם), 88, 252-257, 509, 1037, 1061, 1683-1687, 2129-2132, 2292-2297, 2406-2408, 2656-2659, 2788-2790, 2939, 3002-3003, 3339-3340, 3496-3498, 3685, 3875, 4259, 4773-4782, 4931-4937, 5720-5722, 5772-5777, 5906, 6076-6078, 7302, 8223-8225, 8295-8310, 8349-8358, 9064, 9370, 10857-10858, 10870, 10890-10904, 11209, 11312, 11495, 11570-11572, 12092, 12128, 12485, 12644-12645, 12679-12685, 12797-12799, 12860-12866, 13120-13122, 13345-13351, 14648, 14740, 14959-14964, 15320, 17370-17372
Josef b. Soli (יוסף בן סולי), 8278-8284, 12686-12687, 16528-16529
Josef b. Yehuda (יוסף בן יהודה), 12245-12246
Josef Ibn Abitur (יוסף אבן אביתור), 338-339, 3335-3337, 4223, 4482-4486, 4489-4492, 4555-4573, 4605-4608, 4908-4910, 5588-5592(?), 5917-5919, 6942-6962, 9771-9777, 10746-10748, 12452-12454, 12996-12997, 13123-13136, 13140-13180, 14741-14745
Josef Shabbetai b. Isaac (יוסף שבתי בן יצחק), 4783-4786
Josef Zabara (יוסף זבארה) 8177-8178

Levi al-Tiban (לוי אלתבאן), 11822-11824, 13415-13421, 13465-13468, 13650-13653
Levi b. Jacob (לוי בן יעקב), 1768-1772

Matatya b. Isaac (מתתיה בן יצחק), 7862
Meir (מאיר), 6481-6486, 16589-16597
Meir b. Baruch (מאיר בן ברוך), 2325-2326
Meir b. Elazar of Lombardia (מאיר בן אלעזר מלומבארד), 3920-3921
Meir b. Isaac (מאיר ב"ר יצחק), 266, 785, 1052-1056, 1442-1445, 2038-2043, 2233-2261, 3011-3031, 3517-3521, 3614-3619, 3686-3688, 4328-4344, 4735, 4911-4913, 5642-5659, 6208-6226, 7100-7112, 7349, 8005-8018, 8192-8211, 8361-8385, 8558-8560, 9023-9038, 9065-9088, 9174-9182, 10855-10856, 10862-10869, 13053-13055, 13525-13548, 13552-13581, 14345, 14597-14614, 15087, 15205-15215, 17518-17519, 17521-17530, 17662-17663, 17800-17810, 17841-17869
Meir b. Mose (מאיר ב"ר משה), 4756
Meir haKohen (מאיר הכהן), 2433, 11311, 15368

INDEX OF POETS

Menahem (מנחם), 327-329, 1038-1051(?), 1473-1477, 7364-7366, 8612-8615, 13060-13062, 15107-15111, 15201

Menahem b. Abitar (מנחם בן אביתר), 8939-8945

Menahem b. Jacob (מנחם ב"ר יעקב), 1542-1545, 2379-2384, 5558-5559(?), 9183-9186, 15030, 15217-15220

Menahem b. Makhir (מנחם ב"ר מכיר), 1109-1113, 1226-1231, 1626-1630, 2211-2232, 3167-3170, 3190-3193, 3750-3753, 4212-4215, 6110-6111, 8616-8621, 10313-10316, 14635-14637, 16326-16342

Menahem Vardimas b. Perets (מנחם ורדימשי ברבי פרץ), 513

Meshullam (משולם), 9778-9781

Meshullam b. Qalonymos (משולם ב"ר קלונימוס), 1204-1225, 1290-1324, 1631-1649, 3032-3040, 3118-3158, 3307-3323, 3564-3599, 3623-3664, 3713-3724, 3754-3782, 3814-3844, 3997-4030, 4260-4292, 4757-4758, 5660-5673, 5685-5719, 5920-5959, 6044-6075, 6487-6523, 7076-7099, 7738-7759, 7834-7859, 8607-8611, 8753-8785, 9230-9235, 9891-9906, 10020-10030, 10140 10172, 10311-10312, 10336-10367, 10585-10610, 10628-10661, 12646-12650, 14305-14344, 14474-14506, 14527-14549, 14596, 15238-15264, 15409-15440, 15824-15844, 16222-16248, 17154-17194, 17532-17559

Mordekhai (מרדכי), 16385

Mordekhai b. Jacob (מרדכי בר יעקב), 15091

Mordekhai b. Shabbetai (מרדכי בן שבתי), 10559-10563, 14185-14189, 15027-15029, 15062-15069, 15173-15180

Mordekhai b. Yehuda Dato (מרדכי בן יהודה דאטו), 7863-7864, 13424, 14796-14797

Mose (משה), 2919-2921, 7070-7072, 9868-9870, 14586, 15112, 15360-15365

Mose b. Aaron (משה בן אהרן), 8311-8312

Mose b. Benjamin (משה בן בנימין), 15229-15232

Mose b. Ḥisdai (משה ב"ר חסדאי), 322-326

Mose b. Isaac (משה ב"ר יצחק), 14352-14353

Mose b. Meshullam (משה ב"ר משולם), 1650-1652

Mose b. Natan (משה בר נתן), 14965-14966

Mose b. Qalonymos (משה בן קלונימוס), 2107-2124, 3665-3684, 7914-7934, 14279-14297, 17391-17408

Mose b. Samuel (משה בר שמואל), 4349-4365, 5148-5149

Mose b. Samuel b. Absalom (משה בן שמואל בן אבשלום), 1548-1564, 2631-2634, 8386-8395, 8879-8901, 14629, 14800-14802, 17721-17725

Mose Ibn Ezra (משה אבן עזרא), 650-654, 747-750, 1021-1023, 2434-2438, 2635-2639, 3081-3085, 3215-3219, 3541-3543, 3610-3613, 4315-4327, 4543-4547, 4791-4793, 4902-4905, 4966-4969, 5093-5097, 5414-5415, 6967-6973, 7113-7116, 7345-7348, 7367-7371, 7446-7450, 7458, 8020-8024, 9089-9092, 9202-9203, 9225-9229, 9488-9491, 9570-9573, 9698-9702, 9726-9729, 9791-9818, 10323-10334, 10517-10526, 10584, 10624-10627, 10662-10665, 11175-11193, 11222-11225, 11292-11298, 11496-11500, 11514-11515, 11569, 11683-11689, 11938-11956, 12492-12494, 13278-13283, 13285-13295, 13339-13343, 13482-13498, 14096-14105, 14115-14119, 14180-14184, 14192-14202, 14210-14236, 14346-14347, 14350-14351, 14433-14436, 14575-14579, 14798-14799, 14995-14999, 15019-15022, 15035-15039, 15070-15073, 15075-15086, 15092-15096, 15100-15106, 15181-15199, 15270-15274, 15276-15280, 15339-15343, 15366-15367, 15890-15894, 16129-16135, 16317-16321, 16776-16790, 17038-17044, 17500-17509

Mose Levi (משה לוי), 6766-6784

Mose Sofer (משה סופר), 13056-13059

Mose Zakut (משה זכות), 834, 10437, 10459, 11009, 11574, 12954

Naqdan b. Samuel (נקדן ב"ר שמואל), 4830
Natanel b. Josef (נתנאל ב"ר יוסף), 17531

Qalonymos b. Yehuda (קלונימוס ב"ר יהודה), 534-553, 2323-2324, 2660, 3516, 6148-6150, 9055-9063, 11016-11020, 13586-13587, 14473, 15166, 15991
Qalonymos of Lucca (קלונימוס מלוקא), 10749-10750(?)

Saadya (סעדיה), 333-337, 1325-1341, 2889-2893, 3042-3056, 4631-4635, 4637-4641, 6143-6147, 7002-7020, 8622-8626
Saadya Gaon (סעדיה גאון), 137-140, 382-387, 3197-3201, 5435-5436, 7501-7502, 10470-10515, 11105-11111, 13718-13798, 13801-13865, 13989-14083, 15474-15744, 17195-17198, 17299-17303, 17754-17798, 17913-17917
Salomo (שלמה), 3096, 4692, 5090-5092, 6991-6994, 8079-8082, 10583, 13284, 14630-14634, 15900(?), 16575-16579, 16602-16644, 16863, 16993-17012, 17113-17130
Salomo b. Abraham (שלמה בן אברהם), 7399
Salomo b. Isaac (שלמה ב"ר יצחק), 812-826, 2210, 2648-2655, 7760, 17835-17840
Salomo b. Isaac Gerondi (שלמה בן יצחק גירונדי), 4539-4542
Salomo b. Menahem (שלמה בר מנחם), 16858-16861
Salomo b. Nahman (שלמה בן נחמן), 3057-3059
Salomo b. Samuel (שלמה ב"ר שמואל), 4734
Salomo b. Samuel b. Yoel (שלמה בר שמואל בר יואל), 12801-12802
Salomo b. Shimshon (שלמה ברבי שמשון), 8285
Salomo b. Yehuda (שלמה בן יהודה), 10701-10702, 17109-17112
Salomo b. Yehuda Giat (שלמה בן יהודה גיאת), 16719
Salomo Alqabets (שלמה אלקבץ), 13654-13669

Salomo haBabli (שלמה הבבלי), 171-195, 1386-1388, 1397-1422, 2125-2128, 2163-2172, 2262-2291, 2348-2375, 2814-2826, 3220-3240, 3692-3712, 3783-3808, 3883-3904, 4031-4089, 4574-4592, 5354-5372, 5446-5469, 5493-5512, 6085-6109, 7174-7199, 8696-8707, 9917-9933, 13601-13624, 15380-15402, 15845-15871, 16136-16161, 16409-16416, 17247-17272, 17332-17356, 17727-17753, 17814-17832, 17948-17967
Salomo Ibn Gabirol (שלמה אבן גבירול) 955-971, 2529-2544, 3916-3919, 4906-4907, 5997-6000, 8212-8222, 8933-8938, 10696-10699, 13378-13387, 15026, 15298-15302, 16354-16358, 16378-16381, 16423-16425, 16427, 16439-16446, 16491-16496, 16498-16504, 16530-16534, 16580-16588, 16600-16601, 16698-16718, 16721-16751, 16765-16775, 16792-16808, 16838, 16862, 16865-16934, 16951-16954, 16964-16966, 16971-16992, 17013-17027, 17032-17036, 17095, 17104-17108, 17706-17710
Samuel (שמואל), 745, 1004, 1015-1017, 7117, 9250-9252, 16497, 16694-16697, 16813-16824, 17028-17031, 17045, 17103
Samuel b. Abraham (שמואל ב"ר אברהם), 16752-16759
Samuel b. Mose (שמואל בן משה), 8606
Samuel b. Qalonymos (שמואל ב"ר קלונימוס) [only doubtful ascriptions], 5864-5868, 8187-8191, 8631-8636, 10692-10695, 14555-14559
Samuel b. Yehuda (שמואל בן יהודה), 2306, 5875-5876, 10703
Samuel b. Yehuda b. Natanel (שמואל בן יהודה בן נתנאל), 9639
Samuel Duwlin heḤazzan (שמואל דוולין החזן), 16384
Samuel Isaac (שמואל יצחק), 16791
Samuel Kohen (שמואל כהן), 14638-14644, 16506-16527
Saul Kaspi (שאול כספי), 8715-8717
Shaaltiel b. Levi (שאלתיאל בן לוי), 16325

INDEX OF POETS

Shalem Shabazi (שלם שבזי), 197-198, 223(?), 249-251, 1423-1424, 1446, 1454, 3332-3334, 3338, 3341, 3345-3347, 3350-3352, 3620, 4159-4161, 5321-5323, 5329-5331, 5437-5438, 5526, 7128, 7353-7354, 7396-7398, 7869, 8019, 8078, 8603, 9606, 9640, 9646, 9934-9935, 10014, 10060, 10368, 11313-11318, 11470, 11641, 11913, 12455, 12602-12603, 13213, 13463, 14155, 14207, 14255, 14304, 14572-14573, 15023, 15200, 15202, 15216, 15282, 15303-15304, 15819, 15946-15948, 16315, 16382-16383, 16438, 16490, 16810-16811, 16864, 16959-16960, 17096, 17145

Shefatia b. Amitai (שפטיה בר אמתי), 12913-12918

Shemarya (שמריה), 5129-5131, 16760-16764

Shemaya (שמעיה), 16389-16391

Shemaya b. David (שמעיה בן דוד), 10700

Shemtov b. Ardotiel b. Isaac (שמטוב בן ארדוטיאל בן יצחק), 16180

Shimshon (שמשון), 282-287

Silano (סילנו), 7303-7304

Simḥa Isaac b. Mose (שמחה יצחק בן משה), 867-870(?)

Simon b. Avun (שמעון ב"ר אבון), 17046-17062

Simon b. Isaac (שמעון ב"ר יצחק), 554-578, 1249-1289, 1455-1471, 1724-1732, 1745-1767, 2327-2347, 2385-2393, 2464-2517, 3262-3279, 3355-3369, 3385-3414, 3522-3540, 3600-3609, 4200-4211, 4687-4691, 4701-4717, 5098-5117, 5416-5429, 5531-5542, 6027-6042, 6151-6186, 7233-7252, 7785-7800, 8313-8320, 8846-8878, 9253-9257, 9452-9487, 9492-9522, 9907-9916, 10061-10071, 10666-10686, 10871-10889, 10905-10916, 10987-11006, 11269-11279, 13299-13321, 14587-14595, 14701-14739, 14832-14875, 15088-15090, 15167-15172, 15872-15888, 16359-16377, 16392-16408, 16418-16422, 16429-16437, 16459-16489, 16535-16574, 16839-16857, 17063-17094, 17357-17369, 17560-17599, 17644-17661, 17932-17947

Simon Levi (שמעון לוי), 9874-9875

Suleiman (סולימן), 15322-15326

Uri b. Raphael of Engburgo (אורי ב"ר רפאל מענגבורגו), 2378

Yannai (יניי), 2187-2199, 2844-2864, 8786-8819(?), 10741-10744, 12803-12807, 13233, 13582-13585, 15221-15225

Yehoshafat haGer (יהושפט הגר), 11573

Yehuda (יהודה), 1803-1810, 3488-3489, 4663-4686, 4825-4826, 10582, 11460-11468, 11754, 11914, 11957-11958, 14876-14880, 16073-16083

Yehuda b. David Ibn Yiḥya (יהודה בר דוד אבן יחיא), 11690-11691

Yehuda b. Jacob (יהודה בן יעקב), 11915

Yehuda b. Menahem (יהודה בן מנחם), 6113-6116, 7172-7173, 8226-8227, 9148-9149

Yehuda b. Qalonymos (יהודה ב"ר קלונימוס), 12630

Yehuda b. Samuel (יהודה בן שמואל), 4828-4829

Yehuda b. Samuel heḤasid (יהודה בן שמואל החסיד), 4822-4823, 4923

Yehuda b. Zerubabel (יהודה בן זרובבל), 378

Yehuda haKohen (יהודה הכהן), 1744

Yehuda haLevi (יהודה הלוי), 199-222, 360-377, 701-704, 945-954, 976-982, 986, 2186, 3342-3344, 4798-4803, 4890-4901, 4938-4961, 4979-5006, 5150-5170, 5960-5961, 6082, 7356-7360, 7870-7890, 8396-8401, 8461-8464, 8832-8836(?), 8928-8932, 9002, 9150-9151, 9153-9172, 9311-9315, 9410-9429, 9962-9966, 9971-9975, 10567-10568, 11370-11392, 11421-11456, 11469, 11471-11494, 11551-11568, 11582-11610, 11616-11640, 11658-11682, 11697-11731, 11733-11736, 11762-11766, 11793-11821, 11959-11971, 11987-12091, 12205, 12210-12211, 12216, 12219-12244, 12266-

12293, 12303-12320, 12327-12344,
12357-12376, 12385-12404, 12410-
12431, 12442-12443, 12495-12543,
12545-12600, 12606-12629, 12631-
12639, 12660-12678, 12690-12736,
12740-12744, 12770-12776, 12829-
12859, 12868-12888, 12894-12912,
12957-12986, 13390-13414, 13499-
13500, 13671-13692, 14091-14095,
14203-14206, 14257-14276, 14508-
14515, 14560-14566, 14626-14628,
15268, 15286-15293, 15376, 15441-
15442, 15897-15899, 16264-16286,
16322-16324

Yehuda Samuel Abbas (יהודה שמואל עבאס),
15378-15379, 15775-15812

Yeḥiel (יחיאל), 12444-12445

Yequtiel b. Josef (יקותיאל ב"ר יוסף), 4736-4738

Yequtiel b. Mose (יקותיאל בר משה), 12651-12656

Yeshua b. Jacob (ישוע בן יעקב), 11642-11656, 12777-12792

Yeshua Qishlari (ישוע קשלארי), 11972-11986

Yiḥya al-Daudi (יחיי אל דאודי), 15369-15370

Yiḥya alŽahary (יחיא אלצ'הארי), 5560

Yoav (יואב), 11771-11774

Yoel b. Isaac haLevi (יואל ב"ר יצחק הלוי), 4224-4225, 4962-4963, 6191-6192

Yoḥanan haKohen (יוחנן הכהן), 2299-2305, 2646-2647, 2971-2972, 11737-11738

Yosi b. Yosi (יוסי בן יוסי), 1493-1540, 2307-2310, 5835-5863, 7021-7063, 7658-7704, 9316-9332

Yuspiya (יוספיה), 12217-12218

Zebadya (זבדיה), 629-649, 4835-4843, 7778-7783, 17911-17912

Zeraḥya (זרחיה), 944

Zeraḥya haLevi bar Isaac of Gerona (זרחיה הלוי ב"ר יצחק גירונדי), 11010-11012, 11021-11025, 11028-11032, 11120, 11777

INDEX OF COMMENTATORS

Aaron b. Hayyim haKohen (אהרן ב"ר
חיים הכהן) compiler, 13, 38, 126,
168-169, 191, 244, 263, 266, 277,
311, 359, 441, 454, 513, 553, 574,
607, 628, 647, 722, 742, 756, 785,
844-845, 866, 1051, 1095, 1223,
1247-1248, 1285, 1319-1320, 1380,
1420, 1439, 1470, 1534-1535, 1560,
1622, 1648, 1680, 1730, 1764-1765,
1801, 1892, 1993, 2086, 2106,
2124, 2153-2154, 2156, 2172, 2199,
2209, 2259, 2288, 2345, 2372,
2393, 2456, 2479, 2512-2513, 2544,
2604-2605, 2723, 2733, 2740, 2756,
2771, 2784, 2812, 2823, 2842,
2860, 2887, 2915, 2958, 2999,
3031, 3078, 3093, 3152-3153, 3238,
3278, 3300, 3330, 3378, 3410,
3516, 3521, 3539, 3563, 3594-3595,
3658-3659, 3683, 3710, 3748, 3776,
3806, 3839-3840, 3870-3871, 3903,
3921, 3976-3977, 3992-3993, 4024-
4025, 4055-4056, 4084-4085, 4105,
4158, 4194, 4247-4248, 4289, 4308,
4343, 4478, 4591, 4660, 4681,
4690, 4716, 4738, 4757, 4841,
4863, 4888, 4913, 4928, 5047,
5115, 5214, 5283, 5312, 5369,
5410, 5464-5465, 5510, 5628-5629,
5639, 5718-5719, 5746-5747, 5769,
5785, 5828-5830, 5858, 5860, 5903,
5953-5954, 6020, 6041, 6043, 6071-
6072, 6105, 6135, 6142, 6182,
6226, 6486, 6516-6517, 6623, 6862,
6909, 6925, 7057-7058, 7069, 7098-
7099, 7127, 7141-7142, 7196, 7295,
7324, 7390, 7425, 7575, 7595,
7638, 7698-7699, 7735, 7758, 7774,
7784, 7823-7824, 7857, 7909, 7934,
7953, 7976, 7996, 8049, 8076,
8110, 8134, 8175, 8211, 8261,
8345, 8418, 8505, 8550-8552, 8663,
8702, 8748, 8781, 8815-8816, 8900,
8996, 9038, 9063, 9137, 9216,
9295-9296, 9352, 9395, 9449, 9483,
9521, 9599, 9695, 9747, 9754,
9866, 9906, 9916, 10041, 10071,
10167, 10223-10225, 10296, 10309-
10310, 10321-10322, 10363-10364,
10398-10399, 10430-10431, 10458,
10557-10558, 10607, 10655-10656,
10684, 10690-10691, 10790, 10832,
10853, 10856, 10869, 10889,
10916, 10958, 11005, 11020,
11160, 11279, 11356-11357, 11865-
11866, 11925, 12148, 12481,
12649, 13042, 13062, 13210,
13271-13272, 13375, 13454, 13501,
13579, 13620-13621, 13643-13644,
14150, 14177, 14296, 14338-14339,
14417-14418, 14471, 14502-14503,
14549, 14647, 14693, 14735,
14782, 14802, 14871, 14921-14922,
14953-14954, 15090, 15262-15263,
15319, 15357, 15363, 15435-15436,
15766, 15843, 15868, 15887,
15940-15941, 15967-15968, 16031,
16101, 16159, 16177, 16199,
16232, 16248, 16407, 16414,
16489, 16570, 16687-16688, 16863,
17061-17062, 17073, 17092, 17153,
17188-17189, 17240, 17269, 17294-
17296, 17327, 17352, 17366,
17436, 17465, 17496, 17556,
17595, 17641, 17679, 17694,
17750, 17808, 17828-17829, 17863,
17926, 17946, 17964, 17994, 18004

Aaron b. Mordekhai (אהרן בן מרדכי)
compiler, 10548

Abraham b. Azriel (אברהם ב"ר עזריאל),
12, 51, 88, 188, 229-231, 242, 261,
326, 331-332, 357, 397, 530, 604-
605, 626, 644, 801-802, 823, 833,
842, 1055-1056, 1113, 1230-1231,
1437, 1444-1445, 1486, 1492, 1629-
1630, 1705-1706, 1744, 1761, 1819,

2042-2043, 2149, 2170, 2208, 2210,
2228-2229, 2254, 2295, 2369, 2400,
2405, 2537, 2559, 2655, 2659,
2786, 2913, 2991-2992, 2997-2998,
3003, 3030, 3040, 3116-3117, 3169-
3170, 3193, 3209-3210, 3233-3234,
3296-3297, 3367-3368, 3377, 3404-
3406, 3430-3432, 3440, 3448, 3458,
3469, 3476, 3487, 3495, 3618-3619,
3687-3688, 3707, 3732-3733, 3752-
3753, 3802-3803, 3900, 4051, 4081,
4103, 4211, 4214-4215, 4244, 4305-
4306, 4340-4341, 4358-4359, 4448,
4587-4588, 4598, 4751, 4755, 4786,
4860-4861, 4965, 5025-5026, 5044,
5065, 5079-5080, 5227, 5233, 5317,
5366-5367, 5408, 5462, 5507, 5525,
5540, 5558-5559, 5587, 5623-5624,
5655-5656, 5675, 5717, 5783, 5822-
5823, 5874, 5906, 6102, 6111,
6221-6222, 6227, 6240, 6485, 6622,
6861, 6866-6867, 6908, 6923, 6975,
7108, 7124-7125, 7193, 7318, 7582,
7771, 7783, 7797-7798, 7819, 7861,
8178, 8181-8182, 8206-8207, 8292,
8306, 8320, 8342, 8620-8621, 8695,
8712-8713, 8745, 8968-8969, 8992-
8993, 9037, 9083-9084, 9181-9182,
9198, 9249, 9257, 9557-9558, 9725,
9762, 9781, 9941-9942, 10038,
10162, 10204, 10296, 10315-10316,
10359, 10395, 10425, 10466-10467,
10534, 10554-10556, 10563, 10575,
10651, 10868, 11074, 11215,
11229, 11231, 11248, 11351,
11418-11419, 11462-11463, 11753,
11818, 12215, 12220-12222, 12249,
12259-12260, 12409, 12605, 12630,
12762, 12802, 12918, 12952,
13055, 13058-13059, 13229-13230,
13459-13460, 13479, 13545, 13572,
13595-13596, 13616, 13636-13637,
14189, 14352-14353, 14413, 14431,
14636-14637, 14917, 14950, 15029,
15069, 15079, 15180, 15212-15213,
15468-15469, 16339-16340, 16355-
16356, 16410-16411, 16422, 16425,
16458, 16492, 16617-16618, 16644,
16696-16697, 16758-16759, 16825,

16861-16862, 16971, 17009-17010,
17029-17030, 17107-17108, 17111-
17112, 17144, 17152, 17265-17266,
17292, 17349, 17432-17433, 17527,
17677, 17690-17691, 17705, 17725,
17745-17747, 17825, 17859, 17924-
17925, 17961, 18003

Abraham Ḥaldiq (אברהם חלדיק), 2977,
3390, 3405

Alexander Sander Faber (אלכסנדר סנדר
פייבר), 9602

Amram b. Elqayim (עמרם בן אלקיים),
3247, 11757-11758, 15444-15445

Benjamin b. Abraham Anaw (בנימין ב"ר
אברהם ענו), 135-136, 2431-2432,
2867-2868, 3353-3354, 3931-3932,
3943-3944, 5529-5530, 5679-5680,
5971-5972, 6999-7001, 8328-8330,
8359-8360, 8371-8373

Berakha b. Josef haKohen (ברכה בן יוסף
הכהן), 288-290, 705-707, 867-870,
983-985, 1390-1396, 1968-1974,
2161-2162, 2459-2462, 2545-2548,
3203-3208, 3689-3691, 3725-3727,
3876-3878, 3906-3915, 3945-3947,
4108-4110, 4196-4198, 4293-4295,
4432-4437, 4439-4441, 4548-4550,
4601-4604, 4794-4797, 4804-4807,
5121-5123, 5256-5258, 5543-5546,
6079-6081, 6188-6190, 6196-6198,
7340-7342, 9217-9224, 9297-9298,
9308-9310, 9366-9368, 9371-9379,
9603-9605, 9886-9888, 9959-9961,
10009-10011, 12987-12990, 14516-
14526, 14550-14553, 14973-14975

Daniel b. Salomo haRofe (דניאל בן שלמה
הרופא) compiler, 491, 688, 1150,
1615, 1871, 1886, 2024, 2159,
2282, 2424, 2598, 2971, 3866,
4180-4181, 4286, 4472, 4527, 5031,
5212, 5640, 6115, 6281, 7172,
8226, 8544, 8809, 9148, 9322,
9641, 10955, 11087, 11775, 11859,
13035, 13107, 13975, 14686,
15231, 15935, 16681, 17553, 17786

INDEX OF COMMENTATORS 973

David b. Josef Abudraham (דוד בן יוסף אבודרהם), 314-315, 388-393, 506-507, 761-763, 955-956, 958-963, 1472, 2538-2543, 3621-3622, 3809-3813, 3916-3919, 4227-4228, 4251-4254, 4610, 4642-4643, 4896, 4898-4901, 4970-4971, 5090-5092, 5374, 5414-5415, 5433-5434, 5869-5870, 6193-6195, 6241-6246, 6531, 6533-6535, 6718, 7645, 7648-7651, 8216-8219, 8229-8231, 8279-8280, 8399-8401, 8665-8669, 8682, 8715-8717, 8919-8922, 8929-8932, 8935-8938, 9202-9203, 9334, 9339-9343, 9608-9609, 9773-9777, 10012-10013, 10333-10334, 10522-10526, 10584, 10619-10621, 10696-10699, 10747-10748, 11296-11298, 11414-11415, 11471-11472, 11514-11515, 11529-11531, 11569, 11584-11586, 11688-11689, 11735-11736, 11755-11756, 11793-11794, 11876-11877, 11890-11893, 11899-11902, 12122-12123, 12327-12328, 12377-12378, 12437-12440, 12492-12498, 12555-12556, 12925-12928, 12963-12967, 12996-12997, 13285-13286, 13292-13293, 13503-13506, 14086-14090, 14096-14098, 14215-14219, 14346-14347, 14350-14351, 14798-14799, 15031-15034, 15084, 15092, 15203-15204, 15781-15787, 16132-16133, 16528-16532, 16580-16581, 16587-16588, 16620, 16698-16699, 16772-16775, 16805-16808, 16952-16954, 17032, 17043-17044, 17600-17601

David b. Mose (דוד ב"ר משה) compiler, 118, 163, 185, 226, 325, 354, 387, 431, 453, 482, 548, 601, 622-623, 641, 679, 719, 799, 820, 832, 876, 1032, 1087, 1139, 1189, 1244, 1278, 1311, 1373, 1528, 1704, 1760, 1846, 1918, 2018, 2037, 2078, 2146, 2207, 2399, 2505, 2593, 2654, 2680, 2755, 2770, 2783, 2909, 2987-2988, 3143, 3293, 3374, 3400-3401, 3428, 3510, 3586, 3650, 3704, 3768, 3798, 3832, 3862, 3882, 3905, 3971, 4048, 4075, 4224-4225, 4230, 4282, 4337, 4402, 4520, 4675, 4754, 4768, 4833-4834, 4856, 4962-4963, 5043, 5087, 5210, 5219, 5232, 5254, 5393, 5458-5459, 5586, 5620, 5669, 5737, 5855, 5913, 5945, 6064, 6175, 6191-6192, 6230, 6239, 6272, 6484, 6507, 6619, 6922, 6993-6994, 7051, 7075, 7097, 7123, 7288, 7303, 7314-7315, 7482, 7535, 7592, 7630, 7690, 7782, 7794, 7816, 7851, 8080, 8130, 8170, 8490, 8538, 8560, 8611, 8742, 8774, 8804, 8868, 8989, 9001, 9034, 9126-9127, 9293, 9476, 9515, 9545, 9554, 9665, 9939-9940, 10160, 10201, 10268-10269, 10356, 10392, 10422, 10562, 10601, 10612, 10648, 10731, 10782, 10809, 10949, 10979, 11152, 11214, 11227-11228, 11306, 11348, 11854, 12171, 12214, 12654, 12949, 13029-13030, 13076, 13101, 13231, 13267, 13315, 13450, 13614-13615, 13898, 13967, 14145, 14188, 14330, 14359, 14410, 14494, 14542, 14615, 14620, 14642, 14681, 14700, 14727, 14775, 14814, 14862, 14914, 14947, 15028, 15068, 15078, 15135, 15179, 15257, 15430, 15930, 15963, 16230, 16245, 16485, 16562, 16586, 16615, 16677, 16695, 16727, 16757, 16812, 16860, 17058, 17141, 17151, 17180, 17229, 17261, 17322, 17526, 17550, 17588, 17689, 17741-17742, 17778, 17822, 17857, 17901, 17912, 17957, 18002

Elazar b. Yehuda of Worms (אלעזר ב"ר יהודה מוורמייזא), 433, 474, 562, 673, 1134, 1182, 1496, 1690, 1836, 1912, 2012, 2081, 2134, 2144, 2675, 2877, 4396, 4515, 4677, 5064, 6265, 7109-7112, 7175, 7475, 7633, 7693, 8493, 8871, 8945,

9130, 10205-10211, 10273-10279, 10673, 10754(?), 10844, 10952, 10994, 11155, 12630, 13095, 13451, 13891, 13960, 14684, 14730, 14777, 14816, 14864, 16487, 16565, 17233, 17772, 17800, 18010

Eliezer b. Natan (אליעזר ב"ר נתן) [including doubtful attributions], 4, 61, 82, 151, 451, 484-487, 681-684, 1026, 1142-1145, 1191-1194, 1227, 1236, 1261, 1298, 1508, 1665, 1694, 1785, 1848-1851, 1882, 1920-1923, 2020-2021, 2058, 2202, 2230-2232, 2253, 2396, 2576, 2632, 2641, 2682-2683, 2746, 2762, 2776, 3029, 3128, 3235-3237, 3550, 3574, 3633, 3717, 3759, 3822, 3852, 3957, 4172, 4270, 4404-4407, 4521-4524, 4589-4590, 5027-5029, 5039, 5052, 5084, 5203, 5250, 5298, 5596, 5657-5659, 5666, 5700, 5728, 5841, 5889, 5929, 6053, 6161, 6223-6225, 6274-6277, 6296, 6495, 6630, 7034, 7074, 7270, 7484-7487, 7517, 7557, 7586, 7612, 7671, 7719, 7842, 8037, 8061, 8095, 8121, 8158, 8208-8210, 8245, 8475, 8520, 8617, 8641, 8710, 8762, 8794, 8856, 8898-8899, 8944, 8955, 9085-9088, 9461, 9500, 9680, 10148, 10184, 10246, 10314, 10344, 10378, 10409, 10542, 10593, 10636, 10716, 10765, 10799-10800, 10840, 10898, 10930, 10967, 11134, 11168, 11330, 11742, 11837, 12248, 12406, 12468, 13102-13103, 13200, 13260, 13305, 13353, 13389, 13546-13547, 13573-13574, 13638-13640, 13901-13903, 13914-13915, 13933-13934, 13969-13971, 14132, 14166, 14315, 14394, 14483, 14535, 14711, 14758, 14845, 14901, 14937, 15214-15215, 15247, 15417, 15913, 16017, 16227, 16240, 16341-16342, 16469, 16546, 16660, 17051, 17148, 17163, 17482, 17540, 17572, 17685, 17717, 17780-17782, 17883, 17920, 17979, 17999

Eliyahu Carmi (אליהו כרמי), 1586, 3178-3180, 4743-4744, 4799, 7357, 9311, 11118, 11211, 11659, 11763, 12129, 12549-12550, 12771, 14509-14511, 15108, 15268, 15287-15289, 16499-16500, 17023

Ephraim b. Jacob of Bonn (אפרים ב"ר יעקב מבון), 1169, 1634(?), 1899, 2182, 3278(?), 3527, 3539, 6030, 6041, 9283, 9401, 10317(?), 10541, 10869(?), 10889(?), 11273, 11279, 13533, 13878, 16361, 16395, 16407, 17946

Hayyim Galipapa (חיים בן גליפפה), 4223
Ḥat Ḥazzan of Padova (חת חזן מפדובה), 10213-10216, 10286-10289

Ibn Shoshan (אבן שושן), 16879
Isaac b. Abraham Wanneh (יצחק בן אברהם ונה), 138-140, 196, 205-222, 232-233, 335-337, 341-342, 361-378, 380-381, 510-512, 764-784, 808-811, 849-850, 873-874, 877-880, 893-910, 912-914, 916-929, 937-943, 953-954, 966-975, 981-982, 1005-1009, 1016-1017, 1326-1341, 1452-1453, 1571-1584, 1688, 1714-1723, 1734-1735, 1737-1738, 1943-1960, 2524-2526, 2561-2562, 2891-2893, 2924-2937, 2968-2970, 3043-3056, 3094-3095, 3097, 3187-3189, 3199-3201, 3416-3419, 3421-3422, 3488-3489, 4106, 4119-4132, 4134-4148, 4256-4258, 4317-4327, 4428-4431, 4493, 4546-4547, 4559-4572, 4615-4629, 4633-4635, 4639-4641, 4685-4686, 4721-4732, 4739-4741, 4760-4763, 4814-4819, 4915-4917, 4945-4961, 4988-5006, 5036, 5048-5049, 5089, 5118-5119, 5131-5134, 5139-5144, 5154-5170, 5173-5176, 5179-5192, 5260, 5324-5325, 5327-5328, 5338-5353, 5380-5383, 5386-5387, 5413, 5471-5492, 5514-5516, 5556, 5577-5579, 5681-5684,

INDEX OF COMMENTATORS

5789-5802, 5997-6000, 6025-6026, 6117-6118, 6145-6147, 6322-6354, 6380-6415, 6440-6469, 6478-6480, 6529-6530, 6536, 6543-6545, 6568-6598, 6634-6638, 6667-6701, 6709-6711, 6730-6762, 6769-6784, 6786-6790, 6813-6849, 6871-6877, 6886-6889, 6895-6901, 6911-6914, 6930-6939, 6969-6973, 6983-6988(?), 7005-7020, 7070-7072, 7151-7168, 7170-7171, 7255, 7330-7338, 7350-7352, 7361-7363, 7436-7445, 7454, 7501-7502, 7829-7833, 7867-7868, 7874-7890, 8136, 8139-8148, 8281-8284, 8464, 8561-8565, 8569-8584, 8587-8588, 8590-8602, 8604-8605, 8624-8626, 8673-8675(?), 8677-8679, 8687-8689, 8720-8728, 8826-8830, 8833-8836, 8842-8845, 9005-9022, 9042-9054, 9156-9172, 9191-9193, 9199, 9201, 9237-9240, 9396-9398, 9413-9429, 9535-9536, 9542-9544, 9610-9611, 9618-9619, 9624-9638, 9643-9645, 9650-9663, 9706-9719, 9721-9722, 9752, 9785-9789, 9802-9818, 9837-9850, 9870, 9951-9955, 9967-9970, 9972-9975, 9985-10002, 10004-10005, 10019, 10045-10046, 10048-10058, 10072-10075, 10081-10099, 10102, 10104, 10106-10120, 10122-10139, 10439-10442, 10481-10513, 10567-10568, 10580, 10582, 10616-10618, 10701-10702, 11011-11012, 11033-11036, 11039-11043, 11109-11110, 11114, 11181-11193, 11203-11207(?), 11299-11301, 11374-11391, 11395-11409, 11439-11459, 11464-11468, 11478-11494, 11503-11506, 11536-11548, 11553-11568, 11579-11581, 11592-11610, 11622-11640, 11644-11656, 11667-11682, 11691-11692, 11699-11713, 11715-11734, 11747-11750, 11759-11761, 11772-11774, 11778-11781, 11790-11792, 11799-11815, 11819-11824, 11872-11875, 11879-11881, 11903-11910, 11916-11918, 11927-11929, 11941-11958, 11964-11971, 11973-11986, 11996-12015, 12022-12040, 12046-12065, 12073-12091, 12093-12094, 12154-12166, 12179-12200, 12207-12209, 12226-12244, 12256-12258, 12263, 12275-12293, 12305-12320, 12326, 12329-12344, 12360-12376, 12381-12384, 12391-12404, 12415-12430, 12489-12491, 12503-12522, 12526-12543, 12565-12583, 12585-12600, 12611-12628, 12637-12639, 12663-12678, 12686-12687, 12694-12712, 12719-12736, 12778-12792, 12813-12828, 12836-12854, 12872-12888, 12891-12893, 12897-12912, 12931-12934, 12937-12941, 12971-12986, 12991-12992, 13144-13155, 13217-13221(?), 13249-13251, 13274-13277, 13294-13295, 13324-13338, 13386-13387, 13396-13414, 13417-13421, 13466-13468, 13485-13498, 13511-13524, 13651-13653, 13670, 13674-13692, 13694, 13701-13704, 13733-13765, 13772-13796, 13811-13842, 13847-13865, 13999-14030, 14048-14080, 14102-14105, 14108-14109, 14117-14119, 14121-14122, 14195-14202, 14208-14209, 14222-14236, 14259-14278, 14298, 14300-14303, 14369-14383, 14562-14566, 14568-14570, 14582-14585, 14624-14625, 14632-14634, 14882-14894, 14969-14972, 15021-15022, 15094-15096, 15098-15099, 15104-15106, 15143, 15146-15155, 15184-15199, 15305, 15310-15313(?), 15321, 15324-15338, 15358-15359, 15366-15367, 15369-15373, 15378-15379, 15403-15404, 15408, 15441-15442, 15449-15463, 15470-15473, 15483-15514, 15528-15559, 15575-15607, 15611-15630, 15634-15655, 15668-15696, 15711-15742, 15748, 15771-15774, 15794-15812, 15992-15994, 16000, 16076-16083, 16206-16221, 16259, 16263, 16267-16286, 16290, 16292-16297, 16301-16311, 16322-16324, 16344-16351, 16353, 16379-16381, 16386-16388, 16391, 16440-16446, 16496-16497, 16510-16527,

16576-16579, 16590-16599, 16601,
16627-16643, 16702-16718, 16736-
16751, 16761-16764, 16777-16790,
16794-16798, 16800-16804, 16809,
16815-16824, 16827-16837, 16924-
16933(?), 16935-16936, 16938,
16976-16992, 17019-17021, 17102,
17114-17130, 17196-17198, 17273-
17275, 17301-17303, 17376-17390,
17515-17517, 17726, 17799, 17833-
17834, 17915-17917, 18019-18021

Isaac b. Jacob (יצחק ב"ר יעקב) compiler,
178, 269, 349, 384, 542, 581, 595,
616, 635, 715, 795, 817, 830, 856,
1429, 1552, 1726, 1755, 1815,
2141, 2174, 2360, 2388, 2651,
2817, 2902, 2979, 2996, 3088,
3242, 3288, 3305, 3372, 3394,
3426, 3505, 3699, 3792, 3984-3985,
4041, 4069, 4095, 4151, 4238,
4301, 4331, 4352, 4495, 4669,
4788, 4836, 4851, 5236, 5360,
5406, 5442, 5453, 5501, 5612-5613,
5636, 5779, 5814-5815, 5910, 6095,
6112, 6615, 6856, 7066, 7103,
7135, 7184, 7311, 7343, 7765,
7788, 7810, 8276, 8287, 8293,
8317, 8337, 8558, 8606, 8698,
8736, 8966, 8984, 9029, 9059,
9183, 9362, 9550, 9756, 9826,
10006, 10015, 10033, 10462,
11241, 11922, 12139, 12213,
12758, 12915, 12943, 13224,
13461, 13599, 13607, 14357,
14639, 14800, 15064, 15088,
15175, 15361, 15466, 16251,
16409, 16432, 16609, 16724,
16755, 17068, 17098, 17138,
17256, 17283-17284, 17341, 17361,
17426, 17711, 17736, 17817,
17851, 17952

Isaac b. Mordekhai Qimḥi (יצחק בן
מרדכי קמחי), 7131-7133, 7200-
7205(?), 12201, 12351-12356(?),
16867, 17304(?)

Isaac b. Mose Duran (יצחק בן משה דורן),
3098

Isaac b. Salomo Ḥadab (יצחק בן שלמה
חדב), 16889

Isaac b. Samuel haSephardi (יצחק בן
שמואל הספרדי), 5436

Isaac b. Todros of Barcelona (יצחק בן
טודרוס), 16880-16881, 16890-16893

Isaac of Bohemia (יצחק מבהם), 2634

Jacob (יעקב), 17861

Jacob b. Raphael haLevi (יעקב בן רפאל
הלוי), 3041, 7355, 9790, 13693

Josef (יוסף), 144, 1232, 1656, 1776,
3950, 5289, 7079, 7547, 7583,
7709, 8028, 8086, 8117, 8151,
8236, 8513, 8885, 9671, 9753,
10339, 10372, 10402, 11323,
11830, 12460-12461, 13191, 13254,
14125, 14387, 14896, 14931,
15318, 15906, 16008, 16652,
17048, 17473, 17971

Josef b. Abrahm of Montelitz (יוסף בן
אברהם דמונטליץ), 328-329, 651-654,
748-750, 885-889, 947-950, 977-
980, 986, 1022-1023, 1101-1104,
1474-1477, 1587-1590, 1769-1772,
2308-2310, 2435-2438, 2636-2639,
2964-2966, 3082-3085, 3181-3184,
3217-3219, 3542-3543, 3611-3613,
4444-4447, 4449-4452, 4540-4545,
4745-4748, 4770-4772, 4791-4793,
4800-4803, 4891-4894, 4902-4905,
4967-4969, 4974-4975, 4980-4983,
5094-5097, 7114-7116, 7346-7348,
7358-7360, 7368-7371, 7447-7450,
8021-8024, 8613-8615, 8924-8927,
9089-9092, 9226-9229, 9312-9315,
9489-9491, 9571-9573, 9698-9702,
9726-9727, 9767-9770, 9792-9798,
9820-9823, 9963-9966, 10324-
10327, 10329-10332, 10518-10521,
10577-10579, 10624-10627, 10663-
10665, 10836-10839, 10986, 11022-
11025, 11029-11032, 11119, 11176-
11179, 11223-11225, 11285-11291,
11293-11295, 11366-11369, 11410-
11413, 11423-11430, 11496-11500,
11521-11524, 11612-11615, 11660-
11663, 11684-11687, 11693, 11764-
11766, 11886-11889, 11895-11898,
11934-11937, 12118-12121, 12131-

INDEX OF COMMENTATORS

12134, 12247, 12295-12298, 12433-12436, 12447, 12545-12548, 12551-12554, 12633-12636, 12741-12744, 12747-12750, 12764-12767, 12772-12775, 12856-12859, 12920-12923, 12958-12961, 13280-13283, 13288-13291, 13340-13343, 13645-13649, 14092-14095, 14111-14114, 14181-14184, 14203-14206, 14211-14214, 14434-14436, 14512-14515, 14576-14579, 14742-14745, 14792-14795, 14819-14822, 14996-14999, 15019, 15036-15039, 15071-15073, 15081-15083, 15101-15103, 15109-15111, 15234-15237, 15271-15274, 15277-15280, 15290-15297, 15299-15302, 15776-15780, 15889, 15891-15894, 15995-15997, 16125-16131, 16261-16262, 16318-16321, 16501-16504, 16767-16771, 16967-16970, 17024-17027, 17039-17042, 17045, 17501-17504, 17506-17509, 17707-17710, 17811-17813, 17928-17931

Josef b. Josef Ibn Naḥmiash (יוסף בן יוסף אבן נחמיאש), 9338

Josef Garad (יוסף גרד), 87, 703-704, 746, 2298, 3343-3344, 4977-4978, 5334-5335, 5961, 6308, 6555, 6651, 6795, 7406-7407, 9150-9151, 9187, 9639, 11015, 11027, 11120, 11165-11166, 11309-11310, 11392, 11508, 11510-11511, 11518, 11695-11696, 11883-11884, 11931-11932, 12097, 12099, 12126-12127, 12211, 12301, 12322-12323, 12347-12348, 12443, 12487-12488, 12641-12642, 12658-12659, 12738-12739, 13215, 13500, 14627-14628, 15769-15770, 15816-15817, 16003-16004, 16894, 16962-16963

Josef Qara (יוסף קרא), 1401, 1420, 8896, 17849

Meir b. Mose Buchritz (מאיר בן משה בוכריץ), 1546, 15999, 16002

Meir Meili of Narbonne (מאיר מעילי מנרבונה), 3335, 4551, 6187, 6362, 6425, 6540, 6552, 6648, 6715, 6793, 13125, 13136-13138, 13158, 13162, 13165, 13167, 13171, 13178

Menahem b. Mose Tamar (מנחם בן משה תמר), 15201

Mordekhai b. Josef of Rocco Martino (מרדכי בן יוסף רוקא מרטינא), 224, 340, 514, 701, 944-945, 1733, 1736, 2560, 2938, 3342, 3415, 3420, 4832, 4976, 5259, 5326, 5333, 5960, 6024, 7118, 7319, 7391, 7405, 8462, 8718, 9607, 9720, 10622, 10700, 10703, 11010, 11014, 11026, 11235, 11308, 11469, 11507, 11509, 11517, 11690, 11694, 11743, 11871, 11882, 11915, 11930, 12096, 12098, 12135, 12205, 12210, 12261-12262, 12300, 12321, 12345-12346, 12442, 12486, 12640, 12657, 12737, 12740, 13214, 13388, 13499, 14626, 15091, 15286, 15443, 15768, 15815, 15895, 15899, 16001, 16316, 16358, 16719, 16961, 17036, 17103

Mordekhai b. Mose (מרדכי בן משה), 15900

Mordekhai b. Yehuda Dato (מרדכי בן יהודה דאטו), 7863-7864, 14796-14797

Mose (משה), 8003

Mose b. Hayyim Pesante (משה בן חיים פיזנטי), 1924-1925, 4366-4367, 4482, 4489, 4555-4556, 4605, 4908, 5588-5589, 6306, 6358-6359, 6421-6422, 6473-6474, 6538, 6548-6549, 6604-6605, 6644-6645, 6713, 6881-6882, 6926-6927, 6945-6946, 6950, 6955-6956, 6959-6960, 6963, 9613, 9647, 9943, 11098, 11105, 11112, 11525, 12202, 13124, 13129-13130, 13140-13141, 13160-13161, 13166, 13170, 13175-13176, 13695, 13706, 13708-13709, 13799, 13916, 14032-14033, 16871

Mose b. Samuel Ibn Tibbon (משה בן שמואל אבן תיבון), 16868, 16874, 16886, 16895-16900

Mose Muati (משה מועטי), 3248, 3251-3255, 15446

Mose Nahman (משה נחמן), 11198
Mose Nigrin (משה ניגרין), 8917, 16180, 16951
Mose b. Mordekhai Zakut (משה בן מרדכי זכות), 834

Naftali Hirsh Trebitsh (נפתלי הירש טריביש), 1699, 10194
Natan b. Isaac (נתן בר יצחק), 11777
Natan b. Yehuda (נתן בן יהודה), 4190

Raphael Salomo b. Yacob haKohen Prato (רפאל שלמה בן יעקב הכהן פרטו), 16901-16902

Salomo b. Isaac (שלמה ב"ר יצחק), 1520, 7043, 7571(?), 7682(?)
Salomo b. Samuel Rofe (שלמה בן שמואל רופא), 1616, 1872, 2105, 2283, 2859, 4473, 5033, 8545, 8810, 9269, 11088, 11860, 15936, 16682
Samḥun b. Salomo Ḥaloah (סמחון בן שלמה חלואה), 1961, 4370, 4486, 4492, 4573, 4608, 4910, 5592, 5919, 6355, 6416-6417, 6470, 6477, 6542, 6599-6600, 6609, 6639, 6641-6642, 6702-6703, 6707, 6763, 6765, 6850, 6878, 6890, 6940, 6944, 6949, 6953, 6958, 6962, 6966, 6990, 9547, 9621, 9664, 9956, 10059, 10335, 10581, 11103, 11111, 11115, 11212, 11549, 12204, 12454, 12867, 13127, 13134-13135, 13139, 13156, 13159, 13164, 13169, 13173, 13180-13181, 13705, 13707, 13713, 13797, 13800, 14081, 14586, 15112, 16505, 17037
Samuel b. David of Siena (שמואל בן דוד מסיינא), 8005
Samuel b. Elisha of Shear Arie (שמואל בר אלישע משאר אריה), 1613
Samuel b. Salomo of Faliza (שמואל בן שלמה מפליזה), 4777-4778
Samuel Ḥazzan of Erfurt (שמואל חזן מערפורט), 3888
Shabbetai b. Yashayahu haKohen Bilbo (שבתי בן ישעיהו הכהן בילבו), 9596

Simḥa b. Samuel (שמחה בן שמואל), 3941, 5981, 5996, 8384, 8436, 11267, 12115, 14614
Simon b. Tsemaḥ Duran (שמעון בן צמח דורן), 1929, 1962(?), 4368, 4484(?), 5590, 6356, 6360, 6363-6364, 6418, 6423, 6428, 6471, 6475, 6550, 6553, 6601, 6646, 6649, 6704, 6794, 6851, 6883, 6928, 6941, 6947, 9946, 9957, 10514, 11527, 11550, 13142, 13157, 13177, 13697, 13710, 13766, 13843, 14034, 14082, 15515, 15697, 15743, 16869, 16875, 16901-16905

Tobia b. Eliezer (טוביה בן אליעזר) [attributed to] 11044

Yehoshua Raphael b. Israel Benvenisti (יהושע רפאל בן ישראל בנבנשת), 8220-8221, 9325, 9344
Yehoshua Segre (יהושע סגרי), 488, 685, 1146, 2022, 2179, 2684, 4346, 4408, 4525, 6278, 13105, 13936, 13973, 17784
Yehuda b. Eliezer Zvi (יהודה בן אלייעזר צבי), 498, 695, 1156, 1199, 1933, 2030, 2256, 2690, 3934, 4417, 4532, 5974, 5990, 6286, 7210, 7494, 8377, 8429, 10899, 11173, 11260, 13080, 13114, 13120, 13576, 13982, 14608, 17792, 18014
Yehuda Leib Karlburg (יהודה לייב קרלבורג), 4972
Yehuda Toledano (יהודה טולדנו), 1930, 4369, 4485, 4491, 4557, 4607, 4909, 5591, 5918, 6365, 6427, 6476, 6541, 6554, 6607, 6650, 6717, 6929, 6943, 6948, 6952, 6957, 6961, 6965, 9616, 9648, 9945, 10369, 11037, 11102, 11107, 11117, 11528, 13126, 13132-13133, 13143, 13163, 13168, 13172, 13179, 13698, 13712
Yiḥya b. Josef Tsalaḥ (יחיא בן יוסף צאלח), 5557, 5560, 6419, 6472, 6602, 6640, 6705, 6708, 6764, 6791, 6852-6853, 6879, 6902, 6915,

INDEX OF COMMENTATORS

6989, 7913, 8831, 9958, 10438,
10515, 11208, 13767, 13798,
13844, 14031, 14083, 14190,
15314, 15516, 15560, 15608,
15656, 15698, 15744, 16934,
16937, 16939

Zakharya David Shabbetai Segre (זכריה
דויד שבתי סגרי), 490, 687, 1149,
1196, 1853, 1927-1928, 2023, 2685,
4409, 4526, 6280, 6424, 6539,
6551, 6606, 6647, 6714, 7489,
7862, 9614, 10437, 10459, 11009,
11099, 11106, 11113, 11526,
11574, 11664, 12452, 12954,
13077, 13106, 13905, 13974,
14035, 16791, 17785, 18013